MATTHEW HENRY'S NEW TESTAMENT
COMMENTARY

Matthew Henry's New Testament Commentary

Edited and introduced by David Winter

Hodder & Stoughton
LONDON SYDNEY AUCKLAND

First published in this one-volume edition in Great Britain 1995

1   3   5   7   9   10   8   6   4   2

British Library Cataloguing in Publication Data
A record for this book is available from the British Library

ISBN 0 340 64181 9

Printed and bound in Great Britain by
Cox & Wyman Ltd, Reading, Berkshire.

Hodder and Stoughton
A Division of Hodder Headline PLC
338 Euston Road
London NW1 3BH

CONTENTS

BOOK TWO – ACTS TO REVELATION

INTRODUCTION TO THE
NEW EDITION

Since this abridged version of Matthew Henry's New Testament Commentary was first published in 1974, it has proved very popular on both sides of the Atlantic. It may seem surprising that a commentary written two centuries ago should still speak so effectively to people at the end of the second millennium. Henry lived in a different culture, almost a different world from us, yet his ability to open up the Scriptures to the 'ordinary' reader is as real now as it was when the commentary was first written. His work is valued by preachers, because it is a fertile field for the cultivation of sermon ideas. It is valued by those turning to the Bible for inspiration, guidance and help in their daily lives, because his main concern all the while is to apply Scripture, rather than simply to explain it. It is also valued by those who find the Bible hard to understand, because he has an almost unique ability to unravel its various levels of meaning and draw out its essential message. Matthew Henry speaks to the whole person: body, mind and spirit.

In view of this, one may well ask why it is necessary to abridge his work at all. Many people still have his commentaries, in numerous volumes and hundreds of thousands of words, and turn to them with profit. Yet for most modern readers it is all a bit too overwhelming. Matthew Henry tends to pile example upon example. He frequently repeats himself, especially when dealing with parallel passages in the Gospels. Many of his illustrations, drawn from such sources as the master-servant relationship in the time of Queen Anne, are frankly irrelevant to the present-day reader.

Not only that, but there are also long passages of polemic, many on issues which are not regarded by most Christians today as proper causes for such intemperate language – things like baptism, ordination and, of course, the claims of the Roman Catholic Church. Most of these passages have been omitted from this edition, not because it is necessarily wrong to express such opinions, but because for most Christians today an essentially devotional commentary is the wrong place for them.

Matthew Henry approached his work in a radically different way from modern writers of biblical commentaries. Unlike them, he was not very interested in questions of dating, authorship or textual criticism. His overriding concern was less with why, when and how than with what. What has God said? And what does it mean to me, now, as I read it in my present situation? Biblical scholarship has advanced since his day and he is, frankly, sometimes an unreliable guide to the text, but he is an unequalled interpreter of its message. He sees himself as a servant of the Scriptures, rather than as a judge or analyst of them. His task is to see that the Bible feeds the reader's spirit, and no one comes up dry from Henry's well.

There is also a kind of poetry in his commentary that is foreign to most modern writers. Dealing with the words in Matthew's account of the transfiguration, for instance, 'His face did shine as the sun', Henry writes: 'The face of Moses shone as the moon, with a borrowed reflected light, but Christ's shone as the sun, with an innate inherent light, which was the more sensibly glorious, because it suddenly broke out as it were, from behind a black cloud.' The comparison is apt, the language lean and lucid. Any preachers worth their salt will be noting the idea in the margin of their Bibles.

So Matthew Henry lives on to speak to another generation. His painstaking work, which offers illumination for every single phrase and sentence in the Scriptures, is still without rival in its own field. He loves the Bible and wants us to love it too. My hope is that this abridged version will help to make his work known to those who might be put off by large volumes of closely printed type. He really is too good to miss.

David Winter
January 1995

BOOK ONE

THE FOUR GOSPELS

THE GOSPEL ACCORDING TO

ST. MATTHEW

We have before us *the Gospel according to St. Matthew*. The penman was by birth a Jew, by calling a publican, till Christ commanded his attendance, and then he left *the receipt of custom*, to follow him, and was one of those that accompanied him *all the time that the Lord Jesus went in and out, beginning from the baptism of John unto the day that he was taken up*, Acts i. 21, 22. He was therefore a competent witness of what he has here recorded. He is said to have written this history about eight years after Christ's ascension.

CHAPTER ONE
THE GENEALOGY (*vv.* 1–17)

In calling Christ *the son of David*, and *the son of Abraham* (*v.* 1), Matthew shows that God is faithful to his promise, and will make good every word that he has spoken; and this, 1. Though the performance be long deferred. Note, Delays of promised mercies, though they exercise our patience, do not weaken God's promise. 2. Though it begin to be despaired of. This *son of David*, and *son of Abraham*, who was to be the glory of his Father's house, was born when the seed of Abraham was a despised people, recently become tributary to the Roman yoke, and when the house of David was buried in obscurity.

Note, God's time for the performance of his promises is when it labours under the greatest improbabilities.

Some particulars we may observe in this genealogy.

1. The line is brought down, not to Mary the mother of our Lord, but to *Joseph the husband of Mary* (*v.* 16); for the Jews always reckoned their genealogies by the males: yet Mary was of the same tribe and family with Joseph, so that, both by his mother and by his supposed father, he was of the house of David; yet his interest in that dignity is derived by Joseph, to whom really according to the flesh he had no relation, to show that the kingdom of the Messiah is not founded in a natural descent from David.

2. The centre in whom all these lines meet is *Jesus, who is called Christ, v.* 16. *Jesus* is called *Christ*, that is, the *Anointed*, the same with the *Hebrew* name *Messiah*. He is called *Messiah the Prince* (Dan. ix. 25), and often God's *Anointed* (Ps. ii. 2). Under this character he was expected: *Art thou the Christ*—the *anointed one?*—*anointed with the oil of gladness above his fellows*; and from this name of his, which is as ointment poured forth, all his followers are called *Christians*, for they also have *received the anointing*.

1

THE BIRTH OF JESUS
(vv. 18–25)

The mystery of Christ's incarnation is to be adored, not pried into. If we *know not the way of the Spirit* in the formation of common persons, nor *how the bones are formed in the womb of* any one *that is with child* (Eccles. xi. 5), much less do we know how the blessed Jesus was formed in the womb of the blessed virgin. Some circumstances attending the birth of Christ we find here which are not in Luke, though it is more largely recorded there. Here we have:

I. Mary's espousals to Joseph. Mary, the mother of our Lord, *was espoused to Joseph*, not completely married, but contracted. Christ was born of a virgin, but a betrothed virgin, 1. To put respect upon the marriage state, and to recommend it as *honourable among all*, against that doctrine of devils which *forbids to marry*, and places perfection in the single state. Who more highly favoured than Mary was in her espousals? 2. To save the credit of the blessed virgin, which otherwise would have been exposed. 3. That the blessed virgin might have one to be the guide of her youth, the companion of her solitude and travels, a partner in her cares, and a help meet for her.

II. Her pregnancy of the promised seed; *before they came together*, she *was found with child*, which really was *of the Holy Ghost*. The marriage was deferred so long after the contract that she appeared to be *with child* before the time camè for the solemnizing of the marriage, though she was contracted before she conceived. Probably, it was after her return from her cousin Elizabeth, with whom she continued *three months* (Luke i. 56), that she was perceived by Joseph to be with child, and did not herself deny it. Note, Those in whom Christ is formed will show it: it will be *found to be* a work of God which he will own. Now we may well imagine, what a perplexity this might justly occasion to the blessed virgin. Yet we do not find that she tormented herself about it; but, being conscious of her own innocence, she kept her mind calm and easy, and committed her cause to *him that judgeth righteously*.

III. Joseph's perplexity, and his care what to do in this case. We may well imagine what a great trouble and disappointment it was to him to find one he had such an opinion of, and value for, come under the suspicion of such a heinous crime.

Observe, 1. The extremity which he studied to avoid. He was *not willing to make her a public example*. He might have done so; for, by the law, a *betrothed virgin*, if she played the harlot, was to be stoned to death, Deut. xxii. 23, 24. How good is it to *think on things*, as Joseph did here! Were there more of deliberation in our censures and judgments, there would be more of mercy and moderation in them.

Some persons of a rigorous temper would blame Joseph for his clemency: but it is here spoken of to his praise; because *he was a just man*, therefore he was not willing to expose her. He was a *religious, good man*; and therefore inclined to be merciful as God is, and to *forgive*

2

as one that was *forgiven*. Note, It becomes us, in many cases, to be gentle towards those that come under suspicion of having offended, to hope the best concerning them, and make the best of that which at first appears bad, in hopes that it may prove better.

2. The expedient he found out for avoiding this extremity. He was *minded to put her away privily*, that is, to give a bill of divorce into her hand before two witnesses, and so to hush up the matter among themselves.

IV. Joseph's discharge from this perplexity by a messenger sent from heaven, *vv.* 20, 21. *While he thought on these things* and knew not what to determine, God graciously directed him what to do, and made him easy. Note, Those who would have direction from God must *think on things* themselves, and consult with themselves. It is the *thoughtful*, not the *unthinking*, whom God will guide. God's comforts most delight the soul *in the multitude* of its perplexed *thoughts*. The message was sent to Joseph by an *angel of the Lord*, probably the same angel that brought to Mary the tidings of the conception—the angel Gabriel. This angel appeared to Joseph *in a dream* when he was asleep, as God sometimes spoke unto the fathers.

1. Joseph is here *directed* to proceed in his intended marriage. *Fear not to take Mary for thy wife*; so it may be read. From whatever cause his fears arose, they were all silenced with this word.

2. He is here *informed* concerning that *holy thing* with which his espoused wife was now pregnant. That which is conceived in her is of

a divine original. He is so far from being in danger of sharing in an impurity by marrying her, that he will thereby share in the highest dignity he is capable of. Two things he is told,

(1) That she had conceived *by the power of the Holy Ghost*; not by the power of nature.

(2) That she should bring forth *the Saviour of the world* (*v.* 21). *She shall bring forth a Son*; what he shall be is intimated,

[1] In the name that should be given to her Son: *Thou shalt call his name Jesus, a Saviour*. Jesus is the same name as Joshua, the termination only being changed, for the sake of conforming it to the Greek. Christ is our Joshua; both the *Captain of our salvation*, and the *High Priest of our profession*, and, in both, our Saviour—a Joshua who comes in the stead of Moses, and does that for us which *the law could not do, in that it was weak*.

[2] In the reason of that name: *For he shall save his people from their sins*; not the nation of the Jews only (he came to *his own*, and they *received him not*), but all who were given him by *the Father's choice*, and all who have given themselves to him by *their own*.

V. The fulfilling of the scripture in all this. This evangelist, writing among the Jews, more frequently observes this than any other of the evangelists. Here the Old Testament prophecies had their accomplishment in our Lord Jesus, by which it appears that this was he that should come, and we are to look for no other; for this was he *to whom all the prophets bore witness*.

1. The sign given is that the

Messiah shall be *born of a virgin* (Isa. vii. 14). *A virgin shall conceive*, and, by her, he shall be manifested *in the flesh*. The word *Almah* signifies a *virgin* in the strictest sense, such as Mary professes herself to be (Luke i. 34), *I know not a man*; nor had it been any such wonderful sign as it was intended for, if it had been otherwise. It was intimated from the beginning that the Messiah should be born of a virgin, when it was said that he should be the *seed of the woman*; so the seed of the woman as not to be the seed of any man. Christ was born of a virgin not only because his birth was to be *supernatural*, and altogether extraordinary, but because it was to be *spotless*, and pure, and without any stain of sin.

2. The truth proved by this sign is, that he is the Son of God, and the Mediator between God and man: for *they shall call his name Immanuel*; that is, he shall be *Immanuel*; as when it is said, *He shall be called*, it is meant, he shall be, *the Lord our righteousness*. *Immanuel* signifies *God with us*; a mysterious name, but very precious; God *incarnate* among us, and so God *reconcilable* to us, at peace with us, and taking us into covenant and communion with himself. By the light of *nature*, we see God as a God *above us*; by the light of the *law*, we see him as a God *against us*; but by the light of the gospel, we see him as *Immanuel*, God *with us*, in our own nature, and (which is more) in our interest. Herein the Redeemer *commended his love*. With Christ's name, *Immanuel*, we may compare the name given to the gospel church (Ezek. xlviii. 35).

Jehovah Shammah—*The Lord is there*; the Lord of hosts is with us.

VI. Joseph's obedience to the divine precept (*v.* 24). *Being raised from sleep* by the impression which the dream made upon him, *he did as the angel of the Lord had bidden him*, though it was contrary to his former sentiments and intentions; *he took unto him his wife*; he did it speedily, without delay, and cheerfully, without dispute; he was not disobedient to the heavenly vision. Extraordinary direction like this we are not now to expect; but God has still ways of making known his mind in doubtful cases, by hints of providence, debates of conscience, and advice of faithful friends; by each of these, applying the general rules of the written word, we should, therefore, in all the steps of our life, particularly the great turns of it, such as this of Joseph's, take direction from God, and we shall find it safe and comfortable to do as he bids us.

VII. The accomplishment of the divine promise (*v.* 25). *She brought forth her first-born* son. The circumstances of it are more largely related, Luke ii. 1, etc.

It is here further observed, 1. That Joseph, though he solemnized the marriage with Mary, his espoused wife, kept at a distance from her while she was with child of this Holy thing; he *knew her not till she had brought him forth*. 2. That Christ was the *first-born*; and so he might be called though his mother had not any other children after him, according to the language of scripture. Nor is it without a mystery that Christ is called her *first-born*, for he is the *first-born of*

4

every creature, that is, the Heir of all things; and he is the *first-born among many brethren*, that in all things he may have the pre-eminence.

THE WISE MEN (*vv.* 1-12)

It was a *mark of humiliation* put upon the Lord Jesus that, though he was the *Desire of all nations*, yet his coming into the world was little observed and taken notice of, his birth was obscure and unregarded: herein he emptied himself, and made himself of no reputation.

The first who took notice of Christ after his birth were the shepherds (Luke ii. 15, etc.), who saw and heard glorious things concerning him, and *made them known abroad*, to the amazement of all that heard them, *vv.* 17, 18. After that, Simeon and Anna spoke of him, by the Spirit, to all that were disposed to heed what they said, Luke ii. 38. Now, one would think, these hints should have been taken by the men of Judah and the *inhabitants of Jerusalem*, and they should with both arms have embraced the long-looked-for Messiah; but, for aught that appears, he continued nearly two years after at Bethlehem, and no further notice was taken of him till these wise men came. Observe,

I. When this enquiry was made concerning Christ. It was *in the days of Herod the king*. This Herod was an Edomite, made king of Judea by Augustus and Antonius, the then chief rulers of the Roman state, a man made up of falsehood and cruelty; yet he was complimen-ted with the title of *Herod the Great*. Christ was born in the 35th year of his reign.

II. Who and what these *wise men* were; they are here called *Magicians*. Some take it in a good sense; the *Magi* among the *Persians* were their philosophers and their priests; nor would they admit any one for their king who had not first been enrolled among the *Magi*; others think they dealt in unlawful arts; the word is used of Simon, the sorcerer (Acts viii. 9, 11), and of Elymas, the sorcerer (Acts xiii. 6), nor does the scripture use it in any other sense. Well, whatever sort of wise men they were before, now they began to be *wise men* indeed when they set themselves to enquire after Christ.

This we are sure of, 1. That they were Gentiles, and not belonging to the commonwealth of Israel. The Jews regarded not Christ, but these Gentiles enquired him out. 2. That they were *scholars*. They dealt in arts, curious arts; good scholars should be good Christians, and *then* they complete their *learning* when they *learn Christ*. 3. That they were *men of the east*, who were noted for their *soothsaying*, Isa. ii. 6. Arabia is called the land of *the east* (Gen. xxv. 6), and the *Arabians* are called *men of the east*, Judg. vi. 3.

III. What induced them to make this enquiry. The birth of Christ was notified to the Jewish shepherds by *an angel*, to the Gentile philosophers by a *star*; to both God spoke in their own language, and in the way they were best acquainted with. Some think that the light which the shepherds saw shining round about them, the night after Christ was born, was the very same which to the wise men, who lived at such a distance, appeared as a star; but this we cannot easily admit, because the same star which they had seen in the _east_ they saw a great while after, leading them to the house where Christ lay; it was a candle set up on purpose to guide them to Christ. The idolaters worshipped the stars as the _host of heaven_, especially the _eastern_ nations, whence the planets have the names of their idol-gods; we read of a particular _star_ they had in veneration, Amos v. 26. Thus the stars that had been misused came to be put to the right use, to lead men to Christ; the gods of the heathen became his servants.

IV. How they prosecuted this enquiry. So impatient were they to be better acquainted with him, that they took a long journey on purpose to enquire after him. Note, Those who truly desire to know Christ, and find him, will not regard pains or perils in seeking after him. _Then shall we know, if we follow on to know the Lord._

V. How this enquiry was treated at Jerusalem. News of it at last came to court; and _when Herod heard it he was troubled_, v. 3. He could not be a stranger to the prophecies of the _Old Testament_, concerning the Messiah and his kingdom, and the times fixed for his appearing by Daniel's weeks; but, having himself reigned so long and so successfully, he began to hope that those promises would for ever fail, and that his kingdom would be established and perpetuated in spite of them. What a damp therefore must it needs be upon

him, to hear talk of this King being born, now, when the time fixed for his appearing had come!

But though Herod, an Edomite, was troubled, one would have thought Jerusalem should rejoice greatly to hear that her King comes; yet, it seems, _all Jerusalem_, except the few there that _waited for the consolation of Israel, were troubled with_ Herod, and were apprehensive of I know not what ill consequences of the birth of this new king, that it would involve them in war, or restrain their lusts; they, for their parts, desired no king but Herod; no, not the Messiah himself.

VI. What assistance they met with in this enquiry from the scribes and the priests, _vv._ 4–6. It was generally known that Christ should be _born at Bethlehem_ (John vii. 42); but Herod would have counsel's opinion upon it, and therefore applies himself to the proper persons; and _demands of them_ what was the place, according to the scriptures of the Old Testament, _where Christ should be born_? Many a good question is put with an ill design, so was this by Herod.

The priests and scribes agree that the Messiah must be _born in Bethlehem, the city of David_, here called _Bethlehem of Judea_, to distinguish it from another city of the same name in the land of Zebulun, Josh. xix. 15. _Bethlehem_ signifies _the house of bread_; the fittest place for him to be born in who is the true manna, _the bread which came down from heaven_, which was _given for the life of the world_. The proof they produce is taken from Mic. v. 2, where it is foretold that though

Bethlehem be little among the thousands of Judah (so it is in *Micah*), no very populous place, yet it shall be found *not the least among the princes of Judah* (so it is here); for Bethlehem's honour lay not, as that of other cities, in the multitude of the people, but in the magnificence of the princes it produced.

VII. The bloody project and design of Herod, occasioned by this enquiry, *vv.* 7, 8.

Now, 1. See how cunningly he laid the project (*vv.* 7, 8). *He privily called the wise men,* to talk with them about this matter. He would not openly own his fears and jealousies; it would be his disgrace to let the wise men know them, and dangerous to let the people know them. Sinners are often tormented with secret fears, which they keep to themselves. Herod learns of the wise men the *time when the star appeared,* that he might take his measures accordingly; and then employs them to enquire further, and bids them bring him an account.

2. See how strangely he was fooled and infatuated in this, that he trusted it with the wise men, and did not choose some other managers, that would have been true to his interests. It was but seven miles from Jerusalem; how easily might he have sent spies to watch the wise men, who might have been as soon there to destroy the child as they to worship him!

VIII. We have here (*vv.* 9–12) the wise men's humble attendance upon this new-born *King of the Jews,* and the honours they paid him.

See how they found out Christ by the same star that they had seen in their own country, *vv.* 9, 10. Observe, 1. How graciously God directed them. By the first appearance of the star they were given to understand where they might enquire for this King, and then it disappeared, and they were left to take the usual methods for such an enquiry. Note, Extraordinary helps are not to be expected where ordinary means are to be had. Well, they had traced the matter as far as they could; they were upon their journey to Bethlehem, but that is a populous town, where shall they find him when they come thither? Here they were at a loss, at their wit's end, but not at their faith's end; they believed that God, who had brought them thither by his word, would not leave them there; nor did he; for, behold, *the star which they saw in the east went before them.* Note, If we go on as far as we can in the way of our duty, God will direct and enable us to do that which of ourselves we cannot do. 2. Observe how joyfully they followed God's direction (*v.* 10). *When they saw the star, they rejoiced with exceeding great joy.* Now they saw they were not deceived, and had not taken this long journey in vain. What a transport of joy these wise men were in upon this sight of the star; none know so well as those who, after a long and melancholy night of temptation and desertion, under the power of a *Spirit of bondage,* at length *receive the spirit of adoption, witnessing with their spirits that they are the children of God;* this is light out of darkness; it is life from the dead.

IX. See how they made their

address to him when they had found him, *v.* 11. We may well imagine their expectations were raised to find this royal babe, though slighted by the nation, yet honourably attended at home; and what a disappointment it was to them when they found a cottage was his palace, and his own poor mother all the retinue he had! However, these wise men were so wise as to see through this veil, and in this despised babe to discern *the glory as of the Only-begotten of the Father*; they did not think themselves balked or baffled in their enquiry; but, as having found the King they sought, they presented themselves first, and then their gifts, to him.

1. They presented themselves to him: *they fell down, and worshipped him.* We do not read that they gave such honour to Herod, though he was in the height of his royal grandeur; but to this babe they gave this honour, not only as to a king (then they would have done the same to Herod), but as to a God.

2. *They presented their gifts to him.* In the eastern nations, when they did homage to their kings, they made them presents; thus the subjection of the kings of Sheba to Christ is spoken of (Ps. lxxii. 10), *They shall bring presents, and offer gifts.* See Isa. lx. 6. Note, With ourselves, we must give up all that we have to Jesus Christ; and if we be sincere in the surrender of ourselves to him, we shall not be unwilling to part with what is dearest to us, and most valuable, to him and for him; nor are our gifts accepted, unless we first present ourselves to him living sacrifices. Some think there

was a significancy in their gifts; they offered him *gold*, as a king, paying him tribute, to *Cæsar, the things that are Cæsar's; frankincense*, as God, for they honoured God with the smoke of incense; and *myrrh*, as a Man that should die, for *myrrh* was used in embalming dead bodies.

X. See how they left him when they had made their address to him, *v.* 12. We do not find that the wise men promised to come back to Herod, and, if they had, it must have been with the usual proviso, *If God permit*; God did not permit them, and prevented the mischief Herod designed to the Child Jesus, and the trouble it would have been to the wise men to have been made involuntarily accessory to it. They were *warned not to return to Herod,* nor to Jerusalem. *They departed into their own country another way,* to bring the tidings to their countrymen; but it is strange that we never hear any more of them, and that they or theirs did not afterwards attend *him* in the temple, whom they had worshipped in the cradle. However, the direction they had from God in their return would be a further confirmation of their faith in this Child, as *the Lord from heaven.*

CHRIST IN EGYPT (*vv.* 13–15)

We have here Christ's flight into Egypt to avoid the cruelty of Herod.

Now here observe, I. The command given to Joseph concerning it, *v.* 13. Joseph knew neither the danger the child was in, nor how to escape it; but God, by *an angel,* tells him both *in a dream,* as before he directed him in like manner what to do, *ch.* i. 20. Joseph, before his alliance to Christ, had not been wont to converse with angels as now. Those who are spiritually related to Christ by faith have that communion and correspondence with Heaven which before they were strangers to.

1. Joseph is here told what their danger was: *Herod will seek the young child to destroy him.* Note, God is acquainted with all the cruel projects and purposes of the enemies of his church.

2. He is directed what to do, to escape the danger; *Take the young child, and flee into Egypt.* Thus early must Christ give an example to his own rule (*ch.* x. 23): *When they persecute you in one city, flee to another.* He that came to die for us, when *his hour was not yet come,* fled for his own safety.

This as a trial of the faith of Joseph and Mary. They might be tempted to think, "If this child be the Son of God, as we are told he is, has he no other way to secure himself than by such a mean and inglorious retreat as this?" They had been lately told that he should be *the glory of his people Israel*; and is the land of Israel so soon become too hot for him? But we find not that they made any such objections; their faith, being tried, was found firm.

God intimates the continuance of his care and guidance, when he saith, *Be thou there until I bring thee word,* so that he must expect to hear from God again, and not stir without fresh orders. Thus God will keep his people still in a dependence upon him.

II. Joseph's obedience to this command, *v.* 14. The journey would be inconvenient and perilous both to the young child and to his mother; they were but poorly provided for it, and were likely to meet with cold entertainment in Egypt: yet Joseph *was not disobedient to the heavenly vision,* made no objection, nor was dilatory in his obedience. As soon as he had received his orders, he immediately *arose,* and went away *by night,* the same night, as it should seem, that he received the orders. Note, Those that would make *sure* work of their obedience must make *quick* work of it.

Joseph took the young child and his mother. Some observe, that *the young child* is put first, as the principal person, and Mary is called, not *the wife of Joseph,* but, which was her greater dignity, *the mother of the young child.*

III. The fulfilling of the scripture in all this—that scripture (Hos. xi. 1), *Out of Egypt have I called my son.* Of all the evangelists, Matthew takes most notice of the fulfilling of the scripture in what concerned Christ, because his gospel was first published among the Jews, with whom that would add much strength and lustre to it. Now this word of the prophet undoubtedly referred to the deliverance of Israel out of Egypt, in which God owned them for his son, his first-born (Exod. iv. 22); but it is here applied, by way of analogy, to Christ, the Head of the church. Note, The scripture has many accomplishments, so full and copious is it, and so well ordered in all things. God is every day fulfilling the scripture.

RETURN TO NAZARETH
(vv. 16–23)

Here is, I. Herod's resentment of the departure of the wise men, which made him *exceeding wroth*; and he is the more desperate and outrageous for his being disappointed.

II. Herod was now about seventy years old, so that an infant, at this time *under two years old*, was not likely ever to give him any disturbance. Nor was he a man over fond of his own children, or of their preferment, having formerly slain two of his own sons, Alexander and Aristobulus, and his son Antipater after this, but five days before he himself died; so that it was purely to gratify his own brutish lusts of pride and cruelty that he did this. All is fish that comes to his net.

Observe, What large measures he took, 1. As to time; He *slew all from two years old and under*. It is probable that the blessed Jesus was at this time not a year old; yet Herod took in all the infants *under two years old*, that he might be sure not to miss of his prey. He cares not how many heads fall, which he allows to be innocent, provided that escape not which he supposes to be guilty. 2. As to place; He kills all the male children, not only *in Bethlehem*, but *in all the coasts thereof*, in all the villages of that city. This was being *overmuch wicked*, Eccl. vii. 17. But we must look upon this murder of the infants under another character: it was their martyrdom. How early did persecution commence against Christ and his kingdom! *Think ye that he came to send peace on the earth?* No, *but a sword*, such a sword as this, *ch.* x. 34, 35. A passive testimony was hereby given to the Lord Jesus. They shed their blood for him, who afterwards shed his for them. These were the infantry of *the noble army of martyrs*.

III. The fulfilling of the scripture in this (vv. 17, 18); *Then was fulfilled* that prophecy (Jer. xxxi. 15), *A voice was heard in Ramah.* See and adore the fullness of the scripture! That prediction was accomplished in Jeremiah's time, when Nebuzaradan, after he had destroyed Jerusalem, brought all his prisoners to Ramah (Jer. xl. 1), and there disposed of them as he pleased, for the sword, or for captivity. Then was the cry *in Ramah heard* to Bethlehem (for those two cities, the one in Judah's lot, and the other in Benjamin's, were not far asunder); but now the prophecy is again fulfilled in the great sorrow that was for the death of these infants. The scripture was fulfilled,

1. In the place of this mourning. The noise of it was heard from Bethlehem to Ramah; for Herod's cruelty extended itself to *all the coasts of Bethlehem*, even into the lot of Benjamin, among the children of Rachel.

2. In the degree of this mourning. It was *lamentation and weeping, and great mourning*; all little enough to express the sense they had of this aggravated calamity. Here was a representation of this world we live in. We hear in it *lamentation, and weeping, and mourning,* and see *the tears of the oppressed*, some upon one account, and some upon an-

other. Our way lies through a *vale of tears*.

IV. We have here (*vv.* 19–23) Christ's return out of Egypt into the *land of Israel* again. Christ was *sent to the lost sheep of the house of Israel*, and therefore to them he must return. Observe,

What it was that made way for his return—the death of Herod, which happened not long after the murder of the infants; some think not above three months. Such quick work did divine vengeance make!

V. The orders given from heaven concerning their return, and Joseph's obedience to those orders, *vv.* 19–21. God had sent Joseph into Egypt, and there he staid till the same that brought him thither ordered him thence. Note, In all our removes, it is good to see our way plain, and God going before us; we should not move either one way or the other without order.

VI. The further direction he had from God, which way to steer, and where to fix in the land of Israel, *vv.* 22, 23. God could have given him these instructions with the former, but God reveals his mind to his people by degrees, to keep them still waiting on him, and expecting to hear further from him. These orders Joseph received *in a dream,* probably, as those before, by the ministration of an angel.

Now the direction given this holy, royal family, is, 1. That it might not settle in Judea, *v.* 22. Joseph might think that Jesus, being *born in Bethlehem,* must be brought up there; yet he is prudently *afraid* for *the young Child,* because *he hears that Archelaus reigns in* Herod's stead, not over all

the kingdom as his father did, but only over Judea, the other provinces being put into other hands. See what a succession of enemies there is to fight against Christ and his church! If one drop off, another presently appears, to keep up the old enmity. But for this reason Joseph must not take the young Child into Judea.

2. That it must settle in Galilee, *v.* 22. There Philip now ruled, who was a mild, quiet, man. Note, The providence of God commonly so orders it, that his people shall not want a quiet retreat from the storm and from the tempest; when one climate becomes hot and scorching, another shall be kept more cool and temperate. Galilee lay far north; Samaria lay between it and Judea; thither they were sent, to Nazareth, a city upon a hill, in the centre of the lot of Zebulun; there the mother of our Lord lived, when she conceived that *holy thing*; and, probably, Joseph lived there too, Luke i. 26, 27. Thither they were sent, and there they were well known, and were among their relations; the most proper place for them to be in. There they continued, and from thence our Saviour was called *Jesus of Nazareth,* which was to *the Jews a stumbling-block,* for, *Can any good thing come* out of *Nazareth*?

In this is said to be fulfilled what was *spoken by the prophets, He shall be called a Nazarene,* which may be looked upon, (1) As a name of honour and dignity, though primarily it signifies no more than *a man of Nazareth*; there is an allusion or mystery in it, speaking Christ to be, [1] The *Man, the Branch,* spoken of, Isaiah xi. 1. The word there is *Netzar*, which signifies either a *branch*, or *the city of Nazareth*; in being denominated from that *city*, he is declared to be that Branch. [2] It speaks him to be the *great Nazarite*; of whom the legal Nazarites were a type and figure (especially Samson, Judg. xiii. 5), and Joseph, who is called a *Nazarite among his brethren* (Gen. xlix. 26). Not that Christ was, *strictly*, *a Nazarite*, for he drank wine, and touched dead bodies; but he was *eminently* so, both as he was singularly holy, and as he was by a solemn designation and dedication set apart to the honour of God in the work of our redemption, as Samson was to save Israel.

CHAPTER THREE
JOHN THE BAPTIST

Matthew says nothing of the conception and birth of John the Baptist, which is largely related by St. Luke, but finds him at full age, as if dropt from the clouds to preach in the wilderness. For above three hundred years the church had been without prophets; those lights had been long put out, that *he* might be the more desired, who was to be the great prophet. After Malachi there was no prophet, nor any pretender to prophecy, till John the Baptist, to whom therefore the prophet Malachi points more directly than any of the Old Testament prophets had done (Mal. iii. 1); *I send my messenger.*

The beginning of the gospel in a wilderness, speaks comfort to the deserts of the Gentile world. Now must the prophecies be fulfilled, *I will plant in the wilderness the cedar*, Isa. xli. 18, 19. The wilderness shall be *a fruitful field*, Isa. xxxii. 15. And the *desert shall rejoice*, Isa. xxxv. 1, 2. The Septuagint reads, *the deserts of Jordan*, the very wilderness in which John preached.

John came, not fighting, nor disputing, but *preaching* (*v.* 1); for by the foolishness of preaching, Christ's kingdom must be set up.

I. The doctrine he preached was that of repentance (*v.* 2); *Repent ye.* He preached this in *Judea*, among those that were called *Jews*, and made a profession of religion; for even they needed repentance. He preached it, not in Jerusalem, but in the wilderness of Judea, among the plain country people; for even those who think themselves most out of the way of temptation, and furthest from the vanities and vices of the town, cannot wash their hands in innocency, but must do it in repentance. John Baptist's business was to call men to *repent* of their sins; *Bethink yourselves*; "Admit a second *thought*, to correct the errors of the first—an *afterthought*. Consider your ways, *change your minds*; you have thought amiss; *think again*, and *think aright*." Note, True penitents have *other thoughts* of God and Christ, and sin and holiness, and this world and the other, than they have had, and stand otherwise affected toward them. The change of the *mind* produces a change of the *way*. Those who are truly sorry for what they have done amiss, will be careful to do so no more. This repentance is a necessary duty, in obedience to the command of God (Acts xvii. 30); and a necessary preparative and qualification for the comforts of the gospel of Christ.

II. The argument he used to enforce this call was, *For the kingdom of heaven is at hand* (*v.* 2). It is a *kingdom* of which Christ is the Sovereign, and we must be the willing, loyal subjects of it. It is a kingdom of *heaven*, not of this world, a spiritual kingdom: its original from heaven, its tendency to heaven. John preached this as *at hand*; then it was at the door; to us it is come, by the pouring out of the Spirit, and the full exhibition of the riches of gospel-grace. Now, (1) This is a great *inducement* to us *to repent*. There is nothing like the consideration of divine grace to break the heart, both *for sin* and *from sin*. That is evangelical repentance, that flows from a sight of Christ, from a sense of his love, and the hopes of pardon and forgiveness through him. (2) It is a *great encouragement* to us *to repent*; "Repent, for your sins shall be pardoned upon your repentance. Return to God in a way of duty, and he will, through Christ, return to you in a way of mercy.'

1. As the *voice of one crying in the wilderness* (*v.* 3). John owned it himself (John i. 23); *I am the voice*, and that is all, God is the Speaker, who makes known his mind by John, as a man does by his voice. The word of God must be received as such (1 Thes. ii. 13); what else is Paul, and what is Apollos, but the voice!

2. As one whose business it was to *prepare the way of the Lord, and to make his paths straight*; so it was said of him before he was born, that he should *make ready a people prepared for the Lord* (Luke i. 17), as Christ's harbinger and forerunner: he was such a one as intimated the nature of Christ's kingdom, for he came not in the gaudy dress of a herald at arms, but in the homely one of a hermit. Officers are sent before great men to clear the way; so John prepares the way of the Lord. Note, There is a great deal to be done, to make way for Christ into a soul, to *bow the heart* for the reception of the Son of David (2 Sam. xix. 14); and nothing is more needful, in order to this, than the discovery of sin, and a conviction of the insufficiency of our own righteousness.

They, who expected the Messiah as a temporal prince, would think that his forerunner must come in great pomp and splendour; but it proves quite contrary; he shall be *great in the sight of the Lord*, but mean in the eye of the world; to intimate that the glory of Christ's kingdom was to be spiritual, and the subjects of it such as ordinarily were either *found* by *it*, or *made* by it, poor and despised, who derived their honours, pleasures, and riches, from another world.

1. His *dress* was *plain*. This same John had *his raiment of camel's hair, and a leathern girdle about his loins*; he did not go in *long clothing*, as the *scribes*, or *soft clothing*, as the courtiers, but in the clothing of a country husbandman; for he lived in a country place, and suited his *habit* to his *habitation*. Note, It is good for us to accommodate ourselves to the place and condition which God, in his providence, has put us in.

2. His *diet* was *plain*; his *meat*

was *locusts* and *wild honey*; not as if he never ate anything else; but these he frequently fed upon, and made many meals of them, when he retired into solitary places, and continued long there for contemplation. He was so entirely taken up with spiritual things, that he could seldom find time for a set meal.

Then went out to him Jerusalem, and all Judea (v. 5). Great multitudes came to him from the city, and from all parts of the country; some of all sorts, men and women, young and old, rich and poor, Pharisees and publicans; they *went out to him*, as soon as they heard of his preaching the *kingdom of heaven*, that they might hear what they heard so much of. This was an evidence that it was now a time of great expectation; it was generally thought that the *kingdom of God* would presently *appear* (Luke xix. 11), and therefore, when John showed himself to Israel, lived and preached in this way, so very different from the Scribes and Pharisees, they were ready to say of him, that he was *the Christ* (Luke iii. 15); and this occasioned such a confluence of people about him. It appears later that of the many who came to John's Baptism, there were few who adhered to it; witness the cold reception Christ had in Judea, and about Jerusalem.

Those who received his doctrine, and submitted to his discipline, were *baptized of him in Jordan (v. 6),* thereby professing their repentance, and their belief that the kingdom of the Messiah was at hand. 1. They testified their repentance by *confessing their sins*; a general confession, it is probable, they made to

John that they were *sinners*, that they were polluted by sin, and needed cleansing; but to God they made a confession of particular sins, for he is the party offended. The Jews had been taught to *justify* themselves; but John teaches them to *accuse* themselves, and not to rest, as they used to do, in the general confession of sin made for all Israel, once a year, upon the day of atonement. 2. The benefits of the *kingdom of heaven*, now *at hand*, were thereupon sealed to them by baptism. He washed them with water, in token of this—that from all their iniquities God would *cleanse them*. It was usual with the Jews to baptize those whom they admitted proselytes to their religion, especially those who were only *Proselytes of the gate*, and were not circumcised, as the *Proselytes of righteousness* were. The *ceremonial law* consisted in *divers washings or baptisms* (Heb. ix. 10); but John's baptism refers to the remedial law, the law of repentance and faith. He is said to baptize them in Jordan, that river which was famous for Israel's passage through it, and Naaman's cure; yet it is probable that John did not baptize in that river at first, but that afterward, when the people who came to his baptism were numerous, he removed to Jordan. By baptism he obliged them to live a holy life, according to the profession they took upon themselves.

The doctrine John preached was that of repentance, in consideration of the *kingdom of heaven* being *at hand*. Application is the life of preaching, so it was of John's preaching.

Observe, 1. To whom he applied it; to the Pharisees and Sadducees that came to his baptism, *v.* 7. To others he thought it enough to say, *Repent, for the kingdom of heaven is at hand*; but when he saw these Pharisees and Sadducees come about him, he found it necessary to explain himself, and deal more closely. These were two of the three noted sects among the Jews at that time, the third was that of the Essenes, whom we never read of in the gospels, for they affected retirement, and declined busying themselves in public affairs. The Pharisees were zealots for the ceremonies, for the power of the church, and the traditions of the elders; the Sadducees ran into the other extreme, and were little better than deists, denying the existence of spirits and a future state. 2. What the application was. It is directed to their consciences. Though his education was private, he was not bashful when he appeared in public, nor did he fear the face of man, for he was full of the Holy Ghost, and of power.

He begins harshly, calls them not Rabbi, gives them not the titles, much less the applauses, they had been used to. 1. The *title* he gives them is, *O generation of vipers* (*v.* 7). Christ gave them the same title; *ch.* xii. 34; xxiii. 33. The *alarm* he gives them is, *Who has warned you to flee from the wrath to come?* This intimates that they were in danger of the wrath to come; and that their case was so nearly desperate, and their hearts so hardened in sin (the Pharisees by their parade of religion, and the Sadducees by their arguments against religion)

that it was next to a miracle to effect anything hopeful among them.

"*Bring forth therefore fruits meet for repentance*" (*v.* 8). "*Therefore*, because you are *warned to flee from the wrath to come*, let the terrors of the Lord persuade you to a holy life."

Here is a word of caution, not to trust to their external privileges, so as with them to shift off these calls to repentance (*v.* 9); *Think not to say within yourselves, We have Abraham to our father*. Note, There is a great deal which carnal hearts are apt to say within themselves, to put by the convincing, commanding power of the word of God, which ministers should labour to meet with and anticipate; vain thoughts which lodge within those who are called to *wash their hearts*, Jer. iv. 14.

Their pretence was; "*We have Abraham to our father*; we are not sinners of the Gentiles; it is fit indeed that *they* should be called to repent; but we are Jews, a holy nation, a peculiar people, what is this to us?"

How foolish and groundless this pretence was; they thought that being the seed of Abraham, they were the only people God had in the world, and therefore that, if they were cut off, he would be at a loss for a church; but John shows them the folly of this conceit; *I say unto you* (whatever you say within yourselves), that *God is able of these stones to raise up children unto Abraham*. He was now baptizing in Jordan at Bethabara (John i. 28), *the house of passage*, where the children of *Israel passed over*; and

John the Baptist

there were the twelve stones, one for each tribe, which Joshua set up for a memorial, Josh. iv. 20. It is not unlikely that he pointed to those stones, which God could raise to be, more than in representation, the *twelve tribes of Israel.*

Here is a word of terror to the careless and secure Pharisees and Sadducees, and other Jews, that knew not the signs of the times, nor the day of their visitation, *v.* 10. "Now look about you, now that *the kingdom of God is at hand,* and be made sensible."

"How strict and short your trial is; *Now the axe* is carried before you, now it is *laid to the root of the tree,* now you are upon *your good behaviour,* and are to be so but a *while*; now you are marked for ruin, and cannot avoid it but by a speedy and sincere repentance. Now you must expect that God will make quicker work with you by his judgments than he did formerly, and that they will *begin at the house of God*: where God allows more means, he allows less time."

With the warning, a word of instruction concerning Jesus Christ, in whom all John's preaching centred. Christ's ministers preach, not themselves, but him. Here is,

1. The dignity and pre-eminence of Christ above John. See how meanly he speaks of himself, that he might magnify Christ (*v.* 11); "*I indeed baptize you with water,* that is the utmost I can do." But *he that comes after me is mightier than I.* Though John had much power, for he came in the *spirit and power of Elias,* Christ had more; though John was truly great, great in the sight of the Lord (not a greater was

born of woman), yet he thinks himself unworthy to be in the meanest place of attendance upon Christ, *whose shoes I am not worthy to bear.*

When it was prophesied that John should be sent as Christ's forerunner (Mal. iii. i, 2), it immediately follows, *The Lord, whom ye seek, shall suddenly come,* and shall *sit as a refiner, v.* 3. And after the coming of Elijah, *the day comes that shall burn as an oven* (Mal. iv. 1), to which the Baptist seems here to refer. Christ will come to make a distinction,

(1) By the powerful working of his grace; *He shall baptize you,* that is, some of you, *with the Holy Ghost and with fire.* Note, [1] It is Christ's prerogative to baptize *with the Holy Ghost.* This he did in the extraordinary gifts of the Spirit conferred upon the apostles, to which Christ himself applies these words of John, Acts i. 5. This he does in the graces and comforts of the Spirit given to them that ask him, Luke xi. 13; John vii. 38, 39; See Acts xi. 16. [2] They who are baptized with the Holy Ghost are baptized as *with fire*; the seven spirits of God appear as *seven lamps of fire,* Rev. iv. 5. Is fire enlightening? So the Spirit is a Spirit of illumination. Is it warming? And do not their hearts burn within them? Is it consuming? And does not the Spirit of judgment, as a *Spirit of burning,* consume the dross of their corruptions? Does fire make all it seizes like itself? And does it move upwards? So does the Spirit make the soul holy like itself, and its tendency is heaven-ward. Christ says *I am come to send fire,* Luke xii. 49.

(2) By the final determinations of his judgment (*v.* 12); *Whose fan is in his hand.* His ability to distinguish, as the eternal wisdom of the Father, who sees all by a true light, and his authority to distinguish, as the Person to whom all judgment is committed, is the *fan* that is *in his hand*, Jer. xv. 7.

THE BAPTISM OF JESUS

Our Lord Jesus, from his childhood till now, when he was almost thirty years of age, had lain hid in Galilee, as it were, buried alive; but now, after a long and dark night, behold, *the Sun of righteousness* rises in glory.

Now in this story of Christ's baptism we may observe,

1. How hardly John was persuaded to admit of it, *vv.* 14, 15. It was an instance of Christ's great humility, that he would offer himself *to be baptized of John*; that he *who knew no sin* would submit to the baptism of repentance. Note, As soon as ever Christ began to preach, he preached humility, preached it by his example, preached it to all, especially to young ministers. Christ was designed for the highest honours, yet in his first step he thus abases himself. Note, Those who would rise high must begin low. Now here we have,

1. The objection that John made against baptizing Jesus, *v.* 14. *John forbade him*, as Peter did, when Christ went about to wash his feet, John xiii. 6, 8. Note, Christ's gracious condescensions are so surprising, as to appear at first incredible to the strongest believers.

(1) John thinks it necessary that he should be baptized of Christ; *I have need to be baptized of thee* with the baptism of the Holy Ghost, as of fire, for that was Christ's baptism, *v.* 11.

(2) He therefore thinks it very preposterous and absurd, that Christ should be baptized by him; *Comest thou to me?* Does the holy Jesus, that is separated from sinners, come to be baptized by a sinner, as a sinner, and among sinners? How can this be?

2. The overruling of this objection (*v.* 15); *Jesus said, Suffer it to be so now.* Christ accepted his humility, but not his refusal; he will have the thing done; and it is fit that Christ should take his own method, though we do not understand it, nor can give a reason for it. See,

(1) How Christ insists upon it; It must *be so now.* He does not deny that *John had need to be baptized of* him, yet he will now be *baptized of John. Let it be yet so; suffer it to be so now.* Note, Every thing is beautiful in its season. But why *now*? Why yet? [1] Christ is *now* in a state of humiliation: he has emptied himself, and *made himself of no reputation.* [2] John's baptism is now in reputation, it is that by which God is now doing his work; that is the present dispensation, and therefore Jesus will now be baptized with water; but his baptizing with the Holy Ghost is reserved for hereafter, *many days hence*, Acts i. 5. [3] it must *be so now*, because now is the time for Christ's appearing in public, and this will be a fair opportunity for it, See John i. 31–34.

(2) The reason he gives for it;

Thus it becomes us to fulfil all righteousness. Our Lord Jesus looked upon it as a thing well becoming him, *to fulfil all righteousness*, that is (as Dr. Whitby explains it), to own every divine institution, and to show his readiness to comply with all God's righteous precepts. *Thus it becomes* him to justify God, and approve his wisdom, in sending John to prepare his way by the baptism of repentance. *Thus it becomes us* to countenance and encourage every thing that is good, by pattern as well as precept. Thus Jesus began *first to do, and then to teach*; and his ministers must take the same method. Thus *Christ filled up the righteousness of the ceremonial law*, which consisted in divers washings; thus he recommended the gospel-ordinance of baptism to his church, put honour upon it, and showed what virtue he designed to put into it.

With the will of Christ, and this reason for it, John was entirely satisfied, and *then he suffered him*. The same modesty which made him at first decline the honour Christ offered him, now made him do the service Christ enjoined him.

How solemnly Heaven was pleased to grace the baptism of Christ with a special display of glory (*vv.* 16, 17); *Jesus when he was baptized, went up straightway out of the water*. Others that were baptized stayed to *confess their sins* (*v.* 6); but Christ, having no sins to confess, *went up* immediately *out of the water*; so we read it, but not right: for it is *from the water*; from the brink of the river, to which he went down to be washed with water, that is, to have his head or face washed (John xiii. 9). *He went up straightway*, as one that entered upon his work with the utmost cheerfulness and resolution; he would lose no time. *How was he straightened till it was accomplished!*

Now, when he was coming *up out of the water*, and all the company had their eye upon him,

1. *Lo! the heavens were opened unto him*, so as to discover something above and beyond the starry firmament, at least, to him.

2. *He saw the Spirit of God descending like a dove*, or *as a dove, and* coming or *lighting upon him*. Christ saw it (Mark i. 10), and John saw it (John i. 33, 34), and it is probable that all the standers-by saw it; for this was intended to be his public inauguration.

(1) *The Spirit of God descended, and lighted on him*. In the beginning of the old world, *the Spirit of God moved upon the face of the waters* (Gen. i. 2), *hovered* as a bird upon the nest. So here, in the beginning of this new world, Christ, as God, needed not to receive the Holy Ghost, but it was foretold that *the Spirit of the Lord should rest upon him* (Isa. xi. 2; lxi. 1), and here he did so.

(2) He *descended on him like a dove*; whether it was a real, living dove, or, as was usual in visions, the representation or similitude of a dove, is uncertain. Of all fowl none was so significant as the dove. [1] The Spirit of Christ is a dove-like spirit; not like *a silly dove, without heart* (Hos. vii. 11), but like an innocent dove, without gall. [2] The dove was the only fowl that was offered in sacrifice (Lev. i. 14),

and Christ by the Spirit, *the eternal Spirit, offered himself without spot to God.* [3] The tidings of the decrease of Noah's flood were brought by a dove, with an olive-leaf in her mouth; fitly therefore are the glad tidings of peace with God brought by the Spirit as *a dove.* It speaks God's *good will towards men*; that his thoughts towards us are *thoughts of good, and not of evil.*

3. To explain and complete this solemnity, *there came a voice from heaven*, which, we have reason to think, was heard by all that were present.

(1) See here how God owns our Lord Jesus; *This is my beloved Son.* Observe, [1] The relation he stood in to him; He *is my Son.* Jesus Christ is the Son of God, *by eternal generation*, as he was *begotten of the Father before all worlds* (Col. i. 15; Heb. i. 3); and by supernatural conception; he was *therefore* called *the Son of God*, because he *was conceived by the power of the Holy Ghost* (Luke i. 35); yet this is not all; he is the Son of God by special designation to the work and office of the world's Redeemer. [2] The affection the Father had for him; He *is my beloved Son*; his dear Son, *the Son of his love* (Col. i. 13); he had lain in his bosom from all eternity (John i. 18), had been *always his delight* (Prov. viii. 30), but particularly as Mediator, and in undertaking the work of man's salvation, he was his *beloved Son.* He is *my Elect, in whom my soul delights.* See Isa. xlii. 1. Because he consented to the covenant of redemption, and delighted to do that *will of God, therefore the Father loved him.* John x. 17; iii. 35.

(2) See here how ready he is to own us in him: He *is my beloved Son*, not only *with* whom, but *in* whom, I am well pleased. He is pleased with all that are in him, and are united to him by faith. Hitherto God had been displeased with the children of men, but now his anger is turned away, and he has made us *accepted in the Beloved*, Eph. i. 6.

CHAPTER FOUR
TEMPTATION OF JESUS

Concerning Christ's temptation, observe,

I. The time when it happened: *Then*; there is an emphasis laid upon that. Immediately after *the heavens were opened* to him, and *the Spirit descended on him*, and he was declared to be the Son of God, and the Saviour of the world, the next news we hear of him is, he is *tempted*; for *then* he is best able to grapple with the temptation.

Then, when he was newly come from a solemn ordinance, when he was baptized, *then* he was *tempted.* Note, After we have been admitted into communion with God, we must expect to be set upon by Satan. The enriched soul must double its guard. *Then*, when he began to show himself publicly to Israel, *then* he was *tempted*, so as he never had been while he lived in privacy.

II. The place where it was; *in the wilderness*; probably in the great wilderness of *Sinai*, where Moses and Elijah *fasted forty days*, for no part of *the wilderness* of Judea was so abandoned to wild beasts as this is said to have been, Mark i. 13. Christ withdrew into the wilderness, 1. To gain advantage to himself. Retirement gives an opportunity for meditation and communion with God; even they who are called to the most active life must yet have their contemplative hours, and must find time to be alone with God. Those are not fit to speak of the things of God in public to others, who have not first conversed with those things in secret by themselves. 2. To give advantage to the tempter, that he might have a readier access to him than he could have had in company. Those who, under pretence of sanctity and devotion, retire into dens and deserts, find that they are not out of reach of their spiritual enemies, and that there they lack the benefit of the communion of saints. Christ retired, (1) That Satan might have leave to do his worst. To make his victory the more illustrious, he gave the enemy sun and wind on his side, and yet baffled him. (2) That he might have an opportunity to do his best himself, that he might be exalted in his own strength; for so it was written, *I have trod the wine-press alone*, and of the people there was none with me. Christ entered the lists without a second.

III. The preparatives for it, which were two.

1. He was directed to the combat; he did not wilfully thrust himself upon it, but he *was led up of the Spirit to be tempted of the Devil.*

Now Christ's temptation is, (1) An instance of his own condescension and humiliation, because he would humble himself, *in all things to be made like unto his brethren*; thus he *gave his back to the smiters*. (2) An occasion of Satan's confusion. There is no conquest without a combat. Christ was tempted, that he might overcome the tempter. Satan tempted the first Adam, and triumphed over him; but he shall not always triumph, the second Adam shall overcome him and *lead captivity captive*. (3) Matter of comfort to all the saints. In the temptation of Christ it appears that our enemy is subtle, spiteful, and very daring in his temptations; but it also appears that he is not invincible. Though he is *a strong man armed*, yet the Captain of our salvation is *stronger than he*.

2. He was dieted for the combat, as wrestlers, who are *temperate in all things* (1 Cor. ix. 25); but Christ beyond any other, for he *fasted forty days and forty nights*, in compliance with the type and example of Moses the great lawgiver, and of Elias, the great reformer, of the Old Testament. Christ did not need to fast for mortification (he had no corrupt desires to be subdued); yet he *fasted*, (1) That herein he might humble himself, and might seem as one abandoned, *whom no man seeketh after*. (2) That he might give Satan both occasion and advantage against him; and so make his victory over him the more illustrious. (3) That he might sanctify and recommend fasting to us, when God in his providence calls to it, or when we are reduced to straits, and are destitute of daily food, or when it is requisite for the keeping under of the body, or the

quickening of prayer, those excellent preparatives for temptation.

IV. The temptations themselves (*vv.* 3–10). That which Satan aimed at, in all his temptations, was, to bring him to *sin against God*, and so to render him for ever incapable of being a Sacrifice for the sin of others. Now, whatever the colours were, that which he aimed at was, to bring him, 1. To despair of his Father's goodness. 2. To presume upon his Father's power. 3. To alienate his Father's honour, by giving it to Satan. In the two former, that which he tempted him *to*, seemed innocent, and therein appeared the subtlety of the tempter; in the last, that which he tempted him *with*, seemed desirable. The two former are artful temptations, which there was need of great wisdom to discern; the last was a strong temptation, which there was need of great resolution to resist; yet he was baffled in them all.

1. Christ began to be hungry, and therefore the motion seemed very proper, to turn *stones* into *bread* for his necessary support. Note, It is one of the wiles of Satan to take advantage of our outward condition, in that to plant the battery of his temptations. [2] Christ was newly declared to be *the Son of God*, and here the Devil tempts him to doubt of that; *If thou be the Son of God.*

"If God were thy Father, he would not see thee starve, for *all the beasts of the forest are his*, Ps. l. 10, 12. It is true there *was a voice from heaven, This is my beloved Son*, but surely it was delusion, and thou wast imposed upon by it; for either

God is not thy Father, or he is a very unkind one." But see how unreasonable this suggestion was, and how easily answered. If Christ seemed to be a mere Man now, because he was hungry, why was he not confessed to be more than a Man, even the *Son of God*, when for *forty days he fasted*, and was not hungry?

Secondly, "Thou hast now an opportunity to show that thou art *the Son of God. If thou* art *the Son of God*, prove it by this, *command that these stones*" (a heap of which, probably, lay now before him) "*be made bread, v.* 3. John Baptist said but the other day, that God *can out of stones raise up children to Abraham*, a divine power therefore can, no doubt, out of stones, make bread for those children; if therefore thou hast that power, exert it now in a time of need for thyself."

See how this temptation was resisted and overcome.

[1] Christ refused to comply with it. He would not *command these stones to be made bread*; not because he could not; his power, which soon after this turned *water into wine*, could have turned *stones* into *bread*; but he would not. And why would he not? *First*, That looked like questioning the truth of the voice he heard from heaven, or putting that upon a new trial which was already settled. *Secondly*, That looked like distrusting his Father's care of him, or limiting him to one particular way of providing for him. *Thirdly*, That looked like setting up for himself; or, *Fourthly*, That looked like gratifying Satan, by doing a thing at his motion.

[2] He was ready to reply to it

(*v.* 4); *He answered and said, It is written.* This is observable, that Christ answered and baffled all the temptations of Satan with, *It is written.* He is himself the eternal Word, and could have produced the mind of God without having recourse to the writings of Moses; but he put honour upon the scripture, and, to set us an example, he appealed to what was written in the law; and he says this to Satan, taking it for granted that he knew well enough what was written.

This answer, as all the rest, is taken out of the book of *Deuteronomy*, which signifies *the second law*, and in which there is very little ceremonial; the Levitical sacrifices and purifications could not drive away Satan, though of divine institution, but moral precepts and evangelical promises, mixed with faith, are *mighty, through God,* for the vanquishing of Satan. This is here quoted from Deut. viii. 3, where the reason given why God fed the Israelites with manna is, because he would teach them that *man shall not live by bread alone.* This Christ applies to his own case.

2. He tempted him to presume upon his Father's power and protection.

Now in this second attempt we may observe,

(1) What the temptation was, and how it was managed. In general, finding Christ so confident of his Father's care of him, in point of nourishment, he endeavours to draw him to presume upon that care in point of safety.

Now in this temptation we may observe,

[1] How he made way for it. He took Christ, not by force and against his will, but moved him to go, and went along with him, to Jerusalem. Intending to solicit Christ to an ostentation of his own power, and a vain-glorious presumption upon God's providence, he fixes him on a public place in Jerusalem, a populous city, and *the joy of the whole earth*; in the temple, one of the wonders of the world, continually gazed upon with admiration by some one or other. There he might make himself remarkable, and be taken notice of by every body, and prove himself the Son of God; not, as he was urged in the former temptation, in the obscurities of a wilderness, but before multitudes, upon the most eminent stage of action.

[2] How he moved it; "*If thou be the Son of God,* now show thyself to the world, and prove thyself to be so; *cast thyself down,* and then," *First,* "Thou wilt be admired, as *under the special protection of heaven.*" *Secondly,* "Thou wilt be received, as coming *with a special commission from heaven.* All Jerusalem will see and acknowledge, not only that thou art more than a man, but that thou art that *Messenger,* that *Angel of the covenant,* that should *suddenly come to the temple* (Mal. iii. 1), and from thence descend into the streets of the holy city; and thus the work of convincing the Jews will be cut short, and soon done."

[3] How he backed this motion with a scripture; *For it is written, He shall give his angels charge concerning thee.* The devil would persuade Christ to *throw himself down,* hoping that he would be his

own murderer, and that there would be an end of him and his undertaking, which he looked upon with a jealous eye; to encourage him to do it, he tells him, that there was no danger, that the good angels would protect him, for so was the promise (Ps. xci. 11), *He shall give his angels charge over thee.* In this quotation,

First, There was *something right.* It is true, there is such a promise of the ministration of the angels, for the protection of the saints.

Secondly, There was a great deal *wrong in it*; and perhaps the devil had a particular spite against this promise, and perverted it, because it often stood in his way, and baffled his mischievous designs against the saints. See here, 1. How he *misquoted* it; and that was *bad.* The promise is, They shall *keep thee*; but how? *In all thy ways*; not otherwise; if we go *out of our way,* out of the way of our duty, we forfeit the promise, and put ourselves out of God's protection. If Christ had *cast himself down,* he had been *out of his way,* for he had no call so to expose himself. 2. How he *misapplied* it; and that was *worse.* Scripture is abused when it is pressed to patronize sin; and when men thus wrest it to their own temptation, they do it to *their own destruction,* 2 Pet. iii. 16. This promise is firm, and stands good; but the devil made an ill use of it, when he used it as an encouragement to presume upon the divine care.

(2) How Christ overcame this temptation; he resisted and overcame it, as he did the former, with, *It is written.* The devil's *abusing* of scripture did not prevent Christ

from using it, but he immediately urges, Deut. vi. 16, *Thou shalt not tempt the Lord thy God.* Satan said, *It is written*; Christ says, *It is written*; not that one scripture contradicts another. God is one, and his word one, and he in one mind, but that is a promise, this is a precept, and therefore that is to be explained and applied by this; for scripture is the best interpreter of scripture; and they who prophesy, who expound scripture, must do it according to the proportion of faith (Rom. xii. 6), consistently with practical godliness.

If Christ should *cast himself down,* it would be the tempting of God, [1] As it would be *requiring a further confirmation* of that which was so well confirmed. [2] As it would be *requiring a special preservation* of him, in doing that which he had no call to. If we expect that because God has promised not to forsake us, therefore he should follow us out of the way of our duty; that because he has promised to supply our wants, therefore he should humour us, and please our fancies; that because he has promised to keep us, we may wilfully thrust ourselves into danger, and may expect the desired end, without using the appointed means; this is presumption, this is tempting God.

3. He tempted him to the most *black and horrid idolatry,* with the offer of the *kingdoms of the world, and the glory of them.*

In this temptation, we may observe,

[1] What he *showed him—all the kingdoms of the world.* In order to this, he took him to an *exceeding high mountain*; in hopes of prevail-

ing, as Balak with Balaam, he changed his ground. Hence observe, concerning *Satan's temptations*, that, *First*, They often *come in at the eye*, which is blinded to the things it should see, and dazzled with the vanities it should be turned from. The first sin began in the eye, Gen. iii. 6. We have therefore need to make a covenant with our eyes, and to pray that God would *turn them away from beholding vanity*. *Secondly*, That temptations commonly take rise from the world, and the things of it. The *lust of the flesh*, and of *the eye*, with the *pride of life*, are the topics from which the devil fetches most of his arguments. *Thirdly*, That it is a *great cheat* which the devil puts upon poor souls, in his temptations. He deceives, and so destroys; he imposes upon men with shadows and false colours; shows the world and the glory of it, and hides from men's eyes the sin and sorrow and death which stain the pride of all this glory, the cares and calamities which attend great possessions, and the thorns which crowns themselves are lined with. *Fourthly*, That the *glory of the world* is the most *charming* temptation to the *unthinking* and *unwary*, and that by which men are most imposed upon.

[2] What he *said to him* (v. 9); *All these things will I give thee, if thou wilt fall down and worship me*. See, *First*, How *vain the promise* was. *All these things will I give thee*. He seems to take it for granted, that in the former temptations he had in part gained his point, and proved that Christ was not the *Son of God*, because he had not given him those evidences of it which he demanded;

so that here he looks upon him as a mere man. The fallacy of this promise lies in that, *All this will I give thee*. And what was *all that*? It was but a map, a picture, a mere fantasy, that had nothing in it real or solid, and this he would give him; a goodly prize! Yet such are Satan's offers. The *nations of the earth* had been, long before, promised to the Messiah; if he be *the Son of God*, they belong to him; Satan pretends now to be a good angel, probably one of those that were set over kingdoms, and to have received a commission to deliver possession to him according to promise.

Secondly, How *vile* the *condition* was; *If thou will fall down, and worship me*. Note, The devil is fond of being worshipped. All the worship which the heathen performed to their gods, was directed to the devil (Deut. xxxii. 17), who is therefore called the *god of this world*, 2 Cor. iv. 4; 1 Cor. x. 20. What temptation could be more hideous, more black?

4. See how Christ warded off the thrust, baffled the assault, and came off a conqueror. He rejected the proposal,

[1] With *abhorrence* and *detestation*; *Get thee hence, Satan*. The two former temptations had something of colour, which would admit of a consideration, but this was so gross as not to bear a parley; it appears abominable at the first sight, and therefore is immediately rejected. Some temptations have their wickedness written in their forehead, they are open before-hand; they are not to be disputed with, but rejected; "*Get thee hence,*

Satan. Away with it, I cannot bear the thought of it!" Note, It is good to be *peremptory* in resisting temptation, and to *stop our ears* to Satan's charms.

[2] With an argument fetched from scripture. The argument is very suitable, and exactly to the purpose, taken from Deut. vi. 13, and x. 20. *Thou shalt worship the Lord thy God, and him only shalt thou serve.* Christ does not dispute whether he were an angel of light, as he pretended, or not; but though he were, yet he must not be worshipped, because that is an honour due to God only. Our Saviour has recourse to the fundamental law in this case, which is indispensable, and universally obligatory. Religious worship is due to God only, and must not be given to any creature; it is a flower of the crown which cannot be alienated, a branch of God's glory which he will not give to another, and which he would not give to his own Son, by obliging all men to *honour the Son, even as they honour the Father*, if he had not been God, *equal to him*, and *one with him*.

V. We have here the end and issue of this combat, *v.* 11. Though the children of God may be exercised with many and great temptations, yet God will not suffer them to be tempted above the strength which either they have, or he will put into them, 1 Cor. x. 13. It is but for a season that they are in heaviness, through manifold temptations.

Now the issue was glorious, and much to Christ's honour: for,

1. The devil was baffled, and quitted the field; *Then the devil*

leaveth him, forced to do so by the power that went along with that word of command, *Get thee hence, Satan*. He made a shameful and inglorious retreat, and came off with disgrace.

2. The holy angels came and attended upon our victorious Redeemer; *Behold, angels came and ministered unto him.* They came in a visible appearance, as the devil had done in the temptation. It is worth taking notice of: (1) That as there is a world of wicked, malicious spirits that fight against Christ and his church, and all particular believers, so there is a world of holy, blessed spirits engaged and employed for them. In reference to our *war with devils*, we may take abundance of comfort from our *communion with angels*. (2) That Christ's victories are the angels' triumphs. (3) That the angels ministered to the Lord Jesus, not only food, but whatever else he wanted after this great fatigue. See how the instances of Christ's condescension and humiliation were balanced with tokens of his glory.

Lastly, Christ, having been thus signalized and made great in the invisible world by the voice of the Father, the descent of the Spirit, his victory over devils, and his dominion over angels, was doubtless qualified to appear in the visible world as the Mediator between God and man; for *consider how great this man was!*

PREACHING IN GALILEE
(*vv.* 12–17)

We have here an account of Christ's preaching in the synagogues of Galilee, for he came into the world to be a Preacher; the great salvation which he wrought out, he himself began to publish (Heb. ii. 3) to show how much his heart *was* upon it, and ours *should* be.

I. The time; *When Jesus had heard that John was cast into prison*, then he *went into Galilee*, v. 12. Note, The cry of the saints' sufferings comes up into the ears of the Lord Jesus. If John be cast into prison, Jesus hears it, takes cognizance of it, and steers his course accordingly: *he remembers the bonds* and afflictions that abide his people. Observe, 1. Christ did *not* go into the country, *till he heard of* John's imprisonment; for he must have time given him to *prepare the way of the Lord*, before the Lord himself appear. Providence wisely ordered it, that John should be *eclipsed* before Christ *shone forth*; otherwise the minds of people would have been distracted between the two; one would have said, *I am of John*, and another, *I am of Jesus*. John must be Christ's harbinger, but not his rival.

II. The place where he preached; in Galilee, a remote part of the country, that lay furthest from Jerusalem, and was there looked upon with contempt, as rude and boorish. The inhabitants of that country were reckoned stout men, fit for soldiers, but not polite men, or fit for scholars. Thither Christ went, there he set up the standard of his gospel; and in this, as in other things, he humbled himself. Observe,

1. The particular city he chose for his residence; not Nazareth, where he had been bred up; no, he left Nazareth; but he *came and dwelt in Capernaum*, which was a city of Galilee, but many miles distant from Nazareth, a great city and of much resort. Capernaum is glad of Nazareth's leavings. If Christ's own countrymen be not˙gathered, yet he will be glorious. "And thou, Capernaum, hast now a day of it; thou art now lifted up to heaven; be wise for thyself, and know the time of thy visitation."

2. The prophecy that was fulfilled in this, *vv.* 14–16. It is quoted from Isa. ix. 1, 2, but with some variation. The punishment of the Jewish nation for rejecting the gospel should be sorer than either (see Isa. viii. 21, 22); for those captivated places had some reviving in their bondage, and saw a great light again, *ch.* ix. 2. This is Isaiah's sense; but the Scripture has many fulfillings; and the evangelist here takes only the latter clause, which speaks of the return of the light of liberty and prosperity to those countries that had been in the darkness of captivity, and applies it to the appearing of the gospel among them.

III. The text he preached upon (*v.* 17): *From that time*, that is, from the time of his coming into Galilee, into the land of Zebulun and Naphtali, from that time, he began to preach. He had been preaching, before this, in Judea, and had made and baptized many disciples (John iv. 1); but his preaching was not so public and constant as now it began to be. The work of the ministry is so great and awful, that it is fit to be entered upon by steps and gradual advances.

The subject which Christ dwelt upon now in his preaching (and it was indeed the sum and substance of all his preaching), was the very same that John had preached upon (*ch.* iii. 2); *Repent, for the kingdom of heaven is at hand*; for the gospel is the same for substance under various dispensations; the commands the same, and the reasons to enforce them the same; an *angel from heaven* dares not preach any other gospel (Gal. i. 8), and will preach this, for it is the *everlasting gospel. Fear God, and,* by repentance, *give honour to him,* Rev. xiv. 6, 7. *Repent, for the kingdom of heaven is at hand.* [1] This he preached *first* upon; he began with this. As John prepared Christ's way, so Christ prepared his own, and made way for the further discoveries he designed, with the doctrine of repentance. [2] This he preached *often* upon; wherever he went, this was his subject, and neither he nor his followers ever reckoned it worn threadbare, as those would have done, that have *itching ears,* and are fond of novelty and variety more than that which is truly edifying. Note, That which has been preached and heard before, may yet very profitably be preached and heard again; but then it should be preached and heard better, and with new affections; what Paul had said before, he said again, *weeping,* Phil. iii. 1, 18. [3] This he preached as gospel; "Repent, review your ways, and return to yourselves." Note, The doctrine of repentance is right gospel-doctrine. Not only the austere Baptist, who was looked upon as a melancholy, morose man, but

the sweet and gracious Jesus, whose lips dropped as a honey-comb, preached repentance; for it is an unspeakable privilege that room is left for repentance. [4] The reason is still the same; The *kingdom of heaven is at hand*; for it was not reckoned to be fully come, till the pouring out of the Spirit after Christ's ascension.

FOUR DISCIPLES CALLED
(*vv.* 18–22)

When Christ began to preach, he began to *gather disciples,* who should now be the *hearers,* and hereafter the *preachers,* of his doctrine, who should now be witnesses *of* his miracles, and hereafter *concerning* them. Now, in these verses, we have an account of the first disciples that he called into fellowship with himself.

And this was an instance, 1. Of *effectual calling* to Christ. In all his preaching he gave a common call to all the country, but in this he gave a special and particular call to those that were given him by the Father. 2. It was an instance of *ordination,* and appointment to the work of the ministry. When Christ, as a Teacher, set up his great school, one of his first works was to appoint ushers, or under masters, to be employed in the work of instruction. Now he began to give gifts unto men, to put the treasure into earthen vessels. It was an early instance of his care for his church.

Now we may observe here,

I. *Where* they were called—by the *sea of Galilee,* where Jesus was walking, Capernaum being situated near that sea. Galilee was a remote part of the nation, the inhabitants

27

were less cultivated and refined, their very language was broad and uncouth to the curious, their *speech betrayed them*. They who were picked up at the sea of Galilee, had not the advantages and improvements, no, not of the more polished Galileans; yet thither Christ went, to call his apostles that were to be the prime ministers of state in his kingdom, for he *chooses the foolish things of the world, to confound the wise*.

II. *Who* they were. We have an account of the call of two pairs of brothers in these verses—Peter and Andrew, James and John; the two former, and, probably, the two latter also, had had acquaintance with Christ before (John i. 40, 41), but were not till now called into a close and constant attendance upon him. We may observe concerning them,

1. That they were *brothers*. Note, It is a blessed thing, when they who are *kinsmen according to the flesh* (as the apostle speaks, Rom. ix. 3), are brought together into a spiritual alliance to Jesus Christ.

2. That they were *fishers*. Being fishers, (1) They were *poor men*: if they had had estates, or any considerable stock in trade, they would not have made fishing their trade, however they might have made it their recreation. (2) They were *unlearned men*. Note, Christ sometimes chooses to endow those with the gifts of grace who have least to show of the gifts of nature. (3) They were *men of business*, who had been bred up to labour. Note, Diligence in an honest calling is pleasing to Christ, and no hindrance to a holy life. (4) They were men that were

accustomed to *hardships* and hazards. Note, Those who have learned to bear hardships, and to run hazards, are best prepared for the fellowship and discipleship of Jesus Christ. Good soldiers of Christ must endure hardness.

III. *What they were doing*. Peter and Andrew were then using their nets, they were fishing; and James and John were *mending their nets*, which was an instance of their industry and good husbandry.

IV. *What the call was* (v. 19); *Follow me, and I will make you fishers of men*. They had followed Christ before, as ordinary disciples (John i. 37), but so they might follow Christ, and follow their calling too; therefore they were called to a more close and constant attendance, and must leave their calling. Note, Even they who have been called to follow Christ, have need to be called to follow on, and to follow nearer, especially when they are designed for the work of the ministry. Observe,

1. What Christ intended them for; *I will make you fishers of men*; this alludes to their former calling. Note, (1) Ministers are *fishers of men*, not to destroy them, but to save them, by bringing them into another element. They must fish, not for wrath, wealth, honour, and preferment, to gain them to themselves, but for souls, to gain them to Christ. *They watch for your souls* (Heb. xiii. 17), *and seek not yours, but you*, 2 Cor. xii. 14, 16. (2) It is Jesus Christ that makes them so; *I will make you fishers of men*. It is he that qualifies men for this work, calls them to it, authorizes them in it, and gives them success in it;

gives them commission to fish for souls, and wisdom to win them. Those ministers are likely to have comfort in their work, who are thus made by Jesus Christ.

2. What they must do to achieve this; *Follow me.* They must separate themselves to a diligent attendance on him, and set themselves to a humble imitation of him; must follow him as their Leader. Note, (1) Those whom Christ employs in any service for him, must first be fitted and qualified for it. (2) Those who would *preach Christ*, must first *learn* Christ, and learn of him.

V. What was the *success* of this call. Peter and Andrew *straightway left their nets* (*v.* 20); and James and John *immediately left the ship and their father* (*v.* 22); *and they* all *followed him.* Note, Those who would follow Christ aright, must *leave all* to follow him. Now,

1. This instance of the power of the Lord Jesus gives us good encouragement to depend upon the sufficiency of his grace. How strong and effectual is his word! *He speaks, and it is done.*

2. This instance of the pliableness of the disciples, gives us a good example of obedience to the command of Christ. Being called, they obeyed, and, like Abraham, *went out not knowing whither they went,* but knowing very well whom they followed.

THE GREAT PHYSICIAN
(*vv.* 23–25)

See here, I. What an industrious preacher Christ was; He *went about all Galilee, teaching in their synagogues, and preaching the gospel of the kingdom. The kingdom of* *heaven,* that is, of grace and glory, is emphatically *the kingdom, the kingdom* that was now to come; that kingdom which shall survive, as it doth surpass, all the kingdoms of the earth. *The gospel* is the charter of that kingdom, containing the King's coronation oath, by which he has graciously obliged himself to pardon, protect, and save the subjects of that kingdom; it contains also their oath of allegiance, by which they oblige themselves to observe his statutes and seek his honour; this is *the gospel of the kingdom*; this Christ was himself the Preacher of, that our faith in it might be confirmed.

II. What a powerful physician Christ was; he *went about* not only *teaching,* but *healing,* and both with his word. *He sent his word, and healed them.* Now observe,

1. What diseases he cured—all without exception. He *healed all manner of sickness, and all manner of disease.*

None was too bad, none too hard, for Christ to heal with a word's speaking.

2. What patients he had. See here, what flocking there was to him from all parts; great multitudes of people came, not only *from Galilee* and the country about, but even *from Jerusalem* and *from Judea,* which lay a great way off; for *his fame went throughout all Syria,* not only among all the people of the Jews, but among the neighbouring nations.

Christ both *taught and healed.* They who came for cures, met with instruction concerning *the things that belonged to their peace.* It is well if any thing will bring people to Christ; and they who come to him will find more in him than they expected.

Now concerning the cures which Christ wrought, let us, once for all, observe the *miracle*, the *mercy*, and the *mystery*, of them.

(1) The *miracle* of them. They were wrought in such a manner, as plainly spake them to be the immediate products of a divine and supernatural power, and they were God's seal to his commission. He appeals to these as credentials, *ch.* xi. 4, 5; John v. 36. It was expected that the Messiah should work miracles (John vii. 31); miracles of this nature (Isa. xxxv. 5, 6); and we have this indisputable proof of his being the Messiah; never was there any man that did thus; and therefore his healing and his preaching generally went together, for the former confirmed the latter; thus here he *began to* do *and to* teach, Acts i. 1.

(2) The *mercy* of them. The miracles that Moses wrought, to prove his mission, were most of them plagues and judgments, to intimate the terror of that dispensation, though from God; but the miracles that Christ wrought, were most of them cures, and all of them (except the cursing of the barren fig-tree) blessings and favours; for the gospel dispensation is founded, and built up in love, and grace, and sweetness.

(3) The *mystery* of them. Christ, by curing *bodily diseases*, intended to show, that his great errand into the world was to cure *spiritual maladies*. He is the *Sun of righteousness*, that *arises with* this *healing under his wings*. As the Converter of sinners, he is the *Physician of souls*, and has taught us to call him so, *ch.* ix. 12, 13. Sin is the *sickness*, *disease*, and *torment* of the soul; Christ *came to take away sin*, and so to heal these.

CHAPTER FIVE

THE SERMON ON THE MOUNT:
THE PREACHER, THE PEOPLE
(*vv.* 1, 2)

We have here a general account of this sermon.

I. *The Preacher* was our Lord Jesus, the Prince of preachers, the great Prophet of his church, who *came into the world*, to be *the Light of the world*. His text was, *Repent, for the kingdom of heaven is at hand*. This is a sermon on the former part of that text, showing what it is to *repent*; it is to reform, both in judgment and practice; and he here tells us wherein, in answer to that question (Mal. iii. 7), *Wherein shall we return?* He afterward preached upon the latter part of the text, when, in various parables, he showed what the kingdom of heaven is like, *ch.* xiii.

II. *The place* was a mountain in Galilee. As in other things, so in this, our Lord Jesus was but ill accommodated; he had no convenient place to preach in, any more than *to lay his head* on. By which Christ would intimate that there is no such distinguishing holiness of places now, under the gospel, as there was under the law; but that it is *the will of God that men should pray* and preach *every where*, any where, provided it be decent and convenient.

III. *The hearers* were *his disciples*, who *came unto him*; came at his call, as appears by comparing Mark iii. 13, Luke vi. 13. To them he directed his speech, because they followed him for love and learning, while others attended him only for cures. *He taught them*, because they were willing to be *taught* (*the meek will he teach his way*); because they would *understand* what he taught, which to others was foolishness; and because they were to teach others; and it was therefore requisite that they should have a clear and distinct knowledge of these things themselves. But though this discourse was directed to the disciples, it was in the hearing of *the multitude*; for it is said (*ch.* vii. 28), *The people were astonished*. No bounds were set about *this mountain*, to keep the people off, as were about *mount Sinai* (Exod. xix. 12); for, through Christ, we have access to God, not only to speak to him, but to hear from him. Nay, he had an eye to *the multitude*, in preaching this sermon. When the fame of his miracles had brought a vast crowd together, he took the opportunity of so great a confluence of people, to instruct them.

IV. *The solemnity* of his sermon is intimated in that word, *when he was set*. Christ preached many times occasionally, and by interlocutory discourses; but this was a set sermon, when he had placed himself so as to be best heard. He sat down as a Judge or Lawgiver.

THE BEATITUDES (*vv.* 3–12)

Christ begins his sermon with blessings, for *he came into the world to bless us* (Acts iii. 26). The Old Testament ended with a curse (Mal. iv. 6), the gospel begins with a blessing; for *hereunto are we called, that we should inherit the blessing*. Each of the blessings Christ here pronounces has a double intention: 1. To show who they are that are to be accounted truly happy, and what their characters are. 2. What that is wherein true happiness consists, in the promises made to persons of certain characters, the performance of which will make them happy. Now,

1. This is designed to rectify the ruinous mistakes of a blind and carnal world. The general opinion is, *Blessed are they* that are rich, and great, and honourable in the world. Now our Lord Jesus comes to correct this fundamental error, to advance a new hypothesis, and to give us quite another notion of blessedness and blessed people, which, however paradoxical it may appear to those who are prejudiced, yet is in itself, and appears to be to all who are savingly enlightened, a rule and doctrine of eternal truth and certainty, by which we must shortly be judged.

2. It is designed to remove the discouragements of the weak and poor who receive the gospel, by assuring them that his gospel did not make only those happy that were eminent in gifts, graces, comforts, and usefulness.

3. It is designed to invite souls to Christ, and to make way for his law into their hearts. Christ pronounced these blessings, not at the end of his sermon, to dismiss the people, but at the beginning of it, to prepare them for what he had further to say to them.

Our Saviour here gives us eight characters of blessed people; which represent to us the principal graces of a Christian. On each of them a present blessing is pronounced; *Blessed are* they; and to each a future blessedness is promised, which is variously expressed, so as to suit the nature of the grace or duty recommended.

Do we ask then who are happy? It is answered,

I. *The poor in spirit* are happy, *v.* 3. There is a poor-spiritedness that is so far from making men blessed that it is a sin and a snare—cowardice and base fear, and a willing subjection to the lusts of men. But this poverty of spirit is a gracious disposition of soul, by which we are emptied of self, in order to our being filled with Jesus Christ. To be *poor in spirit* is, 1. To be contentedly poor, willing to be empty of worldly wealth, if God orders that to be our lot. 2. It is to be humble and lowly in our own eyes. To be *poor in spirit*, is to think meanly of ourselves, of what we are, and have, and do; the poor are often taken in the Old Testament for the humble and self-denying, as opposed to those that are at ease, and the proud; it is to be as little children in our opinion of ourselves, weak, foolish, and insignificant, *ch.* xviii. 4; xix. 14. It is to look with a holy contempt upon ourselves, to value others and undervalue ourselves in comparison of them. It is to be willing to make ourselves cheap, and mean, and little, to do good; to *become all things to all men*. It is to acknowledge that God is great, and we are mean; that he is holy and we are sinful; that he is

all and we are nothing, less than nothing, worse than nothing; and to humble ourselves before him, and under his mighty hand. 3. It is to come off from all confidence in our own righteousness and strength, that we may depend only upon the merit of Christ for our justification, and the spirit and grace of Christ for our sanctification.

Now, (1) This poverty in spirit is put first among the Christian graces. The philosophers did not reckon humility among their moral virtues, but Christ puts it first.

(2) They are *blessed.* Now they are so, in this world. God looks graciously upon them. They are his little ones, and have their angels. To them he gives more grace; they live the most comfortable lives, and are easy to themselves and all about them, and nothing comes amiss to them; while high spirits are always uneasy.

(3) *Theirs is the kingdom of heaven.* The kingdom of *grace* is composed of such; they only are fit to be members of Christ's church, which is called *the congregation of the poor* (Ps. lxxiv. 19); the kingdom of *glory* is prepared for them.

II. *They that mourn* are happy (*v.* 4); *Blessed are they that mourn.* This is another strange blessing, and fitly follows the former. The poor are accustomed to mourn, the graciously poor mourn graciously. We are apt to think, Blessed are the *merry*; but Christ, who was himself a great mourner, says, Blessed are the *mourners*. There is a sinful mourning, which is an enemy to blessedness—*the sorrow of the world*. There is a natural mourning, which may prove a friend to blessedness, by the grace of God working with it, and sanctifying the afflictions to us, for which we mourn. But there is a gracious mourning, which qualifies for blessedness. 1. A penitential mourning for our own sins; this is *godly sorrow*, a sorrow according to God; sorrow for sin, with an eye to Christ, Zech. xii. 10. 2. A sympathizing mourning for the afflictions of others; the mourning of those who *weep with them that weep*, are sorrowful *for the solemn assemblies, for the desolations of Zion* (Zeph. iii. 18; Ps. cxxxvii. 1), especially who look with compassion on perishing souls, and *weep over* them, as Christ *over Jerusalem*.

Now these gracious mourners, (1) *Are blessed*, for they are like the Lord Jesus, who *was a man of sorrows*, and of whom we never read that he laughed, but often that he wept. (2) *They shall be comforted*. Though perhaps they are not immediately comforted, yet plentiful provision is made for their comfort; light is sown for them; and in heaven, it is certain, *they shall be comforted*, as Lazarus, Luke xvi. 25.

III. *The meek* are happy (*v.* 5); *Blessed are the meek*. The meek are those who quietly submit themselves to God, to his word and to his rod, who follow his directions, and comply with his designs, and are *gentle towards all men* (Tit. iii. 2); who can bear provocation without being inflamed by it; are either silent, or return a soft answer; who can be cool when others are hot; and in their patience keep possession of their own souls, when they can scarcely keep possession of any thing else.

They are the meek, who are rarely and hardly provoked, but quickly and easily pacified; and who would rather forgive twenty injuries than revenge one, having the rule of their own spirits.

These meek ones are here represented as happy, even in this world. 1. They are *blessed*, for they are like the blessed Jesus, in that wherein particularly they are to learn of him, *ch.* xi. 29. They are *blessed*, for they have the most comfortable, undisturbed enjoyment of themselves, their friends, their God; they are fit for any relation, any condition, any company; fit to live, and fit to die. 2. *They shall inherit the earth*; it is quoted from Ps. xxxvii. 11, and it is almost the only express temporal promise in all the New Testament. Meekness, however ridiculed and run down, has a real tendency to promote our health, wealth, comfort, and safety, even in this world. *The meek* and quiet are observed to live the most easy lives, compared with the froward and turbulent.

IV. *They that hunger and thirst after righteousness* are happy, *v.* 6. 1. *Righteousness* is here put for all spiritual blessings. See Ps. xxiv. 5; *ch.* vi. 33. They are purchased for us by *the righteousness of Christ*; conveyed and secured by the imputation of that righteousness to us; and confirmed by the faithfulness of God. 2. These we must *hunger and thirst after*. We must truly and really desire them, as one who is hungry and thirsty desires meat and drink. *Hunger and thirst* are appetites that return frequently, and call for fresh satisfactions; so these holy desires rest not in any thing attained, but are carried out toward renewed pardons, and daily fresh supplies of grace.

Those who thus *hunger and thirst* after spiritual blessings, *are blessed* in those desires, and *shall be filled* with those blessings.

V. The *merciful* are happy, *v.* 7. This, like the rest, is a paradox; for the merciful are not taken to be the wisest, nor are likely to be the richest; yet Christ pronounces them *blessed*. Those are the *merciful*, who are piously and charitably inclined to pity, help, and succour persons in misery. We must not only bear our own afflictions patiently, but we must, by Christian sympathy, partake of the afflictions of our brethren; pity must be shown (Job vi. 14), and *bowels of mercy put on* (Col. iii. 12).

Now, as to the merciful, 1. They are *blessed*; so it was said in the Old Testament; *Blessed is he that considers the poor*, Ps. xli. 1. Herein they resemble God, whose goodness is his glory; in being *merciful as he is merciful*, we are, in our measure, *perfect as he is perfect*. One of the purest and most refined delights in this world, is that of *doing good*. In this word, *Blessed are the merciful*, is included that saying of Christ, which otherwise we find not in the gospels, *It is more blessed to give than to receive*, Acts xx. 35. 2. *They shall obtain mercy*; mercy *with men*, when they need it; *he that watereth, shall be watered also himself* (we know not how soon we may stand in need of kindness, and therefore should be kind); but especially mercy *with God*, for *with the merciful he will show himself merciful*, Ps. xviii. 25.

VI. The *pure in heart* are happy (*v.* 8); *Blessed are the pure in heart, for they shall see God*. This is the most comprehensive of all the beatitudes; here holiness and happiness are fully described and put together.

1. Here is the most *comprehensive character* of the blessed; they are the *pure in heart*. Note, True religion consists in heart-purity. Those who are inwardly pure, show themselves to be under the power of *pure and undefiled* religion. True Christianity lies in the heart, in the *purity of the heart*; the *washing* of that *from wickedness*, Jer. iv. 14. We must lift up to God, not only clean hands, but a pure heart, Ps. xxiv. 4, 5; 1 Tim. i. 5. *Create in me such a clean heart, O God!*

2. Here is the most *comprehensive comfort* of the blessed; They shall see God. Note, (1) It is the perfection of the soul's happiness to *see God; seeing him*, as we may by faith in our present state, is a *heaven upon earth*; and seeing him as we shall in the future state, is the *heaven of heaven*. (2) The happiness of seeing God is promised to those, and those only, who are *pure in heart*. None but the *pure* are capable of *seeing* God, nor would it be a felicity to the impure. What pleasure could an unsanctified soul take in the vision of a holy God? As *he* cannot endure to look upon their iniquity, so *they* cannot endure to look upon his purity.

VII. The *peace-makers* are happy, *v.* 9. The wisdom that is from above is first *pure*, and then *peaceable*; the blessed ones are *pure* toward God, and *peaceable* toward men; for with reference to both, conscience must be kept *void of offence*. The *making of peace* is sometimes a *thankless office*, and it is the lot of him who parts a fray, to have *blows on both sides*; yet it is a good office, and we must be forward to it. Some think that this is intended especially as a lesson for ministers, who should do all they can to reconcile those who are at variance, and to promote Christian love among those under their charge.

Now, (1) Such persons are *blessed*; for they have the satisfaction of *enjoying themselves*, by keeping the peace, and of being truly serviceable to others, by disposing them to peace. They are working together with Christ, who came into the world to *slay all enmities*, and to proclaim *peace on earth*. (2) *They shall be called the children of God*; it will be an evidence to themselves that they are so; God will own them as such, and herein they will resemble him. The children of this world love to fish in troubled waters, but the children of God are the peacemakers, the *quiet in the land*.

VIII. Those who are *persecuted for righteousness' sake*, are happy. This is the greatest paradox of all, and peculiar to Christianity; and therefore it is put last, and more largely insisted upon than any of the rest, *vv*. 10–12. Observe here,

1. The case of suffering saints described; and it is a hard case, and a very piteous one.

(1) They are persecuted; hunted, pursued, run down, as dangerous beasts are, that are sought for to be destroyed. Christ has told us that it would be so with the Christian church, and we are not to think it

strange, 1 John iii. 13. He has left us an example.

(2) They are *reviled, and have all manner of evil said against them falsely*. Nicknames, and names of reproach, are fastened upon them, upon particular persons; sometimes to make them despicable, that they may be trampled upon; sometimes to make them formidable, that they may be powerfully assailed.

(3) All this is *for righteousness' sake* (*v*. 10); *for my sake*, *v*. 11. If for *righteousness' sake*, then for *Christ's sake*, for he is closely interested in the work of righteousness. This precludes those from this blessedness who suffer *justly*, and are evil spoken of *truly* for their real crimes; let such be ashamed and confounded, it is part of their punishment; it is not the suffering, but the cause, that makes the martyr.

2. The comforts of suffering saints laid down.

(1) They *are blessed*; for they now, in their life-time, receive *their evil things* (Luke xvi. 25), and receive them upon a good account. They are *blessed*, for it is an honour to them (Acts v. 41); it is an opportunity of glorifying Christ, of doing good, and of experiencing special comforts and visits of grace and tokens of his presence, 2 Cor. i. 5; Dan. iii. 25; Rom. viii. 29.

(2) They shall be *recompensed*; Theirs is *the kingdom of heaven*. They have at present a sure title to it, and sweet foretastes of it; and shall ere long be in possession of it.

(3) "*So persecuted they the prophets that were before you, v*." 12. They were *before you* in excellency,

above what you are yet arrived at; they were *before you* in time, that they might be examples to you of *suffering affliction* and *of patience*, James v. 10. They were in like manner persecuted and abused; and can you expect to go to heaven in a way by yourselves? That grace which was *sufficient for them*, to carry them through their sufferings, shall not be *deficient to you*.

(4) Therefore *rejoice and be exceeding glad*, v. 12. It is not enough to be patient and content under these sufferings - as under common afflictions, and not to render railing for railing; but we must rejoice, because the honour and dignity, the pleasure and advantage, of suffering for Christ, are much more considerable than the pain or shame of it.

SALT AND LIGHT (*vv.* 13–16)

Christ had lately called his disciples, and told them that they should be *fishers of men*; here he tells them further what he designed them to be —*the salt of the earth*, and *lights of the world*, that they might be indeed what it was expected they should be.

I. *Ye are the salt of the earth.* What could they do in so large a province as *the whole earth*? Nothing, if they were to work by force of arms and dint of sword; but, being to work silently as salt, one handful of that salt would diffuse its savour far and wide; would go a great way, and work insensibly and irresistibly as leaven, *ch.* xiii. 33. The doctrine of the gospel is as *salt*; it is penetrating, *buick*, and *powerful* (Heb. iv. 12); it reaches *the heart*, Acts ii. 37. It is

cleansing, it is relishing, and preserves from putrefaction.

If Christians be such as they should be they are *as good salt*, white, and small, and broken into many grains, but very useful and necessary. If they be not, they are as *salt* that has *lost its savour*. If you, who should season others, are yourselves unsavoury, void of spiritual life, relish, and vigour; if a Christian be so, especially if a minister be so, his condition is very sad; for *Wherewith shall it be salted?* Salt is a remedy .for *unsavoury meat*, but there is no remedy for *unsavoury salt*. Christianity will give a man a relish; but if a man can take up and continue the profession of it, and yet remain flat and foolish, and graceless and insipid, no other doctrine, no other means, can be applied, to make him savoury. If Christianity do not do it, nothing will.

II. *Ye are the light of the world*, v. 14. Christ calls himself *the Light of the world* (John viii. 12), and Christians are *workers together with him*, and have some of his honour put upon them.

This similitude is here explained in two things:

1. As *the lights of the world*, they are illustrious and conspicuous, and have many eyes upon them. A city that is *set on a hill cannot be hid.* The disciples of Christ, especially those who are forward and zealous in his service, become remarkable, and are taken notice of as beacons.

2. As the *lights of the world*, they are intended to illuminate and give light to others (*v.* 15), and therefore, (1) They shall be *set up* as lights. Christ having lighted these

candles, they shall not be put under a bushel, not confined always, as they are now, to the cities of Galilee, or the lost sheep of the house of Israel, but they shall be sent into all the world. (2) They must *shine* as lights, [1] By their *good preaching*. The knowledge they have, they must communicate for the good of others; not put it *under a bushel*, but spread it. [2] By their *good living*. They must be *burning and shining lights* (John v. 35); must evidence, in their whole manner of life, that they are indeed the followers of Christ, James iii. 13.

See here, *First, How* our light must shine. We must do good works *that may be seen* to the edification of others, but not *that they may be seen* to our own ostentation.

Secondly, For what *end* our light must shine—"That those who see your good works may be brought, not to glorify *you* (which was the thing the Pharisees aimed at, and it spoiled all their performances), but to *glorify your Father which is in heaven*." Note, The glory of God is the great thing we must aim at in every thing we do in religion, 1 Pet. iv. 11. The sight of our *good works* will do this, by furnishing them, 1. With *matter for praise*. "Let them see *your good works*, that they may see the power of God's grace in you, and may thank him for it, and give him the glory of it, who has given such power unto men." 2. With *motives to piety*. "Let them see your good works, that they may be convinced of the truth and excellency of the Christian religion, may be provoked by a holy emulation to imitate your good works, and so may glorify God."

THE OLD AND THE NEW LAW (*vv.* 17–32)

Those to whom Christ preached, and for whose use he gave these instructions to his disciples, were such as in their religion had an eye, 1. To the *scriptures* of the *Old Testament* as their *rule*, and therein Christ here shows them they were in the right: 2. To the scribes and Pharisees as their *example*, and therein Christ here shows them they were in the wrong; for,

I. The rule which Christ came to establish exactly agreed with the scriptures of the *Old Testament*, here called *the law* and *the prophets*.

1. He protests against the thought of cancelling and weakening the *Old Testament*; *Think not that I am come to destroy the law and the prophets*. The Saviour of souls is the *destroyer* of nothing but the *works of the devil*, of nothing that comes from God, much less of those excellent dictates which we have from Moses and the prophets. No, he came to *fulfil* them. That is, [1] To obey the commands of the law, for he was *made under the law*, Gal. iv. 4. He in all respects yielded obedience to the law, honoured his parents, sanctified the sabbath, prayed, gave alms, and did that which never any one else did, obeyed perfectly, and never broke the law in any thing. [2] To make good the promises of the law, and the predictions of the prophets, which all bore witness to him. [3] To answer the types of the law; thus (as Bishop Tillotson expresses it), he did not make *void*, but made

good, the ceremonial law, and manifested himself to be the Substance of all those shadows. [4] To fill up the defects of it, and so to complete and perfect it.

2. He asserts the perpetuity of it. "*Verily I say unto you*, I, the *Amen*, the faithful Witness, solemnly declare it, that *till heaven and earth pass*, when time shall be no more, and the unchangeable state of recompences shall supersede all laws, *one jot, or one tittle*, the least and most minute circumstance, *shall in no wise pass from the law till all be fulfilled*."

3. He gives it in charge to his disciples, carefully to preserve the law, and shows them the danger of the neglect and contempt of it (*v.* 19). It is a dangerous thing, in doctrine or practice, to dis-annul the least of God's commands; to break them, that is, to go about either to *contract the extent*, or *weaken the obligation* of them; whoever does so, will find it is at his peril. It is impudence enough to break the command, but it is a greater degree of it to teach men so (*v.* 19). This plainly refers to those who at this time sat in Moses' seat, and by their comments corrupted and perverted the text.

II. The righteousness which Christ came to establish by this rule, must exceed that of the scribes and Pharisees, *v.* 20. This was strange doctrine to those who looked upon the scribes and Pharisees as having arrived at the highest pitch of religion. The scribes were the most noted teachers of the law, and the Pharisees the most celebrated professors of it, and they both sat in Moses' chair

(*ch.* xxiii. 2). It was therefore a great surprise to hear that they must be better than they, or they should not go to heaven; and therefore Christ here avers it with solemnity; *I say unto you*, It is so. We must do more than they, and better than they, or we shall come short of heaven. They were *partial in the law*, and laid most stress upon the ritual part of it; but we must be *universal*, and not think it enough to give the priest his tithe, but must give God our hearts. They minded only the *outside*, but we must make conscience of *inside* godliness. They aimed at the *praise* and *applause of men*, but we must aim at *acceptance with God*: they were *proud* of what they did in religion, and trusted to it as *a righteousness*; but we, when we have done all, must *deny ourselves*, and say, We are *unprofitable servants*, and trust only to the *righteousness of Christ*; and thus we may go beyond the scribes and Pharisees.

THE SIXTH COMMANDMENT

Christ having laid down these principles, that Moses and the prophets were still to be their rulers, but that the scribes and Pharisees were to be no longer their rulers, proceeds to expound the law in some particular instances, and to vindicate it from the corrupt glosses which those expositors had put upon it. He adds nothing new, only limits and restrains some permissions which had been abused: and as to the precepts, shows the breadth, strictness, and spiritual nature of them. In these verses (*vv.* 21–26), he explains the law of the sixth commandment, according to the true intent and full extent of it.

Here is the *command itself* laid down (*v.* 12); *We have heard it*, and remember it. *Killing* is here forbidden, killing ourselves, killing any other, directly or indirectly, or being any way accessory to it. The law of God, the God of life, is a hedge of protection about our lives. It was one of the precepts of Noah, Gen. ix. 5, 6.

Here is the exposition of this command which the Jewish teachers contented themselves with; their comment upon it was, *Whosoever shall kill, shall be in danger of the judgment.* This was all they had to say upon it, that wilful murderers were liable to the sword of justice, and casual ones to the judgment of the city of refuge. Now this gloss of theirs upon this commandment was faulty, for it intimated, 1. That the law of the sixth commandment was only external, and forbade no more than the act of murder, and laid no restraint upon the inward lusts, from which *wars and fightings come.* This was indeed *the fundamental error* of the Jewish teachers, that the divine law prohibited only the sinful act, not the sinful thought. Another mistake of theirs was, that this law was merely *political* and *municipal*, given for them, and intended as a directory for their courts, and no more; as if they only were the people, and the wisdom of the law must die with them.

And here is the exposition which Christ gave of this commandment.

Christ tells them that *rash anger is heart-murder* (*v.* 22); *Whosoever is angry with his brother without a* *cause*, breaks the sixth commandment. Anger is a natural passion; there are cases in which it is lawful and laudable; but it is then *sinful*, when we are angry without cause.

2. He tells them, that giving opprobrious language to our brother is tongue-murder, calling him, *Raca*, and, *Thou fool.* When this is done with mildness and for a good end, to convince others of their vanity and folly, it is not sinful. Thus James says, *O vain man*; and Paul, *Thou fool*; and Christ himself, *O fools, and slow of heart.* But when it proceeds from anger and malice within, it is the smoke of that fire which is kindled from hell, and falls under the same character.

He tells them, that how light soever they made of these sins, they would certainly be reckoned for; he *that is angry with his brother shall be in danger of the judgment* and anger of God; he that calls him *Raca, shall be in danger of the council*, of being punished by the Sanhedrim for reviling an Israelite; *but whosoever saith, Thou fool*, thou profane person, thou child of hell, *shall be in danger of hell-fire*, to which he condemns his brother; so the learned Dr. Whitby.

From all this it is here inferred, that we ought carefully to preserve Christian love and peace with all our brethren, and that if at any time a breach happens, we should labour for a reconciliation, by confessing our fault, humbling ourselves to our brother, begging his pardon, and making restitution, or offering satisfaction for wrong done in word or deed, according as the nature of the thing is; and that we should do this quickly.

THE SEVENTH COMMANDMENT

We have (in *vv.* 27–32) an exposition of the seventh commandment, given us by the same hand that made the law, and therefore was fittest to be the interpreter of it: it is the law against uncleanness, which fitly follows upon the former; *that* laid a restraint upon sinful passions, *this* upon sinful appetites, both which ought always to be under the government of reason and conscience, and if indulged, are equally pernicious.

The command is here laid down (*v.* 17), *Thou shalt not commit adultery*; which includes a prohibition of all other acts of uncleanness, and the desire of them: but the Pharisees, in their expositions of this command, made it to extend no further than the act of adultery, suggesting, that if the iniquity was only *regarded in the heart*, and went no further, God could not hear it, would not regard it (Ps. lxvi. 18), and therefore they thought it enough to be able to say that they were *no adulterers*, Luke xviii. 11.

But we are here taught, that there is such a thing as *heart-adultery*, adulterous thoughts and dispositions, which never proceed to the act of adultery or fornication; and perhaps the defilement which these give to the soul, that is here so clearly asserted, was not only included in the seventh commandment, but was signified and intended in many of those ceremonial pollutions under the law, for which they were to *wash their clothes, and bathe their flesh in water. Whosoever looketh on a woman to lust after her,* has committed adultery with her in his heart, *v.* 28.

Such looks are so very dangerous and destructive to the soul, that it is better to lose the eye and the hand that thus offend than to give way to the sin, and perish eternally in it (*vv.* 29, 30).

There are some sins from which we need to be *saved with fear*, particularly *fleshly lusts*, which are such *natural brute beasts* as cannot be checked, but by being frightened; cannot be kept from a forbidden tree, but by *cherubim, with a flaming sword*.

Men's divorcing their wives upon dislike, or for any other cause except adultery, however tolerated and practised among the Jews, was a violation of the seventh commandment, as it opened a door to adultery, *vv.* 31, 32. Here observe,

(1) How the matter now stood with reference to divorce. *It hath been said* (he does not say as before, *It hath been said by them of old time*, because this was not a precept, as those were, though the Pharisees were willing so to understand it (*ch.* xix. 7), but only a permission), "*Whosoever shall put away his wife, let him give her a bill of divorce*". Thus the law had prevented rash and hasty divorces; and perhaps at first, when writing was not so common among the Jews, that made divorces rare things; but in process of time they became very common, and this direction how to do it, when there was just cause for it, was construed into a permission of it for any cause, *ch.* xix. 3.

(2) How this matter was rectified and amended by our Saviour. He

reduced the ordinance of marriage to its primitive institution: *They two shall be one flesh*, not to be easily separated, and therefore divorce is not to be allowed, except in case of adultery, which breaks the marriage covenant; but he that puts away his wife upon any other pretence, *causeth her to commit adultery*, and him also that shall marry her when she is thus divorced. Note, Those who lead others into temptation to sin, or leave them in it, or expose them to it, make themselves guilty of their sin, and will be accountable for it. This is one way of being *partaker with adulterers*, Ps. l. 18.

THE THIRD COMMANDMENT
(*vv.* 33–37)

We have here an exposition of the third commandment, which we are the more concerned rightly to understand, because it is particularly said, that *God will not hold him guiltless*, however he may hold himself, who breaks this commandment, by *taking the name of the Lord God in vain*. Now as to this command.

I. It is agreed on all hands that it forbids perjury, forswearing, and the violation of oaths and vows, *v.* 33. This was said to them of old time, and is the true intent and meaning of the third commandment. *Thou shall not* use, or *take up, the name of God* (as we do by an oath) *in vain*, or *unto vanity*, or *a lie*.

II. It is here added, that the commandment does not only forbid false swearing, but all rash, unnecessary swearing: *Swear not at all*, *v.* 34; Compare Jam. v. 12. Not that all swearing is sinful; so far

from that, if rightly done, it is a part of religious worship, and we in it *give unto God the glory due to his name*. See Deut. vi. 13; x. 20; Isa. xlv. 23; Jer. iv. 2. We find Paul confirming what he said by such solemnities (2 Cor. i. 23), when there was a necessity for it. In swearing, we pawn the truth of something known, to confirm the truth of something doubtful or unknown; we appeal to a greater knowledge, to a higher court, and imprecate the vengeance of a righteous Judge, if we swear deceitfully.

Now the mind of Christ in this matter is,

1. That we must *not swear at all*, but when we are duly called to it, and justice or charity to our brother, or respect to the commonwealth, make it necessary for *the end of strife* (Heb. vi. 16).

2. That we must not swear lightly and irreverently, in common discourse: it is a very great sin to make a ludicrous appeal to the glorious Majesty of heaven, which, being a sacred thing, ought always to be very serious.

3. That we must in a special manner avoid promissory oaths, of which Christ more particularly speaks here, for they are oaths that are to be performed. The influence of an affirmative oath immediately ceases, when we have faithfully discovered the truth, and the whole truth; but a promissory oath binds so long, and may be so many ways broken, by the surprise as well as strength of a temptation, that it is not to be used but upon great necessity.

4. That we must not swear by

any creature. It should seem there were some, who, in civility (as they thought) to the name of God, would not make use of that in swearing, but would swear *by heaven* or *earth*, &c. This Christ forbids here (*v.* 34), and shows that there is nothing we can swear by, but it is some way or other related to God, who is the Fountain of all beings, and therefore that it is as dangerous to swear by them, as it is to swear by God himself.

5. That therefore in all our communications we must content ourselves with, *Yea, yea,* and *Nay, nay,* *v.* 37. In ordinary discourse, if we affirm a thing, let us only say, *Yea,* it is so; and, if need be, to evidence our assurance of a thing, we may double it, and say, *Yea, yea,* indeed it is so: *Verily, verily,* was our Saviour's *yea, yea.* So if we deny a thing, let it suffice to say, No; or if it be requisite, to repeat the denial, and say, No, no; and if our fidelity be known, that will suffice to gain us credit; and if it be questioned, to back what we say with swearing and cursing, is but to render it more suspicious.

THE LAW OF RETALIATION
(*vv.* 38–42)

In these verses the law of retaliation is expounded, and in a manner repealed. Observe,

I. What the *Old Testament permission* was, in case of injury. It was not a command, that every one should of necessity require such satisfaction; but they might lawfully insist upon it, if they pleased; *an eye for an eye, and a tooth for a tooth.* This we find, Exod. xxi. 24; Lev. xxiv. 20; Deut. xix. 21.

But some of the Jewish teachers, who were not the most compassionate men in the world, insisted upon it as necessary that such revenge should be taken, even by private persons themselves, and that there was no room left for remission, or the acceptance of satisfaction.

II. What the *New Testament precept* is, as to the complainant himself, his duty is, to *forgive the injury* as done to himself, and no further to insist upon the punishment of it than is necessary to the public good: and this precept is consonant to the meekness of Christ, and the gentleness of his yoke.

Two things Christ teaches us here:

1. We must not be revengeful (*v.* 39); *I say unto you, that ye resist not evil;*—the evil person that is injurious to you. Yet this does not repeal the law of self-preservation, and the care we are to take of our families; we may *avoid evil,* and may *resist* it, so far as is necessary to our own security; but we must not *render evil for evil,* must not bear a grudge, nor avenge ourselves, nor study to be even with those that have treated us unkindly, but we must go beyond them by forgiving them, Prov. xx. 22; xxiv. 29; xxv. 21, 22. Rom. xii. 17.

Three things our Saviour specifies, to show that Christians must patiently yield to those who bear hard upon them, rather than contend; and these include others.

(1) A blow on the cheek, which is an injury to me in my body; *"Whosoever shall smite thee on thy right cheek,* which is not only a

hurt, but an affront and indignity (2 Cor. xi. 20), if a man in anger or scorn thus abuse thee, "*turn to him the other cheek*." Though this may perhaps, with some base spirits, expose us to the like affront another time, and so it is, in effect, to *turn the other cheek*, yet let not that disturb us, but let us trust God and his providence to protect us in the way of our duty. Perhaps, the forgiving of one injury may prevent another, when the avenging of it would but draw on another; some will be overcome by submission, who by resistance would but be the more exasperated, Prov. xxv. 22.

(2) The loss of a coat, which is a wrong to me in my estate (*v.* 40); *If any man will sue thee at the law, and take away thy coat.* It is a hard case. Though judges be just and circumspect, yet it is possible for bad men who make no conscience of oaths and forgeries, by course of law to force off the coat from a man's back. *Marvel not at the matter* (Eccl. v. 8), but, in such a case, rather than go to law by way of revenge, rather than exhibit a cross bill, or stand out to the utmost, in defence of that which is thy undoubted right, *let him* even take *thy cloak also.*

(3) The going a mile by constraint, which is a wrong to me in my liberty (*v.* 41); "*Whosoever shall compel thee to go a mile*, to run an errand for him, or to wait upon him, grudge not at it, but *go with him two miles* rather than fall out with him:" say not, "I would do it, if I were not compelled to it, but I hate to be forced;" rather say, "Therefore I will do it, for otherwise there will be a quarrel;" and it

is better to serve him, than to serve thy own lusts of pride and revenge.

The sum of all is, that Christians must not be litigious; small injuries must be submitted to, and no notice taken of them; and if the injury be such as requires us to seek reparation, it must be for a good end, and without thought of revenge: though we must not invite injuries, yet we must meet them cheerfully in the way of duty, and make the best of them.

2. We must be charitable and beneficent (*v.* 42); must not only do no hurt to our neighbours, but labour to do them all the good we can. What God says to us, we should be ready to say to our poor brethren, *Ask, and it shall be given you.*

THE LAW OF LOVE
(*vv.* 43–48)

We have here, lastly, an exposition of that great fundamental law, *Thou shalt love thy neighbour*, which was the fulfilling of the law.

I. See here how this law was corrupted by the comments of the Jewish teachers, *v.* 43. God said, *Thou shalt love thy neighbour*; and by *neighbour* they understood those only of their own country, nation, and religion; and those only that they were pleased to look upon as their friends: yet this was not the worst; from this command, *Thou shalt love thy neighbour*, they were willing to infer what God never designed; *Thou shalt hate thine enemy*; and they looked upon whom they pleased as their enemies, thus making void the great command of God by their traditions, though there were express laws to

the contrary, Exod. xxiii. 4, 5;
Deut. xxiii. 7.

II. See how it is cleared by the
command of the Lord Jesus, who
teaches us another lesson: *"But I
say unto you, I,* who come to be the
great Peace-Maker, the general
Reconciler, who loved you when
you were strangers and enemies, *I
say, Love your enemies," v.* 44.
We are here told,

1. That we must *speak* well of
them: *Bless them that curse you.*
They, in whose tongues is *the law
of kindness,* can give good words
to those who give bad words to
them.

2. That we must *do* well to them:
"Do good to them that hate you, and
that will be a better proof of love
than good words. Be ready to do
them all the real kindness that you
can, and glad of an opportunity to
do it, in their bodies, estates, names,
families; and especially to do good
to their souls."

3. We must *pray for them*: *Pray
for them that despitefully use you,
and persecute you.* We must pray
that God will forgive them, that
they may never fare the worse for
any thing they have done against
us, and that he would make them to
be at peace with us; and this is one
way of making them so.

Two reasons are here given to
enforce this command (which
sounds so harsh) of *loving our
enemies.* We must do it,

[1] That we may be *like God our
Father*; "that ye may be, may
approve yourselves to be, *the
children of your Father which is in
heaven."* Can we write after a
better copy? It is a copy in which
love to the worst of enemies is

reconciled to, and consistent with,
infinite purity and holiness.

[2] That we may herein *do more
than others, vv.* 46, 47. *First, Publicans love their friends.* Nature inclines them to it; interest directs
them to it. The publicans were men
of no good fame, yet they were
grateful to such as had helped them
to their places, and courteous to
those they had a dependence upon;
and shall we be no better than they?
In doing this we serve ourselves
and consult our own advantage;
and what reward can we expect for
that, unless a regard to God, and a
sense of duty, carry us further than
our natural inclination and worldly
interest? *Secondly,* We must therefore love our enemies, that we may
exceed them. If we must go beyond
scribes and Pharisees, much more
beyond publicans. Note, Christianity is something more than
humanity. We *know* more than
others; we *talk* more of the things
of God than others; we *profess,*
and have *promised,* more than
others; God has done more for us,
and therefore justly expects more
from us than from others; the glory
of God is more concerned in us
than in others; but *what do we more
than others?* In this especially we
must do more than others, that
while every one will render *good for
good,* we must render *good for evil*;
and this will speak a nobler
principle, and is consonant to a
higher rule, than the most of men
act by.

Lastly, Our Saviour concludes
this subject with this exhortation
(*v.* 48), *Be ye therefore perfect, as
your Father which is in heaven is
perfect.* Which may be understood,

1. In general, including all those things wherein we must be *followers of God as dear children.* Or, 2. In this particular before mentioned, of *doing good to our enemies*; see Luke vi. 36. It is God's perfection to *forgive injuries* and to *entertain strangers*, and to do good to the evil and unthankful, and it will be ours to be like him.

CHAPTER SIX
DOING ALMS (*vv.* 1–4)

As we must do better than the scribes and Pharisees in avoiding heart-sins, heart-adultery, and heart-murder, so likewise in maintaining and keeping up heart-religion, doing what we do from an inward, vital principle, that we may be approved of God, not that we may be applauded of men; that is, we must watch against hypocrisy, which was the leaven of the Pharisees, as well as against their doctrine, Luke xii. 1. *Almsgiving, prayer*, and *fasting*, are three great Christian duties—the three foundations of the law, say the Arabians: by them we do homage and service to God with our three principal interests; by *prayer* with our *souls*, by *fasting* with our *bodies*, by *alms-giving* with our *estates.*

Now in these verses we are cautioned against hypocrisy in giving alms.

Two things are here supposed,

I. The *giving of alms* is a great duty, and a duty which all the disciples of Christ, according to their ability, must abound in.

II. That it is such a duty as has a great reward attending it, which is lost if it be done in hypocrisy.

This being supposed, observe now,

1. What was the *practice of the hypocrites* about this duty. They did it indeed, but not from any principle of obedience to God, or love to man, but in pride and vain-glory. Not that it is unlawful to give alms *when men see us*; we may do it, we must do it, but not *that men may see us*; we should rather choose those objects of charity that are less observed. The hypocrites, if they gave alms at their own houses, *sounded a trumpet*, under pretence of calling the poor together to be served, but really to proclaim their charity, and to have that taken notice of and made the subject of discourse.

Now the judgment that Christ passes upon this is very observable; *Verily I say unto you, they have their reward.* At first view this seems a promise—If they have their reward they have enough, but two words in it make it a threatening.

(1) It is a reward, but it is *their* reward; not the reward which God promises to them that do good, but the reward which they promise themselves, and a poor reward it is.

(2) It is a reward, but it is a *present reward*, they *have* it; and there is none reserved for them in the future state.

2. What is the *precept of our Lord Jesus* about it, *vv.* 3, 4. He that was himself such an example of humility, pressed it upon his disciples, as absolutely necessary to the acceptance of their performances. "*Let not thy left hand know what thy right hand doeth* when thou givest alms." It is intimated,

(1) That we must not let *others* know what we do; no, not those that stand *at our left hand*, that are very near us. (2) That we must not observe it too much *ourselves*: the left hand is a part of ourselves; we must not within ourselves take notice too much of the good we do, must not applaud and admire ourselves.

3. What is the *promise to those who are thus sincere and humble* in their alms-giving. Let *thine alms be in secret*, and then *thy Father who seeth in secret* will observe them. But this is not all; not only the observation and praise, but the recompence is of God, *himself shall reward thee openly*. Observe how emphatically it is expressed; *himself shall reward*, he will himself be the Rewarder, Heb. xi. 6. If the work be not open, the reward shall, and that is better.

PRAYING (*vv.* 5-8)

In *prayer* we have more immediately to do with God than in *giving alms*, and therefore are yet more concerned to be *sincere*, which is what we are here directed to. *When thou prayest* (*v.* 5). It is taken for granted that all the disciples of Christ *pray*.

Now there were two great faults they were guilty of in prayer, against each of which we are here cautioned—vain-glory (*vv.* 5, 6); and vain repetitions, *vv.* 7, 8.

I. We must not be *proud* and *vain-glorious* in prayer, nor aim at the praise of men. In all their exercises of devotion, it was plain, the chief thing they aimed at was to be commended by their neigh-bours, and thereby to make an interest for themselves.

The *product* of all this is—*they have their reward*; they have all the recompence they must ever expect from God for their service, and a poor recompence it is. What will it avail us to have the good word of our fellow-servants, if our Master do not say, *Well done?*

What is the *will of Jesus Christ* in opposition to this? Humility and sincerity are the two great lessons that Christ teaches us.

Observe, (1) The directions here given about it.

[1] Instead of praying in *the synagogues* and in the *corners of the streets, enter into thy closet*, into some place of privacy and retirement.

[2] Instead of doing it to be *seen of men, pray to thy Father who is in secret; to me, even to me*, Zech. vii. 5, 6. By *secret* prayer we give God the glory of his universal presence (Acts xvii. 24), and may take to ourselves the comfort of it.

(2) The encouragements here given us to it.

[1] Thy Father *seeth in secret*; his eye is upon thee to accept thee, when the eye of no man is upon thee to applaud thee.

[2] He *will reward thee openly*; they have their reward that do it openly, and you shall not lose yours for doing it in secret. It is called a *reward*, but it is *of grace*, not *of debt*; what merit can there be in begging? The Pharisees had their reward *before all the town*, and it was a *mere flash and shadow*; true Christians shall have theirs *before all the world*, angels and men, and it shall be a *weight of glory*.

II. We must not *use vain repetitions* in prayer, *vv.* 7, 8. Now observe,

1. What the *fault* is that is here reproved and condemned; it is making a mere lip-labour of the duty of prayer, the service of the tongue, when it is not the service of the soul. This is expressed here by two phrases, (1) *Vain repetitions*— tautology, idle babbling over the same words again and again to no purpose. It is not all repetition in prayer that is here condemned, but vain repetitions. Christ himself prayed, saying the same words (*ch.* xxvi. 44), out of a more than ordinary fervour and zeal, Luke xxii. 44. But the superstitious rehearsing of a tale of words, or the barren and dry going over of the same things again and again, merely to drill out the prayer to such a length, and to make a show of affection when really there is none; these are the vain repetitions here condemned. (2) *Much speaking*, an affectation of prolixity in prayer, either out of pride or superstition, or an opinion that God needs either to be informed or argued with by us, or out of mere folly and impertinence, because men love to *hear themselves talk.* Not that all long prayers are forbidden; Christ prayed all night, Luke vi. 12. But merely to prolong the prayer, as if that would make it more pleasing or more prevailing with God, is that which is here condemned; it is not much *praying* that is condemned; no, we are bid to *pray always,* but much *speaking*.

2. What reasons are given against this.

(1) This is the way of the heathen, *as the heathen do*; and it ill becomes Christians to worship their God as the Gentiles worship theirs.

(2) "It need not be your way, *for your Father* in heaven *knoweth what things ye have need of before ye ask him.*" Consider, [1] The God we pray to is our Father by creation, by covenant; and therefore our addresses to him should be easy, natural, and unaffected; children do not use to make long speeches to their parents when they want anything. [2] He is a Father that knows our case and knows our wants better than we do ourselves. We need not be long, nor use many words in representing our case; God knows it better than we can tell him, only he will know it *from us* (*what will ye that I should do unto you?*).

THE LORD'S PRAYER
(*vv.* 9–15)

When Christ had condemned what was amiss, he directs to do better; for his are reproofs of instruction. Because we know not what to pray for as we ought, he here helps our infirmities, by putting words into our mouths; *after this manner therefore pray ye, v.* 9. Not that we are tied up to the use of this form only, or of this always, as if this were necessary to the consecrating of our other prayers; we are here bid to pray after this manner, with these words, or to this effect.

The Lord's prayer (as indeed every prayer) is a letter sent from earth to heaven. Here is the inscription of the letter, the person to whom it is directed, *our Father*; the place where, *in heaven*; the contents of it in several errands of request; the close, *for thine is the kingdom*; the seal, *Amen*; and if you will, the date too, *this day*.

Plainly thus: there are three parts of the prayer.

I. *The preface, Our Father who art in heaven*. Before we come to our business, there must be a solemn address to him with whom our business lies; *Our Father*.

1. We must address ourselves to him as *our Father*, and must call him so. He is a common Father to all mankind by creation, Mal. ii. 10; Acts xvii. 28. He is in a special manner a Father to the saints, by adoption and regeneration (Eph. i. 5; Gal. iv. 6); and an unspeakable privilege it is.

2. As our Father *in heaven*: so in heaven as to be every where else, for the heaven cannot contain him; yet so in heaven as there to manifest his glory, for it is his throne (Ps. ciii. 19), and it is to believers a throne of grace: thitherward we must direct our prayers, for Christ the Mediator is now in heaven, Heb. viii. 1.

II. *The petitions*, and those are six; the three first relating more immediately to God and his honour, the three last to our own concerns, both temporal and spiritual.

1. *Hallowed be thy name*. It is the same word that in other places is translated *sanctified*. In these words, (1) We give glory to God; it may be taken not as a petition, but as an adoration. We must begin our prayers with praising God, and it is very fit he should be first served, and that we should give glory to God, before we expect to receive

mercy and grace from him. (2) We fix our end, and it is the right end to be aimed at, and ought to be our chief and ultimate end in all our petitions, that God may be glorified; all our other requests must be in subordination to this, and in pursuance of it.

2. *Thy kingdom come*. This petition has plainly a reference to the doctrine which Christ preached at this time, which John Baptist had preached before, and which he afterwards sent his apostles out to preach—*the kingdom of heaven is at hand*. What God has promised we must pray for; for promises are given, not to supersede, but to quicken and encourage prayer; and when the accomplishment of a promise is near and at the door, when the kingdom of heaven is at hand, we should then pray for it the more earnestly.

3. *Thy will be done in earth as it is in heaven*. We pray that God's kingdom being come, we and others may be brought into obedience to all the laws and ordinances of it. We make Christ but a titular Prince, if we call him King, and do not do his will: having prayed that he may rule us, we pray that we may in every thing be ruled by him, and that it may *be done on earth*, in this place of our trial and probation (where our work must be done, or it never will be done), *as it is done in heaven*, that place of rest and joy.

4. *Give us this day our daily bread*. Because our natural being is necessary to our spiritual well-being in this world, therefore, after the things of God's glory, kingdom, and will, we pray for the

necessary supports and comforts of this present life, which are the gifts of God, and must be asked of him, —*Bread for the day approaching*, for all the remainder of our lives.

Every word here has a lesson in it: (1) We ask for *bread*; that teaches us sobriety and temperance; we ask for *bread*, not dainties, not superfluities; that which is wholesome, though it be not nice. (2) We ask for *our* bread; that teaches us honesty and industry: we do not ask for the bread out of other people's mouths, not *the bread of deceit* (Prov. xx. 17), not *the bread of idleness* (Prov. xxxi. 27), but the bread honestly gotten. (3) We ask for our *daily* bread; which teaches us not to *take thought for the morrow* (*v.* 34), but constantly to depend upon divine Providence, as those that live from hand to mouth. (4) We beg of God to *give* it us, not sell it us, nor lend it us, but *give* it. The greatest of men must be beholden to the mercy of God for their *daily* bread, (5) We pray, "Give it to *us*; not to me only, but to others in common with me." This teaches us charity, and a compassionate concern for the poor and needy. It intimates also, that we ought to pray with our families; we and our households eat together, and therefore ought to pray together. (6) We pray that God would give it us *this day*: as duly as the day comes, we must pray to our heavenly Father, and reckon we could as well go a day without meat, as without prayer.

5. *And forgive us our debts, as we forgive our debtors*. This is connected with the former; *and forgive*,

intimating, that unless our sins be pardoned, we can have no comfort in life, or the supports of it. Here we have,

(1) A petition; *Father in heaven forgive us our debts*, our debts to thee. Note, [1] Our sins are our debts. A debtor is liable to process, so are we; a malefactor is a debtor to the law, so are we. [2] Our heart's desire and prayer to our heavenly Father every day should be, that he would *forgive us our debts*; that the obligation to punishment may be cancelled and vacated, that we may *not come into condemnation*.

(2) An argument to enforce this petition; *as we forgive our debtors*. This is not a plea of merit, but a plea of grace. Note, Those that come to God for the forgiveness of their sins against him, must make conscience of forgiving those who have offended them, else they curse themselves when they say the Lord's prayer.

6. *And lead us not into temptation, but deliver us from evil*. This petition is expressed,

(1) Negatively: *Lead us not into temptation*. Having prayed that the guilt of sin may be removed, we pray, as is fit, that we may never return again to folly, that we may not be tempted to it. It is not as if God tempted any to sin; but, "Lord, do not let Satan loose upon us; chain up that *roaring lion*, for he is subtle and spiteful; Lord, do not leave us to ourselves (Ps. xix. 13), for we are very weak."

(2) Positively: *But deliver us from evil; from the evil one*, the devil, the tempter; "keep us, that either we may not be assaulted by him, or

we may not be overcome by those assaults".

III. The conclusion: *For thine is the kingdom, and the power and the glory, for ever. Amen.* Some refer this to David's doxology, 1 Chron. xxix. 11. *Thine, O Lord, is the greatness.* It is,

1. A form of plea to enforce the foregoing petitions. It is our duty to plead with God in prayer, to fill our mouth with arguments (Job xxiii. 4) not to move God, but to affect ourselves; to encourage our faith, to excite our fervency, and to evidence both.

2. It is a form of praise and thanksgiving. The best pleading with God is praising of him; it is the way to obtain further mercy, as it qualifies us to receive it. Observe, how full this doxology is, *The kingdom, and the power, and the glory,* it is all thine.

Most of the petitions in the Lord's prayer had been commonly used by the Jews in their devotions, or words to the same effect: but that clause in the fifth petition, *As we forgive our debtors,* was perfectly new, and therefore our Saviour here shows for what reason he added it. God, in forgiving us, has a peculiar respect to our forgiving those that have injured us; and therefore, when we pray for pardon, we must mention our making conscience of that duty, not only to remind ourselves of it, but to bind ourselves to it. See that parable, *ch.* xviii. 23–35. Selfish nature is loth to comply with this, and therefore it is here inculcated, *vv.* 14, 15.

1. In a promise. *If ye forgive, your heavenly Father will also for-give.* Not as if this were the only condition required; there must be repentance and faith, and new obedience; but as where other graces are in truth, there will be this, so this will be a good evidence of the sincerity of our other graces.

2. In a threatening. *"But if you forgive not* those that have injured you, that is a bad sign you have not the other requisite conditions, but are altogether unqualified for pardon: and therefore *your Father,* whom you call Father, and who, as a father, offers you his grace upon reasonable terms, will nevertheless *not forgive you.*

FASTING (*vv.* 16–18)

We are here cautioned against hypocrisy in fasting, as before in almsgiving, and in prayer.

I. It is here supposed that religious fasting is a duty required of the disciples of Christ, when God, in his providence, calls to it. It is a laudable practice, and we have reason to lament that it is so generally neglected among Christians. Anna was much in fasting, Luke ii. 37. Cornelius fasted and prayed, Acts x. 30. The primitive Christians were much in it, see Acts xiii. 3; xiv. 23. Private fasting is supposed, 1 Cor. vii. 5. It is an act of self-denial, and mortification of the flesh, a holy revenge upon ourselves, and humiliation under the hand of God.

II. We are cautioned not to do this *as the hypocrites* did it, lest we lose the reward of it; and the more difficulty attends the duty, the greater loss it is to lose the reward of it.

Now, 1. The *hypocrites* pretended

fasting, when there was nothing of that contrition or humiliation of soul in them, which is the life and soul of the duty.

2. They proclaimed their fasting, and managed it so that all who saw them might take notice that it was a fasting-day with them. Note, It is sad that men, who have, in some measure, mastered their pleasure, which is sensual wickedness, should be ruined by their pride, which is spiritual wickedness, and no less dangerous. Here also *they have their reward*, that praise and applause of men which they court and covet so much; *they have* it, and it is their all.

III. We are directed how to manage a private fast; we must keep it private, *vv.* 17, 18. "And while thou deniest thyself thy bodily refreshments, do it so as that it may not be taken notice of, no, not by those that are nearest to thee; look pleasant, *anoint thine head and wash thy face*, as thou dost on ordinary days, on purpose to conceal thy devotion; and thou shalt be no loser in the praise of it at last; for though it be not of men, it shall be of God." Fasting is the humbling of the soul (Ps. xxxv. 13), that is the inside of the duty; let that therefore be thy principal care, and as to the outside of it, covet not to let it be seen.

TREASURE (*vv.* 19–24)

We must take heed of hypocrisy and worldly-mindedness, in the choice we make of our treasure, our end, and our masters.

I. In choosing the *treasure* we *lay up*. Something or other every man has which he makes his *treasure*,

his portion, which his heart is upon, to which he carries all he can get, and which he depends upon for futurity. Now Christ designs not to deprive us of our treasure, but to direct us in the choice of it; and here we have,

1. A *good caution* against making *the things that are seen*, that *are temporal*, our best things, and placing our happiness in them. *Lay not up for yourselves treasures upon earth*.

2. Here is a *good reason* given why we should not look upon anything *on earth* as our *treasure*, because it is liable to loss and decay: (1) From corruption within. That which is treasure *upon earth moth and rust do corrupt*. Note, Worldly riches have in themselves a principle of corruption and decay; they wither of themselves, and *make themselves wings*. (2) From violence without. *Thieves break through and steal*. Every hand of violence will be aiming at the house where *treasure* is laid up; nor can anything be laid up so safe, but we may be spoiled of it. It is folly to make that our *treasure* which we may so easily be robbed of.

3. *Good counsel*, to make the joys and glories of the other world, those *things not seen* that *are eternal*, our best things, and to place our happiness in them. *Lay up for yourselves treasures in heaven*. It is a great encouragement to us to *lay up* our *treasure in heaven*, that there it is safe; it will not decay of itself, no *moth* nor *rust* will *corrupt* it; nor can we be by force or fraud deprived of it; *thieves do not break through and steal*. It is a happiness above and beyond the changes and

chances of time, _an inheritance incorruptible_.

4. A _good reason_ why we should thus choose, and an evidence that we have done so (_v._ 21), _Where your treasure is_, on earth or in heaven, _there will your heart be_. The _heart_ follows the _treasure_, as the needle follows the loadstone, or the sunflower the sun.

This direction about laying up our _treasure_, may very fitly be applied to the foregoing caution, of not doing what we do in religion _to be seen of men_. Our _treasure_ is our alms, prayers, and fastings, and the reward of them; if we have done these only to gain the applause of men, we have _laid up this treasure on earth_, have lodged it in the hands of men, and must never expect to hear any further of it. But if we have prayed and fasted and given alms in truth and uprightness, with an eye to God and to his acceptance, and have approved ourselves to him therein, we have laid up that treasure _in heaven_.

II. We must take heed of hypocrisy and worldly-mindedness in choosing the _end we look at_. Our concern as to this is represented by two sorts of eyes which men have, a _single eye_ and an _evil eye_, _vv._ 22, 23.

1. _The eye_, that is, _the heart_ (so some) if that _be single, free and bountiful_ (so the word is frequently rendered, as Rom. xii. 8; 2 Cor. viii. 2, ix. 11. 13; Jam. i. 5, and we read of a _bountiful eye_, Prov. xxii. 9) will direct the man to Christian actions, his whole life _will be full of light_, full of the evidences and instances of true Christianity, that _pure religion and undefiled before God and the Father_ (Jam. i. 27), _full of light_, of good works, which are our _light shining before men_; but _if the heart be evil_, covetous, and hard, and envious, griping and grudging (such a temper of mind is often expressed by an _evil eye_, _ch._ xx. 15; Mark vii. 22; Prov. xxiii. 6, 7), _the body will be full of darkness_, the whole way of life will be heathenish and unchristian.

2. _The eye_, that is, _the understanding_ (so some); the practical judgment, the conscience, which is to the other faculties of the soul, as _the eye_ is to the _body_, to guide and direct their motions; now _if this eye be single_, if it make a true and right judgment, it will rightly guide the affections and actions, which will all be _full of the light_ of grace and comfort; _but if this be evil_ and corrupt, and instead of leading the inferior powers, is led, and bribed, and biassed by them, if this be erroneous and misinformed, the heart and life must needs be _full of darkness_, and the whole way of life corrupt.

3. _The eye_, that is, _the aims_ and _intentions_; by _the eye_ we set our end before us, the mark we shoot at, the place we go to, we keep that in view, and direct our motion accordingly; in every thing we do in religion, there is something or other that we have in our _eye_; now _if our eye be single_, if we aim honestly, fix right ends, and move rightly towards them, if we aim purely and only at the glory of God, seek his honour and favour, and direct all entirely to him, then _the eye is single. But if this eye be evil_, if, instead of aiming only at the

glory of God, and our acceptance with him, we look aside at the applause of men, and while we profess to honour God, contrive to honour ourselves, and seek our own things under colour of *seeking the things of Christ*, this spoils all, and the foundations being thus out of course, there can be nothing but *confusion and every evil work* in the superstructure.

III. We must take heed of hypocrisy and worldly-mindedness in choosing the master we serve, *v.* 24. *No man can serve two masters.* Serving *two masters* is contrary to *the single eye*; for *the eye* will be to the master's hand, Ps. cxxiii. 1, 2. Our Lord Jesus here exposes the cheat which those put upon their own souls, who think to divide between God and the world, to have a *treasure on earth*, and a *treasure in heaven* too, to please God and please men too. Why not? says the hypocrite; it is good to have two strings to one's bow. No, says Christ, this will not do; it is but a supposition that *gain is godliness*, 1 Tim. vi. 5. Here is,

1. A general maxim laid down; it is likely it was a proverb among the Jews, *No man can serve two masters*, much less two gods; for their commands will some time or other cross or contradict one another, and their occasions interfere.

2. The application of it to the business in hand. *Ye cannot serve God and Mammon. Mammon* is a Syriac word, that signifies gain; so that whatever in this world is, or is accounted by us to be, *gain* (Phil. iii. 7), is *mammon*. He does not say, We *must* not or we *should* not, but we *cannot serve God and Mammon*;

we *cannot* love both (1 John ii. 15; Jam. iv. 4); or hold to both, or hold by both in observance, obedience, attendance, trust, and dependence, for they are contrary, the one to the other.

PRIORITIES (*vv.* 25–34)

There is scarcely any one sin against which our Lord Jesus more largely and earnestly warns his disciples, or against which he arms them with more variety of arguments, than the sin of disquieting, distracting, distrustful cares about the things of this life, which are a bad sign that both the *treasure* and the heart are *on the earth*; and therefore he thus largely insists upon it. Here is,

I. The prohibition laid down. It is the repeated command of the Lord Jesus to his disciples, that they should not divide and pull in pieces their own minds with care about the world.

But the *thought* here forbidden is, 1. A disquieting, tormenting *thought*, which hurries the mind hither and thither, and hangs it in suspense; which disturbs our joy in God, and is a damp upon our hope in him; which breaks the sleep, and hinders our enjoyment of ourselves, of our friends, and of what God has given us. 2. A distrustful, unbelieving *thought*. God has promised to provide for those that are his all things needful for life as well as godliness, *the life that now is*, food and a covering: not dainties, but necessaries. Observe the cautions here,

(1) *Take no thought for your life.* Life is our greatest concern for this world; *All that a man has will he*

give for his life; yet take no thought about it. [1] Not about the *continuance* of it; refer it to God to *lengthen* or *shorten* it as he pleases; *my times are in thy hand*, and they are in a good hand. [2] Not about the *comforts* of this life; refer it to God to embitter or sweeten it as he pleases. .

(2) *Take no thought for the morrow*, for the time to come. Be not solicitous for the future, how you shall live next year, or when you are old, or what you shall leave behind you. As we must not *boast of* tomorrow, so we must not *care for* tomorrow, or the events of it.

II. The reasons and arguments to enforce this prohibition. Consider then,

1. *Is not the life more than meat, and the body than raiment? v.* 25. Yes, no doubt it is; so he says who had reason to understand the true value of present things, for he made them, he supports them, and supports us by them; and the thing speaks for itself. Note, (1) Our *life* is a greater blessing than our *livelihood.* Food and raiment are in order to life, and the *end* is more noble and excellent than the *means.* (2) This is an encouragement to us to trust God for *food* and *raiment*, and so to ease ourselves of all perplexing cares about them. God has given us life, and given us the body; it was an act of power, it was an act of favour, it was done without our care: what cannot he do for us, who did that?—what will he not? If we take care about our souls and eternity, which are more than the body, and its life, we may leave it to God to provide for us food and raiment, which are less.

2. *Behold the fowls of the air*, and *consider the lilies of the field.* Here is an argument taken from God's common providence toward the inferior creatures, and their dependence, according to their capacities, upon that providence. A fine pass fallen man has come to, that he must be sent to school to the *fowls of the air*, and that they must *teach him!* Job xii. 7, 8.

(1) Look upon the *fowls*, and learn to trust God *for food* (*v.* 26), and disquiet not yourselves with thoughts *what you shall eat*.

(2) Look upon the *lilies*, and learn to trust God for *raiment*. That is another part of our care, *what we shall put on.* Now to ease us of this care, let us *consider the lilies of the field*; not only *look upon* them (every eye does that with pleasure), but *consider* them.

3. *Which of you*, the wisest, the strongest of you, *by taking thought, can add one cubit to his stature?* (*v.* 27), to *his age*, so some; but the measure of a cubit denotes it to be meant of the stature, and the age at longest is but a span, Ps. xxxix. 5. Let us consider, (1) We did not arrive at the stature we are of by our own care and thought, but by the providence of God. Now he that made our bodies, and made them of such a size, surely will take care to provide for them. (2) We cannot alter the stature we are of, if we would: what a foolish and ridiculous thing would it be for a man of low stature to perplex himself, to break his sleep, and beat his brains, about it, and to be continually taking thought how he might be a cubit higher; when, after all, he knows he cannot effect it, and

therefore he had better be content and take it as it is! Now as we do in reference to our bodily stature, so we should do in reference to our worldly estate. [1] We should not covet an abundance of the wealth of this world. [2] We must reconcile ourselves to our state, as we do to our stature; we must set the conveniences against the inconveniences, and so make a virtue of necessity: what cannot be remedied must be made the best of.

4. *After all these things do the Gentiles seek*, v. 32. Thoughtfulness about the world is a *heathenish* sin, and unbecoming *Christians*. The *Gentiles* seek *these things*, because they know not *better things*; they are eager for this world, because they are strangers to a better; they seek these things with care and anxiety, because they are *without God in the world*, and understand not his providence.

5. *Your heavenly Father knows ye have need of all these things*; these necessary things, food and raiment; he knows our wants better than we do ourselves; though he be in heaven, and his children on earth, he observes what the least and poorest of them has occasion for (Rev. ii. 9), *I know thy poverty*. Therefore, we should ease ourselves of the burden of care, by casting it upon God, because it is he *that careth for us* (1 Pet. v. 7), and what needs all this ado? If he care, why should we care?

6. *Seek first the kingdom of God, and his righteousness, and all these things shall be added unto you*, v. 33. Here is a double argument against the sin of *thoughtfulness; take no thought* for your life, the life of the body. Thoughtfulness for our souls is the most effectual cure of thoughtfulness for the world. Observe here,

[1] The great duty required: it is the sum and substance of our whole duty: "*Seek first the kingdom of God*; mind religion as your great and principal concern." Now observe, *First*, The object of this seeking; *The kingdom of God, and his righteousness*; we must mind heaven as our end, and holiness as our way. "Seek the comforts of the kingdom of grace and glory as your felicity, aim at the *kingdom of heaven*; press towards it; give diligence to make it sure; resolve not to take up short of it; seek for this glory honour, and immortality; prefer heaven and heavenly blessings far before earth and earthly delights." We make nothing of our religion, if we do not make heaven of it. And with the *happiness* of this kingdom, seek the *righteousness* of it; *God's righteousness*, the righteousness which he requires to be wrought *in* us, and wrought *by* us, such as exceeds that of the scribes and Pharisees; we must *follow peace and holiness*, Heb. xii. 14. *Secondly*, The order of it. *Seek first the kingdom of God*. Let your care for your souls and another world take place of all other cares: and let all the concerns of this life be made subordinate to those of the life to come: we must seek the things of Christ more than our own things; and if ever they come in competition, we must remember to which we are to give the preference.

[2] The gracious promise annexed; *all these things*, the necessary supports of life, *shall be added unto*

you; shall be *given over and above*; so it is in the margin. You shall have what you seek, the *kingdom of God and his righteousness*, for never any sought *in vain*, that sought *in earnest*; and besides that, you shall have food and raiment, by way of overplus.

7. *The morrow shall take thought for the things of itself: sufficient unto the day is the evil thereof*, *v.* 34. We must not perplex ourselves inordinately about future events, because every day brings along with it its own burden of cares and grievances. So that we are here told,

(1) That *thoughtfulness* for the morrow is *needless*; *Let the morrow take thought for the things of itself*. If wants and troubles be renewed with the day, there are aids and provisions renewed likewise; *compassions*, that are *new every morning*, Lam. iii. 22, 23. The meaning is, let us *mind present duty*, and then *leave events to God*; do the *work of the day in its day*, and then let *tomorrow bring its work along with it*.

(2) That thoughtfulness for the morrow is one of those *foolish and hurtful lusts*, which those that will be rich fall into, and one of the *many sorrows*, wherewith they *pierce themselves through. Sufficient unto the day is the evil thereof*. What a folly is it to take that trouble upon ourselves this day by care and fear, which belongs to another day, and will be never the lighter when it comes? Let us not pull that upon ourselves all together at once, which Providence has wisely ordered to be borne by parcels.

CENSURE AND REPROOF
(*vv.* 1–6)

Our Saviour is here directing us how to conduct ourselves in reference to the faults of others.

I. A caution *against judging*, *vv.* 1, 2. Now observe,

1. The prohibition; *Judge not*. We must judge ourselves, and judge of our own acts, but we must not judge our brother. We must not sit in the judgment-seat, to make our word a law to every body. We must not make the worst of people, nor infer such invidious things from their words and actions as they will not bear. We must not judge uncharitably, unmercifully, nor with a spirit of revenge, and a desire to do mischief. We must not judge of a man's state by a single act, nor of what he is in himself by what he is to us, because in our own cause we are apt to be partial. We must not judge the hearts of others, nor their intentions, for it is God's prerogative to try the heart, and we must not step into his throne; nor must we judge of their eternal state. Counsel him, and help him, but do not judge him.

2. The reason to enforce this prohibition. *That ye be not judged*. This intimates, (1) That if we presume to judge others, we may expect to be ourselves judged. (2) That if we be modest and charitable in our censures of others, and decline judging them, and judge ourselves rather, *we shall not be judged of the Lord*. As God will forgive those that forgive their brethren; so he will not judge those

that will not judge their brethren; the *merciful shall find mercy*.

The judging of those that judge others is according to the law of retaliation; *With what judgment ye judge, ye shall be judged*, v. 2. What would become of us, if God should be as exact and severe in judging us, as we are in judging our brethren; if he should weigh us in the same balance?

II. Some cautions, *about reproving*. Now observe here,

1. It is not everyone who is fit to reprove. Those who are themselves guilty of the same faults of which they accuse others, or of worse, bring shame upon themselves, and are not likely to do good to those whom they reprove, *vv*. 3–5. Here is,

(1) A just reproof to the censorious, who quarrel with their brother for small faults, while they allow themselves in great ones. Note, [1] There are degrees in sin: some sins are comparatively but as *motes*, others as *beams*; some as a *gnat*, others as a *camel*: not that there is any sin little, for there is no little God to sin against: if it be a *mote* (or *splinter*, for so it might better be read), it is in the eye; if a *gnat*, it is in the throat; both painful and perilous, and we cannot be easy or well till they are got out. [2] Our own sins ought to appear greater to us than the same sins in others: that which charity teaches us to call but a *splinter in our brother's eye*, true repentance and godly sorrow will teach us to call a *beam in our own*. [3] There are many that have *beams in their own eyes*, and yet do not consider it. They are under the guilt and dominion of very great

sins, and yet are not aware of it, but justify themselves, as if they needed no repentance nor reformation. [4] It is common for those who are most sinful themselves, and least sensible of it, to be most forward and free in judging and censuring others: the Pharisees, who were most haughty in justifying themselves, were most scornful in condemning others. But, [5] Men's being so severe upon the faults of others, while they are indulgent of their own, is a mark of hypocrisy. *Thou hypocrite*, v. 5. [6] The consideration of what is amiss in ourselves, though it ought not to keep us from administering friendly reproof, ought to keep us from magisterial censuring, and to make us very candid and charitable in judging others.

(2) Here is a good rule for reprovers, *v.* 5. Go in the right method, *first cast the beam out of thine own eye*. A man's *of*fence will never be his *de*fence: but I must first reform myself, that I may thereby help to reform my brother, and may qualify myself to reprove him.

2. It is not everyone who is fit to be reproved; *Give not that which is holy unto the dogs*, v. 6. This may be considered, either, (1) As a rule to the disciples in preaching the gospel; not that they must not preach it to any who were wicked and profane. (Christ himself preached to publicans and sinners), but the reference is to such as they found obstinate after the gospel was preached to them, such as blasphemed it, and persecuted the preachers of it; let them not spend much time among such, for it would

be lost labour, but let them turn to others, Acts xiii. 41. So Dr. Whitby. Or, (2) As a rule to all in giving reproof. Our zeal against sin must be guided by discretion, and we must not go about to give instructions, counsels, and rebukes, much less comforts, to hardened scorners, to whom it will certainly do no good, but who will be exasperated and enraged at us. See here what is the evidence of men's being *dogs* and *swine*. Those are to be reckoned such, who *hate reproofs* and reprovers, and fly in the face of those who, in kindness to their souls, show them their sin and danger. These sin against the remedy; who shall heal and help those that will not be healed and helped?

ASKING ARIGHT (*vv.* 7–11)

Our Saviour, in the foregoing chapter, had spoken of prayer as a commanded duty, by which God is honoured, and which, if done aright, shall be rewarded; here he speaks of it as the appointed means of obtaining what we need, especially grace to obey the precepts he had given, some of which are so displeasing to flesh and blood.

I. Here is a precept in three words to the same purport, *Ask, Seek, Knock* (*v.* 7); that is, in one word, "Pray; pray often, pray with sincerity and seriousness; pray, and pray again; make conscience of prayer, and be constant in it; make a business of prayer, and be earnest in it. *Ask*, as a beggar asks alms." Those that would be rich in grace, must betake themselves to the poor trade of begging,

and they shall find it a thriving trade. *Seek* as for a thing of value that we have lost, or as the merchantman that *seeks goodly pearls. Seek by prayer*, Dan. ix. 3. *Knock*, as he that desires to enter into the house knocks at the door." We would be admitted to converse with God, would be taken into his love, and favour, and kingdom; sin has shut and barred the door against us; by prayer, we knock; *Lord, Lord, open to us.*

II. Here is a promise annexed: *our labour* in prayer, if indeed we do labour in it, *shall not be in vain.* Now here,

1. The promise is made, and made so as exactly to answer the precept, *v.* 7. God will meet those that attend on him; *Ask, and it shall be given you. Seek,* and *ye shall find,* and then you do not lose your labour; God is himself *found of those that seek* him, and if we find him we have enough. "*Knock, and it shall be opened*; the door of mercy and grace shall no longer be shut against you as enemies and intruders, but opened to you as friends and children."

2. It is repeated, *v.* 8. It is to the same purport, yet with some addition. (1) It is made to extend to all that pray aright; "Not only you my disciples shall receive what you pray for, but *every one that asketh, receiveth*, whether Jew or Gentile, young or old, rich or poor, high or low, master or servant, learned or unlearned, they are all alike welcome to *the throne of grace*, if they come in faith: *for God is no respecter of persons.* (2) It is made so as to amount to a grant, in words of the present tense, which

is more than a promise for the future. *Every one that asketh*, not only *shall* receive, but *receiveth*. Christ hereby puts his *fiat* to the petition; and he having all power, that is enough.

3. It is illustrated, by a similitude taken from earthly parents, and their innate readiness to give their children what they ask. Christ appeals to his hearers, *What man is there of you*, though never so morose and ill-humoured, *whom if his son ask bread, will he give him a stone?* vv. 9, 10. Whence he infers (*v.* 11), *If ye then, being evil*, yet grant your children's requests, *much more will your heavenly Father give you the good things you ask*. Now this is of use,

(1) To *direct* our prayers and expectations. [1] We must come to God, as children to a *Father in heaven*, with reverence and confidence. [2] We must come to him for *good things*, for those he *gives to them that ask him*; which teaches us to refer ourselves to him; we know not what is good for ourselves (Eccl. vi. 12), but he knows what is good for us, we must therefore leave it with him; *Father, thy will be done*.

(2) To *encourage* our prayers and expectations. We may hope that we shall not be denied and disappointed. The world often gives *stones for bread*, and *serpents for fish*, but God never does; nay, we shall be heard and answered, for children are by their parents.

THE WAY TO LIFE
(*vv.* 12–14)

Our Lord Jesus here presses upon us that righteousness towards men which is an essential branch of true religion, and that religion towards God which is an essential branch of universal righteousness.

I. We must make righteousness our rule, and be ruled by it, *v.* 12. *Therefore*, lay this down for your principle, to do as you would be done by. Now here we have,

1. The rule of justice laid down; *Whatsoever ye would that men should do to you, do you even so to them*. This is grounded upon that great commandment, *Thou shalt love thy neighbour as thyself*. (1) We must do that to our neighbour which we ourselves acknowledge to be fit and reasonable. (2) We must put other people upon the level with ourselves, and reckon we are as much obliged to them, as they to us. (3) We must, in our dealings with men, suppose ourselves in the same particular case and circumstances with those we have to do with, and deal accordingly. If I were making such a one's bargain, labouring under such a one's infirmity and affliction, how should I desire and expect to be treated?

2. A reason given to enforce this rule; *This is the law and the prophets*. It is the summary of that second great commandment, which is one of the two, *on which hang all the law and the prophets*, ch. xxii. 40. We have not this in so many words, either in *the law* or *the prophets*, but it is the concurring language of the whole. All that is there said concerning our duty towards our neighbour (and that is no little) may be reduced to this rule.

II. We must make religion our business, and be intent upon it; we must be strict and circumspect in our conversation, which is here represented to us as entering in at a *strait gate*, and walking on in a *narrow way*, vv. 13, 14. Observe here,

1. The account that is given of the bad way of sin, and the good way of holiness. There are but two ways, right and wrong, good and evil; the way to heaven, and the way to hell; in the one of which we are all of us walking: no middle place hereafter, no middle way now.

Here is, (1) An account given us of the way of sin and sinners; both what is the best, and what is the worst of it.

[1] That which allures multitudes into it, and keeps them in it; *the gate is wide, and the way broad*, and there are many travellers in that way. You may go in at this gate with all your lusts about you; it gives no check to your appetites, to your passions. It is a *broad way*, for there is nothing to hedge in those that walk in it, but they wander endlessly; a *broad way*, for there are many paths in it; there is choice of sinful ways, contrary to each other, but all paths in this *broad way. Secondly*, "You will have abundance of company in that way: *many there be that go in* at this gate, and walk in this way." If we *follow the multitude*, it will be *to do evil*: if we go with the crowd, it will be the wrong way.

[2] That which should affright us all from it is, that it *leads to destruction*. Death, eternal death, is at the end of it (and the way of sin tends to it),—everlasting *destruction from the presence of the Lord*. Whether it be the high way of open profaneness, or the back way of close

hypocrisy, if it be a way of sin, it will be our ruin, if we repent not.

(2) Here is an account given us of the way of holiness.

[1] What there is in it that frightens many from it.

First, That *the gate is strait*. Conversion and regeneration are *the gate*, by which we enter into this way, in which we begin a life of faith and serious godliness; out of a state of sin into a state of grace we must pass, by the new birth, John iii. 3, 5. This is a *strait gate*, hard to find, and hard to get through; like a passage between two rocks, 1 Sam. xiv. 4. There must be *a new heart, and a new spirit*, and *old things must pass away.*

Secondly, That *the way is narrow.* We are not in heaven as soon as we have got through *the strait gate*, not in Canaan as soon as we have got through the Red Sea; no, we must go through a wilderness, must travel a *narrow way*, must endure hardness, must wrestle and be in an agony, must watch in all things, and walk with care and circumspection.

Thirdly, The *gate* being so *strait and the way so narrow*, it is not strange that there are but *few that find it*, and choose it. Many pass it by, through carelessness. Others look upon it, but shun it; they like not to be so limited and restrained. Those that are going to heaven are but few, compared to those that are going to hell; a remnant, a little flock.

[2] Let us see what there is in this way, which, notwithstanding this, should invite us all to it; it *leads to life*, to present comfort in the favour of God, which is the life of

the soul; to eternal bliss, the hope of which, at the end of our way, should reconcile us to all the difficulties and inconveniences of the road.

2. The great concern and duty of every one of us, in consideration of all this; *Enter ye in at the strait gate*. The matter is fairly stated; life and death, good and evil, are set before us; both the ways, and both the ends: now let the matter be taken entire, and considered impartially, and then choose you this day which you will walk in. It is true, we can neither go in, nor go on, without the assistance of divine grace; but it is as true, that grace is freely offered, and shall not be wanting to those that seek it, and submit to it. Conversion is hard work, but it is needful, and, blessed be God, it is not impossible if we strive, Luke xiii. 24.

FALSE PROPHETS
(*vv.* 15–20)

We have here a caution against *false prophets*, to take heed that we be not deceived and imposed upon by them.

They are false teachers and *false prophets*, 1. Who produce false commissions, who pretend to have immediate warrant and direction from God to set up for *prophets*, and to be divinely inspired, when they are not so. Here is,

I. A good reason for this caution, *Beware of* them, for they are *wolves in sheep's clothing*, *v.* 15.

1. We have need to be very cautious, because their pretences are very fair and plausible, and such as will deceive us, if we be not upon our guard. They pretend to be sheep, and outwardly appear so innocent, harmless, meek, useful' and all that is good, as to be excelled by none. They and their errors are gilded with the specious pretences of sanctity and devotion· Satan turns himself *into an angel of light*, 2 Cor. xi. 13, 14.

2. Because under these pretensions their designs are very malicious and mischievous; *inwardly they are ravening wolves*. Every *hypocrite* is a *goat* in sheep's clothing; but a *false prophet* is a *wolf* in sheep's clothing; not only not a sheep, but the worst enemy the sheep has, that comes not but to tear and devour, to *scatter the sheep* (John x. 12), to drive them from God, and from one another, into crooked paths.

II. Here is a good rule to go by in this caution; we must *prove all things* (1 Thess. v. 21), *try the spirits* (1 John iv. 1), and here we have a touchstone; *ye shall know them by their fruits*, 16–20. Observe,

1. The illustration of this comparison, of the fruit's being the discovery of the tree. You cannot always distinguish them by their bark and leaves, nor by the spreading of their boughs, but *by their fruits ye shall know them*. An apple may be stuck, or a bunch of grapes may hang, upon a thorn; so may a good truth, a good word or action, be found in a bad man, but you may be sure it never grew there.

2. The application of this to the false prophets.

(1) By way of terror and threatening (*v.* 19); *Every tree that brings not forth good fruit is hewn down*. This very saying John the Baptist had used, *ch.* iii. 10. God will deal with them as men deal with dry

trees that cumber the ground. Compare this with Ezek. xxxi. 12, 13; Dan. iv. 14; John xv. 6.

(2) By way of trial; *By their fruits ye shall know them.*

[1] *By the fruits* of their persons, their words and actions, and the course of their conversation. If you would know whether they be right or not, observe how they live; their works will testify for them or against them.

[2] *By the fruits* of their doctrine. What do they tend to? What affections and practices will they lead those into, that embrace them? If *the doctrine be of God*, it will tend to promote serious piety, humility, charity, holiness, and love, with other Christian graces; but if, on the contrary, the doctrines these prophets preach have a manifest tendency to make people proud, worldly, and contentious, to make them loose and careless, unjust or uncharitable, factious or disturbers of the public peace; if it indulge carnal liberty, and take people off from governing themselves and their families by the strict rules of *the narrow way*, we may conclude, that *this persuasion comes not of him that calleth us*, Gal. v. 8.

TRUE AND FALSE
(*vv.* 21–29)

We have here the conclusion of this long and excellent sermon, the scope of which is to show the indispensable necessity of obedience to the commands of Christ.

I. He shows, by a plain remonstrance, that an outward profession of religion, however remarkable, will not bring us to heaven, unless there be a correspondent way of life, *vv.* 21–23. Observe here,

1. Christ's law laid down, *v.* 21. *Not every one that saith, Lord, Lord, shall enter into the kingdom of heaven, into the kingdom of grace* and glory. Christ here shows,

(1) That it will not suffice to say, *Lord, Lord.* This is not to take us off from saying, *Lord, Lord*; from praying, and being earnest in prayer, from professing Christ's name, and being bold in professing it, but from resting in these, in the *form of godliness*, without *the power.*

(2) That it is necessary to our happiness that we *do the will of* Christ, which is indeed *the will of* his *Father in heaven.*

2. The hypocrite's plea against the strictness of this law, offering other things in lieu of obedience, *v.* 22. They put in their plea with great importunity, *Lord, Lord*; and with great confidence, appealing to Christ concerning it; *Lord*, dost not thou know, (1) That *we have prophesied in thy name?* Note, A man may be a preacher, may have gifts for the ministry, and an external call to it, and perhaps some success in it, and yet be a wicked man; may help others to heaven, and yet come short himself. (2) That *in thy name we have cast out devils?* A man might *cast devils out* of others, and yet have a devil, nay, and be a devil himself. (3) That *in thy name we have done many wonderful works.* There may be a faith of miracles, where there is no justifying faith; none of that *faith which works by love* and obedience.

3. The rejection of this plea as

frivolous. The same that is the Law-Maker (*v.* 21) is here the Judge according to that law (*v.* 23), and he will overrule the plea, will overrule it publicly; he *will profess to them* with all possible solemnity, as sentence is passed by the Judge, *I never knew you*, and therefore *depart from me, ye that work iniquity.*—Observe, (1) Why, and upon what ground, he rejects them and their plea—because they were *workers of iniquity.* (2) How it is expressed; *I never knew you*; "I never owned you as my servants, no, not when you *prophesied in* my *name*, when you were in the height of your profession, and were most extolled." This intimates, that if he had ever known them, as *the Lord knows them that are his*, had ever owned them and loved them as his, he would have known them, and owned them, and *loved them, to the end*; but he *never* did *know* them, for he always knew them to be hypocrites, and rotten at heart, as he did Judas; therefore, says he, *depart from me.*

II. He shows, by a parable, that hearing these sayings of Christ will not make us happy, if we do not make conscience of doing them; but that if we hear them and do them, we are *blessed in our deed*, *vv.* 24–27.

1. The hearers of Christ's word are here divided into two sorts; some that hear, and do what they hear; others that hear and do not.

(1) Some that *hear his sayings and do them*: blessed be God that there are any such, though comparatively few. To hear Christ is not barely to give him the hearing, but to obey him. Observe, It is not enough to *hear* Christ's *sayings*, and understand them, *hear* them, and remember them, *hear* them, and talk of them, repeat them, dispute for them; but we must *hear, and do* them. *This do, and thou shalt live.* Those only *that hear, and do*, are *blessed* (Luke xi. 28; John xiii. 17), and are akin to Christ, *ch.* xii. 50.

(2) There are others who *hear* Christ's *sayings and do them not*; their religion rests in bare hearing, and goes no further. Those who only *hear* Christ's *sayings, and do them not*, sit down in the midway to heaven, and that will never bring them to their journey's end.

2. These two sorts of hearers are here represented in their true characters, and the state of their case, under the comparison of two builders; one was *wise*, and *built upon a rock*, and his building stood in a storm; the other *foolish*, and *built upon the sand*, and his building fell.

III. In the two last verses, we are told what impressions Christ's discourse made upon the hearers. It was an excellent sermon; and it is probable that he said more than is here recorded; and doubtless the delivery of it from the mouth of him, into whose lips grace was poured, did mightily set it off. Now,

1. *They were astonished at his doctrine*; it is to be feared that few of them were brought by it to follow him: but for the present, they were filled with wonder. Note, It is possible for people to admire good preaching, and yet to remain in ignorance and unbelief; to be astonished, and yet not sanctified.

2. The reason was because he taught them *as one having authority, and*

not as the scribes. The scribes pretended to as much authority as any teachers whatsoever, and were supported by all the external advantages that could be obtained, but their preaching was mean, and flat, and jejune: they spake as those that were not themselves masters of what they preached: the word did not come from them with any life or force; they delivered it as a schoolboy says his lesson; but Christ delivered his discourse, as a judge gives his charge. He did indeed, *dominari in conscionibus—deliver his discourses with a tone of authority*; his lessons were laws; his word a word of command. Christ, upon the mountain, showed more true authority, than the scribes in Moses's seat. Thus when Christ teaches by his Spirit in the soul, he teaches with authority. He says, *Let there be light, and there is light.*

THE LEPER CLEANSED
(vv. 1–4)

The first verse refers to the close of the foregoing sermon: the people that heard him were *astonished at his doctrine*; and the effect was, that *when he came down from the mountain, great multitudes followed him.* It is pleasing to see people so well affected to Christ, as to think they can never hear enough of him; so well affected to the best things, as thus to flock after good preaching, and to *follow the Lamb* whithersoever he goes.

In these verses we have an account of Christ's *cleansing a leper.* It should seem, by comparing Mark i. 40, and Luke v. 12, that this passage, though placed, by St. Matthew, after the sermon on the mount, because he would give account of his doctrine first, and then of his miracles, happened some time before; but that is not at all material. This is fitly recorded with the first of Christ's miracles, 1. Because the leprosy was looked upon, among the Jews, as a particular mark of God's displeasure: hence we find Miriam, Gehazi, and Uzziah, smitten with leprosy for some one particular sin; and therefore Christ, to show that he came to turn away the wrath of God, by taking away sin, began with the cure of a leper. 2. Because this disease, as it was supposed to come immediately from the hand of God, so also it was supposed to be removed immediately by his hand, and therefore it was not attempted to be cured by physicians, but was put under the inspection of the priests, the Lord's ministers, who waited to see what God would do. The law discovered sin (for by the law is the knowledge of sin), and pronounced sinners unclean; it shut them up (Gal. iii. 23), as the priest did the leper, but could go no further; it could not *make the comers thereunto perfect.* But Christ takes away sin; cleanses us from it, and so *perfecteth for ever them that are sanctified.* Now here we have,

I. The leper's address to Christ: *Lord, if thou wilt, thou canst make me clean.* The cleansing of him may be considered,

1. As a temporal mercy; a mercy to the body, delivering it from a disease, which, though it did not threaten life, embittered it.

2. As a typical mercy. Sin is the leprosy of the soul; it shuts us out from communion with God, to which that we may be restored, it is necessary that we be cleansed from this leprosy, and this ought to be our great concern.

II. Christ's answer to this address, which was very kind, v. 3.

1. *He put forth his hand and touched him.* There was a ceremonial pollution contracted by the touch of a leper; but Christ would show, that when he conversed with sinners, he was in no danger of being infected by them, for the prince of this world had nothing in him. If we touch pitch, we are defiled; but Christ was *separate from sinners*, even when he lived among them.

2. He said, *I will, be thou clean.* He did not say, as Elisha to Naaman, *Go, wash in Jordan*; did not put him upon a tedious, troublesome, chargeable course of physic, but spake the word and healed him. (1) Here is a word of kindness, *I will*; I am as willing to help thee, as thou art to be helped. Note, They who by faith apply themselves to Christ for mercy and grace, may be sure that he is willing, freely willing, to give them the mercy and grace they come to him for. (2) A word of power, *Be thou clean*. Both a power of authority, and a power of energy, are exerted in this word. Christ heals by a word of command to us; *Be thou clean*; "Be willing to be clean, and use the means; cleanse thyself from all filthiness;" but there goes along with this a word of command concerning us, a word that does the work; *I will that thou be clean.*

Such a word as this is necessary to the cure, and effectual for it; and the Almighty grace which speaks it, shall not be wanting to those who truly desire it.

III. The happy change hereby wrought: *Immediately his leprosy was cleansed.* Nature works gradually, but the God of nature works immediately; he speaks, it is done; and yet he works effectually; he *commands, and it stands fast.*

IV. The after-directions Christ gave him. It is fit that they who are cured by Christ should ever after be ruled by him.

1. *See thou tell no man*; "Tell no man till thou hast shown thyself to the priest, and he has pronounced thee clean; and so thou hast a legal proof, both that thou wast before a leper, and art now thoroughly cleansed." Christ would have his miracles to appear in their full light and evidence, and not to be published till they could appear so.

2. *Go show thyself to the priest*, according to the law, Lev. xiv. 2. Christ took care to have the law observed, lest he should give offence, and to show that he will have order kept up, and good discipline and respect paid to those that are in office.

3. *Offer the gift that Moses commanded*, in token of thankfulness to God, and recompence to the priest for his pains; and this *for a testimony unto them*.

THE CENTURION'S SERVANT
(vv. 5–13)

We have here an account of Christ's curing the centurion's servant of a palsy. This was done at Capernaum, where Christ now dwelt, *ch.*

iv. 13. Christ went about doing good, and came home to do good too; every place he came to was the better for him.

The persons Christ had now to do with were,

1. A *centurion*; he was a suppliant, a Gentile, a Roman, an officer of the army; probably commander-in-chief of that part of the Roman army which was quartered at Capernaum, and kept garrison there. (1) Though he was a soldier (and a little piety commonly goes a great way with men of that profession), yet he was a godly man; he was eminently so. Note, God has his remnant among all sorts of people. (2) Though he was a Roman soldier, and his very dwelling among the Jews was a badge of their subjection to the Roman yoke, yet Christ, who was *King of the Jews*, favoured him; and therein has taught us to do good to our enemies, and not needlessly to interest ourselves in national enmities. (3) Though he was a Gentile, yet Christ countenanced him. Now good old Simeon's word began to be fulfilled, that he should be *a light to lighten the Gentiles*, as well as *the glory of his people Israel*.

2. *The centurion's servant*; he was the patient. In this also it appears, that there is no respect of persons with God; for *in Christ Jesus*, as there is *neither circumcision nor uncircumcision*, so there is *neither bond nor free*. He is as ready to heal the poorest servant, as the richest master; for himself *took upon him the form of a servant*, to show his regard to the meanest.

Now in the story of the cure of this servant, we may observe an intercourse or interchanging of graces, very remarkable between Christ and the centurion. See here,

I. The grace of the centurion working towards Christ. Observe,

1. His affectionate address to Jesus Christ, which speaks,

(1) A pious regard to our great Master, as one able and willing to succour and relieve poor petitioners. He came to him *beseeching him*, not as Naaman the Syrian (a centurion too) came to Elisha, demanding a cure, taking state, and standing upon points of honour; but with cap in hand as a humble suitor.

(2) A charitable regard to his poor servant. We read of many that came to Christ for their children, but this is the only instance of one that came to him for a servant: *Lord, my servant lieth at home sick*. The centurion's servants were very dutiful to him (*v.* 9), and here we see what made them so; he was very kind to them, and that made them the more cheerfully obedient to him. Observe, How pathetically he represents his servant's case as very sad; he is *sick of the palsy*, a disease which commonly makes the patient senseless of pain, but this person was *grievously tormented*; being young, nature was strong to struggle with the stroke, which made it painful.

2. Observe his great humility and self-abasement: *Lord, I am not worthy that thou shouldst come under my roof* (*v.* 8), which speaks mean thoughts of himself, and high thoughts of our Lord Jesus. He does not say, "My servant is not worthy that thou shouldst come into his chamber, because it is in

the garret;" But *I am not worthy that thou shouldst come into my house*. The centurion was a great man, yet he owned his unworthiness before God.

3. Observe his great faith. The more humility the more faith; the more diffident we are of ourselves, the stronger will be our confidence in Jesus Christ. He had an assurance of faith not only that Christ could cure his servant, but,

(1) That he could cure him at a distance. There needed not any physical contact, as in natural operations, nor any application to the part affected; but the cure, he believed, might be wrought, without bringing the physician and patient together.

(2) That he could cure him with a *word*, not send him a medicine, much less a charm; but *speak the word only*, and I do not question but *my servant shall be healed*. With men, saying and doing are two things; but not so with Christ, who is therefore the *Arm of the Lord*, because he is the *eternal Word*.

The centurion's faith in the power of Christ he here illustrates by the dominion he had, as a centurion, over his soldiers, as a master over his servants; he says to one, *Go, and he goes*, &c. Thus could Christ speak, and it is done; such a power had he over all bodily diseases. Now, [1] Such servants we all should be to God: we must go and come at his bidding, according to the directions of his word, and the disposals of his providence; run where he sends us, return when he remands us, and do what he appoints. *What saith my Lord unto his servant?* When his will crosses

our own, his must take place, and our own be set aside. [2] Such servants bodily diseases are to Christ. They seize us when he sends them; they leave us when he calls them back; they have that effect upon us, upon our bodies, upon our souls, that he orders. It is a matter of comfort to all that belong to Christ, for whose good his power is exerted and engaged, that every disease has his commission, executes his command, is under his control, and is made to serve the intentions of his grace. They need not fear sickness, nor what it can do, who see it in the hand of so good a Friend.

II. Here is the grace of Christ appearing towards this centurion; for to the gracious he will show himself gracious.

1. He complies with his address at the first word. He did but tell him his servant's case, and was going on to beg a cure, when Christ prevented him, with this good word, and comfortable word, *I will come and heal him* (v. 7).

2. He commends his faith, and takes occasion from it to speak a kind word of the poor Gentiles, *vv*. 10–12. See what great things a strong but self-denying faith can obtain from Jesus Christ, even of general and public concern.

PETER'S MOTHER-IN-LAW
(*vv*. 14–17)

Here we have,

I. A particular account of the cure of *Peter's wife's mother*, who was ill *of a fever*; in which observe,

1. The *case*, which was nothing extraordinary; fevers are the most common illnesses; but, the

patient being a near relation of Peter's, it is recorded as an instance of Christ's peculiar care of, and kindness to, the families of his disciples.

2. The *cure, v.* 15. (1) How it was *effected; He touched her hand*; not to know the disease, as the physicians do, by the pulse, but to heal it. This was an intimation of his kindness and tenderness; he is *himself touched with the feeling of our infirmities*; it likewise shows the way of spiritual healing, by the exerting of the power of Christ with his word, and the application of Christ to ourselves.

II. Here is a general account of the many cures that Christ wrought. This cure of Peter's mother-in-law brought him abundance of patients. "He healed such a one; why not me? Such a one's friend, why not mine?" Now we are here told,

1. What he did, *v.* 16. (1) *He cast out devils; cast out the* evil *spirits with his word.* (2) *He healed all that were sick;* all without exception, though the patient was ever so mean, and the case ever so bad.

2. How the scripture was herein fulfilled, *v.* 17. The accomplishment of the Old-Testament prophecies was the great thing Christ had in his eye, and the great proof of his being the Messiah: among other things, it was written of him (Isa. liii. 4), *Surely he hath borne our griefs, and carried our sorrows*: it is referred to, 1 Pet. ii. 24, and there it is construed, *he hath borne our sins*; here it is referred to, and is construed, *he hath borne our sicknesses*; our sins make our sicknesses our griefs; Christ bore away sin by the merit of his death, and bore away sickness

by the miracles of his life; nay, though those miracles are ceased, we may say, that *he bore our sicknesses* then, *when he bore our sins in his own body upon the tree*; for sin is both the cause and the sting of sickness.

TWO DISCIPLES
(*vv.* 18–22)

Here is Christ's communication with two, who, upon his remove to *the other side*, were loth to stay behind, and had a mind to follow him, not as others, who were his followers at large, but to come into close discipleship, which the most were shy of; for it carried such a face of strictness as they could not like, nor be well reconciled to; but here is an account of two who seemed desirous to come into communion, and yet were not right; which is here given as a specimen of the hindrances by which many are kept from closing with Christ, and cleaving to him; and a warning to us, to set out in following Christ, so as that we may not come short; to lay such a foundation, as that our building may stand.

1. Here is one that was *too hasty in promising*; and he was *a certain scribe* (*v.* 19), a scholar, a learned man, one of those who studied and expounded the law. Now observe,

(1) How he expressed his forwardness; *Master, I will follow thee, whithersoever thou goest.* I know not how any man could have spoken better. Now we should think ourselves sure of such a man as this; and yet it appears, by Christ's answer, that his resolution was rash, his ends low and carnal. Note, There are many resolutions

for religion, produced by some sudden pangs of conviction, and taken up without due consideration, that prove abortive, and come to nothing: soon ripe, soon rotten.

(2) How Christ tried his forwardness, whether it were sincere or not, *v.* 20. He let him know that this *Son of man*, whom he is so eager to follow, *has not where to lay his head*, *v.* 20.

It is strange that such a declaration should be made on this occasion. When a scribe offered to follow Christ, one would think he would have encouraged him, and said, *Come, and I will take care of thee*; one scribe might be capable of doing him more credit and service than twelve disciples: but Christ saw his heart, and answered to the thoughts of that, and therein teaches us all how to come to Christ. *First*, The scribe's resolve seems to have been sudden; and Christ would have us, when we take upon us a profession of religion, to *sit down and count the cost* (Luke xiv. 28), to do it intelligently, and with consideration, and choose the way of godliness, not because we know no other, but because we know no better. *Secondly*, His resolve seems to have been from a worldly, covetous principle. He saw what abundance of cures Christ wrought, and concluded that he had large fees, and would get an estate quickly, and therefore he would follow him in hopes of growing rich with him; but Christ rectifies his mistake, and tells him, he was so far from growing rich, that he had not a place to *lay his head on*; and that if he follow him, he cannot expect to fare better than he fared.

2. Here is another that was too *slow in performing*. Delay in execution is as bad, on the one hand, as precipitancy in resolution is on the other hand; when we have taken time to consider, and then have determined, let it never be said, we left that to be done to-morrow, which we could do today. Now observe here,

(1) The excuse that this disciple made, to defer an immediate attendance on Christ (*v.* 21); "*Lord, suffer me first to go and bury my father.*" His father (some think) was now sick, or dying, or dead; others think, he was only aged, and not likely in a course of nature, to continue long; and he desired leave to attend upon him in his sickness, at his death, and to his grave, and then he would be at Christ's service. This seemed a reasonable request, and yet it was not right. He had not the zeal he should have had for the work, and therefore pleaded this, because it seemed a plausible plea.

(2) Christ's disallowing of this excuse (*v.* 22). His excuse is laid aside as insufficient; *Let the dead bury their dead*. It is a proverbial expression; "Let one dead man bury another: rather let them lie unburied, than that the service of Christ should be neglected. *Let the dead* spiritually *bury the dead* corporally; let worldly offices be left to worldly people; do not thou encumber thyself with them. Burying the dead, and especially a dead father, is a good work, but it is not thy work at this time: it may be done as well by others, that are not called and qualified, as thou art, to be employed for Christ; thou hast

something else to do, and must not defer that."

STORM ON THE LAKE
(*vv.* 23–27)

Now observe here,

I. The peril and perplexity of the disciples in this voyage; and in this appeared the truth of what Christ had just now said, that those who follow him must count upon difficulties, *v.* 20.

1. *There arose a very great storm*, *v.* 24. Christ could have prevented this storm, and have ordered them a pleasant passage, but that would not have been so much for his glory and the confirmation of their faith as their deliverance was: this storm was *for their sakes*, as John xi. 4. The church is *tossed with tempests* (Isa. liv. 11); it is only the upper region that enjoys a perpetual calm, this lower one is ever and anon disturbed and disturbing.

2. Jesus Christ *was asleep in this storm*. We never read of Christ's sleeping but at this time; he was in watchings often, and continued all night in prayer to God: this was a sleep, not of security, like Jonah's in a storm, but of holy serenity, and dependence upon his Father. He slept at this time, to try the faith of his disciples, whether they could trust him when he seemed to slight them. He slept not so much with a desire to be refreshed, as with a design to be awaked.

3. The poor disciples, though used to the sea, were in a great fright, and in their fear *came to* their Master, *v.* 25. Whither else should they go? It was well they had him so near them. They *awoke him* with

their prayers; *Lord, save us, we perish*.

II. The power and grace of Jesus Christ put forth for their succour: then the Lord Jesus awaked, as one refreshed, Ps. lxxviii. 65. Christ may sleep when his church is in a storm, but he will not outsleep himself: the time, the set time to favour his distressed church, will come, Ps. cii. 13.

1. He rebuked the disciples (*v.* 26); *Why are ye fearful, O ye of little faith?* He does not chide them for disturbing him with their prayers, but for disturbing themselves with their fears. Christ reproved them first, and then delivered them; this is his method, to prepare us for a mercy, and then to give it us.

2. *He rebukes the wind*; the former he did as the God of *grace*, and the Sovereign of the heart, who can do what he pleases *in* us; this he did as the God of *nature*, the Sovereign of the world, who can do what he pleases *for* us. It is the same *power that stills the noise of the sea*, and the tumult of fear, Ps. lxv. 7.

CASTING OUT DEVILS
(*vv.* 28–34)

The scope of this chapter is to show the divine power of Christ, by the instances of his dominion over bodily diseases, which to us are irresistible; over winds and waves, which to us are yet more uncontrollable; and lastly, over devils, which to us are most formidable of all. Christ has not only all *power in heaven and earth* and all deep places, but has the keys of hell too.

Now, besides the general instance which this gives us of Christ's power over Satan, and his design against him to disarm and dispossess him, we have here especially discovered to us the way and manner of evil spirits in their enmity to man. Observe, concerning this legion of devils, What work they made where they *were*, and where they *went*.

I. What work they made where they *were*; which appears in the miserable condition of these two that were possessed by them ; and some think, these two were man and wife, because the other Evangelists speak but of one.

1. They dwelt among *the tombs*; thence they came when they met Christ. The devil having *the power of death*, not as judge, but as executioner, he delighted to converse among the trophies of his victory, the dead bodies of men; but there, where he thought himself in the greatest triumph and elevation, as afterwards in Golgotha, the place of a skull, did Christ conquer and subdue him.

2. They were *exceeding fierce*; not only ungovernable themselves, but mischievous to others, frightening many, having hurt some; *so that no man durst pass that way*.

3. They bid defiance to Jesus Christ, and disclaimed all interest in him, *v.* 29. It is an instance of the power of God over the devils, that, notwithstanding the mischief they studied to do *by* and *to* these poor creatures, yet they could not keep them from meeting Jesus Christ, who ordered the matter so as to meet them. It was his overpowering hand that dragged these unclean spirits into his presence, which they dreaded more than any thing else: his chains could hold them, when

the chains that men made for them could not. But being brought before him, they protested against his jurisdiction, and broke out into a rage, *What have we to do with thee, Jesus, thou Son of God?*

II. Let us now see what work they made where they *went*, when they were turned out of the men possessed, and that was into *a herd of swine*, which *was a good way off*, *v.* 30. These Gadarenes, though living on the other side Jordan, were Jews. What had they to do with *swine*, which by the law were unclean, and not to be eaten nor touched? Probably, lying in the outskirts of the land, there were many Gentiles among them, to whom this *herd of swine* belonged: or they kept them to be sold, or bartered, to the Romans, with whom they had now great dealings, and who were admirers of *swine's* flesh. Now observe,

1. How the devils seized the *swine*. Though they were *a good way off*, and, one would think, out of danger, yet the devils had an eye upon them, to do them a mischief: for they *go up and down, seeking to devour*, seeking an opportunity; and they seek not long but they find.

2. *Whither they hurried them*, when they had seized them. They were not bid to *save their lives*, and, therefore, they were made to *run violently down a steep place into the sea*, where they all perished, to the number of about *two thousand*, Mark v. 13. Note, The possession which the devil gets is for destruction. Thus the devil hurries people to sin, hurries them to that which they have resolved against, and which they know will be shame and

grief to them: with what a force doth the evil spirit *work in the children of disobedience*, when by so many foolish and hurtful lusts they are brought to act in direct contradiction, not only to religion, but to right reason, and their interest in this world!

3. *What effect this had upon the owners.* The report of it was soon brought them by the swine-herds, who seemed to be more concerned for the loss of the swine than any thing else, for they went not to tell *what was befallen to the possessed of the devils*, till the swine were lost, *v.* 33. Christ went not *into the city*, but the news of his being there did, by which he was willing to feel how their pulse beat, and what influence it had upon them, and then act accordingly.

Now, (1) Their curiosity brought them out to see Jesus. The *whole city came out to meet him*, that they might be able to say, they had seen a man who did such wonderful works. Thus many go out, in profession, to meet Christ for company, that have no real affection for him, nor desire to know him.

(2) Their covetousness made them *willing to be rid of him.* Instead of inviting him into their city, or bringing their sick to him to be healed, they desired him *to depart out of their coasts*, as if they had borrowed the words of the devils, *What have we to do with thee, Jesus thou Son of God?* And now the devils had what they aimed at in drowning the swine; *they* did it, and then made the people believe that *Christ* had done it, and so prejudiced them against him. He seduced our first parents, by

possessing them with hard thoughts of God, and kept the Gadarenes from Christ, by suggesting that he came into their country to destroy their cattle, and that he would do more hurt than good; for though he had cured two men, yet he had drowned two thousand swine. Thus the devil sows tares in God's field, does mischief in the Christian church, and then lays the blame upon Christianity, and incenses men against that.

CHAPTER NINE

THE PARALYSED MAN
(*vv.* 1–8)

The first words of this chapter oblige us to look back to the close of that which precedes it, where we find the Gadarenes so resenting the loss of their swine, that they were disgusted with Christ's company, and besought him to *depart out of their coasts*. Now here it follows, *He entered into a ship, and passed over.* They bid him begone, and he took them at their word, and we never read that he came into their coasts again.

He came *into his own city, Capernaum*, the principal place of his residence at present (Mark ii. 1), and therefore called *his own city.* At Capernaum all the circumstances recorded in this chapter happened, and are, therefore put, together here, though, in the harmony of the evangelists, other events intervened. When the Gadarenes desired Christ to depart, they of Capernaum received him. If Christ be affronted by some, there are others in whom he will be glorious; if one will not, another will.

Now the first occurrence, after Christ's return to Capernaum, as recorded in these verses, was the cure of the man sick of the palsy. In which we may observe,

I. The *faith of his friends* in bringing him to Christ. *Jesus saw their faith*, the faith of the paralytic himself, as well as of them that brought him; Jesus saw the habit of faith, though his disability, perhaps, impaired his intellect, and obstructed the actings of it. Now their faith was, 1. A strong faith; they firmly believed that Jesus Christ both could and would heal him; else they would not have brought the sick man to him so publicly, and through so much difficulty. 2. A humble faith; though the sick man was unable to stir a step, they would not ask Christ to make him a visit, but brought him to attend on Christ. It is fitter that we should wait on Christ, than he on us. 3. An active faith; in the belief of Christ's power and goodness, they brought the sick man to him, *lying on a bed*, which could not be done without a deal of pains. Note, a strong faith regards no obstacles in pressing after Christ.

II. The *favour of Christ*, in what he said to him; *Son, be of good cheer, thy sins be forgiven thee.* Christ bids him *be of good cheer*; and then cures him. He would have those to whom he deals his gifts, to be cheerful in seeking him, and in trusting in him; to be of good courage. 3. A good reason for that encouragement; *Thy sins are forgiven thee.* Now this may be considered, (1) as an introduction

to the cure of his bodily disability; "Thy sins are *pardoned*, and therefore thou shalt be healed." Or, (2) As a reason of the command to *be of good cheer*, whether he were cured of his disease or not; "Though I should not heal thee, wilt thou not say thou hast not sought in vain, if I assure thee that *thy sins are pardoned*; and wilt thou not look upon that as a sufficient ground of comfort, though thou shouldst continue *sick of the palsy*?" Note, They who, through grace, have some evidence of the forgiveness of their sins, have reason to be of good cheer, whatever outward troubles or afflictions they are under; see Isa. xxxiii. 24.

III. The *cavil of the scribes* at that which Christ said (*v.* 3); They *said within themselves, This man blasphemeth.* See how the greatest instance of heaven's power and grace is branded with the blackest note of hell's enmity; Christ's pardoning sin is termed blasphemy; nor had it been less, if he had not had commission from God for it.

IV. The conviction which Christ gave them of the unreasonableness of this cavil, before he proceeded.

1. He *charged them with it.* Though they did but say it within themselves, he *knew their thoughts.*

2. He *argued them out of it, vv.* 5, 6. Where observe,

(1) How he *asserts* his authority in the *kingdom of grace.* He undertakes to make out, that the *Son of man*, the Mediator, has *power on earth to forgive sins*; for *therefore* the Father has *committed all judgment to the Son*, and has given him this authority, *because he is the Son of man*, John v. 22, 27. If he has

power to give eternal life, as he certainly has (John xvii. 2), he must have power to forgive sin; for guilt is a bar that must be removed, or we can never get to heaven. What an encouragement is this to poor sinners to repent, that the power of pardoning sin is put into the hands of the *Son of man*, who is bone of our bone! And if he had this *power on earth*, much more now that he is exalted to the Father's right hand, to give *repentance and remission of sins*, and so to be both *a Prince and a Saviour*, Acts v. 31.

(2) How he *proves* it, by his power in the kingdom of nature; his power to cure diseases. Is it not as easy to say, *Thy sins are forgiven thee*, as to say, *Arise and walk?* He that can cure the disease, can, in like manner, forgive the sin. Now, [1] This is a general argument to prove that Christ had a divine mission. His miracles, especially his miraculous cures, confirm what he said of himself, that he was the Son of God; the *power* that appeared in his cures proved him *sent of God*; and the *pity* that appeared in them proved him sent of God *to heal and save*. The God of truth would not set his seal to a lie. [2] It had a particular cogency in this case. The palsy was but a symptom of the disease of sin; now he made it to appear, that he could effectually cure the original disease, by the immediate removal of that symptom; so close a connection was there between the sin and the sickness. He that had power to remove the punishment, no doubt, had power to remit the sin.

V. The immediate cure of the sick man. Christ turned from dis-

puting with them, and spake healing to him. The most necessary arguings must not divert us from doing the good that our *hand finds to do*. He saith to *the sick of the palsy, Arise, take up thy bed, and go to thine house*; and a healing, quickening, strengthening power accompanied this word (*v.* 7): *he arose and departed to his house*.

VI. The impression which this made upon the multitude (*v.* 8); they *marvelled*, and *glorified God*. Though few of this multitude were so convinced, as to be brought to believe in Christ, and to follow him, yet they admired him, not as God, or the Son of God, but as a *man* to whom God *had given such power*.

MATTHEW CALLED
(*vv.* 9–13)

In these verses we have an account of the grace and favour of Christ to poor publicans, particularly to Matthew. What he did to the bodies of people was to make way for a kind design upon their souls. Now observe here,

I. The call of Matthew, the penman of this gospel. Mark and Luke call him Levi; it was ordinary for the same person to have two names. Some think Christ gave him the name of Matthew when he called him to be an apostle; as Simon, he surnamed Peter. Matthew signifies, *the gift of God*. Ministers are God's gifts to the church; their ministry, and their ability for it, are God's gifts to them. Now observe the posture that Christ's call found Matthew in. He was *sitting at the receipt of custom*, for he was a publican, Luke v. 27. He was a custom-house officer at the port of

Capernaum, or an exciseman, or collector of the land-tax. It was a calling of ill fame among serious people; because it was attended with so much corruption and temptation, and there were so few in that business that were honest men. Matthew himself owns what he was before his conversion, as does St. Paul (1 Tim. i. 13), that the grace of Christ in calling him might be the more magnified, and to show, that God has his remnant among all sorts of people. None can justify themselves in their unbelief, by their calling in the world; for there is no *sinful* calling, but some have been saved *out of it*, and no *lawful calling*, but some have been saved *in it*.

We do not find that Matthew looked after Christ, or had any inclination to follow him, though some of his kindred were already disciples of Christ, but Christ came to him with the blessings of his goodness. He is found of those that seek him not. Christ *spoke first*; we have not chosen him, but he hath chosen us. He said, *Follow me*; and the same divine, almighty power accompanied this word to convert Matthew, which attended that word (*v.* 6), *Arise and walk*, to cure the man sick of the palsy.

II. Christ's converse with publicans and sinners upon this occasion; Christ called Matthew, to introduce himself into an acquaintance with the people of that profession. *Jesus sat at meat in the house, v.* 10.

Now observe, 1. When Matthew invited Christ, he invited his disciples to *come along with him*. Note, They that welcome Christ,

must welcome all that are his, for his sake, and let them have a room in their hearts. 2. He invited many publicans and sinners to *meet him*. This was the chief thing Matthew aimed at in this treat, that he might have an opportunity of bringing his old associates acquainted with Christ. He knew by experience what their temptations were, and pitied them; knew by experience what the grace of Christ could do, and would not despair concerning them.

III. The displeasure of the Pharisees at this, *v.* 11. They cavilled at it; *why eateth your Master with publicans and sinners?*

IV. The defence that Christ made for himself and his disciples, in justification of their converse with publicans and sinners. Two things he urges in his defence,

1. The need of the publicans, which called aloud for his help, and therefore justified him in conversing with them for their good. It was the extreme necessity of poor, lost sinners, that brought Christ from the pure regions above, to these impure ones; and the same was it, that brought him into this company which was thought impure. Now,

(1) He proves the need of the publicans: *they that be whole need not a physician, but they that are sick*. The publicans are sick, and they need one to help and heal them, which the Pharisees think they do not.

(2) He proves, that their need did sufficiently justify his conduct, in conversing familiarly with them, and that he ought not to be blamed for it; for that necessity made it *an act of charity*. This he proves

(*v.* 13) by a passage quoted out of Hos. vi. 6, *I will have mercy and not sacrifice.*

2. He urges the nature and end of his own commission. He must keep to his orders, and prosecute that for which he was appointed to be the great Teacher; now, says he, "*I am not come to call the righteous, but sinners to repentance,* and therefore must converse with publicans." Observe, (1) What his errand was; it was to *call to repentance.* This was his first text (*ch.* iv. 17), and it was the tendency of all his sermons. (2) With whom his errand lay; not with *the righteous,* but with *sinners.* That is, [1] If the children of men had not been *sinners,* there had been no occasion for Christ's coming among them. He is the Saviour, not of man as *man,* but of man as *fallen.* [2] Therefore his *greatest business* lies with the *greatest sinners;* the more dangerous the sick man's case is, the more occasion there is for the physician's help. Christ came into the world to *save sinners,* but especially *the chief* (1 Tim. i. 15); to call not those so much, who, though sinners, are comparatively righteous, but the worst of sinners. [3] The more aware any sinners are of their sinfulness, the more welcome will Christ and his gospel be to them; is desired, not to those who would rather have his room; to them Christ will come, for to them he will be welcome.

NEW AND OLD WINE
(*vv.* 14–17)

The objections which were made against Christ and his disciples gave occasion to some of the most profitable of his discourses. Observe,

I. The objection which the disciples of John made against Christ's disciples, for not fasting so often as they did; which they are charged with, as another instance of the looseness of their profession, besides that of eating with publicans and sinners; and it is therefore suggested to them, that they should change that profession for another more strict.

1. How they boasted of their own fasting. *We and the Pharisees fast often.* The disciples of John *fasted often,* partly in compliance with their master's practice, for he came *neither eating nor drinking* (*ch.* xi. 18); and people are apt to imitate their leaders, though not always from the same inward principle; partly in compliance with their master's doctrine of repentance. Now they come to Christ to tell him that they *fasted often,* at least they thought it often.

2. How they blamed Christ's disciples for not fasting so often as they did. *Thy disciples fast not.* They could not but know, that Christ had instructed his disciples to keep their fasts private, and to manage themselves so as that they might not *appear unto men to fast;* and, therefore, it was very uncharitable in them to conclude they did *not fast,* because they did not proclaim their fasts. Note, We must not judge of people's religion by that which falls under the eye and observation of the world.

3. How they brought this complaint to Christ. Note, If Christ's disciples, either by omission or commission, give offence, Christ

himself will be sure to hear of it, and be reflected upon for it. *O, Jesus, are these thy Christians?* Therefore, as we tender the honour of Christ, we are concerned to conduct ourselves well. Observe, The quarrel with Christ was brought to the disciples (*v.* 11), the quarrel with the disciples was brought to Christ (*v.* 14), this is the way of sowing discord and killing love, to set people against ministers, ministers against people, and one friend against another.

II. The apology which Christ made for his disciples in this matter. When they had nothing to say for themselves, he had something ready to say for them.

But thou shalt answer, Lord, for me.
                                                Herbert.

Two things Christ pleads in defence of their *not fasting*.

1. That it was not a season proper for that duty (*v.* 15): *Can the children of the bride-chamber mourn, as long as the bridegroom is with them?* Observe, Christ's answer is so framed, as that it might sufficiently justify the practice of his own disciples, and yet not condemn the institution of John, or the practice of his disciples.

Now his argument is taken from the common usage of joy and rejoicing during the continuance of marriage solemnities; when all instances of melancholy and sorrow are looked upon as improper and absurd, as it was at Samson's wedding, Judges xiv. 17. The disciples of Christ had *the bridegroom with them*, which the disciples of John had not; their master was now cast into prison, and lay there in continual danger

of his life, and therefore it was seasonable for them to *fast often*. Such a day would come upon the disciples of Christ, when the bridegroom should be taken from them, when they should be deprived of his bodily presence, and *then should they fast*.

2. That they had not strength sufficient for that duty. This is set forth in two similitudes, one of putting *new cloth into an old garment*, which does but pull the old to pieces (*v.* 16); the other of putting *new wine into old bottles*, which does but burst the bottles, *v.* 17. Christ's disciples were not able to bear these severe exercises so well as those of John and of the Pharisees, who led an austere life. Christ's disciples, being taken immediately from their callings, had not been used to such religious austerities, and were unfit for them, and would by them be rather unfitted for their other work.

JAIRUS'S DAUGHTER
(*vv.* 18–26)

We have here two passages of history put together; that of the raising of Jairus's daughter to life, and that of the curing of the woman that had *the bloody issue*, as he was going to Jairus's house, which is introduced in a parenthesis, in the midst of the other. Here is,

I. The ruler's address to Christ, *v.* 18. *A certain ruler*, a ruler of the synagogue, *came and worshipped him. Have any of the rulers believed on him?* Yes, here was one, a church ruler, whose faith condemned the unbelief of the rest of the rulers. This ruler had a little daughter, of twelve years old, just dead, and this breach made upon his family comforts was the occasion of his coming to Christ. Now observe,

1. His humility in this address to Christ. He came with his errand to Christ himself, and did not send his servant.

2. His faith in this address; "*My daughter is even now dead*", and though any other physician would come too late, yet Christ comes not too late; he is a Physician after death, for he is *the resurrection and the life*; "*O come* then, *and lay thy hand upon her, and she shall live.*"

II. The readiness of Christ to comply with his address, *v.* 19. *Jesus* immediately *arose*, left his company, *and followed him*; he was not only willing to grant him what he desired, in raising his daughter to life, but to gratify him so far as to come to his house to do it.

III. The healing of the poor woman's bloody issue. I call her a poor woman, not only because her case was piteous, but because, though she had had something in the world, she had *spent it all upon physicians*, for the cure of her trouble, and was no better. This *woman was diseased with a constant issue of blood twelve years* (*v.* 20); a disease, which was not only weakening and wasting, and under which the body must needs languish; but which also rendered her ceremonially unclean, and shut her *out from the courts of the Lord's house*; but it did not cut her off from approaching to Christ. Observe,

1. The woman's great faith in Christ, and in his power. Her disease was of such a nature, that

her modesty would not suffer her to speak openly to Christ for a cure, as others did, but by a peculiar impulse of the Spirit of faith, she believed him to have such an overflowing fulness of healing virtue, that the very *touch of his garment* would be her cure.

2. Christ's great favour to this woman. He did not suspend (as he might have done) his healing influences, but suffered this bashful patient to steal a cure unknown to anyone else, though she could not think to do it unknown to him. He *turned about* to see for her (*v.* 22), and soon discovered her. Now here,

(1) He *puts gladness into her heart*, by that word, *Daughter, be of good comfort*. She feared being chidden for coming clandestinely, but she is encouraged.

(2) He puts honour upon her faith. That grace of all others gives most honour to Christ, and therefore he puts most honour upon it; *Thy faith has made thee whole*. Thus *by faith she obtained a good report*. And as of all graces Christ puts the greatest honour upon faith, so of all believers he puts the greatest honour upon those that are most humble; as here on this woman, who had more faith than she thought she had.

IV. The posture in which he found the ruler's house, *v.* 23. — He *saw the people and the minstrels*, or musicians, *making a noise*. The house was in a hurry: such work does death make, when it comes into a family; and, perhaps, the necessary cares that arise at such a time, when our dead is to be decently buried out of our sight, give some useful diversion to that grief which is apt to prevail and play the tyrant. The people in the neighbourhood came together to condole on account of the loss, to comfort the parents, to prepare for, and attend on, the funeral, which the Jews were not wont to defer long. The musicians were among them, according to the custom of the Gentiles, with their doleful, melancholy tunes, to increase the grief, and stir up the lamentations of those that attended on this occasion. Notice is taken of this, to show that the girl was really dead, in the undoubted apprehension of all about her.

V. The rebuke that Christ gave to this hurry and noise, *v.* 24. He said, *Give place.* He gives a good reason why they should not thus disquiet themselves and one another; *The maid is not dead but sleepeth.* 1. This was eminently true of this maid, that was immediately to be raised to life; she was really dead, but not so to Christ, who knew within himself what he would do, and could do, and who had determined to make her death but as a sleep.

Now could it be thought that such a comfortable word as this, from the mouth of our Lord Jesus, should be ridiculed as it was? *They laughed him to scorn.* These people lived in Capernaum, knew Christ's character, that he never spake a rash or foolish word; they knew how many mighty works he had done; so that if they did not understand what he meant by this, they might at least have been silent in expectation of the issue.

VI. The raising of the damsel to life by the power of Christ, *v.* 25.

Christ went in and *took her by the hand,* as it were to awake her, and to help her up, prosecuting his own metaphor of her being asleep. He *took her by the hand, and the maid arose.* So easily, so effectually was the miracle wrought; not by prayer, as Elijah did (1 Kings xvii. 21), and Elisha (2 Kings iv. 33), but by a touch. They did it as servants, he as a Son, as a God, *to whom belong the issues from death.* Note, Jesus Christ is the Lord of souls, he commands them forth, and commands them back, when and as he pleases. Dead souls are not raised to spiritual life, unless Christ *take them by the hand*: it is done in the *day of his power.* He helps us up, or we lie still.

VII. The general notice that was taken of this miracle, though it was wrought privately; *v.* 26, *the fame thereof went abroad into all that land*: it was the common subject of discourse.

TWO BLIND MEN
(*vv.* 27–34)

In these verses we have an account of two more miracles wrought together by our Saviour.

I. The giving of sight to two blind men, *vv.* 27–31. Christ is the Fountain of light as well as life; and as, by raising the dead, he showed himself to be the same that at first *breathed into man the breath of life,* so, by giving sight to the blind, he showed himself to be the same that at first *commanded the light to shine out of darkness.* Observe,

1. The importunate address of the blind men to Christ. Observe,

(1) The title which these blind men gave to Christ; *Thou Son of David, have mercy on us.* The promise made to David, that of his loins the Messiah should come, was well known, and the Messiah was therefore commonly called *the Son of David.* At this time there was a general expectation of his appearing; these blind men know, and own, and proclaim it in the streets of Capernaum, that he is come, and that this is he. They could not see him and his miracles, but *faith comes by hearing.*

(2) Their petition, *Have mercy on us.* It was foretold that the *Son of David* should be *merciful* (Ps. lxxii. 12, 13), and in him *shines the tender mercy of our God,* Luke i. 78.

(3) Their importunity in this request; they *followed him, crying.* It seems, he did not take notice of them at first, for he would try their faith, which he knew to be strong; would quicken their prayers, and make his cures the more valued, when they did not always come at the first word. Christ would not heal them publicly in the streets, for this was a cure he would have kept private (*v.* 30), but *when he came into the house,* they *followed him* thither, and *came to him.* Note, Christ's doors are always open to believing and importunate petitioners; it seemed rude in them to rush into the house after him, when he desired to retire; but, such is the tenderness of our Lord Jesus, that they were not more bold than welcome.

2. The confession of faith, which Christ drew from them upon this occasion. When they came to him for mercy, he asked them, *Believe ye that I am able to do this?* Note, Faith is the great condition of Christ's favours. They who would receive the *mercy* of Christ, must firmly believe the *power* of Christ. What we would have him do for us, we must be fully assured that he is *able to do.*

To this question they give an immediate answer, without hesitation: they said, *Yea, Lord.*

3. The cure that Christ wrought on them; *he touched their eyes, v.* 29. This he did to encourage their faith, which, by his delay, he had tried, and to show that he gives sight to blind souls by the operations of his grace accompanying the word, *anointing the eyes with eye-salve*: and he put the cure upon their faith, *According to your faith be it unto you.* This speaks, (1) His knowledge of the sincerity of their faith, and his acceptance and approbation of it. (2) His insisting upon their faith as necessary; "If you believe, take what you come for." Note, They who apply themselves to Jesus Christ, shall be dealt with *according to their faith*; not according to their *fancies*, nor according to their *profession*, but *according to their faith.*

4. The charge he gave them to keep it private (*v.* 30), *See that no man know it.* He gave them this charge, (1) To set us an example of that humility and lowliness of mind, which he would have us to learn of him. (2) Some think that Christ, in keeping it private, showed his displeasure against the people of Capernaum, who had seen so many miracles, and yet believed not.

(3) He did it in discretion, for his own preservation; because the more he was proclaimed, the more jealous would the rulers of the Jews be of his growing interest among the people. (4) Dr. Whitby gives another reason, which is very considerable, why Christ sometimes concealed his miracles, and afterwards forbid the publishing of his transfiguration; because he would not indulge that pernicious conceit which obtained among the Jews, that their Messiah should be a temporal prince, and so give occasion to the people to attempt the setting up of his kingdom, by tumults and seditions, as they offered to do, John vi. 15. And he observes, that the miracles which Christ wrought among the Gentiles and the Gadarenes, were ordered to be published, because with them there was not that danger.

But honour is like the shadow, which, as it flees from those that follow it, so it follows those that flee from it (*v.* 31); *They spread abroad his fame.*

II. The healing of a *dumb man,* that was *possessed with a devil.* And here observe,

1. His case, which was very sad. He was under the power of the devil in this particular instance, that he was disabled from speaking, *v.* 32.

2. His cure, which was very sudden (*v.* 33), *When the devil was cast out, the dumb spake.* Note, Christ's cures strike at the root, and remove the effect by taking away the cause; they open the lips, by breaking Satan's power in the soul.

3. The consequences of this cure.

(1) *The multitudes marvelled;* and well they might; though *few believed, many wondered.*

(2) *The Pharisees* blasphemed, *v.* 34. When they could not gainsay the convincing evidence of these miracles, they fathered them upon the devil, as if they had been wrought by compact and collusion: *he casteth out devils* (say they) by *the prince of the devils*—a suggestion horrid beyond expression.

THE SCATTERED SHEEP
(*vv.* 35–38)

Here is a preface, or introduction, to the account in the following chapter, of his sending forth his apostles. *He* took notice of *the multitude* (*v.* 36); not only of the crowds that *followed him,* but of the vast numbers of people with whom (as he passed along) he observed the country to be replenished; he noticed what nests of souls the towns and cities were, and how thick of inhabitants; what abundance of people there were in every synagogue, and what places of concourse the openings of the gates were: so very populous was that nation now grown; and it was the effect of God's blessing on Abraham. Seeing this,

1. He pitied them, and was concerned for them (*v.* 36); *He was moved with compassion on them;* not upon a temporal account, as he pitied the blind, and lame, and sick; but upon a spiritual account; he was concerned to see them ignorant and careless, and ready to perish for lack of vision. The most Christian compassion is compassion to souls; it is most Christ-like.

See what moved this pity. (1)

They fainted; they were destitute, vexed, wearied. *They strayed*, so some; were loosed one from another; *The staff of bands was broken*, Zech. xi. 14. They wanted help for their souls, and had none at hand that was good for anything. (2) *They were scattered abroad, as sheep having no shepherd*. That expression is borrowed from 1 Kings xxii. 17, and it sets forth the sad condition of those that are destitute of faithful guides to go before them in the things of God.

He excited his disciples to pray for them. His pity put him upon devising means for the good of these people. It appears (Luke vi. 12, 13) that upon this occasion, before he sent out his apostles, he did himself spend a great deal of time in prayer. Note, Those we pity we should pray for. Having spoken to God for them he turns to his disciples, and tells them,

(1) How the case stood; *The harvest truly is plenteous, but the labourers are few*. People desired good preaching, but there were few good preachers. There was a great deal of work to be done, and a great deal of good likely to be done, but there wanted hands to do it. [1] It was an encouragement, that *the harvest* was so *plenteous*. [2] It was a pity when it was so that *the labourers* should be so *few*; loiterers many, but *labourers* very *few*.

(2) What was their duty in this case (*v.* 38); *Pray ye therefore the Lord of the harvest*. When things look discouraging, we should pray more, and then we should complain and fear less. Note, [1] God is *the Lord of the harvest; my Father is the Husbandman*, John xv. 1. It is

the vineyard of the Lord of hosts, Isa. v. 7. It is for him and to him, and to his service and honour, that *the harvest* is gathered in. [2] Ministers are and should be *labourers* in God's *harvest*; the ministry is a *work* and must be attended to accordingly; it is *harvest-work*, which is needful work; work that requires every thing to be done in its season, and diligence to do it thoroughly; but it is pleasant work; they *reap in joy*. [3] It is God's work to *send forth labourers*; Christ makes ministers (Eph. iv. 11); the office is of his appointing, the qualifications of his working, the call of his giving. [4] All that love Christ and souls, should show it by their earnest prayers to God, especially when *the harvest is plenteous, that he would send forth* more skilful, faithful, wise, and industrious *labourers into his harvest*.

CHAPTER TEN

THE DISCIPLES (*vv.* 1–4)

Here we are told, I. Who they were that Christ ordained to be his apostles or ambassadors; they were his disciples, *v.* 1. He had called them some time before to be disciples, his immediate followers and constant attendants, and he then told them that they should be made fishers of men, which promise he now performed. Note, Christ commonly confers honours and graces by degrees; the light of both, like that of the morning, *shines more and more*.

II. What the commission was that he gave them.

1. He *called them to him, v.* 1. He had called them to come *after* him

before; now he calls them to come *to* him, admits them to a greater familiarity, and will not have them to keep at such a distance as they had hitherto observed. They that *humble themselves* shall thus be *exalted*. It is observable, that when the disciples were to be *instructed*, they *came unto* him of their own accord, *ch.* v. 1. But now they were to be *ordained*, he *called them*.

2. He *gave them power, authority* in his name, to command men to obedience, and for the confirmation of that authority, to command devils too into a subjection. Note, The design of the gospel was to *conquer the devil* and to *cure the world*. These preachers were sent out destitute of all external advantages to recommend them; they had no wealth, nor learning, nor titles of honour, and they made a very mean figure; it was therefore requisite that they should have some extraordinary power to advance them above the scribes.

He gave them power to *heal all manner of sickness*. He authorized them to work miracles for the confirmation of their doctrine, to prove that it was of God; and they were to work useful miracles for the illustration of it, to prove that it is not only faithful, but well *worthy of all acceptation*; that the design of the gospel is to heal and save.

III. The number and names of those that were commissioned; they are made apostles, that is, messengers. An angel, and an apostle, both signify the same thing—one *sent on an errand*, an ambassador. All faithful ministers are sent of Christ, but they that

were first, and immediately, sent by him, are eminently called *apostles*, the prime ministers of state in his kingdom. Yet this was but the infancy of their office; it was when Christ *ascended on high* that he *gave some apostles*, Eph. iv. 11. Christ himself is called an apostle (Heb. iii. 1), for he was *sent by the Father*, and so sent them, John xx. 21. The prophets were called God's messengers.

There are some of these twelve apostles, of whom we know no more, from the scripture, than their names; as Bartholomew, and Simon the Canaanite; and yet they were faithful servants to Christ and his church. Note, all the good ministers of Christ are not alike famous, nor their actions alike celebrated.

They are named by couples; for at first they were sent forth *two and two*, because *two are better than one*; they would be serviceable to each other, and the more serviceable jointly to Christ and souls.

Judas Iscariot is always named last, and with that black brand upon his name, *who also betrayed him*; which intimates that from the first, Christ knew what a wretch he was, that he had a devil, and would prove a traitor; yet Christ took him among the apostles, that it might not be a surprise and discouragement to his church, if, at any time, the vilest scandals should break out in the best societies.

THEIR INSTRUCTIONS
(*vv.* 5–15)

We have here the instructions that Christ gave to his disciples, when he gave them their commission. Observe,

I. The people to whom he sent them. These ambassadors are directed what places to go to.

1. Not to the Gentiles nor the Samaritans. They must not *go into the way of the Gentiles*, nor into any road out of the land of Israel, whatever temptations they might have. The Gentiles must not have the gospel brought them, till the Jews have first refused it. As to the Samaritans, who were the posterity of that mongrel people that the king of Assyria planted about Samaria, their country lay between Judea and Galilee, so that they could not avoid *going into the way* of the Samaritans, but they must *not enter into any of their cities*. Christ had declined manifesting himself to the Gentiles or Samaritans, and therefore the apostles must not preach to them. If the gospel be hid from any place, Christ thereby hides himself from that place. This restraint was upon them only in their first mission, afterwards they were appointed to go *into all the world*, and teach *all nations*.

2. But *to the lost sheep of the house of Israel*. To them Christ appropriated his own ministry (*ch.* xv. 24), for he was a *minister of the circumcision* (Rom. xv. 8): and, therefore, to them the apostles, who were but his attendants and agents, must be confined. The first offer of salvation must be made to the Jews, Acts iii. 26.

II. The preaching work which he appointed them. He did not send them forth without an errand; no, *As ye go, preach, v.* 7. They were to be itinerant preachers: wherever they come they must proclaim the beginning of the gospel, saying, *The kingdom of heaven is at hand.* Not that they must say nothing else, but this must be their text; on this subject they must enlarge: let people know, that the kingdom of the Messiah, who is the Lord from heaven, is now to be set up according to the scriptures; from whence it follows, that men must *repent* of their sins and forsake them, that they might be admitted to the privileges of that kingdom.

III. The power he gave them to work miracles for the confirmation of their doctrine, *v.* 8. When he sent them to preach the same doctrine that he had preached, he empowered them to confirm it, by the same divine seals, which could never be set to a lie. This is not necessary now the kingdom of God is come; to call for miracles now is to lay again the foundation when the building is reared. The point being settled, and the doctrine of Christ sufficiently attested, by the miracles which Christ and his apostles wrought, it is tempting God to ask for more signs. They are directed here,

1. To use their power in doing good: not "Go and remove mountains," or "fetch fire from heaven," but, *Heal the sick, cleanse the lepers.*

2. In *doing good freely; Freely ye have received, freely give.* Those that had power to heal all diseases, had an opportunity to enrich themselves; who would not purchase such easy certain cures at any rate? Therefore they are cautioned not to make a gain of the power they had to work miracles: they must cure *gratis*, further to exemplify the nature and complexion of the

gospel kingdom, which is made up, not only of grace, but of free grace.

IV. The provision that must be made for them in this expedition.

1. They must make no provision for it themselves, *vv.* 9, 10. *Provide neither gold nor silver*. Christ would teach them, (1) To act *under the conduct of human prudence*. They were now to make but a short excursion, and were soon to return to their Master, and to their head-quarters again, and, therefore, why should they burden themselves with that which they would have no occasion for? (2) To act in *dependence upon Divine Providence*. They must be taught to live, without *taking thought for life, ch.* vi. 25, &c. Those whom he employs, as they are taken under special protection, so they are entitled to special provisions. Christ's hired servants shall have *bread enough and to spare*; while we abide faithful to God and our duty, and are in care to do our work well, we may cast all our other care upon God.

2. They might expect that those to whom they were sent would *provide for them* what was necessary, *v.* 10. The *workman is worthy of his meat*. They must not expect to be fed by miracles, as Elijah was: but they might depend upon God to incline the hearts of those they went among, to be kind to them, and provide for them.

V. The proceedings they were to observe in dealing with any place, *vv.* 11–15.

1. They are here directed how to conduct themselves toward those that were *strangers to them*; How to do,

(1) In *strange towns and cities*:

when you come to a town, *enquire who* in it *is worthy*. [1] It is supposed that there were some such in every place, as were better disposed than others to receive the gospel, and the preachers of it; though it was a time of general corruption and apostasy. [2] They must enquire out such; not enquire for the best inns; public houses were no proper places for them that neither took money with them (*v.* 9), nor expected to receive any (*v.* 8); but they must look out for accommodations in private houses, with those that would entertain them well, and expect no other recompence for it but a prophet's reward, an apostle's reward, their praying and preaching. [3] In the house of those they found worthy, they must continue; which intimates that they were to make so short a stay at each town, that they needed not change their lodging, but whatever house providence brought them to at first, there they must continue till they left that town.

(2) In strange houses. When they had found the house of one they thought worthy, they must at their entrance salute it.

When they had saluted the family after a godly sort, they must, by the return, judge concerning the family, and proceed accordingly. If *the house be worthy, let your peace come* and rest *upon it; if not, let it return to you, v.* 13. It seems then, that after they had enquired for the *most worthy* (*v.* 11), it was possible they might light upon those that were unworthy.

The case is put (*v.* 14) of those that *would not receive them, nor hear their words*. The apostles might think, that now they had such a doctrine to preach, and such a power to work miracles for the confirmation of it, no doubt but they should be universally entertained and made welcome: they are, therefore, told before, that there would be those that would slight them, and put contempt on them and their message. Note, The best and most powerful preachers of the gospel must expect to meet with some, that will not so much as give them the hearing, nor show them any token of respect.

Now in this case we have here,

(1) The directions given to the apostles what to do. They must *depart out of that house or city*. At their departure they must *shake off the dust of their feet*.

(2) The *doom passed* upon such *wilful recusants, v.* 15. It shall be *more tolerable, in the day of judgment, for the land of* Sodom, as wicked a place as it was.

COUNSEL AND COMFORT
(*vv.* 16–42)

All these verses relate to the sufferings of Christ's ministers in their work, which they are here taught to expect, and prepare for; they are directed also how to bear them, and how to go on with their work in the midst of them.

I. We have here predictions of trouble: which the disciples should meet with in their work: Christ foresaw *their* sufferings as well as his own, and yet will have them go on, as he went on himself; and he foretold them, not only that the troubles might not be a surprise to them, and so a shock to their faith, but that, being the accomplishment

of a prediction, they might be a confirmation to their faith. ·

He tells them what they should suffer, and from whom.

1. *What they should suffer;* hard things to be sure; for, *Behold, I send you forth as sheep in the midst of wolves, v.* 16. And what may a flock of poor, helpless, unguarded sheep expect, in the midst of a herd of ravenous wolves, but to be worried and torn? Note, Wicked men are like wolves, in whose nature it is to devour and destroy. God's people, and especially his ministers, are like sheep among them, of a contrary nature and disposition, exposed to them, and commonly an easy prey to them.

(1) They must expect to be hated, *v.* 22. *Ye shall be hated for my name's sake;* that is the root of all the rest, and a bitter root it is.

(2) They must expect to be apprehended and arraigned as malefactors. They must look for trouble, not only from inferior magistrates in the councils, but from governors and kings, the supreme magistrates. We find this often fulfilled in the *acts of the apostles.*

(3) They must expect to be put to death (*v.* 21); *They shall deliver them to death,* to death in state, with pomp and solemnity, when it shows itself most as *the king of terrors.* They were put to death as criminals, so the enemies meant it, but really as sacrifices (Phil. ii. 17; 2 Tim. iv. 6); as burnt offerings, sacrifices of acknowledgment to the honour of God, and in his truth and cause.

(4) They must expect, in the midst of these sufferings, to be

branded with the most odious and ignominious names and characters that could be. The blackest of all the ill characters they give them is here stated; they call them Beelzebub, the name of the prince of the devils, *v.* 25.

(5) These sufferings are here represented by a sword and division, *vv.* 34, 35. *Think not that I am come to send peace*, temporal peace and outward prosperity; they thought Christ came to give all his followers wealth and power in the world; "no," says Christ, "I did not come with a view to give them *peace*; *peace* in heaven they may be sure of, but not *peace* on earth." Christ came to give us *peace* with God, *peace* in our consciences, *peace* with our brethren, but *in the world ye shall have tribulation*.

These hard things Christ's disciples must suffer,

(1) From men (*v.* 17). The nature of man, if it be not sanctified, is the worst nature in the world next to that of devils. *They are men*, and therefore subordinate, dependent, dying creatures; *they are men*, but *they are but men* (Ps. ix. 20), and *who art thou, that thou shouldst be afraid of a man that shall die?* Isa. li. 12.

(2) From professing men, men that *have a form of godliness*, and make a show of religion. *They will scourge you in their synagogues*, their places of meeting for the worship of God, and for the exercise of their church-discipline: so that they looked upon the scourging of Christ's ministers to be a branch of their religion.

(3) From great men, and men in authority. The Jews did not only

scourge them, which was the utmost their remaining power extended to, but when they could go no further themselves, they delivered them up to the Roman powers, as they did Christ, John xviii. 30. *Ye shall be brought before governors and kings* (*v.* 18), who, having more power, are in a capacity of doing the more mischief. *Governors and kings* receive their power from Christ (Prov. viii. 15), and should be his servants, and his church's protectors and nursing-fathers, but they often use their power against him, and are rebels to Christ, and oppressors of his church. *The kings of the earth* set themselves against his kingdom, Ps. ii. 1, 2; Acts iv. 25, 26.

(4) From all men (*v.* 22). *Ye shall be hated of all men*, of all wicked men, and these are the generality of men, *for the whole world lies in wickedness*. As far as the apostasy from God goes, so far the enmity against the saints goes; sometimes it appears more general than at other times, but there is something of this poison lurking in the hearts of all *the children of disobedience*.

(5) From those of their own kindred. *The brother shall deliver up the brother to death*, *v.* 21. In general, *a man's foes shall be they of his own household* (*v.* 36). They who should be his friends will be incensed against him for embracing Christianity, and especially for adhering to it when it comes to be persecuted, and will join with his persecutors against him. Note, The strongest bonds of relative love and duty have often been broken through, by an enmity against Christ and his doctrine.

II. With these predictions of trouble, we have here prescriptions of counsels and comforts for a time of trial. Let us gather up what he says,

1. By way of counsel and direction in several things.

(1) *Be ye wise as serpents*, *v.* 16. The disciples of Christ are hated and persecuted as *serpents*, and their ruin is sought, and, therefore, they need the *serpent's* wisdom.

(2) *Be ye harmless as doves.* It must be the continual care of all Christ's disciples, to be innocent and inoffensive in word and deed, especially in consideration of the enemies they are in the midst of. We have need of a *dove-like* spirit, when we are beset with birds of prey, that we may neither provoke them nor be provoked by them.

(3) *Beware of men*, *v.* 17. Ever since our Master was betrayed with a kiss, by one of his own disciples, we have need to *beware of men, of false brethren.*

(4) *Take no thought how or what ye shall speak*, *v.* 19. The disciples of Christ must be more thoughtful how to *do* well than how to *speak* well; how to *keep* their integrity than how to *vindicate* it.

(5) *When they persecute you in this city, flee to another*, *v.* 23. He that flies may fight again. It is no inglorious thing for Christ's soldiers to quit their ground, provided they do not quit their colours: they may go out of the way of *danger*, though they must not go out of the way of *duty.*

(6) *Fear them not* (*v.* 26), because *they can but kill the body* (*v.* 28). Note, it is the duty and interest of Christ's disciples, not to fear the

greatest of their adversaries. They who truly fear God, need not fear man; and they who are afraid of the least sin, need not be afraid of the greatest trouble.

Fear him who is able to destroy both soul and body in hell. Note, First, *Hell* is the destruction both of *soul and body*; not of the *being* of either, but the *well-*being of both; it is the ruin of the whole man; if the soul be lost, the body is lost too. Secondly, This destruction comes from the power of God: he *is able to destroy*; it is a destruction from his *glorious power* (2 Thess. i. 9); *he will* in it *make his power known*; not only his authority to sentence, but his ability to execute the sentence, Rom. ix. 22.

(7) *What I tell you in darkness, that speak ye in light* (*v.* 27). The particular instructions which he gave his disciples after his resurrection, concerning *the things pertaining to the kingdom of God*, were whispered in the ear (Acts i. 3), for then *he never showed himself openly.* But they must deliver their embassy publicly, *in the light*, and *upon the house-tops*; for the doctrine of the gospel is what all are concerned in (Prov. i. 20, 21; viii. 2, 3), therefore *he that hath ears to hear, let him hear.*

2. By way of comfort and encouragement.

(1) Here is one word peculiar to their present mission, *v.* 23. *Ye shall not have gone over the cities of Israel, till the Son of man be come.* They were to preach that *the kingdom of the Son of man*, the Messiah, was *at hand*; they were to pray, *Thy kingdom come*: now they should *not have gone over all the cities of*

Israel, thus praying and thus preaching, before that kingdom should come, in the exaltation of Christ, and the pouring out of the Spirit.

(2) Here are many words that relate to their work in general, and the troubles they were to meet with in it; and *they are good words and comfortable words.*

[1] That their sufferings were *for a testimony against them and the Gentiles*, *v.* 18. God's people, and especially God's ministers, are his witnesses (Isa. xliii. 10), not only in their *doing* work, but in their *suffering* work. Hence they are called martyrs — *witnesses* for Christ, that his truths are of undoubted certainty and value; and, being witnesses for him, they are witnesses against those who oppose him and his gospel.

[2] That upon all occasions they should have God's special presence with them, and the immediate assistance of his Holy Spirit, particularly when they should be called out to bear their testimony *before governors and kings; it shall be given you* (said Christ) *in that same hour what ye shall speak.* They cannot but come off well, who have such an advocate; to whom God says, as he did to Moses (Exod. iv. 12), *Go, and I will be with thy mouth, and with thy heart.*

[3] That *he that endures to the end shall be saved*, *v.* 22. Here it is very comfortable to consider, First, that there will be an *end* of these troubles; they may last long, but will not last always. Christ comforted himself with this, and so may his followers; *The things concerning me have an end*, Luke xxii. 37.

Secondly, That while they continue, they may be *endured*; as they are not *eternal*, so they are not *intolerable*; they may be borne, and borne · *to the end*, because the sufferers shall be borne up under them, in everlasting arms.

[4] That whatever hard usage the disciples of Christ meet with, it is no more than what their Master met with before (*vv.* 24, 25). *The disciple is not above his master.* Let us not think it strange, if they who hated him hate his followers, for his sake; nor think it hard if they who are shortly to be · made *like him in glory*, be now made *like him in sufferings.* Christ began in the *bitter cup*, let us be willing to pledge him; his bearing the cross made it easy for us.

[5] That *there is nothing covered that shall not be revealed*, *v.* 26. We understand this, First, Of the revealing of the gospel to all the world. The *ends of the earth must see this salvation.* Or, Secondly, Of the clearing up of the innocency of Christ's suffering servants, that are called Beelzebub; their true character is now invidiously disguised with false colours, but however their innocency and excellency are now *covered*, they *shall be revealed*: sometimes it is in a great measure done in this world, when the righteousness of the saints is made, by subsequent events, to *shine forth as the light*: however, it will be done at the great day, when their glory shall be manifested to all the world, angels and men, to whom they are now *made spectacles*, 1 Cor. iv. 9.

[6] That the providence of God is in a special manner conversant about the saints, in their suffering,

vv. 29–31. It is good to have recourse to our first principles, and particularly to the doctrine of God's universal providence, extending itself to all the creatures, and all their actions, even the smallest and most minute. The light of nature teaches us this, and it is comfortable to all men, but especially to all good men, who can in faith call this God their Father, and for whom he has a tender concern. He that feeds the sparrows, will not starve the saints. *Fear ye not, therefore, v.* 31. There is enough in the doctrine of God's providence to silence all the fears of God's people: *Ye are of more value than many sparrows.*

But the very hairs of your head are all numbered. This is a proverbial expression, denoting the account which God takes and keeps of all the concernments of his people, even of those that are most minute, and least regarded. If God numbers their hairs, much more does he number their heads, and take care of their lives, their comforts, their souls. It intimates, that God takes more care of them, than they do of themselves.

The foundation of their discipleship was laid in such a temper and disposition, as would make sufferings very light and easy to them; and it was upon the condition of a preparedness for suffering, that Christ took them to be his followers, *vv.* 37–39. He told them at first, that they were *not worthy of* him, if they were not willing to part with all for him. If religion be worth *any* thing, it is worth *every* thing: and, therefore, all who believe the truth of it, will soon come up to the price of it; and they who make it their

business and bliss, will make everything else to yield to it.

Our nearest and dearest relations; *father or mother, son or daughter.* Between these relations, because there is little room left for envy, there is commonly more room for love, and, therefore, these are instanced, as relations which are most likely to affect us. Children must love their parents, and parents must love their children; but if they love them better than Christ, they are unworthy of him.

Secondly, our ease and safety. We must *take up our cross* and *follow him,* else we are *not worthy* of him. They who would *follow Christ,* must expect *their cross* and *take it up.*

Thirdly, life itself, *v.* 39. *He that findeth his life shall lose it;* he that thinks he has found it when he has saved it, and kept it, by denying Christ, *shall lose it* in an eternal death; but *he that loseth his life for Christ's sake,* that will part with it rather than deny Christ, *shall find it,* to his unspeakable advantage, an eternal life. They are best prepared for the life to come, that sit most loose to this present life.

He that receiveth me, receiveth him that sent me. Not only Christ takes it as done to himself, but through Christ God does so too. By entertaining Christ's ministers, they entertain not *angels unawares,* but Christ, nay, and God himself, and *unawares* too, as appears, *ch.* xxv. 37. *When saw we thee an hungered?*

That though the kindness done to Christ's disciples be never so small, yet if there be occasion for it, and ability to do no more, it shall be accepted, though it be *but a cup of* cold water given to one of these little ones, v. 42. They are little ones, poor and weak, and often stand in need of refreshment, and glad of the least. The extremity may be such, that a cup of cold water may be a great favour. Note, Kindnesses shown to Christ's disciples are valued in Christ's books, not according to the cost of the gift, but according to the love and affection of the giver.

That kindness to Christ's disciples which he will accept, must be done with an eye to Christ, and for his sake. A prophet must be received in the name of a prophet, and a righteous man in the name of a righteous man, and one of those little ones in the name of a disciple; not because they are learned, or witty, nor because they are our relations or neighbours, but because they are righteous, and so bear Christ's image; because they are prophets and disciples, and so are sent on Christ's errand.

CHAPTER ELEVEN

A MESSAGE FOR JOHN
(vv. 1–6)

Now John Baptist, hearing of Christ's works, sent two of his disciples to him; and what passed between them and him we have here an account of. Here is,

I. The question they had to propose to him: Art thou he that should come, or do we look for another? This was a serious and important question; Art thou the Messiah promised, or not? Art thou the Christ? Tell us. 1. It is taken for granted that the Messiah should come. 2. They intimate, that if this

be not he, they would look for another. Note, We must not be weary of looking for him that is to come, nor ever say, we will no more expect him till we come to enjoy him. 3. They intimate likewise, that if they be convinced that this is he, they will not be sceptics, they will be satisfied, and will look for no other. 4. They therefore ask, Art thou he? John had said for his part, I am not the Christ, John i. 20. Now, (1) Some think that John sent this question for his own satisfaction. It is true he had borne a noble testimony to Christ; he had declared him to be the Son of God (John i. 34), the Lamb of God (v. 29), and he that should baptize with the Holy Ghost (v. 33), and sent of God (John iii. 34), which were great things. But he desired to be further and more fully assured, that he was the Messiah that had been so long promised and expected. (2) John's doubt might arise from his own present circumstances. He was a prisoner, and might be tempted to think, if Jesus be indeed the Messiah, whence is it that I, his friend and forerunner, am brought into this trouble, and am left to be so long in it. It was perhaps a shock to his faith in Christ. Note, [1] Where there is true faith, yet there may be a mixture of unbelief. The best are not always alike strong. [2] Troubles for Christ, especially when they continue long unrelieved, are such trials of faith as sometimes prove too hard to be borne up against. [3] The remaining unbelief of good men may sometimes, in an hour of temptation, strike at the root, and call in question the most fundamental truths which were thought to be well settled. *Will the Lord cast off for ever?* But, (3) Others think that John sent his disciples to Christ with this question, not so much for his own satisfaction as for theirs. Now, [1] They were weak in knowledge, and wavering in their faith, and needed instruction and confirmation. Now John would have their mistakes rectified, and wished them to be as well satisfied as he himself was. [2] John was all along industrious to turn over his disciples to Christ. Perhaps he foresaw his death approaching, and therefore would bring his disciples to be better acquainted with Christ, under whose guardianship he must leave them.

II. Here is Christ's answer to this question, *vv.* 4–6. It was not so direct and express, as when he said, *I that speak unto thee am he*; but it was a real answer, an answer in fact.

1. He points them to what they heard and saw, which they must tell John, that he might from thence take occasion the more fully to instruct and convince them out of their own mouths. Go and tell him *what you hear* and *see*. Note, Our senses may and ought to be appealed to in those things that are their proper objects.

(1) *What you see* of the *power of Christ's miracles*. They are to be considered, [1] As the *acts of a divine power*. None but the God of nature could thus overrule and outdo the power of nature. It is particularly spoken of as God's prerogative to *open the eyes of the blind*, Ps. cxlvi. 8. Miracles are therefore the broad seal of heaven, and the doctrine they are affixed

to must be of God, for his power will never contradict his truth; nor can it be imagined that he should set his seal to a lie; and they leave no room to doubt that he was sent of God, and that his doctrine was his that *sent him*. [2] As the *accomplishment of a divine prediction*. It was foretold (Isa. xxxv. 5, 6), that our God should come, and that then *the eyes of the blind should be opened*. Now if the works of Christ agree with the words of the prophet, as it is plain they do, then no doubt but this is our God whom we have waited for, who shall *come with a recompence*; this is he who is so much wanted.

(2) Tell him *what you hear* of the *preaching of his gospel*, which accompanies his miracles. Faith, though confirmed by seeing, comes by hearing. Note, It is a proof of Christ's divine mission that his doctrine is gospel indeed; good news to those who are truly humbled in sorrow for their sins, and truly humble in the denial of self.

2. He pronounces a *blessing* on those that *were not offended in him*, *v.* 6. So clear are these evidences of Christ's mission, that they who are not wilfully prejudiced against him, and scandalized in him (so the word is), cannot but receive his doctrine, and so be *blessed in him*.

JOHN HONOURED
(*vv.* 7–15)

Concerning this commendation of John, observe.

I. That Christ spoke thus honourably of John, not in the hearing of John's disciples, but *as they departed*, just after they were gone,

Luke vii. 24. He would not so much as seem to flatter John, nor have these praises of him reported to him.

II. That what Christ said concerning John, was intended not only for his praise, but for the people's profit, to revive the remembrance of John's ministry, which had been well attended, but which was now (as other such things used to be) strangely forgotten: they did for a season, and but *for a season, rejoice in his light*, John v. 35.

III. Let us see what the commendation of John was. They know not what answer to make to Christ's question; well, says Christ, "I will tell you what a man John the Baptist was."

1. "He was a firm, resolute man, and not *a reed shaken with the wind*; *you* have been so in your thoughts of him, but *he* was not so. He was not wavering in his principles, nor uneven in his conversation; but was remarkable for his steadiness and constant consistency with himself."

2. He was a *self-denying* man, and *mortified* to this world. "Was he a man *clothed in soft raiment*? If so, you would not have gone *into the wilderness* to see him, but to the *court*. You went to see one that had *his raiment of camel's hair*, and a *leathern girdle about his loins*; his mien and habit showed that he was dead to all the pomps of the world and the pleasures of sense; his clothing agreed with the *wilderness* he lived in, and the doctrine he preached there, that of repentance.

3. His greatest commendation of all was his office and ministry, which was more his honour than any personal endowments or quali-

fications could be; and therefore this is most enlarged upon in a full encomium.

(1) He was *a prophet*, yea, and *more than a prophet* (*v.* 9); so he said of him who was the great Prophet, to whom all the prophets bear witness. John said of himself, he was not *that prophet*, that great prophet, the Messiah himself; and now Christ (a very competent Judge) says of him, that he was *more than a prophet*. He owned himself inferior to Christ, and Christ owned him superior to all other prophets. They *saw Christ's day* at a distance, and their vision was yet for a great while to come; but John saw the day dawn, he saw the sun rise, and told the people of the Messiah, as one that stood among them. They spake of Christ, but he pointed to him; they said, *A virgin shall conceive*: he said, *Behold the Lamb of God!*

(2) He was the same that was predicted to be Christ's forerunner (*v.* 10); *This is he of whom it is written*. He was prophesied of by the other prophets, and therefore was greater than they. Malachi prophesied concerning John, *Behold, I send my messenger before thy face*. That which advanced John above the *Old-Testament* prophets was, that he went immediately before Christ. Note, The nearer any are to Christ, the more truly honourable they are.

(3) There *was not a greater born of women* than John the Baptist, *v.* 11. Christ knew how to value persons according to the degrees of their worth, and he prefers John before all that went before him, before all that were *born of women*

by ordinary generation. Of all that God had raised up and called to any service in his church, John is the most eminent, even beyond Moses himself; for he began to preach the gospel doctrine of remission of sins to those who are truly penitent; and he had more signal revelations from heaven than any of them had; for he *saw heaven opened*, and the *Holy Ghost descend*.

Yet this high encomium of John has a surprising limitation, *notwithstanding, he that is least in the kingdom of heaven is greater than he*. [1] In the kingdom *of glory*. John was a *great* and *good* man, but he was yet in a state of infirmity and imperfection, and therefore came short of glorified saints, and the *spirits of just men made perfect*. [2] By the *kingdom of heaven* here, is rather to be understood the *kingdom of grace*, the gospel dispensation in the perfection of its power and purity. John came to the dawning of the gospel-day, and therein excelled the foregoing prophets, but he was taken off before the noon of that day, before the rending of the veil, before Christ's death and resurrection, and the pouring out of the Spirit; so that the least of the apostles and evangelists, having greater discoveries made to them, and being employed in a greater embassy, is *greater than John*.

(4) The great commendation of John the Baptist was, that God owned his ministry, and made it wonderfully successful for the breaking of the ice, and the preparing of people for the *kingdom of heaven. From the days of* the first

appearing of *John the Baptist*, until now (which was not much above two years), a great deal of good was done; so quick was the motion when it came near to Christ the Centre.

(5) The ministry of John was the *beginning of the gospel*, as it is reckoned, Mark i. 1; Acts i. 22. This is shown here in two things:

[1] In John the Old Testament dispensation began to die, *v*. 13. So long that ministration continued in full force and virtue, but then it began to decline. The law was given by Moses long ago, and there had been no prophets for three hundred years before John, and yet they are both said to *prophecy until John*, because the law was still observed, and Moses and the prophets still read. Their prophecies of a Christ to come became out of date, when John said, *He is come*.

[2] In him the New-Testament day began to dawn; for (*v*. 14) *This is Elias, that was for to come*. John was as the loop that coupled the two Testaments. The concluding prophecy of the Old Testament was, *Behold, I will send you Elijah*, Mal. iv. 5, 6. Those words prophesied until John, and then, being turned into a history, they ceased to prophesy. First, Christ speaks of it as a great truth, that John the Baptist is the Elias of the New Testament; one that should come in the spirit and power of Elias (Luke i. 17), like him in temper and conversation, that should press repentance with terrors, and especially as it is in the prophecy, that should *turn the hearts of the fathers to the children*. Secondly, He speaks of it as a truth, which would

not be easily apprehended by those whose expectations fastened upon the temporal kingdom of the Messiah, and introductions to it agreeable. Christ suspects the welcome of it, *if ye will receive it*. Christ is a Saviour, and John an Elias, to those who will receive the truth concerning them.

Lastly, Our Lord Jesus closes this discourse with a solemn demand of attention (*v.* 15): *He that hath ears to hear, let him hear*; which intimates, that those things were dark and hard to be understood, and therefore needed attention, but of great concern and consequence, and therefore well deserved it.

WORDS OF WARNING
(*vv.* 16–24)

Christ was going on in the praise of John the Baptist and his ministry, but here stops on a sudden, and turns that to the reproach of those who enjoyed both that, and the ministry of Christ and his apostles too, in vain. As to that generation, we may observe to whom he *compares them* (*vv.* 16–19), and as to the particular places he instances in, we may observe with whom he *compares them, vv.* 20–24.

I. As to that *generation*, the body of the Jewish people at that time. There were many indeed that pressed into the kingdom of heaven; but the generality continued in unbelief and obstinacy.

This our Lord Jesus here sets forth in a parable, yet speaks as if he were at a loss to find out a similitude proper to represent this, *Whereunto shall I liken this generation?* The similitude is taken from some common custom among the Jewish children at their play, who, as is usual with children, imitated the fashions of grown people at their marriages and funerals, *rejoicing* and *lamenting*; but being all a jest, it made no impression; no more did the ministry either of John the Baptist or of Christ upon that generation. He especially reflects on the scribes and Pharisees, who had a proud conceit of themselves; therefore to humble them he compares them to children, and their behaviour to children's play.

In the explanation of the parable is set forth the different temper of John's ministry and of Christ's, who were the two great lights of that generation.

(1) On the one hand, John came *mourning to them, neither eating nor drinking*; not conversing familiarly with people, nor ordinarily eating in company, but alone, in his cell in the wilderness, where *his meat was locusts and wild honey*.

(2) On the other hand, *the Son of man came eating and drinking*, and so he *piped unto them*. Christ conversed familiarly with all sorts of people, not affecting any peculiar strictness or austerity; he was affable and easy of access, not shy of any company, was often at feasts, both with Pharisees and publicans, to try if this would win upon those who were not wrought upon by John's reservedness: those who were not awed by John's frowns, would be allured by Christ's smiles; from whom St. Paul learned to become *all things to all men*, 1 Cor. ix. 22. Now our Lord Jesus, by his freedom, did not at all condemn John, any more than

John did condemn him, though their deportment was so very different.

The various methods which God takes for the conversion of sinners, are with many fruitless and ineffectual: "*Ye have not danced, ye have not lamented*; you have not been suitably affected either with the one or with the other." If people will be neither bound by laws, nor invited by promises, nor frightened by threatenings, will neither be awakened by the *greatest* things, nor allured by the *sweetest* things, nor startled by the most *terrible* things, nor be made sensible by the *plainest* things; if they will hearken to the voice neither of scripture, nor reason, nor experience, nor providence, nor conscience, nor interest, what more can be done? The cause of this great unfruitfulness and perverseness of people under the means of grace, is that they are *like children sitting in the markets*; they are foolish as children. *The market-place they sit in* is to some a place of idleness (*ch.* xx. 3); to others a place of worldly business (Jam. iv. 13); to all a place of noise or diversion; so that if you ask the reason why people get so little good by the means of grace, you will find it is because they are slothful and trifling, and do not love to take pains; or because their heads, and hands, and hearts are full of the world, the cares of which *choke the word*, and choke their souls at last (Ezek. xxxiii. 31; Amos viii. 5); and they study to divert their own thoughts from every thing that is serious. Thus *in the markets* they are, and there they *sit*; in these things their hearts rest, and by them they resolve to abide.

Though the means of grace be thus slighted and abused by many, by the most, yet there is a remnant that through grace do improve them, and answer the designs of them, to the glory of God, and the good of their own souls. *But wisdom is justified of her children.* Christ is *Wisdom*; in him *are hid treasures of wisdom*; the saints are the *children God has given* him, Heb. ii. 13. The gospel is *wisdom*, it is *the wisdom from above*: true believers are begotten again by it, and born from above too: they are wise *children*, wise for themselves, and their true interests; not *like the foolish children that sat in the markets*.

II. As to the particular *places* in which Christ was most conversant. What he said in general of that *generation*, he applied in particular to those *places*, to affect them. *Then began he to upbraid them, v.* 20. Now observe,

1. The sin charged upon them: that *they repented not.* Note, Wilful impenitency is the great damning sin of multitudes that enjoy the gospel, and which (more than any other) sinners will be upbraided with to eternity. The great doctrine that both John the Baptist, and Christ, and the apostles preached, was repentance; the great thing designed, both in the *piping* and in the *mourning*, was to prevail with people to change their minds and ways, to leave their sins and turn to God; and this they would not be brought to.

2. The aggravation of the sin; they were *the cities in which most of*

his mighty works were done; for thereabouts his principal residence had been for some time. By Christ's *mighty works* they should have been prevailed with, not only to receive his doctrine, but to obey his law; the curing of bodily diseases should have been the healing of their souls, but it had not that effect. Christ came *into the world to bless us*; but if that blessing be slighted, he has woes in reserve, and his woes are of all others the most terrible. These two cities were situate upon *the sea of Galilee*, the former on the east side, and the latter on the west, rich and populous places; Bethsaida was lately advanced to a city by Philip the tetrarch; out of it Christ took at least three of his apostles: thus highly were these places favoured! Yet because they *knew not the day of their visitation*, they fell under these woes, which stuck so close to them, that soon after this they decayed, and dwindled into mean, obscure villages. So fatally does sin ruin cities, and so certainly does the word of Christ take place!

Capernaum is here condemned with an emphasis (*v.* 23), *"And thou, Capernaum, hold up thy hand, and hear thy doom."*

We have here Capernaum's doom,

[1] Put absolutely; Thou *which art exalted to heaven shalt be brought down to hell*. Note, Those who enjoy the gospel in power and purity, are thereby *exalted to heaven*; they have therein a great honour for the present, and a great advantage for eternity; they are lifted up toward *heaven*; but if, notwithstanding, they still *cleave to the earth*, they may thank themselves that they are not lifted up *into heaven*.

[2] We have it here put in comparison with the doom of Sodom— a place more remarkable, both for sin and ruin, than perhaps any other; and yet Christ here tells us,

First, That Capernaum's means would have saved Sodom. If these miracles had been done among the Sodomites, as bad as they were, they would have repented, and *their city would have remained unto this day* a monument of sparing mercy, as now it is of destroying justice, Jude 7.

Secondly, That Sodom's ruin will therefore be less at the great day than Capernaum's. Sodom will have many things to answer for, but not the sin of neglecting Christ, as Capernaum will.

COME UNTO ME (*vv.* 25–30)

I. Christ here returns thanks to God for his favour to those *babes* who had the mysteries of the gospel *revealed to them* (*vv.* 25, 26).

Now in this thanksgiving of Christ, we may observe,

1. The titles he gives to God; *O Father, Lord of heaven and earth.* When we come to God as a Father, we must withal remember, that he is *Lord of heaven and earth*; which obliges us to come to him with reverence, as to the sovereign Lord of all, and yet with confidence, as one able to do for us whatever we need or can desire; to defend us from all evil and to supply us with all good.

2. The thing he gives thanks for: *Because thou hast hid these things from the wise and prudent, and* yet

97

revealed them to babes. These things; he does not say what things, but means the great things of the gospel, *the things that belong to our peace,* Luke xix. 42.

The great things of the everlasting gospel have been and are hid from many that were *wise and prudent*, that were eminent for learning and worldly policy; some of the greatest scholars and the greatest statesmen have been the greatest strangers to gospel mysteries.

While *the wise and prudent men* of the world are in the dark about gospel mysteries, even the *babes in Christ* have the sanctifying saving knowledge of them: *Thou hast revealed them unto babes.* Such the disciples of Christ were; men of mean birth and education; no scholars, no artists, no politicians unlearned and ignorant men, Acts iv. 13.

3. This difference between *the prudent* and the *babes* is of God's own making. [1] It is he that has *hid these things from the wise and prudent*. God is not the Author of their ignorance and error, but he leaves them to themselves, and their sin becomes their punishment, and the Lord is righteous in it. See John xii. 39, 40; Rom. xi. 7, 8; Acts xxviii. 26, 27. Had they honoured God with the wisdom and prudence they had, he would have given them the knowledge of these better things; but because they served their lusts with them, he has *hid their hearts from this understanding.* [2] It is he that has *revealed them unto babes.* Things revealed belong to our children (Deut. xxix. 29), and to them he *gives an understanding* to

receive these things, and the impressions of them. Thus *he resists the proud*, and *gives grace to the humble*, Jam. iv. 6.

This way of dispensing divine grace is to be acknowledged by us, as it was by our Lord Jesus, with all thankfulness. We must thank God, [1] That *these things* are *revealed*; the mystery hid from ages and generations is manifested; that they are *revealed*, not to a few, but to be published to all the world. [2] That they are *revealed to babes*; that the meek and humble are beautified with this salvation; and this honour put upon those whom the world pours contempt upon. [3] It magnifies the mercy to them, that *these things* are *hid from the wise and prudent*: distinguishing favours are most obliging.

II. Christ here makes a gracious offer of the benefits of the gospel to all, and these are the things which are *revealed to babes, v.* 25, &c.

Two things he here lays before us, *v.* 27.

[1] His commission from the Father: *All things are delivered unto me of my Father.* Christ, as God, is equal in power and glory with the Father; but as Mediator he receives his power and glory from the Father; has *all judgment committed to him.*

(2) His intimacy with the Father: *No man knoweth the Son but the Father, Neither knoweth any man the Father save the Son.* This gives us a further satisfaction, and an abundant one. It must therefore be a great encouragement to us to be assured, that they understood one another very well in this affair; that the Father knew the Son, and the

Son knew the Father, and both perfectly (a mutual consciousness we may call it, between the Father and·the Son), so that there could be no mistake in the settling of this matter.

After so solemn a preface, we may well expect something very great; and it is *a faithful saying*, and well *worthy of all acceptation*; *words whereby we may be saved*. We are here invited to Christ as our Priest, Prince, and Prophet, to be saved, and, in order to that, to be ruled and taught by him.

(1) We must come to Jesus Christ as our Rest, and repose ourselves in him (*v. 28*), *Come unto me all ye that labour*. Observe, [1] The character of the persons invited; *all that labour, and are heavy laden*. This is a word in season to him that is weary, Isa. l. 4. Those who complain of the burden of the ceremonial law, which was an intolerable yoke, and was made much more so by the tradition of the elders (Luke xi. 46), let them come to Christ, and they shall be made easy; he came to free his church from this yoke, to cancel the imposition of those carnal ordinances, and to introduce a purer and more spiritual way of worship; but it is rather to be understood of the burden of sin, both the guilt and the power of it.

[2] The invitation itself: *Come unto me*. That glorious display of Christ's greatness which we had (*v. 27*), as Lord of all, might frighten us from him, but see here how he holds out *the golden sceptre*, that we may touch the top of it and may live. *Come* and *cast that burden upon* him, under which thou art

heavy laden. This is the gospel call, *The Spirit saith, Come*; and *the bride saith, Come; Let him that is athirst come; Whoever will, let him come*.

[3] The blessing promised to those that do come: *I will give you rest*. Note, Jesus Christ will give assured rest to those weary souls, that by a lively faith come to him for it; *rest* from the terror of sin, in a well-grounded peace of conscience; *rest* from the power of sin, in a regular order of the soul, and its due government of itself; a *rest* in God, and a complacency of soul, in his love. Ps. xi. 6, 7. This is that *rest which remains for the people of God* (Heb. iv. 9), begun in grace, and perfected in glory.

(2) We must come to Jesus Christ as our Ruler, and submit ourselves to him (*v. 29*). *Take my yoke upon you*. This must go along with the former, for Christ is exalted to be both a *Prince and a Saviour*, a *Priest upon his throne*. The *rest* he promises is a release from the drudgery of sin, not from the service of God, but an obligation to the duty we owe to him.

Now this is the hardest part of our lesson, and therefore it is qualified (*v. 30*). *My yoke is easy and my burden is light*; you need not be afraid of it.

[1] The *yoke* of Christ's commands is an *easy yoke*; not only *easy*, but gracious, so the word signifies; it is sweet and pleasant; there is nothing in it to gall the yielding neck, nothing to hurt us, but, on the contrary, much to refresh us. It is a *yoke* that is lined with love. Such is the nature of all Christ's commands, so reasonable

in themselves, so profitable to us, and all summed up in one word, and that a sweet word, love.

[2] The *burden* of Christ's cross is a *light burden*, very *light*: afflictions from Christ, which befall us as men; afflictions for Christ, which befall us as Christians; the latter are especially meant. This *burden* in itself is *not joyous, but grievous*; yet as it is Christ's, it is *light*. As afflictions abound, and are prolonged, consolations abound, and are prolonged too.

(3) We must come to Jesus Christ as our Teacher, and set ourselves to learn of him, *v.* 29. Some make the following words, *for I am meek and lowly in heart*, to be the particular lesson we are required to learn from the example of Christ. We must learn of him to be *meek* and *lowly*, and must mortify our pride and passion, which render us so unlike to him. We must so *learn of Christ* as to *learn Christ* (Eph. iv. 20), for he is both Teacher and Lesson, Guide and Way, and All in All.

Two reasons are given why we must *learn of Christ*.

[1] *I am meek and lowly in heart*, and therefore fit to teach you.

First, He is *meek*, and can have *compassion on the ignorant*, whom others would be in a passion with. Secondly, *He is lowly in heart*. He condescends to teach poor scholars, to teach novices; he chose disciples, not from the court, nor the schools, but from the seaside. This humility and meekness, as it qualifies him to be a Teacher, so it will be the best qualification of those who are to be taught by him; *for the meek will he guide in judgment*, Ps. xxv. 9.

[2] *You shall find rest to your souls*. The way of duty is the way of rest. The *understanding* finds *rest* in the *knowledge of* God and Jesus Christ, and is there abundantly satisfied, finding *that* wisdom in the gospel which has been sought for in vain throughout the whole creation, Job xxviii. 12. The truths Christ teaches are such as we may venture our souls upon. The affections find rest in the love of God and Jesus Christ, and meet with that in them which gives them an abundant satisfaction; quietness and assurance for ever.

LORD OF THE SABBATH
(*vv.* 1–13)

The Jewish teachers had corrupted many of the commandments, by interpreting them more loosely than they were intended; a mistake which Christ discovered and rectified (*ch.* v.) in his sermon on the mount: but concerning the fourth commandment, they had erred in the other extreme, and interpreted it too strictly.

Christ's industrious explanation of the fourth commandment, intimates its perpetual obligation to the religious observation of *one day in seven*, as a *holy sabbath*. He would not expound a law that was immediately to expire, but doubtless intended hereby to settle a point which would be of use to his church in all ages; and so it is to teach us, that our Christian sabbath, though under the direction of the fourth commandment, is not under the injunctions of the Jewish elders.

It is usual to settle the meaning of

a law by judgments given upon cases that happen in fact, and in like manner is the meaning of this law settled. Here are two passages of story put together for this purpose, happening at some distance of time from each other, and of a different nature, but both answering this intention.

I. Christ, by justifying his disciples in plucking the ears of corn on the sabbath-day, shows that *works of necessity* are *lawful* on that day.

(1) He justifies them by precedents, which were allowed to be good by the Pharisees themselves.

[1] He urges an ancient instance of David, who in a case of necessity did that which otherwise he ought not to have done (*vv.* 3, 4).

[2] He urges a daily instance of the priests, which they likewise *read in the law*, and according to which was the constant usage, *v.* 5. *The priests in the temple* did a great deal of servile work on the sabbath day; and yet it was never reckoned any transgression of the fourth commandment, because the temple-service required and justified it.

(2) He justifies them by arguments, three cogent ones.

[1] *In this place is one greater than the temple*, *v.* 6.

[2] *God will have mercy and not sacrifice*, *v.* 7. Ceremonial duties must give way to moral, and the natural, royal law of love and self-preservation must take place of ritual observances. This is quoted from Hos. vi. 6.

[3] *The Son of man is Lord even of the sabbath day*, *v.* 8. That law, as all the rest, is put into the hand of Christ, to be altered, enforced, or

dispensed with, as he sees good. It was by *the Son* that God *made the world*, and by him he instituted the sabbath in innocency; by him he gave the ten commandments at mount Sinai, and as Mediator he is entrusted with the institution of ordinances, and to make what changes he thought fit; and particularly, as being *Lord of the sabbath*, he was authorized to make such an alteration of that day, as that it should become the Lord's day, the Lord Christ's day.

Christ having thus silenced the Pharisees, and got clear of them (*v.* 9), *departed*, and *went into their synagogue*, the synagogue of these Pharisees, in which they presided, and toward which he was going, when they picked this quarrel with him.

II. Christ, by *healing the man that had the withered hand on the sabbath day*, shows that works of mercy are lawful and proper to be done on that day. The work of necessity was done by the disciples, and justified by him; the work of mercy was done by himself; the works of mercy were his works of necessity; it was his *meat and drink* to *do good*. *I must preach*, says he, Luke iv. 43. This cure is recorded for the sake of the time when it was wrought, on the sabbath.

CHRIST'S HUMILITY
(*vv.* 14–21)

As in the midst of Christ's greatest humiliations, there were proofs of his dignity, so in the midst of his greatest honours, he gave proofs of his humility; and when the mighty works he did gave him an opportunity of making a figure, yet he made it appear that *he emptied himself*, and *made himself of no reputation*. Here we have,

I. The cursed malice of the Pharisees against Christ (*v.* 14); being enraged at the convincing evidence of his miracles, they *went out, and held a council against him, how they might destroy him.*

II. Christ's absconding upon this occasion, and the privacy he chose, to decline, not his work, but his danger; because *his hour was not yet come* (*v.* 15), *he withdrew himself from thence.*

Christ studied to reconcile usefulness and privacy; he *healed them all*, and yet (*v.* 16), *charged them that they should not make him known*; which may be looked upon, 1. As an act of prudence; it was not so much the miracles themselves, as the public discourse concerning them, that enraged the Pharisees (*vv.* 23, 24); therefore Christ, though he would not omit doing good, yet would do it with as little noise as possible, to avoid offence to them and peril to himself. 2. It may be looked upon as an act of righteous judgment upon the Pharisees, who were unworthy to hear of any more of his miracles, having made so light of those they had seen. By shutting their eyes against the light, they had forfeited the benefit of it. 3. As an act of humility and self-denial. Christ would have his disciples to be the reverse of those who did all their works *to be seen of men.*

III. The fulfilling of the scriptures in all this, *v.* 17. Christ retired into privacy and obscurity, that though he was eclipsed, the word of God might be fulfilled, and so illustrated

and glorified, which was the thing his heart was upon. The scripture here said to be fulfilled is Isa. xlii. 1–4, which is quoted at large, *vv.* 18–21. The scope of it is to show how mild and quiet, and yet how successful, our Lord Jesus should be in his undertaking; instances of both which we have in the foregoing passages.

CONQUEST OF SATAN
(*vv.* 22–37)

In these verses we have,

I. Christ's glorious conquest of Satan, in the gracious cure of one who, by the divine permission, was under his power, and in his possession, *v.* 22. Here observe,

1. The man's case was very sad; he was *possessed with a devil*. More cases of this kind occurred in Christ's time than usual, that Christ's power might be the more magnified, and his purpose the more manifested, in opposing and dispossessing Satan; and that it might the more evidently appear, that he *came to destroy the works of the devil*. This poor man that was possessed was blind and dumb; a miserable case! he could neither see to help himself, nor speak to others to help him.

2. His cure was very strange, and the more so, because sudden; *he healed him*. Note, Christ's mercy is directly opposite to Satan's malice; his favours, to the devil's mischiefs. When Satan's power is broken in the soul, the eyes are opened to see God's glory, and the lips opened to speak his praise.

II. The conviction which this gave to the people, to *all the people*: they *were amazed*. Christ had wrought divers miracles of this kind before; but his works are not the less wonderful, nor the less to be wondered at, for their being often repeated. They inferred from it, "*Is not this the Son of David?* The Messiah promised, that was to spring from the loins of David? Is not this he that should come?" We may take this, 1. As an *enquiring* question; they asked, *Is not this the Son of David?* But they did not stay for an answer: the impressions were cogent, but they were transient. Or, 2. as an *affirming* question; *Is not this the Son of David?* "Yes, certainly it is, it can be no other; such miracles as these plainly evince that the kingdom of the Messiah is now setting up." And they were the people, the vulgar sort of the spectators, that drew this inference from Christ's miracles. So plain and easy was the way made to this great truth of Christ being the Messiah and Saviour of the world, that the common people could not miss it; the *wayfaring men, though fools, could not err therein.* See Isa. xxxv. 8.

III. The blasphemous cavil of the Pharisees, *v.* 24. The Pharisees were a sort of men that pretended to more knowledge in, and zeal for, the divine law, than other people; yet they were the most inveterate enemies to Christ and his doctrine. And when they heard the people say, *Is not this the Son of David?* they were extremely irritated, more at that than at the miracle itself; this made them jealous of our Lord Jesus, and apprehensive, that as *his* interest in the people's esteem increased, *theirs* must of course be

eclipsed and diminished. They said, "*This fellow does not cast out devils, but by Beelzebub the prince of the devils,* and therefore is not the Son of David." Observe,

1. How scornfully they speak of Christ, *this fellow*; as if that precious name of his, which is *as ointment poured forth,* were not worthy to be taken into their lips.

2. How blasphemously they speak of his miracles; they could not deny the matter of fact; it was as plain as the sun, that devils were cast out by the word of Christ; nor could they deny that it was an extraordinary thing, and supernatural. Being thus forced to grant the premises, they had no other way to avoid the conclusion, that *this is the Son of David,* than by suggesting that *Christ cast out devils by Beelzebub*; that there was a compact between Christ and the devil. No surmise could be more palpably false and vile than this; that he, who is Truth itself, should be in combination with the father of lies, to cheat the world. This was the last refuge, or subterfuge rather, of an obstinate infidelity, that was resolved to stand it out against the clearest conviction.

IV. Christ's reply to this base insinuation, *vv.* 25–30. Here are three arguments by which he demonstrates the unreasonableness of this suggestion.

1. It would be very strange, and highly improbable, that Satan should be cast out by such a compact, because then Satan's *kingdom would be divided against itself*; which, considering his subtlety, is not a thing to be imagined, *vv.* 25, 26.

(1) Here is a known rule laid down, that in all societies a common ruin is the consequence of mutual quarrels: *Every kingdom divided against itself is brought to desolation.*

(2) The application of it to the case in hand (*v.* 26), *If Satan cast out Satan*; if the prince of the devils should be at variance with the inferior devils, the whole kingdom and interest would soon be broken. *The works of the devil*, as a rebel against God, and a tyrant over the souls of men, were destroyed by Christ; and therefore it was the most absurd thing imaginable, to think that Beelzebub should at all countenance such a design, or come into it: if he should fall in with Christ, *how should then his kingdom stand?*

2. It was not at all strange, or improbable, that devils should be cast out by the Spirit of God; for,

(1) *How* otherwise *do your children cast them out?* There were those among the Jews who, by invocation of the name of the most high God, or the God of Abraham, Isaac, and Jacob, did sometimes cast out devils. Josephus speaks of some of his time that did it; we read of *Jewish exorcists* (Acts xix. 13), and of some that *in Christ's name cast out devils*, though they did not follow him (Mark ix. 38), or were not faithful to him, *ch.* vii. 22. These the Pharisees condemned not, but imputed what they did to the Spirit of God, and valued themselves and their nation upon it. It was therefore merely from spite and envy to Christ, that they would own that others cast out devils by the Spirit of God, but suggest that

he did it by compact with Beelzebub.

(2) This casting out of devils was a certain token and indication of the approach and appearance of the kingdom of God (*v.* 28); "But if it be indeed that *I cast out devils by the Spirit of God*, as certainly I do, then you must conclude, that though you are unwilling to receive it, yet the kingdom of the Messiah is now about to be set up among you." Other miracles that Christ wrought proved him *sent of God*, but this proved him sent of God to destroy the devil's kingdom and his works.

3. The comparing of Christ's miracles, particularly this of casting out devils, with his doctrine, and the design and tendency of his holy religion, evidenced that he was so far from being in league with Satan, that he was at open enmity and hostility against him (*v.* 29); *How can one enter into a strong man's house, and plunder his goods*, and carry them away, *except he first bind the strong man? And then he* may do what he pleases with his goods. The world, that sat in darkness, and lay in wickedness, was in Satan's possession, and under his power, as a house in the possession and under the power of a strong man; so is every unregenerate soul; there Satan resides, there he rules. Now, (1) The design of Christ's gospel was to spoil the devil's house, which, as a strong man, he kept in the world; *to turn the people from darkness to light*, from sin to holiness, from this world to a better, *from the power of Satan unto God* (Acts xxvi. 18); to alter the property of souls. (2)

Pursuant to this design, he bound the strong man, when he cast out unclean spirits by his word: thus he wrested the *sword* out of the devil's hand, that he might wrest the *sceptre* out of it. The doctrine of Christ teaches us how to construe his miracles, and when he showed how easily and effectually he could cast the devil out of people's bodies, he encouraged all believers to hope that, whatever power Satan might usurp and exercise in the souls of men, Christ by his grace would break it: he will spoil him, for it appears that he can bind him.

4. It is here intimated, that this holy war, which Christ was carrying on with vigour against the devil and his kingdom, was such as would not admit of a neutrality (*v.* 30), *He that is not with me is against me.* In the little differences that may arise between the disciples of Christ among themselves, we are taught to lessen the matters in variance, and to seek peace, by accounting those who *are not against us, to be with us* (Luke ix. 50); but in the great quarrel between Christ and the devil, no peace is to be sought, nor any such favourable construction to be made of any indifference in the matter; he that is not hearty *for* Christ, will be reckoned with as really *against* him: he that is cold in the cause, is looked upon as an enemy.

V. Here is a discourse of Christ's upon this occasion, concerning tongue-sins; *Wherefore I say unto you.* He seems to turn from the Pharisees to the people, from disputing to instructing; and from the sin of the Pharisees he warns the people concerning three sorts of tongue-sins; for others' harms are admonitions to us.

1. Blasphemous words against the Holy Ghost are the worst kind of tongue-sins, and unpardonable, *vv.* 31, 32.

(1) Here is a gracious assurance of the pardon of all sin upon gospel terms: this Christ says to us, and it is a comfortable saying, that the greatness of sin shall be no bar to our acceptance with God, if we truly repent and believe the gospel: *All manner of sin and blasphemy shall be forgiven unto men.*

(2) Here is an exception of *the blasphemy against the Holy Ghost,* which is here declared to be the only unpardonable sin. See here,

[1] What this sin is; it is *speaking against the Holy Ghost.* See what malignity there is in tongue-sins, when the only unpardonable sin is so. *But Jesus knew their thoughts, v.* 25. It is not all speaking against the person or essence of the Holy Ghost, or some of his more private operations, or merely the resisting of his internal working in the sinner himself, that is here meant; for *who then should be saved?* This blasphemy is excepted, not for any defect of mercy in God or merit in Christ, but because it inevitably leaves the sinner in infidelity and impenitency. We have reason to think that none are guilty of this sin, who believe that Christ is *the Son of God,* and sincerely desire to have part in his merit and mercy: and those who fear they have committed this sin, give a good sign that they have not.

[2] What the sentence is that is passed upon it; *It shall not be forgiven, neither in this world, nor in*

the world to come. As in the then present state of the Jewish church, there was no sacrifice of expiation for *the soul that sinned presumptuously*; so neither under the dispensation of gospel grace, which is often in scripture called *the world to come*, shall there be any pardon to *such as tread underfoot the blood of the covenant, and do despite to the Spirit of grace*: there is no cure for a sin so directly against the remedy. It was a rule in our old law, No sanctuary for sacrilege. Or, *It shall be forgiven neither now*, in the sinner's own conscience, *nor in the great day*, when the pardon shall be published. Or, this is a sin that exposes the sinner both to temporal and eternal punishment, both to present wrath and *the wrath to come*.

2. Christ speaks here concerning other wicked words, the products of corruption reigning in the heart, and breaking out thence, *vv.* 33–35.

(1) The heart is the *root*, the language is the *fruit* (*v.* 33); if the nature of the tree be good, it will bring forth fruit accordingly. Where grace is the reigning principle in the heart, the language will be the language of Canaan; and, on the contrary, whatever lust reigns in the heart it will break out.

(2) The heart is the *fountain*, the words are the streams (*v.* 34); *Out of the abundance of the heart the mouth speaks*, as the streams are the overflowings of the spring.

(3) The heart is the *treasury*, the words are the things brought out of that treasury (*v.* 35); and from hence men's characters may be drawn, and may be judged of.

[1] It is the character of a *good*

man, that he has a *good treasure in his heart*, and from thence *brings forth good things*, as there is occasion. Graces, comforts, experiences, good knowledge, good affections, good resolutions, these are a *good treasure in the heart*; the word of God hidden there, the law of God written there, divine truths dwelling and ruling there, are a treasure there, valuable and suitable, kept safe and kept secret, as the stores of the good householder, but ready for use upon all occasions.

[2] It is the character of *an evil man*, that he has an *evil treasure in his heart*, and out of it *bringeth forth evil things*. Lusts and corruptions dwelling and reigning in the heart are an evil treasure, out of which the sinner brings forth bad words and actions, to the dishonour of God, and the hurt of others. See Gen. vi. 5, 12; Matt. xv. 18–20; Jam. i. 15. But *treasures of wickedness* (Prov. x. 2) will be *treasures of wrath*.

3. Christ speaks here concerning *idle words*, and shows what evil there is in them (*vv.* 36, 37); much more is there in such wicked words as the Pharisees spoke. It concerns us to think much of the day of judgment, that *that* may be a check upon our tongues; and let us consider,

(1) How particular the account will be of tongue-sins in that day: even *for every idle word*, or discourse, *that men speak, they shall give account*. This intimates, [1] That God takes notice of every word we say, even that which we ourselves do not notice. See Psalm cxxxix. 4. *Not a word in my tongue*

but thou knowest it: though spoken without regard or design, God takes cognizance of it. [2] That vain, idle, impertinent talk is displeasing to God, which tends not to any good purpose, is not good to any use of edifying; it is the product of a vain and trifling heart. [3] We must shortly account for these idle words; they will be produced in evidence against us, to prove us unprofitable servants, that have not improved the faculties of reason and speech, which are part of the talents we are entrusted with.

(2) How strict the judgment will be upon that account (*v.* 37); *By thy words thou shalt be justified or condemned*; a common rule in men's judgments, and here applied to God's.

A WICKED GENERATION
(*vv.* 38–45)

It is probable that these Pharisees with whom Christ is here in discourse were not the same that cavilled at him (*v.* 24), and would not credit the signs he gave; but another set of them, who saw that there was no reason to discredit them, but would not content themselves with the signs he gave, nor admit the evidence of them, unless he would give them such further proof as they should demand. Here is,

1. Their address to him, *v.* 38. They compliment him with the title of *Master*, pretending respect for him, when they intended to abuse him; all are not indeed Christ's servants, who call him *Master*. Their request is, *We would see a sign from thee*. It was highly reasonable that they should see a

sign, that he should by miracles prove his divine mission: see Exod. iv. 8, 9. He came to take down a model of religion that was set up by miracles, and therefore it was requisite he should produce the same credentials; but it was highly unreasonable to demand a sign now, when he had given so many signs already, that did abundantly prove him *sent of God*.

II. His answer to this address, this insolent demand.

1. He condemns the demand, as the language of *an evil and adulterous generation, v.* 39. He fastens the charge, not only on *the scribes and Pharisees*, but the whole nation of the Jews; they were all like their leaders, a seed and succession of evil-doers: they were an evil generation indeed, that not only hardened themselves against the conviction of Christ's miracles, but set themselves to abuse him, and put contempt on his miracles.

2. He refuses to give them any other sign than he has already given them, but *that of the prophet Jonas*.

Justly might Christ have said, They shall never see another miracle: but see his wonderful goodness; (1) They shall have the same signs still repeated, for their further benefit, and more abundant conviction. (2) They shall have one sign of a different kind from all these, and that is, *the resurrection of Christ from the dead by his own power*, called here *the sign of the prophet Jonas*; this was yet reserved for their conviction, and was intended to be the great proof of Christ's being the Messiah; for by that he was *declared to be the Son of God with power*, Rom. i. 4.

Now this sign of the prophet Jonas he further explains here: (*v.* 40). *As Jonas was three days and three nights in the whale's belly,* and then came out again safe and well, thus Christ shall be so long in the grave, and then shall rise again.

3. Christ takes this occasion to represent the sad character and condition of that generation in which he lived, a generation that would not be reformed, and therefore could not but be ruined; and he gives them their character, as it would stand in the day of judgment, under the full discoveries and final sentences of that day. Persons and things now appear under false colours; characters and conditions are here changeable: if therefore we would make a right estimate, we must take our measures from the last judgment; things are really, what they are eternally.

Now Christ represents the people of the Jews,

(1) As a generation that would be condemned by *the men of Nineveh,* whose *repenting at the preaching of Jonas* would *rise up in judgment* against them, *v.* 41. Christ's resurrection will be the sign of the prophet Jonas to them: but it will not have so happy an effect upon them, as that of Jonas had upon the Ninevites, for they were by it brought to such a repentance as prevented their ruin; but the Jews will be hardened in an unbelief that shall hasten their ruin; and in the day of judgment, the repentance of the Ninevites will be mentioned as an aggravation of the sin, and consequently the condemnation of those to whom Christ preached then, and of those to whom Christ is preached now; for this reason, because Christ is greater than Jonah.

(2) As a generation that would be condemned by the queen of the south, the queen of Sheba, *v.* 42. The Ninevites would shame them for not repenting, the queen of Sheba for not believing in Christ. She came from a far country to hear the wisdom of Solomon; yet people will not be persuaded to come and hear the wisdom of Christ, though he is in every thing greater than Solomon.

(3) As a generation that were resolved to continue in the possession, and under the power, of Satan, notwithstanding all the methods that were used to dispossess him and rescue them. They are compared to one out of whom the devil is gone, but returns with double force, *vv.* 43–45. The devil is here called *the unclean spirit,* for he has lost all his purity, and delights in and promotes all manner of impurity among men. Now,

[1] The parable represents his possessing men's bodies: Christ having lately cast out a devil, and they having said *he had a devil,* gave occasion to show how much they were under the power of Satan. This is a further proof that Christ did not cast out devils by compact with the devil, for then he would soon have returned again; but Christ's ejectment of him was final, and such as barred a re-entry: we find him charging the evil spirit to *go out, and enter no more,* Mark ix. 25.

[2] The application of the parable makes it to represent the case of the body of the Jewish church and

nation: *So shall it be with this wicked generation*, that now resist, and will finally reject, the gospel of Christ. The devil, who by the labours of Christ and his disciples had been cast out of many of the Jews, sought for rest among the heathen, from whose persons and temples the Christians would everywhere expel him: so Dr. Whitby: or finding nowhere else in the heathen world such pleasant, desirable habitations, to his satisfaction, as here in the heart of the Jews: so Dr. Hammond: he shall therefore enter again into them, for Christ had not found admission among them, and they, by their prodigious wickedness and obstinate unbelief, were still more ready than ever to receive him; and then he shall take a durable possession here, and the state of this people is likely to be more desperately damnable (so Dr. Hammond) than it was before Christ came among them, or would have been if Satan had never been cast out.

The body of that nation is here represented, *First*, As an apostate people. After the captivity in Babylon, they began to reform, left their idols, and appeared with some face of religion; but they soon corrupted themselves again: though they never relapsed into idolatry, they fell into all manner of impiety and profaneness, grew worse and worse, and added to all the rest of their wickedness a wilful contempt of, and opposition to, Christ and his gospel. *Secondly*, As a people marked for ruin. A new commission was passing the seals against that hypocritical nation, the people of God's wrath (like that,

Isa. x. 6), and their destruction by the Romans was likely to be greater than any other, as their sins had been more flagrant: then it was *that wrath came upon them to the uttermost*, 1 Thess. ii. 15, 16.

MOTHER AND BROTHERS
(vv. 46–50)

Observe, I. How Christ was interrupted in his preaching by *his mother and his brethren*, that *stood without, desiring to speak with him* (vv. 46, 47); which desire of theirs was conveyed to him through the crowd.

1. He was as yet talking to the people. Note, Christ's preaching was talking; it was plain, easy, and familiar, and suited to their capacity and case. What Christ had delivered had been cavilled at, and yet he went on.

2. His mother and brethren stood outside desiring to speak with him, when they should have been standing inside, desiring to hear him. They had the advantage of his daily converse in private, and therefore were less mindful to attend upon his public preaching.

3. They not only would not hear him themselves, but they interrupted others that *heard him gladly*. The devil was a sworn enemy to our Saviour's preaching. He had sought to baffle his discourse by the unreasonable cavils of the scribes and Pharisees, and when he could not gain his point that way, he endeavoured to break it off by the unseasonable visits of relations.

II. How he resented this interruption, vv. 48–50.

1. He would not hearken to it; he was so intent upon his work, that

no natural or civil respects should take him off from it. *Who is my mother and who are my brethren?* Not that natural affection is to be put off, or that, under pretence of religion, we may be disrespectful to parents, or unkind to other relations; but *every thing is beautiful in its season*, and the less duty must stand by, while the greater is done. When our regard to our relations comes in competition with the service of God, and the improving of an opportunity to *do good*, in such a case, we must *say to our Father, I have not seen him*, as Levi did, Deut. xxxiii. 9.

2. He took that occasion to prefer his disciples, who were his spiritual kindred, before his natural relations as such: which was a good reason why he would not leave preaching to speak with his brethren. He would rather be profiting his disciples, than pleasing his relations. Observe,

(1) The description of Christ's disciples. They are such as *do the will of his Father*; not only hear it, and know it, and talk of it, but *do it*; for doing the will of God is the best preparative for discipleship (John vii. 17), and the best proof of it (*ch.* vii. 21); *that* denominates us his disciples indeed. Christ does not say, "Whosoever shall do my will," for he came not to seek or do his own will distinct from his Father's: his will and his Father's are the same; but he refers us to his Father's will, because now in his present state and work he referred himself to it, John vi. 38.

(2) The dignity of Christ's disciples: *The same is my brother, and sister, and mother*. His disciples,

that had left all to follow him, and embraced his doctrine, were dearer to him than any that were akin to him according to the flesh. They had preferred Christ before their relations; they *left their father* (*ch.* iv. 22; x. 37); and now to make them amends, and to show that there was no love lost, he preferred them before his relations.

CHAPTER THIRTEEN

PREACHING IN PARABLES
(*vv.* 1–23)

We have here Christ preaching, and may observe,

1. *When* Christ preached this sermon; it was the same day that he preached the sermon in the foregoing chapter: so unwearied was he in doing good, and working the works of him that sent him.

2. *To whom* he preached; there were *great multitudes gathered together to him*, and they were the auditors; we do not find that any of the scribes or Pharisees were present. They were willing to hear him when he preached in the synagogue (*ch.* xii. 9, 14), but they thought it below them to hear a sermon by the sea-side, though Christ himself was the preacher: and truly he had better have their room than their company, for now they were absent, he went on quietly and without contradiction.

3. *Where* he preached this sermon.

(1) His meeting-place was the sea-side. He went out of the house (because there was no room for the audience) into the open air. As he had not a house of his own to live in, so he had not a chapel of his

own to preach in. By this he teaches us in the external circumstances of worship not to covet that which is stately, but to make the best of the conveniences which God in his providence allots to us.

(2) His pulpit was a ship; not like Ezra's pulpit, that was *made for the purpose* (Neh. viii. 4); but converted to this use for want of a better. No place amiss for such a Preacher, whose presence dignified and consecrated any place: let not those who preach Christ be ashamed, though they have mean and inconvenient places to preach in.

4. *What* and *how* he preached. (1) *He spake many things unto them.* Many more it is likely than are here recorded, but all excellent and necessary things, things that belong to our peace, things pertaining to the kingdom of heaven. (2) What he spake was in parables. A parable sometimes signifies any wise, weighty saying that is instructive; but here in the gospels it generally signifies a continued similitude or comparison, by which spiritual or heavenly things were described in language borrowed from the things of this life. Now,

I. We have here the general reason why Christ taught in parables. The disciples were a little surprised at it, for hitherto, in his preaching, he had not much used them, and therefore they ask, *Why speakest thou to them in parables?*

1. This reason is laid down (*v.* 11): *Because it is given unto you to know the mysteries of the kingdom of heaven, but to them it is not given.* That is, (1) The disciples had knowledge, but the people had not.

You know already something of these mysteries, and need not in this familiar way to be instructed; but the people are ignorant, are yet but babes, and must be taught as such by plain similitudes, being yet incapable of receiving instruction in any other way: for though they have eyes, they know not how to use them; so some. Or, (2) The disciples were well inclined to the knowledge of gospel mysteries, and would search into the parables, and by them would be led into a more intimate acquaintance with those mysteries; but the carnal hearers that rested in bare hearing, and would not be at the pains to look further, nor to ask the meaning of the parables, would be never the wiser, and so would justly suffer for their remissness. A parable is a shell that keeps good fruit *for* the diligent, but keeps it *from* the slothful.

2. This reason is further illustrated by the rule God observes in dispensing his gifts; he bestows them on those who improve them, but takes them away from those who bury them.

(1) Here is a promise to him that has true grace, pursuant to the election of grace, and uses what he has; he shall have more abundance: God's favours are earnests of further favours; where he lays the foundation, he will build upon it.

(2) Here is a threatening to him that has not, that has no desire of grace, that makes no right use of the gifts and graces he has: has no root, no solid principle; that has, but uses not what he has; from him shall be *taken away* that which he has or seems to have.

3. This reason is particularly explained, with reference to the two sorts of people Christ had to do with.

(1) Some were willingly ignorant; and such were amused by the parables (*v.* 13); *because they seeing, see not*. They had shut their eyes against the clear light of Christ's plainer preaching, and therefore were noiw left in the dark.

Now n this the scripture would be fulfilled, *vv.* 14, 15. It is quoted from Isa. vi. 9, 10. The evangelical prophet that spoke most plainly of gospel grace, foretold the contempt of it, and the consequences of that contempt. Here is,

First. A description of sinners' wilful blindness and hardness, which is their sin. *This people's heart is waxed gross*; it is *fattened*, so the word is; which denotes both sensuality and senselessness (Ps. cxix. 70).

Secondly. A description of that judicial blindness, which is the just punishment of this. To hear God's word, and see his providences, and yet not to understand and perceive his will, either in the one or in the other, is the greatest sin and the greatest judgment that can be.

Thirdly, The woeful effect and consequence of this; *Lest at any time they should see*. They will not see because they will not turn; and God says that they shall not see, because they shall not turn: *Lest they should be converted, and I should heal them*.

Note, 1. That seeing, hearing, and understanding, are necessary to conversion; for God, in working grace, deals with men as men, as rational agents; he draws with the cords of a man, changes the heart

by opening the eyes, and turns *from the power of Satan unto God*, by turning first *from darkness to light*, Acts xxvi. 18. 2. All those who are truly converted to God, shall certainly be healed by him. "If they be converted I shall heal them, I shall save them": so that if sinners perish, it is not to be imputed to God, but to themselves; they foolishly expected to be healed, without being converted. 3. It is just with God to deny his grace to those who have long and often refused the proposals of it, and resisted the power of it.

(2) Others were effectually called to be the disciples of Christ, and were truly desirous to be taught of him; and they were instructed, and made to improve greatly in knowledge, by these parables, especially when they were expounded; and by them the things of God were made more plain and easy, more intelligible and familiar, and more apt to be remembered (*vv.* 16, 17). *Your eyes see, your ears hear*. Now this Christ speaks of,

[1] As a blessing; "*Blessed are your eyes for they see, and your ears for they hear*; it is your happiness, and it is a happiness for which you are indebted to the peculiar favour and blessing of God." It is a promised blessing, that in the days of the Messiah *the eyes of them that see shall not be dim*, Isa. xxxii. 3. The eyes of the meanest believer that knows experimentally the grace of Christ, are more blessed than those of the greatest scholars, the greatest masters in experimental philosophy, that are strangers to God; who, like the other gods they serve, *have eyes, and see not*.

[2] As a transcendent blessing, desired by, but not granted to, many prophets and righteous men, *v.* 17. Though they were the favourites of Heaven, with whom God's secret was, yet they have not seen the things which they desired to see, because God had determined not to bring them to light yet; and his favours shall not anticipate his counsels. There was then, as there is still, a *glory to be revealed*; something in reserve, *that they without us should not be made perfect*, Heb. xi. 40. *Thirdly*, For the exciting of our thankfulness, and the quickening of our diligence. It is good for us to see that our improvements be proportionable to our advantages.

II. We have, in these verses, one of the parables which our Saviour put forth; it is that of the *sower and the seed*; both the parable itself, and the explanation of it.

The parable of the sower is plain enough, *vv.* 3–9. The exposition of it we have from Christ himself, who knew best what was his own meaning.

Let us therefore compare the parable and the exposition.

(1) The seed sown is the word of God, here called *the word of the kingdom* (*v.* 19). The gospel comes *from* that kingdom, and conducts *to* that kingdom; the word of the gospel is the word of the kingdom; it is the word of the King, and where that is, *there is power*; it is a law, by which we must be ruled and governed. This word is the seed sown, which seems a dead, dry thing, but all the product is virtually in it. It is *incorruptible seed* (1 Pet. i. 23); it is the gospel that

brings forth fruit in souls, Col. i. 5, 6.

(2) The sower that scatters the seed is our Lord Jesus Christ, either by himself, or by his ministers; see *v.* 37. The people are God's husbandry, his tillage, so the word is; and ministers are *labourers together with God*, 1 Cor. iii. 9.

(3) The ground in which this seed is sown is the hearts of the children of men, which are differently qualified and disposed, and accordingly the success of the word is different.

Now observe the characters of these four sorts of ground.

[1] The highway ground, *vv.* 4–19. They had pathways through their cornfields (*ch.* xii. 1), and the seed that fell on them never entered, and so the birds picked it up.

Observe, *First*, What kind of hearers are compared to *the highway ground*; such as *hear the word and understand it not*; and it is their own fault that they do not. They take no heed to it, take no hold of it; they do not come with any design to get good, as the highway was never intended to be sown.

Secondly, How they come to be unprofitable hearers. The *wicked one*, that is, the devil, *cometh and catcheth away that which was sown.* —Such mindless, careless, trifling hearers are an easy prey to Satan; who, as he is the great murderer of souls, so he is the great thief of sermons, and will be sure to rob us of the word, if we take not care to keep it.

[2] The *stony ground. Some fell upon stony places* (*vv.* 5, 6), which

Preaching in Parables

represents the case of hearers that go further than the former, who receive some good impressions of the word, but they are not lasting, *vv.* 20, 21.

First, How far they went. 1. They *hear the word*; they turn neither their backs upon it, nor a deaf ear to it. Note, Hearing the word, though ever so frequently, ever so gravely, if we rest in that, will never bring us to heaven. 2. They are *quick in hearing,* swift to hear, he is ready to receive it, *forthwith it sprung up* (*v.* 5), it sooner appeared above ground than that which was sown in the good soil. Note, Hypocrites often get the start of true Christians in the shows of profession, and are often too hot to hold. He *receiveth it straightway,* without trying it; swallows it without chewing, and then there can never be a good digestion. Those are most likely to *hold fast that which is good,* that *prove all things,* 1 Thess. v. 21. 3. They receive it with joy. Note, There are many that are very glad to hear a good sermon, that yet do not profit by it. 4. They *endure for awhile,* like a violent motion, which continues as long as the impression of the force remains, but ceases when that has spent itself.

Secondly, How they fell away, so that no fruit was brought to perfection; no more than the corn, that having no depth of earth from which to draw moisture, is scorched and withered by the heat of the sun. And the reason is,

1. They have *no root in themselves,* no settled, fixed principles in their judgments, no firm resolution in their wills, nor any rooted habits in their affections: nothing firm that will be either the sap or the strength of their profession.

2. Times of trial come, and then they come to nothing. *When tribulation and persecution arise because of the word, he is offended*; it is a stumbling-block in his way which he cannot get over, and so he flies off, and this is all his profession comes to.

[3] The thorny ground, *Some fell among thorns; and the thorns sprung up,* which intimates that they did not appear, or but little, when the corn was sown, but afterwards they proved choking to it, *v.* 7. This went further than the former, for it had root; and it represents the condition of those who do not quite cast off their profession, and yet come short of any saving benefit by it; the good they gain by the word, being insensibly overcome and overborne by the things of this world. Prosperity destroys the word in the heart, as much as persecution does; and more dangerously, because more silently: the stones spoiled the root, the thorns spoil the fruit.

Now what are these choking thorns?

First, The cares of this world. Care for another world would quicken the springing of this seed, but care for this world chokes it. Note, Worldly cares are great hindrances to our profiting by the word of God, and our proficiency in religion. They eat up that vigour of soul which should be spent in divine things; divert us from duty, distract us in duty, and do us most mischief of all afterwards; quenching the sparks of good affections,

114

and bursting the cords of good resolutions; those who *are careful and cumbered about many things,* commonly neglect *the one thing needful.*

Secondly, The deceitfulness of riches. Observe, It is not so much riches, as *the deceitfulness of riches,* that does the mischief: now they cannot be said to be deceitful to us unless we put our confidence in them, and raise our expectations from them, and then it is that they choke the good seed.

[4] The good ground (*v.* 18); *Others fell into good ground,* and it is pity but that good seed should always meet with good soil, and then there is no loss; such are *good hearers of the word, v.* 23.

Now that which distinguished this good ground from the rest, was in one word, fruitfulness. By *this* true Christians are distinguished from hypocrites, that they *bring forth the fruits of righteousness; so shall ye be my disciples,* John xv. 8. He does not say that this good ground has no stones in it, or no thorns; but there were none that prevailed to hinder its fruitfulness. Saints, in this world, are not perfectly free from the remains of sin; but happily freed from the reign of it.

The hearers represented by the good ground are,

First, Intelligent hearers; they *hear the word and understand it;* they understand not only the sense and meaning of the word, but their own concern in it; they understand it as a man of business understands his business. God in his word deals with men as men, in a rational way, and gains possession of the will and

affections by opening the understanding.

Secondly, Fruitful hearers, which is an evidence of their good understanding: which *also beareth fruit.* Fruit is to every seed its own body, a substantial product in the heart and life, agreeable to the seed of the word received.

Thirdly, Not all alike fruitful; *some a hundred-fold, some sixty, some thirty.* Note, Among fruitful Christians, some are more fruitful than others: where there is true grace, yet there are degrees of it; some are of greater attainments in knowledge and holiness than others; all Christ's scholars are not in the same form. But if the ground be good, and the fruit right, the heart honest, and the life of a piece with it, those who bring forth but thirty-fold shall be graciously accepted of God, and it will be fruit abounding to their account, for *we are under grace, and not under the law.*

Lastly, He closes the parable with a solemn call to attention (*v.* 9), *Who hath ears to hear, let him hear.*

THE TARES (*vv.* 24–43)

In these verses, we have, I. Another reason given why Christ preached by parables, *vv.* 34, 35. *All these things he spoke in parables,* because the time was not yet come for the more clear and plain discoveries of the mysteries of the kingdom. Christ, to keep the people attending and expecting, preached in *parables, and without a parable spake he not unto them;* namely, at this time and in this sermon. Here is, 1. The matter of Christ's preaching; he preached *things which had been kept secret from the foundation of the world.* The mystery of the gospel had been *hid in God,* in his councils and decrees, *from the beginning of the world.* Eph. iii. 9. Compare Rom. xvi. 25; 1 Cor. ii. 7; Col. i. 26.

2. The manner of Christ's preaching; he preached by parables; wise sayings, but figurative, and which help to engage attention and a diligent search.

II. The parable of the *tares,* and the exposition of it; they must be taken together, for the exposition explains the parable and the parable illustrates the exposition.

Observe, 1. The disciples' request to their Master to have this parable expounded to them (*v.* 36); *Jesus sent the multitude away;* and it is to be feared many of them went away no wiser than they came; they had heard a sound of words, and that was all.

2. The exposition Christ gave of the parable, in answer to their request; so ready is Christ to answer such desires of his disciples. Now the drift of the parable is, to represent to us the present and future state of the kingdom of heaven, the gospel church: Christ's care of it, the devil's enmity against it, the mixture that there is in it of good and bad in this world, and the separation between them in the other world. Note, The visible church is the kingdom of heaven; though there be many hypocrites in it, Christ rules in it as a King; and there is a remnant in it, that are the subjects and heirs of heaven.

Let us go over the particulars of the exposition of the parable.

(1) *He that sows the good seed is the Son of man.* Jesus Christ is the Lord of the field, *the Lord of the harvest,* the Sower of good seed.

(2) *The field is the world;* the world of mankind, a large field, capable of bringing forth good fruit; the more is it to be lamented that it brings forth so much bad fruit: the world here is the visible church, scattered all the world over, not confined to one nation.

(3) *The good seed are the children of the kingdom,* true saints. They are, [1] The *children of the kingdom;* not in profession only, as the Jews were (*ch.* viii. 12), but in sincerity; Jews inwardly, Israelites indeed, incorporated in faith and obedience to Jesus Christ the great King of the church. [2] They are the good seed, precious as seed, Ps. cxxvi. 6. The seed is that from which fruit is expected; what fruit of honour and service God has from this world he has from the saints, whom he has *sown unto himself in the earth,* Hos. ii. 23.

(4) *The tares are the children of the wicked one.* Here is the character of sinners, hypocrites, and all profane and wicked people. They are tares in the field of this world; they do no good, they do hurt; unprofitable in themselves, and hurtful to *the good seed,* both by temptation and persecution: they are weeds in the garden, have the same rain, and sunshine, and soil, with the good plants, but are good for nothing: the *tares are among the wheat.* Note, God has so ordered it, that good and bad should be mixed together in this world, that the good may be exercised, the bad left inexcusable,

116

and a difference made between earth and heaven.

(5) *The enemy that sowed the tares is the devil*; a sworn enemy to Christ and all that is good, to the glory of the good God, and the comfort and happiness of all good men. He is an enemy to the field of the world, which he endeavours to make his own, by sowing his tares in it.

Now concerning the sowing of the tares, observe in the parable,

[1] That they were sown *while men slept*. Magistrates slept, who by their power, ministers slept, who by their preaching, should have prevented this mischief. Note, Satan watches all opportunities, and lays hold of all advantages, to propagate vice and profaneness. The prejudice he does to particular persons is when reason and conscience sleep, when they are off their guard; we have therefore need to *be sober, and vigilant*.

[2] The enemy, when he had sown the tares, *went his way* (*v.* 25), that it might not be known who did it. Note, When Satan is doing the greatest mischief, he studies most to conceal himself.

[3] The tares appeared not till *the blade sprung up, and brought forth fruit, v.* 26. There is a great deal of secret wickedness in the hearts of men, which is long hid under the cloak of a plausible profession, but breaks out at last.

[4] The servants, when they were aware of it, complained to their master (*v.* 27); *Sir, didst thou not sow good seed in thy field?* No doubt he did; whatever is amiss in the church, we are sure it is not of Christ: considering the

seed which Christ sows, we may well ask, with wonder, *Whence* should *these tares come?*

[5] The Master was soon aware whence it was (*v.* 28); *An enemy has done this.* He does not lay the blame upon the servants; they could not help it, but had done what was in their power to prevent it. Note, The ministers of Christ, that are faithful and diligent, shall not be judged of Christ, and therefore should not be reproached by men, for the mixture of bad with good, hypocrites with the sincere, in the field of the church.

[6] The servants were very forward to have these tares rooted up. "*Wilt thou that we go* and do it presently?" Note, The over-hasty and inconsiderate zeal of Christ's servants, before they have consulted with their Master, is sometimes ready, with the hazard of the church, to root out all that they presume to be tares.

[7] The Master very wisely prevented this (*v.* 29); *Nay, lest while ye gather up the tares, ye root up also the wheat with them.* Note, It is not possible for any man infallibly to distinguish between tares and wheat, but he may be mistaken; and therefore such is the wisdom and grace of Christ, that he will rather permit the tares, than any way endanger the wheat.

(6) *The harvest is the end of the world, v.* 39. At the end of the world, there will be a great harvest-day, a day of judgment; at harvest all is ripe and ready to be cut down: both good and bad are ripe at the great-day, Rev. vi. 11. It is *the harvest of the earth*, Rev. xiv. 15.

At harvest the reapers cut down all before them; not a field, not a corner, is left behind; so at the great day all must be judged (Rev. xx. 12, 13); God has *set a harvest* (Hos. vi. 11), and it shall not fail, (Gen. viii. 22). At harvest every man reaps as he sowed; every man's ground, and seed, and skill, and industry, will be manifested: see Gal. vi. 7, 8.

(7) *The reapers are the angels:* they shall be employed, in the great day, in executing Christ's righteous sentences, both of approbation and condemnation, as ministers of his justice, *ch.* xxv. 31.

(8) Hell-torments are the *fire*, into which the *tares* shall then be cast, and in which they shall be burned.

[1] The tares will then be gathered out: *The reapers* (whose primary work it is to gather in the corn) shall be charged first to *gather out the tares.* Note, Though good and bad are together in this world undistinguished, yet at the great day they shall be parted; no tares shall then be among the wheat; no sinners among the saints.

[2] They will then be *bound in bundles, v.* 30. Sinners of the same sort will be bundled together in the great day: a bundle of atheists, a bundle of epicures, a bundle of persecutors, and a great bundle of hypocrites.

[3] They will *be cast into a furnace of fire*; such will be the end of wicked, mischievous people, that are in the church as *tares in the field*; they are fit for nothing but fire; to it they shall go, it is the fittest place for them.

(9) Heaven is the *barn* into which all God's wheat shall be gathered in that harvest-day.

In the explanation of the parable, this is gloriously represented (*v.* 43); *Then shall the righteous shine forth as the sun in the kingdom of their Father.* Here they are obscure and hidden (Col. iii. 3), their beauty is eclipsed by their poverty, and the meanness of their outward condition; their own weaknesses and infirmities, and the reproach and disgrace cast upon them, cloud them; but then they shall shine forth as the sun from behind a dark cloud; at death they shall shine forth to themselves; at the great day they will shine forth publicly before all the world.

Our Saviour concludes, as before, with a demand of attention; *Who hath ears to hear, let him hear.* These are things which it is our happiness to hear of, and our duty to hearken to.

III. Here is the parable of the *grain of mustard-seed, vv.* 31, 32. The scope of this parable is to show, that the beginnings of the gospel *would be small, but that its latter end would greatly increase.*

Now concerning the work of the gospel, observe.

1. That it is commonly very weak and small at first, *like a grain of mustard-seed, which is one of the least of all seeds.*

2. That yet it is growing and coming on. *A grain of mustard-seed* is small, but, however, it is seed, and has in it a disposition to grow. Grace will be getting ground, shining more and more, Prov. iv. 18.

3. That it will at last come to a great degree of strength and usefulness; *when it is grown to some*

maturity, *it becomes a tree*, much larger in those countries than in ours. The church, like the *vine brought out of Egypt*, has taken root, and *filled the earth*, (Ps. lxxx. 9–11).

IV. Here is the parable of the *leaven*, v. 33. The scope of this is much the same with that of the foregoing parable, to show that the gospel should prevail and be successful by degrees, but silently and insensibly; the preaching of the gospel is like leaven, and works like leaven in the hearts of those who receive it.

The leaven hid in the dough, works there, it ferments; *the word is quick and powerful*, Heb. iv. 12. The leaven works speedily, so does the word, and yet gradually. Hide but the leaven in the dough, and all the world cannot hinder it from communicating its taste and relish to it, and yet none sees how it is done, but by degrees *the whole is leavened*.

(1) Thus it was in the world. The apostles, by their preaching, hid a handful of leaven in the great mass of mankind, and it had a strange effect; it put the world into a ferment, and in a sense turned it *upside down* (Acts xvii. 6).

(2) Thus it is in the heart. When the gospel comes into the soul, [1] It works a change, not in the substance; the dough is the same, but in the quality; it makes us to savour otherwise than we have done, and other things to savour with us otherwise than they used to do, Rom. viii. 5. [2] It works a universal change; it diffuses itself into all the powers and faculties of the soul, and alters the property even of the members of the body, Rom. vi. 13. [3] This change is such as makes the soul to partake of the nature of the word, as the dough does of the leaven.

FOUR PARABLES (*vv.* 44–52)

We have four short parables in these verses.

I. That of the *treasure hid in the field*. Hitherto he had compared *the kingdom of heaven* to small things, because its beginning was small; but, lest any should thence take occasion to think meanly of it, in this parable and the next he represents it as of great value in itself, and of great advantage to those who embrace it, and are willing to come up to its terms; it is here likened *to a treasure hid in the field*, which, if we will, we may make our own.

II. That of *the pearl of price* (*vv.* 45, 46), which is to the same purport with the former, of the treasure.

Jesus Christ is a *Pearl of great price*, a Jewel of inestimable value, which will make those who have it rich, truly rich, rich toward God; in having him, we have enough to make us happy here and for ever.

A true Christian is a spiritual *merchant*, that seeks and finds this pearl of price; that does not take up with any thing short of an interest in Christ, and, as one that is resolved to be spiritually rich, trades high: *He went and bought that pearl*; did not only bid for it, but purchased it. What will it avail us to know Christ, if we do not know him as ours, *made to us wisdom*? (1 Cor. i. 30.)

Those who would have a saving

interest in Christ, must be willing to part with all for him, leave all to follow him. A man may buy gold too dear, but not this pearl of price.

III. That of the *net cast into the sea, vv.* 47-49.

1. Here is the parable itself. Where note, (1) The world is a vast sea. (2) The preaching of the gospel is the casting of a net into this sea, to catch something out of it, for his glory who has the sovereignty of the sea. Ministers are *fishers of men,* employed in casting and drawing this net. (3) This net gathers of every kind, as large dragnets do. In the visible church there is a deal of trash and rubbish, dirt and weeds and vermin, as well as fish. (4) There is a time coming when this net will be full, and drawn to the shore; a set time when the gospel shall have fulfilled that for which it was sent, and we are sure it shall not return void, Isa. lv. 10, 11. (5) When the net is full and drawn to the shore, there shall be a separation between the good and bad that were gathered in it. Hypocrites and true Christians shall then be parted; the good shall be gathered into vessels, as valuable, and therefore to be carefully kept, but the bad shall be cast away, as vile and unprofitable; and miserable is the condition of those who are cast away in that day.

2. Here is the explanation of the latter part of the parable, the former is obvious and plain enough: we see gathered in the visible church, *some of every kind*: but the latter part refers to that which is yet to come, and is therefore more particularly explained, *vv.* 49, 50.

So shall it be at the end of the world; then, and not till then, will the dividing, discovering day be. We must not look for the net full of all good fish; the vessels will be so, but in the net they are mixed. See here, (1) The distinguishing of the wicked from the righteous. The angels of heaven shall come forth to do that which the angels of the churches could never do; they shall *sever the wicked from among the just.* (2) The doom of the wicked when they are thus severed. They shall be *cast into the furnace.*

IV. Here is the parable of the *good householder,* which is intended to rivet all the rest.

1. The occasion of it was the good proficiency which the disciples had made in learning, and their profiting by this sermon in particular.

2. The scope of the parable itself was to give his approbation and commendation of their proficiency.

(1) He commends them as *scribes instructed unto the kingdom of heaven.* They were now learning that they might teach, and the teachers among the Jews were the scribes.

(2) He compares them to a good householder, who *brings forth out of his treasure things new and old*; fruits of last year's growth and this year's gathering, abundance and variety, for the entertainment of his friends, Cant. vii. 13. Christ himself received that he might give; so must we, and we shall have more. In bringing forth, things new and old do best together; old truths, but new methods and expressions, especially new affections.

PROPHET AT HOME
(*vv.* 53–58)

We have here Christ in his own country. He went about doing good, yet left not any place till he had finished his testimony there at that time. His own countrymen had rejected him once, yet he came to them again. His treatment this time was much the same as before, scornful and spiteful. Observe,

I. How they expressed their contempt of him. When he *taught them in their synagogue, they were astonished*; not that they were taken with his preaching, or admired his doctrine in itself, but only that it should be his; looking upon him as unlikely to be such a teacher. Two things they upbraided him with.

1. His want of academical education. Thus they turned that against him which was really for him; for if they had not been wilfully blind, they must have concluded him to be divinely assisted and commissioned, who without the help of education gave such proofs of extraordinary wisdom and power.

2. The meanness and poverty of his relations, *vv.* 55, 56.

(1) They upbraid him with his father. *Is not this the carpenter's son?* Yes, it is true he was reputed so: and what harm in that? No disparagement to him to be the son of an honest tradesman.

(2) They upbraid him with his mother; and what quarrel have they with her? Why, truly, *his mother is called Mary*, and that was a very common name, and they all knew her, and knew her to be an ordinary person; and this is turned

to his reproach, as if men had nothing to be valued by but foreign extraction, noble birth, or splendid titles; poor things to measure worth by.

(3) They upbraid him with his brethren, whose names they knew, and had them ready enough to serve this turn; James, and Joses, and Simon, and Judas, good men but poor men, and therefore despised; and Christ for their sakes.

(4) His sisters too are all with us; they should therefore have loved him and respected him the more, because he was one of themselves, but therefore they despised him.

II. See how he resented this contempt, *vv.* 57, 58.

1. It did not trouble his heart. It appears he was not much concerned at it; he *despised the shame*, Heb. xii. 2.

2. It did for the present (to speak with reverence), in effect, tie his hands: *He did not many mighty works there, because of their unbelief.* Note, Unbelief is the great obstruction to Christ's favours.

CHAPTER FOURTEEN
THE DEATH OF JOHN (*vv.* 1–12)

We have here the story of John's martyrdom. Observe,

I. The occasion of relating this story here, *vv.* 1, 2. Here is,

1. The account brought to Herod of the miracles which Christ wrought. Herod the tetrarch or chief governor of Galilee *heard of the fame of Jesus*. Christ's disciples were now sent abroad to preach, and to work miracles in his name,

and this spread the fame of him more than ever; which was an indication of the spreading of the gospel by their means after his ascension.

2. The construction he puts upon this (*v.* 2); *He said to his servants* that told him of the fame of Jesus, as sure as we are here, *this is John the Baptist; he is risen from the dead.* Observe here concerning Herod.

(1) How he was disappointed in what he intended by beheading John. He thought if he could get that troublesome fellow out of the way, he might go on in his sins, undisturbed and uncontrolled; yet no sooner is that effected, than he hears of Jesus and his disciples preaching the same pure doctrine that John preached; and, which is more, even the disciples confirming it by miracles in their Master's name.

(2) How he was filled with causeless fears, merely from the guilt of his own conscience.

(3) How, notwithstanding this, he was hardened in his wickedness; for though he was convinced that John was a prophet, and one owned of God, yet he does not express the least remorse or sorrow for his sin in putting him to death. The devils believe and tremble, but they never believe and repent.

II. The story itself of the imprisonment and martyrdom of John. As the first Old-Testament saint, so the first New-Testament minister, died a martyr. And if Christ's forerunner was thus treated, let not his followers expect to be caressed by the world. Observe here,

1. John's faithfulness in reproving Herod, *vv.* 3, 4.

The particular sin he reproved him for was, marrying his brother Philip's wife, not his widow (that had not been so criminal), but his wife. Philip was now living, and Herod inveigled his wife from him, and kept her for his own. Here was a complication of wickedness, adultery, incest, besides the wrong done to Philip, who had had a child by this woman. See Ps. 1. 20. For this sin John reproved him; not by tacit and oblique allusions, but in plain terms. *It is not lawful for thee to have her.*

2. The imprisonment of John for his faithfulness, *v.* 3. Faithful reproofs, if they do not profit, usually provoke; if they do not do good, they are resented as affronts, and they that will not bow to the reproof, will fly in the face of the reprover and hate him.

3. The restraint that Herod lay under from further venting of his rage against John, *v.* 5.

(1) He would have put him to death. Perhaps that was not intended at first when he imprisoned him, but his revenge by degrees boiled up to that height.

(2) That which hindered him was his *fear of the multitude, because they counted John as a prophet.* It was not because he feared God (if the fear of God had been before his eyes he would not have imprisoned him), nor because he feared John, though formerly he had had a reverence for him (his lusts had overcome that), but because he feared the people; he was afraid for himself, his own safety, and the safety of

his government, his abuse of which he knew had already rendered him odious to the people, whose resentments being so far heated already would be apt, upon such a provocation as the putting of a prophet to death, to break out into a flame.

4. The contrivance of bringing John to his death.

Herodias laid the plot; her implacable revenge thirsted after John's blood, and would be satisfied with nothing less. Herodias contrived how to bring about the murder of John so artificially as to save Herod's credit, and so to pacify the people. Here we have,

(1) The humouring of Herod by the damsel's dancing upon a birth-day.

(2) The rash and foolish promise which Herod made to this wanton girl, to give her whatsoever she would ask: and this promise confirmed with an oath, *v.* 7.

(3) The bloody demand the young lady made of John the Baptist's head, *v.* 8. She was before instructed of her mother.

(4) Herod's grant of this demand (*v.* 9); *The king was sorry*, at least took on him to be so, but, *for the oath's sake, he commanded it to be given her.*

Thus was that voice silenced, that burning and shining light extinguished; thus did that prophet, that Elias, of the New Testament, fall a sacrifice to the resentments of an imperious, whorish woman. Thus did he, who was great in the sight of the Lord, *die as a fool dieth, his hands were bound, and his feet put into fetters; and as a man falleth before wicked men*, so he

fell, a true martyr to all intents and purposes: dying, though not for the profession of his faith, yet for the performance of his duty. However, though his work was soon done, *it was done and his testimony finished*, for till then none of God's witnesses are slain. And God brought this good out of it, that hereby his disciples, who while he lived, though in prison, kept close to him, now after his death heartily closed with Jesus Christ.

The disciples *buried the body*, and brought the news in tears to our Lord Jesus. The disciples of John had fasted often while their master was in prison, their *bridegroom was taken away from them*, and they prayed earnestly for his deliverance, as the church did for Peter's, Acts xii. 5. They had free access to him in prison, which was a comfort to them, but they wished to see him at liberty, that he might preach to others; but now on a sudden all their hopes are dashed. Disciples weep and lament, when the world rejoices.

FEEDING FIVE THOUSAND
(*vv.* 13–21)

This passage of story, concerning Christ's feeding *five thousand men with five loaves and two fishes*, is recorded by all the four Evangelists, which very few, if any, of Christ's miracles are: this intimates that there is something in it worthy of special remark. Observe,

I. The great resort of people to Christ, when he was retired *into a desert place*, *v.* 13. He withdrew into privacy when he heard, not of John's death, but of the thoughts

Herod had concerning him, that he was *John the Baptist risen from the dead*, and therefore so feared by Herod as to be hated; he departed further off, to get out of Herod's jurisdiction.

II. The tender compassion of our Lord Jesus towards those who thus followed him, *v.* 14. He did not only pity them, but he helped them; many of them were *sick, and he, in compassion to them, healed them*; for he came into the world to be the great Healer. After awhile, they were all hungry, *and he, in compassion to them, fed them.*

III. The motion which the disciples made for the dismissing of the congregation, and Christ's setting aside the motion. 1. The *evening* drawing on, the disciples moved it to Christ to send the multitude away; they thought there was a good day's work done, and it was time to disperse. See how loth Christ is to part with those who are resolved to cleave to him! *They need not depart*; nor will Christ put his willing followers upon a needless expense, but will make their attendance cheap to them.

But if they be hungry, they have need to depart, for that is a necessity which has no law, therefore *give you them to eat.*

IV. The slender provision that was made for this great multitude; and here we must compare the number of invited guests with the bill of fare.

1. The number of the guests was *five thousand of men, besides women and children*; and it is probable the women and children might be as many a⸱ the men, if not more.

2. The bill of fare was very disproportionable to the number of the guests, but *five loaves and two fishes*. This provision the disciples carried about with them for the use of the family, now they *were retired into the desert*. Christ could have fed them by miracle, but to set us an example of providing for those of our own households, he will have their own camp victualled in an ordinary way.

V. The liberal distribution of this provision among the multitude (*vv.* 18, 19); *Bring them hither to me*. Note, The way to have our creature-comforts, comforts indeed to us, is to bring them to Christ; for every thing is sanctified by his word, and by prayer to him: that is likely to prosper and do well with us, which we put into the hands of our Lord Jesus, that he may dispose of it as he pleases, and that we may take it back from his hand, and then it will be doubly sweet to us. What we give in charity, we should bring to Christ first, that he may graciously accept it from us, and graciously bless it to those to whom it is given; this is *doing it as the Lord*.

VI. The plentiful satisfaction of all the guests with this provision. Though the disproportion was so great, yet there was enough and to spare.

1. There was enough: *They did all eat, and were filled*. Note, Those whom Christ feeds, he fills; so runs the promise (Ps. xxxvii, 19), *They shall be satisfied*.

2. There was to spare; *They took up of the fragments that remained,*

twelve baskets full, one basket for each apostle: thus what they gave they had again, and a great deal more with it. This was to manifest and magnify the miracle, and to show that the provision Christ makes for those who are his is not bare and scanty, but rich and plenteous; *bread enough, and to spare* (Luke xv. 17), an overflowing fulness.

It is the same divine power, though exerted in an ordinary way, which multiplies *the seed sown in the ground* every year, and makes *the earth yield her increase*; so that what was brought out by handfuls, is brought home in sheaves. *This is the Lord's doing*; it is *by Christ* that all natural things consist, and *by the word of his power* that they are upheld.

WALKING ON THE SEA
(vv. 22–33)

We have here the story of another miracle which Christ wrought for the relief of his friends and followers, his *walking upon the water to his disciples*. In the foregoing miracle he acted as the Lord of nature, improving its powers for the supply of those who were in want; in this, he acted as the Lord of nature, correcting and controlling its powers for the succour of those who were in danger and distress. Observe,

I. Christ's dismissing of his disciples and *the multitude*, after he had fed them miraculously. He *constrained his disciples to get into a ship, and to go before him unto the other side*, v. 22. St. John gives a particular reason for the hasty breaking up of this assembly,

because the people were so affected with the miracle of the loaves, that they were about *to take him by force, and make him a King* (John vi. 15); to avoid which, he immediately scattered the people, sent away the disciples, lest they should join with them, and he himself withdrew, John vi. 15.

II. Christ's retirement hereupon (*v.* 23); *He went up into a mountain apart to pray*. Observe here,

1. That he was alone; *he went apart into a solitary place, and was there all alone*. Though he had so much work to do with others, yet he chose sometimes to be alone, to set us an example.

2. That he was alone at prayer; that was his business in this solitude, to pray. Though Christ, as God, was Lord of all, and was prayed to, yet Christ, as Man, had *the form of a servant*, of a beggar, and prayed.

3. That he was long alone. *The night* came on, and it was a stormy, tempestuous night, yet he continued *instant in prayer*.

III. The condition that the poor disciples were in at this time: *Their ship was now in the midst of the sea, tossed with waves, v.* 24. We may observe here,

1. That they were got into the midst of the sea when the storm rose. We may have fair weather at the beginning of our voyage, and yet meet with storms before we arrive at the port we are bound for. Therefore *let not him that girdeth on the harness boast as he that puts it off*, but after a long calm expect some storm or other.

2. The disciples were now where Christ sent them, and yet met with

this storm. Note, It is no new thing for Christ's disciples to meet with storms in the way of their duty, and to be sent to sea then when their Master foresees a storm; but let them not take it unkindly; what he does they *know not now, but they shall know hereafter*, that Christ designs hereby to manifest himself with the more wonderful grace to them and for them.

3. It was a great discouragement to them now that they had not Christ with them, as they had formerly when they were in a storm. Thus Christ used his disciples first to less difficulties, and then to greater, and so trains them up by degrees to live *by faith, and not by sense*.

4. Though *the wind was contrary*, and they were tossed with waves, yet being ordered by their Master *to the other side*, they did not tack about and come back again, but made the best of their way forward.

IV. Christ's approach to them in this condition (*v.* 25); and in this we have an instance,

1. Of his goodness, that he went unto them, as one that took cognizance of their case, and was under a concern about them, as a father about his children.

2. Of his power, that he *went unto them, walking on the sea*. This is a great instance of Christ's sovereign dominion over all the creatures; they are all under his feet, and at his command; they forget their natures, and change the qualities that we call essential. We need not enquire how this was done, whether by condensing the surface of the water, or by sus-

pending the gravitation of his body, which was transfigured as he pleased; it is sufficient that it proves his divine power, for it is God's prerogative to *tread upon the waves of the sea* (Job ix. 8), as it is *to ride upon the wings of the wind*.

V. Here is an account of what passed between Christ and his distressed friends upon his approach.

1. Between him and all the disciples. We are here told,

(1) How their fears were raised (*v.* 26); *When they saw him walking on the sea, they were troubled, saying, It is a spirit; It is an apparition*; so it might much better be rendered. It seems, the existence and appearance of spirits were generally believed in by all except the Sadducees, whose doctrine Christ had warned his disciples against; yet, doubtless, many supposed apparitions have been merely the creatures of men's own fear and fancy. These disciples said, *It is a spirit*; when they should have said, *It is the Lord*; it can be no other.

(2) How these fears were silenced, *v.* 27. He straightway relieved them, by showing them their mistake; when they were wrestling *with the waves*, he delayed his succour for some time; but he hastened his succour against their fright, as much the more dangerous; he straightway laid that storm with his word, *Be of good cheer; it is I; be not afraid*.

[1] He rectified their mistake, by making himself known to them; *It is I*.

[2] He encouraged them against their fright; *It is I*, and therefore,

First, *Be of good cheer*. If Christ's disciples be not cheerful in a storm, it is their own fault, he would have them so. *Secondly*, *Be not afraid*; 1. "Be not afraid of me, now that you know it is I; surely you will not fear, for you know I mean you no hurt."

2. Between him and Peter, *vv.* 28–31, where observe,

(1) Peter's courage, and Christ's countenancing that.

[1] It was very bold in Peter, that he would venture to come to Christ *upon the water* (*v.* 28); *Lord, if it be thou, bid me come unto thee*.

[2] It was very kind and condescending in Christ, that he was pleased to own him in it, *v.* 29. He might have condemned the proposal as foolish and rash; nay, and as proud and assuming; "Shall Peter pretend to do as his Master does?" But Christ knew that it came from a sincere and zealous affection to him, and graciously accepted of it.

First, He bid him *come*. When the Pharisees asked a sign, they had not only a repulse, but a reproof, for it, because they did it with a design to tempt Christ; when Peter asked a sign, he had it, because he did it with a resolution to trust Christ.

Secondly, He bore him out when he did come; *Peter walked upon the water*.

He walked upon the water, not for diversion or ostentation, but to go to Jesus; and in that he was thus wonderfully borne up.

(2) Here is Peter's cowardice, and Christ's reproving him and succouring him. Christ bid him come, not only that he might walk upon the water, and so know Christ's power, but that he might sink, and so know his own weakness; for as he would encourage his faith, so he would check his confidence, and make him ashamed of it. Observe then,

[1] Peter's great fear (*v.* 30); He *was afraid.* The strongest faith and the greatest courage have a mixture of fear.

Here is, *First*, The cause of this fear; *He saw the wind boisterous*. While Peter kept his eye fixed upon Christ, and upon his word and power, he *walked upon the water* well enough; but when he took notice withal of the danger he was in, and observed how *the floods lift up their waves*, then he feared. Note, Looking at difficulties with an eye of sense more than at precepts and promises with an eye of faith is at the bottom of all our inordinate fears, both as to public and personal concerns.

Secondly, The effect of this fear; *He began to sink*. While faith kept up, he kept above water: but when faith staggered, *he began to sink*. Note, The sinking of our spirits is owing to the weakness of our faith; we are upheld (but it is as we are saved) *through faith* (1 Pet. i. 5); and therefore, when our *souls are cast down and disquieted*, the sovereign remedy is, *to hope in God*, Ps. xliii. 5.

Thirdly, The remedy he had recourse to in this distress, the old, tried, approved remedy, and that was prayer: he cried, *Lord, save me*.

[2] Christ's great favour to Peter, in this fright. Though there was a

mixture of presumption with Peter's faith in his first adventure, and of unbelief with his faith in his after-fainting, yet Christ did not cast him off; for,

First, He saved him; *he answered him with the saving strength of his right hand* (Ps. xx. 6), for immediately *he stretched forth his hand, and caught him.*

Secondly, He rebuked him; for as many as he loves and saves, he reproves and chides; *O thou of little faith, wherefore didst thou doubt?*

VI. The *ceasing of the storm*, v. 32. When Christ was come into the ship, they were presently at the shore. Christ *walked upon the water* till he came to the ship, and then went into that, when he could as easily have walked to the shore; but when ordinary means are to be had, miracles are not to be expected.

When they were come into the ship, immediately the storm ceased, for it had done its work, its trying work. When Christ comes into a soul, he makes winds and storms to cease there, and commands peace. Welcome Christ, and *the noise of her waves will soon be quelled*. The way to be still is, to know that he is God, that he is the *Lord with us*.

VII. The adoration paid to Christ hereupon (*v.* 33); *They that were in the ship came and worshipped him, and said, Of a truth, thou art the Son of God.*

WHOLESALE MIRACLES
(*vv.* 34–36)

We have here an account of miracles by wholesale, which Christ wrought on the other side of the water, in the land of Gennesaret. Whithersoever Christ went, he was doing good. Gennesaret was a tract of land that lay between Bethsaida and Capernaum, and either gave the name to, or took the name from, this sea, which is called (Luke v. 1) *The lake of Gennesaret*; it signifies the valley of branches. Observe here,

1. How *the men of that place* were brought to Christ; they *had knowledge of him.*

They *had knowledge of him*, that is, of his being among them, and that he would be but awhile among them. It is better to know that there *is* a prophet among us than that there *has been* one, Ezek. ii. 5.

2. How they brought others to Christ, by giving notice to their neighbours of Christ's being come into those parts; *They sent out into all that country*. Note, those that have got the knowledge of Christ themselves, should do all they can to bring others acquainted with him too.

3. What their business was with Christ; not only, perhaps not chiefly, if at all, to be taught, but to have their sick healed; *They brought unto him all that were diseased*. If love to Christ and his doctrine will not bring them to him, yet self-love would. Did we but rightly seek our own things, the things of our own peace and welfare, we should seek the things of Christ.

4. How they made their application to him; *They besought him that they might only touch the hem of his garment, v.* 36. They applied

themselves to him, (1) With great importunity; they besought him. (2) With great humility; they came to him as those that were sensible of their distance, humbly beseeching him to help them; and their desiring to touch the hem of his garment, intimates that they thought themselves unworthy that he should take any particular notice of them, that he should so much as speak to their case, much less touch them for their cure; but they will look upon it as a great favour, if he will give them leave to *touch the hem of his garment*. (3) With great assurance of the all-sufficiency of his power, not doubting but that they should be healed, even by touching the hem of his garment. It was in this country and neighbourhood that the woman with the bloody issue was cured by *touching the hem of his garment*, and was commended for her faith (*ch*. ix. 20–22); and thence, probably, they took occasion to ask this.

When we mix faith with the word, apply it to ourselves, depend upon it, and submit to its influences and commands, then we touch the hem of Christ's garment. It is but thus touching, and we are made whole. On such easy terms are spiritual cures offered by him, that he may truly be said to heal *freely*; so that if our souls die of their wounds, it is not owing to our Physician, it is not for want of skill or will in him; but it is purely owing to ourselves. He *could* have healed us, he *would* have healed us, but we *would not be healed*; so that our blood will lie upon our own heads.

CHAPTER FIFTEEN
HYPOCRITES (*vv*. 1–9)

Evil manners, we say, beget good laws. The intemperate heat of the Jewish teachers for the support of their hierarchy, occasioned many excellent discourses of our Saviour's for the settling of the truth, as here.

I. Here is the cavil of the scribes and Pharisees at Christ's disciples, for *eating with unwashen hands*.

Observe, 1. What was the *tradition of the elders*—That people should often wash their hands, and always at meat. This they placed a great deal of religion in, supposing that the meat they touched with unwashen hands would be defiling to them. The Pharisees practised · this themselves, and with a great deal of strictness imposed it upon others, not under civil penalties, but as matter of conscience, and making it a sin against God if they did not do it.

2. What was the transgression of this tradition or injunction by the disciples; it seems, they did not wash their hands when they ate bread. The custom was innocent enough, and had a decency in its civil use. But when it came to be practised and imposed as a religious rite and ceremony, and such a stress laid upon it, the disciples, though weak in knowledge, yet were so well taught as not to comply with it, or observe it; no not when the scribes and Pharisees had their eye upon them.

3. What was the complaint of the scribes and Pharisees against them. They quarrel with Christ

about it, supposing that he allowed them in it, as he did, no doubt, by his own example; "*Why do thy disciples transgress* the canons of the church? And why dost thou suffer them to do it?" It was well that the complaint was made to Christ; for the disciples themselves, though they knew their duty in this case, were perhaps not so well able to give a reason for what they did as were to be wished.

II. Here is Christ's answer to this cavil, and his justification of the disciples in that which was charged upon them as a transgression.

Two ways Christ replies upon them;

1. By way of recrimination, *vv.* 3–6. They were spying motes in the eyes of his disciples, but Christ shows them a beam in their own.

(1) The charge in general is, *You transgress the commandment of God by your tradition.* They called it the *tradition of the elders,* laying stress upon the antiquity of the usage, and the authority of them that imposed it, as the church of Rome does upon fathers and councils; but Christ calls it *their* tradition.

(2) The proof of this charge is in a particular instance, that of their transgressing the fifth commandment.

[1] Let us see what the command of God is (*v.* 4), what the precept, and what the sanction of the law is.

The precept is, *Honour thy father and thy mother.* Our Saviour here supposes it to mean the duty of children's maintaining their parents, and ministering to their wants, if there be occasion, and being every way serviceable to their comfort. *Honour widows,* that is, maintain them, 1 Tim. v. 3.

The sanction of this law in the fifth commandment, is, a promise, *that thy days may be long*; but our Saviour waives that, lest any should thence infer it to be only a thing commendable and profitable, and insists upon the penalty annexed to the breach of this commandment in another scripture, which denotes the duty to be highly and indispensably necessary; *He that curseth father or mother, let him die the death*: this law we have, Exod. xxi. 17.

[2] Let us see what was the contradiction which the tradition of the elders gave to this command. It was not direct and downright, but implicit; their casuists gave them such rules as furnished them with an easy evasion from the obligation of this command, *vv.* 5, 6. You hear what God saith, *but ye say* so and so.

First, What their tradition was; That a man could not in any case bestow his worldly estate better than to give it to the priests, and devote it to the service of the temple: and that when any thing was so devoted, it was not only unlawful to alienate it, but all other obligations, though ever so just and sacred, were thereby superseded, and a man was thereby discharged from them.

Secondly, How they allowed the application of this to the case of children. When their parents' necessities called for their assistance, they pleaded, that all they could spare from themselves and their children, they had devoted to the treasury of the temple; *It is a gift, by whatsoever thou mightest be profited by me,* and therefore their parents must expect nothing from them.

2. The other part of Christ's answer is by way of reprehension; and that which he here charges them with, is hypocrisy; *Ye hypocrites, v.* 7.

Now Christ fetches his reproof from Isa. xxix. 13. *Well did Esaias prophesy of you.* Isaiah spoke it of the men of that generation to which he prophesied, yet Christ applies it to these scribes and Pharisees. Isaiah prophesied not of them only, but of all other hypocrites, against whom that word of his is still levelled, and stands in force. The prophecies of scripture are every day in the fulfilling.

This prophecy exactly deciphers a hypocritical nation, Isa. ix. 17; x. 6. Here is,

(1) The description of hypocrites, in two things.

[1] In their own performances of religious worship, *v.* 8, when they *draw nigh to God with their mouth, and honour him with their lips, their heart is far from him.*

[2] In their prescriptions to others. This is an instance of their hypocrisy, that *they teach for doctrines the commandments of men.* The Jews paid the same respect to oral tradition that they did to the word of God. When men's inventions are tacked to God's institutions, and imposed accordingly, this is hypocrisy, a mere human religion.

(2) The doom of hypocrites; it is put in a little compass; *In vain do they worship me.* Their worship does not attain the end for which it was appointed; it will neither please God, nor profit themselves. If it be not *in spirit,* it is not *in truth,* and so it is all nothing.

INNER DEFILEMENT
(*vv.* 10–20)

Christ having proved that the disciples, in eating with unwashen hands, were not to be blamed, as transgressing the traditions and injunctions of the elders, comes here to show that they were not to be blamed, as having done any thing that was in itself evil. In the former part of his discourse he overturned the authority of the law, and in this the reason of it. Observe,

I. The solemn introduction to this discourse (*v.* 10); *He called the multitude.*

II. The truth itself laid down (*v.* 11), in two propositions.

1. *Not that which goes into the mouth defileth the man.* It is not the kind or quality of our food, not the condition of our hands, that affects the soul with any moral pollution or defilement. *The kingdom of God is not meat and drink,* Rom. xiv. 17. That defiles the man, by which guilt is contracted before God, and the man is rendered offensive to him, and disfitted for communion with him; now what we eat, if we do not eat unreasonably and immoderately, does not this; for *to the pure all things are pure,* Tit. i. 15.

2. *But that which comes out of the mouth, this defiles a man.* We are polluted, not by the meat we

eat with unwashen hands, but by the words we speak from an unsanctified heart. It is not the disciples that defile themselves with what they eat, but the Pharisees that defile themselves with what they speak spitefully and censoriously of them.

III. The offence that was taken at this truth and the account brought to Christ of that offence (*v.* 12).

1. It was not strange that the Pharisees should be offended at this plain truth, for they were men made up of error and enmity, mistake and malice.

2. The disciples thought it strange that their Master should say that which he knew would give so much offence. But he knew what he said, and to whom he said it, and what would be the effect of it; and would teach us, that though in indifferent things we must be tender of giving offence, yet we must not, for fear of that, evade any truth or duty.

IV. The doom passed upon the Pharisees and their corrupt traditions. Two things Christ here foretells concerning them.

1. The rooting out of them and their traditions (*v.* 13): *Every plant which my heavenly Father hath not planted, shall be rooted up.* Not only the corrupt opinions and superstitious practices of the Pharisees, but their sect, and way, and constitution, were plants not of God's planting. Those plants that are not of God's planting, shall not be of his protecting, but shall undoubtedly be rooted up. What is not of God shall not stand, Acts v. 38.

2. The ruin of them; and their followers, who had their persons and principles in admiration, *v.* 14. Where,

(1) Christ bids his disciples *let them alone.* "Have no converse with them or concern for them; neither court their favour, nor dread their displeasure." The case of those sinners is sad indeed, whom Christ orders his ministers to let alone.

(2) He gives them two reasons for it. *Let them alone;* for,

[1] They are proud and ignorant; two bad qualities that often meet, and render a man incurable in his folly, Prov. xxvi. 12. *They are blind leaders of the blind.* They are grossly ignorant in the things of God, and strangers to the spiritual nature of the divine law; and yet so proud, that they think they see better and further than any, and therefore undertake to be leaders of others, to show others the way to heaven, when they themselves know not one step of the way.

[2] They are posting to destruction, and will shortly be plunged into it; *Both shall fall into the ditch.* This must needs be the end of it, if both be so blind, and yet both so bold, venturing forward, and yet not aware of danger. Both will be involved in the general desolation coming upon the Jews, and both drowned in eternal destruction and perdition. The blind leaders and the blind followers will perish together.

V. Instruction given to the disciples concerning the truth Christ had laid down, *v.* 10.

Here is, 1. Their desire to be better instructed in this matter (*v.* 15); in this request as in many others, Peter was their speaker; the rest, it is probable, putting him on to speak, or intimating their concurrence; *Declare unto us this parable.* What Christ said was plain, but, because it agreed not with the notions they had imbibed, though they would not contradict it, yet they call it a parable, and cannot understand it.

2. The reproof Christ gave them for their weakness and ignorance (*v.* 16); *Are ye also yet without understanding?* As many as Christ loves and teaches, he thus rebukes.

3. The explanation Christ gave them of this doctrine of pollutions. Though he chided them for their dullness, he did not cast them off, but pitied them, and taught them, as Luke xxiv. 25–27. He here shows us,

(1) What little danger we are in of pollution from that which *entereth in at the mouth, v.* 17. What there is of dregs and defilement in our meat, nature (or rather the God of nature) has provided a way to clear us of it; *it goes in at the belly, and is cast out into the draught,* and nothing remains to us but pure nourishment.

(2) What great danger we are in of pollution from that which *proceeds out of the mouth* (*v.* 18), out of the abundance of the heart: compare *ch.* xii. 34. Now here we have,

[1] The corrupt fountain of that which proceeds out of the mouth; it comes from the heart; that is the spring and source of all sin, Jer. viii. 7. It is the heart that is so desperately wicked (Jer. xvii. 9);

for there is no sin in word or deed, which was not first in the heart.

[2] Some of the corrupt streams which flow from this fountain, specified; though they do not all *come out of the mouth,* yet they all come out of the man, and are the fruits of that wickedness which is in the heart, and is wrought there, Ps. lviii. 2.

First, Evil thoughts, sins against all the commandments. These are the first-born of the corrupt nature, the beginning of its strength, and do most resemble it. Carnal fancies and imaginations are evil thoughts, wickedness in the contrivance, wicked plots, purposes, and devices of mischief to others, Mic. ii. 1.

Secondly, Murders, sins against the sixth commandment; these come from a malice in the heart against our brother's life, or a contempt of it.

Thirdly, Adulteries and *fornications,* sins against the seventh commandment; these come from the wanton, unclean, carnal heart; and the lust that reigns there, is conceived there, and brings forth these sins, Jam. i. 15. There is adultery in the head first, and then in the act, *ch.* v. 28.

Fourthly, Thefts, sins against the eighth commandment; cheats, wrongs, robberies, and all injurious contracts; the fountain of all these is in the heart, that is it that is *exercised in these covetous practices* (2 Pet. ii. 14), that is set upon riches, Ps. lxii .10. *Achan coveted, and then took,* Joshua vii. 20, 21.

Fifthly, False witness, against the ninth commandment; this comes from a complication of falsehood and covetousness, or falsehood and malice in the heart.

Sixthly, Blasphemies, speaking evil of God, against the third commandment; speaking evil of our neighbour, against the ninth commandment; these come from a contempt and disesteem of both in the heart; thence *the blasphemy against the Holy Ghost* proceeds (*ch.* xii. 31, 32); these are the overflowing of the gall within.

Now *these are the things which defile a man, v.* 20. The mind and conscience are defiled by sin, and that makes everything else so, Tit. i. 15.

These therefore are the things we must carefully avoid, and all approaches toward them, and not lay stress upon the washing of the hands.

A DAUGHTER HEALED
(*vv.* 21–28)

We have here that famous story of Christ's *casting the devil out of the woman of Canaan's daughter.*

I. *Jesus went thence.* Note, Justly is the light taken from those that either play by it, or rebel against it.

II. When he went thence, he *departed into the coasts of Tyre and Sidon*; not to those cities (they were excluded from any share in *Christ's mighty works, ch.* xi. 21, 22), but into that part of the land of Israel which lay that way. Here it was, that this miracle was wrought, in the story of which we may observe.

1. The address of the woman of Canaan to Christ, *v.* 22. She was a Gentile, *a stranger to the commonwealth of Israel*; probably one of the posterity of those accursed nations that were devoted by that word, *Cursed be Canaan.*

Her address was very importunate, she *cried* to Christ, as one in earnest; cried, as being at some distance from him, not daring to approach too near, being a Canaanite, lest she should give offence. In her address,

(1) She relates her misery; *My daugher. is grievously vexed with a devil.* There were degrees of that misery, and this was the worst sort. It was a common case at that time, and very calamitous.

(2) She requests for mercy; *Have mercy on me, O Lord, thou Son of David.* In calling him *Lord, the Son of David*, she owns him to be the Messiah: that is the great thing which faith should fasten upon, and fetch comfort from.

Her petition is, *Have mercy on me.* She does not limit Christ to this or that particular instance of mercy, but mercy, mercy is the thing she begs: she pleads not merit, but depends upon mercy; *Have mercy upon me.*

2. The discouragement she met with in this address; in all the story of Christ's ministry we do not meet with the like. He was wont to countenance and encourage all that came to him, and either *to answer before they called,* or *to hear while they were yet speaking*; but here was one otherwise treated: and what could be the reason of it? (1) Some think that Christ showed himself backward to gratify this poor woman, because he would not give offence to the Jews, by being as free and as forward in his favour to the Gentiles as to them. Or rather,

(2) Christ treated her thus, to try her; he knows what is in the heart, knew the strength of her faith, and how well able she was, by his grace, to break through such discouragements; he *therefore* met her with them, *that the trial of her faith might be found unto praise, and honour, and glory,* 1 Pet. i. 6, 7.

Observe the particular discouragements given her:

[1] When she cried after him, *he answered her not a word, v.* 23. But Christ knew what he did, and *therefore* did not answer, that she might be the more earnest in prayer.

[2] When the disciples spake a good word for her, he gave a reason why he refused her, which was yet more discouraging.

First, It was some little relief, that the disciples interposed on her behalf; they said, *Send her away, for she crieth after us.* Continued importunity may be uneasy to men, even to good men; but Christ loves to be cried after.

Secondly, Christ's answer to the disciples quite dashed her expectations; "*I am not sent, but to the lost sheep of the house of Israel.*" He doth not only not answer her, but he argues against her, and stops her mouth with a reason. It is true, she is a *lost sheep,* and hath as much need of his care as any, but she is not *of the house of Israel,* to whom he was first sent (Acts iii. 26), and therefore not immediately interested in it, and entitled to it.

Thirdly, When she continued her importunity, he insisted upon the unfitness of the thing, and gave her not only a repulse, but a

seeming reproach too (*v.* 26); *It is not meet to take the children's bread and to cast it to dogs.* This seems to cut her off from all hope, and might have driven her to despair, if she had not had a very strong faith indeed. Gospel grace and miraculous cures (the appurtenances of it), were children's bread; they belonged to them *to whom pertained the adoption* (Rom. ix. 4). The Gentiles were looked upon by the Jews with great contempt, were called and counted *dogs*; and, in comparison with the house of Israel, who were so dignified and privileged, Christ here seems to allow it, and therefore thinks it not meet that the Gentiles should share in the favours bestowed on the Jews. But see how the tables are turned; after the bringing of the Gentiles into the church, the Jewish zealots for the law are called *dogs,* Phil. iii. 2.

Now this Christ urges against this woman of Canaan; "How can she expect to eat of the children's bread, who is not of the family?" Note, 1. Those whom Christ intends most signally to honour, he first humbles and lays low in a sense of their own meanness and unworthiness. We must first see ourselves to be as dogs, *less than the least of all God's mercies,* before we are fit to be dignified and privileged with them. 2. Christ delights to exercise great faith with great trials, and sometimes reserves the sharpest for the last, that, *being tried, we may come forth like gold.* 3. Here is the strength of her faith and resolution, in breaking

A Daughter Healed

through all these discouragements.

She breaks through all these discouragements.

(1) With a holy earnestness of desire in prosecuting her petition. This appeared upon the former repulse (*v.* 25); *Then came she, and worshipped him, saying, Lord, help me.* [1] She continued to pray. What Christ said, silenced the disciples; you hear no more of them; they took the answer, but the woman did not. [2] She improved in prayer. Instead of blaming Christ, or charging him with unkindness, she seems rather to suspect herself, and lay the fault upon herself. She fears lest, in her first address, she had not been humble and reverent enough, and therefore now *she came, and worshipped him,* and paid him more respect than she had done; or she fears that she had not been earnest enough, and therefore now she cries, *Lord, help me.* [3] She waives the question, whether she was of those to whom Christ was sent or no; she will not argue that with him, though perhaps she might have claimed some kindred to the house of Israel; but, "Whether an Israelite or no, I come to the Son of David for mercy, and *I will not let him go, except he bless me.*" [4] Her prayer is very short, but comprehensive and fervent, *Lord, help me.* Take this, *First,* As lamenting her case: "If the Messiah be sent only to the house of Israel, the *Lord help me,* what will become of me and mine." Or, *Secondly,* As begging grace to assist her in this hour of temptation. She found it hard to keep up her faith when it

was thus frowned upon, and therefore prays, "*Lord, help me*; Lord, strengthen my faith now; *Lord, let they right hand uphold me,* while my soul is *following hard after thee,*" Ps. lxiii. 8. Or, *Thirdly,* As enforcing her original request, "*Lord, help me*; Lord, give me what I come for." She believed that Christ could and would help her, though she was not of the house of Israel; else she would have dropt her petition. Still she keeps up good thoughts of Christ, and will not quit her hold.

(2) With a holy skilfulness of faith, suggesting a very surprising plea. Christ had placed the Jews with the children, *as olive-plants round about* God's *table,* and had put the Gentiles with the dogs, under the table; and she doth not deny the aptness of the similitude. *Truth, Lord; yet the dogs eat of the crumbs.* Now, here,

[1] Her acknowledgment was very humble: *Truth, Lord.* Note, You cannot speak so meanly and slightly of a humble believer, but he is ready to speak as meanly and slightly of himself.

[2] Her improvement of this into a plea was very ingenious; *Yet the dogs eat of the crumbs.* It was by a singular acumen, and spiritual quickness and sagacity, that she discerned matter of argument in that which looked like a slight.

Her plea is, *Yet the dogs eat of the crumbs.* We poor Gentiles cannot expect the stated ministry and miracles of the Son of David, that belongs to the Jews; but they begin now to be weary of their meat, and to play with it, they find fault with it, and crumble it away; surely then some of the broken meat may fall to a poor Gentile. Observe here,

First, Her humility and necessity made her glad of crumbs.

Secondly, Her faith encouraged her to expect these crumbs. Why should it not be at Christ's table as at a great man's, where the dogs are fed as sure as the children?

4. The happy issue and success of all this. She came off with credit and comfort from this struggle; and, though a Canaanite, approved herself a true daughter of Israel, who, *like a prince, had power with God, and prevailed.*

(1) He commended her faith. *O woman, great is thy faith.*

(2) He cured her daughter; "*Be it unto thee even as thou wilt*: I can deny thee nothing, take what thou camest for."

The event was answerable to the word of Christ; *Her daughter was made whole from that very hour*; from thenceforward was never vexed with the devil any more; the mother's faith prevailed for the daughter's cure. Though the patient was at a distance, that was no hindrance to the efficacy of Christ's word. *He spake, and it was done.*

FOUR THOUSAND FED
(*vv.* 29–39)

Here is, I. A general account of Christ's cures, his curing by wholesale. The tokens of Christ's power and goodness are neither scarce nor scanty; for there is in him an overflowing fulness.

Now, (1) Such was the goodness of Christ, that he admitted all sorts of people; the poor as well as the rich are welcome to Christ, and with him there is room enough for all comers. He never complained of crowds or throngs of seekers, or looked with contempt upon the vulgar, the *herd*, as they are called; for the souls of peasants are as precious with him as the souls of princes.

Such was the power of Christ, that he healed all sorts of diseases; those that came to him, brought their sick relations and friends along with them, and *cast them down at Jesus' feet, v.* 30. Whatever our case is, the only way to find ease and relief, is, to lay it at Christ's feet, to spread it before him, and refer it to his cognizance, and then submit it to him, and refer it to his disposal.

Here were *lame, blind, dumb, maimed, and many others*, brought to Christ. See what work sin has made! It has turned the world into an hospital: what various diseases are human bodies subject to! See what work the Saviour makes! He conquers those hosts of enemies to mankind.

II. Here is a particular account of his feeding *four thousand men* with *seven loaves, and a few little fishes*, as he had lately fed *five thousand with five loaves*. The guests indeed were now not quite so many as then, and the provision a little more; which does not intimate that Christ's arm was shortened, but that he wrought his miracles as the occasion required, and not for ostentation, and therefore he suited them to the occasion: both then and now he took as many as were to be fed, and made use of all that was at hand to feed them with. When once the utmost powers of nature are exceeded, we must say, *This is the finger of God*; and it is neither here nor there how far they are outdone; so that this is no less a miracle than the former.

CHAPTER SIXTEEN

SIGNS OF THE TIMES (vv. 1–4)

We have here Christ's discourse with the Pharisees and Sadducees.

I. Their demand, and the design of it.

1. The demand was of a sign from heaven; this they desired him to show them; pretending they were very willing to be satisfied and convinced, when really they were far from being so, but sought excuses from an obstinate infidelity. That which they pretended to desire was,

(1) Some other sign than what they had yet had. They had great plenty of signs; every miracle Christ wrought was a sign, for *no man could do what he did unless God were with him*. But this will not serve, they must have a sign of their own choosing; they despised those signs which relieved the necessity of the sick and sorrowful, and insisted upon some sign which would gratify the curiosity of the proud.

(2) It must be a sign from heaven. They would have such miracles to prove his commission, as were wrought at the giving of the law upon mount Sinai: thunder, and lightning, and the voice of words, were the sign from heaven they required.

2. The design was to tempt him; not to be taught by him, but to ensnare him. If he should show them a sign from heaven, they would attribute it to a confederacy with the *prince of the power of the air*; if he should not, as they supposed he would not, they would have that to say for themselves, *why they did not believe on him*.

II. Christ's reply to this demand: In his answer,

1. He condemns their overlooking of the signs they had, vv. 2, 3. They were seeking for the signs of the kingdom of God, when it was already among them.

To expose this, he observes to them,

(1) Their skilfulness and sagacity in other things, particularly in natural prognostications of the weather.

(2) Their sottishness and stupidity in the concerns of their souls; *Can ye not discern the signs of the times?*

[1] "Do you not see that the Messiah is come?" The sceptre was departed from Judah, Daniel's weeks were just expiring, and yet they regarded not. The miracles Christ wrought, and the gathering of the people to him, were plain indications that the *kingdom of heaven was at hand*, that this was *the day of their visitation*.

[2] "Do you not foresee your own ruin coming for rejecting him? You will not entertain the gospel of peace, and can you not evidently discern that hereby you pull an inevitable destruction upon your own heads?"

2. He refuses to give them any other sign (*v.* 4), as he had done before in the same words, *ch.* xii. 39. Those that persist in the same iniquities, must expect to meet with the same reproofs.

This discourse broke off abruptly; *he left them and departed.* Christ will not tarry long with those that tempt him, but justly withdraws from those that are disposed to quarrel with him. He left them as irreclaimable; *Let them alone.* He left them to themselves, left them in the hand of their own counsels; *so he gave them up to their own hearts' lust.*

EVIL LEAVEN (*vv.* 5–12)

We have here Christ's discourse with his disciples concerning bread, in which, as in many other discourses, he speaks to them of spiritual things under a similitude, and they misunderstand him of carnal things. The occasion of it was, their forgetting to victual their ship, and to take along with them provisions for their family on the other side the water.

1. Here is the caution Christ gave them, to *beware of the leaven of the Pharisees.* He had now been discoursing with the Pharisees and Sadducees, and saw them to be men of such a spirit, that it was necessary to caution his disciples to have nothing to do with them. Disciples are in most danger from hypocrites; against those that are openly vicious they stand upon their guard, but against Pharisees, who are great pretenders to devotion, and Sadducees, who pretend to a free and impartial search after truth, they commonly lie unguarded: and therefore the caution is doubled, *Take heed, and beware.*

The corrupt principles and practices of the Pharisees and Sadducees are compared to leaven; they were souring, and swelling, and spreading, like leaven; they fermented wherever they came.

II. Their mistake concerning this caution, *v.* 7. They thought Christ hereby upbraided them with their improvidence and forgetfulness, that they were so busy attending to his discourse with the Pharisees, that *therefore* they forgot their private concerns.

III. The reproof Christ gave them for this.

1. He reproves their distrust of his ability and readiness to supply them in this strait (*v.* 8); "*O ye of little faith,* why are ye in such perplexity because ye have *taken no bread,* that ye can mind nothing else, that ye think your Master is as full of it as you, and apply everything he saith to that?" See how easily Christ forgave his disciples' carelessness, though it was in such a material point as taking bread; and do likewise. But that which he chides them for is their little faith.

(1) He would have them to depend upon him for supply, though it were in a wilderness, and not to disquiet themselves with anxious thoughts about it.

(2) He is displeased at their solicitude in this matter. The weakness and shiftlessness of good people in their worldly affairs is that for which men are apt to condemn them; but it is not such an offence to Christ as their

inordinate care and anxiety about those things.

(3) The aggravation of their distrust was the experience they had so lately had of the power and goodness of Christ in providing for them, *vv*. 9, 10. Though they had no bread with them, they had him with them who could provide bread for them. If they had not the cistern, they had the Fountain. *Do ye not yet understand, neither remember?*

2. He reproves their misunderstanding of the caution he gave them (*v*. 11); *How is it that you do not understand?* Note, Christ's disciples may well be ashamed of the slowness and dullness of their apprehensions in divine things; especially when they have long enjoyed the means of grace; *I spake it not unto you concerning bread.* He took it ill, (1) That they should think him as thoughtful about bread as they were; whereas his *meat and drink were to do his Father's will.* (2) That they should be so little acquainted with his way of preaching, as to take that literally which he spoke by way of parable; and should thus make themselves like the multitude, who, when Christ spoke to them in parables, seeing, saw not, and hearing, heard not, *ch*. xiii. 13.

IV. The rectifying of the mistake by this reproof (*v*. 12);| *Then understood they* what he meant. He did not tell them expressly what he meant, but repeated what he had said, that they should beware of the leaven; and so obliged them, by comparing this with his other discourses, to arrive at the sense of it in their own thoughts. Thus

Christ teaches by the Spirit of wisdom in the heart, opening the understanding to the Spirit of revelation in the word.

PETER'S CONFESSION
(*vv*. 13–20)

We have here a private conference which Christ had with his disciples concerning himself. It was in the coasts of Cesarea Philippi, the utmost borders of the land of Canaan northward; there in that remote corner, perhaps, there was less flocking after him than in other places, which gave him leisure for this private conversation with his disciples.

Christ is here catechising his disciples.

I. He enquires what the opinions of others were concerning him; *Who do men say that I, the Son of man, am?*

1. He calls himself the *Son of man*; which may be taken either, (1) As a title common to him with others. He was called, and justly, *the Son of God,* for so he was (Luke i. 35); but he called himself the Son of man; for he is really and truly "Man, made of a woman." Or, (2) As a title peculiar to him as Mediator. He is made known, in Daniel's vision, as the *Son of man,* Dan. vii. 13. I am the Messiah, that Son of man that was promised. But,

2. He enquires what people's sentiments were concerning him: "*Who do men say that I am? The Son of Man?*" (So I think it might better be read). "Do they own me for the Messiah?"

3. To this question the disciples

gave him an answer (*v.* 14), *Some say, thou art John the Baptist,* &c. There were some that said, he was the *Son of David* (*ch.* xii. 23), and the great Prophet, John vi. 14. The disciples, however, do not mention that opinion, but only such opinions as were wide of the truth, which they had gathered up from their countrymen.

II. He enquires what *their* thoughts were concerning him; "*But who say ye that I am? v.* 15. Ye tell me what other people say of me; can ye say better?" 1. The disciples had themselves been better taught than others; had, by their intimacy with Christ, greater advantages of getting knowledge than others had. 2. The disciples were trained up to teach others, and therefore it was highly requisite that they should understand the truth themselves: "Ye that are to preach the gospel of the kingdom, what are your notions of him that sent you?" Note, Ministers must be examined before they be sent forth, especially what their sentiments are of Christ, and who they say that he is; for how can they be owned as ministers of Christ, that are either ignorant or erroneous concerning Christ? This is a question we should every one of us be frequently putting to ourselves, "*Who* do we say, *what* kind of one do we say, that *the Lord Jesus is*? Is he precious to us? Is he in our eyes the chief of ten thousand? Is he the Beloved of our souls?" It is well or ill with us, according as our thoughts are right or wrong concerning Jesus Christ.

Well, this is the question; now let us observe,

(1) Peter's answer to this question, *v.* 16. To the former question concerning the opinion others had of Christ, several of the disciples answered, according as they had heard people talk; but to this Peter answers in the name of all the rest, they all consenting to it, and concurring in it.

Peter's answer is short, but it is full, and true, and to the purpose; *Thou art the Christ, the Son of the living God.* Here is a confession of the Christian faith, addressed to Christ, and so made an act of devotion. Here is a confession of the true God as the living God, in opposition to dumb and dead idols, and of *Jesus Christ, whom he hath sent,* whom to know is *life eternal.* This is the conclusion of the whole matter.

[1] The people called him *a Prophet, that Prophet* (John vi. 14); but the disciples own him to be the Christ, the anointed One; the great Prophet, Priest, and King of the church; the true Messiah promised to the fathers, and depended on by them as *He that shall come.* It was a great thing to believe this concerning one whose outward appearance was so contrary to the general idea the Jews had of the Messiah.

[2] He called himself the *Son of Man;* but they owned him to be *the Son of the living God.* The *people's* notion of him was, that he was the ghost of a dead man, Elias or Jeremias; but *they* know and believe him to be *the Son of the living God,* who has life in himself, and has given to his Son

to have life in himself, and to be the *Life of the world*.

(2) Christ's approbation of his answer (*vv.* 17–19); in which Peter is replied to, both as a believer and as an apostle.

[1] As a believer, *v.* 17. Christ shows himself well pleased with Peter's confession, that it was so clear and express, without *ifs* or *ands*, as we say. But,

First, Peter had the happiness of it; *Blessed art thou, Simon Bar-jona*. He reminds him of his rise and original, the meanness of his parentage, the obscurity of his extraction; he was *Bar-jonas—The son of a dove*; so some. Let him remember *the rock out of which he was hewn*, that he may see he was not born to this dignity, but preferred to it by the divine favour; it was free grace that made him to differ. Having reminded him of this, he makes him sensible of his great happiness as a believer; *Blessed art thou. Blessed are your eyes*, ch. xiii. 16. All happiness attends the right knowledge of Christ.

Secondly, God must have the glory of it; "*For flesh and blood have not revealed it to thee*. Thou hadst this neither by the invention of thy own wit and reason, nor by the instruction and information of others; this light sprang neither from nature nor from education, but from my Father who is in heaven." Note, 1. The Christian religion is a revealed religion, has its rise in heaven; it is a religion from above, given by inspiration of God, not the learning of philosophers, nor the politics of statesmen. 2. Saving faith is the gift of God,

and, wherever it is, is wrought by him, as the Father of our Lord Jesus Christ, for his sake, and upon the score of his mediation, Phil. i. 29. *Therefore* thou art blessed, because *my Father has revealed it to thee*.

[2] Christ replies to him as an apostle òr minister, *vv.* 18, 19. Peter, in the name of the church, had confessed Christ, and to him therefore the promise intended for the church is directed.

Upon occasion of this great confession made of Christ, which is the church's homage and allegiance, he signed and published this royal, this divine charter, by which that body politic is incorporated.

Now the purport of this charter is,

First, To establish the being of the church; *I say also unto thee*. It is Christ that makes the grant, he who is the church's Head, and Ruler, to whom all judgment is committed, and from whom all power is derived; he who makes it pursuant to the authority received from the Father, and his undertaking for the salvation of the elect. The grant is put into Peter's hand; "I say it to *thee*." The Old Testament promises relating to the church were given immediately to particular persons, eminent for faith and holiness, as to Abraham and David; which yet gave no supremacy to them, much less to any of their successors; so the New-Testament charter is here delivered to Peter as an agent, but to the use and behoof of the church in all ages, according to the purposes therein specified and contained. Now it is here promised,

1. That Christ would build his church upon a rock. This body politic is incorporated by the style and title of *Christ's church*. It is a number of the children of men called out of the world, and set apart from it, and dedicated to Christ.

(1) The Builder and Maker of the church is Christ himself; *I will build it*. By the working of his Spirit with the preaching of his word he adds souls to his church, and so builds it up with living stones, 1 Pet. ii. 5.

(2) The foundation on which it is built is, *this Rock*. Let the architect do his part ever so well, if the foundation be rotten, the building will not stand; let us therefore see what the foundation is, and it must be meant of Christ, for *other foundation can no man lay*. See Isa. xxviii. 16.

[1] The church is built upon a *rock*; a firm, strong, and lasting foundation, which time will not waste, nor will it sink under the weight of the building.

[2] It is built upon *this* rock; thou art *Peter*, which signifies *a stone* or *rock*; Christ gave him that name when he first called him (John i. 42), and here he confirms it. From the mention of this significant name, occasion is taken for this metaphor of *building upon a rock*.

First, Some by this rock understand Peter himself as an apostle, the chief, though not the prince, of the twelve, senior among them, but not superior over them. The church is built upon the foundation of the apostles, Eph. ii. 20. The first stones of that building were laid in and by their ministry; hence their names are said to be *written in the foundations* of the new Jerusalem, Rev. xxi. 14. Now Peter being that apostle by whose hand the first stones of the church were laid, both in Jewish converts (Acts ii), and in the Gentile converts (Acts x.), he might in some sense be said to be the rock on which it was built. *Cephas* was one that seemed to be a pillar, Gal. ii. 9. But it sounds very harsh, to call a man that only lays the first stone of a building, which is a transient act, the foundation on which it is built, which is an abiding thing.

Secondly, Others, by this *rock*, understand *Christ*; "*Thou art Peter*, thou hast the name of a *stone*, but *upon this rock*, pointing to himself, *I will build my church*." Perhaps he laid his hand on his breast, as when he said, *Destroy this temple* (John ii. 19), when he *spoke of the temple of his body*. But this must be explained by those many scriptures which speak of Christ as the only Foundation of the church; see 1 Cor. iii. 11; 1 Pet. ii. 6. Christ is both its Founder and its Foundation; he draws souls, and draws them to himself; to him, they are united, and on him they rest and have a constant dependence.

Thirdly, Others by this *rock* understand this confession which Peter made of Christ, and this comes all to one with understanding it of Christ himself. It was a good confession which Peter witnessed, *Thou art the Christ, the Son of the living God*; the rest concurred with him in it. "Now," saith Christ, "this is that great truth *upon which I will build my church*." 1. Take away this truth itself, and the universal church falls to the ground. If Christ be not the Son of God, Christianity is a cheat, and the church is a mere chimera; *our preaching is vain, your faith is vain, and you are yet in your sins*, 1 Cor. xv. 14–17. If Jesus be not the Christ, those that own him are not of the church, but deceivers and deceived. 2. Take away the faith and confession of this truth from any particular church, and it ceases to be a part of Christ's church, and relapses to the state and character of infidelity.

2. Christ here promises to preserve and secure his church, when it is built; *The gates of hell shall not prevail against it*; neither against this truth, nor against the church which is built upon it.

(1) This implies that the church has enemies that fight against it, and endeavour its ruin and overthrow, here represented by *the gates of hell, that is*, the city of hell; (which is directly opposite to this heavenly city, this *city of the living God*), the devil's interest among the children of men. These fight against the church by opposing gospel truths, corrupting gospel ordinances, persecuting good ministers and good Christians; drawing or driving, persuading by craft or forcing by cruelty, to that which is inconsistent with the purity of religion; this is the design of the gates of hell, to root out the name of Christianity (Ps. lxxxiii. 4), *to devour the man-child* (Rev. xii. 9), to raze this city to the ground.

(2) This assures us that the enemies of the church shall not gain their point. While the world stands, Christ will have a church in it, in which his truths and ordinances shall be owned and kept up, in spite of all the opposition of the powers of darkness; *They shall not prevail against it*, Ps. cxxix. 1, 2.

Secondly, The other part of this charter is, to settle the order and government of the church, *v.* 19. When a city or society is incorporated, officers are appointed and empowered to act for the common good. A city without government is a chaos. Now this constituting of the government of the church, is here expressed by the delivering of the keys, and, with them, a power to bind and loose. This is not to be understood of any peculiar power that Peter was invested with, as if he were sole door-keeper of the kingdom of heaven, and had that key of David which belongs only to the Son of David; no, this invests all the apostles and their successors with a ministerial power to guide and govern the church of Christ, as it exists in particular congregations or churches, according to the rules of the gospel.

Now, 1. The power here delegated is a spiritual power; it is a power *pertaining to the kingdom of heaven*, that is, to the church, that part of it which is militant here on earth, to the gospel dispensation.

2. It is the *power* of the keys that is given, alluding to the custom of investing men with authority in such a place, by delivering to them the keys of the place.

3. It is a power to *bind and loose*,

that is (following the metaphor of the keys), to shut and open.

4. It is a power which Christ has promised to own the due administration of; he will ratify the sentences of his stewards with his own approbation; *It shall be bound in heaven, and loosed in heaven*: not that Christ hath hereby obliged himself to confirm all church-censures, right or wrong; but such as are duly passed according to the word, such are sealed in heaven; that is, the word of the gospel, in the mouth of faithful ministers, is to be looked upon, not as the word of man, but as the word of God, and to be received accordingly, 1 Thes. ii. 13; John xii. 20.

Now *the keys of the kingdom of heaven are*,

(1) The key of *doctrine*, called the key of *knowledge*. Now the apostles had an extraordinary power of this kind; some things forbidden by the law of Moses were now to be allowed, as the eating of such and such meats; some things allowed there were now to be forbidden, as divorce; and the apostles were empowered to declare this to the world, and men might take it upon their words. When Peter was first taught himself, and then taught others, *to call nothing common or unclean*, this power was exercised. There is also an ordinary power hereby conveyed to all ministers, to preach the gospel as appointed officers; to tell people, in God's name, and according to the scriptures, *what is good, and what the Lord requires of them*: and they who *declare the whole counsel of God*, use these keys well, Acts xx. 27.

(2) The key of *discipline*, which is but the application of the former to particular persons, upon a right estimate of their characters and actions. It is not legislative power that is hereby conferred, but judicial; the judge doth not make the law, but only declares what is law, and upon an impartial enquiry into the merits of the cause, gives sentence accordingly. Such is *the power of the keys*, wherever it is lodged, with reference to church-membership and the privileges thereof.

Lastly, Here is the charge which Christ gave his disciples, to keep this private for the present (*v.* 20); *They must tell no man that he was Jesus the Christ*. What they had professed to him, they must not yet publish to the world, for several reasons; 1. Because this was the time of preparation for his kingdom: the great thing now preached, was, that *the kingdom of heaven was at hand*. 2. Christ would have his Messiahship proved by his works, and would rather *they* should testify of him than that his *disciples* should, because their testimony was but as his own, which he insisted not on. See John v. 31, 34.

PETER REBUKED (*vv.* 21–23)

We have here Christ's discourse with his disciples concerning his own sufferings; in which observe,

I. Christ's foretelling of his sufferings. Now he *began* to do it, and from this time he frequently spake of them.

From that time, when they had

made that full confession of Christ, that he was the Son of God, then he began to show them this. When he found them knowing in one truth, he taught them another; *for to him that has, shall be given*. Now observe,

1. What he foretold concerning his sufferings, the particulars and circumstances of them, and all surprising.

(1) The place where he should suffer. He must go to Jerusalem, the head city, the holy city, and suffer there. Though he lived most of his time in Galilee, he must die at Jerusalem; there all the sacrifices were offered, there therefore *he* must die, *who is the great sacrifice*.

(2) The persons by whom he should suffer; *the elders, and chief priests, and scribes*; these made up the great sanhedrim, which sat at Jerusalem, and was had in veneration by the people. Those that should have been most forward in owning and admiring Christ, were the most bitter in persecuting him.

(3) What he should suffer; *he must suffer many things, and be killed*.

(4) What should be the happy issue of all his sufferings; he shall *be raised again the third day*. As the prophets, so Christ himself, when he testified beforehand his sufferings, testified withal the glory that should follow, 1 Pet. i. 11. His rising again the third day proved him to be the Son of God, notwithstanding his sufferings; and therefore he mentions that, to keep up their faith.

2. Why he foretold his sufferings.

(1) To show that they were the product of an eternal counsel and consent; were agreed upon between the Father and the Son from eternity; *Thus it behoved Christ to suffer*. The matter was settled in *the determinate counsel and foreknowledge*, in pursuance of his own voluntary susception and undertaking for our salvation; his sufferings were no surprise to him, did not come upon him as a snare, but he had a distinct and certain foresight of them, which greatly magnifies his love, John xviii. 4. (2) To rectify the mistakes which his disciples had imbibed concerning the external pomp and power of his kingdom. Believing him to be the Messiah, they counted upon nothing but dignity and authority in the world; but here Christ reads them another lesson, tells them of the cross and sufferings. Those that follow Christ must be dealt plainly with, and warned not to expect great things in this world. (3) It was to prepare them for the share, at least, of sorrow and fear, which they must have in his sufferings.

II. The offence which Peter took at this, he said, *Be it far from thee, Lord*: probably he spake the sense of the rest of the disciples, as before, for he was chief speaker. *He took him, and began to rebuke him.*

1. It did not become Peter to contradict his Master, or take upon him to advise him; he might have wished, *that, if it were possible, this cup might pass away*, without saying so peremptorily, *This shall not be*, when Christ had said, *It must be*.

2. It savoured much of fleshly

wisdom, for him to appear so warmly against suffering, and to startle thus at the offence of the cross. It is the corrupt part of us, that is thus solicitous to sleep in a whole skin. We are apt to look upon sufferings as they relate to this present life, to which they are uneasy; but there are other rules to measure them by, which, if duly observed, will enable us cheerfully to bear them, Rom. viii. 18.

III. Christ's displeasure against Peter for this suggestion of his, *v.* 23. We do not read of any thing said or done by any of his disciples, at any time, that he resented so much as this, though they often offended.

Observe, 1. How he expressed his displeasure: He turned upon Peter, and (we may suppose) with a frown said, *Get thee behind me, Satan*. Just now, he had said, *Blessed art thou, Simon*, and had even laid him in his bosom; but here, *Get thee behind me, Satan*; and there was cause for both. Note, A good man may by a surprise of temptation soon grow very unlike himself. He answered him as he did Satan himself, *ch.* iv. 10.

2. What was the ground of this displeasure; why did Christ thus resent a motion that seemed not only harmless, but kind? Two reasons are given:

(1) *Thou art an offence to me— Thou art my hindrance* (so it may be read); "thou standest in my way." Christ was hastening on in the work of our salvation, and his heart was so much upon it, that he took it ill to be hindered, or

tempted to start back from the hardest and most discouraging part of his undertaking. Peter was not so sharply reproved for disowning and denying his Master in his sufferings as he was for dissuading him from them; though that was the defect, this the excess, of kindness.

(2) *Thou savourest not the things that are of God, but those that are of men.* Note, [1] *The things that are of God,* that is, the concerns of his will and glory, often clash and interfere with *the things that are of men,* that is, with our own wealth, pleasure, and reputation. [2] Those that inordinately fear, and industriously decline suffering for Christ, when they are called to it, savour more of the things of man than of the things of God; they relish those things more themselves, and make it appear to others that they do so.

LAW OF DISCIPLESHIP
(*vv.* 24–28)

Christ, having shown his disciples that *he* must suffer, and that he was ready and willing to suffer, here shows them that *they* must suffer too, and must be ready and willing. It is a weighty discourse that we have in these verses.

I. Here is the law of discipleship laid down, and the terms fixed, upon which we may have the honour and benefit of it, *v.* 24. He said this to his disciples, not only that they might instruct others concerning it, but that by this rule they might examine their own sincerity. Observe,

1. What it is to be a disciple of Christ; it is to come after him.

When Christ called his disciples, this was the word of command, *Follow me*. A true disciple of Christ is one that doth follow him in duty, and shall follow him to glory.

2. What are the great things required of those that will be Christ's disciples; *If any man will come—If any man be willing* to come. It denotes a deliberate choice, and cheerfulness and resolution in that choice. Many are disciples more by chance or the will of others than by any act of their own will; but Christ will have his people volunteers, Ps. cx. 3.

Now what are these terms?

(1) *Let him deny himself*. Peter had advised Christ to spare himself, and would be ready, in the like case, to take the advice; but Christ tells them all, they must be so far from *sparing* themselves, that they must *deny* themselves. Herein they must come after Christ, for his birth, and life, and death, were all a continued act of self-denial, a self-emptying, Phil. ii. 7, 8. If self-denial be a hard lesson, and against the grain to flesh and blood, it is no more than what our Master learned and practised before us and for us, both for our redemption and for our instruction; and *the servant is not above his lord*.

(2) *Let him take up his cross*. The cross is here put for all sufferings, as men or Christians; providential afflictions, persecutions for righteousness' sake, every trouble that befals us, either for doing well or for not doing ill. The troubles of Christians are fitly called *crosses*, in allusion to the death of the cross, which Christ was obedient to; and it should reconcile us to troubles, and take off the terror of them, that they are what we bear in common with Christ, and such as he hath borne before us. That which we have to do, is, not only to bear the cross (that a stock, or a stone, or a stick may do), not only to be silent under it, but we must *take up* the cross, must improve it to some good advantage. We should not say, "This is an evil, and I must bear it, because I cannot help it;" but, "This is an evil, and I will bear it, because it shall work for my good." When we *rejoice in our afflictions, and glory in them*, then we take up the cross. This fitly follows upon denying ourselves; for he that will not deny himself the pleasures of sin, and the advantages of this world for Christ, when it comes to the push, will never have the heart to take up his cross.

(2) *Let him follow me*, in this particular of taking up the cross. Suffering saints must look unto Jesus, and take from him both direction and encouragement in suffering. Do we bear the cross? We therein follow Christ, who bears it *before* us, bears it *for* us, and so bears it *from* us.

II. Self-denial, and patient suffering, are hard lessons, which will never be learned if we consult with flesh and blood; let us therefore consult with our Lord Jesus, and see what advice he gives us; and here he gives us,

1. Some considerations proper to engage us to these duties of self-denial and suffering for Christ. Consider,

(1) The weight of that eternity which depends upon our present choice (*v.* 25); *Whosoever will save his life*, by denying Christ, *shall lose it; and whosoever is* content to *lose his life*, for owning Christ, *shall find it.* Here are *life and death, good and evil, the blessing and the curse, set before us.* Observe,

[1] The misery that attends the most plausible apostasy. *Whosoever will save his life* in this world, if it be by sin, he *shall lose it* in another; he that forsakes Christ, to preserve a temporal life and avoid a temporal death, will certainly come short· of eternal life, and will be hurt of the second death, and eternally held by it.

[2] The advantage that attends the most perilous and expensive constancy; *Whosoever will lose his life for Christ's sake* in this world, *shall find it* in a better, infinitely to his advantage. The loss of other comforts, for Christ, may possibly be made up in this world (Mark x. 30); the loss of life cannot, but it shall be made up in the other world, in an eternal life; the believing prospect of which hath been the great support of suffering saints in all ages. An assurance of the life they should find, in lieu of the life they hazarded, hath enabled them to triumph over death in all its terrors; to go smiling to a scaffold, and stand singing to a stake, and to call the utmost instances of their enemies' rage but *a light affliction.*

[3] The worth of the soul which lies at stake, and the worthlessness of the world in comparison of it (*v.* 26). *What is a man profited, if he gain the whole world and lose his own soul?* The same word which is translated *his life (v.* 25), for the *soul* is the *life*, Gen. ii. 7. This alludes to that common principle, that, whatever a man gets, if he lose his life, it will do him no good, he cannot enjoy his gains. But it looks higher, and speaks of the soul as immortal, and a loss of it beyond death, which cannot be compensated by the gain of the whole world. Here is *the whole world* set in the scale against *one soul*, and *Tekel* written upon it; it is weighed in the balance, and found too light to weigh it down. This is Christ's judgment upon the matter, and he is a competent Judge; he had reason to know the price of *souls*, for he redeemed them; nor would he under-rate the world, for he made it.

What shall a man give in exchange for his soul? Note, If once the soul be lost, it is lost for ever. There is no *counter-price*, that can be paid, or will be accepted. Therefore it is good to be wise in time, and do well for ourselves.

2. Here are some considerations proper to encourage us in self-denial and suffering for Christ.

(1) The assurance we have of Christ's glory, at his second coming to judge the world, *v.* 27. If we look to the end of all these things, the period of the world, and the posture of souls then, we shall thence form a very different idea of the present state of things. If we see things as they *will* appear then, we shall see them as they *should* appear now.

The great encouragement to steadfastness in religion is taken from the second coming of Christ, considering it.

(2) The near approach of his kingdom in this world, *v.* 28. It was so near, that there were some attending him who should live to see it. As Simeon was assured that he should not see death till he had seen the Lord's Christ come in the flesh; so some here are assured that they shall not taste death (death is a sensible thing, its terrors are seen, its bitterness is tasted) till they had seen the Lord's Christ coming in his kingdom. At the end of time, he shall come in his Father's glory; but now, in the fulness of time, he was to come in his own kingdom, his mediatorial kingdom. Some little specimen was given of his glory a few days after this, in his transfiguration (*ch.* xvii. 1); then he tried his robes. But this points at Christ's coming by the pouring out of his Spirit, the planting of the gospel church, the destruction of Jerusalem, and the taking away of the place and nation of the Jews, who were the most bitter enemies to Christianity. Here was *the Son of man coming in his kingdom.* Many then present lived to see it, particularly John, who lived till after the destruction of Jerusalem, and saw Christianity planted in the world. Let *this* encourage the followers of Christ to suffer for him.

CHAPTER SEVENTEEN
THE TRANSFIGURATION
(*vv.* 1–13)

We have here the story of Christ's transfiguration; he had said that

the *Son of man should* shortly *come in his kingdom,* with which promise all the three evangelists industriously connect this story; as if Christ's transfiguration were intended for a specimen and an earnest of the kingdom of Christ, and of that light and love of his, which therein appears to his select and sanctified ones. Peter speaks of this as *the power and coming of our Lord Jesus* (2 Pet. i. 16); because it was an emanation of his power, and a previous notice of his coming, which was fitly introduced by such prefaces.

Now concerning Christ's transfiguration, observe,

I. The circumstances of it, which are here noted, *v.* 1.

1. The time; *six days* after he had the solemn conference with his disciples, *ch.* xvi. 21. St. Luke saith, *It was about eight days after,* six whole days intervening, and this the eighth day, that day seven-night.

2. The place; it was *on the top of a high mountain apart.* Christ chose a mountain, (1) As a secret place. Christ chose a retired place to be transfigured in, because his appearing publicly in his glory was not agreeable to his present state; and thus he would show his humility, and teach us that privacy much befriends our communion with God.

3. The witnesses of it. He took with him Peter and James and John. (1) He took three, a competent number to testify what they should see; for *out of the mouth of two or three witnesses shall every word be established.* (2) He took these three because they were the

chief of his disciples, the first three of the worthies of the Son of David; probably they excelled in gifts and graces; they were Christ's favourites, singled out to be the witnesses of his retirements. They were present when he raised the damsel to life, Mark v. 37. They were afterward to be the witnesses of his agony, and this was to prepare them for that.

II. The manner of it (*v.* 2); *He was transfigured before them*. The substance of his body remained the same, but the accidents and appearances of it were greatly altered; he was not turned into a spirit, but his body, which had appeared in weakness and dishonour, now appeared in power and glory. *He was transfigured, he was metamorphosed*. Christ was both God and man; but, in the days of his flesh, he took on him the *form of a servant*—Phil. ii. 7. He drew a veil over the glory of his godhead; but now, in his transfiguration, he put by that veil, appeared in the form of God (Phil. ii. 6), and gave his disciples a glimpse of his glory, which could not but change his form.

The great truth which we declare, is, that *God is Light* (1 John i. 5), *dwells in light* (1 Tim. vi. 16), *covers himself with light*, Ps. civ. 2. And therefore when Christ would appear in the *form of God*, he appeared *in light*, the most glorious of all visible beings, the first-born of the creation, and most nearly resembling the eternal Parent. Christ is *the Light*; while he was in the world, he *shined in darkness*, and therefore *the world knew him not* (John i. 5, 10); but, at this

time, that Light shined out of the darkness.

Now his transfiguration appeared in two things:

1. *His face did shine as the sun.* The face is the principal part of the body, by which we are known; therefore such a brightness was put on Christ's face, that face which afterward *he hid not from shame and spitting*. It shone as the sun when he goes forth in his strength, so clear, so bright; for he is the Sun of righteousness, the Light of the world. The face of Moses shone but as the moon, with a borrowed reflected light, but Christ's shone as the sun, with an innate inherent light, which was the more sensibly glorious, because it suddenly broke out, as it were, from behind a black cloud.

2. *His raiment was white as the light.* All his body was altered, as his face was; so that beams of light, darting from every part through his clothes, made them white and glittering. The shining of the face of Moses was so weak, that it could easily be concealed by a thin veil; but such was the glory of Christ's body, that his clothes were enlightened by it.

III. The companions of it. He will come, at last, *with ten thousands of his saints*; and, as a specimen of that, there now *appeared unto them Moses and Elias talking with him, v.* 3. Observe, 1. There were glorified saints attending him, that, when there were *three to bear record on earth*, Peter, James, and John, there might be some to bear record from heaven too. 2. These two were Moses and Elias, men very eminent in their day. In them the law and the prophets honoured Christ, and bore testimony to him. Moses and Elias appeared to the disciples; they saw them, and heard them talk, and, either by their discourse or by information from Christ, they knew them to be Moses and Elias; glorified saints shall know one another in heaven.

IV. The great pleasure and satisfaction that the disciples took in the sight of Christ's glory. Peter, as usual, spoke for the rest; *Lord, it is good for us to be here*. Peter here expresses,

1. The delight they had in this converse; *Lord, it is good to be here*. This intimates a thankful acknowledgment of his kindness in admitting them to this favour.

2. The desire they had of the continuance of it; *Let us make here three tabernacles*. There was in this, as in many other of Peter's sayings, a mixture of weakness and of goodwill, more zeal than discretion.

(1) Here was a zeal for this converse with heavenly things, a laudable complacency in the sight they had of Christ's glory.

It argued great respect for his Master and the heavenly guests, with some commendable forgetfulness of himself and his fellow-disciples, that he would have tabernacles for Christ, and Moses, and Elias, but none for himself. He would be content to lie in the open air, on the cold ground, in such good company.

(2) Yet in this zeal he betrayed a great deal of weakness and ignorance. What need had Moses and Elias of tabernacles? They

belonged to that blessed world, *where they hunger no more, nor doth the sun light upon them*. Christ had lately foretold his sufferings, and bidden his disciples expect the like; Peter forgets this, or, to prevent it, will needs be building tabernacles in the mount of glory, out of the way of trouble.

Yet it is some excuse for the incongruity of Peter's proposal, not only that *he knew not what he said* (Luke ix. 33), but also that he submitted the proposal to the wisdom of Christ; *If thou wilt, let us make tabernacles*.

Now to this which Peter said, there was no reply made; the disappearing of the glory would soon answer it. They that promise themselves great things on this earth will soon be undeceived by their own experience.

V. The glorious testimony which God the Father gave to our Lord Jesus, in which *he received from him honour and glory* (2 Pet. i. 17), when *there came this voice from the excellent glory*.

Now concerning this testimony from heaven to Christ, observe.

1. How it came, and in what manner it was introduced.

(1) There was a cloud. We find often in the Old Testament, that a cloud was the visible token of God's presence; he came down upon mount Sinai in a cloud (Exod. xix. 9), and so to Moses, Exod. xxxiv. 5; Numb. xi. 25. He took possession of the tabernacle in a cloud, and afterwards of the temple; where Christ was in his glory, the temple was, and there God showed himself present.

(2) It was a bright cloud. Under

the law it was commonly a thick and dark cloud that God made the token of his presence; he came down upon mount Sinai in a thick cloud (Exod. xix. 16), and said he would *dwell in thick darkness*; see 1 Kings viii. 12. But *we are now come, not to the mount that was covered in blackness and darkness* (Heb. xii. 18), but to the mount that is crowned with a bright cloud.

(3) It overshadowed them. This cloud was intended to break the force of that great light which otherwise would have overcome the disciples, and have been intolerable; it was like the veil which Moses put upon his face when it shone. God, in manifesting himself to his people, considers their frame.

(4) *There came a voice out of the cloud,* and it was the voice of God, who now, as of old, *spake in the cloudy pillar,* Ps. xcix. 7. This voice came from the excellent glory (2 Pet. i. 17), the glory which excelleth, in comparison of which the former had no glory; though the excellent glory was clouded, yet thence came a voice, for *faith comes by hearing.*

2. What this testimony from heaven was; *This is my beloved Son, hear ye him.* Here we have,

(1) The great gospel mystery revealed; *This is my beloved Son, in whom I am well pleased.* This was the very same that was spoken from heaven at his baptism (*ch.* iii. 17); and it was the best news that ever came from heaven to earth since man sinned. Moses and Elias were sometimes instruments of reconciliation between

God and Israel; Moses was a great intercessor, and Elias a great reformer; but in Christ God is reconciling the world; his intercession is more prevalent than that of Moses, and his reformation more effectual than that of Elias.

This repetition of the same voice that came from heaven at his baptism was no vain repetition; but, like the doubling of Pharaoh's dream, was to show the thing was established. What God hath thus spoken once, yea twice, no doubt he will stand to, and he expects we should take notice of it.

(2) The great gospel duty required, and it is the condition of our benefit by Christ; *Hear ye him.* God is well pleased with none in Christ but those that hear him. It is not enough to give him the hearing (what will that avail us?) but we must hear him and believe him, as the great Prophet and Teacher; hear him, and be ruled by him, as the great Prince and Lawgiver; hear him, and heed him.

Moses and Elias were now with him; the law and the prophets; hitherto it was said, *Hear them,* Luke xvi. 29. The disciples were ready to equal them with Christ, when they must have tabernacles for them as well as for him. They had been talking with Christ, and probably the disciples were very desirous to know what they said, and to hear something more from them; No, saith God, *hear him,* and that is enough; him, and not Moses and Elias, who were present, and whose silence gave consent to this voice; they had nothing to say to the contrary;

whatever interest they had in the world as prophets, they were willing to see it all transferred to Christ, that in *all things he might have the pre-eminence*.

VI. The fright which the disciples were put into by this voice, and the encouragement Christ gave them.

1. The disciples *fell on their faces, and were sore afraid*. Ever since man sinned, and heard God's voice in the garden, extraordinary appearances of God have ever been terrible to man, who, knowing he has no reason to expect any good, has been afraid to hear any thing immediately from God.

2. Christ graciously raised them up with abundance of tenderness. Observe here, (1) What he did; *he came, and touched them*. His approaches banished their fears; and when they apprehended that they were apprehended of Christ, there needed no more to make them easy. (2) What he said; *Arise, and be not afraid*. Considering what they had seen and heard, they had more reason to rejoice than to fear, and yet, it seems, they needed this caution. Observe, After they had an express command from heaven to hear Christ, the first word they had from him was, *Be not afraid*, hear that.

VII. The disappearing of the vision (*v.* 8); *They* lift up themselves, and then *lift up their eyes*, and *saw no man, save Jesus only*. Note, Christ will tarry with us when Moses and Elias are gone. The *prophets do not live for ever* (Zech. i. 5), and we see the period of our ministers' conversation; but

Jesus Christ is the same yesterday, to-day, and for ever, Heb. xiii. 7, 8.

VIII. The discourse between Christ and his disciples as they came down from the mountain, *vv.* 9–13.

Here is, (1) The charge that Christ gave the disciples to keep the vision very private for the present (*v.* 9); *Tell it to no man till the Son of man is risen*. If they had proclaimed it, the credibility of it would have been shocked by his sufferings, which were now hastening on. But let the publication of it be adjourned till after his resurrection, and then that and his subsequent glory will be a great confirmation of it.

(2) An objection which the disciples made against something Christ had said (*v.* 10); "*Why then say the scribes that Elias must first come?* If Elias make so short a stay, and is gone so suddenly, and we must say nothing of him; why have we been taught our of the law to expect his public appearance in the world immediately before the setting up of the Messiah's kingdom? Must the coming of Elias be a secret, which everybody looks for?" Or thus; "If the resurrection of the Messiah, and with it the beginning of his kingdom, be at hand, what becomes of that glorious preface and introduction to it, which we expect in the coming of Elias?"

(3) The solving of this objection. [1] Christ allows the prediction (*v.* 11); "*Elias truly shall first come, and restore all things*; so far you are in the right."

[2] He asserts the accomplishment. The scribes say true, that

Elias shall come; but I say unto you, what the scribes could not say, that *Elias is come*, *v.* 12. Note, God's promises are often fulfilled, and men perceive it not, but enquire, *Where is the promise?* when it is already performed. *Elias is come, and they knew him not*; they knew him not to be the Elias promised, the forerunner of the Messiah. But it is no wonder that the morning star was not observed, when he who is the Sun itself, was *in the world, and the world knew him not*.

Because they knew him not, *they have done to him whatsoever they listed*; if they had known, they would not have crucified Christ, or beheaded John. 1 Cor. ii. 8. They ridiculed John, persecuted him, and at last put him to death; which was Herod's doing, but is here charged upon the whole generation of unbelieving Jews, and particularly the scribes, who, though they could not prosecute John themselves, were pleased with what Herod did. He adds, *Likewise also shall the Son of man suffer of them*.

(4) The disciples' satisfaction in Christ's reply to their objection (*v.* 13); *They understood that he spake unto them of John the Baptist*. He did not name John, but gives them such a description of him as would put them in mind of what he had said to them formerly concerning him; *This is Elias*.

THE LUNATIC BOY
(*vv.* 14–21)

We have here the miraculous cure of a child that was lunatic and vexed with a devil. Observe,

I. A melancholy representation of the case of this child, made to Christ by the afflicted father. This was immediately upon his coming down from the mountain where he was transfigured.

Two things the father of the child complains of.

1. The distress of his child (*v.* 15); *Lord, have mercy on my son*. Now, (1) The nature of this child's disease was very sad; *He was lunatic and sore vexed*. A lunatic is properly one whose distemper lies in the brain, and returns with the change of the moon. The devil, by the divine permission, either caused this distemper, or at least concurred with it, to heighten and aggravate it. (2) The effects of the disease were very deplorable; *He oft falls into the fire, and into the water*. If the force of the disease made him to fall, the malice of the devil made him to fall into the fire or water; so mischievous is he where he gains possession and power in any soul. He *seeks to devour*, 1 Pet. v. 8.

2. The disappointment of his expectation from the disciples (*v.* 16); *I brought him to thy disciples, and they could not cure him*. Christ gave his disciples power to cast out devils (*ch.* x. 1, 8), and therein they were successful (Luke x. 17); yet at this time they failed in the operation, though there were nine of them together, and before a great multitude. Christ permitted this, (1) To keep them humble, and to show their dependence upon him, that without him they could do nothing. (2) To glorify himself and his own power.

II. The rebukes that Christ gave to the people first, and then to the devil.

1. He chid those about him (*v.* 17); *O faithless and perverse generation!* This is not spoken to the disciples, but to the people, and perhaps especially to the scribes, who are mentioned in Mark ix. 14, and who, as it should seem, insulted over the disciples, because they had now met with a case that was too hard for them.

Two things he upbraids them with. (1) His presence with them so long; "*How long shall I be with you?* Will you always need my bodily presence, and never come to such maturity as to be fit to be left, the people to the conduct of the disciples, and the disciples to the conduct of the Spirit and of their commission? Must the child be always carried, and will it never learn to go alone?" (2) His patience with them so long; *How long shall I suffer you?* Note, [1] The faithlessness and perverseness of those who enjoy the means of grace are a great grief to the Lord Jesus. Thus did he suffer the manners of Israel of old, Acts xiii. 18. [2] The longer Christ has borne with a perverse and faithless people, the more he is displeased with their perverseness and unbelief; and he is God, and not man, else he would not suffer so long, nor bear so much, as he doth.

2. He cured the child, and set him to rights again. He called, *Bring him hither to me.* Note, When all other helps and succours fail, we are welcome to Christ, and may be confident in him and in his power and goodness.

See here an emblem of Christ's undertaking as our Redeemer.

(1) He breaks the power of Satan (*v.* 18); *Jesus rebuked the devil*, as one having authority, who could back with force his word of command.

(2) He redresses the grievances of the children of men; *The child was cured from that very hour.* It was an immediate cure, and a perfect one.

III. Christ's discourse with his disciples hereupon.

1. They ask the reason why they could not cast out the devil at this time (*v.* 19); *They came to Jesus apart.*

2. Christ gives them two reasons why they failed.

(1) It was *because of their unbelief*, *v.* 20. When he spake to the father of the child and to the people, he charged it upon their unbelief; when he spake to his disciples, he charged it upon theirs; for the truth was, there were faults on both sides. Though they had faith, yet that faith was weak and ineffectual.

Our Lord Jesus takes this occasion to show them the power of faith, that they might not be defective in that, another time, as they were now; *If ye have faith as a grain of mustard-seed, ye shall do wonders,* *v.* 20. Some make the comparison to refer to the quality of the mustard-seed, which is, when bruised, sharp and penetrating; "If you have an active growing faith, not dead, flat, or insipid, you will not be baffled thus." But it rather refers to the quantity; "If you had but a grain of true faith, though so little that it were like that which is the least of all seeds, you would do wonders." Faith in general is a firm assent to, a compliance with, and a confidence in, all divine revelation. The faith here required, is that which had for its object that particular revelation by which Christ gave his disciples power to work miracles in his name, for the confirmation of the doctrine they preached. It was a faith in this revelation that they were defective in; either doubting the validity of their commission, or fearing that it expired with their first mission, and was not to continue when they were returning to their Master; or that it was some way or other forfeited or withdrawn.

It is good for us to be diffident of ourselves and of our own strength; but it is displeasing to Christ, when we distrust any power derived from him or granted by him.

If you have ever so little of this faith in sincerity, if you truly rely upon the powers committed to you, *ye shall say to this mountain, Remove*. This is a proverbial expression, denoting that which follows, and no more, *Nothing shall be impossible to you*.

(2) Because there was something in the kind of the malady, which rendered the cure more than ordinarily difficult (*v.* 21); *"This kind goes not out but by prayer and fasting*. This possession, which works by a falling-sickness, or this kind of devils that are thus furious, is not cast out ordinarily but by great acts of devotion, and therein ye were defective." Fasting and prayer are proper means for the

bringing down of Satan's power against us, and the fetching in of divine power to our assistance. Fasting is of use to put an edge upon prayer; it is an evidence and instance of humiliation which is necessary in prayer, and is a means of mortifying some corrupt habits, and of disposing the body to serve the soul in prayer.

A PROPHECY (*vv.* 22, 23)

Christ here foretells his own sufferings; he began to do it before (*ch.* xvi. 21); and, finding that it was to his disciples a hard saying, he saw it necessary to repeat it. There are some things which *God speaketh once, yea twice, and yet man perceiveth it not*. Observe here,

1. What he foretold concerning himself—that he should be betrayed and killed. He perfectly knew, before, all things that should come to him, and yet undertook the work of our redemption, which greatly commends his love; nay, his clear foresight of them was a kind of ante-passion, had not his love to man made all easy to him.

2. How the disciples received this; *They were exceedingly sorry*. Herein appeared their love to their Master's person, but with all their ignorance and mistake concerning his undertaking. Peter indeed durst not say any thing against it, as he had done before (*ch.* xvi. 22), having then been severely chidden for it; but he, and the rest of them, greatly lamented it, as it would be their own loss, their Master's grief, and the sin and ruin of them that did it.

PAYING TRIBUTE (*vv.* 24–27)

We have here an account of Christ's paying tribute.

I. Observe how it was demanded, *v.* 24. Christ was now at Capernaum, his headquarters, where he mostly resided; he did not keep from thence, to decline being called upon for his dues, but he rather came thither, to be ready to pay them.

1. The tribute demanded was not any civil payment to the Roman powers, that was strictly exacted by the publicans, but the church-duties, the half shekel, about fifteen pence, which were required from every person for the service of the temple, and the defraying of the expenses of the worship there; it is called *a ransom for the soul*, Exod. xxx. 12, &c. This was not so strictly exacted now as sometimes it had been, especially not in Galilee.

2. The demand was very modest; the collectors stood in such awe of Christ, because of his mighty works, that they durst not speak to him about it, but applied themselves to Peter, whose house was in Capernaum, and probably in his house Christ lodged; he therefore was fittest to be spoken to as the housekeeper, and they presumed he knew his Master's mind. Their question is, *Doth not your master pay tribute?* Some think that they sought an occasion against him, designing, if he refused, to represent him as disaffected to the temple-service, and his followers as lawless people, that would pay *neither toll, tribute, nor custom*, Ezra. iv. 13. It should

rather seem, they asked this with respect, intimating, that if he had any privilege to exempt him from this payment, they would not insist upon it.

Peter presently passed his word for his Master; "*Yes*, certainly; my *Master pays tribute*; it is his principle and practice; you need not fear moving it to him."

II. How it was disputed (*v.* 25), not with the collectors themselves, lest they should be irritated, but with Peter, that he might be satisfied in the reason why Christ paid tribute, and might not mistake about it. He brought the collectors into the house; but Christ anticipated him, to give him a proof of his omniscience, and that no thought can be withholden from him. The disciples of Christ are never attacked without his knowledge.

Now, 1. He appeals to the way of the kings of the earth, which is, to take tribute of strangers, of the subjects of their kingdom, or foreigners that deal with them, but not of their own children that are of their families; there is such a community of goods between parents and children, and a joint-interest in what they have, that it would be absurd for the parents to levy taxes upon the children, or demand any thing from them; it is like one hand taxing the other.

2. He applies this to himself; *Then are the children free.* Christ is the Son of God, and Heir of all things; the temple is his temple (Mal. iii. 1), his Father's house (John ii. 16), in it *he is faithful as a Son in his own house* (Heb. iii. 6), and therefore not obliged to pay this tax for the service of the temple.

III. How it was paid, notwithstanding, *v.* 27.

1. For what reason Christ waived his privilege, and paid this tribute, though he was entitled to an exemption—*Lest we should offend them*. Few knew, as Peter did, that he was *the Son of God*; and it would have been a diminution to the honour of that great truth, which was yet a secret, to advance it now, to serve such a purpose as this. Therefore Christ drops that argument, and considers, that if he should refuse this payment, it would increase people's prejudice against him and his doctrine, and alienate their affections from him, and therefore he resolves to pay it.

2. What course he took for the payment of this tax; he furnished himself with money for it out of the mouth of a fish (*v.* 27), wherein appears,

(1) The poverty of Christ; he had not fifteen pence at command to pay his tax with, though he cured so many that were diseased; it seems, he did all gratis; *for our sakes he became poor*, 2 Cor. viii. 9.

(2) The power of Christ, in fetching money out of a fish's mouth for this purpose. Whether his omnipotence put it there, or his omniscience knew that it was there, it comes all to one; it was an evidence of his divinity, and that he is Lord of hosts.

CHAPTER EIGHTEEN

A LESSON IN HUMILITY
(*vv.* 1–6)

As there never was a greater pattern of humility, so there never was a greater preacher of it, than Christ; he took all occasions to command it, to commend it, to his disciples and followers.

I. The occasion of this discourse concerning humility was an unbecoming contest among the disciples for precedency; they *came to him, saying*, among themselves (for they were ashamed to ask him, Mark ix. 34), *Who is the greatest in the kingdom of heaven?*

1. They suppose that all who have a place in that kingdom are great, for it is a kingdom of priests.

2. They suppose that there are degrees in this greatness. All the saints are honourable, but not all alike so; *one star differs from another star in glory*.

3. They suppose it must be some of them, that must be prime ministers of state. To whom should King Jesus delight to do honour, but to them who had left all for him, and were now his companions in patience and tribulation?

4. They strive who it should be, each having some pretence or other to it.

II. The discourse itself, which is a just rebuke to the question, *Who shall be greatest?*

Christ here teacheth them to be humble.

1. By a sign (*v.* 2); *He called a little child to him, and set him in the midst of them*. Christ often taught by signs or sensible representations (comparisons to the eye), as the prophets of old.

2. By a sermon upon this sign; in which he shows them and us,

(1) The necessity of humility, *v.* 3. His preface is solemn, and

commands both attention and assent; *Verily I say unto you, I, the Amen, the faithful Witness*, say it, *Except ye be converted, and become as little children, ye shall not enter into the kingdom of heaven.* Here observe,

[1] What it is that he requires and insists upon.

First, "You must be converted, you must be of another mind, and in another frame and temper, must have other thoughts, both of yourselves and of the kingdom of heaven, before you be fit for a place in it. The pride, ambition, and affectation of honour and dominion, which appear in you, must be repented of, mortified, and reformed, and you must come to yourselves." *Secondly,* You must *become as little children.* Note, Converting grace makes us like little children, not foolish as children (1 Cor. xiv. 20), nor fickle (Eph. iv. 14), nor playful (*ch.* xi. 16); but, *as children,* we must *desire the sincere milk of the word* (1 Pet. ii. 2); as children, we must be anxious for nothing, but leave it to our heavenly Father to care for us (*ch.* vi. 31); we must, as children, be harmless and inoffensive, and void of malice (1 Cor. xiv. 20), governable, and under command (Gal. iv. 2); and (which is here chiefly intended) we must be humble as little children, who have no great aims at great places, or projects to raise themselves in the world; they *exercise not themselves in things too high for them*; and we should in like manner, *behave, and quiet ourselves,* Ps, cxxxi. 1, 2.

[2] What stress he lays upon this; Without this, *you shall not enter into the kingdom of heaven.* Note, Disciples of Christ have need to be kept in awe by threatenings, that they may fear *lest they seem to come short,* Heb. iv. 1. The disciples, when they put that question (*v.* 1), thought themselves sure of the kingdom of heaven; but Christ awakens them to be jealous of themselves. They were ambitious of being *greatest in the kingdom of heaven*; Christ tells them, that, except they came to a better temper, they should never come thither.

(2) He shows the honour and advancement that attend humility (*v.* 4), thus furnishing a direct but surprising answer to their question. He that humbles himself as a little child, though he may fear that hereby he will render himself contemptible, as men of timid minds, who thereby throw themselves out of the way of preferment, yet *the same is greatest in the kingdom of heaven.*

(3) The special care Christ takes for those that are humble; he espouses their cause, protects them, interests himself in their concerns, and will see that they are not wronged, without being righted.

Those that thus humble themselves will be afraid,

[1] That nobody will receive them; but (*v.* 5), *Whoso shall receive one such little child in my name, receiveth me.* Whatever kindnesses are done to such, Christ takes as done to himself.

[2] They will be afraid that everybody will abuse them; the basest men delight to trample upon the humble. This objection

he obviates (*v.* 6), where he warns all people, as they will answer it at their utmost peril, not to offer any injury to one of Christ's little ones. This word makes a wall of fire about them; he that touches them, touches the apple of God's eye.

HOW SCANDALS COME
(*vv.* 7–14)

Our Saviour here speaks of offences, or scandals,

I. In general, *v.* 7. Having mentioned the offending of little ones, he takes occasion to speak more generally of offences. Now, concerning offences, Christ here tells them,

(1) That they were certain things; *It must needs be, that offences come.* When we are sure there is danger, we should be the better armed.

(2) That they would be woeful things, and the consequence of them fatal. Here is a double woe annexed to offences:

[1] A woe to the careless and unguarded, to whom the offence is given; *Woe to the world because of offences.* The obstructions and oppositions given to faith and holiness in all places are the bane and plague of mankind, and the ruin of thousands. This present world is an evil world, it is so full of offences, of sins, and snares, and sorrows; a dangerous road we travel, full of stumbling-blocks, precipices, and false guides. Woe to the world.

[2] A woe to the wicked, who wilfully give the offence; *But woe to that man by whom the offence comes.* Though it must needs be,

that the offence will come, that will be no excuse for the offenders.

II. In particular, Christ here speaks of offences given,

1. By us to ourselves, which is expressed by our hand or foot offending us; in such a case, it must be *cut off, vv.* 8, 9. This Christ had said before (*ch.* v. 29, 30), where it especially refers to seventh-commandment sins; here it is taken more generally. Now observe,

(1) What it is that is here enjoined. We must part with an *eye,* or a *hand,* or a *foot,* that is, that, whatever it is, which is dear to us, when it proves unavoidably an occasion of sin to us. We must think nothing too dear to part with, for the keeping of a good conscience.

(2) Upon what inducement this is required; *It is better for thee to enter into life maimed, than, having two hands, to be cast into hell.* The argument is taken from the future state, from heaven and hell; thence are fetched the most cogent dissuasives from sin. If the right hand of the old man be cut off, and its right eye plucked out, its chief policies blasted and powers broken, it is well; but there is still an eye and a hand remaining, with which it will struggle. They that are Christ's have nailed the flesh to the cross, but it is not yet dead; its life is prolonged, but its *dominion taken away* (Dan. vii. 12), and the deadly wound given it, that shall not be healed.

1. Concerning offences given by us to others, especially Christ's little ones, which we are here

charged to take heed of, pursuant to what he had said, *v.* 6. Observe,

(1) The caution itself; *Take heed that ye despise not one of these little ones.* This is spoken to the disciples. As Christ will be displeased with the enemies of his church, if they wrong any of the members of it, even the least, so he will be displeased with the great ones of the church, if they despise the little ones of it.

[1] We must not despise them, not think meanly of them, as lambs despised, Job xii. 5. We must not impose upon the consciences of others, nor bring them into subjection to our humours, as they do who say to men's souls, *Bow down, that we may go over.* There is a respect owing to the conscience of every man who appears to be conscientious.

[2] We must take heed that we do not despise them; we must be afraid of the sin, and be very cautious what we say and do, lest we should through inadvertency give offence to Christ's little ones, lest we put contempt upon them, without being aware of it.

(2) The reasons to enforce the caution. We must not look upon these little ones as contemptible, because really they are considerable. To prove that the little ones which believe in Christ are worthy to be respected, consider,

[1] The ministration of the good angels about them; *In heaven their angels always behold the face of my Father.* This Christ saith to us, and we may take it upon *his* word, who came from heaven to let us know what is done there by the world of angels.

[2] The gracious design of Christ concerning them (*v.* 11); *For the Son of man is come to save that which was lost.* This is a reason, *First*, Why the little ones' angels have such a charge concerning them, and attend upon them; it is in pursuance of Christ's design to save them. *Secondly*, Why they are not to be despised; because Christ came to save them, to save them that are lost, the little ones that are lost in their own eyes (Isa. lxvi. 3), that are at a loss within themselves. This is a good reason why the least and weakest believers should not be despised or offended. If Christ put such a value upon them, let us not undervalue them.

[3] The tender regard which our heavenly Father has to these little ones, and his concern for their welfare. This is illustrated by a comparison, *vv.* 12–14. Observe the gradation of the argument; the angels of God are their servants, the Son of God is their Saviour, and, to complete their honour, God himself is their Friend. *None shall pluck them out of my Father's hand*, John x. 28.

Here is, *First*, The comparison, *vv.* 12, 13. The owner that had lost one sheep out of a hundred, does not slight it, but diligently enquires after it, is greatly pleased when he has found it, and has in that a sensible and affecting joy, more than in the ninety and nine that wandered not. The fear he was in of losing that one, and the surprise of finding it, add to the joy. Now this is applicable, 1. To the state of fallen man in general; he is strayed like a lost sheep, the angels that stood were as the ninety-nine that never went astray; wandering man is sought upon the mountains, which Christ, in great fatigue, traversed in pursuit of him, and he is found; which is matter of joy. Greater joy there is in heaven for returning sinners than for remaining angels. 2. To particular believers, who are offended and put out of their way by the stumbling-blocks that are laid in their way, or the wiles of those who seduce them out of the way. Now though but one of a hundred should hereby be driven off, as sheep easily are, yet that one shall be looked after with a great deal of care, the return of it welcomed with a great deal of pleasure; and therefore the wrong done to it, no doubt, will be reckoned for with a great deal of displeasure. If there be joy in heaven for the finding of one of these little ones, there is wrath in heaven for the offending of them.

Secondly, The application of this comparison (*v.* 14); *It is not the will of your Father, that one of these little ones should perish.* More is implied than is expressed. It is not his will that any should perish, but, 1. It is his will, that these little ones should be saved; it is the will of his design and delight: he has designed it, and set his heart upon it, and he will effect it; it is the will of his precept, that all should do what they can to further it, and nothing to hinder it. 2. This care extends itself to every particular member of the flock, even the meanest. We think if but *one* or *two* be

offended and ensnared, it is no great matter, we need not mind it; but God's thoughts of love and tenderness are above ours. 3. It is intimated that those who do any thing by which any of these little ones are brought into danger of perishing, contradict the will of God, and highly provoke him.

Observe, Christ called God, *v.* 19, *my Father which is in heaven*; he calls him, *v.* 14, *your Father which is in heaven*; intimating that he is not ashamed to call his poor disciples *brethren*; for have not he and they one Father? *I ascend to my Father and your Father* (John xx. 17); therefore ours because his.

HEARING COMPLAINTS
(*vv.* 15-20)

Christ, having cautioned his disciples not to give offence, comes next to direct them what they must do in case of offences given them.

I. Let us apply it to the quarrels that happen, upon any account, among Christians. If thy brother trespass against thee, by grieving thy soul (1 Cor. viii. 12), by affronting thee, or putting contempt or abuse upon thee; if he blemish thy good name by false reports or tale-bearing; if he encroach on thy rights, or be any way injurious to thee in thy estate; if he be guilty of any of those trespasses that are specified, Lev. vi. 2, 3; if he transgress the laws of justice, charity, or relative duties; these are trespasses against us, and often happen among Christ's disciples, and sometimes, for want of prudence, are of very mischievous consequence. Now observe what is the rule prescribed in this case,

1. *Go, and tell him his fault between thee and him alone.* Let this be compared with, and explained by, Lev. xix. 17, *Thou shalt not hate thy brother in thy heart.* This agrees with Prov. xxv. 8, 9, "*Go not forth hastily to strive,* but *debate thy cause with thy neighbour himself,* argue it calmly and amicably; and *if he shall hear thee,* well and good, *thou hast gained thy brother,* there is an end of the controversy, and it is a happy end; let no more be said of it, but let the falling out of friends be the renewing of friendship."

2. "*If he will not hear thee,* if he will not own himself in a fault, nor come to an agreement, yet do not despair, but try what he will say to it, if thou take *one or two more,* not only to be witnesses of what passes, but to reason the case further with him; he will be the more likely to hearken to them because they are disinterested; and if reason will rule him, the word of reason in the mouth of two or three witnesses will be better spoken to him and more regarded by him, and perhaps it will influence him to acknowledge his error, and to say, *I repent.*"

3. "If *he shall neglect to hear them,* and will not refer the matter to their arbitration, then *tell it to the church,* to the ministers, elders, or other officers, or the most considerable persons in the congregation you belong to, make them the referees to accommodate the matter, and do not presently appeal to the magistrate, or fetch a writ for him."

4. "If he will not *hear the church,* will not stand to their award, but persists in the wrong he has done thee, and proceeds to do thee further wrong, *let him be to thee as a heathen man, and a publican*; take the benefit of the law against him, but let that always be the last remedy."

II. Let us apply it to scandalous sins, which are an offence to the little ones, of bad example to those that are weak and pliable, and of great grief to those that are weak and timorous. Now let us see,

(1) What is the case supposed? *If thy brother trespass against thee.* [1] "The offender is a brother, one that is in Christian communion, that is baptized." Note, Church discipline is for church members. *Them that are without God judges,* 1 Cor. v. 12, 13. When any trespass is done against us, it is good to remember that the trespasser is a brother, which furnishes us with a qualifying consideration. [2] "The offence is a trespass against thee; if thy brother sin against thee (so the word is), if he do anything which is offensive to thee as a Christian."

(2) What is to be done in this case. We have here,

[1] The rules prescribed, *vv.* 15–17. Proceed in this method:

First, "*Go and tell him his fault between thee and him alone.* Do not stay till he comes to thee, but go to him, as the physician visits the patient, and the shepherd goes after the lost sheep."

"*Tell him his fault, argue the case with him*" (so the word signifies); "and do it with reason and argument, not with passion." Christian reproof is an ordinance of Christ for the bringing of sinners to repentance, and must be managed as an ordinance. "Let the reproof be private, between thee and him alone; that it may appear you seek not his reproach, but his repentance."

"*If he shall hear thee*"—that is, "heed thee—if he be wrought upon by the reproof, it is well, *thou hast gained thy brother*; thou hast helped to save him from sin and ruin, and it will be thy credit and comfort," Jam. v. 19, 20.

Secondly, If that doth not prevail, *then take with thee one or two more, v.* 16.

"*Take with thee one or two more*; 1. To assist thee; they may speak some pertinent convincing word which thou didst not think of, and may manage the matter with more prudence than thou didst." 2. "To affect him; he will be the more likely to be humbled for his fault, when he sees it witnessed against by *two or three*." Deut. xix. 15. 3. "To be witnesses of his conduct, in case the matter should afterward be brought before the church."

Thirdly, *If he neglect to hear them*, and will not be humbled, *then tell it to the church, v.* 17. The church must receive the complaints of the offended, and rebuke the sins of the offenders, and judge between them, after an impartial enquiry made into the merits of the cause.

Fourthly, "*If he neglect to hear*

the church*, if he slight the admonition, and will neither be ashamed of his faults, nor amend them, *let him be unto thee as a heathen man and a publican*; let him be cast out of the communion of the church, secluded from special ordinances, degraded from the dignity of a church member, let him be put under disgrace, and let the members of the society be warned to withdraw from him, that he may be ashamed of his sin, and they may not be infected by it, or made chargeable with it." Christ has appointed this method for the vindicating of the church's honour, the preserving of its purity, and the conviction and reformation of those that are scandalous. But when by this he is humbled and reclaimed, he must be welcomed into communion again, and all shall be well.

[2] Here is a warrant signed for the ratification of all the church's proceedings according to these rules, *v.* 18. What was said before to Peter is here said to all the disciples, and in them to all the faithful office-bearers in the church, to the world's end. While ministers preach the word of Christ faithfully, and in their government of the church strictly adhere to his laws they may be assured that he will own them, and stand by them, and will ratify what they say and do, so that it shall be taken as said and done by himself.

Now it is a great honour which Christ here puts upon the church, that he will condescend not only to take cognizance of their sentences, but to confirm them; and in the following verses we have two things laid down as the ground of this.

(1) God's readiness to answer the church's prayers (*v.* 19); *If two of you shall agree* harmoniously, *touching anything that they shall ask, it shall be done for them.* Apply this,

[1] In general, to all the requests of the faithful praying seed of Jacob; they shall not *seek God's face in vain.* Many promises we have in scripture of a gracious answer to the prayers of faith, but this gives a particular encouragement to joint-prayer; "the requests which two of you agree in, much more which many agree in."

[2] In particular, to those requests that are put up to God about binding and loosing; to which this promise seems more especially to refer. Observe, *First,* That the power of church discipline is not here lodged in the hand of a single person, but two, at least, are supposed to be concerned in it. *Secondly,* It is good to see those who have the management of church discipline, agreeing in it. Heats and animosities, among those whose work it is to remove offences, will be the greatest offence of all. *Thirdly,* Prayer must evermore go along with church discipline. Pass no sentence, which you cannot in faith ask God to confirm.

(2) The presence of Christ in the assemblies of Christians, *v.* 20. Every believer has the presence of Christ with him; but the promise here refers to the meetings where two or three are gathered in his name, not only for discipline, but for religious worship, or any act of Christian communion. Assemblies of Christians for holy purposes are hereby appointed, directed, and encouraged.

[1] They are hereby appointed; the church of Christ in the world exists most visibly in religious assemblies; it is the will of Christ that these should be set up, and kept up, for the honour of God, the edification of men, and the preserving of a face of religion upon the world.

[2] They are hereby directed to gather together in Christ's name. In the exercise of church discipline, they must *come together in the name of Christ,* 1 Cor. v. 4. That name gives to what they do an authority on earth, and an acceptableness in heaven.

[3] They are hereby encouraged with an assurance of the presence of Christ; *There am I in the midst of them.* By his common presence he is in all places, as God; but this is a promise of his special presence. Where his saints are, his sanctuary is, and there he will dwell; it is his rest (Ps. cxxxii. 14), it is his walk (Rev. ii. 1); he is in the midst of them, to quicken and strengthen them, to refresh and comfort them, as the sun in the midst of the universe. He is in the midst of them, that is, in their hearts; it is a spiritual presence, the presence of Christ's Spirit with their spirits, that is here intended.

And though there be but two or three, the smallest number that can be, yet, if Christ make one among them, who is the principal one, their meeting is as honourable and comfortable as if they were two or three thousand.

PERSONAL WRONGS
(*vv*. 1–35)

This part of the discourse concerning offences is certainly to be understood of personal wrongs, which it is in our power to forgive. Now observe,

I. Peter's question concerning this matter (*v*. 21); *Lord, how oft shall my brother trespass against me, and I forgive him?* Will it suffice to do it *seven times*?

1. He takes it for granted that he must forgive; Christ had before taught his disciples this lesson (*ch*. vi. 14, 15), and Peter has not forgotten it.

2. He thinks it a great matter to forgive till seven times; he means not *seven times a day*, as Christ said (Luke xvii. 4), but seven times in his life; supposing that if a man had any way abused him seven times, though he were ever so desirous to be reconciled, he might then abandon his society, and have no more to do with him. Perhaps Peter had an eye to Prov. xxiv. 16. *A just man falleth seven times*; or to the mention of *three transgressions*, and *four*, which God would no more pass by, Amos ii. 1.

II. Christ's direct answer to Peter's question; *I say unto thee, Until seven times* (he never intended to set up any such bounds), but, *Until seventy times seven*; a certain number for an indefinite one, but a great one. God multiplies his pardons, and so should we, Ps. lxxviii. 38, 40. It intimates that we should make it our constant practice to forgive injuries, and should accustom ourselves to it till it becomes habitual.

III. A further discourse of our Saviour's, by way of parable, to show the necessity of forgiving the injuries that are done to us. The parable is a comment upon the fifth petition of the Lord's prayer, *Forgive us our trespasses, as we forgive them that trespass against us.*

There are three things in the parable.

1. The master's wonderful clemency to his servant who was indebted to him; he forgave him ten thousand talents, out of pure compassion to him, *vv*. 23–27. Where observe,

(1) Every sin we commit is a debt to God; not like a debt to an equal, contracted by buying or borrowing, but to a superior; like a debt to a prince when a recognizance is forfeited, or a penalty incurred by a breach of the law or a breach of the peace; like the debt of a servant to his master, by withholding his service, wasting his lord's goods, breaking his indentures, and incurring the penalty. We are all debtors; we owe satisfaction, and are liable to the process of the law.

(2) There is an account kept of these debts, and we must shortly be reckoned with for them.

(3) The debt of sin is a very great debt; and some are more in debt, by reason of sin, than others. When he *began to reckon*, one of the first defaulters appeared to owe *ten thousand talents*. There is no evading the enquiries of divine justice; your sin will be sure to find you out.

(4) The debt of sin is so great,

that we are not able to pay it; *He had not to pay*. Sinners are insolvent debtors; the scripture, *which concludeth all under sin*, is a statute of bankruptcy against us all.

(5) If God should deal with us in strict justice; we should be condemned as insolvent debtors, and God might exact the debt by glorifying himself in our utter ruin.

(6) Convinced sinners cannot but humble themselves before God, and pray for mercy. *The servant*, under this charge, and this doom, *fell down* at the feet of his royal master, *and worshipped him*; or, as some copies read it, *he besought him*; his address was very submissive and very importunate; *Have patience with me, and I will pay thee all*, v. 26. This servant doth not deny the debt, nor seek evasions, nor go about to abscond.

But, [1] He begs time; *Have patience with me*. Patience and forbearance are a great favour, but it is folly to think that these alone will save us; reprieves are not pardons.

[2] He promises payment; *Have patience awhile, and I will pay thee all*. He that *had nothing to pay* with (*v.* 25) fancied he could pay *all*. See how close pride sticks, even to awakened sinners; they are convinced, but not humbled.

(7) The God of infinite mercy is very ready, out of pure compassion, to forgive the sins of those that humble themselves before him (*v.* 27); *The lord of that servant*, when he might justly have ruined him, mercifully released him; and, since he could not be

satisfied by the payment of the debt, he would be glorified by the pardon of it. The servant's prayer was, *Have patience with me*; the master's grant is a discharge in full.

2. The servant's unreasonable severity toward his fellow-servant, notwithstanding his lord's clemency toward him, *vv.* 28–30.

See here, (1) How small the debt was, how very small, compared with the *ten thousand talents* which his lord forgave him; *He owed him a hundred pence*, about three pounds and half a crown of our money. Note, Offences done to men are nothing to those which are committed against God.

(2) How severe the demand was; *He laid hands on him, and took him by the throat*.

(3) How submissive the debtor was; *His fellow servant*, though his equal, yet knowing how much he lay at his mercy, *fell down at his feet*, and humbled himself to him for this trifling debt, as much as he did to his lord for that great debt; for *the borrower is servant to the lender*, Prov. xxii. 7. The poor man's request is, *Have patience with me*; he honestly confesses the debt, and puts not his creditor to the charge of proving it, only begs time.

(4) How implacable and furious the creditor was (*v.* 30); *He would not have patience with him*, would not hearken to his fair promise, but without mercy *cast him into prison*.

(5) How much concerned the rest of the servants were; *They were very sorry* (*v.* 31), sorry for the creditor's cruelty, and for the

debtor's calamity. Note, The sins and sufferings of our fellow-servants should be matter of grief and trouble to us.

(6) How notice of it was brought to the master; *They came, and told their lord.* They durst not reprove their fellow-servant for it, he was so unreasonable and outrageous; but they went to their lord, and besought him to appear for the oppressed against the oppressor.

3. The master's just resentment of the cruelty his servant was guilty of. Now observe here,

(1) How he reproved his servant's cruelty (*vv.* 32, 33); *O thou wicked servant.* Note, Unmercifulness is wickedness, it is great wickedness. [1] He upbraids him with the mercy he had found with his master; *I forgave thee all that debt.* Those that will use God's favours, shall never be upbraided with them, but those that abuse them, may expect it, *ch.* xi. 20. [2] He thence shows him the obligation he was under to be merciful to his fellow-servant; *Shouldst not thou also have had compassion on thy fellow-servant, even as I had pity on thee?* Note, It is justly expected, that such as have received mercy, should show mercy. He shows him, *First*, That he should have been more compassionate to the distress of his fellow servant, because he had himself experienced the same distress. *Secondly*, That he should have been more conformable to the example of his master's tenderness, having himself experienced it, so much to his advantage.

(2) How he revoked his pardon

and cancelled the acquittance, so that the judgment against him revived (*v.* 34); *He delivered him to the tormentors, till he should pay all that was due unto him.* See how the punishment answers the sin; he that would not forgive shall not be forgiven; *He delivered him to the tormentors*; the utmost he could do to his fellow servant was but to cast him into prison, but he was himself delivered to the tormentors.

Lastly, Here is the application of the whole parable (*v.* 35); *So likewise shall my heavenly Father do also unto you.* The title Christ here gives to God was made use of, *v.* 19, in a comfortable promise; *It shall be done for them of my Father which is in heaven*; here it is made use of in a terrible threatening. If God's governing be fatherly, it follows thence, that it is righteous, but it does not therefore follow that it is not rigorous, or that under his government we must not be kept in awe by the fear of the divine wrath. When we pray to God as *our Father in heaven*, we are taught to ask for *the forgiveness of sins, as we forgive our debtors.* Observe here,

1. The duty of forgiving; we must *from our hearts* forgive.

2. The danger of not forgiving; *So shall your heavenly Father do.* (1) This is not intended to teach us that God reverses his pardons to any, but that he denies them to those that are unqualified for them, according to the tenour of the gospel. (2) This is intended to teach us, that *they shall have judgment without mercy, that have*

showed no mercy, Jam. ii. 13. It is indispensably necessary to pardon and peace, that we not only *do justly*, but *love mercy*.

We have here the law of Christ in the case of divorce, occasioned, as some other declarations of his will, by a dispute with *the Pharisees*. Observe here,

I. The case proposed by the Pharisees (*v.* 3); *Is it lawful for a man to put away his wife?* This they asked, tempting him, not desiring to be taught by him. Some time ago, he had, in Galilee, declared his mind in this matter, against that which was the common practice (*ch.* v. 31, 32); and if he would, in like manner, declare himself now against divorce, they would make use of it for the prejudicing and incensing of the people of this country against him, who would look with a jealous eye upon one that attempted to cut them short in a liberty they were fond of.

Their question is, *Whether a man may put away his wife for every cause.* That it might be done for some cause, even for that of fornication, was granted; but may it be done, as now it commonly was done, by the looser sort of people, for every cause; for any cause that a man shall think fit to assign, though ever so frivolous; upon every dislike or displeasure?

II. Christ's answer to this question; though it was proposed to tempt him, yet, being a case of

conscience, and a weighty one, he gave a full answer to it, not a direct one, but an effectual one; laying down such principles as undeniably prove that such arbitrary divorces as were then in use, which made the matrimonial bond so very precarious, were by no ·means lawful. Christ himself would not give the rule without a reason, nor lay down his judgment without scripture proof to support it. Now his argument is this; "If husband and wife are by the will and appointment of God joined together in the strictest and closest union, then they are not to be lightly, and upon every occasion, separated; if the knot be sacred, it cannot be easily untied." Now, to prove that there is such a union between man and wife, he urges three things.

1. The creation of Adam and Eve. *Ye have read* (but have not considered) *that he which made them at the beginning, made them male and female*, Gen. i. 27; v. 2. *He made them male and female*, one female for one male; so that Adam could not divorce his wife, and take another, for there was no other to take. It likewise intimated an inseparable union between them; Eve was a rib out of Adam's side, so that he could not put her away, but he must put away a piece of himself, and contradict the manifest indications of her creation.

2. The fundamental law of marriage, which is, that *a man shall leave father and mother, and shall cleave to his wife, v.* 5. The relation between husband and wife is nearer than that between parents · and children; now, if the

filial relation may not easily be violated, much less may the marriage union be broken. See here the power of a divine institution, that the result of it is a union stronger than that which results from the highest obligations of nature.

3. The nature of the marriage contract; it is a union of persons; *They twain shall be one flesh*, so that (*v.* 6) *they are no more twain, but one flesh*. A man's children are pieces of himself, but his wife is himself. They two shall be one, therefore there must be but one wife, for God made but one Eve for one Adam, Mal. ii. 15.

From hence he infers, *What God hath joined together, let not man put asunder*. Note (1) Husband and wife are of God's joining together; *he hath yoked them together*, so the word is, and it is very significant. God himself instituted the relation between husband and wife in the state of innocence. Marriage and the sabbath are the most ancient of divine ordinances. Though marriage be not peculiar to the church, but common to the world, yet, being stamped with a divine institution, and here ratified by our Lord Jesus, it ought to be managed *after a godly sort, and sanctified by the word of God, and prayer*. It is a general rule that man must not go about to *put asunder what God hath joined together*.

III. An objection started by the Pharisees against this; an objection not destitute of colour and plausibility (*v.* 7); "*Why did Moses command to give a writing of divorcement*, in case a man did put away his wife?"

IV. Christ's answer to this objection, in which,

1. He rectifies their mistake concerning the law of Moses; they called it a *command*, Christ calls it but a *permission*, a *toleration*.

But Christ tells them there was a reason for this toleration, not at all to their credit; *It was because of the hardness of your hearts*, that you were permitted to *put away your wives*. Moses complained of the people of Israel in his time, that *their hearts were hardened* (Deut. ix. 6; xxxi. 27), hardened against God; this is here meant of their being hardened against their relations; they were generally violent and outrageous, which way soever they took, both in their appetites and in their passions; and therefore if they had not been allowed to put away their wives, when they had conceived a dislike of them, they would have used them cruelly, would have beaten and abused them, and perhaps have murdered them.

2. He reduces them to the original institution; *But from the beginning it was not so*. Truth was from the beginning; we must therefore enquire for *the good old way* (Jer. vi. 16), and must reform, not by later patterns, but by ancient rules.

3. He settles the point by an express law; *I say unto you* (*v.* 9); and it agrees with what he said before (*ch.* v. 32); there it was said in preaching, here in dispute, but it is the same, for Christ is constant to himself. Now, in both these places,

(1) He allows divorce, in case of

adultery; the reason of the law against divorce being this, *They two shall be one flesh*. If the wife play the harlot, and make herself one flesh with an adulterer, the reason of the law ceases, and so does the law. By the law of Moses adultery was punished with death, Deut. xxii. 22. Now our Saviour mitigates the rigour of that, and appoints divorce to be the penalty.

(2) He disallows it in all other cases; *Whosoever puts away his wife, except for fornication, and marries another, commits adultery.* This is a direct answer to their query, that it is not lawful. In this, as in other things, gospel times are *times of reformation*, Heb. ix. 10. The law of Christ tends to reinstate man in his primitive integrity; the law of love, conjugal love, is no new commandment, but was from the beginning.

V. Here is a suggestion of the disciples against this law of Christ (*v.* 10); *If the case of the man be so with his wife, it is better not to marry*. It seems, the disciples themselves were loth to give up the liberty of divorce, thinking it a good expedient for preserving comfort in the married state; and therefore, like sullen children, if they have not what they would have, they will throw away what they have.

VI. Christ's answer to this suggestion (*vv.* 11, 12), in which,

1. He allows it good for some not to marry; *He that is able to receive it, let him receive it*. Christ allowed what the disciples said, *It is good not to marry*; not as an objection against the prohibition

of divorce, as they intended it, but as giving them a rule (perhaps no less unpleasing to them), that they who have the gift of continence, and are not under any necessity of marrying, do best if they continue single (1 Cor. vii. 1); for they that are unmarried have opportunity, if they have but a heart, to care more *for the things of the Lord, how they may please the Lord* (1 Cor. vii. 32–34), being less encumbered with the cares of this life, and having a greater vacancy of thought and time to mind better things. The increase of grace is better than the increase of the family, and fellowship with the Father and with his Son Jesus Christ is to be preferred before any other fellowship.

2. He disallows it, as utterly mischievous, to forbid marriage, because *all men cannot receive this saying*; indeed few can, and therefore the crosses of the married state must be borne, rather than that men should run themselves into temptation, to avoid them; *better marry than burn*.

Christ here speaks of a twofold unaptness to marriage.

(1) That which is a calamity by the providence of God; such as those labour under who are born eunuchs, or made so by men, who, being incapable of answering one great end of marriage, ought not to marry.

(2) That which is a virtue by the grace of God; such is theirs who *have made themselves eunuchs for the kingdom of heaven's sake*. This is meant of an unaptness for marriage, not in body (which some, through mistake of this scripture,

have foolishly and wickedly brought upon themselves), but in mind. Those have thus made themselves eunuchs who have attained a holy indifference to all the delights of the married state, have a fixed resolution, in the strength of God's grace, wholly to abstain from them; and by fasting, and other instances of mortification, have subdued all desires toward them.

Now, [1] This affection to the single state must be given of God; for none can receive it, *save they to whom it is given.*

[2] The single state must be chosen for the kingdom of heaven's sake. Note, That condition is best for us, and to be chosen and stuck to accordingly, which is best for our souls, and tends most to the preparing of us for, and the preserving of us to, the kingdom of heaven.

CHILDREN WELCOME
(*vv.* 13–15)

We have here the welcome which Christ gave to some little children that were brought to him. Observe,

I. The faith of those that brought them. How many they were, that were brought, we are not told; but they were so little as to be taken up in arms, a year old, it may be, or two at most.

They desired that he would put his hands on them, and pray. Imposition of hands was a ceremony used especially in paternal blessings; Jacob used it when he blessed and adopted the sons of Joseph, Gen. xlviii. 14. It intimates something of love and familiarity

mixed with power and authority, and bespeaks an efficacy in the blessing. Whom Christ prays for in heaven, he *puts his hand upon* by his Spirit. Note, (1) Little children may be brought to Christ as needing, and being capable of receiving, blessings from him, and having an interest in his intercession. (2) Therefore they should be brought to him. We cannot do better for our children than to commit them to the Lord Jesus, to be wrought upon, and prayed for, by him. We can but beg a blessing for them, it is Christ only that can command the blessing.

II. The fault of the disciples in rebuking them. They discountenanced the address as vain and frivolous, and reproved them that made it as impertinent and troublesome.

III. The favour of our Lord Jesus. See how he carried it here.

1. He rebuked the disciples (*v.* 14); *Suffer little children, and forbid them not*; and he rectifies the mistake they went upon, *Of such is the kingdom of heaven.* Note, (1) The children of believing parents belong to the kingdom of heaven, and are members of the visible church. (2) That for this reason they are welcome to Christ, who is ready to entertain those who, when they cannot come themselves, are brought to him.

2. *He received the little children,* and did as he was desired; *he laid his hands on them,* that is, *he blessed them.* The strongest believer lives not so much by apprehending Christ as by being apprehended of him (Phil. iii. 12), not so much by knowing God as by

being known of him (Gal. iv. 9); and this the least child is capable of. If they cannot stretch out their hands to Christ, yet he can lay his hands on them, and so make them his own, and own them for his own.

THE RICH RULER (*vv*. 16–22)

Here is an account of what passed between Christ and a hopeful young gentleman that addressed himself to him upon a serious errand; he is said to be a *young man* (*v*. 20); and I called him a *gentleman*, not only because he had great possessions, but because he was a ruler (Luke xviii. 18), a magistrate, a justice of peace in his country; it is probable that he had abilities beyond his years, else his youth would have debarred him from the magistracy.

Now concerning this young gentleman, we are told how fair he bid for heaven and came short.

I. How fair he bid for heaven, and how kindly and tenderly Christ treated him, in favour to good beginnings. Here is,

1. The gentleman's serious address to Jesus Christ (*v*. 16); *Good Master, what good thing shall I do, that I may have eternal life?* Not a better question could be asked, nor more gravely.

(1) He gives Christ an honourable title, *Good Master*. It signifies not a ruling, but a teaching Master. His calling him *Master*, bespeaks his submissiveness, and willingness to be taught; and *good Master*, his affection and peculiar respect to the Teacher, like that of Nicodemus, *Thou art a Teacher come from God.*

(2) He comes to him upon an errand of importance (none could be more so), and he came not to tempt him, but sincerely desiring to be taught by him. His question is, *What good thing shall I do, that I may have eternal life?* By this it appears, [1] That he had a firm belief of eternal life; he was no Sadducee. [2] That he was concerned to make it sure to himself that he should live eternally, and was desirous of that life more than of any of the delights of this life. [3] That he was sensible something must be done, some good thing, for the attainment of this happiness. [4] That he was, or at least thought himself, willing to do what was to be done for the obtaining of this eternal life.

2. The encouragement that Jesus Christ gave to this address. It is not his manner to send any away without an answer, that come to him on such an errand, for nothing pleases him more, *v*. 17. In his answer,

(1) He tenderly assists his faith; for, doubtless, he did not mean it for a reproof, when he said, *Why callest thou me good?* But he would seem to find that faith in what he said, when he called him *good Master*, which the gentleman perhaps was not conscious to himself of; he intended no more than to own and honour him as a good man, but Christ would lead him to own and honour him as a good God; for *there is none good but one, that is God.*

(2) He plainly directs his practice, in answer to his question. He started that thought of his being good, and therefore God, but did

not stay upon it, lest he should seem to divert from, and so to drop, the main question, as many do in needless disputes and strifes of words. Now Christ's answer is, in short, this, *If thou wilt enter into life, keep the commandments.*

[1] The end proposed is, entering into life. The young man, in his question, spoke of eternal life. Christ, in his answer, speaks of *life*; to teach us, that eternal life is the only true life. He desired to know how he might *have* eternal life; Christ tells him how he might *enter into it*: we *have* it by the merit of Christ, a mystery which was not as yet fully revealed, and therefore Christ waives that; but the way of *entering into it*, is, by obedience, and Christ directs us in that. By the former we *make* our title, by this, as by our evidence, we *prove* it; it is *by adding to faith virtue*, that an *entrance* (the word here used) is *ministered to us into the everlasting kingdom*, 2 Pet. i. 5, 11.

[2] The way prescribed is, keeping the commandments. Note, Keeping the commandments of God, according as they are revealed and made known to us, is the only way to life and salvation; and sincerity herein is accepted through Christ as our gospel perfection, provision being made of pardon, upon repentance, wherein we come short.

[3] At his further instance and request, he mentions some particular commandments which he must keep (*vv.* 18, 19); *The young man saith unto him, Which?* In answer to this, Christ specifies several, especially the command-

ments of the second table; not as if the first were of less account, but, 1. Because they that now sat in Moses's seat, either wholly neglected, or greatly corrupted, these precepts in their preaching. 2. Because he would teach him, and us all, that moral honesty is a necessary branch of true Christianity, and to be minded accordingly.

II. See here how he came short, though he bid thus fair, and wherein he failed; he failed by two things.

1. By pride, and a vain conceit of his own merit and strength; this is the ruin of thousands, who keep themselves miserable by fancying themselves happy. When Christ told him what commandments he must keep, he answered very scornfully, *All these things have I kept from my youth up, v.* 20.

It was commendable also, that he desired to know further what his duty was; *What lack I yet?* He was convinced that he wanted something to fill up his works before God, and was therefore desirous to know it, because, if he was not mistaken in himself, he was willing to do it. Having not yet attained, he thus seemed to press forward. And he applied himself to Christ, whose doctrine was supposed to improve and perfect the Mosaic institution. He desired to know what were the peculiar precepts of his religion, that he might have all that was in them to polish and accomplish him. Who could bid fairer?

But, (2) Even in this that he said, he discovered his ignorance and folly. [1] Taking the law in its spiritual sense, as Christ expounded it, no doubt, in many things he had offended against all these commands. Had he been acquainted with the extent and spiritual meaning of the law, instead of saying, *All these have I kept*; *what lack I yet?* he would have said, with shame and sorrow, "All these have I broken, what shall I do to get my sins pardoned?" [2] Take it how you will, what he said savoured of pride and vainglory, and had in it too much of that boasting which is excluded by the law of faith (Rom. iii. 27), and which excludes from justification, Luke xviii. 11, 14.

2. He came short by an inordinate love of the world, and his enjoyments in it. This was the fatal rock on which he split. Observe,

(1) How he was tried in this matter (*v.* 21); *Jesus said unto him, If thou wilt be perfect, go and sell that thou hast.* Christ waived the matter of his boasted obedience to the law, and let that drop, because this would be a more effectual way of discovering him than a dispute of the extent of the law. What Christ said to him, he thus far said to us all, that, if we would approve ourselves Christians indeed, and would be found at last the heirs of eternal life, we must do these two things:

[1] We must practically prefer the heavenly treasures before all the wealth and riches in this world. That glory must have the pre-eminence in our judgment and esteem before this glory. Now, as an evidence of this, *First*, We must dispose of what we have in this world, for the honour of God, and

in his service: "*Sell that thou hast, and give to the poor.* If the occasions of charity be very pressing, sell thy possessions that thou mayest have to give to them that need; as the first Christians did, with an eye to this precept, Acts iv. 34." A gracious contempt of the world, and compassion of the poor and afflicted ones in it, are in all a necessary condition of salvation.

Christ knew that covetousness was the sin that did most easily beset this young man, that, though what he had he had got honestly, yet he could not cheerfully part with it, and by this he discovered his insincerity. *Secondly*, We must depend upon what we hope for in the other world as an abundant recompence for all we have left, or lost, or laid out, for God in this world; *Thou shalt have treasure in heaven.* We must, in the way of chargeable duty, trust God for a happiness out of sight, which will make us rich amends for all our expenses in God's service.

[2] We must devote ourselves entirely to the conduct and government of our Lord Jesus; *Come, and follow me.* To sell all, and give to the poor, will not serve, unless we come, and follow Christ. If I give all my goods to feed the poor, and have not love, it profits me nothing. Well, on these terms, and on no lower, is salvation to be had; and they are very easy and reasonable terms, and will appear so to those who are brought to be glad of it upon any terms.

(2) See how he was discovered. This touched him in a tender part (*v.* 22); *When he heard that*

saying, he went away sorrowful, for he had great possessions.

[1] He was a rich man, and loved his riches, and therefore went away. He did not like eternal life upon these terms. Note, *First*, Those who have much in the world are in the greatest temptation to love it, and to set their hearts upon it. *Secondly*, The reigning love of this world keeps many from Christ, who seem to have some good desires toward him.

Yet something of honesty there was in it, that, when he did not like the terms, he went away, and would not pretend to that, which he could not find in his heart to come up to the strictness of; since he could not be a complete Christian, he would not be a hypocrite.

[2] Yet he was a thinking man, and well-inclined, and therefore *went away sorrowful*. He had a leaning toward Christ, and was loth to part with him. Thus this man's wealth was *vexation of spirit* to him, then when it was his temptation. What then would the sorrow be afterward, when his possessions would be gone, and all hopes of eternal life gone too?

THE EYE OF THE NEEDLE
(vv. 23–30)

We have here Christ's discourse with his disciples upon occasion of the rich man's breaking with Christ.

I. Christ took occasion from thence to show the difficulty of the salvation of rich people, vv. 23–26.

1. That it is a very hard thing

for a rich man to get to heaven, such a rich man as this here.

Now, (1) This is vehemently asserted by our Saviour, vv. 23, 24. He said this to his disciples, who were poor, and had but little in the world, to reconcile them to their condition with this, that the less they had of worldly wealth, the less hindrance they had in the way to heaven. This saying is ratified, v. 23. *Verily I say unto you.* He that has reason to know what the way to heaven is, for he has laid it open, he tells us that this is one of the greatest difficulties in that way. It is repeated, v. 24. *Again I say unto you.* Thus he speaks once, yea, twice, that which man is loth to perceive and more loth to believe.

[1] He saith that it is a hard thing for a rich man to be a good Christian, and to be saved; to enter into the kingdom of heaven, either here or hereafter. Rich people have a great account to make up for their estates, their interest, their time, and their opportunities of doing and getting good, above others. It must be a great measure of divine grace that will enable a man to break through these difficulties.

[2] He saith that the conversion and salvation of a rich man is so extremely difficult, that *it is easier for a camel to go through the eye of a needle*, v. 24. This is a proverbial expression, denoting a difficulty altogether unconquerable by the art and power of man; nothing less than the almighty grace of God will enable a rich man to get over this difficulty. *First*, The way to heaven is very

fitly compared to a *needle's eye*, which is hard to hit and hard to get through. *Secondly*, A rich man is fitly compared to a *camel*, a beast of burden, for he has riches, as a camel has his load, he carries it, but it is another's, he has it from others, spends it for others, and must shortly leave it to others.

(2) This truth is very much wondered at, and scarcely credited by the disciples (*v.* 25); *They were exceedingly amazed, saying, Who then can be saved?* Many surprising truths Christ told them, which they were astonished at, and knew not what to make of; this was one, but their weakness was the cause of their wonder. Since so many are rich, and have great possessions, and so many more would be rich, and are well affected to great possessions; who can be saved? If riches are a hindrance to rich people, are not pride and luxury incident to those that are not rich, and as dangerous to them? and who then can get to heaven? This is a good reason why rich people should strive against the stream.

2. That, though it be hard, yet it is not impossible, for the rich to be saved (*v.* 26); *Jesus beheld them*, turned and looked wistfully upon his disciples, to shame them out of their fond conceit of the advantages rich people had in spiritual things. He beheld them as men that had got over this difficulty, and were in a fair way for heaven, and the more so because poor in this world; *and he said unto them, with men this is impossible, but with God all things are possible*. This is a great truth in general, that God is able to do that which quite exceeds all created power; that nothing is too hard for God, Gen. xviii. 14; Numb. xi. 23. When men are at a loss, God is not, for his power is infinite and irresistible; but this truth is here applied, (1) To the salvation of any. *Who can be saved?* say the disciples. None, saith Christ, by any created power. *With men this is impossible:* the wisdom of man would soon be nonplussed in contriving, and the power of man baffled in effecting, the salvation of a soul. But *with God all things are possible*. (2) To the salvation of rich people especially; it is impossible with men that such should be saved, but with God even this is possible; not that rich people should be saved *in* their worldliness, but that they should be saved *from* it.

II. Peter took occasion from hence to enquire what *they* should get by it, who had come up to these terms, upon which this young man broke with Christ, and had left all to follow him, *vv.* 27, &c. We have here the disciples' expectations from Christ, and his promises to them.

1. We have their expectations from Christ; Peter, in the name of the rest, signifies that they depended upon him for something considerable in lieu of what they had left for him; *Behold, we have forsaken all, and have followed thee; what shall we have therefore?* Christ had promised the young man, that, if he would sell all, and come and follow him, he should *have treasure in heaven*; now Peter desires to know,

(1) Whether they had sufficiently come up to those terms: they had not sold all (for they had many of

them wives and families to provide for), but they had *forsaken all*; they had not given it to the poor, but they had renounced it as far as it might be any way a hindrance to them in serving Christ.

(2) Whether therefore they might expect *that treasure* which the young man shall have if he will sell all. "Lord," saith Peter, "shall *we* have it, who have left all?"

2. We have here Christ's promises to them, and to all others that tread in the steps of their faith and obedience.

(1) To his immediate followers, *v.* 28. They had signalized their respect to him, as the first that followed him, and to them he promises not only *treasure*, but *honour*, in heaven; and here they have a grant or patent for it from him who is the fountain of honour in that kingdom; *Ye which have followed me in the regeneration shall sit upon twelve thrones.*

[1] The *preamble* to the patent, or the *consideration* of the grant, which, as usual, is a recital of their services; "You have followed me in the regeneration, and therefore this will I do for you." The time of Christ's appearing in this world was a time of regeneration, of reformation (Heb. ix. 10), when old things began to pass away, and all things to look new. The disciples had followed Christ when the church was yet in the embryo state, when few did; and therefore on them he will put particular marks of honour.

[2] The *date* of their honour, which fixes the time when it should commence; not immediately from the day of the date of *these presents*, no, they must continue a while in obscurity, as they were. But *when the Son of man shall sit in the throne of his glory*; and to this some refer that, *in the regeneration*; "You who now have followed me, shall, in the regeneration, be thus dignified." Christ's second coming will be a regeneration, when there shall be *new heavens, and a new earth, and the restitution of all things.* All that partake of the regeneration in grace (John iii. 3) shall partake of the regeneration in glory; for as grace is the first resurrection (Rev. xx. 6), so glory is the second regeneration.

[3] The honour itself hereby granted; *Ye also shall sit upon twelve thrones, judging the twelve tribes of Israel.*

The general intendment of this promise is, to show the glory and dignity reserved for the saints in heaven, which will be an abundant recompence for the disgrace they suffered here in Christ's cause. There are higher degrees of glory for those that have done and suffered most. The apostles in this world were hurried and tossed, there they shall sit down at rest and ease; here *bonds, and afflictions, and deaths, did abide them,* but there they *shall sit on thrones of glory*; here they were dragged to the bar, there they shall be advanced to the bench; here the twelve tribes of Israel trampled upon them, there they shall tremble before them. And will not this be recompence enough to make up all their losses and expenses for Christ? Luke xxii. 29.

[4] The ratification of this grant; it is firm, it is inviolably immutably sure; for Christ hath said, "*Verily I say unto you, I the Amen, the*

faithful Witness, who am empowered to make this grant, I have said it, and it cannot be disannulled."

(2) Here is a promise to all others that should in like manner leave all to follow Christ. It was not peculiar to the apostles, to be thus preferred, but *this honour have all his saints*. Christ will take care they shall none of them lose by him (*v.* 29); *Every one that has forsaken* anything for Christ, *shall receive*.

CHAPTER TWENTY

THE VINEYARD (*vv.* 1–16)

This parable of the labourers in the vineyard is intended,

I. To represent to us *the kingdom of heaven* (*v.* 1), that is, the way and method of the gospel dispensation.

II. In particular, to represent to us that concerning the kingdom of heaven, which he had said in the close of the foregoing chapter, that *many that are first shall be last, and the last, first*; with which this parable is connected; that truth, having in it a seeming contradiction, needed further explanation.

Nothing was more a mystery in the gospel dispensation than the rejection of the Jews and the calling in of the Gentiles; so the apostle speaks of it (Eph. iii. 3–6); that the Gentiles should be fellow-heirs: nor was any thing more provoking to the Jews than the intimation of it. Now this seems to be the principal scope of this parable, to show that the Jews should be first called into the vineyard, and many of them should come at the call; but, at length, the gospel should be preached to the Gentiles, and they

should receive it, and be admitted to equal privileges and advantages with the Jews; should be *fellow-citizens with the saints*, which the Jews, even those of them that believed, would be very much disgusted at, but without reason.

But the parable may be applied more generally, and shows us, 1. That God is debtor to no man; a great truth, which the contents in our Bible give as the scope of this parable. 2. That many who begin last, and promise little in religion, sometimes, by the blessing of God, arrive at greater attainments in knowledge, grace, and usefulness, than others whose entrance was more early, and who promised fairer. Thus *many that are last, shall be first*. Some make it a caution to the disciples, who had boasted of their timely and zealous embracing of Christ; they had left all to follow him; but let them look to it, that they keep up their zeal; let them press forward and persevere; else their good beginnings will avail them little; they that seemed to be *first*, would be *last*. Sometimes those that are converted later in their lives, outstrip those that are converted earlier. Paul was *as one born out of due time, yet came not behind the chiefest of the apostles*, and outdid those that were in Christ before him. Something of affinity there is between this parable and that of the prodigal son, where he that returned from his wandering, was as dear to his father as he was, that never went astray; *first and last alike*. 3. That *the recompence of reward* will be given to the saints, not according to the time of their conversion, but according to the preparations for it by grace in this world; not according to the seniority (as Gen. xliii. 33), but *according to the measure of the stature of the fulness of Christ.* Christ had promised the apostles, who followed him *in the regeneration,* at the beginning of the gospel dispensation, great glory (*ch.* xix. 38); but he now tells them that those who are in like manner faithful to him, even in the latter end of the world, shall have the same reward, shall *sit with Christ on his throne,* as well as the apostles, Rev. ii. 26–iii. 21. Sufferers for Christ in the latter days, shall have the same reward with the martyrs and confessors of the primitive times, though they are more celebrated; and faithful ministers now, the same with the first fathers.

Here is the application of the parable (*v.* 16), in that observation which occasioned it (*ch.* xix. 30); *So the first shall be last, and the last first.* There were many that followed Christ now in the regeneration, when the gospel kingdom was first set up, and these Jewish converts seemed to have got the start of others; but Christ, to obviate and silence their boasting, here tells them,

1. That they might possibly be outstripped by their successors in profession, and, though they were before others in profession, might be found inferior to them in knowledge, grace, and holiness. The Gentile church, which was as yet unborn, the Gentile world, which as yet stood *idle in the market-place,* would produce greater numbers of eminent, useful Christians, than were found among the Jews. More and more excellent shall be *the children of the desolate than those of the married wife,* Isa. liv. 1. Who knows but that the church, in its old age, may be more fat and flourishing than ever, to show that the Lord is upright? Though primitive Christianity had more of the purity and power of that holy religion than is to be found in the degenerate age wherein we live, yet what *labourers* may be *sent into the vineyard in the eleventh hour of the* church's *day,* in the Philadelphian period, and what plentiful effusions of the Spirit may then be, above what has been yet, who can tell?

2. That they had reason to fear, lest they themselves should be found hypocrites at last; for *many are called but few chosen.* This is applied to the Jews (*ch.* xxii. 14); it was so then, it is too true still; many are called with a common call, that are not chosen with a saving choice. All that are chosen from eternity, are effectually called, *in the fulness of time* (Rom. viii. 30), so that in making our effectual calling sure we *make sure our election* (2 Pet. i. 10); but it is not so as to the outward call; *many are called,* and yet refuse (Prov. i. 24), nay, as they are called *to* God, so they go *from* him (Hos. xi. 2, 7), by which it appears that they were not chosen, for *the election will obtain,* Rom. xi. 7. Note, There are but few *chosen* Christians, in comparison with the many that are only *called* Christians; it therefore highly concerns us to build our hope for heaven upon the rock of an eternal choice, and not upon the sand of an external call; and we should fear

lest we be found but seeming Christians, and so should really come short; nay, lest we be found blemished Christians, and so should *seem to come short*, Heb. iv. 1.

AMBITION CORRECTED
(*vv.* 17–28)

This is the third time that Christ gave his disciples notice of his approaching sufferings; he was now going up to Jerusalem to celebrate the passover, and to offer up himself the great Passover; both must be done at Jerusalem: there *the passover must be kept* (Deut. xii. 5), and there a prophet must perish, because there the great sanhedrim sat, who were judges in that case, Luke xiii. 33.

There follows the request of the two disciples to Christ, and the rectifying of the mistake upon which that was grounded, *vv.* 20–23. The sons of Zebedee were James and John, two of the first three of Christ's disciples; Peter and they were his favourites; John was the disciple whom Jesus loved; yet none were so often reproved as they; whom Christ loves best he reproves most, Rev. iii. 19.

I. Here is the ambitious address they made to Christ—that they might sit, the one on his right hand, and the other on his left, in his kingdom, *vv.* 20, 21. It was a great degree of faith, that they were confident of his kingdom, though now he appeared in meanness; but a great degree of ignorance, that they still expected a temporal kingdom, with worldly pomp and power, when Christ had so often told them

of sufferings and self-denial. Now observe,

1. There was policy in the management of this address, that they put their mother on to present it, that it might be looked upon as her request, and not theirs. Though proud people think well of themselves, they would not be thought to do so, and therefore affect nothing more than *a show of humility* (Col. ii. 18), and others must be put on to court that honour for them, which they are ashamed to court for themselves.

2. There was pride at the bottom of it, a proud conceit of their own merit, a proud contempt of their brethren, and a proud desire of honour and preferment; pride is a sin that most easily besets us, and which it is hard to get clear of. It is a holy ambition to strive to excel others in grace and holiness; but it is a sinful ambition to covet to exceed others in pomp and grandeur.

II. Christ's answer to this address (*vv.* 22, 23), directed not to the mother, but to the sons that set her on. Christ's answer is very mild; they were overtaken in the fault of ambition, but Christ *restored them with the spirit of meekness.* Observe,

1. How he reproved the ignorance and error of their petition; *Ye know not what ye ask.* (1) They were much in the dark concerning the kingdom they had their eye upon; they dreamed of a temporal kingdom, whereas Christ's kingdom is not of this world. They knew not what it was to sit on his right hand, and on his left; they talked of it as blind men do of colours. (2) They were much in the dark concerning

the way to that kingdom. *They* know not what they ask, who ask for the end, but overlook the means, and so put asunder what God has joined together. The disciples thought, when they had left what little *all* they had for Christ, and had gone about the country awhile preaching the gospel of the kingdom, all their service and sufferings were over, and it was now time to ask, *What shall we have?* As if nothing were now to be looked for but crowns and garlands; whereas there were far greater hardships and difficulties before them than they had yet met with. They imagined their warfare was accomplished when it was scarcely begun.

2. How he repressed the vanity and ambition of their request.

(1) He leads them to the thoughts of their sufferings, which they were not so mindful of as they ought to have been.

Observe, [1] How fairly he puts the matter to them, concerning these difficulties (*v.* 22); "You would stand candidates for the first post of honour in the kingdom; but *are you able to drink of the cup that I shall drink of?* You talk of what great things you must have when you have done your work; but are you able to hold out to the end of it? Put the matter seriously to yourselves. These same two disciples once knew not what manner of spirit they were of, when they were disturbed with anger, Luke ix. 55; and now they were not aware what was amiss in their spirits when they were lifted up with ambition. Christ sees that pride in us which we discern not in ourselves.

Note, *First,* That to suffer for Christ is *to drink of a cup,* and *to be baptized with a baptism.* In this description of sufferings, 1. It is true, that affliction doth abound. It is supposed to be a bitter cup, that is drunk of, wormwood and gall, those waters of a full cup, that are wrung out to God's people (Ps. lxxiii. 10); a cup of trembling indeed, but not of fire and brimstone, the portion of the cup of wicked men, Ps. xi. 6. It is supposed to be a baptism, a washing with the waters of affliction; some are dipped in them, the waters compass them about even to the soul (Jonah ii. 5); others have but a sprinkling of them; both are baptisms, some are overwhelmed in them, as in a deluge, others ill wet, as in a sharp shower. But, 2. Even in this, *consolation doth more abound.* It is but a cup, not an ocean; it is but a draught, bitter perhaps, but we shall see the bottom of it; it is a cup in the hand of a Father (John xviii. 11); and it is full of mixture, Ps. lxxv. 8. It is but a baptism; if dipped, that is the worst of it, not drowned; perplexed, but not in despair.

Secondly, It is to drink of the same cup that Christ drank of, and to be baptized with the same baptism that he was baptized with. Christ is beforehand with us in suffering, and in that as in other things left us an example.

Thirdly, It is good for us to be often putting it to ourselves, whether we are able to drink of this cup, and to be baptized with this baptism. We must expect suffering, and not look upon it as a hard thing to suffer well and as becomes us. Are we able to suffer cheerfully, and in the worst of times still to hold fast our integrity? The truth is, Religion, if it be worth any thing, is worth every thing; but it is worth little, if it be not worth suffering for. Now let us sit down, and count the cost of dying for Christ rather than denying him, and ask, Can we take him upon these terms?

[2] See how boldly they engage for themselves; they said, *We are able*, in hopes of sitting on his right hand, and on his left; but at the same time they fondly hoped that they should never be tried. As before they knew not what they asked, so now they knew not what they answered. *We are able*; they would have done well to put in, "*Lord, by thy strength*, and *in thy grace, we are able*, otherwise we are not." But the same that was Peter's temptation, to be confident of his own sufficiency, and presume upon his own strength, was here the temptation of James and John; and it is a sin we are all prone to. They knew not what Christ's cup was, nor what his baptism, and therefore they were thus bold in promising for themselves. But those are commonly most confident, that are least acquainted with the cross.

[3] See how plainly and positively their sufferings are here foretold (v. 23); *Ye shall drink of my cup.* Sufferings foreseen will be the more easily borne, especially if looked upon under a right notion, as drinking of his cup, and being baptized with his baptism. Christ began in suffering for us, and expects we should pledge him, in suffering for him. Christ will have us know the worst, that we may make the best of our way to

heaven; *Ye shall drink*; that is, ye shall suffer. James drank the bloody cup first of all the apostles, Acts xii. 2. John, though at last he died in his bed, if we may credit the ecclesiastical historians, yet often drank of this bitter cup, as when he was banished into the isle of Patmos (Rev. i. 9), and when (as they say) at Ephesus he was put into a cauldron of boiling oil, but was miraculously preserved. He was, as the rest of the apostles, in deaths often. He took the cup, offered himself to the baptism, and it was accepted.

(2) He leaves them in the dark about the degrees of their glory. To carry them cheerfully through their sufferings, it was enough to be assured that they should have *a place in his kingdom*. The lowest seat in heaven is an abundant recompence for the greatest sufferings on earth. But as to the preferments there, it was not fit there should be any intimation given for whom they were intended; for the infirmity of their present state could not bear such a discovery with any evenness; "*To sit on my right hand and on my left is not mine to give*, and therefore it is not for you to ask it or to know it; *but it shall be given to them for whom it is prepared of my Father.*"

III. Here are the reproof and instruction which Christ gave to the other ten disciples for their displeasure at the request of James and John. He had much to bear with in them all, they were so weak in knowledge and grace, yet he bore their manners.

1. The fret that the ten disciples were in (v. 24). *They were moved*

with indignation against the two brethren; not because they were desirous to be preferred, which was their sin, and for which Christ was displeased with them, but because they were desirous to be preferred *before them*, which was a reflection upon them.

2. The check that Christ gave them, which was very gentle, rather by way of instruction what they should be, than by way of reprehension for what they were.

He called them unto him, which intimates great tenderness and familiarity. What he had to say concerned both the two disciples and the ten, and therefore he will have them all together. And he tells them, that, whereas they were asking which of them should have dominion in a temporal kingdom, there was really no such dominion reserved for any of them. For,

(1) They must not be *like the princes of the Gentiles*. Principality doth no more become ministers than Gentilism doth Christians.

Observe, [1] What is the way of the princes of the Gentiles (*v.* 25); to *exercise dominion and authority* over their subjects, and (if they can but win the upper hand with a strong hand) over one another too.

[2] What is the will of Christ concerning his apostles and ministers, in this matter.

First, "*It shall not be so among you.* The constitution of the spiritual kingdom is quite different from this. You are to teach the subjects of this kingdom, to instruct and beseech them, to counsel and comfort them, to take pains with them, and suffer with them, not to exercise dominion or

authority over them; you are not to *lord it over God's heritage* (1 Pet. v. 3), but to labour in it."

Secondly, How then shall it be among the disciples of Christ? Something of greatness among them Christ himself had intimated, and here he explains it; "*He that will be great among you*, that *will be chief*, that would really be so, and would be found to be so at last, *let him be your minister, your servant,*" *vv.* 26, 27. Here observe, 1. That it is the duty of Christ's disciples to serve one another, for mutual edification. This includes both humility and usefulness. 2. It is the dignity of Christ's disciples faithfully to discharge this duty. The way to be great and chief is to be humble and serviceable.

(2) They must be like the Master himself; and it is very fit that they should, that, while they were in the world, they should be as he was when he was in the world; for to both the present state is a state of humiliation, the crown and glory were reserved for both in the future state. Let them consider that the *Son of man came not to be ministered to, but to minister, and to give his life a ransom for many, v.* 28. Our Lord Jesus here sets himself before his disciples as a pattern of those two things before recommended, humility, and usefulness.

[1] Never was there such an example of humility and condescension as there was in the life of Christ, who came not to be *ministered unto, but to minister.*

[2] Never was there such an example of beneficence and usefulness as there was in the death of Christ, who *gave his life a ransom*

for many. He lived as a servant, and went about doing good; but he died as a sacrifice, and in that he did the greatest good of all.

Now this is a good reason why we should not strive for precedency, because the cross is our banner, and our Master's death is our life. It is a good reason why we should study to do good, and, in consideration of the love of Christ in dying for us, not hesitate *to lay down our lives for the brethren,* 1 John iii. 16. Ministers should be more forward than others to serve and suffer for the good of souls, as blessed Paul was, Acts xx. 24; Phil. ii. 17. The nearer we are all concerned in, and the more we are advantaged by, the humility and humiliation of Christ, the more ready and careful we should be to imitate it.

TWO BLIND MEN
(vv. 29–34)

We have here an account of the cure of two poor blind beggars; in which we may observe,

I. Their address to Christ, *vv.* 29, 30. And in this,

1. The circumstances of it are observable. It was as Christ and his disciples departed from Jericho; of that devoted place, which was rebuilt under a curse, Christ took his leave with this blessing, for he received gifts even for the rebellious. It was in the presence of *a great multitude that followed him*; Christ had a numerous, though not a pompous, attendance, and did good to them, though he did not take state to himself. Two blind men concurred in their request; for joint-prayer is pleasing to Christ,

ch. xviii. 19. These joint-sufferers were joint-suitors; being companions in the same tribulation, they were partners in the same supplication.

When they heard that Jesus passed by, they asked no further questions, who were with him, or whether he was in haste, but immediately *cried out.* Note, It is good to improve the present opportunity, to make the best of the price now in the hand, because, if once let slip, it may never return; these blind men did so, and did wisely; for we do not find that Christ ever came to Jericho again. *Now is the accepted time.*

2. The address itself is more observable; *Have mercy on us, O Lord, thou Son of David,* repeated again, *v.* 31. Four things are recommended to us for an example in this address; for, though the eye of the body was dark, the eye of the mind was enlightened concerning truth, duty, and interest.

(1) Here is an example of importunity in prayer. They cried out as men in earnest; men in want are earnest, of course.

(2) Of humility in prayer; in that word, *Have mercy on us,* not specifying the favour, or prescribing what, much less pleading merit, but casting themselves upon, and referring themselves cheerfully to, the Mediator's mercy, in what way he pleases; "Only have mercy." This is that which our hearts must be upon, when we come to *the throne of grace, that we may find mercy,* Heb. iv. 16; Ps. cxxx. 7.

(3) Of faith in prayer; in the title they gave to Christ, which was in the nature of a plea; *O Lord, thou*

Son of David; they confess that *Jesus Christ is Lord*, and therefore had authority to command deliverance for them. Surely it was by the Holy Ghost that they called Christ *Lord*, 1 Cor. xii. 3.

(4) Of perseverance in prayer, notwithstanding discouragement. *The multitude rebuked them*, as noisy, clamorous, and impertinent, and bid them *hold their peace*, and not disturb the Master, who perhaps at first himself seemed not to regard them. In following Christ with our prayers, we must expect to meet with hindrances and manifold discouragements from within and from without, something or other that bids us hold our peace. Such rebukes are permitted, that faith and fervency, patience and perseverance, may be tried.

II. The answer of Christ to this address of theirs. The multitude rebuked them; but Christ encouraged them.

1. *He stood still, and called them*, *v*. 32. He was now going up to Jerusalem, and was straitened till his work there was accomplished; and yet he stood still to cure these blind men.

2. He enquired further into their case; *What will ye that I shall do unto you?* This implies, (1) A very fair offer; "Here I am; let me know what you would have, and you shall have it." What would we more? He is able to do for us, and as willing as he is able; *Ask, and it shall be given you*. (2) A condition annexed to this offer, which is a very easy and reasonable one—that they should tell him what they would have him do for them. One would think this a strange question, anyone might tell

what they would have. Christ knew well enough; but he would know it from them, whether they begged only for an alms, as from a common person, or for a cure, as from the Messiah.

They soon made known their request to him, such a one as they never made to anyone else; *Lord, that our eyes may be opened*.

3. He cured them; when he encouraged them to seek him, he did not say, *Seek in vain*. What he did was an instance,

(1) Of his pity; *He had compassion on them*. Misery is the object of mercy. They that are poor and blind are *wretched and miserable* (Rev. iii. 17), and the objects of compassion. It was the tender mercy of our God, that gave light and sight to them that sat in darkness, Luke i. 78, 79.

(2) Of his power; *He that formed the eye, can he not heal it?* Yes, he can, he did, he did it easily, he touched their eyes; he did it effectually, *Immediately their eyes received sight*. Thus he not only proved that he was sent of God, but showed on what errand he was sent —to give sight to those that are spiritually blind, *to turn them from darkness to light*.

Lastly, These blind men, when they had received sight, *followed him*. Note, None follow Christ blindfold. He first by his grace opens men's eyes, and so draws their hearts after him.

CHAPTER TWENTY-ONE

PALM SUNDAY (*vv*. 1–11)

All the four evangelists take notice of this passage of Christ's *riding in triumph into Jerusalem*, five days before his death. The passover was on the fourteenth day of the month, and this was the tenth; on which day the law appointed that the paschal lamb should be taken up (Exod. xii. 3), and set apart for that service; on that day therefore Christ our Passover, who was to be sacrificed for us, was publicly showed. So that this was the prelude to his passion. He had lodged at Bethany, a village not far from Jerusalem, for some time; at a supper there the night before Mary had *anointed his feet*, John xii. 3. But, as is usual with ambassadors, he deferred his public entry till some time after his arrival.

Now here we have,

I. The provision that was made for this solemnity; and it was very poor and ordinary, and such as bespoke his *kingdom* to be *not this world*. But in this public appearance,

1. The preparation was sudden and offhand. For his glory in the other world, and ours with him, preparation was made before the foundation of the world, for that was the glory his heart was upon; his glory in this world he was dead to, and therefore, though he had it in prospect, did not forecast for it, but took what came next.

2. It was very mean. He sent only for an ass and her colt, *v.* 2. Yet some think that he had herein an eye to the custom in Israel for the judges to ride upon white asses (Judg. v. 10), and their sons on ass-colts, Judg. xii. 14. And Christ would thus enter, not as a Conqueror, but as the Judge of Israel, *who for judgment came into this world.*

3. It was not his ˏown, but borrowed. Though he had not a house of his own, yet, one would think, like some wayfaring men that live upon their friends, he might have had an ass of his own, to carry him about; but for our sakes he became in all respects poor, 2 Cor. viii. 9.

The disciples who were sent to borrow this ass are directed to say, *The Lord has need of him.* In the borrowing of this ass,

(1) We have an instance of Christ's knowledge. Though the thing was altogether contingent, yet Christ could tell his disciples where they should find an ass tied, and a colt with her. His omniscience extends itself to the meanest of his creatures; asses and their colts, and their being bound or loosed.

(2) We have an instance of his power over the spirits of men. The hearts of the meanest subjects, as well as of kings, *are in the hand of the Lord. If any man say aught to you, ye shall say, The Lord hath need of him.*

(3) We have an example of justice and honesty, in not using the ass, though for so small a piece of service as riding the length of a street or two, without the owner's consent.

II. The prediction that was fulfilled in this, *vv.* 4, 5. Our Lord Jesus, in all that he did and suffered, had very much his eye upon this, *That the scriptures might be fulfilled.* This particularly which was written of him, Zech. ix. 9, where it ushers in a large prediction of the kingdom of the Messiah, *Tell ye the daughter of Sion, Behold, thy*

King cometh, must be accomplished. Now observe here,

1. How the coming of Christ is foretold; *Tell ye the daughter of Sion*, the church, the holy mountain, *Behold, thy King cometh unto thee*.

2. How his coming is described. When a king comes, something great and magnificent is expected, especially when he comes to take possession of his kingdom. The King, the Lord of hosts, was seen *upon a throne, high and lifted up* (Isa. vi. 1); but there is nothing of that here; *Behold, he cometh to thee, meek, and sitting upon an ass*. When Christ would appear in his glory, it is in his meekness, not in his majesty.

(1) His temper is very mild. He comes not in wrath to take vengeance, but in mercy to work salvation.

(2) As an evidence of this, his appearance is very mean, sitting upon an ass, a creature made not for state, but service, not for battles, but for burdens; slow in its motions, but sure, and safe, and constant. The foretelling of this so long before, and the care taken that it should be exactly fulfilled, intimate it to have a peculiar significancy, for the encouragement of poor souls to apply themselves to Christ.

III. The procession itself, which was answerable to the preparation, both being destitute of worldly pomp, and yet both accompanied with a spiritual power.

Observe, 1. His equipage; *The disciples did as Jesus commanded them* (v. 6); they went to fetch the ass and the colt, not doubting but to find them, and to find the owner willing to lend them.

2. His retinue; there was nothing in this stately or magnificent. Sion's King comes to Sion, and the daughter of Sion was told of his coming long before; yet he is not attended by the gentlemen of the country, nor met by the magistrates of the city in their formalities as one might have expected; he should have had the keys of the city presented to him, and should have been conducted with all possible convenience to *the thrones of judgment, the thrones of the house of David*; but here is nothing of all this; yet he has his attendants, *a very great multitude*; they were only the common people, the mob (the *rabble* we should have been apt to call them), that graced the solemnity of Christ's triumph, and none but such.

Now, concerning this great multitude, we are here told,

(1) What they did; according to the best of their capacity, they studied to do honour to Christ. [1] *They spread their garments in the way*, that he might ride upon them. When Jehu was proclaimed king, the captains put their garments under him, in token of their subjection to him. [2] *Others cut down branches from the trees, and strewed them in the way*, as they used to do at the feast of tabernacles, in token of liberty, victory, and joy; for the mystery of that feast is particularly spoken of as belonging to gospel times, Zech. xiv. 16.

(2) What they said; *They that went before, and they that followed*, were in the same tune; both those

that gave notice of his coming, and those that attended him with their applauses, *cried, saying, Hosanna to the Son of David, v.* 9. When they carried branches about at the feast of tabernacles, they were wont to cry *Hosanna*, and from thence to call their bundles of branches their *hosannas. Hosanna* signifies, *Save now, we beseech thee*; referring to Ps. cxviii. 25, 26, where the Messiah is prophesied of as the *Head-stone of the corner*, though *the builders refused him*; and all his loyal subjects are brought in triumphing with him, and attending him with hearty good wishes to the prosperity of all his enterprises. *Hosanna to the Son of David* is, "This we do in honour of the Son of David."

3. We have here his entertainment in Jerusalem (*v.* 10); *When he was come into Jerusalem, all the city was moved*; every one took notice of him.

Upon this commotion we are further told,

(1) What the citizens said; *Who is this?* [1] They were, it seems, ignorant concerning Christ. Though he was *the Glory of his people Israel*, yet *Israel knew him not*; though he had distinguished himself by the many miracles he wrought among them, yet *the daughters of Jerusalem* knew him not *from another beloved*, Cant. v. 9. The Holy One unknown in the holy city! [2] Yet they were inquisitive concerning him. Who is this that is thus cried up, and comes with so much observation? *Who is this King of glory*, that demands admission into our hearts? Ps. xxiv. 8; Isa. lxiii. 1.

(2) How the multitude answered them; *This is Jesus, v.* 11. The multitude were better acquainted with Christ than the great ones. *The voice of the people*, is sometimes *the voice of God*. Now, in the account they give of him, [1] They were right in calling him *the Prophet, that great Prophet*. [2] Yet they missed it, in saying he was *of Nazareth*; and it helped to confirm some in their prejudices against him.

CLEANSING THE TEMPLE
(*vv.* 12–17)

When Christ came into Jerusalem, he did not go up to the court or the palace, though he came in as a King, but *into the temple*; for his kingdom is spiritual, and *not of this world*; it is in holy things that he rules, in the temple of God that he exercises authority. Now, what did he do there?

I. Thence he drove the buyers and sellers. Abuses must first be purged out, and the plants not of God's planting be plucked up, before that which is right can be established. The great Redeemer appears as a great Reformer, that turns away ungodliness, Rom. xi. 26. Here we are told,

1. What he did (*v.* 12); *He cast out all them that sold and bought*; he had done this once before (John ii. 14, 15), but there was occasion to do it again.

(1) The abuse was, buying and selling, and changing money, in the temple. Note, Lawful things, ill timed and ill placed, may become sinful things. That which was decent enough in another place, and not only lawful, but laudable,

on another day, *defiles the sanctuary*, and *profanes the sabbath*.

(2) The purging out of this abuse. Christ *cast them out that sold*. He did it before *with a scourge of small cords* (John ii. 15); now he did it with a look, with a frown, with a word of command. This was the only act of regal authority and coercive power that Christ did in the days of his flesh; he began with it, John ii. and here ended with it.

2. What he said, to justify himself, and to convict them (*v.* 13); *It is written*. Note, In the reformation of the church, the eye must be upon the scripture, and that must be adhered to as the rule, the pattern in the mount; and we must go no further than we can justify ourselves with, *It is written*.

(1) He shows, from a scripture prophecy, what the temple should be, and was designed to be; *My house shall be called the house of prayer*; which is quoted from Isa. lvi. 7.

(2) He shows, from a scripture reproof, how they had abused the temple, and perverted the intention of it; *Ye have made it a den of thieves*. This is quoted from Jer. vii. 11, *Is this house become a den of robbers in your eyes?* The priests lived, and lived plentifully, upon the altar; but, not content with that, they found other ways and means to squeeze money out of the people; and therefore Christ here calls them *thieves*, for they exacted that which did not belong to them.

II. There, in the temple, *he healed the blind and the lame*, *v.* 14. When he had driven the buyers and sellers out of the temple, he invited the blind and lame into it; for *he fills*

the hungry with good things, but the rich he sends empty away.

There also he silenced the offence which the chief priests and scribes took at the acclamations with which he was attended, *vv.* 15, 16. They that should have been most forward to give him honour, were his worst enemies.

1. They were inwardly vexed at the wonderful things that he did; they could not deny them to be true miracles, and therefore were cut to the heart with indignation at them, as Acts iv. 16; 33.

2. They openly quarrelled at the children's hosannas; they thought that hereby an honour was given him, which did not belong to him, and that it looked like ostentation.

Just now we had Christ preferring the blind and the lame before the buyers and sellers; now here we have him (*v.* 16), taking part with the children against priests and scribes.

Observe, (1) The children were in the temple, perhaps playing there; no wonder, when the rulers make it a *market-place*, that the children make it a place of pastime; but we are willing to hope that many of them were worshipping there.

(2) They were there *crying Hosanna to the Son of David*. This they learned from those that were grown up. Note, *Hosanna to the Son of David* well becomes the mouths of little children, who should learn young the language of Canaan.

(3) Our Lord Jesus not only allowed it, but was very well pleased with it, and quoted a scripture which was fulfilled in it (Ps. viii. 2), or, at least, may be accommodated to it; *Out of the*

mouth of babes and sucklings thou has perfected praise.

Lastly, Christ, having thus silenced them, forsook them, *v.* 17. *He left them*, in prudence, lest they should now have seized him before his hour was come; in justice, because they had forfeited the favour of his presence.

THE BARREN FIG TREE
(*vv.* 19–22)

(1) This cursing of the barren fig-tree, represents the state of hypocrites in general; and so it teaches us, [1] That the fruit of fig-trees may justly be expected from those that have the leaves. Christ looks for the power of religion from those that make profession of it; the favour of it from those that have the show of it; grapes from the vineyard that is planted in a fruitful hill: he hungers after it, his soul *desires the first ripe fruits.* [2] Christ's just expectations from flourishing professors are often frustrated and disappointed; he comes to many, seeking fruit, and finds leaves only, and he discovers it. Many have a name to live, and are not alive indeed; dote on the form of godliness, and yet deny the power of it. [3] The sin of barrenness is justly punished with the curse and plague of barrenness; *Let no fruit grow on thee henceforward for ever.* As one of the chiefest blessings, and which was the first, is, *Be fruitful*; so one of the saddest curses is, *Be no more fruitful.* Thus the sin of hypocrites is made their punishment; they *would* not do good, and therefore they *shall* do none; he that is fruitless, let him be fruitless still,

and lose his honour and comfort. [4] A false and hypocritical profession commonly withers in this world, and it is the effect of Christ's curse; the fig-tree that had no fruit, soon lost its leaves.

(2) It represents the state of the nation and people of the Jews in particular; they were a fig-tree planted in Christ's way, as a church. Now observe, [1] The disappointment they gave to our Lord Jesus. He came among them, expecting to find some fruit, something that would be pleasing to him; he hungered after it; not that he *desired a gift*, he needed it not, *but fruit that might abound to a good account.* But his expectations were frustrated; he found nothing but leaves; they called *Abraham their father, but did not do the works of Abraham*; they professed themselves expectants of the promised Messiah, but, when he came, they did not receive and entertain him. [2] The doom he passed upon them, *that never any fruit should grow upon them*, or be gathered from them, as a church or as a people, *from henceforward for ever.*

2. See the *power* of Christ.

(1) The disciples admired the effect of Christ's curse (*v.* 20); *They marvelled*; no power could do it but his, *who spake, and it was done.* They marvelled at the suddenness of the thing; *How soon is the fig-tree withered away!*

(2) Christ empowered them by faith to do the like (*vv.* 21, 22); as he said (John xiv. 12), *Greater works than these shall ye do.*

Observe, [1] The description of this wonder-working faith; *If ye have faith, and doubt not.* Note,

Doubting of the power and promise of God is the great thing that spoils the efficacy and success of faith.

[2] The power and prevalence of it expressed figuratively; *If ye shall say to this mountain*, meaning the mount of Olives, *Be thou removed, it shall be done.* This is a proverbial expression; intimating that we are to believe that nothing is impossible with God, and therefore that what he has promised shall certainly be performed, though to us it seem impossible.

[3] The way and means of exercising this faith, and of doing that which is to be done by it; *All things whatsoever ye shall ask in prayer, believing, ye shall receive.* Faith is the soul, prayer is the body; both together make a complete man for any service.

THE BAPTISM OF JOHN
(vv. 23–27)

Our Lord Jesus (like St. Paul after him) preached his gospel *with much contention*; his first appearance was in a dispute with *the doctors in the temple, when he was twelve years old*; and here, just before he died, we have him engaged in controversy. Observe,

I. As soon as he came into Jerusalem, he went to the temple, though he had been affronted there the day before, was there in the midst of enemies and in the mouth of danger.

II. In the temple he was teaching; he had called it *a house of prayer* (v. 13), and here we have him preaching there.

III. When Christ was teaching the people, the priests and elders came upon him, and challenged him to produce his orders; the hand of Satan was in this, to hinder him in his work.

Now, in this dispute with them, we may observe,

1. How he was assaulted by their insolent demand; *By what authority doest thou these things, and who gave thee this authority?* Had they duly considered his miracles, and the power by which he wrought them, they needed not to have asked this question; but they must have something to say for the shelter of an obstinate infidelity.

Christ had often said it, and proved it beyond contradiction, and Nicodemus, a master in Israel, had owned it, that he was *a teacher sent of God* (John iii. 2); yet, at this time of day, when that point had been so fully cleared and settled, they come to him with this question.

2. How he answered this demand with another, which would help them to answer it themselves (*vv.* 24, 25); *I also will ask you one thing.* He declined giving them a direct answer, lest they should take advantage against him; but answers them with a question.

Now this question is concerning John's baptism, here put for his whole ministry, preaching as well as baptizing; "Was this *from heaven, or of men?* One of the two it must be; either what he did was of his own head, or he was sent of God to do it." This question was not at all shuffling, to evade theirs; but,

(1) If they answered this question, it would answer theirs: should they say, against their consciences, that John's baptism was of men, yet it would be easy to answer, *John did no miracle* (John x. 41),

Christ did many; but should they say, as they could not but own, that John's baptism was from heaven (which was supposed in the questions sent him, John i. 21, *Art thou Elias, or that prophet?*) then their demand was answered, for he bare testimony to Christ.

(2) If they refused to answer it, that would be a good reason why he should not offer proofs of his authority to men that were obstinately prejudiced against the strongest conviction; it was but to cast pearls before swine.

3. How they were hereby baffled and run aground; they knew the truth, but would not own it, and so were taken in the snare they laid for our Lord Jesus. Observe,

(1) How *they reasoned with themselves*, not concerning the merits of the cause, what proofs there were of the divine original of John's baptism; no, their care was, how to make their part good against Christ.

(2) How they replied to our Saviour, and so dropped the question. They fairly confessed *We cannot tell;* that is, "We will not; *We never knew.*" The more shame for them, while they pretended to be leaders of the people, and by their office were obliged to take cognizance of such things; when they would not confess their knowledge, they were constrained to confess their ignorance. And observe, by the way, when they said, *We cannot tell*, they told a lie, for they knew that John's baptism was of God.

Thus Christ avoided the snare they laid for him, and justified himself in refusing to gratify them;

Neither tell I you by what authority I do these things. If they be so wicked and base as either not to believe, or not to confess, that the baptism of John was from heaven (though it obliged to repentance, that great duty, and sealed the kingdom of God at hand, that great promise), they were not fit to be discoursed with concerning Christ's authority; for men of such a disposition could not be convinced of the truth, nay, they could not but be provoked by it, and therefore *he that is thus ignorant, let him be ignorant still.*

TWO SONS (*vv.* 28–32)

In these verses, we have the parable of the *two sons* sent to work in the vineyard, the scope of which is to show that they who knew not John's baptism to be of God, were shamed even by the publicans and harlots, who knew it, and owned it. Here is,

I. The parable itself, which represents two sorts of persons; some that prove better than they promise, represented by the first of those sons; others that promise better than they prove, represented by the second.

1. They had both one and the same father, which signifies that God is a common Father to all mankind.

2. They had both the same command given them; *Son, go work today in my vineyard.* It is the command of a Father, which carries with it both authority and affection.

3. Their conduct was very different.

(1) One of the sons did better than he said, proved better than he

promised. His answer was bad, but his actions were good.

Note, There are many who in the beginning are wicked and wilful, and very unpromising, who afterward repent and mend, and come to something. Observe, When he repented, he went; that was the *fruit meet for repentance*. The only evidence of our repentance for our former resistance, is, immediately to comply, and set to work; and then what is past, shall be pardoned, and all shall be well.

(2) The other son said better than he did, promised better than he proved; his answer was good but his actions bad.

Many with their mouth show much love, but their heart goes another way. They had a good mind to be religious, but they met with something to be done, that was too hard, or something to be parted with, that was too dear, and so their purposes are to no purpose. Buds and blossoms are not fruit.

II. A general appeal upon the parable; *Whether of them twain did the will of his father? v.* 31. They both had their faults, but the question is, Which was the better of the two, and the less faulty? And it was soon resolved; the first, because his actions were better than his words, and his latter end than his beginning.

III. A particular application of it to the matter in hand, *vv.* 31, 32. The primary scope of the parable is, to show how the publicans and harlots, who never talked of the Messiah and his kingdom, yet entertained the doctrine, and submitted to the discipline, of John the Baptist, his forerunner, when the priests and elders, who were big with expectations of the Messiah, and seemed very ready to go into his measures, slighted John the Baptist, and ran counter to the designs of his mission. But it has a further reach; the Gentiles were *sometimes disobedient*, had been long so, children of disobedience, like the elder son (Tit. iii. 3, 4); yet, when the gospel was preached to them, they became obedient to the faith; whereas the Jews who said, *I go, sir*, promised fair (Exod. xxiv. 7; Josh. xxiv. 24); yet went not; they did but flatter God with their mouth, Ps. lxxviii. 36.

THE WICKED HUSBANDMEN
(*vv.* 33–46)

This parable plainly sets forth the sin and ruin of the Jewish nation; they and their leaders are the husbandmen here; and what is spoken for conviction to them, is spoken for caution to all that enjoy the privileges of the visible church, not to be high-minded, but fear.

I. We have here the privileges of the Jewish church, represented by the letting out of a vineyard to the husbandmen; they were as tenants holding by, from, and under, God the great Householder.

II. God's expectation of rent from these husbandmen, *v.* 34. It was a reasonable expectation; for *who plants a vineyard, and eats not of the fruit thereof?* Note, From those that enjoy church-privileges, both ministers and people, God looks for fruit accordingly. He did not demand more than they could make of it, but some fruit of that which he himself planted—an observance of the laws and statutes he gave them. What could have been done more reasonable? Israel was an empty vine, nay it was become the degenerate plant of a strange vine, and brought forth wild grapes.

III. The husbandmen's baseness in abusing the messengers that were sent to them.

1. When he sent them his servants, they abused them, though they represented the master himself, and spoke in his name. See here what hath all along been the lot of God's faithful messengers, more or less; (1) To suffer; *so persecuted they the prophets*, who were hated with a cruel hatred. (2) It has been their lot to suffer from their Master's own tenants; they were the husbandmen that treated them thus, the chief priests and elders that *sat in Moses's chair*, that professed religion and relation to God; these were the most bitter enemies of the Lord's prophets, that cast them out, and killed them, and said, *Let the Lord be glorified*, Isa. lxvi. 5. See Jer. xx. 1, 2; xxvi. 11.

Now see, [1] How God persevered in his goodness to them. He sent other servants, more than the first; though the first sped not, but were abused. He had sent them John the Baptist, and him they had beheaded; and yet he sent them his disciples, to prepare his way. O the riches of the patience and forbearance of God, in keeping up in his church a despised, persecuted ministry! [2] How they persisted in their wickedness. They *did unto them likewise*. One sin makes way for another of the same kind.

2. At length, he sent them his Son; we have seen God's goodness in sending, and their badness in abusing, the servants; but in the latter instance both these exceed themselves.

(1) Never did grace appear more gracious than in *sending the Son*. This was done *last of all*. Note, All the prophets were harbingers and forerunners to Christ. He was sent last; for if nothing else would work upon them, surely this would; it was therefore reserved for the *last expedient. Surely they will reverence my Son*, and therefore I will send him.

(2) Never did sin appear more sinful than in the abusing of him, which was now to be done in two or three days. Observe,

[1] How it was plotted (*v.* 38); *When they saw the Son:* when he came, whom the people owned and followed as the Messiah, who would either have the rent paid, or distrain for it; this touched their copyhold, and they were resolved to make one bold push for it, and to preserve their wealth and grandeur by taking *him* out of the way, who was the only hindrance of it, and rival with them. *This is the heir, come, let us kill him.*

[2] How this plot was executed, *v.* 39. While they were so set upon killing him, in pursuance of their design to secure their own pomp and power, and while he was so set upon dying, in pursuance of his design to subdue Satan, and save his chosen, no wonder if they soon *caught him, and slew him*, when his hour was come.

IV. Here is their doom read out of their own mouths, *vv.* 40, 41. He puts it to them, *When the Lord of the vineyard cometh, what will he do unto these husbandmen?*

1. Our Saviour, in his question, supposes that *the lord of the vineyard will come*, and reckon with them. God is the Lord of the vineyard; the property is his, and he will make *them* know it, who now *lord it over his heritage*, as if it were all their own. The Lord of the vineyard will come. Persecutors say in their hearts, He *delays his coming*, he *doth not see*, he *will not require*; but they shall find, though he bear long with them, he will not bear always.

2. They, in their answer, suppose that it will be a terrible reckoning; the crime appearing so very black, you may be sure.

(1) That he will *miserably destroy those wicked men*; it is destruction that is their doom. This was fulfilled upon the Jews, in that miserable destruction which was brought upon them by the Romans, and was completed about forty years after this; an unparalleled ruin, attended with all the most dismal aggravating circumstances. It will be fulfilled upon all that tread in the steps of their wickedness; hell is everlasting destruction, and it will be the most miserable destruction to them of all others, that have enjoyed the greatest share of church privileges, and have not improved them.

(2) That he will *let out his vineyard to other husbandmen*. The Jews imagined that no doubt *they were the people*, and wisdom and holiness must *die with them*; and if they were cut off, what would God do for a church in the world? But when God makes use of any to bear up his name, it is not because he

needs them, nor is he at all beholden to them.

V. The further illustration and application of this by Christ himself, telling them, in effect, that they had rightly judged.

1. He illustrates it by referring to a scripture fulfilled in this (*v.* 42); *Did ye never read in the scriptures?* The scripture he quotes is Ps. cxviii. 22, 23, the same context out of which the children fetched their hosannas. The same word yields matter of praise and comfort to Christ's friends and followers, which speaks conviction and terror to his enemies. Such a two-edged sword is the word of God. That scripture, the *Stone which the builders refused is become the head-stone of the corner*, illustrates the preceding parable, especially that part of it which refers to Christ.

(1) The builders' rejecting of the stone is the same with the husbandmen's abusing of the son that was sent to them. The chief priests and the elders were the builders, had the oversight of the Jewish church, which was God's building: and they would not allow Christ a place in their building, would not admit his doctrine or laws into their constitution; they threw him aside as a despised broken vessel, a stone that would serve only for a stepping-stone, to be trampled upon.

(2) The advancing of this stone to be the head of the corner is the same with *letting out the vineyard to other husbandmen*. He who was rejected by the Jews was embraced by the Gentiles; and to that church where there is no difference of circumcision or uncircumcision, *Christ is all, and in all.* His authority

over the gospel church, and influence upon it, his ruling it as the Head, and uniting it as the Cornerstone, are the great tokens of his exhaltation.

(3) The hand of God was in all this; *This is the Lord's doing.* Even the rejecting of him by the Jewish builders was by the determinate counsel and foreknowledge of God; he permitted and overruled it; much more was his advancement to the Head of the corner; his right hand and his holy arm brought it about; it was God himself that *highly exalted him,* and gave him *a name above every name; and it is marvellous in our eyes.*

2. He applies it to them, and application is the life of preaching.

(1) He applies the sentence which they had passed (*v.* 41), and turns it upon themselves; not the former part of it, concerning the miserable destruction of the husbandmen (he could not bear to speak of that), but the latter part, of *letting out the vineyard to others*; because though it looked black upon the Jews, it spoke good to the Gentiles.

(2) He applies the scripture which he had quoted (*v.* 42), to their terror, *v.* 44. This *Stone,* which the *builders refused, is set for the fall of many in Israel*; and we have here the doom of two sorts of people, for whose fall it proves that Christ is set.

[1] Some, through ignorance, stumble at Christ in his estate of humiliation; when this Stone lies on the earth, where the builders threw it, they, through their blindness and carelessness, fall on it, fall over it, and *they shall be broken.*

[2] Others, through malice, oppose Christ, and bid defiance to him in his estate of exaltation, when this Stone is advanced to the head of the corner; and on them *it shall fall,* for they pull it on their own heads, as the Jews did by that challenge, *His blood be upon us and upon our children,* and *it will grind them to powder.*

Lastly, The entertainment which this discourse of Christ met with among the chief priests and elders, that heard his parables.

1. *They perceived that he spake of them* (*v.* 45), and that in what they said (*v.* 41) they had but read their own doom.

2. *They sought to lay hands on him.* Note, When those who hear the reproofs of the word, perceive that it speaks of them, if it do not do them a great deal of good, it will certainly do them a great deal of hurt.

3. They durst not do it, *for fear of the multitude, who took him for a prophet,* though not for the Messiah; this served to keep the Pharisees in awe. The fear of the people restrained them from speaking ill of John (*v.* 26), and here from doing ill to Christ.

CHAPTER TWENTY-TWO

THE WEDDING FEAST
(*vv.* 1–14)

We have here the parable of the guests invited to *the wedding-feast.* In this it is said (*v.* 1), *Jesus answered,* not to what his opposers *said* (for they were put to silence), but to what they *thought,* when they were wishing for an opportunity to *lay hands on him, ch.* xxi. 46.

I. Gospel preparations are here

represented by a feast which a king made *at the marriage of his son*; such is *the kingdom of heaven*, such the provision made for precious souls, in and by the new covenant. The *King* is God, *a great King, King of kings*. Now,

1. Here is *a marriage made for his son*. Christ is the Bridegroom, the church is the bride; the gospel-day is *the day of his espousals*, Cant. iii. 11.

2. Here is *a dinner prepared for this marriage*, *v.* 4. All the privileges of church-membership, and all the blessings of the new covenant, pardon of sin, the favour of God, peace of conscience, the promises of the gospel, and all the riches contained in them, access to the throne of grace, the comforts of the Spirit, and a well-grounded hope of eternal life. These are the preparations for this feast, a heaven upon earth now, and a heaven in heaven shortly.

II. Gospel calls and offers are represented by an invitation to this feast. Those that make a feast will have guests to grace the feast with. God's guests are the children of men. *Lord, what is man*, that he should be thus dignified! *The guests* that were first invited were the Jews; wherever the gospel is preached, this invitation is given; ministers are the *servants* that are sent to invite, Prov. ix. 4, 5.

Now, 1. The guests *are called, bidden* to the wedding. All that are within hearing of the joyful sound of the gospel, to them is the word of this invitation sent.

2. The guests are called upon; for in the gospel there are not only gracious proposals made, but

gracious persuasives. *We persuade men, we beseech them in Christ's stead*, 2 Cor. v. 11, 20. One would think it had been enough to give men an intimation that they had leave to come, and should be welcome; but, because *the natural man discerns not*, and therefore desires not, *the things of the Spirit of God*, we are pressed to accept the call by the most powerful inducements, *drawn with the cords of a man, and all the bonds of love*.

III. The cold treatment which the gospel of Christ often meets with among the children of men, represented by the cold treatment that this message met with and the hot treatment that the messengers met with, in both which the king himself and the royal bridegroom are affronted. This reflects primarily upon the Jews, who rejected the counsel of God against themselves; but it looks further, to the contempt that would, by many in all ages, be put upon, and the opposition that would be given to, the gospel of Christ.

1. The message was basely slighted (*v.* 3); *They would not come*. Note, Making light of Christ, and of the great salvation wrought out by him, is the damning sin of the world. *They were careless*. And the reason why *they made light of the marriage feast* was, because they had other things that they minded more, and had more mind to; *they went their ways, one to his farm, and another to his merchandise*. Note, The business and profit of worldly employments prove to many a great hindrance in closing with Christ: none turn their back on the feast, but with

some plausible excuse or other, Luke xiv. 18.

2. The messengers were basely abused; *The remnant*, or the rest of them, that is, those who did not go to the *farms*, or *merchandise*, were neither husbandmen nor tradesmen, but ecclesiastics, *the scribes, and Pharisees, and chief priests*; these were the persecutors, these *took the servants, and treated them spitefully, and slew them.* The prophets and John the Baptist had been thus abused already, and the apostles and ministers of Christ must count upon the same.

IV. The utter ruin that was coming upon the Jewish church and nation is here represented by the revenge which the king, in wrath, took on these insolent recusants (*v.* 7); *He was wroth.* Now observe here,

1. What was the crying sin that brought the ruin; it was their being *murderers.* He does not say, he destroyed those *despisers of his call,* but *those murderers of his servants*; as if God were more jealous for the lives of his ministers than for the honour of his gospel.

2. What was the ruin itself, that was coming? *He sent forth his armies.* The Roman armies were his armies, of his raising, of his sending against the people of his wrath; and he *gave them a charge to tread them down,* Isa. x. 6. This points out very plainly the destruction of the Jews, and the burning of Jerusalem, by the Romans, forty years after this.

V. The replenishing of the church again, by the bringing in of the Gentiles, is here represented by the furnishing of the feast with guests *out of the high-ways, vv.* 8–10.

Here is, 1. The complaint of the master of the feast concerning those that were first bidden (*v.* 8), *The wedding is ready,* the covenant of grace ready to be sealed, a church ready to be founded; *but they which were bidden,* that is, the Jews, *to whom pertained the covenant and the promises,* by which they were of old invited to the *feast of fat things,* they *were not worthy,* they were utterly unworthy, and, by their contempt of Christ, had forfeited all the privileges they were invited to.

2. The commission he gave to the servants, to invite other guests. The inhabitants of the *city* (*v.* 7) had refused; *Go into the high-ways* then; into *the way of the Gentiles,* which at first they were to decline, *ch.* x. 5. Thus by the fall of the Jews salvation is come to the Gentiles, Rom. xi. 11, 12; Eph. iii. 8.

3. The success of this second invitation; if some will not come, others will (*v.* 10); *They gathered together all, as many as they found.* The servants obeyed their orders.

Now the guests that were gathered were, [1] A multitude, *all, as many as they found*; so many, that the guest-chamber was filled. The sealed ones of the Jews were numbered, but those of other nations *were without number, a very great multitude,* Rev. vii. 9. See Isa. lx. 4, 8. [2] A mixed multitude, *both bad and good*; some that before their conversion were sober and well-inclined, as the devout Greeks (Acts xvii. 4), and Cornelius; others that had run to an excess of riot, as the Corinthians (I Cor. vi. 11).

VI. The case of hypocrites, who are *in* the church, but not *of* it, who have a name to live, but are not alive indeed, is represented by *the guest that had not on a wedding garment*; one of the bad that were gathered in. Concerning this hypocrite observe,

1. His discovery, how he was found out, *v.* 11.

(1) *The king came in to see the guests*, to bid those welcome who came prepared, and to turn those out who came otherwise.

Observe, This hypocrite was never discovered to be without *a wedding garment*, till *the king himself came in to see the guests*. Note, It is God's prerogative to know who are sound at heart in their profession, and who are not.

(2) As soon as he came in, he presently espied the hypocrite; *He saw there a man which had not on a wedding garment*.

2. His trial (*v.* 12); and here we may observe,

(1) How he was arraigned (*v.* 12); *Friend, how camest thou in hither, not having a wedding garment?* A startling question to one that was priding himself in the place he securely possessed at the feast. *Friend!* That was a cutting word; a seeming friend, a pretended friend, a friend in profession, under manifold ties and obligations to be a friend. Note, There are many in the church who are false friends to Jesus Christ, who say that they love him, while their hearts are not with him. *How camest thou in hither?* He does not chide the servants for letting him in (the wedding garment is an inward thing, ministers must go according to that which falls within their cognizance); but he checks his presumption in crowding in, when

he knew that his heart was not upright.

(2) How he was convicted; *he was speechless: he was muzzled* (so the word is used, 1 Cor. ix. 9); the man stood mute, upon his arraignment, being convicted and condemned by his own conscience. They who live within the church, and die without Christ, will not have one word to say for themselves in the judgment of the great day, they will be without excuse.

3. His sentence (*v.* 13); *Bind him hand and foot*, &c.

Lastly, The parable is concluded with that remarkable saying which we had before (*ch.* xx. 16), *Many are called, but few are chosen, v.* 14. Of the many that are called to the wedding feast, if you set aside all those as unchosen that make light of it, and avowedly prefer other things before it; if then you set aside all that make a profession of religion, but the temper of whose spirits and the tenour of whose conversation are a constant contradiction to it; if you set aside all the profane, and all the hypocritical, you will find that they are few, very few, that are chosen; many called to the wedding feast, but few chosen to the wedding garment, that is, to *salvation, by sanctification of the Spirit*. This *is the strait gate, and narrow way*, which *few find*.

TRIBUTE TO CÆSAR
(*vv.* 15–22)

In these verses, we have him attacked by the Pharisees and Herodians with a question about paying tribute to Cæsar. Observe,

I. What the design was, which they proposed to themselves; *They took counsel to entangle him in his talk.*

1. *They took counsel.* It was foretold concerning him, that *the rulers* would *take counsel against him* (Ps. ii. 2); and *so persecuted they the prophets. Come, and let us devise devices against Jeremiah.* See Jer. xviii. 18; xx. 10.

2. That which they aimed at was *to entangle him in his talk.* They saw him free and bold in speaking his mind, and hoped by that, if they could bring him to some nice and tender point, to get an advantage against him.

II. The question which they put to him pursuant to this design, *vv.* 16, 17. Observe,

1. The persons they employed; they did not go themselves, lest the design should be suspected and Christ should stand the more upon his guard; but they sent their disciples, who would look less like tempters, and more like learners.

With them they sent the Herodians, a party among the Jews, who were for a cheerful and entire subjection to the Roman emperor, and to Herod his deputy; and who made it their business to reconcile people to that government, and pressed all to pay their tribute.

2. The preface, with which they were plausibly to introduce the question; it was highly complimentary to our Saviour (*v.* 16); *Master, we know that thou art true, and teachest the way of God in truth.* Note, It is a common thing for the most spiteful projects to be covered with the most specious pretences.

3. The proposal of the case; *What thinkest thou? Is it lawful to give tribute to Cæsar, or not?*

This implies a further question; Has Cæsar a right to demand it?

Now the question was, Whether it was lawful to pay these taxes voluntarily, or, Whether they should not insist upon the ancient liberty of their nation, and rather suffer themselves to be distrained upon? The ground of the doubt was, that they *were Abraham's seed*, and should not by consent be *in bondage to any man*, John viii. 33. God had given them a law, that they should not *set a stranger over them.* Did not that imply, that they were not to yield any willing subjection to any prince, state, or potentate, that was not of their own nation and religion? This was an old mistake, arising from that *pride and* that *haughty spirit* which bring *destruction and a fall.*

However, by this question they hoped to entangle Christ, and, which way soever he resolved it, to expose him to the fury either of the jealous Jews, or of the jealous Romans; they were ready to triumph, as Pharaoh did over Israel, that *the wilderness had shut him in*, and his doctrine would be concluded either injurious to the rights of the church, or hurtful to kings and provinces.

III. The breaking of this snare by the wisdom of the Lord Jesus.

1. He discovered it (*v.* 18); *He perceived their wickedness*; for, *surely in vain is the net spread in the sight of any bird*, Prov. i. 17. A temptation perceived is half conquered, for our greatest danger lies from snakes under the green grass; *and he said, Why tempt ye me, ye hypocrites?*

2. He evaded it; his convicting

them of hypocrisy might have served for an answer: but our Lord Jesus gave a full answer to their question, and introduced it by an argument sufficient to support it, so as to lay down a rule for his church in this matter, and yet to avoid giving offence, and to break the snare.

(1) He forced them, ere they were aware, to confess Cæsar's authority over them, *vv.* 19, 20. *Show me the tribute-money.* He had none of his own to convince them by; it should seem, he had not so much as one piece of money about him, for for our sakes he emptied himself, and became poor. They presently *brought him a penny*, a Roman penny in silver, in value about sevenpence half-penny of our money, the most common piece then in use: it was stamped with the emperor's image and superscription, which was the warrant of the public faith for the value of the pieces so stamped; a method agreed on by most nations, for the more easy circulation of money with satisfaction. The coining of money has always been looked upon as a branch of the prerogative, a flower of the crown, a royalty belonging to the sovereign powers; and the admitting of that as the good and lawful money of a country is an implicit submission to those powers, and an owning of them in money matters.

Christ asked them, *Whose image is this?* They owned it to be Cæsar's, and thereby convicted those of falsehood who said, *We were never in bondage to any*; and confirmed what afterward they said, *We have no king but Cæsar.*

It is a rule in the Jewish Talmud, that "he is the king of the country whose coin is current in the country." Some think that the superscription upon this coin was a memorandum of the conquest of Judea by the Romans, *anno post captum Judæam—the year after that event*; and that they admitted that too.

(2) From thence he inferred the lawfulness of paying tribute to Cæsar (*v.* 21); *Render therefore to Cæsar the things that are Cæsar's*; not, "*Give* it him" (as they expressed it, *v.* 17), but, "*Render* it; Return," or "Restore it." Now by this answer,

[1] No offence was given. It was much to the honour of Christ and his doctrine, that he did not interpose as a Judge or a Divider in matters of this nature, but left them as he found them, for *his kingdom is not of this world*; and in this he hath given an example to his ministers, who deal in sacred things, not to meddle with disputes about things secular, not to wade far into controversies relating to them, but to leave that to those whose proper business it is.

[2] His adversaries were reproved. *First*, Some of them would have had him make it unlawful to give tribute to Cæsar, that they might have a pretence to save their money. Thus many excuse themselves from that which they must do, by arguing whether they may do it or no. *Secondly*, They all withheld from God his dues, and are reproved for that: while they were vainly contending about their civil liberties, they had lost the life and power of religion, and

needed to be put in mind of their duty to God, with that to Cæsar.

[3] His disciples were instructed, and standing rules left to the church.

First, That the Christian religion is no enemy to civil government, but a friend to it. Christ's kingdom doth not clash or interfere with the kingdoms of the earth, in any thing that pertains to their jurisdiction. By Christ kings reign.

Secondly, It is the duty of subjects to render to magistrates that which, according to the laws of their country, is their due.

Thirdly, When we render to Cæsar the things that are Cæsar's, we must remember withal to render to God the things that are God's. If our purses be Cæsar's, our consciences are God's; he hath said, *My son, give me thy heart*: he must have the innermost and uppermost place there; we must render to God that which is his due, out of our time and out of our estates; from them he must have his share as well as Cæsar his; and if Cæsar's commands interfere with God's *we must obey God rather than men*.

Lastly, Observe how they were nonplussed by this answer; they *marvelled, and left him, and went their way*, *v.* 22. They admired his sagacity in discovering and evading a snare which they thought so craftily laid.

MARRIAGES AND HEAVEN
(*vv.* 23–33)

We have here Christ's dispute with the Sadducees concerning the resurrection; it was the same day on which he was attacked by the Pharisees about paying tribute. Observe here,

I. The opposition which the Sadducees made to a very great truth of religion; they say, *There is no resurrection*, as there are some fools who say, *There is no God*. These heretics were called *Sadducees* from one Sadoc, a disciple of Antigonus Sochæus, who flourished about two hundred and eighty-four years before our Saviour's birth. As the Pharisees and Essenes seemed to follow Plato and Pythagoras, so the Sadducees were much of the genius of the Epicureans; they denied the resurrection, they said, There is no future state, no life after this; that, when the body dies, the soul is annihilated, and dies with it; that there is no state of rewards or punishments in the other world; no judgment to come in heaven or hell. They maintained, that, except God, there is no spirit (Acts xxiii. 8), nothing but matter and motion. They would not own the divine inspiration of the prophets, nor any revelation from heaven, but what God himself spoke upon mount Sinai. Now the doctrine of Christ carried that great truth of the resurrection and a future state much further than it had yet been revealed, and therefore the Sadducees in a particular manner set themselves against it. The Pharisees and Sadducees were contrary to each other, and yet confederates against Christ.

II. The objection they made against the truth, which was taken from a supposed case of a woman that had seven husbands successively; now they take it for granted, that, if there be a resurrection, it must be a return to such a state as this we are now in, and to the same circumstances, like the imaginary Platonic year; and if so, it is an invincible absurdity for this woman in the future state to have seven husbands, or else an insuperable difficulty which of them should have her, he whom she had first, or he whom she had last, or he whom she loved best, or he whom she lived longest with.

1. They suggest the law of Moses in this matter (*v.* 24), that the next of kin should marry the widow of him that died childless (Deut. xxv. 5); we have it practised, Ruth iv. 5.

2. They put a case upon this statute, which, whether it were a *case in fact* or only a *moot case*, is not at all material; if it had not really occurred, yet possibly it might. It was of seven brothers, who married the same woman, *vv.* 25–27.

3. They propose a doubt upon this case (*v.* 28); "*In the resurrection, whose wife shall she be of the seven?* You cannot tell whose; and therefore we must conclude *there is no resurrection.*"

III. Christ's answer to this objection; by reproving their ignorance, and rectifying their mistake, he shows the objection to be fallacious and unconcluding.

1. He reproves their ignorance (*v.* 29); *Ye do err, not knowing.* Note, Ignorance is the cause of error; those that are in the dark, miss their way. Now observe,

(1) *They know not the power of God*; which would lead men to infer that there *may be* a resurrection and a future state. God is omnipotent, and can do what he will; and then no room is left for doubting but that he will do what he has promised; and, if so, *why should it be thought a thing incredible with you that God should raise the dead?* Acts xxvi. 8. His power far exceeds the power of nature.

(2) *They know not the scriptures,* which decidedly affirm that there shall be a resurrection and a future state.

2. He rectifies their mistake, and (*v.* 30) corrects those gross ideas which they had of the resurrection and a future state, and fixes these doctrines upon a true and lasting basis. Concerning that state, observe,

(1) It is not like the state we are now in upon earth; *They neither marry, nor are given in marriage.* In our present state marriage is necessary; it was instituted in innocency; whatever intermission or neglect there has been of other institutions, this was never laid aside, nor will be till the end of time. But, in the resurrection, there is no occasion for marriage; whether in glorified bodies there will be any distinction of sexes some too curiously dispute (the ancients are divided in their opinions about it); but, whether there will be a distinction or no, it is certain that there will be no conjunction; where God will be *all in all*, there needs no other *meet-help*; the body will be *spiritual*, and there will be in it no carnal desires to be gratified. The joys of that state are pure and spiritual, and arise from the marriage of all of them to the Lamb, not of any of them to one another.

(2) It is like the state angels are now in, in heaven; *They are as the angels of God in heaven*; they *are* so, that is, undoubtedly they shall be so. The bodies of the saints shall be raised incorruptible and glorious, like the uncompounded vehicles of those pure and holy spirits (1 Cor. xv. 42, &c.), swift and strong, like them.

IV. Christ's argument to confirm this great truth of the resurrection and a future state; the matters being of great concern, he did not think it enough (as in some other disputes) to discover the fallacy and sophistry of the objections, but backed the truth with a solid argument. Now observe,

1. Whence he fetched his argument—from the scripture; that is the great magazine or armoury whence we may be furnished with spiritual weapons, offensive and defensive.

2. What his argument was (*v.* 32); *I am the God of Abraham.* This was not an express proof, *in so many words*; and yet it was really a conclusive argument.

Now the drift of the argument is to prove,

(1) That there is a future state, another life after this, in which the righteous shall be truly and constantly happy. This is proved from what God said; *I am the God of Abraham.*

[1] For God to be any one's God supposes some very extraordinary privilege and happiness; unless we know fully what God is, we could not comprehend the riches of that word, *I will be to thee a God*, that is, a Benefactor like myself.

[2] It is manifest that these good men had no such extraordinary happiness, in *this* life, as might look any thing like the accomplishment of so great a word as that. If no happiness had been reserved for these great and good men on the other side death, that melancholy word of poor Jacob's, when he was old (Gen. xlvii. 9), *Few and evil have the days of the years of my life been*, would have been an eternal reproach to the wisdom, goodness, and faithfulness, of that God who had so often called himself *the God of Jacob.*

[3] Therefore there must certainly be a future state, in which, as God will ever live to be eternally rewarding, so Abraham, Isaac, and Jacob, will ever live to be eternally rewarded.

(2) That the soul is immortal, and the body shall rise again, to be united; if the former point be gained, these will follow; but they are likewise proved by considering the time when God spoke this; it was to Moses at the bush, long after Abraham, Isaac, and Jacob, were dead and buried; and yet God saith, not, "*I was*," or "*have been*," but, *I am the God of Abraham.* Now *God is not the God of the dead, but of the living.* He is a living God, and communicates vital influences to those to whom he is a God. If, when Abraham died, there had been an end of him, there had been an end likewise of God's relation to him as his God; but at that time, when God spoke to Moses, he was the God of Abraham, and therefore Abraham must be then alive; which proves the immortality of the soul in a state of bliss; and that, by consequence, infers the resurrec-

tion of the body; for there is such an inclination in the human soul to its body, as would make a final and eternal separation inconsistent with the bliss of those that have God for *their God*. The Sadducees' notion was, that the union between body and soul is so close, that, when the body dies, the soul dies with it. Now, upon the same hypothesis, if the soul lives, as it certainly does, the body must some time or other live with it.

Lastly, We have the issue of this dispute. The Sadducees were *put to silence* (v. 34), and so put to shame. But the multitude *were astonished at his doctrine*, v. 33.

THE GREAT COMMANDMENT
(vv. 34–40)

Here is a discourse which Christ had with a Pharisee-lawyer, about the great commandment of the law.

This lawyer *asked him a question, tempting him*; not with any design to ensnare him, as appears by St. Mark's relation of the story, where we find that this was he to whom Christ said, *Thou art not far from the kingdom of God*, Mark xii. 34, but only to see what he would say, and to draw on discourse with him, to satisfy his own and his friends' curiosity.

I. The question was, *Master, which is the greatest commandment of the law?* A needless question, when all the things of God's law are great things (Hos. viii. 12).

II. The design was to try him, or tempt him; to try, not so much his knowledge as his judgment. It was a question disputed among the critics in the law. Some would have the

law of circumcision to be the great commandment, others the law of the sabbath, others the law of sacrifices, according as they each stood affected, and spent their zeal; now they would try what Christ said to this question, hoping to incense the people against him, if he should not answer according to the vulgar opinion; and if he should magnify one commandment, they would reflect on him as vilifying the rest.

III. Christ's answer to this question. Now Christ recommends to us those as the great commandments, not which are so exclusive of others, but which are *therefore* great because inclusive of others. Observe,

1. Which these great commandments are (vv. 37–39); not the judicial laws, those could not be the greatest now that the people of the Jews, to whom they pertained, were so little; not the ceremonial laws, those could not be the greatest, now that they were waxen old, and were ready to vanish away; nor any particular moral precept; but the love of God and our neighbour, which are the spring and foundation of all the rest, which (these being supposed) will follow of course.

All the law is fulfilled in one word, and that is, *love*. See Rom. xiii. 10. All obedience begins in the affections, and nothing in religion is done right, that is not done there first. Love is the leading affection, which gives law, and gives ground, to the rest; and therefore that, as the main fort, is to be first secured and garrisoned for God. Man is a creature cut out for love; thus therefore is the law written in the heart, that it is a *law of love*. Love is a short and sweet word; and, if that be *the fulfilling of the law*, surely the yoke of the command is very easy. Love is the rest and satisfaction of the soul; if we walk in this good old way, we shall find rest.

2. Observe what the weight and greatness of these commandments is (v. 40); *On these two commandments hang all the law and the prophets*; that is, This is the sum and substance of all those precepts relating to practical religion which were written in men's hearts by nature, revived by Moses, and backed and enforced by the preaching and writing of the prophets. All hang upon the law of love; take away this, and all falls to the ground, and comes to nothing.

SON OF DAVID (vv. 41–46)

Many questions the Pharisees had asked Christ, by which, though they thought to pose him, they did but *expose* themselves; but now let him ask them a question; and he will do it when they are gathered together, *v.* 41. Now here,

I. Christ proposes a question to them, which they could easily answer; it was a question in their own catechism; "*What think ye of Christ? Whose Son is he?* Whose Son do you expect the Messiah to be, who was promised to the fathers?" This they could easily answer, *The Son of David*.

What think ye of Christ? They had put questions to him, one after another, out of the law; but he comes and puts a question to them upon the promise.

II. He starts a difficulty upon their answer, which they could not so easily solve, *vv.* 43–45. The objection Christ raised was, *If Christ be David's son, how then doth David, in spirit, call him Lord?* He did not hereby design to ensnare them, as they did him, but to instruct them in a truth they were loth to believe—that the expected Messiah is God.

1. It is easy to see that David calls Christ *Lord*, and this in spirit being divinely inspired, and actuated therein by a spirit of prophecy; for it was *the Spirit of the Lord that spoke by him*, 2 Sam. xxiii. 1, 2. David was one of those *holy men that spoke as* they were *moved by the Holy Ghost*, especially in calling Christ *Lord*; for it was then, as it is still (1 Cor. xii. 3), that *no man can say that Jesus is the Lord, but by the Holy Ghost*. Now, to prove that David, in spirit, called Christ *Lord*, he quotes Ps. cx. 1, which psalm the scribes themselves understood of Christ; of him, it is certain, the prophet there speaks, of him and of no other man; and it is a prophetical summary of the doctrine of Christ, it describes him executing the offices of a Prophet, Priest, and King, both in his humiliation and also in his exaltation.

Christ quotes the whole verse, which shows the Redeemer in his exaltation; (1) *Sitting at the right hand of God*. His sitting denotes both rest and rule; his sitting at God's right hand denotes superlative honour and sovereign power. See in what great words this is expressed (Heb. viii. 1); *He is set on the right hand of the throne of the*

Majesty. See Phil. ii. 9; Eph. i. 20. He did not take this honour to himself, but was entitled to it by covenant with his Father, and invested in it by commission from him, and here is that commission. (2) Subduing his enemies. There he shall sit, till they be all made either his friends or his footstool.

But that which this verse is quoted for is, that David calls the Messiah *his Lord*; *the Lord,* Jehovah, *said unto my Lord.* This intimates to us, that in expounding scripture we must take notice of, and improve, not only that which is the main scope and sense of a verse, but of the words and phrases, by which the Spirit chooses to express that sense, which have often a very useful and instructive significance. Here is a good note from that word, *My Lord.*

2. It is not so easy for those who believe not the Godhead of the Messiah, to clear this from an absurdity, if Christ be David's son. It is incongruous for the father to speak of his son, the predecessor of his successor, as his *Lord.* We must hold this fast, that he is David's Lord, and by that explain his being David's son. The seeming differences of scripture, as here, may not only be accommodated, but contribute to the beauty and harmony of the whole.

III. We have here the success of this gentle trial which Christ made of the Pharisees' knowledge, in two things.

1. It puzzled them (*v.* 46); *No man was able to answer him a word.* Either it was their ignorance that they did not know, or their impiety that they would not own, the

Messiah to be God; which truth was the only key to unlock this difficulty.

2. It silenced them, and all others that sought occasion against him; *Neither durst any man, from that day forth, ask him any more* such captious, tempting, ensnaring *questions.*

WOE, SCRIBES AND PHARISEES (*vv.* 1–33)

We find not Christ, in all his preaching, so severe upon any sort of people as upon these *scribes and Pharisees*; for the truth is, nothing is more directly opposite to the spirit of the gospel than the temper and practice of that generation of men, who were made up of pride, worldliness, and tyranny, under a cloak and pretence of religion; yet these were the idols and darlings of the people, who thought, if but two men went to heaven, one would be a Pharisee.

Now, in this discourse,

I. Christ allows their office as expositors of the law; *The scribes and Pharisees sit in Moses's seat* (*v.* 2), as public teachers and interpreters of the law; and, the law of Moses being the municipal law of their state, they were as judges, or a bench of justices; teaching and judging seem to be equivalent, comparing 2 Chron. xvii. 7, 9, with 2 Chron. xix. 5, 6, 8.

Hence he infers (*v.* 3), "*Whatsoever they bid you observe, that observe and do.* As far as they *sit in Moses's seat,* that is, read and preach the law that was given by Moses" (which, as yet, continued in full force, power, and virtue), "and judge according to that law, so far you must hearken to them, as remembrancers to you of the written word."

II. He condemns the men. He had ordered the multitude to do as they taught; but here he annexeth a caution not to do as they did, to beware of their leaven; *Do not ye after their works*. Their traditions were their works, were their idols, the works of their fancy. Or, "Do not according to their example."

Our Saviour here, and in the following verses, specifies diverse particulars of their works, wherein we must not imitate them. In general, they are charged with hypocrisy, dissimulation, or double-dealing in religion; a crime which cannot be enquired of at men's bar, because we can only judge according to outward appearance; but God, who searcheth the heart, can convict of hypocrisy; and nothing is more displeasing to him, for he desireth truth.

He cautions his disciples against being like them; they must not do after their works; "But be not ye called so, for ye shall not be of such a spirit," *v*. 8, &c.

Here is, [1] A prohibition of pride. They are here forbidden,

First, To challenge titles of honour and dominion to themselves, *vv*. 8–10. It is repeated twice; *Be not called Rabbi, neither be ye called Master* or *Guide*: not that it is unlawful to give civil respect to *those that are over us in the Lord*, nay, it is an instance of the honour and esteem which it is our duty to show them; but, 1. Christ's ministers must not affect

the name of *Rabbi* or *Master*, by way of distinction from other people; it is not agreeable to the simplicity of the gospel, for them to covet or accept the honour which they have that are in kings' palaces. 2. They must not assume the authority and dominion implied in those names; they must not be magisterial, nor domineer over their brethren, or over God's heritage, as if they had dominion over the faith of Christians.

(1) *One is your Master, even Christ, v*. 8, and again, *v*. 10. Note, [1] Christ is our Master, our Teacher, our Guide. Mr. George Herbert, when he named the name of *Christ*, usually added, *My Master*. [2] Christ only is our Master, ministers are but ushers in the school.

(2) *All ye are brethren*. Ministers are brethren not only to one another, but to the people; and therefore it ill becomes them to be masters, when there are none for them to master it over but their brethren.

Secondly, They are forbidden to ascribe such titles to others (*v*. 9); "*Call no man your father upon the earth*; constitute no man the father of your religion, that is, the founder, author, director, and governor, of it."

The reason given is, *One is your Father, who is in heaven*. God is our Father, and is All in all in our religion.

[2] Here is a precept of humility and mutual subjection (*v*. 11); *He that is greatest among you shall be your servant*; not only call himself so, but he shall be so. Take it as a promise; "*He* shall be accounted

greatest, and stand highest in the favour of God, that is most submissive and serviceable": or as a precept; "He that is advanced to any place of dignity, trust, and honour, in the church, *let him be your servant.*"

[3] Here is a good reason for all this, *v.* 12. Consider,

First, The punishment intended for the proud; *Whosoever shall exalt himself shall be abased.*

Secondly, The preferment intended for the humble; *He that shall humble himself shall be exalted.*

The gospel has its woes as well as the law, and gospel curses are of all curses the heaviest. These woes (*vv.* 13–16) are the more remarkable, not only because of the authority, but because of the meekness and gentleness, of him that denounced them.

This is here the burden of the song, and it is a heavy burden; *Woe unto you, scribes and Pharisees, hypocrites.*

Now each of these woes against the scribes and Pharisees has a reason annexed to it, containing a separate crime charged upon them, proving their hypocrisy, and justifying the judgment of Christ upon them; for his woes, his curses, are never causeless.

(1) They were sworn enemies to the gospel of Christ, and consequently to the salvation of the souls of men (*v.* 13); *They shut up the kingdom of heaven against men,* that is, they did all they could to keep people from believing in Christ, and so entering into his kingdom.

1. They would not go in themselves; *Have any of the rulers,* or *of*

the Pharisees, believed on him? John vii. 48. No; they were too proud to stoop to his meanness, too formal to be reconciled to his plainness; they did not like a religion which insisted so much on humility, self-denial, contempt of the world, and spiritual worship. Repentance was the door of admission into this kingdom, and nothing could be more disagreeable to the Pharisees, who justified and admired themselves, than to repent, that is, to accuse and abase and abhor themselves; therefore they *went not in themselves*; but that was not all.

2. They would not *suffer them that were entering to go in.* It is bad to keep away from Christ ourselves, but it is worse to keep others from him; yet that is commonly the way of hypocrites: they do not love that any should go beyond them in religion, or be better than they.

(2) They made religion and the form of godliness a cloak and stalking-horse to their covetous practices and desires, *v.* 14. Observe here,

1. What their wicked practices were; they *devoured widows' houses,* either by quartering themselves and their attendants upon them for entertainment, which must be of the best for men of their figure; or by insinuating themselves into their affections, and so getting to be the trustees of their estates, which they could make an easy prey of; for who could presume to call such as they were to an account? The thing they aimed at was to enrich themselves; and, this being their chief and highest end, all considerations of justice and equity were laid

aside, and even widows' houses were sacrificed to this.

2. What was the cloak with which they covered this wicked practice; *For a pretence they made long prayers*; very long indeed, if it be true which some of the Jewish writers tell us, that they spent three hours at a time in the formalities of meditation and prayer, and did it thrice every day, which is more than an upright soul, that makes a conscience of being inward with God in the duty, dares pretend ordinarily to do; but to the Pharisees it was easy enough, who never made a business of the duty, and always made a trade of the outside of it. Note, It is no new thing for the show and form of godliness to be made a cloak to the greatest enormities. But dissembled piety, however it passeth now, will be reckoned for as double iniquity, *in the day when God shall judge the secrets of men.*

3. The doom passed upon them for this; *Therefore ye shall receive the greater damnation.* Note, (1) There are degrees of damnation; there are some whose sin is more inexcusable, *and whose ruin will therefore be more intolerable.* (2) The pretences of religion, with which hypocrites disguise or excuse their sin now, will aggravate their condemnation shortly.

(3) While they were such enemies to the conversion of souls to Christianity, they were very industrious in the perversion of them to their faction. They shut up the kingdom of heaven against those that would turn to Christ, but at the same time *compassed sea and land to make proselytes* to themselves, *v.* 15.

(4) Their seeking their own worldly gain and honour more than God's glory put them upon coining false and unwarrantable distinctions, with which they led the people into dangerous mistakes, particularly in the matter of oaths; which, as an evidence of a universal sense of religion, have been by all nations accounted sacred (*v.* 16); *Ye blind guides.*

Now, to prove their blindness, he specifies the matter of swearing, and shows what corrupt casuists they were.

1. He lays down the doctrine they taught.

[1] They allowed swearing by creatures provided they were consecrated to the service of God, and stood in any special relation to him. They allowed swearing by the temple and the altar, though they were the work of men's hands, intended to be the servants of God's honour, not sharers in it. An oath is an appeal to God, to his omniscience and justice; and to make this appeal to any creature is to put that creature in the place of God. See Deut. vi. 13.

[2] They distinguished between an oath by *the temple* and an oath by the *gold of the temple*; an oath by *the altar* and an oath by *the gift upon the altar*; making the latter binding, but not the former. Here was a double wickedness; *First,* That there were some oaths which they dispensed with, and made light of, and reckoned a man was not bound by to assert the truth, or perform a promise. They ought not to have sworn by the temple or the altar; but, when they had so sworn, they were taken in

the words of their mouth. That doctrine cannot be of the God of truth which gives countenance to the breach of faith in any case whatsoever. Oaths are edge-tools and are not to be jested with. *Secondly*, That they preferred the gold before the temple, and the gift before the altar, to encourage people to bring gifts to the altar, and gold to the treasures of the temple, which they hoped to be gainers by.

2. He shows the folly and absurdity of this distinction (*vv.* 17–19); *Ye fools, and blind.* It was in the way of a necessary reproof, not an angry reproach, that Christ called them *fools*.

To convict them of folly, he appeals to themselves, *Whether is greater, the gold* (the golden vessels and ornaments, or the gold in the treasury), *or the temple that sanctifies the gold; the gift, or the altar that sanctifies the gift?* The temple and altar were dedicated to God fixedly, the gold and gift but secondarily. Christ is our altar (Heb. xiii. 10), our temple (John ii. 21); for it is he that sanctifies all our gifts, and puts an acceptableness in them, 1 Pet. ii. 5.

3. He rectifies the mistake (*vv.* 20–22), by reducing all the oaths they had invented to the true intent of an oath, which is, By the name of the Lord: so that though an oath by the temple, or the altar, or heaven, be formally bad, yet it is binding.

(5) They were very strict and precise in the smaller matters of the law, but as careless and loose in the weightier matters, *vv.* 23, 24. They were *partial in the law* (Mal. ii. 9),

would pick and choose their duty, according as they were interested or stood affected. The partiality of the scribes and Pharisees appears here, in two instances.

1. They observed smaller duties, but omitted greater; they were very exact in paying tithes, till it came to *mint*, *anise*, and *cummin*, their exactness in tithing of which would not cost them much, but would be cried up, and they should buy reputation cheap.

But that which Christ here condemns them for, is, that they *omitted the weightier matters of the law, judgment, mercy, and faith*; and their niceness in paying tithes, was, if not to atone before God, yet at least to excuse and palliate to men the omission of those. All the things of God's law are weighty, but those are most weighty, which are most expressive of inward holiness in the heart; the instances of self-denial, contempt of the world, and resignation to God, in which lies the life of religion. Judgment and mercy toward men, and faith toward God, are the weightier matters of the law, the *good things* which the *Lord our God requires* (Mic. vi. 8); to do justly, and love mercy, and humble ourselves by faith to walk with God. This is the obedience which is better than sacrifice or tithe; judgment is preferred before sacrifice, Isa. i. 11.

2. They avoided lesser sins, but committed greater (*v.* 24); *Ye blind guides;* so he had called them before (*v.* 16), for their corrupt teaching; here he calls them so for their corrupt living, for their example was leading as well as their doctrine; and in this also they

were blind and partial; they *strained at a gnat, and swallowed a camel*. In their doctrine they strained at gnats, warned people against every the least violation of the tradition of the elders. But they made no difficulty of those sins which, in comparison with them, were as a camel to a gnat; when they devoured widows' houses, they did indeed *swallow a camel*.

It is not the scrupling of a little sin that Christ here reproves; if it be a sin, though but a gnat, it must be strained at, but the doing of that, and then swallowing a camel. In the smaller matters of the law to be superstitious, and to be profane in the greater, is the hypocrisy here condemned.

(6) They were all for the outside, and not at all for the inside, of religion. They were more desirous and solicitous to appear pious to men than to approve themselves so toward God. This is illustrated by two similitudes.

1. They are compared to a vessel that is clean washed on the outside, but all dirt within, *vv.* 25, 26.

2. They are compared to *whited sepulchres, vv.* 27, 28.

(1) They were fair outside, like sepulchres, *which appear beautiful outward*. Now the righteousness of the scribes and Pharisees was like the ornaments of a grave, or the dressing up of a dead body, only for show. The top of their ambition was to *appear righteous before men*, and to be applauded and had in admiration by them. But,

(2) They were *foul* within, like sepulchres, *full of dead men's bones, and all uncleanness*: so vile are our bodies, when the soul has deserted

them! Thus were they full of hypocrisy and iniquity. Hypocrisy is the worst iniquity of all other.

(7) They pretended a deal of kindness for the memory of the prophets that were dead and gone, while they hated and persecuted those that were present with them. This is put last, because it was the blackest part of their character. God is jealous for his honour in his laws and ordinances, and resents it if they be profaned and abused; but he has often expressed an equal jealousy for his honour in his prophets and ministers, and resents it worse if they be wronged and persecuted: and therefore, when our Lord Jesus comes to this head, he speaks more fully than upon any of the other (*vv.* 29–37); for he that toucheth his ministers, *toucheth his Anointed*, and toucheth the *apple of his eye*.

THE BLIND FOLLOWERS
(*vv.* 34–39)

We have left the blind leaders fallen into the ditch, under Christ's sentence, into the damnation of hell; let us see what will become of the blind followers, of the body of the Jewish church, and particularly Jerusalem.

I. Jesus Christ designs yet to try them with the means of grace; *I send unto you prophets, and wise men, and scribes.* The connection is strange; "*You are a generation of vipers*, not likely to *escape the damnation of hell*"; one would think it should follow, "Therefore you shall never have a prophet sent to you any more"; but no, "*Therefore I will send unto you prophets*, to see if you will yet at length be wrought upon, or else to leave you inexcusable, and to justify God in your ruin." It is therefore ushered in with a note of admiration, behold!

II. He foresees and foretells the ill usage that his messengers would meet with among them; "*Some of them ye shall kill and crucify*, and yet I will send them." Christ knows beforehand how ill his servants will be treated, and yet sends them, and appoints them their measure of sufferings; yet he loves them nevertheless for his thus exposing them, for he designs to glorify himself by their sufferings, and them after them; he will counterbalance them, though not prevent them. Observe,

1. The cruelty of these persecutors; *Ye shall kill and crucify them.* It is no less than the blood, the life-blood, that they thirst after; their lust is not satisfied with any thing short of their destruction, Exod. xv. 9.

2. Their unwearied industry; *Ye shall persecute them from city to city.* As the apostles went from city to city, to preach the gospel, the Jews dodged them, and haunted them, and stirred up persecution against them, Acts xiv. 19; xvii. 13.

3. The pretence of religion in this; they scourged them in their synagogues, their places of worship, where they kept their ecclesiastical courts; so that they did it as a piece of service to the church; cast them out, and said, *Let the Lord be glorified*, Isa. lxvi. 5; John xvi. 2.

III. He imputes the sin of their fathers to them, because they imitated it; *That upon you may come all the righteous blood shed upon the earth*, vv. 35, 36. Though God bear

long with a persecuting generation, he will not bear always; and patience abused, turns into the greatest wrath.

Observe, 1. The extent of this imputation; it takes in *all the righteous blood shed upon the earth*, that is, the blood shed for righteousness' sake, which has all been laid up in God's treasury, and not a drop of it lost, for *it is precious*, Ps. lxxii. 14.

2. The effect of it; *All these things shall come*; all the guilt of this blood, all the punishment of it, it shall *all come upon this generation.* The destruction shall be so dreadful, as if God had once for all arraigned them for all the righteous blood shed in the world. It shall *come upon this generation*; which intimates, that it shall come quickly; some here shall live to see it.

IV. He laments the wickedness of Jerusalem, and justly upbraids them with the many kind offers he had made them, v. 37. See with what concern he speaks of that city; *O Jerusalem, Jerusalem!* The repetition is emphatical, and bespeaks abundance of commiseration. A day or two before Christ had wept over Jerusalem, now he sighed and groaned over it. Jerusalem, *the vision of peace* (so it signifies), must now be the seat of war and confusion.

1. She persecuted God's messengers; *Thou that killest the prophets, and stonest them that are sent unto thee.* This sin is especially charged upon Jerusalem; because there the Sanhedrim, or great council, sat, who took cognizance of church matters, and therefore a prophet

could not perish but in Jerusalem, Luke xiii. 33.

2. She refused and rejected Christ, and gospel offers. The former was a sin *without* remedy, this *against* the remedy.

V. He reads Jerusalem's doom (*vv.* 38, 39); *Therefore behold your house is left unto you desolate*. Both the city and the temple, God's house and their own, all shall be laid waste. But it is especially meant of the temple, which they boasted of, and trusted to; that holy mountain because of which they were so haughty.

1. Their house shall be *deserted*; *It is left unto you*. Christ was now departing from the temple, and never came into it again, but by this word abandoned it to ruin.

2. It shall be *desolate*; *It is left unto you desolate*; it is left *a wilderness*. (1) It was immediately, when Christ left it, in the eyes of all that understood themselves, a very dismal melancholy place. (2) It was, not long after, destroyed and ruined, and *not one stone left upon another*. The lot of Jerusalem's enemies will now become Jerusalem's lot, *to be made of a city a heap, of a defenced city a ruin* (Isa. xxv. 2), *a lofty city laid low, even to the ground*, Isa. xxvi. 5. The temple, that holy and beautiful house, became desolate. When God goes out, all enemies break in.

Lastly, Here is the final farewell that Christ took of them and their temple; *Ye shall not see me henceforth, till ye shall say, Blessed is he that cometh*. This bespeaks,

1. His departure from them. The time was at hand, when *he should leave the world, to go to his Father*,

and be seen no more. *After his resurrection, he was seen only by a few chosen witnesses*, and they saw him not long, but he soon removed to the invisible world, and there will be *till the time of the restitution of all things*, when his welcome at his first coming will be repeated with loud acclamations; *Blessed is he that cometh in the name of the Lord*. Christ will not be seen again till he *come in the clouds, and every eye shall see him* (Rev. i. 7); and then, even they, who, when time was, rejected and pierced him, will be glad to come in among his adorers.

2. Their continued blindness and obstinacy; *Ye shall not see me*, that is, not see me to be the Messiah (for otherwise they did see him upon the cross), not see the light of the truth concerning me, nor *the things that belong to your peace, till ye shall say, Blessed is he that cometh*. They will never be convinced, till Christ's second coming convince them, when it will be too late to make an interest in him, and nothing will remain *but a fearful looking for of judgment*.

CHAPTER TWENTY-FOUR
WHAT IS THE SIGN?
(*vv.* 1–3)

Here is,

I. Christ's quitting *the temple*, and his public work there. He had said, in the close of the foregoing chapter, *Your house is left unto you desolate*; and here he made his words good; *He went out, and departed from the temple*.

II. His private discourse with his disciples; he left the temple, but he did not leave the twelve, who were the seed of the gospel church, which the casting off of the Jews was the enriching of. When he left the temple, his disciples left it too, and came to him. Observe,

1. *His disciples came to him, to show him the buildings of the temple.* They showed Christ these things, and desired him to take notice of them, either,

(1) As being greatly pleased with them themselves, and expecting he should be so too.

Or, (2) As grieving that this house should be left desolate; they showed him the buildings, as if they would move him to reverse the sentence; "Lord, let not this holy and beautiful house, where our fathers praised thee, be made a desolation."

2. Christ, hereupon, foretells the utter ruin and destruction that were coming upon this place, *v.* 2. *See ye not all these things?* They would have Christ look upon them, and be as much in love with them as they were; he would have them look upon them, and be as dead to them as he was. There is such a sight of these things as will do us good; so to see them as to see through them and see to the end of them.

Christ, instead of reversing the decree, ratifies it; *Verily, I say unto you, there shall not be left one stone upon another.*

3. The disciples, not disputing either the truth or the equity of this sentence, nor doubting of the accomplishment of it, enquire more particularly of the time when it should come to pass, and the signs of its approach, *v.* 3.

[1] Some think, these questions do all point at one and the same thing—the destruction of the temple, and the period of the Jewish church and nation, which Christ had himself spoken of as his coming (*ch.* xvi. 28), and which would be the consummation of the age (for so it may be read), the finishing of that dispensation. Or, they thought the destruction of the temple must needs be the end of the world. If that house be laid waste, the world cannot stand; for the Rabbin used to say that the house of the sanctuary was one of the seven things for the sake of which the world was made; and they think, if so, the world will not survive the temple.

[2] Others think their question, *When shall these things be?* refers to the destruction of Jerusalem, and the other two to the end of the world; or Christ's coming may refer to his setting up his gospel kingdom, and the end of the world to the day of judgment. I rather incline to think that their question looked no further than the event Christ now foretold; but it appears by other passages, that they had very confused thoughts of future events; so that perhaps it is not possible to put any certain construction upon this question of theirs.

But Christ, in his answer, though he does not expressly rectify the mistakes of his disciples (that must be done by the pouring out of the Spirit), yet looks further than their question, and instructs his church, not only concerning the great events of that age, the destruction of Jerusalem, but concerning his second coming at the end of time, which here he insensibly slides into a discourse of, and of that it is plain he speaks in the next chapter, which is a continuation of this sermon.

THE LAST DAYS (vv. 4-31)

The disciples had asked concerning the times, *When shall these things be?* Christ gives them no answer to that, after what number of days and years his prediction should be accomplished, for *it is not for us to know the times* (Acts i. 7); but they had asked, *What shall be the sign?* That question he answers fully, for we are concerned to *understand the signs of the times*, ch. xvi. 3. Now the prophecy primarily respects the events near at hand—the destruction of Jerusalem, the period of the Jewish church and state, the calling of the Gentiles, and the setting up of Christ's kingdom in the world; but this prophecy also under the type of Jerusalem's destruction, looks as far forward as the general judgment.

I. Christ here foretells the going forth of deceivers; he begins with a caution, *Take heed that no man deceive you.*

Three times in this discourse he mentions the appearing of *false prophets*, which was, 1. A presage of Jerusalem's ruin. Justly were they who killed the true prophets, left to be ensnared by false prophets; and they who crucified the true Messiah, left to be deceived and broken by false Christs and pretended Messiahs. 2. It was a trial to the disciples of Christ, and therefore agreeable to their state of probation, *that they which are perfect, may be made manifest.*

Now concerning these deceivers, observe here,

(1) The pretences they should come under. Satan acts most mischievously, when he appears as an angel of light: the colour of the greatest good is often the cover of the greatest evil.

(2) The proof they should offer for the making good of these pretences; *They shall show great signs and wonders* (v. 24), not true miracles, those are a divine seal, and with those the doctrine of Christ stands confirmed. But these were *lying wonders* (2 Thess. ii. 9), wrought by Satan (God permitting him), who is *the prince of the power of the air*.

(3) The success they should have in these attempts,

[1] *They shall deceive many* (v. 5), and again, *v.* 11. Note, The devil and his instruments may prevail far in deceiving poor souls; few find the strait gate, but many are drawn into the broad way; many will be imposed upon by their signs and wonders, and many drawn in by the hopes of deliverance from their oppressions. Note, Neither miracles nor multitudes are certain signs of a true church; for *all the world wonders after the beast*, Rev. xiii. 3.

[2] *They shall deceive, if it were possible, the very elect*, v. 24. This bespeaks, *First*, The strength of the delusion. *Secondly*, The safety of the elect in the midst of this danger, which is taken for granted in that parenthesis, *If it were possible*, plainly implying that it is not possible, for they are *kept by the power of God*, that *the purpose of God, according to the election, may stand.*

(4) The repeated cautions which our Saviour gives to his disciples to stand upon their guard against them; *therefore* he gave them warning, that they might watch (*v.* 25); *Behold, I have told you before.*

[1] We must not believe those who say, *Lo, here is Christ*; or, *Lo, he is there, v.* 23. We believe that the true Christ is at the right hand of God, and that his spiritual presence is *where two or three are gathered together in his name.*

[2] We must not go forth after those that say, *He is in the desert,* or, *He is in the secret chambers, v.* 26. We must not hearken to every empiric and pretender, nor follow every one that puts up the finger to point us to a new Christ, and a new gospel.

II. He foretells wars and great commotions among the nations, *vv.* 6, 7. From the time that the Jews rejected Christ, and he *left their house desolate, the sword did never depart from their house, the sword of the Lord* was never quiet, because he had given it a charge against a hypocritical nation and the people of his wrath, and by it brought ruin upon them.

Here is, 1. A prediction of the event of the day; You will now shortly *hear of wars, and rumours of wars.* See what comes of refusing the gospel! Those that will not hear the messengers of peace, shall be made to hear the messengers of war.

2. A prescription of the duty of the day; *See that ye be not troubled.* Is it possible to hear such sad news, and not be troubled? Yet, where the heart is fixed, trusting in God, it is kept in peace, and is not afraid, no not of the evil tidings of wars,

and rumours of wars; no not the noise of *Arm, arm.*

We must not be troubled, for two reasons.

(1) Because we are bid to expect this: the Jews must be punished, ruin must be brought upon them; by this the justice of God and the honour of the Redeemer must be asserted; and therefore *all those things must come to pass*; the word is gone out of God's mouth, and it shall be accomplished in its season.

(2) Because we are still to expect worse; *The end is not yet*; the end of time is not, and, while time lasts, we must expect trouble, and that the end of one affliction will be but the beginning of another; or, "The end of these troubles is not yet; there must be more judgments than one made use of to bring down the Jewish power. Therefore be not troubled, do not give way to fear and trouble, sink not under the present burden, but rather gather in all the strength and spirit you have, to encounter what is yet before you.

III. He foretells other judgments more immediately sent of God— *famines, pestilences, and earthquakes.* Beside war (and that is enough), there shall be,

1. *Famine,* signified by the *black horse* under the *third seal,* Rev. vi. 5, 6.

2. *Pestilences,* signified by the *pale horse, and death upon him,* and *the grave at his heels,* under the *fourth seal,* Rev. vi. 7, 8. This destroys without distinction, and in a little time lays heaps upon heaps.

3. *Earthquakes in divers places,* or from place to place, pursuing those that flee from them, as they did

from the earthquake *in the days of Uzziah*, Zech. xiv. 5. When we look forward to the eternity of misery that is before the obstinate refusers of Christ and his gospel, we may truly say, concerning the greatest temporal judgments, "They are but the beginning of sorrows; bad as things are with them, there are worse behind."

IV. He foretells the persecution of his own people and ministers, and a general apostasy and decay in religion thereupon, *vv.* 9, 10, 12. Observe,

1. The *cross* itself foretold, *v.* 9. Christ had told his disciples, when he first sent them out, what hard things they should suffer; but they had hitherto experienced little of it, and therefore he reminds them again, that the less they had suffered, the more there was behind to be filled up, Col. i. 24.

(1) They shall be *afflicted* with bonds and imprisonments, *cruel mockings and scourgings*, as blessed Paul (2 Cor. xi. 23–25); not killed outright, but *killed all the day long, in deaths often*, killed so as to feel themselves die, *made a spectacle to the world*, 1 Cor. iv. 9, 11.

(2) They shall be *killed*; so cruel are the church's enemies, that nothing less will satisfy them than the blood of the saints, which they thirst after, suck, and shed, like water.

(3) They shall be *hated of all nations for Christ's name sake*, as he had told them before, *ch.* x. 22. The world was generally leavened with enmity and malignity to Christians.

2. *The offence of the cross, vv.* 10–12. Satan thus carries on his interest by force of arms, though

Christ, at length, will bring glory to himself out of the sufferings of his people and ministers. Three ill effects of persecution are here foretold.

(1) The *apostasy* of some. When the profession of Christianity begins to cost men dear, *then shall many be offended*, shall first fall out with, and then fall off from, their profession.

(2) The *malignity* of others. When persecution is in fashion, envy, enmity, and malice, are strangely diffused into the minds of men by contagion: and charity, tenderness, and moderation, are looked upon as singularities, which make a man like a speckled bird. Then *they shall betray one another*.

(3) The general *declining* and *cooling* of most, *v.* 12. In seducing times, when false prophets arise, in persecuting times, when the saints are hated, expect these two things,

[1] The *abounding* of iniquity; though the world always lies in wickedness, yet there are some times in which it may be said, that *iniquity doth* in a special manner abound.

[2] The *abating* of love; this is the consequence of the former; *Because iniquity shall abound, the love of many shall wax cold.* It is too common for professors of religion to grow cool in their profession, when the wicked are hot in their wickedness; as the church of Ephesus in bad times *left her first love*, Rev. ii. 2–4.

3. Comfort administered in reference to this offence of the cross, for the support of the Lord's people under it (*v.* 13); *He that endures to*

the end, shall be saved. Perseverance wins the crown, through free grace, and shall wear it. *They shall be saved:* perhaps they may be delivered out of their troubles, and comfortably survive them in this world; but it is eternal salvation that is here intended. They that endure to the end of their days, shall then receive the end of their faith and hope, *even the salvation of their souls,* 1 Pet. i. 9; Rom. ii. 7; Rev. iii. 20. The crown of glory will make amends for all; and a believing regard to that will enable us to choose rather to die at a stake with the persecuted, than to live in a palace with the persecutors.

V. He foretells the preaching of the gospel in all the world (*v.* 14); *This gospel shall be preached, and then shall the end come.* Observe here, 1. It is called *the gospel of the kingdom,* because it reveals the kingdom of grace, which leads to the kingdom of glory; sets up Christ's kingdom in this world; and secures ours in the other world. 2. This gospel, sooner or later, is to be preached in all the world, to every creature, and all nations are to be discipled by it; for in it Christ is to be *Salvation to the ends of the earth;* for this end the gift of tongues was *the first-fruits of the Spirit.* 3. The gospel is preached *for a witness to all nations,* that is, a faithful declaration of the mind and will of God concerning the duty which God requires from man, and the recompence which man may expect from God. It is a *record* (1 John v. 11), it is a *witness,* for those who believe, that they shall be saved, and against those who persist in unbelief, that they shall be damned. See Mark xvi. 16. But how does this come in here?

(1) It is intimated that the gospel should be, if not heard, yet at least heard of, throughout the then known world, before the destruction of Jerusalem; that the Old-Testament church should not be quite dissolved till the New Testament was pretty well settled, had got considerable footing, and began to make some figure. Better is the face of a corrupt degenerate church than none at all. Within forty years after Christ's death, the *sound* of the gospel was *gone forth to the ends of the earth,* Rom. x. 18. St. Paul *fully preached the gospel from Jerusalem, and round about unto Illyricum;* and the other apostles were not idle. The persecuting of the saints at Jerusalem helped to disperse them, so that they *went every where, preaching the word,* Acts viii. 1–4. And when the tidings of the Redeemer are sent over all parts of the world, then shall come the end of the Jewish state. Thus, that which they thought to prevent, by putting Christ to death, they thereby procured; all men *believed on him, and the Romans came, and took away their place and nation,* John xi. 48. Paul speaks of the gospel being *come to all the world, and preached to every creature,* Col. i. 6–23.

(2) It is likewise intimated that even in times of temptation, trouble, and persecution, the gospel of the kingdom shall be preached and propagated, and shall force its way through the greatest opposition.

(3) That which seems chiefly intended here, is, that the end of·the

world shall be *then*, and not till then, when the gospel has done its work in the world. The gospel shall be preached, and that work carried on, when you are dead; so that all nations, first or last, shall have either the enjoyment, or the refusal, of the gospel; and *then cometh the end*, when the kingdom *shall be delivered up to God, even the Father*. The world shall stand as long as any of God's chosen ones remain uncalled; but, when they are all gathered in, it will be set on fire immediately.

VI. He foretells more particularly the ruin that was coming upon the people of the Jews, their city, temple, and nation, *vv.* 15, &c.

1. The Romans *setting up the abomination of desolation in the holy place, v.* 15. Now, (1) Some understand by this an image, or statue, set up in the temple by some of the Roman governors, which was very offensive to the Jews, provoked them to rebel, and so brought the desolation upon them. (2) Others choose to expound it by the parallel place (Luke xxi. 20), *when ye shall see Jerusalem compassed with armies*. Jerusalem was the holy city, Canaan the holy land, the Mount Moriah, which lay about Jerusalem, for its nearness to the temple was, they thought, in a particular manner holy ground; on the country lying round about Jerusalem the Roman army was encamped, that was the abomination that made desolate.

2. The means of preservation which thinking men should betake themselves to (*vv.* 16, 20); *Then let them which are in Judea, flee*. Then conclude there is no other way to help yourselves than by flying for the same.

Now those to whom Christ said this immediately, did not live to see this dismal day, none of all the twelve but John only; they needed not to be hidden in the mountains (Christ hid them in heaven), but they left the direction to their successors in profession, who pursued it, and it was of use to them; for when the Christians in Jerusalem and Judea saw the ruin coming on, they all retired to a town called *Pella*, on the other side Jordan, where they were safe; so that of the many thousands that perished in the destruction of Jerusalem, there was not so much as one Christian. See *Euseb. Eccl. Hist.* lib. 3, cap. 5. Thus *the prudent man foresees the evil, and hides himself*, Prov. xxii. 3; Heb. xi. 7. This warning was not kept private. St. Matthew's gospel was published long before that destruction, so that others might have taken the advantage of it; but their perishing through their unbelief of this, was a figure of their eternal perishing through their unbelief of the warnings Christ gave concerning the wrath to come.

3. The greatness of the troubles which should immediately ensue (*v.* 21).

It was a desolation unparalleled, such as *was not since the beginning of the world, nor ever shall be*. Many a city and kingdom has been made desolate, but never any with a desolation like this.

It was a desolation which, if it should continue long, would be intolerable, so that *no flesh should be saved, v.* 22. He doth not say, "No *soul* shall be saved," for the destruction of the flesh may be for *the saving of the spirit in the day of the Lord Jesus*; but temporal lives will be sacrificed so profusely, that one would think, if it last awhile, it would make a full end.

But here is one word of comfort in the midst of all this terror—that *for the elects' sake these days shall be shortened*, not made shorter than what God had determined (for *that which is determined, shall be poured upon the desolate*, Dan. ix. 27), but shorter than what he might have decreed, if he had dealt with them according to their sins; shorter than what the enemy designed, who would have cut all off, if God who made use of them to serve his own purpose, had not set bounds to their wrath; shorter than one who judged by human probabilities would have imagined.

And now comes in the repeated caution, which was opened before, to take heed of being ensnared by false Christs, and false prophets (*vv.* 23, &c.), who would promise them deliverance, as the lying prophets in Jeremiah's time (Jer. xiv. 13; xxiii. 16, 17; xxvii. 16; xxviii. 2), but would delude them. Times of great trouble are times of great temptation, and therefore we have need to double our guard then. If they shall say, *Here is a Christ, or there is one*, that shall deliver us from the Romans, do not heed them, it is all but talk; such a deliverance is not to be expected, and therefore not such a deliverer.

VII. He foretells the sudden spreading of the gospel in the world, about the time of these great events (*vv.* 27, 28); *As the lightning comes out of the east, so shall the coming of the Son of man be.*

1. It seems primarily to be meant of his coming to set up his spiritual kingdom in the world; where the gospel came in its light and power, there the Son of man came, and in a way quite contrary to the fashion of the seducers and false Christs, who came creeping *in the desert*, or the *secret chambers* (2 Tim. iii. 6); whereas Christ comes not with such a *spirit of fear*, but *of power, and of love, and of a sound mind*.

2. Some understand these verses of the coming of the Son of man *to destroy Jerusalem*, Mal. iii. 1, 2, 5. So much was there of an extraordinary display of divine power and justice in that event, that it is called *the coming of Christ*.

Now here are two things intimated concerning it.

(1) That to the most it would be as unexpected as a flash of lightning, which indeed gives warning of the clap of thunder which follows, but is itself surprising. The seducers say, *Lo, here is Christ* to deliver us; or there is one, a creature of their own fancies; but ere they are aware, the wrath of the Lamb, the true Christ, will arrest them, and they shall not escape.

(2) That it might be as justly expected as that the eagle should fly to the carcases; though they put far from them the evil day, yet the desolation will come as certainly as the birds of prey to a dead carcase, that lies exposed in the open field.

3. It is very applicable to the day of judgment, the coming of our Lord Jesus Christ in that day, and *our gathering together unto him*, 2 Thess. ii. 1. Now see here,

(1) How he shall come; *as the lightning*. He shall *come in the clouds*, as the lightning doth, and *every eye shall see him*, as they say it is natural for all living creatures to turn their faces towards the lightning, Rev. i. 7. Christ will appear to all the world, from one end of heaven to the other; nor shall any thing be hid from the light and heat of that day.

(2) How the saints shall be gathered to him; as the eagles are to the carcase by natural instinct, and with the greatest swiftness and alacrity imaginable. Saints, when they shall be fetched to glory, will be carried as on eagles' wings (Exod. xix. 4), as on angels' wings.

VIII. He foretells his second coming at the *end of time*, *vv.* 29–31. *The sun shall be darkened*, &c.

1. Some think this is to be understood only of the destruction of Jerusalem and the Jewish nation.

2. It seems rather to refer to Christ's second coming. The destruction of the particular enemies of the church was typical of the complete conquest of them all; and therefore what will be done really at the great day, may be applied metaphorically to those destructions: but still we must attend to the principal scope of them; and while we are all agreed to expect Christ's second coming, what need is there to put such strained constructions as some do, upon these verses, which speak of·it so clearly, and so agreeably to other scriptures, especially when Christ is here answering an enquiry concerning his coming at the end of the world, which Christ was never shy of speaking of to his disciples?

The only objection against this, is, that it is said to be *immediately after the tribulation of those days*; but as to that, (1) It is usual in the prophetical style to speak of things great and certain as near and just at hand, only to express the greatness and certainty of them. (2) *A thousand years are* in God's sight *but as one day*, 2 Pet. iii. 8. It is there urged, with reference to this very thing, and so it might be said to be immediately after.

Now concerning Christ's second coming, it is here foretold,

[1] That there shall be then a great and amazing change of the creatures, and particularly the *heavenly bodies* (*v.* 29). *The sun shall be darkened, and the moon shall not give her light*. The moon shines with a borrowed light, and therefore if the sun, from whom she borrows her light, is turned into darkness, she must fail of course, and become bankrupt. *The stars shall fall*; and shall lose their light, and disappear, and be as if they were fallen; and *the powers of heaven shall be shaken*.

[2] That *then shall appear the sign of the Son of man in heaven* (*v.* 30), the Son of man himself, as it follows here, *They shall see the Son of man coming in the clouds*. At his first coming, he was *set for a Sign that should be spoken against* (Luke ii. 34), but at his second coming, a sign that should be admired. It will certainly be such a clear convincing sign as will dash infidelity quite out of countenance, and fill their faces with shame, who said, *Where is the promise of his coming?*

[3] That *then all the tribes of the earth shall mourn*, *v.* 30. See Rev. i.

7. *All the kindreds of the earth shall then wail because of him*; some of all the tribes and kindreds of the earth shall mourn; for the greater part will tremble at his approach, while the chosen remnant, one of a family and two of a tribe, shall lift up their heads with joy, knowing that their redemption draws nigh, and their Redeemer.

[4] That *then they shall see the Son of man coming in the clouds of heaven, with power and great glory*.

[5] That *he shall send his angels with a great sound of a trumpet, v.* 31. By the law, trumpets were to be sounded for the calling of assemblies (Numb. x. 2), in praising God (Ps. lxxxi. 3), in offering sacrifices (Numb. x. 10), and in proclaiming the year of jubilee, Lev. xxv. 9. Very fitly therefore shall there be the sound of a trumpet at the last day, when the general assembly shall be called, when the praises of God shall be gloriously celebrated, when sinners shall fall as sacrifices to divine justice, and when the saints shall enter upon their eternal jubilee.

[6] That *they shall gather together his elect from the four winds.* The elect of God are scattered abroad (John xi. 52), there are some in all places, in all nations (Rev. vii. 9); but when that great gathering day comes, there shall not one of them be missing; distance of place shall keep none out of heaven, if distance of affection do not. *Undique ad cœlos tantundem est viæ— Heaven is equally accessible from every place.* See *ch.* viii. 11; Isa. xliii. 6; xlix. 12.

We have here the practical application of the foregoing pre-diction; in general, we must expect and prepare for the events here foretold.

I. We must expect them; "*Now learn a parable of the fig-tree, vv.* 32, 33. The parable of the fig-tree is no more than this, that its budding and blossoming are a presage of summer; for as the *stork* in the heaven, so the trees of the field, *know their appointed time.* The beginning of the working of second causes assures us of the progress and perfection of it. Thus when God begins to fulfil prophecies, he will make an end. There is a certain series in the works of providence, as there is in the works of nature.

Now touching the events foretold here, which we are to expect,

1. Christ here assures us of the certainty of them (*v.* 35); *Heaven and earth shall pass away*; they continue this day indeed, according to God's ordinance, but they shall not continue for ever (Ps. cii. 25, 26; 2 Pet. iii. 10); *but my words shall not pass away.* Note, The word of Christ is more sure and lasting than heaven and earth. *Hath he spoken? And shall he not do it?*

2. He here instructs us as to the time of them, *vv.* 34, 36.

(1) As to *these things*, the wars, seductions, and persecutions, here foretold, and especially the ruin of the Jewish nation; "*This generation shall not pass away, till all these things be fulfilled* (*v.* 34); there are those now alive, that shall see Jerusalem destroyed, and the Jewish church brought to an end."

(2) But as to *that day and hour* which will put a period to time, *that knoweth no man, v.* 36. There-

fore take heed of confounding these two, as *they* did, who, from the words of Christ and the apostles' letters, inferred that *the day of Christ was at hand*, 2 Thess. ii. 2. No, it was not; *this generation*, and many another, *shall pass*, before *that day and hour* come. Note, [1] There is a certain day and hour fixed for the judgment to come; it is called *the day of the Lord*, because so unalterably fixed. [2] That day and hour are a great secret. *No man knows it*; not the wisest by their sagacity, not the best by any divine discovery. This is one of those *secret things* which *belong to the Lord our God*.

II. To this end we must expect these events, that we may prepare for them, *vv.* 37–41. In these verses we have such an idea given us of the judgment day, as may serve to startle and awaken us, that we may not sleep as others do.

It will be a surprising day, and a separating day.

1. It will be a surprising day, as the deluge was to the old world, *vv.* 37–39. That which he here intends to describe, is, the posture of the world at the coming of the Son of man; besides his first coming, to save, he has other comings to judge. He saith (John ix. 39), *For judgment I am come*; and for judgment he will come; for all judgment is committed to him, both that of the word, and that of the sword.

2. It will be a separating day (*vv.* 40, 41); *Then shall two be in the field.* Two ways this may be applied.

(1) We may apply it to the success of the gospel, especially at the first preaching of it; it divided the world; *some believed the things which were spoken*, and were taken to Christ; *others believed not*, and were left to perish in their unbelief.

(2) We may apply it to the second coming of Jesus Christ, and the separation which will be made in that day. He had said before (*v.* 31), that the elect will be *gathered together*. Christ will come unlooked for, will find people busy at their usual occupations, *in the field, at the mill*; and then, according as they are vessels of mercy prepared for glory, or vessels of wrath prepared for ruin, accordingly it will be with them; the one taken *to meet the Lord and his angels in the air, to be for ever with him and them*; the other left to the devil and his angels, who, when Christ has gathered out his own, will sweep up the residue.

III. Here is a general exhortation to us, *to watch, and be ready* against that day comes, enforced by divers weighty considerations, *v.* 42, &c. Observe,

1. The duty required; *Watch, and be ready*, *vv.* 42, 44.

(1) *Watch therefore*, *v.* 42. Note, It is the great duty and interest of all the disciples of Christ to watch, to be awake and keep awake, that they may mind their business. As a sinful state or way is compared to *sleep*, senseless and inactive (1 Thess. v. 6), so a gracious state or way is compared to *watching* and *waking*.

(2) *Be ye also ready*. We wake in vain, if we do not get ready. It is not enough to *look* for such things; but we must therefore *give diligence*, 2 Pet. iii. 11, 14.

2. The reasons to induce us to this watchfulness and diligent pre-

paration for that day; which are two.

(1) Because the time of our Lord's coming is very uncertain. This is the reason immediately annexed to the double exhortation (*vv.* 42, 44); and it is illustrated by a comparison, *v.* 43. If the master of a house had notice that a thief would come such a night, and such a watch of the night (for they divided the night into four watches, allowing three hours to each), and would make an attempt upon his house, though it were the midnight-watch, when he was most sleepy, yet he would be up, and listen to every noise in every corner, and be ready to give him a warm reception. Now, though we know not *just when* our Lord will come, yet, knowing that he *will* come, and come quickly, and without any other warning that what he hath given in his word, it concerns us to watch always.

(2) Because the issue of our Lord's coming will be very happy and comfortable to those that shall be found ready, but very dismal and dreadful to those that shall not, *v.* 45, &c. This is represented by the different state of good and bad servants, when their lord comes to reckon with them. It is likely to be well or ill with us to eternity, according as we are found ready or unready at that day; for Christ comes *to render to every man according to his works*. Now this parable, with which the .chapter closes, is applicable to all Christians, who are in profession and obligation God's servants; but it seems especially intended as a warning to ministers; for the servant spoken of is a *steward*.

THE TEN VIRGINS
(*vv.* 1–13)

I. That in general which is to be illustrated is, *the kingdom of heaven*, the state of things under the gospel, the external kingdom of Christ, and the administration and success of it. The professors of Christianity shall then be likened to these ten virgins, and shall be thus distinguished.

II. That by which it is illustrated, is, a marriage solemnity. It was a custom sometimes used among the Jews on that occasion, that the bridegroom came, attended with his friends, late in the night, to the house of the bride, where she expected him, attended with her bride-maids; who, upon notice given of the bridegroom's approach, were to go out with lamps in their hands, to light him into the house with ceremony and formality, in order to the celebrating of the nuptials with great mirth. And some think that on these occasions they had usually *ten virgins*; for the Jews never held a synagogue, circumcised, kept the passover, or contracted marriage, but ten persons at least were present. Boaz, when he married Ruth, had *ten witnesses*, Ruth iv. 2. Now in this parable,

1. The *Bridegroom* is our Lord Jesus Christ; he is so represented in the 45th Psalm, Solomon's Song, and often in the New Testament.

2. The virgins are the professors of religion, members of the church; but here represented as *her companions* (Ps. xlv. 14), as elsewhere her *children* (Isa. liv. 1), her *ornaments*, Isa. xlix. 18.

3. The office of these virgins is to meet the bridegroom, which is as much their happiness as their duty. They come to wait *upon* the bridegroom when he appears, and in the mean time to wait *for* him. See here the nature of Christianity. As Christians, we profess ourselves to be, (1) Attendants upon Christ, to do him honour, as the glorious Bridegroom, to be to him for a name and a praise, especially then when he shall come to be glorified in his saints. We must follow him as honorary servants do their masters, John xii. 26. Hold up the name, and hold forth the praise of the exalted Jesus; this is our business. (2) Expectants of Christ, and of his second coming. As Christians, we profess, not only to believe and look for, but to love and long for, the appearing of Christ, and to act in our whole conversation with a regard to it. The second coming of Christ is the centre in which all the lines of our religion meet, and to which the whole of the divine life hath a constant reference and tendency.

4. Their chief concern is to have lights in their hands, when they attend the bridegroom, thus to do him honour and do him service. Note, Christians are children of light. The gospel is light, and they who receive it must not only be enlightened by it themselves, but must *shine as lights*, must *hold it forth*, Phil. ii. 15, 16. This in general.

Now concerning these ten virgins, we may observe,

(1) Their different character, with the proof and evidence of it.

[1] Their character was, that *five were wise, and five foolish* (*v.* 2); and *wisdom excelleth folly, as far as light excelleth darkness*; so saith Solomon, a competent judge, Eccl. ii. 13. Sincere Christians are the *wise* virgins, and hypocrites the *foolish ones*, as in another parable they are represented by wise and foolish builders.

[2] The evidence of this character was in the very thing which they were to attend to; by that they are judged of.

First, It was the folly of the foolish virgins, that they *took their lamps, and took no oil with them*, *v.* 3. They had just oil enough to make their lamps burn for the present, to make a show with, as if they intended to meet the bridegroom; but no cruse or bottle of oil with them if the bridegroom tarried; thus hypocrites,

1. They have no principle within. They have a lamp of profession in their hands, but have not in their hearts that stock of sound knowledge, rooted dispositions, and settled resolutions, which is necessary to carry them through the services and trials of the present state.

2. They have no prospect of, nor make provision for, what is to come. They took lamps for a present show, but not oil for after use.

Secondly, It was the wisdom of the wise virgins, that *they took oil in their vessels with their lamps*, *v.* 4. They had a good principle within, which would maintain and keep up their profession. 1. The heart is the vessel, which it is our wisdom to get furnished. 2. Grace is the *oil* which we must have in this *vessel*; in the tabernacle there was constant provision made of *oil for the light,* Exod. xxxv. 14. Our light must shine before men in good works, but this cannot be, or not long, unless there be a fixed active principle in the heart, of faith in Christ, and love to God and our brethren.

(2) Their common fault, during the bridegroom's delay; *They all slumbered and slept, v.* 5. Observe here,

[1] The bridegroom tarried, that is, he did not come out so soon as they expected. But though Christ tarry past *our* time, he will not tarry past the *due* time.

[2] While he tarried, those that waited for him, grew careless, and forgot what they were attending; *They all slumbered and slept*; as if they had given over looking for him; for *when the Son of man cometh,* he will *not find faith,* Luke xviii. 8.

(3) The surprising summons given them, to attend the bridegroom (*v.* 6); *At midnight there was a cry made, Behold, the bridegroom cometh.*

(4) The address they all made to answer this summons (*v.* 7); *They all arose, and trimmed their lamps,* snuffed them and supplied them with oil, and went about with all expedition to put themselves in a posture to receive the bridegroom. Now, [1] This, in the wise virgins, bespeaks an actual preparation for the Bridegroom's coming. [2] In the foolish virgins, it denotes a vain confidence, and conceit of the goodness of their state, and their readiness for another world.

(5) The distress which the foolish virgins were in, for want of *oil, vv.*

8, 9. This bespeaks, [1] The apprehensions which some hypocrites have of the misery of their state, even on this side death, when God opens their eyes to see their folly, and themselves perishing *with a lie in their right hand.* Or, however, [2] The real misery of their state on the other side death, and in the judgment; how far their fair, but false, profession of religion will be from availing them any thing in the great day; see what comes of it.

First, Their lamps are gone out. The lamps of hypocrites often go out in this life; when they who have begun in the spirit, end in the flesh, and the hypocrisy breaks out in an open apostasy, 2 Pet. ii. 20.

Secondly, They wanted oil to supply them when they were going out. Note, Those that take up short of true grace, will certainly find the want of it one time or other. An external profession well humoured may carry a man far, but it will not carry him through; it may light him along this world, but the damps of the valley of the shadow of death will put it out.

Thirdly, They would gladly be beholden to the wise virgins for a supply out of their vessels; *Give us of your oil.* Note, The day is coming, when carnal hypocrites would gladly be found in the condition of true Christians. God would have given them oil, had they asked in time; but there is no buying when the market is over, no bidding when the inch of candle is dropped.

Fourthly, They were denied a share in their companions' oil. It is a sad presage of a repulse with God, when they were thus repulsed by good people. *The wise answered, Not so*; that peremptory denial is not in the original, but supplied by the translators: these wise virgins would rather give a reason without a positive refusal, than (as many do) give a positive refusal without a reason. They were well inclined to help their neighbours in distress; but, We must not, we cannot, we dare not, do it, *lest there be not enough for us and you*; charity begins at home; but *go, and buy for yourselves*. Note, 1. Those that would be saved, must have grace of their own. 2. Those that have most grace, have none to spare; all we have, is little enough for ourselves to appear before God in.

(6) The coming of the bridegroom, and the issue of all this different character of the wise and foolish virgins. See what came of it.

[1] *While they went out to buy, the bridegroom came.* Note, With regard to those that put off their great work to the last, it is a thousand to one, that they have not time to do it then. Getting grace is a work of time, and cannot be done in a hurry.

[2] *They that were ready, went in with him to the marriage.*

[3] *The door was shut*, as is usual when all the company is come, that are to be admitted. The door was shut, *First*, To secure those that were within; that, being now made *pillars in the house of our God, they may go no more out*, Rev. iii. 12. *Secondly*, To exclude those that were out. The state of saints and sinners will then be unalterably fixed, and those that are shut out then, will be shut out for ever.

[4] The foolish virgins came when it was *too late* (*v.* 11); *Afterward came also the other virgins*.

[5] They were *rejected*, as Esau was (*v.* 12); *I know you not*. Note, We are all concerned to *seek the Lord while he may be found*; for there is a time coming when he will not be found.

Lastly, Here is a practical inference drawn from this parable (*v.* 13); *Watch therefore*. We had it before (*ch.* xxiv. 42), and here it is repeated as the most needful caution.

THE PARABLE OF THE TALENTS (*vv.* 14–30)

We have here the parable of the *talents* committed to three servants; this implies that we are in a state of work and business, as the former implies that we are in a state of expectancy.

In this parable, 1. The *Master* is Christ, who is the absolute Owner and Proprietor of all persons and things, and in a special manner of his church; into his hands all things are delivered. 2. The *servants* are Christians, his own servants, so they are called; born in his house, bought with his money, devoted to his praise, and employed in his work.

We have three things, in general, in this parable.

I. The trust committed to these servants; Their master *delivered to them his goods*: having appointed them to work (for Christ keeps no servants to be idle), he left them something to work upon. Now observe here,

(1) On what occasion this trust was committed to these servants; The master was *travelling into a far*

country. This is explained, Eph. iv. 8. *When he ascended on high, he gave gifts unto men*.

(2) In what proportion this trust was committed. He gave to some more, to others less; to one *five* talents, to another *two*, to another *one*; to everyone according to his several ability. When Divine Providence has made a difference in men's ability, as to mind, body, estate, relation, and interest, divine grace dispenses spiritual gifts accordingly, but still the ability itself is from him.

II. The different management and improvement of this trust, which we have an account of, *vv.* 16–18.

1. Two of the servants did well.

(1) They were diligent and faithful; *They went, and traded*; they put the money they were entrusted with, to the use for which it was intended—laid it out in goods, and made returns of it; as soon as ever their master was gone, they immediately applied themselves to their business. Those that have so much work to do, as every Christian has, need to set about it quickly, and lose no time.

(2) They were successful; they doubled their stock, and in a little time made *cent. per cent.* of it: he that had *five talents*, soon made them *other five*.

Observe, The returns were in proportion to the receivings. From those to whom he has given but two talents, he expects only the improvement of two, which may encourage those who are placed in a lower and narrower sphere of usefulness; if they lay out themselves to do good according to the best of

their capacity and opportunity, they shall be accepted, though they do not so much good as others.

2. The third did ill (*v.* 18); *He that had received one talent, went, and hid his lord's money*. The unfaithful servant was he that had but *one* talent: doubtless there are many that have five talents, and bury them all; great abilities, great advantages, and yet do no good with them.

He hid his *lord's* money; had it been his *own*, he might have done as he pleased; but, whatever abilities and advantages we have, they are not our *own*, we are but stewards of them, and must give account to our Lord, whose goods they are. It was an aggravation of his slothfulness, that his fellow-servants were busy and successful in trading, and their zeal should have provoked his. Are others active, and shall we be idle?

III. The account of this improvement, *v.* 19. 1. The account is deferred; it is not *till after a long time* that they are reckoned with; not that the master neglects his affairs, or that God is *slack concerning his promise* (2 Pet. iii. 9); no, he is *ready to judge* (1 Pet. iv. 5); but every thing must be done in its time and order. 2. Yet the day of account comes at last; *The lord of those servants reckoneth with them*. Now here is,

(1) The good account of the faithful servants; and here observe,

[1] The servants *giving up the account* (*vv.* 20, 22); "*Lord, thou deliveredst to me five talents*, and to me *two*; behold, *I have gained five talents*, and *I two* talents *more*."

First, Christ's faithful servants acknowledge with thankfulness his vouchsafements to them; *Lord, thou deliveredst to me* such and such things.

Secondly, They produce, as an evidence of their faithfulness, what they have gained. Note, God's good stewards have something to show for their diligence; *Show me thy faith by thy works.*

[2] The master's acceptance and approbation of their account, *vv.* 21, 23.

First, He commended them; *Well done, good and faithful servant.*

Secondly, He rewards them. The faithful servants of Christ shall not be put off with bare commendation; no, all their work and labour of love shall be rewarded.

Now this reward is here expressed two ways.

1. In one expression agreeable to the parable; *Thou hast been faithful over a few things, I will make thee ruler over many things.* It is usual in the courts of princes, and families of great men, to advance those to higher offices, that have been faithful in lower.

2. In another expression, which slips out of the parable into the thing signified by it; *Enter thou into the joy of thy Lord.*

(2) The bad account of the slothful servant. Observe,

[1] His apology for himself, *vv.* 24, 25. Though he had received but *one* talent, for that one he is called to account. The smallness of our receiving will not excuse us from a reckoning. None shall be called to an account for more than they have received; but for what we have, we must all account. His excuse bespeaks,

1. The sentiments of an enemy; *I knew thee, that thou art a hard man.* This was like that wicked saying of the house of Israel, *The way of the Lord is not equal,* Ezek. xviii. 25. Thus his *defence* is his *offence*. *The foolishness of man perverteth his way,* and then, as if that would mend the matter, *his heart fretteth against the Lord.*

2. The spirit of a slave; *I was afraid*. This ill affection toward God arose from his false notions of him; and nothing is more unworthy of God, nor more hinders our duty to him, than slavish fear.

[2] His Lord's answer to this apology.

First, His conviction, *vv.* 26, 27. Two things he is convicted of.

1. Slothfulness; *Thou wicked and slothful servant.* Those that are idle in the affairs of their souls, are not only idle, but something worse, 1 Tim. v. 13. When men sleep, the enemy sows tares.

2. Self-contradiction (*vv.* 26, 27); *Thou knewest that I reap where I sowed not: thou oughtest therefore to have put my money to the exchangers.* Note, The hard thoughts which sinners have of God, though false and unjust, will be so far from justifying their wickedness and slothfulness, that they will rather aggravate and add to their guilt.

Secondly, His condemnation. The slothful servant is sentenced,

1. To be deprived of his talent (*vv.* 28, 29); *Take therefore the talent from him.* The talents were first disposed of by the Master, as an absolute Owner, but this was now disposed of by him as a Judge; he takes it from the unfaithful

servant, to punish him, and gives it to him that was eminently faithful, to reward him. And the meaning of this part of the parable we have in the reason of the sentence (*v.* 29), *To every one that hath shall be given.* This may be applied, (1) To the blessings of this life—worldly wealth and possessions. These we are entrusted with, to be used for the glory of God, and the good of those about us. Now *he that hath* these things, and useth them for these ends, he *shall have abundance*; perhaps abundance of the things themselves, at least, abundance of comfort in them, and of better things; but *from him that hath not*, that is, that hath these things as if he had them not, had not power to eat of them, or to do good with them. (2) We may apply it to the means of grace. They who are diligent in improving the opportunities they have, God will enlarge them, will *set before them an open door* (Rev. iii. 8); but they who know not the day of their visitation, shall have the things that belong to their peace hid from their eyes.

2. He is sentenced to be *cast into outer darkness, v.* 30. Here,

(1) His character is that of an *unprofitable servant*.

(2) His doom is, to be *cast into outer darkness*. Here, as in what was said to the faithful servants, our Saviour slides insensibly out of the parable into the thing intended by it, and it serves as a key to the whole; for, *outer darkness, where there is weeping and gnashing of teeth*, is, in Christ's discourses, the common periphrasis of the miseries of the damned in hell. This will be

the portion of the slothful servant.

SHEEP AND GOATS
(*vv.* 31–46)

We have here a description of the process of the last judgment in the great day. There are some passages in it that are parabolical; as the separating between the sheep and the goats, and the dialogues between the judge and the persons judged: but there is no thread of similitude carried through the discourse, and therefore it is rather to be called a draught or delineation of the final judgment, than a parable; it is, as it were, the explanation of the former parables. And here we have,

I. The placing of the judge upon the judgment-seat (*v.* 31); *When the Son of man shall come.*

II. The appearing of all the children of men before him (*v.* 32); *Before him shall be gathered all nations.*

III. The distinction that will then be made between the precious and the vile; *He shall separate them one from another*, as the tares and wheat are separated at the harvest, the good fish and the bad at the shore, the corn and chaff in the floor. This separation will be so exact, that the most inconsiderable saints shall not be lost in the crowd of sinners, nor the most plausible sinner hid in the crowd of saints (Ps. i. 5), but every one shall go to his own place. This is compared to a shepherd's dividing between the sheep and the goats; it is taken from Ezek. xxxiv. 17, *Behold, I judge between cattle and cattle.*

IV. The process of the judgment concerning each of these.

1. Concerning the godly, on the right hand. Their cause must be first despatched, that they may be assessors with Christ in the judgment of the wicked, whose misery will be aggravated by their seeing Abraham, and Isaac, and Jacob, admitted into the kingdom of heaven, Luke xiii. 28. Observe here,

(1) The *glory* conferred upon them; the sentence by which they shall be not only acquitted, but preferred and rewarded (*v.* 34).

(2) The ground of this (*vv.* 35, 36), *For I was an hungered, and ye gave me meat*. We cannot hence infer that any good works of ours merit the happiness of heaven, by any intrinsic worth or excellency in them: our goodness extends not unto God; but it is plain that Jesus Christ will judge the world by the same rule by which he governs it, and therefore will reward those that have been obedient to that law; and mention will be made of their obedience, not as their title, but as their evidence of an interest in Christ, and his purchase.

Now the good works here mentioned are such as we commonly call works of charity to the poor: not but that many will be found on the right hand who never were in a capacity to feed the hungry, or clothe the naked, but were themselves fed and clothed by the charity of others; but one instance of sincere obedience is put for all the rest, and it teaches us this in general, that faith working by love is all in all in Christianity; *Show me thy faith by thy works*: and nothing will abound to a good account hereafter, but the fruits of righteousness in a good conversation now. Works of charity and beneficence, according as our ability is, are necessary to salvation; and there will be more stress laid upon them in the judgment of the great day, than is commonly imagined; these must be the proofs of our love, and of our professed subjection to the gospel of Christ, 2 Cor. ix. 13. But they that show no mercy, shall have judgment without mercy.

Now this reason is modestly excepted against by the righteous, but is explained by the Judge himself.

1. It is questioned by the righteous, *vv.* 37–39. Not as if they were loth to inherit the kingdom, or were ashamed of their good deeds, or had not the testimony of their own consciences concerning them: but, (1) The expressions are parabolical, designed to introduce and impress these great truths, that Christ has a mighty regard to works of charity, and is especially pleased with kindnesses done to his people for his sake. Or, (2) They bespeak the humble admiration which glorified saints will be filled with, to find such poor and worthless services, as theirs are, so highly celebrated, and richly rewarded: *Lord, when saw we thee an hungered, and fed thee?* Note, Gracious souls are apt to think meanly of their own good deeds; especially as unworthy to be compared with the glory that shall be revealed.

2. It is explained by the Judge himself (*v.* 40); *Inasmuch as ye have done it to these my brethren, to the least, to one of the least of them, ye have done it unto me*. The good works of the saints, when they are produced in the great day, (1) Shall

all be remembered; and not the least, not one of the least, overlooked, no not a cup of cold water. (2) They shall be interpreted most to their advantage, and the best construction that can be put upon them. As Christ makes the best of their infirmities, so he makes the most of their services.

2. Here is the process concerning the wicked, those on the left hand. And in that we have,

(1) The sentence passed upon them, *v.* 41. It was a disgrace to be set on the left hand; but that is not the worst of it, he shall say to them, *Depart from me, ye cursed.*

(2) The reason of this sentence assigned.

Now, [1] All that is charged upon them, on which the sentence is grounded, is, omission; as, before, the servant was condemned, not for wasting his talent, but for burying it; so here, he doth not say, "I was hungry and thirsty, for you took my meat and drink from me; I was a stranger, for you banished me; naked, for you stripped me; in prison, for you laid me there": but, "When I was in these distresses, you were so selfish, so taken up with your own ease and pleasure, made so much of your labour, and were so loth to part with your money, that you did not *minister* as you might have done to my relief and succour. You were like those epicures that were at ease in Zion, and were not *grieved for the affliction of Joseph*," Amos vi. 4–6. Note, Omissions are the ruin of thousands.

[2] It is the omission of works of charity to the poor. They are not sentenced for omitting their sacri-

fices and burnt-offerings (they abounded in these, Ps. l. 8), but for omitting the weightier matters of the law, *judgment, mercy, and faith.*

Lastly, Here is the execution of both these sentences, *v.* 46. Execution is the life of the law, and Christ will take care that that be done according to the sentence.

1. *The wicked shall go away into everlasting punishment.* Sentence will then be executed speedily, and no reprieve granted, nor any time allowed to move in arrest of judgment. The execution of the wicked is first mentioned; for first the tares are gathered and burned.

2. *The righteous shall go away into life eternal;* that is, they shall *inherit the kingdom, v.* 34. Note, (1) Heaven is life, it is all happiness. The life of the soul results from its union with God by the mediation of Jesus Christ, as that of the body from its union with the soul by the animal spirits. The heavenly life consists in the vision and fruition of God, in a perfect conformity to him, and an immediate uninterrupted communion with him. (2) It is *eternal* life. There is no death to put a period to the life itself, nor old age to put a period to the comfort of it, or any sorrow to embitter it. Thus life and death, good and evil, the blessing and the curse, are set before us, that we may choose our way; and so shall our end be.

THE PLOT OF THE PRIESTS
(vv. 1–5)

Here is, 1. The notice Christ gave his disciples of the near approach of his sufferings, *vv.* 1, 2. While his enemies were preparing trouble for him, he was preparing himself and his followers for it. He had often told them of his sufferings at a distance, now he speaks of them as at the door; *after two days.*

2. The plot of the chief priests, and scribes, and elders of the people, against the life of our Lord Jesus, *vv.* 3–5. Many consultations had been held against the life of Christ; but this plot was laid deeper than any yet, for the grandees were all engaged in it. The chief priests, who presided in ecclesiastical affairs; the elders, who were judges in civil matters, and the scribes, who, as doctors of the law, were directors to both—these composed the sanhedrim, or great council that governed the nation, and these were confederate against Christ.

CHRIST ANOINTED
(*vv.* 6–13)

In this passage of story, we have,

I. The singular kindness of a good woman to our Lord Jesus in anointing his head, *vv.* 6, 7. The woman that did this, is supposed to have been Mary, the sister of Martha and Lazarus. And Dr. Lightfoot thinks it was the same that was called *Mary Magdalene.* She had a *box of ointment very precious*, which she *poured upon the head* of Christ as he sat at meat. This, among us, would be a strange sort of compliment. But it was then accounted the highest piece of respect; for the smell was very grateful, and the ointment itself refreshing to the head. David had his *head anointed*, Ps. xxiii. 5;

Luke vii. 46. Now this may be looked upon,

1. As an act of faith in our Lord Jesus, the Christ, the Messiah, the anointed. To signify that she believed in him as God's anointed, whom he had set king, she anointed him, and made him her king.

2. As an act of love and respect to him. Some think that this was she who *loved much* at first, and *washed Christ's feet with her tears* (Luke vii. 38, 47); and that she had not left her first love, but was now as affectionate in the devotions of a grown Christian as she was in those of a young beginner.

II. The offence which the disciples took at this. They *had indignation* (*vv.* 8, 9), were vexed to see this ointment thus spent, which they thought might have been better bestowed.

1. See how they expressed their offence at it. They said, *To what purpose is this waste?*

2. See how they excused their offence at it, and what pretence they made for it; *This ointment might have been sold for much, and given to the poor.* Note, It is no new thing for bad affections to shelter themselves under specious covers; for people to shift off works of piety under colour of works of charity.

III. The reproof Christ gave to his disciples for the offence at this good woman (*vv.* 10, 11); *Why trouble ye the woman?* He here took part with a good, honest, zealous, well-meaning woman, against all his disciples, though they seemed to have so much reason on their side; so heartily does he espouse the cause of the *offended little ones*, ch. xviii. 10.

Observe his reason; *You have the poor always with you.* Note,

1. There are some opportunities of doing and getting good which are constant, and which we must give constant attendance to the improvement of.

2. There are other opportunities of doing and getting good, which come but seldom, which are short and uncertain, and require more peculiar diligence in the improvement of them, and which ought to be preferred before the other; "*Me ye have not always*, therefore use me while ye have me."

IV. Christ's approbation and commendation of the kindness of this good woman. He calls it a *good work* (*v.* 10), and says more in praise of it than could have been imagined; particularly,

1. That the meaning of it was mystical (*v.* 12); *She did it for my burial.* (1) Some think that she *intended* it so, and that the woman better understood Christ's frequent predictions of his death and sufferings than the apostles did; for which they were recompensed with the honour of being the first witnesses of his resurrection. (2) However, Christ interpreted it so; and he is always willing to make the best, to make the most of his people's well-meant words and actions. This was as it were the embalming of his body; because the doing of that after his death would be prevented by his resurrection, it was therefore done before; for it was fit that it should be done some time, to show that he was still the Messiah, even when he seemed to be triumphed over by death.

2. That the memorial of it should be honourable (*v.* 13); *This shall be told for a memorial.* This act of faith and love was so remarkable, that the preachers of Christ crucified, and the inspired writers of the history of his passion, could not choose but take notice of this passage, proclaim the notice of it, and perpetuate the memorial of it.

THE TREACHERY OF JUDAS
(*vv.* 14–16)

Immediately after an instance of the greatest kindness done to Christ, follows an instance of the greatest unkindness; such mixture is there of good and bad among the followers of Christ; he hath some faithful friends, and some false and feigned ones. What could be more base than this agreement which Judas here made with the chief priests, to betray Christ to them?

I. The traitor was Judas Iscariot; he is said to be *one of the twelve*, as an aggravation of his villainy.

II. Here is the proffer which he made to the chief priests; he *went to them, and said, What will ye give me? v.* 15. They did not send for him, nor make the proposal to him; they could not have thought that one of Christ's own disciples should be false to him.

III. Here is the bargain which the chief priests made with him; *they covenanted with him for thirty pieces of silver.* It should seem, Judas referred himself to them, and was willing to take what they were willing to give; he catches at the first offer, lest the next should be worse.

IV. Here is the industry of Judas, in pursuance of his bargain (*v.* 16); *he sought opportunity to betray him,* his head was still working to find out how he might do it effectually.

THE PASSOVER (*vv.* 17–25)

We have here an account of Christ's keeping the passover. Being made under the law, he submitted to all the ordinances of it, and to this among the rest; it was kept in remembrance of Israel's deliverance out of Egypt, the birth-day of that people; it was a tradition of the Jews, that in the days of the Messiah they should be redeemed on the very day of their coming out of Egypt; and it was exactly fulfilled, for Christ died the day after the passover, in which day they began their march.

I. The time when Christ ate the passover, was the usual time appointed by God, and observed by the Jews (*v.* 17); *the first day of the feast of unleavened bread*, which that year happened on the fifth day of the week, which is our Thursday.

II. The place where, was particularly appointed by himself to the disciples, upon their enquiry (*v.* 17): they asked, *Where wilt thou that we prepare the passover?*

1. They took it for granted that their Master would eat the passover, though he was at this time persecuted by the chief priests, and his life sought; they knew that he would not be put by his duty, either by frightenings without or fears within. Those do not follow Christ's example who make it an excuse for their not attending on the Lord's supper, our gospel passover, that they have many troubles and many enemies, are full of care and fear; for, if so, they have the more need of that ordinance, to help to silence their fears, and comfort them under their troubles, to help them in forgiving their enemies, and casting all their cares on God.

2. They knew very well that there must be preparation made for it, and that it was their business, as his servants, to make preparation; *Where wilt thou that we prepare?*

3. They knew that he had no house of his own wherein to eat the passover; in this, as in other things, *for our sakes he became poor*. Among all Zion's palaces there was none for Zion's King; but his kingdom was not of this world. See John i. 11.

4. They would not pitch upon a place without direction from him, and from him they had direction; he sent them to *such a man* (*v.* 18), who probably was a friend and follower of his, and to his house he invited himself and his disciples.

III. The preparation was made by the disciples (*v.* 19); *They did as Jesus had appointed*. Note, Those who would have Christ's presence with them in the gospel passover, must strictly observe his instructions, and do as he directs.

IV. They ate the passover according to the law (*v.* 20). By the law, they were to *take a lamb for a household* (Exod. xii. 3, 4), which were to be not less than ten, nor more than twenty; Christ's disciples were his household. Note, They whom God has charged with families, must have their houses with them in serving the Lord.

V. We have here Christ's discourse with his disciples at the passover-supper. The usual subject of discourse at that ordinance, was the deliverance of Israel out of

Egypt (Exod. xii. 26, 27); but the great Passover is now ready to be offered, and the discourse of that swallows up all talk of the other, Jer. xvi. 14, 15. Here is,

1. The general notice Christ gives his disciples of the treachery that should be among them (*v.* 21); *One of you shall betray me.*

2. The disciples' feelings on this occasion, *v.* 22. How did they take it?

(1) *They were exceeding sorrowful.* [1] It troubled them much to hear that their Master should be betrayed. [2] It troubled them more to hear that one of them should do it. [3] It troubled them most of all, that they were left at uncertainty which of them it was, and each of them was afraid for himself, lest, as Hazael speaks (2 Kings viii. 13), he was the *dog* that should *do this great thing*.

(2) *They began every one of them to say, Lord, is it I?*

3. Further information given them concerning this matter (*vv.* 23, 24), where Christ tells them, (1) That the traitor was a familiar friend; *He that dippeth his hand with me in the dish*, that is, One of you that are now with me at the table. He mentions this, to make the treachery appear the more exceeding sinful.

4. The conviction of Judas, *v.* 25. (1) He asked, *Is it I?* to avoid coming under the suspicion of guilt by his silence. He knew very well that it was he, and yet wished to appear a stranger to such a plot. (2) Christ soon answered this question; *Thou hast said*, that is, It is as thou hast said. This is not spoken out so plainly as Nathan's, *Thou*

art the man; but it was enough to convict him, and, if his heart had not been wretchedly hardened, to have broken the neck of his plot, when he saw it discovered to his Master, and discovered by him.

THE LORD'S SUPPER
(*vv.* 26–30)

We have here the institution of the great gospel ordinance of the Lord's supper, which was received of the Lord. Observe,

I. The time when it was instituted —*as they were eating*. At the latter end of the passover-supper, before the table was drawn, because, as a feast upon a sacrifice, it was to come in the room of that ordinance. Christ is to us the Passover-sacrifice by which atonement is made (1 Cor. v. 7); *Christ our Passover is sacrificed for us*. This ordinance is to us the passover-supper, by which application is made, and commemoration celebrated, of a much greater deliverance than that of Israel out of Egypt. All the legal sacrifices of propitiation being summed up in the death of Christ, and so abolished, all the legal feasts of rejoicing were summed up in this sacrament, and so abolished.

II. The institution itself. A sacrament must be instituted; it is no part of moral worship, nor is it dictated by natural light, but has both its being and significancy from the institution, from a divine institution; it is his prerogative who established the covenant, to appoint the seals of it. In which,

1. The body of Christ is signified and represented by bread; he had said formerly (John vi. 35), *I am the bread of life*, upon which metaphor

this sacrament is built; as the life of the body is supported by bread, which is therefore put for all bodily nourishment (*ch.* iv. 4; vi. 11), so the life of the soul is supported and maintained by Christ's mediation.

(1) *He took bread, the loaf*; some loaf that lay ready at hand, fit for the purpose; it was, probably, unleavened bread; but, that circumstance not being taken notice of, we are not to bind ourselves to that, as some of the Greek churches do. His taking the bread was a solemn action, and was, probably, done in such a manner as to be observed by them that sat with him, that they might expect something more than ordinary to be done with it.

(2) *He blessed it*; set it apart for this use by prayer and thanksgiving. We do not find any set form of words used by him upon this occasion; but what he said, no doubt, was accommodated to the business in hand, that new testament which by this ordinance was to be sealed and ratified.

(3) *He brake it*; which denotes, [1] The breaking of Christ's body for us, that it might be fitted for our use; *He was bruised for our iniquities*, as *bread-corn is bruised* (Isa. xxviii. 28). [2] The breaking of Christ's body to us, as the father of the family breaks the bread to the children.

(4) *He gave it to his disciples*, as the Master of the family, and the Master of this feast; it is not said, He gave it *to the apostles*, though they were so, and had been often called so before this, but *to the disciples*, because all the disciples of Christ have a right to this ordinance; and those shall have the benefit of it who are his disciples indeed; yet he gave it to them as he did the multiplied loaves, by them to be handed to all his other followers.

(5) *He said, Take, eat; this is my body*, v. 26. He here tells them,

[1] What they should do with it; *"Take, eat*; accept of Christ as he is offered to you, receive the atonement, approve of it, consent to it, come up to the terms on which the benefit of it is proposed to you; submit to his grace and to his government." Believing on Christ is expressed by *receiving him* (John i. 12), and *feeding upon him*, John vi. 57, 58. Meat looked upon, or the dish ever so well garnished, will not nourish us; it must be fed upon: so must the doctrine of Christ.

[2] What they should have with it; *This is my body*, not *this bread*, but *this eating and drinking*. Believing carries all the efficacy of Christ's death to our souls. *This is my body*, spiritually and sacramentally; this signifies and represents my body. He employs sacramental language, like that, Exod. xii. 11.

2. The blood of Christ is signified and represented by the wine; to make it a complete feast, here is not only bread to strengthen, but wine to *make glad the heart* (*vv.* 27, 28).

This cup he gave to the disciples,

(1) With a command; *Drink ye all of it*. Thus he welcomes his guests to his table, obliges them all to drink of his cup. Why should he so expressly command them all to drink, and to see that none let it pass them, and press that more expressly in this than in the other part of the ordinance? Surely it was

because he foresaw how in after-ages this ordinance would be dismembered by the prohibition of the cup to the laity.

(2) With an explication; *For this is my blood of the New Testament.* Therefore drink it with appetite, delight, because it is so rich a cordial. Hitherto the blood of Christ had been represented by the blood of beasts, real blood: but, after it was actually shed, it was represented by the blood of grapes, metaphorical blood; so wine is called in an Old-Testament prophecy of Christ, Gen. xlix. 10, 11.

Now observe what Christ saith of his blood represented in the sacrament.

[1] *It is my blood of the New Testament.* The Old Testament was confirmed by the *blood of bulls and goats* (Heb. ix. 19, 20; Exod. xxiv. 8); but the New Testament with the blood of Christ, which is here distinguished from that; *It is my blood of the New Testament.* The covenant God is pleased to make with us, and all the benefits and privileges of it, are owing to the merits of Christ's death.

[2] *It is shed*; it was not shed till next day, but it was now upon the point of being shed, it is as good as done.

[3] *It is shed for many.* Christ came to confirm *a covenant with many* (Dan. ix. 27), and the intent of his death agreed.

[4] *It is shed for the remission of sins,* that is, to purchase remission of sins for us. The redemption which we have through his blood, is *the remission of sins,* Eph. i. 7. The new covenant which is procured and ratified by the blood of Christ, is a charter of pardon, an act of indemnity, in order to a reconciliation between God and man; for sin was the only thing that made the quarrel, and *without shedding of blood is no remission,* Heb. ix. 22. The pardon of sin is that great blessing which is, in the Lord's supper, conferred upon all true believers; it is the foundation of all other blessings, and the spring of everlasting comfort, *ch.* ix. 2, 3.

He takes leave of such communion; *I will not drink henceforth of this fruit of the vine,* that is, now that I am no more in the world (John xvii. 11); I have had enough of it, and am glad to think of leaving it, glad to think that this is the last meal.

Secondly, He assures them of a happy meeting again at last. It is a long, but not an everlasting, farewell; *until that day when I drink it new with you.*

Lastly, Here is the close of the solemnity with a hymn (*v.* 30); *They sang a hymn* or psalm; whether the psalms which the Jews usually sang at the close of the passover-supper, which they called *the great hallel,* that is, Ps. cxiii. and the five that follow it, or whether some new hymn more closely adapted to the occasion, is uncertain; I rather think the former; had it been new, John would not have omitted to record it.

BEFORE THE COCK CROW
(*vv.* 31–35)

We have here Christ's discourse with his disciples upon the way, as they were going to the mount of Olives. Observe,

I. A prediction of the trial which

both he and his disciples were now to go through. He here foretells,

1. A dismal scattering storm just arising, *v.* 31.

(1) That they should *all be offended because of Christ that very night*; that is, they would all be so frightened with the sufferings, that they would not have the courage to cleave to him in them, but would all basely desert him. [1] There are some temptations and offences, the effects of which are general and universal among Christ's disciples; *All you shall be offended.* [2] We have need to prepare for sudden trials, which may come to extremity in a very little time. [3] The cross of Christ is the great stumbling-block to many that pass for his disciples; both the cross he bore for us (1 Cor. i. 23), and that which we are called out to bear for him, *ch.* xvi. 24.

(2) That herein the scripture would be fulfilled; *I will smite the Shepherd.* It is quoted from Zech. xiii. 7.

2. He gives them the prospect of a comfortable gathering together again after this storm (*v.* 32); "*After I am risen again, I will go before you.* Though you will forsake me, I will not forsake you; though you fall, I will take care you shall not fall finally: we shall have a meeting again in Galilee, *I will go before you,* as the shepherd before the sheep."

II. The presumption of Peter, that he should keep his integrity, whatever happened (*v.* 33); *Though all men be offended, yet will I never be offended.* Peter had a great stock of confidence, and was upon all occasions forward to speak, especially to speak for himself;

sometimes it did him a kindness, but at other times it betrayed him, as it did here.

III. The particular warning Christ gave Peter of what he would do, *v.* 34. He imagined that in the hour of temptation he should come off better than any of them, and Christ tells him that he should come off worse. The warning is introduced with a solemn asseveration; "*Verily, I say unto thee*; take my word for it, who know thee better than thou knowest thyself."

GETHSEMANE (*vv.* 36–46)

Hitherto, we have seen the preparatives for Christ's sufferings; now, we enter upon the bloody scene. In these verses we have the story of his agony in the garden. This was the beginning of sorrows to our Lord Jesus. Observe,

I. The place where he underwent this mighty agony; it was *in a place called Gethsemane.* The name signifies, *torculus olei—an olive-mill,* a press for olives, like a wine-press, where they *trod the olives,* Mic. vi. 15. And this was the proper place for such a thing, at the foot of the mount of Olives. There our Lord Jesus began his passion; there it pleased the Lord to bruise him, and crush him, that fresh oil might flow to all believers from him, that we might partake of the root and fatness of that *good Olive.* There he trod the wine-press of his Father's wrath, and trod it alone.

II. The company he had with him, when he was in this agony.

1. He took all the twelve disciples with him to the garden, except Judas, who was at this time otherwise employed.

2. He took only Peter, and James, and John, with him into that corner of the garden where he suffered his agony. He left the rest at some distance, perhaps at the garden door, with this charge, *Sit ye here, while I go and pray yonder.*

III. The agony itself that he was in; *He began to be sorrowful and very heavy.* It is called an agony (Luke xxii. 44), a conflict. It was not any bodily pain or torment that he was in, nothing occurred to hurt him; but, whatever it was, it was from within; he troubled himself, John xi. 33.

But what was the cause of this? What was it that put him into this agony? Certainly, it was nothing of despair or distrust of his Father, much less any conflict or struggle with him. As the Father loved him because he laid down his life for the sheep, so he was entirely subject to his Father's will in it. But,

1. He engaged in an encounter with the powers of darkness; so he intimates (Luke xxii. 53); *This is your hour, and the power of darkness:* and he spoke of it just before (John xiv. 30, 31).

2. He was now *bearing the iniquities* which the Father laid upon him, and, by his sorrow and amazement, he accommodated himself to his undertaking. The sufferings he was entering upon were for our sins; they were all made to meet upon him, and he knew it.

3. He had a full and clear prospect of all the sufferings that were before him. He foresaw the treachery of Judas, the unkindness of Peter, the malice of the Jews, and their base ingratitude. He knew that he should now in a few hours be scourged, spit upon, crowned with thorns, nailed to the cross; death in its most dreadful appearances, death in pomp, attended with all its terrors, looked him in the face; and this made him sorrowful, especially because it was the wages of our sin, which he had undertaken to satisfy for.

IV. His complaint of this agony. Finding himself under the arrests of his passion, he goes to his disciples (*v.* 38), and,

1. He acquaints them with his condition; *My soul is exceedingly sorrowful, even unto death.* It gives some little ease to a troubled spirit, to have a friend ready to unbosom itself to, and give vent to its sorrows.

2. He bespeaks their company and attendance; *Tarry ye here, and watch with me.*

V. What passed between him and his Father when he was in this agony; *Being in an agony, he prayed.* Prayer is never out of season, but it is especially seasonable in an agony.

The prayer itself; wherein we may observe three things,

(1) The title he gives to God; *O my Father.* Thick as the cloud was, he could see God as a Father through it.

(2) The favour he begs; *If it be possible, let this cup pass from me.* He calls his sufferings a *cup*; not a river, not a sea, but a cup, which we shall soon see the bottom of. When we are under troubles, we should make the best, the least, of them, and not aggravate them. His sufferings might be called a *cup*, because allotted him, as at feasts a

cup was set to every mess. He begs that this cup might *pass from him*, that is, that he might avoid the sufferings now at hand; or, at least, that they might be shortened. This intimates no more than that he was really and truly Man, and as a Man he could not but be averse to pain and suffering. This is the first and simple act of man's will—to start back from that which is sensibly grievous to us, and to desire the prevention and removal of it. The law of self-preservation is impressed upon the innocent nature of man, and rules there till over-ruled by some other law; therefore Christ admitted and expressed a reluctance to suffer, to show that he was *taken from among men* (Heb. v. 1), was touched with *the feeling of our infirmities* (Heb. iv. 15), and *tempted as we are; yet without sin.*

(3) His entire submission to, and acquiescence in, the will of God; *Nevertheless, not as I will, but as thou wilt.* Not that the human will of Christ was adverse or averse to the divine will; it was only, in its first act, diverse from it; to which, in the second act of the will, which compares and chooses, he freely submits himself. Note, In conformity to this example of Christ, we must drink of the bitter cup which God puts into our hands, be it ever so bitter; though nature struggle, grace must submit. We then are disposed as Christ was, when our wills are in every thing melted into the will of God, though ever so displeasing to flesh and blood; *The will of the Lord be done*, Acts xxi. 14.

4. The repetition of the prayer; *He went away again the second*

time, and prayed (v. 42), and again the third time (v. 44), and all to the same purport; only, as it is related here, he did not, in the second and third prayer, expressly ask that the cup might pass from him, as he had done in the first.

He prayed, saying, Thy will be done. Note, Prayer is the offering up, not only of our desires, but of our resignations, to God.

But what answer had he to this prayer? Certainly it was not made in vain; he that heard him *always*, did not deny him *now*. It is true, the cup did not pass from him, for he withdrew that petition, and did not insist upon it (if he had, for aught I know, the cup had passed away); but he had an answer to his prayer; for, (1) *He was strengthened with strength in his soul*, in the day when he cried (Ps. cxxxviii. 3); and that was a real answer, Luke xxii. 43. (2) He was delivered from that which he feared, which was, lest by impatience and distrust he should offend his Father, and so disable himself to go on with his undertaking, Heb. v. 7. In answer to his prayer, God provided that he should not fail or be discouraged.

VI. What passed between him and his three disciples at this time; and here we may observe,

1. The fault they were guilty of; that when he was in his agony, sorrowful and heavy, sweating and wrestling and praying, they were so little concerned, that they could not keep awake; he comes, and *finds them asleep, v. 40.*

2. Christ's favour to them, notwithstanding. Persons in sorrow are too apt to be cross and peevish with those about them, and to lay it

grievously to heart, if they but seem to neglect them; but Christ in his agony is as meek as ever, and carries it as patiently toward his followers as toward his Father, and is not apt to take things ill.

When Christ's disciples put this slight upon him, he gave them a gentle reproof, for as many as he loves he rebukes; he directed it to Peter, who used to *speak* for them; let him now *hear* for them. The reproof was very melting; *What! could ye not watch with me one hour?* He speaks as one amazed to see them so stupid; every word, when closely considered, shows the aggravated nature of the case. How small a thing it was that he expected from them—only to *watch with him.* If he had bid them do some great thing, had bid them be in an agony with him, or die with him, they thought they could have done it; and yet they could not do it, when he only desired them to *watch with him,* 2 Kings v. 13. How short a time it was that he expected it—but *one hour*; they were not set upon the guard whole nights, as the prophet was (Isa. xxi. 8), only *one hour.* Sometimes he *continued all night in prayer to God,* but did not then expect that his disciples should watch with him; only now, when he had but one hour to spend in prayer.

He gave them good counsel; *Watch and pray, that ye enter not into temptation,* v. 41. Note, When we find ourselves entering into temptation, we have need to watch and pray.

(4) He kindly excused for them; *The spirit indeed is willing, but the flesh is weak.* We do not read of one word they had to say for themselves (the sense of their own weakness stopped their mouth); but then he had a tender word to say on their behalf, for it is his office to be an Advocate; in this he sets us an example of that love *which covers a multitude of sins.* He considered their frame, and did not chide them, for he remembered that they were but flesh; *and the flesh is weak though the spirit be willing,* Ps. lxxviii. 38, 39.

(5) Though they continued dull and sleepy, he did not any further rebuke them for it; for, though we daily offend, yet he will not always chide.

THE ARREST (*vv.* 47–56)

We are here told how the blessed Jesus was seized, and taken into custody; this followed immediately upon his agony, *while he yet spake.*

Now concerning the apprehension of the Lord Jesus, observe,

I. Who the persons were, that were employed in it. 1. Here was *Judas, one of the twelve,* at the head of this infamous guard: *he was guide to them that took Jesus* (Acts i. 16); without his help they could not have found him in this retirement. The rest were the servants and officers of the High Priest, and they were Jews; they that were at variance with each other, agreed against Christ, and Roman guards.

II. How they were armed for this enterprise.

1. What weapons they were armed with; They came *with swords and staves.* The Roman soldiers, no doubt, had swords; the servants of the priests, those of

them that had not swords, brought staves or clubs.

2. What warrant they were armed with; *They came from the chief priests, and elders of the people*; this armed multitude was sent by them upon this errand. It was a sign that he was supported by a divine power, for by all earthly powers he was not only deserted, but opposed; Pilate upbraided him with it; *Thine own nation and the chief priests delivered thee to me*, John xviii. 35.

III. The manner how it was done, and what passed at that time.

1. How Judas betrayed him; he did his business effectually, and his resolution in this wickedness may shame us who fail in that which is good.

2. How the officers and soldiers secured him; *Then came they, and laid hands on Jesus, and took him*; they made him their prisoner. *How were they not afraid to stretch forth their hands against the Lord's Anointed?* They could not have taken him, if he had not surrendered himself, and been *delivered by the determinate counsel and foreknowledge of God*, Acts ii. 23.

Our Lord Jesus was made a prisoner, because he would in all things be treated as a malefactor, punished for our crime, and as a surety under arrest for our debt. The yoke of our transgressions was bound by the Father's hand upon the neck of the Lord Jesus, Lam. i. 14.

3. How Peter fought for Christ, and was checked for his pains. It is here only said to be *one of them that were with Jesus in the garden*; but John xviii. 10, we are told that

it was Peter who signalized himself upon this occasion. Observe,

(1) Peter's rashness (*v.* 51); He *drew his sword*. They had but two swords among them all (Luke xxii. 38), and one of them, it seems, fell to Peter's share; and now he thought it was time to draw it, and he laid about him as if he would have done some great matter; but all the execution he did was the cutting off an ear from a servant of the High Priest; designing, it is likely, to cleave him down the head, because he saw him more forward than the rest in laying hands on Christ, he missed his blow.

(2) The rebuke which our Lord Jesus gave him (*v.* 52); *Put up again thy sword into its place*. As Christ forbade his disciples the sword of justice (*ch.* xx. 25, 26), so here the sword of war. Christ bade Peter put up his sword, and never bade him draw it again; yet that which Peter is here blamed for is his doing it unseasonably; the hour was come for Christ to suffer and die, he knew Peter knew it, the *sword of the Lord was drawn against him* (Zech. xiii. 7), and for Peter to draw his sword for him, was like, *Master, spare thyself*.

Three reasons Christ gives to Peter for this rebuke:

[1] His drawing the sword would be dangerous to himself and to his fellow-disciples; *They that take the sword, shall perish with the sword*; they that use violence, fall by violence; and men hasten and increase their own troubles by blustering bloody methods of self-defence.

[2] It was needless for him to draw his sword in defence of his Master, who, if he pleased, could

summon into his service all the hosts of heaven (*v.* 53); "*Thinkest thou that I cannot now pray to my Father, and he shall send* from heaven effectual succours? Peter, if I would put by these sufferings, I could easily do it without thy hand or thy sword."

[3] It was the wrong time; *For how then shall the scriptures be fulfilled, that thus it must be? v.* 54. It was written, that Christ should be *led as a lamb to the slaughter*, Isa. liii. 7. Should he summon the angels to his assistance, he would not be led to the slaughter at all; should he permit his disciples to fight, he would not be led as a lamb quietly and without resistance; therefore he and his disciples must yield to the accomplishment of the predictions.

4. We are next told how Christ argued the case with them that came to take him (*v.* 55); though he did not resist them, yet he did reason with them. *Are ye come out*, (1) With rage and enmity, *as against a thief*, as if I were an enemy to the public safety, and deservedly suffered this? (2) With all this power and force, as against the worst of thieves, that dare the law, bid defiance to public justice, and add rebellion to their sin?

He further expostulates with them, by reminding them how he had behaved himself hitherto toward them, and they toward him. [1] Of his public appearance; *I sat daily with you in the temple teaching.* And, [2] Of their public connivance; *Ye laid no hold on me.* How comes then this change? They were very unreasonable, in treating him as they did.

But all this was done (so it follows, *v.* 56) *that the scriptures of the prophets might be fulfilled.* Note, The scriptures are in the fulfilling every day; and all those scriptures which speak of the Messiah, had their full accomplishment in our Lord Jesus.

5. How he was, in the midst of this distress, shamefully deserted by his disciples; *They all forsook him, and fled, v.* 56.

THE TRIAL (*vv.* 57–68)

We have here the arraignment of our Lord Jesus in the ecclesiastical court, before the great sanhedrim. Observe,

I. The sitting of the court; the scribes and the elders were assembled, though it was in the dead time of the night, when other people were fast asleep in their beds; yet, to gratify their malice against Christ, they denied themselves that natural rest, and sat up all night, to be ready to fall upon the prey which Judas and his men, they hoped, would *seize*.

II. The setting of the prisoner to the bar; they that had *laid hold on Jesus, led him away*, hurried him, no doubt, with violence, led him as a trophy of their victory, led him as a victim to the altar; he was brought into Jerusalem through that which was called the *sheep-gate*, for that was the way into town from the mount of Olives; and it was so called because the sheep appointed for sacrifice were brought that way to the temple; very fitly therefore is Christ led that way, who is the Lamb of God, that takes away the sin of the world. Christ was led first to the High Priest, for by the law all sacrifices were to be first *presented to the priest, and delivered into his hand*, Lev. xvii. 5.

III. The cowardice and faint-heartedness of Peter (*v.* 58); *But Peter followed afar off*. This comes in here, with an eye to the following story of his denying him. He forsook him as the rest did, when he was seized, and what is here said of his following him is easily reconcilable with his forsaking him; such following was no better than forsaking him.

IV. The trial of our Lord Jesus in this court.

1. They examined witnesses against him, though they were resolved, right or wrong, to condemn him; yet, to put the better colour upon it, they would produce evidence against him. The crimes properly cognizable in their court, were, false doctrine and blasphemy; these they endeavoured to prove upon him. And observe here,

(1) Their search for proof; *They sought false witness against him*; they had seized him, bound him, abused him, and after all have to seek for something to lay to his charge, and can show no cause for his commitment. They tried if any of them could allege seemingly from their own knowledge any thing against him; and suggested one calumny and then another, which, if true, might touch his life.

(2) Their success in this search; in several attempts they were baffled, but at last they met with *two* witnesses, who, it seems, agreed in their evidence, and therefore were hearkened to, in hopes that now the point was gained. The words they swore against him,

were, that he should say, *I am able to destroy the temple of God, and to build it in three days*, *v.* 61. Now by this they designed to accuse him, [1] As an enemy to the temple, and one that sought for the destruction of it, which they could not bear to hear of; for they valued themselves by *the temple of the Lord* (Jer. vii. 4), and, when they abandoned other idols, made a perfect idol of that. Stephen was accused for *speaking against this holy place*, Acts vi. 13, 14. [2] As one that dealt in witchcraft, or some such unlawful arts, by the help of which he could rear such a building in three days: they had often suggested that he was in league with Beelzebub. Now, as to this, *First*, The words were misrecited; he said, *Destroy ye this temple* (John ii. 19), plainly intimating that he spoke of a temple which his enemies would seek to destroy; they come, and swear that he said, *I am able to destroy* this temple, as if the design against it were his. He said, *In three days I will raise it up*— *I will raise it to life.* They come, and swear that he said, *I am able to build it*; which is properly used of a house temple. *Secondly*, The words were misunderstood; *he spoke of the temple of his body* (John ii. 21), and perhaps when he said, ·*this temple*, pointed to, or laid his hane upon, his own body; but they sword that he said the *temple of God*, meaning this holy place.

(3) Christ's silence under all these accusations, to the amazement of the court, *v.* 62. The High Priest, the judge of the court, arose in some heat, and said, "*Answerest thou nothing?*" But *Jesus held his peace* (*v.* 63), not as one sullen, or

as one self-condemned, or as one astonished and in confusion; not because he lacked something to say, or knew not how to say it, but that the scripture might be fulfilled (Isa. liii. 7); *As the sheep is dumb before the shearer*, and before the butcher, *so he opened not his mouth.*

2. They examined our Lord Jesus himself upon an oath like that *ex officio*; and, since they could not accuse him, they will try, contrary to the law of equity, to make him accuse himself.

(1) Here is the interrogatory put to him by the High Priest.

Observe, [1] The question itself; *Whether thou be the Christ, the Son of God?* That is, Whether thou pretend to be so? For they will by no means admit it into consideration, whether he be really so or no.

[2] The solemnity of the proposal of it; *I adjure thee by the living God, that thou tell us.* If he should refuse to answer when he was thus adjured, they would charge him with contempt of the blessed name of God.

(2) Christ's answer to this interrogatory (*v.* 64), in which,

[1] He owns himself to be *the Christ the Son of God. Thou hast said*; that is, "It is as thou hast said"; for in St. Mark it is, *I am.* Hitherto, he seldom professed himself expressly to be the Christ, the Son of God; the tenor of his doctrine bespoke it, and his miracles proved it: but now he would not omit to make a confession of it, *First*, Because that would have looked like a disowning of that truth which he came into the world to bear witness to. *Secondly*, It would have looked like declining

his sufferings, when he knew the acknowledgment of this would give his enemies all the advantage they desired against him.

[2] He refers himself, for the proof of this, to his second coming, and indeed to his whole estate of exaltation. It is probable that they looked upon him with a scornful disdainful smile, when he said, *I am*"; "A likely fellow," thought they, "to be the Messiah, who is expected to come in so much pomp and power"; and to that this *nevertheless* refers. "Though now you see me in this low and abject state, and think it a ridiculous thing for me to call myself the Messiah, *nevertheless* the day is coming when I shall appear otherwise." *Hereafter ye shall see the Son of man sitting on the right hand of power, to judge the world.*

V. His conviction upon this trial; *The High Priest rent his clothes*, according to the custom of the Jews, when they heard or saw any thing done or said, which they looked upon to be a reproach to God; as Isa. xxxvi. 22; xxxvii. 1; Acts xiv. 14. Caiaphas would be thought extremely tender of the glory of God (*Come, see his zeal for the Lord of hosts*); but, while he pretended an abhorrence of blasphemy, he was himself the greatest blasphemer; he now forgot the law which forbade the High Priest in any case to rend his clothes, unless we will suppose this an excepted case.

Observe, 1. The crime he was found guilty of; *blasphemy. He hath spoken blasphemy*; that is, he hath spoken reproachfully of the living God; that is the notion we have of blasphemy; because we by sin had reproached the Lord, therefore Christ, when *he was made Sin for us*, was condemned as a blasphemer for the truth he told them.

2. The evidence upon which they found him guilty; *Ye have heard the blasphemy*; why should we trouble ourselves to examine *witnesses* any further? He owned the fact, that he did profess himself the *Son of God*; and then they made blasphemy of it, and convicted him upon his confession.

VI. His sentence passed, upon this conviction, *v.* 66.

Here is, 1. Caiaphas's appeal to the bench; *What think ye?*

2. Their concurrence with him; they said, *He is guilty of death*; perhaps they did not all concur: it is certain that Joseph of Arimathea, if he was present, dissented (Luke xxiii. 51); so did Nicodemus, and, it is likely, others with them; however, the majority carried it that way.

VII. The abuses and indignities done to him after sentence passed (*vv.* 67, 68); *Then*, when he was found guilty, they *spat in his face*. Because they had not power to put him to death, and could not be sure that they should prevail with the governor to be their executioner, they would do him all the mischief they could, now that they had him in their hands.

PETER'S DENIAL (*vv.* 69–75)

We have here the story of Peter's denying his Master, and it comes in as a part of Christ's sufferings. Our Lord Jesus was now in the High Priest's hall, not to be tried, but baited rather; and then it would have been some comfort to him to see his friends near him. But we do not find any friend he had about the court, save Peter only, and it would have been better if he had been at a distance. Observe how he fell, and how he got up again by repentance.

I. His sin, which is here impartially related, to the honour of the penmen of scripture, who dealt faithfully. Observe,

1. The immediate occasion of Peter's sin. He sat without in the palace, among the servants of the High Priest. Note, Bad company is to many an occasion of sin.

2. The temptation to it. He was challenged as a retainer to Jesus of Galilee. First one maid, and then another, and then the rest of the servants, charged it upon him; *Thou also wert with Jesus of Galilee*, *v.* 69. And again, *This fellow was with Jesus of Nazareth*, *v.* 71. And again (*v.* 73), *Thou also art one of them, for thy speech betrayeth thee* to be a Galilean; whose dialect and pronunciation differed from that of the other Jews.

3. The sin itself. When he was charged as one of Christ's disciples, he denied it, was ashamed and afraid to own himself so, and would have all about him to believe that he had no knowledge of him, nor any kindness or concern for him.

This is written for warning to us, that we sin not after the similitude of Peter's transgression; that we never, either directly or indirectly, deny Christ the Lord that bought us, by rejecting his offers, resisting his Spirit, dissembling our knowledge of him, and being ashamed of him and his words, or afraid of suffering for him and with his suffering people.

4. The aggravations of this sin, which it may be of use to take notice of, that we may observe the like transgressions in our own sins. Consider, (1) Who he was: an apostle, one of the first three, that had been upon all occasions the most forward to speak to the honour of Christ. The greater profession we make of religion, the greater is our sin if in any thing we walk unworthily. (2) What fair warning his Master had given him of his danger; if he had regarded this as he ought to have done, he would not have run himself into the temptation. (3) How solemnly he had promised to adhere to Christ in this night of trial; he had said again and again, "*I will never deny thee*; no, I will die with thee first"; yet he broke these bonds in sunder, and his word was yea and nay. (4) How soon he fell into this sin after the Lord's supper. There to receive such an inestimable pledge of redeeming love, and yet the same night, before morning, to disown his Redeemer, was indeed *turning aside quickly*. (5) How weak comparatively the temptation was; it was not the judge, nor any of the officers of the court, that charged him with being a disciple of Jesus, but a silly maid or two, that probably designed him no hurt, nor would have done him any if he had owned it. (6) How often he repeated it; even after the cock had crowed once he continued in the temptation, and a second and third time relapsed into the sin. Is this Peter? *How art thou fallen!*

II. Peter's repentance for this sin, *v.* 75. The former is written for our admonition, that we may not sin; but, if at any time we be overtaken, this is written for our imitation, that we may make haste to repent. Now observe,

1. What it was, that brought Peter to repentance.

(1) *The cock crew* (*v.* 74); a common contingency; but, Christ having mentioned the crowing of *the cock* in the warning he gave him, that made it a means of bringing him to himself.

(2) *He remembered the words of the Lord*; this was it that brought him to himself, and melted him into tears of godly sorrow; a sense of his ingratitude to Christ, and the slight regard he had had to the gracious warning Christ had given him. Note, A serious reflection upon the words of the Lord Jesus will be a powerful inducement to repentance, and will help to break the heart for sin.

2. How his repentance was expressed; *He went out, and wept bitterly*.

(1) His sorrow was secret; he went out, out of the High Priest's hall, vexed at himself that ever he came into it, now that he found what a snare he was in, and got out of it as fast as he could.

(2) His sorrow was serious; *He wept bitterly*. Sorrow for sin must not be slight, but great and deep, like that for an only son. Those that have sinned sweetly, must weep bitterly; for, sooner or later, sin will be bitterness. Those that have truly sorrowed for sin, will sorrow upon every remembrance of it; yet not so as to hinder, but rather to

increase, their joy in God and in his mercy and grace.

THE DEATH OF JUDAS
(vv. 1–10)

We left Christ in the hands of the chief priests and elders, condemned to die, but they could only show their teeth; about two years before this the Romans had taken from the Jews the power of capital punishment; they could put no man to death, and therefore early in the morning another council is held, to consider what is to be done. And here we are told what was done in that morning-council, after they had been for two or three hours consulting with their pillows.

I. Christ is delivered up to Pilate, that he might execute the sentence they had passed upon him.

II. The money which they had paid to Judas for betraying Christ, is by him delivered back to them, and Judas, in despair, hangs himself. The chief priests and elders supported themselves with *this*, in prosecuting Christ, that his own disciple betrayed him to them; but now, in the midst of the prosecution, that string failed them, and even *he* is made to them a *witness* of Christ's innocency and a monument of God's justice; which served, 1, For glory to Christ in the midst of his sufferings, and a specimen of his victory over Satan who had entered into Judas. 2. For warning to his persecutors, and to leave them the more inexcusable. If their heart had not been fully set in them to do this evil, what Judas said and did, one would think, should have stopped the prosecution.

See here how Judas *repented*: not like Peter, who repented, believed, and was pardoned: no, he repented, despaired, and was ruined.

AT THE BAR OF PILATE
(vv. 11–25)

We have here an account of what passed in Pilate's judgment-hall, when the blessed Jesus was brought thither early in the morning. Though it was no court-day, Pilate immediately took his case before him. We have here,

I. The trial Christ had before Pilate.

1. His arraignment; *Jesus stood before the governor*, as the prisoner before the judge.

2. His indictment; *Art thou the king of the Jews?* It was plain that he was not so *de facto—actually*; "But dost thou lay any claim to the government, or pretend a right to rule the Jews?"

3. His plea; *Jesus said unto him, "Thou sayest. It is as thou sayest,* though not as thou meanest; I am a king, but not such a king as thou dost suspect me to be." Thus before Pilate he witnessed a good confession, and was not ashamed to own himself a king, though it looked ridiculous, nor afraid, though at this time it was dangerous.

4. The evidence (v. 12); He was *accused of the chief priests*. Pilate found *no fault in him*; whatever was said, nothing was proved, and therefore what was wanting in matter they made up in noise and violence, and followed him with repeated accusations, the same as they had given in before; but by

the repetition they thought to force a belief from the governor.

5. The prisoner's silence as to the prosecutors' accusations; *He answered nothing*, (1) Because there was no occasion; nothing was alleged but what carried its own confutation along with it. (2) He was now taken up with the great concern that lay between him and his Father, to whom he was offering up himself a Sacrifice, to answer the demands of his justice, which he was so intent upon, that he minded not what they said against him. (3) His hour was come, and he submitted to his Father's will; *Not as I will, but as thou wilt*. He knew what his Father's will was, and therefore silently *committed himself to him that judgeth righteously*.

Now, [1] Pilate pressed him to make some reply (*v.* 13); *Hearest thou not how many things they witness against thee?* What these things were, may be gathered from Luke xxiii. 3, 5, and John xix. 7. Pilate, having no malice at all against him, was desirous he should clear himself, urges him to it, and believes he could do it. We have,

II. The outrage and violence of the people, in pressing the governor to crucify Christ. The chief priests had a great interest in the people, they called them *Rabbi, Rabbi*, made idols of them, and oracles of all they said; and they made use of this to incense them against him, and by the power of the mob gained the point which they could not otherwise carry. Now here are two instances of their outrage.

1. Their preferring Barabbas before him, and choosing to have him released rather than Jesus.

The proposal was made by Pilate the governor (*v.* 17); *Whom will ye that I release unto you?* It is probable that the judge had the nomination of two, one of which the people were to *choose*. Pilate proposed to them to have Jesus *released*; he was convinced of his innocency, and that the prosecution was malicious; yet had not the courage to acquit him, as he ought to have done, by his own power, but would have him released by the people's election, and so he hoped to satisfy both his own *conscience*, and the *people* too; whereas, finding no fault in him, he ought not to have *put him upon the country*, or brought him *into peril of his life*.

While Pilate was thus labouring the matter, he was confirmed in his unwillingness to condemn Jesus, by a message sent him from his wife (*v.* 19), by way of caution; *Have thou nothing to do with that just man* (together with the reason), *for I have suffered many things this day in a dream because of him*. Probably, this message was delivered to Pilate publicly, in the hearing of all that were present, for it was intended to be a warning not to him only, but to the prosecutors. Observe,

[1] The special providence of God, in sending this dream to Pilate's wife; it is not likely that she had heard any thing, before, concerning Christ, at least not so as to occasion her dreaming of him, but it was immediately from God: perhaps she was one of the *devout and honourable women*, and had some sense of religion; yet God revealed himself by dreams to some

that had not, as to Nebuchadnez-zar.

[2] The tenderness and care of Pilate's wife, in sending this caution, thereupon, to her husband; *Have nothing to do with that just man.*

(5) The chief priests and the elders were busy, all this while, to influence the people in favour of Barabbas, *v.* 20. They *persuaded the multitude*, both by themselves and their emissaries, whom they sent abroad among them, *thdt they should ask Barabbas, and destroy Jesus*; suggesting that this Jesus was a deceiver, in league with Satan, an enemy to their church and temple; that, if he were let alone, the Romans would come, and take away their place and nation; that Barabbas, though a bad man, yet, having not the interest that Jesus had, could not do so much mischief. Thus they managed the mob, who otherwise were well affected to Jesus, and, if they had not been so much at the beck of their priests, would never have done such a preposterous thing as to prefer Barabbas before Jesus.

(6) Being thus over-ruled by the priests, at length they made their choice, *v.* 21. *Whether of the twain* (saith Pilate) *will ye that I release unto you?* He hoped that he had gained his point, to have Jesus released. But, to his great surprise, they said *Barabbas*; as if his *crimes* were *less*, and therefore he less *deserved to die*; or as if his *merits* were *greater*, and therefore he better *deserved to live*. This was it that Peter charged so home upon them (Acts iii. 14); *Ye desired a murderer to be granted to you*; yet

multitudes who choose the world, rather than God, for their ruler and portion, thus *choose their own delusions.*

2. Their pressing earnestly to have Jesus crucified, *vv.* 22, 23. Pilate, being amazed at their choice of Barabbas, was willing to hope that it was rather from a fondness for him than from an enmity to Jesus; and therefore he puts it to them, "*What shall I do then with Jesus?* Shall I release him likewise, for the greater honour of your feast, or will you leave it to me? No, *they all said, Let him be crucified.* That death they desired he might die, because it was looked upon as the most scandalous and ignominious; and they hoped thereby to make his followers ashamed to own him, and their relation to him.

Now, as to this demand, we are further told,

(1) How Pilate objected against it; *Why, what evil hath he done?* A proper question to ask before we censure any in common discourse, much more for a judge to ask before he pass a sentence of death.

(2) How they *insisted* upon it; *They cried out the more, Let him be crucified.* They do not go about to show any evil he had done, but, right or wrong, he must be *crucified.* Quitting all pretensions to the proof of the premises, they resolve to hold the conclusion, and what was wanting in evidence to make up in clamour; this unjust judge was wearied by importunity into an unjust sentence, as he in the parable into a just one (Luke xviii. 4, 5), and the cause carried purely by noise.

III. Here is the *devolving* of the *guilt* of Christ's blood upon the *people* and *priests*.

1. Pilate endeavours to transfer it from himself, v. 24.

(1) He sees it *to no purpose to contend*. What he said, [1] Would do no good; *he could prevail nothing*; he could not convince them what an unjust unreasonable thing it was for him to condemn a man whom he believed innocent, and whom they could not prove guilty. See how strong the stream of lust and rage sometimes is; neither authority nor reason will prevail to give check to it. Nay, [2] It was more likely to *do hurt*; he saw that rather a *tumult was made*.

(2) This puts him into a *great strait*, betwixt the peace of his own mind, and the peace of the city; he is loth to condemn an innocent man, and yet loth to *disoblige* the people, and raise a devil that would not be soon laid. Had he steadily and resolutely adhered to the sacred laws of justice, as a judge ought to do, he had not been in any perplexity; the matter was plain and past dispute, that a man in whom was found *no fault*, ought not to be crucified, upon any pretence whatsoever, nor must an unjust thing be done, to gratify any man or company of men in the world.

(3) Pilate thinks to trim the matter, and to pacify both the people and his own conscience too, by *doing it*, and yet *disowning* it, *acting* the thing, and yet *acquitting* himself from it at the same time.

Now Pilate endeavours to clear himself from the guilt,

[1] By a *sign*; He *took water, and washed his hands before the multitude*; not as if he thought thereby to cleanse himself from any guilt contracted before God, but to acquit himself before the people, from so much as contracting any guilt in this matter; as if he had said, "If it be done, bear witness that it is none of my doing."

[2] By a *saying*; in which, *First*, He *clears* himself; *I am innocent of the blood of this just person*. What nonsense was this, to condemn him, and yet protest that he was innocent of his blood!

2. The priests and people *consented* to take the guilt *upon themselves*; they all said, "*His blood be on us, and on our children.*" What a desperate word was this, and how little did they think what was the direful import of it, or to what an abyss of misery it would bring them and theirs! Christ had lately told them, that upon them would come *all the righteous blood shed upon the earth*, from that of the righteous Abel; but as if that were too little, they here imprecate upon themselves the guilt of that blood which was more precious than all the rest, and the guilt of which would lie heavier.

THE SCOURGING (*vv.* 26–32)

Here is,

I. The sentence passed, and the warrant signed for his execution; and this *immediately*, the same hour.

Jesus was *scourged*; this was an ignominious cruel punishment, especially as it was inflicted by the Romans, who were not under the moderation of the Jewish law, which forbade scourgings, above forty stripes; this punishment was most unreasonably inflicted on one that was sentenced to die: the *rods* were not to introduce the axes, but to supersede them.

3. He was then *delivered to be crucified*; though his chastisement was in order to our peace, yet there is no peace made but by the *blood of his cross* (Col. i. 20); therefore the scourging is not enough, he must be *crucified*; a kind of death used only among the Romans; the manner of it is such, that it seems to be the result of wit and cruelty in combination, each putting forth itself to the utmost, to make death in the highest degree terrible and miserable.

II. The barbarous treatment which the soldiers gave him, while things were getting ready for his execution. When he was condemned, he ought to have had some time allowed him to prepare for death. There was a law made by the Roman senate, in Tiberius's time, perhaps upon complaint of this and the like precipitation, that the execution of criminals should be deferred at least *ten days* after sentence. *Sueton in Tiber. cap.* 25. But there were scarcely allowed so many minutes to our Lord Jesus; nor had he any breathing-time during those minutes; it was a *crisis*, and there were no *lucid intervals* allowed him; *deep called unto deep*, and the storm continued without any intermission.

When he was *delivered* to be *crucified*, that was enough; they that *kill the body*, yield that there is no more that they *can do*, but Christ's enemies will *do more*, and, if it be possible, wrap up a thousand deaths in one. Though Pilate pronounced him innocent, yet his soldiers, his guards, set themselves to abuse him, being swayed more by the fury of the people *against him*, than by their master's testimony *for him*; the Jewish *rabble* infected the Roman soldiery, or perhaps it was not so much in spite to him, as to make *sport* for themselves, that they thus abused him. They understood that he *pretended to a crown; to taunt* him with that gave them some diversion, and an opportunity to make themselves and one another merry.

III. The conveying of him to the place of execution. After they had mocked and abused him, as long as they thought fit, they then *took the robe off from him*; to signify their divesting him of all the kingly authority they had invested him with, by putting it on him; and they put his own raiment on him, because that was to fall to the soldiers' share, that were employed in the execution. They took off the robe, but no mention is made of their taking off the *crown of thorns*, whence it is commonly supposed (though there is no certainty of it) that he was crucified with that on his head; for as he is a Priest upon his throne, so he was a King upon his cross. Christ was led to be crucified in *his own raiment*, because he himself was to *bear our sins in his own body upon the tree*. And here,

1. They *led him away* to be *crucified*; he was led *as a lamb to the slaughter*, as a sacrifice to the altar. We may well imagine how they hurried him on, and dragged him along, with all the speed

possible, lest anything should intervene to prevent the glutting of their cruel rage with his precious blood. It is probable that they now loaded him with taunts and reproaches, and treated him as the off-scouring of all things. They led him away *out of the city*; for Christ, that he might sanctify the people with his own blood, *suffered without the gate* (Heb. xiii. 12), as if he that was the glory of them that *waited for redemption* in Jerusalem was not worthy to live among them. To this he himself had an eye, when in the parable he speaks of his being *cast out of the vineyard*, ch. xxi. 39.

2. They compelled Simon of Cyrene *to bear his cross*, v. 32. It seems, at first he *carried the cross* himself, as Isaac carried the wood for the burnt-offering, which was to burn him. And this was intended, as other things, both for pain and shame to him. But after a while they *took the cross* off from him, either, (1) In compassion to him, because they saw it was too great a load for him. We can hardly think that they had any consideration of that, yet it teaches us that God *considers the frame* of his people, and will not *suffer them to be tempted above what they are able*; he gives them some breathing-time, but they must expect that the cross will return, and the lucid intervals only give them space to prepare for the next fit. But, (2) Perhaps it was because he could not, with the cross on his back, go forward so fast as they would have him. Or, (3) They were afraid, lest he should faint away under the load of his cross, and die, and so prevent what their malice further intended to do against him:

thus even the *tender mercies of the wicked* (which seem to be so) *are* really *cruel*. Taking the cross off from him, they *compelled* one Simon of Cyrene to bear it, pressing him to the service by the authority of the governor or the priests. It was a reproach, and none would do it but by compulsion. Some think that this Simon was a disciple of Christ, at least a well-wisher to him, and that they knew it, and therefore put this upon him. Note, All that will approve themselves disciples indeed, must follow Christ, *bearing his cross* (*ch.* xvi. 24), *bearing his reproach*, Heb. xiii. 13. We must know the *fellowship of his sufferings for us*, and patiently submit to all the sufferings for him we are called out to; for those only shall *reign with him*, that *suffer with him*; shall sit with him in his kingdom, that drink of *his cup*, and are baptized with *his baptism*.

THE CRUCIFIXION
(vv. 33–49)

We have here the crucifixion of our Lord Jesus.

I. The place where our Lord Jesus was put to death.

1. They came to a place called *Golgotha*, near adjoining to Jerusalem, probably the common place of execution.

2. There they *crucified* him (v. 35), nailed his hands and feet to the cross, and then reared it up, and him hanging on it; for so the manner of the Romans was to crucify. Let our hearts be touched with the feeling of that exquisite pain which our blessed Saviour now endured, and let us look upon him who was thus pierced, and mourn. Was ever

sorrow like unto his sorrow? And when we behold what manner of death he died, let us in that behold with *what manner of love* he *loved us*.

II. The barbarous and abusive treatment they gave him, in which their wit and malice vied which should excel. As if death, so great a death, were not bad enough, they contrived to add to the bitterness and terror of it.

1. By the drink they provided for him before he was nailed to the cross, *v*. 34. It was usual to have a cup of spiced wine for those to drink of, that were to be put to death, according to Solomon's direction (Prov. xxxi. 6, 7), *Give strong drink to him that is ready to perish*; but with that cup which Christ was to drink of, they mingled *vinegar and gall*, to make it sour and bitter. This signified, (1) The *sin of man*, which is a *root of bitterness, bearing gall and wormwood*, Deut. xxix. 18. (2) It signified the *wrath of God*, that cup which his Father *put into his hand*, a bitter cup indeed, like the *bitter water which caused the curse*, Numb. v. 18. This drink they offered him, as was literally foretold, Ps. lxix. 21. And, [1] He *tasted thereof*, and so had the *worst* of it, took the bitter taste into his mouth; he let no bitter cup go by him untasted, when he was making atonement for all our sinful tasting of forbidden fruit; now he was *tasting* death in its full bitterness. [2] He *would not drink it*, because he would not have the *best of it*; would have nothing like an opiate to lessen his sense of pain, for he would die so as to *feel himself die*, because he had so much

work to *do*, as our High Priest, in his suffering work.

2. By the dividing of his garments, *v*. 35. When they nailed him to the cross, they *stripped* him of his garments, at least his *upper garments*; for by sin we were made naked, to our shame, and thus he purchased for us white raiment to cover us. If we be at any time stripped of our comforts for Christ, let us bear it patiently; he was stripped for us. The clothes of those that are executed are the executioner's fee: four soldiers were employed in crucifying Christ, and they must each of them have a share: his upper garment, if it were divided, would be of no use to any of them, and therefore they agreed to *cast lots* for it.

They now *sat down, and watched him*, *v*. 36. The chief priests were careful, no doubt, in setting this guard, lest the people, whom they still stood in awe of, should rise, and rescue him. But Providence so ordered it, that those who were appointed to *watch* him, thereby became unexceptionable witnesses for him; having the opportunity to see and hear that which extorted from them that noble confession (*v*. 54), *Truly this was the Son of God*.

3. By the *title* set up over his head, *v*. 37. It was usual for the vindicating of public justice, and putting the greater shame upon malefactors that were executed, not only by a crier to proclaim before them, but by a writing also over their heads to notify what was the crime for which they suffered; so they set up over Christ's head his accusation written, to give public

notice of the charge against him; *This is Jesus the King of the Jews.* This they designed for his reproach, but God so overruled it, that even his accusation redounded to his honour. Pilate, instead of accusing Christ as a Criminal, proclaimed him a *King*, and that *three times*, in three inscriptions. Thus God makes men to serve *his* purposes, quite beyond *their own*.

4. By his companions with him in suffering, *v.* 38. There were *two thieves crucified with him* at the same time, in the same place, under the same guard; two highway-men, or robbers upon the road, as the word properly signifies. It is probable that this was appointed to be *execution-day*; and therefore they hurried the prosecution of Christ in the morning, that they might have him ready to be executed with the other criminals.

5. By the blasphemies and revilings with which they loaded him when he was hanging upon the cross; though we read not that they cast any reflections on the thieves that were crucified with him.

The taunts and jeers they uttered are here recorded.

First, They upbraided him with his *destroying of the temple*. "*Thou that destroyest the temple*, that vast and strong fabric, try thy strength now in plucking up that *cross*, and drawing those *nails*, and so *save thyself*; if thou hast the power thou hast boasted of, this is a proper time to exert it, and give proof of it; for it is supposed that every man will do his utmost to *save himself*."

Secondly, They upbraided him with his saying that he was *the Son of God*; If thou be so, say they, *come down from the cross.* Now they take the devil's words out of his mouth, with which he tempted him in the wilderness (*ch.* iv. 3, 6), and renew the same assault; *If thou be the Son of God.* They think that now, or never, he must prove himself to be the *Son of God*; forgetting that he had proved it by the miracles he wrought, particularly his raising of the dead; and unwilling to wait for the complete proof of it by his own resurrection, to which he had so often referred himself and them; which, if they had observed it, would have anticipated the offence of the cross. This comes of judging things by the present aspect of them, without a due remembrance of what is *past*, and a patient expectation of *what may further be produced.*

(2) The *chief priests and scribes*, the church rulers, and the *elders*, the state rulers, they mocked him, *v.* 41. They did not think it enough to invite the rabble to do it, but gave Christ the dishonour, and themselves the diversion, of reproaching him in their own proper persons. They should have been in the temple at their devotion, for it was the first day of the feast of unleavened bread, when there was to be a *holy convocation* (Lev. xxiii. 7); but they were here at the place of execution, spitting their venom at the Lord Jesus. How much below the grandeur and gravity of their character was this!

Two things the priests and elders upbraided him with.

[1] That he could not *save himself*, *v.* 42. He had been before abused in his prophetical and

kingly office, and now in his priestly office as a Saviour. *First*, They take it for granted that he *could not* save himself, and therefore had not the power he pretended to, when really he *would not* save himself, because he would die to *save us*. They should have argued, "He *saved others*, therefore he *could* save himself, and if he do not, it is for some good reason." But, *Secondly*, They would insinuate, that, because he did not now save himself, therefore all his pretence to save others was but sham and delusion, and was never really done; though the truth of his miracles was demonstrated beyond contradiction. *Thirdly*, They upbraid him with being *the King of Israel*. They dreamed of the external pomp and power of the Messiah, and therefore thought *the cross* altogether disagreeable to the King of Israel, and inconsistent with that character. Many people would like the *King of Israel* well enough, if he would but *come down from the cross*, if they could have his kingdom without the tribulation through which they must *enter into* it. But the matter is settled; if no cross, then no Christ, no crown. Those that would reign with him, must be willing to suffer with him, for Christ and his cross are *nailed together* in this world. *Fourthly*, They challenged him to *come down from the cross*. And what had become of us then, and the work of our redemption and salvation? If he had been provoked by these scoffs to *come down from the cross*, and so to have left his undertaking *unfinished*, we had been for ever *undone*. But his unchangeable love and resolution set him above, and

fortified him against, this temptation, so that he did not *fail*, nor was *discouraged*. *Fifthly*, They promised that, if he would *come down from the cross, they would believe him*. Let him give them that proof of his being the Messiah, and they will own him to be so.

[2] That God, *his Father*, would *not save him* (v. 43); *He trusted in God*, that is, he pretended to do so; for he said, *I am the Son of God*. Those who call God *Father*, and themselves *his children*, thereby profess to put a confidence in him, Ps. ix. 10. Now they suggest, that he did but deceive himself and others, when he made himself so much the *darling of heaven*; for, if he had been the Son of God (as *Job's* friends argued concerning him), he would not have been *abandoned to* all this misery, much less *abandoned in* it.

(3) To complete the reproach, the *thieves also that were crucified with him* were not only not reviled as he was, as if they had been saints compared with him, but, though fellow-sufferers with him, joined in with his prosecutors, and *cast the same in his teeth*; that is, one of them did, who said, *If thou be the Christ, save thyself and us*, Luke xxiii. 39.

Well, thus our Lord Jesus having undertaken to satisfy the justice of God for the wrong done him in his honour by sin, he did it by suffering *in his honour*; not only by divesting himself of that which was due to him as the Son of God, but by submitting to the utmost indignity that could be done to the worst of men; because he was made sin for us, he was thus made a curse for us, to make reproach easy to us, if at any time we suffer it, and have all manner of evil said against us falsely, for righteousness' sake.

III. We have here the frowns of heaven, which our Lord Jesus was under, in the midst of all these injuries and indignities from men. Concerning which, observe,

1. How this was signified—by an extraordinary and miraculous eclipse of the sun, which continued for *three hours*, v. 45. There was darkness *over all the earth*; so most interpreters understand it, though our translation confines it to *that land*. An extraordinary light gave intelligence of the birth of Christ (*ch.* ii. 2), and therefore it was proper that an extraordinary darkness should notify his death, for he is the *Light of the world*. Never were there three such hours since the day that God created man upon the earth, never such a dark and awful scene; the *crisis* of that great affair of man's redemption and salvation.

2. How he complained of it (*v.* 46); *About the ninth hour*, when it began to clear up, after a long and silent conflict. *Jesus cried, Eli, Eli, lama sabachthani?* The words are related in the Syriac tongue, in which they were spoken, because worthy of double remark, and for the sake of the perverse construction which his enemies put upon them, in putting *Elias* for *Eli*. Now observe here,

(1) Whence he borrowed this complaint—from Ps. xxii. 1. It is not probable (as some have thought) that he repeated the whole psalm; yet hereby he intimated that the whole was to be applied to him, and that David, in spirit, there

spoke of his humiliation and exaltation.

(2) How he uttered it—*with a loud voice*; which bespeaks the extremity of his pain and anguish, the strength of nature remaining in him, and the great earnestness of his spirit in this expostulation. Now the scripture was fulfilled (Joel iii. 15, 16); *The sun and the moon shall be darkened. The Lord shall also roar out of Zion, and utter his voice from Jerusalem.* David often speaks of his *crying aloud* in prayer, Ps. lv. 17.

(3) What the complaint was— *My God, My God, why hast thou forsaken me?*

Note, [1] That our Lord Jesus was, in his sufferings, for a time, *forsaken by his Father.* So he saith himself, who we are sure was under no mistake concerning his own case. Not that the union between the divine and human nature was in the least weakened or shocked; no, he was *now by the eternal Spirit offering himself*: nor as if there were any abatement of his Father's love to him, or his to his Father; we are sure that there was upon his mind no horror of God, or despair of his favour, nor any thing of the torments of hell; but his Father forsook him; that is, *First*, He delivered him up into the hands of his enemies, and did not appear to deliver him out of their hands. He let loose the powers of darkness against him, and suffered them to do their worst. *Secondly*, He withdrew from him the present comfortable sense of his complacency in him. When *his soul* was first *troubled*, he had a *voice from heaven* to comfort him (John xii.

27, 28); when he was in his agony in the garden, there appeared an angel from heaven strengthening him; but now he had neither the one nor the other. God hid his face from him, and for awhile withdrew his rod and staff in the darksome valley. *Thirdly*, He let out upon his soul an afflicting sense of his wrath against man for sin. Christ was made *Sin* for us, a *Curse* for us; and therefore, though God loved him as a Son, he frowned upon him as a Surety.

[2] That Christ's being *forsaken* of his Father was the most grievous of his sufferings, and that which he complained most of.

[3] That our Lord Jesus, even when he was thus forsaken of his Father, kept hold of him as his God, notwithstanding; *My God, my God*; though forsaking me, yet *mine*. Christ was God's *servant* in carrying on the work of redemption, to him he was to make satisfaction, and by him to be carried through and crowned, and upon that account he calls him *his God*; for he was now *doing his will*. See Isa. xlix. 5–9.

(4) See how his enemies impiously bantered and ridiculed this complaint (*v.* 47); *They said, This man calleth for Elias*. Some think that this was the ignorant mistake of the Roman soldiers, who had heard talk of Elias, and of the Jews' expectation of the coming of Elias, but knew not the signification of *Eli, Eli*, and so made this blundering comment upon these words of Christ, perhaps not hearing the latter part of what he said, for the noise of the people. But others think that it was the wilful mistake

of some of the Jews, who knew very well what he said, but were disposed to abuse him, and make themselves and their companions merry, and to misrepresent him as one who, being forsaken of God, was driven to trust in creatures; perhaps hinting also, that he who had pretended to be himself the Messiah, would now be glad to be beholden to Elias, who was expected to be only the harbinger and forerunner of the Messiah.

IV. The cold comfort which his enemies ministered to him in this agony, which was like all the rest.

1. Some *gave him vinegar to drink* (*v.* 48); instead of some cordial-water to revive and refresh him under this heavy burden, they tantalized him with that which did not only add to the reproach they were loading him with, but did too sensibly represent that cup of trembling which his Father had *put into his hand*.

2. Others, with the same purpose of disturbing and abusing him, refer him to Elias (*v.* 49); "*Let be, let us see whether Elias will come to save him*."

THE DEATH OF CHRIST
(*vv.* 50–56)

We have here, at length, an account of the death of Christ, and several remarkable passages that attended it.

I. The *manner* how he breathed his last (*v.* 50); between the third and the sixth hour, that is, between nine and twelve o'clock, as we reckon, he was nailed to the cross, and soon after the ninth hour, that is, between three and four o'clock in the afternoon, he *died*. That was the time of the offering of the evening sacrifice, and the time when the paschal lamb was killed; and Christ our Passover was sacrificed for us and offered himself in the evening of the world a sacrifice to God of a sweet-smelling savour.

Two things are here noted concerning the manner of Christ's dying.

1. That he *cried with a loud voice*, as before, *v.* 46. Now,

(1) This was a sign, that, after all his pains and fatigues, his life was *whole* in him, and nature *strong*.

(2) It was significant. This *loud voice* shows that he attacked our spiritual enemies with an undaunted courage, and such a bravery of resolution as bespeaks him hearty in the cause and daring in the encounter. Christ's loud cry was like a trumpet blown over the sacrifices.

2. That then he *yielded up the ghost*. This is the usual periphrasis of dying; to show that the Son of God upon the cross did truly and properly die by the violence of the pain he was put to. His *soul* was separated from his *body*, and so his body was left really and truly dead. He had undertaken to make his soul an *offering for sin*; and he did it, when he *yielded up the ghost*, and voluntarily resigned it.

II. The miracles that attended his death.

1. *Behold, the veil of the temple was rent in twain*. Just as our Lord Jesus expired, at the time of the offering of the evening-sacrifice, and upon a solemn day, when the priests were officiating in the temple, and might themselves be eye-witnesses of it, *the veil of the temple was rent* by an invisible power; that veil which parted between the *holy place* and the *most holy*.

(1) It was in correspondence with the temple of Christ's body, which was now in the dissolving. This was the true temple, in which dwelt *the fulness of the Godhead*; when Christ *cried with a loud voice, and gave up the ghost*, and so dissolved that temple, the literal temple did, as it were, echo to that cry, and answer the stroke, by *rending its veil*.

(2) It signified the revealing and unfolding of the mysteries of the Old Testament. The veil of the temple was for concealment, as was that on the face of Moses, therefore it was called the *veil of the covering*. But now, at the death of Christ, all was laid open, the mysteries were unveiled, so that now he that runs may read the meaning of them. Now we see that the mercy-seat signified *Christ* the great *Propitiation*; the pot of *manna* signified Christ the Bread of life. Thus *we all with open face behold, as in a glass* (which helps the sight, as the veil hindered it), *the glory of the Lord. Our eyes see the salvation*.

(3) It signified the uniting of Jew and Gentile, by the removing of the partition wall between them, which was the ceremonial law, by which the Jews were distinguished from all other people (as a *garden enclosed*), were brought near to God, while others were made to *keep their distance*.

(4) It signified the consecrating and laying open of *a new and living way* to God. The veil kept people off from drawing near to the most holy place, where the *Shechinah*

was. But the rending of it signified that Christ by his death opened a way to God, [1] *For himself.* Though he did not personally ascend into the holy place not made with hands till above forty days after, yet he immediately acquired a right to enter, and had a virtual admission. [2] *For us in him*: so the apostle applies it, Heb. x. 19, 20. We have *boldness to enter into the holiest, by that new and living way which he has consecrated for us through the veil.* We have free access through Christ to the throne of grace, or mercy-seat, now, and to the throne of glory hereafter, Heb. iv. 16; vi. 20.

2. The *earth did quake;* not only mount Calvary, where Christ was crucified, but the *whole land,* and the adjacent countries.

3. The *rocks rent;* the hardest and firmest part of the earth was made to feel this mighty shock.

4. The *graves were opened.* This matter is not related so fully as our curiosity would wish; for the scripture was not intended to gratify that; it should seem, the same earthquake that rent the rocks, *opened the graves,* and many bodies of *saints which slept, arose.* Death to the saints is but the *sleep* of the body, and the *grave* the bed it *sleeps in*; they awoke by the power of the Lord Jesus, and (*v.* 53) came *out of the graves after his resurrection, and went into Jerusalem, the holy city, and appeared unto many.*

III. The conviction of his enemies that were employed in the execution (*v.* 54), which some make no less than another miracle, all things considered. Observe,

1. The persons convinced; *the centurion, and they that were with him watching Jesus*; a captain and his company, that were set on the guard on this occasion. (1) They were *soldiers,* whose profession is commonly hardening, and whose breasts are commonly not so susceptible as some others of the impressions either of fear or pity. But there is no spirit too big, too bold, for the power of Christ to break and humble. (2) They were *Romans, Gentiles,* who knew not the scriptures which were now fulfilled; yet they only were convinced.

2. The means of their conviction; they perceived *the earthquake,* which frightened them, and saw the other *things that were done.* These were designed to assert the honour of Christ in his sufferings, and had their end on these soldiers, whatever they had on others.

3. The expressions of this conviction, in two things.

(1) The *terror* that was *struck* upon them; they *feared greatly*; feared lest they should have been buried in the darkness, or swallowed up in the earthquake.

(2) The *testimony* that was *extorted* from them; they said, *Truly this was the Son of God*; a noble confession; Peter was blessed for it, *ch.* xvi. 16, 17. The best of his disciples could not have said more at any time, and at this time they had not faith and courage enough to say thus much.

IV. The attendance of his friends, that were witnesses of his death, *vv.* 55, 56. Observe,

1. Who they were; *many women who followed him from Galilee.* Not his apostles (only elsewhere we

264

find John by the cross, John xix. 26), their hearts failed them, they durst not appear, for fear of coming under the same condemnation. But here were a company of women, some would have called them *silly* women, that *boldly* stuck to Christ, when the rest of his disciples had basely deserted him.

2. What they did; they were *beholding afar off*.

(1) They stood *afar off*. Whether their own fear or their enemies' fury kept them at a distance, is not certain; however, it was an aggravation of the sufferings of Christ, that his *lovers and friends stood aloof from his sore*, Ps. xxxviii. 11; Job xix. 13.

(2) They were there *beholding*, in which they showed a concern and kindness for Christ; when they were debarred from doing any other office of love to him, they looked a look of love toward him.

THE BURIAL (*vv.* 57–66)

We have here an account of Christ's *burial*, and the manner and circumstances of it, concerning which observe, 1. The *kindness* and *good will* of his friends that *laid him in the grave*. 2. The *malice* and *ill will* of his enemies that were very solicitous to keep him there.

I. His friends gave him a *decent burial*. Observe,

1. In general, that Jesus Christ was *buried*; when his precious soul was gone to paradise, his blessed body was deposited in the chambers of the grave, that he might answer the type of Jonas, and fulfil the prophecy of Isaias; he *made his grave with the wicked*. Thus in all things he must be made *like unto his*

brethren, sin only excepted, and, like us, unto dust *he must return*. He was buried, to make his death the more certain, and his resurrection the more illustrious. Pilate would not deliver his body to be buried, till he was well assured that he was really dead; while the witnesses lay *unburied*, there were some hopes concerning them, Rev. xi. 8. But Christ, the great Witness, is as one *free among the dead, like the slain that lie in the grave*. He was *buried*, that he might take off the terror of the grave, and make it easy to us, might warm and perfume that cold noisome bed for us, and that we might be *buried with him*.

2. The particular circumstances of his burial here related.

(1) The time *when* he was buried; *when the evening was come*; the same evening that he died, before sun-set, as is usual in burying malefactors. It was not deferred till the next day, because it was *the sabbath*; for burying the dead is not proper work either for a day of rest or for a day of rejoicing, as the sabbath is.

(2) The person that took care of the funeral was Joseph of Arimathea. The apostles had all fled, and none of them appeared to show this respect to their Master, which the disciples of John *showed* to him after he was beheaded, who *took up his body, and buried it, ch.* xiv. 12. The women that followed him durst not move in it; then did God stir up this good man to do it; for what work God has to do, he will find out instruments to do it.

(3) The grant of the dead body procured from Pilate, *v.* 58. Joseph *went to* Pilate, the proper person to

be applied to on this occasion, who had the disposal of the body. In Joseph's petition, and Pilate's ready grant of it, *honour* was done to Christ, and a testimony borne to his *integrity*.

(4) The dressing of the body in its grave-clothes (*v.* 59); though he was an honourable counsellor, yet he himself *took the body*, as it should seem, into his own arms, from the infamous and accursed tree (Acts xiii. 29); for where there is true love to Christ, no service will be thought too mean to stoop to for him. Having taken it, he wrapped it in a *clean linen cloth*; for burying in linen was then the common usage, which Joseph complied with.

(5) The depositing of it in the sepulchre, *v.* 60. Here there was nothing of that pomp and solemnity with which the grandees of the world are *brought to the grave, and laid in the tomb*, Job xxi. 32. A private funeral did best befit him whose kingdom came not with observation.

[1] He was laid in a *borrowed* tomb, in Joseph's burying place; as he had not a house of his own, wherein to *lay his head* while he lived, so he had not a grave of his own, wherein to *lay his body* when he was dead, which was an instance of his poverty.

[2] He was laid in a *new tomb*, which Joseph, it is likely, designed *for himself*; it would, however, be *never the worse* for *his* lying in it, who was to rise so quickly, but a *great deal the better* for *his* lying in it, who has altered the property of the grave, and made it *anew* indeed, by turning it into a *bed of*

rest, nay into a *bed of spices*, for all the saints.

[3] In a tomb that was *hewn out of a rock*; the ground about Jerusalem was generally rocky. Providence ordered it that Christ's sepulchre should be in a solid entire rock, that no room might be left to suspect his disciples had access to it by some underground passage, or broke through the back wall of it, to steal the body; for there was no access to it but by the door, which was watched.

[4] A *great stone was rolled to the door of his sepulchre*; this also was according to the custom of the Jews in burying their dead, as appears by the description of the grave of Lazarus (John xi. 38), signifying that those who are dead, are *separated* and *cut off from all the living*; if the grave were his prison, now was the prison-door locked and bolted.

(6) The company that attended the funeral; and that was very *small* and *mean—Mary Magdalene, and the other Mary*, *v.* 56. These, as they had attended him *to the cross*, so they followed him to *the grave*; as if they composed themselves to sorrow, they *sat over against the sepulchre*, not so much to fill their eyes with the sight of what was done, as to empty them in rivers of tears.

II. His enemies did what they could to prevent his resurrection; what they did herein was *the next day that followed the day of the preparation*, *v.* 62. On that day, the *chief priests and Pharisees*, when they should have been at their devotions, asking pardon for the sins of the week past, were dealing with Pilate about securing the sepulchre, and so *adding rebellion to their sin*. They that had so often quarrelled with Christ for works of the greatest mercy on that day, were themselves busied in a work of the greatest malice. Observe here,

(1) Their address to *Pilate*; they were vexed that the body was given to one that would bury it decently; but, since it must be so, they desire a guard may be set on the sepulchre.

[1] Their petition sets forth, that *that deceiver* (so they call him who is truth itself) *had said, After three days I will rise again*. He had said so, and his disciples *remembered* those very words for the confirmation of their faith, but his persecutors remember them for the provocation of their rage and malice.

[2] It further sets forth their jealousy; *lest his disciples come by night, and steal him away, and say, He is risen*.

First, That which *really* they were afraid of, was, his *resurrection*; that which is most Christ's honour and his people's joy, is most the terror of his enemies.

Secondly, That which they took on them to be afraid of, was, lest *his disciples should come by night, and steal him away*, which was a very improbable thing; for, 1. They had not the courage to own him while he lived, when they might have done him and themselves real service; and it was not likely that his death should put courage into such cowards. 2. What could they promise themselves by stealing away his body, and making people believe he was risen; when, if he should not rise, and so prove himself a deceiver, his disciples, who had left all for him in this world, in

dependence upon a recompence in the other world, would of all others suffer most by the imposture, and would have had reason to throw the first stone at his name?

[3] In consideration hereof, they humbly move to have a guard set upon the sepulchre till the third day; *Command that the sepulchre be made sure*.

(2) Pilate's answer to this address (v. 65); *Ye have a watch, make it sure, as sure as you can*. He was ready to gratify Christ's friends, in allowing them the body, and his enemies, in setting a guard upon it, being desirous to please all sides, while perhaps he laughed in his sleeve at both for making such ado, *pro* and *con*, about the dead body of a man, looking upon the hopes of one side and the fears of the other to be alike ridiculous.

(3) The wonderful care they took, hereupon, to secure the sepulchre (v. 66); *They sealed the stone*. But not trusting too much to that, withal they *set a watch*, to keep *his disciples* from coming to *steal him away*, and, if possible, to hinder *him* from coming out of the grave. To guard the sepulchre against the poor weak disciples, was folly, because *needless*; but to think to guard it against the power of God was folly, because *fruitless* and to no purpose; and yet they thought they had *dealt wisely*.

CHAPTER TWENTY-EIGHT

THE RESURRECTION
(vv. 1–10)

For the proof of Christ's resurrection, we have here the testimony of *the angel*, and of *Christ* himself,

The Resurrection

concerning his resurrection. Now we may think that it would have been better, if the matter had been so ordered, that a competent number of witnesses should have been present, and have seen the stone rolled away by the angel, and the dead body reviving, as people saw Lazarus come out of the grave, and then the matter had been past dispute; but let us not prescribe to Infinite Wisdom, which ordered that the witnesses of his resurrection should see him *risen*, but not see him *rise*. Christ gave such proofs of his resurrection as were *corroborated* by the scriptures, and by the *word* which he had *spoken* (Luke xxiv. 6, 7–44; Mark xvi. 7); for here we must *walk by faith, not by sight*. We have here,

I. The *coming* of the *good women* to the *sepulchre*.

Observe, 1. *When* they came; *in the end of the sabbath, as it began to dawn toward the first day of the week, v.* 1. This fixes the time of Christ's resurrection.

(1) He arose the *third day* after his death; that was the time which he had often pre-fixed, and he kept within it. He was buried in the evening of the sixth day of the week, and arose in the morning of the first day of the following week, so that he lay in the grave about thirty-six or thirty-eight hours. He lay so long, to show that he was really and truly dead; and no longer, that he might not *see corruption*. He arose the third day, to answer the type of the prophet Jonas (*ch.* xii. 40), and to accomplish that prediction (Hos. vi. 2), *The third day he will raise us up, and we shall live in his sight*.

(2) He arose *after the Jewish sabbath*, and it was the passover-sabbath; all that day he lay in the grave, to signify the abolishing of the Jewish feasts and the other parts of the ceremonial law, and that his people must be dead to such observances, and take no more notice of them than he did when he *lay in the grave*. Christ on *the sixth day finished* his work; he said, *It is finished*; on the seventh day he rested, and then on the first day of the next week did as it were begin a new world, and enter upon new work.

(3) He arose upon the *first day of the week*; on the first day of the first week God *commanded the light to shine out of darkness*; on this day therefore did he who was to be the Light of the world, shine out of the darkness of the grave; and the seventh-day sabbath being buried with Christ, it arose again in the first-day sabbath, called the *Lord's day* (Rev. i. 10), and no other day of the week is from henceforward mentioned in all the New Testament than this, and this often, as the day which Christians religiously observed in solemn assemblies, to the honour of Christ, John xx. 19, 26; Acts xx. 7; 1 Cor. xvi. 2.

(4) He arose *as it began to dawn* toward that day; as soon as it could be said that the *third day* was come, the time prefixed for his resurrection, he *arose*; after his withdrawings from his people, he returns with all convenient *speed*, and *cuts the work* as *short in righteousness* as may be.

2. Who they were, that came to the sepulchre; *Mary Magdalene and the other Mary*, the same that

268

attended the funeral, and *sat over against the sepulchre*, as before they *sat over against the cross*; still they studied to express their love to Christ; still they were enquiring after him. Then shall we *know*, if we thus *follow on to know*. No mention is made of the Virgin Mary being with them; it is probable that the *beloved disciple*, who had taken her to his own home, hindered her from *going to the grave to weep there*.

3. What they *came to do*: the other evangelists say that they came to anoint the body; Matthew saith that they came to *see the sepulchre*, whether it was as they left it; hearing perhaps, but not being sure, that the chief priests had set a guard upon it. They went, to show their good-will in another visit to the dear remains of their beloved Master, and perhaps not without some thoughts of his resurrection, for they could not have quite forgotten all he had said of it.

II. The appearance of an angel of the Lord to them, *vv.* 2–4. We have here an account of the manner of the resurrection of Christ, as far as it was fit that we should know.

1. There was a *great earthquake*. When he died, the earth that *received him*, shook for fear; now that he arose, the earth that *resigned him*, leaped for joy in his exaltation.

2. The *angel of the Lord descended from heaven*. The angels frequently attended our Lord Jesus, at his birth, in his temptation, in his agony; but upon the cross we find no angel attending him: when his Father *forsook him*, the angels withdrew from him; but now that

he is resuming the glory he had before the foundation of the world, now, behold, the *angels of God worship him*.

3. He came, and rolled back the stone from the door, and sat upon it. Our Lord Jesus could have *rolled back the stone* himself by his own power, but he chose to have it done by an angel, to signify that having undertaken to make satisfaction for our sin, imputed to him, and being under arrest pursuant to that imputation, he did not *break prison*, but had a fair and *legal discharge*, obtained from heaven; he did not break prison, but an officer was sent on purpose to *roll away the stone*, and so to open the prison door, which would never have been done, if he had not made a *full satisfaction*.

4. That his *countenance was like lightning, and his raiment white as snow*, *v.* 3. This was a visible representation, by that which we call *splendid* and *illustrious*, of the *glories* of the invisible world, which know no *difference of colours*. When Christ died, the court of heaven *went into deep mourning*, signified by the *darkening of the sun*; but when he arose, they again put on the *garments of praise*.

5. That *for fear of him the keepers did shake, and became as dead men*, *v.* 4. They were posted here, to *keep a dead man in his grave*—as easy a piece of service surely as was ever assigned them, and yet it proves too hard for them. They were told that they must expect to be assaulted by a company of feeble faint-hearted disciples, who for fear of them would soon *shake* and become as *dead men*, but are amazed when they find themselves attacked by a

mighty angel, whom they dare not look in the face.

III. The message which this angel delivered to the women, *vv.* 5–7.

1. He *encourages them against their fears*, *v.* 5. "*Fear not ye*. Let not the news I have to tell you, be any surprise to you, for you were told before that your Master would rise; let it be no terror to you, for his resurrection will be your consolation; fear not any hurt, that I will do you, nor any evil tidings I have to tell you. *Fear not ye, for I know that ye seek Jesus.* I know you are friends to the cause. I do not come to frighten you, but to encourage you."

2. He *assures them of the resurrection of Christ*; and there was enough in that to silence their fears (*v.* 6); He *is not here, for he is risen.*

Two things the angel refers these women to, for the confirmation of their faith, touching Christ's resurrection.

[1] To his *word* now *fulfilled*, which they might *remember; He is risen, as he said.* This he vouches as the proper object of faith; "He said that he *would rise*, and you know that he is the *Truth* itself, and therefore have reason to expect that he *should rise*; why should you be backward to *believe* that which he told you would be?"

[2] To his *grave* now *empty*, which they might *look into*; "*Come, see the place where the Lord lay.* Compare what you have *heard*, with what you *see*, and, putting both together, you will *believe*."

3. He *directs them* to go *carry the tidings* of it to his disciples (*v.* 7); Go *quickly, and tell his disciples.* It is probable that they were for

entertaining themselves with the sight of the sepulchre and discourse with the angels. It was good to be here, but they have other work appointed them; *this is a day of good tidings*, and though they have the *first taste* of it, yet they must not have the *monopoly* of it, must not hold their peace, any more than those lepers, 2 Kings vii. 9. They must go *tell the disciples.*

They were directed to appoint the disciples to *meet him in Galilee.* There were other appearances of Christ to them before that in *Galilee*, which were sudden and surprising; but he would have one to be solemn and public, and gave them notice of it before.

Lastly, The angel solemnly affirms upon his word the truth of what he had related to them; "*Lo, I have told you*, you may be assured of it, and depend upon it; *I* have told you, who dare not tell a lie. *The word spoken by angels was steadfast*, Heb. ii. 2.

IV. The women's *departure* from the *sepulchre*, to bring notice to the disciples, *v.* 8. And observe,

1. What frame and temper of spirit they were in; They *departed with fear and great joy*; a strange mixture, fear and joy at the same time, in the same soul. To hear that Christ was risen, was matter of joy; but to be led into his grave, and to see an angel, and talk with him about it, could not but cause fear. It was good news, but they were *afraid* that it was too *good* to be true. But observe, it is said of their joy, It was *great* joy; it is not said so of their fear.

2. What haste they made; *They did run.*

3. What errand they went upon; They ran, to *bring his disciples word.*

V. Christ's appearing to the women, to confirm the testimony of the angel, *vv.* 9, 10. These zealous good women not only heard the first tidings of him, but had the first sight of him, after his resurrection.

Here is, 1. Christ's surprising appearance to the women; *As they went to tell his disciples, behold, Jesus met them.*

2. The salutation wherewith he accosted them; *All hail.* We use the old *English form of salutation,* wishing *all health* to those we meet; for so *All hail* signifies, and is expressive of the Greek form of salutation here used, answering to that of the Hebrew, *Peace be unto you.*

3. The affectionate respect they paid him; *They came, and held him by the feet, and worshipped him.*

4. The encouraging words Christ said to them, *v.* 10. Now observe here,

(1) How he rebukes their fear; *Be not afraid.* They must not fear being imposed upon by these repeated notices of his resurrection, nor fear any hurt from the appearance of one from the dead; for the news, though strange, was both *true* and *good.*

(2) How he repeats their message; "*Go, tell my brethren,* that they must prepare for a journey into Galilee, and there *they shall see me.*"

A DECEPTION (*vv.* 11–15)

For the further proof of the resurrection of Christ, we have here the confession of the adversaries that were upon the guard; and there are two things which strengthen this testimony—that they were *eyewitnesses,* and did themselves see the glory of the resurrection, which none else did—and that they were *enemies,* set there to oppose and obstruct his resurrection.

The sham was *ridiculous,* and carried along with it its own confutation. If *they slept,* how could they know any thing of the matter, or say who came? If *any one* of them was awake to *observe it,* no doubt, he would awake them all to *oppose it*; for that was the only thing they had in charge. It was altogether improbable that a company of poor, weak, cowardly, dispirited men should expose themselves for so inconsiderable an achievement as the rescue of the dead body. Why were not the houses where they lodged diligently searched, and other means used to discover the dead body; but this was so thin a lie as one might easily see through. But had it been ever so plausible, (2) It was a wicked thing for these priests and elders to hire those soldiers to tell a deliberate lie (if it had been in a matter of ever so small importance), against their consciences. Those know not what they do, who draw others to commit one wilful sin; for that may debauch conscience, and be an inlet to many. But, (3) Considering this as intended to overthrow the great doctrine of Christ's resurrection, this was a sin against the last remedy, and was, in effect, a blasphemy *against the Holy Ghost,* imputing *that* to the roguery of the disciples, which was done by *the power of the Holy Ghost.*

But lest the soldiers should object the penalty they incurred by the Roman law for *sleeping upon the guard*, which was very severe (Acts xii. 19), they promised to interpose with the governor; "*We will persuade him, and secure you.*"

Well, thus was the plot laid; now what success had it?

[1] Those that were *willing to deceive*, took the money, and did as they were taught.

The great argument to prove Christ to be the Son of God, is, his resurrection, and none could have more convincing proofs of the truth of that than these soldiers had; they saw the angel descend from heaven, saw the stone rolled away, saw the body of Christ come out of the grave, unless the consternation they felt hindered them; and yet they were so far from being convinced by it themselves, that they were hired to belie him, and to hinder others from believing in him.

[2] Those that were willing to be deceived, not only credited, but propagated, the story; This *saying is commonly reported among the Jews until this day*. The sham took well enough, and answered the end.

THE GREAT COMMISSION
(*vv.* 16–20)

This evangelist passes over several other appearances of Christ, recorded by Luke and John, and hastens to this, which was of all other the most solemn, as being promised and appointed again and again before his death, and after his resurrection. Observe,

I. How the disciples attended his appearance, according to the appointment (*v.* 16); *They went into Galilee*, a long journey to go for one sight of Christ, but it was worth while. They had seen him several times at Jerusalem, and yet they went into Galilee, to see him there.

II. How they were affected with the appearance of Christ to them, *v.* 17. Now was the time that he was *seen of above five hundred brethren at once*, 1 Cor. xv. 6. We are told,

1. That they *worshipped him*; many of them did so, nay, it should seem, they all did that, they gave divine honour to him, which was signified by some outward expressions of adoration. Note, All that see the Lord Jesus with an eye of faith are obliged to *worship him*.

2. But *some doubted*, some of those that were then present. These doubts were afterward removed, and their faith grew up to a full assurance, and it tended much to the honour of Christ, that the disciples *doubted* before they *believed*; so that they cannot be said to be credulous, and willing to be imposed upon; for they first *questioned*, and *proved all things*, and then *held fast* that which was *true*, and which they found to be so.

III. What Jesus Christ said to them (*vv.* 18–20); *Jesus came, and spoke unto them*. Christ now delivered to his apostles the great charter of his kingdom in the world, was sending them out as his ambassadors, and here gives them their credentials.

In opening this great charter, we may observe two things.

1. The commission which our Lord Jesus received himself from the Father. Being about to *authorize* his apostles, if any ask by what

authority he doeth it, and who gave him that authority, here he tells us, *All power is given unto me in heaven and in earth*; a very great word, and which none but he could say. Hereby he asserts his universal dominion as Mediator, which is the great foundation of the Christian religion. He has *all power*. Observe, (1) *Whence* he hath this power. He did not assume it, or usurp it, but it was *given* him, he was legally entitled to it, and invested in it, by a grant from him who is the Fountain of all being, and consequently of all power. God *set him King* (Ps. ii. 6), inaugurated and enthroned him, Luke i. 32. (2) *Where* he has this power; in *heaven and earth*, comprehending the universe. Christ is the sole universal Monarch, he is *Lord of all*, Acts x. 36.

2. The commission he gives to those whom he sent forth; *Go ye therefore*. This commission is given, (1) To the *apostles* primarily, the chief ministers of state in Christ's kingdom, the architects that laid the foundation of the church. Now those that had followed Christ in the regeneration, were *set on thrones* (Luke xxii. 30); *Go ye*. It is not only a word of command, like that, *Son, go work*, but a word of encouragement, *Go*, and *fear not, have I not sent you?* (2) It is given to their successors, the ministers of the gospel, whose business it is to transmit the gospel from age to age, to the end of the world in time, as it was theirs to transmit it from nation to nation, to the end of the world in place, and no less necessary. The Old-Testament promise of a gospel ministry is made to a succession (Isa. lix.

21); and this must be so understood, otherwise how could Christ be with them always to the *consummation of the world*? Christ, at his ascension, gave not only apostles and prophets, but *pastors and teachers*, Eph. iv. 11. Now observe,

[1] How far his commission is extended; to *all nations*. Go, and disciple *all nations*. Not that they must go all together into every place, but by consent disperse themselves in such manner as might best *diffuse* the light of the gospel. Now this plainly signifies it to be the will of Christ, *First*, That the covenant of peculiarity, made with the Jews, should now be cancelled and disannulled. *Secondly*, That salvation by Christ should be offered to all, and none excluded that did not by their unbelief and impenitence exclude themselves.

[2] What is the principal intention of this commission; to *disciple* all nations. "*Admit them disciples*; do your utmost to make the nations Christian nations"; not, "Go to the nations, and denounce the judgments of God against them, as Jonah against Nineveh, and as the other Old-Testament prophets" (though they had reason enough to expect it for their wickedness), "but go, and *disciple them*."

[3] Their instructions for executing this commission.

First, They must *admit disciples* by the *sacred rite of baptism*; "Go into all nations, preach the gospel to them, work miracles among them, and persuade them to come in themselves, and bring their children with them, into the church of Christ, and then admit them and theirs into the church, by washing them with water."

Secondly, This baptism must be administered *in the name of the Father, and of the Son, and of the Holy Ghost*. That is, 1. *By authority from heaven*, and not *of man*; for his ministers act by authority from the three persons in the Godhead, who all concur, as to our *creation*, so to our *redemption*; they have their commission under the great seal of heaven, which puts an honour upon the ordinance, though to a carnal eye, like him that instituted it, it has *no form or comeliness*. 2. *Calling upon the name* of the Father, Son, and Holy Ghost. Every thing is sanctified by prayer, and particularly the waters of baptism. But, 3. It is *into the name* of *Father, Son, and Holy Ghost*; this was intended as the *summary* of the first principles of the Christian religion, and of the new covenant, and according to it the ancient creeds were drawn up. By our being baptized, we solemnly profess, (1) Our *assent* to the scripture-revelation concerning *God, the Father, Son, and Holy Ghost*. (2) Our *consent* to a covenant-relation to God, *the Father, Son, and Holy Ghost*. Baptism is a *sacrament*, that is, it is *an oath*. It is an oath of *abjuration*, by which we renounce the world and the flesh, as rivals with God for the throne in our hearts; and an oath of *allegiance*, by which we resign and give up *ourselves* to God, to be *his*, our own selves, our whole selves, *body, soul, and spirit*, to be governed by his will, and made happy in his favour.

Thirdly, Those that are thus baptized, and enrolled among the disciples of Christ, must be taught (v. 20); *Teaching them to observe all things, whatsoever I have commanded you*. This denotes two things.

(1) The duty of *disciples*, of all *baptized Christians*; they must observe all things whatsoever Christ has commanded, and, in order to that, must submit to the teaching of those whom he sends.

(2) The duty of the apostles of Christ, and his ministers; and that is, to *teach* the commands of Christ, to expound them to his disciples, to press upon them the necessity of obedience, and to assist them in applying the general commands of Christ to particular cases.

3. Here is the assurance he gives them of his spiritual presence with them in the execution of this commission; *And lo, I am with you always, even unto the end of the world*. Observe,

The favour promised them; *I am with you*. Not, *I will be* with you, but *I am*.

They shall have his *constant* presence; *always, all days*, every day. There is no day, no hour of the day, in which our Lord Jesus is not present with his churches and with his ministers; if there were, that day, that hour, they were undone. Since his resurrection he had appeared to them *now and then*, once a week it may be, and scarcely that. But he assures them that they shall have his spiritual presence continued to them without intermission.

Two solemn farewells we find our Lord Jesus giving to his church, and his parting word at both of them is very encouraging; one was here, when he closed up his personal converse with them, and then his parting word was, "*Lo, I am with you always*; I leave you, and yet still I am with you"; the other was, when he closed up the canon of the scripture by the pen of his beloved disciple, and then his parting word was, "*Surely, I come quickly*. I leave you for awhile, but I will be with you again shortly," Rev. xxii. 20. By this it appears that he did not part in anger, but in love, and that it is his will we should keep up both our communion with him and our expectation of him.

275

ST. MARK

CHAPTER ONE
JOHN THE BAPTIST
(vv. 1–8)

We may observe here,

I. What the New Testament is— the *divine* testament, to which we *adhere* above all that is *human*; the new testament, which we *advance* above that which was old. It is *the gospel of Jesus Christ the Son of God, v.* 1. 1. It is *gospel*; it is God's word, and is *faithful* and *true*; see Rev. xix. 9; xxi. 5; xxii. 6. It is a *good word*, and well *worthy of all acceptation*; it brings us glad tidings. 2. It is the *gospel of Jesus Christ*, the *anointed Saviour*, the Messiah promised and expected.

II. What the *reference* of the New Testament is to the Old, and its *coherence* with it. The gospel of Jesus Christ *begins*, and so we shall find it *goes on*, just *as it is written in the prophets* (*v.* 2); for it *saith no other things than those which the prophets and Moses said should come* (Acts xxvi. 22).

Quotations are here borrowed from two prophecies—that of Isaiah, which was the *longest*, and that of Malachi, which was the *latest* (and there were above three hundred years between them), both of whom spoke to the same purport concerning *the beginning of the gospel of Jesus Christ*, in the ministry of John.

1. Malachi, in whom we had the Old-Testament *farewell*, spoken very plainly (*ch.* iii. 1) concerning John Baptist, who was to give the New Testament *welcome. Behold, I send my messenger before thy face, v.* 2. Christ himself had taken notice of this, and applied it to John (Matt. xi. 10), who was God's *messenger*, sent to *prepare Christ's way*.

2. Isaiah, the most evangelical of all the prophets, *begins* the evangelical part of his prophecy with this, which points to the *beginning of the gospel of Christ* (Isa. xl. 3); *The voice of him that crieth in the wilderness, v.* 3. Matthew had taken notice of this, and applied it to John, *ch.* iii. 3.

III. What the *beginning of the New Testament* was. The gospel began in John Baptist; for *the law and the prophets were, until John*, the only divine revelation, but then the *kingdom of God began to be preached*, Luke xvi. 16. Peter begins *from the baptism of John*, Acts i. 22. The gospel did not begin *so soon* as the *birth* of Christ, for he took time to *increase in wisdom and stature*, not so late as his entering upon his public ministry, but half a year before, when John began to preach the same doctrine that Christ afterward preached. His baptism was the dawning of the *gospel day*.

In the success of John's preaching, and the disciples he admitted by baptism, there was the *beginning of a gospel church*. He baptized *in the wilderness*, and declined going into the cities; but *there went out unto him all the land of Judea, and they of Jerusalem*, inhabitants both of city and country, families of them, and *were all baptized of him*. They entered themselves his disciples, and bound themselves to his discipline; in token of which, they *confessed their sins*; he admitted them his disciples, in token of which, he *baptized* them. Many of these afterward became followers of Christ, and preachers of his gospel, and this grain of mustard-seed became a *tree*.

BAPTISM OF JESUS
(vv. 9–13)

We have here a brief account of Christ's baptism and temptation, which were largely related Matt. iii. and iv.

CHRIST IN GALILEE
(vv. 14–22)

Here is, I. A general account of Christ's preaching in Galilee. John gives an account of his preaching in Judea, before this (*ch.* ii. and iii.), which the other evangelists had omitted, who chiefly relate what occurred in Galilee, because that was the least known at Jerusalem. Observe,

1. When Jesus began to preach in Galilee; *After that John was put in prison*. When he had *finished* his testimony, then Jesus *began* his.

2. What he preached; *The gospel of the kingdom of God*. Christ came to set up the kingdom of God among men, that they might be brought into *subjection to it*, and might obtain *salvation in it*; and he set it up by the preaching of his gospel, and a power going along with it.

Observe, (1) The great *truths* Christ preached; *The time is fulfilled, and the kingdom of God is at hand*. This refers to the Old Testament, in which the kingdom of the Messiah was promised, and the time fixed for the introducing of it. They were not so well versed in those prophecies, nor did they so well observe the signs of the times, as to understand it themselves, and therefore Christ gives them notice of it.

(2) The great *duties* inferred from thence. Christ tells them, in the prospect of that kingdom approaching, they must *repent, and believe the gospel*. They had broken the *moral law*, and could not be saved by a *covenant of innocency*, for both Jew and Gentile are concluded *under guilt*. They must therefore take the benefit of a *covenant of grace*, must submit to a *remedial law*, and this is it—*repentance towards God, and faith towards our Lord Jesus Christ*.

II. Christ appearing as a teacher, here is next his *calling of disciples*, vv. 16–20. Observe, 1. Christ will have followers. 2. The instruments Christ chose to employ in setting up his kingdom, were the *weak* and *foolish things of the world*; not called from the great sanhedrim, or the schools of the rabbin, but picked up from among the tarpaulins *by the sea-side, that the excellency of the power* might appear to be wholly *of God*, and not at all *of them*. 3. Though Christ needs not the help of man, yet he is pleased to make use of it in setting up his kingdom, that he might deal with us not in a formidable but in a familiar way, and that in his kingdom the *nobles and governors may be of ourselves*, Jer. xxx. 21. 4. Christ puts honour upon those who, though mean in the world, are *diligent in their business*, and *loving to one another*; so those were, whom Christ called. 5. The business of ministers is to *fish for souls*, and *win them to Christ*. 6. Those whom Christ calls, must *leave all*, to follow him; and by his grace he inclines them to do so. *Not that we must needs go out of the world* immediately, but we must sit loose to the world, and forsake every thing that is inconsistent with our duty to Christ, and that cannot be kept without prejudice to our souls.

III. Here is a·particular account of his preaching in Capernaum, one of the *cities* of Galilee. Observe, 1. When Christ *came into Capernaum*, he *straightway* applied himself to his work there, and took the *first* opportunity of preaching the gospel. Those will think themselves concerned not to *lose time*, who consider what a deal of work they have to do, and what a little time to do it in. 2. Christ religiously observed the sabbath day, though not by tying himself up to the tradition of the elders, in all the niceties of the *sabbath-rest*, yet (which was far better) by applying himself to, and abounding in, the *sabbath-work*, in order to which the sabbath-rest was instituted. 3. Sabbaths are to be sanctified in *religious assemblies*, if we have opportunity; it is a *holy day*, and

must be honoured with a *holy convocation*; this was the *good old way*, Acts xiii. 27; xv. 21. 4. In *religious assemblies* on sabbath-days, the gospel is to be preached, and those to be *taught*, who are willing to learn the *truth as it is in Jesus*. 5. Christ was a non-such preacher; he did not preach *as the scribes*, who expounded the law of Moses by rote, as a school-boy says his lessons, but were neither *acquainted* with it (Paul himself, when a Pharisee, was ignorant of the law), nor *affected* with it; it came not *from the heart*, and therefore came not *with authority*. But Christ taught *as one that had authority*, as one that knew the mind of God, and was commissioned to declare it. 6. There is much in the doctrine of Christ, that is *astonishing*; the more we hear it, the more cause we shall see to *admire it*.

A SABBATH HEALING
(*vv.* 23–28)

As soon as Christ began to preach, he began to work miracles for the confirmation of his doctrine; and they were such as intimated the design and tendency of his doctrine, which were to conquer Satan, and cure sick souls.

In these verses, we have,

I. Christ's *casting the devil* out of a man that was possessed, in the synagogue at Capernaum. Now here we have,

1. The rage which the unclean spirit expressed at Christ; *He cried out*, as one in an agony, at the presence of Christ, and afraid of being dislodged; thus the *devils believe and tremble*, have a horror

of Christ, but no hope in him, nor reverence for him.

2. The victory which Jesus Christ obtained over the unclean spirit; *for this purpose was the Son of God manifested, that he might destroy the works of the devil,* and so he makes it to appear; nor will he be turned back from prosecuting this war, either by his flatteries or by his menaces. It is in vain for Satan to beg and pray, *Let us alone;* his power must be broken, and the poor man must be relieved; and therefore, (1) Jesus *commands.* As he taught, so he healed, *with authority.* Jesus *rebuked him;* he chid him and threatened him, imposed silence upon him; *Hold thy peace; be muzzled.* (2) The unclean spirit *yields,* for there is no remedy (*v.* 26); He *tore him,* put him into a *strong convulsion;* that one could have thought he had been pulled in pieces; when he would not *touch* Christ, in fury at him he grievously disturbed this poor creature.

II. The impression which this miracle made upon the minds of the people, *vv.* 27, 28.

1. It astonished them that saw it; *They were all amazed.* It was evident, beyond contradiction, that the man was possessed — witness the tearing of him, and the *loud voice* with which the *spirit cried;* it was evident that he was *forced out* by the authority of Christ; this was surprising to them, and put them upon considering with themselves, and enquiring of one another, "*What is this new doctrine?*"

2. It raised his reputation among all that heard it; *Immediately his fame spread abroad into the whole*

adjacent region of Galilee, which was a third part of the land of Canaan.

HEALING AND PRAYING
(*vv.* 29–45)

In these verses, we have,

I. A particular account of one miracle that Christ wrought, in the cure of Peter's wife's mother, who was ill of a fever. This passage we had before, in Matthew.

II. A general account of many cures he wrought — diseases healed, devils expelled. It was on the *evening of the sabbath,* when the *sun did set,* or *was set;* perhaps many scrupled bringing their sick to him, till the sabbath was over, but their weakness therein was no prejudice to them in applying to Christ. Though he proved it *lawful to heal on the sabbath days,* yet, if any stumbled at it, they were welcome at another time.

III. His *retirement* to his *private devotion* (*v.* 35); *He prayed,* prayed alone; to set us an example of secret prayer. Though as God he was *prayed to,* as man he *prayed.* Though he was glorifying God, and doing good, in his public work, yet he found time to be alone with his Father; and thus *it became him to fulfil all righteousness.*

IV. His *return* to his *public* work. The disciples thought they were *up early,* but found their Master was up *before them,* and they enquired which way he went, *followed him* to his *solitary place,* and there *found him* at prayer, *vv.* 36, 37. They told him that he was much wanted, that there were a great many patients waiting for him; *All men seek for thee.* "No," saith Christ, "Capernaum must not have the monopoly of the Messiah's preaching and miracles. *Let us go into the next towns*, the *villages* that lie about here, *that I may preach there also*, and work miracles there, *for therefore came I forth*, not to be constantly resident in one place, but to *go about doing good.*"

We also have here the story of Christ's *cleansing* a *leper*, which we had before, Matt. viii. 2–4.

CHAPTER TWO
A PARALYTIC HEALED
(*vv.* 1–12)

Christ, having been for some time preaching about in the country, here returns to Capernaum, his headquarters, and makes his appearance there, in hopes that by this time the talk and crowd would be somewhat abated. Now observe,

I. The great resort there was to him. *There was no room to receive them*, they were so numerous, *no not so much as about the door*. A blessed sight, to see people thus flying like a cloud to Christ's house, though it was but a poor one, and *as the doves to their windows!*

II. The good entertainment Christ gave them, the best his house would afford, and better than any other could; he *preached the word unto them*, *v.* 2. Many of them perhaps came only for cures, and many perhaps only for curiosity, to get a sight of him; but when he had them together he *preached to them*.

III. The presenting of a poor cripple to him, to be helped by him. The patient was one *sick of the palsy*, it should seem not as that,

Matt. viii. 6, *grievously tormented*, but perfectly disabled, so that he was *borne of four*, was carried upon *a bed*, as if he had been upon *a bier*, by four persons. These kind relations or neighbours thought, if they could but carry this poor man once to Christ, they should not need to carry him any more; and therefore made hard shift to get him to him; and when they could not otherwise get to him, they *uncovered the roof where he was*, *v.* 4. This bespoke both their *faith* and their *fervency* in this address to Christ. Hereby it appeared that they were in earnest, and would not go away, nor *let Christ go without a blessing*. Gen. xxxii. 26.

IV. The kind word Christ said to this poor patient; *He saw their faith*; perhaps not so much his, for his disability hindered him from the exercise of faith, but *theirs* that brought him. In curing the centurion's servant, Christ took notice of it as an instance of *his faith*, that he did not bring him to Christ, but believed he could cure him at a distance; here he commended *their faith*, because they did bring their friend through so much difficulty. Note, True faith and strong faith may work variously, conquering sometimes the objections of reason, sometimes those of sense; but, however manifested, it shall be accepted and approved by Jesus Christ. Christ said, *Son, thy sins be forgiven thee*. Note, 1. Sin is the procuring cause of all our pains and sicknesses. The word of Christ was to take his thoughts off from the disease, which was the effect, and to lead them to the sin, the cause, that he might be more concerned about that, to get that pardoned. 2. God doth *then* graciously take away the sting and malignity of sickness, when he forgives sin. Pardon of sin strikes at the root of all diseases, and either cures them, or alters their property.

V. The cavil of the scribes at that which Christ said, and a demonstration of the unreasonableness of their cavil. They were expositors of the law, and their doctrine was *true* —that it is blasphemy for any creature to undertake the pardon of sin, and that it is God's prerogative, Isa. xliii. 25. But, as is usual with such teachers, their application was *false*, and was the effect of their ignorance and enmity to Christ. It is *true, None can forgive sins but God only*; but it is false that therefore Christ cannot, who had abundantly proved himself to have a divine power. But Christ *perceived in his spirit that they so reasoned within themselves*; this proves him to be God, and therefore confirmed what was to be proved, that he had authority to *forgive sins*; for he *searched* the heart, and knew *what was in man*, Rev. ii. 23. Now he proves his power to *forgive sin*, by demonstrating his power to cure the *man sick of the palsy, vv.* 9–11. He would not have pretended to do *the one*, if he could not have done *the other; that ye may know that the Son of man*, the Messiah, *has power on earth to forgive sin*, that I have that power, *Thou that art* sick of the palsy, *arise, take up thy bed*. Now, 1. This was a *suitable* argument in itself. He could not have cured the disease, which was the effect, if he could not have taken away the sin,

which was the cause. 2. It was suited to them. These carnal scribes would be more affected with such a suitable effect of a pardon as the cure of the disease, and be sooner convinced by it, than by any other more spiritual consequences; therefore it was proper enough to appeal, whether it is easier to say, *Thy sins are forgiven thee*, or to say, *Arise, and walk?* The removing of the punishment as such, was the remitting of the sin; he that could go so far in the cure, no doubt could perfect it. See Isa. xxxiii. 24.

VI. The cure of the sick man, and the impression it made upon the people, *v.* 12. *They were all amazed*, as well they might, and *glorified God*, as indeed they ought; saying, *"We never saw it on this fashion;* never were such wonders as these done before in our time."

FOLLOW ME (*vv.* 13–17)

Here is,

I. Christ preaching by the *seaside* (*v.* 13), whither he went *for room*, because he found, upon second trial, no house or street large enough to contain his auditory; but upon the strand there might come as many as would.

II. His calling Levi; the same with Matthew, who had a place in the custom-house at Capernaum, from which he was denominated a *publican*; his place fixed him by the waterside, and thither Christ went to meet with him, and to give him an effectual call. This Levi is here said to be *the son of Alpheus* or *Cleophas*, husband to that Mary who was sister or near kinswoman to the virgin Mary, and if so, he was own brother to James the less, and Jude, and Simon the Canaanite, so that there were four brothers of them apostles. It is probable that Matthew was but a loose extravagant young man, or else, being a Jew, he would never have been a publican. However, Christ called him to *follow him*. Paul, though a Pharisee, had been one of the chief of sinners, and yet was called to be an apostle. With God, through Christ, there is mercy to pardon the greatest sins, and grace to sanctify the greatest sinners.

III. His familiar converse with *publicans and sinners, v.* 15. We are here told, 1. That Christ *sat at meat in Levi's house*, who invited *him and his disciples* to the farewell-feast he made to his friends, when he left all to attend on Christ: such a feast he made, as Elisha did (1 Kings xix. 21), to show, not only with what cheerfulness in himself, but with what thankfulness to God, he quitted all, in compliance with Christ's call. Fitly did he make the *day of his espousals* to Christ a festival day. 2. That *many publicans and sinners* sat with Christ in Levi's house (for *there were many* belonging to that custom-house); and *they followed him.* They followed Levi; so some understand it, supposing that, like Zaccheus, he was *chief among the publicans*, and was *rich*; and for that reason, the inferior sort of them attended him for what they could get. I rather take it, that they *followed Jesus* because of the report they had heard of him. The publicans are here and elsewhere ranked with *sinners*, the worst of *sinners*. (1) Because commonly they *were such*; so general were the corruptions in the execution of that office.

(2) Because the Jews had a particular antipathy to them and their office, as an affront to the liberty of their nation and a badge of their slavery.

IV. The *offence* which the scribes and Pharisees took at this, *v.* 16. They would not come to hear him preach, which they might have been convinced and edified by; but they would come themselves to *see him* sit with publicans and sinners, which they would be provoked by.

V. Christ's justification of himself in it, *v.* 17. He stood to what he did, and would not withdraw, though the Pharisees were offended, as Peter afterwards did, Gal. ii. 12. They thought Christ's character should separate him from them; "No," saith Christ, "my commission directs me to them; *I came not to call the righteous, but sinners to repentance."*

THE DISCIPLES JUSTIFIED
(vv. 18–28)

Christ had been put to *justify* himself in conversing with *publicans and sinners*: here he is put to justify his disciples; and in what they do according to his will he will justify them, and bear them out.

I. He justifies them in their *not fasting*, which was turned to their reproach by the Pharisees.

Two things Christ pleads in excuse of his disciples *not fasting*.

1. That these were *easy days* with them, and fasting was not so *seasonable* now as it would be hereafter, *vv.* 19, 20.

2. That these were *early days* with them, and they were not so able for the severe exercises of

religion as hereafter they would be. The Pharisees had long accustomed themselves to such austerities; and John Baptist himself came neither eating nor drinking. His disciples from the first inured themselves to hardships, and thus found it easier to bear strict and frequent fasting, but it was not so with Christ's disciples; their Master came *eating and drinking*, and had not bred them up to the difficult services of religion as yet, for it was all in good time. To put them upon such frequent fasting at first, would be a discouragement to them, and perhaps drive them off from following Christ; it would be of as ill consequence as *putting new wine into old casks*, or sewing *new cloth* to that which is worn thin and threadbare, *vv.* 21, 22.

II. He justifies them in *plucking the ears of corn on the sabbath day*, which, I will warrant you, a disciple of the Pharisees would not dare to have done; for it was contrary to an express tradition of their elders.

Observe, 1. What a poor breakfast Christ's disciples had on a sabbath-day morning, when they were going to church (*v.* 23); they *plucked the ears of corn*, and that was the best they had. The Jews made it a piece of religion, to eat dainty food on sabbath days, but the disciples were content with any thing.

2. How even this was *grudged them* by the Pharisees, upon supposition that it was not lawful to *pluck the ears of corn* on the sabbath day, that that was as much a servile work as *reaping* (*v.* 24): *Why do they on the sabbath day that which is not lawful?*

3. How Christ defended them in what they did.

(1) By example. They had a good precedent for it in David's eating the *show-bread*, when he was hungry, and there was no other bread to be had (*vv.* 25, 26).

(2) By argument. To reconcile them to the disciples' *plucking the ears of corn*, let them consider,

[1] Whom the sabbath was *made for* (*v.* 27); *it was made for man, and not man for the sabbath*. This we had not in Matthew. The sabbath is a sacred and divine institution; but we must receive and embrace it as a privilege and a benefit, not as a task and a drudgery.

[2] Whom the sabbath was *made by* (*v.* 28); "*The Son of man is Lord also of the sabbath*; and therefore he will not see the kind intentions of the institution of it frustrated by your impositions." Note, The sabbath days are *days of the Son of man*; he is the Lord of the day, and to his honour it must be observed.

CHAPTER THREE

MORE MIRACLES (*vv.* 1–12)

Here, as before, we have our Lord Jesus busy at work *in the synagogue* first, and then by *the sea side*. Now here we have some account of what he did.

I. When he *entered again into the synagogue*, he improved the opportunity he had there, of doing good, and having, no doubt, preached a sermon there, he wrought a miracle for the confirmation of it, or at least for the confirmation of this truth—that *it is lawful to do good on the sabbath day*. We had the narrative, Matt. xii. 9.

1. The patient's case was piteous; he had a *withered hand,* by which he was disabled to work for his living; and those that are so, are the most proper objects of charity; let those be helped that cannot help themselves.

2. The spectators were very unkind, both to the patient and to the Physician; instead of interceding for a poor neighbour, they did what they could to hinder his cure: for they intimated that if Christ cured him now on the sabbath day, they would accuse him as a *Sabbath breaker.*

3. Christ dealt very fairly with the spectators, and dealt with them *first,* if possible to *prevent* the offence.

(1) He laboured to convince their judgment. He bade the man *stand forth* (v. 3), that by the sight of him they might be moved with compassion toward him, and might not, for shame, account his cure a crime. And then he appeals to their own consciences; though the thing *speaks itself,* yet *he* is pleased to speak it; "*Is it lawful to do good on the sabbath days,* as I design to do, *or to do evil,* as you design to do? Whether is better, to *save life* or to *kill?*"

(2) When they rebelled against the light, he *lamented their stubbornness* (v. 5); *He looked round about on them with anger, being grieved for the hardness of their hearts.*

4. Christ dealt very kindly with the patient; he bade him *stretch forth his hand,* and it was immediately *restored.*

5. The enemies of Christ dealt very barbarously with him. Such a work of *mercy* should have engaged their love *to him,* and such a work of *wonder* their faith *in him.* But, instead of that, the Pharisees, who pretended to be oracles in the church, and the Herodians, who pretended to be the supporters of the state, though of opposite interests one to another, *took counsel together against him, how they might destroy him.*

II. When he withdrew *to the sea,* he did good there. While his enemies sought to *destroy him,* he quitted the place; to teach us in troublous times to shift for our own safety; but see here,

1. How he was followed into his retirement. When some had such an enmity to him, that they drove him out of their country, others had such a value for him, that they followed him wherever he went; and the enmity of their leaders to Christ did not cool their respect to him.

2. What abundance of good he did in his retirement. He did not withdraw to be idle, nor did he send back those who rudely crowded after him when he withdrew, but took it kindly, and gave them what they came for; for he never said to any that sought him diligently, *Seek ye me in vain.* (1) Diseases were effectually cured; He *healed many*; divers sorts of patients, ill of divers sorts of diseases; though numerous, though various, he *healed them.* (2) *Devils* were effectually *conquered*; those whom unclean spirits had got possession of, *when they saw him,* trembled at his presence, and they also *fell down before him,* not to supplicate his favour, but to deprecate his wrath, and by their

own terrors were compelled to own that *he was the Son of God, v.* 11. (3) Christ sought not applause to himself in doing those great things, for *he strictly charged* those for whom he did them, *that they should not make him known (v.* 12).

THE TWELVE CALLED
(vv. 13–21)

In these verses, we have,

I. The choice Christ made of the *twelve apostles* to be his constant followers and attendants, and to be sent abroad as there was occasion, to preach the gospel. Observe,

1. The introduction to this *call* or *promotion* of disciples; He *goes up into a mountain*, and his errand thither was *to pray*. Ministers must be set apart with solemn prayer for the pouring out of the Spirit upon them; though Christ had authority to confer the gifts of the Holy Ghost, yet, to set us an example, he prayed for them.

2. The rule he went by in his choice, and that was his own good pleasure; *He called unto him whom he would.* Christ calls *whom he will*; for he is a free agent, and his grace is his own.

3. The efficacy of the call; He *called them* to separate themselves from the crowd, and stand by him, and they *came unto him.*

4. The end and intention of this call; He *ordained them* (probably by the imposition of hands, which was a ceremony used among the Jews), *that they should be with him* constantly, to be witnesses of *his doctrine, manner of life, and patience,* that they might *fully know it,* and be able to give an account of it; and especially that they might attest the truth of his miracles; they must be *with him,* to receive instructions *from him,* that they might be qualified to give instructions *to others.*

5. The power he gave them to work miracles; and hereby he put a very great honour upon them, beyond that of the great men of the earth. He ordained them to *heal sicknesses and to cast out devils.* This showed that the power which Christ had to work these miracles was an *original* power; that he had it not *as a Servant,* but *as a Son in his own house,* in that he could confer it upon others, and invest them with it.

6. Their number and names; *He ordained twelve,* according to the number of the twelve tribes of Israel. They are here named not just in the same order as they were in Matthew, nor by couples, as they were there; but as there, so here, Peter is put first and Judas last.

7. Their retirement with their Master, and close adherence to him; *They went into a house.*

II. The continual crowds that attended Christ's movements (*v.* 20); The *multitude cometh together again,* unsent for, and unseasonably pressing upon him, some with one errand and some with another; so that he and his disciples could not get time *so much as to eat bread,* much less for a set and full meal. Yet he did not shut his doors against the petitioners, but bade them welcome, and gave to each of them *an answer of peace.*

III. The care of his relations concerning him (*v.* 21); *When his friends* in Capernaum heard how he was followed, and what pains he took, they *went out, to lay hold on* him, and fetch him home, for they said, *He is beside himself.* 1. Some understand it of an absurd preposterous care, which had more in it of reproach to him than of respect; and so we must take it as we read it, *He is beside himself*; either they suspected it themselves, or it was suggested to them, and they gave credit to the suggestion, that he was *gone distracted*, and therefore his friends ought to bind him, and put him in a dark room, to bring him to his right mind again. 2. Others understand it of a *well-meaning* care; and then they read *"He fainteth*, he has no time to *eat bread*, and therefore his strength will fail him; he will be stifled with the crowd of people, and will have his spirits quite exhausted with constant speaking, and the virtue that *goes out of him* in his miracles; and therefore let us use a friendly violence with him, and get him a little *breathing-time.*" In his preaching-work, as well as his suffering-work, he was attacked with, *Master, spare thyself.* Note, They who go on with vigour and zeal in the work of God, must expect to meet with hindrances, both from the groundless disaffection of their enemies, and the mistaken affections of their friends, and they have need to stand upon their guard against both.

BLASPHEMY AGAINST THE HOLY SPIRIT (*vv.* 22–29)

I. Here is, The impudent impious brand which the scribes fastened upon Christ's casting out devils, they they might evade and invalidate the conviction of it, and have a poor excuse for not yielding to it.

These *scribes came down from Jerusalem, v.* 22. They could not deny but that he cast out devils, which plainly bespoke him sent of God; but they insinuated that *he had Beelzebub* on his side, was in league with him, and by *the prince of the devils cast out devils.* There is a trick in the case; Satan is not *cast out*, he only *goes out* by consent. There was nothing in the manner of Christ's *casting out devils*, that gave any cause to suspect this; he did it *as one having authority*; but so they will have it, who resolve not to believe him.

II. The rational answer which Christ gave to this objection, demonstrating the absurdity of it.

1. Satan is so *subtle*, that he will never voluntarily quit his possession; *If Satan cast out Satan, his kingdom is divided against itself*, and it *cannot stand, vv.* 23–26.

2. Christ is so *wise*, that, being engaged in war with him, he will attack his forces wherever he meets them, whether in the bodies or souls of people, *v.* 27. It is plain, Christ's design is to *enter into the strong man's house*, to take possession of the interest he has in the world, and to *spoil his goods*, and convert them to his own service; and therefore it is natural to suppose that he will thus *bind the strong man*, will forbid him to *speak* when he would, and to *stay* where he would, and thus show that he has gained a victory over him.

III. The awful warning Christ gave them to take heed how they spoke such dangerous words as these; however they might make light of them, as only conjectures, and the language of *free-thinking*, if they persisted in it, it would be of fatal consequence to them; it would be found a sin against the last remedy, and consequently *unpardonable*; for what could be imagined possible to bring *them* to repentance for their sin in blaspheming Christ, who would set aside such a *strong* conviction with such a *weak* evasion?

A FAMILY MISUNDERSTANDING
(*vv.* 31–35)

Here is, 1. The *disrespect* which Christ's *kindred, according to the flesh,* showed to him, when he was preaching (and they knew very well that he was then in his element); they not only *stood without,* having no desire to come in, and hear him, but they sent in a message to *call him out to them* (*vv.* 31, 32), as if he must leave his work, to hearken to their *impertinences.*

2. The *respect* which Christ showed to his spiritual kindred upon this occasion. Now, as at other times, he put a *comparative neglect* upon his mother, which seemed purposely designed to obviate and prevent the extravagant respect which men in aftertimes would be apt to pay her. *Our* respect ought to be guided and governed by Christ's; now the virgin Mary, or Christ's mother, is not here regarded as superior to ordinary believers, on whom Christ here puts a *superlative* honour. He looked upon those that *sat about* him, and pronounced those of them that not only heard, but did, the will of God, to be to him as *his brother, and sister, and mother*; as much esteemed, loved,

and cared for, as his nearest relations, *vv.* 33–35. This is a good reason why we should *honour those that fear the Lord,* and choose them for our people; why we should be not hearers of the word only, but doers of the work, that we may share with the saints in this honour.

THE SOWER (*vv.* 1–20)

I. The *way of teaching* that Christ used with the *multitude* (*v.* 2); He *taught them many things,* but it was *by parables* or similitudes, which would *tempt them to hear.*

II. The way of *expounding* that he used with his *disciples; When he was alone* by himself, not only the *twelve,* but others that were *about him with the twelve,* took the opportunity to *ask him* the meaning of the parables, *v.* 10. And he told them what a distinguishing favour it was to them, that they were made acquainted with the *mystery of the kingdom of God, v.* 11. *The secret of the Lord was with them.*

In particular, we have here,

1. The parable of the sower, as we had it, Matt. xiii. 3, &c.

2. The exposition of it to the disciples. Here is a question Christ put to them before he expounded it, which we had not in Matthew (*v.* 13); "*Know ye not this parable?* Know ye not the meaning of it? *How then will ye know all parables?*" (1) "If ye know not this, which is so plain, how will ye understand other parables, which will be more dark and obscure?" (2) "If ye know not this, which is intended for your direction in hearing the word, that ye may profit by it; how

shall ye profit by what ye are further to hear? This parable is to teach you to be attentive to the word, and affected with it, that you may *understand* it. If ye receive not this, ye will not know how to use the key by which ye must be let into all the rest."

PARABLES OF THE KINGDOM
(vv. 21–34)

The lessons which our Saviour designs to teach us here by parables and figurative expressions are these:—

I. That those who *are good* ought to consider the obligations they are under to *do good*; that is, as in the parable before, to *bring forth fruit*. Those who are lighted as candles, should set themselves *on a candlestick*; that is, should improve all opportunities of doing good, as those that were made for the glory of God, and the service of the communities they are members of; we are not born for ourselves.

II. *If any man have ears to hear, let him hear*, v. 23. Let him give the gospel of Christ a fair hearing; but that is not enough, it is added (v. 24), *Take heed what ye hear*, and give a due regard to that which ye do hear; *Consider what ye hear*, so Dr. Hammond reads it. Note, What we hear, doth us no good, unless we consider it. To enforce this caution, consider,

1. As we deal with God, God will deal with us, so Dr. Hammond explains these words, "*With what measure ye mete, it shall be measured to you.* If ye be faithful servants to him, he will be a faithful Master to

you: *with the upright he will show himself upright.*"

2. As we improve the talents we are entrusted with, we shall increase them; if we make use of the knowledge we have, for the glory of God and the benefit of others, it shall sensibly grow, as stock in trade doth by being turned; *Unto you that hear, shall more be given; to you that have, it shall be given, v. 25.* If the disciples *deliver* that to the church, which they have *received of the Lord*, they shall be *led* more into the *secret of the Lord.* Gifts and graces multiply by being exercised; and God has promised to bless the *hand of the diligent.*

3. If we do not *use*, we *lose*, what we have; *From him that hath not*, that doeth no good with what he hath, and so hath it in vain, is as if he had it not, *shall be taken even that which he hath.*

III. The good seed of the gospel sown in the world, and sown in the heart, doth by degrees produce wonderful effects, but without noise (vv. 26, &c.); *So is the kingdom of God*; so is the gospel, when it is sown, and received, as seed in good ground.

1. It will *come up*; though it seem lost and buried under the clods, it will find or make its way through them.

2. The husbandman cannot describe how it comes up; it is one of the mysteries of nature; It *springs and grows up, he knows not how, v. 27.*

3. The husbandman, when he hath sown the seed, doth nothing toward the springing of it up; *He sleeps, and rises, night and day*;

goes to sleep *at night*, gets up *in the morning*, and perhaps never so much as thinks of the corn he hath sown, or ever looks upon it, but follows his pleasures or other business, and yet *the earth brings forth fruit of itself*, according to the ordinary course of nature, and by the concurring power of the God of nature. Thus the *word of grace*, when it is received in faith, is in the heart a *work of grace*, and the preachers contribute nothing to it. The Spirit of God is carrying it on when *they sleep*, and can do no business (Job xxxiii. 15, 16), or when they rise to go about other business.

4. It grows gradually; *first the blade, then the ear, after that the full corn in the ear, v.* 28. When it is sprung up, it will go forward; nature will have its course, and so will grace.

5. It comes to perfection at last (*v.* 29); *When the fruit is brought forth*, that is, when it is *ripe*, and ready to be *delivered* into the owner's hand; then he *puts in the sickle*.

IV. The work of grace is small in its beginnings, but comes to be great and considerable at last (*vv.* 30–32); *"Whereunto shall I liken the kingdom of God*, as now to be set up by the Messiah? How shall I make you to understand the designed method of it?"* Christ speaks as one considering and consulting with himself, how to illustrate it with an apt similitude; *With what comparison shall we compare it?* Shall we fetch it from the motions of the sun, or the revolutions of the moon? No, the comparison is borrowed from this earth, it is *like a grain of mustard-seed*; he had compared it before to *seed sown*, here to *that seed*, intending thereby to show,

1. That the beginnings of the *gospel kingdom* would be very small, like that which is *one of the least of all seeds*.

2. That the perfection of it will be very great; *When it grows up, it becomes greater than all herbs.* The gospel kingdom in the world, shall increase and spread to the remotest nations of the earth, and shall continue to the latest ages of time.

After the parables thus specified the historian concludes with this general account of Christ's preaching—that *with many such parables he spoke the word unto them* (*v.* 33); probably designing to refer us to the larger account of the parables of this kind, which we had before, Matt. xiii.

THE STORM STILLED
(*vv.* 35–41)

This miracle which Christ wrought for the relief of his disciples, in stilling the storm, we had before (Matt. viii. 23, &c.); but it is here more fully related.

CHAPTER FIVE
LEGION EXPELLED
(*vv.* 1–20)

We have here an instance of Christ's dispossessing the strong man armed, and disposing of him as he pleased, to make it appear that he was *stronger than he*.

In Matthew, they were said to be *two* possessed with devils; here it is said to be a *man* possessed with an unclean spirit. If there were *two*, there was one, and Mark doth not say that there was *but one*; so that this difference cannot give us any just offence; it is probable that one of them was much more remarkable than the other, and said what was said. Now observe here,

I. The miserable condition that this poor creature was in; he was under the power of an *unclean spirit*, the devil got possession of him, and the effect of it was not, as in many, a silent melancholy, but a raging frenzy; he was raving mad; his condition seems to have been worse than any of the possessed, that were Christ's patients.

1. He had *his dwelling among the tombs*, among the graves of dead people. Their tombs were out of the cities, in *desolate places* (Job iii. 4); which gave the devil great advantage: for *woe to him that is alone*.

2 He was very strong and ungovernable; *No man could bind him*, as it is requisite both for their own good, and for the safety of others, that those who are distracted should be. Not only cords would not hold him, but *chains* and *fetters of iron* would not, *vv*. 3, 4.

3. He was a terror and torment to himself and to all about him, *v*. 5. The devil is a *cruel* master to those that are *led captive* by him, a perfect tyrant; this wretched creature was *night and day in the mountains and in the tombs, crying, and cutting himself with stones*.

II. His application to Christ (*v*. 6); *When he saw Jesus afar off*, coming ashore, he *ran and wor-*

shipped him. He usually *ran upon* others with *rage*, but he *ran to* Christ with *reverence*. That was done by an invisible hand of Christ, which could not be done with chains and fetters; his fury was all on a sudden curbed.

III. The word of command Christ gave to the unclean spirit, to quit his possession (*v*. 8); *Come out of him, thou unclean spirit*. He made the man desirous to be relieved, when he enabled him to *run, and worship him*, and then put forth his power for his relief.

IV. The dread which the devil had of Christ. The *man ran*, and *worshipped Christ*; but it was the devil in the man, that *cried with a loud voice* (making use of the poor man's tongue), *What have I to do with thee? v*. 7.

V. The account Christ took from this unclean spirit of his name. This we had not in Matthew. Christ asked him, *What is thy name?* Not but that Christ could call all the *fallen* stars, as well as the *morning* stars, by their names; but he demands this, that the standers by might be affected with the vast numbers and power of those malignant infernal spirits, as they had reason to be, when the answer was, *My name is Legion, for we are many*; a *legion* of soldiers among the Romans consisted, some say, of six thousand men, others of twelve thousand and five hundred; but the number of a legion with them, like that of a regiment with us, was not always the same.

VI. The request of this legion, that Christ would suffer them to go into a herd of swine that was *feeding nigh unto the mountains* (*v.* 11), those mountains which the demoniacs haunted, *v.* 5. Their request was, 1. That he *would not send them away out of the country* (*v.* 10). 2. That he would suffer them to *enter into the swine*, by destroying which they hoped to do more mischief to the souls of all the people in the country, than they could by entering into the body of any particular person, which therefore they did not ask leave to do, for they knew Christ would not grant it.

VII. The permission Christ gave them to enter into the swine, and the immediate destruction of the swine thereby; *He gave them leave* (*v.* 13), he did not forbid or restrain them, he let them do as they had a mind. The consequence of the devils entering into the swine, was, that they all *ran mad* presently, and ran headlong into the adjoining sea, where they were all drowned, to the number of *two thousand*. The man they possessed did only *cut himself*, for God had said, *He is in your hands, only save his life*. But thereby it appeared, that, if he had not been so restrained, the poor man would have *drowned himself*.

VIII. The report of all this dispersed through the country immediately. They that *fed the swine*, hastened to the owners, to give an account of their charge, *v.* 14. This drew the people together, to see what was done.

IX. An account of the conduct of the poor man after his deliverance. 1. He *desired that he might go along with Christ* (*v.* 18),

perhaps for fear lest the evil spirit should again seize him; or, rather, that he might receive instruction from him, being unwilling to stay among those heathenish people that desired him to depart. 2. Christ *would not suffer him* to go with him, lest it should savour of ostentation, and to let him know that he could both protect and instruct him at a distance. And besides, he had other work for him to do; he must go home to his friends, and tell them what *great things the Lord had done for him*, the Lord Jesus had done; that Christ might be honoured, and his neighbours and friends might be edified, and invited to believe in Christ.

TWO MIRACLES (*vv.* 21–43)

The Gadarenes having desired Christ to leave their country, he did not stay to trouble them long, but presently went by water, as he came, back *to the other side* (*v.* 21), and there *much people gathered to him*. Now among the many that applied themselves to him,

I. Here is one, that comes *openly to beg* a cure for a sick child; and it is no less a person than one of the *rulers of the synagogue*, one that presided in the synagogue-worship or, as some think, one of the judges of the consistory court, which was in every city, consisting of *twenty-three*. He was not named in Matthew, he is here, *Jairus*, or *Jair*, Judg. x. 3. The case is this, He has a *little daughter*, about twelve years old, the darling of the family, and she *lies a dying*; but he believes that if Christ will but come, and *lay his hands upon her,* she will return even from the gates of the grave. He said, at first, when he came, *She lies a dying* (so Mark); but afterward, upon fresh information sent him, he saith, *She is even now dead* (so Matthew); but he still prosecutes his suit; see Luke viii. 42–49. Christ readily agreed, and went with him, *v.* 24.

II. Here is another, that comes *clandestinely* to *steal* a cure (if I may so say) for herself; and she got the relief she came for. This cure was wrought by *the way,* as he was going to raise the ruler's daughter, and was followed by a crowd. See how Christ improved his time, and lost none of the precious moments of it. Many of his discourses, and some of his miracles, are dated *by the way-side*; we should be doing good, not only when we *sit in the house,* but when we *walk by the way,* Deut. vi. 7. We dealt with these two miracles at Matt. ix. 18–26

THE GIRL RAISED

Diseases and deaths came into the world by the sin and disobedience of the first Adam; but by the grace of the second Adam both are conquered. Christ, having healed an incurable disease, here goes on to triumph over death, as in the beginning of the chapter he had triumphed over an outrageous devil.

I. The melancholy news is brought to Jairus, that his *daughter is dead,* and therefore, if Christ be as other physicians, he comes too late. While 'here is life, there is hope, and room for the use of means; but when life is gone, it is past recall; *Why troublest thou the*

Master any further? v. 35. Ordinarily, the proper thought in this case, is, "The matter is determined, the will of God is done, and I submit, I acquiesce; *The Lord gave, and the Lord hath taken away. While the child was alive, I fasted and wept; for I said, Who can tell but* God will yet be gracious to me, and *the child shall live?* But *now that it is dead, wherefore should I weep? I shall go to it, but it shall not return to me."* With such words we should *quiet ourselves* at such a time, that our souls may be *as a child that is weaned from his mother*: but here the case was extraordinary; the death of the child doth not, as usually, put an end to the narrative.

II. Christ encourageth the afflicted father yet to hope that his application to Christ on the behalf of his child should not be in vain. Christ had staid to work a cure by the way, but he shall be no sufferer by that, nor loser by the gain of others; *Be not afraid, only believe.* We may suppose Jairus at a pause, whether he should ask Christ to go on or no; but have we not as much occasion for the grace of God, and his consolations, and consequently of the prayers of our ministers and Christian friends, when death is in the house, as when sickness is? Christ therefore soon determines this matter; "*Be not afraid* that my coming will be to no purpose, only believe that I will make it turn to a good account." Note, 1. We must not despair concerning our relations that are dead, nor *sorrow for* them *as those that have no hope.* See what is said to Rachel, who refused to be comforted concerning her children, upon the presumption that they *were not; Refrain thy voice from weeping, and thine eyes from tears; for there is hope in thine end, that thy children shall come again,* Jer. xxxi. 16, 17. Therefore fear not, faint not. 2. Faith is the only remedy against disquieting grief and fear at such a time: let that silence them, *Only believe.* Keep up a confidence in Christ, and a dependence upon him, and he will do what is for the best. Believe the resurrection, and then be not afraid.

III. He went with a select company to the house where the dead child was and raised her.

All who saw them, and heard of them, admired the miracles, and him that wrought them; *They were astonished with a great astonishment.* They could not but acknowledge that there was something extraordinary and very great, and yet they knew not what to make of it, or to infer from it. Their wonder should have worked forward to a lively faith, but it rested in a *stupor* or *astonishment.*

Christ endeavoured to conceal it; *He charged them straitly, that no man should know it.* It was sufficiently known to a competent number, but he would not have it as yet *proclaimed* any further; because his own resurrection was to be the great instance of his power over death, and therefore the divulging of other instances must be reserved till that great proof was given: let one part of the evidence be kept private, till the other part, on which the main stress lies, be made ready.

CHAPTER SIX
CHRIST IN NAZARETH
(*vv* 1–6)

Here, I. Christ makes a visit to *his own country,* the place not of his birth, but of his education; that was *Nazareth;* where his relations were. He had been in danger of his life among them (Luke iv. 29), and yet he came among them again; so strangely doth he wait to be gracious, and seek the salvation of his enemies.

II. There he *preached* in their *synagogue,* on the *sabbath day, v.* 2. It seems, there was not such flocking to him there as in other places, so that he had no opportunity of preaching till they came together on the sabbath day; and then he expounded a portion of scripture with great clearness.

III. They could not but own that which was very honourable concerning him. 1. That he spoke with great *wisdom,* and that this wisdom was *given to him,* for they knew he had no learned education. 2. That he did *mighty works,* did them with his own hands, for the confirming of the doctrine he taught. They acknowledged the two great proofs of the divine original of his gospel—the *divine wisdom* that appeared in the contrivance of it, and the *divine power* that was exerted for the ratifying and recommending of it; and yet, though they could not deny the premises, they would not admit the conclusion.

IV. They studied to disparage him, and to raise prejudices in the minds of people against him, notwithstanding. All this *wisdom,* and all these *mighty works*, shall be of no account, because he had a home-education, had never travelled, nor been at any university, or bred up at the feet of any of their doctors (*v.* 3); *Is not this the Carpenter?* In Matthew, they upbraid him with being the carpenter's son, his supposed father Joseph being of that trade. But, it seems, they could say further, *Is not this the Carpenter?* our Lord Jesus, it is probable, employing himself in that business with his father, before he entered upon his public ministry, at least, sometimes in journey-work. 1. He would thus *humble himself*, and make himself of no reputation, as one that had taken upon him the form of a servant, and came to minister. Thus low did our Redeemer stoop, when he came to redeem us out of our low estate. 2. He would thus teach us to *abhor idleness*, and to find *ourselves something to do* in this world; and rather to take up with mean and laborious employments, and such as no more is to be got by than a bare livelihood, than indulge ourselves in sloth. 3. He would thus put an honour upon despised mechanics, and encourage those who eat the labour of their hands, though great men look upon them with contempt.

Another thing they upbraided him with, was, the meanness of his relations; "*He is the son of Mary*; his *brethren* and *sisters* are here *with us*; we know his family and kindred"; and therefore, though they were *astonished* at his doctrine (*v.* 2), yet they were *offended* at his person (*v.* 3), were prejudiced against him, and looked upon him with contempt; and for that reason would not receive his doctrine, though ever so well recommended. May we think that if they had not known his pedigree, but he had dropped among them from the clouds, without father, without mother, and without descent, they would have entertained him with any more respect? Truly, no; for in Judea, where this was not known, that was made an objection against him (John ix. 29); *As for this fellow, we know not from whence he is*. Obstinate unbelief will never want excuses.

V. Let us see how Christ bore this contempt.

1. He partly *excused it*, as a common thing, and what might be expected, though not reasonably or justly (*v.* 4); *A prophet is not despised anywhere but in his own country*.

2. He did *some good* among them, notwithstanding the slights they put upon him, for he is kind even to the evil and unthankful; *He laid his hands upon a few sick folks, and healed them*.

3. Yet he *could there do* no such mighty works, at least not so many, as in other places, because of the unbelief that prevailed among the people, by reason of the prejudices which their leaders instilled into them against Christ, *v.* 5. It is a strange expression, as if unbelief tied the hands of omnipotence itself; he *would have done* as many miracles there as he had done elsewhere, but he could not, because people would not make application to him, nor sue for his favours; he could have

wrought them, but they forfeited the honour of having them wrought for them.

4. He *marvelled because of their unbelief, v. 6.* We never find Christ wondering but at the *faith* of the Gentiles that were strangers, as the *centurion* (Matt. viii. 10), and the woman of Samaria, and at the unbelief of Jews that were his own countrymen.

5. He *went round about the villages, teaching.* If we cannot do good where we would, we must do it where we can, and be glad if we may have any opportunity, though but in the villages, of serving Christ and souls.

MIRACLES—AND HEROD'S REACTION (*vv.* 7–29)

Here is the commission given to the twelve apostles, to preach and work miracles; it is the same which we had more largely, Matt. x.

Here is also the opinion of Herod concerning him. He heard of *his name* and fame, of what he said and what he did; and he said, "It is certainly John Baptist, *v.* 14. As sure as we are here, *It is John, whom I beheaded, v.* 16. He is *risen from the dead*; and though while he was with us *he did no miracle*, yet, having removed for awhile to another world, he is come again with greater power, and *now mighty works do show forth themselves in him.*"

Note, 1. Where there is an *idle faith*, there is commonly a *working fancy*. The people said, It is a prophet risen from the dead; Herod said, It is *John Baptist risen from the dead.*

2. They who fight against the cause of God, will find themselves baffled, even when they think themselves conquerors; they cannot gain their point, for the word of the Lord endures for ever.

3. A guilty conscience needs no accuser or tormentor but itself. Herod charges himself with the murder of John, which perhaps no one else dare charge him with; *I beheaded him*; and the terror of it made him imagine that Christ was John risen.

4. There may be the terrors of strong conviction, where there is not the truth of a saving conversion.

Here is also a narrative of Herod's putting John Baptist to death, which is brought in upon this occasion, as it was in Matthew.

FEEDING FIVE THOUSAND (*vv.* 30–44)

In these verses, we have,

I. The return to Christ of the apostles whom he had sent forth (*v.* 7), to preach, and work miracles. They had dispersed themselves into several quarters of the country for some time, but when they had made good their several appointments, by consent they *gathered themselves together*, to compare notes, and came to Jesus, the centre of their unity, to give him an account of what they had done pursuant to their commission: they *told him all things*, both *what they had done, and what they had taught.*

II. The tender care Christ took for their repose, after the fatigue they had (*v.* 31); *He said unto them*, perceiving them to be almost spent, and out of breath,

Come ye yourselves apart into a desert place, and rest awhile. It should seem that John's disciples came to Christ with the mournful tidings of their master's death, much about the same time that his own disciples came to him with the report of their negotiation. Note, Christ takes cognizance of the *frights* of some, and the *toils* of others, of his disciples, and provides suitable relief for both, rest for those that are tired, and refuge for those that are terrified.

III. The diligence of the people to follow him. It was rude to do so, when he and his disciples were desirous, for such good reason, to *retire*; and yet they are not blamed for it, nor bid to go back, but bid welcome.

IV. The entertainment Christ gave them (*v.* 34); *When he saw much people,* instead of being moved with displeasure, because they disturbed him when he desired to be private, as many a man, many a good man, would have been, he was *moved with compassion toward them,* and looked upon them with concern, because *they* were *as sheep having no shepherd,* they seemed to be well-inclined, and manageable as sheep, and willing to be taught, but they had *no shepherd,* none to lead and guide them in the right way, none to feed them with good doctrine: and therefore, in compassion to them, he not only *healed their sick,* as it is in Matthew, but he *taught them many things,* and we may be sure that they were all true and good, and fit for them to learn.

V. The provision he made for them all; all his hearers he generously made his guests, and treated them at a *splendid* entertainment: so it might truly be called, because a *miraculous* one.

1. The disciples moved that they should be *sent home.*

2. Christ ordered that they should all be fed (*v.* 37); *Give ye them to eat.*

3. The disciples objected against it as impracticable; *Shall we go, and buy two hundred penny-worth of bread, and give them to eat?*

4. Christ effected it, to universal satisfaction. They had brought with them *five loaves,* for the victualling of their ship, and *two fishes* perhaps they caught as they came along; and that is the bill of fare. This was but a little for Christ and his disciples, and yet this they must give away. We often find Christ entertained at other people's tables, dining with one friend, and supping with another: but here we have him supping a great many at his own charge, which shows that, when others *ministered to him of their substance,* it was not because he could not supply himself otherwise (if he was *hungry,* he needed not *tell them*); but it was a piece of humiliation, that he was pleased to submit to, nor was it agreeable to the intention of miracles, that he should work them for himself. Observe,

A blessing was craved upon the meat; *He looked up to heaven, and blessed.* And by virtue of this blessing the bread strangely multiplied, and so did the fishes, for they did *all eat, and were filled,* though they were to the number of *five thousand, vv.* 42, 44. This miracle was significant, and shows that Christ came into the world, to be the great feeder as well as the great healer; not only to restore, but to preserve and nourish, spiritual life; and in him there is enough for all that come to him, enough to fill the soul, to fill the treasures; none are sent empty away from Christ, but those that come to him full of themselves.

WALKING ON THE WATER
(vv. 45–56)

This passage of story we had Matt. xiv. 22, &c., only what was there related concerning Peter, is omitted here.

The disciples were more surprised and astonished at this miracle than did become them, and there was that at the bottom of their astonishment, which was really culpable; *They were sore amazed in themselves*, were in a perfect ecstasy; as if it were a new and unaccountable thing, as if Christ had never done the like before, and they had no reason to expect he should do it now; they ought to admire the power of Christ, and to be confirmed hereby in their belief of his being the Son of God: but why all this confusion about it? It was because they *considered not the miracle of the loaves*; had they given that its due weight, they would not have been so much surprised at this; for his multiplying the bread was as great an instance of his power as his walking on the water. They were strangely stupid and unthinking, and their heart was hardened, or else they would not have thought it a thing incredible

that Christ should command a calm. It is for want of a right understanding of Christ's former works, that we are transported at the thought of his present works, as if there never were the like before.

CHAPTER SEVEN

TRADITIONS OF MEN
(vv. 1–23)

One great design of Christ's coming, was, to set aside the ceremonial law which God made, and to put an end to it; to make way for which he begins with the ceremonial law which men had made, and added to the law of God's making, and discharges his disciples from the obligation of that; which here he doth fully, upon occasion of the offence which the Pharisees took at them for the violation of it. These Pharisees and scribes with whom he had this argument, are said to *come from Jerusalem* down to Galilee—fourscore or a hundred miles, to pick quarrels with our Saviour there, where they supposed him to have the greatest interest and reputation. Had they come so far to be taught by him, their zeal had been commendable; but to come so far to oppose him, and to check the progress of his gospel, was great wickedness. It should seem that the scribes and Pharisees at Jerusalem pretended not only to a pre-eminence above, but to an authority over, the country clergy, and therefore kept up their visitations and sent inquisitors among them, as they did to John when he appeared, John i. 19.

Now in this passage we may observe,

I. What the tradition of the elders was: by it all were enjoined to *wash their hands* before meat; a cleanly custom, and no harm in it; and yet as such to be over-nice in it discovers too great a care about the body, which is *of the earth*; but they placed religion in it, and would not leave it indifferent, as it was in its own nature; people were at their liberty to do it or not to do it; but they interposed their authority, and commanded all to do it upon pain of excommunication; this they kept up as a *tradition of the elders*.

II. What the practice of Christ's disciples was; they knew what the law was, and the common usage; but they understood themselves so well that they would not be bound up by it: they ate bread with *defiled*, that is, with *unwashen*, *hands*, *v.* 2.

III. The offence which the Pharisees took at this; They *found fault* (*v.* 2). They do not ask, Why do not thy disciples *do as we do?* (Though that was what they meant, coveting to make themselves the standard.) But, Why do not they *walk according to the tradition of the elders? v.* 5. To which it was easy to answer, that, by receiving the doctrine of Christ, they had *more understanding than all their teachers*, yea *more than the ancients*, Ps. cxix. 99, 100.

IV. Christ's vindication of them; in which,

1. He argues with the Pharisees concerning the authority by which this ceremony was imposed.

(1) He reproves them for their hypocrisy in pretending to honour God, when really they had no such design in their religious observances (*vv.* 6, 7).

(2) He reproves them for placing religion in the inventions and injunctions of their elders and rulers; They *taught for doctrines the traditions of men*.

(3) He reproves them for *laying aside the commandment of God*, and overlooking that, not urging that in their preaching, and in their discipline conniving at the violation of that, as if that were no longer of force, *v.* 8.

This he gives them a particular instance of, and a flagrant one— God commanded children to *honour their parents*, not only by the law of Moses, but, antecedent to that, by the law of nature; and whoso *revileth*, or *speaketh evil of*, father or mother, *let him die the death*, *v.* 10. But if a man will but conform himself in all points to the tradition of the elders, they will find him out an expedient by which he may be discharged from this obligation, *v.* 11. If his parents be in want, and he has wherewithal to help them, but has no mind to do it, let him swear by the *Corban*, that is, by the *gold of the temple*, and the *gift upon the altar*, that his parents shall not be profited by him, that he will not relieve them; and, if they ask any thing of him, let him tell them this, and it is enough; as if by the obligation of this wicked vow he had discharged himself from the obligation of God's holy law. He concludes, *And many such like things do ye*. Where will men stop, when once they have made the word of God give way to their tradition?

2. He instructs the people concerning the principles upon which this ceremony was grounded.

Now that which he goes about to set them right in, is, what the pollution is, which we are in danger of being damaged by, *v.* 15. (1) Not by the *meat we eat*, though it be eaten with unwashen hands; that is but from without, and goes through a man. But, (2) It is by the breaking out of the corruption that is in our hearts; the mind and conscience are defiled, guilt is contracted, and we become odious in the sight of God by that which *comes out* of us; our wicked thoughts and affections, words and actions, these defile us, and these only. Our care must therefore be, to *wash our heart from wickedness*.

3. He gives his disciples, in private, an explication of the instructions he gave the people. They *asked* him, when they had him by himself, *concerning the parable* (*v.* 17); for to them, it seems, it was a parable. Now, in answer to their enquiry, (1) He reproves their dullness; "*Are ye so without understanding also? Are ye dull also*, as dull as the people that *cannot* understand, as dull as the Pharisees that *will not*? Are ye *so* dull?" He doth not expect they should understand every thing; "But are ye so weak as not to understand *this*?" (2) He explains this truth to them, that they might *perceive* it, and then they would *believe* it, for it carried its own evidence along with it. If we understand the spiritual nature of God and of his law, and what it is that is offensive to him, and disfits us for communion with him, we shall soon perceive, [1]

That that which we eat and drink cannot defile us, so as to call for any religious washing. But, [2] It is that which *comes out from* the heart, the corrupt heart, that defiles us. As by the ceremonial law, whatsoever (almost) comes out of a man, defiles him (Lev. xv. 2; Deut. xxiii. 13), so what comes out from the *mind* of a man is that which defiles him before God, and calls for a religious washing (*v.* 21); *From within, out of the heart of men*, which they boast of the *goodness* of, and think is the best part of them, thence that which defiles proceeds, thence comes all the mischief.

A GREEK WOMAN
(*vv.* 24–30)

Observe, 1. The application made to Christ by a poor woman in distress and trouble. She was a Gentile, a Greek, *a stranger to the commonwealth of Israel, an alien to the covenant of promise*; she was by extraction a Syrophenician, and not in any degree proselyted to the Jewish religion; she had a *daughter*, a *young* daughter, that was possessed *with the devil*. Her address was, (1) Very humble, pressing, and importunate; *She heard of him, and came, and fell at his feet*. (2) It was very particular; she tells him what she wanted.

2. The discouragement he gave to this address (*v.* 27); He said unto her, "*Let the children first be filled*; let the Jews have all the miracles wrought for them, that they have occasion for, who are in a particular manner God's chosen people; and let not that which was intended for them, be thrown to those who are

not of God's family, and who have not that knowledge of him, and interest in him, which they have, and who are as *dogs in comparison of them*, vile and profane, and who are as *dogs to them*, snarling at them, spiteful toward them, and ready to worry them."

3. The turn she gave to this word of Christ, which made against her, and her improvement of it, to make for her, *v.* 28. She said, "*Yes, Lord,* I own it is true that the *children's bread* ought not to be cast to the dogs; but they were never denied the *crumbs* of that bread, nay it belongs to them, and they are allowed a place *under the table*, that they may be ready to receive them. I ask not for a *loaf*, no, nor for a *morsel*, only for a *crumb*; do not refuse me that."

4. The grant Christ thereupon made of her request. Is she thus humble, thus earnest? For *this saying, Go thy way*, thou shalt have what thou camest for, *the devil is gone out of thy daughter, v.* 29. This encourages us to *pray* and not to *faint*, to continue instant in prayer, not doubting but to prevail at last; the vision at the end shall *speak, and not lie.*

BE OPENED! (*vv.* 31–37)

Now here we have the story of a cure that Christ wrought, which is not recorded by any other of the evangelists; it is of one that was *deaf* and *dumb*.

I. His case was sad, *v.* 32. There were those that brought to him one that was *deaf*; some think, born deaf, and then he must be dumb of course; others think that by some distemper or disaster he was be-

come deaf, or, at least, thick of hearing; and he had an *impediment in his speech*. He was μογιλάλος some think that he was quite dumb; others, that he could not speak but with great difficulty to himself, and so as scarcely to be understood by those that heard him. He was *tongue-tied*, so that he was perfectly unfit for conversation, and deprived both of the pleasure and of the profit of it; he had not the satisfaction either of hearing other people talk, or of telling his own mind. Let us take occasion from hence to give thanks to God for preserving to us the sense of hearing, especially that we may be capable of hearing the word of God; and the faculty of speech, especially that we may be capable of speaking God's praises; and let us look with compassion upon those that are deaf or dumb, and treat them with great tenderness. They that brought this poor man to Christ, besought him that he would *put his hand upon him*, as the prophets did upon those whom they *blessed* in the name of the Lord. It is not said, They besought him to *cure him*, but to *put his hand upon him*, to take cognizance of his case, and put forth his power to do to him as he pleased.

II. His cure was solemn, and some of the circumstances of it were singular.

1. Christ *took him aside from the multitude, v.* 33. Ordinarily, he wrought his miracles publicly before all the people, to show that they would bear the strictest scrutiny and inspection; but this he did privately, to show that he did not seek his own glory, and to

teach us to avoid every thing that savours of ostentation. Let us learn of Christ to be humble, and to do good where no eye sees, but his that is *all eye*.

2. He used more significant actions, in the doing of this cure, than usual. (1) He *put his fingers into his ears*, as if he would *syringe* them, and fetch out that which stopped them up. (2) He spit upon his own finger, and then *touched his tongue*, as if he would moisten his mouth, and so loosen that with which his tongue was tied; these were no causes that could in the least contribute to his cure, but only signs of the exerting of that power which Christ had in himself to cure him, for the encouraging of his faith, and theirs that brought him. The application was all from himself, it was his own *fingers* that he put into his ears, and his own *spittle* that he put upon his tongue; for he alone heals.

3. He *looked up to heaven*, to give his Father the praise of what he did; for he sought his praise, and did his will, and, as Mediator, acted in dependence on him, and with an eye to him. Thus he signified that it was by a divine power, a power he had as the Lord from heaven, and brought with him thence, that he did this; for the *hearing ear* and the *seeing eye* the *Lord has made*, and can remake even *both of them*. He also hereby directed his patient who could *see*, though he could not *hear*, to look up to heaven for relief. Moses with his stammering tongue is directed to look that way (Exod. iv. 11); *Who hath made man's mouth? Or who maketh the dumb or deaf, or the*

seeing or the blind? Have not I the Lord?

4. He sighed; not as if he found any difficulty in working this miracle, or obtaining power to do it from his Father; but thus he expressed his pity for the miseries of human life, and his sympathy with the afflicted in their afflictions, as one that was himself *touched with the feeling of their infirmities*.

5. He said, *Ephphatha*; that is, *Be opened*. This was nothing that looked like *spell* or *charm*, such as they used, who had *familiar spirits*, who *peeped and muttered*, Isa. viii. 19. Christ speaks as one having authority, and power went along with the word. *Be opened*, served both parts of the cure; "Let the *ears* be *opened*, let the *lips* be *opened*, let him hear and speak freely, and let the restraint be taken off"; and the effect was answerable (*v.* 35); *Straightway his ears were opened, and the string of his tongue was loosed*, and all was well: and happy he who, as soon as he had his hearing and speech, had the blessed Jesus so near him, to converse with.

Now this cure was, (1) A proof of Christ's being the Messiah; for it was foretold that by his power the *ears of the deaf should be unstopped*, and the *tongue of the dumb* should be made to *sing*, Isa. xxxv. 5, 6. (2) It was a specimen of the operations of his gospel upon the minds of men. The great command of the gospel, and grace of Christ to poor sinners, is *Ephphatha—Be opened*. Grotius applies it thus, that the internal impediments of the mind are removed by the Spirit of Christ, as those bodily impediments were by the word of his power. He *opens the heart*, as he did Lydia's, and thereby opens the ear to receive the word of God, and opens the mouth in prayer and praises.

6. He ordered it to be kept very private, but it was made very public. (1) It was his humility, that he *charged them they should tell no man*, v. 36. Most men will proclaim their own goodness, or, at least, desire that others should proclaim it; but Christ, though he was himself in no danger of being puffed up with it, knowing that we are, would thus set us an example of self-denial, as in other things, so especially in praise and applause. We should take pleasure in doing good, but not in its being known. (2) It was their zeal, that, though he charged them to say nothing of it, yet they published it, before Christ would have had it published. But they meant honestly, and therefore it is to be reckoned rather an act of indiscretion than an act of disobedience, v. 36. But they that told it, and they that heard it, were *beyond measure astonished*; they were exceedingly affected with it, and this was said by every body, it was the common verdict, *He hath done all things well* (v. 37); whereas there were those that hated, and persecuted him as an *evil-doer*, they are ready to witness for him, not only that he has done no evil, but that he has done a great deal of good, and has done it well, modestly and humbly, and very devoutly, and all gratis, *without money and without price*, which added much to the lustre of his good works. He *maketh both the deaf to hear, and the dumb to speak*; and that is *well*, it is well for them, it is well for their relations, to whom they had been a burden; and therefore *they* are inexcusable who speak ill of him.

CHAPTER EIGHT

THE LEAVEN OF THE PHARISEES (vv. 1–21)

We had the story of a miracle very like this (*vv.* 1–9) before, in this gospel (*ch.* vi. 35), and of this same miracle (Matt. xv. 32), and here is little or no addition or alteration as to the circumstances.

Still Christ is upon motion; now he visits the parts of Dalmanutha, that no corner of the land of Israel might say that they had not had his presence with them. He came thither *by ship* (*v.* 10); but, meeting with occasions of dispute there, and not with opportunities of doing good, he *entered into the ship again* (*v.* 13), and came back. In these verses, we are told,

I. How he refused to gratify the Pharisees, who challenged him to give them a *sign from heaven*.

1. They demanded of him a *sign from heaven*, as if the signs he gave them on earth, which were more familiar to them, and were more capable of being examined and enquired into, were not sufficient. There was a sign *from heaven* at his baptism, in the descent of the dove, and the voice (Matt. iii. 16, 17); it was public enough; and if they had attended John's baptism as they ought to have done, they might themselves have seen it. Afterward, when he was nailed to the cross, they prescribed a new sign; *Let him come down from the cross, and we will believe him*; thus obstinate infidelity will still have something

to say, though ever so unreasonable. They demanded this sign, *tempting him*; not in hopes that he would give it them, that they might be satisfied, but in hopes that he would not, that they might imagine themselves to have a pretence for their infidelity.

2. He denied them their demand; He *sighed deeply in his spirit, v.* 12. He *groaned* (so some), being grieved for the *hardness of their hearts,* and the little influence that his preaching and miracles had had upon them. (1) He expostulates with them upon this demand; "*Why doth this generation seek after a sign*; this generation, that is so unworthy to have the gospel brought to it, and to have any sign accompanying it; *this generation,* that so greedily swallows the traditions of the elders, without the confirmation of any sign at all?" (2) He refuses to answer their demand; *Verily, I say unto you, there shall no sign,* no such sign, *be given to this generation.* He denied them, and then *left them,* as men not fit to be talked with; if they will not be convinced, they shall not; leave them to their strong delusions.

II. How he warned his disciples against the leaven of the Pharisees and of Herod. Observe here,

1. What the caution was (*v.* 15); "*Take heed, beware,* lest ye partake of the *leaven of the Pharisees,* lest ye embrace the tradition of the elders, which they are so wedded to, lest ye be proud, and hypocritical, and ceremonious, like them."

2. How they misunderstood this caution. It seems, at their putting to sea this time, they had *forgotten to take bread,* and *had not in their ship*

more than one loaf, v. 14. When therefore Christ bid them *beware of the leaven of the Pharisees,* they understood it as an intimation to them, not to apply themselves to any of the Pharisees for relief, when they came to the other side, for they had lately been offended at them for eating with *unwashen hands*.

3. The reproof Christ gave them for their uneasiness in this matter, as it argued a disbelief of his power to supply them, notwithstanding the abundant experience they had had of it. The reproof is given with some warmth, for he knew their hearts, and knew they needed to be thus soundly chidden; "*Perceive ye not yet, neither understand,* that which you have had so many demonstrations of? *Have ye your hearts yet hardened,* so as that nothing will make any impression upon them, or bring them to compliance with your Master's designs? *Do ye not remember* that which was done but the other day, *when I broke the five loaves among the five thousand,* and soon after, the *seven loaves among the four thousand?* Do ye not remember *how many baskets full ye took up* of the fragments?" Yes, they did remember, and could tell that they took up *twelve* baskets full one time, and *seven* another; "Why then," saith he, "*how is it that ye do not understand?* As if he that multiplied *five* loaves, and *seven,* could not multiply one."

A TWO-STAGE HEALING
(*vv.* 22–26)

This cure is related only by this evangelist, and there is something singular in the circumstances.

I. Here is a *blind man* brought to Christ by his friends, with a desire that he would *touch him*, v. 22. Here appears the faith of those that brought him—they doubted not but that one touch of Christ's hand would recover him his sight; but the man himself showed not that earnestness for, or expectation of, a cure that other blind men did.

II. Here is Christ *leading* this blind man, v. 23. He did not bid his friends lead him, but (which bespeaks his wonderful condescension) he himself *took him by the hand, and led him*. Never had poor blind man such a Leader. He led him *out of the town*. Had he herein only designed privacy, he might have led him into a house, into an inner chamber, and have cured him there; but he intended hereby to upbraid Bethsaida with the *mighty works* that had *in vain* been done *in her* (Matt. xi. 21), and was telling her, in effect, she was unworthy to have any more done within her walls. Perhaps Christ took the blind man *out of the town*, that he might have a larger prospect in the *open fields*, to try his sight with, than he could have in the *close streets*.

III. Here is the cure of the blind man, by that blessed Oculist, who came into the world to *preach the recovering of sight to the blind* (Luke iv. 18), and to *give* what he *preached*. In this cure we may observe, 1. That Christ used a *sign*; he *spat on his eyes* (spat *into* them, so some), and *put his hand upon him*. He could have cured him, as he did others, with a word speaking, but thus he was pleased to assist his faith which was very weak, and to help him against his *unbelief*.

2. That the cure was wrought *gradually*, which was not usual in Christ's miracles. He *asked him if he saw aught*, v. 23. And he *looked up*; so far he *recovered his sight*, that he could open his eyes, and he said, *I see men as trees walking*; he could not distinguish men from trees, otherwise than that he could discern them to move. But, 3. It was soon completed; Christ never doeth *his work* by the halves, nor leaves it till he can say, *It is finished*. He *put his hands again upon his eyes*, to disperse the remaining darkness, and then bade him look up again, and he *saw every man clearly*, v. 25. Now Christ took this way, (1) Because he would not *tie himself to a method*, but would show with what liberty he acted in all he did. He did not cure by *rote*, as I may say, and in a *road*, but *varied* as he thought fit. (2) Because it should be to the patient *according to his faith*; and perhaps this man's faith was at first very weak, but afterward gathered strength, and accordingly his cure grew. (3) Thus Christ would show how, and in what method, those are healed by his grace, who by nature are *spiritually blind*; at first, their knowledge is confused, they see *men as trees walking*; but, like the light of the morning, it *shines more and more to the perfect day*, and then they *see all things clearly*, Prov. iv. 18.

IV. The directions Christ gave the man he had cured, not to *tell it to any in the town of Bethsaida*, nor so much as to *go into the town*, where probably there were some expecting him to come back, who had seen Christ lead him out of the town, but, having been eye-witnesses of so many miracles, had not so much as the curiosity to follow him: let not these be gratified with the sight of him when he was cured, who would not show so much respect to Christ as to go a step out of the town, to see this cure wrought. Bethsaida, in the day of her visitation, would not know the things that belonged to her peace, and now they are *hid from her eyes*. They will not see, and therefore shall not see.

THE MEANING OF THE MIRACLES
(*vv.* 27–38)

We have read a great deal of the doctrine Christ preached, and the miracles he wrought, which were many, and strange, and well-attested, of various kinds, and wrought in several places, to the astonishment of the multitudes that were eye-witnesses of them. It is now time for us to pause a little, and to consider what these things mean; the wondrous works which Christ then forbade the publishing of, being recorded in these sacred writings, are thereby published to all the world, to us, to all ages; now what shall we think of them? Is the record of those things designed only for an amusement, or to furnish us with matter for discourse? No, certainly *these things are written, that we may believe that Jesus is the Christ the Son of God* (John xx. 31); and this discourse which Christ had with his disciples, will assist us in making the necessary reflections upon the miracles of Christ, and a right use of them. Three things we are here taught to infer from the miracles Christ wrought.

I. They *prove* that he is *the true Messiah*, the Son of God, and Saviour of the world: this the works he did witnessed concerning him; and this his disciples, who were the eye-witnesses of those works, here profess their belief of; which cannot but be a satisfaction to us in making the same inference from them.

1. Christ enquired of them what the sentiments of the people were concerning him; *Who do men say that I am? v.* 27. Note, Though it is a small thing for us to be judged of men, yet it may sometimes do us good to know what people say of us, not that we may seek our own glory, but that we may hear of our faults. Christ asked them, not that he might be informed, but that they might observe it themselves, and inform one another.

2. The account they gave him, was such as plainly intimated the *high opinion* the people had of him. Though they came short of the truth, yet they were convinced by his miracles that he was an extraordinary person, sent from the invisible world with a divine commission. It is probable that they would have acknowledged him to be the Messiah, if they had not been possessed by their teachers with a notion that the Messiah must be a temporal Prince, appearing in external pomp and power, which the figure Christ made, would not comport with; yet (whatever the Pharisees said, whose copyhold was touched by the strictness and spirituality of his doctrine) none of the people said that he was a Deceiver, but some said that *he was John Baptist*, others *Elias*, others

one of the prophets, *v.* 28. All agreed that he was one *risen from the dead*.

3. The account they gave him of their own sentiments concerning him, intimated their abundant satisfaction in him, and in their having left all to follow him, which now, after some time of trial, they see no reason to repent; *But whom say ye that I am?* To this they have an answer ready, *Thou art the Christ*, the Messiah often promised, and long expected, *v.* 29. To be a Christian indeed, is, sincerely to believe that Jesus is the Christ, and to act accordingly; and that he is so, plainly appears by his wondrous works. This they knew, and must shortly publish and maintain; but for the present they must keep it secret (*v.* 30), till the proof of it was completed, and they were completely qualified to maintain it, by the pouring out of the Holy Ghost; and then *let all the house of Israel know assuredly that God has made this same Jesus, whom ye crucified, both Lord and Christ*, Acts ii. 36.

II. These miracles of Christ *take off the offence of the cross*, and assure us that Christ was, in it, not conquered, but a Conqueror. Now that the disciples are convinced that Jesus is the Christ, they may bear to hear of his sufferings, which Christ now *begins* to give them notice of, *v.* 31.

1. Christ *taught* his disciples that he must *suffer many things*, Though they had got over the vulgar error of the Messiah's being a temporal Prince, so far as to believe their Master to be the Messiah, notwithstanding his present meanness, yet still they retained it, so far as to

expect that he would *shortly* appear in outward pomp and grandeur, and *restore the kingdom to Israel*; and therefore, to rectify that mistake, Christ here gives them a prospect of the contrary, that he must be *rejected of the elders, and the chief priests*, and *the scribes*, who, they expected, should be brought to own and prefer him; that, instead of being crowned, *he must be killed*, he must be crucified, and *after three days he must rise again* to a heavenly life, and to be *no more in this world*. This he spoke *openly* (*v.* 32).

2. Peter opposed it; *He took him, and began to rebuke him.* Here Peter showed more love than discretion, a zeal for Christ and his safety, but not according to knowledge. Our Lord Jesus allowed his disciples to be free with him, but Peter here took too great a liberty.

3. Christ checked him for his opposition (*v.* 33); He *turned about*, as one offended, and *looked on his disciples*, to see if the rest of them were of the same mind, and concurred with Peter in this, that, if they did, they might take the reproof to themselves, which he was now about to give to Peter; and he said, *Get thee behind me, Satan.* Peter little thought to have had such a sharp rebuke for such a kind dissuasive, but perhaps expected as much commendation now for his love as he had lately had for his faith. Note, Christ sees that amiss in what we say and do, which we ourselves are not aware of, and knows what manner of spirit we are of, when we ourselves do not.

III. Here is that which all are concerned to know, and consider, if they expect Christ should heal *their souls*.

1. They must not be *indulgent* of the *ease of the body*; for (*v.* 34), "*Whosoever will come after me* for spiritual cures, as these people do for bodily cures, *let him deny himself*, and live a life of self-denial, mortification, and contempt of the world; let him not pretend to be his own physician, but renounce all confidence in himself and his own righteousness and strength, and let him *take up his cross*, conforming himself to the pattern of a crucified Jesus, and accommodating himself to the will of God in all the afflictions he lies under; and thus let him continue to *follow me*"; as many of those did, whom Christ healed. Those that will be Christ's patients must attend on him, converse with him, receive instruction and reproof from him, as those did that *followed* him, and must resolve they will never forsake him.

2. They must not be *solicitous*, no, not for *the life of the body*, when they cannot keep it without quitting Christ, *v.* 35. Are we invited by the words and works of Christ to follow him? Let us sit down, and count the cost, whether we can prefer our advantages by Christ before life itself, whether we can bear to think of losing our life *for Christ's sake and the gospel's*.

(1) We must *not dread the loss of our lives*, provided it be *in the cause of Christ* (*v.* 35); *Whosoever will save his life*, by declining Christ, and refusing to come to him, or by disowning and denying him after he has in profession come to Christ,

he shall *lose it*, shall lose the comfort of his natural life, the root and fountain of his spiritual life, and all his hopes of eternal life; such a bad bargain will he make for himself. But whosoever *shall lose his life*, shall be truly willing to lose it, shall venture it, shall lay it down when he cannot keep it without denying Christ, he shall *save it*, he shall be an unspeakable gainer; for the loss of his life shall be made up to him in a better life.

(2) We must *dread the loss of our souls*, yea, though we should *gain the whole world* by it (*vv.* 36, 37); *For what shall it profit a man, if he should gain the whole world*, and all the wealth, honour, and pleasure, in it, by denying Christ, and *lose his own soul*? "True it is," said Bishop Hooper, the night before he suffered martyrdom, "that *life is sweet*, and *death is bitter*, but *eternal death is more bitter*, and *eternal life is more sweet*." As the happiness of heaven with Christ, is enough to countervail the loss of life itself for Christ, so the gain of all the world *in sin*, is not sufficient to countervail the ruin of the soul *by sin*.

What that is that men do, to *save their lives*, and *gain the world*, he tells us (*v.* 38), and of what fatal consequence it will be to them; *Whosoever therefore shall be ashamed of me, and of my words, in this adulterous and sinful generation, of him shall the Son of man be ashamed.* Something like this we had, Matt. x. 33. But it is here expressed more fully. Those that are ashamed of Christ in this world where he is despised, he will be ashamed of in that world where he is eternally

The Transfiguration

adored. *They* shall not share with him in his glory then, that were not willing to share with him in his disgrace now.

THE TRANSFIGURATION
(*vv.* 1–29)

Here is, I. A prediction of Christ's kingdom now near approaching, *v.* 1. That which is foretold, is, 1. That the *kingdom of God* would *come*, and would come so as to be *seen*: the kingdom of the Messiah shall be set up in the world by the utter destruction of the Jewish polity, which stood in the way of it; this was the restoring of the kingdom of God among men, which had been in a manner lost by the woeful degeneracy both of Jews and Gentiles. 2. That it would come *with power*, so as to make its own way, and bear down the opposition that was given to it. It came *with power*, when vengeance was taken on the Jews for crucifying Christ, and when it conquered the idolatry of the Gentile world. 3. That it would come while some now *present were alive*; There are some *standing here, that shall not taste of death*, till they *see* it; this speaks the same with Matt. xxiv. 34, This *generation shall not pass, till all these things be fulfilled*. Those that were standing here with Christ, should see it, when the others could not discern it to be the kingdom of God, for it came not with observation.

II. A specimen of that kingdom in the transfiguration of Christ, *six days* after Christ spoke that prediction. He had begun to give notice to his disciples of his death and sufferings; and, to prevent their offence at that, he gives them this glimpse of his glory, to show that his sufferings were voluntary, and what a virtue the dignity and glory of his person would put into them, and to prevent the *offence of the cross*.

We have had this, and the following miracle—the demon expelled from a boy—in Matt. xvii. 1–21.

THE APOSTLES REPROVED
(*vv.* 30–40)

Here, I. Christ foretells his own approaching sufferings. He *passed through Galilee* with more expedition than usual, and *would not that any man should know it* (*v.* 30); because he had done many mighty and good works among them in vain, they shall not be invited to see them and have the benefit of them, as they had been. The time of his sufferings drew nigh, and therefore he was willing to be private awhile, and to converse only with his disciples, to prepare them for the approaching trial, *v.* 31. He said to them, *The Son of man is delivered* by the determinate counsel and foreknowledge of God *into the hands of men* (*v.* 31), and *they shall kill him*. But still it is observable that when Christ spoke of his death, he always spoke of his resurrection, which took away the reproach of it from himself, and should have taken away the grief of it from his disciples. But they *understood not that saying, v.* 32. The words were plain enough, but they could not be reconciled to the thing, and therefore would suppose them to have some mystical meaning which they did not understand, and they were *afraid to ask him*; not because he was difficult of access, or stern to those who consulted him, but either because they were loth to know the truth, or because they expected to be chided for their backwardness to receive it. Many remain ignorant because they are ashamed to enquire.

II. He rebukes his disciples for magnifying themselves. When he came to Capernaum, he privately asked his disciples what it was that they *disputed among themselves by the way*, *v.* 33. He knew very well what the dispute was, but he would know it *from them*, and would have them to confess their fault and folly in it.

Now, (1) They were willing to *cover this fault* (*v.* 34); they *held their peace*. As they would not *ask* (*v.* 32), because they were ashamed to own their ignorance, so here they would not *answer* because they were ashamed to own their pride. (2) He was willing to *amend this fault* in them, and to bring them to a better temper; and therefore *sat down*, that he might have a solemn and full discourse with them about this matter; he *called the twelve to him*, and told them, [1] That ambition and affectation of dignity and dominion, instead of gaining them preferment in his kingdom, would but postpone their preferment; *If any man desire* and aim *to be first*, he *shall be last*; he that exalteth himself, shall be abased, and men's *pride* shall *bring them low*. [2] That there is no preferment to be had under him, but an opportunity for, and an obligation to, so

much the more labour and condescension; *If any man desire to be first*, when he is so, he must be much the more busy and serviceable to every body. [3] That those who are most humble and self-denying, do most resemble Christ, and shall be most tenderly owned by him. This he taught them by a sign; *He took a child in his arms*, that had nothing of pride and ambition in it. "Look you," saith he; "*whosoever shall receive* one like this child, *receives me*."

III. He rebukes them for *villifying all but themselves*; while they are striving which of them should be greatest, they will not allow those who are not in communion with them to be any thing. Observe,

1. The account which John gave him, of the restraint they had laid upon one from making use of the name of Christ, because he was not of their society.

2. The rebuke he gave to them for this (*v.* 39); *Jesus said*, "*Forbid him not*, nor any other that does likewise." Two reasons Christ gives why such should not be forbidden. (1) Because we cannot suppose that any man who makes use of Christ's name in working miracles, should blaspheme his name, as the scribes and Pharisees did. There were those indeed that did *in Christ's name cast out devils*, and yet in other respects were *workers of iniquity*; but they did not *speak evil of Christ*. (2) Because those that differed in communion, while they agreed to fight against Satan under the banner of Christ, ought to look upon one another as on the same side, notwithstanding that difference. *He that is not against us is on our part.*

As to the great controversy between Christ and Beelzebub, he had said, *He that is not with me is against me*, Matt. xii. 30. He that will not own Christ, owns Satan. But as to those that own Christ, though not in the same circumstances, that follow him, though *not with us*, we must reckon that though these differ from us, they are not against us, and therefore are *on our part*, and we must not be any hindrance to their usefulness.

OFFENCES (*vv.* 41–50)

Here, I. Christ promiseth a reward to all those that are any way kind to his disciples (*v.* 41); "*Whosoever shall give you a cup of water*, when you need it, and it will be a refreshment to you, *because ye belong to Christ*, and are of his family, *he shall not lose his reward.*"

II. He threatens those that *offend* his *little ones*, that wilfully are the occasion of sin or trouble to them, *v.* 42. Whosoever shall grieve any true Christians, though they be of the weakest, shall oppose their *entrance* into the ways of God, or discourage and obstruct their *progress* in those ways, shall either restrain them from doing good, or draw them in to commit sin, it were *better for him that a millstone were hanged about his neck, and he were cast into the sea*: his punishment will be very great, and the death and ruin of his soul more terrible than such a death and ruin of his body would be. See Matt. xviii. 6.

III. He warns all his followers to take heed of ruining their own souls. This charity must begin at home; if we must take heed of doing any thing to hinder others

from good, and to occasion their sin, much more careful must we be to avoid every thing that will take us off from our duty, or lead us to sin; and that which doth so we must part with, though it be ever so dear to us. This we had twice in Matthew, *ch.* v. 29, 30, and *ch.* xviii. 8, 9. It is here urged somewhat more largely and pressingly; certainly this requires our serious regard, which is so much insisted upon.

CHAPTER TEN
DIVORCE LAWS (*vv.* 1–12)

Here we have our Lord Jesus in the *coasts* of Judea, by the further side of Jordan eastward, as we found him, not long since, in the utmost borders westward, near Tyre and Sidon. Thus was his circuit like that of the sun, from whose light and heat nothing is hid. Now here we have him,

I. *Resorted to* by the *people*, *v.* 1. Wherever he was, they flocked after him in crowds; they came to him *again*, as they had done when he had formerly been in these parts, and, *as he was wont, he taught them again*. Note, Preaching was Christ's constant practice; it was what he was used to, and, wherever he came, he did *as he was wont*. In Matthew it is said, *He healed them*; here it is said, *He taught them*: his cures were to confirm his doctrine, and to recommend it, and his doctrine was to explain his cures, and illustrate them. His *teaching* was *healing* to poor souls.

II. We have him *disputed with* by the Pharisees, who envied the progress of his spiritual arms, and did all they could to obstruct and oppose it; to divert him, to perplex him, and to prejudice the people against him.

Here is, 1. A question they started concerning divorce (v. 2); *Is it lawful for a man to put away his wife?*

2. Christ's reply to them with a question (v. 3); *What did Moses command you?* This he asked them, to testify his respect to the law of Moses, and to show that he came not to destroy it; and to engage them to a universal impartial respect for Moses's writings and to compare one part of them with another.

3. The fair account they gave of what they found in the law of Moses, expressly concerning divorce, v. 4. They own that Moses only *suffered*, or *permitted*, a man to write his wife a *bill of divorce*, and to put *her away*, Deut. xxiv. 1.

4. The answer that Christ gave to their question, in which he abides by the doctrine he had formerly laid down in this case (Matt. v. 32), *That whosoever puts away his wife, except for fornication, causeth her to commit adultery.* And to clear this he here shows,

(1) That the reason why Moses, in his *law*, permitted divorce, was such, as that they ought not to make use of that permission; for it was only *for the hardness of their hearts* (v. 5), lest, if they were not permitted to divorce their wives, they should murder them; so that none must put away their wives but such as are willing to own that their hearts were so hard as to need this permission.

(2) That the account which Moses, in this *history, gives* of the institution of marriage, affords

such a reason against divorce, as amounts to a prohibition of it. So that if the question be, *What did Moses command?* (v. 3), it must be answered, "Though by a temporary proviso he allowed divorce to the Jews, yet by an eternal reason he forbade it to all the children of Adam and Eve, and that is it which we must abide by."

Now from all this he infers, that men ought not to *put* their wives *asunder* from them, whom God has put so near to them. The bond which God himself has tied, is not to be lightly untied.

5. Christ's discourse with his disciples, in private, about this matter, vv. 10–12. No more is here related of this private conference, than the law Christ laid down in this case—That it is adultery for a man to put away his wife, and marry another; it is adultery *against the wife* he puts away, it is a wrong to her, and a breach of his contract with her, v. 11. He adds, *If a woman shall put away her husband,* that is, elope from him, leave him by consent, and *be married to another,* she *commits adultery* (v. 12), and it will be no excuse at all for her to say that it was with the consent of her husband. Wisdom and grace, holiness and love, reigning in the heart, will make those commands easy which to the carnal mind may be as a heavy yoke.

CHILDREN BROUGHT TO CHRIST (vv. 13–16)

Here we have,

I. Little children brought to Christ, v. 13. Their parents, or whoever they were that had the nursing of them, brought them to him, that he should *touch them*, in token of his commanding and conferring a blessing on them. It doth not appear that they needed any bodily *cure*, nor were they capable of being *taught*: but it seems, 1. They that had the care of them were mostly concerned *about their souls*, their better part, which ought to be the principal care of all parents for their children; for that is the principal part, and it is well with them, if it be well with their souls. 2. They believed that Christ's blessing would do their souls good; and therefore to him they brought them, that he might *touch* them, knowing that he could reach their hearts, when nothing their parents could say to them, or do for them, would reach them.

II. The *dis*couragement which the disciples gave to the bringing of children to Christ; *They rebuked them that brought them*; as if they had been sure that they knew their Master's mind in this matter, whereas he had lately cautioned them not to *despise the little ones*.

III. The *en*couragement Christ gave to it. 1. He took it very ill that his disciples should keep them off; *When he saw it, he was much displeased, v.* 14. 2. He ordered that they should be *brought to him*, and nothing said or done to hinder them; suffer *little children*, as soon as they are capable, to *come to me*, to offer up their supplications to me, and to receive instructions from me. Little children are welcome betimes to the throne of grace with their Hosannas. 3. He owned them as members of his church, as they had been of the

Jewish church. He came to set up the *kingdom of God* among men, and took this occasion to declare that that kingdom admitted *little children* to be the subjects of it, and gave them a title to the privileges of subjects. 4. That there must be something of the temper and disposition of little children found in all that Christ will own and bless. We must *receive the kingdom of God as little children* (*v.* 15); that is, we must stand affected to Christ and his grace as little children do to their parents, nurses, and teachers. 5. He received the children, and gave them what was desired (*v.* 16); *He took them up in his arms*, in token of his affectionate concern for them; *put his hands upon them*, as was desired, and *blessed them.* See how he outdid the desires of these parents; they begged he would touch them, but he did more. He *blessed* them with the spiritual blessings he came to give. Our children are happy, if they have but the *Mediator's blessing* for their portion. It is true, we do not read that he baptized these children, baptism was not fully settled as the door of admission into the church till after Christ's resurrection; but he asserted their visible church-membership, and by another sign bestowed those blessings upon them, which are now appointed to be conveyed and conferred by baptism, the seal of the promise, which is *to us* and *to our children.*

A HOPEFUL YOUTH
(*vv.* 17–31)

Here is a *hopeful meeting* between Christ and a *young man*; such he is said to be (Matt. xix. 20, 22), and a *ruler* (Luke xviii. 18), a person of quality. Some circumstances here are, which we had not in Matthew, which makes his address to Christ very promising.

1. He came *running* to Christ, which was an indication of his humility; he laid aside the gravity and grandeur of a ruler, when he came to Christ: thus too he manifested his earnestness and importunity; he *ran* as one *in haste*, and longing to be in conversation with Christ.

2. He came to him when he was *in the way*, in the midst of company: he did not insist upon a private conference with him by night, as Nicodemus did, though like him he was a ruler.

3. He *kneeled to him*, in token of the great value and veneration he had for him, as a teacher come from God, and his earnest desire to be taught by him.

4. His address to him was serious and weighty; *Good Master, what shall I do, that I may inherit eternal life?* Most men enquire for good to be *had* in this world (Ps. iv. 6), *any good*; he asks for *good to be done* in this world, in order to the enjoyment of the greatest good in the other world; not, Who will make us to *see good*? But, "Who will make us to *do good*?"

The rest of the account is as in Matt. xix.

THE CUP OF SUFFERING
(*vv.* 32–45)

Here is, I. Christ's prediction of his own sufferings; this string he harped much upon, though in the ears of his disciples it sounded very harsh and unpleasing.

1. See here how bold he was; when they were going up to Jerusalem, *Jesus went before them*, as the *captain of our salvation*, that was now to be *made perfect through sufferings*, *v.* 32. Thus he showed himself forward to go on with his undertaking, even when he came to the hardest part of it.

2. See here how timorous and faint-hearted his disciples were; *As they followed, they were afraid*, afraid for themselves, as being apprehensive of their own danger; and justly might they be *ashamed* of their being thus *afraid*. Their Master's courage should have put spirit into them.

3. See here what method he took to silence their fears. He did not go about to make the matter better than it was, nor to feed them with hopes that he might escape the storm, but told them *again* what he had often told them before, the *things that should happen to him*. He knew the worst of it, and therefore went on thus boldly, and he will let them know the worst of it. Come, *be not afraid*; for, (1) There is no remedy, the matter is determined, and cannot be avoided. (2) It is only the *Son of man* that shall suffer; their time of suffering was not at hand, he will now provide for their security. (3) He *shall rise again*; the issue of his sufferings will be glorious to himself, and advantageous to all that are his, *vv.* 33, 34.

II. The check he gave to two of his disciples for their ambitious request. This story is much the same here as we had in Matt. xx. 20.

Only there they are said to have made their request by their mother, here they are said to make it themselves; she introduced them, and presented their petition, and then they seconded it, and assented to it.

III. The check he gave to the rest of the disciples, for their uneasiness at it. *They began to be much displeased*, to have *indignation about James and John*, *v.* 41. They were angry at them for affecting precedency, not because it did so ill become the disciples of Christ, but because each of them hoped to have it himself. He shows them,

1. That dominion was generally *abused in the world* (*v.* 42); *They that seem to rule over the* Gentiles, that have the name and title of rulers, *they exercise lordship over them*, that is all they study and aim at, not so much to protect them and provide for their welfare, as to *exercise authority upon them*.

2. That therefore it ought not to be *admitted into the church*; "*It shall not be so among you*; those that shall be put under your charge, must be as sheep under the charge of the *shepherd*, who is to tend them and feed them, and be a servant to them, not as horses under the command of the driver, that works them and beats them, and gets his pennyworths out of them. He that affects to be great and chief, that thrusts himself into a secular dignity and dominion, *he shall be servant of all*, he shall be mean and contemptible in the eyes of all that are wise and good; *he that exalteth himself shall be abased*." Or rather, "He that would be *truly* great and

chief, he must lay out himself to do good to all, must stoop to the meanest services, and labour in the hardest services. Those not only shall be most *honoured* hereafter, but are most *honourable* now, who are most useful." To convince them of this, he sets before them his own example (*v.* 45): "The *Son of man* submits first to the greatest hardships and hazards, and then enters into his glory, and can you expect to come to it any other way; or to have more ease and honour than he has?" (1) He takes upon him *the form of a servant*, comes not to be *ministered to*, and waited upon, but *to minister*, and wait to be gracious. (2) He becomes *obedient to death*, and to its dominion, for he *gives his life a ransom for many*; did he die for the benefit of good people, and shall not we study to live for their benefit?

BLIND BARTIMEUS
(*vv.* 46–52)

This passage of story agrees with that, Matt. xx. 29, &c. Only that there we were told of *two* blind men; here, and Luke xviii. 35, only of *one*: but if there were *two*, there was *one*. This one is named here, being a *blind beggar that* was much talked of; he was called *Bartimeus*, that is, the *son of Timeus*; which, some think, signifies *the son of a blind man*; he was the blind son of a blind father, which made the case the worse, and the cure the more wonderful, and the more proper to typify the spiritual cures wrought by the grace of Christ, on those that not only are born blind, but are born of those that are blind.

CHAPTER ELEVEN
CHRIST ENTERS JERUSALEM
(*vv.* 1–11)

We have here the story of the public entry Christ made into Jerusalem, four or five days before his death. And he came into town thus remarkably, 1. To show that he was not afraid of the power and malice of his enemies in Jerusalem. He did not steal into the city *incognito*, as one that durst not show his face; no, they needed not send spies to search for him, he comes in with observation. This would be an encouragement to his disciples that were timorous, and cowed at the thought of their enemies' power and rage; let them see how bravely their Master sets them all at defiance. 2. To show that he was not cast down or disquieted at the thoughts of his approaching sufferings. He came, not only publicly, but cheerfully, and with acclamations of joy. Though he was now but taking the field, and *girding on the harness*, yet, being fully assured of a complete victory, he thus triumphs as though he had put it off.

The account is as in Matt. xxi. 1–11.

THE FIG-TREE (*vv.* 12–26)

Here is, I. Christ's cursing the fruitless fig-tree. He had a convenient resting-place at Bethany, and therefore thither he went at resting-time; but his work lay at Jerusalem, and thither therefore he returned in the morning, at working-time; and so intent was he upon his work, that he went out from Bethany without breakfast, which,

before he was gone far, he found the want of, and *was hungry* (*v.* 12), for he was subject to all the sinless infirmities of our nature. Finding himself in want of food, he went to a *fig-tree*, which he saw at some distance, and which being well *adorned* with green leaves he hoped to find *enriched* with some sort of fruit. But he *found nothing but leaves*; he hoped to find some fruit, *for* though *the time of* gathering in *figs* was near, it *was not yet*; so that it could not be pretended that it had had fruit, but that it was gathered and gone; for the season had not yet arrived. Or, He found none, for indeed it *was not a season of figs*, it was no good fig-year. But this was worse than any other fig-tree, for there was not so much as one fig to be found upon it, though it was so full of leaves. However, Christ was willing to make an example of it, not to the *trees*, but to the *men*, of that generation, and therefore cursed it with that curse which is the reverse of the first blessing, *Be fruitful*; he said unto it, *Never let any man eat fruit of thee hereafter for ever*, *v.* 14. This was intended to be a type and figure of the doom passed upon the Jewish church, to which he came, *seeking fruit, but found none* (Luke xiii. 6, 7); and though it was not, according to the doom in the parable, immediately cut down, yet, according to this in the history, *blindness* and *hardness* befell them (Rom. xi. 8, 25), so that they were from henceforth *good for nothing*. The *disciples heard* what sentence Christ passed on this tree, and took notice of it.

II. His clearing the temple of the

market-people that frequented it, and of those that made it a thoroughfare. We do not find that Christ met with food elsewhere, when he missed of it on the fig-tree; but the zeal of God's house so ate him up, and made him forget himself, that he came, hungry as he was, to Jerusalem, and went straight to the temple, and began to reform those abuses which the day before he had marked out; to show that when the Redeemer came to Zion, his errand was, to *turn away ungodliness from Jacob* (Rom. xi. 26), and that he came not, as he was falsely accused, to *destroy* the temple, but to purify and refine it, and reduce his church to its primitive rectitude.

We have had the account in Matt. xxi. 12–17.

III. His discourse with his disciples, upon occasion of the fig-tree's withering away which he had cursed. At *even*, as usual, he *went out of the city* (v. 19), to Bethany; but it is probable that it was in the dark, so that they could not see the fig-tree; but the next morning, as they *passed by*, they observed the *fig-tree dried up from the roots, v.* 20. More is *included* many times in Christ's curses than is *expressed*, as appears by the effects of them. The curse was no more than that it should never bear fruit again, but the effect goes further, *it is dried up from the roots*. If it bear no fruit, it shall bear no leaves to cheat people. Now observe,

1. How the disciples were affected with it. Peter remembered Christ's words, and said, with surprise, *Master, behold, the fig-tree which thou cursedst is withered away, v.* 21. And this seemed very strange to the disciples, and scarcely credible, that the Jews, who had been so long God's own, his only professing people in the world, should be thus abandoned; they could not imagine how that *fig-tree* should *so soon wither away*: but this comes of rejecting Christ, and being rejected by him.

2. The good instructions Christ gave them from it; for of *those* even this *withered* tree was *fruitful*.

(1) Christ teacheth them from hence to *pray in faith* (v. 22); *Have faith in God*. They admired the power of Christ's word of command; "Why," saith Christ, "a lively active faith would put as great a power into your prayers, *vv.* 23, 24. *Whosoever shall say to this mountain*, this mount of Olives, *Be removed, and be cast into the sea*; if he has but any word of God, general or particular, to build his faith upon, and if he *shall not doubt in his heart, but shall believe that those things which he saith*, according to the warrant he has from what God hath said, *shall come to pass, he shall have whatsoever he saith.*" Through the strength and power of God in Christ, the greatest difficulty shall be got over, and the thing shall be effected.

(2) To this is added here that necessary qualification of the prevailing prayer, that we freely forgive those who have been any way injurious to us, and be in charity with all men (*vv.* 25, 26); *When ye stand praying*, forgive. This ought to be remembered in prayer, because one great errand we have to the throne of grace, is, to pray for the pardon of our sins: and care

about it ought to be our daily care, because prayer is a part of our daily work. Our Saviour often insists on this, for it was his great design to engage his disciples to love one another.

A QUESTION OF AUTHORITY
(*vv.* 27-33)

We have here Christ examined by the great Sanhedrim concerning his authority; for they claimed a power to call prophets to an account concerning their mission. The great men were vexed to see him followed and heard with attention, and therefore *came to him* with some solemnity, and did as it were arraign him at the bar with this question, *By what authority doest thou these things? v.* 28. Now observe,

I. How they designed hereby to run him aground, and embarrass him. If they could make it out before the people, that he had not a *legal mission*, that he was not duly *ordained*, though he was ever so well qualified, and preached ever so profitably and well, they would tell the people that they *ought not to hear him.*

II. How he effectually ran them aground, and embarrassed them, with this question, "What are your thoughts concerning *the baptism of John? Was it from heaven, or of men?* By what authority did John preach, and baptize, and gather disciples? *Answer me, v.* 30.

1. If they own the baptism of John to be *from heaven*, as really it was, they *shame themselves*; for Christ will presently turn it upon them, *Why did ye not then believe him*, and receive his baptism?

2. If they say, "*It is of men*, he was not sent of God, but his doctrine and baptism were inventions of his own;" they *expose themselves*, the people will be ready to do them a mischief, or at least clamour upon them; for *all men counted John that he was a prophet indeed*, and therefore they could not bear that he should be reflected on. Now by this dilemma to which Christ brought them, (1) They were confounded and baffled, and forced to make a dishonourable retreat; to pretend ignorance—*We cannot tell* (and that was mortification enough to those proud men), but really to discover the greatest malice and wilfulness. What Christ did by his wisdom, we must labour to do by our well doing—*put to silence the ignorance of foolish men*, 1 Pet. ii. 15. (2) Christ came off with honour, and justified himself in refusing to give them an answer to their imperious demand; *Neither tell I you by what authority I do these things.* They did not deserve to be told; for it was plain that they contended not for truth, but victory; nor did *he* need to *tell them*, for the works which he did, told them plainly that he had authority from God to do what he did; since no man could do those miracles which he did unless God were with him.

CHAPTER TWELVE
THE HUSBANDMEN
(*vv.* 1-12)

Christ had formerly in parables showed how he designed to set up the gospel church; now he begins in parables to show how he would lay aside the Jewish church, which it might have been grafted into the *stock of*, but was built upon the *ruins of*. This parable we had just as we have it here, Matt. xxi. 33.

GOD AND CÆSAR
(*vv.* 13–17)

When the enemies of Christ, who thirsted for his blood, could not find occasion against him from what he said against them, they tried to ensnare him by putting questions to him. Here we have him tempted, or *at*tempted rather, with a question about the lawfulness of paying tribute to Cæsar. We had this narrative, Matt. xxii. 15.

I. The persons they employed were the *Pharisees* and the *Herodians*, men that in this matter were contrary to one another, and yet concurred against Christ, *v.* 13. The Pharisees were great sticklers for the liberty of the Jews, and, if he should say, It is lawful to give tribute to Cæsar, they would incense the common people against him, and the Herodians would, underhand, assist them in it. The Herodians were great sticklers for the Roman power, and, if he should discountenance the paying of tribute to Cæsar, they would incense the governor against him, yea, and the Pharisees, against their own principles, would join with them in it. It is no new thing for those that are at variance in other things, to join in a confederacy against Christ.

II. The pretence they made was, that they desired him to resolve them a case of conscience, which was of great importance in the present juncture; and they take on

them to have a high opinion of his ability to resolve it, *v.* 14.

III. The question they put was, *Is it lawful to give tribute to Cæsar, or not?* They would be thought desirous to know their duty. *As a nation that did righteousness, they ask of God the ordinances of justice,* when really they desired nothing but to know what he would say, in hopes that, which side soever he took of the question, they might take occasion from it to accuse him.

IV. Christ determined the question, and evaded the snare, by referring them to their national concessions already made, by which they were precluded from disputing this matter, *vv.* 15–17. He knew they intended to ensnare him, and therefore contrived the matter so as to ensnare them, and to oblige them by their own words to do what they were unwilling to do, which was, to pay their taxes honestly and quietly, and yet at the same time to screen himself against their exceptions. He made them acknowledge that the current money of their nation was Roman money, had the emperor's image on one side, and his *superscription* on the reverse; and if so, 1. *Cæsar* might command their money for the public benefit, because he has the custody and conduct of the state, wherein he ought to have his charges borne; *Render to Cæsar the things that are Cæsar's*. 2. Cæsar might not command their consciences, nor did he pretend to it; he offered not to make any alteration in their religion. "Pay your tribute, therefore, without murmuring or disputing, but be sure to *render to God the things that are*

God's." Perhaps he referred to the parable he had just now put forth, in which he had condemned them for not *rendering* the fruits to the Lord of the vineyard, *v.* 2. All that heard Christ, *marvelled* at the discretion of his answer, and how ingeniously he avoided the snare; but I doubt none were brought by it, as they ought to be, to render to God themselves and their devotions.

GOD OF THE LIVING
(*vv.* 18–27)

The Sadducees, who were the deists of that age, here attack our Lord Jesus, it should seem, not as the scribes, and Pharisees, and chief-priests, with any malicious design upon his person; they were not bigots and persecutors, but sceptics and infidels, and their design was upon his doctrine, to hinder the spreading of that: they denied that there was any resurrection, any world of spirits, any state of rewards and punishments on the other side of death: now those great and fundamental truths which they denied, Christ had made it his business to establish and prove, and had carried the notion of them much further than ever it was before carried; and therefore they set themselves to perplex his doctrine. The incident we have had at Matt. xxii. 22–33.

THE HOPEFUL SCRIBE
(*vv.* 28–34)

The scribes and Pharisees were (however bad otherwise) enemies to the Sadducees; now one would have expected that, when they heard Christ argue so well against the Sadducees, they would have countenanced him, as they did Paul when he appeared against the Sadducees (Acts xxiii. 9); but it had not that effect: because he did not fall in with them in the ceremonials of religion, his agreeing with them in the essentials, gained him no manner of respect with them. Only we have here an account of *one* of them, a scribe, who had so much civility in him as to take notice of Christ's answer to the Sadducees, and to own that he had *answered well*, and much to the purpose (*v.* 28); and we have reason to hope that he did not join with the other scribes in persecuting Christ; for here we have his application to Christ for instruction, and it was such as became him; not tempting Christ, but desiring to improve his acquaintance with him.

I. He enquired, *Which is the first commandment of all? v.* 28. He doth not mean the first in *order*, but the first in *weight* and *dignity*.

II. Christ gave him a direct answer to this enquiry, *vv.* 29–31. Those that sincerely desire to be instructed concerning their duty, Christ will *guide in judgment*, and *teach his way*. He tells him,

1. That the great commandment of all, which is indeed inclusive of all, is, that of *loving God with all our hearts*. Now here in, Mark, our Saviour prefixes to this command the great doctrinal truth upon which it is built (*v.* 29); *Hear, O Israel, The Lord our God is one Lord*; if we firmly believe this, it will follow, that we shall love him *with all our heart*. He is Jehovah, who has all amiable perfections in himself; he is *our God*, to whom we

stand related and obliged; and therefore we ought to *love him*, to set our affections on him, let out our desire toward him, and take a delight in him; and he is *one Lord*, therefore he must be loved with our *whole heart*; he has the sole *right to us*, and therefore ought to have the sole *possession of us*. If he be one, our hearts must be one with him, and since there is no God besides, no rival must be admitted with him upon the throne.

2. That the second great commandment is, to *love our neighbour as ourselves* (*v.* 31), as truly and sincerely as we love ourselves, and in the same instances, and we must show it by *doing as we would be done by*. As we must therefore love God better than ourselves, because he is Jehovah, a being infinitely better than we are, and must love him with *all our heart*, because he is *one Lord*, and there is no other like him; so we must *love our neighbour as ourselves*, because he is of the same nature with ourselves; our hearts are fashioned alike, and my neighbour and myself are of one body, of one society, that of the world of mankind; and if a fellow-Christian, and of the same sacred society, the obligation is the stronger.

III. The scribe consented to what Christ said, and descanted upon it, *vv.* 32, 33. 1. He commends Christ's decision of this question; *Well, Master, thou hast said the truth.* Christ's assertions needed not the scribe's attestations; but this scribe, being a man in authority, thought it would put some reputation upon what Christ said, to have it commended by him; and it shall be brought in evidence against those who persecuted Christ, as a deceiver, that one of themselves, even a scribe of their own, confessed that he *said the truth*, and said it *well*. And thus must we subscribe to Christ's sayings, must set to our seal that they are true. 2. He comments upon it. Christ had quoted that great doctrine, that *the Lord our God is one Lord*; and this he not only assented to, but added, "*There is none other but he*; and therefore we must have no other God besides." This excludes all rivals with him, and secures the throne in the heart entire for him. Christ had laid down that great law, of loving God *with all our heart*; and this also he explains— that it is loving him *with the understanding*, as those that know what abundant reason we have to love him. Christ had said, "To love God and our neighbour is the greatest commandment of all"; "Yea," saith the scribe, "it is better, it is *more than all whole-burnt-offerings and sacrifices*, more acceptable to God, and will turn to a better account to ourselves." There were those who held, that the law of *sacrifices* was the *greatest commandment* of all; but this scribe readily agreed with our Saviour in this—that the law of love to God and our neighbour is greater than that of *sacrifice*, even than that of *whole-burnt-offerings*, which were intended purely for the honour of God.

IV. Christ approved of what he said, and encouraged him to proceed in his enquiries of him, *v.* 34. 1. He owned that he understood well, as far as he went; so far, so good. 2. He owned that he stood fair for a further advance; *"Thou art not far from the kingdom of God,* the kingdom of grace and glory, thou art in a likely way to be a Christian, a disciple of Christ. For the doctrine of Christ insists most upon these things, and is designed, and has a tendency direct, to bring thee to this."* Note, There is hope of those who make a good use of the light they have, and go as far as that will carry them, that by the grace of God they will be led further, by the clearer discoveries God has to make to them.

LORD OF DAVID (*vv.* 35–40)

Here Christ shows the people how weak and defective the scribes were in their preaching, and how unable to solve the difficulties that occurred in the scriptures of the Old Testament, which they undertook to expound. Of this he gives an instance, which is not so fully related here as it was in Matthew.

THE POOR WIDOW (*vv.* 41–44)

This passage of story was not in Matthew, but is here and in Luke; it is Christ's commendation of the poor widow, that cast *two mites* into the treasury, which our Saviour busy as he was in preaching, found leisure to take notice of. Observe,

I. There was a *public fund* for charity, into which contributions were brought, and out of which distributions were made; a poor-box, and this in *the temple*; for works of charity and works of piety very fitly go together; where God is honoured by our worship, it is proper he should be honoured by the relief of his poor; and we often find *prayers* and *alms* in conjunction, as Acts x. 2, 4.

II. Jesus Christ had *an eye* upon it; *He sat over against the treasury, and beheld how the people cast money into it*; not grudging either that he had none to cast in, or had not the disposal of that which was cast in, but observing what was cast in. Note, Our Lord Jesus takes notice of what we contribute to pious and charitable uses; whether we give liberally or sparingly; whether cheerfully or with reluctance and ill-will: nay, he looks at the heart; he observes what principles we act upon, and what our views are, in giving alms; and whether we do it as unto the Lord, or only to be seen of men.

III. He saw *many that were rich cast in much*: and it was a good sight to see rich people charitable, to see *many* rich people so, and to see them not only cast in, but cast in *much*.

IV. There was a *poor widow that cast in two mites, which make a farthing* (*v.* 42); and our Lord Jesus highly commended her; *called his disciples* to him, and bid them take notice of it (*v.* 43); told them that she could very ill spare that which she gave, she had scarcely enough for herself, it was *all her living,* all she had to live upon for that day, and perhaps a great part of what she had earned by her labour the day before; and that forasmuch as he knew she did it from a truly charitable disposition, he reckoned it more than all that put together, which the rich people threw in; for they did *cast in of their abundance, but she of her want, v.* 44. Now many would have been ready to censure this *poor widow*, and to think she did ill; why should she give to others, when she had little enough for herself? Charity begins at home; or, if she would give it, why did she not bestow it upon some poor body that she knew? And yet our Saviour commends her, and therefore we are sure that she did very well and wisely. If Christ saith, *Well-done*, no matter who saith otherwise; and we must hence learn, 1. That *giving alms*, is an excellent good thing, and highly pleasing to the Lord Jesus; and if we be humble and sincere in it, he will graciously accept of it, though in some circumstances there may not be all the discretion in the world. 2. Those that have but a *little*, ought to give alms out of *their little*. Those that live by their labour, from hand to mouth, must *give to those that need*, Eph. iv. 28. When we can cheerfully provide for others, out of our own necessary provision, as the widow of Sarepta for Elijah, and Christ for his five thousand guests, and trust God to provide for us some other way, *this is thank-worthy*.

CHAPTER THIRTEEN
GREAT BUILDINGS
(*vv*. 1–4)

We may here see,

I. How apt many of Christ's own disciples are to idolize things that look *great*, and have been long looked upon as *sacred*. They had heard Christ complain of those who had made the temple a *den of thieves*; and yet, when he quitted it, for the wickedness that remained in it, they court him to be as much in love as they were with the stately structure and adorning of it. One of them said to him, "Look, Master, *what manner of stones, and what buildings are here*," v. 1.

II. How little Christ values external pomp, where there is not real purity; "*Seest thou these great buildings*" (saith Christ), "and admirest thou them? I tell thee, the time is at hand when *there shall not be left one stone upon another, that shall not be thrown down*," v. 2. And the sumptuousness of the fabric shall be no security to it, no nor move any compassion in the Lord Jesus towards it.

III. As he was returning to Bethany, he *sat upon the mount of Olives, over against the temple*, where he had a full view of it; and there four of the disciples agreed to *ask him privately*, what he meant by the destroying of the temple, which they understood no more than they did the predictions of his own death, so inconsistent was it with their scheme. Probably, though these four proposed the question, yet Christ's discourse, in answer to it, was in the hearing of the rest of the disciples, yet *privately*, that is, apart from the multitude. Their enquiry is, "*When shall these things be?* What presages shall there be of them, and how may we prognosticate their approach?"

THE FUTURE (*vv*. 5–13)

Our Lord Jesus, in reply to their question, sets himself, not so much to satisfy their curiosity as to direct their consciences; leaves them still in the dark concerning the *times* and *seasons*, which the father has kept in his own power, and which *it was not for them to know*; but gives them the cautions which were needful, with reference to the events that should now shortly come to pass.

I. They must take heed that they be not *deceived* by the *seducers* and *impostors* that should now shortly arise (*vv.* 5, 6). After the Jews had rejected the true Christ, they were imposed upon, and so *exposed* by many false Christs, but never before; those false Christs *deceived many*; Therefore *take heed lest they deceive you*.

II. They must take heed that they be not *disturbed* at the noise of wars, which they should be alarmed with, *vv.* 7, 8. Sin introduced *wars*, and they come *from men's lusts*. But at some times the nations are more distracted and wasted with wars than at other times; so it shall be now; Christ was born into the world when there was a general peace, but soon after he went out of the world there were general wars; *Nation shall rise against nation, and kingdom against kingdom*. 1. "Let it be no *surprise* to you; you are bid to expect it, and *such things must needs be*." 2. "Let it be no *terror* to you, as if your interest were in danger of being overthrown, or your work obstructed by these wars; you have no concern in them, and therefore need not be apprehensive of any damage by them." 3. "Let it not be looked upon as an omen of the approaching period of the world, for the *end is not yet*", *v.* 7. 4. "Let it not be looked upon as if in them God had done his worst; be not troubled at the wars you shall hear

of, for they are but *the beginnings of sorrows*, and therefore, instead of being disturbed at *them*, you ought to *prepare for worse*; for there shall also be *earthquakes in divers places*, which shall bury multitudes in the ruins of their own houses, and there *shall be famines*, by which many of the poor shall perish for want of bread, and *troubles* and commotions; so that there shall be no peace to him that *goes out* or *comes in*. The world shall be full of *troubles*, but *not be ye troubled*; without are *fightings*, within are *fears*, but *fear not ye their fear*."

III. They must take heed that they be not *drawn away* from Christ, and from their duty to him, by the sufferings they should meet with for Christ's sake. Observe,

1. What the trouble is which they must expect.

(1) They shall be *hated of all men*; trouble enough! The world hated them because they loved them.

(2) Their own *relations* shall *betray them*, those to whom they were most nearly allied, and on whom therefore they depended for protection; "They *shall betray you*, shall inform against you, and be your prosecutors."

(3) Their *church-rulers* shall inflict *their censures* upon them; "You shall be *delivered up* to the great Sanhedrim at Jerusalem, and to the inferior courts and consistories in other cities, and shall be *beaten in the synagogues* with forty stripes at a time, as offenders against the law which was read in the synagogue."

(4) *Governors* and *kings* shall use their power against them. They

must resist unto blood, and still resist.

2. What they shall have to comfort themselves with, in the midst of these great and sore troubles.

(1) That the work they were called to should be carried on and prosper, notwithstanding all this opposition which they should meet with in it (*v.* 10).

(2) That their sufferings, instead of obstructing their work, should forward it; "Your being *brought before governors and kings* shall be for a *testimony of them* (so some read it, *v.* 9); it shall give you an opportunity of preaching the gospel to those before whom you are brought as criminals, to whom otherwise you could not have access." Or, as we read it, It shall be for a testimony *against them*, against both the judges and the prosecutors, who pursue those with the utmost rage that appear, upon examination, to be not only innocent but excellent persons.

(3) That, when they were brought before kings and governors for Christ's sake, they should have special assistance from heaven, to plead Christ's cause and their own (*v.* 11); "*Take no thought beforehand what ye shall speak*, but *whatsoever shall be given you in that hour*, whatsoever shall be suggested to you, and put into your minds, and into your mouths that *speak ye*, and fear not the success of it, because it is *off-hand*, for *it is not ye that speak*, purely by the strength of your own wisdom, consideration, and resolution, but it is *the Holy Ghost*."

(4) That heaven at last would *make amends for all.* Perseverance gains the crown. The salvation here promised is more than a deliverance from evil, it is an everlasting blessedness, which shall be an abundant recompence for all their services and sufferings. All this we have, Matt. x. 17, &c.

THE ABOMINATION
(*vv.* 14–23)

Here we have a prediction of that ruin which came upon them within less than forty years after this: we had it before, Matt. xxiv. 15, &c.

THE SECOND COMING
(*vv.* 24–27)

These verses seem to point at Christ's second coming, to judge the world; the disciples, in their question, had confounded the *destruction* of Jerusalem and the *end of the world* (Matt. xxiv. 3), which was built upon a mistake, as if the temple must needs stand as long as the world stands; this mistake Christ rectifies, and shows that the *end of the world in those days*, those other days you enquire about, the day of Christ's coming, and the day of judgment, shall be *after that tribulation*, and not coincident with it. Let those who live to see the Jewish nation destroyed, take heed of thinking that, because the Son of man doth not visibly come in the clouds *then*, he will never *so* come; no, he will come *after that*. And here he foretells,

1. The final dissolution of the present frame and fabric of the world; even of that part of it which seems least liable to change, the upper part, the purer and more refined part; *The sun shall be dark-*

ened, and the *moon* shall no more give *her light*; for they shall be quite outshone by the glory of the Son of man, Isa. xxiv. 23. The *stars of heaven*, that from the beginning had kept their place and regular motion, shall fall as leaves in autumn; and the *powers that are in heaven*, the heavenly bodies, the fixed stars, *shall be shaken*.

2. The visible appearance of the Lord Jesus, to whom the judgment of that day shall be committed (v. 26); *Then shall they see the Son of man coming in the clouds*. Probably he will come over that very place where he sat when he said this; for the clouds are in the lower region of the air. He shall come with *great power and glory*, such as will be suited to the errand on which he comes. *Every eye shall then see him*.

3. The gathering together of all the elect to him (v. 27); He shall *send his angels*, and *gather together his elect* to him, to *meet him in the air*, 1 Thess. iv. 17.

THE FIG TREE (vv. 28–37)

We have here the application of this prophetical sermon; *now learn* to look forward in a right manner.

I. "As to the *destruction* of Jerusalem, *expect* it to come very *shortly*; as when the *branch of the fig-tree becomes soft*, and the *leaves sprout forth*, ye expect that summer will come shortly," v. 28. "*This generation* that is now rising up, shall not all be worn off before *all these things* come to pass, which I have told you of, relating to Jerusalem, and they shall begin to take effect now shortly.

II. "As to the *end of the world*, do not enquire when it will come, for it is not a question fit to be asked, for of *that day*, and *that hour, knoweth no man*; it is a thing at a great distance; the exact time is fixed in the counsel of God, but is not revealed by any word of God, either to *men* on earth, or to *angels in heaven*." But it follows, *neither the Son*; but is there any thing which the Son is ignorant of? There were those in the primitive times, who taught from this text, that there were some things that Christ, as man, was *ignorant* of; and from thence were called *Agnoetæ*; they said, "It was no more absurd to say so, than to say that his human soul suffered grief and fear"; and many of the orthodox fathers approved of this. "It is certain (says Archbishop Tillotson) that Christ, as God, could not be ignorant of any thing; but the divine wisdom which dwelt in our Saviour, did communicate itself to his human soul, according to the divine pleasure, so that his human nature might sometimes not know some things; therefore Christ is said to grow in wisdom (Luke ii. 52), which he could not be said to do, if the human nature of Christ did necessarily know all things by virtue of its union with the divinity." Dr. Lightfoot explains it thus; Christ calls himself the Son, as Messiah. Now the Messiah, as such, was the Father's servant (Isa. xlii. 1), sent and deputed by him, and as such a one he refers himself often to his Father's will and command, and owns he *did nothing of himself* (John v. 19); in like manner he might be said to *know nothing of himself*. The revelation of Jesus Christ was what *God gave unto him*, Rev. i. 1. He thinks, therefore, that we are to distinguish between those excellencies and perfections of his, which resulted from the personal union between the divine and human nature, and those which flowed from the anointing of the Spirit; from the former flowed the infinite dignity of his person, and his perfect freedom from all sin; but from the latter flowed his power of working miracles, and his foreknowledge of things to come. What therefore (saith he) was to be revealed by him to his church, he was pleased to take, not from the union of the human nature with the divine, but from the revelation of the Spirit, by which he yet knew not this, but *the Father* only knows it; that is, God only, the Deity; for (as Archbishop Tillotson explains it) it is not used here *personally*, in distinction from the Son and the Holy Ghost, but as the Father is, *The Fountain of Deity*.

III. "As to both, your duty is to *watch and pray*. Therefore the time is kept a secret, that you may be engaged to stand always upon your guard (*v.* 33)." This he illustrates, in the close, by a parable.

1. Our Master is gone away, and left us something in trust, in charge, which we must give account of, *v.* 34. He is *as a man taking a far journey*; for he is gone to be away a great while, he has *left his house* on earth, and left his servant, in their offices, given *authority* to some, who are to be overseers, and *work* to others, who are to be labourers. They that have *authority* given them, in that had *work* assigned

them, for those that have the greatest *power* have the most *business*; and to them to whom he gave *work*, he gave some sort of *authority*, to do that work. And when he took his last leave, he *appointed the porter to watch*, to be sure to be ready to open to him at his return; and in the mean time to take care to whom he opened his gates, not to thieves and robbers, but only to his Master's friends and servants. Thus our Lord Jesus, when he *ascended on high*, left something for all his servants to do, expecting they should all do him service in his absence, and be ready to receive him at his return. *All* are appointed to work, and some authorized to rule.

2. We ought to be always upon our watch, in expectation of his return, *v.* 35–37. (1) Our Lord *will come*, and will come as the *Master of the house*, to take account of his servants, of their work, and of the improvement they have made. (2) We know not *when he will come*; and he has very wisely kept us at uncertainty, that we might be always ready. We know not *when he will come*, just at what precise time; the *Master of the house* perhaps will come *at even*, at nine at night; or it may be *at midnight*, or at *cock-crowing*, at three in the morning, or perhaps not till six. This is applicable to his coming to us in particular, at our death, as well as to the general judgment. (3) Our great care must be, that, whenever our Lord comes, he do not *find us sleeping*, secure in ourselves, off our guard, indulging ourselves in ease and sloth, mindless of our work and duty, and

thoughtless of our Lord's coming; *ready* to say, He will not come, and *unready* to meet him. (4) His coming will indeed be *coming suddenly*; it will be a great *surprise* and *terror* to those that are careless, and asleep, it will come upon them as a thief in the night. (5) It is therefore the indispensable duty of all Christ's disciples, to *watch*, to be awake, and keep awake; "*What I say unto you* four (*v.* 37), I *say unto all* the twelve, or rather to *you* twelve, I say unto all my disciples and followers; what I say to you of this generation, I say to all that shall believe in me, through your word, in every age, *Watch, watch,* expect my second coming, prepare for it, that you may be found in peace, without spot, and blameless."

<hr/>

CHAPTER FOURTEEN
CHRIST ANOINTED
(*vv.* 1–11)

We have here instances,

I. Of the *kindness of Christ's friends*, and the provision made of respect and honour for him.

1. Here was *one friend*, that was so kind as to *invite him to sup with him*; and he was so kind as to accept the invitation, *v.* 3.

2. Here was *another friend*, that was so kind as to *anoint his head* with very precious ointment as he *sat at meat*. This was an extraordinary piece of respect paid him by a good woman that thought nothing too good to bestow upon Christ, and to do him honour. It is observable that she took care to pour it all out upon Christ's head. Christ must be honoured with *all*

we have, and we must not think to keep back any part of the price. Do we give him the *precious ointment* of our best affections? Let him have them *all*; love him *with all the heart*.

Now, (1) There were those who put a *worse construction* upon this than it *deserved*. They called it a *waste of the ointment, v.* 4. Because they could not have found in their hearts to put themselves to such an expense for the honouring of Christ, they thought that she was *prodigal*, who did.

(2) Our Lord Jesus put a *better construction* upon it than, for aught that appears, was *designed*. Probably, she intended no more, than to show the great honour she had for him, before all the company, and to complete his entertainment. But Christ makes it to be an act of *great faith*, as well as *great love* (*v.* 8); "*She is come aforehand, to anoint my body to the burying*, as if she foresaw that my resurrection would prevent her doing it afterward." This funeral rite was a kind of presage of, or prelude to, his death approaching. See how Christ's heart was filled with the thoughts of his death, how every thing was construed with a reference to that, and how familiarly he spoke of it upon all occasions.

(3) He recommended this piece of heroic piety to the applause of the church in all ages; *Wherever this gospel shall be preached, it shall be spoken of, for a memorial of her, v.* 9.

II. Of the *malice of Christ's enemies*, and the preparation made by them to do him mischief.

1. The chief priests, his *open*

enemies, consulted how they might *put him to death*, vv. 1, 2. The feast of the *passover* was now at hand, and at *that* feast he must be crucified.

2. Judas, his *disguised enemy*, contracted with them for the betraying of him, vv. 10, 11. He is said to be *one of the twelve* that were Christ's family, intimate with him, trained up for the service of his kingdom; and he *went to the chief priests*, to tender his service in this affair.

(1) That which he proposed to them, was, to *betray Christ* to them, and to give them notice when and where they might find him, and seize him, without making an *uproar among the people*, which they were afraid of, if they should seize him when he appeared *in public*, in the midst of his admirers.

(2) That which he proposed to himself, was, to *get money* by the bargain; he had what he aimed at, when *they promised to give him money*. Covetousness was Judas's master-lust, *his own iniquity*, and that betrayed him to the sin of betraying his Master; the devil suited his temptation to *that*, and so conquered him.

(3) Having secured the money, he set himself to make good his bargain; he sought *how he might conveniently betray him*.

THE UPPER ROOM
(vv. 12–31)

In these verses we have,

I. Christ's eating the passover with his disciples, the night before he died, with the joys and comforts of which ordinance he prepared himself for his approaching sorrows, the full prospect of which did not indispose him for that solemenity.

1. Christ ate the passover at the *usual time* when the other Jews did, as Dr. Whitby has fully made out, and not, as Dr. Hammond would have it, the night before.

2. He directed his disciples how to find the place where he intended to eat the passover; and hereby gave such another proof of his infallible knowledge of things distant and future (which to us seem altogether *contingent*), as he had given when he sent them for the ass on which he rode in triumph (*ch.* xi. 6).

3. He ate the passover in an *upper room furnished, laid with carpets* (so Dr. Hammond); it would seem to have been a very handsome *dining-room*. Christ was far from affecting any thing that looked stately in eating his common meals; on the contrary, he chose that which was homely, sat down on the grass: but, when he was to keep a sacred feast, in honour of that he would be at the expense of as good a room as he could get. God looks not at *outward pomp*, but he looks at the tokens and expressions of *inward reverence* for a divine institution, which, it is to be feared, those lack, who, to save charges, deny themselves decencies in the worship of God.

4. He ate it *with the twelve*, who were his family, to teach those who have the charge of families, not only families of *children*, but families of *servants*, or families of *scholars*, or *pupils*, to keep up religion among them, and worship God with them.

II. Christ's discourse with his disciples, as they were *eating* the passover.

1. They were *pleasing* themselves with the society of *their Master*; but he tells them that they must now presently lose him; *The Son of man is betrayed*; and they knew, for he had often told them, what followed—If he be *betrayed*, the next news you will hear of him, is, that he is *crucified* and *slain*; God hath determined it concerning him, and he agrees to it; *The Son of man goes, as it is written of him. v.* 21.

2. They were *pleasing* themselves with the society *one of another*, but Christ casts a damp upon the joy of that, by telling them, *One of you that eateth with me shall betray me, v.* 18. Christ said this, if it might be, to startle the conscience of Judas, and to awaken him to repent of his wickedness, and to draw back (for it was not too late) from the brink of the pit. But for aught that appears, he who was *most concerned in* the warning, was *least concerned at* it. All the rest were affected with it.

III. The institution of the Lord's supper.

1. It was instituted in the close of a *supper*, when they were sufficiently fed with the *paschal lamb*, to show that in the Lord's supper there is no *bodily repast* intended; to preface it with such a thing, is to revive Moses again. But it is food for *the soul* only, and therefore a very little of that which is for the body, as much as will serve for a *sign*, is enough. It was at the close of the *passover-supper*, which by this was evangelized, and then

superseded and set aside. Much of the doctrine and duty of the eucharist is illustrated to us by the law of the passover (Exod. xii.); for the Old-Testament institutions, though they do not *bind us*, yet *instruct* us, by the help of a gospel-key to them. And these two ordinances lying here so near together, it may be good to compare them, and observe how much shorter and plainer the institution of the Lord's supper is, than that of the passover was.

2. It was instituted by the *example* of Christ himself; not with the ceremony and solemnity of a law, as the ordinance of baptism was, after Christ's resurrection (Matt. xxviii. 19), but by the practice of our Master himself, because intended for those who are already his disciples, and taken into covenant with him: but it has the obligation of a law, and was intended to remain in full force, power, and virtue, till his second coming.

3. It was instituted with *blessing* and *giving of thanks*; the gifts of common providence are to be so received (1 Tim. iv. 4, 5), much more the gifts of special grace. He *blessed* (*v.* 22), and *gave thanks, v.* 23. At his other meals, he was wont to *bless*, and *give thanks* (*ch.* vi. 41; viii. 7) so remarkably, that he was known by it, Luke xxiv. 30, 31. And he did the same at this meal.

4. It was instituted to be a *memorial* of his *death*; and therefore he *broke* the bread, to show how it pleased the Lord to *bruise him*; and he called the *wine*, which is the blood of the grape, the *blood*

of the New Testament. The death Christ died was a *bloody death,* and frequent mention is made of the *blood,* the *precious* blood, as the price of our redemption; for the blood is *the life,* and made *atonement for the soul,* Lev. xvii. 11–14. The pouring out of the blood was the most sensible indication of the *pouring out of his soul,* Isa. liii. 12. It is called the *blood of the New Testament;* for the covenant of grace became a *testament,* and of force by the death of Christ, the testator, Heb. ix. 16. It is said to be *shed for many,* to justify *many* (Isa. liii. 11), to bring *many* sons to glory, Heb. ii. 10. It was sufficient for *many,* being of infinite value; it has been of use to *many;* we read of a great multitude which no man could number, that had all *washed their robes, and made them white in the blood of the Lamb* (Rev. vii. 9–14); and still it is a *fountain opened.* How comfortable is this to poor repenting sinners, that the blood of Christ is *shed for many!* And if for *many,* why not for *me?* If for sinners, sinners of the Gentiles, the chief of sinners, then *why not for me?*

5. It was instituted to be a *ratification* of the covenant made with us in him, and a sign of the conveyance of those benefits to us, which were purchased for us by his death; and therefore he broke the bread *to them* (v. 22), and said, *Take, eat* of it: he gave the cup *to them,* and ordered them to *drink of it,* v. 23. Apply the doctrine of Christ crucified to yourselves, and let it be *meat* and *drink* to your souls, strengthening, nourishing, and refreshing, to you, and the support and comfort of your spiritual life.

6. It was instituted with an eye to the happiness of heaven, and to be an earnest and fore-taste of that, and thereby to put our mouths out of taste for all the pleasures and delights of sense (v. 25); *I will drink no more of the fruit of the vine,* as it is a bodily refreshment. I have done with it.

7. It was closed with a *hymn,* v. 26. Though Christ was in the midst of his enemies, yet he did not, for fear of them, omit this sweet duty of singing psalms.

IV. Christ's discourse with his disciples, as they were returning to Bethany by moonlight.

1. Christ here foretells that in his sufferings he should be *deserted* by all his disciples; *"You will all be offended because of me, this night.* I know you will (v. 27), and what I tell you now, is no other than what the scripture has told you before; *I will smite the shepherd,* and then *the sheep will be scattered."*

But Christ encourages them with a promise that they shall rally again, shall return both to their duty and to their comfort (v. 28); *"After I am risen,* I will *gather you in* from all the places *whither you are scattered,* Ezek. xxxiv. 12. I will *go before you into Galilee,* will see our friends, and enjoy one another there."

2. He foretells that he should be *denied* particularly by Peter.

(1) Peter is confident that he should not *do so ill* as the rest of the disciples (v. 29); *Though all should be offended,* all his brethren here present, *yet will not I.* He supposes himself not only stronger

than others, but so much stronger, as to be able to receive the shock of a temptation, and bear up against it, *all alone*; to *stand*, though nobody stood *by him*. It is bred in the bone with us, to *think well* of ourselves, and *trust* to *our own hearts*.

(2) Christ tells him that he will *do worse* than any of them. They will all *desert* him, but he will *deny* him; not once, but *thrice*; and that presently; "*This day, even this night before the cock crow twice*, thou wilt *deny* that ever thou hadst any knowledge of me, or acquaintance with me, as one ashamed and afraid to own me."

(3) He stands to his promise; "*If I should die with thee, I will not deny thee*; I will adhere to thee, though it cost me my life:" and, no doubt, he thought as he said. But he that thinks he stands, must learn to take heed lest he fall; and he that *girdeth on the harness*, not boast *as though he had put it off*.

WATCH AND PRAY (*vv.* 32–42)

Christ is here entering upon his sufferings, and begins with those which were the sorest of all his sufferings, those in his *soul*. Here we have him in his *agony*; this melancholy story we had in Matthew *ch. xxvi*; this *agony* in soul was the *wormwood and the gall* in the *affliction and misery*; and thereby it appeared that no sorrow was *forced upon him*, but that it was what he *freely* admitted.

THE BETRAYAL (*vv.* 43–52)

We have here the *seizing* of our Lord Jesus by the officers of the chief priests. This was what his

enemies had long aimed at, they had often sent to *take him*; but he had escaped out of their hands, because *his hour was not come*, nor could they now have taken him, had he not freely surrendered himself. He began first to suffer *in his soul*, but afterward suffered in his body, that he might satisfy for sin, which begins in the heart, but afterward makes the members of the body *instruments of unrighteousness*.

I. Here is a band of rude miscreants employed to *take* our Lord Jesus and make him a prisoner; *a great multitude with swords and staves*.

II. Men of no less figure than the *chief priests, and the scribes*, and *the elders*, sent them, and set them on work, who pretended to expect the Messiah, and to be ready to welcome him; and yet, when he *is come*, and has given undeniable proofs that it is he that *should come*, because he doth not make court to them, nor countenance and support their pomp and grandeur, because he appears not as a temporal prince, but sets up a spiritual kingdom, and preaches repentance, reformation, and a holy life, and directs men's thoughts, and affections, and aims, to another world, they set themselves against him, and, without giving the credentials he produces an impartial examination, resolve to run him down.

III. Judas betrayed him *with a kiss*; abusing the freedom Christ used to allow his disciples of kissing his cheek at their return when they had been any time absent. He called him, *Master, Master, and kissed him*; he said, *Rabbi, Rabbi,* as if he had been now more respectful to him than ever.

IV. They arrested him, and made him their prisoner (*v.* 46).

V. Peter laid about him in defence of his Master, and wounded one of the assailants, being for the present mindful of his promise, to venture his life with his Master. He was *one of them that stood by*, of them that *were with him* (so the word signifies), of *those three* disciples that were *with him* in the garden; he *drew a sword*, and aimed, it is likely, to cut off the head, but missed his blow, and only *cut off the ear*, of a servant of the high priest, *v.* 47.

VI. Christ argues with them that had seized him, and shows them the absurdity of their proceedings against him. 1. That they came out *against him*, as against a *thief*, whereas he was *innocent* of any crime; he *taught daily in the temple*, and if he had any wicked design, there it would some time or other have been discovered. 2. That they came to take him thus *privately*, whereas he was neither *ashamed* nor *afraid* to appear *publicly* in the temple. But this was not all. 3. They came *with swords and staves*, as if he had been in arms against the government, and must have the *posse comitatus* raised to reduce him.

VII. He reconciled himself to all this injurious, ignominious treatment, by referring himself to the Old-Testament predictions of the Messiah. I am hardly used, *but* I submit, for *the scriptures must be fulfilled*, *v.* 49.

VIII. All Christ's disciples, here-

upon, deserted him (*v.* 50); *They all forsook him, and fled*. They were very confident that they should adhere to him; but even good men know not what they will do, till they are tried.

IX. The noise disturbed the neighbourhood, and some of the neighbours were brought into danger by the riot, *vv.* 51, 52. This passage of story we have not in any other of the evangelists. Here is an account of a *certain young man*, who, as it should seem, was no disciple of Christ, nor, as some have imagined, a servant of the house wherein Christ had eaten the passover, who *followed him* to see what would become of him, but some young man that lived near the garden, perhaps in the house to which the garden belonged. Now observe concerning him.

1. How he was *frightened out of his bed*, to be a *spectator* of Christ's sufferings.

2. See how he was *frightened into his bed* again, when he was in danger of being made a *sharer* in Christ's sufferings. His own disciples had run away from him; but this young man, having no concern for him, thought he might securely attend him, especially being so far from being armed, that he was not so much as clothed; but *the young men*, the Roman soldiers, who were called to assist, *laid hold of him*, for all was fish that came to their net. Perhaps they were now vexed at themselves, that they had suffered the disciples to *run away*, and they being got out of their reach they resolved to seize the first they could *lay their hands on.* Finding himself in danger, he *left*

the linen cloth by which they had *caught hold of him*, and *fled away naked*.

CHRIST BEFORE CAIAPHAS
(*vv.* 53–65)

We have here Christ's arraignment, trial, conviction, and condemnation, in the *ecclesiastical* court, before the great sanhedrim, of which the *high priest* was president, or judge of the court; the same Caiaphas that had lately adjudged it expedient he should be put to death, guilty or not guilty (John xi. 50), and who therefore might justly be excepted against as partial.

I. Christ is hurried away to his *house*, his *palace* it is called, such state did he live in. And there, though in the dead of the night, *all the chief priests, and elders, and scribes*, that were in the secret, were *assembled*, ready to receive the prey; so sure were they of it.

II. *Peter followed* at a distance, such a degree of cowardice was his late courage dwindled into, *v.* 54. But when he came to the high priest's palace, he *sneakingly* went, and *sat with the servants*, that he might not be suspected to belong to Christ. The high priest's fire side was no proper place, nor his servants proper company, for Peter, but it was his *entrance into a temptation*.

III. Great diligence was used to procure, for love or money, false witnesses against Christ.

IV. He was at length charged with words spoken some years ago, which, as they were represented, seemed to threaten *the temple*, which they had made no better than an idol of (*vv.* 57, 58); but the witnesses to this matter did not agree (*v.* 59).

V. He was urged to be his own accuser (*v.* 60); The *high priest stood up* in a heat, and said, *Answerest thou nothing?* This he said under pretence of justice and fair dealing, but really with a design to ensnare him, that they might *accuse him*, Luke xi. 53, 54; xx. 20. Still Christ *answered nothing*. But,

VI. When he was asked *whether he was the Christ*, he confessed, and denied not, that *he was*, *vv.* 61, 62. He asked, *Art thou the Son of the Blessed?* that is, the Son of *God*? for, as Dr. Hammond observes, the Jews, when they named *God*, generally added, *blessed for ever*; and thence *the Blessed* is the title of *God*, a peculiar title, and applied to Christ, Rom. ix. 5. And for the proof of his being the *Son of God*, he binds them over to his second coming; "*Ye shall see the Son of man sitting on the right hand of power*; that *Son of man* that now appears so mean and despicable, whom you *see* and trample upon (Isa. liii. 2, 3), you shall shortly see and *tremble before*."

VII. The high priest, upon this confession of his, convicted him as *a blasphemer* (*v.* 63); He *rent his clothes*.

VIII. They agreed that he was a blasphemer, and, as such, was guilty of a capital crime, *v.* 64. The question *seemed* to be put fairly, *What think ye?* But it was really *prejudged*, for the high priest had said, *Ye have heard the blasphemy*; he gave judgment first, who, as president of the court, ought to have voted last. So they *all condemned him* to be *guilty of death*; what friends he had in the great sanhedrim, did not appear, it is probable that they had not notice.

IX. They set themselves to abuse him, and, as the Philistines with Samson, to make sport with him, *v.* 65. If they did not think it below them to abuse Christ, shall we think any thing below us, by which we may do him honour?

PETER'S DENIAL (*vv.* 66–72)

We have here the story of Peter's denying Christ.

1. It began in *keeping at a distance* from him. Peter had followed *afar off* (*v.* 54), and now was *beneath in the palace*, at the lower end of the hall. Those that are *shy* of Christ, are in a fair way to *deny* him, that are shy of attending on holy ordinances, shy of the communion of the faithful, and loth to be seen on the side of despised godliness.

2. It was occasioned by his associating with the high priest's servants, and sitting among them.

3. The temptation was, his being charged as a disciple of Christ; *Thou also wert with Jesus of Nazareth, v.* 67. *This is one of them* (*v.* 69), *for thou art a Galilean*, one may know that by thy speaking broad, *v.* 70. Yet, all things considered, the temptation could not be called *formidable*; it was only a *maid* that casually cast her eye upon him, and, for aught that appears, without design of giving him any trouble, said, *Thou art one of them*, to which he needed not to have made any reply, or might have said, "And if I be, I hope that is no treason."

4. The sin was very great; he denied Christ before men, at a time when he ought to have confessed and owned him, and to have appeared in court a witness for him.

5. His repentance was very speedy. He repeated his denial thrice, and the third was worst of all, for then he *cursed* and *swore*, to confirm his denial; and that third blow, which, one would think, should have *stunned him*, and knocked him down, *startled him*, and roused him up. Then the *cock crew* the second time, which put him in mind of his Master's words, the warning he had given him, with that particular circumstance of the *cock crowing twice*; by recollecting that, he was made sensible of his sin and the aggravations of it; and when he thought thereon, he wept. Some observe that this evangelist, who wrote, as some have thought, by St. Peter's direction, speaks as fully of Peter's sin as any of them, but more briefly of his *sorrow*, which Peter, in modesty, would not have to be magnified, and because he thought he could never sorrow enough for so great a sin.

BEFORE PILATE (*vv.* 1–13)

Here we have, I. A *consultation* held by the great Sanhedrim for the effectual prosecution of our Lord Jesus.

II. The delivering of him up a prisoner to Pilate; they *bound him*. He was to be the great sacrifice, and sacrifices must be bound with cords, Ps. cxviii. 27.

III. The examining of him by

Pilate upon interrogatories (*v.* 2); "*Art thou the king of the Jews?* Dost thou pretend to be so, to be that Messiah whom the Jews expect as a temporal prince?"— "Yea," saith Christ, "it is as *thou sayest*, I am that Messiah, but not such a one as they expect."

IV. The articles of impeachment exhibited against him, and his silence under the charge and accusation. The chief priests forgot the dignity of their place, when they turned informers, and did in person *accuse Christ of many things* (*v.* 3), and witness against him, *v.* 4. These priests were very eager and noisy in their accusation; but Christ *answered nothing*, *v.* 3. When Pilate urged him to clear himself, and was desirous he should (*v.* 4), yet still he stood mute (*v.* 5), he *answered nothing*, which Pilate thought very strange. He gave Pilate a direct answer (*v.* 2), but would not answer the prosecutors and witnesses, because the things they alleged, were notoriously false, and he knew Pilate himself was convinced they were so.

V. The proposal Pilate made to the people, to have Jesus released to them, since it was the custom of the feast to grace the solemnity with the release of one prisoner. There was indeed another prisoner, *one Barabbas*, that had an interest, and would have some votes; but he questioned not but Jesus would out-poll him.

VI. The unanimous outrageous clamours of the people to have *Christ put to death*, and particularly to have him *crucified*. It was a great surprise to Pilate, when he found the people so much under the influence of the priests, that they all agreed to desire that Barabbas might be *released*, *v.* 11. Pilate opposed it all he could; "*What will ye that I shall do to him whom ye call the King of the Jews?* Would not ye then have him released too?" *v.* 12. No, say they, *Crucify him.* The priests having put that in their mouths, they insist upon it; when Pilate objected, *Why, what evil has he done?* (a very material question in such a case), they did not pretend to answer it, but *cried out the more exceedingly*, as they were more and more instigated and irritated by the priests, *Crucify him, crucify him.*

THE SCOURGING (*vv.* 15–21)

Here, I. Pilate, to gratify the Jews' malice, delivers Christ to be *crucified*, *v.* 15. *Willing to content the people*, to *do enough* for them (so the word is), and make them easy, that he might keep them quiet, he *released Barabbas unto them*, who was the scandal and plague of their nation, and *delivered Jesus* to be *crucified*, who was the glory and blessing of their nation.

Christ was *crucified*, for that was, 1. A *bloody* death, and *without blood no remission*, Heb. ix. 22. Christ was to lay down *his life* for us, and therefore shed *his blood*. Blood *made atonement for the soul* (Lev. xvii. 11), and therefore in every sacrifice of propitiation special order was given for the *pouring out* of the blood, and the *sprinkling* of that before the Lord. Now, that Christ might answer all these types, he *shed his blood*. 2. It was a *painful* death; the pains were exquisite and acute, for death made its assaults upon the vitals by the exterior parts, which are *quickest of sense*. Christ died, so as that he might feel *himself die*, because he was to be both the priest and the sacrifice; so that he might be *active* in dying, because he was to *make his soul an offering* for sin. 3. It was a *shameful* death, the death of slaves, and the vilest malefactors; so it was accounted among the Romans. The *cross* and the *shame* are put together. God having been injured in his honour by the sin of man, it is *in his honour* that Christ makes him *satisfaction*, not only by denying himself in, and divesting himself of, the honours due to his divine nature, for a time, but by submitting to the greatest reproach and ignominy the human nature was capable of being loaded with. Yet this was not the worst. 4. It was a *cursed* death; thus it was branded by the Jewish law (Deut. xxi. 23); *He that is hanged, is accursed of God*, is under a particular mark of God's displeasure.

II. Pilate, to gratify the gay humour of the Roman soldiers, delivered him to them, to be abused and spitefully treated, while they were preparing for the execution.

III. The soldiers, at the hour appointed, led him away from Pilate's judgment-hall to the place of execution (*v.* 20), as a sheep to the slaughter; he was *led forth with the workers of iniquity*, though he did no sin. But lest his death, under the load of his cross, which he was to carry, should prevent the further cruelties they intended, they compelled one Simon of Cyrene to carry his cross for him. He *passed by, coming out of the country* or out of the *fields*, not thinking of any such matter.

THE CRUCIFIXION
(*vv.* 22–32)

We have here the *crucifixion* of our Lord Jesus.

I. The *place where* he was crucified; it was called *Golgotha— the place of a skull*: some think, because of the heads of malefactors that were there cut off: it was the common place of execution, as Tyburn, for he was in all respects numbered with the transgressors.

II. The *time when* he was crucified; it was the *third hour, v.* 25. He was brought before Pilate about the sixth hour (John xix. 14), according to the Roman way of reckoning, which John uses, with which ours at this day agrees, that is at six o'clock in the morning; and then, at the *third hour*, according to the Jews' way of reckoning, that is, about nine of the clock in the morning, or soon after, they nailed him to the cross.

III. The indignities that were done him, when he was nailed to the cross; as if that had not been ignominious enough, they added several things to the ignominy of it.

1. It being the custom to give *wine* to persons that were to be *put to death*, they *mingled* his with *myrrh*, which was *bitter*, and made it *nauseous*; he *tasted* it, but would not drink it; was willing to admit the bitterness of it, but not the benefit of it.

2. The garments of those that were crucified, being, as with us, the executioners' fee, the soldiers

cast lots upon his garments (*v.* 24), threw dice for them: so making themselves merry with his misery, and sitting at their sport while he was hanging in pain.

3. They set a superscription over his head, by which they intended to reproach him, but really did him both justice and honour, *The king of the Jews, v.* 26. Here was no crime alleged, but his sovereignty owned.

4. They crucified *two thieves* with him, *one on his right hand, the other on his left*, and him in the midst as the worst of the three (*v.* 27); so great a degree of dishonour did they hereby intend him. In that famous prediction of Christ's sufferings (Isa. liii. 12), it was foretold that he should be numbered with the *transgressors*, because he was made *sin for us*.

5. The spectators, that is, the generality of them, instead of condoling with him in his misery, added to it by insulting over him. Surely never was such an instance of barbarous inhumanity toward the vilest malefactor: but thus the devil showed the utmost rage against him, and thus he submitted to the greatest dishonours that could be done him.

CHRIST'S DYING (*vv.* 33–41)

Here we have an account of Christ's dying, how his enemies abused him, and God honoured him at his death.

I. There was a thick *darkness* over *the whole land* (some think over the whole earth), for three hours, from noon till three of the clock.

II. Toward the close of this darkness, our Lord Jesus, in the agony of his soul, cried out, *My God, my God, why hast·thou forsaken me? v.* 34. The darkness signified the present cloud which the human soul of Christ was under, when he was making it an *offering for sin*.

III. Christ's prayer was bantered by them that stood by (*vv.* 35, 36); because he cried, *Eli, Eli*, or (as Mark has it, according to the Syriac dialect) *Eloi, Eloi*, they said, *He calls for Elias*, though they knew very well what he said, and what it signified, *My God, My God*. Thus did they represent him as *praying to saints*, either because he had abandoned God, or God had abandoned him; and hereby they would make him more and more odious to the people. One of them *filled a sponge with vinegar*, and reached it up to him upon a reed; "Let him cool his mouth, with that it is drink good enough for him," *v.* 36. This was intended for a further affront and abuse to him; and whoever it was that checked him who did it, did but add to the reproach; "*Let him alone*;·he has called for Elias: *let us see whether Elias will come to take him down*; and if not, we may conclude that he also hath abandoned him."

IV. Christ did again *cry with a loud voice*, and so *gave up the ghost, v.* 37. He was now commending his soul into his Father's hand; and though God is not moved with any *bodily exercise*, yet this loud voice signified the great strength and ardency of affection wherewith he did it.

V. Just at that instant that Christ, died upon *mount Calvary*, the veil of the *temple* was *rent in twain from the top to the bottom, v.* 38. This bespoke a great deal, 1. Of terror to the unbelieving Jews; for it was a presage of the utter destruction of their church and nation, which followed not long after. 2. It bespeaks a great deal of comfort to all believing Christians, for it signifies the consecrating and laying open to us of a *new and living way into the holiest* by the *blood of Jesus.*

VI. The centurion who commanded the detachment which had the oversight of the execution was convinced, and confessed that this Jesus was the *Son of God, v.* 39. But what reason had he to say so? I answer, 1. He had reason to say that he suffered *unjustly*, and had a great deal of wrong done him. 2. He had reason to say that he was a *favourite of heaven*, and one for whom the almighty power was particularly engaged, seeing how Heaven did him honour at his death, and frowned upon his persecutors. This he expresses by such words as denote his eternal generation as God, and his special designation to the office of Mediator, though he meant not so. Our Lord Jesus, even in the depth of his sufferings and humiliation, was the Son of God, and was declared to be so *with power.*

VII. There were some of his friends, the good women especially, that attended him (*v.* 40, 41). These women had followed Christ *from Galilee*, though they were not required to attend the feast, as the males were; but it is probable that they came, in expectation that his temporal kingdom would now shortly be set up, and big with

hopes of preferment for themselves, and their relations under him. It is plain that the mother of Zebedee's children was so (Matt. xx. 21); and now to see *him* upon a cross, whom they thought to have seen upon a throne, could not but be a great disappointment to them. Note, Those that follow Christ, in expectation of great things in this world by him, and by the profession of his religion, may probably live to see themselves sadly disappointed.

THE FUNERAL (*vv.* 42–47)

We are here attending the funeral of our Lord Jesus, a solemn, mournful funeral. O that we may by grace be planted in the likeness of it! Observe,

I. How the body of Christ was *begged*. It was, as the dead bodies of malefactors are, at the disposal of the government. Those that hurried him to the cross, designed that he should make *his grave with the wicked*; but God designed he should make it *with the rich* (Isa. liii. 9), and so he did.

II. How the body of Christ was *buried*. Pilate gave Joseph leave to take down the body, and do what he pleased with it. It was a wonder the chief priests were not too quick for him, and had not first begged the body of Pilate, to expose it and drag it about the streets, but that remainder of their wrath did God restrain, and gave that invaluable prize to Joseph, who knew how to value it; and the hearts of the priests were so influenced, that they did not oppose it.

1. Joseph bought *fine linen* to wrap the body in, though in such a

case old linen that had been worn might have been thought sufficient.

2. He *took down* the body, mangled and macerated as it was, and *wrapt it in the linen* as a treasure of great worth.

3. He *laid it in a sepulchre* of his own, in a private place. This sepulchre was *hewn out of a rock*, for Christ died to make the grave a *refuge* and shelter to the saints, and being hewn out of a rock, it is a *strong* refuge. *O that thou wouldest hide me in the grave!* Christ himself is a *hiding place* to his people, that is, *as the shadow of a great rock*.

4. He *rolled a stone to the door of the sepulchre*, for so the manner of the Jews was to bury.

5. Some of the good women attended the funeral, and *beheld where he was laid*, that they might come after the sabbath to anoint the dead body, because they had not time to do it now.

CHAPTER SIXTEEN

EASTER MORNING
(vv. 1–8)

Never was there such a *sabbath* since the sabbath was first instituted as this was, which the first words of this chapter tell us was *now past*; during all this sabbath our Lord Jesus lay in the grave. It was *to him* a sabbath of *rest*, but a *silent* sabbath; it was to his disciples a melancholy sabbath, spent in tears and fears. Never were the sabbath services in the temple such an *abomination to God*, though they had been often so, as they were now, when the chief priests, who presided in them, had their hands full of blood, the blood of Christ.

Well, this sabbath is over, and the first day of the week is the first day of a new world. We have here,

I. The affectionate visit which the good women that had attended Christ, now made to his sepulchre —not a *superstitious* one, but a *pious* one. They had *bought sweet spices* too, and came not only to *bedew* the dead body with their tears (for nothing could more renew their grief than this), but to *perfume* it with their *spices, v.* 1. Nicodemus had bought a very large quantity of *dry spices, myrrh* and *aloes*, which served to dry the wounds, and dry up the blood, John xix. 39. But these good women did not think that enough; they bought spices, perhaps of another kind, some perfumed oils, to *anoint him*.

II. The care they were in about the rolling away of the stone, and the superseding of that care *(vv.* 3, 4); *They said among themselves*, as they were coming along, and now drew near the sepulchre, *Who shall roll us away the stone from the door of the sepulchre? For it was very great*, more than they with their united strength could move. And there was another difficulty much greater than this, to be got over, which they knew nothing of, to wit, a guard of soldiers set to *keep* the sepulchre. But their gracious love to Christ carried them to the sepulchre; and see how by the time they came thither, both these difficulties were removed, both the *stone* which they *knew of*, and the *guard* which they *knew not of*. They *saw that the stone was rolled away*, which was the first thing that amazed them.

339

III. The assurance that was given them by an angel, that the Lord Jesus was risen from the dead, and had taken leave of his sepulchre, and had left him there to tell those so who came thither to enquire after him.

1. They *entered into the sepulchre*, at least, a little way in, and saw that the body of Jesus was not there where they had left it the other night.

2. They saw a *young man sitting on the right side* of the sepulchre. This angel was *sitting* on *the right hand* as they went into the sepulchre, *clothed with a long white garment*, a garment down to the feet, such as great men were arrayed with. The sight of him might justly have encouraged them, but they were *affrighted*.

3. He silences their fears by assuring them that here was cause enough for triumph, but none for trembling (*v.* 6); *He saith to them, Be not affrighted.* "We cannot as yet show you *him*, but hereafter you will see him, and you may here see *the place where they laid him.* You see he is gone hence, not stolen either by his enemies or by his friends, but *risen.*"

4. He orders them to give speedy notice of this to his disciples.

(1) They must tell the *disciples*, that *he is risen.* "O, go quickly to them," saith the angel, "tell them that *their Master is risen*; this will put some life and spirit into them, and keep them from sinking into despair."

(2) They must be sure to tell Peter. This is particularly taken notice of by this evangelist, who is supposed to have written by Peter's direction. If it were told the disciples, it would be told Peter, for, as a token of his repentance for disowning his Master, he still associated with his disciples; yet he is particularly named: *Tell Peter*, for, [1] It will be good news to him, more welcome to him than to any of them; for he is in sorrow for sin, and no tidings can be more welcome to true penitents than to hear of the resurrection of Christ, because he rose again for *their justification.* [2] He will be afraid, lest the joy of this good news do not belong to him. To obviate that, "Go to Peter by name, and tell him, he shall be as welcome as any of the rest to *see* him in Galilee." Note, A sight of Christ will be very welcome to a true penitent, and a true penitent shall be very welcome to a sight of Christ, for there is joy in heaven concerning him.

(3) They must appoint them all, and Peter by name, to give him the meeting in Galilee, as *he said unto you*, Matt. xxvi. 32. Note, [1] All the meetings between Christ and his disciples are of his own appointing. [2] Christ never forgets his appointment, but will be sure to meet his people with the promised blessing in every place where he records his name. [3] In all meetings between Christ and his disciples, he is the most forward. *He goes before you.*

TWO APPEARANCES
(*vv.* 9–13)

We have here a very short account of two of Christ's appearances, and the little credit which the report of them gained with the disciples.

I. He appeared to Mary Magdalene, to her first in the garden, which we have a particular narrative of, John xx. 14.

2. They could not give credit to the report she brought them. They heard that *he was alive*, and had been seen of her. The story was plausible enough, and yet *they believed not*. They would not say that she made the story herself, or designed to deceive them; but they fear that she is *imposed upon*, and that it was but a fancy that she *saw him*. Had they believed the *frequent* predictions of it from his own mouth, they would not have been now so incredulous of the report of it.

II. He appeared to two of the disciples, *as they went into the country*, *v.* 12. This refers, no doubt, to that which is largely related (Luke xxiv. 13, &c.), of what passed between Christ and the two disciples *going to Emmaus*. He is here said to have appeared to them in *another form*, in another dress than what he usually wore, in the form of a *traveller*, as, in the garden, in such a dress, that Mary Magdalene took him for the gardener; but that he had really his own countenance, appears by this, that *their eyes were holden, that they should not know him*; and when that restraint on *their* eyes was taken off, immediately they *knew him*, Luke xxiv. 16–31. Now,

1. These *two* witnesses gave in their *testimony* to this proof of Christ's resurrection; *They went and told it to the residue*, *v.* 13. Being *satisfied* themselves, they were desirous to give their brethren the *satisfaction* they had, that they might be comforted as they were.

2. This did not gain credit with all; *Neither believed they them.* They suspected that their eyes also deceived them.

CONVICTION AND COMMISSION (*vv.* 14–18)

Here is, I. The *conviction* which Christ gave his apostles of the truth of his resurrection (*v.* 14); He *appeared to them* himself, when they were all together, *as they sat at meat*, which gave him an opportunity to *eat and drink with them*, for their full satisfaction; see Acts x. 41. And still, when he appeared to them, he *upbraided them with their unbelief and hardness of heart*, for even at the general meeting in *Galilee, some doubted*, as we find Matt. xxviii. 17.

II. The *commission* which he gave them to set up his kingdom among men by the preaching of his *gospel*, the glad tidings of reconciliation to God through a Mediator. Now observe,

1. *To whom* they were to preach *the gospel*. Hitherto they had been sent only to *the lost sheep of the house of Israel*, and were forbidden to go into the *way of the Gentiles*, or into any city of the Samaritans; but now their commission is enlarged, and they are authorized to *go into all the world*, into all parts of the world, the habitable world, and to *preach the gospel* of Christ to *every creature*, to the Gentiles as well as to the Jews; to every human creature that is capable of receiving it.

2. What is the *summary of the gospel* they are to preach (*v.* 16). "Now go and tell them," (1) "That if they *believe the gospel*, and give up themselves to be Christ's

disciples; if they *renounce* the devil, the world, and the flesh, and be *devoted* to Christ as their prophet, priest, and king, and to God in Christ as their God in covenant, and evidence by their constant adherence to this covenant their sincerity herein, they *shall be saved* from the guilt and power of sin, it shall not *rule* them, it shall not *ruin* them. He that is a true Christian, shall be saved through Christ." *Baptism* was appointed to be the *inaugurating* rite, by which those that embraced Christ owned him; but it is here put rather for the *thing signified* than for the sign, for Simon Magus *believed* and was *baptized*, yet was not *saved*, Acts viii. 13. *Believing with the heart, and confessing with the mouth the Lord Jesus* (Rom. x. 9), seem to be much the same with this here. Or thus, We must *assent* to gospel-truths, and *consent* to gospel-terms. (2) "*If they believe not*, if they receive not the record God gives concerning his Son, they cannot expect any other way of salvation, but must inevitably perish; *they shall be damned*, by the sentence of a *despised* gospel, added to that of a broken law."

3. What power they should be endowed with, for the confirmation of the doctrine they were to preach (*v.* 17); *These signs shall follow them that believe*. It added much to the glory and evidence of the gospel, that the preachers not only wrought miracles themselves, but conferred upon others a power to work miracles, which power *followed* some of them that believed, wherever they went to preach. They shall do wonders *in Christ's name*, the

same name into which they were baptized, in the virtue of power derived from him, and fetched in by prayer.

EPILOGUE (*vv.* 19, 20)

Here is, 1. Christ *welcomed* into the *upper world* (*v.* 19): *After the Lord had spoken* what he had to say to his disciples, he *went up into heaven*, in a cloud. Whatever God does concerning us, gives to us, or accepts from us, it is *by his Son*. Now he is glorified with the glory he had before the world.

2. Christ *welcomed* in this *lower world*; his being *believed on in the world*, and *received up into glory*, are put together, 1. Tim. iii. 16. (1) We have here the apostles working diligently for him; they *went forth, and preached every where* far and near. (2) We have here God *working* effectually *with them*, to make their labours successful, by *confirming the word with signs following*, partly by the miracles that were wrought upon the *bodies* of people, which were divine seals to the Christian doctrine, and partly by the influence it had upon the *minds* of people, through the operation of the Spirit of God, see Heb. ii. 4. These were properly *signs following* the word—the reformation of the world, the destruction of idolatry, the conversion of sinners, the comfort of saints; and these signs still follow it, and that they may do so more and more, for the honour of Christ and the good of mankind, the evangelist prays, and teaches us to say *Amen*. Father in heaven, thus let thy name be hallowed, and let thy kingdom come.

THE GOSPEL ACCORDING TO

ST. LUKE

CHAPTER ONE
PREFACE (vv. 1-4)

Complimentary prefaces and dedications, the language of flattery and the food and fuel of pride, are justly condemned by the wise and good; but it doth not therefore follow, that such as are useful and instructive are to be run down; such is this, in which St. Luke dedicates his gospel to his friend Theophilus, not as to his *patron*, though he was a man of honour, to protect it, but as to his *pupil*, to learn it, and hold it fast. It is not certain who this Theophilus was; the name signifies a *friend of God*; some think that it does not mean any particular person, but every one that is a *lover of God*.

Now observe here, I. Why St. Luke wrote this gospel. It is certain that he was moved by the Holy Spirit, not only *to* the writing, but *in* the writing of it; but in both he was moved as a reasonable creature, and not as a mere machine; and he was made to consider,

1. That the things he wrote of were things that were *most surely believed among all Christians*, and therefore things which they ought to be instructed in, that they may know what they believe, and things which ought to be transmitted to posterity (who are as much concerned in them as we are); and,

in order to that, to be committed to writing, which is the surest way of conveyance to the ages to come.

2. That it was requisite there should be a *declaration made in order* of those things; that the history of the life of Christ should be *methodized*, and committed to writing, for the greater certainty of the conveyance. When things are *put in order*, we know the better where to *find them* for *our own* use, and how to *keep* them for the benefit of *others*.

3. That there were *many who had undertaken* to *publish* narratives of the *life of Christ*, many well-meaning people, who *designed* well, and *did* well, and what they published had *done good*, though not done by divine inspiration, nor so well done as might be, nor intended for perpetuity.

4. That the truth of the things he had to write was *confirmed* by the *concurring testimony* of those who were competent and unexceptionable witnesses of them; what had been published in writing already, and what he was now about to publish, agreed with that which had been delivered by word of mouth, over and over, by those who from the beginning were *eye-witnesses and ministers of the word*, v. 2.

II. Observe why he sent it to *Theophilus*: "I wrote unto thee these things *in order*, not that thou mayest

343

give reputation to the work, but that thou mayest be edified by it (*v.* 4); *that thou mightest know the certainty of those things wherein thou hast been instructed.*" 1. It is implied, that he had been *instructed* in these things either before his baptism, or since, or both, according to the rule, Matt. xxviii. 19, 20. 2. It was intended that he should *know the certainty of those things*, should understand them more clearly and believe them more firmly. There is a *certainty* in the gospel of Christ, there is that therein which we may build upon; and those who have been well instructed in the things of God when they were young should afterwards give diligence to *know the certainty* of those things, to know not only what we believe, but why we believe it, that we may be able to give a *reason of the hope that is in us.*

ZACHARIAS AND THE ANGEL (*vv.* 5–25)

The two preceding evangelists had agreed to begin the gospel with the baptism of John and his ministry, which commenced about six months before our Saviour's public ministry, and therefore this evangelist, designing to give a more particular account than had been given of our Saviour's conception and birth, determines to do so of John Baptist, who in both was his harbinger and forerunner, the morning-star to the Sun of righteousness. Now observe here,

I. The account given of *his parents* (*v.* 5): They lived *in the days of Herod the king*, who was a foreigner, and a deputy for the Romans, who had lately made Judea a province of the empire.

Now the father of John Baptist was a priest, a son of Aaron; his name *Zacharias*.

Now that which is observed concerning Zacharias and Elisabeth is,

1. That they were a very religious couple (*v.* 6): *They were both righteous before God*; they were so in his sight whose judgment, we are sure, is *according to truth*; they were sincerely and really so.

2. That they had been long *childless, v.* 7. Elisabeth was *barren*, and they began to despair of ever having children, for they were both now *well stricken in years*, when the women that have been most fruitful *leave off bearing*. Many eminent persons were born of mothers that had been long childless, as Isaac, Jacob, Joseph, Samson, Samuel, and so here John Baptist, to make their birth the more remarkable and the blessing of it the more valuable to their parents, and to show that when God keeps his people long waiting for mercy he sometimes is pleased to recompense them for their patience by *doubling* the worth of it when it comes.

II. The appearing of an angel to his father Zacharias, as he was ministering in the temple, *vv.* 8–11. Zechariah the prophet was the last of the Old Testament that was conversant with angels, and Zacharias the priest the first in the New Testament. Observe,

1. How Zacharias was employed in the service of God (*v.* 8): He *executed the priest's office, before God, in the order of his course*; it

was his *week of waiting*, and he was *upon duty*.

While Zacharias was burning incense in the temple, *the whole multitude of the people were praying without*, v. 10. Now observe here, (1) That the true Israel of God always were a *praying* people; and prayer is the great and principal piece of service by which we give honour to God, fetch in favours from him, and keep up our communion with him. (2) That *then*, when ritual and ceremonial appointments were in full force, as this of *burning incense*, yet moral and spiritual duties were required to go along with them, and were principally looked at. (3) That it is not enough for us to be where God is worshipped, if our hearts do not join in the worship, and go along with the minister, in all the parts of it. (4) All the prayers we offer up to God here in his courts are acceptable and successful only in virtue of the incense of Christ's intercession in the temple of God above.

2. How, when he was thus employed, he was *honoured* with a messenger, a special messenger sent from heaven to him (v. 11): *There appeared unto him an angel of the Lord*.

3. What impression this made upon Zacharias (v. 12): *When Zacharias saw him*, it was a surprise upon him, even to a degree of terror, for he was *troubled*, and *fear fell upon him*, v. 12.

III. The message which the angel had to deliver to him, v. 13. He began his message, as angels generally did, with, *Fear not*. "Fear not, but compose thyself, that thou

mayest with a sedate and even spirit receive the message I have to deliver to thee." Let us see what that is.

1. The *prayers* he has often made shall now receive an *answer of peace: Fear not, Zacharias, for thy prayer is heard*. (1) If he means his particular prayer *for a son* to build up his family, it must be the prayers he had formerly made for that mercy, when he was likely to have children; but we may suppose, now that he and his wife were both *well stricken in years*, as they had done expecting it, so they had done praying for it: like Moses, it *sufficeth them*, and they *speak no more to God of that matter*, Deut. iii. 26. But, (2) If he means the prayers he was *now making*, and offering up with his incense, we may suppose that those were according to the duty of his place, for the Israel of God and their welfare, and the performance of the promises made to them concerning the Messiah and the coming of his kingdom: "This prayer of thine is now *heard*; for thy wife shall shortly conceive him that is to be the Messiah's forerunner." Or, (3) In general, "The prayers thou *now* makest, and all thy prayers, are accepted of God, and *come up for a memorial* before him" (as the angel said to Cornelius, when he visited him at prayer, Acts x. 30, 31); "and this shall be the sign that thou art accepted of God, Elisabeth shall *bear thee a son*." ،

2. He shall have a son in his old age, by Elisabeth his wife, who had been long barren, that by his birth, which was *next* to miraculous, people might be prepared to receive

and believe a virgin's bringing forth of a son, which was *perfectly* miraculous. He is directed what name to give his son: *Call him John*, in Hebrew *Johanan*, a name we often meet with in the Old Testament: it signifies *gracious*.

3. This son shall be the joy of his family and of all his relations, *v.* 14. He shall be another Isaac, thy laughter; and some think that is partly intended in his name, *John*. He shall be a *welcome child.*

4. This son shall be a distinguished *favourite of Heaven*, and a distinguished *blessing to the earth*. The honour of having *a son* is nothing to the honour of having *such a son*.

(1) He shall be *great in the sight of the Lord*; those are great indeed that are so in God's sight, not those that are so in the eye of a vain and carnal world.

(2) He shall be a Nazarite, set apart to God from every thing that is *polluting*; in token of this, according to the law of Nazariteship, he *shall drink neither wine nor strong drink*,—or, rather, neither *old* wine nor *new*; for most think that the word here translated *strong drink* signifies some sort of wine, perhaps those that we call *made wines*, or any thing that is *intoxicating*. Those that would be *eminent* servants of God, and employed in *eminent* services, must learn to live a life of self-denial and mortification, must be dead to the pleasures of sense, and keep their minds from every thing that is darkening and disturbing to them.

(3) He shall be abundantly fitted and qualified for those great and eminent services to which in due time he shall be called: *He shall be filled with the Holy Ghost, even from his mother's womb*, and as soon as it is possible he shall appear to have been so.

(4) He shall be instrumental for the conversion of many souls to God, and the preparing of them to receive and entertain the gospel of Christ, *vv.* 16, 17.

He shall go *in the spirit and power of Elias*. That is, *First*, He shall be such a man as Elias was, and do such works as Elias did,—shall, like him, wear a hairy garment and a leathern girdle, and live retired from the world,—shall, like him, preach the necessity of repentance and reformation to a very corrupt and degenerate age,—shall, like him, be bold and zealous in reproving sin and witnessing against it even in the greatest, and be hated and persecuted for it by a Herod and his Herodias, as Elijah was by an Ahab and his Jezebel. He shall be carried on in his work, as Elijah was, by a divine *spirit* and *power*, which shall crown his ministry with wonderful success. As Elias went *before* the *writing* prophets of the Old Testament, and did as it were *usher* in that *signal* period of the Old-Testament dispensation by a little *writing* of his own (2 Chron. xxi. 12), so John Baptist went before Christ and his apostles, and introduced the gospel dispensation by preaching the substance of the gospel doctrine and duty, *Repent, with an eye to the kingdom of heaven. Secondly*, He shall be that very person who was prophesied of by Malachi under the name of Elijah (Mal. iv. 5), who should be sent *before the coming of the day of* the Lord. Behold, I *send you a prophet, even Elias*, not Elias the Tishbite (as the LXX. have corruptly read it, to favour the Jews' traditions), but a prophet *in the spirit and power of Elias*, as the angel here expounds it.

He shall *turn many of the children of Israel to the Lord their God*, shall incline their hearts to receive the Messiah, and bid him welcome, by awakening them to a sense of sin and a desire of righteousness.

Hereby he shall *turn the hearts of the fathers to the children*, that is, of the Jews to the Gentiles; shall help to conquer the rooted prejudices which the Jews have against the Gentiles, which was done by the gospel, as far as it prevailed, and was begun to be done by John Baptist, who came *for a witness, that all through him might believe*, who baptized and taught Roman soldiers as well as Jewish Pharisees, and who cured the pride and confidence of those Jews who gloried in their having Abraham to their father, and told them that God would *out of stones raise up children unto Abraham* (Matt. iii. 9), which would tend to *cure* their enmity to the Gentiles. He shall *turn the hearts of the fathers with the children*, that is, the hearts of old and young, shall be instrumental to bring some of every age to be *religious*, to work a great reformation in the Jewish nation, to bring them *of from* a ritual traditional religion which they had rested in, and to bring them up to *substantial serious* godliness: and the effect of this will be, that enmities will be slain and discord made to cease; and they that are at variance, being

united in his baptism, will be better reconciled one to another.

Hereby he shall *make ready a people prepared for the Lord*, shall dispose the minds of people to receive the doctrine of Christ, that thereby they may be *prepared* for the comforts of his coming.

IV. Zacharias's unbelief of the angel's prediction, and the rebuke he was laid under for that unbelief. He heard all that the angel had to say, and should have bowed his head, and worshipped the Lord, saying, *Be it unto thy servant according to the word* which thou hast spoken; but it was not so. We are here told,

1. What his unbelief spoke, *v.* 18. He said to the angel, *Whereby shall I know this?* This was not a humble petition for the confirming of his faith, but a peevish objection against what was said to him as altogether incredible; as if he should say, "I can never be made to believe this."

2. How his unbelief was *silenced*, and he *silenced* for it.

(1) The angel *stops his mouth*, by *asserting* his authority. Doth he ask, *Whereby shall I know this?* Let him know it by this, *I am Gabriel, v.* 19. He puts his name to his prophecy, doth as it were sign it with his own hand. He is Gabriel, who *stands in the presence of God*, an immediate attendant upon the throne of God. "Though I am now talking with thee here, yet *I stand in the presence of God*. I know his eye is upon me, and I dare not say any more than I have warrant to say."

(2) The angel *stops his mouth* indeed, by *exerting his power*: "That thou mayest object no more,

behold thou shalt be dumb," v. 20. Thou shalt be both *dumb* and *deaf;* the same word signifies both, and it is plain that he lost his hearing as well as his speech, for his friends *made signs* to him (v. 62), as well as he to them, v. 22.

V. The return of Zacharias to the people, and at length to his family, and the conception of this child of promise, the son of his old age.

1. The people stayed, expecting Zacharias to come out of the temple, because he was to pronounce the blessing upon them in the name of the Lord.

2. When he came out, he was *speechless,* v. 22. He was now to have dismissed the congregation with a blessing, but was dumb and not able to do it.

3. He made a shift to give them to understand that he had *seen a vision,* by some awful signs he made, for he *beckoned to them,* and *remained speechless,* v. 22.

4. He stayed out the *days of his ministration;* for, his lot being to *burn incense,* he could do that, though he was *dumb* and *deaf.* When we cannot perform the service of God so well as we would, yet, if we perform it as well as we can, God will accept of us in it.

5. He then returned to his family, and his *wife conceived,* vv. 23, 24. She conceived by virtue of the promise, and, being aware of it, *she hid herself five months.* Now Elisabeth triumphs, that not only this reproach is taken away, but great glory is put upon her instead of it: *Thus hath the Lord dealt with me,* beyond any thought or expectation of mine, *in the days wherein he looked on me.* Note, In God's

gracious dealings with us we ought to observe his gracious regards to us. He has *looked on us* with compassion and favour, and therefore has thus *dealt with us.*

THE ANNUNCIATION
(vv. 26–37)

We have here notice given us of all that it was fit we should know concerning the incarnation and conception of our blessed Saviour, six months after the conception of John. The same angel, Gabriel, that was employed in making known to Zacharias God's purpose concerning *his son,* is employed in this also; for in this, the same glorious work of redemption, which was *begun* in that, is *carried on.*

I. We have here an account given of the mother of our Lord, of whom he was to be born, whom, though we are not to pray to, yet we ought to praise God for.

1. Her name was *Mary,* the same name with *Miriam,* the sister of Moses and Aaron; the name signifies *exalted,* and a great elevation it was to her indeed to be thus *favoured* above all the daughters of the house of David.

2. She was a daughter of the royal family, lineally descended from David, and she herself and all her friends knew it, for she went under the title and character of the *house of David,* though she was poor and low in the world.

3. She was *a virgin,* a pure unspotted one, but *espoused* to one of the same royal stock, like her, however, of low estate; so that upon both accounts there was (as it was fit there should be) an equality between them; his name

348

was Joseph; he also was *of the house of David*, Matt. i. 20. Christ's mother was a *virgin*, because he was not to be born by ordinary generation, but miraculously; it was necessary that he should be so, that, though he must partake of the nature of man, yet not of the corruption of that nature: but he was born of a *virgin espoused*, made up to be married, and contracted, to put honour upon the married state, that that might not be brought into contempt (which was an ordinance in innocency) by the Redeemer's being born of a virgin.

4. She lived in Nazareth, a *city of Galilee*, a remote corner of the country, and in no reputation for religion or learning, but which bordered upon the heathen, and therefore was called *Galilee of the Gentiles*.

II. The *address* of the angel to her, *v*. 28. We are not told what she was doing, or how employed, when the angel came *unto her*; but he surprised her with this salutation, *Hail, thou that art highly favoured.* This was intended to raise in her, 1. A value for *herself*; and, though it is very rare that any need to have any sparks struck into their breast with such design, yet in some, who like Mary pore only on their *low estate*, there is occasion for it. 2. An expectation of great news, not from abroad, but from above. Heaven designs, no doubt, uncommon favours for one whom an angel makes court to with such respect.

(1) She is dignified: "Thou art *highly favoured*. God, in his choice of thee to be the mother of the Messiah, has put an honour upon thee peculiar to thyself, above that of Eve, who was the mother of *all living*."

(2) She has the presence of God with her: "*The Lord is with thee*, though poor and mean, and perhaps now forecasting how to get a livelihood and maintain a family in the married state."

(3) She has the blessing of God upon her: "*Blessed art thou among women.*" She explains this herself (*v*. 48), *All generations shall call me blessed.*

III. The consternation she was in, upon this address (*v*. 29). *When she saw him*, and the glories with which he was surrounded, she was *troubled* at the sight of him, and much more *at his saying.* She *cast in her mind what manner of salutation this should be.* Was it from heaven or of men? Was it to amuse her? was it to ensnare her? was it to banter her? or was there something substantial and weighty in it?

IV. The message itself which the angel had to deliver to her. Some time the angel gives her to *pause*; but, observing that this did but increase her perplexity, he went on with his errand, *v*. 30. To what he had said she made no reply; he therefore confirms it: "*Fear not, Mary*, I have no other design than to assure thee that *thou hast found favour with God.*" Note, Those that have *found favour with God* should not give way to disquieting distrustful fears.

1. Though she is a *virgin*, she shall have the honour of being a *mother*: "*Thou shalt conceive in thy womb, and bring forth a son*, and thou shalt have the naming of him; thou shalt *call his name Jesus*," *v*. 31.

2. Though she lives in *poverty* and *obscurity*, yet she shall have the honour to be the mother of the Messiah; her son shall be named *Jesus—a Saviour*, such a one as the world *needs*, rather than such a one as the Jews *expect*.

(1) He will be very *nearly allied* to the *upper world*. He *shall be great*, truly great, incontestably great; for he shall be called *the Son of the Highest*, the Son of God who is *the Highest*; of the same nature, as the son is of the same nature with the father; and very dear to him, as the son is to the father.

(2) He will be very *highly preferred* in the *lower world*; for, though born under the most disadvantageous circumstances possible, and appearing in the form of a servant, yet *the Lord God shall give unto him the throne of his father David, v.* 32. He assures her, [1] That his kingdom shall be *spiritual*: he shall *reign over the house of Jacob*, not *Israel according to the flesh*, for they neither came into his interests nor did they continue long a people; it must therefore be a *spiritual* kingdom, the house of Israel *according to promise*, that he must *rule over*. [2] That it shall be eternal: he shall reign *for ever*, and *of his kingdom there shall be no end*.

V. The further information given her, upon her enquiry concerning the birth of this prince.

1. It is a just enquiry which she makes: "*How shall this be?*" *v.* 34. "How can I now presently conceive a child" (for so the angel meant) "when I *know not a man*; must it therefore be otherwise than by ordinary generation? If so, let me know *how*?"

2. It is a satisfactory answer that is given to it, *v.* 35. (1) She shall conceive by *the power of the Holy Ghost*, whose proper work and office it is to *sanctify*, and therefore to sanctify the virgin for this purpose.

(2) She must *ask no questions* concerning the way and manner how it shall be wrought; for the Holy Ghost, as the *power of the Highest*, shall *overshadow* her, as the *cloud* covered the tabernacle when the glory of God took possession of it, to conceal it from those that would too curiously observe the motions of it, and pry into the mystery of it. The formation of every babe in the womb, and the entrance of the spirit of life into it, is a mystery in nature; none knows *the way of the spirit, nor how the bones are formed in the womb of her that is with child*, Eccl. xi. 5. We were *made in secret*, Ps. cxxxix. 15, 16. Much more was the formation of the child Jesus a *mystery*; without controversy, *great was the mystery of godliness, God manifest in the flesh*, 1 Tim. iii. 16. It is a *new thing created in the earth* (Jer. xxxi. 22), concerning which we must not covet to be *wise above what is written*.

(3) The child she shall conceive is a *holy thing*, and therefore must not be conceived by *ordinary generation*, because he must not share in the common corruption and pollution of the human nature.

3. It was a further encouragement to her faith to be told that *her cousin Elisabeth*, though stricken in years, was *with child, v.* 36. Here is an age of wonders beginning, and therefore be not surprised.

VI. Her acquiescence in the will of God concerning her, *v.* 38. She owns herself, 1. A believing subject to the divine authority: "*Behold, the handmaid of the Lord*. Lord, I am at thy service, at thy disposal, to do what thou commandest me." She objects not the danger of spoiling her marriage, and blemishing her reputation, but leaves the issue with God, and submits entirely to his will. 2. A believing expectant of the divine favour. She is not only content that it should be so, but humbly desires that it may be so: *Be it unto me according to thy word*.

Hereupon, *the angel departed from her*; having completed the errand he was sent upon, he returned, to give account of it, and receive new instructions.

MARY'S SONG (*vv.* 39–56)

We have here an interview between the two happy mothers, Elisabeth and Mary. Here is,

I. The visit which Mary made to Elisabeth. Mary was the *younger*, and younger with child; and therefore, if they must come together, it was fittest that Mary should take the journey, not insisting on the preference which the greater dignity of her conception gave her, *v.* 39.

II. The meeting between Mary and Elisabeth. Mary entered into the house of Zacharias; but he, being *dumb* and *deaf*, kept his chamber, it is probable, and saw no company; and therefore she *saluted Elisabeth* (*v.* 40), told her that she was come to make her a visit, to know her state, and *rejoice with her* in her joy.

Now, at their first coming together, for the confirmation of the faith of both of them, there was something very extraordinary. Mary knew that Elisabeth was with child, but it does not appear that Elisabeth had been told any thing of her cousin Mary's being designed for the mother of the Messiah; and therefore what knowledge she appears to have had of it must have come by a *revelation*, which would be a great encouragement to Mary.

1. The babe *leaped in her womb*, *v.* 41. It is very probable that she had been several weeks *quick* (for she was six months gone), and that she had often felt the child stir; but this was a more than ordinary motion of the child, which alarmed her to expect something very extraordinary.

2. Elisabeth was herself *filled with the Holy Ghost*, or a Spirit of prophecy, by which, as well as by the particular suggestions of the Holy Ghost she was filled with, she was given to understand that the Messiah was at hand, in whom prophecy should revive, and by whom the Holy Ghost should be more plentifully poured out than ever, according to the expectations of those who *waited for the consolation of Israel*. The uncommon motion of the babe in her womb was a token of the extraordinary emotion of her spirit under a divine impulse.

III. The welcome which Elisabeth, by the Spirit of prophecy, gave to Mary, the mother of our Lord; not as to a common friend making a common visit, but as to one of whom the Messiah was to be born.

1. She congratulates her on her

honour, and, though perhaps she knew not of it till *just now*, she acknowledges it with the greatest assurance and satisfaction. She said, *Blessed art thou among women*, the same word that the angel had said (*v.* 28); for thus this will of God, concerning honouring the Son, should be done *on earth* as it is *done in heaven*. But Elisabeth adds a reason, *Therefore blessed art thou* because *blessed is the fruit of thy womb*; thence it was that she derived this excelling dignity.

2. She acknowledges her condescension, in making her this visit (*v.* 43): *Whence is this to me, that the mother of my Lord should come to me?* Observe, (1) She calls the virgin Mary the *mother of her Lord* (as David, in spirit, called the Messiah Lord, *his Lord*), for she knew he was to be *Lord of all*. (2) She not only bids her welcome to her house, though perhaps she came but in mean circumstances, but reckons this visit a great favour, which she thought herself unworthy of.

3. She acquaints her with the concurrence of the babe in her womb, in this welcome to her (*v.* 44). He *leaped* as it were *for joy* that the Messiah, whose harbinger he was to be, would himself come so soon after him.

4. She commends her faith, and encourages it (*v.* 45): *Blessed is she that believed.* They are *blessed* who *believe* the word of God, for that word will not fail them; *there shall*, without doubt, *be a performance of those things which are told her from the Lord.*

IV. Mary's song of praise, upon this occasion.

1. Here are the expressions of joy and praise, and God alone the object of the praise and centre of the joy. Some compare this song with that which her name-sake Miriam, the sister of Moses, sung, upon the triumphant departure of Israel out of Egypt, and their triumphant passage through the Red Sea; others think it better compared with the song of Hannah, upon the birth of Samuel, which, like this, passes from a family mercy to a public and general one. *This* begins, like *that*, My heart rejoiceth in the Lord, 1 Sam. ii. 1. Observe how Mary here speaks of God.

(1) With great reverence of him, as *the Lord*: "*My soul doth magnify the Lord*; I never saw him so *great* as now I find him so *good*."

(2) With great complacency in him as *her Saviour: My spirit rejoiceth in God my Saviour*. This seems to have reference to the Messiah, whom she was to be the mother of. She calls him *God her Saviour*; for the angel had told her that he should be the *Son of the Highest*, and that his name should be *Jesus, a Saviour*; this she fastened upon, with application to herself: *He is God my Saviour.*

2. Here are just causes assigned for this joy and praise.

(1) Upon *her own* account, *vv.* 48, 49. [1] Her *spirit rejoiced in the Lord*, because of the *kind* things he had done for her: his *condescension* and *compassion* to her. *He has regarded the low estate of his handmaiden*; that is, he has *looked* upon her *with pity*, for so the word is commonly used. [2] Her *soul magnifies* the Lord, because of the

wonderful things he has done for her (v. 49): *He that is mighty has done to me great things.* A *great* thing indeed, that a *virgin* should *conceive.* A *great* thing indeed, that Messiah, who had been so long ago promised to the church, and so long expected by the church, should now at length be born. He that is *mighty*, even he *whose name is holy*, has *done to me great things.* Glorious things may be expected from him that is both *mighty* and *holy*; who *can do every thing*, and *will* do every thing *well* and *for the best.*

(2) Upon the account of *others.* The virgin Mary, as the mother of the Messiah, is become a kind of public person, wears a public character, and is therefore immediately endued with another spirit, a more public spirit than before she had, and therefore *looks abroad*, looks *about her*, looks *before her*, and takes notice of God's various dealings with the children of men (vv. 50, &c.), as Hannah (1 Sam. ii. 3, etc.). In this she has especially an eye to the coming of the Redeemer and God's manifesting himself therein.

[1] It is a certain truth that *God has mercy in store*, mercy in reserve, *for all that have a reverence for his majesty*, and a due regard to his sovereignty and authority. But never did this appear so as in sending his Son into the world to save us (v. 50): *His mercy is on them that fear him*; it has always been so; he has ever looked upon *them* with an eye of *peculiar favour* who have looked up to him with an eye of *filial fear.*

[2] It has been a common obser-vation that God in his providence puts *contempt* upon the *haughty* and *honour* upon the *humble*; and this he has done remarkably in the whole economy of the work of man's redemption. This doth especially appear in the methods of gospel grace.

(1.) In the *spiritual honours* it dispenses. When the proud Pharisees were rejected, and Publicans and sinners went *into the kingdom of heaven* before them,—when the Jews, who *followed after the law of righteousness*, did not attain it, and the Gentiles, who never thought of it, attained to righteousness (Rom. ix. 30, 31),—when God chose not the *wise men after the flesh*, not the *mighty*, or the *noble*, to preach the gospel, and plant Christianity in the world, but the *foolish* and *weak* things of the world, and things that were despised (1 Cor. i. 26, 27)—then he *scattered the proud*, and *put down the mighty*, but *exalted them of low degree.*

(2.) In the *spiritual riches* it dispenses, v. 53. (1) Those who see their need of Christ, and are importunately desirous of righteousness and life in him, he *fills* with *good things*, with the *best things.* (2) Those who are rich, who are not *hungry*, who, like Laodicea, think they have *need of nothing*, are full of themselves and their own righteousness, and think they have a sufficiency in themselves, those he *sends away* from his door, they are not welcome to him, he sends them *empty* away, they come *full of self*, and are sent away *empty of Christ.*

[3] It was always expected that the Messiah should be, in a special

manner, the strength and glory of his people Israel, and so he is in a peculiar manner (*v.* 54): *He hath helped his servant Israel.* The sending of the Messiah, on whom *help* was *laid* for poor sinners, was the greatest kindness that could be done, the greatest help that could be provided for his people Israel, and that which magnifies it is,

First, That it is *in remembrance of his mercy,* the mercifulness of his nature, the mercy he has in store for *his servant Israel.*

Secondly, That it is *in performance of his promise.* It is a mercy not only designed, but declared (*v.* 55); it was *what he spoke to our fathers.*

Lastly, Mary's return to Nazareth (*v.* 56), after she had continued with Elisabeth about *three months,* so long as to be fully satisfied concerning herself that she was *with child,* and to be confirmed therein by her cousin Elisabeth.

THE BIRTH OF JOHN
(*vv.* 57–66)

In these verses, we have,

I. The birth of John Baptist, *v.* 57. Though he was conceived in the womb by miracle, he continued in the womb according to the ordinary course of nàture (so did our Saviour).

II. The great joy that was among all the relations of the family, upon this extraordinary occasion (*v.* 58): *Her neighbours and her cousins heard of it*; for it would be in every body's mouth, as next to miraculous.

III. The dispute that was among them concerning the naming him (*v.* 59): *On the eighth day,* as God had appointed, they *came together,* to *circumcise the child.*

Now it was the custom, when they circumcised their children, to *name them,* because, when *Abram* was circumcised God gave him a new name, and called him *Abraham*; and it is not unfit that they should be left *nameless* till they are by name *given up to God.* Now,

1. *Some* proposed that he should be called by his father's name, *Zacharias.*

2. The *mother* opposed it, and would have him called *John*; having learned, either by inspiration of the Holy Ghost (as is most probable), or by information in writing from her husband, that God appointed this to be his name (*v.* 60).

3. The *relations* objected to that (*v.* 61).

4. They appealed to the *father,* and would try if they could possibly get to know his mind; for it was his office to *name the child, v.* 62. They *made signs* to him, by which it appears that he was *deaf* as well as *dumb*; nay, it should seem, *mindless* of any thing, else one would think they should at first have desired him to write down his child's name, if he had ever yet communicated any thing by writing since he was *struck.* Whereupon he made signs to them to give him a *table-book,* such as they then used, and with the pencil he wrote these words, *His name is John, v.* 63. Not, "It shall be so," or, "I would have it so," but, "It is so." The matter is determined already; the *angel* had given him that name.

5. He thereupon recovered the use of his speech (*v.* 64): *His mouth*

was opened immediately. The time prefixed for his being silenced was *till the day that these things shall be fulfilled* (*v*. 20); not *all the things* going before concerning John's ministry, but those which relate to his birth and name (*v*. 13). That time was now expired, whereupon the restraint was taken off, and God gave him the *opening of the mouth again*, as he did to Ezekiel, *ch*. iii. 27.

6. These things were told all the country over, to the great amazement of all that heard them, *vv*. 65, 66. They said *within* themselves, and said *among* themselves, "*What manner of child shall this be?* What will be the fruit when these are the buds, or rather when the *root* is out of such a *dry ground*?"

Lastly, It is said, *The hand of the Lord was with him*; that is, he was taken under the special protection of the Almighty, from his birth, as one designed for something great and considerable, and there were many instances of it.

THE SONG OF ZACHARIAS
(*vv*. 67–80)

We have here the song wherewith Zacharias *praised God* when his *mouth* was *opened*; in it he is said to *prophesy* (*v*. 67), and so he did in the strictest sense of *prophesying*; for he foretold things to come concerning the kingdom of the Messiah, to which all the prophets bear witness. Observe,

I. How he was qualified for this: *He was filled with the Holy Ghost*, was endued with more than ordinary measures and degrees of it, for this purpose; he was divinely inspired.

II. What the matter of his song

was. He is wholly taken up with the kingdom of the Messiah, and the public blessings to be introduced by it. The Old-Testament prophecies are often expressed in *praises* and *new songs*, so is this beginning of New-Testament prophecy: *Blessed be the Lord God of Israel*. The *God of the whole earth shall he be called*; yet Zacharias, speaking of the work of redemption, called him the *Lord God of Israel*, because to Israel the prophecies, promises, and types, of the redemption had hitherto been given, and to them the first proffers and proposals of it were now to be made.

Now Zacharias here blesses God,

1. For the work of *salvation* that was to be wrought out by the Messiah himself, *vv*. 68–75. This it is that *fills him*, when he is *filled with the Holy Ghost*, and it is that which all who have the *Spirit of Christ* are *full of*.

(1) In sending the Messiah, God has *made a gracious visit* to his people, whom for many ages he had seemed to neglect, and to be estranged from; he hath *visited them* as a friend, to take cognizance of their case.

(2) He has *wrought out redemption* for them: *He has redeemed his people*. This was the errand on which Christ *came into the world*, to redeem those that were sold *for* sin, and sold *under* sin; even God's own people, his Israel, his son, his *first-born*, his *free-born*, need to be *redeemed*, and are undone if they be not. Christ redeems them by *price* out of the hands of God's justice, and redeems them by *power* out of the hands of Satan's tyranny, as Israel out of Egypt.

(3) He has fulfilled the *covenant of royalty* made with the most famous *Old-Testament prince*, that is, David. Glorious things had been said of his family, that on him, as a *mighty one*, *help* should be *laid*, that *his horn should be exalted*, and his *seed* perpetuated, Ps. lxxxix. 19, 20, 24, 29. But that family had been long in a manner *cast off* and *abhorred*, Ps. lxxxix. 38. Now here it is gloried in, that, according to the promise, the *horn* of David should again be *made to bud*; for, Ps. cxxxii. 17, he *hath raised up a horn of salvation for us in the house of his servant David* (*v.* 69), there, where it was promised and expected to arise.

He has fulfilled all the precious promises made to the church by the most famous *Old-Testament prophets* (*v.* 70). *As he spoke by the mouth of his holy prophets*. His doctrine of salvation by the Messiah is confirmed by an appeal to the prophets, and the greatness and importance of that salvation thereby evidenced and magnified; it is the same that they spoke of, which therefore ought to be expected and welcomed; it is what they *enquired and searched diligently after* (1 Pet. i. 10, 11), which therefore ought not to be slighted or thought meanly of.

Now what is this *salvation* which was prophesied of?

First, It is a *rescue* from the malice of *our enemies*; it is *a salvation out of our enemies*, from among them, and *out of the power of them that hate us* (*v.* 71). He shall *save his people from their sins*, that they may not have dominion over them, Matt. i. 21.

Secondly, It is a *restoration* to the *favour of God*; it is to *perform the mercy promised to our forefathers*, *v.* 72. Observe, 1. That which was promised to the fathers, and is performed to us, is *mercy*, pure mercy; nothing in it is owing to our *merit* (we deserve wrath and the curse), but all to the *mercy* of God, which *designed* us grace and life. 2. God herein had an eye to *his covenant*, his *holy* covenant, that covenant with Abraham: I *will be a God to thee and thy seed*.

Thirdly, It is a qualification for, and an encouragement to, the service of God. Thus was *the oath he sware to our Father Abraham*, That he would *give us* power and grace to *serve him*, in an acceptable manner to him and a comfortable manner to ourselves, *vv.* 74, 75. We are hereby enabled, 1. To serve God *without fear*. We are *therefore* put into a state of *holy safety* that we might serve God with a *holy security* and *serenity of mind*, as those that are *quiet from the fears of evil*. 2. To serve him in *holiness and righteousness*, which includes the whole duty of man towards God and our neighbour. It is both the intention and the direct tendency of the gospel to renew upon us that image of God in which man was at first made, which consisted *in righteousness and true holiness*, Eph. iv. 24. 3. To serve him, *before him*, in the duties of his *immediate* worship, wherein we present ourselves *before the Lord*, to serve him as those that have an eye always upon him, and see his eye always upon us, upon our inward man, that is serving him *before him*. 4. To serve him *all the days of our life*. The design of the gospel is to engage us to constancy and perseverance in the service of God, by showing us how much depends upon our not drawing back, and by showing us how Christ *loved us to the end*, and thereby engaged us to *love him to the end*.

2. He *blessed God* for the work of *preparation* for this salvation, which was to be done by John Baptist (*v.* 76): *Thou child*, though now but a child of eight days old, shalt be called *the prophet of the Highest*. John's business was,

(1) To prepare people for the salvation, by preaching repentance and reformation as great gospel duties: *Thou shalt go before the face of the Lord*, and but a little before him, to *prepare his ways*, to call people to make room for him, and get ready for his entertainment.

(2) To give people a general idea of the salvation, that they might know, not only what to do, but what to expect; for the doctrine he preached was that the *kingdom of heaven* is at hand.

In the last verse, we have a short account of the younger years of John Baptist. Though he was the son of a priest, he did not, like Samuel, go up, when he was a child, to minister before the Lord; for he was to prepare the way for a better priesthood. But we are here told,

[1.] Of his *eminence* as to the *inward man*: The *child grew* in the capacities of his mind, much more than other children; so that he *waxed strong in spirit*, had a strong judgment and strong resolution.

[2.] Of his *obscurity* as to the *outward man*: *He was in the deserts*; not that he lived a hermit, cut off

from the society of men. No, we have reason to think that he went up to Jerusalem at the *feasts*, and frequented the synagogues on the sabbath day, but his constant residence was in some of those scattered houses that were in the wilderness of Zuph or Maon, which we read of in the story of David.

CHAPTER TWO

THE BIRTH OF JESUS

(*vv.* 1–7)

The *fulness of time* was now come, when God would send forth his Son, *made of a woman*, and *made under the law*; and it was foretold that he should be born at Bethlehem. Now here we have an account of the time, place, and manner of it.

I. The time when our Lord Jesus was born. Several things may be gathered out of these verses which intimate to us that it was the *proper time*.

1. He was born at the time when the *fourth monarchy* was in its height, just when it was become, more than any of the three before it, a *universal monarchy*. Now this was the time when the Messiah was to be born, according to Daniel's prophecy (Dan. ii. 44): *In the days of these kings*, the kings of the fourth monarchy, *shall the God of heaven set up a kingdom which shall never be destroyed*.

2. He was born when Judea was become a province of the empire, and tributary to it; as appears evidently by this, that when all the Roman empire was taxed, the Jews were taxed among the rest. Now just at this juncture, the

Messiah was to be born, for so was dying Jacob's prophecy, that Shiloh should come when the *sceptre was departed from Judah*, and the *law-giver from between his feet*, Gen. xlix. 10. This was the *first taxing* that was made in Judea, the first badge of their servitude; therefore now Shiloh must come, to set up his kingdom.

3. There is another circumstance, as to the time, implied in this general enrolment of all the subjects of the empire, which is, that there was now universal peace in the empire. The temple of Janus was now shut, which it never used to be if any wars were on foot; and now it was fit for the Prince of peace to be born, in whose days *swords should be beaten into plough-shares*.

II. The place where our Lord Jesus was born is very observable. He was born at *Bethlehem*; so it was foretold (Mic. v. 2), the scribes so understood it (Matt. ii. 5, 6), so did the common people, John vii. 42.

That which Augustus designed was either to gratify his *pride* in knowing the numbers of his people, and proclaiming it to the world, or he did it in *policy*, to strengthen his interest, and make his government appear the more formidable; but Providence had another reach in it. All the world shall be at the trouble of being *enrolled*, only that Joseph and Mary may. This brought them up from Nazareth in Galilee to Bethlehem in Judea, because they were *of the stock and lineage of David* (*vv.* 4, 5). Divers ends of Providence were served by this.

1. Hereby the virgin Mary was brought, *great with child*, to Bethlehem, to be *delivered* there, according to the prediction; whereas she had designed to lie in at Nazareth. See how *man purposes and God disposes*; and how Providence orders all things for the fulfilling of the scripture, and makes use of the projects men have for serving their own purposes, quite beyond their intention, to serve his.

2. Hereby it appeared that Jesus Christ was of the *seed* of David; for what brings his mother to Bethlehem now, but because she *was of the stock and lineage of David?*

3. Hereby it appeared that he was *made under the law*; for he became a subject of the Roman empire as soon as he was born, a *servant of rulers*, Isa. xlix. 7.

III. The circumstances of his birth, which were very mean, and under all possible marks of contempt.

1. He was under some abasements in common with other children; he was *wrapped in swaddling clothes*, as other children are when they are new-born, as if he could be bound, or needed to be kept straight. The Ancient of days became an infant of a span long.

2. He was under some abasements peculiar to himself.

(1) He was born *at an inn*. That son of David that was the glory of his father's house had no inheritance that he could command, no not in the city of David, no nor a friend that would accommodate his mother in distress with lodgings to be brought to bed in. Christ was born *in an inn*, to intimate that he came into the world but to sojourn here for awhile, as in an inn, and to teach us to do likewise.

(2) He was born *in a stable*; so some think the word signifies which we translate *a manger*, a place for cattle to stand to be fed in. His being born in a stable and laid in a manger was an instance, [1] Of the poverty of his parents. Had they been rich, room would have been made for them; but, being poor, they must *shift* as they *could.* [2] Of the corruption and degeneracy of manners in that age; that a woman in reputation for virtue and honour should be used so barbarously. If there had been any common humanity among them, they would not have turned a woman in travail into a stable. [3] It was an instance of the humiliation of our Lord Jesus. We were become by sin like an out-cast infant, helpless and forlorn; and such a one Christ was.

THE SHEPHERDS (*vv.* 8–20)

We had in Matthew an account of the notice given of the arrival of this ambassador, this prince from heaven, to the wise men, who were Gentiles, by a star; here we are told of the notice given of it to the shepherds, who were Jews, by an angel: to each God chose to speak in the language they were most conversant with.

I. See here how the shepherds were employed; they were *abiding in the fields* adjoining to Bethlehem, and *keeping watch over their flocks by night, v.* 8. Observe, 1. They were not *sleeping* in their beds, when this news was brought them (though many had very acceptable intelligence from heaven in *slumbering upon the bed*), but *abiding in the fields*, and *watching*. Those that

would hear from God must *stir up themselves*. They were broad awake, and therefore could not be deceived in what they saw and heard, so as those may be who are half asleep. 2. They were employed now, not in acts of devotion, but in the business of their calling; they were *keeping watch over their flock*, to secure them from thieves and beasts of prey, it being probably in the summer time, when they kept their cattle out all night, as we do now, and did not house them. Note, We are not out of the way of divine visits when we are sensibly employed in an honest calling, and abide with God in it.

II. How they were surprised with the appearance of an angel (*v.* 9). This made them *sore afraid*, put them into a great consternation, as fearing some evil tidings.

III. What the message was which the angel had to deliver to the shepherds, *vv.* 10–12. 1. "*Fear not*, for we have nothing to say to you that needs be a terror to you; you *need not* fear your enemies, and *should not* fear your friends." 2. He furnishes them with abundant matter for joy: "Behold, I *evangelize to you great joy*; I solemnly declare it, and you have reason to bid it welcome, for it shall bring *joy to all people*, and not to the people of the Jews only; that *unto you is born this day*, at this time, *a Saviour*, the Saviour that has been so long expected, *which is Christ the Lord, in the city of David*," *v.* 11. Jesus is the Christ, the Messiah, the Anointed; he is *the Lord*, Lord of all; he is a sovereign prince; nay, he is God, for *the Lord*, in the Old Testament, answers to *Jehovah*. He is a Saviour, and he will be a Saviour to those only that accept of him for their Lord. "The Saviour *is born*, he is born *this day*; and, since it is matter of *great joy to all people*, it is not to be kept secret, you may proclaim it, may tell it to whom you please. He is born in the place where it was foretold he should be born, in the *city of David*; and he is born *to you*; to you Jews he is sent in the first place, to *bless you*, to you *shepherds*, though poor and mean in the world." This refers to Isa. ix. 6, *Unto us a child is born, unto us a son is given*. To *you* men, not to *us* angels; he took not on him the nature of angels. This is matter of *joy* indeed to all people, great joy. Long-looked for is come at last. Let heaven and earth rejoice before this Lord, *for he cometh*. 3. He gives them a sign for the confirming of their faith in this matter. "How shall we find out this child in Bethlehem, which is now full of the descendants from David?" "You will find him by this token: he is lying in a *manger*, where surely never any new-born infant was laid before." They expected to be told, "You shall find him, though a babe, dressed up in robes, and lying in the best house in the town, lying in state, with a numerous train of attendants in rich liveries." "No, you will find him wrapped in *swaddling clothes*, and *laid in a manger*. When Christ was here upon earth, he *distinguished* himself, and made himself remarkable, by nothing so much as the instances of his *humiliation*."

IV. The angels' *doxology* to God, and *congratulations* of men, upon this solemn occasion, *vv*. 13, 14.

The message was no sooner delivered by one angel (that was sufficient to go express) than suddenly there was with that angel *a multitude of the heavenly hosts*; sufficient, we may be sure, to make a *chorus*, that were heard by the shepherds, *praising God*; and certainly their song was not like that (Rev. xiv. 3) which *no man could learn*, for it was designed that we should all learn it. 1. Let God have the honour of this work: *Glory to God in the highest*. God's goodwill to men, manifested in sending the Messiah, redounds very much to his praise; and angels in the highest heavens, though not immediately interested in it themselves, will celebrate it to his honour, Rev. v. 11, 12. *Glory to God*, whose kindness and love designed this favour, and whose wisdom contrived it in such a way as that one divine attribute should not be glorified at the expense of another, but the honour of all effectually secured and advanced. Other works of God are for his glory, but the redemption of the world is for his *glory in the highest*. 2. Let men have the joy of it: *On earth peace, good-will toward men*. God's *good-will* in sending the Messiah introduced peace in this lower world, slew the enmity that sin had raised between God and man, and resettled a peaceable correspondence. If God be at peace with us, all peace results from it: peace of conscience, peace with angels, peace between Jew and Gentile. Peace is here put for *all good*, all that good which flows to us from the incarnation of Christ. All the *good* we have, or hope, is owing

to God's *good-will*; and, if we have
the comfort of it, he must have the
glory of it. Nor must any *peace*, any
good, be expected in a way inconsistent with the glory of God;
therefore not in any way of sin, nor
in any way but by *a Mediator*.
Here was the *peace proclaimed* with
great solemnity; whoever will, let
them come and take the benefit of
it. It is on earth peace, to *men of
good-will* (so some copies read it),
ἐν ἀνθρώποις εὐδοκίας; to men
who have a *good-will to God*, and
are willing to be reconciled; or to
men whom God has a *good-will to*,
though vessels of his mercy. See
how well affected the angels are to
man, and to his welfare and
happiness; how well pleased they
were in the incarnation of the Son
of God, though he passed by their
nature; and ought not we much
more to be affected with it? This is
a *faithful saying*, attested by an
innumerable company of angels,
and well *worthy of all acceptation,
That the good-will of God toward
men is glory to God in the highest,
and peace on the earth*.

V. The visit which the shepherds
made to the new-born Saviour.
1. They consulted about it, *v.* 15.
While the angels were singing their
hymn, they could attend to that
only; but, *when they were gone
away from them into heaven* (for
angels, when they appeared, never
made any long stay, but returned as
soon as they had despatched their
business), *the shepherds said one to
another, Let us go to Bethlehem*.
Note, When extraordinary messages from the upper world are no
more to be expected, we must set
ourselves to improve the advan-

tages we have for the confirming of
our faith, and the keeping up of our
communion with God in this lower
world. And it is no reflection upon
the testimony of angels, no nor
upon a divine testimony itself, to
get it corroborated by observation
and experience. But observe, These
shepherds do not speak doubtfully,
"Let us go see whether it be so or
no"; but with assurance, *Let us go
see this thing which is come to pass*;
for what room was left to doubt of
it, when *the Lord had* thus *made it
known to them?* The *word spoken by
angels was steadfast* and unquestionably true. 2. They immediately
made the visit, *v.* 16. They lost no
time, but *came with haste* to the
place, which, probably, the angel
directed them to more particularly
than is recorded ("Go to the stable
of such an inn"); and there *they
found Mary and Joseph*, and *the
babe lying in the manger*. The
poverty and meanness in which
they found *Christ the Lord* were no
shock to their faith, who themselves
knew what it was to live a life of
comfortable communion with God
in very poor and mean circumstances. We have reason to think
that the shepherds told Joseph and
Mary of the vision of the angels
they had seen, and the song of the
angels they had heard, which was a
great encouragement to them, more
than if a visit had been made them
by the best ladies in the town. And
it is probable that Joseph and Mary
told the shepherds what visions
they had had concerning the child;
and so, by communicating their
experiences to each other, they
greatly strengthened one another's
faith.

VI. The care which the shepherds took to spread the report of this (v. 17): *When they had seen it*, though they saw nothing in the child that should induce them to believe that he was *Christ the Lord*, yet the circumstances, how mean soever they were, agreeing with the sign that the angel had given them, they were abundantly satisfied. They made *known abroad* the whole story of what was *told them*, both by the *angels*, and by Joseph and Mary, *concerning this child*, that he was the Saviour, even *Christ the Lord*, that in him there is *peace on earth*, and that he was *conceived by the power of the Holy Ghost*, and *born of a virgin*. This they told every body, and agreed in their testimony concerning it. And now if, when he *is in the world*, the world knows him not, it is *their own fault*, for they have sufficient notice given them.

VII. The use which those made of these things, who did believe them, and receive the impression of them. 1. The virgin Mary made them the matter of her *private meditation*. She said little, but *kept all these things*, and *pondered them in her heart*, v. 19. 2. The shepherds made them the matter of their more *public praises*. If others were not affected with those things, yet they themselves were (v. 20): *They returned, glorifying and praising God*, in concurrence with the holy angels.

THE PRESENTATION
(vv. 21–24)

Our Lord Jesus, being *made of a woman*, was *made under the law*, Gal. iv. 4.

Now here we have two instances of his being *made under* that *law*, and submitting to it.

I. He was *circumcised* on the very day that the law appointed (v. 21): *When eight days were accomplished*, that day seven-night that he was born, they *circumcised* him. Christ was circumcised, (1) That he might own himself of the seed of Abraham, and of that nation *of whom, as concerning the flesh, Christ came*, and who was to *take on him the seed of Abraham*, Heb. ii. 16. (2) That he might own himself a surety for our sins, and an undertaker for our safety. Circumcision (saith Dr. Goodwin) was our *bond*, whereby we acknowledged ourselves *debtors to the law*; and Christ, by being circumcised, did as it were set his hand to it, being *made sin for us*. The ceremonial law consisted much in sacrifices; Christ hereby obliged himself to offer, not the blood of bulls or goats, but his own blood, which none that ever were circumcised before could oblige themselves to. (3) That he might justify, and put an honour upon, the dedication of the infant seed of the church to God, by that ordinance which is the instituted seal of the covenant, and of the righteousness which is by faith, as circumcision was (Rom. iv. 11), and baptism is. And certainly his being circumcised at eight days old doth make much more for the dedicating of the seed of the faithful by baptism in their infancy than his being baptized at thirty years old doth for the deferring of it till they are grown up. The change of the ceremony alters not the substance. At his circumcision, according to the custom, he had his name given him; he was called *Jesus* or *Joshua*, for he was *so named of the angel* to his mother Mary *before he was conceived in the womb* (Luke i. 31), and to his supposed father Joseph after, Matt. i. 21.

II. He was *presented* in the temple. This was done with an eye to the law, and at the time appointed by the law, when he was forty days old, *when the days of her purification were accomplished*, v. 22. Now, according to the law,

1. The child Jesus, being a first-born son, was *presented to the Lord*, in one of the courts of the temple. The law is here recited (*v.* 23): *Every male that opens the womb shall be called holy to the Lord*, because by a special writ of protection the first-born of Israel were preserved, when the first-born of the Egyptians were slain by the destroying angel; so that Christ, as first-born, was a priest by a title surer than that of Aaron's house.

2. The mother brought her offering, *v.* 24. When she had presented that son of hers unto the Lord who was to be the great sacrifice, she might have been excused from offering any other; but so *it is said in the law of the Lord*, that law which was yet in force, and therefore so it must be done, she must offer *a pair of turtle-doves, or two young pigeons*; had she been of ability, she must have brought a *lamb for a burnt-offering*, and a *dove for a sin-offering*; but, being poor, and not able to reach the price of a lamb, she brings *two doves*, one for a *burnt-offering and the other for a sin-offering* (see Lev. xii. 6, 8), to teach us in every address to God, and

particularly in those upon special occasions, both to give thanks to God for his mercies to us and to acknowledge with sorrow and shame our sins against him; in both we must give glory to him, nor do we ever want matter for both. Christ was not *conceived* and *born* in sin, as others are, so that there was not that occasion in his case which there is in others; yet, because he was made under the law, he complied with it. *Thus it became him to fulfil all righteousness.* Much more doth it become the best of men to join in confessions of sin; for *who can say, I have made my heart clean?*

SIMEON AND ANNA
(*vv.* 25–40)

Even when he humbles himself, still Christ has honour done him to balance the offence of it. Simeon and Anna now do him honour, by the inspiration of the Holy Ghost.

I. A very honourable testimony is borne to him by Simeon. Now observe here,

1. The account that is given us concerning this Simeon, or Simon.

(1) That he was *just* and *devout*, *just* towards men and *devout* towards God; these two must always go together, and each will befriend the other, but neither will atone for the defect of the other. (2) That he *waited for the consolation of Israel*, that is, for the coming of the Messiah, in whom alone the nation of Israel, that was now miserably harassed and oppressed, would find *consolation.* He was long a coming, and they who believed he would come continued *waiting, desiring* his coming, and *hoping* for it with

patience; I had almost said, with some degree of *impatience* waiting till it came. (3) The *Holy Ghost* was upon him, not only as a Spirit of holiness, but as a Spirit of prophecy; he was *filled with the Holy Ghost*, and enabled to speak things above himself. (4) He had a gracious promise made him, that before he died he should have a sight of the Messiah, *v.* 26.

2. The seasonable coming of Simeon into the temple, at the time when Christ was presented there, *v.* 27. Just then, when Joseph and Mary brought in the child, to be registered as it were in the church-book, among the first-born, Simeon came, by direction of *the Spirit*, into the temple.

3. The abundant satisfaction wherewith he welcomed this sight: *He took him up in his arms* (*v.* 28), he *embraced* him with the greatest affection imaginable, laid him in his bosom, as near his heart as he could, which was as full of joy as it could hold.

4. The solemn declaration he made hereupon: *He blessed God*, and said, *Lord, now let thou thy servant depart in peace, vv.* 29–32.

(1) He has a pleasant prospect *concerning himself*, and (which is a great attainment) is got quite above the love of life and fear of death; nay, he is arrived at a holy contempt of life, and desire of death: "*Lord, now let thou thy servant depart*, for mine eyes have seen the salvation I was promised a sight of before I died." Here is, [1] An acknowledgment that God had been *as good as his word*; there has not failed one tittle of his good promises, as Solomon owns,

1 Kings viii. 56. Note, Never any that hoped in God's word were made ashamed of their hope. [2] A thanksgiving for it. He *blessed God* that he saw that salvation in his arms which many prophets and kings desired to see, and might not. [3] A confession of his faith, that this child in his arms was the *Saviour*, the *Salvation* itself; *thy salvation*, the salvation of thine appointing, the salvation *which thou hast prepared* with a great deal of contrivance. And, while it has been thus long *in the coming*, it hath still been *in the preparing*. [4] It is a farewell to this world: "*Now let thy servant depart*; now mine eyes have been blessed with this sight, let them be closed, and see no more in this world." The eye is not satisfied with seeing (Eccl. i. 8), till it hath *seen Christ*, and then it is.

(2) He has a pleasant prospect concerning the world, and concerning the church. This salvation shall be,

[1] A blessing to the world. It is *prepared before the face of all people*, not to be hid in a corner, but to be made known; to be a *light to lighten the Gentiles* that now sit in darkness: they shall have the knowledge of him, and of God, and another world through him. This has reference to Isa. xlix. 6, *I will give thee for a light to the Gentiles*; for Christ came to be the light of the world, not a candle in the Jewish candlestick, but the *Sun of righteousness*.

[2] A blessing to the church: *the glory of thy people Israel*. It was an honour to the Jewish nation that the Messiah sprang out of one of

their tribes, and was born, and lived, and died, among them. And of those who were Israelites indeed, of the spiritual Israel, he was indeed *the glory*, and will be so to eternity, Isa. lx. 19.

5. The prediction concerning this child, which he delivered, with his blessing, to Joseph and Mary. They *marvelled at those things* which were still more and more fully and plainly spoken concerning this child, *v.* 33. And because they were affected with, and had their faith strengthened by, that which was said to them, here is more said to them.

(1) Simeon shows them what reason they had to *rejoice*; for he *blessed them* (*v.* 34), he pronounced them blessed who had the honour to be related to this child, and were entrusted with the bringing him up. He *prayed* for them, that God would *bless* them, and would have others do so too.

(2) He shows them likewise what reason they had to *rejoice with trembling*, according to the advice given of old, with reference to the Messiah's kingdom, Ps. ii. 11. Lest Joseph, and Mary especially, should be *lifted up* with the abundance of the revelations, here is a *thorn in the flesh* for them, an allay to their joy; and it is what we sometimes need.

[1] It is true, Christ shall be a blessing to Israel; but there are those in Israel whom he is *set for the fall of*, whose corruptions will be provoked, who will be prejudiced and enraged against him, and offended, and whose sin and ruin will be aggravated by the revelation of Jesus Christ. Men will be judged of by the thoughts of

their hearts, their thoughts concerning Christ; are they for *him*, or are they for his *adversaries*? The *word of God* is a discerner of the *thoughts* and *intents of the heart*, and by it we are discovered to ourselves, and shall be judged hereafter.

[2] It is true, Christ shall be a comfort to his mother; but be not thou too proud of it, for *a sword shall pass through thine own soul also*. He shall be a suffering Jesus; and, *First*, "Thou *shalt suffer with him*, by sympathy, more than any other of his friends, because of the nearness of thy relation, and strength of affection, to him." When he was abused, it was *a sword in her bones*. When she stood by his cross, and saw him dying, we may well think her inward grief was such that it might truly be said, *A sword pierced through her soul*, it cut her to the heart. *Secondly*, Thou shalt *suffer for him*. Many understand it as a prediction of her martyrdom; and some of the ancients say that it had its accomplishment in that.

II. He is taken notice of by one *Anna*, or *Ann*, a *prophetess*, that one of each sex might bear witness to him in whom both *men* and *women* are invited to believe, that they may be saved. Observe,

1. The account here given of this Anna, who she was. She was, (1) *A prophetess*; the Spirit of prophecy now began to revive, which had ceased in Israel above three hundred years. (2) She was *the daughter of Phanuel*; her father's name (says Grotius) is mentioned, to put us in mind of Jacob's *Phanuel*, or *Penuel* (Gen. xxxii 30), that now the mystery of

that should be unfolded, when in Christ we should as it were see God face to face, and our lives be preserved; and her name signifies *gracious.* (3) She was of *the tribe of Asher,* which was in Galilee; this, some think, is taken notice of to refute those who said, *Out of Galilee ariseth no prophet,* when no sooner did prophecy revive but it appeared from Galilee. (4) She was of *a 'great age,* a widow of about eighty-four years. (5) She was a constant resident *in* or at least attendant *on* the temple. Some think she had lodgings in the courts of the temple, either in an alms-house, being maintained by the temple charities; or, as a prophetess, she was lodged there, as in a proper place to be consulted and advised with by those that desired to know the mind of God; others think her not *departing from the temple* means no more, than that she was constantly there at the time of divine service: when any good work was to be done, she was ready to join in it.

2. The testimony she bore to our Lord Jesus (*v.* 38): *She came in at that instant* when the child was presented, and Simeon discoursed concerning him; she, who was so *constant* to the temple, could not miss the opportunity.

Now, (1) She *gave thanks likewise to the Lord,* just as Simeon, perhaps like him, wishing now to depart in peace.

(2) She, as a prophetess, instructed others concerning him: She *spoke of him to all them* that believed the Messiah would come, and with him *looked for redemption in Jerusalem.* Redemption was the thing wanted, waited for, and wished for; redemption *in Jerusalem,* for thence the *word of the Lord was to go forth,* Isa. ii. 3.

Lastly, Here is a short account of the infancy and childhood of our Lord Jesus.

1. *Where* he spent it, *v.* 39. When the ceremony of presenting the child, and purifying the mother, was all over, they *returned into Galilee.*

2. *How* he spent it, *v.* 40. In all things *it behoved him to be made like unto his brethren,* and therefore he passed through infancy and childhood as other children did, yet without sin; nay, with manifest indications of a divine nature in him. As other children, he *grew* in stature of body, and the improvement of understanding in his human soul, that his *natural* body might be a figure of his *mystical* body, which, though animated by a perfect spirit, yet *maketh increase of itself* till it comes to the *perfect man,* Eph. iv. 13, 16.· But, (1) Whereas other children are weak in understanding and resolution, he was *strong in spirit.* By the Spirit of God his human soul was endued with extraordinary· vigour, and all his faculties performed their offices in an extraordinary manner. He reasoned strongly, and his judgment was penetrating. (2) Whereas other children have *foolishness bound in their hearts,* which appears in what they say or do, he was *filled with wisdom,* not by any advantages of instruction and education, but by the operation of the Holy Ghost; every thing he said and did was wisely said, and wisely done, above his years. (3) Whereas other

children show that the corruption of nature is in them, and *the tares of sin* grow up with the *wheat of reason*, he made it appear that nothing but *the grace of God was upon him* (the wheat sprang up without tares), and that, whereas other children are by nature children of wrath, he was *greatly beloved*, and high in the favour of God; and God loved him, and cherished him, and took a particular care of him.

THE BOY CHRIST
(vv. 41–52)

We have here the only passage of story recorded concerning our blessed Saviour, from his infancy to the day of his showing to Israel at twenty-nine years old, and therefore we are concerned to make much of this, for it is in vain to wish we had more. Here is,

I. Christ's *going up with his parents* to Jerusalem, at the feast of the passover, vv. 41, 42. 1. It was their constant practice to attend there, according to the law, though it was a long journey, and they were poor, and perhaps not well able, without straitening themselves, to bear the expenses of it. 2. The child Jesus, at *twelve years old*, went up with them. The Jewish doctors say that at twelve years old children must begin to fast from time to time, that they may learn to fast on the day of atonement; and that at thirteen years old a child begins to be *a son of the commandment*, that is, obliged to the duties of adult church-membership, having been from his infancy, by virtue of his circumcision, *a son of the covenant*.

II. Christ's *tarrying behind his parents at Jerusalem*, unknown to them, in which he designed to give an early specimen of what he was reserved for.

1. His parents did not return till they had *fulfilled the days*; they had stayed there all the seven days at the feast, though it was not absolutely necessary that they should stay longer than the two first days, after which many went home.

2. The child *tarried behind in Jerusalem*, not because he was loth to go home, or shy of his parents' company, but because he had business to do there, and would let his parents know that he had a *Father in heaven*, whom he was to be *observant* of more than of *them*; and respect to *him* must not be construed disrespect *to them*.

3. His parents went the *first day's journey* without any suspicion that he was left behind, for they *supposed him to have been in the company*, v. 44. On these occasions, the crowd was very great, especially the first day's journey, and the roads full of people; and they concluded that he came along with some of their neighbours, and they *sought him among their kindred and acquaintance*, that were upon the road, going down.

4. When they found him not at their quarters at night, they *turned back again*, next morning, *to Jerusalem, seeking him*.

5. The *third day* they found him *in the temple*, in some of the apartments belonging to the temple, where the doctors of the law kept, not their courts, but their conferences rather, or their schools for

disputation; and there they found him *sitting in the midst of them* (v. 46), not standing as a *catechumen* to be examined or instructed by them, for he had discovered such measures of knowledge and wisdom that they admitted him to sit among them as a fellow or member of their society. This is an instance, not only that he was *filled with wisdom* (v. 40), but that he had both a desire to increase it and a readiness to communicate it; and herein he is an example to children and young people, who should learn of Christ to delight in the company of those they may get good by, and choose to *sit in the midst of* the doctors rather than in the midst of the players. Let them begin at *twelve years old*, and sooner, to enquire after knowledge, and to associate with those that are able to instruct them; it is a hopeful and promising presage in youth to be desirous of instruction. Many a youth at Christ's age now would have been playing with the *children in the temple*, but he was sitting with the *doctors in the temple*. (1) He *heard* them. Those that would *learn* must be *swift to hear*. (2) He *asked them questions*; whether, as a teacher (he had authority so to ask) or as a learner (he had humility so to ask) I know not, or whether as an associate, or joint-searcher after truth, which must be found out by mutual amicable disquisitions. (3) He returned *answers* to them, which were very surprising and satisfactory, v. 47. And his wisdom and *understanding* appeared as much in the questions he asked as in the answers he gave, so that all who heard him *were astonished*:

they never heard one so young, nor indeed any of their greatest doctors, talk sense at the rate that he did; like David, he had *more understanding than all his teachers*, yea, *than the ancients*, Ps. cxix. 99, 100.

6. His mother talked with him privately about it. When the company broke up, she took him aside, and examined him about it with a deal of tenderness and affection, v. 48. Joseph and Mary were both *amazed* to find him there, and to find that he had so much respect showed him as to be admitted to *sit among the doctors*, and to be taken notice of. His father knew he had only the name of a father, and therefore said nothing. But, (1) His mother told him how ill they took it: *"Son, why hast thou thus dealt with us?* Why didst thou put us into such a fright?"* They were ready to say, as Jacob of Joseph, *"A wild beast has devoured him*; or, He is fallen into the hands of some more cruel enemy, who has at length found out that he was the young child whose life Herod had sought some years ago." A thousand imaginations, we may suppose, they had concerning him, each more frightful than another. "Now, why hast thou given us occasion for these fears? *Thy father and I have sought thee, sorrowing*; not only troubled that we lost thee, but vexed at ourselves that we did not take more care of thee, to bring thee along with us." (2) He gently reproved their inordinate solicitude about him (v. 49): *"How is it that you sought me?* You might have depended upon it, I would have followed you home when I had

done the business I had to do here. I could not be lost in Jerusalem. Wist ye not that I *ought to be in my Father's house*?" so some read it; "where else should the Son be, who *abideth in the house for ever*? I ought to be," [1] "*Under my Father's care* and protection; and therefore you should have cast the care of me upon him, and not have burdened yourselves with it." Christ is a shaft hid in his Father's quiver, Isa. xlix. 2. He takes care of his church likewise, and therefore let us never despair of its safety. [2] "*At my Father's work*" (so we take it): "I must be *about my Father's business*, and therefore could not go home as soon as you might. *Wist ye not?* Have you not already perceived that concerning me, that I have devoted myself to the service of religion, and therefore must employ myself in the affairs of it?"

Lastly, Here is their return to Nazareth. This glimpse of his glory was to be short. It was now over, and he did not urge his parents either to come and settle at Jerusalem or to settle him there (though that was the place of improvement and preferment, and where he might have the best opportunities of showing his wisdom), but very willingly retired into his obscurity at Nazareth, where for many years he was, as it were, buried alive. Doubtless, he came up to Jerusalem, to worship at the feasts. three times a year, but whether he ever went again into the temple, to dispute with the doctors there, we are not told; it is not improbable but he might. But here we are told,

1. That he was *subject to his*

parents. Though once, to show that he was *more than a man*, he withdrew himself from his parents, to attend his heavenly Father's business, yet he did not, as yet, make that his constant practice, nor for many years after, but was *subject to them*, observed their orders, and went and came as they directed, and, as it should seem, worked with his father at the trade of a carpenter.

2. That his mother, though she did not perfectly understand her son's sayings, yet *kept them in her heart*, expecting that hereafter they would be explained to her, and she should fully understand them, and know how to make use of them.

3. That he improved, and came on, to admiration (*v.* 52): *He increased in wisdom and stature*. In the perfections of his divine nature there could be no increase; but this is meant of his human nature, his body increased in *stature* and bulk, he grew in the growing age; and his soul increased *in wisdom*, and in all the endowments of a human soul. And he increased in *favour with God and man*, that is, in all those graces that rendered him acceptable to God and man.

CHAPTER THREE

JOHN'S MINISTRY (*vv.* 1–14)

John's baptism introducing a new dispensation, it was requisite that we should have a particular account of it. Glorious things were said of John, what a distinguished favourite of Heaven he should be, and what a great blessing to this earth (*ch.* i. 15, 17); but we lost him in the deserts, and there he remains until *the day of his showing unto Israel, ch.* i. 80. And now at last that day dawns, and a welcome day it was to them that waited for it more than they that waited for the morning. Observe here,

I. The date of the beginning of John's baptism, when it was that he appeared; this is here taken notice of, which was not by the other evangelists, that the truth of the thing might be confirmed by the exact fixing of the time. And it is dated,

1. By the government of the heathen, which the Jews were under, to show that they were a conquered people, and therefore it was time for the Messiah to come to set up a spiritual kingdom, and an eternal one, upon the ruins of all the temporal dignity and dominion of David and Judah.

(1) It is dated by the reign of the Roman emperor; it was in the fifteenth year of Tiberius Cæsar, the third of the twelve Cæsars, a very bad man, given to covetousness, drunkenness, and cruelty.

(2) It is dated by the governments of the viceroys that ruled in the several parts of the Holy Land under the Roman emperor, which was another badge of their servitude, for they were all foreigners.

2. By the government of the Jews among themselves, to show that they were a corrupt people, and that therefore it was time that the Messiah should come, to reform them, *v.* 2. Annas and Caiaphas were the high priests. God had appointed that there should be but one high priest at a time, but here were two, to serve some ill turn or

other: one served one year and the other the other year; so some.

II. The origin and tendency of John's baptism.

1. The origin of it was *from heaven: The word of God came unto John, v.* 2. He received full commission and full instructions from God to do what he did.

2. The scope and design of it were to bring all the people of his country off from their sins and home to their God, *v.* 3. *He came* out of the wilderness *into all the country*, with some marks of distinction, *preaching* a new *baptism*; not a sect, or party, but a *profession*, or distinguishing badge. The sign, or ceremony, was such as was ordinarily used among the Jews, *washing with water*, by which proselytes were sometimes admitted, or disciples to some great master; but the meaning of it was, *repentance for the remission of sins*: that is, all that submitted to his baptism,

(1) Were thereby obliged to *repent of their sins,* to be *sorry* for what they had done amiss, and to *do so no more*.

(2) They were thereby assured of the pardon of their sins, upon their repentance.

III. The fulfilling of the scriptures in the ministry of John. The other evangelists had referred us to the same text that is here referred to, that of Esaias, *ch.* xl. 3.

IV. The general warnings and exhortations which he gave to those who submitted to his baptism, *vv.* 7-9. In Matthew he is said to have preached these same things to *many of the Pharisees and Sadducees*, that *came to his baptism*

(Matt. iii. 7–10); but here he is said to have spoken them *to the multitude, that came forth to be baptized of him, v.* 7. This was the purport of his preaching to all that came to him, and he did not alter it in compliment to the Pharisees and Sadducees, when they came, but dealt as plainly with them as with any other of his hearers. And as he did not flatter the *great*, so neither did he compliment the *many*, or make his court to them, but gave the same reproofs of sin and warnings of wrath to the *multitude* that he did to the Sadducees and Pharisees; for, if they had not the same faults, they had others as bad.

V. The particular instructions he gave to several sorts of persons, that enquired of him concerning their duty: the *people*, the *publicans*, and the *soldiers*. Some of the Pharisees and Sadducees came to his baptism; but we do not find them asking, *What shall we do?* They thought they knew what they had to do as well as he could tell them, or were determined to do what they pleased, whatever he told them. But the *people*, the *publicans*, and the *soldiers*, who knew that they had done amiss, and that they ought to do better, and were conscious to themselves of great ignorance and unacquaintedness with the divine law, were particularly inquisitive: *What shall we do?* Now John gives answer to each, according to their place and station.

(1) He tells the *people* their duty, and that is to be charitable (*v.* 11): *He that has two coats*, and, consequently, one to spare, let him *give*, or *lend* at least, *to him that has none*, to keep him warm. Perhaps he saw among his hearers some that were overloaded with clothes, while others were ready to perish in rags, and he puts those who had superfluities upon contributing to the relief of those that had not necessaries. The gospel requires *mercy*, and not sacrifice; and the design of it is to engage us to do all the good we can. *Food and raiment* are the two supports of life; he that hath *meat* to spare, let him give to him that is destitute of *daily food*, as well as he that hath clothes to spare: what we have we are but stewards of, and must use it, accordingly, as our Master directs.

(2) He tells the *publicans* their duty, the collectors of the emperor's revenue (*v.* 13): *Exact no more than that which is appointed you.* They must do justice between the government and the merchant, and not oppress the people in levying the taxes, nor any way make them heavier or more burdensome than the law had made them. They must not think that because it was their office to take care that the people did not defraud the prince they might therefore, by the power they had, bear hard upon the people; as those that have ever so little a branch of power are apt to abuse it: "No, keep to your *book of rates*, and reckon it enough that you collect for Cæsar the things that are Cæsar's, and do not enrich yourselves by taking more." The public revenues must be applied to the public service, and not to gratify the avarice of private persons. Observe, He does not direct the publicans to quit their places, and to go no more to the receipt of custom; the employment

is in itself lawful and necessary, but let them be just and honest in it.

(3) He tells the *soldiers* their duty, *v.* 14. Some think that these soldiers were of the Jewish nation and religion: others think that they were Romans; for it was not likely either that the Jews would serve the Romans or that the Romans would trust the Jews in their garrisons in their own nation; and then it is an early instance of Gentiles embracing the gospel and submitting to it. Military men seldom seem inclined to religion; yet these submitted even to the Baptist's strict profession, and desired to receive the *word of command* from him: *What must we do?* Those who more than other men have their lives in their hands, and are in deaths often, are concerned to enquire what they shall do that they may be *found in peace.* In answer to this enquiry, John does not bid them lay down their arms, and desert the service, but cautions them against the sins that soldiers were commonly guilty of; for this is fruit meet for repentance, to *keep ourselves from our iniquity.* [1] They must not be injurious to *the people* among whom they were quartered, and over whom indeed they were set: "*Do violence to no man.* Your business is to keep the peace, and prevent men's doing violence to one another; but do not you *do violence* to any. *Shake no man*" (so the word signifies); "do not put people into fear; for the sword of war, as well as that of justice, is to be a terror only to evil doers, but a protection to those that do well. Be not rude in your quarters; force not money from

people by frightening them. Shed not the blood of war in peace; offer no incivility either to man or woman, nor have any hand in the barbarous devastations that armies sometimes make." Nor must they *accuse any falsely* to the government, thereby to make themselves formidable, and get bribes. [2] They must not be injurious to their *fellow-soldiers*; for some think that caution, not to *accuse falsely*, has special reference to them: "Be not forward to complain one of another to your superior officers, that you may be revenged on those whom you have a pique against, or undermine those above you, and get into their places." *Do not oppress any*; so some think the word here signifies, as used by the LXX. in several passages of the Old Testament. [3] They must not be given to mutiny, or contend with their generals about their pay: "*Be content with your wages.* While you have what you agreed for, do not murmur that it is not more." It is discontent with what they have that makes men oppressive and injurious; they that never think they have enough themselves will not scruple at any the most irregular practices to make it more, by defrauding others.

JOHN'S BAPTISM (*vv.* 15–20)

We are now drawing near to the appearance of our Lord Jesus publicly; the Sun will not be long after the morning-star. We are here told,

I. How the people took occasion, from the ministry and baptism of John, to think of the Messiah, and to think of him as at the door, as now come. Thus the way of the Lord was *prepared*, and people were prepared to bid Christ welcome. Now when they observed what an excellent doctrine John Baptist preached, what a divine power went along with it, and what a tendency it had to reform the world, 1. They began presently to consider that now was the time for the Messiah to appear. 2. Their next thought was, "Is not this he that should come?" *All* thinking *men mused*, or reasoned, *in their hearts*, concerning John, *whether he were the Christ or not*.

II. How John disowned all pretensions to the honour of being himself the Messiah, but confirmed them in their expectations of him that really was the Messiah, *vv.* 16, 17. John's office, as a crier or herald, was to give notice that the *kingdom of God* and the King of that kingdom were *at hand*; and therefore, when he had told all manner of people severally what they must do ("You must do this, and you must do that"), he tells them one thing more which they must all do: they must expect the Messiah now shortly to appear. And this serves as an *answer* to their *musings* and debates concerning himself. Though he knew not their thoughts, yet, in declaring this, he *answered* them.

1. He declares that the utmost he could do was to *baptize* them *with water*. He had no access to *the Spirit*, nor could command *that* or work upon *that*; he could only exhort them to *repent*, and assure them of forgiveness, upon repentance; he could not work repent-

ance in them, nor confer remission on them.

2. He consigns them, and turns them over, as it were, to Jesus Christ, for whom he was sent to *prepare the way*, and to whom he was ready to transfer all the interest he had in the affections of the people, and would have them no longer to *debate* whether John was the Messiah or no, but to look for him that was really so.

(1) John owns the Messiah to have a greater *excellency* than he had, and that he was in all things preferable to him; he is one the *latchet of whose shoe* he does not think himself *worthy to loose*; he does not think himself worthy to be the meanest of his servants, to help him on and off with his shoes.

(2) He owns him to have a greater *energy* than he had: "He is *mightier than I*, and does that which I cannot do, both for the comfort of the faithful and for the terror of hypocrites and dissemblers."

The evangelist concludes his account of John's preaching with an *et cætera* (*v.* 18): *Many other things in his exhortation preached he unto the people*, which are not recorded.

III. How full a stop was put to John's preaching. When he was in the midst of his usefulness, going on thus successfully, he was imprisoned by the malice of Herod (*vv.* 19, 20): *Herod the tetrarch being reproved by him*, not only for living in incest with his brother Philip's wife, but for the many other *evils which Herod had done* (for those that are wicked in one instance are commonly so in many others), he could not *bear it*, but contracted an antipathy to him for his plain dealing, and *added* this wickedness to all the rest, which was indeed *above all*, that he *shut up John in prison*, put that burning and shining light under a bushel.

CHRIST'S PEDIGREE

The evangelist mentioned John's imprisonment before Christ's being baptized, though it was nearly a year after it, because he would finish the story of John's ministry, and then introduce that of Christ. Now here we have,

I. A short account of Christ's baptism, which had been more fully related by St. Matthew. Jesus came, to be baptized of John, and he was so, *vv.* 21, 22.

II. A long account of Christ's pedigree, which had been more briefly related by St. Matthew. Here is,

1. His age: *He now began to be about thirty years of age.* So old Joseph was when he stood before Pharaoh (Gen. xli. 46), David when he began to reign (2 Sam. v. 4), and at this age the priests were to enter upon the full execution of their office, Num. iv. 3.

2. His pedigree, *vv.* 23, &c. Matthew had given us somewhat of this. He goes no higher than Abraham, but Luke brings it as high as Adam. Matthew designed to show that Christ was the son of Abraham, in whom *all the families of the earth are blessed*, and that he was heir to the throne of David; and therefore he begins with Abraham, and brings the genealogy down to Jacob, who was the father of Joseph, an heir-male of the house of David: but Luke, de-

signing to show that Christ was the *seed of the woman*, that should break the serpent's head, traces his pedigree upward as high as Adam, and begins it with Eli, or Heli, who was the father, not of Joseph, but of the virgin Mary.

THE TEMPTATION
(*vv.* 1–13)

We have already had this report in full in Matthew.

Christ gave the devil opportunity to say and do all he could against him; he let him try all his force, and yet defeated him.

He then quitted the field: He *departed from him.* He saw it was to no purpose to attack him; he had *nothing in him* for his fiery darts to fasten upon; he had no blind side, no weak or unguarded part in his wall, and therefore Satan gave up the cause. Note, If we resist the devil, he will flee from us.

Yet he continued his malice against him, and departed with a resolution to attack him again; he departed but *for a season*, or till the season when he was again to be let loose upon him, not as a *tempter*, to draw him to *sin*, and so to strike at *his head*, which was what he now aimed at and was wholly defeated in; but as a *persecutor*, to bring him to *suffer* by Judas and the other wicked instruments whom he employed, and so to *bruise his heel*, which it was told him (Gen. iii. 15) he should have to do, and would do, though it would be the breaking of his *own head*. He *departed now* till that season came which Christ calls the *power of darkness* (*ch.* xxii. 53), and when the prince of this world would again *come*, John xiv. 30.

CHRIST IN THE SYNAGOGUE
(*vv.* 14–30)

Observe,

I. What is here said in general of his preaching, and the entertainment it met with *in Galilee*, a remote part of the country, distant from Jerusalem; it was a part of Christ's humiliation that he began his ministry there.

But, 1. Thither he came *in the power of the Spirit*. The same Spirit that qualified him for the exercise of his prophetical office strongly inclined him to it. He was not to wait for a call from men, for he had light and life in himself. 2. There he *taught in their synagogues*, their places of public worship, where they met, not, as in the temple, for ceremonial services, but for the moral acts of devotion, to read, expound, and apply, the word, to pray and praise, and for church-discipline; these came to be more frequent since the captivity, when the ceremonial worship was near expiring. 3. This he did so as that he gained a great reputation. *A fame of him went through all that region* (*v.* 14), and it was a good fame; for (*v.* 15) he *was glorified of all*.

II. Of his preaching at Nazareth, the city where he was brought up; and the entertainment it met with there. And here we are told how he *preached* there, and how he was *persecuted*.

How he preached there. In that observe,

(1) The opportunity he had for it: *He came to Nazareth when he* had gained a reputation in other places, in hopes that thereby something at least of the contempt and prejudice with which his countrymen would look upon him might be worn off.

(2) The call he had to it. [1] He *stood up to read*. [2] The *book of the prophet Esaias* was *delivered to him*, either by the ruler of the synagogue or by the minister mentioned (*v.* 20), so that he was no intruder, but duly authorized *on this occasion*. The second lesson for *that* day being in the prophecy of Esaias, they gave him that volume to read in.

(3) The text he preached upon. Now the book being *delivered to him*, [1] He *opened* it. The books of the Old Testament were in a manner *shut up* till Christ opened them, Isa. xxix. 11. [2] Now his text was taken out of Isa. lxi. 1, 2, which is here quoted at large, *vv.* 18, 19. There was a providence in it that that portion of scripture should be read that day, which speaks so very plainly of the Messiah, that they might be left inexcusable who *knew him not*, though they heard *the voices of the prophets* read *every sabbath day*, which bore witness of him, Acts xiii. 27. This text gives a full account of Christ's undertaking, and the work he came into the world to do.

He was qualified and commissioned,

1. To be a great *prophet*. He was *anointed to preach*; that is three times mentioned here, for that was the work he was now entering upon. Observe, (1) To *whom* he was to preach: to the *poor*; to those that were *poor in the world*. (2) *What* he

was to *preach*. In general, he must preach *the gospel*. Not only to preach to them, but to make that preaching effectual; to bring it, not only to their ears, but to their hearts, and deliver them into the mould of it. Three things he is to preach:—

[1] *Deliverance to the captives.* The gospel is a proclamation of liberty, like that to Israel in Egypt and in Babylon.

[2] *Recovering of sight to the blind.* He came not only by the word of his gospel to bring *light* to them that sat *in the dark*, but by the power of his grace to give sight to them that were *blind*.

[3] *The acceptable year of the Lord, v. 19.* He came to let the world know that the God whom they had offended was willing to be reconciled to them, and to *accept* of them upon new terms; that there was yet a way of making their services acceptable to him; that there is now a time of *good will toward men*.

2. Christ came to be a great *Physician*; for he was sent to *heal the broken-hearted*, to comfort and cure afflicted consciences, to give peace to those that were troubled and humbled for sins, and under a dread of God's wrath against them for them, and to bring them to rest who were weary and heavy-laden, under the burden of guilt and corruption.

3. To be a great *Redeemer*. He not only proclaims liberty to the captives. He came in God's name to discharge poor sinners that were debtors and prisoners to divine justice.

(4) Here is Christ's *application* of

this text to himself (*v.* 21): "*This day is this scripture fulfilled in your ears.* This, which Isaiah wrote by way of prophecy, I have now read to you by way of history." It now began to be fulfilled in Christ's entrance upon his public ministry; *now*, in the report they heard of his preaching and miracles in other places; *now*, in his preaching to them in their own synagogue. It is most probable that Christ went on, and showed particularly how this scripture was fulfilled in the doctrine he preached concerning *the kingdom of heaven at hand*; that that was preaching liberty, and sight, and healing, and all the blessings of *the acceptable year of the Lord.* Many other gracious words proceeded out of his mouth, which these were but the *beginning* of: for Christ often preached long sermons, which we have but a short account of. This was enough to introduce a great deal: *This day is this scripture fulfilled.*

(5) Here is the *attention* and *admiration* of the auditors.

[1] Their *attention* (*v.* 20): *The eyes of all them that were in the synagogue* (and, probably, there were a great many) *were fastened on him.*

[2] Their *admiration* (*v.* 22): *They all bore him witness* that he spoke admirably well, and to the purpose. They all commended him, and *wondered at the gracious words that proceeded out of his mouth*; and yet, as appears by what follows, they did not *believe in him*.

(6) Christ's anticipating an objection which he knew to be in the minds of many of his hearers. Observe,

[1] What the objection was (v. 23): "*You will surely say to me, Physician, heal thyself.*"

[2] How he answers this objection against the course he took.

First, By a plain and positive reason why he would not make Nazareth his headquarters (v. 24), because it generally holds true *that no prophet is accepted in his own country,* at least not so well, nor with such probability of doing good, as in some other country; experience seals this. For this reason, Christ declined working miracles, or doing any thing extraordinary, at Nazareth, because of the rooted prejudices they had against him there.

Secondly, By pertinent examples of two of the most famous prophets of the Old Testament, who chose to dispense their favours among foreigners rather than among their own countrymen, and that, no doubt, by divine direction.

How he was *persecuted* at Nazareth.

(1) That which provoked them was his taking notice of the favour which God by Elijah and Elisha showed to the Gentiles: *When they heard these things, they were filled with wrath* (v. 28), they were *all so*; a great change since v. 22, when they *wondered at the gracious words that proceeded out of his mouth*; thus uncertain are the opinions and affections of the multitude, and so very fickle.

(2) They were provoked to that degree that they made an attempt upon his life. This was a severe trial, now at his setting out, but a specimen of the usage he met with

when he *came to his own,* and they received him not.

(3) Yet he escaped, because his hour was not yet come: He *passed through the midst of them,* unhurt. Either he blinded their eyes, as God did those of the Sodomites and Syrians, or he bound their hands, or filled them with confusion, so that they could not do what they designed; for his work was not done, it was but just begun; his hour was not yet come, when it was come, he freely surrendered himself.

A DEMON EXPELLED
(vv. 31–44)

When Christ was expelled Nazareth, he came to Capernaum, another city of Galilee. The account we have in these verses of his preaching and miracles there we had before, Mark i. 21, &c.

CHAPTER FIVE
THE DRAUGHT OF FISHES
(vv. 1–11)

This passage of story fell, in order of time, before the two miracles we had in the close of the foregoing chapter, and is the same with that which was more briefly related by Matthew and Mark, of Christ's calling Peter and Andrew to be *fishers of men,* Matt. iv. 18, and Mark i. 16. They had not related this miraculous draught of fishes at that time, having only in view the calling of his disciples; but Luke gives us that story as one of the many signs which Jesus did in the presence of his disciples, which *had not been written* in the foregoing books, John xx. 30, 31. Observe here,

I. What vast *crowds* attended Christ's preaching: *The people pressed upon him to hear the word of God* (*v.* 1), insomuch that no house would contain them, but he was forced to draw them out to the *strand*. Christ was a popular preacher; and though he was able, at *twelve*, to *dispute* with the *doctors*, yet he chose, at *thirty*, to preach to the capacity of the *vulgar*. See how the people relished *good preaching*, though under all external disadvantages: they pressed to *hear the word of God*; they could perceive it to be the *word of God*, by the divine power and evidence that went along with it, and therefore they coveted to hear it.

II. What poor *conveniences* Christ had for preaching: *He stood by the lake of Gennessareth* (*v.* 1), upon a level with the crowd, so that they could neither see him nor hear him. So Christ *entered* into that *ship* that belonged to Simon, and begged of him that he would lend it him for a pulpit. There he *sat down*, and *taught the people* the good knowledge of the Lord.

III. What a particular acquaintance Christ, hereupon, fell into with these fishermen. They had had some conversation with him before, which began at John's baptism (John i. 40, 41); they were with him at *Cana of Galilee* (John ii. 2), and in Judea (John iv. 3); but as yet they were not called to attend him constantly, and therefore here we have them at their calling, and now it was that they were called into a more intimate fellowship with Christ.

1. When Christ had done preaching, he ordered Peter to apply himself to the business of his calling again: *Launch out into the deep, and let down your nets, v.* 4.

2. Peter having *attended* upon Christ in his *preaching*, Christ will *accompany* him in his *fishing*.

3. Christ ordered Peter and his ship's crew to *cast their nets into the sea*, which they did, in obedience to him, though they had been hard at it all night, and had *caught nothing, vv.* 4, 5. We may observe here

(1) How melancholy their business had now been: "*Master, we have toiled all the night*, when we should have been asleep in our beds, *and have taken nothing*, but have had our labour for our pains."

(2) How ready their obedience was to the command of Christ: *Nevertheless, at thy word, I will let down the net.* [1] Though they had *toiled all night*, yet, if Christ bid them, they will renew their toil, for they know that they who *wait on him shall renew their strength*, as work is renewed upon their hands; for every fresh service they shall have a fresh supply of *grace sufficient*. [2] Though they have *taken nothing*, yet, if Christ bid them *let down for a draught*, they will hope to take *something*. Note, We must not abruptly quit the callings wherein we are called because we have not the success in them we promised ourselves.

4. The draught of fish they caught was so much beyond what was ever known that it amounted to a miracle (*v.* 6): They *enclosed a great multitude of fishes*, so that *their net broke*, and yet, which is strange, they did not lose their draught.

Now by this vast draught of fishes, (1) Christ intended to show his *dominion* in the *seas* as well as on the *dry land*, over its *wealth* as over its *waves*. (2) He intended hereby to confirm the doctrine he had just now preached out of Peter's ship. (3) He intended hereby to repay Peter for the loan of his boat; for Christ's gospel will be sure to make amends, rich amends, for its kind entertainment. (4) He intended hereby to give a specimen, to those who were to be his ambassadors to the world, of the success of their embassy, that though they might for a time, and in one particular place, *toil* and *catch nothing*, yet they should be instrumental to bring in many to Christ, and enclose many in the gospel net.

5. The impression which this miraculous draught of fishes made upon Peter was very remarkable.

(1) All *concerned* were *astonished*, and the more *astonished* for their being *concerned*. All the boat's crew were *astonished at the draught of fishes which they had taken* (v. 9); *and so were also James and John, who were partners with Simon* (v. 10), and who, for aught that appears, were not so well acquainted with Christ, before this, as Peter and Andrew were. Now they were the more *affected* with it, [1] Because they *understood* it better than others did. [2] Because they were most *interested* in it, and *benefited* by it. Peter and his part-owners were gainers by this great draught of fishes; it was a rich booty for them and therefore it transported them, and their *joy* was a *helper* to their *faith*.

(2) Peter, above all the rest, was astonished to such a degree that he *fell down at Jesus's knees*, as he sat in the stern of his boat, and said, as one in an ecstasy or transport, that knew not where he was or what he said, *Depart from me, for I am a sinful man, O Lord*, v. 8. Not that he feared the weight of the fish would sink him because he was a sinful man, but that he thought himself unworthy of the favour of Christ's presence in his boat, and worthy that it should be to him a matter rather of terror than of comfort. [1] His acknowledgment was very just, and what it becomes us all to make: *I am a sinful man, O Lord.* [2] His inference from it was what *might have been* just, though really it was not so. If I be a *sinful man*, as indeed I am, I ought to say, "*Come to me, O Lord*, or let me come to thee, or I am undone, *for ever undone.*" But, considering what reason *sinful men* have to tremble before the holy Lord God and to dread his wrath, Peter may well be excused, if, in a sense of his own sinfulness and vileness, he cried out on a sudden, *Depart from me.*

6. The occasion which Christ took from this to intimate to Peter (v. 10), and soon after to James and John (Matt. iv. 21), his purpose to make them his apostles, and instruments of planting his religion in the world. When by Peter's preaching *three thousand souls* were, *in one day*, added to the church, then the type of this great draught of fishes was abundantly answered.

Lastly, The fishermen's farewell to their calling, in order to their constant attendance on Christ (v. 11): *When they had brought their ships to land*, instead of going to seek for a market for their fish, that they might make the best hand they could of this miracle, they *forsook all and followed him*, being more solicitous to serve the interests of Christ than to advance any secular interests of their own. It is observable that they *left all to follow Christ*, when their calling prospered in their hands more than ever it had done and they had had uncommon success in it. When *riches increase*, and we are therefore most in temptation to *set our hearts* upon them, then to quit them for the service of Christ, this is *thank-worthy*.

TWO HEALED (vv. 12–26)

Here is the cleansing of a leper, vv. 12–14. This narrative we had both in Matthew and Mark. It is here said to have been *in a certain city* (v. 12); it was in Capernaum, but the evangelist would not name it, perhaps because it was a reflection upon the government of the city that a leper was suffered to be *in it*.

Here is also, I. A general account of Christ's preaching and miracles, v. 17. 1. He was *teaching on a certain day*, not in the *synagogue*, but in a *private house*. 2. There he *taught*, he *healed* (as before, v. 15): *And the power of the Lord was to heal them*. It was *mighty* to heal them; it was *exerted* and *put forth* to heal them, to heal those whom he *taught* (we may understand it so), to heal their souls, to cure them of their spiritual diseases, and to give them a new life, a new nature.

II. A particular account of the cure of the man *sick of the palsy*, which was related much as it is here by both the foregoing evangelists.

NEW WINE, OLD BOTTLES
(vv. 27–39)

All this, except the last verse, we had before in Matthew and Mark; it is not the story of any *miracle in nature* wrought by our Lord Jesus, but it is an account of some of the *wonders of his grace*, which, to those who understand things aright, are no less cogent proofs of Christ's being sent of God than the other.

Christ would train up his followers gradually to the discipline of his family; for no man, having *drank old wine*, will *of a sudden*, straightway, *desire new*, or relish it, but will say, *The old is better*, because he has been *used to it*, v. 39. The disciples will be tempted to think their old way of living better, till they are by degrees trained up to this way whereunto they are called. Or, turn it the other way: "Let them be *accustomed* awhile to religious exercises, and then they will *abound* in them as much as you do: but we must not be too hasty with them."

CHAPTER SIX
SABBATH HEALING (vv. 1–11)

These two passages of story we had both in Matthew and Mark, and they were there laid together (Matt. xii. 1; Mark ii. 23; iii. 1), because, though happening at some distance of time from each other, both were designed to rectify the mistakes of the scribes and Pharisees concerning the sabbath day, on the *bodily rest* of which they laid greater stress and required greater strictness than the Law-giver intended.

APOSTLES CHOSEN (*vv.* 12–19)

In these verses, we have our Lord Jesus in *secret*, in *his family*, and in *public*; and in all three acting like himself.

I. In *secret* we have him *praying to God*, *v.* 12. This evangelist takes frequent notice of Christ's retirements, to give us an example of secret prayer, by which we must keep up our communion with God daily, and without which it is impossible that the soul should prosper.

II. In his *family* we have him nominating his immediate attendants, that should be the constant auditors of his doctrine and eye-witnesses of his miracles, that hereafter they might be sent forth as *apostles*, his *messengers* to the world, to preach his gospel to it, and plant his church in it, *v.* 13. The number of the apostles was *twelve*. Their names are here recorded; it is the *third time* that we have met with them, and in each of the *three* places the *order* of them differs, to teach both ministers and Christians not to be nice in precedency. He that in Mark was called *Thaddeus*, in Matthew *Lebbeus*, whose surname was *Thaddeus*, is here called *Judas the brother of James*, the same that wrote the epistle of Jude. Simon, who in Matthew and Mark was called the *Canaanite*, is here called *Simon*

Zelotes, perhaps for his great zeal in religion.

III. In *public* we have him *preaching* and *healing*, the two great works between which he divided his time, *v.* 17. He came down with the twelve from the mountain, and *stood in the plain*, ready to receive those that resorted to him; and there were presently gathered about him, not only the *company of his disciples*, who used to attend him, but also a great *multitude of people*, a mixed multitude *out of all Judea and Jerusalem*. 1. They *came to hear him*, and he *preached* to them. Those that have not good preaching near them had better travel far for it than be without it. 2. They came to be *cured* by him, and he *healed* them. Some were troubled *in body*, and some *in mind*; some had *diseases*, some had *devils*; but both the one and the other, upon their application to Christ, were *healed*, for he has power over *diseases* and *devils* (*vv.* 17, 18), over the effects and over the causes.

BLESSINGS AND WOES (*vv.* 20–26)

Here begins a practical discourse of Christ, which is continued to the end of the chapter, most of which is found in the *sermon upon the mount*, Matt. v. and vii. Some think that this was preached at some other time and place, and there are other instances of Christ's preaching the same things, or to the same purport, at different times; but it is probable that this is only the evangelist's abridgment of that sermon, and perhaps that in

Matthew too is but an abridgment; the beginning and the conclusion are much the same; and the story of the cure of the centurion's servant follows presently upon it, both there and here, but it is not material. In these verses, we have,

I. Blessings pronounced upon *suffering saints*, as *happy* people, though the world *pities them* (*v.* 20).

II. *Woes* denounced against *prospering sinners as miserable people*, though the world *envies them*. These we had not in Matthew. It should seem, the best exposition of *these woes*, compared with the foregoing *blessings*, is the parable of the *rich man* and Lazarus. Lazarus had the blessedness of those that are *poor*, and *hunger*, and *weep*, now, for in Abraham's bosom all the promises made to them who did so were *made good* to him; but the rich man had the *woes* that follow here, as he had the character of those on whom these woes are entailed.

1. Here is a *woe* to them that are *rich*, that is, that *trust in riches*, that have abundance of this world's wealth, and, instead of serving God with it, serve their lusts with it; woe to them, for *they have received their consolation*, that which they placed their happiness in, and were willing to take up with for a portion, *v.* 24. (1) It is the *folly* of carnal worldlings that they make the things of this world *their consolation*, which were intended only for their *convenience*. (2) It is their misery that they are *put off* with them as *their consolation*. Let them know it, to their terror, when they are parted from these things, there is an end of all their comfort,

a final end of it, and nothing remains to them but everlasting misery and torment.

2. Here is a *woe* to them that are *full* (*v.* 25), that are *fed to the full*, and have *more than heart could wish* (Ps. lxxiii. 7). They are *full of themselves*, without God and Christ. Woe to such, for *they shall hunger*, they shall shortly be *stripped* and *emptied* of all the things they are so proud of; and, when they shall have *left behind them* in the world all those things which are their fulness, they shall *carry away with them* such appetites and desires as the world they remove to will afford them no gratifications of; for all the delights of sense, which they are now so full of, will in hell be *denied*, and in heaven *superseded*.

3. Here is a *woe* to them that *laugh now*, that have always a *disposition to be merry*, and always something to *make merry with*. *Woe unto such*, for it is but *now*, for a little time, that they *laugh*; they shall *mourn and weep* shortly, shall *mourn and weep* eternally, in a world where there is nothing but *weeping and wailing*, endless, easeless, and remediless sorrow.

4. Here is a *woe* to them *whom all men speak well of*, that is, who make it their great and only care to gain the praise and applause of men, who value themselves upon that more than upon the favour of God and his acceptance (*v.* 26): "The false prophets indeed, that flattered your fathers in their wicked ways, that *prophesied smooth things* to them, were caressed and spoken well of; and, if you be in like manner cried up,

you will be justly suspected to deal deceitfully as they did."

MORE PRECEPTS (*vv.* 27–49)

Verses 27–36 agree with Matt. v. 38, to the end of that chapter: *I say unto you that hear* (v. 27), to all you that hear, and not to disciples only, for these are lessons of universal concern. *He that has an ear, let him hear*. Those that diligently hearken to Christ shall find he has something to say to them well worth their hearing.

The sayings of Christ in *vv.* 37–49 we had before in Matthew; some of them in *ch.* vii., others in other places. They were sayings that Christ often used; they needed only to be mentioned, it was easy to apply them. Grotius thinks that we need not be critical here in seeking for the coherence: they are golden sentences, like Solomon's proverbs or parables.

CHAPTER SEVEN

THE CENTURION'S SERVANT (*vv.* 1–10)

Some difference there is between this story of the cure of the centurion's servant as it is related here and as we had it in Matt. viii. 5, &c. There it was said that the centurion came to Christ; here it is said that he sent to him first some of the *elders of the Jews* (v. 3), and afterwards some other *friends*, v. 6.

This miracle is here said to have been wrought by our Lord Jesus *when he had ended all his sayings in the audience of the people*, v. 1. What Christ said he said *publicly*; whoever would might come and hear him: *In secret have I said*

nothing, John xviii. 20. Now, to give an undeniable proof of the *authority* of his *preaching word*, he here gives an incontestable proof of the *power* and *efficacy* of his *healing word*.

THE WIDOW'S SON (*vv.* 11–18)

We have here the story of Christ's raising to life a widow's son at Nain, that was dead and in the carrying out to be buried, which Matthew and Mark had made no mention of; only, in the general, Matthew had recorded it, in Christ's answer to the disciples of John, that *the dead were raised* up, Matt. xi. 5. Observe,

I. Where, and when, this miracle was wrought. It was the *next day after* he had cured the centurion's servant, *v.* 11. Christ was doing good *every day*, and never had cause to complain that he had *lost a day*. It was done at the gate of a small city, or town, called *Nain*, not far from Capernaum, probably the same with a city called *Nais*, which Jerome speaks of.

II. Who were the witnesses of it. It is as well attested as can be, for it was done in the sight of two crowds that met in or near the gate of the city.

III. How it was wrought by our Lord Jesus.

1. The person raised to life was a *young man*, cut off by death in the beginning of his days. That he was really dead was universally agreed. There could be no collusion in the case; for Christ was *entering into the town*, and had not seen him till now that he met him upon the bier. He was *carried out* of the city; for the Jews' burying-places were without their cities, and at some

distance from them. This young man was the *only son of his mother*, and *she a widow*. She depended upon him to be the staff of her old age, but he proves a broken reed; every man at his best estate is so. *Much people of the city was with her*, *condoling* with her loss, to *comfort* her.

2. Christ showed both his *pity* and his *power* in raising him to life, that he might give a specimen of both, which shine so brightly in man's redemption.

(1) See how *tender* his *compassions* are towards the afflicted (*v.* 13): *When the Lord saw* the poor widow following her son to the grave, *he had compassion on her*. Christ said, *Weep not*; and he could give her a reason for it which no one else could: "Weep not for a *dead son*, for he shall presently become a *living one*." This was a reason peculiar to her case; yet there is a reason common to all that sleep in Jesus, which is of equal force against inordinate and excessive grief for their death— that they shall rise again, shall rise in glory; and therefore we must *not sorrow as those that have no hope*, 1 Thess. iv. 13.

(2) See how *triumphant* his *commands* are over even death itself (*v.* 14): *He came, and touched the bier*, or coffin, in or upon which the dead body lay; for to him it would be no pollution. Hereby he intimated to the bearers that they should not proceed; he had something to say to the dead young man. Hereupon *they that bore him stood still*, and probably let down the bier from their shoulders to the ground, and opened the coffin, if it

was closed up; and then with solemnity, as one that had authority, and to whom belonged the issues from death, he said, *Young man, I say unto thee, Arise*. The young man was *dead*, and could not arise by any power of his own (no more can those that are spiritually dead in trespasses and sins); yet it was no absurdity at all for Christ to bid him *arise*, when a power went along with that word to *put life* into him. Christ's dominion over death was evidenced by the immediate effect of his word (*v.* 15): *He that was dead sat up*, without any help. Another evidence of life was that he *began to speak*; for whenever Christ gives us spiritual life he *opens the lips* in prayer and praise. And, *lastly*, he would not oblige this young man, to whom he had given a new life, to go along with him as his disciple, to minister to him (though he owned him even his own self), much less as a trophy or show to get honour by him, but *delivered him to his mother*, to attend her as became a dutiful son; for Christ's miracles were miracles of mercy, and a great act of mercy this was to this widow.

IV. What influence it had upon the people (*v.* 16): *There came a fear on all*; it frightened them all, to see a dead man start up alive out of his coffin in the open street, at the command of a man; they were all struck with wonder at this miracle, and *glorified God*. The Lord and his goodness, as well as the Lord and his greatness, are to be feared. The inference they drew from it was, "*A great prophet is risen up among us*, the great prophet that we have been long looking for; doubtless, he is one divinely inspired who can thus breathe life into the dead, and in him *God hath visited his people*, to redeem them, as was expected," Luke i. 68. This would be *life from the dead* indeed to all them that waited for the consolation of Israel.

TRIBUTE TO JOHN (*vv.* 19–35)

All this discourse concerning John Baptist, occasioned by his sending to ask whether he was the Messiah or no, we had, much as it is here related, Matt. xi. 2–19.

AT SIMON'S HOUSE (*vv.* 36–50)

When and where this passage of story happened does not appear; this evangelist does not observe order of time in his narrative so much as the other evangelists do. Who this woman was that here testified so great an affection to Christ does not appear; it is commonly said to be Mary Magdalene, but I find no ground in scripture for it: she is described (*ch.* viii. 2 and Mark xvi. 9) to be one *out of whom Christ had cast seven devils*; but that is not mentioned here, and therefore it is probable that it was not she. Now observe here,

I. The civil entertainment which a Pharisee gave to Christ, and his gracious acceptance of that entertainment (*v.* 36): *One of the Pharisees desired him that he would eat with him*. It appears that this Pharisee did not believe in Christ, for he will not own him to be a *prophet* (*v.* 39), and yet our Lord Jesus accepted his invitation, *went into his house, and sat down to meat*, that they might see he took the same liberty with Pharisees that he

did with publicans, in hopes of *doing them good*.

II. The great respect which a poor penitent sinner showed him, when he was at meat in the Pharisee's house. It was a woman in the city *that was a sinner*, a Gentile a *harlot*, I doubt, known to be so, and infamous. She *knew that Jesus sat at meat in the Pharisee's house*, and, having been converted from her wicked course of life by his preaching, she came to acknowledge her obligations to him, having no opportunity of doing it in any other way than by *washing* his feet, and anointing them with some sweet ointment that she brought with her for that purpose. The way of sitting at table then was such that their feet were partly *behind them*. Now this woman did not look Christ in the face, but came *behind him*, and did that part of a *maid-servant*, whose office it was to *wash the feet* of the guests (1 Sam. xxv. 41) and to prepare the ointments.

Now in what this good woman did, we may observe,

1. Her *deep humiliation* for sin. She stood behind him *weeping*; her eyes had been the inlets and outlets of sin, and now she makes them fountains of tears.

2. Her *strong affection* for the Lord Jesus. This was what our Lord Jesus took special notice of, that she *loved much*, *vv.* 42, 47. She *washed his feet*, in token of her ready submission to the meanest office in which she might *do him honour*. Nay, she washed them with *her tears*, tears of joy; she was in a transport, to find herself so near her Saviour, whom her soul loved.

She *kissed his feet*. It was a kiss of adoration as well as affection. *She wiped them with her hair*, as one entirely devoted to his honour. She anointed his feet in token of her consent to God's design in anointing his head with the *oil of gladness*. Note, All true penitents have a dear love to the Lord Jesus.

III. The offence which the Pharisee took at Christ, for admitting the respect which this poor penitent paid him (*v.* 39): *He said within himself* (little thinking that Christ knew what he thought), *This man, if he were a prophet*, would then have so much *knowledge* as to perceive that *this woman is a sinner*, is a Gentile, is a woman of ill fame, and so much *sanctity* as *therefore* not to suffer her to come so near him; for can one of such a character approach a prophet, and his heart not rise at it?

IV. Christ's justification of the woman in what she did to him, and of himself in admitting it. Christ knew what the Pharisee spoke *within himself*, and made answer to it: *Simon, I have something to say unto thee, v.* 40. Though he was kindly entertained at his table, yet even there he reproved him for what he saw amiss in him, and would not *suffer sin upon him*. Now Christ, in his answer to the Pharisee, reasons thus:—It is true this woman has been a sinner: he knows it; but she is a *pardoned* sinner, which supposes her to be a *penitent* sinner. What she did to him was an expression of her *great love* to her Saviour, by whom her sins were forgiven. If she was pardoned, who had been *so great a sinner*, it might reasonably be expected that she

should love her Saviour more than others, and should give greater proofs of it than others; and if this was the fruit of her love, and flowing from a sense of the pardon of her sins, it became him to accept of it, and it ill became the Pharisee to be offended at it. Now Christ has a further intention in this. The Pharisee doubted whether he was a *prophet* or no, nay, he did in effect deny it; but Christ shows that he was more than a prophet, for he is one that has *power on earth to forgive sins*, and to whom are due the affections and thankful acknowledgments of penitent pardoned sinners. Now, in his answer,

⊦. He by a parable forces Simon to acknowledge that the greater sinner this woman had been the greater love she ought to show to Jesus Christ when her *sins* were *pardoned, vv.* 41–43. A man had *two debtors* that were both insolvent, but one of them owed him *ten times* more than the other. He very freely *forgave them both*, and did not take the advantage of the law against them, did not order them and their children to be sold, or *deliver them to the tormentors*. Now they were both sensible of the great kindness they had received; but *which of them, will love him most*? Certainly, saith the Pharisee, he to *whom he forgave most*; and herein he rightly judged. Now we, being obliged to *forgive*, as we are and hope to be *forgiven*, may hence learn the duty between debtor and creditor.

(1) The *debtor*, if he have *any thing to pay*, ought to make satisfaction to his *creditor*. No man can reckon any thing *his own*, or

have any comfortable enjoyment of it, but that which is so when *all his debts are paid*.

(2) If God in his providence have disabled the debtor to pay his debt, the creditor ought not to be severe with him, nor to go to the utmost rigour of the law with him, but *freely to forgive him. Summum jus est summa injuria—The law stretched into rigour becomes unjust*. Let the unmerciful creditor read that parable, Matt. xviii. 23, &c., and tremble; for *they* shall have judgment without mercy that show no mercy.

(3) The debtor that has found his creditors merciful ought to be very grateful to them; and, if he cannot otherwise recompense them, ought to love them. We may learn here, [1] That *sin is a debt*, and *sinners are debtors* to God Almighty. [2] That some are deeper in debt to God, by reason of sin, than others are: *One owed five hundred pence and the other fifty*. The Pharisee was the less debtor, yet he a debtor too, which was more than he thought himself, but rather that God was his debtor, Luke xviii. 10, 11. [3] That, whether our debt be more or less, it is *more* than we are able to pay: *They had nothing to pay*, nothing at all to make a composition with; for the debt is great, and we have nothing at all to pay it with. [4] That the God of heaven is *ready* to forgive, *frankly* to *forgive*, poor sinners, upon gospel terms, though their debt be ever so great. [5] That those who have their sins *pardoned* are obliged to *love him* that pardoned them; and the more is forgiven them, the more they should love him.

2. He applies this parable to the different temper and conduct of the Pharisee and the sinner towards Christ. Though the Pharisee would not allow Christ to be a prophet, Christ seems ready to allow him to be in a justified state, and that he was one *forgiven*, though to him *less was forgiven*. He did indeed show some love to Christ, in inviting him to his house, but nothing to what this poor woman showed. "Observe," saith Christ to him, "she is one that has much forgiven her, and therefore, according to thine own judgment, it might be expected that she should love much more than thou dost, and so it appears. *Seest thou this woman? v*. 44. (1) "Thou didst not so much as order a basin of water to be brought, to wash my feet in, when I came in, wearied and dirtied with my walk, which would have been some refreshment to me; but she has done much more: *she has washed my feet with tears*, tears of affection to me, tears of affliction for sin, and has *wiped them with the hairs of her head*, in token of her great love to me." (2) "Thou didst not so much as kiss my cheek" (which was a usual expression of a hearty and affectionate welcome to a friend); "but *this woman has not ceased to kiss my feet* (v. 45), thereby expressing both a humble and an affectionate love." (3) "Thou didst not provide me a little common oil, as usual, to anoint my head with; but she has bestowed a box of precious *ointment* upon *my feet* (v. 46), so far has she outdone thee."

3. He silenced the Pharisee's cavil: *I say unto thee*, Simon, *her*

sins, which are many, are forgiven,
v. 47. He owns that she had been
guilty of *many sins*: "But they are
forgiven her, and therefore it is no
way unbecoming in me to accept her
kindness. They *are forgiven, for she
loved much.*" It should be rendered,
therefore she loved much; for it is
plain, by the tenour of Christ's
discourse, that her loving much was
not the *cause,* but the *effect,* of her
pardon, and of her comfortable
sense of it; for *we love God* because
he first loved us; he did not forgive
us because we first loved him. "But
to whom little is forgiven, as is
to thee, *the same loveth little,* as
thou dost." Hereby he intimates to
the Pharisee that his love to Christ
was so little that he had reason to
question whether he loved him at
all in sincerity; and, consequently,
whether indeed his sins, though
comparatively *little,* were forgiven
him.

4. He silenced her fears, who
probably was discouraged by the
Pharisee's conduct, and yet would
not so far yield to the discouragement as to fly off. (1) Christ said
unto her, *Thy sins are forgiven, v.* 48.
(2) Though there were those present who quarrelled with Christ, in
their own minds, for presuming to
forgive sin, and to pronounce
sinners absolved (*v.* 49), as those
had done (Matt. ix. 3), yet he *stood
to what he had said;* for as he had
there proved that he had *power to
forgive sin,* by curing the man sick
of the palsy, and therefore would
not here take notice of the cavil, so
he would now show that he had
pleasure in forgiving sin, and it was
his delight; he loves to speak
pardon and peace to penitents: *He*

*said to the woman, Thy faith hath
saved thee, v.* 50.

CHAPTER EIGHT
WOMEN DISCIPLES (*vv.* 1-3)

We are here told,

I. *What* Christ *made* the *constant
business* of his *life*—it was *preaching;* in that work he was indefatigable, and went about doing
good (*v.* 1).

II. *Whence* he *had* the *necessary
supports* of life: He lived upon the
kindness of his friends. There were
certain women, who frequently
attended his ministry, that *ministered to him of their substance, vv.*
2, 3.

1. They were such, for the most
part, as had been *Christ's patients,*
and were the monuments of his
power and mercy; they had been
*healed by him of evil spirits and
infirmities.* He is the physician both
of body and soul, and those who
have been *healed by him* ought to
study what they shall *render to him.*

2. One of them was Mary
Magdalene, out of whom had been
cast seven devils; a certain number
for an uncertain. Some think that
she was one that had been *very
wicked,* and then we may suppose
her to be the woman that *was a
sinner* mentioned just before, ch.
vii. 37.

3. Another of them was *Joanna
the wife of Chuza, Herod's steward.*
She had been his wife (so some),
but was now a widow, and left in
good circumstances. If she was now
his wife, we have reason to think
that her *husband,* though preferred
in Herod's court, had received the
gospel, and was very willing that

his wife should be both a hearer of Christ and a contributor to him.

4. There were many of them that *ministered to Christ of their substance*. It was an instance of the meanness of that condition to which our Saviour humbled himself that he needed it, and of his great humility and condescension that he accepted it. Though he was rich, yet for our sakes *he became poor*, and lived upon alms.

THE SOWER (*vv.* 4–21)

The former paragraph began with an account of Christ's industry in *preaching* (*v.* 1); this begins with an account of the people's industry in hearing, *v.* 4.

Now in these verses we have,

I. Necessary and excellent rules and cautions for hearing the word, in the parable of *the sower* and the explanation and application of it, all which we had twice before more largely.

II. Needful instructions given to those that are appointed to preach the word, and to those also that have heard it. 1. Those that have *received the gift* must *minister the same*; for a *candle* must not be *covered with a vessel* nor *put under a bed, v.* 16. Ministers and Christians are to be lights in the world, *holding forth the word of life*. Their light must shine before men; they must not only *be good*, but *do good*. 2. We must expect that what is now done *in secret*, and from unseen springs, will shortly be *manifested* and *made known, v.* 17. What is committed to you *in secret* should be made manifest *by you*; for your Master did not give you talents to be buried, but to be traded with.

Let that which is now hid be *made known*; for, if it be not manifested *by you*, it will be manifested *against you*, will be produced in evidence of your treachery. 3. The gifts we have will either be continued to us, or taken from us, according as we do, or do not, make use of them for the glory of God and the edification of our brethren: *Whosoever hath, to him shall be given, v.* 18.

III. Great encouragement given to those that prove themselves faithful *hearers of the word*, by being *doers of the work*, in a particular instance of Christ's respect to his disciples, in preferring them even before his nearest relations (*vv.* 19–21), which passage of story we had twice before.

FOUR MIRACLES (*vv.* 22–56)

We have here two illustrious proofs of the power of our Lord Jesus which we had before—his power over the *winds*, and his power over the *devils*. See Mark iv. v.

We also have here two miracles interwoven, as they were in Matthew and Mark—the raising of Jairus's daughter to life, and the cure of the woman that had an issue of blood, as he was going in a crowd to Jairus's house.

CHAPTER NINE

THE DISCIPLES SENT OUT (*vv.* 1–9)

We have here, I. The method Christ took to spread his gospel, to diffuse and enforce the light of it. He had *himself* travelled about, preaching and healing; but he could be only in one place at a time, and therefore now he *sent* his twelve disciples abroad, who by this time were pretty well instructed in the nature of the present dispensation, and able to instruct others and *deliver to them* what they had *received from the Lord*. For the confirming of their doctrine, because it was new and surprising, and very different from what they had been taught by the scribes and Pharisees, and because so much depended upon men's receiving, or not receiving it, he empowered them to work miracles (*vv.* 1, 2): He *gave them authority over all devils*, to dispossess them, and cast them out, though ever so numerous, so subtle, so fierce, so obstinate. He authorized and appointed them likewise to *cure diseases*, and to *heal the sick*, which would make them welcome wherever they came, and not only convince people's judgments, but gain their affections. This was their commission. Now observe,

1. What Christ directed them to do, in prosecution of this commission at this time, when they were not to *go far* or be *out long*. (1) They must not be solicitous to recommend themselves to people's esteem by their outward appearance. (2) They must depend upon Providence, and the kindness of their friends, to furnish them with what was convenient for them. (3) They must not change their lodgings, as suspecting that those who entertained them were *weary* of them; they have no reason to be so, for the ark is a guest that always pays well for its entertainment: "*Whatsoever house ye enter into there abide* (*v.* 4)."

(4) They must put on authority, and speak *warning* to those who *refused* them as well as comfort to those that *received* them, *v.* 5.

2. What they did, in prosecution of this commission (*v.* 6): *They departed* from their Master's presence; yet, having still his spiritual presence with them, his *eye* and his *arm* going along with them, and, thus borne up in their work, they *went through the towns*, some or other of them, all the towns within the circuit appointed them, *preaching the gospel, and healing every where*. Their work was the same with their Master's, doing good both to souls and bodies.

II. We have here Herod's perplexity and vexation at this. When the country sees such as these *healing the sick* in the name of Jesus it gives it an alarm. Now observe,

1. The *various speculations* it *raised* among the *people*, who, though they thought not *rightly*, yet could not but think *honourably*, of our Lord Jesus, and that he was an extraordinary person, one come from the other world; that either John Baptist, who was lately persecuted and slain for the cause of God, or *one of the old prophets*, that had been persecuted and slain long since in that cause, was *risen again*, to be recompensed for his sufferings by this honour put upon him; or that Elias, who was taken alive to heaven in a fiery chariot, *had appeared* as an express from heaven, *vv.* 7, 8.

2. The *great perplexity* it *created* in the mind of Herod: *When he had heard of all that was done* by

Christ, his guilty conscience flew in his face, and he was ready to conclude with them that *John was risen from the dead*. He *desired to see him*; and why did he not go and see him? Probably, because he thought it *below him* either to go to him or to send for him; he had enough of John Baptist, and cared not for having to do with any more such reprovers of sin. He desired to see him, but we do not find that ever he did, till he saw him at his bar, and then *he and his men of war set him at nought*, Luke xxiii. 11.

REFRESHMENT (*vv.* 10–17)

We have here, I. The account which the twelve gave their Master of the success of their ministry. They were not long out; but, *when they returned, they told him all that they had done*, as became servants who were sent on an errand. They told him *what they had done*, that, if they had done anything amiss, they might mend it next time.

II. Their *retirement*, for a little *breathing*: He *took them, and went aside privately into a desert place*, that they might have some relaxation from business and not be always upon the stretch.

III. The *resort* of the people to him, and the kind *reception* he gave them. They *followed* him, though it was into a *desert place*; for that is no desert where Christ is. 1. He *spoke unto them of the kingdom of God*, the laws of that kingdom with which they must be bound, and the privileges of that kingdom with which they might

be blessed. 2. He *healed them that had need of healing*, and, in a sense of their need, made their application to him.

IV. The plentiful provision Christ made for the multitude that attended him. With *five loaves* of bread, and *two fishes*, he fed *five thousand men*. This narrative we had twice before, and shall meet with it again; it is the only miracle of our Saviour's that is recorded by all the four evangelists.

PETER'S CONFESSION
(*vv.* 18–27)

In these verses, we have Christ discoursing with his disciples about the great things that *pertained to the kingdom of God*; and one circumstance of this discourse is taken notice of here which we had not in the other evangelists—that Christ was *alone praying*, and his *disciples with him*, when he entered into this discourse, *v.* 18. Observe, 1. Though Christ had much public work to do, yet he found some time to be *alone* in private, for converse with himself, with his Father, and with his disciples. 2. When Christ was alone he was *praying*. It is good for us to improve our solitude for devotion, that, *when we are alone*, we may *not be alone*, but may have *the Father with us*. 3. When Christ was alone, praying, his *disciples were with him*, to join with him in his prayer; so that this was a family-prayer.

He discourses with them,

I. Concerning himself; and enquires,

1. What *the people* said of him:

Who say the people that I am?
Christ knew better than they did,
but would have his disciples
made sensible, by the mistakes of
others concerning him, how happy
they were that were led into the
knowledge of him and of the truth
concerning him. Some said that
he was John Baptist, who was
beheaded but the other day;
others Elias, or *one of the old
prophets*; any thing but what he
was.

2. What *they* said of him. "Now
see what an advantage you have
by your discipleship; you know
better." "So we do," saith Peter,
"thanks be to our Master for it;
we know that thou art *the Christ
of God*, the *Anointed* of God, the
Messiah promised." Now one
would have expected that Christ
should have charged his disciples
who were so fully apprized and
assured of this truth, to publish it
to every one they met with; but
no, he *strictly charged them to
tell no man that thing* as yet,
because there is a time for all
things. After his resurrection, which
completed the proof of it, Peter
made the temple ring of it, that
*God had made this same Jesus
both Lord and Christ* (Acts ii. 36);
but as yet the evidence was not
ready to be summed up, and
therefore it must be concealed;
while it was so, we may conclude
that the belief of it was not necessary to salvation.

II. Concerning his own *sufferings* and *death*, of which he had
yet said little. Now that his
disciples were well established in
the belief of his being the Christ,
and able to bear it, he speaks of

them expressly, and with great
assurance, *v.* 22.

III. Concerning their sufferings
for him. So far must they be from
thinking how to *prevent* his sufferings that they must rather
prepare for their own.

1. We must *accustom* ourselves
to all instances of *self-denial* and
patience, v. 23.

2. We must *prefer the salvation
and happiness of our souls* before
any *secular concern* whatsoever.
Observe, In Matthew and Mark
the dreadful issue is a man's
losing his own soul, here it is
losing himself, which plainly intimates that *our souls* are *ourselves*.

3. We must therefore *never be
ashamed* of Christ and his gospel,
nor of any disgrace or reproach
that we may undergo for our
faithful adherence to him and it,
v. 26. *For whosoever shall be
ashamed of me and of my words,
of him shall the Son of man be
ashamed*, and justly. Observe here,
How Christ, to support himself
and his followers under present
disgraces, speaks *magnificently* of
the lustre of his second coming, in
prospect of which he *endured the
cross, despising the shame.* (1) He
shall come *in his own glory*. This
was not mentioned in Matthew
and Mark. He shall come in the
glory of the Mediator, *all that
glory* which the Father *restored to
him*, which he had with God
before the worlds were. (2) He
shall come *in his Father's glory*.
The Father will judge the world
by him, having committed all
judgment to him; and therefore
will publicly own him in the
judgment as the *brightness of his*

glory and the *express image* of his person. (3) He shall come in *the glory of the holy angels*. They shall all *attend* him, and *minister* to him, and add every thing they can to the lustre of his appearance. What a figure will the blessed Jesus make in that day! Did we believe it, we should never be ashamed of him or his words now.

Lastly, To encourage them in suffering for him, he assures them that *the kingdom of God* would now *shortly be set up,* notwithstanding the great opposition that was made to it, *v.* 27. "Though the second coming of the Son of man is at a great distance, the kingdom of God shall come in its power in the present age, while some here present are alive." They *saw the kingdom of God* when the Spirit was poured out, when the gospel was preached to all the world and nations were brought to Christ by it; they saw the kingdom of God triumph over the Gentile nations in their *conversion,* and over the Jewish nation in its *destruction.*

THE TRANSFIGURATION
(vv. 28–36)

We have here the narrative of Christ's transfiguration, which was designed for a specimen of that glory of his in which he will come to judge the world, of which he had lately been speaking, and, consequently, an encouragement to his disciples to suffer for him, and never to be ashamed of him. We had this account before in Matthew and Mark.

Here are divers circumstances

added and explained, which are very material.

1. We are *here* told that Christ had this honour put upon him when he was *praying*: He *went up into a mountain to pray,* as he frequently did (*v.* 28), and *as he prayed* he was *transfigured.* When Christ *humbled* himself to pray, he was thus *exalted.*

2. Luke does not use the word *transfigured* (which Matthew and Mark used), perhaps because it had been used so much in the Pagan theology, but makes use of a phrase equivalent, *the fashion of his countenance was another thing from what it had been*: his face shone far beyond what Moses's did when he came down from the mount; and *his raiment* was *white and glistering*: it was—*bright like lightning* (a word used only here), so that he seemed to be arrayed all with light, to *cover himself with light as with a garment.*

3. It was said in Matthew and Mark that Moses and Elias *appeared to them*; here it is said that they *appeared in glory,* to teach us that saints departed are *in glory,* are in a *glorious* state; they shine in glory.

4. We are here told what was the subject of the discourse between Christ and the two great prophets of the Old Testament: *They spoke of his decease, which he should accomplish at Jerusalem—his exodus, his departure*; that is, *his death.*

5. We are here told, which we were not before, that the disciples were *heavy with sleep, v.* 32. These three were now asleep, when Christ was in *his glory,* as after-

wards they were, when he was in *his agony*; see the *weakness* and *frailty* of human nature, even in the best, and what need they have of the grace of God.

Lastly, The apostles are here said to have kept this vision private. They *told no man in those days*, reserving the discovery of it for another opportunity, when the evidences of Christ's being the Son of God were completed in the pouring out of the Spirit, and that doctrine was to be published to all the world. As there is a time *to speak*, so there is a time to *keep silence*. Every thing is beautiful and useful in its season.

THE LUNATIC BOY
(vv. 37–50)

This passage of story in Matthew and Mark follows immediately upon that of Christ's transfiguration, and his discourse with his disciples after it; but here it is said to be *on the next day, as they were coming down from the hill*, which confirms the conjecture that Christ was transfigured *in the night*, and, it should seem, though they did not *make tabernacles* as Peter proposed, yet they found some shelter to repose themselves in all night, for it was not till next day that they *came down from the hill*, and then he found things in some disorder among his disciples, though not so bad as Moses did when he came down from the mount. When wise and good men are in their beloved retirements, they would do well to consider whether they are not wanted in their *public stations*.

FIRE FROM HEAVEN
(vv. 51–56)

This passage of story we have not in any other of the evangelists, and it seems to come in here for the sake of its affinity with that next before, for in this also Christ rebuked his disciples, because they envied for his sake. There, under colour of zeal for Christ, they were for silencing and restraining separatists; here, under the same colour, they were for putting infidels to death; and, as for *that*, so for *this* also, Christ reprimanded them, for a spirit of bigotry and persecution is directly contrary to the spirit of Christ and Christianity. Observe here,

I. The *readiness* and *resolution* of our Lord Jesus, in prosecuting his great undertaking for our redemption and salvation. Of this we have an instance, *v.* 51: *When the time was come that he should be received up, he stedfastly set his face to go to Jerusalem.* Observe 1. There was a time fixed for the sufferings and death of our Lord Jesus, and he knew well enough when it was, and had a clear and certain foresight of it, and yet was so far from keeping out of the way that then he appeared most publicly of all, and was most busy, knowing that his time was short. 2. When he saw his death and sufferings approaching, he looked through them and beyond them, to the glory that should follow; he looked upon it as the time when he should be *received up into glory* (1 Tim. iii. 16), received up into the highest heavens, to be enthroned there. 3. On this prospect of the joy set before him, he *stedfastly set his face to go to Jerusalem*, the place where he was to suffer and die. He *did not fail nor was discouraged*, but *set his face as a flint, knowing* that he should be not only *justified*, but glorified (Isa. 1. 7), not only not *run down*, but *received up*. How should this shame us *for*, and shame *us out of*, our backwardness to do and suffer for Christ!

II. The *rudeness* of the Samaritans in a *certain village* (not named, nor deserving to be so) who would not *receive him*, nor suffer him to stay in their town, though his way lay through it. Observe here, 1. How *civil* he was to them: *He sent messengers before his face*. 2. How *uncivil* they were to him, *v.* 53. They did not *receive him*, would not suffer him to come into their village, but ordered their watch to keep him out.

III. The *resentment* which James and John expressed of this affront, *v.* 54. When these two heard this message brought, they were all in a flame presently, and nothing will serve them but Sodom's doom upon this village: "Lord," say they, "give us leave to command fire to come down from heaven, not to *frighten* them only, but to *consume* them."

IV. The *reproof* he gave to James and John for their fiery, furious zeal (*v.* 55): He *turned* with a just displeasure, and *rebuked them*.

1. He shows them in particular their mistake: *Ye know not what manner of spirit ye are of*; that is,

(1) "You *are not aware* what an *evil spirit* and disposition you are of; how much there is of pride, and passion, and personal revenge, covered under this pretence of zeal for your Master." Note, There may be much corruption lurking, nay, and stirring too, in the hearts of good people, and they themselves not be sensible of it. (2) "You *do not consider* what a *good spirit*, directly contrary to this, you *should be of*. Surely you have yet to learn, though you have been so long learning, what the spirit of Christ and Christianity is. Have you not been taught to *love your enemies*, and to *bless them that curse you*, and to call for grace from heaven, not fire from heaven, upon them?"

2. He shows them the general design and tendency of his religion (*v.* 56): *The Son of man* is not himself come, and therefore does not send you abroad *to destroy men's lives, but to save them*.

V. His *retreat* from this village. Christ would not only not punish them for their rudeness, but would not insist upon his right of travelling the road (which was as free to him as to his neighbours), would not attempt to force his way, but quietly and peaceably *went to another village*, where they were not so stingy and bigoted, and there refreshed himself, and went on his way.

THE COST OF FOLLOWING
(*vv.* 57–62)

We have here an account of three different persons who offered themselves to follow Christ, and the answers that Christ gave to each of them. The two former we had an account of in Matt. viii. 19–22.

Here is another that is willing to follow Christ, but he must have a *little time* to *talk with his friends* about it.

Observe, 1. His request for a dispensation, *v.* 61. He said, *"Lord, I will follow thee*; I design no other, I am determined to do it; but *let me first go bid them farewell that are at home.*" This seemed reasonable. But that which was amiss in this is, (1) That he looked upon his following Christ as a melancholy, troublesome, dangerous thing; it was to him as if he were *going to die*, and therefore he must take *leave* of all his friends, never to *see them again*, or never *with any comfort*; whereas, in following Christ, he might be more a comfort and blessing to them than if he had continued with them. (2) That he seemed to have his worldly concerns more upon his heart than he ought to have, and than would consist with a close attendance to his duty as a follower of Christ. He seemed to hanker after his relations and family concerns, and he could not part easily and suitably from them, but they stuck to him. (3) That he was willing to enter into a temptation from his purpose of following Christ. To go and bid them *farewell* that were *at home at his house* would be to expose himself to the strongest solicitations imaginable to alter his resolution; for they would all be against it, and would *beg* and. *pray* that he would not *leave them.* Now it was presumption in him to thrust himself into such a

temptation. Those that resolve to walk with their Maker, and follow their Redeemer, must resolve that they will not so much as parley with their tempter.

2. The rebuke which Christ gave him for this request (*v.* 62): *"No man, having put his hand to the plough*, and designing to make good work of his ploughing, will *look back*, or look behind him, for then he makes balks with his plough, and the ground he ploughs is *not fit* to be sown; so thou, if thou hast a design to follow me and to reap the advantages of those that do so, yet if thou *lookest back* to a worldly life again and hankerest after that, if thou *lookest back* as Lot's wife did to Sodom which seems to be alluded to here, *thou art not fit for the kingdom of God.*" Note, Those who begin with the work of God must resolve to *go on* with it, or they will make nothing of it. Looking back inclines to *drawing back*, and *drawing back* is to *perdition.* Those are not fit for heaven who, having set their faces heavenward, face about. But he, and he only, that *endures to the end, shall be saved.*

CHAPTER TEN
THE SEVENTY SENT OUT
(*vv.* 1–16)

We have here the sending forth of seventy disciples, two and two, into divers parts of the country, to preach the gospel, and to work miracles in those places which Christ himself designed to visit, to make way for his entertainment. This is not taken notice of by the other evangelists: but the instructions here given them are much the same with those given to the twelve. Observe,

I. Their number: they were seventy. As in the choice of twelve apostles Christ had an eye to the twelve patriarchs, the twelve tribes, and the twelve princes of those tribes, so here he seems to have an eye to the *seventy* elders of Israel. Now,

1. We are glad to find that Christ had so many followers fit to be sent forth; his labour was not altogether in vain, though he met with much opposition. Many of those that were the companions of the apostles, whom we read of in the Acts and the Epistles, we may suppose, were of these seventy disciples.

2. We are glad to find there was work for so many ministers, hearers for so many preachers: thus the grain of mustard-seed began to *grow*, and the savour of the leaven to diffuse itself in the meal, in order to the leavening of the whole.

II. Their work and business: He sent them *two and two*, that they might strengthen and encourage one another. *If one fall, the other will help to raise him up.* He sent them, not to all the cities of Israel, as he did the *twelve*, but only *to every city and place whither he himself would come* (v. 1), as his harbingers; and we must suppose, though it is not recorded, that Christ soon after went to all those places whither he now sent them, though he could stay but a little while in a place. Two things they were ordered to do, the same that

Christ did wherever he came:—
1. They must *heal the sick* (v. 9), heal them *in the name of Jesus*, which would make people long to see this Jesus, and ready to entertain him whose name was so powerful. 2. They must publish the approach of the kingdom of God, its approach *to them*: "Tell them this, *The kingdom of God is come nigh to you*, and you now stand fair for an admission into it, if you will but look about you. Now is the *day of your visitation*, know and understand it." It is good to be made sensible of our advantages and opportunities, that we may lay hold of them. When the *kingdom of God comes nigh us*, it concerns us to go forth to meet it.

THE SUCCESS OF THE SEVENTY (vv. 17–24)

Now here we are told,

1. What account they gave him of the success of their expedition: *They returned again with joy* (v. 17); not complaining of the fatigue of their journeys, nor of the opposition and discouragement they met with, but rejoicing in their success, especially in casting out unclean spirits: *Lord, even the devils are subject unto us through thy name.* ⟳

II. What acceptance they found with him, and how he received this account.

1. He confirmed what they said, as agreeing with his own observation (v. 18): "My heart and eye went along with you; I took notice of the success you had, and I *saw Satan fall as lightning from*

The Success of the Seventy

heaven." Note, Satan and his kingdom fell before the preaching of the gospel. "I see how it is," saith Christ, "as you get ground the devil loseth ground." He falls *as lightning falls from heaven,* so suddenly, so irrecoverably, so visibly, that all may perceive it, and say, "See how Satan's kingdom totters, see how it tumbles." They triumphed in casting devils out of the bodies of people; but Christ sees and rejoices in the fall of the devil from the interest he has in the souls of men, which is called his power *in high places,* Eph. vi. 12.

2. He repeated, ratified, and enlarged their commission: *Behold I give you power to tread on serpents, v.* 19. Note, To him that hath, and useth well what he hath, more shall be given. They had employed their power vigorously against Satan, and now Christ entrusts them with greater power.

3. He directed them to turn their joy into the right channel (*v.* 20): "*Notwithstanding in this rejoice not, that the spirits are subject unto you,* that they have been so, and shall be still so, but *rather rejoice because your names are written in heaven,* because you are chosen of God to eternal life, and are the children of God through faith." Christ, who knew the counsels of God, could tell them that their *names were written in heaven,* for it is the *Lamb's book of life* that they are written in. Note, Power to become the children of God is to be valued more than a power to work miracles; for we read of those who did *in Christ's name cast out devils,* as Judas did, and yet will be disowned by Christ in the great day.

4. He offered up a solemn thanksgiving to his Father, for employing such mean people as his disciples were in such high and honourable services, *vv.* 21, 22. This we had before (Matt. xi. 25–27), only here it is prefixed that *in that hour Jesus rejoiced.* It was fit that particular notice should be taken of *that* hour, because there were so few such, for he was a *man of sorrows.* In *that hour* in which he saw Satan fall, and heard of the good success of his ministers, *in that hour he rejoiced.*

THE GOOD SAMARITAN
(*vv.* 25–37)

We have here Christ's discourse with a lawyer about some points of conscience, which we are all concerned to be rightly informed in, and are so here, from Christ, though the questions were proposed with no good intention.

I. We are concerned to know what that good is which we should do in *this* life, in order to attain *eternal life.* A question to this purport was proposed to our Saviour by a *certain lawyer,* or *scribe,* only with a design to *try* him, not with a desire to be instructed by him, *v.* 25. The lawyer *stood up,* and *asked him, Master, what shall I do to inherit eternal life?* Now this question being started, observe,

1. How Christ turned him over to the divine law, and bade him follow the direction of that. Though he knew the thoughts and intents of his heart, he did not

answer him according to the folly of that, but according to the wisdom and goodness of the question he asked. He answered him with a question: *What is written in the law? How readest thou? v.* 26.

2. What a good account he gave of the law, of the principal commandments of the law, to the observance of which we must bind ourselves if we would inherit eternal life. He did not, like a Pharisee, refer himself to the tradition of the elders, but, like a good textuary, fastened upon the two first and great commandments of the law, as those which he thought must be most strictly observed in order to the obtaining of *eternal life*, and which included all the rest, *v.* 27. (1) We must *love God with all our hearts*, must look upon him as the best of beings, in himself most amiable, and infinitely perfect and excellent; as one whom we lie under the greatest obligations to, both in gratitude and interest. We must prize him, and value ourselves by our relation to him; must please ourselves in him, and devote ourselves entirely to him. Our love to him must be sincere, hearty, and fervent; it must be a superlative love, a love that is as strong as death, but an intelligent love, and such as we can give a good account of the grounds and reasons of. It must be an *entire* love; he must have our *whole* souls, and must be served with *all that is within us*. We must love nothing *besides him*, but what we love *for him* and in subordination to him. (2) We must love our neighbours as *ourselves*, which we

shall easily do, if we, as we ought to do, love God *better than ourselves*. We must wish well to all and ill to none; must do all the good we can in the world and no hurt, and must fix it as a rule to ourselves to do to others as we would they should do to us; and this is to love our neighbour *as ourselves*.

3. Christ's approbation of what he said, *v.* 28. Though he came to tempt him, yet what he said that was good Christ commended: *Thou hast answered right*. So far is right; but the hardest part of this work yet remains: "*This do, and thou shalt live*; thou shalt *inherit eternal life*.

4. His care to avoid the conviction which was now ready to fasten upon him. He was *willing to justify himself*, and therefore cared not for carrying on that discourse, but saith, in effect, as another did (Matt. xix. 20), *All these things have I kept from my youth up*.

II. We are concerned to know who is our neighbour, whom by the second great commandment we are obliged to love. This is another of this lawyer's queries, which he started only that he might *drop* the former, lest Christ should have forced him, in the prosecution of it, to *condemn himself*, when he was resolved to *justify* himself. Now observe,

1. What was the corrupt notion of the Jewish teachers in this matter. Dr. Lightfoot quotes their own words to this purport: "Where he saith, *Thou shalt love thy neighbour, he excepts all Gentiles*, for they are not *our neighbours*,

but those only that are of our own nation and religion."

2. How Christ corrected this inhuman notion, and showed, by a parable, that whomsoever we *have need* to receive kindness *from*, and *find ready* to show us the kindness *we need*, we cannot but look upon as *our neighbour*; and therefore ought to look upon all those as such who need our kindness, and to show them kindness accordingly, though they be not of our own nation and religion. Now observe,

(1) The parable itself, which represents to us a poor Jew in distressed circumstances, succoured and relieved by a good Samaritan. Let us see here,

[1] How he was *abused* by his *enemies*. The honest man was travelling peaceably upon his lawful business in the road, and it was a great road that led from Jerusalem to Jericho, *v.* 30. This poor man *fell among thieves*. They not only took his money, but stripped him of his clothes, and, that he might not be able to pursue them, or only to gratify a cruel disposition (for otherwise *what profit was there in his blood?*) they *wounded him*, and left him *half dead*, ready to die of his wounds.

[2] How he was *slighted* by those who should have been his friends, who were not only men of his own nation and religion, but one a priest and the other a Levite, men of a public character and station; nay, they were men of professed sanctity, whose offices obliged them to tenderness and compassion (Heb. v. 2), who ought to have taught others their duty in such a case as this, which was to *deliver them that were drawn unto death*; yet they would not themselves do it. It is sad when those who should be examples of charity are prodigies of cruelty, and when those who should, by displaying the mercies of God, open the bowels of compassion in others, shut up their own.

[3] How he was *succoured* and *relieved* by a *stranger*, a *certain Samaritan*, of that nation which of all others the Jews most despised and detested and would have no dealings with. This man had some humanity in him, *v.* 33. The priest had his heart hardened against one of *his own people*, but the Samaritan had his opened towards one of *another* people. *When he saw him he had compassion on him*, and never took into consideration what country he was of. See how friendly this good Samaritan was. *First*, He *went to* the poor man, whom the priest and Levite kept at a distance from; he enquired, no doubt, how he came into this deplorable condition, and condoled with him. *Secondly*, He did the surgeon's part, for want of a better. He *bound up his wounds*, making use of his own linen, it is likely, for that purpose; and poured *in oil and wine*, which perhaps he had with him; wine to wash the wound, and oil to mollify it, and close it up. He did all he could to ease the pain, and prevent the peril, of his wounds, as one whose heart bled with them. *Thirdly*, He *set him on his own beast*, and went on foot himself, and *brought him to an inn. Fourthly*, He *took care of him* in the inn,

got him to bed, had food for him that was proper, and due attendance, and, it may be, prayed with him. Nay, *Fifthly,* As if he had been his own child, or one he was obliged to look after, when he left him next morning, he left money with the landlord, to be laid out for his use, and passed his word for what he should spend more.

Now this parable is applicable to another purpose than that for which it was intended; and does excellently set forth the kindness and love of God our Saviour towards sinful miserable man. We were like this poor distressed traveller. Satan, our enemy, had *robbed* us, *stripped* us, *wounded* us; such is the mischief that sin hath done us. We were by nature more than *half dead,* twice dead, in trespasses and sins; utterly unable to help ourselves, for we were without strength. The law of Moses, like the priest and Levite, the ministers of the law, *looks upon us,* but has no compassion on us, gives us no relief, *passes by on the other side,* as having neither pity nor power to help us; but then comes the blessed Jesus, that good Samaritan (and they said of him, by way of reproach, *he is a Samaritan*), he has compassion on us, he binds up our bleeding wounds (Ps. cxlvii. 3; Isa. lxi. 1), pours in, not *oil and wine,* but that which is infinitely more precious, *his own blood.* He takes care of us, and bids us put all the expenses of our cure upon his account; and all this though he was none of us, till he was pleased by his voluntary condescension to make himself so, but infinitely

above us. This magnifies the riches of his love, and obliges us all to say, "How much are we indebted, and what shall we render?"

(2) The application of the parable. [1] The truth contained in it is extorted from the lawyer's own mouth. "Now tell me," saith Christ, *"which of these three was neighbour to him that fell among thieves* (v. 36), the priest, the Levite, or the Samaritan? Which of these did the neighbour's part?" To this the lawyer would not answer, as he ought to have done, "Doubtless, the Samaritan was"; but, *"He that showed mercy on him*; doubtless, he was a good neighbour to him, and very neighbourly, and I cannot but say that it was a good work thus to save an honest Jew from perishing." [2] The duty inferred from it is pressed home upon the lawyer's own conscience: *Go, and do thou likewise.*

MARTHA AND MARY
(vv. 38–42)

We may observe in this story,

I. The entertainment which Martha gave to Christ and his disciples at her house, v. 38. Observe,

1. Christ's coming to the village where Martha lived: *As they went* (Christ and his disciples together), he and they with him *entered into a certain village.* This village was *Bethany,* nigh to Jerusalem, whither Christ was now going up, and he took this in his way.

2. His reception at Martha's house: *A certain woman, named Martha, received him into her*

house, and made him welcome, for she was the housekeeper.

II. The attendance which Mary, the sister of Martha, gave upon the word of Christ, *v.* 20. She *heard his word*. It seems, our Lord Jesus, as soon as he came into Martha's house, even before entertainment was made for him, addressed himself to his great work of preaching the gospel. He presently took the chair with solemnity; for Mary sat to hear him, which intimates that it was a continued discourse.

III. The care of Martha about her domestic affairs: But Martha *was cumbered about much serving* (*v.* 40), and that was the reason why she was not where Mary was— sitting at Christ's feet, to hear his word. She was providing for the entertainment of Christ and those that came with him. Observe here,

1. Something *commendable*, which must not be overlooked. (1) Here was a commendable *respect to our Lord Jesus*; for we have reason to think it was not for ostentation, but purely to testify her good-will to him, that she made this entertainment. (2) Here was a commendable *care of her household affairs*.

2. Here was something *culpable*, which we must take notice of too. (1) She was for *much serving*. Her heart was upon it, to have a very sumptuous and splendid entertainment; great plenty, great variety, and great exactness, according to the fashion of the place. (2) She was *cumbered* about it; she was just *distracted* with it. Note, Whatever cares the providence of God casts upon us we must not be

cumbered with them, nor be disquieted and perplexed by them. *Care* is good and duty; but *cumber* is sin and folly. (2) She was *then cumbered about much serving* when she should have been with her sister, sitting at Christ's feet to hear his word.

IV. The *complaint* which Martha made to Christ against her sister Mary, for not *assisting* her, upon this occasion, in the *business of the house* (*v.* 40): "*Lord, dost thou not care that my sister*, who is concerned as well as I in having things done well, *has left me to serve alone*? Therefore dismiss her from attending thee, and bid her come and help me." Now,

1. This complaint of Martha's may be considered as a *discovery* of her *worldliness*: it was the language of her inordinate care and cumber.

2. It may be considered as a discouragement of Mary's piety and devotion. Her sister should have *commended* her for it, should have told her that she was in the right; but, instead of this, she *condemns* her as wanting in her duty.

V. The reproof which Christ gave to Martha for her inordinate care, *v.* 41. She appealed to him, and he gives judgment against her: *Martha, Martha, thou art careful and troubled about many things*, whereas but *one thing is needful*.

1. He reproved her, though he was at this time her guest. Her fault was her over-solicitude to entertain him, and she expected he should justify her in it, yet he publicly checked her for it.

2. When he reproved her, he

called her by her name, *Martha*;
for reproofs are *then* most likely
to do good when they are *particular*, applied to particular persons and cases, as Nathan's to
David, *Thou art the man.*

3. Christ reproves her, both for
the *intenseness* of her care ("Thou
art *careful and troubled, divided*
and *disturbed* by thy care"), and
for the *extensiveness of it*, "about
many things; thou dost *grasp* at
many *enjoyments*, and so art
troubled at many *disappointments*.
Poor Martha, thou hast many
things to fret at, and this puts thee
out of humour, whereas less ado
would serve."

4. That which aggravated the
sin and folly of her care was that
but one thing is needful. There is
need of *one heart* to attend upon
the word, not divided and hurried
to and fro, as Martha's was at
this time. *The one thing needful* is
certainly meant of · that which
Mary made her choice—*sitting at*
Christ's feet, to hear his word.

VI. Christ's approbation and
commendation of Mary for her
serious piety: *Mary hath chosen
the good part.* Mary said nothing
in her own defence; but, since
Martha has appealed to the
Master, to him she is willing to
refer it, and will abide by his
award; and here we have it.

1. She had justly given the
preference to that which best
deserved it; for *one thing is needful,*
this one thing that she has done, to
give up herself to the guidance of
Christ, and *receive the law* from
his mouth.

2. She had herein wisely done
well for herself. Christ *justified*

Mary against her sister's clamours.
But this was not all; he *applauded*
her for her wisdom: *She hath
chosen the good part*; for she
chose to be with Christ, to take
her part with him; she chose the
better business, and the better
happiness, and took a better way
of *honouring* Christ and of *pleasing*
him, by receiving his word into her
heart, than Martha did by providing for his entertainment in her
house.

CHAPTER ELEVEN
PRAYER (*vv.* 1–13)

Prayer is one of the great laws of
natural religion. That man is a
brute, is a monster, that never
prays, that never gives glory to his
Maker, nor feels his favour, nor
owns his dependence upon him.
One great design therefore of
Christianity is to *assist us in
prayer*, to enforce the duty upon
us, to instruct us in it, and encourage us to expect advantage by
it. Now here,

I. We find Christ himself *praying
in a certain place*, probably where
he used to pray, *v.* 1. As God, he
was *prayed to*; as man, he *prayed*;
and, though he was a Son, yet
learned he this obedience. This
evangelist has taken particular
notice of Christ's *praying often*,
more than any other of the evangelists: when he was baptized
(*ch.* iii. 21), he was *praying*; he
*withdrew into the wilderness, and
prayed* (*ch.* v. 16); he *went out into
a mountain to pray, and continued
all night in prayer* (*ch.* vi. 12); he
was *alone praying* (*ch.* ix. 18);
soon after, he *went up into a*

mountain to pray, and *as he prayed he was transfigured* (*ch.* ix. 28, 29); and here he was *praying in a certain place*. Thus, like a genuine son of David, he *gave himself unto prayer*, Ps. cix. 4.

II. His disciples applied themselves to him for direction in prayer.

Now, 1. Their request is, "*Lord, teach us to pray*; give us a rule or model by which to go in praying, and put words into our mouths."

2. Their plea is, "*As John also taught his disciples.* He took care to instruct his disciples in this necessary duty, and we would be taught as they were, for we have a better Master than they had."

III. Christ gave them direction, much the same as he had given them before in his sermon upon the mount, Matt. vi. 9, &c. In Mathew he had directed them to pray *after this manner*; here, *When ye pray, say*; which intimates that the Lord's prayer was intended to be used both as a form of prayer and a directory.

There are some differences between the Lord's prayer in Matthew and in Luke, by which it appears that it was not the design of Christ that we should be *tied up* to these very words, for then there would have been no variation.

POWER OVER SATAN
(*vv.* 14–26)

The substance of these verses we had in Matt. xii. 22, &c. Christ is here giving a general proof of his divine mission, by a particular proof of his power over Satan, his conquest of whom was an indication of his great design in coming

into the world, which was, to *destroy the works of the devil*. Here too he gives an earnest of the success of that undertaking. He is here casting out *a devil* that made the poor possessed man *dumb*: in Matthew we are told that he was *blind* and *dumb*. When the devil was forced out by the word of Christ, the *dumb* spoke immediately, echoed to Christ's word, and the lips were opened to show forth his praise.

TRUE BLESSING
(*vv.* 27, 28)

We had not this passage in the other evangelists, nor can we tack it, as Dr. Hammond does, to that of Christ's mother and brethren desiring to speak with him (for this evangelist also has related that in *ch.* viii. 19), but it contains an interruption much like that, and, like that, occasion is taken from it for instruction.

1. The applause which an affectionate, honest, well-meaning woman gave to our Lord Jesus, upon hearing his excellent discourses. While the scribes and Pharisees despised and blasphemed them, this good woman (and probably she was a person of some quality) admired them, and the wisdom and power with which he spoke: *As he spoke these things* (*v.* 27), with a convincing force and evidence, a *certain woman of the company* was so pleased to hear how he had confounded the Pharisees, and conquered them, and put them to shame, and cleared himself from their vile insinuations, that she

could not forbear crying out, "*Blessed is the womb that bore thee*. What an admirable, what an excellent man is this! Surely never was there a greater or better born of a woman: happy the woman that has him for her son. I should have thought myself very happy to have been the mother of one that *speaks as never man spoke*, that has so much of the grace of heaven in him, and is so great a blessing to this earth." This was *well said*, as it expressed her high esteem of Christ, and that for the sake of his doctrine; and it was not amiss that it reflected honour upon the virgin Mary his mother, for it agreed with what she herself had said (*ch.* i. 48), *All generations shall call me blessed*; some even of this generation, bad as it was. Note, To all that believe the word of Christ the person of Christ is precious, and he is *an honour*, 1 Pet. ii. 7. Yet we must be careful, lest, as this good woman, we too much magnify the honour of his natural kindred, and so *know him after the flesh*, whereas we must now henceforth *know him so no more*.

2. The occasion which Christ took from this to pronounce *them* more happy who are his faithful and obedient followers than she was who bore and nursed him. He does not deny what this woman said, nor refuse her respect to him and his mother; but leads her from this to that which was of higher consideration, and which more concerned her: *Yea, rather, blessed are they that hear the word of God, and keep it*, *v.* 28. He thinks them so; and his saying

that they are so makes him so, and should make us of his mind. This is intended partly as a *check* to her, for doting so much upon his bodily presence and his human nature, partly as an *encouragement* to her to hope that she might be as happy as his own mother, whose happiness she was ready to envy, if she would *hear the word of God and keep it*. Note, Though it is a great privilege to hear the word of God, yet those only are truly blessed, that is, blessed of the Lord, that hear it and *keep* it, that keep it in memory, and keep to it as their way and rule.

SIGN OF JONAH
(*vv.* 29–36)

Christ's discourse in these verses shows two things:—

I. What is the *sign* we may *expect* from God for the *confirmation* of our *faith*. The great and most convincing proof of Christ's being sent of God, and which they were yet to wait for, after the many signs that had been given them, was the resurrection of Christ from the dead. Here is,

1. A reproof to the people for demanding other signs than what had already been given them in great plenty. They came *seeking a sign*, they came to gaze, to have something to talk of when they went home; and it is an *evil generation* which nothing will awaken and convince, no, not the most sensible demonstrations of divine power and goodness.

2. A promise that yet there should be *one sign* more given

Sign of Jonah

them, different from any that had yet been given them, even the *sign of Jonas the prophet*, which in Matthew is explained as meaning the *resurrection of Christ*. As Jonas being cast into the sea, and lying there three days, and then coming up alive and preaching repentance to the Ninevites, was a sign to them, upon which they turned from their evil way, so shall the death and resurrection of Christ, and the preaching of his gospel immediately after to the Gentile world, be the last warning to the Jewish nation.

3. A warning to them to improve this sign; for it was at their peril if they did not. (1) The *queen of Sheba* would *rise up in judgment against them*, and condemn *their unbelief*, *v*. 31. She was a stranger to the commonwealth of Israel, and yet so readily gave credit to the report she heard of the glories of a king of Israel, that, notwithstanding the prejudices we are apt to conceive against foreigners, she came from the uttermost parts of the earth to *hear his wisdom*, not only to satisfy her curiosity, but to inform her mind, especially in the knowledge of the true God and his worship, which is upon record, to her honour; and, behold, a *greater than Solomon is here, more than a Solomon is here*; that is, says Dr. Hammond, more of wisdom and more heavenly divine doctrine than ever was in all Solomon's words or writings; and yet these wretched Jews will give no manner of regard to what Christ says to them, though he be in the midst of them. (2) The Ninevites would rise up in judgment against them, and condemn their impenitency (*v*. 32): They *repented at the preaching of Jonas*; but here is preaching which far exceeds that of Jonas, is more powerful and awakening, and threatens a much sorer ruin than that of Nineveh, and yet none are startled by it, to turn *from their evil way*, as the Ninevites did.

II. What is the *sign* that God *expects* from us for the *evidencing* of our faith, and that is the serious practice of that religion which we profess to believe, and a readiness to entertain all divine truths, when brought to us in their proper evidence. Now observe,

1. They had *the light* with all the advantage they could desire.

2. Having the *light*, their concern was to have the *sight*, or else to what purpose had they the light? Be the *object* ever so *clear*, if the *organ* be not *right*, we are never the better: *The light of the body is the eye* (*v*. 34), which receives the light of the candle when it is brought into the room. So the light of the soul is the understanding and judgment, and its power of discerning between good and evil, truth and falsehood. If the *eye of the* soul be *evil*,—if the judgment be *bribed* and *biassed* by the corrupt and vicious dispositions of the mind, by pride and envy, by the love of the world and sensual pleasures,—if the understanding be *prejudiced* against divine truths, and resolved not to admit them, though brought with ever so convincing an evidence,—it is no wonder that the *whole body*, the whole soul, should be *full of*

darkness, *v.* 34. How can they have instruction, information, direction, or comfort, from the gospel, that wilfully shut their eyes against it? and what hope is there of such? what remedy for them? The inference hence therefore is, *Take heed that the light which is in thee be not darkness*, *v.* 35. Take heed that the eye of the mind be not blinded by partiality, and prejudice, and sinful aims. Be sincere in your enquiries after truth, and ready to receive it in the light, and love, and power of it; and not as the men of *this generation* to whom Christ preached, who never sincerely *desired* to know God's will, nor *designed* to do it, and therefore no wonder that they *walked on in darkness*, wandered *endlessly*, and perished *eternally*.

PHARISEES REPROVED
(vv. 37–54)

Christ here says many of those things to a Pharisee and his guests, in a *private* conversation at table, which he afterwards said in a *public* discourse in the temple (Matt. 23); for what he said in public and private was *of a piece*. Here is,

I. Christ's going to dine with a Pharisee that very civilly invited him to his house (*v.* 37): *As he spoke*, even while he was speaking, a *certain Pharisee* interrupted him with a request to him to come and *dine with him*, to come *forthwith*, for it was dinner-time. Note, Christ's disciples must learn of him to be *conversable*, and not *morose*. Though we have need to

be *cautious* what company we keep, yet we need not be *rigid*, nor must we therefore *go out of the world*.

II. The offence which the Pharisee took at Christ, as those of that sort had sometimes done at the disciples of Christ, for not *washing before dinner*, *v.* 38. Was it not strictly commanded by the canons of their church? It was so, and *therefore* Christ would not do it, because he would witness against their assuming a power to impose that as a matter of religion which *God commanded them not*.

III. The sharp reproof which Christ, upon this occasion, gave to the Pharisees, without begging pardon even of the Pharisee whose guest he now was; for we must not flatter our best friends in any evil thing.

1. He reproves them for placing religion so much in those instances of it which are only external, and fall under the eye of man, while those were not only *postponed*, but quite *expunged*, which respect the soul, and fall under the eye of God, *vv.* 39, 40.

2. He reproves them for laying stress upon trifles, and neglecting the weighty matters of the law, *v.* 42.

3. He reproves them for their pride and vanity, and affectations of precedency and praise of men (*v.* 43).

4. He reproves them for their hypocrisy, and their colouring over the wickedness of their hearts and lives with specious pretences (*v.* 44).

IV. The testimony which he bore also against the lawyers or

scribes, who made it their business to *expound* the law according to the tradition of the elders, as the Pharisees did to *observe* the law according to that tradition.

1. There was one of that profession who resented what he said against the Pharisees (*v.* 45): "*Master, thus saying thou reproachest us also,* for we are scribes; and are we therefore hypocrites?"

2. Our Lord Jesus thereupon took them to task (*v.* 46): *Woe unto you also, ye lawyers*; and again (*v.* 52): *Woe unto you, lawyers.*

(1) The lawyers are reproved for making the services of religion more *burdensome* to others, but more *easy* for themselves, than God had made them (*v.* 46).

(2) They are reproved for pretending a veneration for the memory of the prophets whom their fathers killed, when yet they hated and persecuted those in their own day who were sent to them on the same errand, to call them to repentance, and direct them to Christ, *vv.* 47–49.

(3) They are reproved for opposing the gospel of Christ, and doing all they could to obstruct the progress and success of it, *v.* 52.

Lastly, In the close of the chapter we are told how spitefully and maliciously the scribes and *Pharisees* contrived to draw him into a snare, *vv.* 53, 54. Note, Faithful reprovers of sin must expect to have many enemies, and have need to set a watch before the door of their lips, because of *their observers* that watch for their slips.

CHAPTER TWELVE
CHRIST'S PREACHING
(*vv.* 1–12)

We find here, I. A vast auditory that was got together to hear Christ preach. Though in the morning sermon, when they were *gathered thickly together* (*ch.* xi. 29), he had severely reproved them, as an *evil generation that seek a sign,* yet they renewed their attendance on him; so much better could the people bear *their* reproofs than the Pharisees *theirs.*

II. The instructions which he gave his followers, in the hearing of this auditory.

1. He began with a caution against *hypocrisy.*

(1) The description of that sin which he warns them against: *It is the leaven of the Pharisees.* [1] It is *leaven*; it is *spreading* as leaven, *insinuates* itself into the whole man, and all that he does; it is *swelling* and *souring* as leaven, for it puffs men up with pride, embitters them with malice, and makes their service unacceptable to God. [2] It is the leaven of the Pharisees: "It is the sin they are most of them found in. Make not *your* religion a *cloak of maliciousness,* as they do theirs."

(2) A good reason against it: "*For there is nothing covered that shall not be revealed, vv.* 2, 3. It is to no purpose to dissemble, for, sooner or later, truth will come out; and a *lying tongue is but for a moment.*"

2. To this he added a charge to them to be faithful to the trust reposed in them, and not to betray it, through cowardice or base fear.

(1) "The power of your enemies is a limited power (*v.* 4): *I say unto you, my friends*" (Christ's disciples are his friends, he calls them *friends*, and gives them this *friendly* advice), "*be not afraid*; do not disquiet yourselves with tormenting fears of the power and rage of men." Note, Those whom Christ owns for *his friends* need not be afraid of any enemies.

(2) God is to be feared more than the most powerful men: "*I will forewarn you whom you shall fear* (*v.* 5): that you may fear man less, fear God more.*"

(3) The lives of good Christians and good ministers are the particular care of divine Providence, *vv.* 6, 7. To encourage us in times of difficulty and danger, we must have recourse to our first principles, and build upon them. Now a firm belief of the doctrine of God's universal providence, and the extent of it, will be satisfying to us when at any time we are in peril, and will encourage us to trust God in the way of duty.

(4) "You will be owned or disowned by Christ, in the great day, according as you now own or disown him," *vv.* 8, 9. [1] To engage us to *confess Christ before men*, whatever we may lose or suffer for our constancy to him, and how dear soever it may cost us, we are assured that they who *confess Christ* now shall be owned by him in the great day *before the angels of God*, to their everlasting comfort and honour. [2] To deter us from *denying* Christ, and a cowardly *deserting* of his truths and ways, we are here assured that those who *deny Christ*, and

treacherously depart from him, whatever they may save by it, though it were life itself, and whatever they may *gain* by it, though it were a kingdom, will be vast losers at last, for they shall be *denied before the angels of God*.

(5) The errand they were shortly to be sent out upon was of the highest and last importance to the children of men, to whom they were sent, *v.* 10. Let them be bold in preaching the gospel, for a sorer and heavier doom would attend those that rejected them than those that now rejected Christ himself, and opposed him.

(6) Whatever trials they should be called out to, they should be sufficiently furnished for them, and honourably brought through them, *vv.* 11, 12.

THE RICH MAN
(*vv.* 13–21)

We have in these verses,

I. The application that was made to Christ, very unseasonably, by one of his hearers, desiring him to interpose *between him and his brother* in a matter that concerned the estate of the family (*v.* 13): "*Master, speak to my brother*; speak as a prophet, speak as a king, speak with authority; he is one that will have regard to what thou sayest; speak to him, *that he divide the inheritance with me*."

II. Christ's refusal to interpose in this matter (*v.* 14): *Man, who made me a judge or divider over you?* In matters of this nature, Christ will not assume either a *legislative* power to alter the settled rule of inheritances, or a *judicial* power to determine controversies concerning them. Now this shows us what is the nature and constitution of Christ's kingdom. It is a spiritual kingdom, and not of this world. 1. It does not interfere with civil powers, nor take the authority of princes out of their hands. Christianity leaves the matter as it found it, as to civil power. 2. It does not intermeddle with civil rights; it obliges all to do justly, according to the settled rules of equity, but dominion is not founded in grace. 3. It does not *encourage* our *expectations* of worldly advantages by our religion. If this man will be a disciple of Christ, and expects that in consideration of this Christ should give him his brother's estate, he is mistaken; the rewards of Christ's disciples are of another nature. 4. It does not *encourage* our *contests* with our brethren, and our being rigorous and high in our demands, but rather, for peace' sake, to recede from our right.

III. The necessary caution which Christ took occasion from this to give to his hearers. Though he came not to be a *divider* of men's estates, he came to be a director of their consciences about them, and would have all take heed of harbouring that corrupt principle which they saw to be in others the *root* of *so much evil*. Here is,

1. The caution itself (*v.* 15): *Take heed and beware of covetousness*.

2. The reason of it, or an argument to enforce this caution: *For a man's life consisteth not in the abundance of the things which he possesseth*; that is, "our happiness and comfort do not depend upon our having a great deal of the wealth of this world."

3. The illustration of this by a parable which gives us the life and death of a *rich man*, and leaves us to judge whether he was a *happy* man.

(1) Here is an account of his worldly wealth and abundance (*v.* 16): *The ground of a certain rich man brought forth plentifully*.

(2) Here are the workings of his heart, in the midst of this abundance.

[1] What his *cares* and *concerns* were. When he saw an extraordinary crop upon his ground, instead of *thanking God* for it, or rejoicing in the opportunity it would give him of doing the more good, he afflicts himself with this thought, *What shall I do, because I have no room to bestow my fruits?*

[2] What his *projects* and *purposes* were, which were the result of his cares, and were indeed absurd and foolish like them (*v.* 18): "*This will I do*, and it is the wisest course I can take, *I will pull down my barns*, for they are too little, and I will *build greater, and there will I bestow all my fruits and my goods*, and then I shall be at ease." Now here, *First*, It was folly for him to call the fruits of the ground *his* fruits and *his* goods. It is *my corn* (saith God) and *my wine*, Hos. ii. 8, 9. *Secondly*, It was folly for him to *hoard up* what he had, and then to think it *well bestowed*. There will I bestow it *all*; as if none must be bestowed upon the poor, none upon his family, none upon the Levite and *the stranger*, the

fatherless and the widow, but all in the great barn. *Thirdly*, It was folly for him to let his *mind* rise with his *condition*; when his ground brought forth more plentifully than usual, then to talk of bigger barns, as if the next year must needs be as fruitful as this, and much more abundant, whereas the barn might be as much too big the next year as it was too little this. *Fourthly*, It was folly for him to contrive and resolve all this *absolutely* and *without reserve*. This *I will* do: *I will* pull down my barns and *I will* build greater, yea, that *I will*; without so much as that necessary proviso, *If the Lord will, I shall live*, Jam. iv. 13–15.

[3] What his *pleasing hopes* and *expectations* were, when he should have made good these projects. "Then *I will say to my soul, thou hast much goods laid up for many years* in these barns; now *take thine ease*, enjoy thyself, *eat, drink, and be merry*," *v.* 19.

(3) Here is God's sentence upon all this; and we are sure that his judgment is according to truth. God said he did ill for himself: *Thou fool, this night thy soul shall be required of thee, v.* 20. Now observe what God said,

[1] The character he gave him: *Thou fool*.

[2] The sentence he passed upon him, a sentence of death: *This night thy soul shall be required of thee; they shall require thy soul* (so the words are), and then *whose shall those things be which thou hast provided?* He thought he had goods that should be his for many years, but he must part from them *this night*; he thought he should

enjoy them himself, but he must leave them to he knows not who.

First, It is a *force*, an *arrest*; it is the *requiring of the soul*, that soul that thou art making such a fool of. God shall require it; he shall require an account of it. "Man, woman, what hast thou done with they soul. Give an account of that stewardship."

Secondly, It is a *surprise*, an *unexpected* force. It is *this night*, this *present* night, without delay; there is no giving bail, or begging a day. This *pleasant* night, when thou art promising thyself many years to come, now thou must die, and go to judgment.

Thirdly, It is the leaving of all *those things* behind *which they have provided*, which they have laboured for, and prepared for hereafter, with abundance of toil and care. All that which they have placed their happiness in, and built their hope upon, and raised their expectations from, they must leave behind.

Fourthly, It is leaving them to they *know not who*: "Then *whose shall those things be*? Not *thine* to be sure, and thou knowest not what *they* will prove for whom thou didst design them."

Fifthly, It is a demonstration of his folly. Then it will appear that he took pains to lay up treasure in a world he was hastening from, but took no care to lay it up in the world he was hastening to.

Lastly, Here is the application of this parable (*v.* 21): *So is he*, such a fool, a fool in God's judgment, a fool upon record, that *layeth up treasure for himself, and is not rich towards God*. This is the way and this is the end of such a man.

MORE PRECEPTS (vv. 22–40)

Our Lord Jesus is here inculcating some needful useful lessons upon his disciples, which he had before taught them, Matt. vi. 25, &c.; and the arguments here used are much the same, designed for our encouragement to cast all our care upon God, which is the *right way* to *ease* ourselves of it.

He also charges them to get ready, and to keep in a readiness for Christ's coming, when all those who have laid up their treasure in heaven shall enter upon the enjoyment of it, *vv.* 35, &c.

1. Christ is our *Master*, and we are his *servants*, not only *working* servants, but *waiting* servants, servants that are to do him honour, in *waiting* on him, and attending his motions: *If any man serve me, let him follow me. Follow the Lamb whithersoever he goes*. But that is not all: they must do him honour in *waiting for him*, and expecting his return. We must be as men that *wait for their Lord*, that sit up late while he stays out late, to be ready to receive him.

2. Christ our Master, though now *gone from us*, will *return again*. He *will come* to take cognizance of his servants, and, that being a *critical day*, they shall either stay with him or be turned out of doors, according as they are found in that day.

3. The time of our Master's return is uncertain; it will be *in the night*, it will be *far* in the night, when he has long *deferred* his coming, and when many have done

looking for him; in the *second watch*, just before midnight, or in the *third watch*, next after midnight, *v.* 38. His coming to us, at our death, is uncertain, and to many it will be a great surprise; for *the Son of man cometh at an hour that ye think not* (*v.* 40), without giving notice beforehand.

4. That which he expects and requires from his servants is that they be *ready to open to him immediately*, whenever he comes (*v.* 36), that is, that they be in a frame fit to receive him, or rather to be received by him; that they be found *as* his servants, in the posture that becomes them.

5. Those servants will be happy who shall be found ready, and in a good frame, when their Lord shall come (*v.* 37): *Blessed are those servants*.

6. We are *therefore* kept at uncertainty concerning the precise time of his coming that we may be always ready; for it is no thanks to a man to be ready for an attack, if he know beforehand just the time when it will be made: *The good man of the house, if he had known what hour the thief would have come*, though he were ever so careless a man, *would* yet *have watched*, and have frightened away the thieves, *v.* 39. But we do not know at what hour the alarm will be given us, and therefore are concerned to watch at all times, and never to be off our guard.

THE DISCIPLES' RESPONSIBILITY (vv. 41–53)

Here is, I. Peter's question, which he put to Christ upon occasion of the foregoing parable (*v.* 41). Peter desires Christ to explain himself, and to direct the arrow of the foregoing parable to the mark he intended. Lord, said Peter, was it intended for *us*, or for *all*? To this Christ gives a direct answer (Mark xiii. 37): *What I say unto you, I say unto all.* Yet here he seems to show that the apostles were primarily concerned in it.

II. Christ's reply to this question, directed to Peter and the rest of the disciples. Now our Lord Jesus here tells them,

1. What was their *duty* as *stewards*, and what the *trust* committed to them. (1) They are made *rulers of God's household*, under Christ, whose own the house is. (2) Their business is to give God's children and servants *their portion of meat*, that which is proper for them and allotted to them. (3) To give it to them *in due season*, at that time and in that way which are most suitable to the temper and condition of those that are to be fed. (4) Herein they must approve themselves *faithful* and *wise*.

2. What would be their happiness if they approved themselves faithful and wise (*v.* 43): *Blessed is that servant*, (1) That is *doing*, and is not idle, nor indulgent of his ease; even the rulers of the household must be *doing*, and make themselves *servants of all*. (2) That is *so* doing, doing as he should be, giving them their *portion of meat*, by public preaching and personal application. (3) That is *found* so doing when his Lord comes; that perseveres to the end, notwithstanding the difficulties he may meet with in the way.

3. What a dreadful reckoning there would be if they were treacherous and unfaithful, *vv.* 45, 46. If that servant begin to be quarrelsome and profane, he shall be called to an account, and severely punished. We had all this before in Matthew.

III. A further discourse concerning his own sufferings, which he expected, and concerning the sufferings of his followers, which he would have them also to live in expectation of. In general (*v.* 49): *I am come to send fire on the earth.* By this some understand the preaching of the gospel, and the pouring out of the Spirit, holy fire. But, by what follows, it seems rather to be understood of the fire of *persecution.* Christ is not the Author of it, as it is the sin of the incendiaries, the *persecutors*; but he *permits* it, nay, he *commissions* it, as a *refining* fire for the *trial* of the *persecuted.*

1. He must himself suffer many things; he must pass through this fire that was already kindled (*v.* 50): *I have a baptism to be baptized with.* Afflictions are compared both to *fire* and *water*, Ps. lxvi. 12; lxix. 1, 2. Christ's sufferings were both. He calls them a *baptism* (Matt. xx. 22); for he was watered or sprinkled with them. He must be sprinkled with his own blood, and with the blood of his enemies, Isa. lxiii. 3. Christ in his sufferings *devoted* himself to his Father's honour, and *consecrated* himself a priest for evermore, Heb. vii. 27, 28. He longed for the time when he should suffer and die, having an eye to the glorious issue of his sufferings.

2. He tells those about him that they also must bear with hardships and difficulties (v. 51): "*Suppose ye that I came to give peace on earth, to give you a peaceable possession of the earth, and outward prosperity on the earth?*" You will find,

(1) "That the effect of the preaching of the gospel will be *division.*" Not but that the design of the gospel and its proper tendency are to unite the children of men to one another, to knit them together in holy love, and, if all would receive it, this would be the effect of it; but there being multitudes that not only will not receive it, but oppose it, and have their corruptions exasperated by it, and are enraged at those that do receive it, it proves, though not the *cause*, yet the *occasion* of *division.*

(2) "That this *division* will reach into private families, and the preaching of the gospel will give occasion for discord among the nearest relations" (v. 53). Therefore let not the disciples of Christ promise themselves *peace upon earth*, for they are sent forth *as sheep in the midst of wolves.*

SEEING THE SIGN (vv. 54–59)

Having given his disciples *their* lesson in the foregoing verses, here Christ turns to *the people*, and gives them *theirs*, v. 54. Two things he specifies:—

I. Let them learn to *discern the way of God towards them*, that they may *prepare* accordingly. The prognostications here referred to had their origin in repeated observations upon the chain of causes; from what *has been* we conjecture what *will be*. See the benefit of experience; by *taking notice* we may come to *give notice.*

II. Let them hasten to *make their peace with God* in time, before it be too late, vv. 58, 59. This we had upon another occasion, Matt. v. 25, 26.

REPENT—OR PERISH
(vv. 1–5)

We have here, I. Tidings brought to Christ of the death of some Galileans lately, whose blood *Pilate had mingled with their sacrifices*, v. 1. Let us consider,

1. What this tragical story was. It is briefly related here, and is not met with in any of the historians of those times. Josephus indeed mentions Pilate's killing some Samaritans, who, under the conduct of a factious leader, were going in a tumultuous manner to mount Gerizim, where the Samaritans' temple was; but we can by no means allow that story to be the same with this. The Galileans being Herod's subjects, it is probable that this outrage committed upon them by Pilate occasioned the quarrel that was between Herod and Pilate, which we read of in *ch.* xxiii. 12.

2. Why it was related *at this season* to our Lord Jesus. (1) Perhaps merely as a matter of news, which they supposed he had not heard before, and as a thing which they lamented, and believed he would do so too; for the Galileans were their countrymen. (2) Perhaps it was intended as a

confirmation of what Christ had said in the close of the foregoing chapter, concerning the necessity of making our peace with God in time, before we be *delivered to the officer*, that is, to *death*, and so *cast into prison*, and then it will be too late to make agreements. (3) Perhaps they would stir him up, being himself of Galilee, and a prophet, and one that had a great interest in that country, to find out a way to revenge the death of these Galileans upon Herod. (4) Perhaps this was told Christ to *deter* him from going up to Jerusalem, to worship (*v.* 22), lest Pilate should serve him as he had served those Galileans. (5) Christ's answer intimates that they told him this with a spiteful *innuendo*, that, though Pilate was unjust in killing them, yet without doubt they were secretly bad men, else God would not have permitted Pilate thus barbarously to cut them off.

II. Christ's reply to this report, in which,

1. He seconded it with another story, which, like it, gave an instance of people's being taken away by sudden death. It is not long since *the tower of Siloam fell*, and there were eighteen persons killed and buried in the ruins of it.

2. He cautioned his hearers not to make an ill use of these and similar events, nor take occasion thence to censure *great sufferers*, as if they were *therefore* to be accounted *great sinners*: *Suppose ye that these Galileans*, who were slain as they were sacrificing, *were sinners above all the Galileans, because they suffered such things?*

I tell you nay, *vv.* 2, 3. We cannot judge of men's *sins* by their *sufferings* in this world; for many are thrown into the furnace as gold to be purified, not as dross and chaff to be consumed.

3. On these stories he founded a call to repentance, adding to each of them this awakening word, *Except ye repent, ye shall all likewise perish*, *vv.* 3–5. (1) This intimates that we all deserve to *perish* as much as *they did*, and had we been dealt with according to our sins, according to the *iniquity of our holy things*, our blood had been long ere this mingled with our sacrifices by the justice of God. (2) That therefore we are all concerned to *repent*, to be sorry for what we have done amiss, and to do so no more. The judgments of God upon others are loud calls to us to *repent*. (3) That repentance is the way to escape perishing, and it is a sure way: *so iniquity shall not be your ruin*, but upon no other terms. (4) That, if we repent not, we shall certainly perish, as others have done before us.

THE FIG TREE (*vv.* 6–9)

This parable is intended to enforce that word of warning immediately going before, "*Except ye repent, ye shall all likewise perish*; except you be reformed, you will be ruined, as the barren tree, except it bring forth fruit, will be cut down."

I. This parable primarily refers to the nation and people of the Jews. God chose them for his own, made them a people near to him, gave them advantages for knowing and serving him above any other people, and expected answerable returns of duty and obedience from them, which, turning to his praise and honour, he would have accounted *fruit*; but they disappointed his expectations: they did not do their duty; they were a reproach instead of being a credit to their profession. Upon this, he justly determined to abandon them, and cut them off, to deprive them of their privileges, to unchurch and unpeople them; but, upon Christ's intercession, as of old upon that of Moses, he graciously gave them further time and further mercy; tried them, as it were, another year, by sending his apostles among them, to call them to repentance, and in Christ's name to offer them pardon, upon repentance. Some of them were wrought upon to *repent*, and bring forth fruit, and with them all was well; but the body of the nation continued impenitent and unfruitful, and ruin without remedy came upon them; about forty years after they were cut down, and cast into the fire, as John Baptist had told them (Matt. iii. 10), which saying of his this parable enlarges upon.

II. Yet it has, without doubt, a further reference, and is designed for the awakening of all that enjoy the means of grace, and the privileges of the visible church, to see to it that the temper of their minds and the tenour of their lives be answerable to their professions and opportunities, for that is the *fruit* required. Now observe here,

1. The advantages which this fig-tree had. It was *planted in a vineyard*, in better soil, and where it had more care taken of it and more pains taken with it, than other fig-trees had, that commonly grew, not in *vineyards* (those are for vines), but by the *way-side*, Matt. xxi. 19.

2. The owner's expectation from it: *He came, and sought fruit thereon*, and he had reason to expect it. Note, The God of heaven requires and expects *fruit* from those that have a place in his vineyard.

3. The disappointment of his expectation: *He found none*, none at all, not one fig. Note, It is sad to think how many enjoy the privileges of the gospel, and yet do nothing at all to the honour of God, nor to answer the end of his entrusting them with those privileges; and it is a disappointment to him and a grief to the Spirit of his grace.

4. The doom passed upon it: *Cut it down*. He saith this to the *dresser of the vineyard*, to Christ, to whom all judgment is committed, to the ministers who are in his name to declare this doom.

5. The dresser's intercession for it. Christ is the great Intercessor; he ever lives, interceding. Now observe,

(1) What it is he prays for, and that is a reprieve: *Lord, let it alone this year also*.

(2) How he promises to improve this reprieve, if it be obtained: *Till I shall dig about it, and dung it*. Unfruitful Christians must be *awakened* by the terrors of the law, which *break up the fallow ground*, and then encouraged by the promises of the gospel, which

are warming and fattening, as manure to the tree. Both methods must be tried; the one prepares for the other, and all little enough.

(3) Upon what foot he leaves the matter: "Let us try it, and try what we can do with it one year more, *and, if it bear fruit, well, v.* 9. It is possible, nay, there is hope, that yet it may be fruitful."

But he adds, *If not, then after that thou shalt cut it down.* Observe here, [1] That, though God bear long, he will not bear always with unfruitful professors. [2] The longer God has *waited,* and the more cost he has been at upon them, the greater will their destruction be. [3] Cutting down, though it is work that shall be done, is work that God does not take pleasure in. [4] Those that now intercede for barren trees, and take pains with them, if they persist in their unfruitfulness will be even content to see them cut down, and will not have one word more to say for them.

INFIRM WOMAN HEALED
(*vv.* 10–17)

Here is, I. The miraculous cure of a woman that had been long under a spirit of infirmity. Our Lord Jesus spent his *sabbaths* in the *synagogues, v.* 10. Now to confirm the doctrine he preached, and recommend it as faithful, and well worthy of all acceptation, he wrought a miracle, a miracle of mercy.

1. The object of charity that presented itself was a woman in the synagogue that had *a spirit of infirmity eighteen years, v.* 11. She had an infirmity, which an evil

spirit, by divine permission, had brought upon her, which was such that she was *bowed together* by strong convulsions, and could *in no wise lift up herself.*

2. The offer of this cure to one that sought it not bespeaks the preventing mercy and grace of Christ: *When Jesus saw her, he called her to him, v.* 12.

3. The cure effectually and immediately wrought bespeaks his almighty power. He *laid his hands on her,* and said, "*Woman, thou art loosed from thine infirmity*; though thou hast been long labouring under it, thou art at length released from it." Let not those despair whose disease is *inveterate,* who have been long in affliction. God can at length relieve them, therefore though he tarry wait for him. Though it was a *spirit of infirmity,* an evil spirit, that she was under the power of, Christ has a power superior to that of Satan, is *stronger than he.* Though *she could in no wise lift up herself,* Christ could lift her up, and enable her to lift up herself.

4. The present effect of this cure upon the *soul* of the patient as well as upon her *body.* She *glorified God,* gave him the praise of her cure to whom all praise is due. When crooked souls are made straight, they will show it by their glorifying God.

II. The offence that was taken at this by the *ruler of the synagogue,* as if our Lord Jesus had committed some heinous crime, in healing this poor woman. He *had indignation* at it, because it was *on the sabbath day, v.* 14.

III. Christ's justification of him-

Infirm Woman Healed

self in what he had done (*v.* 15): *The Lord then answered him*, as he had answered others who in like manner cavilled at him, *Thou hypocrite*. Christ knew that he had a real enmity to him and to his gospel, that he did but cloak this with a pretended zeal for the sabbath day, and that when he bade the people come on the *six days*, and be healed, he really would not have them be healed any day. Christ could have told him this, but he vouchsafes to reason the case with him; and,

1. He *appeals* to the common practice among the Jews, which was never disallowed, that of *watering* their cattle on the sabbath day.

2. He applies this to the present case (*v.* 16): "Must the *ox* and the *ass* have compassion shown them on the sabbath day, and have so much time and pains bestowed upon them *every* sabbath, to be loosed from the stall, led away perhaps a great way to the water, and then back again, and shall not this woman, only with a touch of the hand and a word's speaking, be *loosed* from a much *greater* grievance than that which the cattle undergo when they are kept a day without water?

IV. The different effect that this had upon those that heard him. And now observe,

1. What a confusion this was to the malice of his persecutors: *When he had said these things, all his adversaries were ashamed* (*v.* 17).

2. What a confirmation this was to the faith of his friends: *All the people*, who had a better sense of things, and judged more impartially

than their rulers, rejoiced *for all the glorious things that were done by him*. The shame of his foes was the joy of his followers.

SIMILES OF THE KINGDOM
(*vv.* 18–22)

Here is, I. The gospel's progress foretold in two parables, which we had before, Matt. xiii. 31–33. The *kingdom of the Messiah* is the *kingdom of God*, for it advances his glory; this kingdom was yet a mystery, and people were generally in the dark, and under mistakes, about it. Now, when we would describe a thing to those that are strangers to it, we choose to do it by similitudes. So Christ undertakes here to show *what the kingdom of God is like* (*v.* 18).

THE LAST AND THE FIRST
(*vv.* 23–30)

We have here,

1. A question put to our Lord Jesus. The question was, *Are there few that are saved? v.* 23: "*If the saved be few?*"

II. Christ's answer to this question, which directs us what use to make of this truth. Ask not, "How many shall be saved?" But, be they more or fewer, "Shall I be one of them?" Not, "What shall become of such and such, and *what shall this man do?*" But, "What shall I do, and what will become of me?" Now in Christ's answer observe,

1. A quickening exhortation and direction: *Strive to enter in at the strait gate*. This is directed not to him only that asked the question, but to all, to us, it is in the plural number: *Strive ye*.

2. Various awakening considerations, to enforce this exhortation.

(1) Think how many take *some pains* for salvation and yet perish because they do not take *enough*, and you will say that there are *few that will be saved* and that it highly concerns us to *strive*: *Many will seek to enter in, and shall not be able*; they *seek*, but they do not *strive*.

(2) Think of the *distinguishing* day that is coming and the *decisions* of that day, and you will say there are *few that shall be saved* and that we are concerned to strive: The *Master of the house* will *rise up, and shut to the door*, v. 25.

(3) Think how many who were very *confident* that they should be *saved* will be rejected in the day of trial, and their confidences will deceive them, and you will say that there are *few* that *shall be saved* and that we are all concerned to *strive*. Consider,

[1] What an *assurance* they had of *admission*, and how far their hope carried them, even to *heaven's gate*. There they *stand and knock*, knock as if they had authority, knock as those that belong to the house, *saying*, "*Lord, Lord, open to us*, for we think we have a right to enter; take us in among the *saved ones*, for we joined ourselves to them."

[2] What *grounds* they had for this *confidence*. Let us see what their plea is, v. 26. *First*, They had been *Christ's guests*, had had an intimate converse with him, and had shared in his favours: *We have eaten and drunk in thy presence*, at thy table. *Secondly*, They had been *Christ's hearers*, had received instruction from him, and were well acquainted with his doctrine and law.

[3] How their confidence will fail them, and all their pleas be rejected as frivolous. Christ will say to them, *I know you not whence you are*, v. 25. And again (v. 27), *I tell you, I know you not, depart from me*. He does not deny that what they pleaded was true; they had *eaten and drunk in his presence*, by the same token that they had no sooner eaten of his bread than they lifted up the heel against him. He had *taught in their streets*, by the same token that they had despised his instruction and would not submit to it. And therefore, *First*, He *disowns* them: "*I know you not*; you do not belong to my family." *Secondly*, He *discards* them: *Depart from me*. It is the hell of hell to depart from Christ, the principal part of the misery of the damned. *Thirdly*, He gives them such a character as is the reason of this doom: *You are workers of iniquity*. This is their ruin, that, under a pretence of piety, they kept up secret haunts of sin, and did the devil's drudgery in Christ's livery.

[4] How terrible their punishment will be (v. 28): *There shall be weeping and gnashing of teeth*, the utmost degree of grief and indignation; and that which is the cause of it, and contributes to it, is a sight of the happiness of those that are saved: *You shall see the patriarchs and prophets in the kingdom of God, and yourselves thrust out*.

(4) Think who are they that shall be saved, notwithstanding:

They shall come from the east and the west; and the last shall be first, vv. 29, 30. Those who *sit down in the kingdom of God* are such as had taken pains to get thither, for they came from far—*from the east and from the west, from the north and from the south*; they had passed through different climates, had broken through many difficulties and discouragements. This shows that they who would enter into that kingdom must *strive.* They who *travel* now in the service of God and religion shall shortly *sit down* to rest in the *kingdom of God.*

A MESSAGE TO HEROD
(vv. 31-35)

Here is, I. A suggestion to Christ of his danger from Herod, now that he was in Galilee, within Herod's jurisdiction (v. 31).

II. His defiance of Herod's rage and the Pharisees' too; he fears neither the one nor the other: *Go you, and tell that fox* so, v. 32. In calling him a *fox*, he gives him his true character; for he was subtle as a fox, noted for his craft, and treachery, and baseness, and preying (as they say of a fox) furthest from his own den. And, though it is a black and ugly character, yet it did not ill become Christ to give it to him, nor was it in him a violation of that law, *Thou shalt not speak evil of the ruler of thy people.* For Christ was a prophet, and prophets always had a liberty of speech in reproving princes and great men.

III. His lamentation for Jerusalem, and his denunciation of wrath against that city, vv. 34, 35. This we had Matt. xxiii. 37-39.

ANOTHER SABBATH MIRACLE (vv. 1-6)

In this passage of story we find,

I. That *the Son of man went into the house of one of the chief Pharisees*, a ruler, it may be, and a magistrate in his country, *to eat bread on the sabbath day*, v. 1.

II. That he *went about doing good.* Here was *a certain man before him who had the dropsy*, v. 2. We do not find that he offered himself, or that his friends offered him to be Christ's patient, but Christ *prevented him* with the blessings of his goodness, and *before he called* he answered him.

III. That he *endured the contradiction of sinners against himself: They watched him*, v. 1. When Christ asked them *whether* they thought it *lawful to heal on the sabbath day* (and herein he is said to *answer* them, for it was an answer to *their thoughts*, and thoughts are *words* to Jesus Christ), they would say neither *yea* nor *nay*, for their design was to *inform against him*, not to be *informed by him.*

IV. That Christ would not be hindered from *doing good* by the *opposition* and *contradiction* of sinners. He *took him, and healed him, and let him go*, v. 4.

V. That our Lord Jesus *did nothing but what he could justify*, to the conviction and confusion of those that quarrelled with him, vv. 5, 6. He still answered their thoughts, and made them *hold their peace* for *shame* who before held their peace for *subtlety*, by an appeal to their own practice, as he had been used to do upon such occasions, that he might show them how in condemning him they condemned themselves.

TABLE TALK (vv. 7–14)

Our Lord Jesus here sets us an example of profitable edifying discourse at our tables, when we are in company with our friends.

I. He takes occasion to reprove *the guests* for striving to *sit uppermost*, and thence gives us a lesson of *humility*.

1. He observed how these lawyers and Pharisees affected the *highest seats*, towards the head-end of the table, *v.* 7.

2. He observed how those who were thus aspiring often exposed themselves, and came off *with a slur*; whereas those who were modest, and seated themselves in the lowest seats, often *gained respect* by it.

3. He applied this generally, and would have us all learn not to *mind high things*, but to content ourselves with mean things, as for other reasons, so for this, because pride and ambition are disgraceful before men: for *whosoever exalteth himself shall be abased*; but humility and self-denial are really honourable: *he that humbleth himself shall be exalted, v.* 11. We see in other instances that *a man's pride will bring him low*, but *honour shall uphold the humble in spirit*, and *before honour is humility*.

II. He takes occasion to reprove the master of the feast for inviting so many *rich people*, who had wherewithal to dine very well at home, when he should rather have *invited the poor*, or, which was all one, have *sent portions to them for whom nothing was prepared*, and who could not afford themselves a good meal's meat. See Neh. viii. 10.

THE GREAT SUPPER
(vv. 15–24)

Here is another discourse of our Saviour's.

I. The occasion of the discourse was given by one of the guests, who, when Christ was giving rules about feasting, said to him, *Blessed is he that shall eat bread in the kingdom of God* (*v.* 15), which, some tell us, was a saying commonly used among the rabbin.

1. But with what design does this man bring it in here? (1) Perhaps this man, observing that Christ reproved first the guests and then the master of the house, fearing he should put the company out of humour, started this, to *divert* the discourse to something else. Or, (2) Admiring the good rules of humility and charity which Christ had now given, but despairing to see them lived up to in the present degenerate state of things, he longs for *the kingdom of God*, when these and other good laws shall prevail, and pronounces them *blessed* who shall have a place in that kingdom. Or, (3) Christ having mentioned *the resurrection of the just*, as a recompence for acts of charity to the poor, he here confirms what he said, "Yea, Lord, they that shall be recompensed in the resurrection of the just, shall *eat bread in the kingdom*,

and that is a greater recompence than being reinvited to the table of the greatest man on earth." Or, (4) Observing Christ to be silent, after he had given the foregoing lessons, he was willing to draw him in again to further discourse, so wonderfully well-pleased was he with what he said.

2. Now what this man said was a plain and acknowledged truth. (1) In the kingdom of grace, in the kingdom of the Messiah, which was expected now shortly to be set up. Christ promised his disciples that they should *eat and drink with him in his kingdom*. (2) In the kingdom of glory, at the resurrection. The happiness of heaven is an *everlasting feast*.

II. The parable which our Lord Jesus put forth upon this occasion, *vv*. 16, &c. Now in the parable we may observe,

1. The free grace and mercy of God, shining in the gospel of Christ; it appears,

(1) In the rich provision he has made for poor souls, for their nourishment, refreshment, and entertainment (*v*. 16): *A certain man made a great supper*.

(2) In the gracious invitation given us to come and partake of this provision. Here is, [1] A general invitation given: He *bade many*. Christ invited the whole nation and people of the Jews to partake of the benefits of his gospel. [2] A particular memorandum given, when the supper time was at hand; the servant was sent round to put them in mind of it: *Come, for all things are now ready*. When the Spirit was poured out, and the gospel church planted,

those who before were invited were more closely pressed to come in at once.

2. The cold entertainment which the grace of the gospel meets with. The invited guests declined coming. They did not say flatly and plainly that they *would not come*, but *they all with one consent began to make excuse*, *v*. 18. (1) Here were *two* that were *purchasers*, who were in such haste to go and see their purchases that they could not find time to go to this supper. (2) Here was one that was *newly married*, and could not leave his wife to go out to supper, no, not for once (*v*. 30): *I have married a wife, and therefore*, in short, *I cannot come*. He pretends that he *cannot*, when the truth is he *will not*. Thus many pretend *inability* for the duties of religion when really they have an *aversion* to them.

3. The account which was brought to the master of the feast of the affront put upon him by his friends whom he had invited, who now showed how little they valued him (*v*. 21).

4. The master's just resentment of this affront: *He was angry*, *v*. 21. Note, The ingratitude of those that slight gospel offers, and the contempt they put upon the God of heaven thereby, are a very great provocation to him, and justly so. Abused mercy turns into the greatest wrath.

5. The care that was taken to furnish the table with guests, as well as food. "Go" (saith he to the servants), "*go first into the streets and lanes of the city*, and bring in *hither the poor and the*

maimed, the halt and the blind;
pick up the common beggars."
They soon gather an abundance of
such guests: *Lord, it is done as
thou hast commanded*. But *yet there
is room* for more guests, and
provision enough for them all.
"Go, then, *secondly, into the
highways and hedges. Compel them
to come in*, not by force of arms,
but by force of arguments. They
will be shy and modest, and will
hardly believe that they shall be
welcome, and therefore be importunate with them and do not
leave them till you have prevailed
with them." This refers to the
calling of the Gentiles, to whom the
apostles were to *turn* when the
Jews refused the offer, and with
them the church was filled. Now
observe here, (1) The provision
made for precious souls in the
gospel of Christ shall appear not
to have been made *in vain*; for,
if some *reject it*, yet others will
thankfully *accept* the offer of it.
(2) Those that are very poor and
low in the world shall be as welcome
to Christ as the rich and great.
(3) Many times the gospel has the
greatest success among those that
are *least likely* to have the benefit
of it, and whose submission to it
was least expected. The publicans
and harlots went into the kingdom
of God before the scribes and
Pharisees; *so the last shall be
first, and the first last*. Let us not be
confident concerning those that are
most forward, nor despair of those
that are least promising. (4) Christ's
ministers must be both very
expeditious and very importunate
in inviting to the gospel feast:
"*Go out quickly* (*v.* 21); lose no

time, because *all things are now
ready*. Call to them to come
to-day, while it is called to-day;
and *compel them to come in*, by
accosting them kindly, and *drawing
them with the cords of a man and
the bands of love*."

COUNTING THE COST
(*vv.* 25–35)

See how Christ in his doctrine
suited himself to those to whom he
spoke, and *gave every one his
portion of meat*. To Pharisees he
preached humility and charity. He
is in these verses directing his
discourse to the multitudes that
crowded after him, and seemed
zealous in following him; and his
exhortation to them is to understand the terms of discipleship,
before they undertook the profession of it, and to consider what
they did. See here.

I. How zealous people were in
their attendance on Christ (*v.* 25):
*There went great multitudes with
him.*

II. How *considerate* he would
have them to be in their *zeal*. Those
that undertake to follow Christ
must count upon the worst, and
prepare accordingly.

1. He tells them what the worst
is that they must count upon,
much the same with what he had
gone through *before* them and *for*
them.

(1) They must be willing to *quit*
that which was *very dear*, and
therefore must come to him
thoroughly *weaned from* all their
creature-comforts, and *dead* to
them, so as cheerfully to part with
them rather than quit their interest
in Christ, *v.* 26. [1] Every good

man loves *his relations*; and yet, if he be a disciple of Christ, he must comparatively *hate them*, must love them *less than Christ*, as Leah is said to be *hated* when Rachel was better loved. Not that their persons must be in any degree hated, but our comfort and satisfaction in them must be lost and swallowed up in our love to Christ. [2] Every man loves *his own life*, no man ever yet *hated it*; and we cannot be Christ's disciples if we do not love him better than our own lives, so as rather to have our lives *embittered* by cruel *bondage*, nay, and *taken away* by cruel *deaths*, than to dishonour Christ, or depart from any of his truths and ways.

(2) That they must be willing to *bear* that which was very *heavy* (v. 27). Though the disciples of Christ are not *all crucified*, yet they all *bear their cross*, as if they counted upon being crucified. They must be content to be put into an ill name, and to be loaded with infamy and disgrace.

2. He bids them count upon it, and then consider of it. It is better never to begin than not to proceed; and therefore before we begin we must consider what it is to proceed. This is to act rationally, and as becomes men, and as we do in other cases. The cause of Christ will bear a scrutiny.

(1) When we take upon us a profession of religion we are like a man that undertakes to *build a tower*, and therefore must consider the *expense of it* (vv. 28–30).

(2) When we undertake to be Christ's disciples we are like a man that *goes to war*, and therefore

must consider the *hazard* of it, and the difficulties that are to be encountered, vv. 31, 32. A king that declares war against a neighbouring prince considers whether he has strength wherewith to make his part good, and, if not, he will lay aside his thoughts of war.

3. He warns them against apostasy and a degeneracy of mind from the truly Christian spirit and temper, for that would make them utterly useless, vv. 34, 35. (1) Good Christians are *the salt of the earth*, and good ministers especially (Matt. v. 13); and this *salt is good* and of great use. (2) Degenerate Christians, who, rather than part with what they have in the world, will throw up their profession, and then of course become carnal, and worldly, and wholly destitute of a Christian spirit, are like *salt that has lost its savour*; it has no manner of virtue or good property in it.

CHAPTER FIFTEEN

THE LOST SHEEP (vv. 1–10)

Here is, I. The diligent attendance of the publicans and sinners upon Christ's ministry. These *drew near*, when perhaps the multitude of the Jews that had followed him had (upon his discourse in the close of the foregoing chapter) *dropped off*; thus afterwards the Gentiles took their turn in hearing the apostles, when the Jews had rejected them.

II. The offence which the *scribes* and *Pharisees* took at this. They *murmured*, and turned it to the reproach of our Lord Jesus: *This man receiveth sinners, and eateth with them*, v. 2. They could not, for shame, condemn him for *preaching to them*, though that was the thing they were most enraged at; and therefore they reproached him for *eating with them*, which was more expressly contrary to the tradition of the elders.

III. Christ's justifying himself in it, by showing that the worse these people were, to whom he preached, the more glory would redound to God, and the more joy there would be in heaven, if by his preaching they were brought to repentance. This he here illustrates by two parables, the explication of both of which is the same.

1. The parable of the *lost sheep*. Something like it we had in Matt. xviii. 12. There it was designed to show the care God takes for the preservation of saints, as a reason why we should not offend them; here it is designed to show the pleasure God takes in the conversion of sinners, as a reason why we should rejoice in it.

This is very applicable to the great work of our redemption. Mankind were gone astray, Isa. liii. 6. The value of the whole race to God was not so much as that of one sheep to him that had a hundred; what loss would it have been to God if they had all been left to perish? There is a world of holy angels that are as the ninety-nine sheep, a noble flock; yet God sends his Son to *seek and save that which was lost*, ch. xix. 10. Christ is said to *gather the lambs in his arms*, and carry *them in his bosom*, denoting his pity and tenderness towards poor sinners; here he is

said to bear them *upon his shoulders*, denoting the power wherewith he supports and bears them up; those can never perish whom he carries upon his shoulders.

He *lays it on his shoulders rejoicing* that he has not lost his labour in seeking; and the joy is the greater because he began to be out of hope of finding it; and he *calls his friends and neighbours*, the shepherds that keep their flocks about him, *saying, Rejoice with me*.

2. The parable of the *lost piece of silver*. (1) The *loser* is here supposed to be *a woman*, who will more passionately grieve for her loss, and rejoice in finding what she had lost, than perhaps a man would do, and therefore it the better serves the purpose of the parable. She has *ten pieces of silver*, and out of them loses only one. Let this keep up in us high thoughts of the divine goodness, notwithstanding the sinfulness and misery of the world of mankind, that there are nine to one, nay, in the foregoing parable there are ninety-nine to one, of God's creation, that retain their integrity, in whom God *is* praised, and never *was* dishonoured. O the numberless beings, for aught we know numberless worlds of beings, that never were lost, nor stepped aside from the laws and ends of their creation!

3. The explication of these two parables is to the same purport (vv. 7, 10): *There is joy in heaven, joy in the presence of the angels of God, over one sinner that repenteth*, as those publicans and sinners did, some of them at least (and, if but

one of them did repent, Christ would reckon it worth his while), more than *over* a great number of *just persons, who need no repentance.*

Now if there is such *joy in heaven,* for the conversion of sinners, then the Pharisees were very much strangers to a heavenly spirit, who did all they could to hinder it and were grieved at it, and who were exasperated at Christ when he was doing a piece of work that was of all others most grateful to Heaven.

THE PRODIGAL SON
(vv. 11–33)

We have here the parable of the prodigal son, the scope of which is the same with those before, to show how pleasing to God the conversion of sinners is, of great sinners, and how ready he is to receive and entertain such, upon their repentance.

I. The parable represents God as a *common Father* to all mankind, to the whole family of Adam. We are all his *offspring,* have all *one Father,* and *one God created us,* Mal. ii. 10.

II. It represents the children of men as of *different* characters, though all related to God as their common Father. He had *two sons,* one of them a solid grave youth, *reserved* and *austere,* sober himself, but not at all *good-humoured* to those about him; such a one would adhere to his education, and not be easily drawn from it; but the other *volatile* and *mercurial,* and impatient of restraint, roving, and willing to try his fortune, and, if he fall into ill hands, likely to be a

rake, notwithstanding his virtuous education. Now this latter represents the publicans and sinners, whom Christ is endeavouring to bring to repentance, and the Gentiles, to whom the apostles were to be sent forth to *preach repentance.* The former represents the Jews in general, and particularly the Pharisees, whom he was endeavouring to reconcile to that grace of God which was offered to, and bestowed upon, sinners.

The *younger son* is the prodigal, whose character and case are here designed to represent that of a sinner, that of every one of us in our natural state, but especially of some. Now we are to observe concerning him,

1. His *riot* and *ramble* when he was a prodigal, and the extravagances and miseries he fell into. We are told,

(1) What his request to his father was (v. 12): *He said to his father,* proudly and pertly enough, *"Father, give me the portion of goods that falleth to me;* not so much as you *think fit* to allot to me, but that which falls to me as *my due."*

(2) How kind his father was to him: *He divided unto them his living.* He computed what he had to dispose of between his sons, and gave the younger son *his share.*

(3) How he managed himself when he had got his portion in his own hands. He set himself to spend it as fast as he could, and, as prodigals generally do, in a little time he made himself a beggar: *not many days after,* v. 13.

Now the condition of the prodigal in this ramble of his

represents to us a *sinful* state, that *miserable* state into which man is *fallen*.

[1] A sinful state is a state of *departure* and *distance* from God. *First*, It is the *sinfulness* of sin that it is an apostasy from God. He *took his journey* from his father's house. Sinners are fled from God. They get as far off him as they can. The world is the *far country* in which they take up their residence, and are as at home; and in the service and enjoyment of it they spend their all. *Secondly*, It is the misery of sinners that they are afar off from God, from him who is the Fountain of all good, and are going further and further from him. What is hell itself, but being *afar off* from God?

[2] A sinful state is a *spending* state: There he *wasted his substance with riotous living* (v. 13), devoured it *with harlots* (v. 30), and in a little time *he had spent all*, v. 14. Wilful sinners *waste* their patrimony; for they misemploy their thoughts and all the powers of their souls, mispend their time and all their opportunities, do not only bury, but embezzle, the talents they are entrusted to trade with for their Master's honour; and the gifts of Providence, which were intended to enable them to serve God and to do good with, are made the food and fuel of their lusts.

[3] A sinful state is a *wanting* state: *When he had spent all* upon his harlots, they left him, to seek such another prey; and *there arose a mighty famine in that land*, every thing was scarce and dear, and he *began to be in want*, v. 14.

Note, Wilful waste brings woeful want. This represents the misery of *sinners*, who have thrown away *their own mercies*, the favour of God, their interest in Christ, the strivings of the Spirit, the admonitions of conscience; these they *gave away* for the pleasure of sense, and the wealth of the world, and then are ready to perish for want of them. Sinners are *wretchedly* and *miserably poor*, and, what aggravates it, they brought themselves into that condition, and keep themselves in it by refusing the supplies offered.

[4] A sinful state is *a vile servile state*. When this young man's riot had brought him to want his want brought him to servitude. *He went, and joined himself to a citizen of that country*, v. 15. The same wicked life that before was represented by *riotous living* is here represented by *servile living*; for sinners are perfect slaves. The devil is the *citizen of that country*; for he is both in city and country. Sinners *join themselves* to him, hire themselves into his service, to do *his work*, to be at *his beck*, and to depend upon him for maintenance and a portion. They that commit sin are the *servants of sin*, John viii. 34.

[5] A sinful state is a state of *perpetual dissatisfaction*. When the prodigal began to be in want, he thought to help himself by *going to service*; and he must be content with the provision which not the house, but the field, afforded; but it is poor provision: *He would fain have filled his belly*, satisfied his hunger, and nourished his body, *with the husks which the*

swine did eat, v. 16. A fine pass my young master had brought himself to, to be fellow-commoner with the swine!

[6] A sinful state is a state which *cannot expect relief from any creature*. This prodigal, when he could not earn his bread by *working*, took to *begging*; but *no man gave unto him*, because they knew he had brought all this misery upon himself, and because he was rakish, and provoking to every body; such poor are *least pitied*. This, in the application of the parable, intimates that those who depart from God cannot be helped by any creature.

[7] A sinful state is a *state of death: This my son was dead*, vv. 24, 32. A sinner is not only dead in law, as he is under a sentence of death, but dead in state too, dead in trespasses and sins, destitute of spiritual life; no union with Christt, no spiritual senses exercised, no living to God, and therefore *dead*.

[8] A sinful state is a *lost state: This my son was lost*—lost to every thing that was good—lost to all virtue and honour—lost to his father's house; they had no joy of him. Souls that are separated from God are *lost* souls; lost as a *traveller* that is out of his way, and, if infinite mercy prevent not, will soon be lost as a ship that is sunk at sea, lost irrecoverably.

[9] A sinful state is a state of *madness* and *frenzy*. This is intimated in that expression (*v.* 17), *when he came to himself*, which intimates that he had been *beside himself*. Surely he was so when he left his father's house, and much

more so when he joined himself to the citizen of that country.

2. We have here his *return* from this *ramble*, his penitent *return* to his father again. When he was brought to the last extremity, then he bethought himself how much it was his interest to go home. The grace of God can soften the hardest heart, and give a happy turn to the strongest stream of corruption. Now observe here,

(1) What was the *occasion* of his return and repentance. It was his *affliction*; when he was in *want*, then he *came to himself*. Note, Afflictions, when they are sanctified by divine grace, prove happy means of turning sinners from the error of their ways.

(2) What was the *preparative* for it; it was *consideration*. He said within himself, he reasoned with himself, when he recovered his right mind, *How many hired servants of my father's have bread enough!* Note, Consideration is the first step towards conversion.

[1] He considered how bad his condition was: *I perish with hunger*. Not only, "I am *hungry*," but, "*I perish with hunger*, for I see not what way to expect relief."

[2] He considered how much better it might be made if he would but return: *How many hired servants of my father's*, the meanest in his family, the very day-labourers, *have bread enough, and to spare*, such a good house does he keep!

(3) What was the *purpose* of it. Since it is so, that his condition is so bad, and may be bettered by returning to his father, his consideration issues, at length, in this

conclusion: *I will arise, and go to my father*. Note, Good purposes are good things, but still good performances are all in all.

[1] He determined what to do: *I will arise and go to my father*. He will not take any longer time to consider of it, but will *forthwith* arise and go.

[2] He determined what to say. Note, In all our addresses to God, it is good to deliberate with ourselves beforehand what we shall say, that we may *order our cause before him*, and *fill our mouth with arguments*.

First, He would confess his fault and folly: *I have sinned*. The confession of sin is required and insisted upon, as a necessary condition of peace and pardon.

Secondly, He would aggravate it, and would be so far from extenuating the matter that he would *lay a load* upon himself for it: I have sinned *against Heaven*, and *before thee*. Let those that are *undutiful* to their *earthly parents* think of this; they sin *against heaven, and before God*. Offences against them are offences against God. Let us all think of this, as that which renders our *sin exceedingly sinful*, and should render us exceedingly sorrowful for it.

Thirdly, He would judge and condemn himself for it, and acknowledge himself to have forfeited all the privileges of the family: *I am no more worthy to be called thy son*, *v.* 19. Note, It becomes sinners to acknowledge themselves unworthy to receive any favour from God, and to humble and abase themselves before him.

Fourthly, He would nevertheless sue for admission into the family, though it were into the meanest post there: "*Make me as one of thy hired servants*; that is good enough, and too good for me." Note, True penitents have a high value for God's house, and the privileges of it, and will be glad of any place, so they may but be in it, though it be but as *doorkeepers*, Ps. lxxxiv. 10.

Fifthly, In all this he would have an eye to his father as a father: "*I will arise, and go to my father, and will say unto him, Father.*" Note, Eyeing God as a Father, and our Father, will be of great use in our repentance and return to him. It will make our sorrow for sin genuine, our resolutions against it strong, and encourage us to hope for pardon.

(4) What was the performance of this purpose: *He arose, and came to his father*. His good resolve he put in execution without delay; he struck while the iron was hot, and did not adjourn the thought to some more convenient season.

3. We have here his reception and entertainment with his father: *He came to his father*; but was he welcome? Yes, heartily welcome. Now here observe,

(1) The great love and affection wherewith the father received the son: *When he was yet a great way off his father saw him*, *v.* 20. He expressed his kindness before the son expressed his repentance; for God precedes us with the blessings of his goodness. Even *before we call he answers*; for he knows what is in our hearts.

(2) The penitent submission which the poor prodigal made to his father (v. 21): He *said unto him, Father, I have sinned*. As it commends the good father's kindness that he showed it before the prodigal expressed his repentance, so it commends the prodigal's repentance that he expressed it after his father had shown him so much kindness. When he had received the kiss which sealed his pardon, yet he said, *Father, I have sinned*.

(3) The splendid provision which this kind father made for the returning prodigal. He was going on in his submission, but one word we find in his purpose to say (v. 19) which we do not find that he did say (v. 21), and that was, *Make me as one of thy hired servants*. We cannot think that he forgot it, much less that he changed his mind, and was now either less desirous to be in the family or less willing to be a hired servant there than when he made that purpose; but his father interrupted him, prevented his saying it: "Hold, son, talk no more of thy unworthiness, thou art heartily welcome, and, though not *worthy to be called a son*, shalt be treated as a *dear son*, as a *pleasant child*." He who is thus entertained at first needs not ask to be made *as a hired servant*.

But this is not all; here is rich and royal provision made for him, according to his birth and quality, far beyond what he did or could expect. He would have thought it sufficient, and been very thankful, if his father had but taken notice of him, and bid him go to the kitchen, and get his dinner with his servants; but God does for those who return to their duty, and cast themselves upon his mercy, abundantly above what they are able to ask or think. The prodigal came home between hope and fear, fear of being rejected and hope of being received; but his father was not only better to him than his fears, but better to him than his hopes—not only *received* him, but received him with respect.

[1] He came home *in rags*, and his father not only *clothed* him, but *adorned* him.

[2] He came home *hungry*, and his father not only *fed him*, but *feasted him* (v. 23). Now he found his own words made good, *In my father's house there is bread enough and to spare*.

(4) The great joy and rejoicing occasioned by his return. The bringing of the fatted calf was designed to be not only a *feast* for him, but a *festival* for the family: "*Let us all eat, and be merry*, for it is a good day; for *this my son was dead*, when he was in his ramble, but his return is as *life from the dead*, he *is alive again*; we thought that he was dead, having heard nothing from him of a long time, but behold *he lives*; he *was lost*, we gave him up for lost, we despaired of hearing of him, but he *is found*."

4. We have here the *repining and envying of the elder brother*, which is described by way of reproof to the scribes and Pharisees, to show them the folly and wickedness of their discontent at the repentance and conversion of the

publicans and sinners, and the favour Christ showed them. Now concerning the elder brother, observe,

(1) How *foolish* and *fretful* he was upon occasion of his brother's reception, and how he was disgusted at it. It seems he was abroad *in the field*, in the country, when his brother came, and by the time he had returned home the *mirth* was *begun: When he drew nigh to the house he heard music and dancing,* either while the dinner was getting ready, or rather after they had eaten and were full, *v.* 25. He enquired *what these things meant* (*v.* 26), and was informed that his brother was come, and his father had made him a feast for his *welcome home,* and great joy there was because he had received him *safe and sound, v.* 27. Now this offended him to the highest degree: *He was angry, and would not go in* (*v.* 28), not only because he was resolved he would not himself join in the mirth, but because he would show his displeasure at it, and would intimate to his father that he should have kept out his younger brother.

Let us observe, 1. He *would not go in,* except his brother were *turned out*; one house shall not hold him and his own brother, no, not his *father's house.* The language of this was that of the Pharisee (Isa. lxv. 5): *Stand by thyself, come not near to me, for I am holier than thou*; and (*ch.* xviii. 11) *I am not as other men are, nor even as this publican.* 2. He would not call him *brother*; but *this thy son,* which sounds arrogantly, and not without reflection upon his father, as if his indulgence had made him a prodigal: "He is *thy son,* thy darling." 3. He *aggravated his brother's faults,* and made the worst of them, endeavouring to incense his father against him: He *is thy son, who hath devoured thy living with harlots.* It is true, he had spent his own portion foolishly enough (whether *upon harlots* or no we are not told before, perhaps that was only the language of the elder brother's jealousy and ill will), but that he had devoured *all his father's living* was false; the father had still a good estate. Now this shows how apt we are, in censuring our brethren, to *make the worst* of every thing, and to set it out in the blackest colours, which is not doing as we would be done by, nor as our heavenly Father does by us, who is not extreme to mark iniquities. 4. He *grudged* him the *kindness* that his father *showed him: Thou hast killed for him the fatted calf,* as if he were such a son as he should be.

(2) Let us now see how *favourable* and *friendly* his father was in *his carriage towards him* when he was thus sour and ill-humoured.

[1] When he would not come in, his *father came out, and entreated him,* accosted him mildly, gave him good words, and desired him to come in. He might justly have said, "If he will not come in, let him stay out, shut the doors against him, and send him to seek a lodging where he can find it. Is not the house my own? and may I not do what I please in it? Is not the fatted calf my own? and may

I not do what I please with it?"
No, as he went to meet the younger
son, so now he goes to court
the elder, did not send a servant
out with a kind message to him,
but went himself. Now, *First*, This
is designed to represent to us the
goodness of God; how strangely
gentle and winning he has been
towards those that were strangely
froward and provoking. *Secondly*,
It is to teach all superiors to be
mild and gentle with their inferiors,
even when they are in a fault and
passionately justify themselves in
it, than which nothing can be more
provoking; and yet even in that
case let fathers *not provoke their
children to more wrath*, and let
masters forebear threatening, and
both show all *meekness*.

[2] His father assured him that
the kind entertainment he gave
his younger brother was neither
any reflection upon him nor should
be any prejudice to him (*v.* 31).

[3] His father gave him a good
reason for this uncommon joy in
the family: *It was meet that we
should make merry and be glad,
v.* 32. He might have insisted
upon his own authority: "It was
my will that the family should
make merry and be glad." It is
better to give a convincing reason,
as the father does here: *It was
meet*, and very becoming, *that we
should make merry* for the return
of a prodigal son, more than for
the perseverance of a dutiful son;
for, though the latter is a greater
blessing to a family, yet the former
is a more emotional pleasure.
Any family would be much more
transported with joy at the raising
of a dead child to life, yea, or

at the recovery of a child from a
sickness that was adjudged mortal,
than for the continued life and
health of many children. We do
not find that the elder brother
made any reply to what his father
said, which intimates that he was
entirely satisfied, and acquiesced
in his father's will, and was well
reconciled to his prodigal brother;
and his father put him in mind
that he was his brother: *This thy
brother*. But as for the scribes and
Pharisees, for whose conviction it
was primarily intended, for aught
that appears they continued the
same disaffection to the sinners of
the Gentiles, and to the gospel of
Christ because it was preached to
them.

CHAPTER SIXTEEN

THE UNJUST STEWARD
(*vv.* 1–17)

Let us consider,

I. The parable itself, in which
all the children of men are represented as *stewards* of what they
have in this world, and we are but
stewards. Whatever we have, the
property of it is God's; we have
only the use of it, and that according to the direction of our
great Lord, and for his honour.
Now,

1. Here is the *dishonesty* of this
steward. He *wasted his lord's
goods*, embezzled them, misapplied
them, or through carelessness suffered them to be lost and damaged;
and for this he was *accused to his
lord, v.* 1. We are all *liable* to the
same charge. We have not made
a due improvement of what God
has entrusted us with in this

world, but have perverted his purpose; and, that we may not be for this *judged of our Lord*, it concerns us to *judge ourselves*.

2. His *discharge* out of his place. His lord *called for him*, and said, "*How is it that I hear this of thee?* I expected better things from thee." The steward cannot deny it, and therefore there is no remedy, he must make up his accounts, and be gone in a little time, *v.* 2.

3. His *after-wisdom*. Now he began to consider, *What shall I do? v.* 3. He would have done well to have considered this before he had so foolishly thrown himself out of a good place by his unfaithfulness; but it is better to *consider* late than never. He must live; which way shall he have a livelihood? (1) He knows that he has not such a degree of industry in him as to get his living by work: "*I cannot dig*; I cannot earn my bread by my labour." But why can he not dig? It does not appear that he is either old or lame; but the truth is, he is *lazy*. His *cannot* is a *will not*; it is not a natural but a moral disability that he labours under. (2) He knows that he has not such a degree of *humility* as to get his bread by begging: *To beg I am ashamed.* This was the language of his pride, as the former of his slothfulness. (3) He therefore determines to make friends of his lord's debtors, or his tenants that were behind with their rent, and had given notes under their hands for it. Now the way he would take to make them his friends was by striking off a considerable part

of their debt to his lord, and giving it in in his accounts so much less than it was. How hard is it to find one that confidence can be reposed in! *Let God be true, but every man a liar.* Though this steward is turned out for dealing dishonestly, yet still he does so. So rare is it for men to mend of a fault, though they smart for it.

4. The approbation of this: *The lord commended the unjust steward, because he had done wisely, v.* 8. It may be meant of *his lord*, the lord of that servant, who, though he could not but be angry at his knavery, yet was pleased with his ingenuity and policy for himself; but, taking it so, the latter part of the verse must be the words of *our Lord*, and therefore I think the whole is meant of him. Christ did, as it were, say, "Now commend me to such a man as this, that knows how to do well for himself, how to improve a present opportunity, and how to provide for a future necessity." He does not commend him because he had done *falsely* to his master, but because he had done *wisely* for himself. Yet perhaps herein he did well for his master too, and but justly with the tenants. Now this forecast of his, for a comfortable subsistence in this world, shames our improvidence for another world: *The children of this world,* who choose and have their portions in it, *are wiser for their generation,* act more considerately, and better consult their worldly interest and advantage, than the *children of light,* who enjoy the gospel, in *their generation,* that is, in the

concerns of their souls and eternity.

II. The application of this parable, and the inferences drawn from it (*v.* 9): "*I say unto you,* you my disciples" (for to them this parable is directed, *v.* 1), "though you have but little in this world, consider how you may do good with that little." Observe,

1. What it is that our Lord Jesus here exhorts us to; to provide for our comfortable reception to the happiness of another world, by making good use of our possessions and enjoyments in this world: "*Make to yourselves friends of the mammon of unrighteousness,* as the steward with his lord's goods made his lord's tenants his friends." It is the wisdom of the men of this world so to manage their money as that they may have the benefit of it hereafter, and not for the present only; therefore they put it out to interest, buy land with it, put it into this or the other fund. Now we should learn of them to make use of our money so as that we may be the better for it hereafter in another world, as they do in hopes to be the better for it hereafter in this world.

2. With what arguments he presses this exhortation to abound in works of piety and charity.

(1) If we do not make a right use of the *gifts of God's providence,* how can we expect from him those present and future comforts which are the *gifts of his spiritual grace?*

(2) We have no other way to prove ourselves the servants of God than by giving up ourselves so entirely to his service as to make *mammon,* that is, all our worldly gain, serviceable to us in his service (*v.* 13): *No servant can serve two masters,* whose commands are so inconsistent as those of God and *mammon* are. If a man will *love* the world, and *hold to that,* it cannot be but he will *hate* God and *despise* him. But, on the other hand, if a man will *love* God, and *adhere* to him, he will comparatively *hate* the world (whenever God and the world come into competition) and will *despise* it, and make all his business and success in the world some way or other conducive to his furtherance in the business of religion; and the things of the world shall be made to help him in serving God and working out his salvation.

3. We are here told what entertainment this doctrine of Christ met with among the Pharisees, and what rebuke he gave them.

(1) They wickedly *ridiculed* him, *v.* 14. *The Pharisees, who were covetous, heard all these things,* and could not contradict him, but *they derided him.* Let us consider this, [1] As their *sin,* and the fruit of their *covetousness,* which was their reigning sin, their own iniquity. [2] As *his suffering.* Our Lord Jesus endured not only the *contradiction* of sinners, but their *contempt;* they *had him in derision* all the day.

(2) He justly reproved them; not for *deriding* him (he knew how to *despise the shame*), but for *deceiving* themselves with the shows and colours of piety, when they were strangers to the power of it, *v.* 15. Here is,

[1] Their *specious outside;* nay, it was a *splendid* one. *First,* They

justified themselves before men; they denied whatever ill was laid to their charge, even by Christ himself.

[2] Their *odious inside*, which was under the eye of God: "He *knows your heart*, and it is in his sight an *abomination*; for it is full of all manner of wickedness."

(3) He turned from them to the publicans and sinners, as more likely to be wrought upon by his gospel than those covetous conceited Pharisees (v. 16).

(4) Yet still he protests against any design to invalidate the law (v. 17): *It is easier for heaven and earth to pass*, to pass away, though the foundations of the earth and the pillars of heaven are so firmly established, *than for one tittle of the law to fail*. The more law is confirmed and ratified, and not one tittle of that fails; the duties enjoined by it are duties still; the sins forbidden by it are sins still.

RICH MAN AND LAZARUS
(vv. 19-31)

As the parable of the prodigal son set before us the grace of the gospel, which is encouraging to us all, so this sets before us the *wrath to come*, and is designed for our awakening; and very fast asleep those are in sin that will not be awakened by it. In this description (for so I shall choose to call it) we may observe,

I. The different condition of a *wicked rich man*, and a *godly poor man*, in this world. We know that as some of late, so the Jews of old, were ready to make prosperity one of the marks of a true

church, of a good man and a favourite of heaven, so that they could hardly have any favourable thoughts of a *poor man*. This mistake Christ, upon all occasions, set himself to correct, and here very fully, where we have,

1. A wicked man, and one that will be for ever miserable, in the height of prosperity (v. 19): *There was a certain rich man*. Now we are told concerning this rich man,

(1) That he was *clothed in purple and fine linen*, and that was his *adorning*. He never appeared abroad but in great magnificence.

(2) He *fared* deliciously and *sumptuously every day*. It is true, eating good meat and wearing good clothes are lawful; but it is as true that they often become the food and fuel of pride and luxury, and so turn into sin to us. The sin of this rich man was not so much his dress or his diet, but his providing only for himself.

2. Here is a godly man, and one that will be for ever happy, in the depth of adversity and distress (v. 20): *There was a certain beggar*, named *Lazarus*. Now observe,

[1] His expectations from the rich man's table: *He desired to be fed with the crumbs*, v. 21. He did not look for a feast from off his table, though he ought to have had one, one of the best; but would be thankful for the crumbs from under the table, the broken meat which was the rich man's leavings; nay, the leavings of his dogs. He was *poor*, but he was *poor in spirit*, contentedly poor. This miserable man was a good man, and in favour with God.

[2] The usage he had from the dogs: *The dogs came and licked his sores*. The rich man kept a kennel of hounds, it may be, or other dogs, for his diversion, and to please his fancy, and these were fed to the full, when poor Lazarus could not get enough to keep him alive.

II. Here is the *different condition* of this *godly poor man*, and this *wicked rich man*, *at* and *after death*.

1. They both died (*v.* 22): The *beggar died*; the *rich man also died*. Death is the common lot of rich and poor, godly and ungodly; there they meet together.

2. The beggar *died first*. God often takes godly people out of the world, when he leaves the wicked to flourish still.

3. The rich man *died and was buried*. Nothing is said of the interment of the poor man. They dug a hole any where, and tumbled his body in, without any solemnity. But the rich man had a pompous funeral, lay in state, had a train of mourners to attend him to his grave, and a stately monument set up over it.

4. The beggar died and was *carried by angels into Abraham's bosom*. How much did the honour done to his soul, by this convoy of it to its rest, exceed the honour done to the rich man, by the carrying of his body with so much magnificence to its grave! Observe (1) His soul *existed* in a state of separation from the body. It did not *die*, or *fall asleep*, with the body; his candle was not put out with him; but lived, and acted, and knew what it did, and what

was done to it. (2) His soul *removed* to another world, to the world of spirits; it returned to God who gave it, to its native country; this is implied in its being *carried*. The spirit of a man goes upward. (3) Angels took care of it; it was *carried by angels*. They are ministering spirits to the heirs of salvation, not only while they live, but when they die. (4) It was carried *into Abraham's bosom*. The Jews expressed the happiness of the righteous at death three ways:—they go *to the garden of Eden*; they go *to be under the throne of glory*; and they go *to the bosom of Abraham*, and it is this which our Saviour here makes use of. Abraham was the *father of the faithful*; and whither should the souls of the faithful be gathered but to him, who, as a tender father, lays them *in his bosom*, especially at their first coming, to bid them welcome, and to refresh them when newly come from the sorrows and fatigues of this world?

5. The next news you hear of the *rich man*, after the account of his *death* and *burial*, is, that *in hell he lifted up his eyes, being in torment, v.* 23.

(1) His state is very miserable. *He is in hell*, in *hades*, in the state of separate souls, and there he is in *the utmost misery* and *anguish* possible. This *rich man* had entirely devoted himself to the pleasures of the *world of sense*, was wholly *taken up* with them, and *took up with them* for his portion, and therefore was wholly unfit for the pleasures of the *world of spirits*; to such a carnal mind as

his they would indeed be no pleasure, nor could he have any relish of them, and therefore he is of course excluded from them.

(2) The misery of his state is aggravated by his knowledge of the happiness of Lazarus: He *lifts up his eyes*, and *sees Abraham afar off*, and *Lazarus in his bosom*. It is the soul that is *in torment*, and they are the eyes of the mind that are lifted up.

III. Here is an account of what passed between the rich man and Abraham in the separate state—a state of separation one from another, and of both from this world. Though it is probable that there will not be, nor are, any such dialogues between glorified saints and damned sinners, yet it is very proper to represent what will be the mind and sentiments both of the one and of the other. Now in this discourse we have,

1. The request which the rich man made to Abraham for some mitigation of his present misery, *v.* 24. Observe here,

(1) The title he gives to Abraham: *Father Abraham*. Note, There are many in hell that can call Abraham *father*, that were Abraham's seed after the flesh, nay, and many that were, in name and profession, the children of the covenant made with Abraham.

(2) The representation he makes to him of his present deplorable condition: *I am tormented in this flame.*

(3) His request to Abraham, in consideration of this misery: *Have mercy on me*. Note, The day is coming when those that make light of divine mercy will beg hard

for it. He that had no mercy on Lazarus, yet expects Lazarus should have mercy on him; "for," thinks he, "Lazarus is better natured than ever I was." The particular favour he begs is, *Send Lazarus, that he may dip the tip of his finger in water, and cool my tongue.*

2. The reply which Abraham gave to this request. In general, he did not grant it. He would not allow him one *drop of water, to cool* his tongue. See how justly this rich man is paid in his own coin. He that denied a crumb is denied a drop. Now it is said to us, *Ask, and it shall be given you*; but, if we let slip this accepted time, we may ask, and it shall not be given us. But this is not all; had Abraham only said, "You shall have nothing to abate your torment," it had been sad; but he says a great deal which would add to his torment, and make the flame hotter, for every thing in hell will be tormenting.

(1) He calls him *son*, a kind and civil title, but here it serves only to aggravate the denial of his request, which shut up the bowels of the compassion of a father from him. He had been a son, but a rebellious one, and now an abandoned disinherited one.

(2) He puts him in mind of what had been both his own condition and the condition of Lazarus, in their *life-time*: *Son, remember*; this is a cutting word. The memories of damned souls will be their tormentors, and conscience will then be awakened and stirred up to do its office, which here they would not suffer it to do.

(3) He puts him in mind of

Lazarus's present bliss, and his own misery: *But now* the tables are turned, and so they must abide for ever; *now he is comforted, and thou art tormented.*

(4) He assures him that it was to no purpose to think of having any relief by the ministry of Lazarus; for (*v.* 26), *Besides all this,* worse yet, *between us and you there is a great gulf fixed,* an impassable one, *a great chasm,* that so there can be no communication between glorified saints and damned sinners. In this world, blessed be God, there is no gulf fixed between a state of nature and grace, but we may pass from the one to the other, from sin to God; but if we die in our sins, if we throw ourselves into the pit of destruction, there is no coming out. It is a pit *in which there is no water,* and *out of which there is no redemption.* The decree and counsel of God have fixed this gulf, which all the world cannot unfix.

3. The further request he had to make to his father Abraham, not for himself, his mouth is stopped.

(1) He begs that Lazarus might be *sent to his father's house,* upon an errand thither: *I pray thee therefore, father, v.* 27. "Send him back *to my father's house*; he knows well enough where it is, has been there many a time, having been denied the crumbs that fell from the table. He knows I have *five brethren* there; if he appear to them, they will *know him,* and will regard what he saith, for they knew him to be an honest man. Let him *testify to them*; let him tell them what condition I am in, and that I brought myself to it

by my luxury and sensuality, and my unmercifulness to the poor. Let him warn them not to tread in my steps, nor to go on in the way wherein I led them, and left them, *lest they also come into this place of torment,*" *v.* 28.

(2) Abraham denies him this favour too. There is no request granted in hell. Abraham leaves them to the testimony of Moses and the prophets, the ordinary means of conviction and conversion; they have the written word, which they may read and hear read.

(3) He urges his request yet further (*v.* 30): "*Nay, father Abraham,* give me leave to press this. It is true, they have Moses and the prophets, and, if they would but give a due regard to them, it would be sufficient; but they do not, they will not; yet it may be hoped, *if one went to them from the dead, they would repent,* that would be a more sensible conviction to them."

(4) Abraham insists upon the denial of it, with a conclusive reason (*v.* 31): "*If they hear not Moses and the prophets,* and will not believe the testimony nor take the warning they give, *neither will they be persuaded though one rose from the dead.* If they regard not the public revelation, which is confirmed by miracles, neither would they be wrought upon by a private testimony to themselves." Let us not therefore desire visions and apparitions, nor seek to the dead, but *to the law and to the testimony* (Isa, viii. 19, 20), for that is *the sure word of prophecy,* upon which we may depend,

CHAPTER SEVENTEEN
OFFENCES (vv. 1–10)

We are here taught,

I. That the *giving of offences* is a *great sin*, and that which we should every one of us avoid and carefully watch against, *vv.* 1, 2. *It is almost impossible but that offences will come*, and therefore we are concerned to provide accordingly; but *woe to him through whom they come*, his doom will be heavy (*v.* 2), more terrible than that of the worst of the malefactors who are condemned to be thrown into the sea, for they perish under a load of guilt more *ponderous* than that of *millstones*. This includes a woe, 1. To persecutors, who offer any injury to the least of Christ's *little ones*, in word or deed, by which they are discouraged in serving Christ, and doing their duty, or in danger of being driven off from it. 2. To seducers, who corrupt the truths of Christ and his ordinances, and so *trouble the minds of the disciples*; for they are those by whom *offences come*. 3. To those who, under the profession of the Christian name, live scandalously, and thereby weaken the hands and sadden the hearts of God's people.

II. That the *forgiving of offences* is a *great duty*, and that which we should every one of us make conscience of (*v.* 3): *Take heed to yourselves*. This may refer either to what goes before, or to what follows: *Take heed that you offend not one of these little ones*. Ministers must be very careful not to say or do anything that may be a discouragement to weak Chris-

tians; there is need of great caution, and they ought to speak and act very considerately, for fear of this: or, "When *your brother trespasses against you*, does you any injury, puts any slight or affront upon you, if he be accessary to any damage done you in your property or reputation, *take heed to yourselves at such a time*, lest you be put into a passion; lest, when your spirits are provoked, you *speak unadvisedly*, and rashly vow revenge (Prov. xxiv. 29): *I will do so to him as he hath done to me*. Take heed what you say at such a time, lest you say amiss."

1. If you are permitted to *rebuke him*, you are advised to do so. Smother not the resentment, but give it vent.

2. You are commanded, upon his repentance, to forgive him, and to be perfectly reconciled to him: *If he repent, forgive him*; forget the injury, never think of it again, much less upbraid him with it.

3. You are to repeat this every time he repeats his trespass, *v.* 4. If he could be supposed to be either so negligent, or so impudent, as to *trespass against thee seven times in a day*, and as often profess himself sorry for his fault, and promise not again to offend in like manner, continue to *forgive him*.

III. That we have all need to get our *faith* strengthened, because, as that grace grows, all other graces grow. Faith in God's pardoning mercy will enable us to get over the greatest difficulties that lie in the way of our forgiving our brother. Christ assured them of the wonderful efficacy of true faith (*v.* 6): "*If ye had faith as a grain of mustard-seed*, so *small* as mustard-seed, you might do wonders much beyond what you now do; nothing would be too hard for you, that was fit to be done for the glory of God, and the confirmation of the doctrine you preach, yea, though it were the *transplanting of a tree* from the earth, *to the sea*. See Matt. xvii. 20. As with God *nothing is impossible*, so are all *things possible to him that can believe*.

IV. That, whatever we do in the service of Christ, we must be very humble, and not imagine that we can merit any favour at his hand, or claim it as a debt; even the apostles themselves, who did so much more for Christ than others, must not think that they had thereby made him their debtor. 1. We are all *God's servants* (his *apostles* and *ministers* are in a special manner *so*), and, as servants, are bound to do all we can for his honour. 2. As God's servants, it becomes us to fill up our time with duty, and we have a variety of work appointed us to do; we ought to make the end of one service the beginning of another. 3. Our principal care here must be to do the duty of our relation, and leave it to our Master to give us the comfort of it, when and how he thinks fit. No servant expects that his master should say to him, *Go and sit down to meat*; it is time enough to do that when we have *done our day's work*. Let us be in care to finish our work, and to do that

well, and then the reward will come in due time. 4. It is fit that Christ should be served before us: *Make ready wherewith I may sup, and afterwards thou shalt eat and drink*. Doubting Christians say that they cannot give to Christ the glory of his love as they should, because they have not yet obtained the comfort of it; but this is wrong. First let Christ have the glory of it, let us attend him with our praises, and then we shall *eat and drink* in the comfort of that love, and in this there is a feast. 5. Christ's servants, when they are to wait upon him, must *gird themselves*, must free themselves from every thing that is entangling and encumbering, and fit themselves with a close application of mind to go on, and go through, with their work; they must *gird up the loins of their mind*. 6. Christ's servants do not so much as merit his thanks for any service they do him: "*Does he thank that servant?* Does he reckon himself indebted to him for it? No, by no means." No good works of ours can merit any thing at the hand of God. 7. Whatever we do for Christ, though it should be more perhaps than some others do, yet it is no more than is our duty to do. 8. The best servants of Christ, even when they do the best services, must humbly acknowledge that they are *unprofitable servants*; though they are not those unprofitable servants that bury their talents, and shall be cast into *utter darkness*, yet as to Christ, and any advantage that can accrue to him by their services, they are *unprofitable*. For God is happy without us, but we are undone without him.

TEN LEPERS (*vv.* 11–19)

We have here an account of the cure of ten lepers, which we had not in any other of the evangelists. Observe,

I. The address of these lepers to Christ. They were ten in a company; for, though they were shut out from society with others, yet those that were infected were at liberty to converse with one another. Now observe, 1. They *met* Christ *as he entered into a certain village.* They did not stay till he had refreshed himself for some time after the fatigue of his journey, but met him as he *entered* the town, weary as he was; and yet he did not put them off, nor adjourn their cause. 2. They *stood afar off,* knowing that by the law their disease obliged them to *keep their distance.* A sense of our spiritual leprosy should make us very humble in all our approaches to Christ. 3. Their request was unanimous, and very importunate (*v.* 13): *They lifted up their voices,* being at a distance, and cried, *Jesus, Master, have mercy on us.*

II. Christ sent them to *the priest,* to be *inspected* by him, who was the judge of the leprosy. He did not tell them positively that they should be *cured,* but bade them *go show themselves to the priests, v.* 14. This was a trial of their obedience, and it was fit that it should be so tried, as Naaman's in a like case: *Go wash in Jordan.*

III. *As they went, they were cleansed,* and so became fit to be looked upon by the priest, and to have a certificate from him that they were clean. Observe, *Then* we may expect God to meet us with mercy when we are found in the way of duty.

IV. One of them, and but one, *returned, to give thanks, v.* 15. When he *saw that he was healed,* instead of going forward to the priest, to be by him declared clean, and so discharged from his confinement, which was all that the rest aimed at, he *turned back* towards him who was the Author of his cure, whom he wished to have the glory of it, before he received the benefit of it. He appears to have been very hearty and affectionate in his thanksgivings: *With a loud voice he glorified God,* acknowledging it to come originally from *him.* But he also made a particular address of thanks to Christ (*v.* 16): *He fell down at his feet,* put himself into the most humble reverent posture he could, and *gave him thanks.*

V. Christ took notice of this one that had thus distinguished himself; for, it seems, he was a Samaritan, whereas the rest were Jews, *v.* 16. The Samaritans were separatists from the Jewish church, and had not the pure knowledge and worship of God among them that the Jews had, and yet it was one of them that *glorified God,* when the Jews forgot, or, when it was moved to them, *refused,* to do it. Now observe here,

1. The particular notice Christ took of him, of the grateful return he made, and the ingratitude of those that were sharers with him in the mercy—that he who

was a *stranger* to the common-wealth of Israel was the only one that *returned to give glory to God, vv,* 17, 18.

2. The great encouragement Christ gave him, *v.* 19. The rest had their *cure,* and had it not *revoked,* as justly it might have been, for their ingratitude, though they had such a good example of gratitude set before them; but he had his cure confirmed particularly with an encomium: *Thy faith hath made thee whole.* The rest were *made whole* by the power of Christ, in compassion to their distress, and in answer to their prayer; but he was made whole *by his faith,* by which Christ saw him distinguished from the rest. Note, Temporal mercies are *then* doubled and sweetened to us when they are *fetched* in by the prayers of faith, and *returned* by the praises of faith.

THE KINGDOM TO COME
(*vv.* 20–37)

We have here a discourse of Christ's concerning the *kingdom of God,* that is, the kingdom of the Messiah, which was now shortly to be *set up,* and of which there was great expectation.

I. Here is the demand of the Pharisees concerning it, which occasioned this discourse.

II. Christ's reply to this demand, directed to the Pharisees first, and afterwards to his own disciples, who knew better how to under-stand it (*v.* 22); what he said to both, he saith to us.

1. That the kingdom of the Messiah was to be a *spiritual kingdom,* and not temporal and

external. They asked *when* it would come. "You know not what you ask," saith Christ; "it may come, and you not be aware of it." For it has not an *external show,* as other kingdoms have, the advancements and revolutions of which are taken notice of by the nations of the earth, and fill the newspapers; so they expected this kingdom of God would do. "No," saith Christ, (1) "It will have a silent entrance, without pomp, without noise; it *cometh not with observation.*" (2) "It has a *spiritual* influence: *The kingdom of God is within you.*" It is not of this world, John xviii. 36. Its glory does not strike men's fancies, but affects their spirits, and its power is over their souls and consciences; from them it receives homage, and not from their bodies only. The *kingdom of God* will not change men's outward condition, but their hearts and lives.

2. That the setting up of this kingdom was a work that would meet with a great deal of *opposition* and *interruption, v.* 22. This looks forward to his disciples in after-ages; they must expect much disappointment; the gospel will not be always preached with equal liberty and success. Ministers and churches will sometimes be under *outward restraints.* Teachers will be removed into corners, and solemn assemblies scattered. Then they will wish to see such days of opportunity as they have formerly enjoyed, sabbath days, sacrament days, preaching days, praying days; these are *days of the Son of man,* in which we hear from him, and converse with him. The time

may come when we may in vain wish for such days. God teaches us to know the worth of such mercies by the want of them. It concerns us, while they are continued, to *improve* them, and in the years of plenty to lay up in store for the years of famine.

3. That Christ and his kingdom are not to be looked for in this or that particular place, but his appearance will be general in all places at once (*vv.* 23, 24). The kingdom of God was not designed to be the glory of one people only, but to *give light to the Gentiles*. The design of the setting up of Christ's kingdom was not to make one *nation great*, but to make *all nations good*—some, at least, of all nations; and this point shall be gained, though the *nations rage*, and the *kings of the earth set themselves* with all their might against it.

4. That the Messiah must *suffer* before he must *reign* (*v.* 25). They thought of having the kingdom of the Messiah set up in external splendour: "No," saith Christ, "we must go by the cross to the crown. The *Son of man must suffer many things*."

5. That the setting up of the kingdom of the Messiah would introduce the destruction of the Jewish nation, whom it would find in a deep sleep of *security*, and drowned in *sensuality*, as the old world was in the days of Noah, and Sodom in the days of Lot, *vv.* 26, &c.

6. That it ought to be the care of his disciples and followers to distinguish themselves from the unbelieving Jews in that day, and,

leaving them, their city and country, to themselves, to flee at the signal given, according to the direction that should be given. This flight of theirs from Jerusalem must be *expeditious*, and must not be retarded by any concern about their worldly affairs (*v.* 31). When they have made their escape, they must not think of returning (*v.* 32): "*Remember Lot's wife*; and take warning by her not only to flee from this Sodom (for so Jerusalem is become, Isa. i. 10), but to persevere in your flight, and do not *look back*, as she did; be not loth to leave a place marked for destruction, whomsoever or whatsoever you leave behind you, that is ever so dear to you."

7. That all good Christians should certainly escape, but many of them very *narrowly*, from that destruction, *vv.* 34–36.

8. That this distinguishing, dividing, discriminating work shall be done in all places, as far as the kingdom of God shall extend, *v.* 37. *Where, Lord?* They had enquired concerning the time, and he would not gratify their curiosity with any information concerning that; they therefore tried him with another question: "*Where, Lord?* Where shall those be *safe* that are *taken*? Where shall those *perish* that are left?" The answer is proverbial, and may be explained so as to answer each side of the question: *Wheresoever the body is, thither will the eagles be gathered together*. (1) Wherever the wicked are, who are marked for perdition, they shall *be found out* by the judgments of God; as wherever a dead carcase is, the birds of prey

will smell it out, and make a prey of it. (2) Wherever the godly are, who are marked for preservation, they *shall be found* happy in the enjoyment of Christ. As the dissolution of the Jewish church shall be extended to all parts, so shall the constitution of the Christian church. Wherever Christ is, believers will flock to him, and meet in him, as eagles about the prey, without being directed or shown the way, by the instinct of the new nature.

CHAPTER EIGHTEEN
THE POOR WIDOW (vv. 1–8)

This parable has its key hanging at the door; the drift and design of it are *prefixed*. Christ spoke it with this intent, to teach us that *men ought always to pray and not to faint*, v. 1.

I. Christ shows, by a parable, the *power of importunity* among men, who will be swayed by that, when nothing else will influence, to do what is just and right. He gives you an instance of an honest cause that succeeded before an unjust judge, not by the equity or compassionableness of it, but purely by *dint of importunity*. Observe here, 1. The bad character of the judge that was in a certain city. He *neither feared God nor regarded man*; he had no manner of concern either for his conscience or for his reputation; he stood in no awe either of the wrath of God against him or of the censures of men concerning him: or, he took no care to do his duty either to God or man; he was a perfect stranger both to godliness

and honour, and had no notion of either. 2. The distressed case of a poor widow that was necessitated to make her appeal to him, being wronged by some one that thought to bear her down with power and terror. She had manifestly right on her side; but, it should seem, in soliciting to have right done her, she tied not herself to the formalities of the law, but made personal application to the judge from day to day at his own house, still crying, *Avenge me of mine adversary*, that is, *Do me justice against mine adversary*; not that she desired to be revenged on him for any thing he had done against her, but that he might be obliged to restore what effects he had of hers in his hands, and might be disabled any more to oppress her. 3. The difficulty and discouragement she met with in her cause: *He would not for awhile*. According to his usual practice, he frowned upon her, took no notice of her cause, but connived at all the wrong her adversary did her; for she had no bribe to give him, no great man whom he stood in any awe of to speak for her, so that he did not at all incline to redress her grievances; and he himself was conscious of the reason of his dilatoriness, and could not but own within himself that he *neither feared God nor regarded man*. 4. The gaining of her point by continually *dunning* this unjust judge (v. 5): "*Because this widow troubleth me*, gives me a continual toil, I will hear her cause, and do her justice; not so much lest by her clamour against me she bring me into an ill name, as lest by her clamour to me she weary me; for she is resolved that she will give me no rest till it is done, and therefore I will do it, to save myself further trouble; as good at first as at last." Thus she got justice done her by continual craving; she begged it at his door, followed him in the streets, solicited him in open court, and still her cry was, *Avenge me of mine adversary*, which he was forced to do, to get rid of her; for his conscience, bad as he was, would not suffer him to send her to prison for an affront upon the court.

II. He applies this for the encouragement of God's praying people to pray with faith and fervency, and to persevere therein.

1. He assures them that God will at length be gracious to them (v. 6): *Hear what the unjust judge saith*, how he owns himself quite overcome by a constant importunity, *and shall not God avenge his own elect*? Observe,

(1) What it is that they desire and expect: that God would *avenge his own elect*. God's own elect meet with a great deal of trouble and opposition in this world; there are *many adversaries* that fight against them; Satan is their great adversary. That which is wanted and waited for is God's preserving and protecting them, and the work of his hands in them; his securing the interest of the church in the world and his grace in the heart.

(2) What it is that is required of God's people in order to the obtaining of this: they must *cry*

day and night to him; not that he needs their remonstrances, or can be moved by their pleadings, but this he has made their duty, and to this he has promised mercy.

(3) What discouragements they may perhaps meet with in their prayers and expectations. He may *bear long with them*, and may not presently appear for them, in answer to their prayers.

(4) What assurance they have that mercy will come at last, though it be delayed, and how it is supported by what the unjust judge saith: If this widow prevail by being importunate, much more shall God's elect prevail. For, [1] This widow was a *stranger*, nothing related to the judge; but God's praying people are his own elect, whom he knows, and loves, and delights in, and has always concerned himself for. [2] She was but *one*, but the praying people of God are *many*, all of whom come to him on the same errand, and agree to ask what they need, Matt. xviii. 19. [3] She came to a *judge* that bade her *keep her distance*; we come to a *Father* that bids us *come boldly* to him, and teaches us to cry, *Abba, Father*. [4] She came to an *unjust judge*; we come to a *righteous Father* (John xvii. 25), one that regards his own glory and the comforts of his poor creatures, especially those in distress, as *widows* and *fatherless*. [5] She came to this judge purely upon her own account; but God is himself engaged in the cause which we are soliciting; and we can say, *Arise, O Lord, plead thine* own cause; and *what wilt thou do to*

thy great name? [6] She had no friend to speak for her, to add force to her petition, and to use interest for her more than her own; but we have an *Advocate with the Father*, his own Son, who *ever lives to make intercession* for us, and has a powerful prevailing interest in heaven. [7] She had no promise of speeding, no, nor any encouragement given her to ask; but we have the golden sceptre held out to us, are told to ask, with a promise that it shall be given to us. [8] She could have access to the judge only at some certain times; but we may cry to God *day and night*, at all hours, and therefore may the rather hope to prevail by importunity. [9] Her importunity was provoking to the judge, and she might fear lest it should set him more against her; but our importunity is pleasing to God; the prayer of the upright is *his delight*, and therefore, we may hope, shall avail much, if it be an effectual fervent prayer.

2. He intimates to them that, notwithstanding this, they will begin to be weary of waiting for him (*v.* 8): "*Nevertheless*, though such assurances are given that God will avenge his own elect, yet, *when the Son of man cometh, shall he find faith on the earth?*" The question implies a strong negation: No, he will not; he himself foresees it.

TWO KINDS OF PRAYER
(*vv.* 9–14)

The scope of this parable likewise is prefixed to it, and we are told (*v.* 9) who they were whom it was levelled at, and for whom it was calculated. He designed it for the conviction of some who *trusted in themselves that they were righteous, and despised others*. Now Christ by this parable would show such their folly, and that thereby they shut themselves out from acceptance with God.

I. Here are both these addressing themselves to the duty of prayer at the same place and time (*v.* 10): *Two men went up into the temple* (for the temple stood upon a hill) *to pray.*

II. Here is the Pharisee's address to God (for a prayer I cannot call it): He *stood* and *prayed thus with himself* (*vv.* 11, 12); *standing by himself, he prayed thus*, so some read it; he was wholly intent upon himself, had nothing in his eye but *self*, his own praise, and not God's glory. We see,

1. That he *trusted to himself that he was righteous*. A great many good things he said of himself, which we will suppose to be true. Now all this was very well and commendable. Miserable is the condition of those who come short of the righteousness of this Pharisee: yet he was not accepted; and why was he not? (1) His giving God thanks for this, though in itself a good thing, yet seems to be a mere formality. He does not say, *By the grace of God I am what I am*, as Paul did, but turns it off with a slight, *God, I thank thee*, which is intended but for a plausible introduction to a proud vainglorious ostentation of himself. (2) He makes his boast of this, and dwells with delight upon this subject, as if all his

business to the temple was to tell God Almighty how very good he was; and he is ready to say, with those hypocrites that we read of (Isa. lviii. 3), *Wherefore have we fasted, and thou seest not?* (3) He *trusted* to it as a righteousness, and not only mentioned it, but pleaded it, as if hereby he had merited at the hands of God, and made him his debtor. (4) Here is not one word of prayer in all he saith. He went *up to the temple to pray*, but forgot his errand, was so full of himself and his own goodness that he thought he had need of nothing, no, not of the favour and grace of God, which, it would seem he did not think worth asking.

2. That he *despised others*. (1) He thought meanly of all mankind but himself: *I thank thee that I am not as other men are*. He speaks indefinitely, as if he were better than any. We may have reason to thank God that we are not as *some men* are, that are notoriously wicked and vile; but to speak at random thus, as if *we* only were good, and all besides us were reprobates, is to judge by wholesale. (2) He thought meanly in a particular manner of this publican, whom he had left behind, it is probable, in the court of the Gentiles, and whose company he had fallen into as he came to the temple. He knew that he was a publican, and therefore very uncharitably concluded that he was an *extortioner, unjust*, and all that is evil. Suppose it had been so, and he had known it, what business had he to take notice of it? There could not be a plainer evidence,

not only of the want of humility and charity, but of reigning pride and malice, than this was.

III. Here is the publican's address to God, which was the reverse of the Pharisee's, as full of *humility* and *humiliation* as his was of *pride* and *ostentation*; as full of *repentance* for sin, and *desire* towards God, as his was of *confidence* in *himself* and his own righteousness and sufficiency.

1. He expressed his repentance and humility in *what he did*; and his gesture, when he addressed himself to his devotions, was *expressive* of great seriousness and humility, and the proper clothing of a broken, penitent, and obedient heart. (1) He *stood afar off*. The Pharisee *stood*, but crowded up as high as he could, to the upper end of the court; the publican *kept at a distance* under a sense of his unworthiness to draw near to God. (2) He *would not lift up so much as his eyes to heaven*, much less his *hands*, as was usual in prayer. The dejection of his looks is an indication of the dejection of his mind at the thought of sin. (3) He *smote upon his breast*, in a holy indignation at himself for sin: "Thus would I smite this wicked heart of mine, the poisoned fountain out of which flow all the streams of sin, if I could come at it."

2. He expressed it *in what he said*. His prayer was *short*. Fear and shame hindered him from saying much; sighs and groans swallowed up his words; but what he said was to the purpose: *God, be merciful to me a sinner*. And blessed be God that we have this

prayer upon record as an answered prayer, and that we are sure that he who prayed it went to his house justified; and so shall we, if we pray it, as he did, through Jesus Christ: *"God, be merciful to me a sinner."*

IV. Here is the publican's *acceptance with God*. We have seen how differently these two addressed themselves to God; it is now worth while to enquire how they sped. There were those who would cry up the Pharisee, by whom he would go to his house applauded, and who would look with contempt upon this sneaking whining publican. But our Lord Jesus, to whom all hearts are open, all desires known, and from whom no secret is hid, who is perfectly acquainted with all proceedings in the court of heaven, assures us that this poor, penitent, brokenhearted publican *went to his house justified, rather than the other.*

The reason given for this is because God's glory is to *resist the proud, and give grace to the humble.* 1. Proud men, who *exalt themselves*, are *rivals with God*, and therefore *they shall* certainly be *abased*. 2. Humble men, who *abase themselves*, are *subject to God*, and they shall be *exalted*. God has preferment in store for those that will take it as a favour, not for those that demand it as a debt.

ACTIONS AND REACTIONS
(*vv.* 15–34)

This passage we had both in Matthew (xix and xx) and Mark;

it very fitly follows here after the story of the publican, as a confirmation of the truth which was to be illustrated by that parable, that those shall be accepted with God, and honoured, who humble themselves, and for them Christ has *blessings in store*, the choicest and best of blessings.

A BLIND BEGGAR
(*vv.* 35–43)

Christ came not only to bring *light* to a *dark* world, and so to set before us the *objects* we are to have in view, but also to give *sight* to blind *souls*, and by healing the *organ* to enable them to view those objects. As a token of this, he cured many of their bodily blindness; we have now an account of one to whom he *gave sight* near Jericho. Mark gives us an account of one, and names him, whom he cured *as he went out of Jericho*, Mark x. 46. Matthew speaks of two whom he cured *as they departed* from Jericho, Matt. xx. 30. Luke says it was *when he was near* to Jericho, which might be when he was going out of it as well as when he was coming into it.

CHAPTER NINETEEN
ZACCHEUS (*vv.* 1–10)

Many, no doubt, were converted to the faith of Christ of whom no account is kept in the gospels; but the conversion of some, whose case had something in it extraordinary, is recorded, as this of Zaccheus. Observe,

I. Who, and what, this Zaccheus was. His name bespeaks him a

Jew. *Zaccai* was a common name among the Jews; they had a famous rabbi, much about this time, of that name. Observe, 1. His calling, and the post he was in: *He was the chief among the publicans*, receiver-general; other publicans were officers under him; he was, as some think, farmer of the customs. We often read of publicans coming to Christ; but here was one that was *chief* of the publicans, was in authority, that enquired after him. God has his remnant among all sorts. Christ came to save even the *chief of sinners*, and therefore even the *chief of publicans*. 2. His circumstances in the world were very considerable: *He was rich*. The inferior publicans were commonly men of broken fortunes, and low in the world; but he that was *chief of the publicans* had raised a good estate. Christ had lately shown how *hard* it is for *rich people to enter into the kingdom of God*, yet presently produces an instance of one rich man that had been lost, and was found, and that not as the prodigal by being reduced to want.

II. How he came in Christ's way, and what was the occasion of his acquaintance with him. 1. He had a great *curiosity to see Jesus*, what kind of a man he was, having heard great talk of him, *v*. 3. 2. He could not get his curiosity gratified in this matter because he was *little*, and the crowd was *great*. Zaccheus was *low of stature*, and over-topped by all about him, so that he could not get a sight of Jesus. Many that are little of stature have large

souls, and are lively in spirit. 3. Because he would not disappoint his curiosity he *forgot his gravity*, as chief of the publicans, and *ran before*, like a boy, and *climbed up into a sycamore-tree, to see him*.

III. The notice Christ took of him, the call he gave him to a further acquaintance (*v*. 5), and the efficacy of that call, *v*. 6. 1. Christ *invited himself* to Zaccheus's house, not doubting of his hearty welcome there. He bade him *make haste, and come down*. Those that Christ calls must *come down*, must humble themselves, and not think to climb to heaven by any righteousness of their own; and they must *make haste* and come down, for delays are dangerous. Zaccheus must not hesitate, but hasten; he knows it is not a matter that needs consideration whether he should welcome such a guest to his house. He must *come down*, for Christ intends this day to *wait at his house*, and stay an hour or two with him. *Behold, he stands at the door and knocks*. 2. Zaccheus was *overjoyed* to have such an honour put upon his house (*v*. 6): *He made haste, and came down, and received him joyfully*; and his receiving him *into his house* was an indication and token of his receiving him *into his heart*.

IV. The offence which the people took at this *kind greeting* between Christ and Zaccheus. Those narrow-souled censorious Jews *murmured*, saying that he was *gone to be a guest with a man that is a sinner*; and were not they themselves sinful men? Was it not Christ's errand into the world to seek and save *men* that are *sinners*? But Zaccheus they think to be a sinner above all men that dwelt in Jericho, such a sinner as was not fit to be conversed with.

V. The proofs which Zaccheus gave publicly that, though he had been a *sinner*, he was now a *penitent*, and a true *convert*, *v.* 8. He does not expect to be justified by his works as the Pharisee who boasted of what he had done, but by his *good works* he will, through the grace of God, evidence the *sincerity* of his *faith* and *repentance*; and here he declares what his determination was. He *stood*, which denotes his saying it deliberately and with solemnity, in the nature of a vow to God. He makes it appear that there is a change *in his heart* (and that is repentance), for there is a change in his way.

1. Zaccheus had a good estate, and, whereas he had been in it hitherto laying up treasure for himself, and doing hurt to himself, now he resolves that for the future he will be all towards God, and do good to others with it: *Behold, Lord, the half of my goods I give to the poor*. Not, "I *will* give it by my will when I die," but, "I *do* give it now."

2. Zaccheus was conscious to himself that he had not got all he had honestly and fairly, but some by indirect and unlawful means, and of what he had got by such means he promises to make restitution: "If *I have taken any thing from any man by false accusation*, or if I have wronged any man in the way of my business as a *publican*, exacting more than was appointed, I promise to

restore him *four-fold*." This was the restitution that a thief was to make, Exod. xxii. 1.

VI. Christ's *approbation* and *acceptance* of Zaccheus's conversion, by which also he cleared himself from any imputation in going to be a guest with him, *vv.* 9, 10.

1. Zaccheus is declared to be now a *happy man*. Now he is turned from sin to God; now he has bidden Christ welcome to his house, and is become an honest, charitable, good man: *This day is salvation come to this house*.

2. What Christ had done to make him, in particular, a happy man, was consonant to the great design and intention of his coming into the world, *v.* 10. With the same argument he had before justified his conversing with publicans, Matt. ix. 13. He came from heaven to earth (a long journey) to *seek* that which was *lost* (which had *wandered and gone astray*), and to bring it back (Matt. xviii. 11, 12), and to *save* that which was lost, which was perishing, and in a manner destroyed and cut off. Christ undertook the cause when it was given up for *lost*; undertook to bring those to themselves that were *lost* to God and all goodness. He seeks those that were not worth seeking; he seeks those that sought him not, and asked not for him, as Zaccheus here.

TRUE SERVANTS (*vv.* 11–27)

Our Lord Jesus is now upon his way to Jerusalem, to his last passover, when he was to suffer and die; now here we are told,

I. How the expectations of his friends were *raised* upon this occasion: *They thought that the kingdom of God would immediately appear*, v. 11. The Pharisees expected it about this time (*ch.* xvii. 20), and, it seems, so did Christ's own disciples; but they both had a mistaken notion of it.

II. How their expectations were *checked*, and the mistakes *rectified* upon which they were founded; and this he does in three things:—

1. They expected that he should appear in his glory now *presently*, but he tells them that he must not be publicly installed in his kingdom for a great while yet. He is like *a certain nobleman who goes into a far country, to receive for himself a kingdom*. Christ must go to heaven, to sit down at the right hand of the Father there, and to receive from him *honour and glory*, before the Spirit was poured out by which his kingdom was to be set up on earth, and before a church was to be set up for him in the Gentile world. He must receive the kingdom, and then *return*.

2. They expected that his apostles and immediate attendants should be advanced to dignity and honour, that they should all be made princes and peers, privy-counsellors and judges, and have all the pomp and preferments of the court and of the town. But Christ here tells them that, instead of this, he designed them to be *men of business*; they must expect no other preferment in this world than that of the trading end of the town; he would set them up with a stock under their hands, that they might employ it themselves, in serving him and the interest of his kingdom among men.

They have a *great work* to do now. Their Master leaves them, to receive his kingdom, and, at parting, he gives each of them a *pound*. This signifies the same thing with the talents in the parable that is parallel to this (Matt. xxv.), all the gifts with which Christ's apostles were endued, and the advantages and capacities which they had of serving the interests of Christ in the world, and others, both ministers and Christians, like them in a lower degree.

3. Another thing they expected was, that, when the kingdom of God should appear, the body of the Jewish nation would immediately fall in with it, and submit to it, and all their aversions to Christ and his gospel would immediately vanish; but Christ tells them that, after his departure, the generality of them would persist in their obstinacy and rebellion, and it would be their ruin.

PALM SUNDAY (*vv.* 28–48)

We have here the same account of Christ's riding in some sort of triumph (such as it was) into Jerusalem which we had before in Matthew (xxi) and Mark.

But also observe,

I. The *tears he shed* for the *approaching ruin* of the *city* (v. 41): *When he was come near, he beheld the city, and wept over it.*

1. What a tender spirit Christ was of; we never read that he

laughed, but we often find him in tears.

2. That Jesus Christ *wept* in the midst of his triumphs, *wept* when all about him were *rejoicing*, to show how little he was elevated with the applause and acclamation of the people.

3. That he *wept over Jerusalem*. Note, There are cities to be wept over, and none to be more lamented than Jerusalem, that had been the holy city, and the joy of the whole earth, if it be degenerated. But why did Christ weep at the sight of Jerusalem?

(1) Jerusalem has not improved the day of her opportunities. He wept, and said, *If thou hadst known, even thou at least in this thy day, the things that belong to thy peace,* the making of thy peace with God, and the securing of thine own spiritual and eternal welfare—but thou *dost not know the day of thy visitation*, v. 44.

(2) Jerusalem cannot escape the day of her desolation. The *things of her peace* are now in a manner hidden from her eyes; they will be shortly. The *peaceful things* are not *hidden from the eyes* of particular persons; but it is too late to think now of the nation of the Jews, *as such*, becoming a Christian nation, by embracing Christ. And therefore they are marked for ruin. And there was scarcely one stone *left upon another*. This was for their crucifying Christ; this was because they *knew not the day of their visitation*. Let other cities and nations take warning.

II. The *zeal he showed* for the *present purification of the temple*. Though it must be destroyed ere

long, it does not therefore follow that no care must be taken of it in the meantime. See Matt. xxi. 12.

CHAPTER TWENTY

TEACHING IN THE TEMPLE
(vv. 1–47)

The whole of this passage we have dealt with already, at Matt. xxi–xxiii. Luke adds no more to this.

CHAPTER TWENTY-ONE

THE POOR WIDOW
(vv. 1–4)

This short passage of story we had before in Mark xii.

JUDGMENTS TO COME
(vv. 5–28)

Most of this is common to Matt. (xxiv) and Mark (xiii), so we confine ourselves to what is unique to Luke.

1. "God will stand by you, and own you, and assist you, in your trials; you are his advocates, and you shall be well furnished with instructions, *vv.* 14, 15. *Settle it in your hearts*, impress it upon them, take pains with them to persuade them *not to meditate before what you shall answer*; do not *depend* upon your own wit and ingenuity, your own prudence and policy, and do not *distrust* or *despair* of the immediate and extraordinary aids of the divine grace. I promise you the special assistance of divine grace: *I will give you a mouth and wisdom.*" This proves Christ to be God; for it is God's prerogative to *give wisdom*, and he it is that *made man's mouth*. Note, *First*, A *mouth* and *wisdom* together com-

pletely fit a man both for services and sufferings; *wisdom* to know what to say, and a *mouth* wherewith to say it as it should be said. *Secondly*, Those that plead Christ's cause may depend upon him to give them *a mouth and wisdom*, which way soever they are called to plead it, especially when they are brought before magistrates for his name's sake. It is not said that he will send an angel from heaven to answer for them, though he could do this, but that he will give them a *mouth* and *wisdom* to enable them to answer for themselves, which puts a greater honour upon them, which requires them to use the gifts and graces Christ furnishes them with, and redounds the more to the glory of God, who *stills the enemy and the avenger out of the mouths of babes and sucklings*. *Thirdly*, When Christ gives to his witnesses a *mouth and wisdom*, they are enabled to say that both for him and themselves which *all their adversaries are not able to gainsay or resist*, so that they are silenced, and put to confusion. This was remarkably fulfilled after the pouring out of the Spirit, by whom Christ gave his disciples this *mouth* and *wisdom*, when the apostles were brought before the priests and rulers, and answered them so as to make them ashamed, Acts iv. v. and vi.

(1) "You shall suffer no real damage by all the hardships they shall put upon you (*v.* 18): *There shall not a hair of your head perish.*" Shall some of them lose their heads, and yet not lose a hair? It is a proverbial expression, denoting the greatest indemnity and security imaginable; it is frequently used both in the Old Testament and New, in that sense. "Not a hair of your head shall perish but," *First*, "I will take *cognizance* of it." To this end he had said (Matt. x. 30), *The hairs of your head are all numbered*; and an account is kept of them, so that none of them shall perish but he will miss it. *Secondly*, "It shall be upon a *valuable consideration.*" We do not reckon that *lost* or *perishing* which is laid out for good purposes, and will turn to a good account. *Thirdly*, "It shall be abundantly recompensed; when you come to balance profit and loss, you will find that nothing has perished, but, on the contrary, that you have great gain in present comforts, especially in the joys of a life eternal;" so that though we may be losers for Christ we shall not, we cannot be losers by him in the end.

(2) "It is therefore your duty and interest, in the midst of your own sufferings and those of the nation, to maintain a holy sincerity and serenity of mind, which will keep you always easy (*v.* 19): *In your patience possess ye your souls*; get and keep possession of your souls." Some read it as a promise, "You *may* or *shall* possess your souls." It comes all to one.

2. Having given them an idea of the times for about thirty-eight years next ensuing, he here comes to show them what all those things would issue in at last, namely, the destruction of Jerusalem, and the utter dispersion of the Jewish nation, which would be a little day of judgment, a type and figure of Christ's second coming, which was not so fully spoken of here as in the

parallel place (Matt. xxiv.), yet glanced at; for the destruction of Jerusalem would be as it were the destruction of the world to those whose hearts were bound up in it.

III. He foretells the terrible havoc that should be made of the Jewish nation (*v.* 22): *Those are the days of vengeance* so often spoken of by the Old-Testament prophets, which would complete the ruin of that provoking people. All their predictions must now be fulfilled, and the blood of all the Old-Testament martyrs must now be required. *All things that are written must be fulfilled* at length.

IV. He describes the issue of the struggles between the Jews and the Romans, and what they will come to at last; in short, 1. Multitudes of them *shall fall by the edge of the sword.* It is computed that in those wars of the Jews there fell by the sword above eleven hundred thousand. And the siege of. Jerusalem was, in effect, a military execution. 2. The rest shall be *led away captive*; not into *one* nation, as when they were conquered by the Chaldeans, which gave them an opportunity of keeping together, but *into all nations,* which made it impossible for them to *correspond* with each other, much less to *incorporate.* 3. Jerusalem itself was *trodden down of the Gentiles.* The Romans, when they had made themselves masters of it, laid it quite waste, as a *rebellious and bad city, hurtful to kings and provinces,* and therefore hateful to them.

V. He describes the great frights that people should generally be in. Many frightful *sights* shall be *in the sun, moon and stars,* prodigies in the heavens, and here in this lower world, the *sea and the waves roaring,* with terrible storms and tempests, such as had not been known, and above the ordinary working of natural causes. The effect of this shall be universal confusion and consternation *upon the earth, distress of nations with perplexity, v.* 25. *Men's hearts shall fail them for fear* (*v.* 26), *men being quite* dispirited, *unsouled,* dying away for fear. When *judgment begins at the house of God,* it will not end there; it shall be as if all the world were falling in pieces; and where can any be secure then? The *powers of heaven shall be shaken,* and then the pillars of the earth cannot but tremble. Thus shall the present Jewish policy, religion, laws, and government, be all entirely dissolved by a series of unparalleled calamities, attended with the utmost confusion.

VI. He encourages all the faithful disciples in reference to the terrors of that day (*v.* 28): "*When these things begin to come to pass,* when Jerusalem is besieged, and everything is concurring to the destruction of the Jews, *then* do you look *up,* when others are looking down, look heavenward, in faith, hope, and prayer, and *lift up your heads* with cheerfulness and confidence, *for your redemption draws nigh.*" 1. When Christ came to destroy the Jews, he came to redeem the Christians that were persecuted and oppressed by them; *then had the churches rest.* 2. When he comes to judge the world at the last day, he will *redeem* all that are his, from all their grievances. When they see that day approaching, they can *lift up their heads with joy*, knowing that *their redemption draws nigh*, their removal to their Redeemer.

VII. Here is one word of prediction that looks further than the destruction of the Jewish nation, which is not easily understood; we have it in *v.* 24: *Jerusalem shall be trodden down of the Gentiles, till the times of the Gentiles be fulfilled.* 1. Some understand it of what is past; so Dr. Hammond. The Gentiles, who have conquered Jerusalem, shall keep possession of it, and it shall be purely Gentile, till the times of the Gentiles be fulfilled, till a great part of the Gentile world shall have become Christian, and many of the Jews shall turn Christians, shall join with the Gentile Christians, to set up a church in Jerusalem, which shall flourish there for a long time. 2. Others understand it of what is yet to come; so Dr. Whitby. Jerusalem shall be possessed by the Gentiles, of one sort or other, for the most part, till the time come when the nations that yet remain infidels shall embrace the Christian faith, when the kingdoms of this world shall become Christ's kingdoms, and then all the Jews shall be converted. Jerusalem shall be inhabited by them, and neither they nor their city any longer trodden down by the Gentiles.

BE READY (*vv.* 29–38)

Here, in the close of this discourse,

I. Christ appoints his disciples to observe the signs of the times. This we had at Matt. xxiv. 32 ff.

He also cautions them against security and sensuality, by which they would unfit themselves for the trying times that were coming on, and make them to be a great surprise and terror to them (*vv.* 34, 35): *Take heed to yourselves.* This is the word of command given to all Christ's disciples: "*Take heed to yourselves,* that you be not overpowered by temptations, nor betrayed by your own corruptions." Note, We cannot be *safe* if we be *secure.* It concerns us at *all* times, but especially at *some* times, to be very cautious. See here, 1. What our *danger* is: that *the day* of death and judgment should *come upon us unawares,* when we do not *expect* it, and are not *prepared* for it. 2. What our *duty* is, in consideration of this danger: we must *take heed lest our hearts be overcharged,* lest they be burdened and overloaded, and so unfitted and disabled to do what must be done in preparation for death and judgment. Two things we must watch against, lest our hearts be overcharged with them:—
(1) The indulging of the appetites of the body, and allowing of ourselves in the gratifications of sense to an excess: *Take heed lest you be overcharged with surfeiting and drunkenness.* (2) The inordinate pursuit of the good things of this world. The heart is overcharged with the *cares of this life.* The former is the snare of those that are given to their pleasures: this is the snare of the men of business, that *will be rich* We have need to guard on both hands, not only lest at the time when death comes, but lest *at any time* our hearts should be thus overcharged. Our caution against sin, and our care of our own souls, must be *constant.*

II. He counsels them to prepare and get ready for this great day, *v.* 36. Here see. 1. What should be *our aim*: that we may be *accounted worthy to escape all these things*; that, when the judgments of God are abroad, we may be preserved from the malignity of them. Yet we must aim not only to *escape that*, but to *stand before the Son of man*; not only to stand *acquitted* before him as our Judge (Ps. i. 5), to have boldness in the day of Christ (that is supposed in our *escaping* all those things), but to *stand before him*, to attend on him as our Master. 2. What should be our *actings* in these aims: *Watch therefore, and pray always*. Watching and praying must go together, Neh. iv. 9. Those that would escape the wrath to come, and make sure of the joys to come, must *watch* and *pray*, and must do so always, must make it the constant business of their lives.

In the last two verses we have an account how Christ disposed of himself during those three or four days between his riding in triumph into Jerusalem and the night in which he was betrayed. 1. He was *all day teaching in the temple*. Christ preached on week-days as well as sabbath days. He was an indefatigable preacher; he preached in the face of opposition, and in the midst of those that he knew sought occasion against him. 2. At night he went out to lodge at a friend's house, in the mount of Olives, about a mile out of town. 3. Early in the morning he was in the temple again, where he had a morning lecture for those that were willing to attend it; and the people were forward to hear one that they saw forward to preach (*v.* 38).

CHAPTER TWENTY-TWO

THE UPPER ROOM
(*vv.* 1–20)

Most of this narrative is also found in Matt. xxvi. and Mark xiv. Again we note the distinctively Lucan material.

The institution of the Lord's supper, *vv.* 19, 20. The *pass. er* and the *deliverance* out of Egypt were *typical* and *prophetic signs* of a Christ to come, who should by dying deliver us from sin and death, and the tyranny of Satan. Therefore the Lord's supper is instituted to be a commemorative sign or memorial of a Christ already come, that *has* by dying delivered us; and it is his death that is in a special manner set before us in that ordinance.

1. The *breaking of Christ's body* as a *sacrifice for us* is here commemorated by the *breaking of bread*; and the sacrifices under the law were called the *bread of our God* (Lev. xxi. 6, 8, 17): *This is my body which is given for you*. And there is a feast upon that sacrifice instituted, in which we are to apply it to ourselves, and to take the benefit and comfort of it. This bread that was given for us is given *to us* to be food for our souls, for nothing can be more *nourishing* and *satisfying* to our souls than the doctrine of Christ's making atonement for sin, and the assurance of our interest in that atonement; this bread that was *broken* and *given for us*, to satisfy for the guilt

of our sins, is *broken* and *given to us*, to satisfy the desire of our souls. And this we do in *remembrance* of what he did for us, when he died for us, and for a *memorial* of what we *do*, in making ourselves *partakers of him*, and joining ourselves to him in an everlasting covenant.

2. The *shedding* of *Christ's blood*, by which the atonement was made (for *the blood made atonement for the soul*, Lev. xvii. 11), as represented by the wine in the cup; and that cup of wine is a sign and token of the New Testament, or new covenant, made with us. It *commemorates* the purchase of the covenant by the blood of Christ, and *confirms* the promises of the covenant, which are all *Yea* and *Amen* in him. This will be reviving and refreshing to our souls, as wine that *makes glad the heart*. In all our commemorations of the shedding of Christ's blood, we must have an eye to it as shed for us; we needed it, we take hold of it, we hope to have benefit by it; *who loved me, and gave himself for me*. And in all our regards to the New Testament we must have an eye to the *blood of Christ*, which gave life and being to it, and seals to us all the promises of it. Had it not been for the blood of Christ, we had never had the New Testament; and, had it not been for the New Testament, we had never known the meaning of Christ's blood shed.

DISCOURSE
WITH THE DISCIPLES
(*vv.* 21–38)

We have here Christ's discourse with his disciples after supper, much of which is new here; and in St. John's gospel we shall find other additions.

I. He discoursed with them concerning him that should betray him, who was now present. 1. He signifies to them that the traitor was now among them, and one of them, *v.* 21. By placing this after the institution of the Lord's supper, though in Matthew and Mark it is placed before it, it seems plain that Judas did receive the Lord's supper, did *eat of that bread* and *drink of that cup*; for, after the solemnity was over, Christ said, *Behold, the hand of him that betrayeth me is with me on the table*. There have been those that have eaten bread with Christ and yet have betrayed him. 2. He foretells that the treason would take effect (*v.* 22): *Truly the Son of man goes as it was determined*, goes to the place where he will be betrayed; for he is delivered up by the counsel and foreknowledge of God, else Judas could not have delivered him up. Christ was not driven to his sufferings, but cheerfully *went to them*. He said, *Lo, I come*. 3. He threatens the traitor: *Woe to that man by whom he is betrayed*. 4. He frightens the rest of the disciples into a suspicion of themselves, by saying that it was one of them, and not naming which (*v.* 23): *They began to enquire among themselves*, to interrogate themselves, to put the question to themselves, *who it was that should do this thing*, that could be so base to so good a Master. The enquiry was not, *Is it you?* or, *Is it such a one?* but, *Is it I?*

II. Concerning the strife that was among them for precedency or supremacy.

1. See what the dispute was: *which of them should be accounted the greatest*. Such and so many contests among the disciples for dignity and dominion, *before* the Spirit was poured upon them, were a sad presage of the like strifes for, and affections of, supremacy in the churches, after the Spirit should be provoked to depart from them.

2. See what Christ said to this dispute.

(1) This was to make themselves like the *kings of the Gentiles*, who affect worldly pomp, and worldly power, *v.* 25.

(2) It was to make themselves unlike the disciples of Christ, and unlike Christ himself: "*You shall not be so,*" *vv.* 26, 27. See here,

[1] What is the rule Christ gave to his disciples: He that is *greater among you*, that is *senior*, to whom precedency is due upon the account of his age, let him be as the *younger*, both in point of *lowness of place* (let him condescend to sit with the younger, and be free and familiar with them) and in point of *labour* and *work*. [2] What was the example which he himself gave to this rule: *Whether is greater, he that sitteth at meat or he that serveth?* he that attendeth or he that is attended on? Now Christ was among his disciples just like one that waited at table. Shall those take upon them the form of princes who call themselves followers of him that *took upon him the form of a servant*?

(3) They ought not to strive for worldly honour and grandeur, because he had better honours in reserve for them, of another nature,

a *kingdom*, a *feast*, a *throne*, for each of them, wherein they should all share alike and should, have no occasion to strive for precedency, *vv.* 28–30. Where observe,

[1] Christ's commendation of his disciples for their faithfulness to him; and this was honour enough for them, they needed not to strive for any greater.

[2] The recompence he designed them for their fidelity: *I appoint, I bequeath, unto you a kingdom*. Or thus, *I appoint to you, as my Father has appointed a kingdom to me, that you may eat and drink at my table*. Understand it, *First*, Of what should be done for them in this world. God gave his Son a *kingdom among men*, the gospel church, of which he is the living, quickening, ruling, Head. This *kingdom* he *appointed* to his apostles and their successors in the ministry of the gospel. Or, *Secondly*, Of what should be done for them in the other world, which I take to be chiefly meant. Let them go on in their services in this world; their preferments shall be in the other world.

III. Concerning Peter's denying him. And in this part of the discourse we may observe,

1. The general notice Christ gives to Peter of the devil's design upon him and the rest of the apostles (*v.* 31): *The Lord said, Simon, Simon*, observe what I say; *Satan hath desired to have you*, to have you all in his hands, *that he may sift you as wheat*. Peter, who used to be the *mouth* of the rest in speaking to Christ, is here made the *ear* of the rest; and what is designed for warning to them all (*all*

you shall be offended, because of me) is directed to Peter, because he was principally concerned, being in a particular manner struck at by the tempter: *Satan has desired to have you.*

2. The particular encouragement he gave to Peter, in reference to this trial: *"I have prayed for thee,* because, though he desires to have them all, he is permitted to make his strongest onset upon thee only: thou wilt be most violently assaulted, *but I have prayed for thee, that thy faith fail not,* that it may not totally and finally fail." Note, (1) If faith be kept up in an hour of temptation, though we may fall, yet we shall not be utterly cast down. Faith will quench Satan's fiery darts. (2) Though there may be many failings in the faith of true believers, yet there shall not be a total and final failure of their faith. It is their seed, their root, remaining in them. (3) It is owing to the mediation and intercession of Jesus Christ that the faith of his disciples, though sometimes sadly shaken, yet is not sunk.

3. The charge he gives to Peter to help others as he should himself be helped of God: *"When thou art converted, strengthen thy brethren;* when thou art recovered by the grace of God, and brought to repentance, do what thou canst to recover others." Note, (1) Those that have fallen into sin must be *converted from it*; those that have turned aside must *return*; those that have left their first love must do their first works. (2) Those that through grace are converted from sin must do what they can to strengthen their brethren that stand, and to prevent *their*

falling; see Ps. li. 1–13; 1 Tim. i. 13.

4. Peter's declared resolution to cleave to Christ, whatever it cost him (v. 33): *Lord, I am ready to go with thee, both into prison and to death.* This was a great word, and yet I believe no more than he meant at this time, and thought he should *make good* too.

5. Christ's express prediction of his denying him thrice (v. 34): "*I tell thee, Peter the cock shall not crow this day before thou even deny that thou knowest me.*" Note, Christ knows us better than we know ourselves, and knows the evil that is in us, and will be done by us, which we ourselves do not suspect.

IV. Concerning the condition of all the disciples.

1. He appeals to them concerning what had been, v. 35, He had owned that they had been faithful servants to him, v. 28. Now he expects, at parting, that they should acknowledge that he had been a kind and careful Master to them ever since they left all to follow him: *When I sent you without purse, lacked you any thing?*

2. He gives them notice of a very great change of their circumstances now approaching. For, (1) He that was their Master was now entering upon his sufferings, which he had often foretold (v. 37). (2) They must therefore expect troubles, and must not think now to have such an easy and comfortable life as they had had; no, the scene will alter. They must now in some degree suffer *with* their Master; and, when he is gone, they must expect to suffer *like* him. The servant is not better than his Lord.

GETHSEMANE (*vv.* 39–53)

We have here the awful story of Christ's *agony in the garden,* just before he was betrayed, which was largely related by the other evangelists.

There are three things in this passage which we had not in the other evangelists:—

1. That, when Christ was in his agony, *there appeared* to him *an angel from heaven, strengthening him, v.* 43. (1) It was an instance of the deep humiliation of our Lord Jesus that he *needed* the assistance of an angel, and would *admit* it. (2) When he was not delivered from his sufferings, yet he was *strengthened* and supported under them, and that was *equivalent.* (3) The angels ministered to the Lord Jesus in his sufferings. He could have had legions of them to rescue him; nay, this one could have done it, could have chased and conquered the whole band of men that came to take him; but he made use of his ministration only to *strengthen him;* and the very visit which this angel made him now in his grief, when his enemies were awake and his friends asleep, was such a seasonable token of the divine favour as would be a very great strengthening to him. Yet this was not all: he probably *said something* to him to strengthen him; put him in mind that his sufferings were in order to his Father's glory, to his own glory, and to the salvation of those that were given him, represented to him the joy set before him, the seed he should see; with these and the like suggestions he encouraged him to go on cheerfully; and what is comforting is strengthening.

2. That, *being in an agony, he prayed more earnestly, v.* 44. As his sorrow and trouble grew upon him, he grew more importunate in prayer; not that there was before any coldness or indifferency in his prayers, but there was now a greater vehemency in them, which was expressed in his voice and gesture.

3. That, in this agony, *his sweat was as it were great drops of blood falling down to the ground.* Sweat came in with sin, and was a branch of the curse, Gen. iii. 19. And therefore, when Christ was made sin and a curse for us, he underwent a grievous sweat, that *in the sweat of his face* we might eat bread, and that he might sanctify and sweeten all our trials to us. There is some dispute among the critics whether this *sweat* is only *compared to* drops of *blood,* being much *thicker* than drops of sweat commonly are, the pores of the body being more than ordinarily opened, or whether *real* blood out of the capillary veins mingled with it, so that it was in colour like blood, and might truly be called a *bloody sweat;* the matter is not great. Some reckon this one of the times when Christ shed his blood for us, *for without the shedding of blood there is no remission.* Every pore was as it were a bleeding wound, and his blood stained all his raiment. This showed the *travail of his soul.*

The other evangelists tell us what was the check Christ gave to Peter for striking the servant of the high priest. Luke here tells us, 1. How Christ excused the blow:

Suffer ye thus far, v. 51. Dr. Whitby thinks he said this to his enemies who came to take him, to pacify them, that they might not be provoked by it to fall upon the disciples, whom he had undertaken the preservation of. 2. How he cured the wound, which was more than amends sufficient for the injury: *He touched his ear, and healed him*. Christ hereby gave them a proof, (1) Of his power. He that could *heal* or could *destroy* if he pleased, which should have obliged them in interest to submit to him. (2) Of his mercy and goodness. Christ here gave an illustrious example to his own rule of *doing good to them that hate us*, as afterwards he did of *praying for them that despitefully use us*. Those who render good for evil do as Christ did.

PETER'S DENIAL (vv. 54–62)

This is recorded and commented upon at Matt. xxvi. 69 ff.

CHRIST BEFORE THE SANHEDRIM
(vv. 63–71)

We are here told, as before in the other gospels,

I. How our Lord Jesus was *abused* by the servants of the high priest.

II. How he was accused and condemned by the great sanhedrim, consisting of the *elders of the people, the chief priests, and the scribes*, who were all up betimes, and got together *as soon as it was day*, about five of the clock in the morning, to prosecute this matter. It is but a short account that we have here of his trial in the ecclesiastical court.

PILATE AND HEROD
(vv. 1–12)

Our Lord Jesus was condemned as a blasphemer in the spiritual court, but it was the most *impotent malice* that could be that this court was actuated by; for, when they had *condemned* him, they knew they could not *put him to death*, and therefore took another course.

I. They accused him before Pilate. The *whole multitude of them arose*, when they saw they could go no further with him in their court, and *led him unto Pilate*.

1. Here is the indictment drawn up against him (v. 2), in which they pretended a zeal for Cæsar, only to ingratiate themselves with Pilate, but it was all *malice* against Christ, and nothing else. They misrepresented him, (1) As making the people *rebel against Cæsar*. Christ had particularly taught that they *ought to give tribute to Cæsar*, though he knew there were those that would be offended at him for it; and yet he is here falsely accused as *forbidding to give tribute to Cæsar*. Innocency is no fence against calumny. (2) As making himself a *rival with Cæsar*, though the very reason why they rejected him, and would not own him to be the Messiah, was because he did not appear in worldly pomp and power, and did not set up for a temporal prince.

2. His pleading to the indictment: *Pilate asked him, Art thou the king of the Jews ?* v. 3. To which he answered, *Thou sayest it*; that is, "It is as thou sayest," Christ's

kingdom is wholly spiritual, and will not interfere with Cæsar's jurisdiction. Or, *"Thou sayest it;* but canst thou prove it? What evidence hast thou for it?"

3. Pilate's declaration of his innocency (*v.* 4): He *said to the chief priests, and the people* that seemed to join with them in the prosecution, *"I find no fault in this man."*

4. The continued fury and outrage of the prosecutors, *v.* 5. Instead of being moderated by Pilate's declaration of his innocency, and considering, as they ought to have done, whether they were not bringing the guilt of innocent blood upon themselves, they were the more exasperated, more exceedingly *fierce.*

II. They accused him before Herod. 1. Pilate removed him and his cause to Herod's court. 2. Herod was very willing to have the examining of him (*v.* 8): *When he saw Jesus he was exceedingly glad.* He had *heard many things of him* in Galilee, where his miracles had for a great while been all the talk of the country; and he *longed to see him,* not for any affection he had for him or his doctrine, but purely out of curiosity. 3. His prosecutors appeared against him before Herod, for they were restless in the prosecution: *They stood, and vehemently accused him* (*v.* 10), *impudently* and *boldly,* so the word signifies. They would make Herod believe that he had poisoned Galilee too with his seditious notions. 4. Herod was very *abusive* to him: He, with *his men of war,* his attendants, and officers, and great men, *set him at nought.* They *made nothing* of him;

so the word is. 5. Herod sent him back to Pilate, and it proved an occasion of the making of them friends, they having been for some time before at variance.

SECOND TRIAL BEFORE PILATE (*vv.* 13–25)

We have here the blessed Jesus run down by the mob, and hurried to the cross in the storm of a popular noise and tumult, raised by the malice and artifice of the *chief priests,* as agents for the prince of the power of the air.

I. Pilate solemnly protests that he believes he has done nothing worthy of death or of bonds.

II. He appeals to Herod concerning him (*v.* 15): *"I sent you to him,* who is supposed to have known more of him than I have done, and he has *sent him back,* not convicted of any thing, nor under any mark of his displeasure; in his opinion, his crimes are not capital."

III. He proposes to release him, if they will but consent to it.

IV. The people choose rather to have Barabbas released, a wretched fellow, that had nothing to recommend him to their favour but the daringness of his crimes.

V. When Pilate urged the second time that Christ should be released, they cried out, *Crucify him, crucify him, vv.* 20, 21.

VI. When Pilate the third time reasoned with them, to show them the unreasonableness and injustice of it, they were the more peremptory and outrageous (*v.* 22).

VII. Pilate's yielding, at length, to their importunity. The voice of the people and of the *chief priests prevailed,* and were too hard for

Pilate, and overruled him to go contrary to his convictions and inclinations.

THE WAY OF SORROW
(vv. 26–31)

We have here the blessed Jesus, the Lamb of God, led as *a lamb to the slaughter*, to the sacrifice. Now as they led him away to death we find,

I. One that was a *bearer*, that carried his cross, *Simon* by name, *a Cyrenian*.

II. Many that were *mourners*; true mourners, who followed him, *bewailing* and *lamenting* him. He diverts their lamentation into another channel, *v.* 28.

1. He gives them a general direction concerning their lamentations: *Daughters of Jerusalem, weep not for me*, but rather let them *weep for themselves and for their children*, with an eye to the destruction that was coming upon Jerusalem, which some of them might live to see and share in the calamities of, or, at least their children would, for whom they ought to be solicitous.

2. He gives them a particular reason why they should *weep for themselves and for their children*: "*For behold* sad times are coming upon your city; it will be destroyed, and you will be involved in the common destruction."

3. He shows how natural it was for them to infer this desolation from his sufferings. *If they do these things in a green tree, what shall be done in the dry? v.* 31. Christ was a *green tree*, fruitful and flourishing; now, if such things were done to

him, we may thence infer what would have been done to the whole race of mankind if he had not *interposed*, and what shall be done to those that continue dry trees, notwithstanding all that is done to make them fruitful.

THE TWO MALEFACTORS
(vv. 32–43)

In these verses we have,

I. Divers passages which we had before in Matthew and Mark concerning Christ's sufferings.

II. Here are two passages which we had not before, and they are very remarkable ones.

1. Christ's prayer for his enemies (*v.* 34): *Father, forgive them*. Seven remarkable words Christ spoke after he was nailed to the cross, and before he died, and this is the first. Observe,

(1) The petition: *Father, forgive them*. Now he made intercession for transgressors, as was foretold (Isa. liii. 12), and it is to be added to his prayer (John xvii.), to complete the specimen he gave of his intercession within the veil: that for saints, this for sinners. Now the sayings of Christ upon the cross as well as his sufferings had a further intention than they seemed to have. This was a mediatorial word, and explicatory of the intent and meaning of his death: "*Father, forgive them*, not only these, but all that shall repent, and believe the gospel"; and he did not intend that these should be forgiven upon any other terms. "Father, that which I am now suffering and dying for is in order to this, that poor sinners may be pardoned."

(2) The plea: *For they know not what they do*; for, *if they had known*, they would not have crucified him, 1 Cor. ii. 8. There was a veil upon his glory and upon their understandings; and how could they see through two veils? They wished his blood on them and their children: but, had they known what they did, they would have unwished it again.

2. The conversion of the thief upon the cross. Christ was crucified between two thieves, and in them were represented the different effects which the cross of Christ would have upon the children of men, to whom it would be *brought near* in the preaching of the gospel. They are all malefactors, all guilty before God. Now the cross of Christ is to some a *savour of life unto life*, to others of *death unto death*.

(1) Here was one of these malefactors that was *hardened to the last*. Near to the cross of Christ, he *railed on him*, as others did (*v.* 39): he said, *If thou be the Christ*, as they say thou art, *save thyself and us*.

(2) Here was the other of them that was *softened at the last*. This malefactor, when just ready to fall into the hands of Satan, was snatched as a brand out of the burning, and made a monument of divine mercy and grace, and Satan was left to roar as a lion disappointed of his prey. This gives no encouragement to any to put off their repentance to their death-bed, or to hope that then they shall find mercy; for, though it is certain that true repentance is never too late, it is as certain that late repentance is seldom true. He never had any offer of Christ, nor day of grace, before now: he was designed to be made a singular instance of the power of Christ's grace now at a time when he was *crucified in weakness*. We shall see the case to be extraordinary if we observe,

[1] The extraordinary operations of God's grace upon him, which appeared in what he said. Here were so many evidences given in a short time of a blessed change wrought in him that more could not have been given in so little a compass.

[2] The extraordinary grants of Christ's favour to him: *Jesus said unto him*, in answer to his prayer, "*Verily I say unto thee*, I the *Amen*, the faithful Witness, I say *Amen* to this prayer, put my *fiat* to it: nay, thou didst have more than thou didst ask, *This day thou shalt be with me in paradise*," *v.* 43.

See here how the happiness of heaven is set forth to us. (1) It is *paradise*, a garden of pleasure, the *paradise of God* (Rev. ii. 7), alluding to the garden of Eden, in which our first parents were placed when they were innocent. (2) It is being *with Christ* there. That is the happiness of heaven, to see Christ, and sit with him, and share in his glory, John xvii. 24. (3) It is immediate upon death: *This day shalt thou be with me*, to-night, before to-morrow. *The souls of the faithful, after they are delivered from the burden of the flesh*, immediately *are in joy and felicity*; the spirits of just men are immediately *made perfect*. Lazarus departs, and is immediately *comforted*; Paul departs, and is immediately with Christ, Phil. i. 23.

CHRIST'S DEATH (*vv.* 44–56)

We have here the dying and burying of the Lord Jesus, as earlier recorded by Matt. xxvii. 45 ff, and Mark.

FIRST DAY OF THE WEEK (*vv.* 1–12)

The manner of the re-uniting of Christ's soul and body in his resurrection is a mystery, one of the *secret things* that *belong not to us*. But that he did indeed rise from the dead, and was thereby proved to be the Son of God, are *things revealed, which belong to us and to our children*. Some of them we have here in these verses, which relate the same story for substance that we had in Matthew and Mark.

I. We have here the affection and respect which the good women that had followed Christ showed to him, after he was dead and buried, *v.* 1. As soon as ever they could, after the sabbath was over, they *came to the sepulchre*, to embalm his body.

II. The surprise they were in, when they found the stone rolled away and the grave empty (*vv.* 2, 3).

III. The plain account which they had of Christ's resurrection from two angels, who appeared to them *in shining garments*, not only white, but bright, and casting a lustre about them. They first saw *one* angel without the sepulchre, who presently *went in*, and sat with another angel in the sepulchre, *one at the head and the other at the feet, where the body of Jesus had lain*; so

the evangelists may be reconciled.

IV. Their satisfaction in this account, *v.* 8. The women seemed to acquiesce; they *remembered his words*, when they were thus put in mind of them, and thence concluded that if he was risen it was no more than they had reason to expect.

V. The report they brought of this to the apostles: *They returned from the sepulchre, and told all these things to the eleven, and to all the rest* of Christ's disciples, *v.* 9. *Their words seemed to them as idle tales, and they believed them not.* One cannot but be amazed at the stupidity of these disciples,—who had themselves so often professed that they believed Christ to be the Son of God and the true Messiah, had been so often told that he must die and rise again, and then enter into his glory, had seen him more than once raise the dead,—that they should be so backward to believe in his raising himself.

VI. The enquiry which Peter made hereupon, *v.* 12. It was Mary Magdalene that brought the report to him, as appears, John xx. 1, 2, where this story of his running to the sepulchre is more particularly related. 1. Peter hastened to the sepulchre upon the report. He now *ran to the sepulchre*, who but the other day *ran from his Master*. 2. He looked into the sepulchre, and took notice how orderly the linen clothes in which Christ was wrapped were taken off, and folded up, and laid by themselves, but the body gone. 3. He went away, as he thought, not much the wiser, *wondering in himself at that which was come to pass*.

THE EMMAUS ROAD
(vv. 13–35)

This appearance of Christ to the *two disciples* going to Emmaus was mentioned, and but just mentioned, before (Mark xvi. 12); here it is largely related. It happened the same day that Christ rose, the first day of the new world that rose with him. One of these two disciples was *Cleopas* or *Alpheus*, said by the ancients to be the brother of Joseph, Christ's supposed father; who the other was is not certain. Now in this passage of story we may observe,

I. The *walk* and *talk* of these two disciples: *They went to a village called Emmaus*, which is reckoned to be about two hours' walk from Jerusalem; it is here said to be about sixty furlongs, seven measured miles, *v.* 13. But as they travelled they *talked together of all those things which had happened*, *v.* 14. They *talked over these things*, reasoning with themselves concerning the probabilities of Christ's resurrection; for, according as these appeared, they would either go forward or return back to Jerusalem.

II. The good company they met with upon the road, when Jesus himself came, and joined himself to them (*v.* 15): *They communed together, and reasoned*, and perhaps were warm at the argument, one hoping that their Master was risen, and would set up his kingdom, the other despairing. *Jesus himself drew near*, as a stranger who, seeing them travel the same way that he *went*, told them that he should be *glad of their company*. But, though

they had Christ with them, they were not at first aware of it (*v.* 16): *Their eyes were held, that they should not know him*. It should seem, there were both an alteration of the *object* (for it is said in Mark that now *he appeared in another form*) and a restraint upon the organ (for here it is said that *their eyes were held* by a divine power).

III. The conference that was between Christ and them, when he knew them, and they knew not him. Now Christ and his disciples, as is usual when friends meet incognito, or in a disguise, are here crossing questions.

1. Christ's first question to them is concerning *their* present *sadness*, which plainly appeared in their countenances. Observe,

(1) They were *sad*; it appeared to a stranger that they were so. [1] They had lost their dear Master, and were, in their own apprehensions, quite disappointed in their expectations from him. They had given up the cause, and knew not what course to take to retrieve it. [2] Though he was risen from the dead, yet either they did not know it or did not believe it, and so they were still in sorrow. [3] Being sad, they had *communications one with another* concerning Christ. Joint-mourners should be mutual comforters; comforts sometimes come best from such.

(2) Christ came up to them, and enquired into the matter of their talk, and the cause of their grief: *What manner of communications are these?* Though Christ had now entered into his state of exaltation, yet he continued tender of his disciples, and concerned for their

comfort. He speaks as one troubled to see their melancholy: *Wherefore look ye so sadly to-day?* Gen. xl. 7.

2. In answer to this, they put a question to him concerning *his strangeness. Art thou only a stranger in Jerusalem, and hast not known the things that are come to pass there in these days?* Observe, (1) Cleopas gave him a civil answer. He does not rudely ask him, "As for what we are talking of, what is that to you?" and bid him go about his business. (2) He is full of Christ himself and of his death and sufferings, and wonders that every body else is not so too: "What! art thou such a stranger in Jerusalem as not to know what has been done to our Master there?" (3) He is very willing to inform this stranger concerning Christ, and to draw on further discourse with him upon this subject. (4) It appears, by what Cleopas says, that the death of Christ made a great noise in Jerusalem, so that it could not be imagined that any man should be such a stranger in the city as not to know of it; it was all the talk of the town, and discoursed of in all companies. Thus the matter of fact came to be universally *known*, which, after the pouring out of the Spirit, was to be *explained*.

3. Christ, by way of reply, asked concerning *their knowledge* (v. 19): *He said unto them, What things?* thus making himself yet more a stranger.

4. They, hereupon, gave him a particular account concerning Christ, and the present posture of his affairs. Observe the story they tell, *v.* 19, &c.

(1) Here is a summary of Christ's

life and *character*. The *things* they are full of are concerning *Jesus of Nazareth* (so he was commonly called), who *was a prophet*, a teacher come from God. He preached a true and excellent doctrine, which had manifestly its rise from heaven, and its tendency towards heaven. He confirmed it by many glorious miracles, miracles of mercy, so that he was *mighty in deed and word before God and all the people*. He had great acceptance with God, and a great reputation in the country.

(2) Here is a modest narrative of his sufferings and death, *v.* 20. "Though he was so dear both to God and man, yet the *chief priests and our rulers*, in contempt of both, *delivered him* to the Roman power, *to be condemned to death*, and *they have crucified him*."

(3) Here is an intimation of their disappointment in him, as the reason of their sadness: "*We trusted that it had been he who should have redeemed Israel, v.* 21. We are of those who not only looked upon him to be a prophet, like Moses, but, like him, a redeemer too." He was depended upon, and great things expected from him, by them that *looked for redemption*, and in it for the consolation of Israel. Now, if *hope deferred makes the heart sick*, hope disappointed, especially such a hope, kills the heart.

(4) Here is an account of their present amazement with reference to his resurrection.

(5) Our Lord Jesus, though not known by face to them, makes himself known to them by his word.

[1] He reproves them for their

incogitancy, and the weakness of their faith in the scriptures of the Old Testament: *O fools, and slow of heart to believe*, v. 25. That which is condemned in them as their *foolishness* is, *First*, Their *slowness to believe*. Believers are branded as fools by atheists, and infidels, and free-thinkers, and their most holy faith is censured as a fond credulity; but Christ tells us that those are *fools* who are *slow of heart to believe*, and are kept from it by prejudices never impartially examined. *Secondly*, Their slowness to believe *the writings of the prophets*. He does not so much blame them for their slowness to believe the testimony of the women and of the angels, but for that which was the cause thereof, their *slowness to believe* the prophets.

[2] He shows them that the sufferings of Christ, which were such a stumbling-block to them, and made them unapt to believe his glory, were really the appointed way to his glory, and he could not go to it any other way (v. 26): "*Ought not the Christ* (the Messiah) to *have suffered these things, and to enter into his glory?* Was it not decreed, and was not that decree *declared*, that the promised Messiah must first suffer and then reign, that he must go by his cross to his crown?" Had they never read the fifty-third of Isaiah and the ninth of Daniel, where the prophets speak so very plainly of the *sufferings of Christ* and the *glory that should follow*? 1 Pet. i. 11.

[3] He expounded to them the scriptures of the Old Testament, which spoke of the Messiah, and showed them how they were fulfilled in Jesus of Nazareth, and now can tell them more concerning him than they could before tell him (v. 27). You cannot go far in any part of scripture but you meet with something that has reference to Christ, some prophecy, some promise, some prayer, some type or other; for he is the true *treasure hid in the field* of the Old Testament. A golden thread of gospel grace runs through the whole web of the Old Testament.

IV. Here is the discovery which Christ at length made of himself to them. *They drew nigh to the village whither they went* (v. 28), where, it should seem, they determined to *take up* for that night. And now,

1. They courted his stay with them: *He made as though he would have gone further*. Christ yielded to their importunity: He *went in, to tarry with them*. Thus ready is Christ to give further instructions and comforts to those who improve what they have received.

2. He manifested himself to them, vv. 30, 31. (1) They began to suspect it was he, when, as they *sat down to meat*, he undertook the office of the Master of the feast, which he performed so like himself, and like what he used to do among his disciples, that by it they discerned him: *He took bread, and blessed it, and brake, and gave to them.* (2) Presently *their eyes were opened*, and then they saw who it was, and *knew him* well enough. See how Christ by his Spirit and grace makes himself known to the souls of his people. [1] He opens the scriptures to them, for they are they which testify of him to those who

search them, and search for him in them. [2] He meets them at his table, in the ordinance of the Lord's supper, and commonly there makes further discoveries of himself to them, is *known to them in the breaking of bread*. But, [3] The work is completed by the opening of the eyes of their mind, and causing the scales to fall off from them, as from Paul's in his conversion.

3. He immediately disappeared: *He vanished out of their sight.* He *withdrew himself* from them, slipped away of a sudden, and went *out of sight*. Or, he *became not visible by them*, was made inconspicuous by them. Such short and transient views have we of Christ in this world; we see him, but in a little while lose the sight of him again. When we come to heaven the vision of him will have no interruptions.

V. Here is the reflection which these disciples made upon this conference, and the report which they made of it to their brethren at Jerusalem.

1. The reflection they each of them made upon the influence which Christ's discourse had upon them (*v.* 32): *They said one to another, Did not our hearts burn within us?* They found the preaching powerful, even when they knew not the preacher. See here, (1) What *preaching* is likely to *do good*—such as Christ's was, *plain preaching*, and that which is familiar and level to our capacity—*he talked with us by the way*; and *scriptural* preaching—*he opened to us the scriptures*, the scriptures relating to himself. (2) What *hearing* is likely to *do good*—that which makes the

heart burn; when we are much affected with the things of God, especially with the love of Christ in dying for us, then we may say, "Through grace our hearts are thus inflamed."

2. The report they brought of this to their brethren at Jerusalem (*v.* 33). Observe, (1) How they found them, just when they came in among them, discoursing on the same subject, and relating another proof of the resurrection of Christ. *The Lord is risen indeed, and hath appeared to Simon, v.* 34. That Peter had a sight of him before the rest of the disciples had appears 1. Cor. xv. 5, where it is said, *He was seen of Cephas, then of the twelve.* (2) How they seconded their evidence with an account of what they had seen (*v.* 35): *They told what things were done in the way.* The words that were spoken by Christ to them in the way, having a wonderful effect and influence upon them, are here called the *things* that were *done in the way*; for the words that Christ speaks are not an empty sound, but *they are spirit and they are life*, and wondrous things are *done* by them.

THE RISEN CHRIST
(*vv.* 36–49)

Five times Christ was seen the same day that he rose: by Mary Magdalene alone in the garden (John xx. 14), by the women as they were going to tell the disciples (Matt. xxviii. 9), by Peter alone, by the two disciples going to Emmaus, and now at night by the eleven, of which we have an account in these verses, as also John xx. 19. Observe,

1. The great *surprise* which his

appearing gave them. 2. The *fright* which they put themselves into upon it (*v.* 37): They were *terrified*, supposing that *they had seen a spirit*, because he came in among them without any noise, and was in the midst of them ere they were aware. The word used (Matt. xiv. 26), when they said *It is a spirit*, is a *spectre*, and *apparition*; but the word here used properly signifies *a spirit*; they supposed it to be a spirit not clothed with a real body.

II. The great *satisfaction* which has discourse gave them, wherein we have,

1. The reproof he gave them for their causeless fears: *Why are you troubled, and why do* frightful *thoughts arise in your hearts? v.* 38.

2. The proof he gave them of his resurrection. Two proofs he gives them:—

(1) He shows them his body, particularly *his hands and his feet.* They saw that he had the shape, and features, and exact resemblance, of their Master; but is it not his ghost? "No," saith Christ, "*behold my hands and my feet.*" He lays down this principle—that a *spirit has not flesh and bones.* He does not tell us what a *spirit* is (it is time enough to know that when we go to the world of spirits), but what it is not: *It has not flesh and bones.*

(2) He *eats* with them, to show that he had a real and true body, and that he was willing to converse freely and familiarly with his disciples, as one friend with another. Peter lays a great stress upon this (Acts x. 41): We *did eat and drink with him after he rose from the dead.*

3. The *insight* he gave them into

the word of God, which they had *heard* and read, by which faith in the resurrection of Christ is wrought in them, and all the difficulties are cleared. (1) He refers them to the *word* which they had *heard* from him when he was with them, and puts them in mind of that as the angel had done (*v.* 44): *These are the words which I said unto you* in private, many a time, *while I was yet with you.* (2) He refers them to the *word* they had read in the Old Testament, to which the word they had heard from him directed them: *All things must be fulfilled which were written.* (3) By an immediate present work upon their minds, of which they themselves could not but be aware he gave them to apprehend the true intent and meaning of the Old-Testament prophecies of Christ, and to see them all fulfilled in him: *Then opened he their understanding, that they might understand the scriptures, v.* 45.

4. The instructions he gave them as *apostles*, who were to be employed in setting up his kingdom in the world. "You are now to enter upon them; *you are* to be *witnesses of these things* (*v.* 48), to carry the notice of them to all the world; not only to *report* them as matter of news, but to *assert* them as evidence upon the trial of the great cause that has been so long depending between God and Satan, the issue of which must be the casting down and casting out of the *prince of this world.* You are fully assured of these things yourselves, you are eye and ear-witnesses of them; go, and assure the world of them; and the same Spirit that has

enlightened you shall go along with you for the enlightening of others."

Whither must they carry these proposals, and how far does their commission extend? They are here told, [1] That they must preach this *among all nations.* The prophets had preached *repentance* and *remission* to the *Jews,* but the apostles must preach them to *all the world.* [2] That they must *begin at Jerusalem.* There they must preach their first *gospel sermon;* there the *gospel church* must be first formed; there the gospel day must dawn, and thence that light shall go forth which must take hold on the ends of the earth.

It is a vast undertaking that they are here called to, a very large and difficult province, especially considering the opposition this service would meet with, and the sufferings it would be attended with. If therefore they ask, *Who is sufficient for these things?* here is an answer ready: *Behold, I send the promise of my Father upon you,* and *you shall be endued with power from on high, v.* 49. He here assures them that in a little time the Spirit should be poured out upon them in greater measures than ever, and they should thereby be furnished with all those gifts and graces which were necessary to their discharge of this great trust; and therefore they must *tarry at Jerusalem,* and not enter upon it till this be done.

EPILOGUE (*vv.* 50–53)

How solemnly Christ took leave of his disciples. Probably, it was very early in the morning that he ascended, before people were stirring; for he never showed himself openly to all the people after his resurrection, but only to *chosen witnesses.* The disciples did not see him rise out of the grave, because his resurrection was capable of being proved by their seeing him alive afterwards; but they saw him *ascend* into heaven, because they could not otherwise have an *ocular* demonstration of his ascension. They were *led out* on purpose to see him ascend, had their eye upon him when he ascended, and were not looking another way. He did not go away in displeasure, but in love; he left a blessing behind him; *he lifted up his hands,* as the high priest did when he blessed the people; see Lev. ix. 22. *While he was blessing them, he was parted from them;* not as if he were taken away before he had said all he had to say, but to intimate that his being parted from them did not put an end to his blessing them, for the intercession which he went to heaven to make for all his is a continuation of the blessing.

How cheerfully his disciples continued their attendance on him, and on God through him, even now that he was parted from them. They *returned to Jerusalem with great joy.* There they were ordered to continue till the Spirit should be poured out upon them, and thither they went accordingly, though it was into the mouth of danger. They abounded in acts of devotion while they were in expectation of the promise of the Father, *v.* 53. (1) They attended the temple-service at the hours of prayer. God had not as yet quite forsaken it, and therefore they did not. (2) Temple-sacrifices, they knew, were superseded by Christ's sacrifice, but the temple-songs they joined in.

The *amen* that concludes seems to be added by the church and every

believer to the reading of the gospel, signifying an assent to the truths of the gospel, and a hearty concurrence with all the disciples of Christ in praising and blessing God. *Amen.* Let him be continually praised and blessed.

472

THE GOSPEL ACCORDING TO

ST. JOHN

CHAPTER ONE
PROLOGUE (vv. 1–5)

The evangelist here lays down the great truth he is to prove, that Jesus Christ is God, one with the Father. Observe,

I. Of whom he speaks—*The Word.* This is an idiom peculiar to John's writings. See 1 John i. 1; v. 7; Rev. xix. 13. Yet some think that Christ is meant by *the Word* in Acts xx. 32; Heb. iv. 12; Luke i. 2. Even the Jews were taught that the *Word of God* was the same with God. The evangelist, in the close of his discourse (*v.* 18), plainly tells us why he calls Christ *the Word—because he is the only begotten Son, who is in the bosom of the Father, and has declared him. Word* is two-fold: *word conceived;* and *word uttered; intelligence* and *utterance.*

1. There is the *word conceived,* that is, *thought,* which is the first and only immediate product and conception of the soul (all the operations of which are performed by *thought*), and it is one with the soul. And thus the second person in the Trinity is fitly called *the Word;* for he is the *first-begotten of the Father,* that eternal essential Wisdom which *the Lord possessed,* as the soul does its thought, *in the beginning of his way,* Prov. viii. 22. There is nothing we are more sure of than *that we think,* yet nothing we are more in the dark about than *how we think;* who can declare the generation of *thought* in the soul? Surely then the generations and births of the eternal mind may well be allowed to be great mysteries of godliness, the bottom of which we cannot fathom, while yet we adore the depth. 2. There is the *word uttered,* and this is *speech,* the chief and most natural indication of the mind. And thus Christ is *the Word,* for *by him* God has in *these last days spoken to us* (Heb. i. 2), and has directed us to *hear him,* Matt. xvii. 5. He has made known God's mind to us, as a man's word or speech makes known his thoughts, as far as he pleases, and no further. Christ is called that *wonderful speaker* (see notes on Dan. viii. 13), the *speaker of things hidden* and *strange.* He is *the Word* speaking *from* God to us, and *to God* for us. John Baptist was *the voice,* but Christ *the Word*: being *the Word,* he is *the Truth,* the *Amen,* the *faithful Witness* of the mind of God.

II. What he saith of him, enough to prove beyond contradiction that *he is God.* He asserts,

1. His existence in the beginning: *In the beginning was the Word.* This bespeaks his existence, not only before his incarnation, but before all time. The Word had a being before the world had a beginning.

He that *was* in the beginning *never* began, and therefore was *ever,—without beginning of time*. So Nonnus.

2. His co-existence with the Father: *The Word was with God, and the Word was God.* Let none say that when we invite them to Christ we would draw them from God, for Christ is *with God* and *is God*; it is repeated in *v.* 2: *the same*, the very same that we believe in and preach, was *in the beginning with God*, that is, he was so from eternity. The Word was with God, (1) In respect of *essence* and *substance*; for *the Word was God*: a distinct person or substance, for he was *with God*; and yet the same in substance, for he *was God*, Heb. i. 3. (2) In respect of *complacency* and *felicity*. There was a glory and happiness which Christ had *with God* before the world was (*ch.* xvii. 5), the Son infinitely happy in the enjoyment of his Father's bosom, and no less the Father's delight, the Son of his love, Prov. viii. 30. (3) In respect of *counsel* and *design*. The mystery of man's redemption by this Word incarnate was *hid in God* before all worlds, Eph. iii. 9.

3. His agency in making the world, *v.* 3. This is here, (1) Expressly asserted: *All things were made by him.* By him, not as a subordinate instrument, but as a co-ordinate agent, God *made the world* (Heb. i. 2), not as the workman cuts by his axe, but as the body sees by the eye. (2) The contrary is denied: *Without him was not any thing made that was made*, from the highest angel to the meanest worm. God the Father did nothing without him in that work.

Now, [1] This proves that *he is God*; for he that *built all things is God*, Heb. iii. 4. [2] This proves the excellency of the Christian religion, that the author and founder of it is the same that was the author and founder of the world. [3] This shows how well qualified he was for the work of our redemption and salvation. Help was laid upon one that was mighty indeed; for it was laid upon him that made all things; and he is appointed the author of our bliss who was the author of our being.

4. The original of life and light that is in him: *In him was life, v, 4.* This further proves that he is God, and every way qualified for his undertaking; for, (1) He has *life in himself*; not only the *true God*, but the *living God*. God is life; he swears by himself when he saith, *As I live.* (2) All living creatures have their life in him; not only all the *matter* of the creation was *made* by him, but all the *life* too that is in the creation is derived from him and supported by him. (3) Reasonable creatures have their *light* from him; that *life* which is *the light of men* comes from him. Life in man is something greater and nobler than it is in other creatures; it is *rational*, and not merely *animal*. When man became a *living soul*, his life was *light*, his capacities such as distinguished him from, and dignified him above, the beasts that perish.

5. The manifestation of him to the children of men. It might be objected, If this eternal Word was all in all thus in the creation of the world, whence is it that he has been so little taken notice of and regarded? To this he answers (*v.* 5),

The light shines, but the darkness comprehends it not. Observe,

The disability of the degenerate world to receive this discovery: *The darkness comprehended it not*; the most of men received the grace of God in these discoveries in vain.[1]

THE WORD REJECTED
(*vv.* 6–14)

The evangelist designs to bring in John Baptist bearing an honourable testimony to Jesus Christ. Now in these verses, before he does this,

I. He gives us some account of the witness he is about to produce. His name was *John*, which signifies *gracious*; his conversation was austere, but he was not the less *gracious*. Now,

1. We are here told concerning him, in general, that he was a *man sent of God*. God gave him both his mission and his message, both his credentials and his instructions.

2. We are here told what his office and business were (*v.* 7): *The same came for a witness*, an eye-witness, a leading witness. Now observe, (1) The matter of his testimony: *He came to bear witness to the light*. Light is a thing which witnesses for itself, and carries its own evidence along with it; but to those who shut their eyes against the light it is necessary there should be those that bear witness to it. Christ's light needs not man's testimony, but the world's darkness

does. (2) The design of his testimony: *That all men through him might believe*; not in him, but in Christ, whose way he was sent to prepare. He taught men to look through him, and pass through him, to Christ; through the doctrine of repentance for sin to that of faith in Christ.

3. We are here cautioned not to mistake him for the light who only came to bear witness to it (*v.* 8): *He was not that light* that was expected and promised, but only was sent to bear witness of that great and ruling light.

II. Before he goes on with John's testimony, he returns to give us a further account of this Jesus to whom John bore record. Having shown in the beginning of the chapter the glories of his Godhead, he here comes to show the graces of his incarnation, and his favours to man as Mediator.

1. Christ was the *true light* (*v.* 9); not as if John Baptist were a false light, but, in comparison with Christ, he was a very small light. Christ is the great light thát deserves to be called so. But how does Christ enlighten every man that comes into the world? (1) By his creating power he enlightens every man with the light of reason; that life which is the light of men is from him; all the discoveries and directions of reason, all the comfort it gives us, and all the beauty it puts upon us, are from Christ. (2) By the publication of his gospel to all nations he does in effect enlighten every man. (3) By the operation of his Spirit and grace he enlightens all those that are enlightened to salvation; and those

---

[1] Editor's note: The author has, in common with most of his contemporaries, misunderstood the Greek here. See RV, RSV, NEB etc.

that are not enlightened by him perish in darkness.

2. Christ *was in the world,* v. 10. The Son of the Highest was here. in this *lower* world; that *light* in this *dark* world; that *holy thing* in this sinful polluted world. He left a world of bliss and glory, and was here in this melancholy miserable world. He undertook to reconcile the world to God, and therefore was *in the world,* to treat about it, and settle that affair; to satisfy God's justice for the world, and discover God's favour to the world. Now observe here, (1) What reason Christ had to expect the most affectionate and respectful welcome possible in this world; for *the world was made by him.* (2) What cold entertainment he met with, notwithstanding: *The world knew him not.* They did not own him, did not bid him welcome, because they did not *know him*; and they did not know him because he did not make himself known in the way that they expected—in external glory and majesty.

3. He *came to his own* (v. 11); not only to the world, which was *his own,* but to the people of Israel, that were peculiarly *his own* above all people; of them he came, among them he lived, and to them he was *first sent.* He was sent to the lost sheep of the house of Israel, for it was he whose own the sheep were. Now observe,

(1) That the generality *rejected* him: *His own received him not.* They had the oracles of God, which told them beforehand *when* and *where* to expect him, and of what tribe and family he should arise. He came among them him-

self, introduced with signs and wonders, and himself the greatest; and therefore it is not said of them, as it was of the world (v. 10), that they *knew him not*; but *his own,* though they could not but know him, yet *received him not*; did not receive his doctrine, did not welcome him as the Messiah, but fortified themselves against him.

(2) That yet there was a remnant who *owned* him, and were faithful to him. Though his own received him not, yet there were those that *received* him (v. 12). Observe here,

[1] The true Christian's *description* and *property*; and that is, that he *receives Christ,* and *believes on his name*; the latter explains the former.

[2] The true Christian's dignity and privilege are twofold:—

First, The *privilege of adoption,* which takes them into the number of God's children: *To them gave he power to become the sons of God.* The Son of God became a Son of man, that the sons and daughters of men might become the sons and daughters of God Almighty.

Secondly, The *privilege of regeneration* (v. 13): *Which were born.* Now here we have an account of the original of this new birth. 1. Negatively. (1) It is not *propagated* by natural generation from our parents. It is *not of blood, nor of the will of the flesh,* nor of *corruptible seed,* 1 Pet. i. 23. Man is called *flesh and blood,* because thence he has his original: but we do not become the children of God as we become the children of our natural parents. (2) It is not *produced* by the natural power of our own will. As it is not of *blood,* nor of *the will of the flesh*, so neither is it of the *will of man*, which labours under a moral impotency of determining itself to that which is good; so that the principles of the divine life are not of our own planting, it is the grace of God that makes us willing to be *his*.

4. The *word was made flesh*, *v*. 14. This expresses Christ's incarnation more clearly than what went before. By his divine presence he always *was in the world*, and by his prophets he *came to his own*. But now that the fulness of time was come he was sent forth after another manner, *made of a woman* (Gal. iv. 4); God manifested in the flesh, according to the faith and hope of holy Job; *Yet shall I see God in my flesh*, Job xix. 26. Observe here,

(1) The *human nature of Christ* with which he was veiled; and that expressed two ways.

[1] *The word was made flesh.* The voice that ushered in the gospel cried, *All flesh is grass* (Isa. xl. 6), to make the Redeemer's love the more wonderful, who, to *redeem* and *save* us, was made flesh, and withered as grass; but the *Word of the Lord*, who was made flesh, *endures for ever*; when made flesh, he ceased not to be the Word of God.

[2] He *dwelt among us*, here in this lower world. Having taken upon him the nature of man, he put himself into the place and condition of other men. But that the eternal Word was *made flesh*, was clothed with a body as we are, and dwelt in this world as we do, this has put an honour upon them both, and should make us willing to abide in the flesh while God has any work

for us to do; for Christ dwelt in this lower world, bad as it is, till he had finished what he had to do here, *ch*. xvii. 4.

(2) The *beams of his divine glory* that *darted* through this *veil of flesh: We beheld his glory, the glory as of the only begotten of the Father, full of grace and truth*. Observe,

[1] Who were the witnesses of this glory: *we*, his disciples and followers, that conversed most freely and familiarly with him; we among whom he *dwelt*. Other men discover their weaknesses to those that are most familiar with them, but it was not so with Christ; those that were most intimate with him saw most of his glory.

[2] What evidence they had of it: *We saw it*. The word signifies a fixed abiding sight, such as gave them an opportunity of making their observations.

[3] What the glory was: *The glory as of the only begotten of the Father*. The glory of the *Word made flesh* was such a glory as became the only *begotten Son of God*, and could not be the glory of any other. God's goodness is his glory, and he went about doing good; he spoke and acted in every thing as an incarnate Deity.

[4] What advantage those he dwelt among had from this. He dwelt among them, *full of grace and truth*. In the old tabernacle wherein God dwelt was the *law*, in *this* was grace; in that were *types*, in this was *truth*.

GRACE FOR GRACE (*vv*. 15–18)

In these verses,

I. The evangelist begins again to give us John Baptist's testimony

Grace for Grace

concerning Christ, *v.* 15. He had said (*v.* 8) that he *came for a witness*; now here he tells us that he did accordingly *bear witness.* Here, Observe,

1. *How he expressed* his testimony: He *cried,* according to the prediction that he should be *the voice of one crying.* This intimates, (1) That it was an open *public* testimony, proclaimed, that all manner of persons might take notice of it, for all are concerned in it. (2) That he was free and hearty in bearing this testimony.

2. What his *testimony* was.

(1) He had given the preference to this Jesus: *He that comes after me,* in the time of his birth and public appearance, is preferred before me; he that *succeeds* me in preaching and making disciples is a more excellent person, upon all accounts; as the prince or peer that *comes after* is preferred before the harbinger or gentleman-usher that makes way for him.

(2) He here gives a good reason for it: *For he was before me, He was my first,* or *first to me*; he was my first Cause, my original.

II. He presently returns again to speak of Jesus Christ, and cannot go on with John Baptist's testimony till *v.* 19. The 16th verse has a manifest connection with *v.* 14, where the incarnate Word was said to be *full of grace and truth.* Now here he makes this the matter, not only of our adoration, but of our thankfulness, because *from the fulness* of his *we all have received. He received gifts for men* (Ps. lxviii. 18), that he might *give gifts to men,* Eph. iv. 8. He was filled, that he might *fill all in all* (Eph. i. 23),

might *fill our treasures,* Prov. viii. 21. Let us see what it is that we have received.

1. We have received *grace for grace.* Our receivings by Christ are all summed up in this one word, *grace.* It is repeated, *grace for grace*; for every stone in this building, as well as *to the top-stone,* we must cry, *Grace, grace.*

2. We have received *grace and truth, v.* 17. He had said (*v.* 14) that Christ was *full of grace and truth*; now here he says that by him *grace and truth* came to us. From Christ we *receive grace*; this is a string he delights to harp upon, he cannot go off from it. Two things he further observes in this verse concerning this grace:—(1) Its *preference* above the law of Moses. (2) Its *connection* with truth: *grace and truth.* The law was only *made known* by Moses, but the *being* of this grace and truth, as well as the discovery of them, is owing to Jesus Christ; this was *made* by him, as the world at first was; and by him this *grace and truth* do *consist.*

3. Another thing we receive from Christ is a clear revelation of God to us (*v.* 18): He hath *declared* God to us, whom *no man hath seen at any time.* This was the grace and truth which came by Christ, the knowledge of God and an acquaintance with him. Observe,

(1) The insufficiency of all other discoveries: *No man hath seen God at any time.*

(2) The all-sufficiency of the gospel discovery proved from its author: *The only-begotten Son, who is in the bosom of the Father, he has declared him.*

JOHN'S TESTIMONY (*vv.* 19–28)

We have here the testimony of John, which he delivered to the messengers who were sent from Jerusalem to examine him. Observe here,

I. Who they were that sent to him, and who they were that were sent: *the Jews at Jerusalem*, the great sanhedrim or high-commission court, which sat at Jerusalem, and was the representative of the Jewish church, who took cognizance of all matters relating to religion.

II. On what errand they were sent; it was to enquire concerning John and *his baptism*.

III. What was the answer he gave them, and his account, both concerning himself and concerning his baptism, in both which he witnessed to Christ.

1. Concerning himself, and what he professed himself to be. He answers their interrogatory,

(1) *Negatively.* He was not that great one whom some took him to be. God's faithful witnesses stand more upon their guard *against undue respect* than against *unjust contempt*.

(2) *Affirmatively. I am the voice of one crying in the wilderness.* Observe,

[1] He gives his answer in the words of scripture, to show that the scripture was fulfilled in him, and that his office was supported by a divine authority.

[2] He gives in his answer in very humble, modest, self-denying expressions. He chooses to apply that scripture to himself which denotes not his dignity, but his duty and dependence, which bespeaks him little.

[3] He gives such an account of himself as might be profitable to them, and might excite and awaken them to hearken to him; for he *was the voice* (see Isa. xl. 3), a voice to alarm, an articulate voice to instruct. He came to prepare and dispose people for the reception and entertainment of Christ and his gospel. It is an allusion to the harbingers of a prince or great man, that cry, *Make room.*

2. Here is his testimony concerning *his baptism.*

(1) The enquiry which the committee made about it: *Why baptizest thou, if thou be not the Christ, nor Elias, nor that prophet?* v. 25. [1] They readily apprehended baptism to be fitly and properly used as a sacred rite or ceremony. [2] They expected it would be used in the days of the Messiah, because it was promised that then there should be a *fountain opened* (Zech. xiii. 1), and *clean water sprinkled*, Ezek. xxxvi. 25. It is taken for granted that Christ, and Elias, and *that prophet*, would baptize, when they came to *purify* a *polluted* world. [3] They would therefore know by what authority John baptized. His denying himself to be Elias, or *that prophet*, subjected him to this further question, *Why baptizest thou?*

(2) The account he gave of it, vv. 26, 27.

[1] He owned himself to be only the minister of the outward sign: "*I baptize with water,* and that is all; I am no more, and do no more, than what you see; I have no other title than *John the Baptist*; I

cannot confer the spiritual grace signified by it."

[2] He directed them to one who was greater than himself, and would do that for them, if they pleased, which he could not do. *First*, He tells them of Christ's *presence among them* now at this time: *There stands one among you*, at this time, *whom you know not.* Note, 1. Much true worth lies hid in this world; obscurity is often the lot of real excellency. Saints are God's *hidden ones*, therefore *the world knows them not.* 2. God himself is often nearer to us than we are aware of. *The Lord* is *in this place*, and *I knew it not.*

Lastly, Notice is taken of the place where all this was done: *In Bethabara beyond Jordan, v.* 28. It was at a great *distance* from Jerusalem, beyond Jordan; probably because what he did *there* would be least offensive to the government.

THE LAMB OF GOD (*vv.* 29–36)

Now here are *two testimonies* borne by John to Christ, but those two *agree in one.*

I. Here is his testimony to Christ on the first day that he saw him coming from the wilderness; and here four things are witnessed by him concerning Christ, when he had him before his eyes:—

1. That he is *the Lamb of God which taketh away the sin of the world, v.* 29. Let us learn here,

(1) That Jesus Christ is the *Lamb of God*, which bespeaks him the great sacrifice, by which atonement is made for sin, and man reconciled to God. He is the Lamb *of God*; he is appointed by *him*

(Rom. iii. 25), he was devoted to him (*ch.* xvii. 19), and he was accepted with him; in him he was well pleased.

(2) That Jesus Christ, as the *Lamb of God, takes away the sin of the world.* This ground of hope we have—Jesus Christ is *the Lamb of God.* [1] He *takes away sin.* He, being Mediator between God and man, takes away that which is, above any thing, offensive to the *holiness* of God, and destructive to the *happiness* of man. [2] He takes away the *sin of the world*; purchases pardon for all those that repent, and believe the gospel, of what country, nation, or language, soever they be. The legal sacrifices had reference only to the sins of Israel, to make atonement for them; but the Lamb of God was offered to be a propitiation for the *sin of the whole world*; see 1 John ii. 2. This is encouraging to our faith; if Christ takes away the sin of the world, then why not my sin? [3] He does this by *taking it upon himself.* He is the Lamb of God, that *bears the sin of the world*; so the margin reads it. He bore sin *for us*, and so bears it *from us*; he *bore the sin of many*, as the scapegoat had the sins of Israel put upon his head, Lev. xvi. 21. God could have taken away the sin by taking away the sinner, as he took away the sin of the old world; but he has found out a way of abolishing the sin, and yet sparing the sinner, by making his Son *sin for us.*

(3) That it is our duty, with an eye of faith, to *behold* the Lamb of God thus taking away the *sin of the world.*

2. That this was he of whom he

had spoken before (*vv.* 30, 31). Observe, (1) This honour John had above all the prophets, that, whereas they spoke of him as one that should come, he saw him already come. *This. is he.* Such a difference there is between present *faith* and future *vision.* (2) John calls Christ *a man*; after me comes a man—a *strong man*: like *the man,* the branch, or the *man of God's right hand.* (3) He refers to what he had himself said of him before: *This is he of whom I said.* (4) He protests against any confederacy or combination with this Jesus: *And I knew him not.* Though there was some relation between them (Elisabeth was cousin to the virgin Mary), yet there was no acquaintance at all between them; John had no personal knowledge of Jesus till he saw him come to his baptism. (5) The great intention of John's ministry and baptism was to introduce Jesus Christ. That he should be *made manifest to Israel, therefore am I come baptizing with water.* Observe, [1] Though John did not know Jesus by face, yet he knew that he should be made manifest. [2] The general assurance John had that Christ *should be made manifest* served to carry him with diligence and resolution through his work, though he was kept in the dark concerning particulars. [3] God reveals himself to his people by degrees. At first, John knew no more concerning Christ but that he should be made manifest; in confidence of that, he came baptizing, and now he is favoured with a sight of him. They who, upon God's word, believe what they do not see, shall shortly see what they

now believe. [4] The ministry of the word and sacraments is designed for no other end than to lead people to Christ, and to make him more and more manifest. [5] Baptism with water made way for the manifesting of Christ, as it supposed our corruption and filthiness, and signified our cleansing by him who is the *fountain opened.*

3. That this was he *upon whom the Spirit descended from heaven like a dove.* For the confirming of his testimony concerning Christ, he here vouches the extraordinary appearance at his baptism, in which God himself bore witness to him. This was a considerable proof of Christ's mission.

Observe, [1] The spirit descended *from heaven,* for every good and perfect gift is *from above.* [2] He descended *like a dove*—an emblem of meekness, and mildness, and gentleness, which makes him *fit to teach.* The dove brought the olive-branch of peace, Gen. viii. 11. [3] The Spirit that descended upon Christ *abode upon him,* as was foretold, Isa. xi. 2. The Spirit did not *move him at times,* as Samson (Judg. xiii. 25), but *at all times.*

4. That he is *the Son of God.* This is the conclusion of John's testimony, that in which all the particulars centre: *I saw, and bore record, that this is the Son of God.* (1) The truth asserted is, *that this is the Son of God.* The voice from heaven proclaimed, and John subscribed to it, not only that he should baptize with the Holy Ghost by a divine authority, but that he has a divine nature. (2) John's testimony to it: "*I saw, and bore record.*" Christ's witnesses

were eye-witnesses, and therefore the more to be credited: they did not speak by hear-say and report, 2 Pet. i. 16.

II. Here is John's testimony to Christ, the next day after, *vv.* 35, 36. Where observe, 1. He took every opportunity that offered itself to lead people to Christ. 2. He repeated the same testimony which he had given to Christ the day before, though he could have delivered some other great truth concerning him; but thus he would show that he was uniform and constant in his testimony, and consistent with himself. 3. He intended this especially for his two disciples that stood with him; he was willing to turn them over to Christ, for to this end he bore witness to Christ in their hearing that they might leave all to follow him, even that they might leave *him.*

ANDREW AND SIMON
(*vv.* 37–42)

We have here the turning over of two disciples from John to Jesus, and one of them fetching in a third, and these are the first-fruits of Christ's disciples; see how small the church was in its beginnings, and what the dawning of the day of its great things was.

I. Andrew and another with him were the two that John Baptist had directed to Christ, *v.* 37.

1. Here is their readiness to go over to Christ: They *heard John speak* of Christ as the *Lamb of God,* and they *followed Jesus.* The strongest and most prevailing argument with a sensible awakened soul to follow Christ is that

it is he, and he only, that *takes away sin.*

2. The kind notice Christ took of them, *v.* 38. They came behind him; but, though he had his back towards them, he was soon aware of them, and *turned,* and *saw them following.*

3. Their modest enquiry concerning the place of his abode: *Rabbi, where dwellest thou?*

4. The courteous invitation Christ gave them to his lodgings: *He saith unto them, Come and see.* Thus should good desires towards Christ and communion with him be countenanced.

5. Their cheerful and (no doubt) thankful acceptance of his invitation: *They came and saw where he dwelt,* and *abode with him that day.* It had been greater modesty and manners than had done them good if they had refused this offer.

II. Andrew brought his brother Peter to Christ. Observe,

1. The *information* which Andrew gave to Peter, with an intimation to come to Christ.

(1) He *found him: He first finds his own brother Simon;* his finding implies his seeking him. Simon came along with Andrew to attend John's ministry and baptism, and Andrew knew where to look for him.

(2) He told him whom they had found: *We have found the Messias. We have found* that pearl of great price that true treasure; and, having found it, he proclaims it as those lepers, 2 Kings vii. 9, for he knows that he shall have never the less in Christ for others sharing. He speaks *intelligently: We have found the Messias,* which was more than

had yet been said. John had said, *He is the Lamb of God, and the Son of God*, which Andrew compares with the scriptures of the Old Testament, and, comparing them together, concludes that he is the Messiah promised to the fathers, for it is now that the fulness of time is come.

(3) He *brought him to Jesus*; would not undertake to instruct him himself, but brought him to the fountain-head, persuaded him to come to Christ and introduced him.

2. The *entertainment* which Jesus Christ gave to Peter, who was never the less welcome for his being influenced by his brother to come, *v.* 42. Observe,

(1) Christ called him by his name: *When Jesus beheld him, he said, Thou art Simon, the son of Jona.* It should seem that Peter was utterly a stranger to Christ, and if so, [1] It was a proof of Christ's omniscience that upon the first sight, without any enquiry, he could tell the name both of him and of his father. However, [2] It was an instance of his condescending grace and favour, that he did thus freely and affably call him by his name. Some observe the signification of these names: *Simon—obedient, Jona—a dove.* An obedient dove-like spirit qualifies us to be the disciples of Christ.

(2) He gave him a new name: *Cephas.* [1] His giving him a name intimates *Christ's favour* to him. A new name denotes some great dignity, Rev. ii. 17; Isa. lxii. 2. [2] The name which he gave him bespeaks his *fidelity* to Christ: *Thou shalt be called Cephas* (that is Hebrew for *a stone*), *which is by*

interpretation Peter; so it should be rendered. Peter's natural temper was stiff, and hardy, and resolute, which I take to be the principal reason why Christ called him *Cephas—a stone.* When Christ afterwards prayed for him, that his faith might not fail, that so he might be firm to Christ himself, and ·at the same time bade him *strengthen his brethren*, and lay out himself for the support of others, then he *made him* what he here called him, *Cephas—a stone.*

PHILIP AND NATHANAEL
(*vv.* 43–51)

We have here the call of Philip and Nathanael.

I. Philip was called immediately by Christ himself, not as Andrew, who was directed to Christ by John, or Peter, who was invited by his brother. God has various methods of bringing his chosen ones home to himself. Philip was brought to be a disciple by the power of Christ going along with that word, *Follow me.* See the nature of true Christianity; it is *following Christ*, devoting ourselves to his *converse* and *conduct*, attending his movements, and treading in his steps. See the efficacy of the grace of Christ making the call of his word to prevail; it is the *rod of his strength.*

II. Nathanael was invited to Christ by Philip, and much is said concerning him. In which we may observe,

1. What passed between Philip and Nathanael. Here is,

(1) The joyful news that Philip brought to Nathanael, *v.* 45. As Andrew before, so Philip here,

having got some knowledge of Christ himself, rests not till he has *made manifest the savour of that knowledge*.

(2) The objection which Nathanael made against this, *Can any good thing come out of Nazareth?* v. 46. Here, [1] His *caution* was commendable, that he did not lightly assent to every thing that was said, but took it into examination; our rule is, *Prove all things*. But, [2] His objection arose from ignorance. If he meant that no good thing could come out of Nazareth it was owing to his ignorance of the divine grace, as if that were less affected to one place than another, or tied itself to men's foolish and ill-natured observations.

(3) The short reply which Philip gave to this objection: *Come and see*. [1] It was his *weakness* that he could not give a satisfactory answer to it; yet it is the common case of young beginners in religion. We may *know* enough to *satisfy* ourselves, and yet not be able to *say* enough to *silence* the cavils of a subtle adversary. [2] It was his *wisdom* and zeal that, when he could not answer the objection himself, he would have him go to one that could: *Come and see.*

2. What passed between Nathanael and our Lord Jesus. He came and *saw*, not in vain.

(1) Our Lord Jesus bore a very honourable testimony to Nathanael's integrity: *Jesus saw him* coming, and met him with favourable encouragement; he said of him to those about him, Nathanael himself being within hearing, *Behold an Israelite indeed*. Observe,

[1] That he *commended* him;

not to flatter him, or puff him up with a good conceit of himself, but perhaps because he knew him to be a *modest* man.

[2] That he commended him for his *integrity*. The whole nation were Israelites in name, but *all are not Israel that are of Israel* (Rom. ix. 6); here, however, was *an Israelite indeed*. 1. A sincere follower of the good example of Israel, whose character it was that he was a *plain man*, in opposition to Esau's character of a *cunning man*. 2. A sincere professor of the faith of Israel; he was true to the religion he professed, and lived up to it: he was really as good as he seemed, and his practice was *of a piece* with his profession.

(2) Nathanael is much surprised at this.

[1] Here is Nathanael's modesty, in that he was soon put out of countenance at the kind notice Christ was pleased to take of him: "*Whence knowest thou me*, me that am unworthy of thy cognizance? *who am I, O Lord God?*" 2 Sam. vii. 18. This was an evidence of his sincerity, that he did not catch at the praise he met with, but declined it.

[2] Here is Christ's further *manifestation* of himself to him: *Before Philip called thee, I saw thee. First*, He gives him to understand that he *knew him*, and so manifests his divinity. *Secondly*, That before Philip called him he saw him under the fig-tree; this manifests a particular kindness for him. 1. His eye was towards him before Philip called him, which was the first time that ever Nathanael was acquainted with Christ. Christ has knowledge

of us before we have any knowledge of him; see Isa. xlv. 4; Gal. iv. 9. 2. His eye was upon him when he was *under the fig-tree*; this was a private token which nobody understood but Nathanael. It is most probable that Nathanael under the fig-tree was employed, as Isaac in the field, in meditation, and prayer, and communion with God. Perhaps then and there it was that he solemnly joined himself to the Lord in an inviolable covenant. Christ saw in secret, and by this public notice of it did in part reward him openly.

(3) Nathanael hereby obtained a full assurance of faith in Jesus Christ, expressed in that noble acknowledgment (*v.* 49): *Rabbi, thou art the Son of God, thou art the king of Israel*; that is, in short, thou art the true Messiah.

(4) Christ hereupon raises the hopes and expectations of Nathanael to something further and greater than all this, *vv.* 50, 51.

He promises him much greater helps for the confirmation and increase of his faith than he had had for the first production of it.

First, In general: "*Thou shalt see greater things than these*, stronger proofs of my being the Messiah"; the miracles of Christ, and his resurrection.

Secondly, In particular: "Not thou only, but you, all you my disciples, whose faith this is intended for the confirmation of, you *shall see heaven opened*." Through Christ we have communion with and benefit by the holy angels, and things in heaven and things on earth are *reconciled* and *gathered together*. Christ is to

us as Jacob's ladder (Gen. xxviii. 12), by whom angels continually ascend and descend for the good of the saints.

CHAPTER TWO
WATER INTO WINE (*vv.* 1–11)

We have here the story of Christ's miraculous conversion of water into wine at a marriage in Cana of Galilee. Now observe,

I. The occasion of this miracle. Observe,

1. The time: the *third day* after he came into Galilee. The evangelist keeps a journal of occurrences, for no day passed without something extraordinary done or said.

2. The place: it was at Cana in Galilee. Christ began to work miracles in an obscure corner of the country, remote from Jerusalem, which was the public scene of action, to show that he *sought not honour from men* (*ch.* v. 41), but would put honour *upon the lowly*.

3. The occasion itself was a *marriage*; probably one or both of the parties were akin to our Lord Jesus. The *mother of Jesus* is said to be *there*, and not to be *called*, as Jesus and his disciples were, which intimates that she was there as one at home. Observe the honour which Christ hereby put upon the ordinance of marriage, that he graced the solemnity of it, not only with his presence, but with his first miracle. Marriages were usually celebrated with festivals (Gen. xxix. 22; Judg. xiv. 10), in token of joy and friendly respect, and for the confirming of love.

4. Christ and his mother and

disciples were principal guests at this entertainment.

II. The miracle itself. In which observe,

1. They *wanted wine, v.* 3. (1) There was *want* at a *feast*; though much was provided, yet all was spent.

2. The *mother of Jesus* solicited him to assist her friends in this strait. We are told (*vv.* 3–5) what passed between Christ and his mother upon this occasion.

(1) She acquaints him with the difficulty they were in (*v.* 3): *She saith unto him, They have no wine.*

(2) He gave her a reprimand for it, for he saw more amiss in it than we do, else he had not treated it thus.—Here is,

[1] The rebuke itself: *Woman, what have I to do with thee?* As many as Christ loves, he rebukes and chastens. The question might be read, *What is that to me and thee?* What is it to us if they do want?

[2] The reason of this rebuke: *Mine hour is not yet come.* For every thing Christ did, and that was done to him, he had *his hour*, the *fixed* time and the *fittest* time, which was punctually observed. "Mine hour for *working miracles* is not yet come." Yet afterwards he wrought this, before the hour, because he foresaw it would confirm the faith of his infant disciples (*v.* 11), which was the end of all his miracles: so that this was an earnest of the many miracles he would work when his *hour was come.*

(3) Notwithstanding this, she encouraged herself with expectations that he would help her friends in this strait, for she bade the

servants *observe his orders, v.* 5. She directed the servants to have an eye *to him* immediately, and not to make their applications to her, as it is probable *they had done.* Note, Those that expect Christ's *favours* must with an implicit obedience observe his *orders.* The way of duty is the way to mercy; and Christ's methods must not be objected against.

(4) Christ did at length miraculously supply them; for he is often better than his word, but never worse.

[1] The miracle itself was *turning water into wine*; the substance of water acquiring a new form, and having all the accidents and qualities of wine.

[2] The circumstances of it magnified it and freed it from all suspicion of cheat or collusion; for,

First, It was done in water-pots (*v.* 6): *There were set there six water-pots of stone.*

Secondly, The water-pots were filled *up to the brim* by the servants at Christ's word, *v.* 7.

Thirdly, The miracle was wrought suddenly, and in such a manner as greatly magnified it.

a. As soon as they had filled the water-pots, presently he said, *Draw out now* (*v.* 8), and it was done, (*a*) Without any ceremony, in the eye of the spectators. (*b*) Without any hesitation or uncertainty in his own breast. As he knew what he *would* do, so he knew what he *could* do, and made no essay in his work; but all was good, very good, even in the beginning.

b. Our Lord Jesus directed the servants, (*a*) *To draw it out*; not to let it alone in the vessel, to be admired, but to *draw it out*, to be drank. Christ's works are all *for use*; he gives no man a talent to be *buried*, but to be *traded with*. (*b*) To present it to *the governor of the feast*.

Fourthly, The wine which was thus miraculously provided was of the best and richest kind, which was acknowledged by the governor of the feast; and that it was really so, and not his fancy, is certain, because he knew not whence it was, *vv*. 9, 10. This the governor of the feast takes notice of to the bridegroom, with an air of pleasantness, as *uncommon*. (1) The common method was otherwise. Good wine is brought out to the best advantage at the beginning of a feast. (2) This bridegroom obliged his friends with a reserve of the best wine for the grace-cup: *Thou hast kept the good wine until now*; not knowing to whom they were indebted for this good wine, he returns the thanks of the table to the bridegroom.

III. In the conclusion of this story (*v*. 11) we are told, 1. That this was *the beginning of miracles* which Jesus did. 2. That herein he *manifested his glory*; hereby he proved himself to be the Son of God, and his glory to be that of the only-begotten of the Father.

THE TEMPLE CLEANSED
(*vv*. 12–22)

Here we have,

I. The short visit Christ made to Capernaum, *v*. 12. It was a large and populous city, about a day's journey from Cana; it is called *his own city* (Matt. ix. 1), because he made it his headquarters in Galilee, and what little rest he had was there.

II. The passover he kept at Jerusalem; it is the *first* after his baptism, and the evangelist takes notice of all the passovers he kept henceforward, which were four in all, the *fourth* that at which he suffered (three years after this), and half a year was now past since his baptism. Christ kept the passover at Jerusalem yearly, ever since he was twelve years old, in obedience to the law; but now that he has entered upon his public ministry we may expect something more from him than before; and two things we are here told he did there:—

1. He *purged the temple*, *vv*. 14–17. Observe here,

(1) The first place we find him in at Jerusalem was the *temple*, and, it should seem, he did not make any public appearance till he came thither; for his presence and preaching there were that glory of the latter house which was to *exceed the glory of the former*, Hag. ii. 9. It was foretold (Mal. iii. 1): *I will send my messenger*, John Baptist; he never preached in the temple, but *the Lord*, *whom ye seek*, he shall *suddenly come to his temple*, suddenly after the appearing of John Baptist; so that this was the time, and the temple the place, when, and where, the Messiah was to be expected.

(2) The first work we find him at in the temple was the *purging* of it; for so it was foretold there (Mal. iii. 2, 3): *He shall sit as a refiner and purify the sons of Levi.* Now was come the *time of reformation*. See here,

[1] What were the corruptions that were to be purged out. He found a market in one of the courts of the temple, that which was called the *court of the Gentiles*, within the *mountain of that house*.

[2] What course our Lord took to purge out those corruptions. He did not complain to the chief priests, for he knew they countenanced those corruptions. But he himself,

First, *Drove out the sheep and oxen*, and those that *sold them*, out of the temple. He never used *force* to drive any *into* the temple, but only to drive those out that profaned it.

Secondly, He *poured out the changers' money*. In *pouring out* the money, he showed his contempt of it; he threw it to the ground, to the earth as it *was*. In *overthrowing* the tables, he showed his displeasure against those that make religion a matter of worldly gain. Money-changers in the temple are the scandal of it.

Thirdly, *He said to them that sold doves* (sacrifices for the poor), *Take these things hence*. The doves, though they took up less room, and were a less nuisance than the oxen and sheep, yet must not be allowed there. The sparrows and swallows were welcome, that were left to God's providence (Ps. lxxxiv. 3), but not the doves, that were appropriated to man's profit.

Fourthly, He gave them a good reason for what he did: *Make not my Father's house a house of merchandise*. Reason for conviction should accompany force for correction.

Fifthly, Here is the remark which his disciples made upon it (*v.* 17): *They remembered that it was written, The zeal of thine house hath eaten me up*. They were somewhat surprised at first to see him to whom they were directed as the *Lamb of God* in such a heat, and him whom they believed to be the *King of Israel* take so little state upon him as to do this himself; but one scripture came to their thoughts, which taught them to reconcile this action both with the meekness of the *Lamb of God* and with the majesty of the *King of Israel*; for David, speaking of the Messiah, takes notice of his *zeal for God's house*, as so great that it even *ate him up*, it made him forget himself, Ps. lxix. 9.

2. Christ, having thus purged the temple, gave a sign to those who demanded it to prove his authority for so doing. Observe here,

(1) Their demand of a sign: *Then answered the Jews*, that is the multitude of the people, with their leaders. Being Jews, they should rather have stood by him, and assisted him to vindicate the honour of their temple; but, instead of this, they objected against it.

(2) Christ's answer to this demand, *v.* 19. He did not immediately work a miracle to convince them, but gave them a sign in something *to come*, the truth of which must appear by the event, according to Deut. xviii. 21, 22.

Now, [1] The sign that he gives them is his own *death* and *resurrection*.

[2] He foretells his death and resurrection, not in plain terms, as he often did to his disciples, but in figurative expressions; as after-

wards, when he gave this for a sign, he called it the *sign of the prophet Jonas*, so here, *Destroy this temple, and in three days I will raise it up.* Thus he spoke in parables to those who were willingly ignorant, that *they might not perceive*, Matt. xiii. 13, 14. Those that will not see shall not see.

[3] He chose to express this by *destroying* and *re-edifying* the temple, *First*, Because he was now to justify himself in purging the temple, which they had profaned. *Secondly*, Because the death of Christ was indeed the destruction of the Jewish temple, the procuring cause of it; and his resurrection was the raising up of another temple, the gospel church, Zech. vi. 12.

(3) Their cavil at this answer: "*Forty and six years was this temple in building*, *v.* 20. Temple work was always slow work, and canst thou make such quick work of it?"

(4) A vindication of Christ's answer from their cavil. The difficulty is soon solved by explaining the terms: *He spoke of the temple of his body*, *v.* 21. Some think that when he said, Destroy *this* temple, he pointed to his own body, or laid his hand upon it; however, it is certain that he *spoke of the temple of his body*. Note, The body of Christ is the true temple, of which that at Jerusalem was a type.

(5) A reflection which the disciples made upon this, long after, inserted here, to illustrate the story (*v.* 22): *When he was risen from the dead*, some years after, *his disciples remembered that he had said this.* We found them, *v.* 17, remembering what had been *written before of him*, and here we find them re-membering what they had *heard from him*.

MANY BELIEVED (*vv.* 23–25)

We have here an account of the success, the poor success, of Christ's preaching and miracles at Jerusalem, while he kept the pass-over there.

Yet *Jesus did not commit himself unto them* (v. 24): *He did not trust himself with them.* It is the same word that is used for *believing* in him. So that to believe in Christ is to *commit ourselves* to him and to his guidance. Christ did not see cause to repose any confidence in these new converts at Jerusalem, where he had many enemies that sought to destroy him, either, 1. Because they were *false*, at least some of them, and would betray him if they had an opportunity, or were strongly tempted to do so. Or, 2. Because they were *weak*, and I would hope that this was the worst of it; not that they were *treacherous* and designed him a mischief.

The reason he did not *commit himself* to them was because he *knew* them (v. 25), knew the wickedness of some and the weakness of others. The evangelist takes this occasion to assert Christ's omnisci-ence.

CHAPTER THREE

CHRIST AND NICODEMUS
(vv. 1–21)

We found, in the close of the fore-going chapter, that few were brought to Christ at Jerusalem; yet here was *one*, a considerable one. It is worth while to go a great way for the salvation though but of *one soul.* Observe,

I. Who this Nicodemus was. Not many mighty and noble are called; yet some are, and here was one. He was a *ruler of the Jews*, a member of the great sanhedrim, a senator, a privy-counsellor, a man of authority in Jerusalem.

II. His solemn address to our Lord Jesus Christ, *v.* 2. See here,

1. When he came: *He came to Jesus by night*, which may be considered, [1] As an act of *prudence* and *discretion.* [2] As an act of *zeal* and *forwardness.* Nicodemus was a man of business, and could not spare time all day to make Christ a visit, and therefore he would rather take time from the diversions of the *evening*, or the rest of the *night*, than not converse with Christ. Or, [3] As an act of *fear* and *cowardice.* He was afraid, or ashamed, to be *seen* with Christ, and therefore came *in the night*.

2. What he said. He tells Christ how far *he had attained*: We *know that thou art a teacher.* Observe,

(1) His *assertion* concerning Christ: *Thou art a teacher come from God.*

(2) His *assurance* of it: *We know*, not only *I*, but *others*; so he took it for granted, the thing being so plain and self-evident. (3) The ground of this assurance: *No man can do those miracles that thou doest, except God be with him.* Here, [1] We are assured of the truth of Christ's miracles, and that they were not counterfeit. Here was Nicodemus, a judicious, sensible, inquisitive man, one that had all the *reason* and *opportunity* imaginable to examine them, so fully satisfied that they were real miracles that he was wrought upon by them to go contrary to his interest, and to the stream of those of his own rank, who were prejudiced against Christ. [2] We are directed what inference to draw from Christ's miracles: Therefore we are to receive him as a *teacher come from God.*

III. The discourse between Christ and Nicodemus hereupon, or, rather, the sermon Christ preached to him; the contents of it, and that perhaps an abstract of Christ's public preaching; see *vv.* 11, 12. Four things our Saviour here discourses of:

1. Concerning the *necessity and nature of regeneration* or the *new birth, vv.* 3–8. Observe,

(1) What it is that is required: to be *born again*; that is, *First*, We must *live a new life.* Birth is the beginning of life; to be *born again* is to begin anew, as those that have hitherto lived either much amiss or to little purpose. We must not think to patch up the old building, but begin from the foundation. *Secondly*, We must *have a new nature*, new principles, new affections, new aims. By our *first birth* we are corrupt, shapen in sin and iniquity; we must therefore undergo a second birth; our souls must be *fashioned* and *enlivened* anew. We must be born *from above*, so the word is used by the evangelist, *ch.* iii. 31; xix. 11; for to be born *from above* supposes being *born again.* But this new birth has its rise *from* heaven (*ch.* i. 13) and its tendency *to* heaven: it is to be born to a *divine* and *heavenly* life, a life of communion with God and the upper world, and, in order to this, it is to

partake of a *divine nature* and bear the *image of the heavenly*.

(2) The indispensable necessity of this: "Except *a man be born again, he cannot see the kingdom of God*, the kingdom of the Messiah begun in *grace* and perfected in *glory*." Except we be *born from above*, we cannot *see* this. That is, *First,* We cannot *understand* the *nature* of it. *Secondly,* We cannot *receive the comfort* of it, cannot expect any benefit by Christ and his gospel, nor have any part or lot in the matter.

This great truth of the necessity of regeneration being thus solemnly laid down,

a. It is objected against by Nicodemus (*v.* 4): *How can a man be born when he is old? Can he enter the second time into his mother's womb, and be born?*

b. It is opened and further explained by our Lord Jesus, *vv.* 5–8. From the objection he takes occasion,

(*a*) To repeat and confirm what he had said (*v.* 5): "*Verily, verily, I say unto thee*, the very same that I said before."

(*b*) To expound and clear what he had said concerning regeneration; for the explanation of which he further shows,

[*a*] The *author* of this blessed change, and who it is that works it. To be born again is to be *born of the Spirit, vv.* 5–8. The change is not wrought by any wisdom or power of our own, but by the power and influence of the blessed Spirit of grace.

[*b*] The *nature* of this change, and what that is which is wrought; it is *spirit, v.* 6. Those that are regenera-

ted are made *spiritual,* and refined from the dross and dregs of sensuality.

[*c*] The *necessity* of this change. *First,* Christ here shows that it is necessary in the *nature of the thing,* for we are not fit to enter into the kingdom of God till we are born again: *That which is born of the flesh is flesh, v.* 6. Here is our malady, with the causes of it, which are such that it is plain there is no remedy but we must be *born again.*

[*d*] This change is illustrated by two comparisons. *First,* The regenerating work of the Spirit is compared to *water, v.* 5. 1. That which is primarily intended here is to show that the Spirit, in sanctifying a soul, (1) *Cleanses* and purifies it as water, takes away its filth, by which it was unfit for the kingdom of God. It is the *washing of regeneration,* Tit. iii. 5. *You are washed,* 1 Cor. vi. 11. See Ezek. xxxvi. 25. (2) Cools and refreshes it, as water does the hunted hart and the weary traveller. The Spirit is compared to water, *ch.* vii. 38, 39; Isa. xliv. 3. 2. It is probable that Christ had an eye to the ordinance of baptism, which John had used and he himself had begun to use, "You must be born again of the Spirit," which regeneration by the Spirit should be signified by washing with water, as the visible sign of that spiritual grace: not that all they, and they only, that are baptized, are saved; but without that new birth which is wrought by the Spirit, and signified by baptism, none shall be looked upon as the *protected privileged* subjects of the *kingdom of heaven. Secondly,*

It is compared to *wind: The wind bloweth where it listeth, so is every one that is born of the Spirit*, v. 8. The same word signifies both the wind and the Spirit. The Spirit came upon the apostles in a *rushing mighty wind* (Acts ii. 2), his *strong* influences on the hearts of sinners are compared to the *breathing of the wind* (Ezek. xxxvii. 9), and his *sweet* influences on the souls of saints to the north and south wind, Cant. iv. 16. This comparison is here used to show, 1. That the Spirit, in regeneration, works *arbitrarily*, and as a free agent. 2. That he works *powerfully*, and with evident effects: *Thou hearest the sound thereof*; though its causes are hidden, its effects are manifest. 3. That he works *mysteriously*, and in secret hidden ways: *Thou canst not tell whence it comes, nor whither it goes*. How it gathers and how it spends its strength is a riddle to us; so the manner and methods of the Spirit's working are a mystery.

2. Here is a discourse concerning the *certainty and sublimity of gospel truths*, which Christ takes occasion for from the weakness of Nicodemus. Here is,

(1) The objection which Nicodemus still made (v. 9): *How can these things be?* Christ's explanation of the doctrine of the necessity of regeneration, it should seem, made it no clearer to him.

(2) The reproof which Christ gave him for his dullness and ignorance: "*Art thou a master in Israel, a teacher*, a tutor, one who sits in Moses's chair, and yet not only unacquainted with the doctrine of regeneration, but incapable of understanding it?"

(3) Christ's discourse, hereupon, of the certainty and sublimity of gospel truths (*vv.* 11–13), to show the folly of those who make strange of these things, and to recommend them to our search. Observe here,

[1] That the truths Christ taught were very *certain* and what we may venture upon (v. 11): *We speak that we do know*. Observe, *First*, That the truths of Christ are of undoubted certainty. He spoke not upon hearsay, but upon the clearest evidence, and therefore with the greatest assurance. *Secondly*, That the unbelief of sinners is greatly aggravated by the infallible certainty of the truths of Christ.

[2] The truths Christ taught, though communicated in language and expressions borrowed from common and earthly things, yet in their own nature were most sublime and heavenly. The things of the gospel are *heavenly* things, out of the road of the enquiries of human reason, and much more out of the reach of its discoveries. Earthly things are despised because they are *vulgar*, and heavenly things because they are *abstruse*; and so, whatever method is taken, still some fault or other is found with it (Matt. xi. 17), but Wisdom is, and will be, *justified of her children*, notwithstanding.

[3] Our Lord Jesus, and he alone, was fit to reveal to us a doctrine thus certain, thus sublime: *No man hath ascended up into heaven but he*, v. 13.

First, None but Christ was able to reveal to us the will of God for our salvation.

Secondly, Jesus Christ is able, and fit, and every way qualified, to reveal the will of God to us; for it is *he that came down from heaven* and *is in heaven*.

3. Christ here discourses of the *great design of his own coming into the world, and the happiness of those that believe in him, vv.* 14–18. Here we have the very marrow and quintessence of the whole gospel, that *faithful saying* (1 Tim. i. 15), that Jesus Christ came to seek and to save the children of men from death, and recover them to life.

[1] Jesus Christ came to save us by *healing* us, as the children of Israel that were stung with fiery serpents were cured and *lived* by looking up to the brazen serpent; we have the story of it, Num. xxi. 6–9. It was the *last* miracle that passed through the hand of Moses before his death. Now in this type of Christ we may observe,

First, The *deadly* and *destructive* nature of *sin*, which is implied here. The guilt of sin is like the *pain* of the biting of a fiery serpent; the power of corruption is like the *venom* diffused thereby.

Secondly, The powerful remedy provided against this fatal malady. The case of poor sinners is deplorable; but is it desperate? Thanks be to God, it is not; there is balm in Gilead. The *Son of man is lifted up*, as the *serpent of brass* was by Moses, which cured the stung Israelites. 1. It was a *serpent of brass* that cured them. It was made in the shape of a *fiery serpent*, and yet had no poison, no sting, fitly representing Christ, who was *made sin for us* and yet knew no sin; was *made in the likeness of sinful flesh* and yet not sinful; as harmless as a serpent of brass. The serpent was a

cursed creature; Christ was made a *curse*. That which cured them reminded them of their plague; so in Christ sin is set before us most fiery and formidable. 2. It was lifted up upon a pole, and so *must* the Son of man be lifted up; thus it *behoved him*, Luke xxiv. 26, 46.

Thirdly, The way of *applying* this remedy, and that is by *believing*, which plainly alludes to the Israelites' *looking up* to the brazen serpent, in order to their being healed by it. If any stung Israelite was either so little sensible of his pain and peril, or had so little confidence in the word of Moses as not to look up to the brazen serpent, justly did he die of his wound; but every one that *looked up to it* did well, Num. xxi. 9. If any so far slight either their disease by sin or the method of cure by Christ as not to embrace Christ upon his own terms, their blood is upon their own head. He hath said, *Look, and be saved* (Isa. xlv. 22), look and live.

Fourthly, The great encouragements given us by faith to look up to him. 1. It was for this end that he was *lifted up*, that his followers might be saved; and he will pursue his end. 2. The offer that is made of salvation by him is general, that *whosoever believes* in him, without exception, might have benefit by him. 3. The salvation offered is complete. (1) They *shall not perish*, shall not die of their wounds; though they may be pained and ill frightened, iniquity shall not be their ruin. But that is not all. (2) They shall *have eternal life*. They shall not only not die of their wounds in the wilderness, but they shall reach Canaan (which they were then just ready to enter into); they shall enjoy the promised rest.

[2] Jesus Christ came to save us by *pardoning us*, that we might not die by the sentence of the law, *vv.* 16, 17.

First, Here is God's *love*, in *giving his Son for the world* (*v.* 16), where we have the great *gospel mystery* revealed: *God so loved the world that he gave his only-begotten Son.* The love of God the Father is the original of our regeneration by the Spirit and our reconciliation by the lifting up of the Son. Note, (1) Jesus Christ is the *only-begotten Son of God.* (2) To achieve the redemption and salvation of man, it pleased God to *give his only-begotten Son.* (3) Herein God has commended his *love to the world*: God so *loved the world*, so really, so richly. Now his creatures shall see that he loves them, and wishes them well. He so loved the world of fallen man as he did not love that of fallen angels; see Rom. v. 8; 1 John iv. 10. Behold, and wonder, that the *great God* should love such a *worthless* world!

Secondly, Here is God's design in sending his Son into the world: it was *that the world through him might be saved.* He came into the world with salvation in *his eye*, with salvation *in his hand*. Therefore the aforementioned offer of life and salvation is sincere, and shall be made good to all that by faith accept it (*v.* 17). 1. He did not come to *condemn the world*. We had reason enough to expect that he should, for it is a guilty world; it is *convicted*, and what cause can be shown why judgment should not be given, and execution awarded, according to law? 2. He came *that the world through him might be saved*, that a door of salvation might be opened to the world, and whoever would might enter in by it. God was in Christ *reconciling the world to himself*, and so *saving* it.

[3] From all this is inferred the happiness of true believers: *He that believeth on him is not condemned, v.* 18. Though he has been a sinner, a great sinner, and *stands convicted*, yet, upon his believing, process is stayed, judgment is arrested, and he is *not condemned*.

4. Christ, in the close, discourses concerning the *deplorable condition of those that persist in unbelief and wilful ignorance, vv.* 18–21.

(1) Read here the doom of those that will not *believe in Christ*: they *are condemned already*. The curse has already taken hold of them; the wrath of God now fastens upon them. They are condemned already, for their own hearts condemn them. Unbelief may truly be called *the great damning sin*, because it leaves us under the guilt of all our other sins; it is a sin against the *remedy*, against our *appeal*.

(2) Read also the doom of those that would not so much as *know him, v.* 19. And *this is the condemnation*, the sin that ruined them, *that light is come into the world, and they loved darkness rather*. Now here observe, [1] That the gospel is light, and, when the gospel came, *light came into the world*. Light is *self-evidencing*, so is the gospel; it proves its own divine origin. [2] It is the unspeakable folly of the most of men that they loved darkness rather than light, rather than *this*

light. [3] The true reason why men love darkness rather than light is *because their deeds are evil.* They love darkness because they think it is an excuse for their evil deeds, and they hate the light because it robs them of the good opinion they had of themselves, by showing them their sinfulness and misery. [4] Wilful ignorance is so far from excusing sin that it will be found, at the great day, to aggravate the condemnation. We must account in the judgment, not only for the knowledge we *had*, and *used not*, but for the knowledge we *might have had*, and *would not*.

On the other hand, upright hearts, that approve themselves to God in their integrity, bid this light welcome (*v.* 21): *He that doeth truth cometh to the light.* It seems, then, that though the gospel had many enemies it had some friends. It is a common observation that *truth seeks no corners.* Those who mean and act honestly dread not a scrutiny, but desire it rather. Now this is applicable to the gospel light; as it *convinces* and *terrifies* evil-doers, so it *confirms* and *comforts* those that walk in their integrity.

Thus far we have Christ's discourse with *Nicodemus*; it is probable that much more passed between them, and it had a good effect, for we find (*ch.* xix. 39) that Nicodemus, though he was puzzled at first, yet afterwards became a faithful disciple of Christ.

JOHN'S WITNESS (*vv.* 22–36)

In these verses we have,

I. Christ's removal into the land of Judea (*v.* 22), and there he tarried with his disciples. *After these things*, after he had had this discourse with Nicodemus, he came into the land of Judea; not so much for *greater privacy* (though mean and obscure places best suited the humble Jesus in his humble state) as for *greater usefulness*. He did not retire into the country for his ease and pleasure, but for more free conversation with his disciples and followers.

II. John's continuance in his work, as long as his opportunities lasted, *vv.* 23, 24. Here we are told,

1. That *John was baptizing*. Christ's baptism was, for substance, the same with John's, for John bore witness to Christ, and therefore they did not at all clash or interfere with one another.

2. That he baptized in Enon near Salim, places we find nowhere else mentioned. He chose a place where there was much water, *many waters*, that is, many *streams* of water; so, that wherever he met with any that were willing to submit to his baptism water was at hand to baptize them with.

3. That thither people *came to him* and *were baptized*. Though they did not come in such vast crowds as they did when he first appeared, yet now he was not without encouragement, but there were still those that attended and owned him.

4. It is noted (*v.* 24) that *John was not yet cast into prison*, to clear the order of the story, and to show that these passages are to come in before Matt. iv. 12.

III. A contest between *John's disciples and the Jews about purify-*

ing, v. 25. See how the gospel of Christ came not to *send peace upon earth*, but *division*. Observe, 1. Who were the disputants: *some of John's disciples, and the Jews* who had not submitted to his baptism of repentance. 2. What was the matter in dispute: *about purifying*, about *religious washing*. Thus objections are made against the gospel from the advancement and improvement of gospel light, as if childhood and manhood were contrary to each other, and the superstructure were against the foundation. There was no reason to object Christ's baptism against John's, for they consisted very well together.

IV. A complaint which John's disciples made to their master concerning Christ and his baptizing, *v.* 26. If these disciples of John had not undertaken to dispute about *purifying*, before they understood the *doctrine of baptism*, they might have answered the objection without being put into a passion. In their complaint, they speak respectfully to their own master, *Rabbi*; but speak very slightly of our Saviour, though they do not name him. 1. They suggest that Christ's setting up a baptism of his own was a piece of presumption, very unaccountable. 2. They suggest that it was a piece of ingratitude to John. He *to whom thou barest witness* baptizes; as if Jesus owed all his reputation to the honourable character John gave of him, and yet had very unworthily improved it to the prejudice of John. But Christ needed not John's testimony, *ch.* v. 36. 3. They conclude that it would be a total eclipse to John's baptism: "*All men come to him*; they that used to follow with us now flock after him, it is therefore time for us to look about us." It was not indeed strange that *all men came to him*. As far as Christ is *manifested* he will be *magnified*; but why should John's disciples grieve at this?

V. Here is John's answer to this complaint which his disciples made, *vv.* 27, &c. His disciples expected that he would have resented this matter as they did; but Christ's *manifestation to Israel* was no *surprise* to John, but what he looked for; it was no *disturbance* to him, but what he wished for.

1. John here *abases himself in comparison with Christ, vv.* 27-30.

(1) *John acquiesces* in the divine disposal, and satisfies himself with that (*v.* 27).

(2) John appeals to the testimony he had formerly given concerning Christ (*v.* 28): You can bear me witness that I said, again and again, *I am not the Christ, but I am sent before him*. See how steady and constant John was in his testimony to Christ, and not as a *reed shaken with the wind*; neither the frowns of the chief priests, nor the flatteries of his own disciples, could make him change his note.

(3) John professes the great satisfaction he had in the advancement of Christ and his interest. He was so far from *regretting* it, as his disciples did, that he *rejoiced* in it. This he expresses (*v.* 29) by an elegant similitude.

(4) He owns it highly fit and necessary that the reputation and interest of Christ should be ad-

vanced, and his own diminished (*v.* 30): *He must increase, but I must decrease.*

2. John Baptist here *advances* Christ, and instructs his disciples concerning him, that, instead of grieving that so many come to him, they might come to him themselves.

(1) He instructs them concerning the *dignity of Christ's person* (*v.* 31): *He that cometh from above, that cometh from heaven, is above all.*

(2) Concerning the *excellency and certainty of his doctrine.* His disciples were displeased that Christ's preaching was admired, and attended upon, more than his; but he tells them that there was reason enough for it. For,

[1] He, for his part, *spoke of the earth,* and so do all those that are *of the earth.*

[2] But he that cometh from heaven is not only in his person, but in his doctrine, above all the prophets that ever lived on earth; none teacheth like him.

From the *certainty* of Christ's doctrine, John takes occasion, [1] To lament the infidelity of the most of men: though he testifies what is infallibly true, yet *no man* receiveth his testimony, that is, very few, next to none, none in comparison with those that refuse it. [2] He takes occasion to commend the faith of the chosen remnant (*v.* 33): *He that hath received his testimony* (and some such there were, though very few) hath *set to his seal that God is true.* God is true, though we do not *set our seal to it;* let God be true, and every man a liar; his

truth needs not our faith to support it, but by faith we do ourselves the honour and justice to subscribe to his truth, and hereby God reckons himself honoured. By believing in Christ we set to our seal, *First,* That God is true to all the promises which he has made *concerning Christ,* that which he spoke by the mouth of *all his holy prophets;* what he *swore to our fathers* is all accomplished, and not one iota or tittle of it fallen to the ground, Luke i. 70, &c. Acts xiii. 32, 33. *Secondly,* That he is true to all the promises he has made *in Christ;* we venture our souls upon God's veracity, being satisfied that he is *true.*

It is recommended to us as a *divine* doctrine; not his own, but *his that sent* him (*v.* 34): *For he whom God hath sent speaketh the word of God,* which he was sent to speak, and enabled to speak; *for God giveth not the Spirit by measure unto him.* The prophets were as messengers that brought letters from heaven; but Christ came under the character of an *ambassador,* and treats with us as such; for, 1. He spoke the *words of God,* and nothing he said savoured of human infirmity; both substance and language were divine. 2. He spoke as no other prophet did; for *God giveth not the Spirit by measure to him.* None can speak the *words of God* without the *Spirit of God,* 1 Cor. ii. 10, 11. The Old-Testament prophets had the Spirit, and in different degrees, 2 Kings ii. 9, 10. But, whereas God gave them the Spirit by *measure* (1 Cor. xii. 4), he gave him to Christ *without measure;* all fulness dwelt in him, the fulness of the Godhead, an immeasurable fulness.

(3) Concerning *the power and authority he is invested with*, which gives him the pre-eminence above all others, and a more excellent name than they.

[1] He is the *beloved Son of the Father* (v. 35): *The Father loveth the Son*. The prophets were faithful as servants, but Christ as a Son.

[2] He is *Lord of all*. The Father, as an evidence of his love for him, *hath given all things into his hand*. Having given *him the Spirit without measure*, he gave him *all things*; for he was hereby qualified to be master and manager of all.

[3] He is the object of that faith which is made the great condition of eternal happiness, and herein he has the pre-eminence above all others: *He that believeth on the Son, hath life*, v. 36. Here is,

First, The blessed state of all true Christians: *He that believes on the Son hath everlasting life*. Grace is glory begun.

Secondly, The wretched and miserable condition of unbelievers: *He that believeth not the Son* is undone. The word includes both *incredulity* and *disobedience*. He is not only under the *wrath of God*, which is as surely *the soul's death* as his favour is *its life*, but it *abides upon him*.

CHAPTER FOUR
THE WOMAN AT THE WELL
(vv. 1-26)

We have here an account of the good Christ did in Samaria, when he *passed through* that country in his way to Galilee. The Samaritans, both in *blood* and *religion* were *mongrel Jews*. They worshipped the God of Israel only, to whom they erected a temple on mount Gerizim, in competition with that at Jerusalem. There was great enmity between them and the Jews. Now observe,

I. Christ's coming into Samaria. He charged his disciples not to *enter into any city of the Samaritans* (Matt. x. 5), that is, not to preach the gospel, or work miracles; nor did he here preach publicly, or work any miracle, his eye being to *the lost sheep of the house of Israel*. What kindness he here did them was *accidental*; it was only a *crumb* of the children's bread that casually *fell from the master's table*.

1. His *road* from Judea to Galilee lay through the *country* of Samaria (v. 4): *He must needs go through Samaria*. There was no other way, unless he would have fetched a compass on the other side *Jordan*, a great way about.

2. His baiting place happened to be at a *city of Samaria*. Now observe,

(1) The place described. It was called *Sychar*; probably the same with *Sichem*, or *Shechem*, a place which we read much of in the Old Testament. [1] Here lay Jacob's ground, the *parcel of ground which Jacob* gave to his son Joseph, whose bones were buried in it, Gen. xlviii. 22; Josh. xxiv. 32. [2] Here was Jacob's well which he digged, or at least used, for himself and his family. We find no mention of this well in the Old Testament; but

the tradition was that it was Jacob's well.

(2) The posture of our Lord Jesus at this place: *Being wearied with his journey, he sat thus on the well*.

II. His discourse with a Samaritan woman, which is here recorded at large, while Christ's dispute with the doctors, and his discourse with Moses and Elias on the mount, are buried in silence. This discourse is reducible to four heads:—

1. They discourse *concerning the water*, vv. 7–15.

(1) Notice is taken of the *circumstances* that gave occasion to this discourse.

[1] There comes a *woman* of Samaria to *draw water*. This intimates her poverty, she had no servant to be a *drawer of water*; and her industry, she would do it herself. The grace of God sometimes brings people unexpectedly under the means of conversion and salvation. He is found of them that sought him not.

[2] His disciples were *gone away into the city to buy meat*. Now this gave Christ an opportunity of discoursing with this woman about spiritual concerns, and he improved it; he often preached to multitudes that crowded after him for instruction, yet here he condescends to teach a single person, a woman, a poor woman, a stranger, a Samaritan, to teach his ministers to do likewise.

(2) Let us observe the *particulars* of this discourse.

[1] Jesus begins with a modest request for a draught of water: *Give me to drink*. He that *for our*

sakes became poor here becomes a beggar, that those who are in want, and cannot dig, may not be ashamed to beg.

[2] The woman, though she does not deny his request, yet quarrels with him because he did not carry on the mood of his own nation (*v.* 9): *How is it?* Observe, *First*, What a mortal feud there was between the Jews and the Samaritans: *The Jews have no dealings with the Samaritans*. *Secondly*, How ready the woman was to upbraid Christ with the haughtiness and ill nature of the Jewish nation: *How is it that thou, being a Jew, askest drink of me?* By his dress or dialect, or both, she knew him to be a Jew, and *thinks it strange* that he runs not to the same excess of riot against the Samaritans with other Jews.

[3] Christ takes this occasion to instruct her in divine things: *If thou knewest the gift of God, thou wouldst have asked, v.* 10. Observe,

First, He waives her objection of the feud between the Jews and Samaritans, and takes no notice of it.

Secondly, He fills her with an apprehension that she had now an opportunity (a fairer opportunity than she was aware of) of gaining that which would be of unspeakable advantage to her.

a. He hints to her what she *should know*, but was ignorant of: *If thou knewest the gift of God*, that is, as the next words explain it, *who it is that saith, Give me to drink*. If thou knewest *who I am*. She saw him to be a Jew, a poor weary traveller; but he would have her know something more concerning him than did yet appear.

b. He hopes concerning her, what she would have done if she had known him: *Thou wouldest have asked.* Note, (*a*) Those that would have any benefit by Christ must ask for it, must be earnest in prayer to God for it. (*b*) Those that have a right knowledge of Christ will seek to him, and if we do not seek unto him it is a sign that we do not know him, Ps. ix. 10.

c. He assures her what he would have done for her if she had applied to him: "He *would have given thee* (and not have upbraided thee as thou dost me) *living water.*" By this living water is meant the *Spirit*, who is not like the water in the bottom of the well, for some of which he asked, but like *living* or *running* water, which was much more valuable. Note, (*a*) The Spirit of grace is as *living water*; see *ch.* vii. 38. Under this similitude the blessings of the Messiah had been promised in the Old Testament, Isa. xii. 3; xxxv. 7; xliv. 3; lv. 1; Zech. xiv. 8. The graces of the Spirit, and his comforts, satisfy the thirsting soul, that knows its own nature and necessity. (*b*) Jesus Christ *can* and *will* give the Holy Spirit to them that ask him; for he *received* that he might *give.*

[4] The woman objects against and cavils at the gracious intimation which Christ gave her (*vv.* 11, 12): *Thou hast nothing to draw with*; and besides, *Art thou greater than our father Jacob?* What he spoke figuratively, she took literally; Nicodemus did so too.

First, She does not think him capable of furnishing her with any water, no, not this in the well that is just at hand: *Thou hast nothing to draw with,* and *the well is deep.*

Secondly, She does not think it possible that he should furnish her with any better water than this which she could come at, but he could not: *Art thou greater than our father Jacob, who gave us the well?*

[5] Christ answers this cavil, and makes it out that the *living water* he had to give was far better than that of Jacob's well, *vv.* 13, 14. Though she spoke perversely, Christ did not cast her off, but instructed and encouraged her. He shows her,

First, That the water of Jacob's well yielded but a *transient* satisfaction and supply: "*Whoso drinketh of this water shall thirst again.*"

Secondly, That the living waters he would give should yield a lasting satisfaction and bliss, *v.* 14. Christ's gifts appear most valuable when they come to be compared with the things of this world; for there will appear no comparison between them. Whoever partakes of the Spirit of grace, and the comforts of the everlasting gospel,

a. He shall *never thirst,* he shall never want that which will abundantly satisfy his soul's desires; they are *longing,* but not *languishing.* A *desiring* thirst he has, nothing more *than* God, still more and more *of* God; but not a *despairing* thirst.

b. Therefore he shall never thirst, because this water that Christ gives *shall be in him a well of water. He* can never be reduced to extremity that has in himself a *fountain* of supply and satisfaction.

[6] The woman (whether in jest or earnest is hard to say) begs of him to give her some of this water (*v.* 15): *Give me this water, that I thirst not.*

2. The next subject of discourse with this woman is *concerning her husband, vv.* 16–18. It was not to let fall the discourse of the water of life that Christ started this, as many who will bring in any *impertinence* in conversation that they may drop a serious subject; but it was with a gracious design that Christ mentioned it. What he had said concerning his grace and eternal life he found had made little impression upon her, because she had not been convinced of sin: therefore, waiving the discourse about the living water, he sets himself to awaken her conscience.

Observe, (1) How discreetly and decently Christ introduces this discourse (*v.* 16): *Go, call thy husband, and come hither.*

(2) How industriously the woman seeks to evade the conviction, and yet insensibly convicts herself, and, ere she is aware, owns her fault; she said, *I have no husband.* Her saying this intimated no more than that she did not care to have her husband spoken of, nor that matter mentioned any more.

(3) How closely our Lord Jesus brings home the conviction to her conscience. It is probable that he said more than is here recorded, for she thought that he told her all that ever she did (*v.* 29), but that which is here recorded is concerning her husbands. Here is, [1] A *surprising narrative* of her *past* way of life. *Thou hast had five husbands.* Doubtless, it was not her *affliction* (the burying of so many husbands), but her *sin*, that Christ intended to upbraid her with; either she had *eloped* (as the law speaks), had run away from her *husbands*, and married others, or by her undutiful, unclean, disloyal conduct, had provoked them to *divorce her*, or by indirect means had, contrary to law, *divorced them.* [2] A severe reproof of her present state of life: *He whom thou now hast is not thy husband.* Either she was never married to him at all, or he had some other wife, or, which is most probable, her former husband, or husbands were living: so that, in short, *she lived in adultery.*

3. The next subject of discourse with this woman is concerning *the place of worship, vv.* 19–24. Observe,

(1) A case of conscience proposed to Christ by the woman, concerning the place of worship, *vv.* 19, 20.

[1] The inducement she had to put this case: *Sir, I perceive that thou art a prophet.* She does not deny the truth of what he had charged her with, but by her silence owns the justice of the reproof. But this is not all; she goes further: *First,* She speaks respectfully to him, calls him *Sir.* Thus should we *honour* those that deal faithfully with us. This was the effect of Christ's meekness in reproving her; he gave her no ill language, and then she gave him

none. *Secondly*, She acknowledges him to be a *prophet*, one that had a correspondence with Heaven.

[2] The case itself that she propounded concerning the *place of religious worship in public*. Some think that she started this to shift off further discourse concerning her sin. Controversies in religion often prove great prejudices to serious godliness; but, it should seem, she proposed it with a good design; she knew she must worship God, and desired to do it aright; and therefore, meeting with a prophet, begs his direction. Observe how she states the case:—

First, As for the Samaritans: *Our fathers worshipped in this mountain*, near to this city and this well; there the Samaritan temple was built by Sanballat.

Secondly, As to the Jews: *You say* that *in Jerusalem is the place where men ought to worship*. The Samaritans governed themselves by the five books of Moses, and (some think) received *only them* as canonical. Now, though they found frequent mention there of the place God would choose, yet they did not find it named there; and they saw the temple at Jerusalem stripped of many of its ancient glories, and therefore thought themselves at liberty to set up another place, altar against altar.

(2) Christ's answer to this case of conscience, *vv.* 21, &c. Those that apply themselves to Christ for instruction shall find him *meek, to teach the meek his way*. Now here,

[1] He puts *a slight* upon the question, as she had proposed it,

concerning the place of worship (*v.* 21). *First*, The object of worship is supposed to continue still the same—*God*, as a Father; under this notion the very heathen worshipped God, the Jews did so, and probably the Samaritans. *Secondly*, But a period shall be put to all scruples and all differences about the place of worship.

[2] He *lays a stress* upon other things, in the matter of religious worship. When he made so light of the place of worship he did not intend to lessen our concern about the thing itself, of which therefore he takes occasion to discourse more fully.

First, As to the present state of the controversy, he *determines* against the Samaritan worship, and in favour of the Jews, *v.* 22. He tells her here, 1. That the Samaritans were certainly *in the wrong*. 2. That the Jews were certainly *in the right*. For, "*We know what we worship*. We go upon sure grounds in our worship, for our people are catechised and trained up in the knowledge of God, as he has revealed himself in the scripture."

Secondly, He describes the evangelical worship which alone God would accept and be well pleased with. Having shown that the place is *indifferent*, he comes to show what is *necessary* and *essential*—that we worship God *in spirit and in truth*, *vv.* 23, 24. The stress is not to be laid upon the *place* where we worship God, but upon the state of *mind* in which we worship him. Observe,

a. The great and glorious revolution which should introduce this change: *The hour cometh, and now is*—the fixed stated time, concerning which it was of old determined when it should come, and how long it should last. The *perfect day is coming*, and now it *dawns*.

b. The blessed change itself. In gospel times the *true worshippers shall worship the Father in spirit and in truth*. As creatures, we worship the Father of *all*: as Christians, we worship *the Father of our Lord Jesus*. Now the change shall be, (*a*) In the *nature* of the worship. Christians shall worship God, not in the ceremonial observances of the Mosaic institution, but in *spiritual* ordinances, consisting less in *bodily exercise*, and animated and invigorated more with divine power and energy. (*b*) In the *temper* and *disposition* of the worshippers; and so the true worshippers are good Christians, distinguished from hypocrites; all *should*, and they will, worship God *in spirit and in truth*. Spirit is sometimes put for the new nature, in opposition to the *flesh*, which is the corrupt nature; and so to worship God *with our spirits* is to worship him *with our graces*, Heb. xii. 28. *In truth*, that is, in sincerity. God requires not only the *inward part* in our worship, but *truth in the inward part*, Ps. li. 6. We must mind the power more than the form, must aim at God's glory, and not to be *seen of men*; draw near with a *true heart*, Heb. x. 22.

Thirdly, He intimates the reasons why God must be thus worshipped.

a. Because in gospel times they, and they only, are accounted the *true* worshippers. The gospel erects a spiritual way of worship, so that the professors of the gospel are not true in their profession, do not live up to gospel light and laws, if they do not worship God *in spirit and in truth*.

b. Because *the Father seeketh such worshippers of him*. This intimates, (*a*) That such worshippers are very rare, and seldom met with, Jer. xxx. 21. (*b*) That God is greatly well pleased with and graciously accepts such worship and such worshippers.

c. Because *God is a spirit*. Christ came to *declare God* to us (*ch.* i. 18), and this he has declared concerning him. Note, (*a*) *God is a spirit*, for he is an infinite and eternal mind, an intelligent being, incorporeal, immaterial, invisible, and incorruptible. It is easier to say what God is not than what he is; a spirit *has not flesh and bones*, but *who knows the way of a spirit?* If God were not *a spirit*, he could not be *perfect*, nor infinite, nor eternal, nor independent, nor the Father of spirits. (*b*) The spirituality of the divine nature is a very good reason for the spirituality of divine worship. If we do not worship God, who is *a spirit, in the spirit*, we neither *give him the glory due to his name*, and so do not perform the *act* of worship, nor can we hope to obtain his favour and acceptance, and so we miss of the *end* of worship, Matt. xv. 8, 9.

4. The last subject of discourse with this woman is concerning the Messiah, *vv.* 25, 26. Observe here,

(1) The faith of the woman, by

which she expected the Messiah: *I know that Messias cometh—and he will tell us all things.* She had nothing to object against what Christ had said; his discourse was, for aught she knew, what might become the Messiah then expected; but *from him* she would receive it, and in the mean time she thinks it best to suspend her belief.

(2) The favour of our Lord Jesus in making himself known to her: *I that speak to thee am he, v.* 26. Christ did never make himself known so expressly to any as he did here to this poor Samaritan, and to the blind man (*ch.* ix. 37); no, not to John Baptist, when he sent to him (Matt. xi. 4, 5); no, not to the Jews, when they challenged him to tell them whether he was the Christ, *ch.* x. 24.

THE HARVEST (*vv.* 27–42)

We have here the remainder of the story of what happened when Christ was in Samaria, after the long conference he had with the woman.

I. The *interruption given to this discourse* by the disciples' coming. 1. They wondered at Christ's converse with this woman, marvelled that he talked thus earnestly (as perhaps they observed at a distance) with a woman, a strange woman alone, especially with a Samaritan woman. 2. Yet they acquiesced in it; they knew it was for some good reason, and some good end, of which he was not bound to give them an account, and therefore none of them asked, *What seekest thou?* or, *Why talkest thou with her?*

II. The notice which the woman gave to her neighbours of the extraordinary person she had happily met with, *vv.* 28, 29. Observe here,

1. How she *forgot her errand to the well, v.* 28. Therefore, because the disciples were come, and broke up the discourse, and perhaps she observed they were not pleased with it, she *went her way.*

2. How she *minded her errand to the town*, for her heart was upon it. She *went into the city*, and said to *the men*, probably the aldermen, the men in authority, whom, it may be, she found met together upon some public business; or to *the men*, that is, to every man she met in the streets; she proclaimed it in the chief places of concourse: *Come, see a man who told me all things that ever I did. Is not this the Christ?* Observe,

(1) How *solicitous* she was to *have her friends and neighbours* acquainted with Christ.

(2) How fair and ingenuous she was in the notice she gave them concerning this stranger she had met with. [1] She *tells them* plainly what induced her to admire him: *He has told me all things that ever I did.* [2] She *invites them* to *come and see* him of whom she had conceived so high an opinion. Not barely, "Come and look upon him" (she does not invite them to him as a *show*), but, "Come and converse with him; come and *hear his wisdom*, as I have done, and you will be of my mind." [3] She

resolves to *appeal to themselves*, and their own sentiments upon the trial? *Is not this the Christ?* She will not impose her faith upon them, but only propose it to them.

(3) What success she had in this invitation: *They went out of the city, and came to him, v.* 30. Though it might seem very improbable that a woman of so *small* a figure, and so *ill* a character, should have the honour of the first discovery of the Messiah among the Samaritans, yet it pleased God to incline their hearts to take notice of her report, and not to slight it as an idle tale.

III. Christ's discourse with his disciples while the woman was absent, *vv.* 31–38. Two things are observable in this discourse:—

1. How Christ *expresses the delight* which he himself had in his work. His work was to *seek and save* that which was lost, to go about doing good. Now with this work we here find him wholly taken up.

2. See here how Christ, having expressed his delight in *his* work, excites his disciples to diligence in *their* work; they were workers *with him*, and therefore should be workers *like him*, and make their work their *meat*, as he did. The work they had to do was to *preach the gospel*, and to set up the kingdom of the Messiah. Now this work he here compares to *harvest work*, the gathering in of the fruits of the earth; and this similitude he prosecutes throughout the discourse, *vv.* 35–38. The disciples were to gather in a harvest of souls for Christ. Now he here suggests three things to them to quicken them to diligence:—

(1) That it was *necessary work*, and the *occasion* for it very urgent and pressing (*v.* 35): *You say, It is four months to harvest*; but I say, *The fields are already white.*

(2) That it was *profitable* and *advantageous* work, which they themselves would be gainers by (*v.* 36): "*He that reapeth receiveth wages*, and so shall you." Christ has undertaken to pay those well whom he employs in his work. He that reapeth, not only *shall* but *does* receive wages. There is a present reward in the service of Christ, and his work is *its own wages.*

(3) That it was *easy work*, and work that was half done to their hands by those that were gone before them: *One soweth, and another reapeth, vv.* 37, 38. This sometimes denotes a grievous judgment upon him that sows, Mic. vi. 15; Deut. xxviii. 30, *Thou shalt sow, and another shall reap*; as Deut. vi. 11, *Houses full of all good things, which thou fillest not.* So here. Moses, and the prophets, and John Baptist, had *paved* the way to the gospel, had sown the good seed which the New-Testament ministers did in effect but gather the fruit of. *I sent you to reap that whereon you bestowed*, in comparison, no *labour.* Isa. xl. 3–5. [1] This intimates *two things* concerning the Old-Testament ministry:—*First*, That it was very much *short* of the New-Testament ministry. Moses and the *prophets* sowed, but they could not be said to *reap*, so little did they see

of the fruit of their labours. *Secondly*, That it was very *serviceable* to the New-Testament ministry, and made way for it. [2] This also intimates *two things* concerning the ministry of the *apostles of Christ*. *First*, That it was a *fruitful* ministry: they were reapers that gathered in a great harvest of souls to Jesus Christ, and did more in seven years towards the setting up of the kingdom of God among men than the prophets of the Old Testament had done in twice so many ages. *Secondly*, That it was much *facilitated*, especially among the Jews, to whom they were first sent, by the writings of the prophets.

IV. The *good effect* which this visit Christ made to the Samaritans had upon them, and the fruit which was now presently gathered among them, *vv.* 39–42. See what impressions were made on them,

1. By the *woman's testimony* concerning *Christ*; though a single testimony, and of one of no good report, and the testimony no more than this, *He told me all that ever I did*, yet it had a good influence upon many. And *two things* they were brought to:—

(1) To *credit* Christ's *word* (*v.* 39): *Many of the Samaritans of that city believed on him for the saying of the woman.*

(2) They were brought to *court his stay* among them (*v.* 40): When they were come to him *they besought him that he would tarry with them*. Now we are told that Christ granted their request.

He *abode there*. Though it was a city of the Samaritans nearly adjoining to their temple, yet,

when he was *invited*, he *tarried* there.

2. We are also told what impressions were made upon them by Christ's own word, and his personal converse with them (*vv.* 41, 42); what he *said* and *did* there is not related, whether he healed their sick or no; but it is intimated, in the effect, that he said and did that which convinced them that he was the Christ; and the labours of a minister are best told by the good fruit of them.

Thus was the seed of the gospel sown in Samaria. What effect there was of this afterwards does not appear, but we find that four or five years after, when Philip preached the gospel in Samaria, he found such blessed remains of this good work now wrought that the *people with one accord gave heed to those things which Philip spoke*, Acts viii. 5, 6, 8. But as some were pliable to good so were others to evil, whom Simon Magus bewitched with his sorceries, *vv.* 9, 10.

THE NOBLEMAN'S SON
(*vv.* 43–54)

In these verses we have,

I. Christ's *coming* into Galilee, *v.* 43. *He went into Galilee*, for there he spent much of his time. Now see here,

1. Whither Christ went; into Gaililee, into the country of Galilee, but not to Nazareth, which was strictly *his own* country. He went among the villages, but declined going to Nazareth, the head city, for a reason here given, which *Jesus himself testified*, who knew the temper of his country-

men, the hearts of all men, and the experiences of all prophets, and it is this, That *a prophet has no honour in his own country*. Men's pride and envy make them scorn to be instructed by those who once were their school-fellows and play-fellows.

2. What entertainment he met with among the Galileans in the country (*v.* 45): They *received him*, bade him welcome, and cheerfully attended on his doctrine.

3. What city he went to. When he would go to a city, he chose to go to Cana of Galilee, *where he had made the water wine* (*v.* 46); thither he went, to see if there were any good fruits of that miracle remaining; and, if there were, to confirm their faith, and water what he had planted.

II. His *curing* the *nobleman's son* that was sick of a fever. This story is not recorded by any other of the evangelists; it comes in Matt. iv. 23.

Observe, 1. Who the *petitioner* was, and who the *patient*: the petitioner was a *nobleman*; the patient was his son: *There was a certain nobleman*. It was fifteen miles from Capernaum where this nobleman lived to Cana, where Christ now was; yet this affliction in his family sent him so far to Christ.

2. How the petitioner made *his application* to the physician. Having heard that *Jesus was come out of Judea to Galilee*, and finding that he did not come towards Capernaum, but turned off towards the other side of the country, he *went to him* himself, and *besought him to come and heal his son*, *v.* 47. See

here, (1) His *tender affection* to his son, that when he was sick he would spare no pains to get help for him. (2) His *great respect* to our Lord Jesus, that he would come himself to wait upon him, when he might have sent a servant. As to the errand he came upon, we may observe a mixture in *his faith*. [1] There was *sincerity* in it; he did believe that Christ could heal his son, though his disease was dangerous. [2] Yet there was *infirmity* in his faith; he believed that Christ could heal his son, but, as it should seem, he thought he could not heal him at a distance, and therefore he besought him that he would *come down* and heal him.

3. The gentle rebuke he met with in this address (*v.* 48): *Jesus said to him*, "I see how it is; *except you see signs and wonders, you will not believe*, as the Samaritans did, though they saw no signs and wonders, and therefore I must work miracles among you." Though he was a *nobleman*, and now in *grief* about his son, and had shown great respect to Christ in coming so far to him, yet Christ gives him a reproof. Men's dignity in the world shall not exempt them from the rebukes of the word or providence.

4. His continued importunity in his address (*v.* 49): *Sir, come down ere my child die. Lord*; so it should be rendered. In this reply of his we have, (1) Something that was commendable: he took the reproof patiently; he spoke to Christ respectfully. (2) Something that was blameworthy, that was his infirmity; for, [1] He seems to take no notice of the reproof

Christ gave him, says nothing to it, by way either of confession or of excuse, for he is so wholly taken up with concern about his child that he can mind nothing else. [2] He still discovered the weakness of his faith in the power of Christ. *First*, He must have Christ to come down, thinking that else he could do the child no kindness. *Secondly*, He believes that Christ could heal a *sick* child, but not that he could raise a *dead* child, and therefore, "O come down, ere my child die," as if then it would be too late.

5. The answer of peace which Christ gave to his request at last (*v.* 50): *Go thy way, thy son liveth*. Observe, His power was exerted by his word. In saying, *Thy son lives*, he showed that he has *life in himself*, and power to *quicken whom he will*.

6. The nobleman's belief of the word of Christ: He *believed*, and *went away*. Though Christ did not gratify him so far as to go down with him, he is satisfied with the method Christ took, and reckons he has gained his point. How quickly, how easily, is that which is lacking in our faith perfected by the word and power of Christ. Now he *sees no sign or wonder*, and yet *believes* the wonder done.

7. The further confirmation of his faith, by comparing notes with his servants at his return. (1) His servants met him with the agreeable news of the child's recovery, *v.* 51. (2) He enquired what hour the child began to recover (*v.* 52); not as if he doubted the influence of Christ's word upon the child's recovery, but he was desirous to

have his faith confirmed. They told him, *Yesterday, at the seventh hour* (at one o'clock in the afternoon, or, as some think this evangelist reckons, at seven o'clock at night) the *fever left him*. So *the father knew that it was at the same hour* when Jesus said to him, *Thy son liveth*.

8. The *happy effect and issue of this*. The bringing of the cure to the family brought salvation to it. (1) The nobleman *himself believed*. (2) His *whole house* believed likewise. [1] Because of the *interest* they all had in the miracle, which preserved the *blossom* and *hopes* of the family; this affected them all, and endeared Christ to them, and recommended him to their best thoughts. [2] Because of the *influence* the master of the family had upon them *all*.

9. Here is the evangelist's remark upon this cure (*v.* 54); *This is the second miracle*, referring to *ch.* ii. 11, where the turning of water into wine is said to be the first; that was soon after his first return out of Judea, this soon after his second.

CHAPTER FIVE

THE POOL OF BETHESDA
(*vv.* 1–16)

This miraculous cure is not recorded by any other of the evangelists, who confine themselves mostly to the miracles wrought in Galilee, but John relates those wrought at Jerusalem. Concerning this observe,

I. *The time when* this cure was wrought: it was at a *feast of the*

Jews, that is, the passover, for that was the most celebrated feast.

II. The *place where* this cure was wrought: at the *pool of Bethesda*, which had a miraculous healing virtue in it, and is here particularly described, *vv.* 2–4.

III. The patient on whom this cure was wrought (*v.* 5): one that *had been infirm thirty-eight years*. 1. His *disease* was *grievous*: He had an *infirmity*, a weakness; he had lost the use of his limbs, at least on one side, as is usual in palsies.

IV. The cure and the circumstances of it briefly related, *vv.* 6–9. 1. *Jesus saw him lie.* Observe, When Christ came up to Jerusalem he visited not the palaces, but the hospitals, which is an instance of his humility, and condescension, and tender compassion, and an *indication* of his great design in coming into the world, which was to seek and save the sick and wounded. There was a great multitude of poor cripples here at Bethesda, but Christ fastened his eye upon this one, and singled him out from the rest, because he was *senior* of the house, and in a more deplorable condition than any of the rest; and Christ delights to help the helpless, and hath mercy *on whom he will have mercy*.

2. He knew and considered *how long he had lain* in this condition. Those that have been long in affliction may comfort themselves with this, that God keeps account *how long*, and knows our frame.

3. He asked him, *Wilt thou be made whole?* A strange question to be asked one that had been so long ill. Christ put it to him,

(1) To *express* his own pity and concern for him. (2) To try him whether he would be beholden for a cure to him against whom the great people were so prejudiced and sought to prejudice others. (3) To teach him to value the mercy, and to excite in him desires after it.

4. The poor impotent man takes this opportunity to renew his complaint, and to set forth the misery of his case, which makes his cure the more illustrious: *Sir, I have no man to put me into the pool, v.* 7. (1) He does not think of any other way of being cured than by these waters, and desires no other friendship than to be helped into *them*; therefore, when Christ cured him, his imagination or expectation could not contribute to it, for he thought of no such thing. (2) He complains for want of friends to help him in: "*I have no man*, no friend to do me that kindness." (3) He bewails his infelicity, that very often when *he* was coming *another stepped in before him*. But a step between him and a cure, and yet he continues impotent.

5. Our Lord Jesus hereupon cures him with a word speaking, though he neither asked it nor thought of it. Here is,

(1) The word he said: *Rise, take up thy bed, v.* 8. [1] He is bidden to *rise and walk*; a strange command to be given to an *impotent* man, that had been long disabled; but this divine word was to be the vehicle of a divine power; it was a command to the disease to *be gone*, to nature to *be strong*, but it is expressed as a command

to him to *bestir himself.* [2] He is bidden to *take up his bed. First,* To make it to appear that it was a *perfect cure,* and purely miraculous. *Secondly,* It was to *proclaim* the cure, and make it public; for, being the sabbath day, whoever carried a burden through the streets made himself very remarkable, and every one would enquire what was the meaning of it; thereby notice of the miracle would spread, to the honour of God. *Thirdly,* Christ would thus witness against the tradition of the elders, which had stretched the law of the sabbath beyond its intention; and would likewise show that he was *Lord of the sabbath,* and had power to make what alterations he pleased about it, and to over-rule the law. *Fourthly,* He would hereby try the faith and obedience of his patient. By carrying his bed publicly, he exposed himself to the censure of the ecclesiastical court, and was liable, at least, to be *scourged in the synagogue.* Now, will he run the hazard of this, in obedience to Christ? Yes, he will. Those that have been *healed by Christ's word* should be *ruled by his word,* whatever it cost them.

(2) The efficacy of this word (*v.* 9): a divine power went along with it, and immediately he was *made whole, took up his bed, and walked.*

V. What became of the poor man after he was cured. We are here told,

1. What passed between him and the Jews who saw him carry his bed on the sabbath day; for on that day this cure was wrought, and it was the sabbath that fell within the passover week, and therefore a *high day, ch.* xix. 31. Now here,

(1) The Jews quarrelled with the man for carrying his bed on the sabbath day, telling him that *it was not lawful, v.* 10.

(2) The man justified himself in what he did by a warrant that would bear him out, *v.* 11. "I do not do it in contempt of the law and the sabbath, but in obedience to one who, by *making me whole,* has given me an undeniable proof that he is greater than either."

(3) The Jews enquired further who it was that gave him this warrant (*v.* 12): *What man is that?* In their question, observe, [1] They resolve to look upon Christ as a *mere man: What man is that?* [2] They resolve to look upon him as a bad *man,* and take it for granted that he who bade this man carry his bed, whatever divine commission he might *produce,* was certainly a delinquent, and as such they resolve to prosecute him.

(4) The poor man was unable to give them any account of him: *He wist not who he was, v.* 13.

[1] Christ was *unknown* to him when he healed him. Probably he had heard of the name of Jesus, but had never seen him, and therefore could not tell that this was he.

[2] For the present he *kept himself unknown*; for as soon as he had wrought the cure he *conveyed himself away,* he *made himself unknown* (so some read it), *a multitude being in that place.* Christ left the miracle to commend

itself, and the man on whom it was wrought to justify it.

2. What passed between him and our Lord Jesus at their next interview, *v.* 14. Observe here,

(1) Where Christ found him: *in the temple*, the place of public worship. There Christ found him the same day, as it should seem, that he was healed; thither he straightway went, *First*, Because he had, *by his infirmity*, been so long *detained* thence. *Secondly*, Because he had *by his recovery* a good errand thither; he went up to the temple to return thanks to God for his recovery. *Thirdly*, Because he had, by *carrying his bed*, seemed to put a contempt on the sabbath, he would thus show that he had an honour for it, and made conscience of sabbath-sanctification, in that on which the chief stress of it is laid, which is the *public worship* of God. Works of necessity and mercy are allowed; but when they are over we must *go to the temple*.

(2) What he said to him. When Christ has cured us, he has not done with us; he now applies himself to the healing of his soul, and this *by the word* too. [1] He gives him a *memento* of his cure: *Behold thou art made whole.* [2] He gives him a caution against sin, in consideration hereof, *Being made whole, sin no more.* This implies that his disease was the punishment of sin; whether of some remarkably flagrant sin, or only of sin in general, we cannot tell, but we know that sin is the procuring cause of sickness, Ps. cvii. 17, 18. [3] He gives him warning of his danger, in case he should return to

his former sinful course: *Lest a worse thing come to thee.*

VI. Now, after this interview between Christ and his patient, observe in the two following verses, 1. The notice which the poor simple man gave to the Jews concerning Christ, *v.* 15. He told them it was Jesus that had *made him whole.* 2. The rage and enmity of the Jews against him: *Therefore did the* rulers of the Jews *persecute Jesus.* This was the pretended crime, *Because he had done these things on the sabbath day.* Thus hypocrites often cover their real enmity against the *power* of godliness with a pretended zeal for the *form* of it.

FROM DEATH TO LIFE
(vv. 17–30)

We have here Christ's discourse upon occasion of his being accused as a sabbath-breaker. Observe,

I. The doctrine laid down, by which he justified what he did on the sabbath day (*v.* 17): *He answered them.* 1. He pleads that he was the *Son of God*, plainly intimated in his calling *God his Father*; and, if so, his holiness was *unquestionable* and his sovereignty *incontestable*; and he might make what alterations he pleased of the divine law. 2. That he was a worker together with God. (1) *My Father worketh hitherto.* The example of God's resting on the seventh day from all his work is, in the fourth commandment, made the ground of our observing it as a *sabbath* or *day of rest.* Now God rested only from such work as he had done the six days before;

otherwise he *worketh hitherto*, he is every day working, sabbath days and week-days; upholding and governing all the creatures, and concurring by his common providence to all the motions and operations of nature, *to his own glory*; therefore, when we are appointed to rest on the sabbath day, yet we are not restrained from doing that which has a direct tendency *to the glory of God*, as the man's carrying his bed had. (2) *I work*; not only therefore I *may* work, *like him*, in doing good on sabbath days as well as other days, but I also *work with him*. As God created all things by Christ, so he supports and governs all by him, Heb. i. 3.

II. The offence that was taken at his doctrine (*v.* 18): *The Jews sought the more to kill him*. They sought to kill him,

1. Because he had broken the sabbath; for, let him say what he would in his own justification, they are resolved, right or wrong, to *find him guilty* of sabbath breaking.

2. Not only so, but he had said also *that God was his Father*. Now they pretend a jealousy for *God's honour*, as before for the sabbath day, and charge Christ with it as a heinous crime that he made himself equal with God; and a heinous crime it had been if he had not really been so.

III. Christ's discourse upon this occasion, which continues without interruption to the end of the chapter.

1. *In general*. He is one with the Father in all he does as Mediator, and there was a perfectly good understanding between them in the whole matter. It is ushered in with a solemn preface (*v.* 19): *Verily, verily, I say unto you*; I the Amen, the Amen, say it. Two things he says in general concerning the Son's oneness with the Father in working:—

[1] That the Son *conforms to the Father* (*v.* 19): *The Son can do nothing of himself but what he sees the Father do*; for *these things does the Son*. The Lord Jesus, as Mediator, is, *First*, *Obedient to his Father's will*; so entirely obedient that he *can do nothing of himself*, in the same sense as it is said, *God cannot* lie, *cannot deny* himself, which expresses the perfection of his truth, not any imperfection in his strength; so here, Christ was so entirely devoted to his Father's will that it was impossible for him in any thing to act separately. *Secondly*, He is *observant of his Father's counsel*; he can, he will, do nothing *but what he sees the Father do*. No man can *find out the work of God*, but the only-begotten Son, who lay in his bosom, sees what he does, is intimately acquainted with his purposes, and has the plan of them ever before him.

[2] That the Father *communicates* to the Son, *v.* 20. Observe,

First, The inducement to it: *The Father loveth the Son*; he declared, *This is my beloved Son*.

Secondly, The instances of it. He shows it, 1. In what he *does* communicate to him: *He shows him all things that himself doth*. 2. In what he *will* communicate; he will *show him*, that is, will appoint and direct him to do *greater works than these.* (1) Works of greater *power* than the *curing of the impotent man*; for he should raise the dead, and should himself rise from the dead. (2) Works of greater *authority* than warranting the man to *carry his bed on the sabbath day.*

2. *In particular.* He proves his equality with the Father, by specifying some of those works which he does that are the peculiar works of God. This is enlarged upon, *vv.* 21–30. He does, and shall do, that which is the peculiar work of God's almighty power— *raising the dead* and *giving life, vv.* 21, 25, 26, 28. He does, and shall do, that which is the peculiar work of God's sovereign dominion and jurisdiction—*judging* and *executing judgment, vv.* 22–24, 27. These two are interwoven, as being nearly connected; and what is said once is repeated and inculcated; put both together, and they will prove that Christ said not amiss when he made himself *equal with God.*

Now observe here,

a. When this resurrection shall be: *The hour is coming*; it is *fixed* to an hour, so very punctual is this great appointment. The judgment is not adjourned *sine die—to some time not yet pitched upon*; no, *he hath appointed a day. The hour is coming.* (*a*) It is *not yet* come, it is not the hour spoken of at *v.* 25, that is coming, and *now is.* Those erred dangerously who said that the *resurrection was past already,* 2 Tim. ii. 18. But, (*b*) It *will certainly* come, it is coming on, nearer every day than other; it is at the door. How

far off it is we know not; but we know that it is infallibly designed and unalterably determined.

b. Who shall be raised: *All that are in the graves,* all that have died from the beginning of time, and all that shall die to the end of time.

c. How they shall be raised. Two things are here told us:— (*a*) The efficient of this resurrection: *They shall hear his voice*; that is, he shall cause them to hear it, as Lazarus was made to hear that word, *Come forth*; a divine power shall go along with the voice, to put life into them, and enable them to obey it. (*b*) The effect of it: *They shall come forth* out of their graves, as prisoners out of their prison-house; they shall *arise out* of the dust, and shake themselves from it; see Isa. lii. 1, 2, 11. But this is not all; they shall *appear* before Christ's tribunal, shall *come forth* as those that are to be tried, *come forth* to the bar, publicly to receive their doom.

d. To what they shall be raised; to a different state of happiness or misery, according to their different character; to a state of retribution, according to what they did in the state of probation.

(*a*) *They that have done good shall come forth to the resurrection of life*; they shall live again, to live for ever.

(*b*) *They that have done evil to the resurrection of damnation*; they shall live again, to be for ever dying.

IV. Observe what is here said concerning the Mediator's *authority to execute judgment, vv.* 22–24, 27. Here is,

[1] Christ's commission or dele-

gation to the office of a judge, which is twice spoken of here (*v.* 22): *He hath committed all judgment to the Son*; and again (*v.* 27): *He hath given him authority.*

First, The *Father judges no man*; not that the Father hath resigned the government, but he is pleased to govern by Jesus Christ; so that man is not under the terror of dealing with God immediately, but has the comfort of access to him by a Mediator.

Secondly, He has committed all judgment to the Son, has constituted him *Lord of all* (Acts x. 36; Rom. xiv. 9). All judgment is committed to our Lord Jesus; for, 1. He is *entrusted* with the administration of the *providential kingdom,* is *head over all things* (Eph. i. 22), head of every man, 1 Cor. xi. 3. All things consist by him, Col. i. 17. 2. He is empowered to make laws immediately to bind conscience. *I say unto you* is now the form in which the statutes of the kingdom of heaven run. *Be it enacted* by the Lord Jesus, and by *his* authority. All the acts now in force are touched with his sceptre. 3. He is authorized to appoint and settle the terms of the new covenant, and to draw up the articles of peace between God and man; it is God in Christ that reconciles the world, and to him he has given power to confer eternal life. The book of life is the Lamb's book; by his award we must stand or fall. 4. He is commissioned to carry on and complete the war with the powers of darkness; to cast out and *give judgment against the prince of this world, ch.* xii. 31. He is commissioned not only to

judge, but to *make war,* Rev. xix. 11. All that will fight *for God against Satan* must enlist themselves under *his* banner. 5. He is constituted sole manager of the judgment of the great day.

Thirdly, He has *given him authority to execute judgment also, v.* 27. Observe, 1. What the authority is which our Redeemer is invested with: *An authority to execute judgment*; he has not only a legislative and judicial power, but an *executive* power too. 2. Whence he has that authority: the Father *gave it to him.* Christ's authority as Mediator is delegated and derived; he acts as the Father's Viceregent, as the Lord's Anointed, the Lord's Christ.

[2] Here are the reasons (reasons of state) for which this commission was given him. He has all judgment committed to him for two reasons:—

First, Because he is the *Son of man*; which denotes these three things:—1. His humiliation and gracious condescension. 2. His affinity and alliance to us. The Father has committed the government of the children of men to him, because, being the *Son of man,* he is of the same nature with those whom he is *set over,* and therefore the more unexceptionable, and the more acceptable, as a Judge. 3. His being the Messiah promised. In that famous vision of his kingdom and glory, Dan. vii. 13, 14, he is called the *Son of man*; and Ps. viii. 4–6 Thou hast made the Son of man have *dominion over the works of thy hands.* He is the Messiah, and therefore is invested with all this power.

Secondly, That all men should honour the Son, v. 23. The honouring of Jesus Christ is here spoken of as God's great design (the Son intended to glorify the Father, and therefore the Father intended to glorify the Son, *ch.* xii. 32); and as man's great duty, in compliance with that design. If God will have the Son honoured, it is the duty of all to whom he is made known to honour him.

[3] Here is the rule by which the Son goes in executing this commission, so those words seem to come in (*v.* 24): *He that heareth and believeth* hath *everlasting life.* Here we have the substance of the whole gospel.

First, The *character* of a Christian: *He that heareth my word, and believeth on him that sent me.* To be a Christian indeed is, 1. To *hear the word of Christ.* It is not enough to be within hearing of it, but we must *attend on* it, as scholars on the instructions of their teachers; and *attend to* it, as servants to the commands of their masters; we must hear and obey it, must abide by the gospel of Christ as the fixed rule of our faith and practice. 2. To *believe on him that sent him*; for Christ's design is to *bring us to God*; and, as he is the first original of all grace, so is he the last object of all faith. Christ is our *way*; God is our rest.

Secondly, The *charter* of a Christian, in which all that are Christians indeed are interested. See what we get by Christ. 1. A charter of pardon: *He shall not come into condemnation.* The grace of the gospel is a full discharge

from the curse of the law. 2. A charter of privileges: He is *passed out of death to life,* is invested in a present happiness in spiritual life and entitled to a future happiness in eternal life.

[4] Here is the righteousness of his proceedings pursuant to this commission, *v.* 30. All judgment being committed to him, we cannot but ask *how he manages it.* And here he answers, *My judgment is just.* All Christ's acts of government, both *legislative* and *judicial,* are exactly agreeable to the rules of equity; see Prov. viii. 8. His judgments are certainly just, for they are directed.

First, By the Father's *wisdom: I can of my ownself do nothing,* nothing without the Father, but *as I hear I judge,* as he had said before (*v.* 19), The Son *can do nothing but what he sees the Father do*; so here, nothing but what he hears the Father *say: As I hear,* 1. From the secret eternal counsels of the Father, *so I judge.* Would we know what we may depend upon in our dealing with God? *Hear the word* of Christ. 2. From the published records of the Old Testament. Christ, in all the execution of his undertaking, had an eye to the scripture, and made it his business to conform to this, and *fulfil* it: *As it was written in the volume of the book.* Thus he taught us to do *nothing of ourselves,* but, *as we hear* from the word of God, *so to judge* of things, and act accordingly.

Secondly, By the Father's *will: My judgment is just,* and cannot be otherwise, *because I seek not my own will,* but *his who sent me.*

CHRIST'S MISSION (vv. 31–47)

In these verses our Lord Jesus proves and confirms the commission he had produced, and makes it out that he was sent of God to be the Messiah.

I. He *sets aside* his own testimony of himself (v. 31). Now, 1. This reflects reproach upon the sons of men, and their veracity and integrity. 2. It reflects honour on the Son of God, and bespeaks his wonderful condescension, that, though he is the *faithful witness*, the truth itself, yet he is pleased to *waive his privilege*, and, for the confirmation of our faith, refers himself to his *vouchers*, that we may have full satisfaction.

II. He produces other witnesses that bear testimony to him that he was sent of God.

1. The Father himself bore testimony to him (v. 32): *There is another that beareth witness.*

2. John Baptist witnessed to Christ, vv. 33, &c. John came to *bear witness of the light* (ch. i. 7); his business was to prepare his way, and direct people to him: *Behold the Lamb of God.*

Two things are added concerning John's testimony:—

[1] That it was a testimony *more than he needed to vouch* (v. 34): *I receive not testimony from man.* Though Christ saw fit to quote John's testimony, it was with a protestation that it shall not be deemed or construed so as to prejudice the prerogative of his self-sufficiency.

[2] That it was a testimony *to the man*, because John Baptist was one whom *they* had a respect for

(v. 35): *He was a light* among you. Observe,

First, The character of John Baptist: *He was a burning and a shining light*. It denotes his *activity*, zeal, and fervency, burning in love to God and the souls of men; fire is always working on itself or something else, so is a good minister.

Secondly, The affections of the people to him: *You were willing for a season to rejoice in his light*. 1. It was a *transport* that they were *in*, upon the appearing of John. 2. It was but *transient*, and soon over: "You were fond of him *for an hour*, for *a season*, as little children are fond of a new thing, you were pleased with John awhile, but soon grew weary of him and his ministry, and said that *he had a devil*, and now you have him in prison." Now, (1) Christ mentions their respect to John, to *condemn* them for their present opposition to himself, to whom John bore witness. If they had continued their veneration for John, as they ought to have done, they would have embraced Christ. (2) He mentions the passing away of their respect, to justify God in depriving them, as he had now done, of John's ministry, and putting that light under a bushel.

3. Christ's own works witnessed to him (v. 36): *I have a testimony greater than that of John*; for *if we believe the witness of men* sent of God, as John was, the *witness of God* immediately, and not by the ministry of men, *is greater*, 1 John v. 9. Now this greater testimony was that of the *works*

which *his Father had given him to finish.*

4. He produces, more fully than before, his Father's testimony concerning him (*v.* 37): *The Father that sent me hath borne witness of me.* Where God demands belief, he will not fail to give sufficient *evidence,* as he has done concerning Christ. That which was to be witnessed concerning Christ was chiefly this, that the God we had offended was willing to accept of him as a Mediator. Now concerning this he has *himself* given us full satisfaction (and he was fittest to do it), declaring himself well-pleased in him; if we be so, the work is done. Now, it might be suggested, if God himself thus bore witness of Christ, how came it to pass that he was not universally received by the Jewish nation and their rulers? To this Christ here answers that it was not to be thought strange, nor could their infidelity weaken his credibility, for two reasons:—[1] Because they were not acquainted with such extraordinary revelations of God and his will: *You have neither heard his voice at any time, nor seen his shape,* or *appearance.* They showed themselves to be as ignorant of God, though they professed relation to him, as we are of a man we never either saw or heard. [2] Because they were not affected, no, not with the ordinary ways by which God had revealed himself to them: *You have not his word abiding in you, v.* 38. They had the scriptures of the Old Testament; might they not by them be disposed to

receive Christ? Yes, if they had had their due influence upon them. But, *First,* The word of God was not in them; it was *among them,* in their country, in their hands, but not *in them,* in their hearts: not ruling in their souls, but only shining in their eyes and sounding in their ears. What did it avail them that they had the oracles of God *committed* to them (Rom. iii. 2), when they had not these oracles *commanding* in them? If they had, they would readily have embraced Christ. *Secondly,* It did not *abide.* Many have the word of God coming into them, and making some impressions for a while, but it does not *abide* with them; it is not constantly in them, as a man at home, but only now and then, as a *wayfaring man.* If the word *abide in* us, if we converse with it by frequent meditation, consult with it upon every occasion, and conform to it in our conversation, we shall then readily receive the witness of the Father concerning Christ; see *ch.* vii. 17.

5. The last witness he calls is the Old Testament, which witnessed of him, and to it he appeals (*vv.* 39, &c.): *Search the scriptures.*

(1) This may be read, either, [1] "*You search the scriptures,* and you do well to do so." Note, It is possible for men to be very studious in the letter of the scripture, and yet to be strangers to the power and influence of it. Or, [2] As we read it: *Search the scriptures;* and so, *First,* It was spoken to *them* in the nature of an *appeal:* "You profess to receive and believe the scripture; here I

will *join issue* with you, let this be the judge, provided you will not *rest in the letter* but will *search* into it." Note, when appeals are made to the scriptures, they must be searched.

(2) Now there are two things which we are here directed to have in our eye, in our searching the scripture: *heaven* our end, and *Christ* our way. [1] We must search the scriptures for *heaven* as our *great end: For in them you think you have eternal life.* [2] We must *search the scriptures* for *Christ*, as the new and living *way* that leads to this *end*. These are *they*, the great and principal witnesses, *that testify of me.*

(3) To this testimony he annexes a reproof of their infidelity and wickedness in four instances; particularly,

[1] Their *neglect of him* and his doctrine: "*You will not come to me, that you might have life, v.* 40. You search the scriptures, you believe the prophets, who you cannot but see testify of me; and yet you will not *come to me*, to whom they direct you."

[2] Their *lack of the love of God* (*v.* 42): "*I know you* very well, *that you have not the love of God in you*. Why should I wonder that you do not come to me, when you lack even the first principle of *natural religion*, which is the *love of God*?"

[3] Another crime charged upon them is their readiness to entertain false Christs and false prophets, while they obstinately opposed him who was the true Messias (*v.* 43).

[4] They are here charged with pride and vain-glory, and unbelief, the effect of them, *v.* 44. Having sharply reproved their unbelief, like a wise physician, he here searches into the cause, lays the axe to the root. They *therefore* slighted and undervalued Christ because they *admired* and *overvalued* themselves.

6. The last witness here called is Moses, *vv.* 45, &c. The Jews had a great veneration for Moses, and valued themselves upon their being the *disciples* of Moses, and pretended to adhere to Moses, in their opposition to Christ; but Christ here shows them,

(1) That Moses was a witness against the unbelieving Jews, *and accused them to the Father: There is one that accuses you, even Moses.* This may be understood either, [1] As showing the difference between the law and the gospel. Or, [2] As showing the manifest unreasonableness of their infidelity. "Moses himself says enough to convict you of, and condemn you for, your unbelief."

(2) That Moses was a witness for Christ and to his doctrine (*vv.* 46, 47): *He wrote of me.* Moses did particularly prophesy of Christ, as the Seed of the woman, the Seed of Abraham, the Shiloh, the great Prophet; the ceremonies of the law of Moses were *figures of him that was to come.* The Jews made Moses the patron of their opposition to Christ; but Christ here shows them their error, that Moses was so far from writing against Christ that he wrote *for him*, and *of him.*

Thus ends Christ's plea for himself, in answer to the charge exhibited against him. What effect it had we know not; it would seem to have had this, their *mouths* were *stopped* for the present, and they could not for shame but drop the prosecution, and yet their *hearts* were *hardened*.

CHAPTER SIX

FEEDING FIVE THOUSAND
(vv. 1–14)

We have here an account of Christ's feeding five thousand men with five loaves and two fishes, which miracle is in *this* respect remarkable, that it is the only passage of the actions of *Christ's life* that is recorded by all the four evangelists. John, who does not usually relate what had been recorded by those who wrote before him, yet relates this, because of the reference the following discourse has to it.

Notice the influence which this miracle had upon the people who tasted of the benefit of it (*v.* 14): *They said, This is of a truth that prophet.* Note, 1. Even the vulgar Jews with great assurance expected the Messiah to come into the world, and to be a *great prophet*. They speak here with assurance of his coming. The Pharisees despised them as *not knowing the law*; but, it should seem, they knew more of him that is the *end of the law* than the Pharisees did. 2. The miracles which Christ wrought did clearly demonstrate that he was the Messiah promised, a teacher come from God, the great prophet, and could not but convince the amazed spectators that this was he that

should come. There were many who were convinced he was that prophet that should come into the world who yet did not cordially receive his doctrine, for they did not continue in it. Such a wretched incoherence and inconsistency there is between the faculties of the corrupt unsanctified soul, that it is possible for men to acknowledge that Christ is that prophet, and yet to turn a deaf ear to him.

WALKING ON THE WATER
(vv. 15–21)

Here is, I. Christ's retirement from the multitude.

1. Observe what induced him to retire; because he perceived that those who acknowledged him to be that prophet that should come into the world would come, and *take him by force, to make him a king, v.* 15. Now here we have an instance,

(1) Of the irregular zeal of some of Christ's followers; nothing would serve but they would make him *a king*. It was intended to carry on a *secular* design; they hoped this might be a fair opportunity of shaking off the Roman yoke, of which they were weary. If they had one to head them who could victual an army cheaper than another could provide for a family, they were sure of the sinews of the war, and could not fail of success, and the recovery of their ancient liberties. Thus is religion often prostituted to a secular interest, and Christ is served only to *serve a turn*, Rom. xvi. 18.

(2) Here is an instance of the humility and self-denial of the

519

Lord Jesus, that, when they would have made him a king, he *departed*; so far was he from countenancing the design that he effectually quashed it.

2. Observe *whither* he retired: *He departed again into a mountain*, the mountain where he had preached (*v.* 3), whence he came down into the plain, to feed the people, and then returned to it alone, to be private.

II. Here is the disciples' distress at sea.

1. Here is their *going down to the sea* in a ship (*vv.* 16, 17).

2. Here is the *stormy wind* arising and *fulfilling the word of God*. They were Christ's disciples, and were now in the way of their duty, and Christ was now in the mount praying for them; and yet they were in this distress. Let it comfort good people, when they happen to be in storms at sea, that the disciples of Christ were so; and let the promises of a gracious God balance the threats of an angry sea. Though in a storm, and *in the dark*, they are no worse off than Christ's disciples were. Clouds and darkness sometimes surround the children of the light, and of the day.

3. Here is Christ's seasonable approach to them when they were in this peril, *v.* 19. *They had rowed* (being forced by the contrary winds to betake themselves to their oars) *about twenty-five or thirty furlongs*. And, when they were got off a good way at sea, they *see Jesus walking on the sea*. See here, (1) The power Christ has over the laws and customs of nature, to control and dispense

with them at his pleasure. It is natural for heavy bodies to sink in water, but Christ walked *upon* the water as upon dry land, which was more than Moses's dividing the water and walking *through* the water. (2) The concern Christ has for his disciples in distress: *He drew nigh to the ship*; for *therefore* he walked upon the water, as he *rides upon the heavens, for the help of his people*, Deut. xxxiii. 26. (3) The relief Christ gives to his disciples in their fears. They *were afraid*, more afraid of an apparition (for so they supposed him to be) than of the winds and waves. But, when they were in this fright, how affectionately did Christ silence their fears with that compassionate word (*v.* 20), *It is I, be not afraid!* When trouble is nigh Christ is nigh.

4. Here is their speedy arrival at the port they were bound for, *v.* 17. (1) They *welcomed* Christ into the ship; they *willingly received him*. (2) Christ brought them safely to the shore: *Immediately the ship was at the land whither they went*. The disciples had rowed hard, but could not make their point till they had got Christ in the ship, and then the work was *done suddenly*.

CHRIST ADDRESSES THE CROWD (*vv.* 22–27)

In these verses we have,

I. The careful enquiry which the people made after Christ, *vv.* 23, 24.

1. They were *much at a loss* for him. He was gone, and they knew not what was become of him.

2. They were very *industrious in seeking* him. They searched the

places thereabouts, and when *they saw that Jesus was not there, nor his disciples* (neither he nor any one that could give tidings of him), they resolved to search elsewhere.

3. They laid hold of the opportunity that offered itself, and *they also took shipping, and came to Capernaum, seeking for Jesus.*

II. The success of this enquiry: *They found him on the other side of the sea,* v. 25.

III. The question they put to him when they found him: *Rabbi, when camest thou hither?* It should seem by *v.* 59 that they found him *in the synagogue.* Their enquiry refers not only to the *time,* but to the *manner,* of his conveying himself thither; not only *When,* but, "*How,* camest thou hither?" for there was no boat for him to come in. They were curious in asking concerning Christ's motions, but not solicitous to observe their own.

IV. The answer Christ gave them, not direct to their question (what was it to them *when* and *how* he came thither?) but such an answer as their case required.

1. He discovers the *corrupt principle* they *acted from* in following him (*v.* 26). These followed Christ, (1) Not for his doctrine's sake: *Not because you saw the miracles.* But, (2) It was for their own bellies' sake: *Because you did eat of the loaves, and were filled*; not because he taught them, but because he fed them. Note, Many follow Christ for *loaves,* and not for *love.*

2. He directs them to better principles (*v.* 27): *Labour for that meat which endures to everlasting life.* His design is,

(1) To moderate our worldly pursuits: *Labour not for the meat that perishes.* This does not forbid honest labour for food convenient, 2 Thess. iii. 12. But we must not make the things of this world our chief care and concern. Note, [1] The things of the world are *meat that perishes.* [2] It is therefore folly for us inordinately to labour after them.

(2) To quicken and excite our gracious pursuits: "Bestow your pains to better purpose, and *labour for that meat* which belongs to the soul," of which he shows,

[1] That it is *unspeakably desirable*: It is meat which *endures to everlasting life*; it is a happiness which will last as long as we must, which not only itself endures eternally, but will nourish us up to everlasting life.

[2] It is *undoubtedly attainable.* We are told to *labour for it,* as if it were to be got by our own industry. But, when we have laboured ever so much for it, we have not merited it as our *hire,* but the Son of man *gives it.* And what more free than gift? It is an encouragement that he who has the giving of it is the *Son of man,* for then we may hope the *sons of men* that seek it, and labour for it, shall not fail to have it. *Secondly,* What authority he has to give it; for *him has God the Father sealed, for him the Father has sealed* (proved and evidenced) *to be God*; so some read it; he has declared him to be the Son of God with power. He has *sealed him,* that is, has given him full authority to deal between God and man, as God's *ambassador* to man and

man's *intercessor* with God, and has proved his commission by miracles. Having given him *authority*, he has given us *assurance* of it; having entrusted him with *unlimited powers*, he has satisfied us with *undoubted proofs* of them; so that as he might go on with confidence in his undertaking for us, so may we in our resignations to him.

BREAD OF HEAVEN
(vv. 28–59)

I. Christ having told them that *they* must *work for the meat* he spoke of, must *labour* for it, they enquire what work they must do, and he answers them, *vv.* 28, 29. 1. Their *enquiry* was *pertinent* enough (*v.* 28): *What shall we do, that we may work the works of God?* Some understand it as a pert question: "What works of God can we do more and better than those we do in obedience to the law of Moses?" But I rather take it as a humble serious question, showing them to be, at least for the present, in a good mind, and willing to know and do their duty. 2. Christ's answer was plain enough (*v.* 29): *This is the work of God that ye believe.* Note, (1) The work of faith is the work of God. They enquire after the *works* of God (in the plural number), being careful about *many things*; but Christ directs them to one work, which includes all, the one thing needful: that *you believe*, which supersedes all the works of the ceremonial law; the work which is necessary to the acceptance of all the other works, and which produces them, for without faith

you cannot please God. (2) That faith is the work of God which closes with Christ, and relies upon him. It is to *believe on him* as one whom God *hath sent*, as God's commissioner in the great affair of peace between God and man, and as such to *rest* upon him, and *resign ourselves* to him. See *ch.* xiv. 1.

II. Christ having told them that the *Son of man* would *give them this meat*, they enquire concerning him, and he answers their enquiry.

1. Their enquiry is after *a sign* (*v.* 30): *What sign showest thou?* But *herein* they missed it,

(1) That they overlooked the many miracles which they had seen wrought by him, and which amounted to an abundant proof of his divine mission.

(2) That they preferred the miraculous feeding of Israel in the wilderness before all the miracles Christ wrought (*v.* 31): *Our fathers did eat manna in the desert*; and, to strengthen the objection, they quote a scripture for it: *He gave them bread from heaven* (taken from Ps. lxxviii. 24), *he gave them of the corn of heaven.* [1] Christ reproved them for their fondness of the miraculous bread, and bade them not set their hearts upon *meat which perisheth.* [2] Christ had fed five thousand men with five loaves, and had given them that as one sign to prove him *sent of God*; but, under colour of *magnifying* the miracles of Moses, they tacitly *undervalue* this miracle of Christ, and *evade* the evidence of it.

2. Here is Christ's reply to this enquiry, wherein,

(1) He *rectifies* their *mistake* concerning the *typical* manna. It was true that their fathers did *eat manna* in the desert. But, [1] It was not Moses that gave it to them, nor were they obliged to him for it; he was but the instrument, and therefore they must look beyond him to God. [2] It was not given them, as they imagined, *from heaven*, from the highest heavens, but only from *the clouds*, and therefore not so much superior to that which had its rise from the earth as they thought. Because the scripture saith, *He gave them bread from heaven*, it does not follow that it was *heavenly bread*, or was intended to be the nourishment of souls. Misunderstanding scripture language occasions many mistakes in the things of God.

(2) He *informs* them concerning the *true* manna, of which that was a type: *But my Father giveth you the true bread from heaven.* That which is truly and properly the *bread from heaven*, of which the manna was but a shadow and figure, is *now given*, not to *your fathers*, who are dead and gone, but *to you* of this present age, for whom the *better things were reserved*: he is *now giving* you that *bread from heaven*, which is *truly* so called.

III. Christ, having replied to their enquiries, takes further occasion from their objection concerning the *manna* to discourse of *himself* under the similitude of *bread*, and of *believing* under the similitude of *eating and drinking*; to which, together with his putting both together in the *eating of his flesh* and *drinking* of his *blood*, and with the remarks made upon it by the hearers, the rest of this conference may be reduced.

1. Christ having spoken of *himself* as the great *gift of God*, and the *true bread* (*v.* 32), largely *explains* and *confirms* this, that we may rightly know him.

(1) He here shows that he is the *true bread*; this he repeats again and again, *vv.* 33, 35, 48–51. *First*, He is the *living bread* (so he explains himself, *v.* 51): *I am the living bread.* Bread is itself a dead thing, and nourishes not but by the help of the faculties of a living body; but Christ is himself *living bread*, and nourishes by his own power. *Secondly*, He gives life *unto the world* (*v.* 33), spiritual and eternal life; the life of the soul in union and communion with God here, and in the vision and fruition of him hereafter; a life that includes in it all happiness. The *manna* did only preserve and support life, did not preserve and perpetuate life, much less restore it; but Christ *gives* life to those that were dead in sin.

(2) He here shows what his undertaking was, and what his errand into the world. Laying aside the metaphor, he speaks plainly, and speaks no proverb, giving us an account of his business among men, *vv.* 38–40.

[1] He assures us, in general, that he came from heaven upon his Father's business (*v.* 38), not to *do his own will, but the will of him that sent him.* That is, *First*, Christ did not come into the world as a *private* person, that acts for himself only, but under a *public character*, to act for others as an ambassador, or plenipotentiary,

authorized by a public commission; he came into the world as God's great agent and the world's great physician. *Secondly*, Christ, when he was in the world, did not carry on any *private* design, nor had any *separate interest* at all, distinct from theirs for whom he acted. The scope of his whole life was to glorify God and do good to men.

[2] He acquaints us, in particular, with that will of the Father which he came to do; he here *declares the decree*, the instructions he was to pursue.

First, The *private instructions* given to Christ, that he should be sure to save all the chosen remnant; and this is the *covenant of redemption* between the Father and the Son (v. 38): *This is the Father's will, who hath sent me*; this is the charge I am entrusted with, that *of all whom he hath given me I should lose none.*" Those whom God chose to be the objects of his special love he lodged as a trust in the hands of Christ. Christ's undertaking for those that are given him extends to the resurrection of their bodies. *I will raise it up again at the last day*, which supposes all that goes before, but this is to crown and complete the undertaking.

Secondly, The *public instructions* which were to be given to the children of men, in what way, and upon what terms, they might obtain salvation by Christ; and this is the *covenant of grace* between God and man. "*This is the will*, the revealed will, *of him that sent me*, the method agreed upon, upon which to proceed with the children of men, that

every one, Jew or Gentile, that *sees the Son, and believes on him*, may have *everlasting life*, and *I will raise him up.*" This is *gospel* indeed, good news. This everlasting life is sure to all those who believe in Christ, and to them only. He that *sees the Son*, and *believes on him*, shall be saved. Some understand this *seeing* as a *limitation* of this condition of salvation to those only that have the revelation of Christ and his grace made to them. Every one that has the opportunity of being acquainted with Christ, and improves this so well as to *believe* in him, shall have everlasting life, so that none shall be condemned for unbelief (however they may be for other sins) but those who have had the gospel preached to them, who, like these Jews here (v. 36), have *seen*, and yet have *not* believed; have known Christ, and yet not trusted in him. But I rather understand *seeing* here to mean the same thing with *believing*. Every one that *sees the Son*, that is, *believes on him*, sees him with an eye of faith, by which we come to be duly acquainted and affected with the doctrine of the gospel concerning him. It is to look upon him, as the stung Israelites upon the brazen serpent. Those who believe in Jesus Christ, shall be raised up by his power at the last day. He had it in charge as his Father's will (v. 39), and here he solemnly makes it his own undertaking.

2. Now Christ discoursing thus concerning himself, as the *bread of life* that came down from heaven, let us see what remarks his hearers made upon it.

(1) When they heard of such a thing as the *bread of God*, which *gives life*, they heartily prayed for it (*v.* 34): *Lord, evermore give us this bread.*

(2) But, when they understood that by this *bread of life* Jesus meant *himself*, then they *despised* it. Whether they were the same persons that had prayed for it (*v.* 34), or some others of the company, does not appear; it seems to be some others, for they are called *Jews.* Now it is said (*v.* 41), *They murmured at him.* This comes in immediately after that solemn declaration which Christ had made of God's will and his own undertaking concerning man's salvation (*vv.* 39, 40), which certainly were some of the most weighty and gracious words that ever proceeded out of the mouth of our Lord Jesus, the most faithful, and best worthy of all acceptation. Now, [1] That which offended them was Christ's asserting his origin to be *from heaven*, *vv.* 41, 42. How is it that he saith, *I came down from heaven?* [2] That which they thought justified them herein was that they knew his extraction on earth: *Is not this Jesus the son of Joseph, whose father and mother we know?* They took it amiss that he should say that he came down from heaven, when he was *one of them.*

3. Christ, having spoken of faith as the great *work of God* (*v.* 29), discourses largely concerning this work, instructing and encouraging us in it.

(1) He shows what it is to *believe in Christ.* [1] To believe in Christ is to *come to Christ.* He

that *comes to* me is the same with him that *believes in me* (*v.* 35), and again (*v.* 37): *He that comes unto me*; so *vv.* 44, 45. [2] It is to *feed upon Christ* (*v.* 51): *If any man eat of this bread.* The former denotes applying ourselves to Christ; this denotes applying Christ to ourselves, with appetite and delight, that we may receive life, and strength, and comfort from him.

(2) He shows what is to be got by believing in Christ.

[1] They shall never want, *never hunger, never thirst, v.* 35. Desires they have, earnest desires, but these so suitably, so seasonably, so abundantly satisfied, that they cannot be called hunger and thirst, which are uneasy and painful.

[2] They shall *never die*, not die eternally; for, *First,* He that believes on Christ *has everlasting life* (*v.* 47); he has the assurance of it, the grant of it, the earnest of it; he has it in the promise and first-fruits. *Secondly,* Whereas they that did *eat manna* died, Christ is such bread as a man may eat of and never die, *vv.* 49, 50. *Not die,* that is, not perish, not come short of the heavenly Canaan, as the Israelites did of the earthly, for want of *faith*, though they had *manna.* This is further explained by that promise in the next words: *If any man eat of this bread, he shall live for ever, v.* 51. This is the meaning of this *never dying*: though he go down *to death*, he shall pass through it to that world where there shall be *no more death.*

(3) He shows what encouragements we have to believe in Christ.

Christ here speaks of some who *had seen him and yet believed not*, v. 36. Two things we are here assured of, to encourage our faith:—

[1] That the Son will bid all those welcome that come to him (v. 37): *Him that cometh to me I will in no wise cast out*. There are two negatives: *I will not, no, I will not*.

[2] That the Father will, without fail, bring all those to him in due time that were given him. Though he lose many of his *creatures*, yet none of his *charge*: *All that the Father gives him shall come to him* notwithstanding. The giving of the chosen remnant to Christ is spoken of (v. 39) as a thing *done*; he *hath given* them. Here it is spoken of as a thing *in the doing*; he *giveth them*; because, *when the first begotten was brought into the world*, it should seem, there was a renewal of the grant; see Heb. x. 5, &c. God was now about to *give him the heathen for his inheritance* (Ps. ii. 8), to put him in possession of *the desolate heritages* (Isa. xlix. 8), to *divide him a portion with the great*, Isa. liii. 12. And though the Jews, who *saw* him, *believed not* on him, yet these (saith he) shall *come to me*; the other sheep, which are not of this fold, shall be *brought*, ch. x. 15, 16. See Acts xiii. 45–48. *They shall come to me*. This is not in the nature of a *promise*, but a *prediction*, that as many as were in the counsel of God ordained to life shall be brought to life by being brought to Christ. He that *formed the spirit of man within him* by his creating power, and *fashions the*

hearts *of men* by his providential influence, knows how to new-mould the soul, and to alter its bent and temper, and make it conformable to himself and his own will, without doing any wrong to its natural liberty (v. 44). It is such a drawing as works not only a *compliance*, but a cheerful compliance, a complacency: *Draw us, and we will run after thee. No man*, in this weak and helpless state, can come to Christ without it. As we *cannot* do any natural action without the concurrence of *common providence*, so we cannot do any action morally good without the influence of *special grace*, in which the *new man* lives, and moves, and has its being, as much as the *mere man* has in the divine providence. The Father, having sent Christ, would not send him on a fruitless errand. Christ having undertaken to bring souls to glory, God promised him to bring them to him, and so to give him possession of those to whom he had given him a right.

4. Christ, having thus spoken of himself as the *bread of life*, and of faith as *the work of God*, comes more particularly to show *what of himself* is this bread, namely, his flesh, and that to believe is to eat of that, vv. 51–58, where he still prosecutes the metaphor of food. Observe, here, the *preparation* of this food: *The bread that I will give is my flesh* (v. 51), *the flesh of the Son of man and his blood*, v. 53. *His flesh is meat indeed, and his blood is drink indeed*, v. 55. Observe, also, the *participation* of this food: We must *eat the flesh of the Son of*

man and drink his blood (*v.* 53); and again (*v.* 54), *Whoso eateth my flesh and drinketh my blood*; and the same words (*vv.* 56, 57), he that *eateth me*. This is certainly a parable or figurative discourse, wherein the actings of the soul upon things spiritual and divine are represented by bodily actions about things sensible, which made the truths of Christ more intelligible to some, and less so to others, Mark iv. 11–12. Now,

(1) Let us see how this discourse of Christ was liable to mistake and misconstruction, that *men might see, and not perceive*. [1] It was misconstrued by the carnal *Jews*, to. whom it was first delivered (*v.* 52). [2] It has been wretchedly misconstrued for the support of the doctrine of transubstantiation. The Lord's supper was not yet instituted, and therefore it could have no reference to that; it is a *spiritual* eating and drinking that is here spoken of, not a *sacramental*. Therefore,

(2) Let us see how this discourse of Christ to be understood.

[1] What is meant by the *flesh and blood of Christ*. It is called (*v.* 53), *The flesh of the Son of man, and his blood, his* as Messiah and Mediator: the *flesh and blood* which he *assumed* in his incarnation (Heb. ii. 14), and which he *gave up* in his *death* and *suffering*: *my flesh which I will give* to be crucified and slain. It is said to be *given for the life of the world*, that is, *First, Instead* of the *life of the world*, which was *forfeited* by sin, Christ gives his own flesh as a ransom or counter-price. *Secondly, In order to* the *life of the world*, to purchase a *general* offer of eternal life to all the world, and the *special* assurances of it to all believers.

[2] What is meant by *eating this flesh* and *drinking* this *blood*, which is so necessary and beneficial; it is certain that it means neither more nor less than believing in Christ. As we partake of meat and drink by eating and drinking, so we partake of Christ and his benefits by faith.

(3) Having thus explained the general meaning of this part of Christ's discourse, the particulars are reducible to two heads:—

[1] The *necessity* of our *feeding upon Christ* (*v.* 53): *Except you eat the flesh of the Son of man, and drink his blood, you have no life in you.* That is, *First,* "It is a certain sign that you *have no* spiritual *life* in you if you have no *desire* towards Christ, nor *delight* in him." *Secondly,* "It is certain that you *can have* no spiritual life, unless you derive it from Christ by faith; separated from him you can do nothing."

[2] The *benefit* and *advantage* of it, in two things:—

First, We shall be *one with Christ,* as our bodies are with our food when it is digested (*v.* 56).

Secondly, We shall *live,* shall live eternally, *by him,* as our bodies live by our food.

a. We shall *live by him* (*v.* 57): *As the living Father hath sent me, and I live by the Father, so he that eateth me, even he shall live by me.* We have here the series and order of the divine life. (*a*) God is the *living Father,* hath life in and of himself. *I am that I am* is his name for ever. (*b*) Jesus Christ, as Mediator, lives *by the Father*; he has life *in himself* (*ch.* v. 26), but he has it of the Father. (*c*) True believers receive this divine life by virtue of their union with Christ, which is inferred from the union between the Father and the Son, as it is compared to it, *ch.* xvii. 21.

b. We shall live *eternally* by him (*v.* 54): *Whoso eateth my flesh, and drinketh my blood*, as prepared in the gospel to be the food of souls, he *hath eternal life*, he hath it now, as *v.* 40. He has that in him which is eternal life begun; he has the earnest and foretaste of it, and the hope of it; he shall live *for ever*, *v.* 58. His happiness shall run parallel with the longest line of eternity itself.

Lastly, The historian concludes with an account *where* Christ had this discourse with the Jews (*v.* 59): *In the synagogue as he taught*, implying that he taught them many other things besides these, but this was that in his discourse which was new.

WORDS OF LIFE (*vv.* 60–71)

We have here an account of the effects of Christ's discourse. Some were offended and others edified by it; some driven *from him* and others brought nearer *to him*.

I. To some it was a *savour of death unto death*. Now here we have,

1. Their murmurings at the doctrine they heard (*v.* 60); not a few, but many of them, were offended at it. Of the several sorts of ground that received the seed, only one in four brought forth fruit. See what they say to it (*v.* 60): *This is a hard saying, who can hear it?*

2. Christ's comments upon their murmurings.

(1) He well enough knew their murmurings, *v.* 61. Their cavils were secret in their own breasts, or whispered among themselves in a corner. But, [1] Christ *knew* them; he saw them, he heard them. [2] He knew it *in himself*, not by any information given him, nor any external indication of the thing, but by his own divine omniscience.

(2) He well enough knew how to answer them: "*Doth this offend you?* Is this a stumbling-block to you?"

[1] He gives them a hint of his ascension into heaven, as that which would give an irresistible evidence of the truth of his doctrine (*v.* 62): *What and if you shall see the Son of man ascend up where he was before?* And what then? Those who stumble at smaller difficulties should consider how they will get over greater. *Secondly*, "When you see the Son of man ascend, this will much more offend you, for then my body will be less capable of being eaten by you in that gross sense wherein you now understand it"; so Dr. Whitby. Let us wait awhile, till the mystery of God shall be finished, and then we shall see that there was no reason to be offended at any of Christ's sayings.

[2] He gives them a general key to this and all such parabolical discourses, teaching them that they are to be understood spiritually, and not after a corporal

and carnal manner: *It is the spirit that quickeneth, the flesh profiteth nothing*, v. 63.

[3] He gives them an intimation of his *knowledge of them*, and that he had expected no better from them, though they called themselves his disciples, vv. 64, 65. Now was fulfilled that of the prophet, speaking of Christ and his doctrine (Isa. liii. 1), *Who hath believed our report? and to whom is the arm of the Lord revealed?* Both these Christ here takes notice of.

II. This discourse was to others a *savour of life unto life. Many went back*, but, thanks be to God, all did not; even then the *twelve* stuck to him. Though the *faith of some be overthrown*, yet the *foundation of God stands sure*. Observe here,

1. The affectionate question which Christ put to the twelve (v. 67): *Will you also go away?*

2. The believing reply which Peter, in the name of the rest, made to this question, vv. 68, 69.

(1) Here is a good resolution to adhere to Christ, and so expressed as to intimate that they would not entertain the least thought of leaving him: "*Lord, to whom shall we go?* It were folly to go from thee, unless we knew where to better ourselves; no, Lord, we like our choice too well to change."

(2) Here is a good reason for this resolution. It was not the inconsiderate resolve of a blind affection, but the result of mature deliberation. The disciples were resolved never to go away from Christ,

[1] Because of the *advantage* they

promised themselves by him: *Thou hast the words of eternal life*.

[2] Because of the assurance they had concerning him (v. 69): *We believe, and are sure, that thou art that Christ*. If he be the promised Messiah, he must *bring in an everlasting righteousness* (Dan. ix. 24), and therefore has the *words of eternal life*, for *righteousness reigns to eternal life*, Rom. v. 21.

3. The melancholy remark which our Lord Jesus made upon this reply of Peter's (vv. 70, 71): *Have not I chosen you twelve, and one of you is a devil?* And the evangelist tells us whom he meant: *he spoke of Judas Iscariot*. Peter had undertaken for them all that they would be faithful to their Master. Now Christ does not condemn his charity (it is always good to hope the best), but he tacitly corrects his confidence. We must not be too sure concerning any. God knows those that are his; we do not.

CHAPTER SEVEN
CHRIST AND HIS BROTHERS
(vv. 1–13)

We have here, I. The reason given why Christ spent more of his time in Galilee than in Judea (v. 1): *because the Jews*, the people in Judea and Jerusalem, sought to *kill him*, for curing the impotent man on the sabbath day, *ch*. v. 16.

II. The approach of the *feast of tabernacles* (v. 2), one of the three solemnities which called for the personal attendance of all the males at Jerusalem; see the institution of it, Lev. xxiii. 34, &c., and the revival of it after a long disuse, Neh. viii. 14.

III. Christ's discourse with his *brethren*, some of his kindred, whether by his mother or his supposed father is not certain; but they were such as pretended to have an interest in him, and therefore interposed to advise him in his conduct. And observe,

1. Their ambition and vain-glory in urging him to make a more public appearance than he did: "*Depart hence*," said they, "*and go into Judea* (v. 3), where thou wilt make a better figure than thou canst here."

2. The prudence and humility of our Lord Jesus, which appeared in his answer to the advice his brethren gave him, *vv.* 6–8. Though there were so many base insinuations in it, he answered them mildly.

(1) He shows the difference between himself and them, in two things:—[1] His *time* was *set*, so was not *theirs*: *My time is not yet come, but your time is always ready*. Understand it of the time of his going up to the feast. It was an indifferent thing to them when they went, for they had nothing of moment to do either where they were, to *detain* them *there*, or where they were going, to *hasten* them *thither*; but every minute of Christ's time was precious, and had its own particular business allotted to it. [2] His *life* was *sought*, so was not *theirs*, *v.* 7. They, in *showing themselves* to the world, did not expose themselves. Christ was not only *slighted*, as inconsiderable in the world (*the world knew him not*), but *hated*, as if he had been hurtful to the world; thus ill was

he requited for his love to the world: reigning sin is a rooted antipathy and enmity to Christ.

(2) He dismisses them, with a design to stay behind for some time in Galilee (*v.* 8): *Go you up to this feast, I go not up yet*. [1] He allows their going to the feast, though they were carnal and hypocritical in it. [2] He denies them his company when they went to the feast, because they were carnal and hypocritical.

3. Christ's continuance in Galilee till his *full time* was come, *v.* 9. He, saying these things to them, *abode still in Galilee*; because of this discourse he continued there.

4. His going up to the feast when his time was come. Observe, (1) *When* he went. *When his brethren were gone up*. He would not go up *with them*, lest they should make a noise and disturbance, under pretence of *showing him to the world*. But he went up *after them*. (2) *How* he went—*as if he were hiding himself: not openly, but as it were in secret*, rather for fear of *giving offence* than of *receiving injury*. He went up to the feast, because it was an opportunity of honouring God and doing good; but he went up as it were in secret, because he would not provoke the government.

5. The great expectation that there was of him among the Jews at Jerusalem, *vv.* 11–14. Having formerly come up to the feasts, and signalized himself by the miracles he wrought, he had made himself the subject of much discourse and observation.

(1) They could not but think of him (*v.* 11): *The Jews sought him*

at the feast, and said, Where is he?

(2) The people differed much in their sentiments concerning him (*v.* 12): *There was much murmuring*, or *muttering* rather, *among the people concerning him.* The enmity of the rulers against Christ, and their enquiries after him, caused him to be so much the more talked of and observed among the people. This ground the gospel of Christ has got by the opposition made to it, that it has been the more enquired into. and, by being *everywhere spoken against*, it has come to be every where *spoken of*, and by this means has been spread the further, and the merits of his cause have been the more *searched into*. This murmuring was not *against* Christ, but *concerning* him.

Now what were the sentiments of the people concerning him? [1] Some said, *He is a good man.* This was a truth, but it was far short of being the *whole truth.* He was not only a *good man*, but more than a man, he was the *Son of God.* [2] Others said, *Nay, but he deceiveth the people*; if this had been true, he had been a very bad man. [3] They were frightened by their superiors from speaking much of him (*v.* 13): *No man spoke openly of him, for fear of the Jews.* Either, *First*, They durst not openly speak *well* of him. While any one was at liberty to censure and reproach him, none durst vindicate him. Or, *Secondly*, They durst not speak *at all* of him openly. Because nothing could justly be said *against* him, they would not suffer any thing to be said *of* him.

AT THE FEAST OF TABERNACLES (*vv.* 14–36)

Here is, I. Christ's public preaching in the temple (*v.* 14): He *went up into the temple, and taught*, according to his custom when he was at Jerusalem.

II. His discourse with the Jews; and the conference is reducible to four heads:

1. Concerning *his doctrine.* See here,

(1) How the Jews *admired* it (*v.* 15): *They marvelled*, saying, *How knoweth this man letters, having never learned?* [1] That Christ *had letters*, though he had never *learned* them; was mighty in the scriptures, though he never had any doctor of the law for his tutor. [2] That Christ's having learning, though he had not been taught it, made him truly great and wonderful; the Jews speak of it here with wonder.

(2) What he *asserted* concerning it; three things:—

[1] That his *doctrine* is *divine* (*v.* 16): *My doctrine is not mine, but his that sent me.* They were offended because he undertook to *teach* though he had never learned, in answer to which he tells them that his doctrine was such as was not to be *learned*, for it was not the product of *human thought* and natural powers enlarged and elevated by reading and conversation, but it was a *divine revelation.*

[2] That the most competent judges of the truth and divine authority of Christ's doctrine are those that with a sincere and upright heart desire and endeavour to do the will of God (*v.* 17): *If*

any man be willing to do the will of God, have his will melted into the *will of God, he shall know of the doctrine whether it be of God or whether I speak of myself*.

2. They discourse concerning the *crime* that was laid to his charge for curing the impotent man, and bidding him carry his bed on the sabbath day, for which they had formerly prosecuted him, and which was still the pretence of their enmity to him.

(1) He argues against them by way of *recrimination*, convicting them of far worse practices, *v.* 19. How could they for shame censure him for a breach of the law of Moses, when they themselves were such notorious breakers of it? *Did not Moses give you the law?*

Here the *people* rudely interrupted him in his discourse, and contradicted what he said (*v.* 20): *Thou hast a devil; who goes about to kill thee?* This intimates, [1] The *good opinion* they had of their rulers, who, they think, would never attempt so atrocious a thing as to kill him; no, such a veneration they had for their elders and chief priests that they would swear for them they would do no harm to an innocent man. [2] The *ill opinion* they had of our Lord Jesus: "*Thou hast a devil*, thou art possessed with a lying spirit, and art a *bad man* for saying so"; so some: or rather, "Thou art melancholy, and art a *weak man*; thou frightenest thyself with causeless fears, as hypochondriacal people are apt to do." Let us not think it strange if the best of men are put under the worst of characters. To this vile

calumny our Saviour returns no direct answer, but seems as if he took no notice of it.

(2) He argues by way of appeal and vindication.

[1] He appeals to *their own sentiments* of this miracle: "*I have done one work, and you all marvel, v.* 21. You cannot choose but marvel at it as truly great, and altogether supernatural; you must all own. it to be marvellous," Or, "Though I have done but *one work* that you have any colour to find fault with, yet you marvel, you are offended and displeased as if I had been guilty of some heinous or enormous crime."

[2] He appeals to their own practice in other instances: "*I have done one work* on the sabbath, and it was done easily, with a word's speaking, and you all marvel, you make a mighty strange thing of it, that a religious man should dare do such a thing, whereas you yourselves *many a time* do that which is a much more servile work on the sabbath day, in the case of circumcision; if it be lawful for you, nay, and your duty, to circumcise a child on the sabbath day, when it happens to be the eighth day, as no doubt it is, much more was it lawful and good for me to heal a diseased man on that day."

He concludes this argument with that rule (*v.* 24): *Judge not according to the appearance, but judge righteous judgment.* This may be applied, either, *First*, In particular, to this work which they quarrelled with as a violation of the law. Or, *Secondly*, In general, to Christ's person and preaching, which they were offended at and prejudiced against. Those things that are false, and designed to impose upon men, commonly appear best when they are judged of *according to the outward appearance*, they appear most plausible *prima facie—at the first glance*. It was this that gained the Pharisees such an interest and reputation, that they *appeared right* unto men (Matt. xxiii. 27, 28), and men judged of them by that appearance, and so were sadly mistaken in them. "But," saith Christ, "be not too confident that all are real saints who are seeming ones." With reference to himself, his *outward appearance* was far short of his real dignity and excellency, for he took upon him the *form of a servant* (Phil. ii. 7), was in the *likeness of sinful flesh* (Rom. viii. 3), had *no form nor comeliness*, Isa. liii. 2. So that those who undertook to judge whether he was the Son of God or no by his *outward appearance* were not likely to *judge righteous judgment*.

3. Christ's discourses with them here concerning *himself*, whence he came, and whither he was going, *vv.* 25–36.

(1) *Whence he came, vv.* 25–31. In the account of this observe,

[1] The objection concerning this stated by some of the inhabitants of Jerusalem, who seem to have been of all others most prejudiced against him, *v.* 25. These people of Jerusalem showed their ill-will to Christ,

First, By their reflecting on the rulers, because they let him alone: *Is not this he whom they seek to kill?*

Secondly, By their exception against his being the Christ, in which appeared more malice than matter, *v.* 27. "If the rulers think him to be the Christ, we neither can nor will believe him to be so, for we have this argument against it, that *we know this man, whence he is; but when Christ comes no man knows whence he is.*"

[2] Christ's answer to this objection, *vv.* 28, 29.

First, He spoke freely and boldly, he *cried in the temple, as he taught,* he spoke this louder than the rest of his discourse, 1. To express his earnestness, being *grieved for the hardness of their hearts.* 2. The priests and those that were prejudiced against him, did not come near enough to hear his preaching, and therefore he must speak louder than ordinary what he will have them to hear.

Secondly, His answer to their cavil is, 1. By way of *concession,* granting that they did or might know his origin as to the flesh: "*You both know me, and you know whence I am.* You know I am of your own nation, and one of yourselves." They knew *whence* he came perhaps, and *where* he had his birth, but he will tell them what they knew not, *from whom* he came. (1) That he did not *come of himself.* (2) That he was sent of his Father; this is twice mentioned: *He hath sent me.* (3) That he was *from his Father—I am from him*; not only sent from him as a servant from his master, but from him by eternal generation, as a son from his father, by essential emanation, as the beams from the sun. (4) *That the Father* who sent him is true; he had promised to give the Messiah, and, though the Jews had forfeited the promise, yet he that made the promise is *true*, and has performed it. (5) That these unbelieving Jews did *not know the Father: He that sent me, whom you know not*. There is much ignorance of God even with many that have a *form of knowledge*; and the true reason why people reject Christ is because they do not *know God*. (6) Our Lord Jesus was intimately acquainted with the Father that *sent him: but I know him*. He knew him so well that he was not at all *in doubt* concerning his mission from him, but perfectly *assured* of it; nor at all *in the dark* concerning the work he had to do, but perfectly *apprized* of it, Matt. xi. 27.

[3] The provocation which this gave to his enemies, who hated him because he *told them the truth, v.* 30. *They sought therefore to take him*, to lay violent hands on him, not only to do him a mischief, but some way or other to be the death of him; but by the restraint of an invisible power it was prevented; nobody touched him, *because his hour was not yet come*; this was not their reason why they did it not, but God's reason why he hindered them from doing it.

[4] The good effect which Christ's discourse had, notwithstanding this, upon some of his hearers (*v.* 31); *Many of the people believed on him.*

(2) *Whither he was going, vv.* 32–36. Here observe,

[1] The design of the Pharisees

and chief priests against him, *v.* 32.

[2] The discourse of our Lord Jesus hereupon (*vv.* 33, 34): *Yet a little while I am with you, and then I go to him that sent me; you shall seek me, and shall not find me; and where I am, thither you cannot come*. These words, like the pillar of cloud and fire, have a *bright* side and a *dark* side.

First, They have a *bright side* towards our Lord Jesus himself, and speak abundance of comfort to him and all his faithful followers that are exposed to difficulties and dangers for his sake. Three things Christ here comforted himself with:—1. That he had but *a little time* to continue here in this troublesome world. 2. That when he should quit this troublesome world, he should *go to him that sent him; I go*. Not, "I am driven away by force," but, "I voluntarily *go*; having finished my embassy, I return to him on whose errand I came. When I have done my work with you, then, and not till then, I go to him *that sent me*, and will *receive me*, will prefer me, as ambassadors are preferred when they return." 3. That, though they persecuted him here, wherever he went, yet none of their persecutions could follow him to heaven: *You shall seek me, and shall not find me.*

Secondly, These words have a *black and dark side* towards those wicked Jews that hated and persecuted Christ. They now longed to be rid of him, *Away with him from the earth*; but let them know, 1. That according to their choice so shall their doom be. They were industrious to *drive him* from them, and their sin shall be their punishment; he will not trouble them long, yet a little while and he will *depart* from them. 2. That they would certainly repent their choice when it was too late. (1) They should in vain seek the presence of the Messiah. Those who rejected the true Messiah when he did come were justly abandoned to a miserable and endless expectation of one that should never come. (2) They should in vain expect a place in heaven: *Where I am*, and where all believers shall be with me, *thither ye cannot come*. Not only because they are *excluded* by the just and irreversible sentence of the judge, and the sword of the angel at every gate of the new Jerusalem, to keep *the way of the tree of life* against those who have *no right to enter*, but because they are disabled by their own iniquity and infidelity: *You cannot come*, because you *will not.*"

[3] Their descant upon this discourse (*vv.* 35, 36): *They said among themselves, Whither will he go?* See here, *First*, Their wilful ignorance and blindness. *Secondly*, Their daring contempt of Christ's threatenings. *Thirdly*, Their inveterate malice and rage against Christ. All they dreaded in his *departure* was that he would be out of the reach of their power: "*Whither will he go, that we shall not find him?*" *Fourthly*, Their proud disdain of the Gentiles, whom they here call the *dispersed of the Gentiles*; meaning either the Jews that were *scattered* abroad among the Greeks (James

i. 1; 1 Pet. i. 1); will he go and make an interest among those silly people? or, the Gentiles *dispersed* over the world, in distinction from the Jews, who were *incorporated* into one church and nation; will he make his court to them? *Fifthly*, Their jealousy of the least intimation of favour to the Gentiles: "Will he go and *teach the Gentiles?*" They now made a *jest* of his going *to teach the Gentiles*; but not long after he did it *in good earnest* by his apostles and ministers, and gathered those *dispersed* people, sorely to the grief of the Jews, Rom. x. 19.

THE LAST DAY OF THE FEAST (*vv.* 37–44)

In these verses we have,

I. Christ's discourse, with the explication of it, *vv.* 37–39. It is probable that these are only short hints of what he enlarged upon, but they have in them the substance of the whole gospel; here is a *gospel invitation* to *come to Christ*, and a *gospel promise* of comfort and happiness in him. Now observe,

1. *When* he gave this invitation: *On the last day* of the feast of tabernacles, *that great day*. The *eighth day*, which concluded that solemnity, was to be a *holy convocation*, Lev. xxiii. 36. Now on this day Christ published this gospel-call, because, (1) Much people were gathered together, and, if the invitation were given to *many*, it might be hoped that *some* would accept of it, Prov. i. 20. (2) The people were now returning to their homes, and he would give

them this to carry away with them as his parting word. Christ made this offer *on the last day of the feast,* [1] To those who had turned a deaf ear to his preaching on the foregoing days of this sacred week; he will try them once more, and, if they will yet hear his voice, they shall live. [2] To those who perhaps might never have such another offer made them.

2. *How* he gave this invitation: *Jesus stood and cried,* which denotes, (1) His great earnestness and importunity. (2) His desire that all might take notice, and take hold of this invitation.

3. The invitation itself is very general: *If any man* thirst, whoever he be, he is invited to Christ be he high or low, rich or poor, young or old, bond or free, Jew or Gentile. It is also very *gracious*: "*If any man thirst, let him come to me and drink.*' If any man desires to be truly and eternally happy, let him apply himself to me, and be ruled by me, and I will undertake to make him so."

(1) The persons invited are such as *thirst,* which may be understood, either, [1] Of their need; either as to their *outward* condition (if any man be destitute of the comforts of this life, or fatigued with the crosses of it, let his poverty and afflictions draw him to Christ for that peace which the world can neither give nor take away), or as to their *inward* state: "If any man want spiritual blessings, he may be supplied by me." Or, [2] Of the *inclination* of their souls and their desires towards a spiritual happiness. If any man hunger and thirst after righteousness, that is, truly desire the good will of God towards him, and the good work of God in him.

(2) The invitation itself: *Let him come to me.* Let him not go to the ceremonial law, nor let him go to the heathen philosophy, which does but beguile men, lead them into a wood, and leave them there; but let him *go to Christ,* admit his doctrine, submit to his discipline, believe in him; come to him as the fountain of living waters, the giver of all comfort.

(3) The satisfaction promised: Let him come *and drink,* he shall have what he comes for, and abundantly more, shall have that which will not only *refresh,* but *replenish,* a soul that desires to be happy."

4. A gracious promise annexed to this gracious call (*v.* 38): *He that believeth on me, out of his belly shall flow*—(1) See here what it is to come to Christ: It is *to believe on him, as the scripture hath said*; it is to receive and entertain him as he is offered to us in the gospel. (2) See how thirsty souls, that come to Christ, shall be made *to drink.* Israel, that believed Moses, drank of the *rock that followed them,* the streams followed; but believers drink of a rock *in them, Christ in them*; he is in them a *well of living water, ch.* iv. 14. Provision is made not only for their *present* satisfaction, but for their *continual perpetual* comfort. Here is, [1] *Living water, running* water, which the Hebrew language calls *living,* because still in motion. [2] *Rivers* of living water, denoting both plenty and

constancy. [3] These flow out *of his belly*, that is, out of his heart or soul, which is the subject of the Spirit's working and the seat of his government. Believers shall have the comfort, not of a vessel of water fetched from a pool, but of a river flowing from themselves. The joy of the law, and the pouring out of the water, which signified this, are not to be compared with the joy of the gospel in the wells of salvation.

5. Here is the evangelist's exposition of this promise (*v.* 39): *This spoke he of the Spirit*: not of any outward advantages accruing to believers (as perhaps some misunderstood him), but of the gifts, graces, and comforts of the Spirit. See how scripture is the best interpreter of scripture. Observe,

(1) It is promised to *all that believe* on Christ that they shall *receive the Holy Ghost*. Some received his miraculous gifts (Mark xvi. 17, 18); all receive his sanctifying graces.

(2) The Spirit dwelling and working in believers is as a *fountain of living* running *water*, out of which plentiful streams flow, cooling and cleansing as water, mollifying and moistening as water, making them fruitful, and others joyful; see *ch.* iii. 5. When the apostles spoke so *fluently* of the things of God, as the Spirit gave them utterance (Acts ii. 4), and afterwards preached and wrote the gospel of Christ with such a *flood* of divine eloquence, then this was fulfilled, *Out of his belly shall flow rivers*.

(3) This plentiful effusion of the Spirit was yet the matter of a promise; for *the Holy Ghost was not yet given, because Jesus was not yet glorified*. See here, [1] That *Jesus was not yet glorified*. [2] That *the Holy Ghost was not yet given*. The Spirit of God was from eternity, for in the beginning he *moved upon the face of the waters*. He was in the Old-Testament prophets and saints, and Zacharias and Elisabeth were both *filled with the Holy Ghost*. This therefore must be understood of that eminent, plentiful, and general effusion of the Spirit which was promised, Joel ii. 28, and accomplished, Acts ii. 1, &c. *The Holy Ghost was not yet given* in that visible manner that was intended. [3] That the reason why *the Holy Ghost was not given* was because *Jesus was not yet glorified*. *First*, The death of Christ is sometimes called his glorification (*ch.* xiii. 31); for in his cross he conquered and triumphed. Now the gift of the Holy Ghost was purchased by the blood of Christ: this was the *valuable consideration* upon which the *grant* was grounded, and therefore till this *price* was *paid* (though many other gifts were bestowed upon its being *secured* to be paid) the Holy Ghost was not given. *Secondly*, There was not so much need of the Spirit, while Christ himself was here upon earth, as there was when he was gone, to supply the want of him. *Thirdly*, The giving of the Holy Ghost was to be both an *answer* to Christ's *intercession* (*ch.* xiv. 16), and an *act* of his *dominion*; and therefore till he is glorified, and enters upon both these, the Holy Ghost is not given. *Fourthly*, The

conversion of the Gentiles was the glorifying of Jesus.

II. The consequence of this discourse: *There was a division among the people because of him,* v. 43. Observe what the debate was:—

1. Some were *taken with him,* and well affected to him. (1) Some of them said, *Of a truth this is the prophet,* that prophet whom Moses spoke of to the fathers, who should be *like unto him.* (2) Others went further, and said, *This is the Christ* (v. 41), not the *prophet* of the Messiah, but the Messiah himself.

2. Others were *prejudiced against him.* No sooner was this great truth started, that *Jesus is the Christ,* than immediately it was contradicted and argued against: and this one thing, that his rise and origin were (as they took it for granted) out of Galilee, was thought enough to answer all the arguments for his being the Christ. For, *shall Christ come out of Galilee?* Has not *the scripture said that Christ comes of the seed of David?* See here, (1) A laudable knowledge of the scripture. They were so far in the right, that the Messiah was to be a *rod out of the stem of Jesse* (Isa. xi. 1), that out of Bethlehem should *arise the Governor,* Mic. v. 2. (2) A culpable ignorance of our Lord Jesus. They speak of it as certain and past dispute that *Jesus was of Galilee,* whereas by enquiring of himself, or his mother, or his disciples, or by consulting the genealogies of the family of David, or the register at Bethlehem, they might have known that he was the

Son of David, and a native of Bethlehem; but *this they willingly are ignorant of.*

3. Others were *enraged against him,* and they *would have taken him,* v. 44. Though what he said was most sweet and gracious, yet they were exasperated against him for it. They *would have taken him*; but no man *laid hands on him,* being restrained by an invisible power, because his hour was not come.

A PROPHET FROM GALILEE?
(vv. 45–53)

The chief priests and Pharisees are here in a close cabal, contriving how to suppress Christ. Now here we are told,

I. What passed between them and their own officers, who returned without him. Observe,

1. The reproof they gave the officers for not executing the warrant they gave them: *Why have you not brought him?*

2. The reason which the officers gave for the non-execution of their warrant: *Never man spoke like this man,* v. 46. Now, (1) This was a very great truth, that *never any man spoke with* that wisdom, and power, and grace, that convincing clearness, and that charming sweetness, wherewith Christ spoke; none of the prophets, no, not Moses himself. (2) The very officers that were sent to take him were taken with him, and acknowledged this. (3) They said this to their lords and masters, who could not endure to hear anything that tended to the honour of Christ and yet could not avoid hearing this.

3. The Pharisees endeavour to secure their officers to their interest, and to beget in them prejudices against Christ, to whom they saw them begin to be well affected. They suggest two things: —

(1) That if they embrace the gospel of Christ they will *deceive themselves* (v. 47): *Are you also deceived?*

(2) That they will *disparage themselves.* Most men, even in their religion, are willing to be governed by the example of those of the *first rank*; these officers therefore, whose preferments, such as they were, gave them a *sense of honour*, are desired to consider,

[1] That, if they become disciples of Christ, they go contrary to those who were persons of quality and reputation.

[2] That they will link themselves with the despicable vulgar sort of people (v. 43): *But this people, who know not the law, are cursed*, meaning especially those that were well-affected to the doctrine of Christ.

II. What passed between them and Nicodemus, a member of their own body, vv. 50, &c. Observe,

1. The just and rational objection which Nicodemus made against their proceedings. Observe,

(1) Who it was that appeared against them; it was Nicodemus, *he that came to Jesus by night, being one of them*, v. 50. Observe, concerning him, [1] That, though he had been with Jesus, and taken him for his teacher, yet he retained his place in the council, and his vote among them. Some impute this to his *weakness* and cowardice,

and think it was his fault that he did not quit his place, but Christ had never said to him, *Follow me*, else he would have done as others that left all to follow him; therefore it seems rather to have been his *wisdom* not immediately to throw up his place, because there he might have opportunity of serving Christ and his interest, and stemming the tide of the Jewish rage, which perhaps he did more than we are aware of. [2] That though at first he came to Jesus *by night*, for fear of being known, and still continued in his post; yet, when there was occasion, he boldly appeared in defence of Christ, and opposed the whole council that were set against him.

(2) What he alleged against their proceedings (v. 51). Observe, [1] He prudently argues from the principles of their own law, and an incontestable rule of justice, that no man is to be condemned *unheard*. [2] Whereas they had reproached the people, especially the followers of Christ, as *ignorant of the law*, he here tacitly retorts the charge upon themselves, and shows how ignorant they were of some of the first principles of the law, so unfit were they to give law to others.

Now we may suppose that the motion Nicodemus made in the house upon this was, That Jesus should be desired to come and give them an account of himself and his doctrine, and that they should favour him with an impartial and unprejudiced hearing; but, though none of them could gainsay his maxim, none of them would second his motion.

2. What was said to this objection. Here is no direct reply given to it; but, when they could not resist the force of his argument, they fell foul upon him, and what was to seek in *reason* they made up in railing and reproach. As to what they said to Nicodemus, we may observe,

(1) How *false* the grounds of their argument were, for, [1] They supposed that Christ was of Galilee, and this was false, and if they would have been at the pains of an impartial enquiry they would have found it so. [2] They suppose that because most of his disciples were Galileans they were all such, whereas he had abundance of disciples in Judea. [3] They suppose that out of Galilee no prophet had *risen*, and for this appeal to Nicodemus's search; yet this was false too: Jonah was of Gath-hepher, Nahum an Elkoshite, both of Galilee.

(2) How *absurd* their arguings were upon these grounds, such as were a shame to *rulers* and *Pharisees*. Supposing no prophet had risen out of Galilee, yet it is not impossible that any should arise thence.

3. The hasty adjournment of the court hereupon. They broke up the assembly in confusion, and with precipitation, and *every man went to his own house.*

CHAPTER EIGHT
THE WOMAN TAKEN IN ADULTERY (*vv.* 1–11)

His dealing with those that brought to him the *woman taken in adultery*, *tempting* him. Observe here,

1. The case proposed to him by the scribes and Pharisees, who herein contrived to pick a quarrel with him, and bring him into a snare, *vv.* 3–6.

(1) They set the prisoner to the bar (*v.* 3): they brought him *a woman taken in adultery.* Those that were *taken in adultery* were by the Jewish law to be put to death, which the Roman powers allowed them the execution of, and therefore she was brought before the ecclesiastical court. The scribes and Pharisees bring her to Christ, and set her in the midst of the assembly, as if they would leave her wholly to the judgment of Christ, he having *sat down*, as a judge upon the bench.

(2) They prefer an indictment against her: *Master, this woman was taken in adultery*, *v.* 4. Here they call him *Master* whom but the day before they had called a *deceiver*, in hopes with their flatteries to have ensnared him, as those, Luke xx. 20. But, though men may be imposed upon with compliments, he that searches the heart cannot.

[1] The crime for which the prisoner stands indicted is no less than adultery, which even in the patriarchal age, before the law of Moses, was looked upon as *an iniquity to be punished by the judges*, Job xxxi. 9–11; Gen. xxxviii. 24. The Pharisees, by their vigorous prosecution of this offender, seemed to have a great zeal against the sin, when it appeared afterwards that they themselves were not free from it; nay, they were within *full of all uncleanness*, Matt. xxiii. 27, 28.

Note, It is common for those that are indulgent to their own sin to be severe against the sins of others.

[2] The proof of the crime was from the notorious evidence of the fact, an incontestable proof; she was *taken in the act*, so that there was no room left to plead not guilty.

(3) They produce the statute in this case made and provided, and upon which she was indicted, *v. 5.* Moses in the law commanded *that such should be stoned.* Moses commanded that they should be *put to death* (Lev. xx. 10; Deut. xxii. 22), but not that they should be stoned, unless the adulteress was espoused, not married, or was a priest's daughter, Deut. xxii. 21.

(4) They pray his judgment in the case. But *this they said tempting him, that they might have to accuse him, v. 6.* [1] If he should confirm the sentence of the law, and let it take its course, they would censure him as inconsistent with himself (he having received publicans and harlots) and with the character of the Messiah, who should be meek, and have salvation, and proclaim a year of release. But, [2] If he should acquit her, and give his opinion that the sentence should not be executed (as they expected he would), they would represent him, *First,* As an enemy to the law of Moses, and *secondly,* As a friend to sinners, and, consequently, a favourer of sin.

2. The method he took to resolve this case, and so to break this snare.

(1) He seemed to slight it, and turned a deaf ear to it: He *stooped down, and wrote on the ground.* It is impossible to tell, and therefore needless to ask, what he wrote; but this is the only mention made in the gospels of Christ's writing.

(2) When they importunately, or rather impertinently, pressed him for an answer, he turned the conviction of the prisoner upon the prosecutors, *v. 7.*

[1] They *continued asking him,* and his seeming not to take notice of them made them the more vehement.

[2] At last he put them all to shame and silence with one word: *He lifted up himself,* and *said unto them, He that is without sin among you, let him first cast a stone at her.*

First, Here Christ avoided the snare which they had laid for him, and effectually saved his own reputation. He neither reflected upon the law nor excused the prisoner's guilt, nor did he on the other hand encourage the prosecution or countenance their heat.

Secondly, In the net which they spread is their own foot taken. They came with design to accuse him, but they were forced to accuse themselves. Christ owns it was fit the prisoner should be prosecuted, but appeals to their consciences whether they were fit to be the prosecutors.

a. He here refers to that rule which the law of Moses prescribed in the execution of criminals, that the *hand of the witnesses must be first upon them* (Deut. xvii. 7), as in the stoning of Stephen, Acts vii. 58. The scribes and Pharisees were the witnesses against this woman. Now Christ puts it to them whether, according to their own law, they would dare to be the executioners.

b. He builds upon an uncontested maxim in morality, that it is very absurd for men to be zealous in punishing the offences of others, while they are every whit as guilty themselves. "If there be any of you who is *without sin*, without sin of this nature, that has not some time or other been guilty of fornication or adultery, let him cast the first stone at her."

[3] Having given them this startling word, he left them to consider of it, *and again stooped down, and wrote on the ground, v.* 8. As when they made their address he seemed to slight their question, so now that he had given them an answer he slighted their resentment of it, not caring what they said to it; nay, they needed not to make any reply; the matter was lodged in their own breasts, let them make the best of it there.

[4] The scribes and Pharisees were so strangely thunderstruck with the words of Christ that they let fall their persecution of Christ, whom they durst no further tempt, and their prosecution of the woman, whom they durst no longer accuse (*v.* 9): *They went out one by one.*

What he said frightened them by sending them to their own consciences; he had *shown them to themselves*, and they were afraid if they should stay till he lifted up himself again his next word would show them to the world, and shame them before men, and therefore they thought it best to withdraw. The order of their departure is taken notice of,

beginning at the eldest, either because they were most guilty, or first aware of the danger they were in of being put to the blush; and if the eldest quit the field, and retreat ingloriously, no marvel if the younger follow them.

[5] When the *self-conceited* prosecutors quitted the field, and *fled for the same*, the *self-condemned* prisoner stood her ground, with a resolution to abide by the judgment of our Lord Jesus.

[6] Here is the conclusion of the trial, and the issue it was brought to: *Jesus lifted up himself, and he saw none but the woman, vv.* 10, 11. The woman, it is likely, stood trembling at the bar, as one doubtful of the issue. Christ was *without sin*, and might cast the first stone; but though none more severe than he against sin, for he is infinitely just and holy, none more compassionate than he to sinners, for he is infinitely gracious and merciful, and this poor malefactor finds him so, now that she *stands upon her deliverance.*

First, The prosecutors are called: *Where are those thine accusers? Hath no man condemned thee?*

Secondly, They do not appear when the question is asked: *Hath no man condemned thee?* She said, *No man, Lord.* She speaks respectfully to Christ, calls him *Lord*, but is silent concerning her prosecutors, says nothing in answer to that question which concerned them, *Where are those thine accusers?* She does not triumph in their retreat nor insult over them as witnesses against themselves, not against her.

Thirdly, The prisoner is therefore

discharged: *Neither do I condemn thee; go, and sin no more.* Consider this,

a. As her discharge from the temporal punishment: "If they do not condemn thee to be *stoned to death,* neither *do I.*"

b. As her discharge from the eternal punishment. For Christ to say, *I do not condemn thee* is, in effect, to say, *I do forgive thee*; and the *Son of man had power on earth to forgive sins,* and could upon good grounds give this absolution. Christ will not condemn those who, though they have sinned, will *go and sin no more,* Ps. lxxxv. 8; Isa. lv. 7. He will not take the advantage he has against us for our former rebellions, if we will but lay down our arms and return to our allegiance.

CHRIST'S CONTRADICTORS
(*vv.* 12–20)

The rest of the chapter is taken up with debates between Christ and contradicting sinners, who cavilled at the most gracious words that proceeded out of his mouth. In these verses we have,

I. A great doctrine laid down, with the application of it.

1. The doctrine is, *That Christ is the light of the world* (*v.* 12). God is light, and Christ is *the image of the invisible God*; God of gods, Light of lights. He was expected to be a *light to enlighten the Gentiles* (Luke ii. 32), and so the *light of the world,* and not of the Jewish church only. The visible light of the world is the sun, and Christ is the *Sun of righteousness.*

2. The inference from this doctrine is, *He that followeth me,* as a traveller follows the light in a dark night, *shall not walk in darkness,* but *shall have the light of life.* It is the happiness of those who follow Christ that they *shall not walk in darkness.* They shall not be left destitute of those instructions in the way of truth which are necessary to keep them from destroying error, and those directions in the way of duty which are necessary to keep them from damning sin. They shall have the *light of life,* that knowledge and enjoyment of God which will be to them the light of spiritual life in this world and of everlasting life in the other world, where there will be no death nor darkness.

II. The objection which the Pharisees made against this doctrine, and it was very trifling and frivolous: *Thou bearest record of thyself; thy record is not true,* *v.* 13. In this objection they went upon the suspicion which we commonly have of men's self-commendation, which is concluded to be the native language of self-love, such as we are all ready to condemn in others, but few are willing to own in themselves. But in this case the objection was very unjust, for, 1. They made that his crime, and a diminution to the credibility of his doctrine, which in the case of one who introduced a divine revelation was necessary and unavoidable. 2. They overlooked the testimony of all the other witnesses, which corroborated the testimony he bore of himself.

III. Christ's reply to this objection, *v.* 14. He is the light of the world, and it is the property of light to be self-evidencing. First principles prove themselves. He urges three things to prove that his testimony, though of himself, was true and cogent.

1. That he was conscious to himself of his own authority, and abundantly satisfied in himself concerning it: *I know whence I came, and whither I go.*

2. That they are very incompetent judges of him, and of his doctrine, and not to be regarded. (1) Because they were *ignorant*, willingly and resolvedly *ignorant*: *You cannot tell whence I came, and whither I go.* (2) Because they were *partial* (*v.* 15): *You judge after the flesh.* When fleshly wisdom gives the rule of judgment, and outward appearances only are given in evidence, and the case decided according to them, then men *judge after the flesh.* (3) Because they were *unjust* and *unfair* towards him, intimated in this: "*I judge no man*; I neither make nor meddle with your political affairs, nor does my doctrine or practice at all intrench upon, or interfere with, your civil rights or secular powers." He thus *judged no man.* Now, if he did not *war after the flesh*, it was very unreasonable for them to *judge him after the flesh.*

3. That his testimony of himself was sufficiently supported and corroborated by the testimony of his Father *with him and for him* (*v.* 16): *And yet, if I judge, my judgment is true.* He did in his doctrine judge (*ch.* ix. 39), though not *politically.* Consider him then,

(1) As a judge, and his own judgment was valid. Now that which makes his judgment unexceptionable is, [1] His Father's concurrence with him: *I am not alone, but I and the Father.* [2] His Father's commission to him: "It is the Father that *sent me.*"

(2) Look upon him as *a witness*, and now he appeared no otherwise (having not as yet taken the throne of judgment), and as such his testimony was true and unexceptionable; this he shows, *vv.* 17, 18, where,

[1] He quotes a maxim of the Jewish law, *v.* 17. That *the testimony of two men is true.*

[2] He applies this to the case in hand (*v.* 18): *I am one that bear witness of myself, and the Father that sent me bears witness of me.* Behold two witnesses! Though in human courts, where two witnesses are required, the criminal or candidate is not admitted to be a witness for himself; yet in a matter purely divine, which can be proved only by a divine testimony, and God himself must be the witness, if the formality of two or three witnesses be insisted on, there can be no other than the eternal Father, the eternal Son of the Father, and the eternal Spirit. Now this proves not only that the Father and the Son are two distinct persons (for their respective testimonies are here spoken of as the testimonies of two several persons), but that these two are one, not only one in their testimony, but equal in power and glory, and therefore the same in substance.

This was the sum of the first conference between Christ and these carnal Jews, in the conclusion of which we are told how their tongues were let loose, and their hands tied.

MORE CONTRADICTIONS
(vv. 21–30)

Christ here gives fair warning to the careless unbelieving Jews to consider what would be the consequence of their infidelity, that they might prevent it before it was too late; for he spoke words of terror as well as words of grace. Observe here,

I. The wrath threatened (v. 21): *Jesus said again unto them* that which might be likely to do them good. Four things are here threatened against the Jews.

1. Christ's departure from them. They said to him, *Depart from us, we desire not the knowledge of thy ways*; and he takes them at their word; but woe to those from whom Christ departs.

2. Their enmity to the true Messiah, and their fruitless and infatuated enquiries after another Messiah when he was gone away, which were both their sin and their punishment.

3. Their final impenitency: *You shall die in your sins.*

4. Their eternal separation from Christ and all happiness in him: *Whither I go you cannot come.* When Christ left the world, he went to a state of perfect happiness; he went to paradise. Thither he took the penitent thief with him, that did not die in his sins; but the impenitent not only *shall not* come to him, but they *cannot*; it is morally impossible, for heaven would not be heaven to those that

die unsanctified and unmeet for it.

II. The jest they made of this threatening. Instead of trembling at this word, they bantered it, and turned it into ridicule (v. 22): *Will he kill himself?*

III. The confirmation of what he had said.

1. *You are from beneath, I am from above; you are of this world, I am not of this world.*

2. He had said, *You shall die in your sins,* and here he stands to it: "Therefore I said, You shall die in your sins, because *you are from beneath*"; and he gives this further reason for it, *If you believe not that I am he, you shall die in your sins, v.* 24. See here, (1) What we are required to believe: *that I am he—that I am,* which is one of God's names, Exod. iii. 14. (2) How necessary it is that we believe this. If we have not this faith, *we shall die in our sins*; for the matter is so settled that without this faith we cannot be saved from the power of sin while we live, and therefore shall certainly continue in it to the last. Unbelief is the damning sin; it is a sin against the remedy.

IV. Here is a further discourse concerning *himself,* occasioned by his requiring faith in himself as the condition of salvation, *vv.* 25–29. Observe,

1. The question which the Jews put to him (v. 25): *Who art thou?*

2. His answer to this question, wherein he directs them three ways for information:—

(1) He refers them to *what he had said* all along: "Do you ask who I am? *Even the same that I said unto you from the beginning.*"

(2) He refers them to his Father's

judgment, and the instructions he had from him (*v.* 26). Here,

[1] He suppresses his accusation of them. He had *many things* to charge them with, and many evidences to produce against them; but for the present he had said enough.

[2] He enters his appeal against them to his Father: *He that sent me.* Here two things comfort him:— *First,* That he had been *true to his Father,* and to the trust reposed in him. *Secondly,* That his Father would be *true to him;* true to the promise that he would *make his mouth like a sharp sword;* true to his purpose concerning him, which was a *decree* (Ps. ii. 7); true to the threatenings of his wrath against those that should reject him.

[3] He refers them to *their own convictions* hereafter, *vv.* 28, 29. He finds they will not understand him, and therefore adjourns the trial till further evidence should come in; they that *will not see shall see,* Isa, xxvi. 11. Now observe here,

a. What they should ere long be *convinced, of:* "*You shall know that I am he,* that Jesus is the true Messiah." Two things they should be convinced of, in order to this:— *First,* That he did nothing *of himself,* not of himself as man, of himself alone, of himself without the Father, with whom he was *one. Secondly,* That as *his Father taught him,* so he *spoke these things,* that he was not *self-taught,* but *taught of God.*

b. When they should be convinced of this: *When you have lifted up the Son of man,* lifted him up upon the cross, as the brazen serpent upon the pole (*ch.* iii. 14), as the sacrifices under the law (for Christ is the great sacrifice), which, when they were offered, were said to be *elevated,* or *lifted up.* Or the expression denotes that his death was his exaltation.

c. What supported our Lord Jesus in the mean time (*v.* 29): *He that sent me is with me,* in my whole undertaking; *for the Father* (the fountain and first spring of this affair, from whom as its great cause and author it is derived) *hath not left me alone,* to manage it myself, hath not deserted the business nor me in the prosecution of it, for *do I always those things that please him.*

V. Here is the good effect which this discourse of Christ's had upon some of his hearers (*v.* 30): *As he spoke these words many believed on him.* Note, 1. Though multitudes perish in their unbelief, yet there is a remnant according to the election of grace, who *believe to the saving of the soul.* 2. The words of Christ, and particularly his *threatening* words, are made effectual by the grace of God to bring in poor souls to believe in him.

TRUE FREEDOM (*vv.* 31–37)

We have in these verses,

I. A comfortable doctrine laid down concerning the *spiritual liberty* of Christ's disciples, intended for the encouragement of *those Jews that believed.* See here,

1. How graciously the Lord Jesus looks to those that *tremble at his word,* and are ready to receive it; he has something to say

to those who have hearing ears, and will not pass by those who set themselves in his way, without speaking to them.

2. How carefully he cherishes the beginnings of grace, and meets those that are coming towards him. In what he said to them, we have two things, which he saith to all that should at any time believe: —

(1) The character of a true disciple of Christ: *If you continue in my word, then are you my disciples indeed.* Those only that *continue in Christ's word* shall be accepted as his *disciples indeed*, that adhere to his word in every instance without partiality, and abide by it to the end without apostasy.

(2) The privilege of a true disciple of Christ. Here are two precious promises made to those who thus approve themselves disciples indeed, *v.* 32.

[1] "*You shall know the truth,* shall know all that truth which it is needful and profitable for you to know, and shall be more confirmed in the belief of it, shall know the certainty of it."

[2] *The truth shall make you free*; that is, *First,* The truth which Christ teaches tends to make men free, Isa. lxi. 1. *Secondly,* The knowing, entertaining, and believing, of this truth does actually *make us free,* free from prejudices, mistakes, and false notions, than which nothing more *enslaves* and *entangles* the soul, free from the dominion of lust and passion; and restores the soul to the government of itself, by reducing it into obedience to its Creator.

II. The offence which the carnal Jews took at this doctrine, and their objection against it. See here,

1. What it was that they were grieved at: it was an *innuendo* in those words, *You shall be made free,* as if the Jewish church and nation were in some sort of bondage, which reflected on the Jews in general, and as if all that did not believe in Christ continued in that bondage, which reflected on the Pharisees in particular.

2. What it was that they alleged against it; whereas Christ intimated that they needed to be made free, they urge, (1) "We are Abraham's seed." Abraham was in covenant with God, and his children by his right, Rom. xi. 28. Now that covenant, no doubt, was a free charter, and invested them with privileges not consistent with a state of slavery, Rom. ix. 4. And therefore they thought they had no occasion with so *great a sum* as they reckoned faith in Christ to be *to obtain this freedom,* when they were thus free-born. (2) *We were never in bondage to any man.* Now observe, [1] How false this allegation was. I wonder how they could have the assurance to say a thing in the face of a congregation which was so notoriously *untrue.* Were not the seed of Abraham in bondage to the Egyptians? Were they not often in bondage to the neighbouring nations in the time of the judges? Were they not seventy years captives in Babylon? Nay, were they not at this time tributaries to the Romans? [2] How foolish the application was. Christ had spoken of a liberty wherewith the *truth* would make them free,

which must be meant of a *spiritual* liberty; and yet they plead against the offer of *spiritual* liberty that they were never in *corporal* bondage, as if, because they were never in bondage to any *man*, they were never in bondage to any *lust*.

III. Our Saviour's vindication of his doctrine from these objections, and the further explication of it, vv. 34–37, where he does these four things:—

1. He shows that, notwithstanding their civil liberties and their visible church-membership, yet it was possible that they might be in a state of bondage (v. 34): *Whosoever commits sin, though he be of Abraham's seed, and was never in bondage to any man, is the servant of sin.*

2. He shows them that, being in a state of bondage, their having a place in the house of God would not entitle them to the inheritance of sons; for (v. 35) *the servant, though he be in the house for awhile, yet, being but a servant, abideth not in the house for ever.*

3. He shows them the way of deliverance out of this state of bondage into the *glorious liberty of the children of God*, Rom. viii. 21. Note,

(1) Jesus Christ in the gospel offers us *our freedom*; he has authority and power to *make free*. [1] To *discharge prisoners*; this he does *in justification*, by making satisfaction for *our guilt* and for *our debts*, for which we were by the law arrested and in execution. [2] He has a power to rescue *bond-slaves*, and this he does in *sanctification*; by the

powerful arguments of his gospel, and the powerful operations of his Spirit, he breaks the power of corruption in the soul, rallies the scattered forces of reason and virtue, and fortifies God's interest against sin and Satan, and so the soul is made free. [3] He has a power to *naturalize strangers and foreigners*, and this he does in *adoption*.

(2) Those whom Christ makes free are *free indeed*. It denotes, [1] The truth and certainty of the promise. The servants of sin promise themselves liberty, and fancy themselves free, when they have broken religion's bands asunder; but they cheat themselves. None are *free indeed* but those whom Christ *makes free*. [2] It denotes the singular excellency of the freedom promised; it is a freedom that deserves the name, in comparison with which all other liberties are no better than slaveries.

4. He applies this to these unbelieving cavilling Jews, in answer to their boasts of relation to Abraham (v. 37): "*I know* very well *that you are Abraham's seed, but now you seek to kill me*, and therefore have forfeited the honour of your relation to Abraham, *because my word hath no place in you*."

Why were they that were Abraham's seed so very inveterate against Abraham's promised seed, in whom they and *all the families of the earth* should be *blessed*? Our Saviour here tells them, It is because *my word hath no place in you*. They *sought to kill him*, and so effectually to *silence* him, not because he had done them any harm, but because they could not bear the convincing, commanding power of his word.

HEARING GOD'S WORDS
(vv. 38–47)

Here Christ and the Jews are still at issue; he sets himself to convince and convert them, while they still set themselves to contradict and oppose him.

I. He here traces the difference between his sentiments and theirs to a different rise and origin (v. 38): *I speak that which I have seen with my Father*, and *you* do *what you have seen with your father*. Here are two fathers spoken of, according to the two families into which the sons of men are divided—God and the devil, and without controversy these are contrary the one to the other.

II. He takes off and answers their vain-glorious boasts of relation to Abraham and to God as their fathers, and shows the vanity and falsehood of their pretensions.

1. They pleaded relation to Abraham, and he replies to this plea. "Abraham's children will do the works of Abraham, but you do not do Abraham's works, therefore you are not Abraham's children."

[1] Those only are reckoned the seed of Abraham, to whom the promise belongs, who *tread in the steps* of his faith and obedience, Rom. iv. 12.

[2] The assumption is evident likewise: *But you do not do* the works of Abraham, for *you seek to kill me, a man that has told you* *the truth, which I have heard of God; this did not Abraham, v.* 40.

[3] The conclusion follows of course (v. 41): "Whatever your boasts and pretensions be, you are not Abraham's children, but father yourselves upon another family (v. 41); there is *a father whose deeds you do*, whose spirit you are of, and whom you resemble."

2. So far were they from owning their unworthiness of relation to Abraham that they pleaded relation to God himself as their Father: "We are *not born of fornication*, we are not bastards, but legitimate sons; *we have one Father, even God.*"

Now our Saviour gives a full answer to this fallacious plea (vv. 42, 43), and proves, by two arguments, that they had no right to call God Father.

First, They did not love Christ: *If God were your Father, you would love me*. He had disproved their relation to Abraham by their going about to kill him (v. 40), but here he disproves their relation to God by their not loving and owning him.

Secondly, They did not understand him. It was a sign they did not belong to God's family that they did not understand the language and dialect of the family. Christ spoke the words of God (*ch.* iii. 34) in the dialect of the kingdom of God; and yet they, who pretended to belong to the kingdom, understood not the idioms and properties of it, but like strangers, and rude ones too, ridiculed it. And the reason why they did not understand

Christ's speech made the matter much worse: *Even because you cannot hear my word*, that is, "You cannot persuade yourselves to hear it attentively, impartially, and without prejudice, as it should be heard."

III. Having thus disproved their relation both to Abraham and to God, he comes next to tell them plainly whose children they were: *You are of your father the devil*, v. 44. If they were not God's children, they were the devil's, for God and Satan divide the world of mankind.

This is a high charge, and sounds very harsh and horrid, that any of the children of men, especially the church's children, should be called *children of the devil*, and therefore our Saviour fully proves it,

1. By a general argument: *The lusts of your father you will do*.

2. By two particular instances, wherein they manifestly resembled the devil—*murder* and *lying*. The devil is an enemy to life, because God is the God of life and life is the happiness of man; and an enemy to truth, because God is the God of truth and truth is the bond of human society.

IV. Christ, having thus proved all murderers and all liars to be the devil's children, leaves it to the consciences of his hearers to say, *Thou art the man*. Two things he charges upon them:—

1. That they would not *believe the word of truth* (v. 45). "*If I say the truth, why do you not believe me?* If you cannot convince me of error, you must own that I *say the truth*, and why do you not

then *give me credit*? Why will you not deal witth me upon trust?"

2. Another thing charged upon them is that they would not hear the words of God (v. 47), which further shows how groundless their claim of relation to God was. Here is,

(1) A doctrine laid down: *He that is of God heareth God's words*; that is, [1] He is *willing* and *ready* to hear them, is sincerely desirous to know what the mind of God is, and cheerfully embraces whatever he knows to be so. [2] He *apprehends* and *discerns* them, he so hears them as to perceive the *voice of God* in them, which the natural man does not, 1 Cor. ii. 14.

(2) The application of this doctrine, for the conviction of these unbelieving Jews: *You therefore hear them not*. If the word of the kingdom do not bring forth fruit, the blame is to be laid upon the soil, not upon the seed, as appears by the parable of the sower, Matt. xiii. 3.

CHRIST INSULTED (vv. 48–50)

Here is, I. The malice of hell breaking out in the base language which the unbelieving Jews gave to our Lord Jesus. Hitherto they had cavilled at his doctrine, and had made invidious remarks upon it; but, having shown themselves uneasy when he complained (vv. 43, 47) that they would not hear him, now at length they fall to downright railing, v. 48. See here,

1. What was the blasphemous character commonly given of our Lord Jesus among the wicked Jews, to which they refer. (1) That

he was a Samaritan, that is, that he was an enemy to their church and nation, one that they hated and could not endure. (2) That *he had a devil*. Either, [1] That he was *in league with the devil*. Or rather, [2] That he was possessed with a devil, or a mad man, and that which he said was no more to be believed than the extravagant rambles of a distracted man, or one in a delirium.

2. How they undertook to justify this character, and applied it to the present occasion: *Say we not well that thou art so?* They value themselves on their enmity to Christ, as if they had never spoken *better* than when they spoke the worst they could of Jesus Christ.

II. The meekness and mercifulness of Heaven shining in Christ's reply to this vile calumny, *vv.* 49, 50.

1. He denies their charge against him: *I have not a devil*; as Paul (Acts xxvi. 25), *I am not mad*. The imputation is unjust; "I am neither actuated by a devil, nor in compact with one"; and this he evidenced by what he did against the devil's kingdom.

2. He asserts the sincerity of his own intentions: But *I honour my Father*.

3. He complains of the wrong they did him by their calumnies: *You do dishonour me*. Christ honoured his Father so as never man did, and yet was himself dishonoured so as never man was; for, though God has promised that those who honour him he will honour, he never promised that men should honour them.

4. He clears himself from the imputation of vain glory, in saying this concerning himself, *v.* 50. See here, (1) His *contempt* of worldly honour: *I seek not mine own glory*. (2) His *comfort* under worldly dishonour: *There is one that seeketh and judgeth*. In two things Christ made it appear that he *sought not his own glory*; and here he tells us what satisfied him as to both. [1] He did not *court* men's respect, but was indifferent to it. [2] He did not *revenge* men's affronts, but was unconcerned at them.

BEFORE ABRAHAM
(*vv.* 51–59)

In these verses we have,

I. The doctrine of the immortality of believers laid down, *v.* 51. Here we have, 1. The *character* of a believer: he is one that *keeps the sayings* of the Lord Jesus. 2. The *privilege* of a believer: *He shall by no means see death for ever*; so it is in the original. Though now they cannot avoid seeing death, and tasting it too, yet they shall shortly be there where it will be *seen no more for ever*, Exod. xiv. 13.

II. The Jews cavil at this doctrine. Instead of laying hold of this precious promise of immortality, which the nature of man has an ambition of (who is there that does not love life, and dread the sight of death?) they lay hold of this occasion to reproach him that makes them so kind an offer: *Now we know that thou hast a devil. Abraham is dead*. Observe here,

1. Their *railing*: "*Now we know that thou hast a devil*, that thou art a madman; thou ravest, and sayest thou knowest no what." See how these swine trample underfoot the precious pearls of gospel promises.

2. Their *reasoning*, and the colour they had to *run him down* thus. In short, they look upon him as guilty of an insufferable piece of arrogance, in making himself greater than *Abraham and the prophets: Abraham is dead*, and *the prophets*, they are dead too. Now their arguing goes upon two mistakes:—[1] They understood Christ of an immortality in this world, and this was a mistake. In the sense that Christ spoke, it was not true that *Abraham and the prophets* were *dead*, for God is still the *God of Abraham* and the *God of the holy prophets* (Rev. xxii. 6); now God is not the God of the dead, but of the living; therefore Abraham and the prophets are still alive, and, as Christ meant it, they had not *seen* nor *tasted* death. [2] They thought none could be greater than Abraham and the prophets, whereas they could not but know that the Messiah would be greater than Abraham or any of the prophets; they did virtuously, but he excelled them all; nay, they borrowed their greatness from him.

III. Christ's reply to this cavil; still he vouchsafes to reason with them, that every mouth may be stopped.

1. In his answer he insists not upon his own testimony concerning himself, but waives it as not sufficient nor conclusive (*v.* 54):

If I honour myself, my honour is nothing.

2. He refers himself to *his* Father, God; and to *their* father, Abraham.

(1) To his Father, *God*: *It is my Father that honoureth me.* By this he means, [1] That he *derived* from his Father all the honour he now claimed. [2] That he *depended* upon his Father for all the honour he further *looked for.* He courted not the applauses of the age, but despised them; for his eye and heart were upon the glory which the Father had promised him, and *which he had with the Father before the world was.* "You *say of him that he is your God, yet you have not known him.*" Here observe,

a. The profession they made of relation to God.

b. Their ignorance of him, and estrangement from him, notwithstanding this profession: *Yet you have not known him.* (*a*) *You know him not at all.* These Pharisees were so taken up with the study of their traditions concerning things foreign and trifling that they never minded the most needful and useful knowledge. Or, (*b*) *You know him not aright*, but mistake concerning him; and this is as bad as not knowing him at all, or worse. Men may be able to dispute subtly concerning God, and yet may think him such a one as themselves, and *not know him.* You say that he is *yours*, and it is natural to us to desire to know *our own*, yet you *know him not.*

(2) Christ refers them to *their* father, whom they boasted so much of a relation to, and that was

Abraham, and this closes the discourse.

[1] Christ asserts Abraham's prospect of him, and respect to him: *Your father Abraham rejoiced to see my day, and he saw it, and was glad, v.* 56. And by this he proves that he was not at all out of the way when he *made himself greater than Abraham.*

[2] The Jews cavil at this, and reproach him for it (*v.* 57): *Thou art not yet fifty years old, and hast thou seen Abraham?*

[3] Our Saviour gives an effectual answer to this cavil, by a solemn assertion of his own seniority even to Abraham himself (*v.* 58): "*Verily, verily, I say unto you*; I do not only say it in private to my own disciples, who will be sure to say as I say, but *to you* my enemies and persecutors; I say it to your faces, take it how you will: *Before Abraham was, I am.*" *Before Abraham was made or born, I am.* The change of the word is observable, and bespeaks Abraham a creature, and himself the Creator; well therefore might he make himself *greater* than Abraham. *Before Abraham he was, First,* As God. *I am,* is the name of God (Exod. iii. 14); it denotes his self-existence; he does not say, *I was,* but *I am,* for he is the first and the last, immutably the same (Rev. i. 8); thus he was not only before Abraham, but before *all worlds, ch.* i. 1; Prov. viii. 23. *Secondly,* As Mediator. He was the appointed Messiah, long before Abraham; the *Lamb slain from the foundation of the world* (Rev. xiii. 8), the channel of conveyance of light, life, and love from God to

man. This supposes his divine nature, that he is the same in himself from eternity (Heb. xiii. 8), and that he is the same to man ever since the fall. If Christ was before Abraham, his doctrine and religion were no novelty, but were, in the substance of them, prior to Judaism, and ought to take place of it.

[4] This great word ended the dispute *abruptly,* and put a period to it. Observe here,

First, How they were *enraged* at Christ for what he said: *They took up stones to cast at him, v.* 59.

Secondly, How he made his *escape* out of their hands. 1. He *absconded*; Jesus hid himself. 2. He *departed,* he *went out of the temple,* going *through the midst of them,* undiscovered, and *so passed by.* As *the kingdom of God comes not,* so it *goes not, with observation.* See Judg. xvi. 20. *Samson wist not that the Lord was departed from him.* Thus it was with these forsaken Jews, God left them, and they never missed him.

CHAPTER NINE

LIGHT SHINES (vv. 1–7)

We have here sight given to a poor beggar that had been blind from his birth. Observe,

I. The notice which our Lord Jesus took of the piteous case of this poor blind man (*v.* 1): *As Jesus passed by he saw a man which was blind from his birth.* If the light is sweet, how melancholy must it needs be for a man, all his days, *to eat in darkness!* He that is *blind* has no *enjoyment* of the light, but he that is *born blind* has no *idea* of it.

II. The discourse between Christ and his disciples concerning this man. Observe,

1. The question which the disciples put to their Master upon this blind man's case, *v.* 2. Now this question of theirs was,

(1) *Uncharitably censorious.* They take it for granted that this extraordinary calamity was the punishment of some uncommon wickedness, and that this man was a sinner above all men that dwelt at Jerusalem, Luke xiii. 4.

(2) It was *unnecessarily curious.* Concluding this calamity to be inflicted for some very heinous crime, they ask, *Who were the criminals, this man or his parents?* And what was this to them? Or what good would it do them to know it?

2. Christ's answer to this question. He was always *apt to teach,* and to rectify his disciples' mistakes.

(1) He gives the reason of this poor man's blindness: *"Neither has this man sinned nor his parents,* but he was born blind, and has continued so to this day, that now at last *the works of God should be made manifest in him,"* *v.* 3. Here Christ, who perfectly knew the secret springs of the divine counsels, told them two things concerning such uncommon calamities:—[1] That they are not always inflicted as punishments of sin. [2] That they are sometimes intended purely *for the glory of God,* and the *manifesting of his works.*

(2) He gives the reason of his own forwardness and readiness to help and heal him, *vv.* 4, 5.

[1] It was his Father's will: *I must work the works of him that sent me.*

[2] Now was his opportunity: I must work *while it is day,* while the time lasts which is appointed to work in, and while the light lasts which is given to work by. Christ himself had *his day.*

[3] The period of his opportunity was at hand, and therefore he would be busy: *The night comes when no man can work.*

[4] His business in the world was to enlighten it (*v.* 5): *As long as I am in the world,* and that will not be long, *I am the light of the world.* He had said this before, *ch.* viii. 12. He is the *Sun of righteousness,* that has not only light in his wings for those that can see, but healing in his wings, or beams, for those that are blind and cannot see, therein far exceeding in virtue that great light which rules *by day.* Christ would cure this blind man, the representative of a blind world, because he came to be *the light of the world,* not only to give *light,* but to give *sight.*

III. The manner of the cure of the blind man, *vv.* 6, 7. In the cure observe,

1. The preparation of the eye-salve. Christ *spat on the ground, and made clay of the spittle.* He could have cured him with a word, as he did others, but he chose to do it in this way to show that he is not *tied* to any method.

2. The application of it to the place: *He anointed the eyes of the blind man with the clay.* Now Christ did this, (1) To magnify his power in making a blind man to see by that method which one

would think more likely to make a seeing man blind. Daubing clay on the eyes would *close them* up, but never *open them*. (2) To give an intimation that it was his mighty hand, the very same that at first made man out of *the clay*; for by him God *made the worlds*, both the great world, and man the little world. (3) To represent and typify the healing and opening of the eyes of the mind by the grace of Jesus Christ. The design of the gospel is to *open men's eyes*, Acts, xxvi. 18. Now the eye-salve that does the work is of Christ's preparing; it is made up, not as this, of his spittle, but of his blood, the blood and water that came out of his pierced side; we must come to Christ for *the eye-salve*, Rev. iii. 18. He only is *able*, and he only is *appointed*, to make it up, Luke iv. 18.

3. The directions given to the patient, *v*. 7. His physician said to him, *Go, wash in the pool of Siloam*. Not that this washing was needful to effect the cure; but, (1) Christ would hereby try his obedience, and whether he would with an implicit faith obey the orders of one he was so much a stranger to. (2) He would likewise try how he stood affected to the tradition of the elders, which taught, and perhaps had taught him (for many that are *blind* are very knowing), that it was not lawful to wash the eyes, no not with spittle medicinally, on the sabbath day, much less to go to a pool of water to wash them. (3) He would hereby represent the method of spiritual healing, in which, though the effect is owing purely to his power and grace, there is duty to be done by us.

4. The patient's obedience to these directions: *He went his way therefore*, and *he washed his eyes*; probably the disciples, or some stander by, informed him that he who bade him do it was that Jesus whom he had heard so much of, else he would not have gone, at his bidding, on that which looked so much like a fool's errand; in confidence of Christ's power, as well as in obedience to his command, he went, and washed.

5. The cure effected: *He came seeing*. There is more glory in this concise narrative, *He went* and *washed*, and *came seeing*, than in Cæsar's *Veni, vidi, vici—I came, I saw, I conquered*.

LIGHT REFLECTS (*vv.* 8–12)

Such a wonderful event as the giving of sight to a man born blind could not but be the talk of the town. Two things are debated in this conference about it:—

I. Whether this was the same man that had before been blind, *v*. 8.

1. The neighbours that lived near the place where he was born and bred, and knew that he had been blind, could not but be amazed when they saw that he had his eye-sight, had it on a sudden, and perfectly; and they said, *Is not this he that sat and begged?*

2. In answer to this enquiry, (1) Some said, *This is he*, the very same man; and these are witnesses to the truth of the miracle, for they had long known him stone-blind. (2) Others, who could not

think it possible that a man born blind should thus on a sudden receive his sight, for that reason, and no other, said, *He is not he, but is like him*, and so, by their confession, if it be he, it is a great miracle that is wrought upon him.

3. This controversy was soon decided by the man himself: *He said, I am he*, the very man that so lately sat and begged. Applying it spiritually, it teaches us that those who are savingly enlightened by the grace of God should be ready to own what they were before that blessed change was wrought, 1 Tim. i. 13, 14.

II. How he came to have his eyes opened, *vv.* 10–12. Two things these neighbours enquire after:—

1. The manner of the cure: *How were thine eyes opened?* In answer to this enquiry the poor man gives them a plain and full account of the matter: *A man that is called Jesus made clay,—and I received sight, v.* 11.

2. The author of it (*v.* 12): *Where is he?* In answer to this, he could say nothing: *I know not.* As soon as Christ had sent him to the pool of Siloam, it should seem, he withdrew immediately (as he did, *ch.* v. 13), and did not stay till the man returned, as if he either doubted of the effect or waited for the man's thanks. For the way of the Spirit is like that of the wind, which thou hearest the sound of, but canst not tell *whence it comes* nor *whither it goes.*

LIGHT REJECTED (*vv.* 13–34)

One would have expected that such a miracle as Christ wrought upon the blind man would have settled his reputation, and silenced and shamed all opposition, but it had the contrary effect; instead of being embraced as a prophet for it, he is prosecuted as a criminal.

I. Here is the information that was given in to the Pharisees concerning this matter: *They brought to the Pharisees him that aforetime was blind, v.* 13.

II. The ground which was pretended for this information, and the colour given to it. That which is good was never maligned but under the imputation of something evil. And the crime objected here (*v.* 14) was that *it was the sabbath day when Jesus made the clay, and opened his eyes.*

III. The trial and examination of this matter by the Pharisees, *v.* 15. Let us see how they teased this man.

1. They interrogated him concerning the cure itself.

(1) They doubted whether he had indeed been *born blind*, and demanded proof of that which even the prosecutors had acknowledged (*v.* 18): They *did not believe*, that is, they would not, that he was *born blind.*

[1] The questions that were put to the parents (*v.* 19): They *asked them* in an imperious threatening way, "*Is this your son?* Dare you swear to it? *Do you say he was born blind?* Are you sure of it? Or did he but pretend to be so, to have an excuse for his begging? *How then doth he now see?* That is impossible, and therefore you had better unsay it."

[2] Their answers to these interrogatories, in which,

First, They fully attest that which they could safely say in this matter; *safely*, that is, upon their own knowledge, and *safely*, that is, without running themselves into trouble (v. 20): *We know that this is our son*; and we know that he was *born blind*.

Secondly, They cautiously decline giving any evidence concerning his cure; partly because they were not themselves eyewitnesses of it, and could say nothing to it *of their own knowledge*; and partly because they found it was a *tender point*, and would not bear to be meddled with.

a. Observe how warily they express themselves (v. 21): "*By what means he now seeth we know not*, or *who has opened his eyes we know not*, otherwise than by *hearsay*; we can give no account either by what means or by whose hand it was done."

b. See the reason why they were so cautious (vv. 22, 23): *Because they feared the Jews*. Here is,

(*a*) The *late law* which the sanhedrim had made. It was agreed and enacted by their authority that, if any man within their jurisdiction did *confess* that Jesus *was Christ, he should be put out of the synagogue*.

(*b*) The influence which this law had upon the parents of the blind man. They declined saying any thing of Christ, and shuffled it off to their son, *because they feared the Jews*. Well, the parents have thus disentangled themselves, and are discharged from any further attendance; let us now go on with the examination of the man himself; the doubt of the man himself; the doubt of the

Pharisees, whether he was *born blind*, was put out of doubt *by them*; and therefore,

(2) They enquired of *him* concerning the *manner of the cure*, and made their remarks upon it, vv. 15, 16.

[1] The same question which his neighbours had put to him *now again the Pharisees asked him, how he had received his sight*.

[2] The same answer, in effect, which he had before given to his neighbours, he here repeats to the Pharisees. In the former account he said, *I washed, and received sight*; but lest they should think it was only a glimpse for the present, which a heated imagination might fancy itself to have, he now says, "*I do see*: it is a complete and lasting cure."

[3] The remarks made upon this story were very different, and occasioned a debate in the court, v. 16.

First, Some took this occasion to censure and condemn Christ for what he had done. Some of the Pharisees said, *This man is not of God*, as he pretends, *because he keepeth not the sabbath day*.

Secondly, Others spoke in his favour, and very pertinently urged, *How can a man that is a sinner do such miracles?* It seems that even in this *council of the ungodly* there were some that were capable of a *free thought*, and were witnesses for Christ, even in the midst of his enemies.

2. After their enquiry concerning the cure, we must observe their enquiry concerning the *author* of it. And here observe,

(1) What the man said of him,

in answer to their enquiry. They ask him (*v.* 17), "*What sayest thou of him, seeing that he has opened thine eyes?*" To this question the poor man makes a short, plain, and direct answer: "*He is a prophet*, he is one inspired and sent of God to preach, and work miracles, and deliver to the world a divine message." This poor blind beggar had a clearer judgment of the things pertaining to the kingdom of God, and saw further into the proofs of a divine mission, than the *masters in Israel*, that assumed an authority to judge of prophets.

(2) What they said of him, in reply to the man's testimony. Having in vain attempted to invalidate the evidence of the fact, and finding that indeed a *notable miracle was wrought*, and they *could not deny it*, they renew their attempt to banter it, and run it down, and do all they can to shake the good opinion the man had of him that opened his eyes, and to convince him that Christ was a bad man (*v.* 24): *Give God the praise, we know that this man is a sinner.* Two ways this is understood: [1] By way of *advice*, to take heed of ascribing the praise of his cure to a sinful man, but to give it all to God, to whom it was due. [2] By way of *adjuration*; so some take it. "We know (though thou dost not, who hast but lately come, as it were, into a new world) that this man is *a sinner*, a great impostor, that cheats the country; this we are sure of, therefore *give God praise*" (as Joshua said to Achan) "by making an ingenuous confession of the fraud and collusion which we are confident there is in this matter; in God's name, man, tell the truth."

3. The debate that arose between the Pharisees and this poor man concerning Christ. They say, *He is a sinner*; he says, *He is a prophet*. Now in the parley between the Pharisees and this poor man we may observe three steps:—

(1) He sticks to the certain matter of fact the evidence of which they endeavour to shake. That which is doubtful is best resolved into that which is plain, and therefore, [1] He adheres to that which to himself at least, and to his own satisfaction, was past dispute (*v.* 25): "*If he be a sinner, I know it not*, I see no reason to say so, but the contrary; for this *one thing I know*, and can be more sure of than you can be of that of which you are so confident, *that whereas I was blind, now I see*, and therefore must not only say that he has been a good friend to me, but that he is a *prophet*; I am both able and bound to speak well of him." The poor man does not here give a nice account of the method of the cure, nor pretend to describe it *philosophically*, but in short, *Whereas I was blind, now I see*. Thus in the work of grace in the soul, though we cannot tell when and how, by what instruments and by what steps and advances, the blessed change was wrought, yet we may take the comfort of it if we can say, through grace, "*Whereas I was blind, now I see*. I did live a carnal, worldly, sensual life, but, thanks be to God, it is now

otherwise with me," Eph. v. 8. [2] They endeavour to baffle and stifle the evidence by a needless repetition of their enquiries into it (v. 26): *What did he to thee? How opened he thine eyes?* They asked these questions, *First,* Because they wanted something to say, and would rather speak *impertinently* than seem to be silenced or run a-ground. *Secondly,* Because they hoped, by putting the man upon repeating his evidence, to catch him tripping in it, or wavering, and then they would think they had gained a good point.

(2) He upbraids them with their obstinate infidelity and invincible prejudices, and they revile him as a disciple of Jesus, vv. 27–29, where the man is more bold with them and they are more sharp upon him than before.

[1] The man boldly upbraids them with their wilful and unreasonable opposition to the evidence of this miracle, v. 27.

[2] For this they scorn and revile him, v. 28. When they could not resist the wisdom and spirit by which he spoke, they broke out into a passion, and scolded him, began to call names, and give him ill language. See what Christ's faithful witnesses must expect from the adversaries of his truth and cause; let them count upon *all manner of evil* to be said of them, Matt. v. 11. The method commonly taken by unreasonable man is to make out with railing what is wanting in truth and reason.

In this argument of theirs observe, 1. How impertinently they allege, in defence of their enmity to Christ, that which none of his followers ever denied: *We know that God spoke unto Moses,* and, thanks be to God, we know it too, more plainly to Moses than to any other of the prophets; but what then? God spoke to Moses, and does it therefore follow that Jesus is an impostor? Moses was a prophet, it is true, and might not Jesus be a prophet also? 2. How absurdly they urge their ignorance of Christ as a reason to justify their contempt of him; *As for this fellow,* this sorry fellow, *we know not whence he is.* It was not long ago that the Jews had made the contrary to this an objection against Christ (*ch.* vii. 27): *We know this man whence he is, but when Christ comes no man knows whence he is.* Thus they could with the greatest assurance either affirm or deny the same thing, according as they saw it would serve their turn.

(3) He reasons with them concerning this matter, and they excommunicate him.

[1] The poor man, finding that he had reason on his side, which they could not answer, grows more bold, and, in prosecution of his argument, is very close upon them.

First, He wonders at their obstinate infidelity (v. 30). Two things he wonders at:—1. That they should be strangers to a man so *famous.* 2. That they should question the divine mission of one that had undoubtedly wrought a divine miracle. When they said, *We know not whence he is,* they meant, "We know not any proof that his doctrine and ministry are from heaven." "Now this is strange," saith the poor man, "that the miracle wrought upon me has not convinced you, and put the matter out of doubt,— that you, whose education and studies give you advantages above others of discerning the things of God, should thus shut your eyes against the light."

Secondly, He argues strongly against them, *vv.* 31–33. They had determined concerning Jesus that he was not of God (*v.* 16), but was a *sinner* (*v.* 24), in answer to which the man here proves not only that he was *not a sinner* (*v.* 31), but that he was *of God,* *v.* 33.

a. He argues here, (*a*) With great knowledge. Though he could not read a letter of the book, he was well acquainted with the scripture and the things of God. (*b*) With great zeal for the honour of Christ, whom he could not endure to hear run down, and evil spoken of. (*c*) With great boldness, and courage, and undauntedness, not terrified by the proudest of his adversaries.

b. His argument may be reduced into form, somewhat like that of David, Ps. lxvi. 18–20.

(*a*) He lays it down for an undoubted truth that none but good men are the favourites of heaven (*v.* 31).

[*b*] The application of these truths is very pertinent to prove that he, at whose word such a divine power was put forth as cured one born blind, was not a bad man, but, having manifestly such an interest in the holy God

as that he *heard him always* (*ch.* xi. 41, 42), was certainly a holy one.

[2] The Pharisees, finding themselves unable either to answer his reasonings or to bear them, fell foul upon him, and with a great deal of pride and passion broke off the discourse, *v.* 34. Here we are told,

First, What they *said.* Having nothing to reply to his argument, they reflected upon his person: *Thou wast altogether born in sin, and dost thou teach us?* They take that amiss which they had reason to take kindly, and are cut to the heart with rage by that which should have pricked them to the heart with penitence.

Secondly, What they did: They *cast him out.* There was a law made that if any confessed Jesus to be the Christ he should be *cast out of the synagogue, v.* 22. But this man had only said of Jesus that he was a prophet, was *of God*: and yet they stretch the law to bring him under the lash of it, as if he had confessed him to be the Christ.

LIGHT ACCEPTED (*vv.* 35–38)

In these verses we may observe,

I. The tender care which our Lord Jesus took of this poor man (*v.* 35). Jesus Christ will graciously find and receive those who for his sake are unjustly rejected and cast out by men. He will be a hiding place to his outcasts, and appear, to the joy of those whom their brethren hated and cast out.

II. The conversation Christ had with him. He had well improved the knowledge he had, and now

Christ gives him further instruction; for he that is faithful in a little shall be entrusted with more, Matt. xiii. 12.

1. Our Lord Jesus examines his faith: "*Dost thou believe on the Son of God?*"

2. The poor man solicitously enquires concerning the Messiah he was to believe in, professing his readiness to embrace him and close with him (*v.* 36): *Who is he, Lord, that I may believe on him?* (1) Some think he did know that Jesus, who cured him, was the Son of God, but did not know which was Jesus, and therefore, supposing this person that talked with him to be a follower of Jesus, desired him to do him the favour to direct him to his master; not that he might satisfy his curiosity with the sight of him, but that he might the more firmly believe in him, and profess his faith, and *know whom he had believed.* See Cant. v. 6, 7; iii. 2, 3. It is Christ only that can direct us to himself. (2) Others think he did know that this person who talked with him was Jesus, the same that cured him, whom he believed a great and good man and a prophet, but did not yet know that he was the Son of God and the true Messiah.

3. Our Lord Jesus graciously reveals himself to him as that Son of God on whom he must believe: *Thou hast both seen him, and it is he that talketh with thee,* v. 37.

4. The poor man readily entertains this surprising revelation, and, in a transport of joy and wonder, he said, *Lord, I believe, and he worshipped him.*

TRUE BLINDNESS (*vv.* 39–41)

Christ, having spoken comfort to the poor man that was persecuted, here speaks conviction to his persecutors, a specimen of the distributions of trouble and rest at the great day, 2 Thess. i. 6, 7. Here is,

I. The account Christ gives of his design in coming into the world (*v.* 39): *For judgment I am* come to order and administer the great affairs of the *kingdom of God among men.*

1. His business into the world was *great*; he came to keep the assizes and general gaol-delivery.

2. This great truth he explains by a metaphor borrowed from the miracle which he had lately wrought. That *those who see not might see, and that those who see might be made blind.* Such a difference of Christ's coming is often spoken of; to some his gospel is a *savour of life unto life,* to others of *death unto death.*

II. The Pharisees cavil at this. They were *with him,* not desirous to learn any good from him, but to form evil against him; and they said, *Are we blind also?*

III. Christ's answer to this cavil, which, if it did not convince them, yet silenced them: *If you were blind you should have no sin; but now you say, We see, therefore your sin remaineth.* They gloried that they were not blind, as the common people, were not so credulous and manageable as they, but would *see with their own eyes,* having abilities, as they thought, sufficient for their own guidance, so that they needed not anybody to lead them. This very thing which they gloried in, Christ here tells them, was their shame and ruin. For,

1. *If you were blind, you would have no sin.* (1) "If you had been really ignorant, your sin had not been so deeply aggravated, nor would you have had so much sin to answer for as now you have."

2. "*But now you say, We see*; now that you have knowledge, and are instructed out of the law, your sin is highly aggravated; and now that you have a conceit of that knowledge, and think you see your way better than any body can show it you, *therefore your sin remains*, your case is desperate, and your disease incurable."

CHAPTER TEN

I AM THE GOOD
SHEPHERD (*vv.* 1–18)

The Pharisees supported themselves in their opposition to Christ with this principle, that they were the *pastors of the church*, and that Jesus, having no commission from them, was an intruder and an impostor, and therefore the people were bound in duty to stick to *them*, against *him*. In opposition to this, Christ here describes who were the false shepherds, and who the true, leaving them to infer what they were.

I. Here is the parable or similitude proposed (*vv.* 1–5); it is borrowed from the custom of that country, in the management of their sheep.

1. In the parable we have,

(1) The evidence of a thief and a robber, that comes to do mischief to the flock, and damage to the owner, *v.* 1. *He enters not by the door,* as having no lawful cause of entry, but *climbs up some other way*, at a window, or some breach in the wall. (2) The character that distinguishes the rightful owner, who has a property in the sheep, and a care for them: *He enters in by the door*, as one having authority (*v.* 2), and he comes to do them some good office or other, to *bind up that which is broken*, and *strengthen that which is sick*, Ezek. xxxiv. 16. (3) The ready entrance that the shepherd finds: *To him the porter openeth*, *v.* 3. (4) The care he takes and the provision he makes for his sheep. The *sheep hear his voice*, when he speaks familiarly to them, when they come into the fold, as men now do to their dogs and horses; and, which is more, he *calls his own sheep by name*, so exact is the notice he takes of them, the account he keeps of them; and he leads them out from the fold to the green pastures; and (*vv.* 4, 5) when he *turns them out* to graze he does not drive them, but (such was the custom in those times) he goes before them, to prevent any mischief or danger that might meet them, and they, being used to it, *follow him*, and are safe. (5) The strange attendance of the sheep upon the shepherd: *They know his voice*, so as to discern his mind by it, and to distinguish it from that of a stranger.

2. Let us observe from this parable, (1) That good men are

fitly compared to sheep. Men, as creatures depending on their Creator, are called the *sheep of his pasture*. (2) The church of God in the world is a *sheepfold*, into which the *children of God* that were scattered abroad are *gathered together* (*ch.* xi. 52). (3) This sheepfold lies much exposed to thieves and robbers; crafty seducers that debauch and deceive, and cruel persecutors that destroy and devour; *grievous wolves* (Acts xx. 29). (4) The great Shepherd of the sheep takes wonderful care of the flock and of all that belong to it. God is the great Shepherd, Ps. xxiii. 1; lxxx. 1. He knows those that are his, calls them by name, marks them for himself, leads them out to fat pastures, makes them both feed and rest there, speaks comfortably to them, guards them by his providence, guides them by his Spirit and word, and goes before them, *to set them in the way of his steps.* (5) The undershepherds, who are entrusted to feed the flock of God, ought to be careful and faithful in the discharge of that trust. (6) Those who are truly the sheep of Christ will be very observant of their Shepherd, and very cautious and shy of strangers.

II. The Jews' ignorance of the drift and meaning of this discourse (*v.* 6): *Jesus spoke this parable* to them, *but they understood not what the things were which he spoke unto them,* were not aware whom he meant by the *thieves and robbers* and whom by the *good Shepherd.*

III. Christ's explication of this parable, opening the particulars of

it fully. Christ, in the parable, had distinguished the shepherd from the robber by this, that he *enters in by the door*. Now, in the explication of the parable, he makes himself to be both *the door* by which the shepherd enters and the shepherd that enters in by the door. Though it may be a solecism in rhetoric to make the same person to be both the *door* and the *shepherd*, it is no solecism in divinity to make Christ to have his authority from himself, as he has life in himself; and *himself* to *enter by his own blood*, as the door, *into the holy place.*

1. Christ is *the door*.

(1) In general, [1] He is as a *door shut*, to keep out thieves and robbers, and such as are not fit to be admitted. [2] He is as a *door open* for passage and communication. *First*, By Christ, as the door, we have our first admission into the flock of God, *ch.* xiv. 6. *Secondly*, We go in and out in a religious conversation, assisted by him, accepted in him; walking up and down in his name, Zech. x. 12. *Thirdly*, By him God comes to his church, visits it, and communicates himself to it. *Fourthly*, By him, as the door, the sheep are at last admitted into the heavenly kingdom, Matt. xxv. 34.

(2) More particularly,

[1] Christ is the door of *the shepherds*, so that none who come not in by him are to be accounted *pastors*.

[2] Christ is the door of *the sheep* (*v.* 9): *By me if any man enter into the sheepfold*, as one of the flock, he *shall be saved*; shall

not only be safe from thieves and robbers, but he shall be happy, he *shall go in and out*. Here are, *First*, Plain directions how to come into the fold: we must come in *by Jesus Christ* as the door. *Secondly*, Precious promises to those who observe this direction. 1. They *shall be saved hereafter*; this is the privilege of *their home*. 2. In the mean time they shall *go in and out and find pasture*; this is the privilege of *their way*.

2. Christ is the *shepherd, vv.* 11, &c. He was prophesied of under the Old Testament as a *shepherd*, Isa. xl. 11; Ezek. xxxiv. 23; xxxvii. 24; Zech xiii. 7. In the New Testament he is spoken of as the *great Shepherd* (Heb. xiii. 20), the *chief Shepherd* (1 v. 4), the *Shepherd and bishop of our souls*, 1 Pet. ii. 25.

(1) Christ is *a shepherd*, and not as the thief, not as those that *came not in by the door*. Observe,

[1] The mischievous design of the thief (*v.* 10): *The thief cometh not* with any good intent, but to *steal, and to kill, and to destroy*.

[2] The gracious design of the shepherd; he is come,

First, To *give life to the sheep*. In opposition to the design of the thief, which is to *kill and destroy* (which was the design of the *scribes* and *Pharisees*) Christ saith, *I am come among men*, 1. That *they might have life*. He came to put life into the flock, the church in general, which had seemed rather like a valley full of dry bones than like a pasture covered over with flocks. 2. That they might have it *more abundantly*. As we read it, it is *comparative*, that they

might have a life *more abundant* than that which was lost and forfeited by sin. But it may be construed without a note of comparison, *that they might have abundance*, or might *have it abundantly*. Life in abundance is *eternal life*, life without death or fear of death, life and *much more*.

Secondly, To *give his life for the sheep*, and this that he might give life *to them* (*v.* 11): *The good shepherd giveth his life for the sheep*. 1. It is the property of every good shepherd to hazard and expose his life for the sheep. 2. It was the prerogative of the great Shepherd to give his life to purchase his flock (Acts xx. 28), to satisfy for their trespass, and to shed his blood to wash and cleanse them.

(2) Christ is *a good shepherd*, and not as a hireling. There were many that were not thieves, aiming to kill and destroy the sheep, but passed for shepherds, yet were very careless in the discharge of their duty, and through their neglect the flock was greatly damaged; *foolish shepherds, idle shepherds*, Zech. xi. 15, 17.

Here are two great instances of the shepherd's goodness.

a. His *acquainting* himself with his flock, with all that belong or in any wise appertain to his flock, which are of two sorts, both known to him:—

(*a*) He is acquainted with all that *are now of his flock* (*vv.* 14, 15), as the good Shepherd (*vv.* 3, 4): *I know my sheep and am known of mine*.

(*b*) He is acquainted with those that are *hereafter to be of this flock* (v. 16): *Other sheep I have, have a right to and an interest in, which are not of this fold*, of the Jewish church; *them also I must bring*.

The happy effect and consequence of this is in two things:—*First*, "They shall hear my voice. Not only my voice shall be heard *among them* (whereas they have not heard, and therefore could not believe, now the *sound* of the gospel shall *go to the ends of the earth*), but it shall be heard *by them*; I will speak, and give to them to hear." Faith comes by hearing, and our diligent observance of the voice of Christ is both a means and an evidence of our being brought to Christ, and to God by him. *Secondly, There shall be one fold and one shepherd.* As there is one shepherd, so there shall be one fold. Both Jews and Gentiles, upon their turning to the faith of Christ, shall be incorporated in one church, be joint and equal sharers in the privileges of it, without distinction.

b. Christ's *offering up himself for his sheep* is another proof of his being a *good shepherd*, and in this he yet more *commended his love*, vv. 15, 17, 18.

(*a*) He declares his purpose of dying for his flock (v. 15): *I lay down my life for the sheep.*

(*b*) He takes off the offence of the cross, which to many is a stone of stumbling, by four considerations:—

[*a*] That his *laying down his life for the sheep* was the condition, the performance of which entitled him to the honours and powers of his exalted state (v. 17).

[*b*] That his laying down his

life was in order to his resuming it: *I lay down my life, that I may receive it again.*

[*c*] That he was perfectly voluntary in his sufferings and death (v. 18): "No one doth or can force my life from me against my will, but I freely *lay it down of myself*, I deliver it as my own act and deed, for I *have* (which no man has) *power to lay it down, and to take it again.*"

[*d*] That he did all this by the express order and appointment of his Father, into which he ultimately resolves the whole affair: *This commandment have I received of my Father.*

THE JEWS DIVIDED
(vv. 19–21)

We have here an account of the people's different sentiments concerning Christ, on occasion of the foregoing discourse. See what the debate was in particular.

I. Some upon this occasion spoke ill of Christ and of his sayings, either openly in the face of the assembly, for his enemies were very impudent, or privately among themselves.

II. Others stood up in defence of him and his discourse, and, though the stream ran strong, dared to swim against it; and, though perhaps they did not believe on him as the Messiah, they could not bear to hear him thus abused. Two things they plead:—1. The excellency of his doctrine: "*These are not the words of him that hath a devil*; they are not idle words; distracted men are not used to talk at this rate." 2. The power of his miracles: *Can a devil*, that is, a man that has a devil, *open the eyes of the blind*? Neither mad men nor bad men can work miracles. Therefore Jesus *had not a devil*.

BELIEVE MY WORKS
(*vv.* 22–38)

We have here another encounter between Christ and the Jews in the temple.

I. We have here the time when this conference was: *It was at the feast of dedication, and it was winter*, a feast that was annually observed by consent, in remembrance of the dedication of a new altar and the purging of the temple, by Judas Maccabæus, after the temple had been profaned and the altar defiled.

II. The place where it was (*v.* 23): *Jesus walked in the temple in Solomon's porch*; so called (Acts iii. 11), not because built by Solomon, but because built in the same place with that which had borne his name in the first temple, and the name was kept up for the greater reputation of it.

III. The conference itself, in which observe,

1. A weighty question put to him by the Jews, *v.* 24. *How long dost thou make us to doubt? If thou be the Christ tell us.*

2. Christ's answer to this question, in which,

(1) He justifies himself as not at all accessary to their infidelity and scepticism, referring them, [1] To what he had said: *I have told you.* He had told them that he was the Son of God, the Son of man, that he had life in himself, that

he had *authority to execute judgment*, &c. And is not this the Christ then? [2] He refers them to his works, to the example of his life, which was not only perfectly pure, but highly beneficent, and of a piece with his doctrine; and especially to his miracles, which he wrought for the confirmation of his doctrine. It was certain that no man could do those miracles except God were with him, and God would not be with him to attest a forgery.

(2) He condemns them for their obstinate unbelief. But the reason he gives is very surprising: "*You believed not, because you are not of my sheep*: you believe not in me, because you belong not to me." [1] "You are not disposed to be my followers, are not of a tractable teachable temper." [2] "You are not *designed* to be my followers; you are not of those that were given me by my Father, to be brought to grace and glory."

(3) He takes this occasion to describe both the gracious disposition and the happy state of those that are his sheep; for such there are, though *they* be not.

[1] To convince them that they were not his sheep, he tells them what were the characters of his sheep. *First*, They *hear his voice* (*v.* 27), for they know it to be his (*v.* 4), and he has undertaken that they shall hear it, *v.* 16. *Secondly*, They *follow him*; they submit to his guidance by a willing obedience to all his commands, and a cheerful conformity to his spirit and pattern. [2] To convince them that it was their great unhappiness and misery not to be of Christ's sheep, he

here describes the blessed state and case of those that are.

First, Our Lord Jesus *takes cognizance* of his sheep: They *hear my voice*, and *I know them*.

Secondly, He has provided a happiness for them, suited to them: *I give unto them eternal life*, v. 28.

Thirdly, He has undertaken for their security and preservation to this happiness.

a. They shall be *saved from everlasting perdition. They shall by no means perish for ever*; so the words are.

b. They cannot be kept from their *everlasting happiness*; it is in reserve, but he that gives it to them will preserve them to it. Christ had himself experienced the power of his Father *upholding* and *strengthening* him, and therefore puts all his followers into his hand too. He that secured the glory of the Redeemer will secure the glory of the redeemed. Further to corroborate the security, that the sheep of Christ may have strong consolation, he asserts the union of these two undertakers: "*I and my Father are one*, and have jointly and severally undertaken for the protection of the saints and their perfection." This denotes more than the harmony, and consent, and good understanding, that were between the Father and the Son in the work of man's redemption. Every good man is so far one with God as to concur with him; therefore it must be meant of the *oneness of the nature* of Father and Son, that they are the same in substance, and equal in power and glory. He proves

that none could pluck them out *of his hand* because they could not pluck them out *of the Father's hand*, which had not been a conclusive argument if the Son had not had the same almighty power with the Father, and consequently been one with him in essence and operation.

IV. The rage, the outrage, of the Jews against him for this discourse: *The Jews took up stones again*, v. 31.

V. Christ's tender expostulation with them upon occasion of this outrage (v. 32). When he could have answered them with fire from heaven, he mildly replied, *Many good works have I shown you from my Father: for which of those works do you stone me?*

VI. Their vindication of the attempt they made upon Christ, and the cause upon which they grounded their prosecution, v. 33.

1. They would not be thought such enemies to their country as to persecute him for a good work: *For a good work we stone thee not.*

2. They would be thought such friends to God and his glory as to prosecute him for blasphemy: *Because that thou, being a man, makest thyself God.* Here is,

(1) A pretended zeal for the law. They seem mightily concerned for the honour of the divine majesty, and to be seized with a religious horror at that which they imagined to be a reproach to it.

(2) A real enmity to the gospel, on which they could not put a greater affront than by representing Christ as a blasphemer. [1] The crime laid to his charge is *blas-*

phemy, speaking reproachfully and despitefully of God. [2] The proof of the crime: *Thou, being a man, makest thyself God.* Now, *First*, Thus far they were in the right, that what Christ said of himself amounted to this—that he was God, for he had said that he was *one with the Father* and that he would *give eternal life*; and Christ does not deny it, which he would have done if it had been a mistaken inference from his words. But, *Secondly*, They were much mistaken when they looked upon him as a *mere man*, and that the Godhead he claimed was a usurpation, and of his own making.

VII. Christ's reply to their accusation of him (for such their vindication of themselves was), and his making good those claims which they imputed to him as blasphemous (*vv.* 34, &c.), where he proves himself to be no blasphemer, by two arguments:—

1. By an argument taken from *God's word.* He appeals to what was *written in their law*, that is, in the Old Testament; whoever opposes Christ, he is sure to have the scripture *on his side.* It is written (Ps. lxxxii. 6), *I have said, You are gods.* It is an argument *from the less to the greater.* If they were gods, much more am I. Observe,

(1) *From what* he argues—from his works, which he had often vouched as his credentials, and the proofs of his mission. As he proved himself sent of God by the *divinity* of his works, so we must prove ourselves allied to Christ by the *Christianity* of ours.

(2) *For what* he argues—*that*

you may know and believe, may believe it intelligently, and with an entire satisfaction, that *the Father is in me and I in him*; which is the same with what he had said (*v.* 30): *I and my Father are one.* The Father was so in the Son as that in him *dwelt all the fulness of the Godhead*, and it was by a divine power that he wrought his miracles; the Son was so in the Father as that he was perfectly acquainted with the whole of his mind, not by communication, but by consciousness, having lain in his bosom. This we must *know*; not know and *explain* (for we cannot by searching find it out to perfection), but know and *believe* it; acknowledging and adoring the depth, when we cannot find the bottom.

MANY BELIEVE (*vv.* 39–42)

We have here the issue of the conference with the Jews. One would have thought it would have convinced and melted them, but their hearts were hardened. Here we are told,

I. How they attacked him by force. Therefore *they sought again to take him, v.* 39. Therefore, 1. Because he had fully answered their charge of blasphemy, and wiped off that imputation, so that they could not for shame go on with their attempts to stone him, therefore they contrived to seize him, and prosecute him as an offender against the state. Or, 2. Because he persevered in the same testimony concerning himself, they persisted in their malice against him.

II. How he avoided them by

flight; not an inglorious retreat, in which there was any thing of human infirmity, but a glorious retirement, in which there was much of a divine power.

III. How he disposed of himself in his retirement: He *went away again beyond Jordan, v.* 40. Now observe,

1. What *shelter* he found there. He went into a private part of the country, and *there he abode*; there he found some rest and quietness, when in Jerusalem he could find none.

2. What *success* he found there. He did not go thither merely for his own security, but to do good there; and he chose to go thither, where John at first baptized (*ch.* i. 28), because there could not but remain some impressions of John's ministry and baptism thereabouts, which would dispose them to receive Christ and his doctrine; for it was not three years since John was baptizing, and Christ was himself baptized here at Bethabara. The event in some measure answered expectation; for we are told,

(1) That they flocked after him (*v.* 41): *Many resorted to him.*

(2) That they reasoned in his favour, and sought arguments to induce them to close with him as much as those at Jerusalem sought objections against him. They said very judiciously, *John did no miracle, but all things that John spoke of this man were true.*

(3) That many believed on him there. Believing that he who wrought such miracles, and in whom John's predictions were fulfilled, was what he declared himself to

be, the Son of God, they gave up themselves to him as his disciples, *v.* 42.

CHAPTER ELEVEN
LAZARUS DIES (*vv.* 1–16)

We have in these verses,

I. A particular account of the parties principally concerned in this story, *vv.* 1, 2. 1. They lived at *Bethany*, a village not far from Jerusalem, where Christ usually lodged when he came up to the feasts. 2. Here was a brother named *Lazarus*; his *Hebrew* name probably was *Eleazar*, which being contracted, and a Greek termination put to it, is made *Lazarus*. 3. Here were two sisters, *Martha* and *Mary*, who seem to have been the housekeepers, and to have managed the affairs of the family, while perhaps Lazarus lived a retired life, and gave himself to study and contemplation. 4. One of the sisters is particularly described to be *that Mary which anointed the Lord with ointment, v.* 2. I think it refers to that anointing of Christ which this evangelist relates (*ch.* xii. 3). This was she *whose brother Lazarus was sick*; and the sickness of those we love is our affliction.

II. The tidings that were sent to our Lord Jesus of the sickness of Lazarus, *v.* 3. *His sisters* knew where Jesus was, a great way off beyond Jordan, and they sent a special messenger to him, to acquaint him with the affliction of their family. The message they sent was very short, not *petitioning*, much less *prescribing* or *pressing*, but barely relating the case with the tender insinuation of a powerful plea, *Lord, behold, he whom thou lovest is sick*. We have great encouragement in our prayers for those who are sick, if we have ground to hope that they are such as Christ loves; and we have reason to love and pray for those whom we have reason to think Christ loves and cares for.

III. An account how Christ entertained the tidings brought him of the illness of his friend.

1. He prognosticated the event and issue of the sickness, and probably sent it as a message to the sisters of Lazarus by the express, to support them while he delayed to come to them. Now one would think it should follow, *When he heard therefore that he was sick* he made all the haste that he could to him; if he loved them, now was a time to show it by hastening to them, for he knew they impatiently expected him. But he took the contrary way to show his love: it is not said, He loved them and *yet* he lingered; but he loved them and *therefore* he lingered; when he heard that his friend was sick, instead of coming post to him, he abode *two days still in the same place where he was*. (1) He *loved them*, that is, had a great opinion of Martha and Mary, of their wisdom and grace, of their faith and patience, above others of his disciples, and therefore he deferred coming to them, that he might try them, that their trial might at last *be found to praise and honour*. (2) He *loved them*, that is, he designed to do something great and extraordinary for them, to

work such a miracle for their relief as he had not wrought for any of his friends; and therefore he delayed coming to them, that Lazarus might be *dead* and *buried* before he came. If Christ had come presently, and cured the sickness of Lazarus, he had done no more than he did for *many*; if he had raised him to life when newly dead, no more than he had done for *some*: but, deferring his relief so long, he had an opportunity of doing more for him than for *any*.

IV. The discourse he had with his disciples when he was about to visit his friends at Bethany, *vv.* 7–16. Two things he discourses about—his own *danger* and Lazarus's *death*.

1. His own danger in going into Judea, *vv.* 7–10.

(1) Here is the notice which Christ gave his disciples of his purpose to go into Judea towards Jerusalem.

(2) Their objection against this journey (*v.* 8): *Master, the Jews of late sought to stone thee, and goest thou thither again?* Here, [1] They remind him of the danger he had been in there not long since. [2] They marvel that he will *go thither again*. "Wilt thou favour those with thy presence that have expelled thee out of their coasts?"

(3) Christ's answer to this objection (*vv.* 9, 10): *Are there not twelve hours in the day?* Man's life is a *day*; this day is divided into various ages, states, and opportunities, as into hours shorter or longer, as God has appointed; the consideration of this should make us not only *very busy*, as to the *work* of life, but also *very*

easy as to the perils of life; our day shall be lengthened out till our work be done, and our testimony finished. This Christ applies to his case, and shows why he must go to Judea, because he had a *clear call* to go. For the opening of this, [1] He shows the comfort and satisfaction which a man has in his own mind while he keeps in the way of his duty, as it is in general prescribed by the word of God, and particularly determined by the providence of God: *If any man walk in the day, he stumbles not.* [2] He shows the pain and peril a man is in who walks not according to this rule (*v.* 10): *If a man walk in the night, he stumbles*; that is, If a man walk in the way of his heart, and the sight of his eyes, and according to the course of this world, he falls into temptations and snares, is liable to great uneasiness, and frightful apprehensions.

2. The death of Lazarus is here discoursed of between Christ and his disciples, *vv.* 11–16, where we have,

(1) The notice Christ gave his disciples of the death of Lazarus, and an intimation that his business into Judea was to look after him, *v.* 11. After he had prepared his disciples for this dangerous march into an enemy's country, he then gives them,

[1] Plain intelligence of the death of Lazarus, though he had received no advice of it: *Our friend Lazarus sleepeth.* He calls the death of a believer a *sleep*: *he sleepeth*. It is good to call death by such names and titles as will help to make it more *familiar* and less *formidable*

to us. The death of Lazarus was in a peculiar sense a sleep, as that of Jairus's daughter, because he was to be raised again speedily; and, since we are sure to *rise again at last*, why should that make any great difference?

[2] Particular intimations of his favourable intentions concerning Lazarus: *but I go, that I may awake him out of sleep.* He could have done it, and yet have staid where he was: he that restored at a distance one that was *dying* (*ch.* iv. 50) could have raised at a distance one that was *dead*; but he would put this honour upon the miracle, to work it by the grave side: *I go, to awake him.*

(2) Their mistake of the meaning of this notice, and the blunder they made about it (*vv.* 12, 13): They said, *Lord, if he sleep, he shall do well.* This intimates, [1] *Some concern* they had for their friend Lazarus; they hoped he would recover; *he shall be saved* from dying at this time. [2] A *greater concern* for themselves; for hereby they insinuate that it was now needless for Christ to go to him, and expose himself and them.

(3) This mistake of theirs rectified (*v.* 13): *Jesus spoke of his death.* See here, [1] How dull of understanding Christ's disciples as yet were. [2] How carefully the evangelist corrects this error: *Jesus spoke of his death.* Those that speak in an unknown tongue, or use similitudes, should learn hence to *explain themselves*, and pray that they may interpret, to prevent mistakes.

(4) The plain and express dec-

laration which Jesus made to them of the death of Lazarus, and his resolution to go to Bethany, *vv*. 14, 15. [1] He gives them notice of the death of Lazarus; what he had before said darkly he now says plainly, and without a figure: *Lazarus is dead, v*. 14. [2] He gives them the reason why he had delayed so long to go and see him: *I am glad for your sakes that I was not there*. If he had been there time enough, he would have healed his disease and prevented his death, which would have been much for the comfort of Lazarus's friends; but then his disciples would have seen no further proof of his power than what they had often seen, and, consequently, their faith had received no improvement. [3] He resolves now to go to Bethany, and take his disciples along with him: *Let us go unto him*.

(5) Thomas exciting his fellow-disciples cheerfully to attend their Master's motions (*v*. 16). *Let us also go that we may die with him; with him*, that is,

[1] With Lazarus, who was now dead; so some take it.

[2] "Let us go and die *with our Master*, who is now exposing himself to death by venturing into Judea"; and so I rather think it is meant.

THE RAISING OF LAZARUS
(*vv*. 17–32)

To Bethany Christ came, and observe,

I. What posture he found his friends there in.

1. He found his friend Lazarus *in the grave, v*. 17. When he came near the town, probably by the burying-place belonging to the town, he was told by the neighbours, or some persons whom he met, that Lazarus had been *four days buried*.

2. He found his friends that survived *in grief*. Martha and Mary were almost swallowed up with sorrow for the death of their brother, which is intimated where it is said that *many of the Jews came to Martha and Mary to comfort them*.

II. What passed between him and his surviving friends at this interview.

1. The interview between Christ and Martha.

(1) We are told that she *went and met him, v*. 20. [1] It should seem that Martha was earnestly expecting Christ's arrival, and enquiring for it. [2] Martha, when the good news was brought that Jesus was coming, threw all aside, and *went and met him*, in token of a most affectionate welcome. She waived all ceremony and compliment to the Jews who came to visit her, and hastened to go and meet Jesus. [3] When Martha went to meet Jesus, Mary *sat still in the house*. Some think she did *not* hear the tidings, being in her drawing-room, receiving visits of condolence, while Martha who was busied in the household-affairs had early notice of it. Perhaps Martha would not tell her sister that Christ was coming, being ambitious of the honour of receiving him first. Others think she *did* hear that Christ was come, but was so overwhelmed with sorrow that she did not care to stir,

choosing rather to indulge her sorrow, and to sit poring upon her affliction, and saying, *I do well to* mourn. Comparing this story with that in Luke x. 38, &c., we may observe the different tempers of these two sisters, and the temptations and advantages of each.

(2) Here is fully related the discourse between Christ and Martha.

[1] Martha's address to Christ, vv. 21, 22.

First, She complains of Christ's long absence and delay. She said it, not only with grief for the death of her brother, but with some resentment of the seeming unkindness of the Master: *Lord, if thou hadst been here, my brother had not died. If thou hadst been here*; whereas she ought to have known that Christ could cure at a distance, and that his gracious operations were not limited to his bodily presence.

Secondly, Yet she corrects and comforts herself with the thoughts of the prevailing interest Christ had in heaven; at least, she blames herself for blaming her Master, and for suggesting that he comes too late: *for I know that even now, desperate as the case is, whatsoever thou wilt ask of God, God will give it to thee.*

[2] The comfortable word which Christ gave to Martha, in answer to her pathetic address (v. 23): *Jesus saith unto her, Thy brother shall rise again.*

[3] The faith which Martha mixed with this word, and the unbelief mixed with this faith, v. 24.

First, She accounts it a *faithful saying* that *he shall rise again at the last day*. Though the doctrine of the resurrection was to have its full proof from Christ's resurrection, yet, as it was already revealed, she firmly believed it, Acts xxiv. 15. 1. That there shall be a *last day*, with which all the days of time shall be numbered and finished. 2. That there shall be a *general* resurrection at that day, when the earth and sea shall give up their dead. 3. That there shall be a *particular* resurrection of each one: "I know that I shall rise again, and this and the other relation that was dear to me." As bone shall return to his bone in that day, so friend to his friend.

Secondly, Yet she seems to think this saying not so well worthy of all acceptation as really it was: "*I know he shall rise again at the last day*; but what are we the better for that now?" As if the comforts of the resurrection to eternal life were not worth speaking of, or yielded not satisfaction sufficient to balance her affliction.

[4] The further instruction and encouragement which Jesus Christ gave her; for he will not quench the smoking flax nor break the bruised reed. He said to her, *I am the resurrection and the life,* vv. 25, 26. Two things Christ possesses her with the belief of, in reference to the present distress; and they are the things which our faith should fasten upon in the like cases.

First, The power of Christ, his sovereign power: *I am the resurrection and the life,* the fountain of life, and the head and author of the resurrection. Martha believed that at his prayer God would give any thing, but he would have her know that by his word he could work any thing. Martha believed a resurrection at the *last day*; Christ tells her that he had that power lodged in his own hand, that the dead were to *hear his voice* (*ch.* v. 25), whence it was easy to infer, He that could raise a world of men that had been dead many ages could doubtless raise one man that had been dead but *four days*.

Secondly, The promises of the new covenant, which give us further ground of hope that *we shall live*. Observe,

a. To whom these promises are made—to those that believe in Jesus Christ, to those that consent to, and confide in, Jesus Christ as the only Mediator of reconciliation and communion between God and man, that receive the record God has given in his word concerning his Son, sincerely comply with it, and answer all the great intentions of it. The condition of the latter promise is thus expressed: *Whosoever liveth and believeth in me*, which may be understood, either, (*a*) Whoever during *life*, while he is here in this state of probation, *believes in me*, shall be happy in me, but after death it will be too late. Or, (*b*) Of *spiritual* life: He that *lives* and *believes* is he that by faith is born again to a heavenly and divine life, to whom *to live is Christ*—that makes Christ the life of his soul.

b. What the promises are (*v.* 25): *Though he die, yet shall he live*,

nay, *he shall never die*, *v.* 26. Man consists of body and soul, and provision is made for the happiness of both.

(*a*) For the *body*; here is the promise of a *blessed resurrection*. Though the body be dead because of sin (there is no remedy but it will die), yet it *shall live again*.

(*b*) For the *soul*; here is the promise of a *blessed immortality*. He that *liveth and believeth*, who, being united to Christ by faith, lives spiritually by virtue of that union, he shall *never die*. Christ asks her, "*Believest thou this?* Canst thou *assent* to it with application? Canst thou take my word for it?"

[5] Martha's unfeigned assent yielded to what Christ said, *v.* 27. We have here Martha's creed, the good confession she witnessed, the same with that for which Peter was commended (Matt. xvi. 16, 17), and it is the *conclusion of the whole matter*.

First, Here is the *guide of her faith*, and that is the word of Christ; without any alteration, exception, or proviso, she takes it entire as Christ had said it: *Yea Lord*, whereby she subscribes to the truth of all and every part of that which Christ had promised, in his own sense: *Even so*. Faith is an echo to divine revelation, returns the same words, and resolves to abide by them: *Yea, Lord*.

Secondly, The *ground of her faith*, and that is the authority of Christ; she believes *this* because she believes that he who saith it is Christ. She has recourse to the foundation for the support of the superstructure. Observe here, *a.* What she believed and confessed concerning Jesus; three things, all to the same effect:— (*a*) That he was the Christ, or Messiah, promised and expected under this name and notion, the *anointed one.* (*b*) That he was the *Son of God*; so the Messiah was called (Ps. ii. 7), not by office only, but by nature. (*c*) That it was *he who should come* into the world.

b. What she inferred hence, and what she alleged this for. If she admits this, that Jesus is the Christ, there is no difficulty in believing that he is the resurrection and the life.

2. The interview between Christ and Mary the other sister. And here observe,

(1) The notice which Martha gave her of Christ's coming (*v.* 28): *When she had so said,* as one that needed to say no more, *she went her way,* easy in her mind, and *called Mary her sister.*

(2) The haste which Mary made to Christ upon this notice given her (*v.* 29): *As soon as she heard* this good news, that the *Master was come,* she *arose quickly,* and came to him.

(3) We are told (*v.* 30) where she found the Master; he was not yet come into Bethany, but was at the town's end, *in that place where Martha met him.*

(4) The misconstruction which the Jews that were with Mary made of her going away so hastily (*v.* 31): They said, *She goes to the grave, to weep there.* Martha bore up better under this affliction than Mary did, who was a woman of a tender and sorrowful spirit; such was her natural temper. Those that

are so have need to watch against melancholy, and ought to be pitied and helped. These comforters found that their formalities did her no service, but that she hardened herself in sorrow: and therefore concluded when she went out, and turned that way, it was to go *to the grave* and *weep there.*

(5) Mary's address to our Lord Jesus (*v.* 32): She came, attended with her train of comforters, and *fell down at his feet,* as one overwhelmed with a passionate sorrow, and said with many tears (as appears *v.* 33), *Lord, if thou hadst been here, my brother had not died,* as Martha said before, for they had often said it to one another. Mary added no more, as Martha did; but it appears, by what follows, that what she fell short in words she made up in tears; she said less than Martha, but wept more; and tears of devout affection have a voice, a loud prevailing voice, in the ears of Christ; no rhetoric like this.

AT THE TOMB (*vv.* 33–44)

Here we have, I. Christ's tender *sympathy* with his afflicted friends, and the share he took to himself in their sorrows, which appeared three ways:—

1. By the inward groans and troubles of his spirit (*v.* 33): *Jesus saw Mary weeping* for the loss of a loving brother, and the *Jews that came with her weeping* for the loss of a good neighbour and friend; when he saw what a *place of weepers,* a *bochim,* this was, *he groaned in the spirit, and was troubled.*

2. His concern for them appeared by his *kind enquiry* after the poor remains of his deceased friend (*v.* 34): Where *have you laid him?*

3. It appeared by *his tears.* Those about him did not tell him where the body was buried, but desired him to *come and see,* and led him directly to the grave, that his eye might yet more affect his heart with the calamity.

(1) As he was going to the grave, as if he had been following the corpse thither, *Jesus wept, v.* 35. A very short verse, but it affords many useful instructions. [1] That Jesus Christ was really and truly man, and partook with the children, not only of flesh and blood, but of a human soul, susceptible of the impressions of joy, and grief, and other affections. Christ gave this proof of his humanity, in both senses of the word; that, as a man, he could weep, and, as a merciful man, he *would weep,* before he gave this proof of his divinity. [2] That he was *a man of sorrows,* and *acquainted with grief,* as was foretold, Isa. liii. 3. We never read that he laughed, but more than once we have him in tears. [3] Tears of compassion well become Christians, and make them most to resemble Christ.

(2) Different constructions were put upon Christ's weeping. [1] Some made a kind and candid interpretation of it, and what was very natural (*v.* 36): *Then said the Jews, Behold how he loved him!* [2] Others made a peevish unfair reflection upon it, as if these tears bespoke his inability to help his friend (*v.* 37): *Could not this man,* who opened the eyes of the blind, have prevented the death of Lazarus? Here it is slily insinuated, *First,* That the death of Lazarus being (as it seemed by his tears) a great grief to him, if he could have prevented it he would, and therefore because he *did not* they incline to think that he *could not. Secondly,* That therefore it might justly be questioned whether he did indeed *open the eyes of the blind,* that is, whether it was not a sham.

II. Christ's approach to the grave, and the preparation that was made for working this miracle.

1. Christ repeats his groans upon his coming near the grave (*v.* 38): *Again groaning in himself, he comes to the grave;* he groaned, (1) Being displeased at the unbelief of those who spoke doubtingly of his power, and blamed him for not preventing the death of Lazarus; he was *grieved for the hardness of their hearts.* (2) Being affected with the fresh lamentations which, it is likely, the mourning sisters made, when they came near the grave, more passionately and pathetically than before, his tender spirit was sensibly touched with their wailings. (3) Some think that he *groaned in spirit* because, to gratify the desire of his friends, he was to bring Lazarus again into this sinful troublesome world, from that rest into which he was newly entered; it would be a kindness to Martha and Mary, but it would be to him like thrusting one out to a stormy sea again who was newly got into a safe and quiet harbour. (4) Christ groaned as

one that would affect himself with the calamitous state of the human nature, as subject to death, from which he was now about to redeem Lazarus.

2. The grave wherein Lazarus lay is here described: *It was a cave, and a stone lay upon it.*

3. Orders are given to remove the stone (*v.* 39): *Take away the stone.* He would have this stone removed that all the standers-by might see the body lie dead in the sepulchre, and that way might be made for its coming out, and it might appear to be a true body, and not a *ghost* or *spectre*.

4. An objection made by Martha against the opening of the grave: *Lord, by this time he stinketh.* He is *four days old* in the other world; a citizen and inhabitant of the grave of four days' standing. Probably Martha perceived the body to smell, as they were removing the stone, and therefore cried out thus.

5. The gentle reproof Christ gave to Martha for the weakness of her faith (*v.* 40): *Said I not unto thee that if thou wouldest believe thou shouldest see the glory of God?* This word of his to her was not before recorded; it is probable that he said it to her when she had said (*v.* 27), *Lord, I believe*: and it is enough that it is recorded here, where it is repeated.

6. The opening of the grave, in obedience to Christ's order, notwithstanding Martha's objection (*v.* 41): *Then they took away the stone.*

III. The miracle itself wrought. Their expectations being raised, our Lord Jesus addresses himself to his work.

1. He applies himself to his *living Father in heaven,* so he had called him (*ch.* vi. 17), and so eyes him here.

(1) The gesture he used was very significant: *He lifted up his eyes,* an outward expression of the elevation of his mind, and to show those who stood by whence he derived his power.

(2) His address to God was with great assurance, and such a confidence as became him: *Father, I thank thee that thou hast heard me.*

[1] He has here taught us, by his own example, *First,* In prayer to call God Father, and to draw nigh to him as children to a father, with a humble reverence, and yet with a holy boldness. *Secondly,* In our *prayers* to *praise him,* and, when we come to beg for further mercy, thankfully to acknowledge former favours.

[2] But our Saviour's thanksgiving here was intended to express the unshaken assurance he had of the effecting of this miracle, which he had in his own power to do in concurrence with his Father.

First, Christ speaks of this miracle as an answer to prayer, 1. Because he would thus *humble himself*; though he was a Son, yet *learned he this obedience,* to ask and receive. 2. Because he was pleased thus to *honour prayer,* making it the key wherewith even he unlocked the treasures of divine power and grace.

Secondly, Christ, being assured that his prayer was answered, professes,

a. His thankful acceptance of

this answer: *I thank thee that thou hast heard me.*

b. His cheerful assurance of a ready answer at any time (*v.* 42): *And I know that thou hearest me always.* Let none think that this was some uncommon favour granted him now, such as he never had before, nor should ever have again; no, he had the same divine power going along with him in his whole undertaking, and undertook nothing but what he knew to be agreeable to the counsel of God's will.

Thirdly, But why should Christ give this public intimation of his obtaining this miracle by prayer? He adds, It is *because of the people who stand by, that they may believe that thou hast sent me*; for *prayer may preach.*

2. He now applies himself to his *dead friend in the earth.* He *cried with a loud voice, Lazarus come forth.*

(1) He could have raised Lazarus by a silent exertion of his power and will, and the indiscernible operations of the Spirit of life; but he did it by a call, a loud call,

[1] To be significant of the power then put forth for the raising of Lazarus, how he *created this new thing*; he *spoke, and it was done.*

[2] To be typical of other works of wonder, and particularly other resurrections, which the power of Christ was to effect. This loud call was a figure, *First,* Of the gospel call, by which dead souls were to be brought out of the grave of sin, which resurrection Christ had formerly spoken of (*ch.* v. 25), and of his word as

the means of it (*ch.* vi. 63), and now he gives a specimen of it.

(2) This *loud call* was but *short*, yet *mighty through God* to the battering down of the strongholds of the grave.

(3) This miracle was wrought, [1] *Speedily.* Nothing intervenes between the command, *Come forth*, and the effect, *He came forth.* Thus the change in the resurrection will be *in a moment, in the twinkling of an eye,* 1 Cor. xv. 52. [2] *Perfectly.* He was so thoroughly revived that he got up out of his grave as strongly as ever he got up out of his bed, and returned not only to life, but health. He was not raised to serve a present turn, but to live as other men. [3] With this additional miracle, as some reckon it, that he came out of his grave, though he was fettered with his grave-clothes, with which he was *bound hand and foot,* and *his face bound about with a napkin* (for so the manner of the Jews was to bury); and he came forth in the same dress wherein he was buried, that it might appear that it was he himself and not another, and that he was not only alive, but strong, and able to walk, after a sort, even in his grave-clothes. Lazarus being *come forth*, hampered and embarrassed with his grave-clothes, we may well imagine that those about the grave were exceedingly surprised and frightened at it; we should be so if we should see a dead body rise; but Christ, to make the thing familiar, sets them to work: "*Loose him,* slacken his grave-clothes, that they may serve for day-clothes till he comes to his house, and then he will go

himself, so clad, without guide or supporter to his own house."

REACTIONS (*vv.* 45–57)

We have here an account of the consequences of this glorious miracle, which were as usual; to some it was a savour of life unto life, to others of death unto death.

I. Some were invited by it, and induced to believe. Many of the Jews, when they *saw the things that Jesus did, believed on him,* and well they might, for it was an incontestable proof of his divine mission.

II. Others were irritated by it, and hardened in their unbelief.

1. The *informers* were so (*v.* 46): *Some of them,* who were eye-witnesses of the miracle, were so far from being convinced that they *went to the Pharisees,* whom they knew to be his implacable enemies, and *told them what things Jesus had done.*

2. The judges, the leaders, the *blind leaders,* of the people were no less exasperated by the report made to them, and here we are told what they did.

(1) A special council is called and held (*v.* 47).

(2) The case is proposed, and shown to be weighty and of great consequence.

[1] The matter to be debated was what course they should take with this Jesus, to stop the growth of his interest.

[2] That which made this matter weighty was the peril they apprehended their church and nation to be in from the Romans (*v.* 48): "If we do not silence him, and take him off, *all men will believe*

on him; and, this being the setting up of a new king, the Romans will take umbrage at it, *and will come* with an army, and *take away our place and nation,* and therefore it is no time to trifle."

(3) Caiaphas makes a malicious but mystical speech in the council on this occasion.

[1] The *malice* of it appears evident at first view, *vv.* 49, 50. He, being the high priest, and so president of the council, took upon him to decide the matter before it was debated. Here,

First, The counsellor was Caiaphas, who was *high priest that same year.*

Secondly, The drift of the advice was, in short, this, That some way or other must be found out to put Jesus to death. We have reason to think that they strongly suspected him to be indeed the Messiah; but his doctrine was so contrary to their darling traditions and secular interest, and his design did so thwart their notions of the Messiah's kingdom, that they resolve, be he who he will, he must be put to death.

Thirdly, This is plausibly insinuated, with all the subtlety as well as malice of the old serpent. 1. He suggests his own sagacity, which we must suppose him as high priest to excel in, though the *Urim* and *Thummim* were long since lost. 2. He takes it for granted that the case is plain and past dispute, and that those are very ignorant who do not see it to be so. 3. He insists upon a maxim in politics, That the welfare of communities is to be preferred before that of particular persons.

It is expedient for us as priests, whose all lies at stake, that *one man die for the people.* Thus far it holds true, that it is *expedient,* and more than so, it is truly *honourable,* for a man to hazard his life in the service of his country (Phil. ii. 17; 1 John iii. 16); but to put an innocent man to death under colour of consulting the public safety is the devil's policy.

[2] The *mystery* that was in this counsel of Caiaphas does not appear at first view, but the evangelist leads us into it (*vv.* 51, 52). Here is a precious comment upon a pernicious text; the counsel of cursed Caiaphas so construed as to fall in with the counsels of the blessed God.

(4) The evangelist explains and enlarges upon Caiaphas's words.

[1] He explains what he said, and shows how it not only was, but was intended to be, accommodated to an excellent purpose. He did not *speak it of himself.* As it was an artifice to stir up the council against Christ, he spoke it of himself, or of the devil rather; but as it was an *oracle,* declaring it the purpose and design of God by the death of Christ to save God's spiritual Israel from sin and wrath, he did not speak it of himself, for he knew nothing of the matter, he *meant not so, neither did his heart think so,* for nothing was in his heart but to destroy and cut off, Isa. x. 7.

First, He *prophesied,* and those that prophesied did not, in their prophesying, *speak of themselves.*

Secondly, He prophesied, *being high priest that year;* not that his being high priest did at all dispose or qualify him to be a prophet; we cannot suppose the pontifical mitre to have first inspired with prophecy the basest head that ever wore it; but, 1. Being high priest, and therefore of note and eminence in the conclave, God was pleased to put this significant word into his mouth rather than into the mouth of any other, that it might be the more observed or the non-observance of it the more aggravated. 2. Being high priest *that year,* that famous year, in which there was to be such a plentiful effusion of the Spirit, more than had ever been yet, according to the prophecy (Joel ii. 28, 29, compared with Acts ii. 17), some drops of the blessed shower light upon Caiaphas, as the crumbs (says Dr. Lightfoot) of the children's bread, which fall from the table among the dogs. This year was the year of the expiration of the Levitical priesthood; and out of the mouth of him who was that year high priest was extorted an implicit resignation of it to him who should not (as they had done for many ages) offer beasts for that nation, but offer himself, and so make an end of the *sin-offering.* This resignation he made *unwittingly,* as Isaac gave the blessing to Jacob.

Thirdly, The matter of his prophecy was *that Jesus should die for that nation,* the very thing to which all the prophets bore witness, who *testified beforehand the sufferings of Christ* (1 Pet. i. 11), that the death of Christ must be the life and salvation of Israel. He so died for *that nation* as that *the whole nation should not perish,* but that *a remnant should be saved*, Rom. xi. 5.

[2] The evangelist enlarges upon this word of Caiaphas (*v.* 52), *not for that nation only*, how much soever it thought itself the darling of Heaven, but *that also he should gather together in one the children of God that were scattered abroad*.

He died to *gather in* those who wandered, and to *gather together in one* those who were scattered; to invite those to him who were at a distance from him, and to unite those in him who were at a distance from each other.

(5) The result of this debate is a resolve of the council to put Jesus to death (*v.* 53): *From that day they took counsel together, to put him to death*.

(6) Christ hereupon absconded, knowing very well what was the vote of their close cabal, *v.* 54.

[1] He suspended his public appearances: *He walked no more openly among the Jews*.

[2] He withdrew into an obscure part of the country, so obscure that the name of the town he retired to is scarcely met with any where else. It was not because he either feared the power of his enemies or distrusted his own power; he had many ways to save himself, and was neither averse to suffering nor unprepared for it; but he retired, *First*, To put a mark of his displeasure upon Jerusalem and the people of the Jews. *Secondly*, To render the cruelty of his enemies against him the more inexcusable. *Thirdly*, His hour was *not yet come*. *Fourthly*, His retirement, for a while, was to make his return into

Jerusalem, when his hour was come, the more remarkable and illustrious.

(7) The strict enquiry made for him during his recess, *vv.* 55–57.

[1] The occasion of it was the approach of the passover, at which they expected his presence, according to custom (*v.* 55).

[2] The enquiry was very solicitous: *They said, What think you, that he will not come to the feast?* *v.* 56.

First, Some think this was said by those who wished well to him, and expected his coming, that they might hear his doctrine and see his miracles.

Secondly, It should rather seem that they were his enemies who made this enquiry after him, who wished for an opportunity to lay hands on him.

[3] The orders issued out by the government for the apprehending of him were very strict, *v.* 57. Yet such was his interest in the affections of some, and such God's hold of the consciences of others, that he continued undiscovered, for the *Lord hid him*.

CHAPTER TWELVE
RETURN TO BETHANY
(*vv.* 1–11)

In these verses we have,

I. The *kind visit* our Lord Jesus paid to his friends at Bethany, *v.* 1. His coming to Bethany now may be considered,

1. As a preface to the passover he intended to celebrate, to which reference is made in assigning the date of his coming: *Six days before the passover*.

2. As a voluntary exposing of himself to the fury of his enemies; now that his hour was at hand he came within their reach, and freely offered himself to them, though he had shown them how easily he could evade all their snares.

3. An instance of his kindness to his friends at Bethany, whom he loved, and from whom he was shortly to be taken away.

II. The *kind entertainment* which his friends there gave him. Lazarus was *one of those that sat at meat*. It proved the truth of his resurrection, as it did of Christ's, that there were those who did *eat and drink with him*, Acts x. 41.

III. The particular respect which Mary showed him, above the rest, in anointing his feet with sweet ointment, *v.* 3. She had a *pound of ointment of spikenard, very costly*, which probably she had by her for her own use; but the death and resurrection of her brother had quite weaned her from the use of all such things, and with this she *anointed the feet of Jesus*, and, as a further token of her reverence for him and negligence of herself, she *wiped them with her hair*, and this was taken notice of by all that were present, for *the house was filled with the odour of the ointment*. See Prov. xxvii. 16.

IV. Judas's dislike of Mary's compliment, or token of her respect to Christ, *vv.* 4, 5, where observe,

1. The person that carped at it was Judas, *one of his disciples*; not one of their nature, but only one of their number.

2. The pretence with which he covered his dislike (*v.* 5). (1) Here

is a foul iniquity gilded over with a specious and plausible pretence, for Satan transforms himself into an angel of light. (2) Here is worldly wisdom passing a censure upon pious zeal, as guilty of imprudence and mismanagement. (3) Here is charity to the poor made a colour for opposing a piece of piety to Christ, and secretly made a cloak for covetousness.

3. The detection and discovery of Judas's hypocrisy herein, *v.* 6. Here is the evangelist's remark upon it, by the direction of him who *searches the heart: This he said, not that he cared for the poor*, as he pretended, *but because he was a thief, and had the bag*.

V. Christ's justification of what Mary did (*vv.* 7, 8): *Let her alone*. For Mary's justification,

1. Christ puts a favourable construction upon what she did, which those that condemned it were not aware of: *Against the day of my burying she has kept this*. Or, *She has reserved this for the day of my embalming*; so Dr. Hammond.

2. He gives a sufficient answer to Judas's objection, *v.* 8. (1) It is so ordered in the kingdom of Providence that *the poor we have always with us*, some or other that are proper objects of charity (Deut. xv. 11); such there will be as long as there are in this lapsed state of mankind so much folly and so much affliction. (2) It is so ordered in the kingdom of grace that the church should not always have the bodily presence of Jesus Christ: "*Me you have not always*, but only now for a

little time." Note, We need wisdom, when two duties come in competition, to know which to give the preference to, which must be determined by the circumstances.

VI. The public notice which was taken of our Lord Jesus here at this supper in Bethany (*v.* 9). 1. They came to see Jesus, whose name was very much magnified, and made considerable by the late miracle he had wrought in raising Lazarus. 2. They came to see Lazarus and Christ together, which was a very inviting sight.

VII. The indignation of the chief priests at the growing interest of our Lord Jesus, and their plot to crush it (*vv.* 10, 11). Here observe,

1. How vain and unsuccessful their attempts against Christ had hitherto been. They had done all they could to alienate the people from him, and exasperate them against him, and yet many of the Jews, their neighbours, their creatures, their admirers, were so overcome by the convincing evidence of Christ's miracles that they *went away* from the interest and party of the priests, went off from obedience to their tyranny, *and believed on Jesus*; and it was by reason of. Lazarus; his resurrection put life into their faith, and convinced them that this Jesus was undoubtedly the Messiah, and had life in himself, and power to give life. This miracle confirmed them in the belief of his other miracles, which they had heard he wrought in Galilee: what was impossible to him that could raise the dead?

2. How absurd and unreasonable

this day's vote was—that Lazarus must be put to death. For, (1) If they had feared God, they would not have done such an act of defiance to him. God will have Lazarus to live by miracle, and they will have him to die by malice. (2) If they had regarded man, they would not have done such an act of injustice to Lazarus, an innocent man, to whose charge they could not pretend to lay any crime.

PALM SUNDAY (*vv.* 12–19)

This story of Christ's riding in triumph to Jerusalem is recorded by all the evangelists, as worthy of special remark. We may observe,

I. The respect that was paid to our Lord Jesus by the common people, *vv.* 12, 13.

II. The posture Christ puts himself into for receiving the respect that was paid him (*v.* 14): *When he had found*, or procured, *a young ass*, he *sat thereon*. It was but a poor sort of figure he made, he alone upon an ass, and a crowd of people about him shouting *Hosanna*.

III. The fulfilling of the scripture in this: *As it is written, Fear not, daughter of Sion*, *v.* 15. This is quoted from Zech. ix. 9. To him bore all the prophets witness, and particularly to this concerning him.

IV. The remark made by the evangelist respecting the disciples (*v.* 16): *They understood not at first* why Christ did this, and how the scripture was fulfilled; but when *Jesus was glorified*, and thereupon the Spirit poured out, then they remembered that *these things were written of him* in the

Old Testament, and that they and others had, in pursuance thereof, *done these things to him*.

V. The reason which induced the people to pay this respect to our Lord Jesus upon his coming into Jerusalem, though the government was so much set against him. It was because of the illustrious miracle he had lately wrought in raising Lazarus.

VI. The indignation of the Pharisees at all this; some of them probably, saw, and they all soon heard of, Christ's public entry. The committee appointed to find out expedients to crush him thought they had gained their point when he had retired unto privacy, and that he would soon be forgotten in Jerusalem, but they now rage and fret when they see they imagined but a *vain thing*.

GREEKS ASK FOR JESUS
(*vv.* 20–26)

Honour is here paid to Christ by certain Greeks that enquired for him with respect.

I. We are told who they were that paid this honour to our Lord Jesus: *Certain Greeks among* the people who *came to worship at the feast, v.* 20. Some think they were *Jews of the dispersion*, some of the twelve tribes that were scattered among the Gentiles, and were called *Greeks*, Hellenist Jews; but others think they were Gentiles, those whom they called *proselytes of the gate*, such as the eunuch and Cornelius.

II. What was the honour they paid him: they desired to be acquainted with him, *v.* 21. Their business is, they would *see Jesus*;

not only see his face, that they might be able to say, when they came home, they had seen one that was so much talked of (it is probable they had seen him when he appeared publicly); but they would have some free conversation with him, and be taught by him, for which it was no easy thing to find him at leisure, his hands were so full of public work.

III. Christ's acceptance of this honour paid him, signified by what he said to the people hereupon, *vv.* 23, &c., where he foretells both the honour which he himself should have in being followed (*vv.* 23, 24) and the honour which those should have that followed him, *vv.* 25, 26. This was intended for the direction and encouragement of these Greeks, and all others that desired acquaintance with him.

1. He foresees that plentiful harvest, in the conversion of the Gentiles, of which this was as it were the first-fruits, *v.* 23. Observe,

(1) The end designed hereby, and that is the glorifying of the Redeemer.

(2) The strange way in which this end was to be attained, and that was by the death of Christ, intimated in that similitude (*v.* 24): "*Verily, verily, I say unto you,* you to whom I have spoken of my death and sufferings, *except a corn of wheat* fall not only *to,* but *into, the ground,* and *die,* and be buried and lost, it *abideth alone,* and you never see any more of it; but *if it die* according to the course of nature (otherwise it would be a miracle) it *bringeth forth much fruit,* God giving to

every seed its own body." Christ is the corn of wheat, the most valuable and useful grain. Now here is,

[1] The necessity of Christ's humiliation intimated. He must *pour out his soul unto death*, else he cannot *divide a portion with the great*, Isa. liii. 12.

[2] The advantage of Christ's humiliation illustrated. He *fell to the ground* in his incarnation, seemed to be buried alive in this earth, so much was his glory veiled; but this was not all: *he died*. The salvation of souls hitherto, and henceforward to the end of time, is all owing to the dying of this *corn of wheat*.

2. He foretells and promises an abundant recompence to those who should cordially embrace him and his gospel and interest, and should make it appear that they do so by their faithfulness in suffering for him or in serving him.

(1) In suffering for him (*v.* 25). This doctrine Christ much insisted on, it being the great design of his religion to wean us from this world, by setting before us another world.

(2) In serving him (*v.* 26). The Greeks desired to see Jesus (*v.* 21), but Christ lets them know that it was not enough to see him, they must *serve him*. He did not come into the world, to be a show for us to gaze at, but a king to be ruled by.

[1] Here is the work which Christ expects from his servants; and it is very easy and reasonable, and such as becomes them.

First, Let them attend their Master's movements: *If any man serve me, let him follow me.*

Secondly, Let them attend their Master's repose: *Where I am, there let my servant be*, to wait upon me. Christ is where his church is, in the assemblies of his saints, where his ordinances are administered; and *there let his servants be*.

[2] Here are the wages which Christ promises to his servants; and they are very rich and noble.

First, They shall be happy with him: *Where I am, there shall also my servant be*. Those that follow him in the way shall be with him in the end.

Secondly, They shall be honoured by his Father. Those that wait on Christ God will put honour upon, such as will be taken notice of another day, though now under a veil.

A VOICE FROM HEAVEN
(*vv.* 27–36)

Honour is here done to Christ by his Father in a voice from heaven, occasioned by the following part of his discourse, and which gave occasion to a further conference with the people. In these verses we have,

I. Christ's address to his Father, upon occasion of the trouble which seized his spirit at this time: *Now is my soul troubled, v.* 27. Observe,

1. Christ's dread of his approaching sufferings: *Now is my soul troubled*. Now the black and dismal scene began, now were the first throes of the travail of his soul, now his agony began, his soul *began to be exceedingly sorrowful.*

2. The strait he seems to be in hereupon, intimated in those words,

And what shall I say? This does not imply his consulting with any other, as if he needed advice, but considering with himself what was fit to be said now.

3. His prayer to God in this strait: *Father, save me from this hour—out of this hour*, praying, not so much that it might not come as that he might be brought through it.

4. His acquiescence in his Father's will, notwithstanding. He presently corrects himself, and, as it were, recalls what he had said: *But for this cause came I to this hour.* Innocent nature got the first word, but divine wisdom and love got the last.

5. His regard to his Father's honour herein. Upon the withdrawing of his former petition, he presents another, which he will abide by: *Father, glorify thy name*, to the same purport with *Father, thy will be done*; for God's will is for his own glory.

II. The Father's answer to this address; for he heard him always, and does still. Observe, 1. How this answer was given. By a voice from heaven. 2. What the answer was. It was an express return to that petition, *Father, glorify thy name: I have glorified it* already, and *I will glorify it yet again.* When we pray as we are taught, *Our Father, hallowed be thy name*, this is a comfort to us, that it is an answered prayer; answered to Christ here, and in him to all true believers.

III. The opinion of the standers-by concerning this voice, *v.* 29. We may hope there were some among them whose minds were so well prepared to receive a divine revelation that they understood what was said and bore record of it. But notice is here taken of the perverse suggestion of the multitude: some of them said that *it thundered*; others, who took notice that there was plainly an articulate intelligible voice, said that certainly *an angel spoke to him.* Now this shows, 1. That it was a real thing, even in the judgment of those that were not at all well affected to him. 2. That they were loth to admit so plain a proof of Christ's divine mission. They would rather say that it was this, or that, or any thing, than that God spoke to him in answer to his prayer.

IV. The account which our Saviour himself gives of this voice.

1. Why it was sent (*v.* 30): "It came *not because of me*, not merely for my encouragement and satisfaction" (then it might have been whispered in his ear privately), "*but for your sakes*". (1) "That all you who heard it may *believe that the Father hath sent me.*" (2) "That you my disciples, who are to follow me in sufferings, may therein be comforted with the same comforts that carry me on."

2. What was the meaning of it.

(1) That by the death of Christ Satan should be conquered (*v.* 31): *Now is the judgment.* He speaks with a divine exultation and triumph.

(2) That by the death of Christ souls should be converted, and this would be the casting out of Satan (*v.* 32): *If I be lifted up from the earth, I will draw all men unto me.* Here observe two things:—

[1] The great design of our Lord Jesus, which was to *draw all men to him*, not the Jews only, who had been long in profession a people *near to God*, but the Gentiles also, who had been *afar off*; for he was to be the *desire of all nations* (Hag. ii. 7), and *to him must the gathering of the people be.*

[2] The strange method he took to accomplish his design by *being lifted up from the earth*. What he meant by this, to prevent mistake, we are told (*v.* 33): *This he spoke signifying by what death he should die*, the death of the cross, though they had designed and attempted to stone him to death. He that was crucified was first nailed to the cross, and then lifted up upon it. He was *lifted up as a spectacle to the world*; lifted up between heaven and earth, as unworthy of either; yet the word here used signifies an honourable advancement—*If I be exalted*; he reckoned his sufferings his honour. Now Christ's drawing all men to him followed his being *lifted up from the earth*. *First*, It followed after it in time. The great increase of the church was after the death of Christ. *Secondly*, It followed upon it as a blessed consequence of it. Note, There is a powerful virtue and efficacy in the death of Christ to draw souls to him.

V. The people's exception against what he said, and their cavil at it, *v.* 34. Christ had called himself the *Son of man* (*v.* 23), which they knew to be one of the titles of the Messiah, Dan. vii. 13. He had also said that the *Son of man must be lifted up* which they understood of his dying, and probably he

explained himself. Now against this,

1. They alleged those scriptures of the Old Testament which speak of the perpetuity of the Messiah, that he should be so far from being cut off in the midst of his days that he should be a *priest for ever* (Ps. cx. 4), and a king *for ever* (Ps. lxxxix. 29, &c.), that he should have *length of days for ever and ever*, and *his years as many generations* (Ps. xxi. 4; lxi. 6), from all which they inferred that the Messiah should not die. Their perverseness in opposing this to what Jesus had said will appear if we consider, (1) That, when they vouched the scripture to prove that the Messiah *abideth for ever*, they took no notice of those texts which speak of the Messiah's death and sufferings. (2) That, when they opposed what Christ said concerning the sufferings of the Son of man, they took no notice of what he had said concerning his glory and exaltation.

2. They asked hereupon, *Who is this Son of man?* This they asked, not with a desire to be instructed, but tauntingly and insultingly, as if now they had baffled him, and run him down.

VI. What Christ said to this exception, or rather what he said *upon* it. "*Yet a little while*, and but a little while, *is the light with you*; therefore be wise for yourselves, and *walk while you have the light*."

1. In general, we may observe here, (1) The concern Christ has for the souls of men, and his desire of their welfare.

2. Particularly we have here,

(1) The advantage they enjoyed in having Christ and his gospel among them, with the shortness and uncertainty of their enjoyment of it: *Yet a little while is the light with you.*

(2) The warning given them to make the best of this privilege while they enjoyed it, because of the danger they were in of losing it: *Walk while you have the light.*

(3) The sad condition of those who have sinned away the gospel, and are come to the period of their day of grace. *They walk in darkness,* and know neither *where* they go, nor *whither* they go; neither the way they are walking in, nor the end they are walking towards.

(4) The great duty and interest of every one of us inferred from all this (*v.* 36): *While you have light, believe in the light.* The Jews had now Christ's presence with them, let them improve it; afterwards they had the first offers of the gospel made to them by the apostles wherever they came; now this is an admonition to them not to out-stand their market, but to accept the offer when it was made to them: the same Christ saith to all who enjoy the gospel.

VII. Christ's retiring from them, hereupon: *These things spoke Jesus,* and said no more at this time, but left this to their consideration, *and departed, and did hide himself from them.* He hid himself from their rage and fury, retreating, it is probable, to Bethany, where he lodged. By this it appears that what he said irritated and exasperated them, and they were made worse by that which should have made them better.

HARD HEARTS (*vv.* 37–41)

We have here the honour done to our Lord Jesus by the Old-Testament prophets, who foretold and lamented the infidelity of the many that believed not on him. Two things are here said concerning this untractable people, and both were foretold by the evangelical prophet Isaiah, that they *did not* believe, and that they *could not* believe.

I. They did not believe (*v.* 37): *Though he had done so many miracles before them,* which, one would think, should have convinced them, yet they believed not, but opposed him.

II. They could not believe, and *therefore* they could not *because Esaias said, He hath blinded their eyes.* This is a hard saying, who can explain it? We are sure that God is infinitely just and merciful, and therefore we cannot think there is in any such an impotency to good, resulting from the counsels of God, as lays them under a fatal necessity of being evil. God damns none by mere sovereignty; yet it is said, *They could not believe.*

1. They *could not* believe, that is, they *would not;* they were obstinately resolved in their infidelity; thus Chrysostom and Austin incline to understand it; and the former gives divers instances of scripture of the putting of an impotency to signify the invincible refusal of the will, as Gen. xxxvii. 4, *They could not speak peaceably to him.* And

ch. vii. 7. This is a *moral* impotency, like that of one that is accustomed to do evil, Jer. xiii. 23. But,

2. They could not because Esaias had said, *He hath blinded their eyes.* Here the difficulty increases; it is certain that God is not the author of sin, and yet,

(1) There is a righteous hand of God sometimes to be acknowledged in the blindness and obstinacy of those who persist in impenitency and unbelief, by which they are justly punished for their former resistance of the divine light and rebellion against the divine law.

Observe the method of conversion implied here, and the steps taken in it. [1] Sinners are brought to *see with their eyes,* to discern the reality of divine things and to have some knowledge of them. [2] To *understand with their heart,* to apply these things to themselves; not only to assent and approve, but to consent and accept. [3] To *be converted,* and effectually turned from sin to Christ, from the world and the flesh to God, as their felicity and portion. [4] Then God will *heal* them, will justify and sanctify them; will *pardon* their sins, which are as bleeding wounds, and mortify their corruptions, which are as lurking diseases. Now when God denies his grace nothing of this is done; the alienation of the mind from, and its aversion to, God and the divine life, grow into a rooted and invincible antipathy, and so the case becomes desperate.

(2) Judicial blindness and hardness are in the word of God threatened against those who wilfully persist in wickedness, and were particularly foretold concerning the Jewish church and nation. Known unto God are all his works, and all ours too. Christ knew before who would betray him, and spoke of it, *ch.* vi. 70. This is a confirmation of the truth of scripture prophecies, and thus even the unbelief of the Jews may help to strengthen our faith. It is also intended for caution to particular persons, to *beware lest that come upon them which was spoken of in the prophets,* Acts xiii. 40.

(3) What God has foretold will certainly come to pass, and so, by a necessary consequence, in order of arguing, it might be said that *therefore* they *could not believe,* because God by the prophets had foretold they would not; for such is the knowledge of God that he cannot be deceived in what he foresees, and such his truth that he cannot deceive in what he foretells, so that the scripture cannot be broken.

Lastly, The evangelist, having quoted the prophecy, shows (*v.* 41) that it was intended to look further than the prophet's own days, and that its principal reference was to the days of the Messiah: *These things said Esaias when he saw his glory, and spoke of him.* 1. We read in the prophecy that this was said to Esaias, Isa. vi. 8, 9. But here we are told that it was said *by him* to the purpose. 2. The vision which the prophet there had of the *glory of God* is here said to be his *seeing the glory* of Jesus Christ: He *saw his glory*. Jesus Christ therefore is equal in power and glory with the Father, and his praises are equally celebrated.

FEAR OF MAN (*vv.* 42, 43)

Some honour was done to Christ by these rulers: for they *believed on him*, were convinced that he was sent of God, and received his doctrine as divine; but they did not do him honour enough, for they had not courage to own their faith in him. Many professed more kindness for Christ than really they had; these had more kindness for him than they were willing to profess. See here what a struggle was in these rulers between their convictions and their corruptions.

A LAST WARNING (*vv.* 44–50)

We have here the honour Christ not assumed, but asserted, to himself, in the account he gave of his mission and his errand into the world. Probably this discourse was not at the same time with that before (for then *he departed, v.* 36), but some time after, when he made another public appearance; and, as this evangelist records it, it was Christ's farewell sermon to the Jews, and his last public discourse; all that follows was private with his disciples. So Christ here takes leave of the temple, with a solemn declaration of three things:—

I. The privileges and dignities of those that believe; this gives great encouragement to us to believe in Christ and to profess that faith. It is a thing of such a nature that we need not be shy either of doing it or of owning it; for,

1. By believing in Christ we are brought into an *honourable acquaintance with God* (*vv.* 44, 45): *He that believes on me*, and so *sees me, believes on him that sent me*, and so *sees him.*

2. We are hereby brought into a comfortable enjoyment of ourselves (*v.* 46): *I am come a light into the world, that whoever believes in me*, Jew or Gentile, *should not abide in darkness.* [1] They do not continue in that dark condition in which they were by nature; they are *light in the Lord.* They were without any true comfort, or joy, or hope, but do not continue in that condition; light is sown for them. [2] Whatever darkness of affliction, disquietment, or fear, they may afterwards be in, provision is made that they may not long abide in it. [3] They are delivered from that darkness which is perpetual, and which *abideth for ever*, that utter darkness where there is not the least gleam of light nor hope of it.

II. The peril and danger of those that believe not, which gives fair warning to take heed of persisting in unbelief (*vv.* 47, 48). Observe,

1. Who they are whose unbelief is here condemned: those who *hear Christ's words* and yet *believe them not*. Those shall not be condemned for their infidelity that never had, nor could have, the gospel; every man shall be judged according to the dispensation of light he was under: *Those that have sinned without law shall be judged without law*. But those

that have heard, or might have heard, and would not, lie open to this doom.

2. What is the constructive malignity of their unbelief: not receiving Christ's word; it is interpreted (*v.* 48) a *rejecting* of Christ.

3. The wonderful patience and forbearance of our Lord Jesus, exercised towards those who slighted him when he was come here upon earth: *I judge him not,* not now. Note, Christ was not quick or hasty to take advantage against those who refused the first offers of his grace, but continued waiting to be gracious.

4. The certain and unavoidable judgment of unbelievers at the great day, the day of the revelation of the righteous judgment of God: unbelief will certainly be a damning sin. (1) There is *one that judgeth them.* Nothing is more dreadful than abused patience, and grace trampled on; though for awhile *mercy rejoiceth against judgment,* yet there will be *judgment without mercy.* (2) Their final judgment is reserved to the *last day*; to that day of judgment Christ here binds over all unbelievers, to answer then for all the contempts they have put upon him. (3) The word of Christ will judge them then: *The words that I have spoken,* how light soever you have made of them, *the same shall judge* the unbeliever *in the last day.*

III. A solemn declaration of the authority Christ had to demand our faith, and require us to receive his doctrine upon pain of damnation, *vv.* 49, 50, where observe,

1. The commission which our Lord Jesus received from the Father to deliver his doctrine to the world (*v.* 49): *I have not spoken of myself,* as a mere man, much less as a common man; *but the Father gave me a commandment what I should say.*

2. The scope, design, and tendency of this commission: *I know that his commandment is life everlasting, v.* 50. The commission given to Christ had a reference to the everlasting state of the children of men, and was in order to their everlasting life and happiness in that state: the instructions given to Christ as a prophet were to reveal eternal life (1 John v. 11); the power given to Christ as a king was to give eternal life, *ch.* xvii. 2. Thus the command given him was life everlasting.

3. Christ's exact observance of the commission and instructions given him, and his steady acting in pursuance of them: *Whatsoever I speak,* it is *as the Father said unto me.* In the midst of all the respect paid to him, this is the honour he values himself upon, that what the Father had said to him that he spoke, and in the manner as he was directed so he spoke.

CHAPTER THIRTEEN

WASHING FEET (*vv.* 1–17)

In these verses we have the story of Christ's washing his disciples' feet; it was an action of a singular nature; no miracle, unless we call it a miracle of humility.

I. Christ washed his disciples' feet that he might give a proof of that great love wherewith he loved them; loved them to the end, vv. 1, 2.

1. It is here laid down as an undoubted truth that our Lord Jesus, *having loved his own that were in the world, loved them to the end*, v. 1.

(1) This is true of the disciples that were his immediate followers, in particular the twelve.

(2) It is true of all believers, for these twelve patriarchs were the representatives of all the tribes of God's spiritual Israel.

2. Christ manifested his love to them by washing their feet, as that good woman (Luke vii. 38) showed her love to Christ by washing his feet and wiping them. Thus he would show that as his love to them was constant so it was condescending.

3. He chose this time to do it, a little before his last passover, for two reasons:—

(1) Because now *he knew that his hour was come*, which he had long expected, *when he should depart out of this world to the Father*. Observe here, [1] The change that was to pass over our Lord Jesus; he must *depart*. This began at his death, but was completed at his ascension. [2] The time of this change: *His hour was come*. It is sometimes called his enemies' hour (Luke xxii. 53), the hour of their triumph; sometimes his hour, the hour of his triumph, the hour he had had in his eye all along. The time of his sufferings was fixed to an hour, and the continuance of them but for an hour. [3] His foresight of it: He *knew that his hour was come*; he knew from the beginning that it

would come, and when, but now he knew that it *was come*.

(2) Because the *devil had. now put it into the heart of Judas to betray him*, v. 2. These words in a parenthesis may be considered, [1] As tracing Judas's treason to its origin; it was a sin of such a nature that it evidently bore the devil's image and superscription. [2] As intimating a reason why Christ now washed his disciples' feet. *First*, Judas being now resolved to betray him, the time of his departure could not be far off; if this matter be determined, it is easy to infer with St. Paul, *I am now ready to be offered*. *Secondly*, Judas being now got into the snare, and the devil aiming at Peter and the rest of them (Luke xxii. 31), Christ would fortify his own against him. *Thirdly*, Judas, who was now plotting to betray him, was *one of the twelve*. Now Christ would hereby show that he did not design to cast them all off for the faults of one.

II. Christ washed his disciples' feet that he might give an instance of his own wonderful humility, and show how lowly and condescending he was, and let all the world know how low he could stoop in love to his own. This is intimated, vv. 3–5.

1. Here is the rightful advancement of the Lord Jesus. Glorious things are here said of Christ as Mediator.

(1) *The Father had given all things into his hands*; had given him a propriety in all, and a power over all, as possessor of heaven and earth, in pursuance of

the great designs of his undertaking; see Matt. xi. 27.

(2) He *came from God*. This implies that he was in the beginning with God, and had a being and glory, not only before he was born into this world, but before the world itself was born.

(3) He *went to God*, to be glorified with him with the same glory which he had with God from eternity.

(4) He *knew* all this; was not like a prince in the cradle, that knows nothing of the honour he is born to, or like Moses, who *wist not that his face shone*; no, he had a full view of all the honours of his exalted state, and yet stooped thus low.

2. Here is the voluntary abasement of our Lord Jesus notwithstanding this. Now that which Christ humbled himself to was to *wash his disciples' feet*.

(1) The action itself was mean and servile, and that which servants of the lowest rank were employed

(2) The condescension was so much the greater that he did this for his own disciples, who in themselves were of a low and despicable condition, not curious about their bodies; their feet, it is likely, were seldom washed, and therefore very dirty. In relation to him, they were his scholars, his servants, and such as should have washed his feet, whose dependence was upon him, and their expectations from him.

(3) He *rose from supper* to do it. Though we translate it (*v.* 2) *supper being ended*, it might be better read, *there being a supper made*, or *he being at supper*, for he sat down again (*v.* 12), and we find him dipping a sop (*v.* 26), so that he did it in the midst of his meal.

(4) He put himself into the garb of a servant, to do it: he *laid aside* his loose and upper *garments*, that he might apply himself to this service the more expedLy.

(5) He did it with all the humble ceremony that could be, went through all the parts of the service distinctly, and passed by none of them; he did it as if he had been used thus to serve; did it himself alone, and had none to minister to him in it. He *girded himself with the towel*, as servants throw a napkin on their arm, or put an apron before them; he *poured water into the basin* out of the water-pots that stood by (*ch.* ii. 6), and then *washed their feet*; and, to complete the service, *wiped them*.

(6) Nothing appears to the contrary but that he washed the feet of Judas among the rest, for he was present, *v.* 26. The blessed Jesus here washed the feet of a sinner, the worst of sinners, the worst to him, who was at this time contriving to betray him.

III. Christ washed his disciples' feet that he might signify to them spiritual washing, and the cleansing of the soul from the pollutions of sin. This is plainly intimated in his discourse with Peter upon it, *vv.* 6–11, in which we may observe,

1. The surprise Peter was in when he saw his Master go about this mean service (*v.* 6). Very willingly would Peter have taken

the basin and towel, and washed his Master's feet, and been proud of the honour, Luke xvii. 7, 8.

2. The immediate satisfaction Christ gave to this question of surprise. This was at least sufficient to silence his objections (v. 7). Here are two reasons why Peter must submit to what Christ was doing:—

(1) Because he was at present in the dark concerning it, and ought not to oppose what he did not understand.

(2) Because there was something considerable in it, of which he should hereafter know the meaning.

3. Peter's peremptory refusal, notwithstanding this, to let Christ wash his feet (v. 8).

4. Christ's insisting upon his offer, and a good reason given to Peter why he should accept it. This may be taken, (1) As a severe caution against disobedience: "*If I wash thee not*, if thou continue refractory, and wilt not comply with thy Master's will in so small a matter, thou shalt not be owned as one of my disciples, but be justly discarded and cashiered for not observing orders." Or, (2) As a declaration of the necessity of spiritual washing; and so I think it is to be understood: "*If I wash not* thy soul from the pollution of sin, *thou hast no part with me*, no interest in me, no communion with me, no benefit by me."

5. Peter's more than submission, his earnest request, to be washed by Christ, v. 9. Observe,

(1) How ready Peter is to recede from what he had said. Now that

the washing of him appeared to be an act of Christ's authority and grace he admits it; but disliked it when it seemed only an act of humiliation.

(2) How importunate he is for the purifying grace of the Lord Jesus, and the universal influence of it, even upon his hands and head.

6. Christ's further explication of this sign, as it represented spiritual washing.

(1) With reference to his disciples that were faithful to him (v. 10): *He that is washed* all over in the bath (as was frequently practised in those countries), when he returns to his house, *needeth not save to wash his feet*, his hands and head having been washed, and he having only dirtied his feet in walking home. Peter had gone from one extreme to the other. At first he would not let Christ wash his feet; and now he overlooks what Christ had done for him in his baptism, and what was signified thereby, and cries out to have his hands and head washed. Now Christ directs him into the meaning; he must have his feet washed, but not his hands and head. [1] See here what is the comfort and privilege of such as are in a justified state; they are washed by Christ, and are *clean every whit*, that is, they are graciously accepted of God, as if they were so; and, though they offend, yet they need not, upon their repentance, be again put into a justified state, for then should they often be baptized. Though we have occasion to repent daily, God's gifts and callings are without

repentance. [2] See what ought to be the daily care of those who through grace are in a justified state, and that is to wash their feet; to cleanse themselves from the guilt they contract daily through infirmity and inadvertence, by the renewed exercise of repentance, with a believing application of the virtue of Christ's blood. The provision made for our cleansing should not make us presumptuous, but the more cautious. *I have washed my feet, how shall I defile them?* From yesterday's pardon, we should fetch an argument against this day's temptation.

(2) With reflection upon Judas: *And you are clean, but not all, vv.* 10, 11.

IV. Christ washed his disciples' feet to set before us an example. This explanation he gave of what he had done, when he had done it, *vv.* 12–17. Observe,

1. With what solemnity he gave an account of the meaning of what he had done (*v.* 12): *After he had washed their feet*, he said, *Know you what I have done?*

2. Upon what he grounds that which he had to say (*v.* 13): "*You call me Master and Lord*, you give me those titles, in speaking of me, in speaking to me, and *you say well*, for *so I am*; you are in the relation of scholars to me, and I do the part of a master to you."

Our calling Christ Master and Lord is an obligation upon us to receive and observe the instructions he gives us.

3. The lesson which he hereby taught: *You also ought to wash one another's feet*, *v.* 14. Doubtless

it is to be understood figuratively; it is an instructive sign, but not sacramental, as the eucharist. This was a parable to the eye; and three things our Master hereby designed to teach us:—
[1] A humble condescension. We must learn of our Master to be *lowly in heart* (Matt. xi. 29), and walk with all lowliness. [2] A condescension to be serviceable. To wash one another's feet is to stoop to the meanest offices of love, for the real good and benefit one of another. [3] A serviceableness to the sanctification one of another: *You ought to wash one another's feet*, from the pollutions of sin. We cannot satisfy for one another's sins, this is peculiar to Christ, but we may help to purify one another from sin.

4. Here is the ratifying and enforcing of this command from the example of what Christ had now done: *If I your Lord and Master have* done it to you, you ought to do it *to one another*. He shows the cogency of this argument in two things:—

(1) I am *your Master*, and you are my disciples, and therefore you ought to *learn of me* (*v.* 15).

(2) I am *your Master*, and you are my disciples, and therefore you cannot think it below you to do that, how mean soever it may seem, which you have seen me do, for (*v.* 16) *the servant is not greater than his Lord, neither he that is sent*, though sent with all the pomp and power of an ambassador, *greater than he that sent him*.

5. Our Saviour closes this part of his discourse with an intimation

of the necessity of their obedience to these instructions: *If you know these things*; or, seeing you know them, *happy are you if you do them*. Most people think, Happy are those that rise and rule. Washing one another's feet will never get estates and preferments; but Christ saith, notwithstanding this, Happy are those that stoop and obey.

JUDAS DEPARTS (vv. 18–30)

We have here the discovery of Judas's plot to betray his Master. Now here,

I. Christ gives them a general intimation of it (*v.* 18): *I speak not of you all*, I cannot expect you will all do these things, for *I know whom I have chosen*, and whom I have passed by; but the scripture will be fulfilled (Ps. xli. 9), *He that eateth bread with me hath lifted up his heel against me*.

II. He gives them a reason why he told them beforehand of the treachery of Judas (*v.* 19): "*Now I tell you before it come*, before Judas has begun to put his wicked plot in execution, *that when it is come to pass you may*, instead of stumbling at it, be confirmed in your *belief that I am he*, he that should come."

III. He gives a word of encouragement to his apostles, and all his ministers whom he employs in his service (*v.* 20): *He that receiveth whomsoever I send receiveth me*. The purport of these words is the same with what we have in other scriptures, but it is not easy to make out their coherence here. Christ had told his disciples that they must humble

and abase themselves. "Now," saith he, "though there may be those that will despise you for your condescension, yet there will be those that will do you honour, and shall be honoured for so doing."

IV. Christ more particularly notifies to them the plot which one of their number was now hatching against him (*v.* 21). He had often spoken of his own sufferings and death, without any such trouble of spirit as he here manifested when he spoke of the ingratitude and treachery of Judas. This touched him in a tender part.

V. The disciples quickly take the alarm. They knew their Master would neither deceive them nor jest with them; and therefore *looked one upon another*, with a manifest concern, *doubting of whom he spoke*.

VI. The disciples were solicitous to get their Master to explain himself, and to tell them particularly whom he meant; for nothing but this can put them out of their present pain, for each of them thought he had as much reason to suspect himself as any of his brethren; now,

1. Of all the disciples John was most fit to ask, because he was the favourite, and sat next his Master (*v.* 23): *There was leaning on Jesus's bosom one of the disciples whom Jesus loved*. It appears that this was John, by comparing ch. xxi. 20, 24.

2. Of all the disciples Peter was most forward to know, *v.* 24. Peter, sitting at some distance, beckoned to John, by some sign or other, to ask. It were a desirable

thing, we should think, to know who in the church will deceive us; yet let this suffice—Christ knows, though we do not.

3. The question was asked accordingly (*v.* 25): *He then, lying at the breast of Jesus*, and so having the convenience of whispering with him, *saith unto him, Lord, who is it?*

4. Christ gave a speedy answer to this question, but whispered it in John's ear; for it appears (*v.* 29) that the rest were still ignorant of the matter. *He it is to whom I shall give a sop, a morsel, a crust, when I have dipped it* in the sauce. And *when he had dipped the sop*, John strictly observing his motions, *he gave it to Judas*.

VII. Judas himself, instead of being convinced hereby of his wickedness, was the more confirmed in it, and the warning given him was to him a *savour of death unto death*; for it follows,

1. The devil hereupon took possession of him (*v.* 27): *After the sop, Satan entered into him*. But,

(1) Was not Satan in him before? How then is it said that now *Satan entered into him*? Judas was all along a devil (*ch.* vi. 70), a son of perdition, but now Satan gained a more full possession of him, had a *more abundant entrance* into him.

(2) How came Satan to enter into him *after the sop*? Perhaps he was presently aware that it was the discovery of him, and it made him desperate in his resolutions. Many are made worse by the gifts of Christ's bounty, and are confirmed in their impenitency

by that which should have led them to repentance. The *coals of fire heaped upon their heads*, instead of melting them, harden them.

2. Christ hereupon dismissed him, and delivered him up to his own heart's lusts: *Then said Jesus unto him, What thou doest, do quickly*. This is not to be understood as either advising him to his wickedness or warranting him in it; but either, (1) As abandoning him to the conduct and power of Satan. Or, (2) As challenging him to do his worst.

3. Those that were at table understood not what he meant, because they did not hear what he whispered to John (*vv.* 28, 29).

4. Judas hereupon sets himself vigorously to pursue his design against him: He *went away*.

A NEW COMMANDMENT
(*vv.* 31–35)

This and what follows, to the end of *ch.* xiv., was Christ's table-talk with his disciples. Now our Lord Jesus discourses with them (and probably discourses much more largely than is here recorded),

I. Concerning the great mystery of his own death and sufferings, about which they were as yet so much in the dark that they could not persuade themselves to expect the thing itself, much less did they understand the meaning of it; and therefore Christ gives them such instructions concerning it as made the offence of the cross to cease.

1. Here is something which Christ instructs them in, concerning

his sufferings, that was very *comforting*.

(1) That he should himself be glorified in them.

(2) That God the Father should be glorified in them. The sufferings of Christ were, [1] The satisfaction of God's justice, and so God was glorified in them. [2] They were the manifestation of his holiness and mercy.

(3) That he should himself be greatly glorified after them, in consideration of God's being greatly glorified by them, *v.* 32.

2. Here is something that Christ instructs them in, concerning his sufferings, which was *awakening*, for as yet they were slow of heart to understand it (*v.* 33).

(1) That his stay in this world, to be with them here, they would find to be very short. Whether we understand this as referring to his death or his ascension it comes much to one; he had but a little time to spend with them.

(2) That their following him to the other world, to be with him there, they would find to be very difficult. Christ tells them here, [1] That when he was gone they would feel the want of him: *You shall seek me*, that is, "you shall wish you had me again with you." [2] That whither he went they *could not come*, which suggests to them high thoughts of him, who was going to an invisible inaccessible world, to dwell in that *light which none can approach unto*; and also low thoughts of themselves, and serious thoughts of their future state. Christ tells them that they could not follow him (as Joshua told the people

that they could not serve the Lord) only to quicken them to so much the more diligence and care.

II. He discourses with them concerning the great duty of brotherly love (*vv.* 34, 35): *You shall love one another*. Three arguments for mutual love are here urged: —

1. The command of their Master (*v.* 34): *A new commandment I give unto you.* He not only commends it as amiable and pleasant, not only counsels it as excellent and profitable, but commands it, and makes it one of the fundamental laws of his kingdom; it goes abreast with the command of believing in Christ, 1 John iii. 23; 1 Pet. i. 22. It is *a new commandment*; that is, (1) It is a renewed commandment; it was a commandment *from the beginning* (1 John ii. 7), as old as the law of nature, it was the second great commandment of the law of Moses; yet, because it is also one of the great commandments of the New Testament, of Christ the new Lawgiver, it is called a new commandment; it is like an old book in a new edition corrected and enlarged. (2) It is an excellent command, as a *new song* is an excellent song, that has an uncommon gratefulness in it. (3) It is an everlasting command; so strangely new as to be always so; as the *new covenant*, which shall never decay (Heb. viii. 13). (4) As Christ gives it, it is *new*. Before it was, *Thou shalt love thy neighbour*; now it is, You shall love *one another*.

2. The example of their Saviour is another argument for brotherly

love: *As I have loved you.* It is this that makes it a *new commandment* —that this rule and reason of *love* (*as I have loved you*) is perfectly new, and such as had been hidden from ages and generations.

3. The reputation of their profession (*v.* 35): *By this shall all men know that you are my disciples, if you have love one to another.* Note, Brotherly love is the badge of Christ's disciples. By this he knows them, by this they may know themselves (1 John iii. 14), and by this others may know them.

PETER WARNED (*vv.* 36–38)

In these verses we have,

I. Peter's curiosity, and the check given to that.

1. Peter's question was bold and blunt (*v.* 36): *Lord, whither goest thou?* referring to what Christ had said (*v.* 33), *Whither I go, you cannot come.*

2. Christ's answer was instructive. Let this suffice, *thou canst not follow me now, but shalt follow me hereafter.* (1) We may understand it of his following him to the cross. (2) We may understand it of his following him to the crown. Christ was now going to his glory, and Peter was very desirous to go with him: "No," saith Christ, "*thou canst not follow me now,* thou art not yet ripe for heaven, nor hast thou finished thy work on earth. The forerunner must *first enter to prepare a place* for thee, but *thou shalt follow me afterwards,* after thou hast fought the good fight, and at the time appointed."

II. Peter's confidence, and the check given to that.

1. Peter makes a daring protestation of his constancy. See here, (1) What an affectionate love Peter had to our Lord Jesus: "*I will lay down my life for thy sake,* and I can do no more." I believe Peter spoke as he thought, and though he was inconsiderate he was not insincere, in his resolution. (2) How ill he took it to have it questioned, intimated in that expostulation, "*Lord, why cannot I follow thee now?* Dost thou suspect my fidelity to thee?"

2. Christ gives him a surprising prediction of his inconstancy, *v.* 38. Jesus Christ knows us better than we know ourselves, and has many ways of discovering those to themselves whom he loves, and will hide pride from. He plainly foretells his cowardice in the critical hour. To stop the mouth of his boasting, lest Peter should say it again, Yea Master, that I will, Christ solemnly asserts it with, *Verily, verily, I say unto thee, the cock shall not crow till thou hast denied me thrice.* Note, The most secure are commonly the least safe; and those most shamefully betray their own weakness that most confidently presume upon their own strength, 1 Cor. x. 12.

CHAPTER FOURTEEN
MANY MANSIONS (*vv.* 1–3)

In these verses we have,

I. A general caution which Christ gives to his disciples against *trouble of heart* (*v.* 1): *Let not your heart be troubled.* They now began to be troubled, were entering into this temptation.

II. Here is a particular direction

to act in faith upon the promise of eternal life, *vv.* 2, 3. He had directed them to trust to God, and to trust in him; but what must they trust God and Christ for? Trust them for a happiness to come when this body and this world shall be no more, and for a happiness to last as long as the immortal soul and the eternal world shall last. Let us see how this is suggested here.

1. Believe and consider that really there is such a happiness: *In my Father's house there are many mansions; if it were not so, I would have told you, v.* 2.

(1) See under what notion the happiness of heaven is here represented: as *mansions,* many mansions in Christ's Father's house. [1] Heaven is a house, not a tent or tabernacle; it is *a house not made with hands, eternal in the heavens.* [2] It is a Father's house: *my Father's house*; and his Father is our Father, to whom he was now ascending. [3] There are *mansions* there; that is, *First,* Distinct dwellings, an apartment for each. *Secondly,* Durable dwellings. The house itself is lasting; our estate in it is not for a term of years, but a perpetuity. [4] There are *many* mansions, for there are many sons to be brought to glory, and Christ exactly knows their number, nor will be stretched for room by the coming of more company than he expects.

(2) See what assurance we have of the reality of the happiness itself, and the sincerity of the proposal of it to us: "*If it were not so, I would have told you.*" If either there were no such mansions,

or none designed for them, who had left all to follow him, he would have given them timely notice of the mistake, that they might have made an honourable retreat to the world again, and have made the best they could of it.

2. Believe and consider that the design of Christ's going away was to prepare a place in heaven for his disciples. He went to prepare a place for us; that is, (1) To take possession for us, as our advocate or attorney, and so to secure our title as indefeasible. (2) To make provision for us as our friend and father.

3. Believe and consider that *therefore* he would certainly come again in due time, to fetch them to that blessed place which he was now going to possess for himself and prepare for them (*v.* 3). Now these are comfortable words indeed. (1) That Jesus Christ will come again; *I do come,* intimating the certainty of it, that he will come and that he is daily coming. (2) That he will come again to receive all his faithful followers to himself. He sends for them privately at death, and gathers them one by one; but they are to make their public entry in solemn state all together at the last day, and then Christ himself will come to receive them, to conduct them in the abundance of his grace, and to welcome them in the abundance of his love. (3) *That where he is there they shall be also.* This intimates what many other scriptures declare, that the quintessence of heaven's happiness is being with Christ *there, ch.* xvii. 24; Phil. i. 23; 1 Thess. iv. 17.

WAY, TRUTH, LIFE (*vv.* 4–11)

Christ, having set the happiness of heaven before them as the end, here shows them himself as the way to it, and tells them that they were better acquainted both with the end they were to aim at and with the way they were to walk in than they thought they were.

This word of Christ gave occasion to two of his disciples to address themselves to him, and he answers them both.

I. Thomas enquired concerning the way (*v.* 5), without any apology for contradicting his Master.

Thomas here shows more modesty than Peter, who thought he could follow Christ now. Peter was the more solicitous to know *whither Christ went.* Thomas here, though he complains that he did not know this, yet seems more solicitous to know *the way.* Had Thomas understood, as he might have done, that Christ was going to the invisible world, the world of spirits, to which spiritual things only have a reference, he would not have said, *Lord, we do not know the way.*

II. Now to this complaint of their ignorance, which included a desire to be taught, Christ gives a full answer, *vv.* 6, 7. Believe in God as the end, and in me as the way (*v.* 1), and you do all you should do.

(1) He speaks of himself as the way, *v.* 6. Dost thou *not know the way? I am the way,* and I only, for *no man comes to the Father but by me.* Great things Christ here saith of himself, showing us,

[1] The nature of his mediation: He is *the way, the truth, and the life.*

First, Let us consider these first distinctly. 1. Christ is *the way, the highway* spoken of, Isa. xxxv. 8. Christ was his own way, for by *his own blood he entered into the holy place.* (Heb. ix. 12), and he is our way, for we enter by him. 2. He is *the truth.* (1) As truth is opposed to figure and shadow. Christ is the substance of all the Old-Testament types, which are therefore said to be *figures of the true,* Heb. ix. 24. Christ is *the true manna* (*ch.* vi. 32), *the true tabernacle,* Heb. viii. 2. (2) As truth is opposed to falsehood and error; the doctrine of Christ is true doctrine. When we enquire for truth, we need learn no more than *the truth as it is in Jesus.* (3) As truth is opposed to fallacy and deceit; he is true to all that trust in him, as true as truth itself, 2 Cor. i. 20. 3. He is *the life;* for we are *alive unto God* only in and *through Jesus Christ,* Rom. vi. 11. Christ formed in us is that to our souls which our souls are to our bodies. Christ is *the resurrection and the life.*

Secondly, Let us consider these jointly, and with reference to each other. Christ is *the way, the truth, and the life;* that is, 1. He is the beginning, the middle, and the end. In him we must set out, go on, and finish. As *the truth,* he is the guide of our way; as *the life,* he is the end of it. 2. He is *the true and living way* (Heb. x. 20); there are *truth and life* in the way, as well as at the end of it. 3. He is *the true way to life*, the only true way; other ways may seem right, but the end of them is *the way of death*.

[2] The necessity of his mediation: *No man cometh to the Father but by me*. Fallen man must come to God as Judge, but cannot come to him as a Father, otherwise than by Christ as Mediator.

(2) He speaks of his Father as the end (*v*. 7). They knew him, and yet did not know him so well as they might and should have known him. They knew him to be the Christ, but did not follow on to know God in him.

II. Philip enquired concerning the Father (*v*. 8), and Christ answered him, *vv*. 9–11, where observe,

1. Philip's request for some extraordinary discovery of the Father.

2. Christ's reply, referring him to the discoveries already made of the Father, *vv*. 9–11.

(1) He refers him to what he had seen, *v*. 9. He upbraids him with his ignorance and inadvertency: "*Have I been so long time with you*, now above three years intimately conversant with you, *and yet hast thou not known me, Philip?* Now, *he that hath seen me hath seen the Father; and how sayest thou then, Show us the Father?* Wilt thou ask for that which thou hast already?" Now here,

[1] He reproves him for two things: *First*, For not improving his acquaintance with Christ, as he might have done, to a clear and distinct knowledge of him.

[2] He instructs him, and gives him a maxim which not only in general magnifies Christ and leads

us to the knowledge of God in him, but justifies what Christ had said (*v*. 7): *You know the Father, and have seen him*; and answered what Philip had asked, *Show us the Father*. Why, saith Christ, the difficulty is soon over, for *he that hath seen me hath seen the Father*. *First*, All that saw *Christ in the flesh might have seen the Father* in him, if Satan had not *blinded their minds*, and kept them from a sight of Christ, *as the image of God*, 2 Cor. iv. 4. *Secondly*, All that saw Christ by faith did *see the Father* in him, though they were not suddenly aware that they did so. In the light of Christ's doctrine they saw God as *the Father of lights*; in the miracles they saw God *as the God of power, the finger of God*. The holiness of God shone in the spotless purity of Christ's life, and his grace in all the acts of grace he did.

(2) He refers him to what he had reason to believe (*vv*. 10, 11): "*Believest thou not that I am in the Father, and the Father in me*, and therefore that in *seeing me* thou hast *seen the Father*? Hast thou not believed this? If not, take my word for it, and believe it now."

[1] See here what it is which we are to believe: *That I am in the Father, and the Father in me*; that is, as he had said (*ch*. x. 30), *I and my Father are one*.

[2] See here what inducements we have to believe this; and they are two:—We must believe it, *First*, For his word's sake: *The words that I speak to you, I speak not of myself*. See *ch*. vii. 16, *My*

doctrine is not mine. Secondly, For his works' sake: *The Father that dwelleth in me, he doeth them;* and therefore *believe me for their sake.* Many works of power, and works of mercy, Christ did, and the Father did them in him; and the work of redemption in general was God's own work.

GREATER WORKS (*vv.* 12–14)

The disciples, as they were full of grief to think of parting with their Master, so they were full of care what would become of themselves when he was gone. Now, to silence these fears, Christ here assures them that they should be clothed with powers sufficient to bear them out. As Christ had *all power*, they, in his name, should have great *power*, *both in heaven and in earth.*

I. Great power on earth (*v.* 12): *He that believeth on me* (as I know you do), *the works that I do shall he do also.*

1. Two things he assures them of:—

(1) That they should be enabled to do such works as he had done, and that they should have a more ample power for the doing of them than they had had when he first sent them forth, Matt. x. 8.

(2) That they should do *greater works than these.* [1] In the kingdom of nature they should work greater miracles. No miracle is little, but some to our apprehension seem greater than others. Christ had healed with the hem of his garment, but Peter with his shadow (Acts v. 15), Paul by the handkerchief that had touched him, Acts xix. 12. [2] In the kingdom of

grace. They should obtain greater victories by the gospel than had been obtained while Christ was upon earth. I think this refers especially to *the gift of tongues;* this was the immediate effect of the *pouring out of the Spirit,* which was a constant miracle upon the mind, in which words are framed, and which was made to serve so glorious an intention as that of spreading the gospel to all nations *in their own language.* This was a greater *sign to them that believed not* (1 Cor. xiv. 22), and more powerful for their conviction, than any other miracle whatever.

2. The reason Christ gives for this is, *Because I go unto my Father,* (1) "*Because I go,* it will be requisite that you should have such a power, lest the work suffer damage by my absence." (2) "*Because I go to the Father,* I shall be in a capacity to furnish you with such a power, for *I go to the Father, to send the Comforter,* from whom *you shall receive power,*" Acts i. 8.

II. Great *power in heaven*: "*Whatsoever you shall ask, that will I do* (*vv.* 13, 14), as Israel, who was a prince with God. Therefore you shall do such mighty works, because you have such an interest in me, and I in *my Father.*"

ANOTHER COMFORTER
(*vv.* 15–17)

Christ not only proposes such things to them as were the matter of their comfort, but here promises to send the Spirit, whose office it should be to be their Comforter, to *impress* these things upon them.

I. He premises to this a memento of duty (*v.* 15): *If you love me, keep my commandments.*

II. He promises this great and unspeakable blessing to them, *vv.* 16, 17.

1. It is promised that they shall have *another comforter*. Observe here,

(1) The blessing promised: "Paraclete". The word is used only here in these discourses of Christ's, and 1 John ii. 1, where we translate it an *advocate*. [1] You shall have another *advocate*. The office of the Spirit was to be Christ's advocate with them and others, to plead his cause, and take care of his concerns, on earth. [2] You shall have another *master* or *teacher*, another *exhorter*. While they had Christ with them he excited and exhorted them to their duty; but now that he is going he leaves one with them that shall do this as effectually, though silently. [3] Another *comforter*. Christ was expected as the consolation of Israel. One of the names of the Messiah among the Jews was *Menahem—the Comforter*. The Targum calls the days of the Messiah *the years of consolation.* Christ comforted his disciples when he was with them, and now that he was leaving them in their greatest need he promises them *another*.

(2) The giver of this blessing: *The Father* shall give him, *my Father* and *your Father*; it includes both. The same that gave the Son to be our Saviour will give his Spirit to be our comforter, pursuant to the same design. The Son is said to send the Comforter (*ch.* xv. 26), but the Father is the prime agent.

(3) How this blessing is procured—by the intercession of the Lord Jesus: *I will pray the Father.* He said (*v.* 14) *I will do it*; here he saith, *I will pray for it*, to show not only that he is both God and man, but that he is both king and priest.

(4) The continuance of this blessing: *That he may abide with you for ever.*

2. This comforter is the *Spirit of truth, whom you know, vv.* 16, 17.

(1) The comforter promised is *the Spirit*, one who should do his work in a spiritual way and manner, inwardly and invisibly, by working on men's spirits.

(2) "He is the *Spirit of truth.* He will *teach you the truth*, will enlighten your minds with the knowledge of it, will strengthen and confirm your belief of it, and will increase your love to it."

(3) He is one *whom the world cannot receive*; but *you know him. Therefore he abideth with you.* The gift of the Holy Ghost is a peculiar gift, bestowed upon the disciples of Christ in a distinguishing way—them, and not the world; it is to them *hidden manna*, and the *white stone*. No comforts comparable to those which make no show, make no noise. This is the favour God bears to his chosen; it is the *heritage of those that fear his name.*

I WILL COME TO YOU
(*vv.* 18–24)

When friends are parting, it is a common request they make to each other, "Pray let us hear from you as often as you can": this Christ engaged to his disciples, that out of sight they should not be out of mind.

I. He promises that he would continue his care of them (*v.* 18): "*I will not leave you orphans*, or *fatherless*; for, though I leave you, yet I leave you this comfort, *I will come to you.*" "I will be coming daily to you in my Spirit"; in the tokens of his love, and visits of his grace, he is still coming. "I will come certainly at the end of time; surely I will come quickly to introduce you into the joy of your Lord."

II. He promises that they should continue their acquaintance with him and interest in him (*vv.* 19, 20). The world sees him no more till his second coming; but his disciples have communion with him in his absence.

1. *You see me*, and shall continue to see me, when *the world sees me no more*. They saw him with their bodily eyes after his resurrection, for he showed himself to them *by many infallible proofs*, Acts i. 8. And *then were the disciples glad when they saw the Lord*. They saw him with an eye of faith after his ascension, sitting at God's right hand, as Lord of all; saw that in him which the world saw not.

2. *Because I live, you shall live also*. That which grieved them was, that their Master was dying, and they counted upon nothing else but to die with him. No, saith Christ, (1) *I live*; this the great God glories in, *I live*, saith the Lord, and Christ saith the same. (2) Therefore *you shall live*

also. Note, The life of Christians is bound up in the life of Christ.

3. You shall have the assurance of this (*v.* 20): *At that day*, when I am glorified, when the Spirit is poured out, *you shall know* more clearly and certainly than you do now that *I am in my Father, and you in me, and I in you*. The knowledge of this union is their unspeakable joy and satisfaction; they were now in Christ, and he in them, but he speaks of it as a further act of grace that they should know it, and have the comfort of it. An interest in Christ and the knowledge of it are sometimes separated.

III. He promises that he would love them, and manifest himself to them, *vv.* 21–24. Here observe,

1. Who they are whom Christ will look upon, and accept, as lovers of him; those that *have his commandments, and keep them.*

2. What returns he will make to them for their love; rich returns; there is no love lost upon Christ. (1) They shall have the Father's love: *He that loveth me shall be loved of my Father*. (2) They shall have Christ's love: *And I will love him*, as God-man, as Mediator. (3) They shall have the comfort of that love: *I will manifest myself to him*. Some understand it of Christ's showing himself alive to his disciples after his resurrection; but, being promised to all that *love him and keep his commandments*, it must be construed so as to extend to them. There is a spiritual manifestation of Christ and his love made to all believers.

3. What occurred upon Christ's making this promise.

(1) One of the disciples expresses his wonder and surprise at it, *v.* 22. Observe, [1] Who it was that said this—*Judas, not Iscariot.* [2] What he said—*Lord how is it?* which intimates either, *First,* the weakness of his understanding. So some take it. Or, *Secondly,* as expressing the strength of his affections, and the humble and thankful sense he had of Christ's distinguishing favours to them: *Lord, how is it?* He is amazed at the condescensions of divine grace, as David, 2 Sam. vii. 18. What is there in us to deserve so great a favour?

(2) Christ, in answer hereto, explains and confirms what he had said, *vv.* 23, 24. He overlooks what infirmity there was in what Judas spoke, and goes on with his comforts.

[1] He further explains the condition of the promise, which was loving him, and keeping his commandments. And, as to this, he shows what an inseparable connection there is between love and obedience; love is the root, obedience is the fruit.

[2] He further explains the promise (*v.* 23): *If a man thus love me, I will manifest myself to him.* 1. Not only, *I will,* but, *We will, I and the Father,* who, in this, *are one.* See *v.* 9. 2. Not only, "*I will show myself to him* at a distance," but, "*We will come to him,* to be near him, to be with him," such are the powerful influences of divine graces and comforts upon the souls of those that love Christ in sincerity. 3. Not only, "I will give him a transient view of me, or make him a short and running

visit," but, *We will take up our abode with him,* which denotes complacency in him and constancy to him.

[3] He gives a good reason both to bind us to observe the condition and encourage us to depend upon the promise. *The word which you hear is not mine, but his that sent me, v.* 24.

PEACE (*vv.* 25–27)

Two things Christ here comforts his disciples with:—
I. That they should be under the tuition of his Spirit, *vv.* 25, 26.
II. That they should be under the influence of his peace (*v.* 27): *Peace I leave with you.* When Christ was about to leave the world he *made his will.* His soul he committed to his Father; his body he bequeathed to Joseph, to be decently interred; his clothes fell to the soldiers; his mother he left to the care of John: but what should he leave to his poor disciples, that had left all for him? Silver and gold he had none; but he left them that which was infinitely better, *his peace.*

THE PRINCE OF THIS WORLD (*vv.* 28–31)

Christ here gives his disciples another reason why their hearts should not be troubled for his going away; and that is, because his heart was not. He comforted himself,
I. That, though he went away, he should *come again.*
II. That he *went to his Father.* His departure had a bright side as well as a dark side. Therefore he sent this message after his

resurrection (*ch.* xx. 17), *I ascend to my Father and your Father*, as most comfortable. 2. The reason of this is, because *the Father is greater than he*, which, if it be a proper proof of that for which it is alleged (as no doubt it is), must be understood thus, that his state with his Father would be much more excellent and glorious than his present state; his returning to his Father (so Dr. Hammond) would be the advancing of him to a much higher condition than that which he was now in. Or thus, His going to the Father himself, and bringing all his followers to him there, was the ultimate end of his undertaking, and therefore greater than the means. 3. The disciples of Christ should show that they love him by their rejoicing in the glories of his exaltation, rather than by lamenting the sorrows of his humiliation.

III. That his going away, compared with the prophecies which went before it, would be a means of confirming the faith of his disciples (*v.* 29): *I have told you before it come to pass* that I must die and rise again, and ascend to the Father, and send the Comforter, *that, when it is come to pass, you might believe.*" See this reason, *ch.* xiii. 19; xvi. 4.

IV. That he was sure of a victory over Satan, with whom he knew he was to have a struggle in his departure (*v.* 30). One reason why he would not talk much with them was because he had now other work to apply himself to: *The prince of this world comes.* He called the devil the *prince of this world, ch.* xii. 31. 2. The assurance

he had of good success in the conflict: *He hath nothing in me, He hath nothing at all.* (1) There was no guilt in Christ to give authority to *the prince of this world* in his terrors. (2) There was no corruption in Christ, to give advantage to *the prince of this world* in his temptations.

V. That his departure was in compliance with, and obedience to, his Father. Satan could not force his life from him, and yet he would die: *that the world may know that I love the Father, v.* 31.

CHAPTER FIFTEEN

THE FRUITS OF THE SPIRIT
(*vv.* 1–8)

Here Christ discourses concerning the fruits, *the fruits of the Spirit*, which his disciples were to bring forth, under the similitude of a vine. Observe here,

I. The doctrine of this similitude; what notion we ought to have of it.

1. That Jesus Christ is *the vine, the true vine.* (1) He is *the vine*, planted in the vineyard, and not a spontaneous product; planted in the earth, for he is *the Word made flesh.* The vine has an unsightly unpromising outside; and Christ had *no form nor comeliness*, Isa. liii. 2. The vine is a spreading plant, and Christ will be known as *salvation to the ends of the earth.* The fruit of the vine honours God and cheers man (Judg. ix. 13), so does the fruit of Christ's mediation; it is *better than gold*, Prov. viii. 19. (2) He is *the true vine*, as truth is opposed to pretence and counterfeit; he is really a fruitful plant, a plant of renown.

2. That believers are branches of this vine, which supposes that Christ is the root of the vine. The root is unseen, and our *life is hid with Christ*; the root bears the tree (Rom. xi. 18), diffuses sap to it, and is all in all to its flourishing and fruitfulness; and in Christ are all supports and supplies. Believers, like the branches of the vine, are weak, and insufficient to stand of themselves, but as they are borne up. See Ezek. xv. 2.

3. That *the Father is the husbandman—the land-worker.* Though *the earth is the Lord's,* it yields him no fruit unless he work it. God has not only a propriety in, but a care of, the vine and all the branches. He *hath planted, and watered, and gives the increase*; for *we are God's husbandry,* 1 Cor. iii. 9. See Isa. v. 1, 2; xxvii. 2, 3.

II. The duty taught us by this similitude, which is to *bring forth fruit,* and, in order to do this, to *abide* in Christ.

1. We must be fruitful. From a vine we look for grapes (Isa. v. 2), and from a Christian we look for Christianity; this is the *fruit,* a Christian temper and disposition, a Christian life and conversation, Christian devotions and Christian designs. To persuade them to this, he urges,

(1) The doom of the unfruitful (*v.* 2): They are *taken away.*

(2) The promise made to the fruitful: *He purgeth them, that they may bring forth more fruit.* The purging of fruitful branches, in order to their greater fruitfulness, is the care and work of the great husbandman, for his own glory.

(3) The benefits which believers

have by the doctrine of Christ, the power of which they should labour to exemplify in a fruitful conversation: *Now you are clean,* *v.* 3. [1] Their society was clean, now that Judas was expelled by that word of Christ. [2] They were each of them clean, that is, sanctified, by the truth of Christ (*ch.* xvii. 17); that faith by which they received the word of Christ *purified their hearts,* Acts xv. 9. The disciples had now been three years under Christ's instruction; and *now you are clean.*

(4) The glory that will redound to God by our fruitfulness, with the comfort and honour that will come to ourselves by it, *v.* 8. And the more fruit we bring forth, the more we abound in that which is good, the more he is glorified.

2. In order to achieve our fruitfulness, we must abide in Christ, must keep up our union with him by faith, and do all we do in religion in the virtue of that union. Here is,

(1) The duty enjoined (*v.* 4): *Abide in me, and I in you.*

(2) The necessity of our abiding in Christ, for our fruitfulness (*vv.* 4, 5). [1] He that is constant in the exercise of faith in Christ and love to him, that lives upon his promises and is led by his Spirit, *bringeth forth much fruit.* [2] It is necessary to our doing any good. It is not only a means of cultivating and increasing what good there is already in us, but it is the root and spring of all good: "*Without me you can do nothing.*"

(3) The fatal consequences of forsaking Christ (*v.* 6): *If any man abide not in me, he is cast forth as a*

branch. This is a description of the fearful state of hypocrites that are *not in Christ*, and of apostates that *abide not in Christ*.

(4) The blessed privilege which those have that *abide in Christ* (*v.* 7): *If my words abide in you, you shall ask what you will* of my Father in my name, *and it shall be done*.

ABIDING IN LOVE (*vv.* 9–17)

Christ, who is love itself, is here discoursing concerning love, a fourfold love.

I. Concerning the Father's love to him; and concerning this he here tells us, 1. That the Father did love him (*v.* 9): *As the Father hath loved me*. 2. That he abode in his Father's love, *v.* 10. He continually loved his Father, and was beloved of him. 3. That therefore he abode in his Father's love because he kept his Father's law: *I have kept my Father's commandments*, as Mediator, and so *abide in his love*.

II. Concerning his own love to his disciples. Though he leaves them, he loves them. And observe here,

1. The pattern of this love: *As the Father has loved me, so have I loved you*. A strange expression of the condescending grace of Christ! As the Father loved him, who was most worthy, he loved them, who were most unworthy.

2. The proofs and products of this love, which are four:—

(1) Christ loves his disciples, for he laid down his life for them (*v.* 13).

(2) Christ loved his disciples, for he took them into a covenant of friendship with himself, *vv.* 14, 15. "If you approve yourselves by your obedience my disciples indeed, *you are my friends*, and shall be treated as friends."

(3) Christ loved his disciples, for he was very free in communicating his mind to them (*v.* 15). The great things relating to man's redemption Christ declared to his disciples, that they might declare them to others; they were the men of his counsel, Matt. xiii. 11.

(4) Christ loved his disciples, for he chose and ordained them to be the prime instruments of his glory and honour in the world (*v.* 16): *I have chosen you, and ordained you*. His love to them appeared,

[1] In their election, their election to their apostleship (*ch.* vi. 70): *I have chosen you twelve*. It did not begin on their side: *You have not chosen me*, but I first *chose you*.

[2] In their ordination: *I have ordained you; "I have put you into the ministry* (1 Tim. i. 12), put you into commission."

[3] His love to them appeared in the interest they had at the throne of grace: *Whatsoever you shall ask of my Father, in my name, he will give it you*. Probably this refers in the first place to the power of working miracles which the apostles were clothed with, which was to be drawn out by prayer.

III. Concerning the disciples' love to Christ, enjoined in consideration of the great love wherewith he had loved them. Three things he exhorts them to:—

1. To continue in his love, *v.* 9. "Continue in your love to me, and in mine to you."

2. To let his joy remain in them, and fill them, *v.* 11. This he designed in those precepts and promises given them.

3. To evidence their love to him by keeping his commandments. "This will be an evidence of the fidelity and constancy of your love to me, and then you may be sure of the continuance of my love to you."

IV. Concerning the *disciples' love one to another*, enjoined as an evidence of their love to Christ, and a grateful return for his love to them. We must keep his commandments, and this is his commandment, that we *love one another*, *v.* 12, and again, *v.* 17. He speaks as if he were about to give them many things in charge, and yet names this only, *that you love one another*; not only because this includes many duties, but because it will have a good influence upon all.

FRUITS OF ENMITY
(*vv.* 18–25)

Here Christ discourses concerning *hatred*, which is the character and genius of the devil's kingdom, as love is of the kingdom of Christ. Observe here,

I. Who they are in whom this hatred is found—the world, the children of this world, as distinguished from the children of God; those who are in the interests of the god of this world, whose image they bear, and whose power they are subject to.

II. Who they are against whom this hatred is levelled—against the disciples of Christ, against Christ himself, and against the Father.

1. The world hates the disciples of Christ: *The world hateth you* (*v.* 19); and he speaks of it as that which they must expect and count upon, *v.* 18, as 1 John iii. 13.

(2) Observe what is here included.

[1] The world's enmity against the followers of Christ: it *hateth them*. Note, Whom Christ blesseth the world curseth.

[2] The fruits of that enmity, two of which we have here, *v.* 20. *First*, They will persecute you, because they hate you, for hatred is a restless passion. *Secondly*, Another fruit of their enmity is implied, that they would reject their doctrine. When Christ says, *If they have kept my sayings, they will keep yours*, he means, They will keep yours, and regard yours, no more than they have regarded and kept mine.

[3] The causes of that enmity. The world will hate them,

First, Because they do not belong to it (*v.* 19). They swim against the stream of the world, and are not conformed to it; they witness against it, and are not conformed to it. This would support them under all the calamities which the world's hatred would bring upon them, that they were hated because they were the choice and the chosen ones of the Lord Jesus, and were not of the world.

Secondly, "Another cause of the world's hating you will be because you do belong to Christ (*v.* 21): *For my name's sake*." Here is the core of the controversy; whatever is pretended, this is the ground of the quarrel, they hate Christ's disciples because they *bear his name*, and *bear up his name* in the world.

Thirdly, After all, it is the world's ignorance that is the true cause of its enmity to the disciples of Christ (*v.* 21): *Because they know not him that sent me.*

2. The world hates Christ himself. And this is spoken of here for two ends:—

(1) To mitigate the trouble of his followers, arising from the world's hatred, and to make it the less strange, and the less grievous (*v.* 18): *You know that it hated me before you.* We read it as signifying priority of time; he began in the bitter cup of suffering, and then left us to pledge him; but it may be read as expressing his superiority over them: "*You know* that it hated me, *your first*, your chief and captain, your leader and commander."

(2) To aggravate the wickedness of this unbelieving world, and to discover its exceeding sinfulness; to hate and persecute the apostles was bad enough, but in them to hate and persecute Christ himself was much worse. The world is generally in an ill name in scripture, and nothing can put it into a worse name than this, that it hated Jesus Christ. There is a world of people that are haters of Christ. Two things he insists upon to aggravate the wickedness of those that hated him:—

[1] That there was the greatest reason imaginable why they should love him; men's good words and good works usually recommend them; now as to Christ,

First, His words were such as merited their love (*v.* 22): "*If I*

had not spoken unto them, to court their love, *they had not had sin*, their opposition had not amounted to a hatred of me, their sin had been comparatively no sin. But now that I have said so much to them to recommend myself to their best affections they have no pretence, no excuse for their sin."

Secondly, His works were such as merited their love, as well as his words (*v.* 24): "*If I had not done among them*, in their country, and before their eyes, such works as *no other man ever did, they had not had sin*; their unbelief and enmity had been excusable, and they might have had some colour to say that my word was not to be credited, if not otherwise confirmed"; but he produced satisfactory proofs of his divine mission, *works which no other man did.*

[2] That there was no reason at all why they should hate him. "*This comes to pass*, this unreasonable hatred of me, and of my disciples for my sake, *that the word might be fulfilled which is written in their law*" (that is, in the Old Testament, which is a law, and was received by them as a law), "*They hated me without a cause*"; this David speaks of himself as a type of Christ, Ps. xxxv. 19; lxix. 4.

3. In Christ the world hates God himself; this is twice said here (*v.* 23): *He that hateth me*, though he thinks his hatred goes no further, yet really he *hates my Father also.* And again, *v.* 24, They have *seen and hated both me and my Father.* God will have all men to honour the Son as

they honour the Father, and therefore what entertainment the Son has, that the Father has.

A DOUBLE WITNESS
(*vv.* 26–27)

I. It is here promised that the blessed Spirit shall maintain the cause of Christ in the world, notwithstanding the opposition it should meet with. We have more in this verse concerning the Holy Ghost than in any one verse besides in the Bible; and, being baptized into his name, we are concerned to acquaint ourselves with him as far as he is revealed.

1. Here is an account of him in his essence, or subsistence rather. He is *the Spirit of truth, who proceedeth from the Father.* Here, (1) He is spoken of as a distinct person; not a quality or property, but a person under the proper name of a *Spirit*, and proper title of the *Spirit of truth*, a title fitly given him where he is brought in testifying. (2) As a divine person, that *proceedeth from the Father*, by out-goings that were of old, *from everlasting.* The *Nicene* Creed says, The Spirit *proceedeth from the Father and the Son*, for he is called the *Spirit of the Son*, Gal. iv. 6. And the Son is here said to *send him.* The Greek church choose rather to say, *from the Father by the Son.*

2. In his mission. (1) He will come in a more plentiful effusion of his gifts, graces, and powers, than had ever yet been. (2) *I will send him to you from the Father.* He had said (*ch.* xiv. 16), *I will pray the Father, and he shall send you the Comforter*, which

bespeaks the Spirit to be the fruit of the intercession Christ makes within the veil: here he says, *I will send him*, which bespeaks him to be the fruit of his dominion within the veil. The Spirit was sent, [1] By Christ as Mediator, now *ascended on high* to *give gifts unto men*, and all power being given to him. [2] From the Father: "Not only from heaven, my Father's house" (the Spirit was given in a *sound from heaven*, Acts ii. 2), "but according to my Father's will and appointment, and with his concurring power and authority." [3] To the apostles to instruct them in their preaching, enable them for working, and carry them through their sufferings. He was given to them and their successors, both in Christianity and in the ministry; to them and their seed, and their seed's seed, according to that promise, Isa. lix. 21.

3. In his office and operations, which are two:—(1) One implied in the title given to him; he is the *Comforter*, or *Advocate.* And advocate for Christ, to maintain his cause against the world's infidelity, a comforter to the saints against the world's hatred. (2) Another expressed: *He shall testify of me.* He is not only an advocate, but a witness for Jesus Christ; he is one of the three that *bear record in heaven*, and the first of the three that *bear witness on earth*, 1 John v. 7, 8.

II. It is here promised that the apostles also, by the Spirit's assistance, should have the honour of being Christ's witnesses (*v.* 27): *And you also shall bear witness of* me, being competent witnesses, for *you have been with* me from the beginning of my ministry. Note. (1) We have great reason to receive the record which the apostles gave of Christ, for they did not speak by hearsay, but what they had the greatest assurance of imaginable, 2 Pet. i. 16; 1 John i. 1, 3. (2) Those are best able to bear witness for Christ that have themselves been with him, by faith, hope, and love, and by living a life of communion with God in him. Ministers must first learn Christ, and then preach him. Those speak best of the things of God that speak experimentally.

CHAPTER SIXTEEN
PERSECUTION FORETOLD
(vv. 1–6)

Christ dealt faithfully with his disciples when he sent them forth on his errands, for he told them the worst of it, that they might sit down and count the cost. He had told them in the chapter before to expect the world's hatred; now here in these verses,

I. He gives them a reason why he alarmed them thus with the expectation of trouble: *These things have I spoken unto you, that you should not be offended*, or *scandalized, v.* 1.

II. He foretells particularly what they should suffer (*v.* 2): "Those that have power to do it shall *put you out of their synagogues*; and this is not the worst, *they shall kill you.*"

1. The sword of ecclesiastical censure; this is drawn against

them by the Jews, for they were the only pretenders to church-power. Note, It has often been the lot of Christ's disciples to be unjustly excommunicated. Many a good truth has been branded with an anathema, and many a child of God *delivered to Satan.*

2. The sword of civil power: "The time cometh, *the hour is come*; now things are likely to be worse with you than hitherto they have been; when you are expelled as heretics, they will *kill you, and think they do God service*, and others will think so too." It is common to patronise an enmity to religion with a colour of duty to God, and service to his church. God's people have suffered the greatest hardships from conscientious persecutors.

III. He gives them the true reason of the world's enmity and rage against them (*v.* 3): "*These things will they do unto you*, not because you have done them any harm, but *because they have not known the Father, nor me*. Let this comfort you, that none will be your enemies but the worst of men."

IV. He tells them why he gave them notice of this now, and why not sooner.

1. Why he told them of it now (*v.* 4), not to discourage them, or add to their present sorrow; nor did he tell them of their danger that they might contrive how to avoid it, but that, "when *the time shall come* (and you may be sure it will come), you may *remember that I told you.*" Note, When suffering times come it will be of use to us to remember what Christ has told us of sufferings.

2. Why he did not tell them of it sooner: "*I spoke not this to you from the beginning* when you and I came to be first acquainted, because *I was with you.* (1) While he was with them, he bore the shock of the world's malice, and stood in the front of the battle. (2) It seems rather to be meant of the promise of *another comforter.* This he had said little of to them *at the beginning,* because he was himself with them to instruct, guide, and comfort them, and then they needed not the promise of the Spirit's extraordinary presence.

V. He expresses a very affectionate concern for the present sadness of his disciples, upon occasion of what he had said to them (*vv.* 5, 6).

1. He had told them that he was about to leave them: *Now I go my way.* He was not driven away by force, but voluntarily departed; his life was not extorted from him, but deposited by him.

2. He had told them what hard things they must suffer when he was gone, and that they must not expect such an easy quiet life as they had had. Now, if these were the legacies he had to leave to them, who had *left all* for him, they would be tempted to think they had made a sorry bargain of it, and were, for the present, in a consternation about it, in which their Master sympathizes with them, yet blames them, (1) That they were careless of the means of comfort, and did not stir up themselves to seek it: *None of you asks me, Whither goest thou?* Peter had started this question (*ch.* xiii. 36), and Thomas had seconded it (*ch.* xiv. 5), but they

did not pursue it, they did not take the answer; they were in the dark concerning it, and did not enquire further, nor seek for fuller satisfaction; they did not continue seeking, continue knocking.

(2) That they were too intent, and pored too much, upon the occasions of their grief: *Sorrow has filled their hearts.* Christ had said enough to fill them with joy (*ch.* xv. 11); but by looking at that only which made against them, and overlooking that which made for them, they were so full of sorrow that there was no room left for joy.

THE COMFORTER (*vv.* 7–15)

Three things we have here concerning *the Comforter's coming*:—

I. That Christ's departure was absolutely necessary to the Comforter's coming, *v.* 7. Now he here tells them,

1. In general, *It was expedient for them that he should go away.* This was strange doctrine, but if it was true it was comfortable enough, and showed them how absurd their sorrow was. *It is expedient,* not only for me, but *for you* also, *that I go away*; though they do not see it, and are loth to believe it, so it is.

2. *It was therefore expedient* because its object was the sending of the Spirit. Now observe,

(1) That Christ's going was so that the Comforter may come.

[1] This is expressed negatively: *If I go not away, the Comforter will not come.* And why not? *First,* So it was settled in the

divine counsels concerning this affair, and the measure must not be altered; *shall the earth be forsaken for them? Secondly*, It is congruous enough that the ambassador extraordinary should be recalled, before the envoy come, that is constantly to reside. *Thirdly*, The sending of the Spirit was to be the fruit of Christ's purchase, and that purchase was to be made by his death, which was his going away. *Fourthly*, It was to be an answer to his intercession within the veil. See *ch.* xiv. 16.

[2] It is expressed positively: *If I depart I will send him to you.* Though he departs, he sends the *Comforter*; nay, he departs on purpose to send him.

(2) That the presence of Christ's Spirit in his church is so much better, and more desirable, than his bodily presence, that it was really expedient for us that he should go away, to send the Comforter.

II. That the coming of *the Spirit* was absolutely necessary to the carrying on of Christ's interests on earth (*v.* 8).

1. See here what the office of the Spirit is, and on what errand he is sent. (1) To *reprove.* The Spirit, by the word and conscience, is a reprover; ministers are reprovers by office, and by them the Spirit reproves. (2) To *convince.* It is a law-term, and speaks the office of the judge in summing up the evidence, and setting a matter that has been long canvassed in a clear and true light.

2. See who they are whom he is to reprove and convince: *The world*, both Jew and Gentile.

3. See what the Spirit shall convince the world of.

(1) *Of sin* (*v.* 9), *because they believe not on me.* [1] The Spirit is sent to convince sinners of sin, not barely to tell them of it. [2] The Spirit, in conviction, fastens especially upon the sin of unbelief, their not believing in Christ, *First*, As the great reigning sin. There was, and is, a world of people, that believe not in Jesus Christ, and they are not sensible that it is their sin. *Secondly*, As the great ruining sin. Every sin is so in its own nature; no sin is so to them that believe in Christ; so that it is unbelief that damns sinners.

(2) *Of righteousness, because I go to my Father, and you see me no more, v.* 10. We may understand this, [1] Of Christ's personal righteousness. He shall convince the world that Jesus of Nazareth was Christ the righteous (1 John ii. 1), as the centurion owned (Luke xxiii. 47), *Certainly this was a righteous man.* [2] Of Christ's righteousness communicated to us for our justification and salvation; that everlasting righteousness which Messiah was to bring in, Dan. ix. 24.

(3) *Of judgment, because the prince of this world is judged, v.* 11. Observe here, [1] The devil, *the prince of this world*, was judged, was discovered to be a great deceiver and destroyer, and as such judgment was entered against him, and execution in part done. He was cast out of the Gentile world when his oracles were silenced and his altars deserted, cast out of the bodies of

many in Christ's name, which miraculous power continued long in the church; he was cast out of the souls of people by the grace of God working with the gospel of Christ; he *fell as lightning from heaven*. [2] This is a good argument wherewith the Spirit convinces the world of judgment, that is, *First*, Of inherent holiness and sanctification, Matt. xii. 18. By *the judgment of the prince of this world*, it appears that Christ is stronger than Satan, and can disarm and dispossess him, and set up his throne upon the ruins of his. *Secondly*, Of a new and better dispensation of things. He shall show that Christ's errand into the world was to set things to right in it, and to introduce times of reformation and regeneration; and he proves it by this, that *the prince of this world*, the great master of misrule, is judged and expelled. *Thirdly*, Of the power and dominion of the Lord Jesus. He shall convince the world that *all judgment is committed to him*, and that he is the *Lord of all*, which is evident by this, that he has judged the prince of this world, has broken *the serpent's head, destroyed him that had the power of death, and spoiled principalities. Fourthly*, Of the final day of judgment: all the obstinate enemies of Christ's gospel and kingdom shall certainly be reckoned with at last, for the devil, their ringleader, is judged.

III. That the coming of the Spirit would be of unspeakable advantage to the disciples themselves.

1. He intimates to them the tender sense he had of their present weakness (*v.* 12).

2. He assures them of sufficient assistances, by the pouring out of the Spirit.

(1) To guide the apostles. He will take care,

[1] That they do not miss their way: *He will guide you*.

[2] That they do not come short of their end: *He will guide them into all truth*. But how into *all truth*? The meaning is,

First, Into the whole truth relating to their embassy.

Secondly, Into nothing but the truth. All that *he shall guide you into* shall be *truth* (1 John ii. 27); *the anointing is truth*. In the following words he proves both these:—1. "The Spirit shall teach nothing but the truth, *for he shall not speak of himself* any doctrine distinct from mine, *but whatsoever he shall hear*, and knows to be the mind of the Father, *that*, and that only, *shall he speak*." This intimates, (1) That the testimony of the Spirit, in the word and by the apostles, is what we may rely upon. (2) That the testimony of the Spirit always concurs with the word of Christ, *for he does not speak of himself*, has no separate interest or intention of his own, but, as in essence so in records, he *is one with the Father and the Son*, 1 John v. 7.

(2) The Spirit undertook to glorify Christ, *vv.* 14, 15. [1] Even the sending, of the Spirit was the glorifying of Christ. God the Father glorified him in heaven, and the Spirit glorified him on earth. [2] The Spirit glorified Christ by leading his followers

into *the truth as it is in Jesus,* Eph. iv. 21.

LASTING JOY (*vv.* 16–22)

Our Lord Jesus, for the comfort of his sorrowful disciples, here promises that he would visit them again.

I. Observe the intimation he gave them of the comfort he designed them, *v.* 16. Here he tells them,

, 1. That they should now shortly lose the sight of him.

2. That yet they should speedily recover the sight of him: *Again a little while, and you shall see me,* and therefore you ought not to *sorrow as those that have no hope.* His farewell was not a final farewell; they should see him again, (1) At his resurrection, soon after his death, when *he showed himself alive,* by many infallible proofs, and this in a very little while, not forty hours. See Hos. vi. 2. (2) By the pouring out of the Spirit, soon after his ascension, which scattered the mists of ignorance and mistake they were almost lost in, and gave them a much clearer insight into the mysteries of Christ's gospel than they had yet had. (3) At his second coming.

3. He assigns the reason: "*Because I go to the Father.*"

It should seem, all this refers rather to his going away at death, and return at his resurrection, than his going away at his ascension, and his return at the end of time; for it was his death that was their grief, not his ascension (Luke xxiv. 52), and between his

death and resurrection it was indeed a *little while.*

II. The perplexity of the disciples upon the intimation given them; they were at a loss what to make of it. (*vv,* 17, 18). When they were at a loss about the meaning of Christ's words, they conferred together upon it, and asked help of one another.

III. The further explication of what Christ had said.

1. See here *why* Christ explained it (*v.* 19); because he *knew they were desirous to ask him,* and designed it.

2. See here *how* he explained it; not by a nice and critical descant upon the words, but by bringing the thing more closely to them; he had told them of *not seeing him, and seeing him,* and they did not apprehend his meaning, and therefore he explains it by their sorrowing and rejoicing, because we commonly measure things according as they affect us (*v.* 20): *You shall weep and lament,* for my departure, *but the world shall rejoice* in it; *and you shall be sorrowful,* while I am absent, *but,* upon my return to you, *your sorrow will be turned into joy.* But he says nothing of the *little while,* because he saw that this perplexed them more than any thing; and it is of no consequence to us to know *the times and the seasons.*

(1) What Christ says here, and *vv.* 21, 22, of their sorrow and joy, is primarily to be understood of the present state and circumstances of the disciples.

(2) It is applicable to all the faithful followers of the Lamb, and describes the common case of

Christians. *Gladness is sown for the upright in heart, that sow in tears,* and without doubt *they will shortly reap in joy.* Their sorrow will not only be followed with joy, but turned into it; for the most precious comforts take rise from pious griefs. This he illustrates by a similitude taken from a woman in travail, to whose sorrows he compares those of his disciples, for their encouragement; for it is the will of Christ that his people should be a comforted people.

First, Here is the similitude or parable itself (*v.* 21): *A woman,* we know, *when she is in travail, hath sorrow,* she is in exquisite pain, *because her hour is come,* the hour which nature and providence have fixed, which she has expected, and cannot escape; *but as soon as she is delivered of the child,* then *she remembers no more the anguish.*

Secondly, The application of the similitude (*v.* 22): "*You now have sorrow,* and are likely to have more, *but I will see you again,* and you me, and then all will be well." Men will attempt to take their joy from them; they would if they could; but they shall not prevail. Some understand it of the eternal joy of those that are glorified; those that have *entered into the joy of the Lord shall go no more out.* I rather understand it of the spiritual joys of those that are sanctified, particularly the apostles' joy in their apostleship.

AN ANSWER TO ASKING
(*vv.* 23–27)

An answer to their askings is here promised, for their further comfort. Now there are two ways of asking: asking by way of enquiry, which is the asking of the ignorant; and asking by way of request, which is the asking of the indigent. Christ here speaks of both.

I. By way of enquiry, they should not need to ask (*v.* 23). In the story *of the apostles' Acts* we seldom find them asking questions, as David, *Shall I do this?* Or, *Shall I go thither?* For they were constantly under a divine guidance.

Now for this he gives a reason (*v.* 25), which plainly refers to this promise, that they should not need to ask questions: "*These things have I spoken unto you in proverbs,* in such a way as you have thought not so plain and intelligible as you could have wished, *but the time cometh when I shall show you plainly,* as plainly as you can desire, *of the Father,* so that you shall not need to ask questions."

1. The great thing Christ would lead them into was the knowledge of God: "*I will show you the Father,* and bring you acquainted with him."

2. Of this he had hitherto spoken to them in proverbs, which are wise and instructive sayings, but figurative, and resting in generals.

3. He would speak to them *plainly—with freedom,* of the Father. When the Spirit was poured out, the apostles attained to a much greater knowledge of divine things than they had before, as appears by the utterance the Spirit gave them, Acts ii. 4.

II. He promises that by way of

request they should ask nothing in vain. Now,

1. Here is an express promise of a grant, *v.* 23. For he says, *Whatsoever you shall ask the Father in my name, he will give it to you.* We had it before, *ch.* xiv. 13. What would we more? The promise is as express as we can desire.

2. Here is an invitation for them to petition. It is thought sufficient if great men permit addresses, but Christ calls upon us to petition, *v.* 24.

(1) He looks back upon their practice hitherto: *Hitherto have you asked nothing in my name.*

(2) He looks forward to their practice for the future: *Ask, and you shall receive, that your joy may be full.*

3. Here are the grounds upon which they might hope to speed (*vv.* 26, 27), which are summed up in short by the apostle (1 John ii. 1): "*We have an advocate with the Father.*"

(1) We have an advocate; as to this, Christ saw cause at present not to insist upon it, only to make the following encouragement shine the brighter: "*I say not unto you that I will pray the Father for you.*" He speaks as if they needed not any further favours, when he had prevailed for the gift of the Holy Ghost to *make intercession within them,* as a Spirit of adoption, crying *Abba, Father;* as if they had no further need of him to pray for them now; but we shall find that he does more for us than he says he will. Men's performances often come short of their promises, but Christ's go beyond them.

(2) We have to do with a Father, which is so great an encouragement that it does in a manner supersede the other. Observe what an emphasis is laid upon this. The Father himself, whose favour you have forfeited, and whose wrath you have incurred, and with whom you need an advocate, he himself now loves you. Observe, [1] Why the Father loved the disciples of Christ: *Because you have loved me, and have believed that I came out from God,* that is, because you are my disciples indeed: not as if the love began on their side, but when by his grace he has wrought in us a love to him he is well pleased with the work of his own hands. [2] What encouragement this gave them in prayer. They need not fear speeding when they came to one that loved them, and wished them well.

CHRIST'S MISSION
(*vv.* 28–33)

Two things Christ here comforts his disciples with:—

I. With an assurance that, though he was leaving the world, he was returning to his Father, from whom he came forth, *vv.* 28–32, where we have,

1. A plain declaration of Christ's mission from the Father, and his return to him (*v.* 28): *I came forth from the Father, and am come,* as you see, *into the world. Again, I leave the world,* as you will see shortly, *and go to the Father.*

(1) These two great truths are here, [1] Contracted, and put into a few words. Brief summaries of Christian doctrine are of great use to young beginners. [2] Compared,

and set the one over against the other. There is an admirable harmony in divine truths; they both corroborate and illustrate one another; Christ's coming and his going do so.

(2) If we ask concerning the Redeemer *whence he came*, and *whither he went*, we are told, [1] That he *came from the Father*, who sanctified and sealed him. [2] That, when he had done his work on earth, he left the world, and went back to his Father at his ascension.

2. The disciples' satisfaction in this declaration (*vv.* 29, 30): *Lo, now speakest thou plainly*. It should seem, this one word of Christ did them more good than all the rest, though he had said many things likely enough to fasten upon them. Two things they improved in by this saying:—

(1) In knowledge: *Lo, now speakest thou plainly*.

(2) In faith: *Now are we sure*. Observe,

[1] What was the matter of their faith: *We believe that thou camest forth from God*.

[2] What was the motive of their faith—his omniscience. This proved him a teacher come from God, and more than a prophet, that he knew all things, which they were convinced of by this that he resolved those doubts which were hid in their hearts, and answered the scruples they had not confessed.

3. The gentle rebuke Christ gave the disciples for their confidence that they now understood him, *vv.* 31, 32. Here we have,

(1) A question, designed to put them upon consideration: *Do you now believe?*

(2) A prediction of their fall, that, how confident soever they were now of their own stability, in a little time they would all desert him, which was fulfilled that very night, when, upon his being seized by a party of the guards, *all his disciples forsook him and fled*, Matt. xxvi. 56.

(3) An assurance of his own comfort notwithstanding: *Yet I am not alone*. He would not be thought to complain of their deserting him, as if it were any real damage to him; for in their absence he should be sure of his Father's presence.

II. He comforts them with a promise of peace in him, by virtue of his victory over the world, whatever troubles they might meet with in it (*v.* 33). Observe,

1. The end Christ aimed at in preaching this farewell sermon to his disciples: *That in him they might have peace*.

2. The entertainment they were likely to meet with in the world: "You shall not have outward peace, never expect it."

3. The encouragement Christ gives them with reference hereto: *But be of good cheer*.

4. The ground of that encouragement: *I have overcome 'the world*. Christ's victory is a Christian's triumph. Never was there such a conqueror of the world as Christ was, and we ought to be encouraged by it, (1) Because Christ has overcome the world before us; so that we may look upon it as a conquered enemy, that has many a time been baffled. Nay, (2) He has conquered it for us, as the captain of our salvation. We are interested in his victory; by his cross the

world is *crucified to us*, which bespeaks it completely conquered and put into our possession; all is yours, even *the world*. Christ having overcome the world, believers have nothing to do but to pursue their victory, and divide the spoil; and this we do by faith, 1 John v. 4. *We are more than conquerors through him that loved us*.

CHAPTER SEVENTEEN

CHRIST'S PRAYER I
(vv. 1–5)

Here we have, I. The circumstances of this prayer, *v*. 1. Observe,

1. The time when he prayed this prayer; when he had *spoken these words*, had given the foregoing farewell to his disciples, he prayed this prayer in their hearing; so that, (1) It was a prayer after sermon; when he had spoken from God to them, he turned to speak to God for them. (2) It was a prayer after sacrament; after Christ and his disciples had eaten the passover and the Lord's supper together, and he had given them a suitable exhortation, he closed the solemnity with this prayer, that God would preserve the good impressions of the ordinance upon them. (3) It was a family-prayer. Christ's disciples were his family. (4) It was a parting prayer. When we and our friends are parting, it is good to part with prayer, Acts xx. 36. (5) It was a prayer that was a preface to his sacrifice, which he was now about to offer on earth, specifying the favours and blessings designed to be purchased by the merit of his death for those that were his.

(6) It was a prayer that was a specimen of his intercession, which he ever lives to make for us within the veil.

(2) The outward expression of fervent desire which he used in this prayer: He *lifted up his eyes to heaven*, as before (*ch*. xi. 41). It is significant of the lifting up of the soul to God in prayer, Ps. xxv. 1.

II. The first part of the prayer itself, in which Christ prays for himself. Observe here,

1. He prays to God as a Father: He *lifted up his eyes, and said, Father*. Note, As prayer is to be made to God only, so it is our duty in prayer to eye him as a Father, and to call him *our Father*. All that have the Spirit of adoption are taught to cry *Abba, Father*, Rom. viii. 15; Gal. iv. 6.

2. He prayed for himself first. Though Christ, as God, was prayed to, Christ, as man, prayed; thus *it became him to fulfil all righteousness. Glorify me, that I may glorify thee*, in doing what is agreed upon to be yet done, *vv*. 1–3. And to the performance of his undertaking hitherto: "*Glorify me, for I have glorified thee*. I have done my part, and now, Lord, do thine," *vv*. 4, 5.

(1) Christ here prays to be *glorified*, in order to *glorify God* (*v*. 1): *Glorify thy Son* according to thy promise, *that thy Son may glorify thee* according to his undertaking. Here observe,

[1] What he prays for—that he might be glorified in this world: "*The hour is come* when all the powers of darkness will combine to vilify thy Son; now, Father, glorify him."

[2] What he pleads to enforce this request.

First, He pleads relation: *Glorify thy Son*; thy Son as God, as Mediator. Note, Those that have received the adoption of sons may in faith pray for the inheritance of sons; if sanctified, then glorified: *Father, glorify thy Son.*

Secondly, He pleads the time: *The hour is come*; the season prefixed to an hour. The hour of Christ's passion was determined in the counsel of God. He had often said his hour was not yet come; but now it was come, and he knew it.

Thirdly, He pleads the Father's own interest and concern herein: *That thy Son may also glorify thee*; for he had consecrated his whole undertaking to his Father's honour. He desired to be carried triumphantly through his sufferings to his glory, that he might glorify the Father two ways:—By *the death of the cross*, which he was now to suffer. 2. By the doctrine of the cross, which was now shortly to be published to the world, by which God's kingdom was to be re-established among men.

Fourthly, He pleads his commission (*vv.* 2, 3); he desires to glorify his Father, in conformity to, and in pursuance of, the commission given him. Now see here the power of the Mediator.

a. The origin of his power: *Thou hast given him power*; he has it from God, *to whom all power belongs.*

b. The extent of his power: He has *power over all flesh.* (*a*) Over all mankind. He has power in and over the world of spirits, the powers of the upper and unseen world are subject to him (1 Peter iii. 22); but,

being now mediating between God and man, he here *pleads his power over all flesh.* (*b*) Over mankind considered as corrupt and fallen, for so he is called *flesh*, Gen. vi. 3. If he had not in this sense been flesh, he had not needed a Redeemer.

c. The grand intention and design of this power: *That he should give eternal life to as many as thou hast given him.* Here is the mystery of our salvation laid open.

(*a*) Here is the Father making over the elect to the Redeemer, and giving them to him as his charge and trust; as the crown and recompence of his undertaking.

(*b*) Here is the Son undertaking to secure the happiness of those that were given him, that he would *give eternal life to them.*

(*c*) Here is the subserviency of the Redeemer's universal dominion to this: He has *power over all flesh*, on purpose that he might give eternal life to the select number. Note, Christ's dominion over the children of men is in order to achieve the salvation of the children of God.

d. Here is a further explication of this grand design (*v.* 3).

(*a*) The great end which the Christian religion sets before us, and that is, eternal life, the happiness of an immortal soul in the vision and fruition of an eternal God.

(*b*) The sure way of attaining this blessed end, which is, by the right knowledge of God and Jesus Christ: *"This is life eternal, to know thee,"* which may be taken two ways: —[*a*] *"Life eternal* lies in the knowledge of God and Jesus Christ.

[b] The knowledge of God and Christ leads to life eternal; this is the way in which Christ gives eternal life, by the knowledge of him that has called us (2 Peter i. 3), and this is the way in which we come to receive it.

(2) Christ here prays to be glorified in consideration of his having glorified the Father hitherto, *vv.* 4, 5. The meaning of the former petition was, Glorify me in this world; the meaning of the latter is, Glorify me in the other world. *I have glorified thee on the earth, and now glorify thou me.*

Thus we must be taught that those, and only those, who glorify God on earth, and persevere in the work God hath given them to do, shall be glorified with the Father, when they must be no more in this world. Not that we can merit that glory, as Christ did, but our glorifying God is required as an evidence of our interest in Christ, through whom eternal life is God's free gift.

CHRIST'S PRAYER II
(*vv.* 6–10)

Christ, having prayed for himself, comes next to pray for those that are his, and he knew them by name, though he did not here name them. Now observe here,

I. Whom he did not pray for (*v.* 9): *I pray not for the world.* Note, There is a world of people that Jesus Christ did not pray for. It is not meant of the world of mankind in general (he prays for that here, *v.* 21, *That the world may believe that thou hast sent me*); nor is it meant of the Gentiles, in distinction from the Jews; but the world is

here opposed to the elect, who are given to Christ out of the world.

II. Whom he did pray for; not for angels, but for the children of men. 1. He prays *for those that were given him,* meaning primarily the disciples that had attended *him in the regeneration*; but it is doubtless to be extended further, to all who come under the same character, who receive and believe the words of Christ, *vv.* 6, 8. 2. He prays *for all that should believe on him* (*v.* 20), and it is not only the petitions that follow, but those also which went before, that must be construed to extend to all believers, in every place and every age; for he has a concern for them all, and calls *things that are not as though they were.*

III. What encouragement he had to pray for them, and what are the general pleas with which he introduces his petitions for them, and recommends them to his Father's favour; they are five:—

1. The charge he had received concerning them: *Thine they were, and thou gavest them me* (*v.* 6), and again (*v.* 9), *Those whom thou hast given me.*

2. The care he had taken of them to teach them (*v.* 6): *I have manifested thy name to them. I have given to them the words which thou gavest to me, v.* 8.

3. The good effect of the care he had taken of them, and the pains he had taken with them (*v.* 6): *They have kept thy word* (*v.* 7), *they have known that all things are of thee* (*v.* 8); *they have received thy words,* and embraced them, have given their assent and consent to them, *and have known surely that I came out*

from thee, and have believed that thou didst send me.

4. He pleads the Father's own interest in them (*v.* 9): *I pray for them, for they are thine*; and this by virtue of a joint and mutual interest, which he and the Father have in what pertained to each: *All mine are thine, and thine are mine.* Between the Father and Son there can be no dispute (as there is among the children of men) about *mine and thine*, for the matter was settled from eternity; *all mine are thine, and thine are mine.*

5. He pleads his own concern in them: *I am glorified in them.* (1) *I have been glorified in them.* What little honour Christ had in this world was among his disciples; he had been glorified by their attendance on him and obedience to him, their preaching and working miracles in his name; and therefore *I pray for them.* (2) "*I am to be glorified in them*, when I am gone to heaven; they are to bear up my name." The apostles preached and wrought miracles *in Christ's name; the Spirit in them glorified Christ* (*ch.* xvi. 14).

CHRIST'S PRAYER III
(*vv.* 11–16)

After the general pleas with which Christ recommended his disciples to his Father's care follow the particular petitions he puts up for them; and, 1. They all relate to spiritual blessings in heavenly things. 2. They are such blessings as were suited to their present state and case, and their various exigencies and occasions. 3. He is large and full in the petitions, orders them before his Father, and *fills his*

mouth with arguments, to teach us fervency and importunity in prayer, to be large in prayer, and dwell upon our errands at the throne of grace, wrestling as Jacob, *I will not let thee go, except thou bless me.*

Now the first thing Christ prays for, for his disciples, is their preservation. He commits them all to his Father's custody. Now observe,

I. The request itself: *Keep them from the world.* There were two ways of their being delivered from the world:—

1. By taking them out of it; and he does not pray that they might be so delivered: *I pray not that thou shouldest take them out of the world.*

2. Another way is by keeping them from the corruption that is in the world; and he prays they may be thus kept, *vv.* 11, 15. Here are three branches of this petition:—

(1) *Holy Father, keep those whom thou hast given me.*

[1] Christ was now leaving them; but let them not think that their defence was departed from them; no, he does here, in their hearing, commit them to the custody of his Father and their Father.

[2] The titles he gives to him he prays to, and them he prays for, enforce the petition. *First*, He speaks to God as a *holy Father.* In committing ourselves and others to the divine care, we may take encouragement, 1. From the attribute of his holiness, for this is engaged for the preservation of his holy ones; he hath *sworn by his holiness*, Ps. lxxxix. 35. 2. From this relation of a Father, wherein he stands to us through Christ. If he be a Father, he will take care of his

own children, will teach them and keep them; who else should? *Secondly*, He speaks of them as those whom the Father had *given him*. What we receive as our Father's gifts, we may comfortably remit to our Father's care.

(2) *Keep* them *through thine own name*: That is, [1] Keep them for thy name's sake; so some. [2] Keep them in thy name; so others; the original is so, "Keep them in the knowledge and fear of thy name; keep them in the profession and service of thy name, whatever it cost them. Keep them in the interest of thy name, and let them ever be faithful to this; keep them in thy truths, in thine ordinances, in the way of thy commandments." [3] Keep them by or through thy name; so others. "Keep them by thine own power, in thine own hand; keep them thyself, undertake for them, let them be thine own immediate care. Keep them by those means of preservation which thou hast thyself appointed, and by which thou hast made thyself known. Keep them by thy word and ordinances; let thy name be their strong tower, thy tabernacle their pavilion."

(3) *Keep them from the evil*, or out of the evil. He had taught them to pray daily, *Deliver us from evil*, and this would encourage them to pray.

II. The reasons with which he enforces these requests for their preservation, which are five:—

1. He pleads that hitherto he had kept them (*v.* 12).

2. He pleads that he was now under a necessity of leaving them, and could no longer watch over

them in the way that he had hitherto done (*v.* 11): "Keep them now, that I may not lose the labour I bestowed upon them while I was with them. Keep them, *that they may be one* with us *as we are* with each other." We shall have occasion to speak of this, *v.* 21.

3. He pleads what a satisfaction it would be to them to know themselves safe, and what a satisfaction it would be to him to see them easy: *I speak this, that they may have my joy fulfilled in themselves*, *v.* 13.

4. He pleads the ill usage they were likely to meet with in the world, for his sake (*v.* 14): "*I have given them thy word* to be published to the world, *and they have received it*, have believed it themselves, and accepted the trust of transmitting it to the world; and therefore *the world hath hated them*, as also because they are *not of the world*, any more than I."

5. He pleads their conformity to himself in a holy non-conformity to the world (*v.* 16): "Father, keep them, for they are of my spirit and mind, *they are not of the world, even as I am not of the world*." Those may in faith commit themselves to God's custody, (1) Who are *as Christ was in this world*, and tread in his steps. God will love those that are like Christ. (2) Who do not engage themselves in the world's interest, nor devote themselves to its service.

CHRIST'S PRAYER IV
(*vv.* 17–19)

The next thing he prayed for for them was that they might be sanctified; not only kept from evil, but made good.

I. Here is the petition (*v.* 17): *Sanctify them through thy truth*, through thy word, for *thy word is truth*; it is true—it is truth itself. He desires they may be sanctified,

1. As Christians. Father, make them holy, and this will be their preservation, 1 Thess. v. 23.

2. As ministers. "*Sanctify them*, set them apart for thyself and service; let their call to the apostleship be ratified in heaven." Prophets were said to be sanctified, Jer. i. 5. Priests and Levites were so. *Sanctify them*; that is, (1) "Qualify them for the office, with Christian graces and ministerial gifts, to make them able ministers of the New Testament." (2) "Separate them to the office, Rom. i. 1. I have called them, they have consented; Father, say *Amen* to it." (3) "Own them in the office; let thy hand go along with them; sanctify them by or in thy truth, as truth is opposed to figure and shadow."

II. We have here two pleas or arguments to enforce the petition for the disciples' sanctification:—

1. The mission they had from him (*v.* 18): "*As thou hast sent me into the world*, to be thine ambassador to the children of men, so now that I am recalled *have I sent them into the world*, as my delegates." Now here,

(1) Christ speaks with great assurance of his own mission: *Thou hast sent me into the world*.

(2) He speaks with great satisfaction of the commission he had given his disciples: "*So have I sent them* on the same errand, and to carry on the same design"; to

preach the same doctrine that he preached, and to confirm it with the same proofs, with a charge likewise to commit to other faithful men that which was committed to them. He gave them their commission (*ch.* xx. 21) with a reference to his own, and it magnifies their office that it comes from Christ, and that there is some affinity between the commission given to the ministers of reconciliation and that given to the Mediator; he is called an *apostle* (Heb. iii. 1), a *minister* (Rom. xv. 8), a *messenger*, Mal. iii. 1. Only they are sent as servants, he as a Son. Now this comes in here as a reason, [1] Why Christ was concerned so much for them, and laid their case so near his heart; because he had himself put them into a difficult office, which required great abilities for the due discharge of it. [2] Why he committed them to his Father; because he was concerned in their cause, their mission being in prosecution of his, and as it were an assignment out of it.

2. The merit he had for them is another thing here pleaded (*v.* 19): *For their sakes I sanctify myself.* Here is, (1) Christ's designation of himself to the work and office of Mediator: *I sanctified myself.* (2) Christ's design of kindness to his disciples herein; it is *for their sakes*, that *they may be sanctified*, that is, that they may be martyrs; so some. But I rather take it more generally, that they may be saints and ministers, duly qualified and accepted of God. And he that designed the end designed also the means, that they might be sanctified *by the truth*, the truth which Christ came into

the world to bear witness to, and died to confirm.

CHRIST'S PRAYER V
(vv. 20–23)

Next to their purity he prays for their unity; for the wisdom from above is *first pure, then peaceable*; and amity is amiable indeed when it is like the ointment on Aaron's holy head, and the dew on Zion's holy hill. Observe,

I. Who are included in this prayer (v. 20): "*Not these only*, not these only that are now my disciples" (the eleven, the seventy, with others, men and women that followed him when he was here on earth), "but *for those also who shall believe on me through their word*, either preached by them in their own day or written by them for the generations to come; I pray *for them all*, that they all may be one in their interest in this prayer, and may all receive benefit by it."

II. What is intended in this prayer (v. 21): *That they all may be one*. The same was said before (v. 11), *that they may be one as we are*, and again, v. 22. The heart of Christ was much upon this. It is the prayer of Christ for all that are his, and we may be sure it is an answered prayer—*that they all may be one*, one in us (v. 21), one *as we are one* (v. 22), made *perfect in one*, v. 23. It includes three things:—

1. That they might all be *incorporated in one body*. As Christ died, so he prayed, to *gather them all in one*, ch. xi. 52; Eph. i. 10.

2. That they might all be animated by one Spirit. This is plainly implied in this—*that they may be one in us*. Union with the Father and Son is obtained and kept up only by the Holy Ghost.

3. That they might all be *knit together* in the bond of love and charity, all of one heart. *That they all may be one*, (1) In judgment and sentiment; not in every little thing—this is neither possible nor needful, but in the great things of God. (2) In disposition and inclination. All that are sanctified have the same divine nature and image; they have all a new heart, and it is *one heart*. (3) They are all one in their designs and aims. Every true Christian, *as far as he is so*, eyes the glory of God as his highest end, and the glory of heaven as his chief good. (4) They are all one in their desires and prayers; though they differ in words and the manner of expressions, yet, having all received the same *spirit of adoption*, and observing the same rule, they pray for the same things in effect. (5) All one in love and affection. Every true Christian has that in him which inclines him to love all true Christians as such. But this prayer of Christ will not have its complete answer till all the saints come to heaven, for then, and not till then, they shall be *perfect in one*, v. 23; Eph. iv. 13.

III. What is intimated by way of plea or argument to enforce this petition; three things:—

1. The oneness that is between the Father and the Son, which is mentioned again and again, vv. 11, 21–23.

2. The design of Christ in all his communications of light and grace to them (v. 22): "*The glory which thou gavest me*, as the trustee or channel of conveyance, *I have*

accordingly *given them*, to this intent, *that they may be one, as we are one*; so that those gifts will be in vain, if they be not one."

3. He pleads the happy influence their oneness would have upon others, and the furtherance it would give to the public good. This is twice urged (v. 21): *That the world may believe that thou hast sent me.* And again (v. 23): *That the world may know it*, for without knowledge there can be no true faith.

[1] In general, it will recommend Christianity to the world, and to the good opinion of those outside. When Christianity, instead of causing quarrels about itself, makes all other strifes to cease, —when it cools the fiery, smooths the rugged, and disposes men to be kind and loving, courteous and beneficent, to all men, studious to preserve and promote peace in all relations and societies, this will recommend it to all that have any thing either of natural religion or natural affection in them.

[2] In particular, it will beget in men good thoughts, *First*, Of Christ: They will know and believe that *thou hast sent me. Secondly*, Of Christians: They will *know that thou hast loved them as thou hast loved me.*

CHRIST'S PRAYER VI
(*vv.* 24–26)

Here is, I. A petition for the glorifying of all those that were given to Christ (v. 24), not only these apostles, but all believers: *Father, I will that they may be with me.* Observe,

1. The connection of this request with those foregoing. He had prayed that God would preserve, sanctify, and unite them; and now he prays that he would crown all his gifts with their glorification.

2. The manner of the request: *Father, I will.* Here, as before, he addresses himself to God as a Father, and therein we must do likewise; but when he says, *I will*, he speaks a language peculiar to himself, and such as does not become ordinary petitioners, but very well became him who paid for what he prayed for.

3. The request itself—that all the elect might come to be with him in heaven at last, to see his glory, and to share in it. Now observe here,

(1) Under what notion we are to hope for heaven? wherein does that happiness consist? three things make heaven:—[1] It is to be where Christ is: *Where I am.* [2] It is to be with him where he is; this is no tautology, but intimates that we shall not only be in the same happy place where Christ is, but that the happiness of the place will consist in his presence; this is *the fulness of its joy.* [3] It is to *behold his glory, which the Father* has given him.

(2) Upon what ground we are to hope for heaven; no other than purely the mediation and intercession of Christ, because he hath said, *Father, I will.*

4. The argument to back this request: *for thou lovedst me before the foundation of the world.* This is a reason, (1) Why he expected this glory himself. Thou wilt *give it to me, for thou lovedst me.* The honour and power given to the Son as Mediator were founded in the Father's love to him (*ch.* v. 20). Or, (2) Why he expected that those

who *were given to him* should be with him to share in his glory: "*Thou lovedst me*, and them in me, and canst deny me nothing I ask for them."

II. The conclusion of the prayer, which is designed to enforce all the petitions for the disciples, especially the last, that they may be glorified. Two things he insists upon, and pleads:—

1. The respect he had to his Father, *v.* 25. Observe,

(1) The title he gives to God: *O righteous Father*. When he prayed that they might be sanctified, he called him *holy Father*; when he prays that they may be glorified, he calls him *righteous Father*; for it is a *crown of righteousness which the righteous Judge shall give*.

(2) The character he gives of the world that lay in wickedness: *The world has not known thee*. Note, Ignorance of God overspreads the world of mankind; this is the darkness they sit in.

(3) The plea he insists upon for himself: *But I have known thee*. Christ knew the Father as no one else ever did. We are unworthy, but he is worthy.

(4) The plea he insists upon for his disciples: *And they have known that thou hast sent me*; and, [1] Hereby they are distinguished from the unbelieving world. [2] Hereby they are interested in the mediation of Christ, and partake of the benefit of his acquaintance with the Father. Knowing Christ as sent of God, they have, in him, known the Father, and are introduced to an acquaintance with him; therefore, "Father, look after them for my sake."

2. The respect he had to his disciples (*v.* 26): "I have led them into the knowledge of thee, and will do it yet more and more; with this great and kind intention, *that the love wherewith thou hast loved me may be in them, and I in them.*"

It is *Christ in us* that is *the* only *hope of glory* that will *not make us ashamed*, Col. i. 27. All our communion with God, the reception of his love to us with our return of love to him again, passes through the hands of the Lord Jesus, and the comfort of it is owing purely to him. Christ had said but a little before, *I in them* (*v.* 23), and here it is repeated (though the sense was complete without it), and the prayer closed with it, to show how much the heart of Christ was set upon it; all his petitions centre in this, and with this *the prayers of Jesus, the Son of David, are ended*: "*I in them*; let me have this, and I desire no more." It is the glory of the Redeemer to dwell in the redeemed: it is his *rest for ever*, and he has desired it. Let us therefore make sure our union with Christ, and then take the comfort of his intercession. *This* prayer had an end, but *that* he ever lives to make.

CHAPTER EIGHTEEN

THE ARREST (*vv.* 1–12)

I. Our Lord Jesus, like a bold champion, takes the field first (*vv.* 1, 2). Observe,

1. That our Lord Jesus entered upon his sufferings *when he had spoken these words*, as Matt. xxvi. 1, *When he had finished all these sayings*. Here it is intimated, (1) That our Lord Jesus took his work

before him. The office of the priest was to teach, and pray, and offer sacrifice. Christ, after teaching and praying, applies himself to make atonement. (2) That having by his sermon prepared his disciples for this hour of trial, and by his prayer prepared himself for it, he then courageously went out to meet it.

2. That *he went forth with his disciples*. Judas knew what house he was in in the city, and he could have stayed and met his sufferings there; but, (1) He would do as he was wont to do, and not alter his method, either to meet the cross or to miss it, when his hour was come. (2) He was as unwilling that there should be *an uproar among the people* as his enemies were, for it was not his way *to strive or cry*. (3) He would set us an example in the beginning of his passion, as he did at the end of it, of retirement from the world.

3. That he went *over the brook Cedron*. He must go over this to go to *the mount of Olives*.

4. That he entered into a garden. This circumstance is taken notice of only by this evangelist, that Christ's sufferings began in a garden. In the garden of Eden sin began; there the curse was pronounced, there the Redeemer was promised, and therefore in a garden that promised seed entered the lists with the old serpent. Christ was buried also in a garden.

5. That he had his disciples with him, (1) Because he used to take them with him when he retired for prayer. (2) They must be witnesses of his sufferings, and his patience under them, that they might with the more assurance and affection

preach them to the world (Luke xxiv. 48), and be themselves prepared to suffer. (3) He would take them into the danger to show them their weakness, notwithstanding the promises they had made of fidelity. Christ sometimes brings his people into difficulties, that he may magnify himself in their deliverance.

6. That Judas the traitor *knew the place*, knew it to be the place of his usual retirement, and probably, by some word Christ had dropped, knew that he intended to be there that night, for want of a better closet.

II. *The captain of our salvation* having taken the field, the enemy presently comes upon the spot, and attacks him (*v.* 3). Observe,

1. The persons employed in this action—*a band of men and officers from the chief priests*, *with Judas*.

2. The preparation they had made for an attack: They came *with lanterns, and torches, and weapons. The weapons of his warfare were spiritual*, and at these *weapons* he had often beaten them, and *put them to silence*, and therefore they have now recourse to other *weapons, swords and staves*.

III. Our Lord Jesus gloriously repulsed the first onset of the enemy, *vv.* 4–6, where observe,

1. How he received them, with all the mildness imaginable towards them, and all the calmness imaginable in himself.

2. See how he terrified them, and obliged them to retire (*v.* 6). Hereby he showed plainly,

(1) What he could have done with them. When he struck them down, he could have struck them

dead; when he spoke them *to the ground*, he could have spoken them to hell, and have sent them, like Korah's company, the next way thither; but he would not do so, [1] Because the hour of his suffering was come, and he would not put it by; he would only show that his life was not forced from him, but *he laid it down of himself*, as he had said. [2] Because he would give an instance of his patience and forbearance with the worst of men, and his compassionate love to his very enemies.

IV. Having given his enemies a repulse, he gives his friends a protection, and that by his word too, *vv.* 7–9, where we may observe,

1. How he continued to expose himself to their rage, *v.* 7. They did not lie long where they fell, but, by divine permission, got up again; it is only in the other world that God's judgments are everlasting.

2. How he contrived to secure his disciples from their rage. He charges them therefore as *one having authority*: "*Let these go their way*; it is at your peril if you meddle with them."

3. Now herein he confirmed the word which he had spoken a little before (*ch.* xvii. 12), *Of those whom thou gavest me, I have lost none*.

V. Having provided for the safety of his disciples, he rebukes the rashness of one of them, and represses the violence of his followers, as he had repulsed the violence of his persecutors, *vv.* 10, 11, where we have,

1. Peter's rashness. He had a sword; and *he smote one of the high priest's servants*, who was probably one of the forwardest, and aiming,

it is likely, to cleave him down the head, missed his blow, and only *cut off his right ear. The servant's name*, for the greater certainty of the narrative, is recorded; it *was Malchus*, or *Malluch*, Neh. x. 4.

2. The rebuke his Master gave him (*v.* 11): *Put up thy sword into the sheath*, or scabbard; it is a gentle reproof, because it was his zeal that carried him beyond the bounds of discretion. Christ did not aggravate the matter, only bade him *do so no more*.

3. The reason for this rebuke: *The cup which my Father has given me, shall I not drink it?* Matthew relates another reason which Christ gave for this rebuke, but John preserves this, which he had omitted; in which Christ gives us, (1) A full proof of his own submission to his Father's will. (2) A fair pattern to us of submission to God's will in every thing that concerns us. [1] It is but a *cup*; a small matter comparatively, be it what it will. [2] It is a cup that is given us; sufferings are gifts. [3] It is given us by a Father, who has a Father's authority, and does us no wrong; a Father's affection, and means us no hurt.

VI. Having entirely reconciled himself to the dispensation, he calmly surrendered, and yielded himself a prisoner, not because he could not have made his escape, but because he would not. One would have thought the cure of Malchus's ear should have made them relent, but nothing would win upon them.

PETER'S DENIAL (*vv.* 13–27)

We have here an account of Christ's arraignment before the high priest, and some circumstances that occurred therein which were omitted by the other evangelists; and Peter's denying him, which the other evangelists had given the story of entire by itself, is interwoven with the other passages. The crime laid to his charge having relation to religion, the judges of the spiritual court took it to fall directly under their cognizance. Both Jews and Gentiles seized him, and so both Jews and Gentiles tried and condemned him, for he died for the sins of both. Let us go over the story in order.

I. Having seized him, they *led him away to Annas first*, before they brought him to the court that was sat, expecting him, in the house of Caiaphas, *v.* 13. 1. They *led him away*, led him in triumph, as a trophy of their victory; led him *as a lamb to the slaughter*, and they led him through the sheep-gate spoken of Neh. iii. 1. 2. They led him away to their masters that sent them. 3. They led him to Annas first. Probably his house lay in the way, and was convenient for them to call at to refresh themselves, and, as some think, to be paid for their service. 4. This Annas was father-in-law to Caiaphas the high priest; this kindred by marriage between them comes in as a reason either why Caiaphas ordered that this piece of respect should be done to Annas, to favour him with the first sight of the prisoner, or why Annas was willing to countenance Caiaphas in a matter his heart was so much upon.

II. Annas did not long detain them, being as willing as any of them to have the prosecution pushed on, and therefore sent him bound to Caiaphas. Observe here,

1. The power of Caiaphas intimated (*v.* 13). He was *high priest that same year*. It was the ruin of Caiaphas that he was high priest that year, and so became a ringleader in the putting of Christ to death.

2. The malice of Caiaphas, which is intimated (*v.* 14) by the repeating of what he had said some time before, that, right or wrong, guilty or innocent, *it was expedient that one man should die for the people*, which refers to the story *ch.* xi. 50.

3. The concurrence of Annas in the prosecution of Christ.

III. In the house of Caiaphas, Simon Peter began to deny his Master, *vv.* 15–18.

1. It was with much ado that Peter got into the hall where the court was sitting, an account of which we have *vv.* 15, 16. Here we may observe,

2. Peter, having got in, was immediately assaulted with the temptation, and foiled by it, *v.* 17. Observe here,

(1) How slight the attack was. It was but a silly maid, of so small account that she was set to keep the door, that challenged him, and she only asked him carelessly, *Art not thou one of this man's disciples?* probably suspecting it by his sheepish look, and coming in timorously.

(2) How speedy the surrender was. Without taking time to re-collect himself, he suddenly answered, *I am not*.

(3) Yet he goes further into the temptation: *And the servants and*

officers stood there, and Peter with them, v. 18.

Peter was much to be blamed, 1. Because he associated with these wicked men, and kept company with them. 2. Because he desired to be thought *one of them,* that he might not be suspected to be a disciple of Christ.

IV. Peter, Christ's friend, having begun to deny him, the high priest, his enemy, begins to accuse him, or rather urges him to accuse himself, *vv.* 19–21. Observe,

1. The articles or heads upon which Christ was examined (*v.* 19): concerning *his disciples and his doctrine.* Observe,

(1) The irregularity of the process; it was against all law and equity.

(2) The intention. The *high priest then,* because he had resolved that Christ must be sacrificed to their private malice under colour of the public good, examined him upon those interrogatories which would touch his life. He examined him, [1] Concerning his disciples, that he might charge him with sedition, and represent him as dangerous to the Roman government, as well as to the Jewish church. [2] Concerning his doctrine, that they might charge him with heresy, and bring him under the penalty of the law against false prophets, Deut. xiii. 9, 10.

2. The appeal Christ made, in answer to these interrogatories. (1) As to his disciples, he said nothing, because it was an impertinent question; if his doctrine was sound and good, his having disciples to whom to communicate it was no more than what was prac-

tised and allowed by their own doctors. (2) As to his doctrine, he said nothing in particular, but in general referred himself to those that heard him, being not only made manifest to God, but made manifest also in their consciences, *vv.* 20, 21.

[1] He tacitly charges his judges with illegal proceedings. *First,* "*Why ask you me now* concerning my doctrine, when you have already condemned it?" They had made an order of court for excommunicating all that owned him (*ch.* ix. 22), had issued out a proclamation for apprehending him; and now they come to ask what his doctrine is! Thus was he condemned, as his doctrine and cause commonly are, unheard. *Secondly,* "*Why ask you me?* Must I accuse myself, when you have no evidence against me?"

[2] He insists upon his fair and open dealing with them in the publication of his doctrine, and justifies himself with this. The crime which the sanhedrim by the law was to enquire after was the clandestine spreading of dangerous doctrines, enticing secretly, Deut. xiii. 6. As to this, therefore, Christ clears himself very fully. *First,* As to the manner of his preaching. He spoke openly. *Secondly,* As to the persons he preached to: *He spoke to the world,* to all that had *ears to hear,* and were willing to hear him, high or low, learned or unlearned, Jew or Gentile, friend or foe, *Thirdly,* As to the places he preached in. When he was in the country, he preached ordinarily in the synagogues — the places of meeting for worship, and on the

sabbath-day—the time of meeting; when he came up to Jerusalem, he preached the same doctrine in the temple at the time of the solemn feasts, when the Jews from all parts assembled there; and though he often preached in private houses, and on mountains, and by the seaside, to show that his word and worship were not to be confined to temples and synagogues, yet what he preached in private was the very same with what he delivered publicly. *Fourthly*, As to the doctrine itself. He *said nothing in secret* contrary to what he said in public, but only by way of repetition and explanation: *In secret have I said nothing*.

[3] He appeals to those that had heard him, and desires that they might be examined what doctrine he had preached, and whether it had that dangerous tendency that was surmised.

V. While the judges were examining him, the servants that stood by were abusing him, *vv.* 22, 23.

1. It was a base affront which one of the officers gave him; though he spoke with so much calmness and convincing evidence, this insolent fellow *struck him with the palm of his hand*, probably on the side of his head or face, saying, *Answerest thou the high priest so?* as if he had behaved himself rudely to the court.

2. Christ bore this affront with wonderful meekness and patience (*v.* 23). Christ could have answered him with a miracle of wrath, could have struck him dumb or dead, or have withered the hand that was lifted up against him. But this was the day of his patience and suffer-ing, and he answered him with the *meekness of wisdom*.

VI. While the servants were thus abusing him, Peter was proceeding to deny him, *vv.* 25–27. It is a sad story, and none of the least of Christ's sufferings.

1. He repeated the sin the second time, *v.* 25.

(1) It was his great folly to thrust himself into the temptation, by continuing in the company of those that were unsuitable for him, and that he had nothing to do with.

(2) It was his great unhappiness that he was again assaulted by the temptation; and no other could be expected, for this was a place, this an hour, of temptation.

(3) It was his great weakness, nay, it was his great wickedness, to yield to the temptation, and to say, *I am not one* of his disciples, as one ashamed of that which was his honour, and afraid of suffering for it, which would have been yet more his honour. See how the *fear of man brings a snare*.

2. He repeated the sin the third time, *vv.* 26, 27. Here he was attacked by one of the servants, who was kinsman to Malchus, who, when he heard Peter deny himself to be a disciple of Christ, gave him the lie with great assurance: "*Did not I see thee in the garden with him?* Witness my kinsman's ear." Peter then denied again, as if he knew nothing of Christ, nothing of the garden, nothing of all this matter.

Immediately the cock crew; and this is all that is here said of his repentance, it being recorded by the other evangelists. The crowing of the cock to others was an accidental thing, and had no significance; but to Peter it was the voice of God, and had a blessed tendency to awaken his conscience, by putting him in mind of the word of Christ.

BEFORE PILATE (*vv.* 28–40)

We have here an account of Christ's arraignment before Pilate, the Roman governor, in the *prætorium* (a Latin word made Greek), the prætor's house, or *hall of judgment*; thither they hurried him, to get him condemned in the Roman court, and executed by the Roman power. Here is,

I. Pilate's conference with the prosecutors. They were called first, and stated what they had to say against the prisoner, as was very fit, *vv.* 29–32.

1. The judge calls for the indictment. Looking upon Pilate as a magistrate, that we may give every one his due, here are three things commendable in him:—(1) His diligent and close application to business. (2) His condescending to the humour of the people, and receding from the honour of his place to gratify their scruples. (3) His adherence to the rule of justice, in demanding the accusation, suspecting the prosecution to be malicious: "*What accusation bring you against this man?*"

2. The prosecutors demand judgment against him upon a general surmise that he was a criminal, not alleging, much less proving, any thing in particular *worthy of death or of bonds* (*v.* 30). Note, It is no new thing for the best of benefactors to be branded and run down as the worst of malefactors.

3. The judge remands him to their own court (*v.* 31): "*Take you him, and judge him according to your own law*, and do not trouble me with him."

4. They disown any authority as judges, and (since it must be so) are content to be prosecutors. They now grow less insolent and more submissive, and own, "*It is not lawful for us to put any man to death*, whatever less punishment we may inflict, and this is a malefactor whom we would have the blood of."

It was necessary that Christ should be put to death by the Romans, that, being *hanged upon a tree*, he might be *made a curse for us* (Gal. iii. 13), and *his hands and feet* might be *pierced*. As the Roman power had brought him to be born at Bethlehem, so now to die upon a cross, and both according to the scriptures.

II. Here is Pilate's conference with the prisoner, *v.* 33, &c., where we have,

1. The prisoner set to the bar. Pilate, after he had conferred with the chief priests at his door, entered into the hall, and called for Jesus to be brought in.

2. His examination. The other evangelists tell us that his accusers had laid it to his charge that *he perverted the nation, forbidding to give tribute to Cæsar*, and upon this he is examined.

(1) Here is a question put to him, with a design to ensnare him and to find out something upon which to ground an accusation: "*Art thou the king of the Jews?*" Some think Pilate asked this with an air of scorn and contempt: "What! *art thou a king*, who makest so mean a

figure?" Since it could not be proved he ever said it, he would constrain him to say it now, that he might proceed upon his own confession.

(2) Christ answers this question with another; not for evasion, but as an intimation to Pilate to consider what he did, and upon what grounds he went (*v.* 34): "*Sayest thou this thing of thyself*, from a suspicion arising in thy own breast, *or did others tell it thee of me*, and dost thou ask it only to oblige them?"

(3) Pilate resents Christ's answer, and takes it very ill, *v.* 35. This is a direct answer to Christ's question, *v.* 34. [1] Christ had asked him whether he spoke of himself. "No," says he; "*am I a Jew*, that thou suspectest me to be in the plot against thee?" [2] Christ had asked him whether others told him. "Yes," says he, "and those *thine own people*, who, one would think, should be biassed in favour of thee." [3] Christ had declined answering that question, *Art thou the king of the Jews?* And therefore Pilate puts another question to him more general, "*What hast thou done?*"

(4) Christ, in his next reply, gives a more full and direct answer to Pilate's former question, *Art thou a king?* explaining in what sense he was a king, but not such a king as was any ways dangerous to the Roman government, not a secular king, for his interest was not supported by secular methods, *v.* 36. Observe,

[1] An account of the nature and constitution of Christ's kingdom: It *is not of this world*. It is expressed negatively to rectify the present mistakes concerning it; but the positive is implied, it is *the kingdom of heaven*, and belongs to another world. Christ is a king, and has a kingdom, but *not of this world*.

[2] An evidence of the spiritual nature of Christ's kingdom produced. If he had designed an opposition to the government, he would have fought them at their own weapons, and would have repelled force with force of the same nature; but he did not take this course: *If my kingdom were of this world, then would my servants fight, that I should not be delivered to the Jews*, and my kingdom be ruined by them. But, *First*, His followers did not offer to fight; there was no uproar, no attempt to rescue him, though the town was now full of Galileans, his friends and countrymen, and they were generally armed; but the peaceable behaviour of his disciples on this occasion was enough *to put to silence the ignorance of foolish men*. *Secondly*, He did not order them to fight; nay, he forbade them, which was an evidence both that he did not depend upon worldly aids (for he could have summoned *legions of angels* into his service, which showed that his *kingdom was from above*), and also that he did not dread worldly opposition.

(5) In answer to Pilate's further query, he replies yet more directly, *v.* 37, where we have, [1] Pilate's plain question: "*Art thou a king then?*" [2] The good confession which our Lord Jesus witnessed before Pontius Pilate, in answer to this (1 Tim. vi. 13): *Thou sayest that I am a king*, that is, It is as thou

sayest, I am a king; for *I came to bear witness of the truth.* He explains himself, and shows how he is a king, as *he came to bear witness of the truth*; he rules in the minds of men by the power of truth. Christ's errand into the world, and his business in the world, were *to bear witness to the truth.* 1. To reveal it, to discover to the world that which otherwise could not have been known concerning God and his will and *good-will to men, ch.* i. 18; xvii. 26. 2. To confirm it, Rom. xv. 8. By his miracles *he bore witness to the truth* of religion, the truth of divine revelation, and of God's perfections and providence, and the truth of his promise and covenant, *that all men through him might believe.* Now by doing this he is a king, and sets up a kingdom.

(6) Pilate, hereupon, puts a good question to him, but does not stay for an answer, *v.* 38. He said, *What is truth?* and *immediately went out again.*

[1] It is certain that this was a good question, and could not be put to one that was better able to answer it.

[2] It is uncertain with what design Pilate asked this question. *First,* Perhaps he spoke it as a learner, as one that began to think well of Christ. *Secondly,* Some think he spoke it as a judge, enquiring further into the cause now brought before him: "Let me into this mystery, and tell me what the truth of it is, the true state of this matter." *Thirdly,* Others think he spoke it as a scoffer, in a jeering way: "Thou talkest of truth; canst thou tell what truth is, or give me a definition of it?" But, though

Christ would not tell Pilate what is truth, he has told his disciples, and by them has told us, *ch.* xiv. 6.

III. The result of both these conferences with the prosecutors and the prisoner (*vv.* 38–40), in two things:—

1. The judge appeared his friend, and favourable to him, for,

(1) He publicly declared him innocent, *v.* 38. This solemn declaration of Christ's innocency was, [1] For the justification and honour of the Lord Jesus. By this it appears that though he was treated as the worst of malefactors he had never merited such treatment. [2] For explaining the design and intention of his death, that he did not die for any sin of his own, even in the judgment of the judge himself, and therefore he died as a sacrifice for our sins, and that, even in the judgment of the prosecutors themselves, *one man should die for the people, ch.* xi. 50. [3] For aggravating the sin of the Jews that prosecuted him with so much violence.

(2) He proposed an expedient for his discharge (*v.* 39): *You have a custom, that I should release to you a prisoner at the passover*; shall it be this king of the Jews? He proposed this, not to the chief priests (he knew they would never agree to it), but to the multitude; it was an appeal to the people, as appears, Matt. xxvii. 15.

2. The people appeared his enemies, and implacable against him (*v.* 40): *They cried all again* and again, *Not this man,* let not him be released, *but Barabbas.* Observe, (1) How fierce and outrageous they were. (2) How foolish and absurd

they were, as is intimated in the short account here given of the other candidate: *Now Barabbas was a robber*, and therefore, [1] A breaker of the law of God; and yet he shall be spared, rather than one who reproved the pride, avarice, and tyranny of the priests and elders. [2] He was an enemy to the public safety and personal property. Thus those do who prefer their sins before Christ. Sin is a robber, every base lust is a robber, and yet foolishly chosen rather than Christ, who would truly enrich us.

CHAPTER NINETEEN
CHRIST EXAMINED
(*vv.* 1–15)

Here is a further account of the unfair trial which they gave to our Lord Jesus.

I. The judge abuses the prisoner, though he declares him innocent, and hopes therewith to pacify the prosecutors; wherein his intention, if indeed it was good, will by no means justify his proceedings, which were palpably unjust.

1. He ordered him to be whipped as a criminal, *v.* 1. (1) *That the scripture might be fulfilled*, which spoke of his being *stricken, smitten, and afflicted*, and *the chastisement of our peace* being *upon him* (Isa. liii. 5), of his giving his back to the smiters (Isa. l. 6), of the ploughers ploughing upon his back, Ps. cxxix. 3. He himself likewise had foretold it, Matt. xx. 19; Mark x. 34; Luke xviii. 33. (2) *That by his stripes we might be healed*, 1 Pet. ii. 4. (3) That stripes, for his sake, might be sanctified and made easy to his followers.

2. He turned him over to his soldiers, to be ridiculed and made sport with as a fool (*vv.* 2, 3).

See here the wonderful condescension of our Lord Jesus in his sufferings for us. Great and generous minds can bear anything better than ignominy, any toil, any pain, any loss, rather than reproach; yet this the great and holy Jesus submitted to for us.

II. Pilate, having thus abused the prisoner, presents him to the prosecutors, in hope that they would now be satisfied, and drop the prosecution, *vv.* 4, 5. Here he proposes two things to their consideration:—

1. That he had not found anything in him which made him obnoxious to the Roman government (*v.* 4).

2. That he had done that to him which would make him the less dangerous to them and to their government, *v.* 5. He brought him out to them, wearing the crown of thorns, his head and face all bloody, and said, "*Behold the man* whom you are so jealous of," intimating that though his having been so popular might have given them some cause to fear that his interest in the country would lessen theirs, yet he had taken an effectual course to prevent it, by treating him as a slave, and exposing him to contempt, after which he supposed the people would never look upon him with any respect, nor could he ever retrieve his reputation again. *Behold the man*. It is good for every one of us, with an eye of faith, to behold the man Christ Jesus in his sufferings. *Behold this king with the crown wherewith his mother*

crowned him, the crown of thorns, Cant. iii. 11. "Behold him, and be suitably affected with the sight. Behold him, and mourn because of him. Behold him, and love him; be still *looking unto Jesus*."

III. The prosecutors, instead of being pacified, were but the more exasperated, *vv*. 6, 7.

1. Observe here their clamour and outrage. It was violent and exceedingly resolute; they will have it their own way, and hazard the governor's favour, the peace of the city, and their own safety, rather than abate of the utmost of their demands.

2. The check Pilate gave to their fury, still insisting upon the prisoner's innocency: "*Take you him and crucify him*, if he must be crucified." This is spoken ironically; he knew they could not, they durst not, crucify him. But Pilate had not courage enough to act according to his conscience; and his cowardice betrayed him into a snare.

3. The further colour which the prosecutors gave to their demand (*v*. 7): *We have a law, and by our law*, if it were but in our power to execute it, *he ought to die, because he made himself the Son of God.* Now here observe, (1) They *made their boast of the law*, even when *through breaking the law they dishonoured God*, as is charged upon the Jews, Rom. ii. 23. (2) They discover a restless and inveterate malice against our Lord Jesus. (3) They pervert the law, and make that the instrument of their malice.

IV. The judge brings the prisoner again to his trial, upon this new suggestion. Observe,

1. The concern Pilate was in,

when he heard this alleged (*v*. 8): When he heard that his prisoner pretended not to royalty only, but to deity, he was *the more afraid*.

2. His further examination of our Lord Jesus thereupon, *v*. 9. That he might give the prosecutors all the fair play they could desire, he resumed the debate, went into the judgment-hall, and asked Christ, *Whence art thou?*

"Where wast thou, and in what world hadst thou a being, before thy coming into this world?"

3. The silence of our Lord Jesus when he was examined upon this head; but *Jesus gave him no answer.* This was not a sullen silence, in contempt of the court, nor was it because he knew not what to say; but, [1] It was a patient silence, that the scripture might be fulfilled, *as a sheep before the shearers is dumb, so he opened not his mouth*, Isa. liii. 7. [2] It was a prudent silence. When the chief priests asked him, *Art thou the Son of the Blessed?* he answered, *I am*, for he knew they went upon the scriptures of the Old Testament which spoke of the Messiah; but when Pilate asked him he knew he did not understand his own question, having no notion of the Messiah, and of his being the *Son of God*, and therefore to what purpose should he reply to him whose head was filled with the pagan theology, to which he would have turned his answer?

4. The haughty check which Pilate gave him for his silence (*v*. 10): "*Speakest thou not unto me?*"

5. Christ's pertinent answer to this check, *v*. 11, where,

[1] He boldly rebukes his arrogance, and rectifies his mistake.

God is the fountain of power; and the *powers that are*, as they are ordained by him and derived from him, so they are subject to him. They ought to go no further than his law directs them; they can go no further than his providence permits them. They are God's hand and his sword, Ps. xvii. 13, 14. Pilate never fancied himself to look so great as now, when he sat in judgment upon such a prisoner as this, who was looked upon by many as the *Son of God* and king of Israel, and had the fate of so great a man at his disposal; but Christ lets him know that he was herein but an instrument in God's hand, and could do nothing against him, but by the appointment of Heaven, Acts iv. 27, 28.

[2] He mildly excuses and extenuates his sin, in comparison with the sin of the ringleaders.

First, It is plainly intimated that what Pilate did was sin, a great sin, and that the force which the Jews put upon him, and which he put upon himself in it, would not justify him.

Secondly, Yet theirs that delivered him to Pilate was the greater sin. By this it appears that all sins are not equal, but some more heinous than others.

V. Pilate struggles with the Jews to deliver Jesus out of their hands, but in vain. We hear no more after this of any thing that passed between Pilate and the prisoner; what remains lay between him and the prosecutors.

1. Pilate seems more zealous than before to get Jesus discharged (*v.* 12): *Thenceforth*, from this time, and for this reason, because Christ

had given him that answer (*v.* 11), which, though it had a rebuke in it, yet he took kindly; and, though Christ found fault with him, he still continued to find no fault in Christ, but *sought to release him*, desired it, endeavoured it.

2. The Jews were more furious than ever, and more violent to get Jesus crucified. In this outcry they sought two things:—(1) To blacken the prisoner as an enemy to Cæsar. (2) To frighten the judge, as no friend to Cæsar. They intimate a threatening that they would inform against him, and get him displaced; and here they touched him in a sensitive and very tender part.

3. When other expedients had been tried in vain, Pilate slightly endeavoured to banter them out of their fury, and yet, in doing this, betrayed himself to them, and yielded to the rapid stream, *vv.* 13–15. After he had stood it out a great while, and seemed now as if he would have made a vigorous resistance upon this attack (*v.* 12), he basely surrendered.

It was the preparation of the passover, and *about the sixth hour*. Observe, 1. The day: It was the preparation of the passover, that is, for the passover-sabbath, and the solemnities of that and the rest of the days of the feast of unleavened bread. This is plain from Luke xxiii. 54, *It was the preparation, and the sabbath drew on*. So that this preparation was for the sabbath. 2. The hour: *It was about the sixth hour*. Some ancient Greek and Latin manuscripts read it about the third hour, which agrees with Mark xv. 25. And it appears by Matt. xxvii. 45 that he was upon the cross before the sixth hour. But it should seem to come in here, not as a precise determination of the time, but as an additional aggravation of the sin of his prosecutors, that they were pushing on the prosecution, not only on a solemn day, the *day of the preparation*, but, from the third to the sixth hour on that day, they were employed in this wickedness; so that for this day, though they were priests, they dropped the temple-service, for they did not leave Christ till the sixth hour, when the darkness began, which frightened them away. Some think that the sixth hour, with this evangelist, is, according to the Roman reckoning and ours, six of the clock in the morning, answering to the Jews' first hour of the day; this is very probable, that Christ's trial before Pilate was at the height about six in the morning, which was then a little after sun-rising.

4. The encounter Pilate had with the Jews, both priests and people, before he proceeded to give judgment, endeavouring in vain to stem the tide of their rage.

[1] He saith unto the Jews, *Behold your king*. This is a reproof to them for the absurdity and malice of their insinuating that this Jesus made himself a king. But Pilate, though he was far from meaning so, seems as if he were the voice of God to them.

[2] They cried out with the greatest indignation, *Away with him, away with him*, which speaks disdain as well as malice.

[3] Pilate, willing to have Jesus released, and yet that it should be their doing, asks them, *Shall I crucify your king?*

[4] The chief priests, that they might effectually renounce Christ, and engage Pilate to crucify him, but otherwise sorely against their will, cried out, *We have no king but Cæsar*. This they knew would please Pilate, and so they hoped to carry their point, though at the same time they hated Cæsar and his government.

GOLGOTHA (*vv.* 16–18)

We have here sentence of death passed upon our Lord Jesus, and execution done soon after.

I. *Pilate gave judgment* against Christ, and signed the warrant for his execution, *v.* 16.

II. Judgment was no sooner given than with all possible expedition the prosecutors, having gained their point, resolved to lose no time lest Pilate should change his mind, and order a reprieve.

1. They immediately hurried away the prisoner. The chief priests greedily flew upon the prey which they had been long waiting for; now it is drawn into their net.

2. To add to his misery, they obliged him, as long as he was able, to carry his cross (*v.* 17), according to the custom among the Romans; hence *Furcifer* was among them a name of reproach. Now Christ's carrying his cross may be considered, (1) As a part of his sufferings; he endured the cross literally. (2) As answering the type which went before him; Isaac, when he was to be offered, carried the wood on which he was to be bound and with which he was to be burned. (3) As very significant of his under-

taking, the Father having *laid upon him the iniquity of us all* (Isa. liii. 6), and he having to *take away sin* by *bearing it in his own body upon the tree*, 1 Pet. ii. 24. (4) As very instructive to us. Our Master hereby taught all his disciples to take up their cross, and follow him.

3. They brought him to the place of execution: He *went forth*, not dragged against his will, but voluntary in his sufferings. He went forth out of the city, for he was *crucified without the gate*, Heb. xiii. 12.

4. There they crucified him, and the other malefactors with him (*v.* 18): *There they crucified him*.

And now let us pause awhile, and with an eye of faith look upon Jesus. Was ever sorrow like unto his sorrow? See him who was clothed with glory stripped of it all, and clothed with shame—him who was the *praise of angels* made a *reproach of men*—him who had been with eternal delight and joy in the bosom of his Father now in the extremities of pain and agony. See him bleeding, see him struggling, see him dying, see him and love him, love him and live to him, and study what we shall render.

FINISHED (*vv.* 19–30)

Here are some remarkable circumstances of Christ's dying more fully related than before, which those will take special notice of who covet to know Christ and him crucified.

I. The title set up over his head. Observe,

1. The inscription itself which Pilate wrote, and ordered to be fixed to the top of the cross, declaring the cause for which he was crucified, *v.* 19. Pilate intended this for his reproach, but God overruled this matter, (1) That it might be a further testimony to the innocency of our Lord Jesus; for here was an accusation which, as it was worded, contained no crime. (2) That it might show forth his dignity and honour.

2. The notice taken of this inscription (*v.* 20): Here are two reasons why the title was so much read:—(1) Because the place where Jesus was crucified, though without the gate, was yet *nigh the city*. (2) Because it was written in Hebrew, and Greek, and Latin, which made it legible by all. God so ordering it that this should be written in the three then most known tongues, it was intimated thereby that Jesus Christ should be a Saviour to all nations, and not to the Jews only.

3. The offence which the prosecutors took at it, *v.* 21. They would not have it written, *the king of the Jews*; but that he said of himself, *I am the king of the Jews*.

4. The judge's resolution to adhere to it: "*What I have written I have written*, and will not alter it to humour them."

Hereby honour was done to the Lord Jesus. Pilate stuck to it with resolution, that he was the king of the Jews. What he had written was what God had first written, and therefore he could not alter it; for thus it was written, that Messiah the prince should be *cut off*, Dan. ix. 26. This therefore is the true cause of his death; he dies because the king of Israel must die, must thus die. When the Jews reject Christ, and will not have him for their king, Pilate, a Gentile, sticks to it that he is a king, which was an earnest of what came to pass soon after, when the Gentiles submitted to the kingdom of the Messiah, which the unbelieving Jews had rebelled against.

II. The dividing of his garments among the executioners, *vv.* 23, 24. Here observe, 1. The shame they put upon our Lord Jesus, in stripping him of his garments before they crucified him. 2. The wages with which these soldiers paid themselves for crucifying Christ. They were willing to do it for his old clothes. Nothing is to be done so bad, but there will be found men bad enough to do it for a trifle. 3. The sport they made about his seamless coat. We read not of any thing about him valuable or remarkable but this, and this not for the richness, but only the variety of it, for it was *woven from the top throughout*; there was no curiosity therefore in the shape, but a designed plainness. The soldiers thought it a pity to rend it, for then it would unravel, and a piece of it would be good for nothing; they would *therefore cast lots for it.* While Christ was in his dying agonies, they were merrily dividing his spoils. 4. The fulfilling of the scripture in this. David, in spirit, foretold this very circumstance of Christ's sufferings, in that passage, Ps. xxii. 18.

III. The care that he took of his poor mother.

1. His mother attends him to his death (*v.* 25): *There stood by the cross,* as near as they could get, *his mother,* and some of his relations and friends with her. (1) See here

the tender affection of these pious women to our Lord Jesus in his sufferings, When all his disciples except John, had forsaken him, they continued their attendance on him (2) We may easily suppose what an affliction it was to these poor women to see him thus abused, especially to the blessed virgin. Now was fulfilled Simeon's word, *A sword shall pierce through thy own soul,* Luke ii. 35. (3) We may justly admire the power of divine grace in supporting these women, especially the virgin Mary, under this heavy trial. We do not find his mother wringing her hands, or tearing her hair, or rending her clothes, or making an outcry; but, with a wonderful composure, *standing by the cross,* and her friends with her. Surely she and they were strengthened by a divine power to this degree of patience; and surely the virgin Mary had a fuller expectation of his resurrection than the rest had, which supported her thus.

2. He tenderly provides for his mother at his death. He saw her standing by, and knew her cares and griefs; and he saw John standing not far off, and so he settled a new relation between his beloved mother and his beloved disciple; for he said to her, "*Woman, behold thy son,* for whom henceforward thou must have a motherly affection"; and to him, "*Behold thy mother,* to whom thou must pay a filial duty." And so *from that hour,* that hour never to be forgotten, *that disciple took her to his own home.* See here,

(1) The care Christ took of his dear mother. He was not so much taken up with a sense of his suffer-

ings as to forget his friends, all whose concerns he bore upon his heart.

(2) The confidence he reposed in the beloved disciple. It is to him he says, *Behold thy mother*, that is, I recommend her to thy care, be thou as a son to her to guide her (Isa. li. 18); and *forsake her not when she is old*, Prov. xxiii. 22.

IV. The fulfilling of the scripture, in the giving of him vinegar to drink, *vv*. 28, 29. Observe,

1. How much respect Christ showed to the scripture (*v*. 28).

(1) It was not at all strange that he was thirsty.

(2) But the reason of his complaining of it is somewhat surprising; it is the only word he spoke that looked like complaint of his outward sufferings. But now he cried, *I thirst*. For, [1] He would thus express *the travail of his soul*, Isa. liii. 11. [2] He would thus take care to see the scripture fulfilled. Now, *First*, The scripture had foretold his thirst, and therefore he himself related it, because it could not otherwise be known, saying, *I thirst*; it was foretold that his tongue should cleave to his jaws, Ps. xxii. 15. *Secondly*, The scripture had foretold that in his thirst he should have vinegar given him to drink, Ps. lxix. 21.

2. See how little respect his persecutors showed to him (*v*. 29).

V. The dying word wherewith he breathed out his soul (*v*. 30): *When he had received the vinegar*, as much of it as he thought fit, *he said, It is finished*; and, with that, *bowed his head, and gave up the ghost*. Observe,

1. What he said, and we may

suppose him to say it with triumph and exultation—*It is finished*, a comprehensive word, and a comfortable one. (1) *It is finished*, that is, the malice and enmity of his persecutors had now done their worst. (2) *It is finished*, that is, the counsel and commandment of his Father concerning his sufferings were now fulfilled; it was a *determinate counsel*, and he took care to see every iota and tittle of it exactly answered, Acts ii. 23. (3) *It is finished*, that is, all the types and prophecies of the Old Testament, which pointed at the sufferings of the Messiah, were accomplished and answered. (4) *It is finished*, that is, the ceremonial law is abolished, and a period put to the obligation of it. (5) *It is finished*, that is, sin is finished, and an end made of transgression, by *the bringing in of an everlasting righteousness*. It seems to refer to Dan. ix. 24. (6) *It is finished*, that is, his sufferings were now finished, both those of his soul and those of his body. (7) *It is finished*, that is, his life was now finished, he was just ready to breathe his last, and *now he is no more in this world*, ch. xvii. 11. (8) *It is finished*, that is, the work of man's redemption and salvation is now completed, at least the hardest part of the undertaking is over; a full satisfaction is made to the justice of God, a fatal blow given to the power of Satan, a fountain of grace opened that shall ever flow, a foundation of peace and happiness laid that shall never fail. Christ had now gone through with his work, and *finished it*, ch. xvii. 4.

2. What he did: *He bowed his head, and gave up the ghost*. He was

voluntary in dying; for he was not only the sacrifice, but the priest and the offerer. His life was not forcibly extorted from him, but freely resigned.

THE PIERCED SIDE
(vv. 31–37)

This passage concerning the piercing of Christ's side after his death is recorded only by this evangelist.

I. Observe the superstition of the Jews, which occasioned it (v. 31). These Jews would be thought to bear a great regard for the sabbath, and yet had no regard to justice and righteousness; they made no conscience of bringing an innocent and excellent person to the cross, and yet scrupled letting a dead body hang upon the cross.

II. The dispatching of *the two thieves that were crucified with him*, v. 32.

III. The trial that was made whether Christ was dead or no, and the putting of it out of doubt.

1. They supposed him to be dead, and therefore *did not break his legs*, v. 33.

2. Because they would be sure he was dead they made such an experiment as would put it past dispute. *One of the soldiers with a spear pierced his side*, aiming at his heart, *and forthwith came thereout blood and water*, v. 34.

(1) The soldier hereby designed to decide the question whether he was dead or no, and by this honourable wound in his side to supersede the ignominious method of dispatch they took with the other two.

(2) But God had a further design herein, which was,

[1] To give an evidence of the truth of his death, in order to the proof of his resurrection. If he was only in a trance or swoon, his resurrection was a sham; but, by this experiment, he was certainly dead.

[2] To give an illustration of the design of his death. There was much of mystery in it, and its being so solemnly attested (v. 35) intimates there was something miraculous in it, that *the blood and water* should come out distinct and separate from the same wound; at least it was very significant; this same apostle refers to it as a very considerable thing, 1 John v. 6, 8.

1. They signified the two great benefits which all believers partake of through Christ—justification and sanctification; blood for remission, water for regeneration; blood for atonement, water for purification.

2. They signified the two great ordinances of baptism and the Lord's supper, by which those benefits are represented, sealed, and applied, to believers; they both owe their institution and efficacy to Christ. It is not the water in the font that will be to us *the washing of regeneration*, but the water out of the side of Christ; not the blood of the grape that will pacify the conscience and refresh the soul, but the blood out of the side of Christ.

IV. The attestation of the truth of this by an eye-witness (v. 35), the evangelist himself.

His record is undoubtedly *true*; for he wrote not only from his own personal knowledge and observation, but from the dictates of the Spirit of truth, that leads into all truth.

V. The accomplishment of the

scripture in all this (*v.* 36): *That the scripture might be fulfilled*, and so both the honour of the Old Testament preserved and the truth of the New Testament confirmed.

CHRIST'S BURIAL
(*vv.* 38–42)

We have here an account of the burial of the blessed body of our Lord Jesus. Here is,

I. The body begged, *v.* 38. This was done by the interest of *Joseph of Ramah*, or *Arimathea*, of whom no mention is made in all the New-Testament story, but only in the narrative which each of the evangelists gives us of Christ's burial, wherein he was chiefly concerned.

II. The embalming prepared, *v.* 39. This was done by Nicodemus, another person of quality, and in a public post. He brought a *mixture of myrrh and aloes*, which some think were bitter ingredients, to preserve the body, others fragrant ones, to perfume it. Here is,
1. The character of Nicodemus, which is much the same with that of Joseph; he was a secret friend to Christ, though not his constant follower. He at first *came to Jesus by night*, but now owned him publicly, as before, *ch.* vii. 50, 51.
2. The kindness of Nicodemus, which was considerable, though of a different nature. Joseph served Christ with his interest, Nicodemus with his purse.

III. The body got ready, *v.* 40. They *took it* into some house adjoining, and, having washed it from blood and dust, *wound it in linen clothes* very decently, with the spices melted down, it is likely, into an ointment, as *the manner of the Jews is to bury*, or to *embalm* (so Dr. Hammond).

IV. The grave pitched upon, in a garden which belonged to Joseph of Arimathea, very near the place where he was crucified. There was a sepulchre, or vault, prepared for the first occasion, but not yet used. Observe,
1. That Christ was buried without the city, for thus the manner of the Jews was to bury, not in their cities, much less in their synagogues.
2. That Christ was buried in a garden. In the garden of Eden death and the grave first received their power, and now in a garden they are conquered, disarmed, and triumphed over.
3. That he was buried in a new sepulchre. This was so ordered, (1) For the honour of Christ; he was not a common person, and therefore must not mix with common dust. (2) For the confirming of the truth of his resurrection, that it might not be suggested that it was not he, but some other that rose now, when many bodies of saints arose.

V. The funeral solemnized (*v.* 42): *There laid they Jesus*, that is, the dead body of Jesus.

Thus without pomp or solemnity is the body of Jesus laid in the cold and silent grave. Here lies our surety under arrest for our debts, so that if he be released his discharge will be ours. Here is the Sun of righteousness set for awhile, to rise again in greater glory, and set no more. Here lies a seeming captive to death, but a real conqueror over death; for here lies death itself slain, and the grave conquered. *Thanks be to God, who giveth us the victory.*

EASTER MORNING
(*vv.* 1–10)

In these verses we have the first step towards the proof of Christ's resurrection, which is, that the sepulchre was found empty. *He is not here*, and, if so, they must tell us where he is, or we conclude him risen.

I. Mary Magdalene, coming to the sepulchre, finds the *stone taken away*.

1. She *came to the sepulchre*, to wash the dead body with her tears, for she *went to the grave, to weep there*, and to *anoint it with the ointment* she had prepared.

2. She came as soon as she could, for she came, (1) Upon the *first day of the week*, as soon as ever the sabbath was gone. (2) She came *early, while it was yet dark*; so early did she set out.

3. She found the stone taken away, which she had seen *rolled to the door of the sepulchre*. Now this was, (1) A surprise to her, for she little expected it. (2) It was the beginning of a glorious discovery; the Lord was risen, though she did not at first apprehend it so.

II. Finding the stone taken away, she hastens back to Peter and John, who probably lodged together at that end of the town, not far off, and acquaints them with it: "*They have taken the Lord out of the sepulchre*, envying him the honour of such a decent burying-place, *and we know not where they have laid him*, nor where to find him, that we may pay him the remainder of our last respects."

III. Peter and John go with all speed to the sepulchre, to satisfy themselves of the truth of what was told them, and to see if they could make any further discoveries, *vv.* 3, 4. Some think that the other disciples were with Peter and John when the news came; for they *told these things to the eleven*, Luke xxiv. 9. (1) He that got foremost in this race was *the disciple whom Jesus loved* in a special manner, and who therefore in a special manner loved Jesus. (2) He that was cast behind was Peter, who had denied his Master, and was in sorrow and shame for it, and this clogged him as a weight; sense of guilt cramps us, and hinders our enlargement in the service of God. When conscience is offended we lose ground.

IV. Peter and John, having come to the sepulchre, prosecute the enquiry, yet improve little in the discovery.

1. John went no further than Mary Magdalene had done. (1) He had the curiosity to look into the sepulchre, and saw it was empty. He *stooped down*, and *looked in*. (2) Yet he had not courage to go into the sepulchre.

2. Peter, though he came last, went in first, and made a more exact discovery than John had done, *vv.* 6, 7.

(1) Observe here the boldness of Peter, and how God dispenses his gifts variously. John could out-run Peter, but Peter could out-dare John.

(2) Observe the posture in which he found things in the sepulchre. [1] Christ had left his grave-clothes

behind him there; what clothes he appeared in to his disciples we are not told, but he never appeared in his grave-clothes, as ghosts are supposed to do; no, he laid them aside. [2] The grave-clothes were found in very good order, which serves for an evidence that his body was not stolen away while men slept.

(3) See how Peter's boldness encouraged John; now he took heart and ventured in (v. 8), and *he saw and believed*; not barely believed what Mary said, that the body was gone (no thanks to him to believe what *he saw*), but he began to believe that Jesus was risen to life again, though his faith, as yet, was weak and wavering.

[1] John followed Peter in venturing. It should seem, he durst not have gone into the sepulchre if Peter had not gone in first.

[2] Yet, it should seem, John got the start of Peter in believing. Peter saw and wondered (Luke xxiv. 12), but John saw and believed. A mind disposed to contemplation may perhaps sooner receive the evidence of divine truth than a mind disposed to action. But what was the reason that they were so slow of heart to believe? The evangelist tells us (v. 9), as yet they *knew not the scripture*, that is, they did not consider, and apply, and duly improve, what they knew of the scripture, that he must *rise again from the dead*.

3. Peter and John pursued their enquiry no further, but desisted, hovering between faith and unbelief (v. 10). It is probable that the rest of the disciples were together; to them they return, to make report of what they had discovered, and to consult with them what was to be done; and, probably, now they appointed their meeting in the evening, when Christ came to them. It is observable that before Peter and John came to the sepulchre an angel had appeared there, rolled away the stone, frightened the guard, and comforted the women; as soon as they were gone from the sepulchre, Mary Magdalene here sees two angels in the sepulchre (v. 12), and yet Peter and John come to the sepulchre, and go into it, and see none. What shall we make of this? Where were the angels when Peter and John were at the sepulchre, who appeared there before and after? [1] Angels appear and disappear at pleasure, according to the orders and instructions given them. They may be, and are really, where they are not visibly; nay, it should seem, may be visible to one and not to another, at the same time, Num. xxii. 23; 2 Kings vi. 17. [2] This favour was shown to those who were early and constant in their enquiries after Christ, and was the reward of those that came first and stayed last, but denied to those that made a transient visit. [3] The apostles were not to receive their instructions from the angels, but from the Spirit of grace. See Heb. ii. 5.

CHRIST AND MARY
(vv. 11–18)

St. Mark tells us that Christ appeared first to Mary Magdalene (Mark xvi. 9); that appearance is here largely related; and we may observe,

I. The constancy and fervency

of Mary Magdalene's affection to the Lord Jesus, *v.* 11.

1. She stayed at the sepulchre, when Peter and John were gone, because there her Master had lain, and there she was likeliest to hear some tidings of him.

2. She stayed there weeping, and these tears loudly bespoke her affection to her Master.

3. *As she wept, she looked into the sepulchre*, that her eye might affect her heart.

II. The vision she had of two angels in the sepulchre, *v.* 12. Observe here,

1. The description of the persons she saw. They were *two angels in white, sitting* (probably on some benches or ledges hewn out in the rock) one at *the head*, and the other at the *feet*, of the grave.

They sat, as it were, reposing themselves in Christ's grave; for angels, though they needed not a restoration, were obliged to Christ for their establishment.

2. Their compassionate enquiry into the cause of Mary Magdalene's grief (*v.* 13): *Woman, why weepest thou?*

3. The melancholy account she gives them of her present distress: *Because they have taken away* the blessed body I came to embalm, *and I know not where they have laid it.* The same story she had told, *v.* 2. In it we may see, (1) The weakness of her faith. (2) The strength of her love. Mary Magdalene is not diverted from her enquiries by the surprise of the vision, nor satisfied with the honour of it; but still she harps upon the same string: *They have taken away my Lord.*

III. Christ's appearing to her

while she was talking with the angels, and telling them her case. In this appearance of Christ to Mary observe,

(1) How he did at first conceal himself from her.

[1] He stood as a common person, and she looked upon him accordingly, *v.* 14. She *knew not that it was Jesus*; not that he appeared in any other likeness, but either it was a careless transient look she cast upon him, and, her eyes being full of care, she could not so well distinguish, or *they were holden, that she should not know him*, as those of the two disciples, Luke xxiv. 16.

[2] He asked her a common question, and she answered him accordingly, *v.* 15.

First, The question he asked her was natural enough, and what any one would have asked her: "*Woman, why weepest thou? Whom seekest thou?*"

Secondly, The reply she made him is natural enough; she does not give him a direct answer, but, *supposing him to be the gardener*, she said, *Sir, if thou hast carried him hence,* pray *tell me where thou hast laid him, and I will take him away.* See here, 1. The error of her understanding. She supposed our Lord Jesus to be the gardener, perhaps because he asked what authority she had to be there. 2. The truth of her affection. See how her heart was set upon finding Christ. She puts the question to every one she meets, like the careful spouse, *Saw you him whom my soul loveth?*

(2) How Christ at length made himself known to her, and, by a

pleasing surprise, gave her infallible assurances of his resurrection. Observe,

[1] How Christ discovered himself to this good woman that was seeking him in tears (v. 16): *Jesus saith unto her, Mary.* It was said with an emphasis, and that air of kindness and freedom with which he was wont to speak to her. Now he changed his voice, and spoke like himself, not like the gardener. Christ's way of making himself known to his people is by his word, his word applied to their souls, speaking to them in particular.

[2] How readily she received this discovery. Observe, *First*, The title of respect she gives him: *My Master—a teaching master.* The Jews called their doctors *Rabbies*, great men. Their critics tell us that *Rabbon* was with them a more honourable title than *Rabbi*; and therefore Mary chooses that, and adds a note of appropriation, *My great Master. Secondly*, With what liveliness of affection she gives this title to Christ. *She turned* from the angels, whom she had in her eye, to look unto Jesus. When *she thought it had been the gardener*, she looked another way while speaking to him; but now that she knew the voice of Christ *she turned herself.*

[3] The further instructions that Christ gave her (v. 17): *"Touch me not*, but go and carry the news to the disciples."

First, He diverts her from the expectation of familiar society and conversation with him at this time: *Touch me not, for I am not yet ascended.* 1. *Touch me not* thus at all, for I am to ascend to heaven. He bade the disciples touch him, for

the confirmation of their faith; he allowed the women to take hold of his feet, and worship him (Matt. xxviii. 9); but Mary, supposing that he was risen, as Lazarus was, to live among them constantly, and converse with them freely as he had done, upon that presumption was about to take hold of his hand with her usual freedom. This mistake Christ rectified; she must believe him, and adore him, as exalted, but must not expect to be familiar with him as formerly. See 2 Cor. v. 16. 2. *"Touch me not*, do not stay to touch me now, stay not now to make any further enquiries, or give any further expressions of joy, for *I am not yet ascended*, I shall not depart immediately, it may as well be done another time; the best service thou canst do now is to carry the tidings to the disciples; lose no time therefore, but go away with all speed."

Secondly, He directs her what message to carry to his disciples: *But go to my brethren, and tell them*, not only that I am risen (she could have told them that of herself, for she had seen him), but that *I ascend.* Observe,

Two full breasts of consolation are here in these words:—

(a) Our joint-relation to God, resulting from our union with Christ, is an unspeakable comfort. Speaking of that inexhaustible spring of light, life, and bliss, he says, He is *my Father, and your Father; my God, and your God.* It is the great condescension of Christ that he is pleased to own the believer's God for his God: *My God, and your God*; mine, that he may be yours; the God of the

Redeemer, to support him (Ps. lxxxix. 26), that he might be the God of the redeemed, to save them.

(*b*) Christ's ascension into heaven, in further prosecution of his undertaking for us, is likewise an unspeakable comfort: "Tell them I must shortly ascend; that is the next step I am to take." Now this was intended to be, [*a*] A word of caution to these disciples, not to expect the continuance of his bodily presence on earth, nor the setting up of his temporal kingdom among men, which they dreamed of. [*b*] A word of comfort to them, and to all *that shall believe in him through their word*; he was then ascending, he is now *ascended to his Father, and our Father*. This was his advancement; he ascended to receive those honours and powers which were to be the recompence of his humiliation; he says it with triumph, that those who love him may rejoice.

Some make those words, *I ascend to my God and your God*, to include a promise of our resurrection, in the virtue of Christ's resurrection; for Christ had proved the resurrection of the dead from these words, *I am the God of Abraham*, Matt. xxii. 32. So that Christ here insinuates, "As he is my God, and hath therefore raised me, so he is your God, and will therefore raise you, and be your God, Rev. xxi. 3. *Because I live, you shall live also*. I now ascend, to honour my God, and you shall ascend to him as your God.

IV. Here is Mary Magdalene's faithful report of what she had seen and heard to the disciples (*v.* 18): *She came and told the disciples, whom she found together, that she had seen the Lord.*

EVIDENCE OFFERED
(*vv.* 19–25)

The infallible proof of Christ's resurrection was his *showing himself alive*, Acts i. 3. In these verses, we have an account of his first appearance to the college of the disciples, on the day on which he rose. Now observe here,

I. When and where this appearance was, *v.* 19. It was *the same day* that he rose, *being the first day of the week*, the day after the Jewish sabbath, at a private meeting of the disciples, ten of them, and some more of their friends with them, Luke xxiv. 33.

II. What was said and done in this visit Christ made to his disciples, and his interview between them. We have five things in this appearance of Christ:—

(1) His kind and familiar salutation of his disciples: *He said, Peace be unto you*. This was not a word of course, though commonly used so at the meeting of friends, but a solemn, uncommon benediction, conferring upon them all the blessed fruits and effects of his death and resurrection. The phrase was common, but the sense was now peculiar. His speaking peace makes peace, *creates the fruit of the lips, peace*; peace with God, peace in your own consciences, peace with one another; all this peace be with you; not peace with the world, but peace in Christ.

(2) His clear and undeniable manifestation of himself to them, *v.* 20. And here observe,

[1] The method he took to convince them of the truth of his resurrection, They now saw him alive

whom multitudes had seen dead two or three days before. Now the only doubt was whether this that they saw alive was the same individual body that had been seen dead; and none could desire a further proof that it was so than the scars or marks of the wounds in the body. Now, *First,* The marks of the wounds, and very deep marks (though without any pain or soreness), remained in the body of the Lord Jesus even after his resurrection, that they might be demonstrations of the truth of it. Conquerors glory in the marks of their wounds. Christ's wounds were to speak on earth that it was he himself. *Secondly,* These marks he showed to his disciples, for their conviction. When Christ manifests his love to believers by the comforts of his Spirit, assures them that *because he lives they shall live also,* then *he shows them his hands and his side.*

[2] The impression it made upon them, and the good it did them. *First,* They were convinced that they saw the Lord; so was their faith confirmed. *Secondly, Then they were glad*; that which strengthened their faith raised their joy; *believing they rejoice.*

(3) The honourable and ample commission he gave them to be his agents in the planting of his church, *v.* 21. Here is,

[1] The preface to their commission, which was the solemn repetition of the salutation before: *Peace be unto you.*

[2] The commission itself, which sounds very great: *As my Father hath sent me, even so send I you.*

First, It is easy to understand how Christ sent them; he appointed them to go on with his work upon earth, and to lay out themselves for the spreading of his gospel, and the setting up of his kingdom, among men. He sent them authorized with a divine warrant, armed with a divine power,—sent them as ambassadors to treat of peace, and as heralds to proclaim it,—sent them as servants to bid to the marriage. Hence they were called *apostles—men sent.*

Secondly, But how Christ sent them as the Father sent him is not so easily understood; certainly their commissions and powers were infinitely inferior to his; but, 1. Their work was of the same kind with his, and they were to go on where he left off. 2. He had a power to send them equal to that which the Father had to send him. Here the force of the comparison seems to lie. By the same authority that the Father sent me do I send you.

(4) The qualifying of them for the discharge of the trust reposed in them by their commission (*v.* 22): *He breathed on them, and said, Receive ye the Holy Ghost.* Observe,

[1] The sign he used to assure them of, and affect them with, the gift he was now about to bestow upon them: *He breathed on them*; not only to show them, by this breath of life, that he himself was really alive, but to signify to them the spiritual life and power which they should receive from him for all the services that lay before them. Christ here seems to refer to the creation of man at first, by the breathing of the breath of life into him (Gen. ii. 7), and to intimate

that he himself was the author of that work, and that the spiritual life and strength of ministers and Christians are derived from him, and depend upon him, as much as the natural life of Adam and his seed. Now this intimates to us, *First*, That the Spirit is the breath of Christ, *proceeding from the Son. Secondly*, That the Spirit is the gift of Christ. The apostles communicated the Holy Ghost by the laying on of hands, those hands being first lifted up in prayer, for they could only beg this blessing, and carry it as messengers; but Christ conferred the Holy Ghost by breathing, for he is the author of the gift, and from him it comes originally.

[2] The solemn grant he made, signified by this sign, "*Receive ye the Holy Ghost*, in part now, as an earnest of what you shall further receive *not many days hence*." Let us see what is contained in this grant. *First*, Christ hereby gives them assurance of the Spirit's aid in their future work, in the execution of the commission now given them: "*I send you*, and you shall have the Spirit to go along with you." *Secondly*, He hereby gives them experience of the Spirit's influences in their present case. He had shown them his hands and his side, to convince them of the truth of his resurrection; but the plainest evidences will not of themselves work faith, witness the infidelity of the soldiers, who were the only eye-witnesses of the resurrection. "Therefore *receive ye the Holy Ghost*, to work faith in you, and to open your understandings."

(5) One particular branch of the power given them by their commis-

sion particularized (*v.* 23): "*Whosoever sins you remit*, in the due execution of the powers you are entrusted with, they are remitted to them, and they may take the comfort of it; *and whosoever sins you retain*, that is, pronounce unpardoned and the guilt of them bound on, *they are retained*, and the sinner may be sure of it, to his sorrow." Now this follows upon their receiving the Holy Ghost; for, if they had not had an extraordinary spirit of discerning, they had not been fit to be entrusted with such an authority; for, in the strictest sense, this is a special commission to the apostles themselves and the first preachers of the gospel, who could distinguish who were in the *gall of bitterness and bond of iniquity*, and who were not. By virtue of this power, Peter struck Ananias and Sapphira dead, and Paul struck Elymas blind. Yet it must be understood as a general charter to the church and her ministers, not securing an infallibility of judgment to any man or company of men in the world, but encouraging the faithful stewards of the mysteries of God to stand to the gospel they were sent to preach, for that God himself will stand to it. Two ways the apostles and ministers of Christ remit and retain sin, and both as having authority:— [1] By sound doctrine. They are commissioned to tell the world that salvation is to be had upon gospel terms, and no other, and they shall find God will say *Amen* to it; so shall their doom be. [2] By a strict discipline, applying the general rule of the gospel to particular persons. "Whom you admit into communion with you, according to the rules of the gospel, God will admit into communion with himself; and whom you cast out of communion as impenitent, and obstinate in scandalous and infectious sins, shall be bound over to the righteous judgment of God."

III. The incredulity of Thomas, when the report of this was made to him, which introduced Christ's second appearance.

1. Here is Thomas's absence from this meeting, v. 24.

2. The account which the other disciples gave him of the visit their Master had made them, v. 25.

3. The objections Thomas raised against the evidence, to justify himself in his unwillingness to admit it. "Tell me not that you have seen the Lord alive; you are too credulous; somebody has made fools of you. For my part, *except I shall* not only *see in his hands the print of the nails*, but put my finger into it, *and thrust my hand* into the wound *in his side*, I am resolved *I will not believe*." Either he will be humoured, and have his fancy gratified, or he will not believe; see Matt. xvi. 1; xxvii. 42.

4. The open avowal of this in the presence of the disciples was an offence and discouragement to them It was not only a sin, but a scandal. As one coward makes many, so does one unbeliever, one sceptic, *making his brethren's heart to faint like his heart*, Deut. xx. 8. Had he only thought this evil, and then laid his hand upon his mouth, to suppress it, his error had remained with himself; but his proclaiming his infidelity, and that so peremptorily, might be of ill consequence to the

rest, who were as yet but weak and wavering.

THOMAS CONVINCED
(*vv.* 26–31)

We have here an account of another appearance of Christ to his disciples, after his resurrection, when Thomas was now with them. And concerning this we may observe,

I. When it was that Christ repeated his visit to his disciples: *After eight days*, that day seven-night after he rose, which must therefore be, as that was, *the first day of the week*.

1. He deferred his next appearance for some time, to show his disciples that he was not risen to such a life as he had formerly lived, to converse constantly with them, but was as one that belonged to another world, and visited this only as angels do, now and then, when there was occasion.

2. He deferred it so long as seven days. And why so? (1) That he might put a rebuke upon Thomas for his incredulity. (2) That he might try the faith and patience of the rest of the disciples. (3) That he might put an honour upon the first day of the week, and give a plain intimation of his will, that it should be observed in his church as the Christian sabbath, the weekly day of holy rest and holy convocations.

II. Where, and how, Christ made them this visit. It was at Jerusalem, for the doors were shut now, as before, for fear of the Jews. Now observe, 1. That Thomas was with them; though he had withdrawn himself once, yet not a second time. 2. That Christ *came* in among them, and *stood in the midst*, and they all knew him, for he showed himself now, just as he had shown himself before (*v.* 19), still the same, and no changling. 3. He saluted them all in a friendly manner, as he had done before; he said, *Peace be unto you.*

III. What passed between Christ and Thomas at this meeting; and that only is recorded, though we may suppose he said a great deal to the rest of them. Here is,

1. Christ's gracious condescension to Thomas, *v.* 27. He singled him out from the rest, and applied himself particularly to him: "*Reach hither thy finger*, and, since thou wilt have it so, *behold my hands*, and satisfy thy curiosity to the utmost about the *print of the nails; reach hither thy hand*, and, if nothing less will convince thee, *thrust it into my side.*" Here we have, (1) An implicit rebuke of Thomas's incredulity, in the plain reference which is here had to what Thomas had said, answering it word for word, for he had heard it, though unseen; and one would think that his telling him of it should put him to the blush. (2) An express condescension to his weakness, which appears in two things:—[1] That he suffers his wisdom to be prescribed to. Great spirits will not be dictated to by their inferiors, especially in their acts of grace; yet Christ is pleased here to accommodate himself even to Thomas's fancy in a needless thing, rather than break with him, and leave him in his unbelief. [2] He suffers his wounds to be raked into, allows Thomas even to thrust his hand into his side, if then at last he would believe.

It is an affecting word with which Christ closes up what he had to say to Thomas: *Be not faithless but believing; do not thou become an unbeliever;* as if he would have been sealed up under unbelief, had he not yielded now.

2. Thomas's believing consent to Jesus Christ. He is now ashamed of his incredulity, and cries out, *My Lord and my God, v.* 28. We are not told whether he did put his finger into the print of the nails; it should seem, he did not, for Christ says (*v.* 29), *Thou hast seen, and believed;* seeing sufficed. And now faith comes off a conqueror, after a struggle with unbelief.

(1) Thomas is now fully satisfied of the truth of Christ's resurrection —that the same Jesus that was crucified is now alive, and this is he.

(2) He therefore believed him to be Lord and God, and we are to believe him so. [1] We must believe his deity—that he is God; not a man made God, but God made man, as this evangelist had laid down his thesis at first, *ch.* i. 1. [2] His mediation—that he is Lord, the one Lord, 1 Cor. viii. 6; 1 Tim. ii. 5. He is sufficiently authorized, as plenipotentiary, to settle the great concerns that lie between God and man, to take up the controversy which would inevitably have been our ruin, and to establish the correspondence that was necessary to our happiness; see Acts ii. 36; Rom. xiv. 9.

(3) He consented to him as his Lord and his God. In faith there must be the consent of the will to gospel terms, as well as the assent of the understanding to gospel truths. We must accept of Christ to

be that to us which the Father hath appointed him. This is the vital act of faith, He is mine, Cant. ii. 16.

(4) He made an open profession of this, before those that had been the witnesses of his unbelieving doubts. He says it to Christ, and, to complete the sense, we must read it, *Thou art* my Lord and my God; or, speaking to his brethren, *This is* my Lord and my God.

3. The judgment of Christ upon the whole (v. 29). Here,

(1) Christ owns Thomas a believer. Sound and sincere believers, though they be slow and weak, shall be graciously accepted of the Lord Jesus.

(2) He upbraids him with his former incredulity. If this must be the only method of proof, how must the world be converted to the faith of Christ? He is therefore justly blamed for laying so much stress upon this.

(3) He commends the faith of those who believe upon easier terms. Thomas, as a believer, was truly blessed; but rather *blessed are those that have not seen*. It is not meant of not seeing the objects of faith (for these are invisible, Heb. xi. 1; 2 Cor. iv. 18), but the motives of faith—Christ's miracles, and especially his resurrection; blessed are those that see not these, and yet believe in Christ.

IV. The remark which the evangelist makes upon his narrative, like an historian drawing towards a conclusion, vv. 30, 31. And here,

1. He assures us that many other things occurred, which were all worthy to be recorded, but are *not written in the book: many signs.* Some refer this to all the signs that

Jesus did during his whole life, all the wondrous words he spoke, and all the wondrous works he did. But it seems rather to be confined to the signs he did after his resurrection, for these were in the presence of the disciples only, who are here spoken of, Acts x. 41.

2. He instructs us in the design of recording what we do find here (v. 31): "These accounts are given in this and the following chapter, *that you might believe* upon these evidences; that you might believe that Jesus is the Christ, the Son of God, declared with power to be so by his resurrection."

CHAPTER TWENTY-ONE
THE SEA OF TIBERIAS
(vv. 1–14)

We have here an account of Christ's appearance to his disciples at the sea of Tiberias. As to the particulars of the story, we may observe,

I. Who they were to whom Christ now showed himself (v. 2): not to all the twelve, but to seven of them only.

II. How they were employed, v. 3. Observe,

1. Their agreement to go a fishing. Some think they did amiss in returning to their boats and nets, which they had left; but then Christ would not have countenanced them in it with a visit.

2. Their disappointment in their fishing. That night they caught nothing, though, it is probable, they *toiled all night,* as Luke v. 5. See the vanity of this world; the hand of the diligent often returns empty.

III. After what manner Christ made himself known to them. It is said (v. 1), *He showed himself*. His body, though a true and real body, was raised, as ours will be, a spiritual body, and so was visible only when he himself was pleased to make it so; or, rather, came and removed so quickly that it was here or there in an instant, *in a moment, in the twinkling of an eye*. Four things are observable in the appearance of Christ to them:—

1. He showed himself to them seasonably (v. 4): *When the morning was now come*, after a fruitless night's toil, Jesus *stood on the shore*. Christ's time of making himself known to his people is when they are most at a loss.

2. He showed himself to them gradually. The disciples, though they had been intimately acquainted with him, *knew not*, all at once, *that it was Jesus*. Little expecting to see him there, and not looking intently upon him, they took him for some common person waiting the arrival of their boat, to buy their fish.

3. He showed himself to them by an instance of his pity, v. 5. He called to them, *Children*,—"*Lads, have you any meat?* Have you caught any fish?" Here, (1) The compellation is very familiar; he speaks unto them as unto his sons, with the care and tenderness of a father: *Children*. (2) The question is very kind: *Have you any meat?*

4. He showed himself to them by an instance of his power; and this perfected the discovery (v. 6): he ordered them to *cast the net on the right side of the ship*, the contrary side to what they had been casting it on; and then they, who were going home empty-handed, were

enriched with a great draught of fishes. Here we have, (1) The orders Christ gave them, and the promise annexed to those orders: *Cast the net* there in such a place, and *you shall find*. He from whom nothing is hid, no, not the *inhabitants under the waters* (Job xxvi. 5), knew on what side of the ship the shoal of fishes was, and to that side he directs them. (2) Their obedience of these orders, and the good success of it. As yet *they knew not that it was Jesus*; however, they were willing to be advised by any body, and did not bid this supposed stranger mind his own business and not meddle with theirs, but took his counsel; in being thus observant of strangers, they were obedient to their Master unawares. And it sped wonderfully well; now they had a draught that paid them for all their pains.

IV. How the disciples received this discovery which Christ made of himself, vv. 7, 8, where we find,

1. That John was the most intelligent and quick-sighted disciple. He whom Jesus loved was the first that said, *It is the Lord*; for those whom Christ loves he will in a special manner manifest himself to: his secret is with his favourites.

2. That Peter was the most zealous and warm-hearted disciple; for as soon as he heard it was the Lord (for which he took John's word) the ship could not hold him, nor could he stay till the bringing of it to shore, but into the sea he throws himself presently, that he might come first to Christ.

3. That the rest of the disciples were careful and honest hearted. Though they were not in such a

transport of zeal as to throw themselves into the sea, like Peter, yet they hastened in the boat to the shore, and made the best of their way (v. 8): *The other disciples*, and John with them, who had first discovered that it was Christ, came slowly, yet they came to Christ.

V. What entertainment the Lord Jesus gave them when they came ashore.

1. He had provision ready for them. When they came to land, wet and cold, weary and hungry, they found a good fire there to warm them and dry them, and fish and bread, competent provision for a good meal. (1) We need not be curious in enquiring whence this fire, and fish, and bread, came, any more than whence the meat came which the ravens brought to Elijah. (2) We may be comforted in this instance of Christ's care of his disciples; he has wherewith to supply all our wants, and *knows what things we have need of*.

2. He called for some of that which they had caught, and they produced it, vv. 10, 11. Observe here,

(1) The command Christ gave them to bring their draught of fish to shore: "Bring of the fish hither, which you have now caught, and let us have some of them."

(2) Their obedience to this command, v. 11. It was said (v. 6), *They were not able to draw the net to shore, for the multitude of fishes*. They had the curiosity to count them, and perhaps it was in order to the making of a dividend; they were in all a *hundred and fifty and three*, and all *great fishes*. These were many more than they needed for their present supply, but they might sell them, and the money would serve to bear their charges back to Jerusalem, whither they were shortly to return.

3. He invited them to dinner. Observing them to keep their distance, and that *they were afraid to ask him, Who art thou?* because they *knew it was their Lord*, he called to them very familiarly, *Come, and dine*.

4. He carved for them, as the master of the feast, v. 13. Observing them to be still shy and timorous, *he comes, and takes bread himself*, and *gives them*, some to each of them, *and fish likewise*.

The evangelist leaves them at dinner, and makes this remark (v. 14): *This is now the third time that Jesus showed himself alive to his disciples*, or the greater part of them. *This is the third day*; so some. On the day he rose he appeared five times; the second day was that day seven-night; and this was the third. Or this was his third appearance to any considerable number of his disciples together; though he had appeared to Mary, to the women, to the two disciples, and to Cephas, yet he had but twice before this appeared to any company of them together.

PETER RE-COMMISSIONED
(vv. 15–19)

We have here Christ's discourse with Peter after dinner, so much of it as relates to himself, in which,

I. He examines his love to him, and gives him a charge concerning his flock, vv. 15–17. Observe,

1. Three times Christ asks Peter whether he loves him or no. The

first time the question is, *Simon, son of Jonas, lovest thou me more than these?* Observe,

[1] How he calls him: *Simon, son of Jonas.* He speaks to him by name, the more to affect him, as Luke xxii. 31. *Simon, Simon.* He does not call him *Cephas*, nor *Peter*, the name he had given him (for he had lost the credit of his strength and stability, which those names signified), but his original name, *Simon.*

[2] How he catechises him: *Lovest thou me more than these?*

First, Lovest thou me? If we would try whether we are Christ's disciples indeed, this must be the enquiry, Do we love him? But there was a special reason why Christ put it now to Peter. 1. His fall had given occasion to doubt of his love. 2. His function would give occasion for the exercise of his *love*. Before Christ would commit his *sheep* to his care, he asked him, *Lovest thou me?*

Secondly, Lovest thou me more than these? 1. "*Lovest thou me more than thou lovest these*, more than thou lovest these persons?" Or, "*more than thou lovest these things*, these boats and nets—more than all the pleasure of fishing, which some make a recreation of—more than the gain of fishing, which others make a calling of." Those only love Christ indeed that love him better than all the delights of sense and all the profits of this world. 2. "*Lovest thou me more than these love me*, more than any of the rest of the disciples love me? And then the question is intended to upbraid him with his vainglorious boast, *Though all men should deny thee, yet will not I.*

"Art thou still of the same mind?" Or, to intimate to him that he had now more reason to love him than any of them had, for more had been forgiven to him than to any of them, as much as his sin in denying Christ was greater than theirs in forsaking him. *Tell me therefore which of them will love him most?* Luke vii. 42.

Thirdly, The second and third time that Christ put this question, 1. He left out the comparison *more than these*, because Peter, in his answer, modestly left it out, not willing to compare himself with his brethren, much less to prefer himself before them. 2. In the last he altered the word, as it is in the original. In the first two enquiries, the original word conveys *Dost thou retain a kindness for me?* In answer to which Peter uses another word, more emphatic—*I love thee dearly.* In putting the question the last time, Christ uses that word: And dost thou indeed love me dearly?

2. Three times Peter returns the same answer to Christ: *Yea, Lord, thou knowest that I love thee.* Observe, [1] Peter does not pretend to love Christ more than the rest of the disciples did. [2] Yet he professes again and again that he loves Christ: *Yea, Lord,* surely *I love thee*; I were unworthy to live if I did not." He had a high esteem and value for him, a grateful sense of his kindness, and was entirely devoted to his honour and interest; his desire was towards him, as one he was undone without; and his delight in him, as one he should be unspeakably happy in. This amounts to a profession of repentance for his sin, for it grieves us to have affronted one we love; and to

a promise of adherence to him for the future: *Lord, I love thee*, and *will never leave thee*. Christ *prayed that his faith might not fail* (Luke xxii. 32), and, because his faith did not fail, his love did not; for faith will work by love. *He was grieved* when Christ asked him the *third time, Lovest thou me? v.* 17. *First*, Because it put him in mind of his threefold denial of Christ, and was plainly designed to do so; *and when he thought thereon he wept. Secondly*, Because it put him in fear lest his Master foresaw some further miscarriage of his, which would be as great a contradiction to his profession of love to him as the former was.

3. Three times Christ committed the care of his flock to Peter: *Feed my lambs; feed my sheep; feed my sheep.* [1] Those whom Christ committed to Peter's care were his lambs and his sheep. The church of Christ is his flock, *which he hath purchased with his own blood* (Acts xx. 28), and he is *the chief shepherd* of it. [2] The charge he gives him concerning them is to feed them. The word used in *vv.* 15, 17 strictly signifies to *give them food*; but the word used in *v.* 16 signifies more largely to do all the offices of a shepherd to them. The particular application to Peter here was designed, *First*, To restore him to his apostleship, now that he repented of his abjuration of it, and to renew his commission, both for his own satisfaction, and for the satisfaction of his brethren. *Secondly*, It was designed to quicken him to a diligent discharge of his office as an apostle. *Thirdly*, What Christ said to him he said to all his disciples;

he charged them all, not only to be fishers of men (though that was said to Peter, Luke v. 10), by the conversion of sinners, but feeders of the flock, by the edification of saints.

II. Christ, having thus appointed Peter his doing work, next appoints him his suffering work. Having confirmed to him the honour of an apostle, he now tells him of further preferment designed him—the honour of a martyr. Observe,

1. How his martyrdom is foretold (*v.* 18): *Thou shalt stretch forth thy hands*, being compelled to it, and *another shall gird thee* (as a prisoner that is pinioned) *and carry thee whither* naturally *thou wouldest not*.

2. The explication of this prediction (*v.* 19), *This spoke he* to Peter, *signifying by what death he should glorify God*, when he had finished his course.

3. The word of command he gives him hereupon: *When he had spoken thus*, observing Peter perhaps to look blank upon it, *he saith unto him, Follow me.* Probably he rose from the place where he had sat at dinner, walked off a little, and bade Peter attend him. This word, *Follow me*, was, (1) A further confirmation of his restoration to his Master's favour, and to his apostleship; for *Follow me* was the first call. (2) It was an explanation of the prediction of his sufferings, which perhaps Peter at first did not fully understand, till Christ gave him that key to it, *Follow me*: "Expect to be treated as I have been, and to tread the same bloody path that I have trodden before thee; *for the disciple is not greater than his Lord*." (3) It was to excite him to, and

encourage him in, faithfulness and diligence in his work as an apostle.

EPILOGUE (vv. 20–25)

In these verses we have,

I. The conference Christ had with Peter concerning John, the beloved disciple, in which we have,

1. The eye Peter cast upon him (v. 20).

2. The enquiry Peter made concerning him (v. 21). John was younger than Peter, and, in the course of nature, likely to survive him: "Lord," says he, "what times shall he be reserved for?" Whereas, if God by his grace enable us to persevere to the end, and finish well, and get safely to heaven, we need not ask, "What shall be the lot of those that shall come after us?"

3. Christ's reply to this enquiry (v. 22), "*If I will that he tarry till I come,* and do not suffer as thou must, *what is that to thee.* Mind thou thy own duty, the present duty, *follow thou me.*"

(1) There seems to be here an intimation of Christ's purpose concerning John, in two things:—[1] That he should not die a violent death, like Peter, but should tarry till Christ himself came by a natural death to fetch him to himself. [2] That he should not die till after Christ's coming to destroy Jerusalem: so some understand his tarrying till Christ comes.

(2) Others think that it is only a rebuke to Peter's curiosity, and that his tarrying till Christ's second coming is only the supposition of an absurdity.

4. The mistake which arose from this saying of Christ, that *that disciple should not die,* but abide with the church to the end of time; together with the suppressing of this motion by a repetition of Christ's words, v. 23. Observe here,

(1) The easy rise of a mistake in the church by misconstruing the sayings of Christ, and turning a supposition to a position. Because John must not die a martyr, they conclude he must not die at all.

(2) The easy rectifying of such mistakes, by adhering to the word of Christ, and abiding by that. So the evangelist here corrects and controls that saying among the brethren, by repeating the very words of Christ. He did not say that that disciple should not die. Let us not say so then; but he said, *If I will that he tarry till I come, what is that to thee?* He said so, and no more. *Add thou not unto his words.* Let the words of Christ speak for themselves, and let no sense be put upon them but what is genuine and natural; and in that let us agree.

II. We have here the conclusion of this gospel, and with it of the evangelical story, vv. 24, 25. This evangelist ends not so abruptly as the other three did, but with a sort of cadency.

1. This gospel concludes with an account of the author or penman of it, connected by a decent transition to that which went before (v. 24): *This is the disciple which testifies of these things* to the present age, and wrote these things for the benefit of posterity, even this same that Peter and his Master had that conference about in the foregoing verses—John the apostle. Observe

here, (1) Those who wrote the history of Christ were not ashamed to put their names to it. John here does in effect subscribe his name. (2) Those who wrote the history of Christ wrote upon their own knowledge, not by hearsay, but what they themselves were eye and ear witnesses of. (3) Those who wrote the history of Christ, as they testified what they had seen, so they wrote what they had first testified. It was published by word of mouth, with the greatest assurance, before it was committed to writing. (4) It was graciously appointed, for the support and benefit of the church, that the history of Christ should be put into writing, that it might with the greater fullness and certainty spread to every place, and last through every age.

2. It concludes with an attestation of the truth of what had been here related: *We know that his testimony is true.* This may be taken either, (1) As expressing the common sense of mankind in matters of this nature, which is, that the testimony of one who is an eye-witness, is of unspotted reputation, solemnly deposes what he has seen, and puts it into writing for the greater certainty, is an unexceptionable evidence. Or, (2) As expressing the satisfaction of the churches *at that time* concerning the truth of what is here related.

Some take it for the subscription of the church of Ephesus, others of the angels or ministers of the churches of Asia to this narrative. Or, (3) As expressing the evangelist's own assurance of the truth of what he wrote, like that (*ch.* xix. 35), *He knows that he saith true.* He speaks of himself in the plural number, *We know,* not for majesty-sake, but for modesty-sake, as 1 John i. 1, *That which we have seen*; and 2 Pet. i. 16.

3. It concludes with an *et cetera*, with a reference to *many other things*; very memorable, said and done by our Lord Jesus, which were well known by many then living, but not thought fit to be recorded for posterity, *v.* 25. There were many things very remarkable and improvable, which, if they should be written at large, with the several circumstances of them, even the world itself, that is, all the libraries in it, could not contain the books that might be written. Thus he concludes like an orator, as Paul (Heb. xi. 32), *What shall I more say? For the time would fail me.*

The evangelist, concluding with *Amen,* thereby sets to his seal, and let us set to ours, an *Amen* of faith, subscribing to the gospel, that it is true, all true; and an *Amen* of satisfaction in what is written, as able to make us wise to salvation. *Amen*; so be it.

BOOK TWO

ACTS TO REVELATION

THE ACTS OF THE APOSTLES

PROLOGUE (vv. 1-5)

In these verses, I. Theophilus is put in mind, and we in him, of St. Luke's gospel.

His gospel is here called *the former treatise which he had made*, which he had an eye to in writing this, intending this for a continuation and confirmation of that.

The contents of his gospel were *that, all that, which Jesus began both to do and teach*; and the same is the subject of the writings of the other three evangelists.

A general hint is given of the instructions he furnished his disciples with, now that he was about to leave them, and they, since *he breathed on them* and *opened their understandings*, were better able to receive them. 1. He instructed them concerning the work they were to do: *He gave commandments to the apostles whom he had chosen.* 2. He instructed them concerning the doctrine they were to preach: *He spoke to them of the things pertaining to the kingdom of God.* He had given them a general idea of that kingdom, and the certain time it should be set up in the world (in his parable, Mark xiii.), but here he instructed them more in the nature of it, as a kingdom of grace in this world and of glory in the other, and opened to them that covenant which is the great charter by which it is incorporated.

A particular assurance is given them that they should now shortly receive the Holy Ghost, with orders given them to expect it (*vv.* 4, 5), he *being assembled together with them*, probably in the interview at the mountain in Galilee which he had appointed before his death; for there is mention of their *coming together again* (*v.* 6), to attend his ascension. Though he had now ordered them to Galilee, yet they must not think to continue there; no, they must return to Jerusalem, and not depart thence.

Now this gift of the Holy Ghost he speaks of,

[1] As *the promise of the Father, which they had heard of him*, and might therefore depend upon. *First*, The Spirit was given by promise, and it was at this time the great promise, as that of the Messiah was before (Luke i. 72), and that of eternal life is now, 1 John ii. 25. *Secondly*, It was *the promise of the Father*, 1. Of Christ's Father. Christ, as Mediator, had an eye to God as his Father, fathering his design, and owning it all along. 2. Of our Father, who, if he give us *the adoption of sons*, will certainly give us *the Spirit of adoption*, Gal. iv. 5, 6.

[2] As the prediction of John Baptist; for so far back Christ here directs them to look (*v.* 5): "You have not only heard it from me, but you had it from John; when he turned you over to me, he said

1

(Matt. iii. 11), *I indeed baptize you with water, but he that comes after me shall baptize you with the Holy Ghost.*" It is a great honour that Christ now does to John, not only to quote his words, but to make this great gift of the Spirit, now at hand, to be the accomplishment of them.

THE ASCENSION (*vv.* 6–11)

In Jerusalem Christ, by his angel, had appointed his disciples to meet him in Galilee; there he appointed them to meet him in Jerusalem again, such a day. Thus he would try their obedience, and it was found ready and cheerful; *they came together*, as he appointed them, to be *the witnesses* of his ascension, of which we have here an account. Observe,

I. The question they asked him at this interview. *Lord, wilt thou at this time restore again the kingdom to Israel?*

Now two things were amiss in this question:

1. Their expectation of the thing itself. They thought Christ would *restore the kingdom to Israel*, that is, that he would make the nation of the Jews as great and considerable among the nations as it was *in the days of David and Solomon.*

2. Their enquiry concerning the time of it: "*Lord, wilt thou* do it *at this time?*" Now herein they missed their mark, [1] That they were inquisitive into that which their Master had never directed nor encouraged them to enquire into. [2] That they were impatient for the setting up of that kingdom in which they promised themselves so great a share, and would anticipate the divine counsels.

II. The check which Christ gave to this question, like that which he had a little before given to Peter's enquiry concerning John, *What is that to thee? v.* 7, *It is not for you to know the times and seasons.* He does not contradict their expectation that the kingdom would be restored to Israel, because that mistake would soon be rectified by the pouring out of the Spirit, after which they never had any more thoughts of the temporal kingdom; and also because there is a sense of the expectation which is true, the setting up of the gospel kingdom in the world; and their mistake of the promise shall not make it of no effect; but he checks their enquiry after the time.

The knowledge of it is reserved to God as his prerogative; it is what *the Father hath put in his own power*; it is hid with him. None besides can reveal the times and seasons to come. *Known unto God are all his works*, but not to us, *ch.* xv. 18.

III. He appoints them their work, and with authority assures them of an ability to go on with it, and of success in it. "*It is not for you to know the times and the seasons*—this would do you no good; but know this (*v.* 8) that you shall receive a spiritual *power*, by the *descent of the Holy Ghost upon you*, and shall not receive it in vain, for *you shall be witnesses unto me* and my glory; and your testimony shall not be in vain, for it shall be received here in Jerusalem, in the country about, and all the world over," *v.* 8. Christ here tells them,

1. That their work should be honourable and glorious: *You shall be witnesses unto me.*

2. That their power for this work

2

should be sufficient. "*But you shall receive the power of the Holy Ghost coming upon you*" (so it may be read), "shall be animated and actuated by a better spirit than your own; you shall have power to preach the gospel, and to prove it out of the scriptures of the Old Testament" (which, when they were *filled with the Holy Ghost*, they did to admiration, *ch*. xviii. 28), "and to confirm it both by miracles and by sufferings."

3. That their influence should be great and very extensive: "*You shall be witnesses* for Christ, and shall carry his cause," (1) "*In Jerusalem*; there you must begin, and many there will receive your testimony; and those that do not will be left inexcusable." (2) "Your light shall thence shine throughout all Judea, where before you have laboured in vain." (3) "Thence you shall proceed *to Samaria*, though at your first mission you were forbidden to preach in *any of the cities of the Samaritans*." (4) "Your usefulness shall reach *to the uttermost part of the earth*, and you shall be blessings to the whole world."

IV. Having left these instructions with them, he leaves them (*v*. 9). We have here Christ's ascending on high; not fetched away, as Elijah was, with *a chariot of fire and horses of fire*, but rising to heaven, as he rose from the grave, purely by his own power, his body being now, as the bodies of the saints will be at the resurrection, a spiritual body, and raised in power and incorruption.

V. The disciples, when he had gone out of their sight, yet still continued *looking up stedfastly to heaven* (*v*. 10), and this longer than it was fit they should; and why so? 1. Perhaps they hoped that Christ would presently come back to them again, to restore the kingdom to Israel, and were loth to believe they should now part with him for good and all. 2. Perhaps they expected to see some change in the visible heavens now upon Christ's ascension, that either *the sun should be ashamed or the moon confounded* (Isa. xxiv. 23), as being out-shone by his lustre; or, rather, that they should show some sign of joy and triumph; or perhaps they promised themselves a sight of the glory of the invisible heavens, upon their opening to receive him. Christ had told them that hereafter they should *see heaven opened* (John i. 51), and why should not they expect it now?

VI. Two angels appeared to them, and delivered them a seasonable message from God. Now we are told what the angels said to them, 1. To check their curiosity: *You men of Galilee, why stand you gazing up into heaven?* Christ's disciples should never stand and gaze, because they have a sure rule to go by, and a sure foundation to build upon. 2. To confirm their faith concerning Christ's second coming. (1) "*This same Jesus* shall come again in his own person, clothed with a glorious body. (2) "*He shall come in like manner*. He is gone away in a *cloud*, and *attended with angels*; and, *behold, he comes in the clouds, and with him an innumerable company of angels!*" When we stand gazing and trifling, the consideration of our Master's second coming should quicken and awaken us; and, when we stand gazing and trembling, the consideration of it should comfort and encourage us.

THE UPPER ROOM
(vv. 12–14)

We are here told, I. Whence Christ ascended—*from the mount of Olives* (v. 12), from that part of it where the town of Bethany stood, Luke xxiv. 50.

II. Whither the disciples returned: They came to Jerusalem, according to their Master's appointment, though there they were in the midst of enemies. At Jerusalem they *went up into an upper room, and there abode*; not that they all lodged and dieted together in one room, but there they assembled every day, and spent time together in religious exercises, in expectation of the descent of the Spirit.

III. Who the disciples were, that kept together. The eleven apostles are here named (v. 13), so is Mary the mother of our Lord (v. 14), and it is the last time that ever any mention is made of her in the scriptures. There were others that are here said to be the brethren of our Lord, *his kinsmen according to the flesh*; and, to make up *the hundred and twenty* spoken of (v. 15), we may suppose that all or most of *the seventy disciples* were with them, that were associates with the apostles, and were employed as evangelists.

IV. How they spent their time: *They all continued with one accord in prayer and supplication.* Those are in the best frame to receive spiritual blessings that are in a praying frame. Christ had promised now shortly to send the Holy Ghost; now this promise was not to supersede prayer, but to quicken and encourage it. God will be enquired of for promised mercies, and the nearer the performance seems to be the more earnest we should be in prayer for it.

DEATH OF JUDAS (vv. 15–26)

The sin of Judas was not only his shame and ruin, but it made a vacancy in the college of the apostles. Now being twelve when they were learners, if they were but eleven when they were to be teachers, it would occasion every one to enquire what had become of the twelfth, and so revive the remembrance of the scandal of their society; and therefore care was taken, before the descent of the Spirit, to fill up the vacancy, of the doing of which we now have an account, our Lord Jesus, probably, having given directions about it, among other things which he spoke *pertaining to the kingdom of God.* Observe,

I. The persons concerned in this affair. 1. The house consisted of *about a hundred and twenty.* The speaker was Peter, who had been, and still was, the most forward man; and therefore notice is taken of his forwardness and zeal, to show that he had perfectly recovered the ground he lost by his denying his Master.

II. The proposal which Peter made for the choice of another apostle. Now in his speech we may observe,

1. The account he gives of the vacancy made by the death of Judas, in which he is very particular, and, as became one that Christ had breathed upon, takes notice of the fulfilling of the scriptures in it.

2. The motion he makes for the choice of another apostle, *vv.* 21, 22. Here observe, (1) How the person must be qualified that must fill up the vacancy. None shall be an apostle but one that has companied with the apostles, and that continually; not that has visited them now and then, but been intimately conversant with them. (2) To what work he is called that must fill up the vacancy: He must be *a witness with us of his resurrection.* By this it appears that others of the disciples were with the eleven when Christ appeared to them, else they could not have been *witnesses with them*, as competent witnesses as they, of his resurrection. The great thing which the apostles were to attest to the world was Christ's resurrection, for this was the great proof of his being the Messiah, and the foundation of our hope in him. See what the apostles were ordained to, not to a secular dignity and dominion, but to preach Christ, and the power of his resurrection.

III. The nomination of the person that was to succeed Judas in his office as an apostle.

1. Two, who were known to have been Christ's constant attendants, and men of great integrity, were set up as candidates for the place (*v.* 23). The two they nominated were *Joseph* and *Matthias*, of neither of whom do we read elsewhere. These two were both of them such worthy men, and so well qualified for the office, that they could not tell which of them was the fitter, but all agreed it must be one of these two.

2. They applied to God by prayer for direction, not which of the seventy, for none of the rest could

stand in competition with these in the opinion of all present, but *which of these two? vv.* 24, 25. (1) They appeal to God as the searcher of hearts. (2) They desire to know which of these God had chosen: *Lord, show us this*, and we are satisfied. (3) They are ready to receive him as a brother whom God hath chosen. (4) The doubt was determined by lot (*v.* 26), which is an appeal to God, and lawful to be used for determining matters not otherwise determinable, provided it be done in a solemn religious manner, and with prayer, the prayer of faith. Matthias was not ordained by the imposition of hands, as presbyters were, for he was chosen by lot, which was the act of God; and therefore, as he must be baptized, so he must be ordained, by the Holy Ghost, as they all were not many days after. Thus the number of the apostles was made up, as afterwards, when James, another of the twelve, was martyred, Paul was made an apostle.

CHAPTER TWO

PENTECOST (*vv.* 1–4)

We have here an account of the descent of the Holy Spirit upon the disciples of Christ. Observe,

I. When, and where, this was done, which are particularly noted, for the greater certainty of the thing.

1. It was *when the day of pentecost was fully come*, in which there seems to be a reference to the manner of the expression in the institution of this feast, (Lev. xxiii. 15). This day was *fully come*, that is, the night preceding, with a part of the

5

day, was fully past. (1) The Holy Ghost came down at the time of a solemn feast, because there was then a great concourse of people to Jerusalem from all parts of the country, and the proselytes from other countries, which would make it the more public, and the fame of it to be spread the sooner and further, which would contribute much to the propagating of the gospel into all nations. (2) This feast of pentecost was kept in remembrance of the giving of the law upon mount Sinai, whence the incorporating of the Jewish church was to be dated, which Dr. Lightfoot reckons to be just one thousand four hundred and forty-seven years before this. Fitly, therefore, is the Holy Ghost given at that feast, in fire and in tongues, for the promulgation of the evangelical law, not as that to one nation, but to every creature. (3) This feast of pentecost happened on the *first day of the week*, which was an additional honour put on that day, and a confirmation of it to be the Christian sabbath.

2. It was when *they were all with one accord in one place*. The disciples were in one place, and they were not as yet so many but that one place, and no large one, would hold them all. And here they were *with one accord*. We cannot forget how often, while their Master was with them, there were *strifes among them, who should be the greatest*; but now all these strifes were at an end, we hear no more of them. Would we have the Spirit *poured out upon us from on high*? Let us be all of one accord, and, notwithstanding variety of sentiments and interests, as no doubt there was among those disciples, let us agree to love one another; for, where *brethren dwell together in unity*, there it is that *the Lord commands his blessing*.

II. How, and in what manner, the Holy Ghost came upon them.

1. Here is an audible summons given them to awaken their expectations of something great, *v.* 2. It is here said, (1) That it came *suddenly*, did not rise gradually, as common winds do, but was at the height immediately. (2) It was *a sound from heaven*, like a thunder-clap, Rev. vi. 1. (3) It was the sound of a wind, for the way of the Spirit is like that of the wind (John iii. 8), *thou hearest the sound thereof, but canst not tell whence it comes nor whither it goes.* (4) It was a *rushing mighty wind*; it was strong and violent, and came not only with a great noise, but with great force, as if it would bear down all before it. This was to signify the powerful influences and operations of the Spirit of God upon the minds of men, and thereby upon the world. (5) *It filled* not only the room, but *all the house where they were sitting*. This wind filling the house would strike an awe upon the disciples, and help to put them into a very serious, reverent, and composed frame, for the receiving of the Holy Ghost.

2. Here is a visible sign of the gift they were to receive. They saw *cloven tongues, like as of fire* (*v.* 3), and *it sat*—he, that is the Spirit (signified thereby), rested upon each of them, as he is said to rest upon the prophets of old. Observe, (1) There was an outward sen-

sible sign, for the confirming of the faith of the disciples themselves, and for the convincing of others. Thus the prophets of old had frequently their first mission confirmed by signs, that all Israel might know them to be established prophets.

(2) The sign given was fire, that John Baptist's saying concerning Christ might be fulfilled, *He shall baptize you with the Holy Ghost and with fire*; with the Holy Ghost as with fire.

(3) This fire appeared in cloven tongues. The operations of the Spirit were many; that of speaking with divers tongues was one, and was singled out to be the first indication of the gift of the Holy Ghost, and to that this sign had a reference. [1] They were tongues; for from the Spirit we have the word of God, and by him Christ would speak to the world, and he gave the Spirit to the disciples, not only to endue them with knowledge, but to endue them with a power to publish and proclaim to the world what they knew; for *the dispensation of the Spirit is given to every man to profit withal*. [2] These tongues were cloven, to signify that God would hereby divide unto all nations the knowledge of his grace, as he is said to have divided to them by his providence the light of the heavenly bodies, Deut. iv. 19. The tongues were divided, and yet they still continued all of one accord; for there may be a sincere unity of affections where yet there is a diversity of expression.

(4) This fire sat upon them for some time, to denote the constant residence of the Holy Ghost with them. The prophetic gifts of old were conferred sparingly and but at some times, but the disciples of Christ had the gifts of the Spirit always with them, though the sign, we may suppose, soon disappeared.

III. What was the immediate effect of this? 1. *They were all filled with the Holy Ghost*, more plentifully and powerfully than they were before. It seems evident to me that not only the twelve apostles, but all the hundred and twenty disciples were *filled with the Holy Ghost* alike at this time—all the seventy disciples, who were apostolic men, and employed in the same work, and all the rest too that were to preach the gospel; for it is said expressly (Eph. iv. 8, 11). *When Christ ascended on high* (which refers to this, *v.* 33), *he gave gifts unto men*, not only *some apostles* (such were the twelve), but *some prophets* and *some evangelists* (such were many of the seventy disciples, itinerant preachers), and some *pastors and teachers* settled in particular churches, as we may suppose some of these afterwards were. The *all* here must refer to the *all* that were together, *v.* 1; *ch.* i. 14, 15. 2. *They began to speak with other tongues*, besides their native language, though they had never learned any other. They spoke not matters of common conversation, but the word of God, and the praises of his name, *as the Spirit gave them utterance*, or gave them to speak *apophthegms*, substantial and weighty sayings, worthy to be had in remembrance. They spoke not from any previous thought or meditation, but *as the Spirit gave them utterance*; he furnished them with the matter as well as the language.

Now this was, (1) A very great miracle; it was a miracle upon the mind (and so had most of the nature of a gospel miracle), for in the mind words are framed. (2) A very proper, needful, and serviceable miracle. The language the disciples spoke was Syriac, a dialect of the Hebrew; so that it was necessary that they should be endued with the gift, for the understanding, both of the original Hebrew of the Old Testament, in which it was written, and of the original Greek of the New Testament, in which it was to be written. But this was not all; they were commissioned to *preach the gospel to every creature, to disciple all nations.* But here is an insuperable difficulty at the threshold. How shall they master the several languages so as to speak intelligibly to all nations? It will be the work of a man's life to learn their languages. And therefore, to prove . that Christ could give authority to preach to the nations, he gives ability to preach to them in their own language. And it should seem that this was the accomplishment of that promise which Christ made to his disciples (John xiv. 12), *Greater works than these shall you do.* For this may well be reckoned, all things considered, a greater work than the miraculous cures Christ wrought. Christ himself did not speak with other tongues, nor did he enable his disciples to do so while he was with them: but it was the first effect of the *pouring out of the Spirit* upon them. And archbishop Tillotson thinks it probable that if the conversion of infidels to Christianity were now sincerely and vigorously attempted, by men of honest minds, God would extraordinarily countenance such an attempt with all fitting assistance, as he did the first publication of the gospel.

NEW WINE (*vv.* 5–13)

We have here an account of the public notice that was taken of this extraordinary gift with which the disciples were all on a sudden endued. Observe,

I. The great concourse of people that there was now at Jerusalem, it should seem more than was usual at the feast of pentecost. *There were dwelling* or abiding *at Jerusalem* Jews that were *devout men, out of every nation under heaven,* whither the Jews were dispersed, or whence proselytes were come. Now, 1. We may here see what were some of those countries whence those strangers came (*vv.* 9–11).

II. The amazement with which these strangers were seized when they heard the disciples speak in their own tongues. It should seem, the disciples spoke in various languages before the people of those languages came to them; for it is intimated (*v.* 6) that the spreading of the report of this abroad was that which *brought the multitude together,* especially those of different countries, who seem to have been more affected with this work of wonder than the inhabitants of Jerusalem themselves.

1. They observe that the speakers are all Galileans, they know no other than their mother tongue (*v.* 7); they are despicable men, from whom nothing learned nor polite is to be expected.

2. They acknowledge that they spoke intelligibly and readily their own language (which they were the most competent judges of), so correctly and fluently that none of their own countrymen could speak it better: *We hear every man in our own tongue wherein we were born* (v. 8), that is, we hear one or other of them speak our native language. (1) The things they heard the apostles discourse of were the *wonderful works of God*. It is probable that the apostles spoke of Christ, and redemption by him, and the grace of the gospel; and these are indeed the *great things of God*, which will be for ever *marvellous in our eyes*. (2) They heard them both praise God for these great things and instruct the people concerning these things, *in their own tongue*, according as they perceived the language of their hearers, or those that enquired of them to be.

3. They wonder at it, and look upon it as an astonishing thing (v. 12): *They were all amazed*, they were in an *ecstasy*, so the word is; and they were in doubt what the meaning of it was, and whether it was to introduce the kingdom of the Messiah, which they were big with the expectation of.

III. The scorn which some made of it who were natives of Judea and Jerusalem, probably the scribes and Pharisees, and chief priests, who always resisted the Holy Ghost; they said, *These men are full of new wine*, or *sweet wine*; they have drunk too much this festival-time, v. 13. And, if they called the Master of the house a wine-bibber, no marvel if they so call those of his household.

PETER'S SERMON
(vv. 14–36)

We have here the first-fruits of the Spirit in the sermon which Peter preached immediately, directed, not to those of other nations in a strange language (we are not told what answer he gave to those that were amazed, and said, *What meaneth this?*) but to the Jews in the vulgar language, even to those that mocked; for he begins with the notice of that (v. 15), and addresses his discourse (v. 14) *to the men of Judea and the inhabitants of Jerusalem*. Observe,

I. His introduction or preface, wherein he craves the attention of the auditory, or demands it rather. He applied himself to *the men of Judea—the men that were Jews*; so it should be read; "and you especially *that dwell at Jerusalem*, who were accessory to the death of Jesus, *be this known unto you*, which you did not know before, and which you are concerned to know now, *and hearken to my words.*"

II. His answer to their blasphemous calumny (v. 15): "*These men are not drunken, as you suppose.* You cannot think they are drunk, for *it is but the third hour of the day*," nine of the clock in the morning; and before this time, on the sabbaths and solemn feasts, the Jews did not eat nor drink.

III. His account of the miraculous effusion of the Spirit, which is designed to awaken them all to embrace the faith of Christ, and to join themselves to his church. Two things he resolves it into:—that it was the fulfilling of the scripture, and the fruit of Christ's resurrection and ascension, and consequently the proof of both.

1. That it was the accomplishment of the prophecies of the Old Testament which related to the kingdom of the Messiah, and therefore an evidence that this kingdom is come, and the other predictions of it are fulfilled. He specifies one, that of *the prophet Joel, ch.* ii. 28. Observe,

(1) The text itself that Peter quotes, *vv.* 17–21. It refers to *the last days*, the times of the gospel, which are called *the last days* because the dispensation of God's kingdom among men, which the gospel sets up, is the last dispensation of divine grace, and we are to look for no other than the continuation of this to the end of time.

(2) The application of this prophecy to the present event (*v.* 16): *This is that which was spoken by the prophet Joel*; it is the accomplishment of that, it is the full accomplishment of it.

2. That it was the gift of Christ, and the product and proof of his resurrection and ascension. From this *gift of the Holy Ghost*, he takes occasion to preach unto them Jesus. Here is,

(1) An abstract of the history of the life of Christ, *v.* 22. He calls him *Jesus of Nazareth*, because by that name he was generally known, but (which was sufficient to roll away that reproach) he was *a man approved of God among you*, censured and condemned by men, but approved of God: God testified his approbation of his doctrine by the power he gave him to work miracles. See what a stress Peter lays upon Christ's miracles. [1] The

matter of fact was not to be denied: "They were done *in the midst of you*, in the midst of your country, your city, your solemn assemblies, *as you yourselves also know*." [2] The inference from them cannot be disputed; the reasoning is as strong as the evidence; if he did those miracles, certainly God approved him, *declared him to be*, what he declared himself to be, *the Son of God* and *the Saviour of the world*; for the God of truth would never set his seal to a lie.

(2) An account of his death and sufferings which they were witness of also but a few weeks ago; and this was the greatest miracle of all, that a man approved of God should thus seem to be abandoned of him; and a man thus approved among the people, and in the midst of them, should be thus abandoned by them too. But both these mysteries are here explained (*v.* 23), and his death considered, [1] As God's act; and in him it was an act of wonderful grace and wisdom. For it was done by *the determinate counsel and foreknowledge of God*, in infinite wisdom, and for holy ends, which Christ himself concurred in, and in the means leading to them. [2] As the people's act; and in them it was an act of prodigious sin and folly; it was fighting against God to persecute one whom he approved as the darling of heaven; and fighting against their own mercies to persecute one that was the greatest blessing of this earth.

(3) An attestation of his resurrection, which effectually wiped away the reproach of his death (*v.* 24): *Whom God raised up*; the same that delivered him *to death*

delivers him *from death*, and thereby gave a higher approbation of him than he had done by any other of *the signs and wonders wrought by him*, or by all put together. This therefore he insists most largely upon.

[1] He describes his resurrection: God *loosed the pains of death, because it was impossible that he should be holden of it*. Christ was imprisoned for our debt, was thrown into the bands of death; but, divine justice being satisfied, it was not possible he should be detained there, either by right or by force; for he had life in himself, and in his own power, and had conquered the prince of death.

[2] He attests the truth of his resurrection (*v.* 32): *God hath raised him up, whereof we all are witnesses*.

[3] He showed it to be the fulfilling of the scripture, and, because the scripture had said that he must rise again before he saw corruption, therefore *it was impossible that he should be holden* by *death* and *the grave; for David speaks* of his being raised, so it comes in, *v.* 25. The scripture he refers to is that of David (Ps. xvi. 8–11), which, though in part applicable to David as a saint, yet refers chiefly to Jesus Christ, of whom David was a type.

To prove that when he spoke of the resurrection he meant it of Christ, he observes that when in another psalm he speaks of the next step of his exaltation he plainly shows that he spoke of another person, and such another as was his Lord (Ps. cx. 1): "*The Lord said unto my Lord*, when he had raised him from the dead, *Sit thou at my right hand*, in the highest dignity and dominion there; be thou entrusted with the administration of the kingdom both of providence and grace; *sit there* as king, *until I make thy foes* either thy friends or *thy footstool*," *v.* 35. Christ rose from the grave to rise higher, and therefore it must be of his resurrection that David spoke, and not his own, in the 16th Psalm; for there was no occasion for him to rise out of his grave who was not to ascend to heaven.

(4) The application of this discourse concerning the death, resurrection, and ascension of Christ.

[1] This explains the meaning of the present wonderful effusion of the Spirit in those extraordinary gifts. *The gift of the Holy Ghost* was, *First*, A performance of divine promises already made; here it is called *the promise of the Holy Ghost*. Christ received *the promise of the Holy Ghost*, that is, the promised gift of the Holy Ghost, and has given it to us; for all *the promises are yea and amen in him. Secondly*, It was a pledge of all divine favours further intended; what you now see and hear is but an earnest of greater things.

[2] This proves what you are all bound to believe, that Christ Jesus is the true Messiah and Saviour of the world. *Therefore let all the house of Israel know assuredly* that this truth has now received its full confirmation, and we our full commission to publish it, *That God has made that same Jesus whom you have crucified both Lord and Christ*. This is the great truth of the gospel which we are to believe, *that that same Jesus*, the very same *that was crucified at Jerusalem*, is he to

whom we owe allegiance, and from whom we are to expect protection, as *Lord and Christ*.

THREE THOUSAND CONVERTS
(vv. 37–41)

In these verses we find the word of God the means of beginning and carrying on a good work of grace in the hearts of many, *the Spirit of the Lord working by it*. Let us see the method of it.

I. They were startled, and convinced, and put upon a serious enquiry, *v.* 37. Peter had charged them with having a hand, a *wicked hand*, in his death, which was likely to have exasperated them against him; yet, when they heard this plain scriptural sermon, they were much affected with it.

1. It put them in pain: *They were pricked in their hearts*.

2. It put them upon enquiry. *Out of the abundance of the heart*, thus pricked, *the mouth spoke*. Observe,

(1) To whom they thus addressed themselves: *To Peter and to the rest of the apostles*.

(2) What the address is: *What shall we do?* [1] They speak as men at a stand, that did not know what to do; in a perfect surprise: "*Is that Jesus* whom we have crucified both *Lord and Christ?* Then what will become of us who crucified him? We are all undone!" [2] They speak as men at a point, that were resolved to do any thing they should be directed to immediately.

II. Peter and the other apostles direct them in short what they must do, and what in so doing they might expect, *vv.* 38, 39.

1. He here shows them the course they must take. (1) *Repent*; this is a plank after shipwreck. "*Repent, repent*; change your mind, change your way; admit an after-thought." (2) *Be baptized every one of you in the name of Jesus Christ*. They must be baptized *in the name of Jesus Christ*. They did believe in the Father and the Holy Ghost speaking by the prophets; but they must also believe in the name of Jesus, that he is the Christ, the Messiah promised to the fathers. (3) This is pressed upon each particular person: *Every one of you*.

2. He gives them encouragement to take this course:—(1) "It shall be for *the remission of sins*. Repent of your sin, and it shall not be your ruin; be baptized into the faith of Christ, and in truth you shall be justified, which you could never be by the law of Moses." (2) "You shall *receive the gift of the Holy Ghost* as well as we; for it is designed for a general blessing." Note, All that receive the remission of sins *receive the gift of the Holy Ghost*. All that are justified are sanctified. (3) "Your children shall still have, as they have had, an interest in the covenant, and a title to the external seal of it. Come over to Christ, to receive those inestimable benefits; for the promise of the remission of sins, and the gift of the Holy Ghost, is *to you and to your children*," *v.* 39. It was very express (Isa. xliv. 3): *I will pour my Spirit upon thy seed*. And (Isa. lix. 21), *My Spirit and my word shall not depart from thy seed, and thy seed's seed*. (4) "Though the promise is still extended to your children as it has been, yet it is not, as it has been,

confined to you and them, but the benefit of it is *designed* for *all that are afar off.*" To this general the following limitation must refer, *even as many of them,* as many particular persons in each nation, *as the Lord our God shall call* effectually into the fellowship of Jesus Christ.

III. These directions are followed with a needful caution (*v.* 40): *With many other words,* to the same purport, *did he testify* gospel truths, and exhort to gospel duties; now that the word began to work he followed it; he had said much in a little (*vv.* 38, 39), and that which, one would think, included all, and yet he had more to say.

IV. Here is the happy success and issue of this, *v.* 41. The Spirit wrought with the word, and wrought wonders by it. These same persons that had many of them been eye-witnesses of the death of Christ, and the prodigies that attended it, and were not wrought upon by them, were yet wrought upon by the preaching of the word, for it is this that is the *power of God unto salvation.* 1. They received the word; and *then* only the word does us good, when we do receive it, embrace it, and bid it welcome. 2. They gladly received it. Herod *heard* the word gladly, but these gladly *received* it. 3. They were baptized; believing with the heart, they made confession with the mouth, and enrolled themselves among the disciples of Christ by that sacred rite and ceremony which he had instituted. 4. Hereby there were added to the disciples to the number of about *three thousand souls that same day.*

THE INFANT CHURCH
(*vv.* 42–47)

We often speak of the primitive church, and appeal to it, and to the history of it; in these verses we have the history of the *truly primitive church,* of the *first days* of it, its state of infancy indeed, but, like that, the state of its greatest *innocence.*

I. They kept close to holy ordinances, and abounded in all instances of piety and devotion, for Christianity, admitted in the power of it, will dispose the soul to communion with God in all those ways wherein he has appointed us to meet him and promised to meet us.

1. They were diligent and constant in their attendance upon the *preaching of the word.* They *continued in the apostles' doctrine,* and never disowned nor deserted it.

2. They kept up the *communion of saints.* They continued *in fellowship* (*v.* 42), and *continued daily with one accord in the temple, v.* 46. They had fellowship with one another in religious worship. They met *in the temple*: there was their rendezvous; for joint-fellowship with God is the best fellowship we can have with one another, 1 John i. 3.

3. They frequently joined in the ordinance of the Lord's supper. They continued *in the breaking of bread,* in celebrating that memorial of their Master's death, as those that were not ashamed to own their relation to, and their dependence upon, Christ and him crucified. They did not think fit to celebrate the eucharist in the temple, for that was peculiar to the Christian institutes, and therefore they adminis-

tered that ordinance in private houses, choosing such houses of the converted Christians as were convenient, to which the neighbours resorted; and they went from one to another of these little synagogues or domestic chapels, houses that had churches in them, and there celebrated the eucharist with those that usually met there to worship God.

4. They continued *in prayers. After* the Spirit was poured out, as well as before, while they were waiting for him, they continued instant in prayer; for prayer will never be superseded till it comes to be swallowed up in everlasting praise.

5. They abounded in thanksgiving; were continually *praising God, v.* 47. This should have a part in every prayer, and not be crowded into a corner. Those that have received the gift of the Holy Ghost will be much in praise.

II. They were loving one to another, and very kind; their charity was as eminent as their piety, and their joining together in holy ordinances knit their hearts to each other, and very much endeared them to one another.

1. They had frequent meetings for Christian converse (*v.* 44). They associated together, and so both expressed and increased their mutual love.

2. They had *all things common.* There was such a concern for one another, and such a readiness to help one another as there was occasion, that it might be said, They had *all things common,* according to the law of friendship; one wanted not what another had; for he might have it for the asking.

3. They were very cheerful, and very generous in the use of what they had. Besides the religion that was in their sacred feasts, (their *breaking bread from house to house*) a great deal of it appeared in their common meals; they did *eat their meat with gladness and singleness of heart.*

4. They raised a fund for charity (*v.* 45): They *sold their possessions and goods*; some sold their lands and houses, others their stocks and the furniture of their houses, and *parted* the money to their brethren, *as every man had need.* This was to destroy, not property (as Mr. Baxter says), but selfishness. Herein, probably, they had an eye to the command which Christ gave to the rich man, as a test of his sincerity, *Sell that thou hast, and give to the poor.*

III. God owned them, and gave them signal tokens of his presence with them (*v.* 43): *Many wonders and signs were done by the apostles* of divers sorts, which confirmed their doctrine, and incontestably proved that it was from God.

But the Lord's giving them power to work miracles was not all he did for them; he *added to the church daily.* The word in their mouths *did wonders,* and God blessed their endeavours for the increase of the number of believers. Note, It is God's work to add souls to the church; and it is a great comfort both to ministers and Christians to see it.

IV. The people were influenced by it; those that were without, the standers by, that were spectators. 1. They *feared them,* and had a veneration for them (*v.* 43). 2. They *favoured them.* Though we have reason to think there were those that despised them and hated them (we are sure the Pharisees and chief priests did), yet far the greater part of the common people had a kindness for them—they *had favour with all the people.* 3. They *fell over* to them. Some or other were daily coming in, though not so many as the first day; and they were such as *should be saved.* Note, Those that God has designed for eternal salvation shall one time or other be effectually brought to Christ: and those that are brought to Christ are *added to the church* in a holy covenant by baptism, and in holy communion by other ordinances.

CHAPTER THREE

LAME MAN HEALED
(vv. 1–11)

We were told in general (*ch.* ii. 43) that *many signs and wonders were done by the apostles,* which are not written in this book; but here we have one given us for an instance.

I. The persons by whose ministry this miracle was wrought were Peter and John, two principal men among the apostles.

II. The time and place are here set down. 1. It was in *the temple,* whither *Peter and John went up together,* because it was the place of concourse. 2. It was *at the hour of prayer,* one of the hours of public worship commonly appointed and observed among the Jews.

III. The patient on whom this miraculous cure was wrought is here described, *v.* 2. He was a poor lame beggar at the temple gate. 1. He was a cripple, not by accident, but born

so; he was *lame from his mother's womb,* as it should seem, by a paralytic distemper, which weakened his limbs; for it is said in the description of his cure (*v.* 7), *His feet and ankle bones received strength.* 2. He was a beggar. Being unable to work for his living, he must live upon alms; such are God's poor. He was *laid daily* by his friends at *one of the gates of the temple,* a miserable spectacle, unable to do any thing for himself but to *ask alms of those that entered into the temple* or came out. 3. He begged of Peter and John (*v.* 3), begged an alms; this was the utmost he expected from them, who had the reputation of being charitable men, and who, though they had not much, yet did good with what they had.

IV. We have here the method of the cure.

1. His expectations were raised. Peter, instead of turning his eyes from him, as many do from objects of charity, turned his eyes to him, nay, he *fastened his eyes upon him,* that his eye might affect his heart with compassion towards him, *v.* 4. John did so too, for they were both guided by one and the same Spirit, and concurred in this miracle; they said, *Look on us.*

2. His expectation of an alms was disappointed. *Peter said, "Silver and gold have I none,* and therefore none to give thee;" yet he intimated that if he had had any he would have given him an alms, not brass, but silver or gold.

3. His expectations, notwithstanding, were quite outdone. Peter had no money to give him; but, (1) He had that which was better, such an interest in heaven, such a power

15

from heaven, as to be able to cure his disease. (2) He gave him that which was better—the cure of his disease, which he would gladly have given a great deal of silver and gold for, if he had had it, and the cure could have been so obtained.

Let us now see how the cure was wrought. [1] Christ *sent his word and healed him* (Ps. cvii. 20); for healing grace is given by the word of Christ: this is the vehicle of the healing virtue derived from Christ. Christ spoke cures by himself; the apostles spoke them in his name. Peter bids a lame man *rise up and walk*, which would have been a banter upon him if he had not premised *in the name of Jesus Christ of Nazareth.* [2] Peter lent his hand, and helped him (*v.* 7). Not that this could contribute any thing to his cure; but it was a sign, plainly intimating the help he should receive from God, if he exerted himself as he was bidden. *His feet and ankle-bones received strength,* which they had not done if he had not attempted to rise, and been helped up; he does his part, and Peter does his, and yet it is Christ that does all: it is he that puts strength into him.

V. Here is the impression which this cure made upon the patient himself, which we may best conceive of it we put our soul into his soul's stead. 1. He leaped up, in obedience to the command, *Arise.* He leaped, as one glad to quit the bed or pad of straw on which he had lain so long lame. 2. He stood, and walked. He stood without either leaning or trembling, stood straight up, and walked without a staff. 3. He *held Peter and John, v.* 11. We need not ask why he held them. I

believe he scarcely knew himself: but it was in a transport of joy that he embraced them as the best benefactors he had ever met with. 4. He *entered with them into the temple.* His strong affection to them held them; but it could not hold them so fast as to keep them out of the temple, whither they were going to preach Christ. 5. He was there *walking, and leaping, and praising God.* All true converts walk and praise God; but perhaps young converts leap more in his praises.

VI. How the people that were eye-witnesses of this miracle were influenced by it we are next told. 1. They were entirely satisfied in the truth of the miracle, and had nothing to object against it. *They knew it was he that sat begging at the beautiful gate of the temple, v.* 10. 2. They were astonished at it: They were *filled with wonder and amazement* (*v.* 10); *greatly wondering, v.* 11. They were in an *ecstasy.* 3. They gathered about Peter and John: *All the people ran together unto them in Solomon's porch.*   •

PETER'S EXPLANATION
(*vv.* 12–26)

We have here the sermon which Peter preached after he had cured the lame man. In the sermon,

I. He humbly disclaims the honour of the miracle as not due to them, who were only the ministers of Christ, or instruments in his hand for the doing of it. Two things he asks them: 1. Why they were so surprised at the miracle itself. It was but a little before that Christ had *raised Lazarus from the dead*; and why should this then seem so strange? 2. Why they gave so much of the praise of it to them, who were only the instruments of it: *Why look you so earnestly on us?* They did not do it by any *power or holiness of their own.* It was not done by any might of their own, any skill they had in physic or surgery, nor any virtue in their word: the power they did it by was wholly derived from Christ.

II. He preaches Christ to them; this was his business, that he might lead them into obedience to Christ.

1. He preaches Christ, as the true Messiah promised to the fathers (*v.* 13).

2. He charges them flatly and plainly with the murder of this Jesus, as he had done before. *You killed the prince of life.* Observe the antithesis: "You preserved *a murderer,* a destroyer of life; and destroyed the Saviour, *the author of life.*"

3. He attests his resurrection as before, *ch.* ii. 32.

4. He ascribes the cure of this impotent man to the power of Christ (*v.* 16). Here, (1) He appeals to themselves concerning the truth of the miracle; the man on whom it was wrought is one *whom you see, and know, and have known.* (2) He acquaints them with the power by which it was wrought. [1] It is done by the name of Christ, not merely by naming it as a spell or charm, but it is done by us as professors and teachers of his name, by virtue of a commission and instructions we have received from him, and a power which he has invested us with. [2] The power of Christ is fetched in *through faith in his name,* a confidence in him, a dependence on him, a believing application to him.

III. He encourages them to hope that, though they had been guilty of putting Christ to death, yet they might find mercy; he does all he can to convince them, yet is careful not to drive them to despair. The guilt was very great, but, 1. He mollifies their crime by a candid imputation of it to their ignorance. 2. He mollifies the effects of their crime—the death of *the prince of life*; this sounds very dreadful, but it was *according to the scriptures* (*v.* 18), the predictions of which, though they did not necessitate their sin, yet did necessitate his sufferings. Now, though this is no extenuation at all of their sin in hating and persecuting Christ *to the death* (this still appears exceedingly sinful), yet it was an encouragement to them to repent, and hope for mercy upon their repentance; not only because in general God's gracious designs were carried on by it, but because in particular the death and sufferings of Christ were for *the remission of sins,* and the ground of that display of mercy for which he now encouraged them to hope.

IV. He exhorts them all to turn Christians, and assures them it would be unspeakably for their advantage to do so; it would be the making of them for ever. This is the application of his sermon.

1. He tells them what they must believe. (1) They must believe that Jesus Christ is the promised seed, that seed in which God had told Abraham *all the kindreds of the earth should be blessed, v.* 25. (2) They must believe that Jesus Christ is a prophet, *that prophet like unto Moses* whom God had promised to

raise up to them from among their brethren, *v.* 22. This refers to that promise, Deut. xviii. 18. (3) They must believe *that times of refreshing will come from the presence of the Lord* (*v.* 19), and that they will be the times of the restitution of all things, *v.* 21. There is a future state, another life after this; those times will come from the presence of the Lord, from his glorious appearance at that day, his coming at the end of time. The presence of the Lord will introduce, [1] *The restitution of all things* (*v.* 21); *the new heavens, and the new earth*, which will be the product of the dissolution of all things (Rev. xxi. 1), the renovation of the whole creation. [2] With this will come *the times of refreshing* (*v.* 19), of consolation to the Lord's people, like a cool shade to those *that have borne the burden and heat of the day*

2. He tells them what they must do. (1) They must *repent*, must bethink themselves of what they have done amiss, must return to their right mind, admit a second thought, and submit to the convictions of it; they must begin anew. (2) They must *be converted*, must face about, and direct both their faces and steps the contrary way to what they had been; they must *return to the Lord their God*, from whom they had revolted. (3) They must hear Christ, the great prophet. Attend his dictates, receive his doctrine, submit to his government.

3. He tells them what they might expect.

(1) That they should have the pardon of their sins; this is always spoken of as the great privilege of all those that embrace the gospel

(*v.* 19): *Repent, and be converted, that your sins may be blotted out*.

(2) That they should have the comfort of Christ's coming (*vv.* 20, 21). For, though *the heavens must receive him till the times of the restitution of all things*; yet, if you *repent and be converted*, you shall find no want of him; some way or other he shall be seen of you.

4. He tells them what ground they had to expect these things, if they were converted to Christ. Though they had denied him, and put him to death, yet they might hope to find favour through him, upon the account of their being Israelites. For,

(1) As Israelites, they had the monopoly of the grace of the Old Testament; they were, above any other, God's favourite nation, and the favours God bestowed upon them were such as had a reference to the Messiah, and his kingdom: *You are the children of the prophets, and of the covenant*.

(2) As Israelites, they had the first offer of the grace of the New Testament. Because *they were the children of the prophets and the covenant*, therefore to them the Redeemer was first sent, which was an encouragement to them to hope that if they did repent, and were converted, he should be yet further sent for their comfort (*v.* 20): *He shall send Jesus Christ*, for to you first he hath sent him, *v.* 26.

CHAPTER FOUR

PETER AND JOHN ARRESTED
(*vv.* 1–4)

I. The apostles, Peter and John, went on in their work, and did not labour in vain. The Spirit enabled the ministers to do their part, and the people theirs.

1. The preachers faithfully deliver the doctrine of Christ: *They spoke unto the people*, to all that were within hearing, *v.* 1.

The hearers cheerfully receive it (*v.* 4): *Many of those who heard the word believed*; not all—perhaps not the most, yet many, *to the number of about five thousand*, over and above the three thousand we read of before.

II. The chief priests and their party now made head against them, and did what they could to crush them; their hands were tied awhile, but their hearts were not in the least changed. It grieved them that the apostles *preached through Jesus the resurrection from the dead*. The Sadducees were grieved that the resurrection from the dead was preached; for they opposed that doctrine, and could not bear to hear of a future state, to hear it so well attested. The chief priests were grieved that they preached the resurrection of the dead through Jesus, that he should have the honour of it.

PETER AND JOHN EXAMINED (*vv.* 5-14)

We have here the trial of Peter and John before the judges of the ecclesiastical court.

I. Here is the court set. An extraordinary court, it should seem, was called on purpose upon this occasion. Here were Annas and Caiaphas, ringleaders in this persecution; Annas the president of the sanhedrim, and Caiaphas the high priest (though Annas is here called so) and *father of the house of judgment*. It should seem that Annas and Caiaphas executed the high priest's office alternately, year for year.

II. The prisoners are arraigned, *v.* 7. 1. They are brought to the bar; they *set them in the midst*, for the sanhedrim sat in a circle, and those who had any thing to do in the court stood or sat in the midst of them (Luke ii. 46), so Dr. Lightfoot. 2. The question they asked them was, "*By what power, or by what name, have you done this?* By what authority do you these things?" (the same question that they had asked their Master, Matt. xxi. 23.)

III. The plea they put in, the design of which was not so much to clear and secure themselves as to advance the name and honour of their Master. Observe,

1. By whom this plea was drawn up: it was dictated by the Holy Ghost, who fitted Peter more than before for this occasion. Mark xiii. 11.

2. To whom it was given in: Peter, who is still the chief speaker, addresses himself to the judges of the court, as the *rulers of the people, and elders of* Israel; for the wickedness of those in power does not divest them of their power.

3. What the plea is: it is a solemn declaration,

(1) That what they did was in the name of Jesus Christ, which was a direct answer to the question the court asked them (*vv.* 9, 10). Here [1] He justifies what he and his colleague had done in curing the lame man. It was a *good deed*; it was a kindness to the man that had begged, but could not work for his

living. [2] He transfers all the praise and glory of this good deed to Jesus Christ. "It is by him, and not by any power of ours, that this man is cured." [3] He charges it upon the judges themselves, that they had been the murderers of this Jesus. [4] He attests the resurrection of Christ as the strongest testimony for him, and against his persecutors. [5] He preaches this to all the bystanders, to be by them repeated to all their neighbours, and commands all manner of persons, from the highest to the lowest, to take notice of it at their peril.

(2) That the name of this Jesus, by the authority of which they acted, is that name alone by which we can be saved. It is not an indifferent thing, but of absolute necessity, that people believe in this name, and call upon it. We are lost if we do not take shelter in this name, and make it our refuge and strong tower; for we cannot be saved but by Jesus Christ, and, if we be not eternally saved, we are eternally lost (v. 12): *Neither is there salvation in any other.* As there is no other name by which diseased bodies can be cured, so there is no other by which sinful souls can be saved.

IV. The stand that the court was put to in the prosecution, by this plea, *vv.* 13, 14.

1. They could not deny the cure of the lame man to be both a good deed and a miracle.

2. They could not, with all their pomp and power, face down Peter and John. Probably there was something extraordinary and very surprising in their looks; they appeared not only undaunted by the rulers, but daring and daunting to them. Now, (1) We are here told what increased their wonder: They *perceived that they were unlearned and ignorant men.* Yet speak to them of the Messiah and his kingdom, and they speak with so much clearness, evidence, and assurance, so pertinently and so fluently, and are so ready in the scriptures of the Old Testament relating to it, that the most learned judge upon the bench is not able to answer them, nor to enter the lists with them. (2) We are told what made their wonder in a great measure to cease: they *took knowledge of them that they had been with Jesus.* When they understood that *they had been with Jesus*, had been conversant with him, attendant on him, and trained up under him, they knew what to impute their boldness to; nay, their boldness in divine things was enough to show with whom they had had their education.

RELEASE (*vv.* 15–22)

We have here the issue of the trial of Peter and John before the council.

I. Here is the consultation and resolution of the court about this matter, and their proceeding thereupon.

1. The prisoners were ordered to withdraw (*v.* 15).

2. A debate arose upon this matter: *They conferred among themselves*; every one is desired to speak his mind freely, and to give advice upon this important affair.

3. They came at last to a resolution, in two things:

(1) That it was not safe to punish the apostles for what they had done.

Very willingly would they have done it, but they had not courage to do it, because the people espoused their cause, and cried up the miracle; and they stood now in as much awe of them as they had done formerly, when they durst not lay hands on Christ *for fear of the people*.

(2) That it was nevertheless necessary to silence them for the future, *vv.* 17, 18. They could not prove that they had said or done any thing amiss, and yet they must no more say nor do what they have done. All their care is that the doctrine of Christ *spread no further among the people*; as if that healing institution were a plague begun, the contagion of which must be stopped. Now, to prevent the further spreading of this doctrine, [1] They charge the apostles never to preach it any more. [2] They threaten them if they do, strictly threaten them: it is at their peril. This court will reckon itself highly affronted if they do, and they shall fall under its displeasure.

II. Here is the courageous resolution of the prisoners to go on in their work, notwithstanding the resolutions of this court, and their declaration of this resolution, *vv.* 19, 20. They do, in effect, tell them that they are resolved to go on in preaching, and justify themselves in it with two things: 1. The command of God. If men's commands and God's interfere God's commands must take place.

III. Here is the discharge of the prisoners (*v.* 21): *They further threatened them*, and thought they frightened them, and then *let them go*.

THE CHURCH GIVES THANKS
(*vv.* 23–31)

We hear no more at present of the chief priests, what they did when they had dismissed Peter and John, but are to attend those *two witnesses*. And here we have,

I. Their return to their brethren, the apostles and ministers, and perhaps some private Christians (*v.* 23).

II. The account they gave them of what had passed. They related it to them, 1. That they might know what to expect both from men and from God in the progress of their work. 2. That they might have it recorded in the history of the church, for the benefit of posterity, particularly for the confirmation of our faith touching the resurrection of Christ. 3. That they might now join with them in prayers and praises; and by such a concert as this God would be the more glorified, and the church the more edified.

III. Their address to God upon this occasion. *They lifted up their voice to God with one accord, v.* 24. Now in this solemn address to God we have,

1. Their adoration of God as the Creator of the world (*v.* 24). Thus we Christians distinguish ourselves from the heathen, that, while they worship gods which they have made, we are worshipping the God that made us and all the world.

2. Their reconciling themselves to the present dispensations of Providence, by reflecting upon those scriptures in the Old Testament which foretold that the kingdom of the Messiah would meet with such opposition as this at the

first setting of it up in the world, vv. 25, 26.

3. Their representation of the present accomplishment of those predictions in the enmity and malice of the rulers against Christ. What was foretold we see fulfilled, vv. 27, 28. See here, (1) The wise and holy designs God had concerning Christ. He is here called the _child Jesus_, as he was called (Luke ii. 27, 43) in his infancy, to intimate that even in his exalted state he is not ashamed of his condescensions for us, and that he continues meek and lowly in heart. In the height of his glory he is the _Lamb of God_, and the _child Jesus_. But he is the _holy child Jesus_ (so he was called, Luke i. 35, _that holy thing_), and _thy_ holy child; the word signifies both a son and a servant. He was the Son of God; and yet in the work of redemption he acted as his Father's servant (Isa. xlii. 1), _My servant whom I uphold_. Now the God that anointed Christ determined what should be done to him, pursuant to that anointing. He was anointed to be a Saviour, and therefore it was determined he should be a sacrifice to make atonement for sin. God's _hand_, which properly denotes his executive power, is here put for his purpose and decree, because with him saying and doing are not two things, as they are with us. (2) The wicked and unholy instruments that were employed in the executing of this design, though they _meant not so, neither did their hearts think so_.

4. Their petition with reference to the case at this time. The enemies _were gathered together against Christ_, and then no wonder that they were so against his ministers: _the disciple is not better than his Master_, nor must expect better treatment; but, being thus insulted, they pray,

(1) That God would take cognizance of the malice of their enemies.

(2) That God, by his grace, would keep up their spirits, and animate them to go on cheerfully with their work.

(3) That God would still give them power to work miracles for the confirmation of the doctrine they preached, which, by _the cure of the lame man_, they found to contribute very much to their success, and would contribute abundantly to their further progress: _Lord, grant us boldness, by stretching forth thy hand to heal_.

IV. The gracious answer God gave to this address, not in word, but in power. 1. God gave them a sign of the acceptance of their prayers (v. 31). The place was shaken, that their faith might be established and unshaken. 2. God gave them greater degrees of his Spirit, which was what they prayed for. Their prayer, without doubt, was accepted, for it was answered: _They were all filled with the Holy Ghost_, more than ever. When _they were filled with the Holy Ghost, they spoke the word with all boldness;_ for _the ministration of the Spirit is given to every man, to profit withal_. Talents must be traded with, not buried.

ALL THINGS IN COMMON (vv. 32-37)

We have a general idea given us in these verses, and it is a very beautiful one, of the spirit and state of this truly primitive church.

I. The disciples loved one another dearly. Observe here, 1. There were multitudes that believed; even in Jerusalem, where the malignant influence of the chief priests was most strong, *there were three thousand* converted on one day, and *five thousand* on another, and, besides these, *there were added to the church daily.* 2. They *were all of one heart, and of one soul.* Though there were many, very many, of different ages, tempers, and conditions, in the world, who perhaps, before they believed, were perfect strangers to one another, yet, when they met in Christ, they were as intimately acquainted as if they had known one another many years.

II. The ministers went on in their work with great vigour and success (*v.* 33). The doctrine they preached was, the resurrection of Christ.

III. The beauty of the Lord our God shone upon them, and all their performances: *Great grace was upon them all*, not only all the apostles, but all the believers.

IV. They were very liberal to the poor, and dead to this world. This was as great an evidence of the grace of God in them as any other, and recommended them as much to the esteem of the people.

1. They insisted not upon property, which even children seem to have a sense of and a jealousy for, and which worldly people triumph in. These believers were so taken up with the hopes of an inheritance in the other world that this was as nothing to them. They did not take away property, but they were indifferent to it. What we have in the world is more God's than our own; we have it from him, must use it for him, and are accountable for it to him.

2. They abounded in charity, so that, in effect, *they had all things common*; for (*v.* 34) *there was not any among them that lacked*, but care was taken for their supply.

3. Many of them sold their estates, to raise a fund for charity. Now,

(1) We are here told what they did with the money that was so raised: They *laid it at the apostles' feet* —they left it to them to be disposed of as they thought fit. Being laid there, it was not hoarded up, but *distribution was made*, by proper persons, *unto every man according as he had need.*

(2) Here is one particular person mentioned that was remarkable for this generous charity: it was *Barnabas*, afterwards Paul's colleague. Observe, [1] The account here given concerning him, *v.* 36. It is probable that he was one of the seventy disciples, and, as he increased in gifts and graces, grew eminent, and was respected by the apostles, who, in token of their value for him, gave him a name, *Barnabas—the son of prophecy* (so it properly signifies), he being endued with extraordinary gifts of prophecy. *A son of exhortation* (so some), one that had an excellent faculty of healing and persuading; we have an instance of it, *ch.* xi. 22–24. *A son of consolation* (so we read it); one that did himself walk very much in *the comforts of the Holy Ghost* —a cheerful Christian, and this enlarged his heart in charity to the poor; or one that

was eminent for comforting the Lord's people, and speaking peace to wounded troubled consciences; he had an admirable facility that way. [2] Here is an account of his charity, and great generosity to the public fund.

ANANIAS AND SAPPHIRA
(*vv.* 1–11)

The chapter begins with a melancholy *but*, which puts a stop to the pleasant and agreeable prospect of things which we had in the foregoing chapters; as every man, so every church, in its best state has its *but*. Observe here,

I. The sin of Ananias and Sapphira his wife. Now their sin was, 1. That they were ambitious of being thought eminent disciples, and of the first rank, when really they were not true disciples. 2. That they were covetous of the wealth of the world, and distrustful of God and his providence. Thus they thought to serve both God and mammon—God, by bringing part of the money to the apostles' feet, and mammon, by keeping the other part in their own pockets. 3. That they thought to deceive the apostles, and make them believe they brought the whole purchase-money, when really it was but a part. They dissembled with God and his Spirit, with Christ and his church and ministers; and this was their sin.

II. The indictment of Ananias, which proved both his condemnation and execution for this sin. When he brought the money, and expected to be commended and encouraged, as others were, Peter took him to task about it. Had it been a sin of infirmity, through the surprise of a temptation, Peter would have taken Ananias aside, and have bidden him go home, and fetch the rest of the money, and repent of his folly in attempting to put this cheat upon them; but he knew *that his heart was fully set in him to do this evil*, and therefore allowed him not space to repent. He here showed him,

1. The origin of his sin: *Satan filled his heart*.

2. The sin itself: *He lied to the Holy Ghost*; a sin of such a heinous nature that he could not have been guilty of it if Satan had not filled his heart.

3. The aggravations of the sin (*v.* 4). Which may be understood two ways: (1) "Thou wast under no temptation *to keep back part of the price*; before it was sold it was thy own, and when it was sold it was in thy own power to dispose of the money at thy pleasure." Or, (2) "Thou wast under no necessity of selling thy land at all, nor bringing any of the money to the apostles' feet. Thou mightest have kept the money, if thou hadst pleased, and the land too, and never have pretended to this piece of perfection."

4. All this guilt, thus aggravated, is charged upon him: *Why hast thou conceived this thing in thine heart?*

III. The death and burial of Ananias, *vv.* 5, 6.

1. He died upon the spot. It does not appear whether Peter designed and expected that this would follow upon what he said to him; it is probable that he did, for to Sapphira his wife Peter particularly spoke death, *v.* 9. This punishment

of Ananias may seem severe, but we are sure it was just. (1) It was designed to maintain the honour of the Holy Ghost, as now lately poured out upon the apostles, in order to the setting up of the gospel kingdom. (2) It was designed to deter others from the like presumptions, now at the beginning of this dispensation.

2. He was buried immediately, for this was the manner of the Jews (*v.* 6).

IV. The reckoning with Sapphira, the wife of Ananias, who perhaps was first in the transgression, and tempted her husband to eat this forbidden fruit. *She came in about three hours after,* expecting to share in the thanks of the house for her coming in, and consenting to the sale of the land, of which perhaps she was entitled to her dower or thirds; for *she knew not what had been done.*

1. She was found guilty of sharing with her husband in his sin, by a question that Peter asked her (*v.* 8). Ananias and his wife agreed to tell the same story, and the bargain being private, and by consent kept to themselves, nobody could disprove them, and therefore they thought they might safely stand in the lie, and should gain credit to it.

2. Sentence was passed upon her, that she should partake in her husband's doom, *v.* 9.

(1) Her sin is opened: *How is it that you have agreed together to tempt the Spirit of the Lord?* Before he passes sentence, he makes her to know her abominations, and shows her the evil of her sin.

(2) Her doom is read: *Behold, the feet of those who have buried*

thy husband are at the door (perhaps he heard them coming, or knew that they could not be long): *and* they *shall carry thee out.*

3. The sentence executed itself. There needed no executioner, a killing power went along with Peter's word, as sometimes a healing power did.

V. The impression that this made upon the people. Notice is taken of this in the midst of the story (*v.* 5): *Great fear came upon all that heard these things,* that heard what Peter said, and saw what followed; or upon all that heard the story of it; for, no doubt, it was all the talk of the city. And again (*v.* 11), *Great fear came upon all the church, and upon as many as heard these things.*

PROGRESS OF THE GOSPEL
(*vv.* 12–16)

We have here an account of the progress of the gospel, notwithstanding this terrible judgment inflicted upon two hypocrites.

I. Here is a general account of the miracles which the apostles wrought (*v.* 12). Now the gospel power returned to its proper channel, which is that of mercy and grace.

II. We are here told what were the effects of these miracles which the apostles wrought.

1. The church was hereby kept together, and confirmed in its adherence both to the apostles and to one another. *They* of the church *were all with one accord in Solomon's porch.* (1) They met in the temple, in the open place that was called Solomon's porch. They all met in public worship; so early was the institution of religious assemblies observed in the church, which must

by no means be forsaken or let fall, for in them a profession of religion is kept up. (2) They were there with one accord, unanimous in their doctrine, worship, and discipline; and there was no discontent nor murmuring about the death of Ananias and Sapphira.

2. It gained the apostles, who were the prime ministers in Christ's kingdom, very great respect. (1) The other ministers kept their distance: *Of the rest* of their company *durst no man join himself to them*, as their equal or an associate with them; though others of them were endued with the Holy Ghost, and spoke with tongues, yet none of them at this time did such signs and wonders as the apostles did: and therefore they acknowledged their superiority, and in every thing yielded to them. (2) All *the people magnified them*, and had them in great veneration, spoke of them with respect, and represented them as the favourites of Heaven, and unspeakable blessings to this earth.

3. The church increased in number (*v.* 14). Observe, (1) Believers are added to the Lord Jesus, joined to him, and so joined to his mystical body, from which nothing can separate us and cut us off, but that which separates us and cuts us off from Christ. (2) Notice is taken of the conversion of *women* as well as *men*; more notice than generally was in the Jewish church.

4. The apostles had abundance of patients, and gained abundance of reputation both to themselves and their doctrine by the cure of them all, *vv.* 15, 16. So many *signs and wonders were wrought by the apostles* that all manner of people

put in for the benefit of them, both in city and country, and had it. (1) In the city: They *brought forth their sick into the streets*. And they *laid them on beds and couches, that at the least the shadow of Peter, passing by, might overshadow some of them*, though it could not reach them all; and, it should seem, it had the desired effect, as the woman's touch of the hem of Christ's garment had; and in this among other things, that word of Christ was fulfilled, *Greater works than these shall you do*. (2) In the country towns: Multitudes came to Jerusalem from *the cities round about, bringing sick folks* that were afflicted in body, and *those that were vexed with unclean spirits*, that were troubled in mind, and they were *healed every one*.

PRISON DOORS OPENED
(*vv.* 17–25)

Never did any good work go on with any hope of success, but it met with opposition.

I. The priests were enraged at them, and shut them up in prison, *vv.* 17, 18. Observe, 1. Who their enemies and persecutors were. The high priest was the ringleader, Annas or Caiaphas, who saw their wealth and dignity, their power and tyranny, that is, their all, at stake, and inevitably lost, if the spiritual and heavenly doctrine of Christ should get ground and prevail among the people. Those that were most forward to join with the high priest herein were the *sect of the Sadducees*, who had a particular enmity to the gospel of Christ, because it confirmed and established the doctrine of the invisible world, the resurrection of the dead, and the future state, which they denied. 2. How they were affected towards them, ill affected, and exasperated to the last degree. 3. How they proceeded against them (*v.* 18). Hereby they designed, (1) To put a restraint upon them; though they could not lay any thing criminal to their charge worthy of death or of bonds, yet while they had them in prison they kept them from going on in their work, and this they reckoned a good point gained. Thus early were the ambassadors of Christ in bonds. (2) To put a terror upon them, and so to drive them off from their work. (3) To put a disgrace upon them, and therefore they chose to clap them up in the common prison, that, being thus vilified, the people might not, as they had done, magnify them.

II. God sent his angel to release them out of prison, and to renew their commission to preach the gospel.

1. The apostles are discharged, legally discharged, from their imprisonment (*v.* 19): *The angel of the Lord by night,* in spite of all the locks and bars that were upon them, *opened the prison doors,* and, in spite of all the vigilance and resolution of the keepers that *stood without before the doors, brought forth* the prisoners (see *v.* 23), gave them authority to go out without crime, and led them through all opposition. This deliverance is not so particularly related as that of Peter (*ch.* xii. 7, &c.); but the miracle here was the very same.

2. They are charged, and legally charged, to go on with their work,

so as thereby to be discharged from the prohibition which the high priest laid under them; the angel bade them, *Go, stand, and speak in the temple to the people all the words of this life, v.* 20.

III. They went on with their work (*v.* 21). 1. It was a great satisfaction to them to have these fresh orders. Perhaps they began to question whether, if they had their liberty, they should preach as publicly in the temple as they had done, because they had been told, when they were *persecuted in one city, to flee to another.* But, now that the angel ordered them to go preach in the temple, their way was plain, and they ventured without any difficulty, entered into the temple, and feared not the face of man. (2) They set themselves immediately to execute them, without dispute or delay.

IV. The high priest and his party went on with their prosecution, *v.* 21. See here,

1. How they were prepared, and how big with expectation, to crush the gospel of Christ and the preachers of it, for they raised the whole posse.

2. How they were disappointed, and had their faces filled with shame. See how they are baffled. (1) The officers come, and tell them that they are not to be found in the prison, *vv.* 22, 23. It occasioned various speculations, some suggesting that they were conjured out of the prison, and made their escape by magic arts; others that the keepers had played tricks with them, knowing how many friends these prisoners had, that were so much the darlings of the people. Some feared that, having made such a

27

wonderful escape, they would be the more followed. (2) Their doubt is, in part, determined; and yet their vexation is increased by another messenger, who brings them word that their prisoners are preaching in the temple (*v.* 25). Prisoners, that have broken prison, usually abscond, for fear of being retaken; but these prisoners, that here made their escape, dare to show their faces even where their persecutors have the greatest influence.

GAMALIEL'S ADVICE
(*vv.* 26–42)

Now here we have,

I. The seizing of the apostles a second time. We may think, if God designed this, "Why were they rescued from their first imprisonment?" But this was designed to humble the pride, and check the fury, of their persecutors; and now he would show that they were discharged, not because they feared a trial, for they were ready to surrender themselves and make their appearance before the greatest of their enemies.

II. Their examination. Being brought before this august assembly, the high priest, as the mouth of the court, told them what it was they had to lay to their charge, *v.* 28. 1. That they had disobeyed the commands of authority, and would not submit to the injunctions and prohibitions given them (*v.* 28). 2. That they had spread false doctrine among the people, or at least a singular doctrine, which was not allowed by the Jewish church, nor agreed with what was delivered from Moses's chair. 3. That they

had a malicious design against the government, and aimed to stir up the people against it, by representing it as wicked and tyrannical, and as having made itself justly odious both to God and man.

III. Their answer to the charge exhibited against them.

1. They justified themselves in their disobedience to the commands of the great sanhedrim, great as it was (*v.* 29): *We ought to obey God rather than men.* God had commanded them to teach in the name of Christ, and therefore they ought to do it, though the chief priests forbade them.

2. They justified themselves in doing what they could to fill Jerusalem with the doctrine of Christ.

(1) The chief priests are told to their faces the indignities they did to this Jesus: "*You slew him and hanged him on a tree,* you cannot deny it." The apostles, instead of making an excuse, or begging their pardon, for bringing the guilt of this man's blood upon them, repeat the charge, and stand to it.

(2) They are told also what honours God put upon this Jesus, and then let them judge who was in the right, the persecutors of his doctrine or the preachers of it. He calls God the *God of our fathers*, not only *ours*, but *yours*, to show that in preaching Christ they did not preach a new god, nor entice people to come and worship other gods; nor did they set up an institution contrary to that of Moses and the prophets, but they adhered to the God of the Jewish fathers; and that name of Christ which they preached answered the promises made to the fathers, and the

covenant God entered into with
them, and the types and figures of
the law he gave them. The God of
Abraham, Isaac, and *Jacob,* is the
*God and Father of our Lord Jesus
Christ*; see what honour he did him.
[1] He *raised him up*; he qualified
him for, and called him to, his
great undertaking, [2] He *exalted
him with his right hand, hath lifted
him up.* [3] "He has appointed him
to be *a prince and a Saviour.*" [4]
He is appointed, as a prince and a
Saviour, to *give repentance to Israel
and remission of sins.* [5] All this is
well attested, *First,* by the apostles
themselves; they are ready to
testify upon oath, if required, that
they saw him alive after his resurrection, and saw him ascend into
heaven. *Secondly,* By the Spirit of
God. And, *Lastly,* The giving of
the Holy Ghost to those that obey
Christ, both for their assistance in
their obedience and as a present
recompence for their obedience, is
a plain evidence that it is the will of
God that Christ should be obeyed;
"judge then whether we ought to
obey you in opposition to him."

IV. The impression which the
apostles' defence of themselves
made upon the court. Instead of
yielding to it, they raged against it,
and were filled, 1. With indignation
at what the apostles said. 2. With
malice against the apostles themselves.

V. The grave advice which Gamaliel, a leading man in the council,
gave upon this occasion, the scope
of which was to moderate the fury
of these bigots, and check the
violence of the prosecution. Now
observe here,

1. The necessary caution he gives

to the council, with reference to the
case before them. It is not a common case, and therefore should not
be hastily determined.

2. The cases he cites, to pave the
way to his opinion. Two instances
he gives of factious seditious men
(such as they would have the
apostles thought to be), whose
attempts came to nothing of themselves; whence he infers that if these
men were indeed such as they
represented them their cause would
sink with its own weight, and
Providence would infatuate and
defeat them, and then they needed
not persecute them.

3. His opinion upon the whole
matter.

(1) That they should not persecute the apostles (*v.* 38).

(2) That they should refer this
matter to Providence: "Wait the
issue, and see what it will come to.
If it be of men, it will come to nought
of itself; *if of God, it will stand,* in
spite of all your powers and
policies." It may be the comfort of
all who are sincerely on God's side,
who have a single eye to his will as
their rule and his glory as their end,
that whatsoever is of God cannot
be overthrown totally and finally,
though it may be very vigorously
opposed; it may be run upon, but
cannot be run down.

VI. The determination of the
council upon the whole matter, *v.*
40. 1. Thus far they agreed with
Gamaliel that they let fall the design
of putting the apostles to death. 2.
Yet they could not forbear giving
some vent to their rage (so outrageous was it) contrary to the convictions of their judgments and
consciences; for, though they were

advised to let them alone, yet, (1) *They beat them*, scourged them as malefactors, stripped them, and whipped them, as they used to do in the synagogues, and notice is taken (*v.* 41) of the ignominy of it. (2) *They commanded them that they should not speak* any more *in the name of Jesus*, that, if they could find no other fault with their preaching, they might have this ground to reproach it, that it was against law, and not only without the permission, but against the express order of their superiors.

VII. The wonderful courage and constancy of the apostles in the midst of all these injuries and indignities done them.

1. They bore their sufferings with an invincible cheerfulness. (*v.* 41).

2. They went on in their work with indefatigable diligence (*v.* 42): They were punished for preaching, and were commanded *not to preach*, and *yet they ceased not to teach and preach*; they omitted no opportunity, nor abated any thing of their zeal or forwardness.

CHAPTER SIX
DEACONS APPOINTED
(*vv.* 1–7)

Having seen the church's struggles with her enemies, and triumphed with her in her victories, we now come to take a view of the administration of her affairs at home; and here we have,

I. An unhappy disagreement among some of the church-members, which might have been of ill consequence, but was prudently accommodated and taken up in time (*v.* 1).

(1) The complainants were *the Grecians*, or Hellenists, *against the Hebrews*—the Jews that were scattered in Greece, and other parts, who ordinarily spoke the Greek tongue, and read the Old Testament in the Greek version, and not the original Hebrew, many of whom being at Jerusalem at the feast embraced the faith of Christ, and were added to the church, and so continued there. These complained against the Hebrews, the native Jews, that used the original Hebrew of the Old Testament.

(2) The complaint of these Grecians was *that their widows were neglected in the daily administration*, that is, in the distribution of the public charity, and the Hebrew widows had more care taken of them.

II. The happy accommodating of this matter, and the expedient pitched upon for the taking away of the cause of this murmuring. Now observe,

1. How the method was proposed by the apostles: They *called the multitude of the disciples unto them*, the heads of the congregations of Christians in Jerusalem, the principal leading men. The twelve themselves would not determine any thing without them, for *in multitude of counsellors there is safety*; and in an affair of this nature those might be best able to advise who were more conversant in the affairs of this life than the apostles were.

(1) The apostles urge that they could by no means admit so great a diversion, as this would be, from their great work (*v.* 2): *It is not reasonable that we should leave the word of God and serve tables.*

(2) They therefore desire *that seven men* might be chosen, well qualified for the purpose, whose business it should be *to serve tables, to be deacons to the tables,* v. 2. Now,

[1] The persons must be duly qualified. The people are to choose, and the apostles to ordain; but the people have no authority to choose, nor the apostles to ordain, men utterly unfit for the office: *Look out seven men*; so many they thought might suffice for the present, more might be added afterwards if there were occasion. These must be, *First, Of honest report,* men free from scandal, that were looked upon by their neighbours as men of integrity. *Secondly,* They must be *full of the Holy Ghost,* must be filled with those gifts and graces of the Holy Ghost which were necessary to the right management of this trust. *Thirdly,* They must be *full of wisdom.* It was not enough that they were honest, good men, but they must be discreet, judicious men, that could not be imposed upon, and would order things for the best, and with consideration.

[2] The people must nominate the persons. They might be presumed to know better, or at least were fitter to enquire, what character men had, than the apostles; and therefore they are entrusted with the choice.

[3] The apostles will ordain them to the service, will give them their charge, that they may know what they have to do and make conscience of doing it, and give them their authority, that the persons concerned may know whom they are to apply to, and submit to, in affairs of that nature.

(3) The apostles engage to addict themselves wholly to their work as ministers, and the more closely if they can but get fairly quit of this troublesome office (v. 4): *We will give ourselves continually to prayer, and to the ministry of the word.*

2. How this proposal was agreed to, and presently put in execution, by the disciples.

(1) They pitched upon the persons. An apostle, who was an extraordinary officer, was chosen by lot, which is more immediately the act of God; but the overseers of the poor were chosen by the suffrage of the people, in which yet a regard is to be had to the providence of God, who has all men's hearts and tongues in his hand. We have a list of the persons chosen. Some think they were such as were before of the seventy disciples; but this is not likely, for they were ordained by Christ himself, long since, *to preach the gospel*; and there was no more reason that they should leave the word of God to serve tables than that the apostles should. It is therefore more probable that they were of those that were converted since the pouring out of the Spirit; for it was promised to all that would be baptized that they should *receive the gift of the Holy Ghost*; and the gift, according to that promise, is that fulness of the Holy Ghost which was required in those that were to be chosen to this service. The first named is *Stephen, a man full of faith and of the Holy Ghost*; he had a strong faith in the doctrine of Christ, and was full of it above most; *full of fidelity, full of courage* (so some), for he was *full of the Holy Ghost*, of his gifts and

31

graces. He was an extraordinary man, and excelled in every thing that was good; his name signifies *a crown*. *Philip* is put next, because he, having *used this office of a deacon well, thereby obtained a good degree*, and was afterwards ordained to the office of an evangelist, a companion and assistant to the apostles, for so he is expressly called, *ch.* xxi. 8.

(2) The apostles appointed them to this work of serving tables for the present, *v.* 6. The people presented them to the apostles, who approved their choice, and ordained them. Having by prayer implored a blessing upon them, they did by the laying on of hands assure them that the blessing was conferred in answer to the prayer; and this was giving them authority to execute that office, and laying an obligation upon the people to be observant of them therein.

III. The advancement of the church hereupon. When things were thus put into good order in the church (grievances were redressed and discontents silenced) then religion got ground, *v.* 7. 1. *The word of God increased*. Now that the apostles resolved to stick more closely than ever to their preaching, it spread the gospel further, and brought it home with the more power. 2. Christians became numerous. 3. *A great company of the priests were obedient to the faith*. *Then* is the word and grace of God greatly magnified when those are wrought upon by it that were least likely, as the priests here, who either had opposed it, or at least were linked in with those that had.

STEPHEN ACCUSED (*vv.* 8–15)

Stephen, no doubt was diligent and faithful in the discharge of his office as distributor of the church's charity. And, being faithful in a little, he was entrusted with more.

I. He proved the truth of the gospel, by working miracles in Christ's name, *v.* 8. 1. He was *full of faith and power*, that is, of a strong faith, by which he was enabled to do great things. Those that are full of faith are full of power, because by faith the power of God is engaged for us.

II. He pleaded the cause of Christianity against those that opposed it, and argued against it (*vv.* 9, 10).

1. We are here told who were his opponents, *v.* 9. They were Jews, but Hellenist Jews, Jews of the dispersion, who seem to have been more zealous for their religion than the native Jews. They were *of the synagogue which is called the synagogue of the Libertines*; the Romans called those *Liberti*, or *Libertini*, who either, being foreigners, were naturalized, or, being slaves by birth, were made freemen. Some think that these Libertines were such of the Jews as had obtained the Roman freedom, as Paul had (*ch.* xxii. 27, 28); and it is probable that he was the most forward man of this synagogue of the Libertines in disputing with Stephen, and engaged others in the dispute, for we find him busy in the stoning of Stephen, and consenting to his death.

2. We are here told how he carried the point in this dispute (*v.* 10): *They were not able to resist the wis-*

dom and the Spirit by which he spoke. They could neither support their own arguments nor answer his. They were not able to resist the *wisdom and the Spirit by which he spoke*, that Spirit of wisdom which spoke by him. They thought they had only disputed with Stephen, and could make their part good with him; but they were disputing with the Spirit of God in him, for whom they were an unequal match.

III. At length, he sealed it with his blood; so we shall find he did in the next chapter; here we have some steps taken by his enemies towards it. When they could not answer his arguments as a disputant, they prosecuted him as a criminal, and suborned witnesses against him, to swear blasphemy upon him. By their rude and violent treatment of him, they would represent him, both to the people and to the government, as a dangerous man, that would either flee from justice if he were not watched, or fight with it if he were not put under a force. Having caught him, they brought him triumphantly into the council, and, as it should seem, so hastily that he had none of his friends with him.

3. How they were prepared with evidence ready to produce against him. They were resolved that they would not be run a-ground, as they were when they brought our Saviour upon his trial, and then had to seek for witnesses. These were got ready beforehand, and were instructed to make oath that they had *heard him speak blasphemous words against Moses and against God* (*v.* 11)—against this *holy place and the law* (*v.* 13); for

they heard him say what Jesus would do to their place and their customs, *v.* 14. It is probable that he had said something to that purport; and yet those who swore it against him are called *false witnesses*, because, though there was something of truth in their testimony, yet they put a wrong and malicious construction upon what he had said, and perverted it.

IV. We are here told how God owned him when he was brought before the council, and made it to appear that he stood by him (*v.* 15). Now Stephen appeared at the bar with the countenance *as of an angel*. 1. Perhaps it intimates no more than that he had an extraordinarily pleasant, cheerful countenance, and there was not in it the least sign either of fear for himself or anger at his persecutors. 2. It should rather seem that there was a miraculous splendour and brightness upon his countenance, like that of our Saviour when he was transfigured—or, at least, that of Moses when he came down from the mount—God designing thereby to put honour upon his faithful witness and confusion upon his persecutors and judges, whose sin would be highly aggravated, and would be indeed a rebellion against the light, if, notwithstanding this, they proceeded against him.

CHAPTER SEVEN
STEPHEN'S DEFENCE
(*vv.* 1–16)

Stephen is now at the bar before the great council of the nation, indicted for blasphemy. Now here,

I. The high priest calls upon him to answer for himself, *v.* 1.

II. He begins his defence, and it is long; but it should seem by his breaking off abruptly, just when he came to the main point (*v.* 50), that it would have been much longer if his enemies would have given him leave to say all he had to say. Observe,

(1) His preface: *Men, brethen, and fathers, hearken.* He gives them, though not flattering titles, yet civil and respectful ones, signifying his expectation of fair treatment with them; from men he hopes to be treated with humanity, and he hopes that brethren and fathers will use him in a fatherly brotherly way.

(2) His entrance upon the discourse.

[1] He begins with the call of Abraham out of Ur of the Chaldees, by which he was set apart for God to be the trustee of the promise, and the father of the Old-Testament church.

First, From this call of Abraham we may observe, 1. That in all our ways we must acknowledge God, and attend the directions of his providence, as of the pillar of cloud and fire. 2. Those whom God takes into covenant with himself he distinguishes from the children of this world.

Secondly, But let us see what this is to Stephen's case. 1. They had charged him as a blasphemer of God, and an apostate from the church; therefore he shows that he is a son of Abraham. 2. They were proud of their being circumcised; and therefore he shows that Abraham was taken under God's

guidance, and into communion with him, before he was circumcised, for that was not till *v.* 8. 3. They had a mighty jealousy for this holy place. "Now," says Stephen, "you need not be so proud of it; for," (1) "You came originally out of *Ur of the Chaldees,*where *your fathers served other gods* (Josh. xxiv. 2), and you were not the first planters of this country." (2) "God appeared in his glory to Abraham a great way off in Mesopotamia, before he came near Canaan, nay, before he dwelt in Charran; so that you must not think God's visits are confined to *this land.*

[2] The unsettled state of Abraham and his seed for many ages after he was called out of Ur of the Chaldees.

[3] The building up of the family of Abraham, with the entail of divine grace upon it, and the disposals of divine Providence concerning it, which take up the rest of the book of Genesis.

Let us now see what this is to Stephen's purpose. 1. He still reminds them of the mean beginning of the Jewish nation, as a check to their priding themselves in the glories of that nation; and that it was by a miracle of mercy that they were raised up out of nothing to what they were, from so small a number to be so great a nation; but, if they answer not the intention of their being so raised, they can expect no other than to be destroyed. Their holy land, which they doted so much upon, their fathers were long kept out of the possession of, and met with dearth and great affliction in it; and therefore let them not think it strange if, after it has been so long polluted with sin, it be at length destroyed. The faith of the patriarchs in desiring to be buried in the land of Canaan plainly showed that they had an eye to the heavenly country, to which it was the design of this Jesus to lead them.

STEPHEN'S DEFENCE
Contd. (*vv.* 17–29)

Stephen here goes on to relate,

I. The wonderful increase of the people of Israel in Egypt; it was by a wonder of providence that in a little time they advanced from a family into a nation.

II. The extreme hardships which they underwent there, *vv.* 18, 19.

III. The raising up of *Moses to be their deliverer*. Stephen was charged with having spoken blasphemous words against Moses, in answer to which charge he here speaks very honourably of him.

IV. The attempts which Moses made to deliver Israel, which they spurned, and would not close in with. This Stephen insists much upon, and it serves for a key to this story (Exod. ii. 11–15), as does also that other construction which is put upon it by the apostle, Heb. xi. 24–26.

Now let us see how this serves Stephen's purpose. 1. They charged him with blaspheming Moses, in answer to which he retorts upon them the indignities which their fathers did to Moses, which they ought to be ashamed of, and humbled for, instead of picking quarrels thus, under pretence of zeal for the honour of Moses, with one that had as great a veneration for him as any

of them had. 2. They persecuted him for disputing in defence of Christ and his gospel, in opposition to which they set up Moses and his law: "But," saith he, "you had best take heed," (1) "Lest you hereby do as your fathers did, refuse and reject one *whom God has raised up to be to you a prince and a Saviour;* you may understand, if you will not wilfully shut your eyes against the light, that God will, by this Jesus, deliver you out of a worse slavery than that in Egypt; take heed then of thrusting him away, but receive him as a ruler and a judge over you." (2) "Lest you hereby fare as your fathers fared, who for this were very justly left to die in their slavery, for the deliverance came not till forty years after. This will be the issue of it, you put away the gospel from you, and it will be *sent to the Gentiles;* you will not have Christ, and you shall not have him, so shall your doom be." Matt. xxiii. 38, 39.

STEPHEN'S DEFENCE
Contd. (*vv.* 30–41)

Stephen here proceeds in his story of Moses; and let any one judge whether these are the words of one that was a blasphemer of Moses or no; nothing could be spoken more honourably of him. Here is,

I. The vision which he saw of the glory of God at the bush (*v.* 30).

II. The declaration which he heard of the covenant of God (*v.* 32). Now the preachers of the gospel preached up this covenant, *the promise made of God unto the fathers; unto which promise those of the twelve tribes* that did continue *serving God hoped to come, ch.*

xxvi. 6, 7. And shall they, under colour of supporting the holy place and the law, oppose the covenant which was made with Abraham and his seed, his spiritual seed, before the law was given, and long before the holy place was built?

III. The commission which God gave him to deliver Israel out of Egypt. The Jews set up Moses in competition with Christ, and accused Stephen as a blasphemer because he did not do so too. But Stephen here shows that Moses was an eminent type of Christ, as he was Israel's deliverer.

IV. His acting in pursuance of this commission, wherein he was a figure of the Messiah. And Stephen takes notice here again of the slights they had put upon him, the affronts they had given him, and their refusal to have him to reign over them, as tending very much to magnify his agency in their deliverance.

V. His prophecy of Christ and his grace, *v.* 37. He not only was a type of Christ (many were so that perhaps had not an actual foresight of his day), but Moses spoke of him (*v.* 37).

VI. The eminent services which Moses continued to do to the people of Israel, after he had been instrumental to bring them out of Egypt, *v.* 38. And herein also he was a type of Christ, who yet so far exceeds him that it is no blasphemy to say, "He has authority to change the customs that Moses delivered."

VII. The contempt that was, after this, and notwithstanding this, put upon him by the people. Those that charged Stephen with speaking against Moses would do well to answer what their own ancestors had done, and they tread in their ancestors' steps.

STEPHEN'S DEFENCE
Cont. (*vv.* 42–50)

Two things we have in these verses:

I. Stephen upbraids them with the idolatry of their fathers, which God gave them up to, as a punishment for their early forsaking him in worshipping the golden calf; and this was the saddest punishment of all for that sin, as it was of the idolatry of the Gentile world *that God gave them up to a reprobate mind.*

II. He gives an answer particularly to the charge exhibited against him relating to the temple, *that he spoke blasphemous words against that holy place*, *vv.* 44–50. He was accused for saying that Jesus would destroy this holy place: "And what if I did say so?" (saith Stephen) "the glory of the holy God is not bound up in the glory of this holy place, but that may be preserved untouched, though this be laid in the dust;" for, 1. It was not till our fathers came into the wilderness, in their way to Canaan, that they had any fixed place of worship. 2. The holy place was at first but a tabernacle, mean and movable, showing itself to be short-lived, and not designed to continue always. 3. That tabernacle was *a tabernacle of witness*, or of testimony, *a figure for the time then present* (Heb. ix. 9), *a figure of good things to come, of the true tabernacle which the Lord pitched, and not men*, Heb. viii. 2. 4. That tabernacle was framed just as God appointed, and *according to the fashion which Moses saw in the mount*, which plainly intimates that it had reference to good things to come. 5. That tabernacle was pitched first in the wilderness; it was not a native of this land of yours (to which you think it must for ever be confined), but was brought in in the next age, by our fathers, who came after those who first erected it, into the possession of the Gentiles, into the land of Canaan, which had long been in the possession of the devoted nations *whom God drove out before the face of our fathers*. And why may not God set up his spiritual temple, as he had done the material tabernacle, in those countries that were now the possession of the Gentiles? That tabernacle was brought in by those who came *with Jesus*, that is, *Joshua*. And I think, for distinction sake, and to prevent mistakes, it ought to be so read, both here and Heb. iv. 8. Yet in naming *Joshua* here, which in Greek is *Jesus*, there may be a tacit intimation that as the Old-Testament Joshua brought in that typical tabernacle, so the New-Testament Joshua should bring in the true tabernacle into the possession of the Gentiles. 6. That tabernacle continued for many ages, *even to the days of David*, above four hundred years, before there was any thought of building a temple, *v.* 45. 7. God had his heart so little upon a temple, or such a holy place as they were so jealous for, that, when David desired to build one, he was forbidden to do it. 8. God often declared that temples made with hands were not his delight, nor could add any thing to the perfection of his rest and joy. Solomon,

when he dedicated the temple, acknowledged that God *dwelleth not in temples made with hands*; he has not need of them, is not benefited by them, cannot be confined to them.

STEPHEN'S DEFENCE
Contd. (*vv.* 51–53)

Stephen was going on in his discourse (as it should seem by the thread of it) to show that, as the temple-service must come to an end, and it would be the glory of both to give way to that worship of the Father in spirit and in truth which was to be established in the kingdom of the Messiah. It is probable that he perceived that they were going to silence him; and therefore he breaks off abruptly in the midst of his discourse, and by that spirit of wisdom, courage, and power, wherewith he was filled, he sharply rebuked his persecutors, and exposed their true character; for, if they will not admit the testimony of the gospel to them, it shall become a testimony against them.

I. They, like their fathers, were stubborn and wilful, and would not be wrought upon by the various methods God took to reclaim and reform them; they were like their fathers, inflexible both to the word of God and to his providences.

II. They, like their fathers, were not only not influenced by the methods God took to reform them, but they were enraged and incensed against them: *You do always resist the Holy Ghost*.

III. They, like their fathers, persecuted and slew those whom God sent unto them to call them to duty, and make them offers of mercy.

They had been the *betrayers and murderers of the just One* himself, as Peter had told them, *ch.* iii. 14, 15; v. 30. They had hired Judas to betray him, and had in a manner forced Pilate to condemn him; and therefore it is charged upon them that they were his betrayers and murderers. To which of the prophets would those have shown any respect who had no regard to the Son of God himself?

IV. They, like their fathers, put contempt upon divine revelation, and would not be guided and governed by it; and this was the aggravation of their sin, that God had given, as to their fathers his law, so to them his gospel, in vain. They would not yield to the plainest demonstrations, any more than their fathers before them did, for they were resolved not to comply with God either in his law or in his gospel.

We have reason to think Stephen had a great deal more to say, and would have said it if they would have suffered him; but they were wicked and unreasonable men with whom he had to do, that could no more hear reason than they could speak it.

STEPHEN MARTYRED
(*vv.* 54–60)

We have here the death of the first martyr of the Christian church.

Let us observe here the wonderful discomposure of the spirits of his enemies and persecutors, and the wonderful composure of his spirit.

I. See the strength of corruption in the persecutors of Stephen— malice in perfection, hell itself broken loose, men become incar-

nate devils, and the serpent's seed spitting their venom.

1. *When they heard these things they were cut to the heart* (*v.* 54), the same word that is used Heb. xi. 37, and translated *they were sawn asunder.* They were put to as much torture in their minds as ever the martyrs were put to in their bodies.

2. They *gnashed upon him with their teeth.* This denotes, (1) Great malice and rage against him. (2) Great vexation within themselves; they fretted to see in him such manifest tokens of a divine power and presence, and it vexed them to the heart.

3. *They cried out with a loud voice* (*v.* 57), to irritate and excite one another, and to drown the noise of the clamours of their own and one another's consciences; when he said, *I see heaven opened,* they cried with a loud voice, that he might not be heard to speak.

4. They *stopped their ears,* that they might not hear their own noisiness; or perhaps under pretence that they could not bear to hear his blasphemies.

5. They *ran upon him with one accord*—the people and the elders of the people, judges, prosecutors, witnesses, and spectators, they all flew upon him, as beasts upon their prey.

6. They *cast him out of the city, and stoned him,* as if he were not worthy to live in Jerusalem; nay, not worthy to live in this world, pretending herein to execute the law of Moses (Lev. xxiv. 16). Now, the stoning of a man being a laborious piece of work, the witnesses took off their upper garments, that they might not hang in

their way, *and they laid them down at a young man's feet, whose name was Saul,* now a pleased spectator of this tragedy. It is the first time we find mention of his name; we shall know it and love it better when we find it changed to *Paul,* and him changed from a persecutor into a preacher. This little instance of his agency in Stephen's death he afterwards reflected upon with regret (*ch.* xxii. 20): *I kept the raiment of those that slew him.*

II. See the strength of grace in Stephen, and the wonderful instances of God's favour to him, and working in him. As his persecutors were full of Satan, so was he *full of the Holy Ghost.* Now here we have a remarkable communion between this blessed martyr and the blessed Jesus in this critical moment. We may observe,

1. Christ's gracious manifestation of himself to Stephen, both for his comfort and for his honour, in the midst of his sufferings.

(1) He, *being full of the Holy Ghost, looked up stedfastly into heaven, v.* 55.

(2) He saw the glory of God (*v.* 55); for *he saw the heavens opened, v.* 56. Some think his eyes were strengthened, and the sight of them so raised above its natural pitch, by a supernatural power, that he saw into the third heavens, though at so vast a distance, as Moses's sight was enlarged to see the whole land of Canaan. Others think it was a representation of the glory of God set before his eyes, as, before, Isaiah and Ezekiel; heaven did as it were come down to him, as Rev. xxi. 2.

(3) He *saw Jesus standing on the right hand of God* (*v.* 55), *the Son of man,* so it is *v.* 56. Now, [1] Here is a proof of the exaltation of Christ to the Father's right hand; the apostles saw him ascend, but they did not see him sit down. We are told that he sat down on the right hand of God; but was he ever seen there? Yes, Stephen saw him there, and was abundantly satisfied with the sight. [2] He is usually said to *sit* there; but Stephen sees him *standing* there, as one more than ordinarily concerned at present for his suffering servant; he stood up as a judge to plead his cause against his persecutors. He stands ready to receive him and crown him, and in the mean time to give him a prospect of the joy set before him. [3] This was intended for the encouragement of Stephen. He sees Christ is for him, and then no matter who is against him.

(4) He told those about him what he saw (*v.* 56): *Behold, I see the heavens opened.* If some were exasperated by it, others perhaps might be wrought upon to consider this Jesus whom they persecuted, and to believe in him.

2. Stephen's pious addresses to Jesus Christ. Two short prayers Stephen offered up to God in his dying moments, and in them as it were breathed out his soul:

(1) Here is a prayer for himself: *Lord Jesus, receive my spirit.* Thus Christ had himself resigned his spirit immediately into the hands of the Father. We are here taught to resign ours into the hands of Christ as Mediator, by him to be recommended to the Father. Stephen saw Jesus standing at the Father's right hand, and he thus

calls to him: "Blessed Jesus, do that for me now which thou standest there to do for all thine, receive my departing spirit into thy hand."

(2) Here is a prayer for his persecutors, *v.* 60.

[1] The circumstances of this prayer are observable; for it seems to have been offered up with something more of solemnity than the former. *First,* He *knelt down,* which was an expression of his humility in prayer. *Secondly,* He *cried with a loud voice,* which was an expression of his importunity.

[2] The prayer itself: *Lord, lay not this sin to their charge.* Herein he followed the example of his dying Master, who prayed thus for his persecutors, *Father, forgive them*; and set an example to all following sufferers in the cause of Christ thus to pray for those that persecute them.

3. His expiring with this: *When he had said this, he fell asleep*; or, as he was saying this, the blow came that was mortal. Note, Death is but a sleep to good people; not the sleep of the soul (Stephen had given that up into Christ's hand), but the sleep of the body; it is its rest from all its griefs and toils; it is perfect ease from toil and pain. Stephen died as much in a hurry as ever any man did, and yet, when he died, he fell asleep.

CHAPTER EIGHT
MORE PERSECUTION
(*vv.* 1–3)

In these verses we have,

   I. Something more concerning Stephen and his death. Accordingly here is, 1. Stephen's death rejoiced in by one—by many, no doubt, but by one in particular, and that was Saul, who was afterwards called Paul; he was *consenting to his death, he consented to it with delight* (so the word signifies); he was pleased with it. 2. Stephen's death bewailed by others (*v.* 2)—*devout men,* which some understand of those that were properly so called, *proselytes,* one of whom Stephen himself probably was. Or, it may be taken more largely; some of the church that were more devout and zealous than the rest went and gathered up the poor crushed and broken remains, to which they gave a decent interment, probably in the *field of blood,* which was bought some time ago to bury strangers in. They buried him solemnly, and made great lamentation over him.

   II. An account of this persecution of the church, which begins upon the martyrdom of Stephen. Observe,

   1. Against whom this persecution was raised: It was *against the church in Jerusalem,* which is no sooner planted than it is persecuted, as Christ often intimated that tribulation and persecution would arise *because of the word.*

   2. Who was an active man in it; none so zealous, so busy, as Saul, a young Pharisee, *v.* 3. As for Saul (who had been twice mentioned before, and now again for a notorious persecutor) *he made havoc of the church*; he did all he could to lay it waste and ruin it; he cared not what mischief he did to the disciples of Christ, nor knew when to stop. He aimed at no less than the cutting off of the gospel Israel, that

the name of it should be no more in remembrance, Ps. lxxxiii. 4.

3. What was the effect of this persecution: *They were all scattered abroad* (v. 1), not all the believers, but all the preachers, who were principally struck at, and against whom warrants were issued out to take them up. The preachers were all scattered *except the apostles*, who, probably, were directed by the Spirit to continue at Jerusalem yet for some time, they being, by the special providence of God, screened from the storm, and by the special grace of God enabled to face the storm.

PHILIP'S MINISTRY
(vv. 4–13)

I. Here is a general account of what was done by them all (v. 4): *They went every where, preaching the word.* They did not go to hide themselves for fear of suffering, no, nor to show themselves as proud of their sufferings; but they went up and down to scatter the knowledge of Christ in every place where they were scatterted. They went every where, into the way of the Gentiles, and the cities of the Samaritans, which before they were forbidden to go into, Matt. x. 5.

II. A particular account of what was done by Philip. Stephen was advanced to the degree of a martyr, Philip to the degree of an evangelist, which when he entered upon, being obliged by it to *give himself to the word and prayer*, he was, no doubt, discharged from the office of a deacon. Now observe,

1. What wonderful success Philip had in his preaching, and what reception he met with.

(1) The place he chose was the city of Samaria.

(2) The doctrine he preached was Christ; for he determined to know nothing else. The Samaritans had an expectation of the Messiah's coming, as appears by John iv. 25. Now Philip tells them that he is come, and that the Samaritans are welcome to him.

(3) The proofs he produced for the confirmation of his doctrine were miracles, v. 6. And the nature of the miracles was such as suited the intention of his commission, and gave light and lustre to it.

(4) The acceptance which Philip's doctrine, thus proved, met with in Samaria (v. 6): *The people with one accord gave heed to those things which Philip spoke.* The common people gave heed to Philip,—*a multitude of them,* not here and there one, but with one accord; they were all of a mind, that it was fit the doctrine of the gospel should be enquired into, and an impartial hearing given to it.

(5) The satisfaction they had in attending on, and attending to, Philip's preaching, and the success it had with many of them (v. 8).

2. What there was in particular at this city of Samaria that made the success of the gospel there more than ordinarily wonderful.

(1) That Simon Magus had been busy there, and had gained a great interest among the people, and *yet they believed the things that Philip spoke.* To unlearn that which is bad proves many times a harder task than to learn that which is good. These Samaritans, though they were not idolaters as the Gentiles, nor prejudiced against the

gospel by traditions received from their fathers, yet had of late been drawn to follow Simon, a conjurer (for so *Magus* signifies) who made a mighty noise among them, and had strangely *bewitched them*.

But Simon Magus himself became a convert to the faith of Christ, in show and profession, for a time. *Is Saul also among the prophets?* Yes (*v.* 13), *Simon himself believed also*. He was convinced that Philip preached a true doctrine, because he saw it confirmed by real miracles, of which he was the better able to judge because he was conscious to himself of the trick of his own pretended ones.

SIMON REBUKED
(*vv.* 14–25)

Two apostles were sent, the two most eminent, to Samaria, 1. To encourage Philip, to assist him, and strengthen his hands. 2. To carry on the good work that was begun among the people, and, with those heavenly graces that had enriched them, to confer upon them spiritual gifts. Now observe,

I. How they advanced and improved those of them that were sincere. It is said (*v.* 16), *The Holy Ghost was as yet fallen upon none of them*, in those extraordinary powers which were conveyed by the descent of the Spirit upon the day of pentecost. They were none of them endued with the gift of tongues, which seems then to have been the most usual immediate effect of the pouring out of the Spirit. See *ch.* x. 45, 46. This was both an eminent sign to those that believed not, and of excellent service to those that did. This, and other such gifts, they had not, *only they were baptized in the name of the Lord Jesus*, and so engaged in him and interested in him, which was necessary to salvation, and in this they had joy and satisfaction (*v.* 8), though they could not speak with tongues. Those that are indeed given up to Christ, and have experienced the sanctifying influences and operation of the Spirit of grace, have great reason to be thankful, and no reason to complain, though they have not those gifts that are for ornament, and would make them bright. But it is intended that they should go on to the perfection of the present dispensation, for the greater honour of the gospel. We have reason to think that Philip had received these gifts of the Holy Ghost himself, but had not a power to confer them; the apostles must come to do this; and they did it not upon all that were baptized, but upon some of them, and, it should seem, such as were designed for some office in the church, or at least to be eminent active members of it; and upon some of them *one gift of the Holy Ghost*, and upon others *another*. See 1 Cor. xii. 4, 8; xiv. 26. Now in order to this, 1. *The apostles prayed for them*, *v.* 15. The Spirit is given, not to ourselves only (Luke xi. 13), but to others also, in answer to prayer: *I will put my Spirit within you* (Ezek. xxxvi. 27), *but I will for this be enquired of*, *v.* 37. We may take encouragement from this example in praying to God to give the renewing graces of the Holy Ghost to those whose spiritual welfare we are concerned for—for our children, for our friends, for our ministers. We should pray, and pray earnestly, *that they may receive the Holy Ghost*; for this includes all blessings. 2. They laid their hands on them, to signify that their prayers were answered, and *that the gift of the Holy Ghost was conferred upon them*; for, upon the use of this sign, *they received the Holy Ghost, and spoke with tongues*. The laying on of hands was anciently used in blessing, by those who blessed with authority. Thus the apostles blessed these new converts, ordained some to be ministers, and confirmed others in their Christianity. We cannot now, nor can any, thus give the Holy Ghost by the laying on of hands; but this may intimate to us that those whom we pray for we should use our endeavours with.

II. How they discovered and discarded him that was a hypocrite among them, and this was Simon Magus; for they knew how to *separate between the precious and the vile*.

(1) Peter shows him his crime (*v*. 20): *Thou hast thought that the gift of God may be purchased with money*; and thus, [1] He had overvalued the wealth of this world. [2] He had undervalued the gift of the Holy Ghost and put it upon a level with the common gifts of nature and providence.

(2) He shows him his character, which is inferred from his crime. And therefore Peter tells him plainly, [1] That his heart was *not right in the sight of God*, *v*. 21. "Though thou professest to believe, and art baptized, yet thou art not sincere." [2] That he is *in the gall of bitterness, and in the bond of iniquity: I perceive that thou art so*,

v. 23. Indwelling sin is *a root of bitterness*, that *bears gall and wormwood*, Deut. xxix. 18. The faculties are corrupted, and the mind embittered against all good, Heb. xii. 15. It intimates likewise the pernicious consequences of sin; the *end is bitter as wormwood*.

(3) He reads him his doom in two things:

[1] He shall sink with his worldly wealth, which he overvalued: *Thy money perish with thee*.

[2] He shall come short of the spiritual blessings which he undervalued (*v*. 21): "*Thou hast neither part nor lot in this matter*."

(4) He gives him good counsel, notwithstanding, *v*. 22. Observe,

[1] What it is that he advises him to: He must do his first works. *First*, He must *repent*,—must see his error and retract it,—must change his mind and way,—must be humbled and ashamed for what he has done. His repentance must be particular: "Repent of this, own thyself guilty in this, and be sorry for it." *Secondly*, He must *pray* to God, must pray that God would give him repentance, and pardon upon repentance.

[2] What encouragement he gives him to do this: *If perhaps the thought of thy heart*, this wicked thought of thine, *may be forgiven thee*. When Peter here puts a *perhaps* upon it, the doubt is of the sincerity of his repentance, not of his pardon if his repentance be sincere.

[3] Simon's request to them to pray for him, *v*. 24. He was startled and put into confusion by that which Peter said, finding that resented thus which he thought

would have been embraced with both arms; and he cries out, *Pray you to the Lord for me, that none of the things which you have spoken come upon me.*

Lastly, Here is the return of the apostles to Jerusalem, when they had finished the business they came about; for as yet they were not to disperse; but, though they came hither to do that work which was peculiar to them as apostles, yet, opportunity offering itself, they applied themselves to that which was common to all gospel ministers. 1. There, in the city of Samaria, they were preachers: *They testified the word of the Lord.* 2. In their road home they were itinerant preachers; as they passed through many villages of the Samaritans they preached the gospel.

THE ETHIOPIAN EUNUCH
(*vv.* 26–40)

We have here the story of the conversion of an Ethiopian eunuch to the faith of Christ, by whom, we have reason to think, the knowledge of Christ was sent into that country where he lived, and that scripture fulfilled, *Ethiopia shall soon stretch out her hands* (one of the first of the nations) *unto God,* Ps. lxviii. 31.

I. Philip the evangelist is directed into the road where he would meet with this Ethiopian, *v.* 26.

II. An account is given of this eunuch (*v.* 27), who and what he was, on whom this distinguishing favour was bestowed. 1. He was a foreigner, *a man of Ethiopia.* 2. He was a person of quality, a great man in his own country, *a eunuch,* not in body, but in office—lord

chamberlain or steward of the household. He *had the charge of all her treasure*; so great a trust did she repose in him. *Not many mighty, not many noble, are called*; but some are. 3. He was a proselyte to the Jewish religion, for *he came to Jerusalem to worship.*

III. Philip and the eunuch are brought together into a close conversation; and now Philip shall know the meaning of his being sent into a desert, for there he meets with a chariot, that shall serve for a synagogue, and one man, the conversion of whom shall be in effect, for aught he knows, the conversion of a whole nation.

1. Philip is ordered to fall into company with this traveller that is going home from Jerusalem towards Gaza, thinking he has done all the business of his journey, when the great business which the overruling providence of God designed in it was yet undone.

2. He finds him reading in his Bible, as he sat in his chariot (*v.* 28). Perhaps the eunuch was now reading over again those portions of scripture which he had heard read and expounded at Jerusalem, that he might recollect what he had heard.

3. He puts a fair question to him: *Understandest thou what thou readest?* Not by way of reproach, but with design to offer him his service.

4. The eunuch in a sense of his need of assistance, desires Philip's company (*v.* 31).

IV. The portion of scripture which the eunuch recited, with some hints of Philip's discourse upon it.

1. The chapter he was reading was the fifty-third of Isaiah, two verses of which are here quoted (*vv.* 32, 33), part of the seventh and eighth verses. These verses foretold concerning the Messiah, (1) That he should die, should be *led to the slaughter*, as sheep that were offered in sacrifice—that his life should be taken from among men, taken from the earth. (2) That he should die wrongfully, should die by violence, should be hurried out of his life, and *his judgment shall be taken away*—no justice done to him; for he must be *cut off, but not for himself*. (3) That he should die patiently. Like *a lamb dumb before the shearer*, nay, and before the butcher too, *so he opened not his mouth*. Never was there such an example of patience as our Lord Jesus was in his sufferings. (4) That yet he should live for ever, to ages which cannot be numbered; for so I understand those words, *Who shall declare his generation?* The Hebrew word properly signifies *the duration of one life*, Eccl. i. 4. Now who can conceive or express how long he shall continue, notwithstanding this; *for his life is taken* only *from the earth*; in heaven he shall live to endless and innumerable ages, as it follows in Isa. liii. 10, *He shall prolong his days*.

2. The eunuch's question upon this is, *Of whom speaketh the prophet this? v.* 34. It is a material question he asks, and a very sensible one.

3. Philip takes this fair occasion given him to open to him the great mystery of the gospel concerning *Jesus Christ, and him crucified.* He *began at this scripture*, took this for his text (as Christ did another passage of the same prophecy, Luke iv. 21), and *preached unto him Jesus, v.* 35. This is all the account given us of Philip's sermon, because it was the same in effect with Peter's sermons, which we have had before.

V. The eunuch is baptized in the name of Christ, *vv.* 36–38. Now here we have,

1. The modest proposal which the eunuch made of himself for baptism (*v.* 36). "*See, here is water,* which perhaps we may not meet with a great while again; *what doth hinder me to be baptized?* Canst thou show any cause why I should not be admitted a disciple and follower of Christ by baptism?" Those who have received the thing signified by baptism should not put off receiving the sign.

2. The fair declaration which Philip made him of the terms upon which he might have the privilege of baptism (*v.* 37): "*If thou believest with all thy heart, thou mayest.*"

3. The confession of faith which the eunuch made in order to his being baptized. It is very short, but it is comprehensive and much to the purpose, and what was sufficient: *I believe that Jesus Christ is the Son of God.* He was before a worshipper of the true God, so that all he had to do now was to *receive Christ Jesus the Lord.* (1) He believes that Jesus is *the Christ*, the true Messiah promised, the *anointed One.* (2) That Christ is *Jesus—a Saviour*, the only Saviour of his people from their sins. And, (3) That this Jesus Christ is the *Son of God*, that he has a divine nature, as the Son is of the same nature with

the Father; and that, being the Son of God, he is the *heir of all things*. This is the principal peculiar doctrine of Christianity, and whosoever believe this with all their hearts, and confess it, they and their seed are to be baptized.

4. The baptizing of him hereupon. If some hypocrites crowd into the church, who afterwards prove a grief and scandal to us, yet we must not therefore make the door of admission any straiter than Christ has made it; they shall answer for their apostasy, and not we.

VI. Philip and the eunuch are separated presently; and this is as surprising as the other parts of the story. One would have expected that the eunuch should have either have staid with Philip, or have taken him along with him into his own country, and, there being so many ministers in those parts, he might be spared, and it would be worth while: but God ordered otherwise.

CHAPTER NINE

CONVERSION OF SAUL
(*vv.* 1–9)

We found mention made of Saul twice or thrice in the story of Stephen, for the sacred penman longed to come to his story; and now we are come to it, not quite taking leave of Peter, but from henceforward being mostly taken up with Paul the apostle of the Gentiles, as Peter was of the circumcision. We are here told,

I. How bad he was, how very bad, before his conversion; just before he was an inveterate enemy to Christianity, did his utmost to root it out, by persecuting all that

embraced it. In other respects he was well enough, as *touching the righteousness which is of the law, blameless*, a man of no ill morals, but a blasphemer of Christ, a persecutor of Christians, and injurious to both, 1 Tim. i. 13. And so ill informed was his conscience that he thought he ought to do what he did against the name of Christ (*ch.* xxvi. 9) and that he did God service in it, as was foretold, John xvi. 2. Saul cannot be easy if he knows a Christian is quiet; and therefore, hearing that the Christians in Damascus were so, he resolves to give them disturbance. In order to this, he applies to the high priest for a commission (*v.* 1) to go to Damascus, *v.* 2.

II. How suddenly and strangely a blessed change was wrought in him, not in the use of any ordinary means, but by miracles. The conversion of Paul is one of the wonders of the church. Here is,

1. The place and time of it: *As he journeyed, he came near to Damascus*; and there Christ met with him.

2. The appearance of Christ to him in his glory. Here it is only said that there *shone round about him a light from heaven*; but it appears from what follows (*v.* 17) that the Lord Jesus was in this light, and appeared to him by the way.

3. The arresting of Saul, and his detachment: *He fell to the earth*, *v.* 4. This may be considered, (1) As the effect of Christ's appearing to him, and of the light which shone round about him. (2) As a step towards this intended advancement. He is designed not only to be a Christian, but to be a minister, an apostle, a great apostle, and

46

therefore he must thus be cast down.

4. The arraigning of Saul. Being by the fall taken into custody, and as it were set to the bar, he heard a voice saying to him (and it was distinguishing, to him only, for though those that were with him heard a sound (*v.* 7) yet they knew not the words, *ch.* xxii. 9), *Saul, Saul, why persecutest thou me?* Observe here,

(1) Saul not only saw a light from heaven, but heard a voice from heaven; wherever the glory of God was seen, the word of God was heard (Exod. xx. 18); and to Moses (Num. vii. 89); and to the prophets.

(2) What he heard was very awakening.

[1] He was called by his name, and that doubled: *Saul, Saul.*

[2] The charge exhibited against him is, *Why persecutest thou me?* Observe, 1. The person sinning: "It is thou; thou, that art hast the knowledge of the scriptures, which, if duly considered, would show thee the folly of it. It is worse in thee than in another." 2. The person sinned against: "It is I, who never did thee any harm, who came from heaven to earth to do thee good, who was not long since crucified for thee; and was not that enough, but must I afresh be crucified by thee?" *Why persecutest thou me?* He thought he was persecuting only a company of, poor, weak, silly people, that were an offence and eye-sore to the Pharisees, little imagining that it was one in heaven that he was all this while insulting; for surely, if he had known, he would not have persecuted the Lord of glory.

5. Saul's question upon his indictment, and the reply to it, *v.* 5.

(1) He makes enquiry concerning Christ: *Who art thou, Lord?* He who had been a blasphemer of Christ's name now speaks to him as his Lord. The question is proper: *Who art thou?* This implies his present unacquaintedness with Christ. Note, There is some hope of people when they begin to enquire after Jesus Christ.

(2) He has an answer immediately, in which we have,

[1] Christ's gracious revelation of himself to him. He is always ready to answer the serious enquiries of those who covet an acquaintance with him: *I am Jesus whom thou persecutest.*

[2] His gentle reproof of him: *It is hard for thee to kick against the pricks,* or *goads*—to spurn at the spur. It is hard, it is in itself an absurd and evil thing, and will be of fatal consequence to him that does it. Those that revolt more and more when they are stricken by the word or rod of God, that are enraged at reproofs and fly in the face of their reprovers, kick against the pricks and will have a great deal to answer for.

6. His surrender of himself to the Lord Jesus at length, *v.* 6. See here,

(1) The frame and temper he was in, when Christ had been dealing with him. [1] He trembled, as one in a great fright. [2] He was astonished, was filled with amazement, as one brought into a new world, that knew not where he was.

(2) His address to Jesus Christ, when he was in this frame: *Lord, what wilt thou have me to do?* The great change in conversion is

wrought upon the will, and consists in the resignation of that to the will of Christ.

(3) The general direction Christ gave him, in answer to this: *Arise, go into the city of Damascus*, which thou art now near to, *and it shall be told thee what thou must do*. It is encouragement enough to have further instruction promised him. Christ manifests himself to his people by degrees; and both what he does and would he have them to do, though they know not now, they shall know hereafter.

7. How far his fellow travellers were affected with this, and what impression it made upon them. They fell to the earth, as he did, but rose without being bidden, which he did not, but lay still till it was said to him, *Arise*; for he lay under a heavier load than any of them did; but when they were up, (1) *They stood speechless*, as men in confusion, and that was all, *v.* 7. (2) *They heard a voice, but saw no man*; they heard Paul speak, but saw not him to whom he spoke, nor heard distinctly what was said to him: which reconciles it with what is said of this matter, *ch.* xxii. 9.

8. What condition Saul was in after this, *vv.* 8, 9. (1) *He arose from the earth*, when Christ commanded him, but probably not without help, the vision had made him so faint and weak. (2) *When his eyes were opened*, he found that his sight was gone. Thus a believing sight of the glory of God in the face of Christ dazzles the eyes to all things here below. Christ, in order to the further discovery of himself and his gospel to Paul, took him off from the sight of other things, which he

must look off, that he may look unto Jesus, and to him only. (3) *They led him by the hand into Damascus*. He was thus taught what need he had of the grace of Christ to lead his soul (being naturally blind and apt to mistake) into all truth. (4) He lay *without sight*, and without food, *neither did eat nor drink for three days*, *v.* 9.

SAUL BAPTIZED (*vv.* 10–22)

I. Ananias is here ordered to go and look after him, to heal and help him; for he that causeth grief will have compassion.

1. The person employed is *Ananias, a certain disciple at Damascus*, not lately driven thither from Jerusalem, but a native of Damascus; for it is said (*ch.* xxii. 12) *that he had a good report of all the Jews who dwelt there, as a devout man according to the law.*

2. The direction given him is to go and enquire at such a house, probably an inn, for one *Saul of Tarsus*. Christ, in a vision, called to Ananias by name, *v.* 10. *Go then*, saith Christ, *into the street which is called Straight, and enquire in the house of Judas* (where strangers used to lodge) *for one called Saul of Tarsus*.

3. Two reasons are given him why he must go and enquire for this stranger, and offer him his service:

(1) Because he prays, and his coming to him must answer his prayer. Observe what condition Saul was now in. He was under conviction of sin, trembling and astonished; the setting of sin in order before us should drive us to prayer. He was under a bodily

affliction, blind and sick; and, *Is any afflicted? Let him pray*. Christ had promised him that it should be further told him what he should do (*v.* 6), and he prays that one may be sent to him to instruct him.

(2) Because he hath seen in a vision such a man coming to him, to restore him to his sight; and Ananias's coming to him must answer his dream, for it was of God (*v.* 12).

II. Ananias objects against going to him, and the Lord answers the objection.

1. Ananias pleads that this Saul was a notorious persecutor of the disciples of Christ, *vv.* 13, 14.

2. Christ overrules the objection (*vv.* 15, 16). The vessel God uses he himself chooses; and it is fit he should himself have the choosing of the instruments he employs (John xv. 16). He is designed, (1) For eminent services: *He is to bear my name before the Gentiles*, is to be the apostle of the Gentiles, and to carry the gospel to heathen nations. (2) For eminent sufferings (*v.* 16). He that has been a persecutor shall be himself persecuted.

III. Ananias presently goes on Christ's errand to Saul, and with good effect.

1. Ananias delivered his message to Saul, *v.* 17. Probably he found him in bed, and applied to him as a patient. (1) *He put his hands on him.* It was promised, as one of the signs that should follow those that believe, that they should lay hands on the sick, and they should recover (Mark xvi. 18), and it was for that intent that he put his hands on him. (2) He called him *brother*, because he was made a partaker of

the grace of God, though not yet baptized. (3) He produces his commission from the same hand that had laid hold on him by the way, and now had him in custody. *The hand that wounded heals.* (4) He assures him that he shall not only have his sight restored, but be filled with the Holy Ghost: he must himself be an apostle, and must in nothing come behind the chief of the apostles, and therefore must receive the Holy Ghost immediately, and not, as others did, by the interposition of the apostles; and Ananias's putting his hands upon him before he was baptized was for the conferring of the Holy Ghost.

2. Ananias saw the good issue of his mission. (1) In Christ's favour to Saul. Saul is delivered from the spirit of bondage by his receiving sight (*v.* 18), which was signified by the falling of scales from his eyes; and this immediately, and forthwith: the cure was sudden, to show that it was miraculous. (2) In Saul's subjection to Christ: He was baptized, and thereby submitted to the government of Christ, and cast himself upon the grace of Christ.

IV. The good work that was begun in Saul is carried on wonderfully; this new-born Christian, though he seemed *as one born out of due time*, yet presently comes to maturity.

1. He received his bodily strength, *v.* 19.

2. He associated with the disciples that were at Damascus, fell in with them, conversed with them, went to their meetings, and joined in communion with them.

3. *He preached Christ in the*

synagogues, v. 20. To this he had an extraordinary call, and for it an extraordinary qualification, God having immediately revealed his Son to him and in him, that he might preach him, Gal. i. 15, 16. He preached concerning Christ, *that he is the Son of God*, his beloved Son, in whom he is well pleased, and with us in him, and not otherwise. *All that heard him were amazed, and said, "Is not this he that destroyed those who called on this name in Jerusalem,* and now does he call on his name himself, and persuade others to call upon it, and strengthen the hands of those that do?"

4. He confuted and confounded those that opposed the doctrine of Christ, v. 22. And we have reason to think he was instrumental in converting many to the faith of Christ, and building up the church at Damascus, which he went hither to make havoc of.

PAUL, THE CHRISTIAN
(vv. 23–31)

As soon as God *had revealed his Son in him, that he might preach him, he went not up to Jerusalem*, to receive instructions from the apostles (as any other convert would have done, that was designed for the ministry), but he went to Arabia (Gal. i. 16) where he would have opportunity of teaching, but not of learning; thence he returned to Damascus, and there, three years after his conversion, this happened, which is here recorded.

I. He met with difficulties at Damascus, and had a narrow escape of being killed there. Saul was no sooner a Christian than a

preacher, no sooner a preacher than a sufferer; so quickly did he rise to the summit of his preferment.

II. He met with difficulties at Jerusalem the first time he went thither, v. 26. He came to Jerusalem. This is thought to be that journey to Jerusalem of which he himself speaks (Gal. i. 18). But I rather incline to think that this was a journey before that. Now observe,

1. How shy his friends were of him (v. 26). (1) See what was the cause of their jealousy of him: *They believed not that he was a disciple*, but that he only pretended to be so, and came among them as a spy or an informer. The disciples of Christ had need to be cautious whom they admit into communion with them. *Believe not every spirit.* (2) See how it was removed (v. 27): *Barnabas took him to the apostles* themselves, who were not so scrupulous as the inferior disciples, *to whom he first assayed to join himself, and he declared to them,* [1] What Christ had done for him. [2] What he had since done for Christ. So it was that, being satisfied himself, he gave satisfaction to the apostles concerning him, he having brought no testimonials from the disciples at Damascus, thinking *he needed not, as some others, epistles of commendation,* 2 Cor. iii. 1.

2. How sharp his enemies were upon him. (1) He was admitted into the communion of the disciples, which was no little provocation to his enemies. (2) He appeared vigorous in the cause of Christ, and this was yet more provoking to them (v. 29). (3) This brought him into peril of his life, with which he narrowly escaped: *The Grecians,*

when they found they could not deal with him in disputation, contrived to silence him another way; *they went about to slay him*, as they did Stephen when *they could not resist the Spirit by which he spoke, ch.* vi. 10. That is a bad cause that has recourse to persecution for its last argument. But notice was given of this conspiracy too, and effectual care taken to secure this young champion (*v.* 30): *When the brethren knew* what was designed against him *they brought him down to Cesarea.*

III. The churches had now a comfortable gleam of liberty and peace (*v.* 31): *Then had the churches rest.* Observe,

1. *The churches had rest.* After a storm comes a calm.

2. They made a good use of this lucid interval. (2) They *walked in the fear of the Lord*—were more exemplary themselves for a holy, heavenly way of life. (3) They *walked in the comfort of the Holy Ghost*—were not only faithful, but cheerful, in religion; they stuck to the ways of the Lord, and sang in those ways.

3. God blessed it to them for their increase in number: They *were multiplied.*

ENEAS HEALED (*vv.* 32–35)

Here we have, I. The visit Peter made to the churches that were newly planted by the dispersed preachers, *v.* 32.

II. The cure Peter wrought on *Eneas*, a man that had been bedridden eight years, *v.* 33. Peter does not pretend to do it himself by any power of his own, but declares it to be Christ's act and deed, directs

him to look up to Christ for help, and assures him of an *immediate* cure—not, "He *will* make thee," but, "He *does* make thee, whole;" and a *perfect* cure—not, "He makes thee *easy*," but "He makes thee *whole*." He does not express himself by way of prayer to Christ that he would make him whole, but as one having authority from Christ, and that knew his mind, he declares him made whole. (2) He ordered him to bestir himself, to exert himself: "*Arise and make thy bed*, that all may see thou art thoroughly cured." (3) Power went along with this word: he arose immediately, and no doubt very willingly made his own bed.

III. The good influence this had upon many (*v.* 35): *All that dwelt at Lydda and Saron saw him, and turned to the Lord.*

DORCAS RAISED (*vv.* 36–43)

Here we have another miracle wrought by Peter, for the confirming of the gospel, and which exceeded the former—the raising of Tabitha to life when she had been for some time dead. Here is,

I. The life, and death, and character of Tabitha, on whom this miracle was wrought, *vv.* 36, 37.

II. The request which her Christian friends sent to Peter to come to them with all speed, not to attend the funeral, but, if it might be, to prevent it, *v.* 38. Lydda, where Peter now was, was nigh to Joppa, and the disciples at Joppa had heard that Peter was there, and that he had raised Eneas from a bed of languishing; and therefore they *sent him two men*, to make the message the more solemn and respectful, *desiring him that he would not delay to come to them*; not telling him the occasion, lest he should modestly decline coming upon so great an errand as to raise the dead: if they can but get him to them, they will leave it to him.

III. The posture in which he found the survivors, when he came to them (*v.* 39). He found the corpse laid in the upper chamber, and attended by widows, probably such as were in the communion of the church, poor widows; there they were,

1. Commending the deceased—a good work, when there was that in them which was truly commendable, and worthy of imitation, and when it is done modestly and soberly, and without flattery of the survivors or any sinister intention, but purely for the glory of God and the exciting of others to that which is virtuous and praiseworthy.

2. They were here lamenting the loss of her: The widows stood by Peter, weeping. They need not weep for·her; she is taken from the evil to come, *she rests from her labours and her works follow her*, besides those she leaves behind her: but they weep for themselves and for their children, who will soon find the want of such a good woman, that has not left her fellow.

IV. The manner in which she was raised to life. 1. Privately. Thus Peter declined everything that looked like vainglory and ostentation; they came to see, but he did not come to be seen. 2. By prayer. In his healing Eneas there was an implied prayer, but in this greater work he addressed himself to God by solemn prayer, as Christ when

he raised Lazarus; but Christ's prayer was with the authority of a Son, who *quickens whom he will*; Peter's with the submission of a servant, who is under direction, and therefore he *knelt down and prayed.* 3. By the word, a quickening word, a word which is spirit and life. When he had prayed, he *turned to the body*, and spoke in his Master's name, according to his example: "*Tabitha, arise*; return to life again." Power went along with his word, and she came to life, *opened her eyes* which death had closed.

V. The good effect of this miracle. 1. Many were by it convinced of the truth of the gospel, that it was from heaven, and not of men, and believed in the Lord, *v.* 42. 2. Peter was hereby induced to continue some time in this city, *v.* 43. Finding that a door of opportunity was opened for him there, he tarried there many days, till he was sent thence, and sent for thence upon business to another place.

CHAPTER TEN

CORNELIUS PRAYS (*vv.* 1–8)

It is not unlikely that some Gentiles might before now have stepped into a synagogue of the Jews, and heard the gospel preached; but the gospel was never yet designedly preached to the Gentiles, nor any of them baptized—Cornelius was the first; and here we have,

I. An account given us of this Cornelius, who and what he was, who was the first-born of the Gentiles to Christ. He was, according to the measure of the light he had, a religious man. It is a very good character that is given of him, *v*. 2. (1) He was possessed with a principle of regard to the true and living God. He was *a devout man and one that feared God*. He believed in one God, the Creator of heaven and earth, and had a reverence for his glory and authority, and a dread of offending him by sin. (2) He kept up religion in his family. He *feared God with all his house*. (3) He was a very charitable man: He *gave much alms to the people*, the people of the Jews, notwithstanding the singularities of their religion. (4) He was much in prayer: He *prayed to God always*. He kept up stated times for prayer, and was constant to them.

II. The orders given him from heaven, by the ministry of an angel, to send for Peter to come to him, which he would never have done if he had not been thus directed to do it. Observe,

1. How, and in what way, these orders were given him. He had a vision, in which an angel delivered them to him. It was about the *ninth hour of the day*, at three of the clock in the afternoon, which is with us an hour of business and conversation; but then, because it was in the temple the time of offering the evening sacrifice, it was made by devout people an *hour of prayer*, to intimate that all our prayers are to be offered up in the virtue of the great sacrifice.

2. What the message was that was delivered to him.

(1) He is assured that God accepts him in walking according to the light he had (*v*. 4). Observe, Prayers and alms must go together. The sacrifices under the law are said to be *for a memorial*. See Lev. ii. 9, 16; v. 12; vi. 15. And prayers and alms are our spiritual offerings, which God is pleased to take cognizance of, and have regard to.

(2) He is appointed to enquire after a further discovery of divine grace, now lately made to the world, *v*. 5, 6. Not, He may do it if he pleases; it will be an improvement and entertainment to him. But, He must do it; it is indispensably necessary to his acceptance with God for the future, though he has been accepted in his services hitherto. He that believed the promise of the Messiah must now believe the performance of that promise. Cornelius has now an angel from heaven talking to him, and yet he must not receive the gospel of Christ from this angel, nor be told by him what he ought to do, but all that the angel has to say is, "Send for Peter, and he shall tell thee."

III. His immediate obedience to these orders, *vv*. 7, 8. He sent with all speed to Joppa, to fetch Peter to him.

PETER'S VISION (*vv*. 9–18)

The scriptures of the Old Testament had spoken plainly of the bringing in of the Gentiles into the church. Christ had given plain intimations of it when he ordered them to *teach all nations*; and yet even Peter himself, who knew so much of his Master's mind, could not understand it, till it was here revealed by vision, *that the Gentiles should be fellow-heirs*, Eph. iii. 6. Now here observe,

I. The circumstances of this vision.

1. It was when the messengers sent from Cornelius were now *nigh the city, v.* 9. Peter knew nothing of their approach, and they knew nothing of his praying; but he that knew both him and them was preparing things for the interview, and facilitating the end of their negociation.

2. It was when *Peter went up upon the housetop to pray,* about noon.

3. It was when he became *very hungry,* and was waiting for his dinner (*v.* 10). Now this hunger was a proper inlet to the vision about meats, as Christ's hunger in the wilderness was to Satan's temptation to turn stones into bread.

II. The vision itself, which was not so plain as that to Cornelius, but more figurative and enigmatical, to make the deeper impression. 1. He *fell into a trance or ecstasy,* not of terror, but of contemplation, with which he was so entirely swallowed up as not only not to be regardful, but not to be sensible, of external things. He saw *a great sheet full of all manner of living creatures, which descended from heaven, and was let down to him to the earth,* that is, to the roof of the house where he now was. By this vision we are taught to see all the benefit and service we have from the inferior creatures coming down to us from heaven; it is the gift of God who made them. Peter was ordered by a voice from heaven to make use of this plenty and variety which God had sent him (*v.* 13): "*Rise, Peter, kill and eat*: without putting any difference between clean and unclean, take which thou

hast most mind to." The distinction of meats which the law made was intended to put a difference between Jew and Gentile, that it might be difficult to them to dine and sup with a Gentile, because they would have that set before them which they were not allowed to eat; and now the taking off of that prohibition was a plain allowance to converse with the Gentiles, and to be free and familiar with them. Now they might fare as they fared, and therefore might eat with them, and be fellow-commoners with them. He stuck to his principles, and would by no means hearken to the motion, though he was hungry (*v.* 14): *Not so, Lord.* God, by a second voice from heaven, proclaimed the repeal of the law in this case (*v.* 15): *What God hath cleansed, that call thou not common.* He that made the law might alter it when he pleased, and reduce the matter to its first state. *This was done thrice, v.* 16. The sheet was drawn up a little way, and let down again the second time, and so the third time, with the same call to him, to kill, and eat, and the same reason, that what God hath cleansed we must not call common; but whether Peter's refusal was repeated the second and third time is not certain; surely it was not, when his objection had the first time received such a satisfactory answer. But at last *the vessel was received up into heaven.*

III. The providence which very opportunely explained this vision, and gave Peter to understand the intention of it, *vv.* 17, 18. 1. What Christ did, Peter knew not just then

54

(John xiii. 7): *He doubted within himself what this vision which he had seen should mean.* 2. Yet he was made to know presently, for *the men who were sent from Cornelius* were just now come to *the house*, and were at *the gate enquiring whether Peter lodged there*; and by their errand it will appear what was the meaning of this vision.

PETER GOES TO CORNELIUS (*vv.* 19–33)

We have here the meeting between Peter the apostle, and Cornelius the centurion. Now here,

I. Peter is directed by the Spirit to go along with Cornelius's messengers (*vv.* 19, 20), and this is the exposition of the vision; now the riddle is unriddled: *While Peter thought on the vision*; he was musing upon it, and then it was opened to him.

II. He receives both them and their message: *He went down to them*, *v.* 21. Peter lodged them, though they were Gentiles, to show how readily he complied with the design of the vision in eating with Gentiles; for he immediately took them to eat with him. Though they were two of them servants, and the other a common soldier, yet Peter thought it not below him to take them into his house.

III. He *went with them* to Cornelius, whom he found ready to receive and entertain him. 1. Peter, when he went with them, was *accompanied by certain brethren from Joppa*, where he now was, *v.* 23. Six of them went along with him, as we find, *ch.* xi. 12. Either Peter desired their company, that

they might be witnesses of his proceeding cautiously with reference to the Gentiles, and of the good ground on which he went, and therefore he invited them (*ch.* xi. 12), or they offered their service to attend him, and desired they might have the honour and happiness of being his fellow-travellers. Now when they came into the house of Cornelius Peter found, (1) That he was expected, and this was an encouragement to him. (2) That he was expected by many, and this was a further encouragement to him. As Peter brought some with him to partake of the spiritual gift he had now to dispense, so *Cornelius had called together*, not only his own family, but *kinsmen and near friends*, to partake with him of the heavenly instructions he expected from Peter, which would give Peter a larger opportunity of doing good.

IV. Here is the first interview between Peter and Cornelius, in which we have, 1. The profound and indeed undue respect and honour which Cornelius paid to Peter (*v.* 25). His worshipping a man was indeed culpable; but, considering his present ignorance, it was excusable, nay, and it was an evidence of something in him that was very commendable—and that was a great veneration for divine and heavenly things. 2. Peter's modest and indeed just and pious refusal of this honour that was done him (*v.* 26). Peter did not entertain a surmise that his great respect for him, though excessive, might contribute to the success of his preaching, and therefore if he will be deceived let him be deceived;

no, let him know that Peter is a man, that *the treasure is in earthen vessels*, that he may value the treasure for its own sake.

V. The account which Peter and Cornelius give to each other, and to the company, of the hand of Heaven in bringing them together. Now,

1. Peter declares the direction God gave to him to come to those Gentiles, *vv.* 28, 29. *"God hath shown me*, by a vision, *that I should not call any man common or unclean*, nor refuse to converse with any man for the sake of his country."

2. Cornelius declares the directions God gave to him to send for Peter, and that it was purely in obedience to those directions that he had sent for him. Now,

(1) Cornelius gives an account of the angel's appearing to him, and ordering him to send for Peter; not as glorying in it, but as that which warranted his expectation of a message from heaven by Peter.

(2) He declares his own and his friends' readiness to receive the message Peter had to deliver (*v.* 33).

PETER'S SERMON (*vv.* 34–43)

We have here Peter's sermon preached to Cornelius and his friends. This excellent sermon of Peter's is admirably suited to the circumstances of those to whom he preached it; for it was a new sermon.

I. Because they were Gentiles to whom he preached. He shows that, notwithstanding this, they were interested in the gospel of Christ, which he had to preach, and entitled to the benefit of it, upon an equal

footing with the Jews. He therefore lays down this as an undoubted principle, *that God is no respecter of persons; doth not know favour in judgment*, as the Hebrew phrase is; which magistrates are forbidden to do (Deut. i. 17; xvi. 19; Prov. xxiv. 23), and are blamed for doing, Ps. lxxxii. 2. God never perverts judgment upon personal regards and considerations, nor countenances a wicked man in a wicked thing for the sake of his beauty, or stature, his country, parentage, relations, wealth, or honour in the world. Now, (1) This was always a truth, before Peter perceived it. Yet now it was made more clear than it had been. Now *in Christ Jesus*, it is plain, *neither circumcision availeth any thing, nor uncircumcision*, Gal. v. 6; Col. iii. 11.

II. Because they were Gentiles inhabiting a place within the confines of the land of Israel, he refers them to what they themselves could not but know concerning the life and doctrine, the preaching and miracles, the death and sufferings of our Lord Jesus: for these were things the report of which spread into every corner of the nation, *vv.* 37, &c.

1. They knew in general, *the word*, that is, the gospel, *which God sent to the children of Israel: That word, I say, you know, v.* 37.

2. They knew the several matters of fact relating to this word of the gospel sent to Israel. (1) They knew the baptism of repentance which John preached by way of introduction to it, and in which the gospel first began, Mark i. 1. (2) They knew that immediately after

John's baptism the gospel of Christ, that word of *peace, was published throughout all Judea,* and that it took its rise from Galilee. (3) They knew that Jesus of Nazareth, when he was here upon earth, *went about doing good.* (4) They knew more particularly that he *healed all that were oppressed of the devil,* and helped them from under his oppressing power. (5) They knew that the Jews put him to death; they *slew* him by *hanging him on a tree.*

3. They did know, or might know, by all this, that he had a commission from heaven to preach and act as he did. This he still harps upon in his discourse, and takes all occasions to hint it to them. Let them know, (1) That this Jesus *is Lord of all*; it comes in in a parenthesis, but is the principal proposition intended to be proved, that Jesus Christ, by whom peace is made between God and man, *is Lord of all*; not only as *God over all blessed for evermore,* but as Mediator, *all power both in heaven and on earth* is put into his hand, and all judgment committed to him. (2) That *God anointed him with the Holy Ghost and with power*; he was both authorized and enabled to do what he did by a divine anointing, whence he was called *Christ—the Messiah, the anointed One.* (3) That *God was with him, v.* 38. His works were wrought in God.

III. Because they had had no more certain information concerning this Jesus, Peter declares to them his resurrection from the dead, and the proofs of it, that they might not think that when he was slain there was an end of him. 1.

The power by which he arose is incontestably divine (*v.* 40). 2. The proofs of his resurrection were incontestably clear; for God *showed him openly.*

IV. He concludes with an inference from all this, that therefore that which they all ought to do was to believe in this Jesus: he was sent to tell Cornelius what he must do, and it is this; his praying and his giving alms were very well, but one thing he lacked, he must believe in Christ. Observe,

1. Why he must believe in him. Faith has reference to a testimony, and the Christian faith is *built upon the foundation of the apostles and prophets,* it is built upon the testimony given by them.

2. What they must believe concerning him. (1) That we are all accountable to Christ as our Judge; this the apostles were commanded to testify to the world, that this Jesus is *ordained of God to be the Judge of the quick and dead, v.* 42. (2) That if we believe in him we shall all be justified by him as our righteousness, *v.* 43. The prophets, when they spoke of the death of Christ, did witness this, *that through his name,* for his sake, and upon the account of his merit, *whosoever believeth in him,* Jew or Gentile, *shall receive remission of sins.*

CORNELIUS BAPTIZED
(*vv.* 44–48)

Here we have,

I. God's owning Peter's word, by conferring the Holy Ghost upon the hearers of it, and immediately upon the hearing of it (*v.* 44). Observe, 1. When the Holy Ghost fell upon them—while Peter was preaching. 2. How it appeared that the Holy Ghost had fallen upon them (v. 46): *They spoke with tongues* which they never learned, perhaps the Hebrew, the holy tongue; as the preachers were enabled to speak the vulgar tongues, that they might communicate the doctrine of Christ to the hearers, so, probably, the hearers were immediately taught the sacred tongue, that they might examine the proofs which the preachers produced out of the Old Testament in the original. Or their being enabled to speak with tongues intimated that they were all designed for ministers, and by this first descent of the Spirit upon them were qualified to preach the gospel to others, which they did but now receive themselves. But, observe, when they spoke with tongues, they *magnified God*, they spoke of Christ and the benefits of redemption, which Peter had been preaching to the glory of God. Thus did they on whom the Holy Ghost first descended, *ch.* ii. 11. Note, Whatever gift we are endued with, we ought to honour God with it, and particularly the gift of speaking, and all the improvements of it. 3. What impression it made upon the believing Jews that were present (v. 45): *Those of the circumcision who believed were astonished*—those six that came along with Peter; it surprised them exceedingly, and perhaps gave them some uneasiness, because *upon the Gentiles also was poured out the gift of the Holy Ghost*, which they thought had been appropriated to their own nation. Had they understood the scriptures of the Old Testament, which

pointed at this, it would not have been such an astonishment to them; but by our mistaken notions of things we create difficulties to ourselves in the methods of divine providence and grace.

II. Peter's owning God's work in baptizing those on whom the Holy Ghost fell. Observe, 1. Though they had received the Holy Ghost, yet it was requisite they should be baptized; though God is not tied to instituted ordinances, we are; and no extraordinary gifts set us above them, but rather oblige us so much the more to conform to them. Some in our days would have argued. 2. Though they were Gentiles, yet, having received the Holy Ghost, they might be admitted to baptism (v. 47).

III. Their owning both Peter's word and God's work in their desire for further advantage by Peter's ministry: *They prayed him to tarry certain days.*

CHAPTER ELEVEN

PETER EXPLAINS (vv. 1–18)

Here we find,

I. Intelligence was presently brought of it to the church in Jerusalem, and thereabouts; for Cesarea was not so far from Jerusalem but that they might presently hear of it. Some for good-will, and some for ill-will, would spread the report of it; so that before he himself had returned to Jerusalem *the apostles and* the *brethren* there and *in Judea heard that the Gentiles also had received the word of God*, that is, the gospel of Christ.

II. That offence was taken at it by the believing Jews (vv. 2, 3).

III. Peter gave such a full and fair account of the matter of fact as was sufficient, without any further argument or apology, both to justify him, and to satisfy them (*v.* 4).

That which put the matter past all dispute was the descent of the Holy Ghost upon the Gentile hearers; this completed the evidence that it was the will of God that he should take the Gentiles into communion.

THE CHURCH AT ANTIOCH
(*vv.* 19–25)

We have here an account of the planting and watering of a church at Antioch, the chief city of Syria, reckoned afterwards the third most considerable city of the empire, only Rome and Alexandria being preferred before it, next to whose patriarch that of Antioch took place. Now concerning the church at Antioch observe,

I. The first preachers of the gospel there were such as were dispersed from Jerusalem by persecution, that persecution which arose five or six years ago (as some compute), at the time of Stephen's death (*v.* 19). Thus the wrath of man is made to praise God. Observe,

1. Those that *fled from persecution* did not flee from their work.

2. They pressed forward in their work, finding that the *good pleasure of the Lord prospered in their hands*.

3. They *preached the word to none but to the Jews only* who were dispersed in all those parts, and had synagogues of their own, in which they met with them by themselves, and preached to them. They did not yet understand that the Gentiles

were to be fellow-heirs, and of the same body; but left the Gentiles either to turn Jews, and so come into the church, or else remain as they were.

4. They particularly applied themselves to the Hellenist Jews, here called the Grecians, that were at Antioch. To them they preached the Lord Jesus. This was the constant subject of their preaching.

5. They had wonderful success in their preaching, *v.* 21. (1) Their preaching was accompanied with a divine power: *The hand of the Lord was with them.* (2) Abundance of good was done: *A great number believed, and turned unto the Lord—* many more than could have been expected, considering the outward disadvantages they laboured under: some of all sorts of people were wrought upon, and brought into obedience to Christ. Observe, What the change was. [1] They believed; they were convinced of the truth of the gospel, and subscribed to the record God had given in it concerning his Son. [2] The effect and evidence of this was that they *turned unto the Lord*. They turned to the Lord Jesus, and he became all in all with them. This was the work of conversion wrought upon them, and it must be wrought upon every one of us.

II. The good work thus begun at Antioch was carried on to great perfection; and the church, thus founded, grew to be a flourishing one, by the ministry of Barnabas and Saul, who built upon the foundation which the other preachers had laid, and *entered into their labours*, John iv. 37, 38.

1. The church at Jerusalem sent

Barnabas thither, to nurse this new-born church, and to strengthen the hands both of preachers and people, and put a reputation upon the cause of Christ there.

2. Barnabas went to fetch Saul, to join with him in the work of the gospel at Antioch. The last news we heard of him was that, when his life was sought at Jerusalem, he was sent away to Tarsus, the city where he was born, and, it should seem, he continued there ever since, doing good, no doubt. But now Barnabas takes a journey to Tarsus on purpose to see what had become of him, to tell him what a door of opportunity was opened at Antioch, and to desire him to come and spend some time with him there, *vv.* 25, 26. And here also it appears that Barnabas was a good sort of a man in two things: (1) That he would take so much pains to bring an active useful man out of obscurity. (2) That he would bring in Saul at Antioch, who, being a *chief speaker* (*ch.* xiv. 12), and probably a more popular preacher, would be likely to eclipse him there, by outshining him; but Barnabas is very willing to be eclipsed when it is for the public service.

3. We are here further told,

(1) What service was now done to the church at Antioch. Paul and Barnabas continued there a whole year, presiding in their religious assemblies, and preaching the gospel, *v.* 26.

(2) What honour was now put upon the church *at Antioch: There the disciples were first called Christians*. Hitherto those who gave up their names to Christ were called *disciples, learners, scholars,* trained up under him, in order to their being employed by him; but henceforward they were called *Christians*. They took their denomination not from the name of his person, *Jesus,* but of his office, *Christ — anointed,* so putting their creed into their names, *that Jesus is the Christ.*

FAMINE RELIEF (*vv.* 27–30)

Now here we have,

I. A visit which some prophets made to Antioch (*v.* 27): *In these days,* during that year that Barnabas and Saul lived at Antioch, there *came prophets from Jerusalem to Antioch.*

II. A particular prediction of a famine approaching, delivered by one of these prophets, his name *Agabus*; we read of him again prophesying Paul's imprisonment, *ch.* xxi. 10, 11. Here he stood up, probably in one of their public assemblies, and prophesied, *v.* 28. Observe, 1. Whence he had his prophecy. What he said was not of himself, but *he signified it by the Spirit, the Spirit of prophecy, that there should be* a famine. 2. What the prophecy was: *There should be great dearth throughout all the world,* by unseasonable weather, that corn should be scarce and dear, so that many of the poor should perish for want of bread. This should be not in one particular country, but *through all the world,* that is, all the Roman empire, which they in their pride, like Alexander before them, called *the world.* 3. The accomplishment of it: *It came to pass in the days of Claudius Cesar*; it began in the second year of his reign, and continued to the fourth, if not longer.

Several of the Roman historians make mention of it, as does also Josephus.

III. The good use they made of this prediction. When they were told of a famine at hand, they did not do as the Egyptians, hoard up corn for themselves; but, as became Christians, laid by for charity to relieve others, which is the best preparative for our own sufferings and want. Observe,

1. What they determined—that *every man, according to his ability,* should *send relief to the brethren that dwelt in Judea, v.* 29. (1) The persons that were recommended to them as objects of charity were *the brethen that dwelt in Judea.* Though we must, as we have opportunity, *do good to all men,* yet we must have a special regard *to the household of faith,* Gal. vi. 10. No poor must be neglected, but God's poor most particularly regarded. (2) The agreement there was among the disciples about it, that *every man* should contribute, *according to his ability,* to this good work.

2. What they did—they did as they determined (*v.* 30). *Which also they did.* They not only talked of it, but they did it.

CHAPTER TWELVE

JAMES MARTYRED (*vv.* 1–4)

Herod, though originally of an Edomite family, yet seems to have been a proselyte to the Jewish religion; for Josephus says he was zealous for the Mosaic rites, a bigot for the ceremonies. He was not only (as Herod Antipas was) tetrarch of Galilee, but had also the government of Judea committed to him by Claudius the emperor, and resided most at Jerusalem, where he was at this time. Three things we are here told he did:

I. He *stretched forth his hands to vex certain of the church, v.* 1. See how he advances gradually. 1. He began with some of the members of the church, certain of them that were of less note and figure; played first at small game, but afterwards flew at the apostles themselves. 2. He began with vexing them only, or afflicting them, imprisoning them, finding them, spoiling their houses and goods, and other ways molesting them; but afterwards he proceeded to greater instances of cruelty.

II. *He killed James the brother of John with the sword, v.* 2. We are here to consider, 1. Who the martyr was: it was *James the brother of John*; so called to distinguish him from the other James the brother of Joses. This who was here crowned with martyrdom was one of the first three of Christ's disciples, one of those that were *the witnesses of his transfiguration and agony,* whereby he was prepared for martyrdom. 2. What kind of death he suffered: he was slain *with the sword,* that is, his head was *cut off with a sword,* which was looked upon by the Romans to be a more disgraceful way of being beheaded than with an axe; so Lorinus. It is strange that we have not a more full and particular account of the martyrdom of this great apostle, as we had of Stephen. But even this short mention of the thing is sufficient to let us know that the first preachers of the gospel were so well assured of the truth of it that they sealed it with their blood, and thereby have encouraged us, if at any time we are called to it, *to resist unto blood too*.

III. He imprisoned Peter, of whom he had heard most, as making the greatest figure among the apostles and whom therefore he would be proud of the honour of taking off. Notice is taken of the time when Herod laid hold on Peter. It was at the feast of the passover, when their celebrating the memorial of their typical deliverance should have led them to the acceptance of their spiritual deliverance; instead of this, they, under pretence of zeal for the law, were most violently fighting against it.

Here is an account of Peter's imprisonment (v. 4). He was *delivered to four quaternions of soldiers*, that is, to sixteen, who were to be a guard upon him, four at a time, that he should not make his escape, nor be rescued by his friends. Thus they thought they had him fast. Herod's design was, *after Easter, to bring him forth unto the people*. He would do this *after Easter, after the passover*, certainly so it ought to be read, for it is the same word that is always so rendered; and to insinuate the introducing of a gospel-feast, instead of the passover, when we have nothing in the New Testament of such a thing, is to mingle Judaism with our Christianity.

PETER RELEASED (vv. 5–19)

We have here an account of Peter's deliverance out of prison, by which the design of Herod against him was defeated, and his life preserved for further service, and a stop given to this bloody torrent. Now,

I. One thing that magnified his deliverance was that it was a signal answer to prayer (v. 5): *Peter was kept in prison* with a great deal of care, so that it was altogether impossible, either by force or by stealth, to get him out. *But prayer was made without ceasing of the church unto God for him*, for prayers and tears are the church's arms; therewith she fights, not only against her enemies, but for her friends: and to these means they have recourse. *Prayer was made without ceasing*; it was *fervent prayer*. It is the word that is used concerning Christ's praying in his agony *more earnestly*; it is *the fervent prayer of the righteous man, that* is effectual, and *availeth much*.

II. Let us observe when his deliverance came. 1. It was the very night before Herod designed to bring him forth, which made it to be so much the greater consolation to his friends and confusion to his enemies. 2. It was when he was *fast bound with two chains, between two soldiers*; so that if he offer to stir he wakes them; and, besides this, though the prison-doors, no doubt, were locked and bolted, yet, to make sure work, *the keepers before the door kept the prison*, that no one might so much as attempt to rescue him. Never could the art of man do more to secure a prisoner. 3. It was when he was *sleeping between the soldiers*, fast asleep.

III. It also magnified his deliverance very much that an *angel was sent from heaven* on purpose to rescue him, which made his escape both practicable and warrantable.

1. *The angel of the Lord came upon him;—stood over him.* He seemed as one abandoned by men, yet not forgotten of his God; *the Lord thinketh upon him.*

2. *A light shone in the prison.* Though it is a dark place, and in the night, Peter shall see his way clear.

3. The angel awoke Peter, by giving him *a blow on his side,* a gentle touch. The language of this stroke was, *Arise up quickly;* not as if the angel feared coming short by his delay, but Peter must not be indulged in it.

4. *His chains fell off from his hands.* It seems they had handcuffed him, to make him sure, but *God loosed his bands.*

5. He was ordered to dress himself immediately, and follow the angel; and he did so, *vv.* 8, 9. Those who are delivered out of a spiritual imprisonment must follow their deliverer, as Israel when they went out of the house of bondage did; they *went out, not knowing whither they went,* but whom they followed.

6. He was led safely by the angel out of danger, *v.* 10. But still there is an iron gate, after all, that will stop them. However, up to that gate they march, and, like the Red Sea before Israel, it *opened to them.*

7. When this was done, *the angel departed from him,* and left him to himself.

IV. Having seen how his deliverance was magnified, we are next to see how it was manifested both to himself and others, and how, being made great, it was made known. We are here told,

1. How Peter came to himself, and so came himself to the knowledge of it, *v.* 11. So many strange and surprising things coming together upon a man just awoke out of sleep put him for the present into some confusion; so that he knew not where he was, nor what he did, nor whether it was fancy or fact; but at length Peter *came to himself,* was thoroughly awake, and found that it was not a dream, but a real thing.

2. How Peter came to his friends, and brought the knowledge of it to them.

(1) He *considered the thing* (*v.* 12), considered how imminent his danger was, how great his deliverance; and now what has he to do?

(2) He went directly to a friend's house, which, it is likely, lay near to the place where he was; it was the house of Mary, a sister of Barnabas, and mother of John Mark, whose house, it should seem, was frequently made use of for the private meeting of the disciples.

(3) There he found *many* that were *gathered together praying,* at the dead time of the night, praying for Peter, who was the next day to come upon his trial, that God would find out some way or other for his deliverance.

(4) He knocked at the gate, and had much ado to get them to let him in (*vv.* 13–16). Now when he knocked there, [1] A *damsel came to hearken*; not to open the door till she knew who was there, a friend or a foe, and what their business was, fearing informers. [2] She knew Peter's voice, having

often heard him pray, and preach, and discourse, with a great deal of pleasure. But, instead of letting him in immediately out of the cold, *she opened not the gate for gladness.* [3] She ran in, and probably went up to an upper room where they were together, and told them that Peter was certainly at the gate, though she had not courage enough to open the gate, for fear she should be deceived, and it should be the enemy. But, when she spoke of Peter's being there, they said, *"Thou art mad*; it is impossible it should be he, for he is in prison."* Sometimes that which we most earnestly wish for we are most backward to believe, because we are afraid of imposing upon ourselves, as the disciples, who, when Christ had risen, *believed not for joy.* However, she stood to it that it was he. Then said they, *It is his angel, v.* 15. *First,* "It is a *messenger* from him, that makes use of his name;" so some take it. *Secondly,* "It is his *guardian angel,* or some other angel that has assumed his shape and voice, and stands at the gate in his resemblance."

(5) At length they let him in (*v.* 16). The iron gate which opposed his enlargement opened of itself, without so much as once knocking at it; but the door of his friend's house that was to welcome him does not open of its own accord, but must be knocked at, long knocked at; lest Peter should be puffed up by the honours which the angel did him, he meets with this mortification, by a seeming slight which his friends put upon him. But, *when they saw him, they were astonished,* were filled with wonder

and joy in him, as much as they were but just now with sorrow and fear concerning him.

(6) Peter gave them an account of his deliverance. *He declared unto them how the Lord Jesus had* by an angel *brought him out of prison*; and it is very likely, having found them praying for his deliverance, he did not part with them till he and they had together solemnly given thanks to God for his enlargement.

(7) Peter sent the account to others of his friends. He would have James and his company to know of his deliverance, not only that they might be eased of their pain and delivered from their fears concerning Peter, but that they might return thanks to God with him and for him.

(8) Peter had nothing more to do for the present than to shift for his own safety, which he did accordingly: He *departed, and went into another place more obscure,* and therefore more safe.

V. Having seen the triumph of Peter's friends in his deliverance, let us next observe the confusion of his enemies thereupon, which was so much the greater because people's expectation was so much raised of the putting of him to death. Herod himself retired upon it: *He went down from Judea to Cesarea, and there abode.* He was vexed to the heart, as a lion disappointed of his prey; and the more because he had so much raised the *expectation of the people of the Jews* concerning Peter, had told them how he would very shortly gratify them with the sight of Peter's head in a charger, which would oblige them as much as John Baptist's did Herodias; it made him ashamed to be robbed of this boasting, and to see himself, notwithstanding his confidence, disabled to make his words good. This is such a mortification to his proud spirit that he cannot bear to stay in Judea, but away he goes to Cesarea.

DEATH OF HEROD
(vv. 20–25)

In these verses we have,

I. The death of Herod. God reckoned with him, not only for his putting James to death, but for his design and endeavour to put Peter to death; for sinners will be called to an account, not only for the wickedness of their deeds, but for the wickedness of their endeavours (Ps. xxviii. 4), for the mischief they have done and the mischief they would have done. It was but a little while that Herod lived after this. Some sinners God makes quick work with.

II. The progress of the gospel after this. 1. *The word of God grew and multiplied*, as seed sown, which comes up with a great increase, thirty, sixty, a hundred fold; wherever the gospel was preached, multitudes embraced it, and were added to the church by it, *v.* 24. After the death of James, the word of God grew; for the church, the more it was afflicted, the more it multiplied, like Israel in Egypt. 2. Barnabas and Saul returned to Antioch as soon as they had despatched the business they were sent upon: *When they had fulfilled their ministry*, had paid in their money to the proper persons, and taken care about the due distribution of

it to those for whom it was collected, they *returned from Jerusalem*. Barnabas and Saul, when they went to *Antioch, took with them John, whose surname was Mark*, at whose mother's house they had that meeting for prayer which we read of *v.* 12. She was sister to Barnabas. It is probable that Barnabas lodged there, and perhaps Paul with him, while they were at Jerusalem, and it was that that occasioned the meeting there at that time (for wherever Paul was he would have some good work doing), and their intimacy in that family while they were at Jerusalem occasioned their taking a son of that family with them when they returned, to be trained up under them, and employed by them, in the service of the gospel.

CHAPTER THIRTEEN.
PAUL AND BARNABAS COMMISSIONED (vv. 1–3)

We have here a divine warrant and commission to Barnabas and Saul to go and preach the gospel among the Gentiles, and their ordination to that service by the imposition of hands, with fasting and prayer.

I. Here is an account of the present state of the church at Antioch, which was planted *ch.* xi. 20.

1. How well furnished it was with good ministers; there were there *certain prophets and teachers* (*v.* 1), men that were eminent for gifts, graces, and usefulness. Barnabas is first named, probably because he was the eldest, and Saul last, probably because he was the youngest; but afterwards the last became first,

and Saul more eminent in the church.

2. How well employed they were (*v.* 2): *They ministered to the Lord, and fasted.* Observe, (1) Diligent faithful teachers do truly minister unto the Lord. Those that instruct Christians serve Christ; they really do him honour, and carry on the interest of his kingdom. (2) Ministering to the Lord, in one way or other, ought to be the stated business of churches and their teachers. What have we to do as Christians and ministers but to *serve the Lord Christ?* Col. iii. 24; Rom. xiv. 18. (3) Religious *fasting* is of use in our ministering to the Lord, both as a sign of our humiliation and a means of our mortification. Though it was not so much practised by the disciples of Christ, *while the bridegroom was with them*, as it was by the disciples of John and of the Pharisees; yet, after the bridegroom was taken away, they abounded in it, as those that had well learned to deny themselves and to endure hardness.

II. The orders given by the Holy Ghost for the setting apart of Barnabas and Saul, while they were engaged in public exercises, the ministers of the several congregations in the city joining in one solemn fast or day of prayer: The *Holy Ghost said*, either by a voice from heaven, or by a strong impulse on the minds of those of them that were prophets, *Separate me Barnabas and Saul for the work whereunto I have called them.* He does not specify the work, but refers to a former call of which they themselves knew the meaning, whether others did or no: as for

Saul, he was particularly told that he must *bear Christ's name to the Gentiles* (*ch.* ix. 15), that *he must be sent to the Gentiles* (*ch.* xxii. 21); the matter was settled between them at Jerusalem before this, that as Peter, James, and John laid out themselves among those of the circumcision, so Paul and Barnabas should *go to the heathen*, Gal. ii. 7–9. Barnabas, it is likely, knew himself designed for this service as well as Paul. Yet they would not thrust themselves into this harvest, though it appeared plenteous, till they received their orders from the Lord of the harvest. The orders were, *Separate me Barnabas and Saul.* Observe here, 1. Christ by his Spirit has the nomination of his ministers; for it is by the Spirit of Christ that they are qualified in some measure for his services, inclined to it, and taken off from other cares inconsistent with it. 2. Christ's ministers are separated to him and to the Holy Ghost: *Separate them to me*; they are to be employed in Christ's work and under the Spirit's guidance, to the glory of God the Father. 3. All that are separated to Christ as his ministers are separated to work; Christ keeps no servants to be idle. 4. The work of Christ's ministers, to which they are to be separated, is work that is already settled, and that which all Christ's ministers hitherto have been called to.

III. Their ordination, pursuant to these orders: not to the ministry in general (Barnabas and Saul had both of them been ministers long before this), but to a particular service in the ministry; which had something peculiar in it, and which required a fresh commission, which commission God saw fit at this time to transmit by the hands of *these prophets and teachers*, for the giving of this direction to the church, that teachers should ordain teachers (for prophets we are not now any longer to expect), and that those who have the dispensing of the oracles of Christ committed to them should, for the benefit of posterity, *commit the same to faithful men, who shall be able also to teach others*, 2 Tim. ii. 2. They implored a blessing upon them in their present undertaking, begged that God would be with them, and give them success; and, in order to do this, that *they might be filled with the Holy Ghost* in their work.

ELYMAS THE SORCERER
(*vv.* 4–13)

In these verses we have,

I. A general account of the coming of Barnabas and Saul to the famous island of Cyprus. Observe, 1. Their being sent forth by the Holy Ghost was the great thing that encouraged them in this undertaking, *v.* 4. 2. They came to Seleucia, the sea-port town opposite to Cyprus, thence crossed the sea to Cyprus, and in that island the first city they came to was Salamis, a city on the east side of the island (*v.* 5); and, when they had sown good seed there, *thence they* went onward *through the isle* (*v.* 6) till they came to Paphos, which lay on the western coast. 3. *They preached the word of God* wherever they came, *in the synagogues of the Jews*; so far were they from excluding them that they gave them the preference, and so left those among them who believed not inexcusable. 4. *They had John for their minister*; not their servant in common things, but their assistant in the things of God.

II. A particular account of their encounter with *Elymas the sorcerer*, whom they met with at Paphos, where the governor resided.

1. There the *deputy*, a Gentile, *Sergius Paulus* by name, encouraged the apostles, and was willing to hear their message.

2. There Elymas, a Jew, a *sorcerer*, opposed them, and did all he could to obstruct their progress. This justified the apostles in *turning to the Gentiles*, that this Jew was so malignant against them.

(1) This Elymas was a pretender *to the gift of prophecy, a sorcerer, a false-prophet*—one that would be taken for a divine, because he was skilled in the arts of divination.

(2) He was hanging on at court, *was with the deputy* of the country.

(3) He made it his business to withstand Barnabas and Saul, as the magicians of Egypt, in Pharaoh's court, *withstood* Moses and Aaron, 2 Tim. iii. 8. He set up himself to be a messenger from heaven, and denied that they were. And *thus he sought to turn away the deputy from the faith* (*v.* 8), to keep him from receiving the gospel, which he saw him inclined to do.

(4) Saul (who is here for the first time called Paul) fell upon him for this with a holy indignation. Now of Paul it is said,

[1] That he was *filled with the Holy Ghost* upon this occasion, filled with a holy zeal against a professed enemy of Christ, which

was one of the graces of the Holy Ghost. What Paul said did not come from any personal resentment, but from the strong impressions which the Holy Ghost made upon his spirit.

[2] He *set his eyes upon him*, to face him down, and to show a holy boldness, in opposition to his wicked impudence. He set his eyes upon him, as an indication that the eye of the heart-searching God was upon him, and saw through and through him.

[3] He gave him his true character, not in passion, but by the Holy Ghost, who knows men better than they know themselves, *v.* 10. He describes him to be, *First*, An agent for hell. *Secondly*, An adversary to heaven.

[4] He charged upon him his present crime, and expostulated with him upon it. Note, *First*, The ways of the Lord are right: they are all so, they are perfectly so. The ways of the Lord Jesus are right, the only right ways to heaven and happiness. *Secondly*, There are those who pervert these right ways, who not only wander out of these ways themselves but mislead others, and suggest to them unjust prejudices against these ways. *Thirdly*, Those who pervert the right ways of the Lord are commonly so hardened in it that, though the equity of those ways be set before them by the most powerful and commanding evidence, yet they will not cease to do it.

[5] He denounced the judgment of God upon him, in a present blindness (*v.* 11). This was designed both for the proof of his crime, as it was a miracle wrought to confirm

the right ways of the Lord, and consequently to show the wickedness of him who would not cease to pervert them, as also for the punishment of his crime.

[6] This judgment was immediately executed. Let not him any more pretend to be a guide to the deputy's conscience who is himself struck blind.

3. Notwithstanding all the endeavours of Elymas *to turn away the deputy from the faith*, he was brought to believe, and this miracle, wrought upon the magician himself, contributed to it.

III. Their departure from the island of Cyprus. When they had done what they had to do, 1. They quitted the country, and *went to Perga*. 2. Then John *Mark quitted them, and returned to Jerusalem*, without the consent of Paul and Barnabas; either he did not like the work, or he wanted to go and see his mother. It was his fault, and we shall hear of it again.

PAUL PREACHES (*vv.* 14–41)

The next place we find them in is another Antioch, said to be in Pisidia, to distinguish it from that Antioch in Syria from which they were sent out. Pisidia was a province of the Lesser Asia, bordering upon Pamphylia; this Antioch, it is likely, was the metropolis of it. Abundance of Jews lived there, and to them *the gospel was to be first preached*; and Paul's sermon to them is what we have in these verses, which, it is likely, is the substance of what was preached by the apostles generally to the Jews in all places. We have here,

I. The appearance which Paul

and Barnabas made in a religious assembly of the Jews at Antioch, *v*. 14.

II. The invitation given them to preach. 1. The usual service of the synagogue was performed (*v*. 15). 2. When that was done, they were asked by *the rulers of the synagogue* to give them a sermon (*v*. 15). It is likely Paul did *often preach in the synagogue*, when he was not thus invited to it by the rulers of the synagogues; for he often preached *with much contention*, 1 Thess. ii. 2. But these were more noble, more generous, than the rulers of the synagogues generally were.

III. The sermon Paul preached in the synagogue of the Jews, at the invitation of the rulers of the synagogue. Every thing is touched in this sermon that might be proper either to convince the judgment or insinuate into the affections of the Jews, to prevail with them to receive and embrace Christ as the promised Messiah.

1. He owns them to be God's favourite people, whom he had taken into special relation to himself, and for whom he had done great things.

(1) That *the God of the whole earth* was, in a particular manner, *the God of this people Israel*.

(2) That he had *chosen their fathers* to be his friends: Abraham was called *the friend of God*.

(3) That he had *exalted that people*, and put a great deal of honour upon them, had advanced them into a people, and raised them from nothing, *when they dwelt as strangers in the land of Egypt*, and had nothing in them to recommend them to the divine favour. They

ought to remember this, and to infer hence that God was no debtor to them.

(4) That he had *with a high hand brought them out of Egypt*, where they were not only strangers, but captives, had delivered them at the expense of a great many miracles, both of mercy to them and judgment on their oppressors.

(5) *That he had suffered their manners forty years in the wilderness*, v. 18. Let not the Jews insist too much upon the privileges of their peculiarity, for they have forfeited them a thousand times.

(6) That he had put them in possession of the land of Canaan (*v*. 19). This was a signal favour of God to them, and he owns that hereby a great honour was put upon them, from which he would not in the least derogate.

(7) That he had raised up men, inspired from heaven, to deliver them out of the hands of those that invaded their rights, and oppressed them after their settlement in Canaan, *vv*. 20, 21. At last, he made David their king, *v*, 22. *When God had removed Saul*, for his mal-administration, *he raised up unto them David to be their king*, and made *a covenant of royalty with him, and with his seed*.

2. He gives them a full account of our Lord Jesus, passing from David to the Son of David, and shows that this Jesus is his promised Seed (*v*. 23): *Of this man's seed*, from that *root of Jesse*, from that *man after God's own heart, hath God, according to his promise, raised unto Israel a Saviour—Jesus*, who carries salvation in his name.

(1) How welcome should the

preaching of the gospel of Christ be to the Jews, and how should they embrace it, as *well worthy of all acceptation.* Now,

(2) Concerning this Jesus, he tells them,

[1] That John the Baptist was his harbinger and forerunner, that great man whom all acknowledged to be a prophet.

[2] That the rulers and people of the Jews, who should have welcomed him, and been his willing, forward, faithful subjects, were his persecutors and murderers. When the apostles preach Christ as *the Saviour*, they are so far from concealing his ignominious death, and drawing a veil over it, that they always *preach Christ crucified*, yea, and (though this added much to the reproach of his sufferings) crucified by his own people, by *those that dwelt in Jerusalem*, the holy city—the royal city, and *their rulers, v.* 27. So Paul saith here, *Because they knew not the voice of the prophets*, therefore *they have fulfilled them*, which implies that if they had understood them they would not have fulfilled them.

[3] That he *rose again from the dead*, and saw no corruption. This was the great truth that was to be preached; for it is the main pillar, by which the whole fabric of the gospel is supported, and therefore he insists largely upon this, and shows,

First, That he rose by consent. When he was imprisoned in the grave for our debt, he did not break prison, but had a fair and legal discharge from the arrest he was under (*v.* 30): *God raised him from the dead*. His enemies laid

him in a sepulchre, with design he should always lay there; but God said, *No*; and it was soon seen whose purpose should stand, his or theirs.

Secondly, That there was sufficient proof of his having risen (*v.* 31): *He was seen many days*, by those that were most intimately acquainted with him; for they *came up with him from Galilee to Jerusalem*, were his constant attendants, and *they are his witnesses unto the people.*

Thirdly, That the resurrection of Christ was the performance of the promise made to the patriarchs; it was not only true news, but good news (*vv.* 32, 33).

Fourthly, That the resurrection of Christ was the great proof of his being the Son of God, and confirms what was written in the second Psalm, *Thou art my Son, this day have I begotten thee.* The reason why it was impossible he should be held by the bands of death was because he was the Son of God, and consequently had *life in himself*, which he could not lay down but with a design to resume it. When his eternal generation is spoken of, it is not improper to say, *This day have I begotten thee*; for *from everlasting to everlasting* is with God as it were one and the same eternal day. Yet it may also be accommodated to his resurrection, in a subordinate sense, "This day have I made it to appear that I have begotten thee, and this day have I begotten all that are given to thee;" for it is said (1 Pet. i. 3) that *the God and Father of our Lord Jesus Christ*, as our God and Father, *hath begotten us again to a lively hope, by the resurrection of Jesus Christ from the dead.*

Fifthly, That his being raised the third day, so as not to see corruption, and to a heavenly life, so as no more to return to corruption, that is, to the state of the dead, as others did who were raised to life, further confirms his being the Messiah promised.

(*a*) It could not be accomplished in David himself (*v.* 36), for *David, after he had served his own generation, by the will of God,* who raised him up to be what he was, *fell asleep, and was laid to his fathers, and saw corruption.* Here we have a short account of the life, death, and burial, of the patriarch David, and his continuance under the power of death. But,

(*b*) It was accomplished in the Lord Jesus (*v.* 37): *He whom God raised again saw no corruption;* for it was in him that the sure mercies were to be reserved for us. He rose the third day, and therefore did not see corruption then; and he rose to die no more, and therefore never did. Of him therefore the promise must be understood, and no other.

Having given them this account of the Lord Jesus, he comes to make application of it.

(*a*) In the midst of his discourse, to engage their attention, he had told his hearers that they were concerned in all this (*v.* 26): *"To you is the word of this salvation sent,* to you first. If you by your unbelief make it a word of rejection to you, you may thank yourselves; but it is sent to you for a word of salvation; if it be not so, it is your own fault."

(*b*) In the close of his discourse he applies what he had said concerning Christ to his hearers. He had told them a long story concerning *this Jesus;* now they would be ready to ask, What is all this to us? And he tells them plainly what it is to them.

[*a*] It will be their unspeakable advantage if they embrace Jesus Christ, and believe this word of salvation. It will relieve them where their greatest danger lies; and that is from the guilt of their sins. Note, 1. The great concern of sinners is to be justified, to be acquitted from guilt and accepted as righteous in God's sight. 2. Those who are truly justified are acquitted from all their guilt; for if any be left charged upon the sinner he is undone. 3. It was impossible for a sinner to be justified by the law of Moses. Not by his moral law, for we have all broken it, and are transgressing it daily, so that instead of justifying us it condemns us. Not by his remedial law, for it was not possible that the *blood of bulls and goats should take away sin,* should satisfy God's offended justice, or pacify the sinner's wounded conscience. It was but a ritual and typical institution. See Heb. ix. 9; x. 1, 4. 4. By Jesus Christ we obtain a complete justification; for by him a complete atonement was made for sin. 5. All that believe in Christ, that rely upon him and give up themselves to be ruled by him, are justified by him, and none but they. 6. What the law *could not do* for us, *in that it was weak,* that the gospel of Christ does; and therefore it was folly, out of a jealousy for the law of Moses and the honour of that institution, to con-

ceive a jealousy of the gospel of Christ and the designs of that more perfect institution.

[*b*] It is at their utmost peril if they reject the gospel of Christ, and turn their backs upon the offer now made them (*vv.* 40, 41). Now the prophecy referred to we have Hab. i. 5, where the destruction of the Jewish nation by the Chaldeans is foretold as an incredible unparalleled destruction; and this is here applied to the destruction that was coming upon that nation by the Romans, for their rejecting the gospel of Christ. Those that will not wonder and be saved shall wonder and perish.

GENTILES CONVERTED
(*vv.* 42–52)

The design of this story being to vindicate the apostles, especially Paul (as he doth himself at large, Rom. xi.), from the reflections of the Jews upon him for preaching the gospel to the Gentiles, it is here observed that he proceeded therein with all the caution imaginable, and upon due consideration, of which we have here an instance.

I. There were some of the Jews that were so incensed against the preaching of the gospel, not to the Gentiles, but to themselves, that they would not bear to hear it, but *went out of the synagogue* while Paul was preaching (*v.* 42), in contempt of him and his doctrine, and to the disturbance of the congregation.

II. The Gentiles were as willing to hear the gospel as those rude and ill-conditioned Jews were to get out of the hearing of it. They begged, 1. That the same offer might be made to them that was made to the Jews. Paul in this sermon had brought the word of salvation to the Jews and proselytes, but had taken no notice of the Gentiles; and therefore they begged that forgiveness of sins through Christ might be preached to them, as it was to the Jews. The Jews' leavings, nay, loathings, were their longings. This justifies Paul in his preaching to them, that he was invited to it, as Peter was sent for to Cornelius.

III. There were some, nay, there were many, both of Jews and proselytes, that were wrought upon by the preaching of the gospel. 1. They submitted to the grace of God, and were admitted to the benefit and comfort of it, which is implied in their being exhorted to continue in it. 2. They were exhorted and encouraged to persevere herein: *Paul and Barnabas, speaking to them* with all the freedom and friendship imaginable, *persuaded them to continue in the grace of God*, to hold fast that which they had received, to continue in their belief of the gospel of grace, their dependence upon the Spirit of grace, and their attendance upon the means of grace.

IV. There was a cheerful attendance upon the preaching of the gospel the *next sabbath day* (*v.* 44): *Almost the whole city* (the generality of whom were Gentiles) *came together to hear the word of God*.

V. The Jews were enraged at this; and not only would not receive the gospel themselves, but were filled with indignation at those that crowded after it (*v.* 45). 1. They grudged the interest the apostles had in the people, were vexed to see the synagogue so full when they were going to preach. 2. They opposed the doctrine the apostles preached. They did it with the utmost spite and rage imaginable: they persisted in their contradiction, and nothing would silence them, they contradicted for contradiction-sake, and denied that which was most evident; and, when they could find no colour of objection, they broke out into ill language against Christ and his gospel, blaspheming him and it.

VI. The apostles hereupon solemnly and openly declare themselves discharged from their obligations to the Jews, and at liberty to bring the word of salvation to the Gentiles, even by the tacit consent of the Jews themselves. 1. They own that the Jews were entitled to the first offer: "*It was necessary that the word of God should first have been spoken to you*, to whom the promise was made, to you *of the lost sheep of the house of Israel*, to whom Christ reckoned himself first sent." 2. They charge them with the refusal of it: *You put it from you*; you will not accept of it; nay, you will not so much as bear the offer of it, but take it as an affront to you." 3. Upon this they ground their preaching the gospel to the uncircumcised: "Since you will not accept eternal life as it is offered, our way is plain, *Lo, we turn to the Gentiles*." 4. They justify themselves in this by a divine warrant (*v.* 47): "*For so hath the Lord commanded us*; the Lord Jesus gave us directions to witness to him in Jerusalem and Judea first, and after that *to the*

utmost part of the earth, to preach the gospel to *every creature*, to *disciple all nations*."

VII. The Gentiles cheerfully embraced that which the Jews scornfully rejected, *vv.* 48, 49. The Jews, the natural branches, were broken off, and the Gentiles, that were branches of the wild olive, were thereupon grafted in, *vv.* 17, 19. Now here we are told how the Gentiles welcomed this happy turn in their favour.

1. They took the comfort of it: *When they heard this they were glad*. It was good news to them that they might have admission into covenant and communion with God by a clearer, nearer, and better way than submitting to the ceremonial law, and being proselyted to the Jewish religion.

2. They gave God the praise of it: *They glorified the word of the Lord*; that is, Christ (so some), the essential Word; they entertained a profound veneration for him, and expressed the high thoughts they had of him. Or, rather, *the gospel*; the more they knew of it, the more they admired it.

3. Many of them became, not only professors of the Christian faith, but sincerely obedient to the faith: *As many as were ordained to eternal life believed*. (1) Those believed to whom God gave grace to believe, whom by a secret and mighty operation he brought into subjection to the gospel of Christ, and made willing in the day of his power. Those came to Christ whom the Father drew, and to whom the Spirit made the gospel call effectual. (2) God gave this grace to believe to all those among them who were

ordained to eternal life (for *whom he had predestinated, them he also called*, Rom. viii. 30); or, *as many as were disposed to eternal life*, as many as had a concern about their eternal state, and aimed to make sure of eternal life, believed in Christ, in whom God hath treasured up that life (1 John v. 11), and who is the only way to it; and it was the grace of God that wrought it in them.

4. When they believed they did what they could to spread the knowledge of Christ and his gospel among their neighbours (*v.* 49).

VIII. Paul and Barnabas, having sown the seeds of a Christian church there, quitted the place, and went to do the like elsewhere. Now here we are told,

1. How *the unbelieving Jews* expelled the apostles out of that country. They first turned their back upon them, and then *lifted up the heel against them* (*v.* 50). When *they could not resist the wisdom and spirit wherewith they spoke*, they had recourse to these brutish methods, the last refuge of an obstinate infidelity. Observe, (1) What method the Jews took to give them trouble: *They stirred up the devout and honourable women* against them. These, according to the genius of their sex, were zealous in their way, and bigoted; and it was easy, by false stories and misrepresentations, to incense them against the gospel of Christ, as if it had been destructive of all religion, of which really it is perfective. (2) How far they carried it, so far that *they expelled them out of their coasts*.

2. How the apostles abandoned and rejected the unbelieving Jews (*v.* 51): *They shook off the dust of their feet against them*. Hereby, (1) They declared that they would have no more to do with them, would take nothing that was theirs; for *they sought not theirs, but them*. (2) They expressed their detestation of their infidelity, and that, though they were Jews by birth, yet, having rejected the gospel of Christ, they were in their eyes no better than heathen and profane. Thus they left a testimony behind them that they had had a fair offer made them of the grace of the gospel, which shall be proved against them in the day of judgment.

3. What frame they left the new converts in *at Antioch* (*v.* 52): *The disciples*, when they saw with what courage and cheerfulness Paul and Barnabas not only bore the indignities that were done them, but went on with their work notwithstanding, they were in like manner inspired.

CHAPTER FOURTEEN
AT ICONIUM (*vv.* 1–7)

In these verses we have,

I. The preaching of the gospel in Iconium, whither the apostles were forced to retire from Antioch.

II. The success of their preaching there: *They so spoke that a great multitude*, some hundreds perhaps, if not thousands, *both of the Jews and also of the Greeks*, that is the Gentiles, *believed*.

III. The opposition that their preaching met with there, and the trouble that was created them; lest they should be puffed up with the multitude of their converts, there was given them this thorn in the flesh. 1. Unbelieving Jews were the first spring of their trouble here, as elsewhere (*v.* 2): they *stirred up the Gentiles*. 2. Disaffected Gentiles, irritated by the unbelieving Jews, were likely to be the instruments of their trouble.

IV. Their continuance in their work there, notwithstanding this opposition, and God's owning them in it *v.* 3. We have here, 1. The apostles working for Christ, faithfully and diligently, according to the trust committed to them. The more they perceived the spite and rancour of the town against the new converts, the more they were animated to go on in their work, and the more needful they saw it to continue among them, *to confirm them in the faith, and to comfort them. They spoke boldly*, and were not afraid of giving offence to the unbelieving Jews. 2. Christ working with the apostles, according to his promise, *Lo, I am with you always*. When they went on in his name and strength, he failed not to give testimony to the word of his grace.

V. The division which this occasioned in the city (*v.* 4): *The multitude of the city was divided* into two parties, and both active and vigorous. Among the rulers and persons of rank, and among the common people, there were some that held with the unbelieving Jews, and others that held with the apostles. Barnabas is here reckoned an apostle, though not one of the twelve, nor called in the extraordinary manner that Paul was, because set apart by special designation of *the Holy Ghost to the service of the Gentiles*.

VI. The attempt made upon the apostles by their enemies. Their evil affection against them broke out at length into violent outrages, *v.* 5. Observe, 1. Who the plotters were: *Both the Gentiles and the Jews, with their rulers*. If the church's enemies can thus unite for its destruction, shall not its friends, laying aside all personal feuds, unite for its preservation? 2. What the plot was. Having now got *the rulers* on their side, they doubted not but to carry their point, and their design was *to use the apostles despitefully*, to expose them to disgrace, and then *to stone them*, to put them to death; and thus they hoped to sink their cause.

VII. The deliverance of the apostles out of the hands of those *wicked and unreasonable men, vv.* 6, 7. They got away to *Lystra and Derbe*; and there, 1. They found safety. 2. They found work, and this was what they went for. In times of persecution ministers may see cause to quit the spot, when yet they do not quit the work.

LAME MAN HEALED
(*vv.* 8–18)

In these verses we have.

I. A miraculous cure wrought by Paul at Lystra upon a cripple that had been lame from his birth, such a one as was miraculously cured by Peter and John, *ch.* iii. 2. That introduced the gospel among the Jews, this among the Gentiles; both that and this were designed to represent the impotency of all the children of men in spiritual things: they are lame from their birth, till the grace of God puts strength into them; for it was when we were yet *without strength* that *Christ died for the ungodly*, Rom. v. 6.

II. The impression which this cure made upon the people: they were amazed at it, had never seen nor heard the like, and fell into an ecstacy of wonder. We find here, 1. The people take them for gods (*v.* 11): *They lifted up their voices* with an air of triumph, saying in their own language (for it was the common people that said it), *in the speech of Lycaonia*, which was a dialect of the Greek, *The gods are come down to us in the likeness of men.* They carried this notion so far here that they pretended to tell which of their gods they were, according to the ideas their poets had given them of the gods (*v.* 12): *They called Barnabas Jupiter*; for, if they will have him to be a god, it is as easy to make him the prince of their gods as not. It is probable that he was the senior, and the more portly comely man, that had something of majesty in his countenance. And *Paul they called Mercury*, who was the messenger of the gods, that was sent on their errands; for Paul, though he had not the appearance that Barnabas had, was *the chief speaker*, and had a greater command of language, and perhaps appeared to have something mercurial in his temper and genius. 2. The priest thereupon prepares *to do sacrifice to them, v.* 13. They *brought oxen*, to be sacrificed *to them, and garlands*, with which to crown the sacrifices. These garlands were made up of flowers and ribbons; and they gilded the horns of the oxen they sacrificed.

III. Paul and Barnabas protest against this undue respect paid them, and with much ado prevent it. Observe,

1. The holy indignation which Paul and Barnabas conceived at this: *When they heard this, they rent their clothes.* We do not find that they rent their clothes when the people vilified them, and spoke of stoning them; they could bear this without disturbance: but when they deified them, and spoke of worshipping them, they could not bear it, but rent their clothes, as being more concerned for God's honour than their own.

2. The pains they took to prevent it.

(1) *They ran in among the people,*as soon as they heard of it, and would not so much as stay awhile to see what the people would do. Their running in, like servants, among the people, showed that they were far from looking upon themselves as gods, or taking state upon them; they did not stand still, expecting honours to be done them, but plainly declined them by thrusting themselves into the crowd.

(2) They reasoned with them, *crying out*, that all might hear, "*Sirs, why do you these things?* Why do you go about to make gods of us? It is the most absurd thing you can do; for,

[1] "Our nature will not admit it: *We also are men of like passions with you.*

[2] "Our doctrine is directly against it. Must we be added to the number of your gods whose business it is to abolish the gods you have? *We preach unto you that you should turn from these vanities unto*

the living God. If we should suffer this, we should confirm you in that which it is our business to convert you from." See here what they preached to the Gentiles.

First, That the gods which they and their fathers worshipped, and all the ceremonies of their worship of them, were *vanities*, idle things, unreasonable, unprofitable, which no rational account could be given of, nor any real advantage gained from.

Secondly, That the God to whom they would have them *turn* is *the living God*. They had hitherto worshipped dead images, that were utterly unable to help them (Isa. lxiv. 9), or (as they now attempted) dying men, that would soon be disabled to help them; but now they are persuaded to worship a living God, who has life in himself, and life for us, and lives for evermore.

Thirdly, That this God is the creator of the world, the fountain of all being and power.

Fourthly, That the world owed it to his patience that he had not destroyed them long ere this for their idolatry (v. 16). Note, 1. God's patience with us hitherto should *lead us to repentance*, and not encourage us to presume upon the continuance of it, while we continue to provoke him. 2. Our having done ill while we were in ignorance will not bear us out in doing ill when we are better taught.

Fifthly, That even when they were not under the direction and correction of the word of God, yet they might have known, and should have known, to do better by the works of God, v. 17. For there were other *witnesses* for God, sufficient

to inform them that he and he only is to be worshipped, and that to him they owed all their services from whom they received all their comforts, and therefore that they were guilty of the highest injustice and ingratitude imaginable, in alienating them from him. God, having *not left himself without witness*, has not left us without a guide, and so has left us without excuse; for whatever is a witness for God is a witness against us, if we give that glory to any other which is due to him only.

Lastly, The success of this prohibition which the apostles gave to *the people* (v. 18). Paul and Barnabas had cured a cripple, and therefore the people deified them, instead of glorifying God for giving them such power, which should make us very cautious that we do not give that honour to another, or take it to ourselves, which is due to God only.

RETURN TO ANTIOCH
(vv. 19–28)

We have here a further account of the services and sufferings of Paul and Barnabas.

I. How Paul was stoned and left for dead, but miraculously came to himself again, vv. 19, 20. Now observe here, 1. How the people were incensed against Paul. *There came certain Jews from Antioch*, hearing, it is likely, and vexed to hear, what respect was shown to Paul and Barnabas at Lystra; and they incensed the people against them, as factious, seditious, dangerous persons, not fit to be harboured. See how restless the rage of the Jews was against the gospel of Christ;

they could not bear that it should have footing any where. 2. To what degree they were incensed by these barbarous Jews: they were irritated to such a degree that the mob rose and *stoned Paul*. 3. How he was delivered by the power of God: When he was *drawn out of the city, the disciples stood round about him* v. 20. It seems there were some here at Lystra that became disciples, that found the mean between deifying the apostles and rejecting them; and even these new converts had courage to own Paul when he was thus run down, though they had reason enough to fear that the same that stoned him would stone them for owning him. They stood round about him, as a guard against the further outrage of the people— stood about him to see whether he were alive or dead; and all of a sudden *he rose up*. Though he was not dead, yet he was ill crushed and bruised, no doubt, and fainted away; so that it was not without a miracle that he came so soon to himself, and was so well as to be able to go into the city.

II. How they went on with their work, notwithstanding the opposition they met with. All the stones they threw at Paul could not beat him off from his work.

1. They went to break up and sow fresh ground at *Derbe*. Thither the next day *Paul and Barnabas departed*, a city not far off; there they preached the gospel, there they *taught many*, v. 21. Nothing is recorded that happened at Derbe.

2. They returned, and went over their work again, watering what they had sown. Let us see what they did,

(1) They *confirmed the souls of the disciples*; that is, they inculcated that upon them which was proper to confirm them, v. 22.

(2) *They exhorted them to continue in the faith*; or, as it may be read, *they encouraged them*. They told them it was both their duty and interest to persevere; to abide in the belief of Christ's being the Son of God, and the Saviour of the world.

(3) That which they insisted most upon was *that we must through much tribulation enter into the kingdom of God*. Not only *they* must, but *we* must; it must be counted upon that all who will go to heaven must expect tribulation and persecution in their way thither. But is this the way to *confirm the souls of the disciples*, and to engage them to *continue in the faith?* One would think it would rather shock them, and make them weary. No, as the matter is fairly stated and taken entire, it will help to confirm them, and fix them for Christ.

(4) *They ordained them elders*, or presbyters, *in every church*. Now at this second visit they settled them in some order, formed them into religious societies under the guidance of a settled ministry, and settled that distinction between those that are taught in the word and those that teach. These elders were *ordained*. The qualifications of such as were proposed or proposed themselves (whether the apostles or the people put them up) were judged of by the apostles, as most fit to judge; and they, having *devoted* themselves, were solemnly set *apart* to the work of the ministry, and bound to it.

(5) *By prayer* joined with *fasting*

they *commended them to the Lord*, to the Lord Jesus, *on whom they believed*.

3. They went on preaching the gospel in other places where they had been, but, as it should seem, had not made so many converts as that now at their return they could form them into churches; therefore thither they came to pursue and carry on conversion-work.

III. How they at length came back to Antioch in Syria, whence they had been sent forth upon this expedition. From Attalia they came by sea to Antioch, *v.* 26. And we are here told,

1. Why they came thither: because *thence they had been recommended to the grace of God*. The brethren having recommended them to the grace of God, for the work *which they fulfilled*, now that they had fulfilled it they thought they owed them an account of it, that they might help them by their praises, as they had been helped by their prayers.

2. What account they gave them of their work (*v.* 27). When they had called them together, they gave them an account of two things: (1) Of the tokens they had had of the divine presence with them in their labours: *They rehearsed all that God had done with them.* They did not tell what *they* had done (this would have savoured of vainglory), but what God had done with them and by them. (2) Of the fruit of their labours among the heathen. They told how *God had opened the door of faith unto the Gentiles*; had not only ordered them to be invited to the gospel feast, but had inclined the hearts of many of them to accept the invitation. Thus the gospel was spread, and it shone more and more, and none was able to shut this door which God had opened; not all the powers of hell and earth.

3. How they disposed of themselves for the present: *There they abode a long time with the disciples* (*v.* 28), longer than perhaps at first they intended, not because they *feared their enemies*, but because they *loved their friends*, and were loth to part from them.

CHAPTER FIFTEEN

DISSENSION AT ANTIOCH
(*vv.* 1–5)

If ever there was a heaven upon earth, surely it was in the church at Antioch at this time, when there were so many excellent ministers there, and blessed Paul among them, building up that church in her most holy faith. But here we have their peace disturbed, and differences arising. Here is,

I. A new doctrine started among them, which occasioned this division, obliging the Gentile converts to submit to circumcision and the ceremonial law, *v.* 1.

1. The persons that urged this were *certain men who came down from Judea*; some think such as had been of the Pharisees (*v.* 5), or perhaps of those priests who were *obedient to the faith*, *ch.* vi. 7. They came from Judea, pretending perhaps to be sent by the apostles at Jerusalem, at least to be countenanced by them.

2. The position they laid down, the thesis they gave, was this, that except the Gentiles who turned

Christians were *circumcised after the manner of Moses*, and thereby bound themselves to all the observances of the ceremonial law, *they could not be saved*.

II. The opposition which Paul and Barnabas gave to this schismatical notion, which limited salvation to the Jews, now that Christ had opened the door of salvation to the Gentiles (*v.* 2): *They had no small dissension and disputation with them*. They would by no means yield to this doctrine, but appeared and argued publicly against it. 1. As faithful servants of Christ, they would not see his truths betrayed. They knew that Christ came to free us from the yoke of the ceremonial law, and to take down that wall of partition between Jews and Gentiles and unite them both in himself. 2. As spiritual fathers to the Gentile converts, they would not see their liberties encroached upon. They had told the Gentiles that if they believed in Jesus Christ they should be saved; and now to be told that this was not enough to save them, except they were circumcised and kept the law of Moses, would be a stumblingblock in their way; and therefore the apostles set themselves against it.

III. They determined that Paul and Barnabas, and some others of their number, should *go to Jerusalem to the apostles and elders*, concerning this doubt. Not that the church at Antioch had any doubt concerning it: they knew the liberty wherewith Christ had made them free; but they sent the case to Jerusalem, 1. Because those who taught this doctrine came from Jerusalem, and pretended to have directions from the apostles there to urge circumcision upon the Gentile converts; it was therefore very proper to send to Jerusalem about it, to know if they had any such direction from the church there. 2. Because those who were taught this doctrine would be the better confirmed in their opposition to it, and in the less danger of being shocked and disturbed by it, if they were sure that *the apostles and elders at Jerusalem* (which was the Christian church that of all others retained the most affection to the law of Moses) were against it. 3. Because the apostles at Jerusalem were fittest to be consulted in a point not yet fully settled; and being most eminent for an infallible spirit, peculiar to them as apostles, their decision would be likely to end the controversy.

IV. Their journey to Jerusalem upon this errand, *v.* 3. They were men that would not lose time, and therefore visited the churches by the way; they passed through Phenice and Samaria, and as they went *declared the conversion of the Gentiles*, and what wonderful success the gospel had had among them, which *caused great joy to all the brethren*.

V. Their hearty welcome at Jerusalem, *v.* 4. 1. The good entertainment their friends gave them. 2. The good entertainment they gave their friends: They *declared all things that God had done with them*, gave them an account of the success of their ministry among the Gentiles, not what they had done, but *what God had done with them*, what he had by his grace in them enabled them to do, and what he had by his grace in their hearers enabled them to receive.

VI. The opposition they met with from the same party at Jerusalem, *v. 5.* When Barnabas and Paul gave an account of the multitude of the Gentiles, and of the great harvest of souls gathered in to Christ there, and all about them congratulated them upon it, *there rose up certain of the sect of the Pharisees,* who received the tidings very coldly, and, though they believed in Christ, yet were not satisfied in the admission of these converts, but thought it was needful to circumcise them.

COUNCIL OF JERUSALEM
(vv. 6–21)

We have here a council called, not by writ, but by consent, on this occasion (*v.* 6): *The apostles and presbyters came together, to consider of this matter.* Now here we have,

I. Peter's speech in this synod. He did not in the least pretend to any primacy or headship in this synod. When both sides had been heard, *Peter rose up,* and addressed himself to the assembly, *Men and brethren,* as did James afterwards, *v.* 13. And here,

1. He put them in mind of the call and commission he had some time ago *to preach the gospel to the Gentiles;* he wondered there should be any difficulty made of a matter already settled.

2. He puts them in mind how remarkably God owned him in preaching to the Gentiles, and gave testimony to their sincerity in embracing the Christian faith (*v.* 8).

3. He sharply reproves those teachers (some of whom, it is likely, were present) who went about to bring the Gentiles under the obligation of the law of Moses, *v.* 10. Here he shows that in this attempt, (1) They offered a very great affront to God: "You tempt him, by calling that in question which he has already settled and determined by no less an indication than that of the gift of the Holy Ghost; you do, in effect, ask, 'Did he know what he did? Or was he in earnest in it? Or will he abide by his own act?'" (2) They offered a very great wrong to the disciples: Christ came to proclaim *liberty to the captives,* and they go about to enslave those whom he has made free. See Neh. v. 8.

4. Whereas the Jewish teachers had urged that circumcision was necessary to salvation, Peter shows it was so far from being so that both Jews and Gentiles were to be saved purely *through the grace of our Lord Jesus Christ,* and in no other way (*v.* 11).

II. An account of what Barnabas and Paul said in this synod, which did not need to be related, for they only gave in a narrative of what was recorded in the foregoing chapters. Observe, 1. What account they gave; they declared, or opened in order, and with all the magnifying and affecting circumstances, what glorious miracles, what signs and wonders, *God had wrought among the Gentiles by them.* Thus God had honoured these apostles whom the Jewish teachers condemned, and had thus honoured the Gentiles whom they contemned. What need had they of any other advocate when God himself pleaded their cause? 2. What attention was given to them: *All the multitude* (who, though they had not votes, yet came together to hear what was said) *kept silence, and gave audience to Paul and Barnabas*; it should seem they took more notice of their narrative than they did of all the arguments that were offered.

III. The speech which James made to the synod. He let Paul and Barnabas say what they had to say, and then he made the application of it.

1. He addresses himself respectfully to those present: "*Men and brethren, hearken unto me.*"

2. He refers to what Peter had said concerning the conversion of the Gentiles (*v.* 14). James observes here, (1) That the *grace of God* was the origin of it; it was God *that visited the Gentiles*; and it was a kind visit. (2) That the glory of God was the end of it: it was *to take out of them a people for his name*, who should glorify him, and in whom he would be glorified.

3. He confirms this with a quotation out of the Old Testament: he could not prove the calling of the Gentiles by a vision, as Peter could, nor by miracles wrought by his hand, as Paul and Barnabas could, but he would prove that it was foretold in the Old Testament, and therefore it must be fulfilled, *v.* 15. *To this agree the words of the prophets*; most of the Old-Testament prophets spoke more or less of the calling in of the Gentiles, even Moses himself, Rom. x. 19. It was the general expectation of the pious Jews that the Messiah should be *a light to enlighten the Gentiles*

(Luke ii. 32): but James waives the more illustrious prophecies of this, and pitches upon one that seemed more obscure: *It is written*, Amos ix. 11, 12, where is foretold, (1) The setting up of the kingdom of the Messiah (*v.* 16): *I will raise up the tabernacle of David, that is fallen.* (2) The bringing in of the Gentiles as the effect and consequence of this (*v.* 17): *That the residue of men might seek after the Lord*; not the Jews only, who thought they had the monopoly of the tabernacle of David, but *the residue of men*, such as had hitherto been left out of the pale of the visible church. The uniting of *Jews and Gentiles in one body*, and all those things that were done in order to achieve it, which were here foretold, were, [1] What God did: *This was the Lord's doing*, whatever instruments were employed in it: and, [2] It was what God delighted in, and was well pleased with; for he is the God of the Gentiles, as well as the Jews, and it is his honour *to be rich in mercy to all that call upon him.*

4. He resolves it into the purpose and counsel of God (*v.* 18): *Known unto God are all his works from the beginning of the world.* He not only foretold the calling of the Gentiles many ages ago by the prophets (and therefore it ought not to be a surprise or stumbling-block to us), but he foresaw and foreordained it in his eternal counsels, which are unquestionably wise and unalterably firm.

5. He gives his advice what was to be done in the present case, as the matter now stood with reference *to the Gentiles* (*v.* 19): *My sentence is; I give it as my opinion*, or judg-

ment; not as having authority over the rest, but as being an adviser with them. Now his advice is,

(1) That circumcision and the observance of the ceremonial law be by no means imposed upon the Gentile converts; no, not so much as recommended nor mentioned to them.

(2) That yet it would be well that in some things, which gave most offence to the Jews, the Gentiles should comply with them. It will please the Jews (and, if a little thing will oblige them, better do so than cross them) if the Gentile converts abstain, [1] *From pollutions of idols, and from fornication,* which are two bad things, and always to be abstained from. [2] *From things strangled, and from blood,* which, though not evil in themselves, as the other two, nor designed to be always abstained from, as those were, had been forbidden by *the precepts of Noah* (Gen. ix. 4), before the giving of the law of Moses; and the Jews had a great dislike to them, and to all those that took a liberty to use them; and therefore, to avoid giving offence, let the Gentile converts abridge themselves of their liberty herein, 1 Cor. viii. 9, 13. Thus we must *become all things to all men.*

6. He gives a reason for his advice—that great respect ought to be shown to the Jews, for they have been so long accustomed to the solemn injunctions of the ceremonial law that they must be borne with, if they cannot presently come off from them (*v.* 21). We must therefore give them time, must meet them half-way; they must be borne

with awhile, and brought on gradually, and we must comply with them as far as we can without betraying our gospel liberty.

COUNCIL DECISIONS
(*vv.* 22–35)

We have here the result of the consultation that was held at Jerusalem about the imposing of the ceremonial law upon the Gentiles. Now observe here,

I. The choice of the delegates that were to be sent with Paul and Barnabas on this errand.

1. They thought fit *to send men of their own company to Antioch, with Paul and Barnabas, v.* 22. This was agreed to by *the apostles and elders, with the whole church,* who, it is likely, undertook to bear their charges, 1 Cor. ix. 7.

2. Those they sent were not inferior persons, who might serve to carry the letters, and attest the receipt of them from the apostles; but *they were chosen men, and chief men among the brethren,* men of eminent gifts, graces, and usefulness; for these are the things which denominate men chief among the brethren, and qualify them to be the messengers of the churches.

II. The drawing up of the letters, circular letters, that were to be sent to the churches, to notify the sense of the synod in this matter.

1. Here is a very condescending, obliging preamble to this decree, *v.* 23. There is nothing in it haughty or assuming.

2. Here is a just and severe rebuke to the judaizing teachers (*v.* 24). (1) They did a great deal of wrong to the apostles and ministers at Jerusalem, in pretending that they

had instructions from them to impose the ceremonial law upon the Gentiles, when there was no colour for such a pretension. (2) They did a great deal of wrong to the Gentile converts, in saying, *You must be circumcised, and must keep the law.* [1] It perplexed them: *"They have troubled you with words,* have occasioned disturbance and disquietment to you." [2] It endangered them; they *subverted* their souls, put them into disorder, and pulled down that which had been built up.

3. Here is an honourable testimony given of the messengers by whom these letters were sent (vv. 25, 26).

4. Here is the direction given what to require from the Gentile converts, where observe,

(1) The matter of the injunction, which is according to the advice given by James.

(2) The manner in which it is worded. [1] They express themselves with something of authority, that what they wrote might be received with respect, and deference paid to it. It is all sweetness and love and good humour, such as became the followers of him who, when he called us to take his yoke upon us, assured us we should find him *meek and lowly in heart.* The difference of the style of the true apostles from that of the false is very observable. Those that were for imposing the ceremonial laws were positive and imperious: *Except you keep it, you cannot be saved* (v. 1), you are excommunicated *ipso facto* —*at once, and delivered to Satan.* The apostles of Christ, who only recommend necessary things, are mild and gentle: *"From which if you*

keep yourselves, you will do well, and as becomes you. *Fare ye well';* we are hearty well-wishers to your honour and peace."

III. The delivering of the letters, and how the messengers disposed of themselves.

1. *When they were dismissed they then came to Antioch.*

2. As soon as they came to Antioch, *they gathered the multitude together, and delivered the epistle to them* (vv. 30, 31).

3. The people were wonderfully pleased with the orders that came from Jerusalem (v. 31): *They rejoiced for the consolation';* and a great consolation it was to the multitude, (1) That they were confirmed in their freedom from the yoke of the ceremonial law, and were not burdened with that, as those upstart teachers would have had them to be. It was a comfort to them to hear that the carnal ordinances were no longer imposed on them, which perplexed the conscience, but could not purify nor pacify it. (2) That those who troubled their minds with an attempt to force circumcision upon them were hereby for the present silenced and put to confusion, the fraud of their pretensions to an apostolical warrant being now discovered. (3) That the Gentiles were hereby encouraged to receive the gospel, and those that had received it to adhere to it. (4) That the peace of the church was hereby restored, and that removed which threatened a division. All this was consolation which they rejoiced in, and blessed God for.

4. They got the strange ministers that came from Jerusalem to give

them each a sermon, and more, *v.* 32.

5. The dismissal of the Jerusalem ministers, *v.* 33. When they had *spent some time among them—having made some stay,* and having made it to good purpose, not having trifled away time, but having filled it up, they were let go in peace from the brethren at Antioch, to the apostles at Jerusalem, with all possible expressions of kindness and respect.

6. The continuance of Silas, notwithstanding, together with Paul and Barnabas, at Antioch. Antioch, being the chief city of Syria, it is probable there was a great resort of Gentiles thither from all parts upon one account or other, as there was of Jews to Jerusalem; so that in preaching there they did in effect preach to many nations, for they preached to those who would carry the report of what they preached to many nations, and thereby prepare them for the apostles' coming in person to preach to them.

DISPUTE OVER MARK
(*vv.* 36–41)

We have seen one unhappy difference among the brethren, which was of a public nature, brought to a good issue; but here we have a private quarrel between two ministers, no less men than Paul and Barnabas, not compromised indeed, yet ending well.

I. Here is a good proposal Paul made to Barnabas to go and review their work among the Gentiles and renew it, to take a circuit among the churches they had planted, and see what progress the gospel made among them.

II. The disagreement between Paul and Barnabas about an assistant; it was convenient to have a young man with them who should attend on them and minister to them, and be a witness of their *doctrine, manner of life, and patience,* and that should be fitted and trained up for further service, by being occasionally employed in the present service. Now, 1. Barnabas would have his nephew John, whose surname was Mark, to go along with them, *v.* 37. He determined to take him, because he was his relation, and, it is likely, was brought up under him, and he had a kindness for him, and was solicitous for his welfare. We should suspect ourselves of partiality, and guard against it in preferring our relations. 2. Paul opposed it (*v.* 38): *He thought not good to take him with them—he did not think him worthy* of the honour, nor fit for the service, who had *departed from them,* clandestinely as it should seem, without their knowledge, or wilfully, without their consent, from Pamphylia (*ch.* xiii. 13), and *went not with them to the work.*

III. The issue of this disagreement: it came to such a height that they separated upon it. Barnabas was peremptory that he would not go with Paul unless they took John Mark with them; Paul was as peremptory that he would not go if John did go with them. Neither would yield, and therefore there is no remedy but they must part. Now here is that which is very humbling, and just matter of lamentation, and yet very instructive. For we see, 1. That the best of men are but men, *subject to like passions* as we are, as these two good men had expressly owned concerning themselves (*ch.* xiv. 15), and now it appeared too true. 2. That we are not to think it strange if there be differences among wise and good men; we were told before that such offences would come, and here is an instance of it. 3. That these differences often prevail so far as to occasion separations. Paul and Barnabas, who were not separated by the persecutions of the unbelieving Jews, nor the impositions of the believing Jews, were yet separated by an unhappy disagreement between themselves.

IV. The good that was brought out of this evil—meat out of the eater, and sweetness out of the strong. It was strange that even the sufferings of the apostles (as Phil. i. 12), but much more strange that even the quarrels of the apostles, should tend to the *furtherance of the gospel of Christ*; yet so it proved here. God would not permit such things to be, if he knew not how to make them to serve his own purposes. 1. More places are hereby visited. 2. More hands are hereby employed in the ministry of the gospel among the Gentiles; for, (1) John Mark, who had been an unfaithful hand, is not rejected, but is again made use of, against Paul's mind, and, for aught we know, proves a very useful and successful hand, though many think it was not the same with that Mark that wrote the gospel, and founded the church at Alexandria, and whom Peter calls his son, 1 Pet. v. 13. (2) Silas who was a new hand, and never yet employed in that work, nor intended to be, but to return to the service of the church at Jerusalem, had not God changed his mind (*vv.* 33, 34), he is brought in, and engaged in that noble work.

V. We may further observe, 1. That the church at Antioch seem to countenance Paul in what he did. Barnabas sailed with his nephew to Cyprus, and no notice was taken of him, nor a recommendation given him. 2. That yet Paul afterwards seems to have had, though not upon second thoughts, yet upon further trial, a better opinion of John Mark than now he had; for he writes to Timothy (2 Tim iv. 11), *Take Mark and bring him with thee, for he is profitable to me for the ministry*; and he writes to the Colossians concerning Marcus, sister's son to Barnabas, that *if he came to them* they should *receive him*, bid him welcome, and employ him (Col. iv. 10).

CHAPTER SIXTEEN
PAUL ENLISTS TIMOTHY
(*vv.* 1–5)

Paul was a spiritual father, and as such a one we have him here adopting Timothy. Here is,

I. His taking Timothy into his acquaintance and under his tuition. And we are here accordingly told, 1. That he was a disciple, one that belonged to Christ, and was baptized, probably in his infancy, when his mother became a believer, as Lydia's household was baptized upon her believing, *v.* 15. Him, that was a disciple of Christ, Paul took to be his disciple, that he might further train him up in the knowledge and faith of Christ; he took him to be brought up for Christ.

2. That his mother was a Jewess originally, *but believed in Christ*; her name was *Eunice*, his grandmother's name was *Lois*. 3. That his father was a Greek, a Gentile. The marriage of a Jewish woman to a Gentile husband (though some would make a difference) was prohibited as much as the marriage of a Jewish man to a Gentile wife, Deut. vii. 3. Now because his father was a Greek he was not circumcised: for the entail of the covenant and the seal of it, as of other entails in that nation, went by the father, not by the mother. 4. That he had gained a very good character among the Christians. Not only those in the place where he was born, but those in the neighbouring cities, admired him, and spoke honourably of him. He had a name for good things with good people. 5. That Paul would have him *to go forth with him*, to accompany him, to give attendance on him, to receive instruction from him, and to join with him in the work of the gospel—to preach for him when there was occasion, and to be left behind in places where he had planted churches. 6. That Paul took him and circumcised him, or ordered it to be done. This was strange. Had not Paul opposed those with all his might that were for imposing circumcision upon the Gentile converts? Had he not at this time the decrees of the council at Jerusalem with him, which witnessed against it? He had, and yet circumcised Timothy, not, as those teachers designed in imposing circumcision, to oblige him to keep the ceremonial law, but only to render his ministry passable, and,

if it might be, acceptable among the Jews that abounded in those quarters. He knew Timothy was a man likely to do a great deal of good among them, being admirably qualified for the ministry, if they were not invincibly prejudiced against him; and therefore, that they might not shun him as one unclean, because uncircumcised, he took him and *circumcised him*. Thus *to the Jews he became as a Jew, that he might gain the Jews*, and *all things to all men, that he might gain some*. It is probable that it was at this time that Paul laid his hands on Timothy, for the conferring of the gift of the Holy Ghost upon him, 2 Tim. i. 6.

II. His confirming the churches which he had planted (*vv.* 4, 5): *He went through the cities* where he had *preached the word of the Lord*, as he intended (*ch.* xv. 36), to enquire into their state. And we are told,

1. That they delivered to them copies of the decrees of the Jerusalem synod.

2. That this was of very good service to them. (1) The churches were hereby *established in the faith*, *v.* 5. (2) They *increased in number daily*. Not a day passed but some or other gave up their names to Christ. And it is a joy to those who heartily wish well to the honour of Christ, and the welfare of the church and the souls of men, to see such an increase.

A MAN OF MACEDONIA
(*vv.* 6-15)

In these verses we have,

I. Paul's travels up and down to do good. 1. He and Silas his col-

A Man of Macedonia

league went throughout Phrygia and the region of Galatia, where, it should seem, the gospel was already planted, but whether by Paul's hand or no is not mentioned; it is likely it was, for in his epistle to the Galatians he speaks of his *preaching the gospel to them at the first*, and how very acceptable he was among them, Gal. iv. 13–15. 2. They were forbidden at this time to preach the gospel in Asia (the country properly so called), because it did not need, other hands being at work there; or because the people were not yet prepared to receive it, as they were afterwards (*ch*. xix. 10), when *all those that dwelt in Asia heard the word of the Lord*; or, as Dr. Lightfoot suggests, because at this time Christ would employ Paul in a piece of new work, which was to preach the gospel to a Roman colony at Philippi, for hitherto the Gentiles to whom he had preached were Greeks. 3. They would have gone into Bithynia, but were not permitted: *the Spirit suffered them not*, *v*. 7. Observe, Though their judgment and inclination were to go into Bithynia, yet, having then extraordinary ways of knowing the mind of God, they were overruled by them, contrary to their own mind. We must now follow providence, and submit to the guidance of that pillar of cloud and fire; and, if this *suffer us not* to do what we assay to do, we ought to acquiesce, and believe it for the best. *The Spirit of Jesus* suffered them not; so many ancient copies read it. The servants of the Lord Jesus ought to be always under the check and conduct of the *Spirit of the Lord Jesus*, by whom he

governs men's minds. 4. They *passed by Mysia*, or passed *through it* (so some), sowing good seed, we may suppose, as they went along; and they came down to Troas, the city of Troy, so much talked of, or the country thereabouts. It should seem that at Troas Luke fell in with Paul, and joined himself to his company; for henceforward, for the most part, when he speaks of Paul's journeys, he puts himself into the number of his retinue, *we* went, *v*. 10.

II. Paul's particular call to Macedonia, that is, to Philippi, the chief city, inhabited mostly by Romans, as appears, *v*. 21. Here we have,

1. The vision Paul had, *v*. 9. Paul had many visions, sometimes to encourage, sometimes, as here, to direct him in his work. An angel appeared to him, to intimate to him that it was the will of Christ he should go to Macedonia. Now observe, (1) The person Paul saw. There stood by him *a man of Macedonia*, who by his habit or dialect seemed so to Paul, or who told him he was so. The angel, some think, assumed the shape of such a man; or, as others think, impressed upon Paul's fancy, when between asleep and awake, the image of such a man: he dreamt he saw such a one. (2) The invitation given him. This honest Macedonian *prayed him, saying, Come over into Macedonia, and help us*; that is, "Come and preach the gospel to us; let us have the benefit of thy labours."

2. The interpretation made of the vision (*v*. 10): They *gathered assuredly from this that the Lord had called them to preach the gospel*

there; and they were ready to go wherever God directed.

III. Paul's voyage to Macedonia hereupon: He *was not disobedient to the heavenly vision*, but followed this divine direction much more cheerfully, and with more satisfaction, than he would have followed any contrivance or inclination of his own.

IV. The cold entertainment which Paul and his companions met with at Philippi. 1. It is a good while before any notice at all is taken of him: *We were in that city abiding certain days*, probably at a public house and at their own charge, for they had no friend to invite them so much as to a meal's meat, till Lydia welcomed them. 2. When they have an opportunity of preaching it is in an obscure place, and to a mean and small auditory, *v.* 13. The place of this meeting is out of the city. It was a place *where prayer was wont to be made*; a chapel, or smaller synagogue. But I rather take it, as we read it, where prayer was appointed or accustomed to be. Those that worshipped the true God, and would not worship idols, met there to pray together, and, according to the description of the most ancient and universal devotion, *to call upon the name of the Lord*. Thither Paul and Silas and Luke went, and *sat down*, to instruct the congregation, that they might the better pray with them. They *spoke unto the women who resorted thither*, encouraged them in practising according to the light they had, and led them on further to the knowledge of Christ.

V. The conversion of *Lydia*, who probably was the first that was wrought upon there to believe in Christ, though not the last. Observe,

1. Who this convert was that there is such particular notice taken of. Four things are recorded of her:

(1) Her name, *Lydia*.

(2) Her calling. She was *a seller of purple*, either of purple dye or of purple cloth or silk. Though she had a calling to mind, yet she was a worshipper of God, and found time to improve advantages for her soul.

(3) The place she was of—*of the city of Thyatira*, which was a great way from Philippi; there she was born and bred, but either married at Philippi, or brought by her trade to settle there. Providence brings Lydia to Philippi, to be under Paul's ministry, and there, where she met with it, she made a good use of it; so should we improve opportunities.

(4) Her religion before the Lord opened her heart. [1] She worshipped God according to the knowledge she had; she was one of the devout women. [2] She heard the apostles. Here, where prayer was made, when there was an opportunity, *the word was preached*; for hearing the word of God is a part of religious worship, and how can we expect God should hear our prayers if we will not hearken to his word? Those that worshipped God according to the light they had looked out for further light; we must improve *the day of small things*, but must not rest in it.

2. What the work was that was wrought upon her: *Whose heart the Lord opened*. Observe here, (1) The author of this work: it was *the Lord*,—the Lord Christ, to whom this judgment is committed,—

the Spirit of the Lord, who is the sanctifier. (2) The seat of this work; it is in the heart that the change is made, it is to the heart that this blessed turn is given; it was the heart of Lydia that was wrought upon. Conversion-work is heart-work; it is a *renewing of the heart, the inward man, the spirit of the mind.* (3) The nature of the work; she had not only her heart touched, but her heart opened.

3. What were the effects of this work on the heart. (1) She took great notice of the word of God. (2) She gave up her name to Jesus Christ, and took upon her the profession of his holy religion: *She was baptized,* and by this solemn rite was admitted a member of the church of Christ. (3) She was very kind to the ministers, and very desirous to be further instructed by them in *the things pertaining to the kingdom of God.*

AN EVIL SPIRIT (*vv.* 16–24)

Paul and his companions, though they were for some time buried in obscurity at Philippi, yet now begin to be taken notice of.

I. *A damsel that had a spirit of divination* caused them to be taken notice of, by proclaiming them to them to be the servants of God. Observe,

1. The account that is given of this damsel: She was actuated by an evil spirit, that dictated ambiguous answers to those who consulted her, which served to gratify their vain desire of knowing things to come, but often deceived them. This damsel *brought her masters much gain by soothsaying.*

2. The testimony which this damsel gave to Paul and his companions. When she met with them she followed them, crying, *"These men are the servants of the most high God,* for *they show unto us the way of salvation."* How came this testimony from the mouth of one that had a spirit of divination? We may take it either, [1] As extorted from this spirit of divination for the honour of the gospel by the power of God; as the devil was forced to say of Christ (Mark i. 24): *I know thee who thou art, the Holy One of God.* Or, [2] As designed by the evil spirit, that subtle serpent, to the dishonour of the gospel; as if these divines were of the same fraternity with their diviners, because they were witnessed to by them, and then the people might as well adhere to those they had been used to.

II. Christ caused them to be taken notice of, by giving them power to cast the devil out of this damsel. Power went along with the word of Christ, before which Satan could not stand, but was forced to quit his hold, and in this case it was a strong hold: *He came out the same hour.*

III. The masters of the damsel that was dispossessed caused them to be taken notice of, by bringing them before the magistrates for doing it, and laying it to their charge as their crime. Observe here,

1. That which provoked them was, that, the damsel being restored to herself, *her masters saw that the hope of their gain was gone, v.* 19.

2. The course they took with them was to incense the higher powers against them, as men fit to be punished.

3. The charge they exhibited against them was that they were the troublers of the land, *v.* 20.

IV. The magistrates, by their proceedings against them, caused them to be taken notice of.

1. By countenancing the persecution they raised the mob upon them (*v.* 22): *The multitude rose up together against them*, and were ready to pull them to pieces.

2. By going on to an execution they further represented them as the vilest malefactors. The magistrates commanded that they should be whipped as vagabonds, by the lictors or beadles who attended the prætors, and carried rods with them for that purpose; this was one of those three times that Paul was beaten with rods, according to the Roman usage, which was not under the compassionate limitation of the number of stripes not to exceed forty, which was provided by the Jewish law. The judges made their commitment very strict: They *charged the jailer to keep them safely*, and have a very watchful eye upon them. *He put them into the inner prison*, the dungeon, into which none were usually put but condemned malefactors, dark at noon-day, damp and cold, dirty, it is likely, and every way offensive, like that into which Jeremiah was let down (Jer. xxxviii. 6); and, as if this were not enough, *he made their feet fast in the stocks*.

JAILER CONVERTED
(*vv.* 25–34)

We have here the designs of the persecutors of Paul and Silas baffled and broken.

I. The persecutors designed to dishearten and discourage the preachers of the gospel, and to make them sick of the cause and weary of their work; but here we find them both hearty and heartened.

1. They were themselves hearty, wonderfully hearty. (1) They prayed together, prayed to God to support them and comfort them in their afflictions. (2) *They sang praises to God.* They praised God; for we must *in every thing give thanks*. We never want matter for praise, if we do not want a heart. And what should put the heart of a child of God out of tune for this duty if a dungeon and a pair of stocks will not do it? (3) Notice is here taken of the circumstance that *the prisoners heard them*. If the prisoners did not hear them pray, yet *they heard them sing praises*. The prisoners were made to hear the prison-songs of Paul and Silas, that they might be prepared for the miraculous favour shown to them all for the sake of Paul and Silas, when *the prison-doors were thrown open*.

2. God heartened them wonderfully by his signal appearances for them, *v.* 26. (1) There was immediately a great earthquake; how far it extended we are not told, but it was such a violent shock in this place *that the very foundations of the prison were shaken*. (2) The prison-doors were thrown open, and the prisoners' fetters were knocked off: *Every man's bands were loosed*. As afterwards God gave to Paul all *those that were in the ship with him* (ch. xxvii. 24), so now he gave him all those that were in the prison with him.

II. It is probable that some of the prisoners, if not all, were converted. But it is only the conversion of the jailer that is recorded.

1. He is afraid he shall lose his life, and Paul makes him easy as to this care, *vv.* 27, 28. (1) He *awoke out of his sleep.* This waking him out of his sleep signified the awakening of his conscience out of its spiritual slumber. The call of the gospel is, *Awake, thou that sleepest* (Eph. v. 14). (2) He saw the prison-doors open, and supposed, as well he might, that the prisoners had fled; and then what would become of him? He knew the Roman law in that case, and it was executed not long ago upon the keepers out of whose hands Peter escaped, *ch.* xii. 19. (3) In his fright *he drew his sword*, and was going *to kill himself*, to prevent a more terrible death. (4) Paul stopped him from his proceeding against himself (*v.* 28): He *cried with a loud voice*, not only to make him hear, but to make him heed, *saying, Do not practise any evil to thyself; Do thyself no harm.*

2. He is afraid he shall lose his soul, and Paul makes him easy as to this care too. One concern leads him to another, and a much greater. Perhaps the heinousness of the sin he was running into helped to alarm him.

(1) Whatever was the cause, he was put into a great consternation. The Spirit of God, that was sent to convince, in order to his being a Comforter, struck a terror upon him, and startled him.

(2) In this consternation, he applied to Paul and Silas for relief. Observe, [1] How reverent and respectful his address to them is: *He called for a light*, because they were in the dark, and that they might see what a fright he was in; *he fell down before them*, as one amazed at the badness of his own condition, and ready to sink under the load of his terror because of it. He gave them a title of respect, *Sirs, lords, masters*; just now it was, *Rogues* and *villains*, and he was their master; but now, *Sirs, lords*, and they are his masters. [2] How serious his enquiry is: *What must I do to be saved? First*, His salvation is now his great concern, and lies nearest his heart, which before was the furthest thing from his thoughts. *Secondly*, He does not enquire concerning others, what they must do; but concerning himself, "What must I do?" *Thirdly*, He is convinced that something must be done, and done by him too, in order to achieve his salvation. *Fourthly*, He is willing to do any thing: "Tell me what I must do, and I am here ready to do it." *Fifthly*, He is inquisitive what he should do, is desirous to know what he should do, and asks those that were likely to tell him. *Sixthly*, He *brought them out*, to put this question to them, that their answer might not be by duress or compulsion, but that they might prescribe to him, though he was their keeper, with the same liberty as they did to others. He brings them out of the dungeon, in hopes they will bring him out of a much worse.

(3) They very readily directed him what he must do, *v.* 31. *Believe in the Lord Jesus Christ.* One would think they should have said, "Repent of thy abusing us, in the

first place." No, that is overlooked and easily passed by, if he will but believe in Christ. Here is the sum of the whole gospel, the covenant of grace in a few words: *Believe in the Lord Jesus Christ, and thou shalt be saved, and thy house.* Here is, [1] The happiness promised: *"Thou shalt be saved."* Though a great sinner, though a persecutor, yet thy heinous transgressions shall be all forgiven through the merits of Christ. [2] The condition required: *Believe in the Lord Jesus Christ.* We must admit the record that God hath given in his gospel concerning his Son, and assent to it as faithful, and well *worthy of all acceptation.* We must approve the method God has taken of reconciling the world to himself by a Mediator; and accept of Christ as he is offered to us, and give up ourselves to be ruled and taught and saved by him. This is the only way and a sure way to salvation. [3] The extension of this to his family: *Thou shalt be saved, and thy house*; that is, "God will be in Christ a God to thee and to thy seed, as he was to Abraham. Believe, and salvation shall *come to thy house*, as Luke xix. 9."

(4) They proceeded to instruct him and his family in the doctrine of Christ (*v.* 32): They *spoke unto him the word of the Lord.* He was, for aught that appears, an utter stranger to Christ, and therefore it is requisite he should be told who this Jesus is, that he may believe in him, John ix. 36.

(5) The jailer and his family were immediately baptized, and thereby took upon them the profession of Christianity, submitted to its laws,

and were admitted to its privileges, upon their declaring solemnly, as the eunuch did, that they believed that *Jesus Christ is the Son of God*: He was *baptized, he and all his, straightway.*

(6) The jailer was hereupon very respectful to Paul and Silas, as one that knew not how to make amends for the injury he had done to them, much less for the kindness he had received from them.

(7) The voice of rejoicing with that of salvation was heard in the jailer's house; never was such a truly merry night kept there before: *He rejoiced, believing in God, with all his house.*

THEY LEAVE PHILIPPI
(*vv.* 35–40)

In these verses we have,

I. Orders sent for the discharge of Paul and Silas out of prison *vv.* 35, 36.

II. Paul's insisting upon the breach of privilege which the magistrates had been guilty of, *v.* 37. It is probable that the magistrates had some intimation that they were Romans, and were made aware that their fury had carried them further than the law would bear them out; and that this was the reason why they gave orders for their discharge. Now observe,

1. Paul did not plead this before he was beaten, though it is probable that it might have prevented it, lest he should seem to be afraid of suffering for the truth which he had preached.

2. He did plead it afterwards, to put an honour upon his sufferings and upon the cause he suffered for, to let the world know that the

preachers of the gospel were not such despicable men as they were commonly looked upon to be, and that they merited better treatment. He insists upon it that they should make them an acknowledgment of their error, and give them a public discharge, to make it the more honourable, as they had done them a public disgrace, which made that the more disgraceful. It was not a point of honour that Paul stood thus stiffly upon, but a point of justice, and not to himself so much as to his cause.

III. The magistrates' submission, and the reversing of the judgment given against Paul and Silas, *vv.* 38, 39. 1. The magistrates were frightened when they were told (though it may be they knew it before) that Paul was a Roman. 2. They *came and besought them* not to take advantage of the law against them, but to overlook the illegality of what they had done and say no more of it: they *brought them out* of the prison, owning that they were wrongfully put into it, and desired them that they would peaceably and quietly *depart out of the city.*

IV. The departure of Paul and Silas from Philippi, *v.* 40. Paul and Silas had an extraordinary call to Philippi; and yet, when they have come thither, they see little of the fruit of their labours, and are soon driven thence. Yet they did. not come in vain. Though the beginnings here were *small, the latter end greatly increased*; now they laid the foundation of a church at Philippi, which became very eminent, had its bishops and deacons, and people that were more generous

to Paul than any other church, as appears by his epistle to the Philippians, *ch.* i. 1; iv. 25. Let not ministers be discouraged, though they see not the fruit of their labours at once; the seed sown seems to be lost under the clods, but it shall come up again in a plentiful harvest in due time.

PAUL AT THESSALONICA
(*vv.* 1–8)

Paul's two epistles to the Thessalonians, the first two he wrote by inspiration, give such a shining character of that church, that we cannot but be glad here in the history to meet with an account of the first founding of the church there.

I. Here is Paul's coming to Thessalonica, which was the chief city of this country, called at this day *Salonech*, in the Turkish dominions.

II. His preaching to the Jews first, in their synagogue at Thessalonica. He found a synagogue of the Jews there (*v.* 1), which intimates that one reason why he passed through those other cities mentioned, and did not continue long in them, was because there were no synagogues in them. But, finding one in Thessalonica, by it he made his entry. 1. It was always his manner to begin with the Jews, to make them the first offer of the gospel, and not to turn to the Gentiles till they had refused it, that their mouths might be stopped from clamouring against him because he preached to the Gentiles. 2. He met them in their synagogue on the sabbath day, in their place and at their time of meeting, and thus he would pay respect to both. 3. He *reasoned with them out of the scriptures.* They agreed with him to receive the scriptures of the Old Testament: so far they were of a mind. But they received the scripture, and therefore thought they had reason to reject Christ; Paul received the scripture, and therefore saw great reason to embrace Christ. 4. He continued to do this *three sabbath days* successively. If he could not convince them the first sabbath, he would try the second and the third; for *precept must be upon precept, and line upon line.* 5. The drift and scope of his preaching and arguing was to prove that *Jesus is the Christ*; this was that which he opened and alleged, *v.* 3. He showed them, (1) That it was necessary the Messiah should *suffer, and die, and rise again*, that the Old-Testament prophecies concerning the Messiah made it necessary he should. (2) That Jesus is the Messiah.

III. The success of his preaching there, *v.* 4. 1. Some of the Jews believed, notwithstanding their rooted prejudices against Christ and his gospel, and they *consorted with Paul and Silas.* 2. Many more of the devout Greeks, and of the chief women, embraced the gospel. These were proselytes of the gate, the *godly among the Gentiles* (so the Jews called them), such as, though they did not submit to the law of Moses, yet renounced idolatry and immorality, worshipped the true God only, and did no man any wrong.

IV. The trouble that was given to Paul and Silas at Thessalonica. Observe,

1. Who were the authors of their trouble: the *Jews who believed not, who were moved with envy, v.* 5. The Jews were in all places the most inveterate enemies to the Christians, especially to those Jews that turned Christians, against whom they had a particular spleen, as deserters.

2. Who were the instruments of the trouble: the Jews made use of *certain lewd persons of the baser sort.* All wise and sober people looked upon them with respect, and valued them, and none would appear against them but such as were the scum of the city, a company of vile men, that were given to all manner of wickedness.

3. In what method they proceeded against them. (1) They *set the city in an uproar*, made a noise to put people in a fright, and then every body ran to see what the matter was; they began a riot, and then the mob was up presently. (2) They *assaulted the house of Jason*, where the apostles lodged, with a design *to bring them out to the people*, whom they had incensed and enraged against them, and by whom they hoped to see them pulled to pieces. (3) When they could not get the apostles into their hands, then they fall upon an honest citizen of their own, who entertained the apostles in his house, his name *Jason*, a converted Jew, and drew him out with some others of the brethren to the rulers of the city. (4) They accused them to the rulers, and represented them as dangerous persons, not fit to be tolerated. [1] That they were enemies to the public peace, and threw every thing into disorder

wherever they came: *Those that have turned the world upside down are come hither also*. In one sense it is true that wherever the gospel comes in its power to any place, to any soul, it works such a change there, gives such a wide change to the stream, so directly contrary to what it was, that it may be said to turn the world upside down in that place, in that soul. But in the sense in which they meant it it is utterly false: they would have it thought that the preachers of the gospel were incendiaries and mischief makers wherever they came, that they sowed discord among relations, set neighbours together by the ears, obstructed commerce, and inverted all order and regularity. [2] That they were enemies to the established government, and disaffected to that, and their principles and practices were destructive to monarchy and inconsistent with the constitution of the state (*v.* 7).

4. The great uneasiness which this gave to the city (*v.* 8). They had no ill opinion of the apostles or their doctrine, could not apprehend any danger to the state from them, and therefore were willing to connive at them; but, if they be represented to them by the prosecutors as enemies to Cæsar, they will be obliged to take cognizance of them, and to suppress them, for fear of the government, and this troubled them.

5. The issue of this troublesome affair. The magistrates here were not so easily incensed against the apostles as the magistrates at Philippi were, but were more considerate and of better temper; so they *took security of Jason and the*

other, bound them to their good behaviour; and perhaps they gave bond for Paul and Silas, that they should be forthcoming when they were called for, if any thing should afterwards appear against them.

THE NOBLE BEREANS
(*vv.* 10–15)

In these verses we have,

I. Paul and Silas removing to Berea, and employed in preaching the gospel there, *v.* 10.

II. The good character of the Jews in Berea (*v.* 11): *These were more noble than those in Thessalonica*.

1. They had a freer thought, and lay more open to conviction, were willing to hear reason, and admit the force of it, and to subscribe to that which appeared to them to be truth, though it was contrary to their former sentiments. This was more noble.

2. They had a better temper, were not so sour, and morose, and ill-conditioned towards all that were not of their mind. They neither prejudged the cause, nor were moved with envy at the managers of it, as the Jews at Thessalonica were, but very generously gave both it and them a fair hearing, without passion or partiality; for,

(1) *They received the word with all readiness of mind*; they were very willing to hear it, presently apprehended the meaning of it, and did not shut their eyes against the light.

(2) *They searched the scriptures daily whether those things were so*. Their readiness of mind to receive the word was not such as that they took things upon trust, swallowed

them upon an implicit faith: no; but since Paul reasoned out of the scriptures, and referred them to the Old Testament for the proof of what he said, they had recourse to their Bibles, turned to the places to which he referred them, read the context, considered the scope and drift of them, compared them with other places of scripture, examined whether Paul's inferences from them were natural and genuine and his arguments upon them cogent, and determined accordingly. Those that rightly study the scriptures, and *meditate therein day and night*, have their minds filled with noble thoughts, fixed to noble principles, and formed for noble aims and designs. *These are more noble.*

III. The good effect of the preaching of the gospel at Berea: it had the desired success; the people's hearts being prepared, a great deal of work was done suddenly, *v.* 12.

IV. The persecution that was raised against Paul and Silas at Berea, which forced Paul thence. 1. *The Jews at Thessalonica* were the mischief-makers at *Berea*. Thus we read before. that the Jews of Antioch and Iconium came to Lystra on purpose to incense the people against the apostles, *ch.* xiv. 19. 2. This occasioned Paul's removal to Athens. By seeking to extinguish this divine fire which Christ had already kindled, they did but spread it the further and the faster. He went out from Berea, in that road which went to the sea, that the Jews, if they enquired after him, might think he had gone to a great distance; but he went by land to Athens, in which there was no culpable dissimulation at all.

PAUL AT ATHENS (*vv.* 16–21)

A scholar that has acquaintance, and is in love, with the learning of the ancients, would think he should be very happy if he were where Paul now was, at Athens, in the midst of the various sects of philosophers, and would have a great many curious questions to ask them, for the explication of the remains we have of the Athenian learning; but Paul, though bred a scholar, and an ingenious active man, does not make this any of his business at Athens. He has other work to mind: it is not the improving of himself in their philosophy that he aims at, he has learned to call it a vain thing, and is above it (Col. ii. 8); his business is, in God's name, to correct their disorders in religion, and *to turn them from the service of idols*, and of Satan in them, to the *service of the true and living God* in Christ.

I. Here is the impression which the abominable ignorance and superstition of the Athenians made upon Paul's spirit, *v.* 16. Observe, 1. The account here given of that city: it was *wholly given to idolatry*. This agrees with the account which the heathen writers give of it, that there were more idols in Athens than there were in all Greece besides put together, and that they had twice as many sacred feasts as others had. 2. The disturbance which the sight of this gave to Paul. Paul was not willing to appear publicly till Silas and Timothy came to him, that out of the mouth of two or three witnesses the word might be established; but in the mean time *his spirit was stirred within him.* He was filled with concern for the glory of God, which he saw given to idols, and with compassion to the souls of men, which he saw thus enslaved to Satan, *and led captive by him at his will.*

II. The testimony that he bore against their idolatry, and his endeavours to bring them to the knowledge of the truth. 1. *He went to the synagogue of the Jews,* who, though enemies to Christianity, were free from idolatry, and joined with them in that among them which was good, and took the opportunity given him there of disputing for Christ, *v.* 17. 2. He entered into conversation with all that came in his way about matters of religion: *In the market,* in the exchange, or place of commerce, *he disputed daily,* as he had occasion, *with those that met with him,* or that he happened to fall into company with, that were heathen, and never came to the Jews' synagogue. The zealous advocates for the cause of Christ will be ready to plead it in all companies, as occasion offers.

III. The enquiries which some of the philosophers made concerning Paul's doctrine. Observe,

1. Who they were the encountered him, that entered into discourse with him, and opposed him. (1) *The Epicureans,* who *thought God altogether such a one as themselves,* an idle inactive being, that minded nothing, nor put any difference between good and evil. (2) *The Stoics,* who thought themselves altogether as good as God, and indulged themselves as much in the pride of life as the Epicureans did in the lusts of the flesh and of the

eye; they made their virtuous man to be no way inferior to God himself, nay to be superior.

2. What their different sentiments were of him; such there were as there were of Christ, *v.* 18. (1) *Some called him a babbler,* and thought he spoke, without any design, whatever came uppermost, as men of crazed imaginations do: (2) *Others* called him *a setter forth of strange gods,* and thought he spoke with design to make himself considerable by that means. And, if he had strange gods to set forth, he could not bring them to a better market than to Athens. From his first coming among them he ever and anon harped upon these two strings which are indeed the principal doctrines of Christianity—Christ and a future state—Christ our way, and heaven our end; and, though he did not call these gods, yet they thought he meant to make them so. Jesus they took for a new god, and the resurrection, for a new goddess.

3. The proposal they made to give him a free, full, fair, and public hearing, *vv.* 19, 20. (1) They look upon it as strange and surprising, and very different from the philosophy that had for many ages been taught and professed at Athens. (2) They desired to know more of it, only because it was new and strange. (3) The place they brought him to for him to make this public declaration of his doctrine; it was *to Areopagus,* the same word that is translated (*v.* 22) *Mars' Hill;* it was the townhouse, or guildhall of their city, where the magistrates met upon public business, and the courts of justice were kept; and it

was as the theatre in the university, or the schools, where learned men met to communicate their notions.

4. The general character of the people of that city given upon this occasion (*v.* 21): *All the Athenians spent their time in nothing else but either to tell or to hear some new thing*, which comes in as the reason why they were inquisitive concerning Paul's doctrine, not because it was *good*, but because it was *new*.

PAUL'S SERMONS AT ATHENS (*vv.* 22–31)

We have here St. Paul's sermon at Athens.

I. He lays down this, as the scope of his discourse, that he aimed to bring them to *the knowledge of the only living and true God*, as the sole and proper object of their adoration. Now,

1. He shows them that they needed to be instructed herein; for they had lost the knowledge of the true God that made them, in the worship of false gods that they had made. *I perceive that in all things you are too superstitious*. He uses a word which among them was taken in a good sense: *You are every way more than ordinarily religious*, so some read it; *you are very devout in your way*.

2. He shows them that they themselves had given a fair occasion for the declaring of this one true God to them, by *setting up an altar, To the unknown God*, which intimated an acknowledgment that there was a God who was yet to them *an unknown God*; and it is sad to think that at Athens, a place which was supposed to have the monopoly of wisdom, the true God

was an unknown God, the only God that was unknown. (1) He tells them that the God he preached to them was one that they did already worship, and therefore he was not a setter forth of new or strange gods: "As you have a dependence upon him, so he has had some kind of homage from you." (2) He was one whom they ignorantly worshipped, which was a reproach to them, who were famous all the world over for their knowledge.

II. He confirms his doctrine of one living and true God, by his works of creation and providence. Now Paul here sets himself, in the first place, to reform the philosophy of the Athenians (he corrects the mistakes of that), and to give them right notions of *the one only living and true God*, and then to carry the matter further than they ever attempted for the reforming of their worship, and the bringing them off from their polytheism and idolatry. Observe what glorious things Paul here says of that God whom he served, and would have them to serve.

1. *He is the God that made the world, and all things therein; the Father almighty, the Creator of heaven and earth*. This was admitted by many of the philosophers; but those of Aristotle's school denied it, and maintained "that the world was from eternity, and every thing always was what now it is." Those of the school of Epicurus fancied "that the world was made by a fortuitous concourse of atoms, which, having been in perpetual motion, at length accidently jumped into this frame." Against both

these Paul here maintains that God by the operations of an infinite power, according to the contrivance of an infinite wisdom, in the beginning of time made the world and all things therein, the origin of which was owing, not as they fancied to an eternal matter, but to an eternal mind.

2. He is therefore *Lord of heaven and earth*, that is, he is their rightful owner, proprietor, and possessor.

3. He is, in a particular manner, the Creator of men, of all men (*v.* 26): *He made of one blood all nations of men*. He made the first man, he makes every man, is the former of every man's body and the Father of every man's spirit. He made them all of one blood, of one and the same nature; *he fashions their heart alike. He hath made them to dwell on all the face of the earth*. He made them not to live in one place, but to be dispersed over all the earth; one nation therefore ought not to look with contempt upon another, as the Greeks did upon all other nations; for those on all the face of the earth are of the same blood.

4. That he is the great benefactor of the whole creation (*v.* 25): *He giveth to all life, and breath, and all things*. He not only *breathed into the first man the breath of life*, but still breathes it into every man.

5. That he is the sovereign disposer of all the affairs of the children of men, according to the counsel of his will (*v.* 26).

6. That *he is not far from every one of us*, *v.* 27. He is every where present, has his eye upon us at all times, and knows us better than we know ourselves.

7. That *in him we live, and move, and have our being*, *v.* 28. (1) *In him we live*; that is, the continuance of our lives is owing to him and the constant influence of his providence. (2) *In him we move*; it is by his providence that our souls move and our thoughts run to and fro. (3) *In him we have our being*; not only from him we had it at first, but in him we have it still.

8. That upon the whole matter we are *God's offspring*; he is *our Father that begat us* (Deut. xxxii. 6, 18), and he hath *nourished and brought us up as children*, Isa. i. 2. The apostle here quotes a saying of one of the Greek poets, Aratus, a native of Cilicia, Paul's countryman, who, in his *Phenomena*, in the beginning of his book, speaking of the heathen *Jupiter*, that is, in the poetical dialect, the supreme *God*, says this of him, *for we are also his offspring*.

III. From all these great truths concerning God, he infers the absurdity of their idolatry, as the prophets of old had done. If this be so, 1. Then God cannot be represented by an image. 2. Then *he dwells not in temples made with hands*, *v.* 24. He is not invited to any temple men can build for him, nor confined to any. 3. Then he is *not worshipped*, he is *not served*, or *ministered unto, with men's hands, as though he needed any thing*, *v.* 25. He that made all, and maintains all, cannot be benefited by any of our services, nor needs them. 4. Then it concerns us all to enquire after God (*v.* 27): *That they should seek the Lord*, that is, fear and worship him in a right manner. Therefore God has kept the children of men in a constant dependence upon him for life and all the comforts of life, that he might keep them under constant obligations to him.

IV. He proceeds to call them all to repent of their idolatries, and to turn from them, *vv.* 30, 31. This is the practical part of Paul's sermon before the university; having declared God to them (*v.* 23), he properly presses upon them *repentance towards God*, and would also have taught them *faith towards our Lord Jesus Christ*, if they had had the patience to hear him. Observe,

1. The conduct of God towards the Gentile world before the gospel came among them: *The times of this ignorance God winked at.* (1) They were times of great ignorance. Human learning flourished more than ever in the Gentile world just before Christ's time; but in the things of God they were grossly ignorant. (2) These times of ignorance God winked at. Understand it, [1] As an act of divine justice. God despised or neglected these times of ignorance, and did not send them his gospel, as now he does. Or rather, [2] As an act of divine patience and forbearance. He winked at these times; he did not restrain them from these idolatries by sending prophets to them, as he did to Israel; he did not punish them in their idolatries, as he did Israel; but gave them the gifts of his providence, *ch.* xiv. 16, 17.

2. The charge God gave to the Gentile world by the gospel, which he now sent among them: *He now commandeth all men every where to repent*—to change their mind and

their way, to be ashamed of their folly and to act more wisely, to break off the worship of idols and bind themselves to the worship of the true God.

3. The great reason to enforce this command, taken from the judgment to come. God commands us to repent, *because he hath appointed a day in which he will judge the world in righteousness* (*v.* 31), and has now under the gospel made a clearer discovery of a state of retribution in the other world than ever before. God will judge the world *by that man whom he hath ordained*, who can be no other than the Lord Jesus, to whom all judgment is committed. God's raising Christ from the dead is the great proof of his being appointed and ordained the Judge of quick and dead. His raising him from the dead was the beginning of his exaltation, his judging the world will be the perfection of it; and he that begins will make an end.

REACTIONS (*vv.* 32–34)

We have here a short account of the issue of Paul's preaching at Athens.

I. Few were the better: the gospel had as little success at Athens as anywhere; for the pride of the philosophers there, as of the Pharisees at Jerusalem, prejudiced them against the gospel of Christ. They heard him patiently till he came to speak of the resurrection of the dead (*v.* 32), and then some of them began to hiss him: they *mocked.*

II. Yet there were some that were wrought upon, *v.* 34. If some would not, others would. There were certain men that adhered to him, and believed. Two are particularly named; one was an eminent man, *Dionysius the Areopagite*, one of that high court or great council that sat in Areopagus, or Mars' Hill—a judge, a senator, one of those before whom Paul was summoned to appear; his judge becomes his convert. The *woman named Damaris* was, as some think, the wife of Dionysius; but, rather, some other person of quality; and, though there was not so great a harvest gathered in at Athens as there was at other places, yet, these few being wrought upon there, Paul had no reason to say he had *laboured in vain*.

CHAPTER EIGHTEEN
PAUL VISITS CORINTH
(*vv.* 1–6)

Corinth was the chief city of Achaia, now a province of the empire, a rich and splendid city. Now here we have,

I. Paul working for his living, *vv.* 2, 3. 1. Though he was bred a scholar, yet he was master of a handicraft trade. He was a tentmaker, an upholsterer. 2. Though he was entitled to a maintenance from the churches he had planted, and from the people to whom he preached, yet he worked at his calling to get bread, which is more to his praise who did not ask for supplies than to theirs who did not supply him unasked, knowing what straits he was reduced to. 3. Though he was himself a great apostle, yet he chose to work with

Aquila and Priscilla, because he found them to be very intelligent in the things of God, as appears afterwards (*v.* 26), and he owns that they had been his *helpers in Christ Jesus*, Rom. xvi. 3. Concerning this Aquila we are here told, (1) That he was a Jew, but born in Pontus, *v.* 2. (2) That he was lately come from Italy to Corinth. (3) That the reason of his leaving Italy was because by a late edict of the emperor Claudius Cæsar all Jews were banished from Rome; for the Jews were generally hated, and every occasion was taken to put hardship and disgrace upon them.

II. We have here Paul preaching to the Jews.

1. He *reasoned with them in the synagogue* publicly *every sabbath*. God invites us to come and reason with him (Isa. i. 18), and challenges sinners to *produce their cause*, and *bring forth their strong reasons*, Isa. xli. 21. Paul was a rational as well as a scriptural preacher.

2. *He persuaded them.* It denotes, (1) The urgency of his preaching. Or, (2) The good effect of his preaching. He persuaded them, that is, he prevailed with them; so some understand it.

3. He was yet more earnest in this matter when his fellow-labourers, his seconds, came up with him (*v.* 5).

III. We have him here abandoning the unbelieving Jews, and turning from them to the Gentiles, as he had done in other places, *v.* 6.

1. Many of the Jews, and indeed the most of them, persisted in their contradiction to the gospel of Christ, and would not yield to the strongest reasonings nor the most

winning persuasions; they *opposed themselves* and *blasphemed*.

2. Paul hereupon declared himself discharged from them, and left them to perish in their unbelief.

3. Having given them over, yet he does not give over his work. Though Israel be not gathered, Christ and his gospel shall be glorious.

PAUL ENCOURAGED
(*vv.* 7–11)

Here we are told,

I. That Paul changed his quarters. He departed out of the synagogue, being driven out by the perverseness of the unbelieving Jews, and he *entered into a certain man's house, named Justus*, *v.* 7. But observe the account of this man and his house. 1. The man was next door to a Jew; he was one that *worshipped God*; he was not an idolater, though he was a Gentile, but was a worshipper of the God of Israel, and him only, as Cornelius. 2. The house was next door to the synagogue, it *joined close to it*, which some perhaps might interpret as done with design to draw people from the synagogue to the meeting; but I rather think it was done in charity, to show that he would come as near to them as he could.

II. That Paul presently saw the good fruit of his labours, both among Jews and Gentiles. 1. *Crispus* a Jew, an eminent one, the *chief ruler of the synagogue, believed on the Lord Jesus, with all his house*, *v.* 8. 2. Many of the Corinthians, who were Gentiles (and some of them persons of bad character, as appears, 1 Cor. vi. 11, *such were*

some of you), *hearing, believed, and were baptized*.

III. That Paul was encouraged by a vision to go on with his work at Corinth (*v.* 9). 1. He renewed his commission and charge to preach the gospel. 2. He assured him of his presence with him, which was sufficient to animate him, and put life and spirit into him. 3. He gave him a warrant of protection to save him harmless. 4. He gave him a prospect of success: "*For I have much people in this city*." The Lord knows those that are his, yea, and those that shall be his; for it is by his work upon them that they become his, and *known unto him are all his works*. Let us not despair concerning any place, when even in Corinth Christ had *much people*.

IV. That upon this encouragement he made a long stay there (*v.* 11). 1. For the bringing in of those that were outside. The people Christ has at Corinth must be called in by degrees, some by one sermon, others by another; *we see not yet all things put under Christ*. 2. For the building up of those that were within. Those that are converted have still need to be *taught the word of God*, and particular need at Corinth to be taught it by Paul himself; for no sooner was the good seed sown in that field than the enemy came and sowed tares, the false apostles, those deceitful workers, of whom Paul in his epistles to the Corinthians complains so much.

PAUL BEFORE GALLIO
(*vv.* 12–17)

We have here an account of some disturbance given to Paul and his friends at Corinth, but no great harm done, nor much hindrance given to the work of Christ there.

I. Paul is accused by the Jews before the Roman governor, *vv.* 12, 13. The governor was *Gallio, deputy of Achaia*, that is, proconsul; for Achaia was a consular province of the empire. Now observe, 1. How rudely Paul is apprehended, and brought before Gallio; *The Jews made insurrection with one accord against Paul*. 2. How falsely Paul is accused before Gallio (*v.* 13): *This fellow persuades men to worship God contrary to the law*. They could not charge him with persuading men not to worship God at all, or to worship other gods (Deut. xiii. 2): but only to worship God in a way contrary to the law. The Romans allowed the Jews in their provinces the observance of their own law; and what then? Must those therefore be prosecuted as criminals who worship God in any other way?

II. Gallio, upon the first hearing, or rather without any hearing at all, dismisses the cause, and will not take any cognizance of it, *vv.* 14, 15. Observe,

1. He shows himself very ready to do the part of a judge in any matter that it was proper for him to take cognizance of. But,

2. He will by no means allow them to make a complaint to him of a thing that was not within his jurisdiction (*v.* 15): "*If it be a question of words and names, and of your law, look you to it*; end it among yourselves as you can, but *I will be no judge of such matters*; you shall neither burden my patience with the hearing of it, nor burden my conscience with giving

judgment upon it;" and therefore, when they were urgent and pressing to be heard, *he drove them from the judgment-seat* (*v.* 16), and ordered another cause to be called.

III. The abuse done to Sosthenes, and Gallio's unconcernedness in it, *v.* 17. 1. The parties put a great contempt upon the court, when *they took Sosthenes and beat him before the judgment-seat*. He is said be a *ruler of the synagogue*, either joint-ruler with Crispus (*v.* 8), or a ruler of one synagogue, as Crispus was of another. As for the Greeks that abused him, it is very probable that they were either Hellenist Jews, or Jewish Greeks, those that joined with the Jews in opposing the gospel (*vv.* 4, 6), and that the native Jews put them on to do it, thinking it would in them be less offensive. They were so enraged against Paul that they beat Sosthenes; and so enraged against Gallio, because he would not countenance the prosecution, that they beat him before the judgment-seat, whereby they did, in effect, tell him that they cared not for him; if he would not be their executioner, they would be their own judges. 2. The court put no less a contempt upon the cause, and the persons too. But *Gallio cared for none of these things*. If by this be meant that he cared not for the affronts of bad men, it was commendable. While he steadily adhered to the laws and rules of equity, he might despise their contempts; but, if it be meant (as I think it is) that he concerned not himself for the abuses done to good men, it carries his indifference too far, and gives us but an ill character of him.

PAUL AT EPHESUS AND JERUSALEM (*vv.* 18–23)

Here is,

I. Paul's departure from Corinth, *v.* 18. 1. He did not go away till some time after the trouble he met with there; from other places he had departed when the storm arose, but not from Corinth, because there it had no sooner risen than it fell again. 2. When he went, he took leave of the brethren solemnly. His farewell sermon would leave impressions upon them. 3. He took *with him Priscilla and Aquila,* because they had a mind to accompany him. 4. At Cenchrea, which was hard by Corinth, the port where those that went to sea from Corinth took ship, either Paul or Aquila (for the original does not determine which) had his head shaved, to discharge himself from the vow of a Nazarite. The Nazarite's head was to be shaved when either his consecration was accidentally polluted, in which case he must begin again, or *when the days of his separation were fulfilled* (Num. vi. 9; xiii. 18), which, we suppose, was the case here. Some throw it upon Aquila, who was a Jew (*v.* 2), and retained perhaps more of his Judaism than was convenient; but I see no harm in admitting it concerning Paul, for concerning him we must admit the same thing (*ch.* xxi. 24, 26), not only in compliance for a time with the Jews, to whom he *became as a Jew* (1 Cor. ix. 20), *that he might win upon them,* but because the vow of the Nazarites, though ceremonial, and as such ready to vanish away, had yet a great deal of moral and very pious

significance, and therefore was fit to die the last of all the Jewish ceremonies.

II. Paul's calling *at Ephesus,* which was the metropolis of the Lesser Asia, and a sea-port. The Jews at Ephesus were so far from driving Paul away that they courted his stay with them (*v.* 20): *They desired him to tarry longer with them,* to instruct them in the gospel of Christ. Paul would not stay with them now: *He consented not*; *but bade them farewell.* He had further to go; he *must by all means keep this feast at Jerusalem*; not that he thought himself bound in duty to it (he knew the laws of the feasts were no longer binding), but he had business at Jerusalem (whatever it was) which would be best done at the time of the feast, when there was a general rendezvous of all the Jews from all parts; which of the feasts it was we are not told, probably it was the passover, which was the most eminent.

III. Paul's visit to Jerusalem; a short visit it was, but it served as a token of respect to that truly mother-church. Paul thought it requisite to show himself among them, that they might not think his success among the Gentiles had made him think himself either above them or estranged from them, or that the honour God had put upon him made him unmindful of the honour he owed to them.

IV. His return through those countries where he had formerly preached the gospel. 1. *He went and spent some time in Antioch,* among his old friends there, whence he was first sent out to preach among the Gentiles, *ch.* xiii. 1. 2. *Thence he* went over the country of Galatia and Phrygia in order, where he had preached the gospel, and planted churches, which, though very briefly mentioned (*ch.* xvi. 6) was yet a glorious work, as appears by Gal. iv. 14, 15, where Paul speaks of his preaching the gospel to the Galatians at the first, and their receiving him *as an angel of God.*

APOLLOS THE JEW (*vv.* 24–28)

The sacred history leaves Paul upon his travels, and goes here to meet Apollos at Ephesus.

I. Here is an account of his character, when he came to Ephesus.

1. He was *a Jew, born at Alexandria* in Egypt, but of Jewish parents.

2. He was a man of excellent good parts, and well fitted for public service. He was *an eloquent man, and mighty in the scriptures* of the Old Testament, in the knowledge of which he was, as a Jew, brought up.

3. He *was instructed in the way of the Lord*; that is, he had some acquaintance with the doctrine of Christ, had obtained some general notions of the gospel and the principles of Christianity, *that Jesus is the Christ,* and *that prophet that should come into the world*; the first notice of this would be readily embraced by one that was so mighty in the scripture as Apollos was, and therefore understood the *signs of the times.* He *was instructed,* κατηχημένος—*he was catechised* (so the word is), either by his parents or by ministers; he was taught something of Christ and the way of salvation by him.

4. Yet he *knew only the baptism of* John; he was instructed in the gospel of Christ as far as John's ministry would carry him, and no further. We cannot but think he had heard of Christ's death and resurrection, but he was not let into the mystery of them, had not had opportunity of conversing with any of the apostles since the pouring out of the Spirit; or he had himself been baptized *only with the baptism of John,* but he was not baptized with the Holy Ghost, as the disciples were at the day of pentecost.

II. We have here the employment and improvement of his gifts at Ephesus.

1. He there made a very good use of his gifts in public. He came, probably, recommended to the synagogue of the Jews as a fit man to be a teacher there, and according to the light he had, and *the measure of the gift given to him,* he was willing to be employed (*v.* 25): *Being fervent in the Spirit, he spoke and taught diligently the things of the Lord.*

2. He there made a good increase of his gifts in private, not so much in study, as in conversation with *Aquila and Priscilla.* They did not take occasion from what they observed of his deficiency either to despise him themselves, or to disparage him to others; did not call him a young raw preacher, not fit to come into a pulpit, but considered the disadvantages he had laboured under, as knowing only the baptism of John; and, having themselves got great knowledge in the truths of the gospel by their long and intimate conversation with Paul, they communicated what they knew to him, and gave him a

clear, distinct, and methodical account of those things which before he had but confused notions of.

III. Here is his preferment to the service of the church of Corinth, which was a larger sphere of usefulness than Ephesus at present was. Paul was gone, was called away to other work, and now there was a fair occasion in this vacancy for Apollos to set in, who was fitted rather to water than to plant, to build up those that were within than to bring in those that were outside.

PAUL AT EPHESUS (*vv.* 1–6)

Ephesus was a city of great note in Asia, famous for a temple built there to Diana, which was one of the wonders of the world: thither *Paul came to preach the gospel while Apollos was at Corinth* (*v.* 1). At his first coming, he met with some disciples there, who professed faith in Christ as the true Messiah, but were as yet in the first and lowest form in the school of Christ, under his usher John the Baptist. They were in number *about twelve* (*v.* 7). Observe here,

I. How Paul catechised them. He was told, probably by Aquila and Priscilla, that they were believers, that they did own Christ, and had given up their names to him; now Paul hereupon takes them under examination.

1. They did believe in the Son of God; but Paul enquires whether they had *received the Holy Ghost*,—whether they believed in the Spirit, whose operations on the minds of men, for conviction, conversion,

and comfort, were revealed some time after the doctrine of Jesus being the Christ,—whether they had been acquainted with, and had admitted, this revelation? This was not all; extraordinary gifts of the Holy Ghost were conferred upon the apostles and other disciples presently after Christ's ascension, which was frequently repeated upon occasion; had they participated in these gifts? "*Have you received the Holy Ghost since you believed?* Have you had that seal of the truth of Christ's doctrine in yourselves?"

2. They owned their ignorance in this matter. They spoke as if they expected it, and wondered they did not hear of it, and were ready to welcome the notice of it.

3. Paul enquired how they came to be baptized, if they knew nothing of the Holy Ghost; for, if they were baptized by any of Christ's ministers, they were instructed concerning the Holy Ghost, and were baptized in his name.

4. They own that they were baptized *unto John's baptism*—that is, as I take it, they were baptized in the name of John, not by John himself (he was far enough from any such thought), but by some weak, well-meaning disciple of his, that ignorantly kept up his name as the head of a party.

5. Paul explains to them the true intent and meaning of John's baptism, as principally referring to Jesus Christ, and so rectifies the mistake of those who had baptized them into the baptism of John, and had not directed them to look any further, but to rest in that.

6. When they were thus shown the error they were led into, they

thankfully accepted the discovery, and *were baptized in the name of the Lord Jesus*, v. 5. It does not therefore follow hence that there was not an agreement between John's baptism and Christ's, or that they were not for substance the same; much less does it follow that those who have been once baptized *in the name of the Father, Son, and Holy Ghost* (which is the appointed form of Christ's baptism), may be again baptized in the same name; for those that were here baptized *in the name of the Lord Jesus* had never been so baptized before.

II. How Paul conferred the extraordinary gifts of the Holy Ghost upon them, v. 6. 1. Paul solemnly *prayed to God* to give them those gifts, signified by his *laying his hands on them*, which was a gesture used in blessing by the patriarchs, especially in conveying the great trust of the promise, as Gen. xlviii. 14. 2. God granted the thing he prayed for: *The Holy Ghost came upon them* in a surprising overpowering manner, and *they spoke with tongues and prophesied*, as the apostles did and the first Gentile converts, *ch.* x. 44. Oh, what a wonderful change was here made on a sudden in these men! those that but just now had *not so much as heard that there was any Holy Ghost* are now themselves filled with the Holy Ghost; for the Spirit, like the wind, blows where and when he listeth.

MIRACLES BY PAUL (*vv.* 8–12)

Paul is here very busy at Ephesus to do good.

I. He begins, as usual, in the Jews' synagogue, and makes the first offer of the gospel to them, that he might gather in the *lost sheep of the house of Israel*, who were now scattered upon the mountains. Observe,

What success his preaching had among them. (1) There were some that were persuaded to believe in Christ; some think this is intimated in the word *persuading*—he prevailed with them. But, (2) Many continued in their infidelity, and were confirmed in their prejudices against Christianity. When Paul called on them before, and preached only some general things to them, they courted his stay among them (*ch.* xviii. 20); but now that he settled among them, and his word came more closely to their consciences, they were soon weary of him.

II. When he had carried the matter as far as it would go in the synagogue of the Jews, and found that their opposition grew more obstinate, he left the synagogue, because he could not safely, or rather because he could not comfortably and successfully, continue in communion with them. Now observe,

1. When Paul departed from the Jews he took the disciples with him, and *separated them, to save them from that untoward generation* (according to the charge Peter gave to his new converts, *ch.* ii. 40).

2. When Paul separated from the synagogue he set up a meeting of his own, he *disputed daily in the school of one Tyrannus*. He left the synagogue of the Jews, that he might go on with the more freedom in his work; still he disputed for Christ and Christianity, and was

ready to answer all opponents
whatsoever in defence of them; and
he had by this separation a double
advantage. (1) That now his opportunities were more frequent. In the
synagogue he could only preach
every sabbath day (*ch.* xiii. 42), but
now he disputed daily, he set up a
lecture every day, and thus redeemed time. (2) That now they were
more open. To the synagogue of
the Jews none might come, nor
could come, but Jews or proselytes;
Gentiles were excluded; but, when
he set up a meeting in the school of
Tyrannus, both Jews and Greeks
attended his ministry, *v.* 10.

3. Here he continued his labours
for *two years*, read his lectures and
disputed daily.

4. The gospel hereby spread far
and near (*v.* 10): *All those that
dwelt in Asia heard the word of the
Lord Jesus.* The gospel is Christ's
word, it is a word concerning
Christ. This they heard, or at least
heard of it. Some of all sects, some
out of all parts both in city and
country, embraced this gospel, and
entertained it, and by them it was
communicated to others; and so
they all *heard the word of the Lord
Jesus*, or might have heard it.

III. God confirmed Paul's doctrine by miracles, which awakened
people's enquiries after it, fixed
their affection to it, and engaged
their belief of it, *vv.* 11, 12. 1. They
were *special miracles*, God exerted
powers that were not according to
the common course of nature.

3. He not only cured the sick that
were brought to him, or to whom
he was brought, but *from his body
were brought to the sick handker-
chiefs or aprons.* Now was fulfilled

that word of Christ to his disciples,
*Greater works than these shall you
do.* We read of one that was cured
by the touch of Christ's garment
when it was upon him, and he
perceived that *virtue went out of
him*; but here were people cured by
Paul's garments when they were
taken from him.

EXORCISTS DEFEATED
(*vv.* 13–20)

I. Here is the confusion of some
of Satan's servants, some *vagabond
Jews*, that were *exorcists*, who
made use of Christ's name profanely and wickedly in their diabolical
enchantments, but were made to
pay dearly for their presumption.
Observe,

1. The general character of those
who were guilty of this presumption. They were Jews, but *vagabond*
Jews, were of the Jewish nation and
religion, but went about from town
to town to get money by conjuring.

2. A particular account of some
at Ephesus that led this course of
life and came thither in their
travels; they were *seven sons of one
Sceva, a Jew, and chief of the
priests, v.* 14.

3. The profaneness they were
guilty of: *They took upon them to
call over evil spirits the name of the
Lord Jesus*; not as those who had a
veneration for Christ and a confidence in his name; but as those who
were willing to try all methods to
carry on their wicked trade.

4. The confusion they were put to
in their impious operations. (1) The
evil spirit gave them a sharp reply
(*v.* 15): *"Jesus I know, and Paul I
know; but who are you?* I know that
Jesus has conquered principalities

and powers, and that Paul has authority in his name to cast out devils; but what power have you to command us in his name, or who gave you any such power?" (2) *The man in whom the evil spirit was* gave them a warm reception, fell foul upon them, *leaped upon them* in the height of his frenzy and rage; so that *they fled out of the house*, not only *naked*, but *wounded*; their clothes pulled off their backs, and their heads broken. This is written for a warning to all those who name the name of Christ, but do not depart from iniquity.

5. The general notice that was taken of this, and the good impression it made upon many (*v.*17). God was glorified; *the name of the Lord Jesus*, by which his faithful servants cast out devils and cured diseases, without any resistance, *was the more magnified*; for now it appeared to be a name above every name.

II. Here is the conversion of others of Satan's servants, with the evidences of their conversion.

1. Those that had been guilty of wicked practices confessed them, *v.* 18. These confessions were not extorted from them, but were voluntary, for the ease of their consciences, upon which the late miracles had struck a terror.

2. Those that had conversed with wicked books burnt them (*v.* 19). It is taken for granted that they were convinced of the evil of these curious arts, and resolved to deal in them no longer; but they did not think this enough unless they burnt their books. (1) Thus they showed a holy indignation at the sins they had been guilty of. (2) Thus they showed their resolution

never to return to the use of those arts, and the books which related to them, again. (3) Thus they showed a contempt of the wealth of this world; for the price of the books was cast up, probably by those that persuaded them not to burn them, and it was found to be *fifty thousand pieces of silver*.

III. Here is a general account of the progress and success of the gospel in and about Ephesus (*v.* 20): *So mightily grew the word of God, and prevailed.*

RIOT AT EPHESUS (*vv.* 21–41)

I. Paul is here brought into some trouble at Ephesus, just when he is forecasting to go thence, and to cut out work for himself elsewhere. See here,

1. How he laid his purpose of going to other places, *vv.* 21, 22. Having spent above two years at Ephesus, (1) He designed a visit to the churches of Macedonia and Achaia, especially of Philippi and Corinth, the chief cities of those provinces, *v.* 21. There he had planted churches, and now is concerned to visit them. He *purposed in the spirit*, either in his own spirit, not communicating his purpose as yet, but keeping it to himself; or by the direction of the Holy Spirit, who was his guide in all his motions, and by whom he was led. (2) Thence he designed to go to Jerusalem, to visit the brethren there; and thence he intended to go to Rome; to see the Christians there, and to do them some service, Rom. i. 11. (3) He sent Timothy and Erastus into Macedonia, to give them notice of the visit he intended them, and to

get their collection ready for the poor saints at Jerusalem.

2. How he was seconded in his purpose, and obliged to pursue it by the troubles which at length he met with at Ephesus.

II. But in the trouble here related, he was worse frightened than hurt. Here is,

1. A great complaint against Paul and the other preachers of the gospel for drawing people off from the worship of Diana, and so spoiling the trade of the silversmiths that worked for Diana's temple.

(1) The complainant is Demetrius, a silversmith, a principal man, it is likely, of the trade, and one that would be thought to understand and consult the interests of it more than others of the company. Whether he worked in other sorts of plate or no we are not told; but the most advantageous branch of his trade was *making silver shrines for Diana*, v. 24.

(2) The persons he appeals to are not the magistrates, but the mob.

(3) His complaint and representation are very full. [1] He lays it down for a principle that the art and mystery of making silver shrines for the worshippers of Diana was very necessary to be supported and kept up (v. 25). [2] He charges it upon Paul that he had dissuaded men from worshipping idols. The words, as they are laid in the indictment, are, that he had asserted, *Those are no gods which are made with hands*, v. 26. [3] He reminds them of the danger which their trade was in of going to decay. Whatever touches this touches them in a sensible tender

part. [4] He pretends a mighty zeal for Diana, and a jealousy for her honour.

2. The popular resentment of this complaint. The charge was managed by a craftsman, and was framed to incense the common people, and it had the desired effect. *The whole city was full of confusion* —the common and natural effect of an intemperate zeal for a false religion.

3. The proceedings of the mob under the power of these resentments, and how far they were carried.

(1) They laid hands on some of Paul's companions, and hurried them into the theatre (v. 29). Those whom they seized were *Gaius and Aristarchus*, of both of whom we read elsewhere. *Gaius was of Derbe*, ch. xx. 4. *Aristarchus* is also there spoken of, and Col. iv. 10. They came with Paul *from Macedonia*, and this was their only crime, that they were Paul's companions in travel, both in services and sufferings.

(2) *Paul*, who had escaped being seized by them, when he perceived his friends in distress for his sake, *would have entered in unto the people*, to sacrifice himself, if there were no other remedy, rather than his friends should suffer upon his account; and it was an evidence of a generous spirit, and that he loved his neighbour as himself.

(3) He was persuaded from it by the kindness of his friends, who overruled him.

(4) The mob was in a perfect confusion (v. 32): *Some cried one thing and some another*, according as their fancies and passions, and

perhaps the reports they received, led them. For the truth was *the greater part knew not wherefore they had come together*.

(5) The Jews would have interested themselves in this tumult (in other places they had been the first movers of such riots) but now at Ephesus they had not interest enough to raise the mob, and yet, when it was raised, they had ill-will enough to set in with it (*v. 33*): *They drew Alexander out of the multitude*, called him out to speak on the behalf of the Jews against Paul and his companions.

(6) This occasioned the prosecutors to drop the prosecution of Paul's friends, and to turn it into acclamations in honour of their goddess (*v. 34*): *When they knew that he was a Jew*, and, as such, an enemy to the worship of Diana (for the Jews had now an implacable hatred to idols and idolatry), whatever he had to say for Paul or against him, they were resolved not to hear him, and therefore set the mob a shouting, "*Great is Diana of the Ephesians*".

4. The suppressing and dispersing of these rioters, by the prudence and vigilance of *the town-clerk*. With much ado he, at length, stilled the noise, so as to be heard, and then made a pacific speech to them, and gave us an instance of that of Solomon, *The words of wise men are heard in quiet more than the cry of him that rules among fools*, as Demetrius did. Eccl. ix. 17.

See here, [1] How the overruling providence of God preserves the public peace, by an unaccountable power over the spirits of men. [2] See how many ways God has of

protecting his people. Perhaps this town-clerk was no friend at all to Paul, nor to the gospel he preached, yet his human prudence is made to serve the divine purpose.

CHAPTER TWENTY

TO TROAS (*vv* 1-6)

These travels of Paul which are thus briefly related, if all in them had been recorded that was memorable and worthy to be written in letters of gold, *the world would not contain the books that would have been* written; and therefore we have only some general hints of occurrences, which therefore ought to be the more precious. Here is,

I. Paul's departure from Ephesus. He had tarried there longer than he had done at any one place since he had been ordained to the apostleship of the Gentiles; and now it was time to think of removing, for he must *preach in other cities also*.

II. His visitation of the Greek churches, which he had planted, and more than once watered, and which appear to have laid very near his heart.

III. The altering of his measures; for we cannot always stand to our purposes. Accidents unforeseen put us upon new counsels, which oblige us to purpose with a proviso. 1. *Paul was about to sail into Syria, to Antioch*, whence he was first sent out into the service of the Gentiles, and which therefore in his journeys he generally contrived to take in his way; but he changed his mind, and resolved *to return to Macedonia*, the same way he came. 2. The reason was because the Jews, expecting he would steer that course as usual, had way-laid him, designing to be the death of him.

IV. His companions in his travels when he went into Asia; they are here named, *v.* 4.

V. His coming to Troas, where he had appointed a general rendezvous of his friends. 1. They went before, and stayed for him at Troas (*v.* 5), designing to go along with him to Jerusalem, as Trophimus particularly did, *ch.* xxi. 29. 2. Paul made the best of his way thither; and, it should seem, Luke was now in company with him; for he says, *We sailed from Philippi* (*v.* 6), and the first time we find him in his company was here at Troas, *ch.* xvi. 11. *The days of unleavened bread* are mentioned only to describe the time, not to intimate that Paul kept the passover after the manner of the Jews.

A MIRACLE AT TROAS
(*vv.* 7–12)

We have here an account of what passed at Troas the last of the seven days that Paul stayed there.

I. There was a solemn religious assembly of the Christians that were there, according to their constant custom, and the custom of all the churches. They *came together upon the first day of the week*, which they called *the Lord's day* (Rev. i. 10), the Christian sabbath, celebrated to the honour of Christ and the Holy Spirit, in remembrance of the resurrection of Christ, and the pouring out of the Spirit, both on the first day of the week.

II. In this assembly Paul gave them a sermon, a long sermon, a farewell sermon, *v.* 7. 1. He gave them a sermon: he *preached to them*. Though they were disciples already, yet it was very necessary they should have the word of God preached to them, in order to their increase in knowledge and grace. 2. It was a farewell sermon, he being *ready to depart on the morrow*. 3. It was a very long sermon: He *continued his speech until midnight*; for he had a great deal to say, and knew not that ever he should have another opportunity of preaching to them.

III. *A young man* in the congregation, that slept at sermon, was killed by a fall *out of the window, but raised to life again*; his name signifies *one that had good fortune— Eutychus, bene fortunatus*; and he answered his name. Observe,

1. The infirmity with which he was overtaken. It is probable his parents brought him, though but a boy, to the assembly, out of a desire to have him well instructed in the things of God by such a preacher as Paul. The particular notice taken of his sleeping makes us willing to hope none of the rest slept, though it was sleeping time and after supper; but this youth fell fast asleep, he was *carried away with it* (so the word is), which intimates that he strove against it, but was overpowered by it, and at last sunk down with sleep.

2. The calamity with which he was seized herein: *He fell down from the third loft, and was taken up dead*.

3. The miraculous mercy shown him in his recovery *to life again, v.* 10. Various speculations, we may suppose, this ill accident had occasioned in the congregation, but

Paul puts an end to them all: *"Trouble not yourselves,* be not in any disorder about it, let it not put you into any hurry, *for his life is in him;* he is not dead, but sleepeth: lay him awhile upon a bed, and he will come to himself, for he is now alive.' Thus, when Christ raised Lazarus, he said, *Father, I thank thee that thou hast heard me.* (3) He returned to his work immediately after this interruption (*v.* 11): *He came up again* to the meeting, they broke bread together in a love-feast, which usually attended the eucharist, in token of their communion with each other, and for the confirmation of friendship among them; and *they talked a long while, even till break of day.* (4) Before they parted *they brought the young man alive* into the congregation, every one congratulating him upon his return to life from the dead, and *they were not a little comforted, v.* 12.

ON VOYAGE (*vv.* 13–16)

Paul is hastening towards Jerusalem, but strives to do all the good he can by the way. He had called at Troas, and done good there; and now he makes a sort of coasting voyage, the merchants would call it a trading voyage, going from place to place, and no doubt endeavouring to make every place he came to the better for him, as every good man should do.

I. He sent his companions by sea to Assos, but he himself was *minded to go afoot, v.* 13. That he might call on his friends by the way, and do good among them, either converting sinners or edifying saints; and in both he was

serving his great Master, and carrying on his great work.

II. At Assos he went on board with his friends. There they *took him in;* for by this time he had enough of his walk, and was willing to betake himself to the other way of travelling.

III. He made the best of his way to Jerusalem. He aimed to be there by the feast of pentecost because it was a time of concourse, which would give him an opportunity of propagating the gospel among the Jews and proselytes, who came from all parts to worship at the feast: and the feast of pentecost had been particularly made famous among the Christians by the pouring out of the Spirit.

FAREWELL TO EPHESUS
(*vv.* 17–35)

These elders, or presbyters, some think, were those twelve who received the Holy Ghost by Paul's hands, *ch.* xix. 6. But, besides these, it is probable that Timothy had ordained other elders there for the service of that church, and the country about; these Paul sent for, that he might instruct and encourage them to go on in the work to which they had laid their hands. And what instructions he gave to them they would give to the people under their charge.

I. He appeals to them concerning both his life and doctrine, all the time he had been in and about Ephesus (*v.* 18): "*You know after what manner I have been with you,* and how I have done the work of an apostle among you." He mentions this as a confirmation of his commission and consequently of the

doctrine he had preached among
them.

1. His spirit and conversation
were excellent and exemplary; they
knew after what manner he had
been among them, and how he had
had his conversation towards them,
in simplicity and godly sincerity (2
Cor. i. 12), how holily, justly, and
unblamably he behaved himself,
and how gentle he was towards
them, 1 Thess. ii. 7, 10.

2. His preaching was likewise
such as it should be, *vv.* 20, 21. He
came to Ephesus to preach the
gospel of Christ among them, and
he had been faithful both to them
and to him that appointed him. He
was a truly evangelical preacher.
He did not preach philosophical
notions, or matters of doubtful
disputation, nor did he preach
politics, or intermeddle at all with
affairs of state or the civil government; but he preached faith and
repentance, the two great gospel
graces, the nature and necessity of
them; these he urged upon all
occasions.

II. He declares his expectation of
sufferings and afflictions in his
present journey to Jerusalem, *vv.*
22–24.

(1) Of holy courage and resolution in our work, notwithstanding
the difficulties and oppositions we
meet with in it; he saw them before
him, but he made nothing of them.
None of these things moved him.
[1] They did not drive him off from
his work; he did not tack about,
and go back again, when he saw the
storm rise, but went on resolutely,
preaching there, where he knew how
dearly it would cost him. [2] They
did not deprive him of his comfort,

nor make him drive on heavily in
his work. In the midst of troubles
he was as one unconcerned.

(2) Of a holy contempt of life,
and the continuance and comforts
of it: *Neither count I my life dear to
myself.* Life is sweet, and is naturally dear to us. *All that a man has
will he give for his life*; but all that
a man has, and life too, will he give
who understands himself aright and
his own interest, rather than lose
the favour of God and hazard
eternal life. Paul was of this mind.

(3) Of a holy concern to go
through with the work of life,
which should be much more our
care than to secure either the outward comforts of it or the countenance of it. Two things this great
and good man is in care about, and
if he gain them it is no matter to
him what becomes of life: [1] That
he may be found faithful to the
trust reposed in him, that he may
*finish the ministry which he has
received of the Lord Jesus*, may do
the work which he was sent into the
world about, or, rather, which he
was sent into the church about. [2]
That he may finish well. He cares
not when the period of his life
comes, nor how, be it ever so soon,
ever so sudden, ever so sad, as to
outward circumstances, so that he
may but *finish his course with joy.*

III. Counting upon it that this
was the last time they should see
him, he appeals to their consciences
concerning his integrity, and demands of them a testimony to it.

1. He tells them that he was now
taking his last leave of them (*v.* 25).

2. He appeals to them concerning
the faithful discharge of his ministry among them (*v.* 26): "*Where-*

fore, seeing my ministry is at an end with you, it concerns both you and me to reflect, and look back;" and, (1) He challenges them to prove him unfaithful, or to have said or done any thing by which he had made himself accessory to the ruin of any precious soul: *I am pure from the blood of all men*, the blood of souls. This plainly refers to that of the prophet (Ezek. xxxiii. 6), where the blood of him that perishes by the sword of the enemy is said to be required at the hand of the unfaithful watchman that did not give warning: 'You cannot say but I have given warning, and therefore no man's blood can be laid at my door." (2) He therefore leaves the blood of those that perish upon their own heads, because they had fair warning given them, but they would not take it. (3) He charges these ministers to look to it that they took care and pains, as he had done: "*I am pure from the blood of all men*, see that you keep yourselves so too."

3. He proves his own fidelity with this (*v.* 27): *For I have not shunned to declare unto you all the counsel of God.* (1) He had preached to them nothing but the counsel of God, and had not added any inventions of his own. (2) He had preached to them the whole counsel of God. As he had preached to them the gospel pure, so he had preached it to them entire. (3) He had not shunned to do it; had not wilfully nor designedly avoided the declaring of any part of the counsel of God.

IV. He charges them as ministers to be diligent and faithful in their work.

1. He commits the care of the church at Ephesus, that is, the saints, the Christians that were there and thereabouts (Eph. i. 1), to them, who, though doubtless they were so numerous that they could not all meet in one place, but worshipped God in several congregations, under the conduct of several ministers, are yet called here *one flock*, because they not only agreed in one faith, as they did with all Christian churches, but in many instances they kept up communion one with another. To these elders or presbyters the apostle here, upon the actual foresight of his own final leaving them, commits the government of this church, and tells then that not he, but *the Holy Ghost, had made them overseers—bishops of the flock.*

2. He commanded them to mind the work to which they were called. Dignity calls for duty; if the Holy Ghost has made them *overseers of the flock*, that is, shepherds, they must be true to their trust. They must feed the church of God, must do all the parts of the shepherd's office, must lead the sheep of Christ into the green pastures, must lay meat before them, must do what they can to heal those that have no appetite to their meat, must feed them with wholesome doctrine, with a tender evangelical discipline, and must see that nothing is wanting that is necessary in order to their being nourished up to eternal life. They must watch (*v.* 31), as shepherds keep watch over their flocks by night, must be awake and watchful, must not give way to spiritual sloth and slumber, but must stir up themselves to their business and closely attend it.

3. He gives them several good reasons why they should mind the business of their ministry.

(1) Let them consider the interest of their Master, and his concern for the flock that was committed to their charge, *v.* 28. It is *the church which he has purchased with his own blood.*

(2) Let them consider the danger that the flock was in of being made a prey to its adversaries, *vv.* 29, 30. "If the flock be thus precious upon the account of its relation to God, and its redemption by Christ, then you are concerned to take heed both to yourselves and to it." Here are reasons for both. [1] *Take heed to the flock*, for wolves are abroad, that seek to devour (*v.* 29): *I know this, that after my departure grievous wolves shall enter in among you. First,* Some understand it of persecutors, that will inform against the Christians, and incense the magistrates against them, and will have no compassion on the flock. *Secondly,* It is rather to be understood of seducers and false teachers. Probably Paul has an eye to those of the circumcision, who preached up the ceremonial law; these he calls *grievous wolves*, for though they came in sheep's clothing, nay, in shepherd's clothing, they made mischief in the congregations of Christians, sowed discord among them, drew away many from the pure gospel of Christ, and did all they could to blemish and defame those that adhered to it. [2] *Take heed to yourselves*, for some shepherds will apostatize (*v.* 30). Some read it, *to draw away disciples after them*—those that are already disciples of Christ, draw them from him to follow them. But, though

there were some such seducers in the church of Ephesus, yet it should seem by Paul's Epistle to that church that that church was not so much infested with false teachers, at least not so much infected with their false doctrine, as some other churches were; but its peace and purity were preserved by the blessing of God on the pains and vigilance of these presbyters.

(3) Let them consider the great pains that Paul had taken in planting this church (*v.* 31): "*Remember that for the space of three years*" (for so long he had been preaching in Ephesus, and the parts adjacent) "*I ceased not to warn every one night and day with tears*; and be not you negligent in building upon that foundation which I was so diligent to lay."

V. He recommends them to divine direction and influence (*v.* 32). They were in care what would become of them, how they should go on in their work, break through their difficulties, and what provision would be made for them and their families. In answer to all these perplexities, Paul directs them to look up to God with an eye of faith, and beseeches God to look down on them with an eye of favour.

VI. He recommends himself to them as an example of indifference to this world, and to every thing in it, which, if they would walk in the same spirit and in the same steps, they would find to contribute greatly to their easy and comfortable passage through it. He had recommended them to God, and to the word of his grace, for spiritual blessings, which, without doubt,

117

are the best blessings; but what shall they do for food for their families, an agreeable subsistence for themselves, and portions for their children? "As to these," Paul says, "do as I did;" and how was that? He here tells them,

1. That he never aimed at worldly wealth (*v.* 33).

2. That he had worked for his living, and taken a great deal of pains to get bread (*v.* 34). When he was to earn his bread, he did it by a manual occupation. Paul had a head and a tongue that he might have got money by, but they were these hands, saith he, *that ministered to my necessities.*

3. That even then, when he worked for the supply of his own necessities, yet he spared something out of what he got for the relief of others; for this he here obliges them to do (*v.* 35). The sentiment of the children of this world is contrary to this; they are afraid of giving. "This giving," they say, "undoes us all;" but they are in hope of getting. *Every one for his gain from his quarter,* Isa. lvi. 11. Clear gain is with them the most blessed thing that can be; but Christ tells us, *It is more blessed* (more excellent in itself, an evidence of a more excellent disposition of mind, and the way to a better blessedness at last) *to give than to receive.* It makes us more like to God, who gives to all, and receives from none; and to the Lord Jesus, *who went about doing good.* It is more blessed to give our pains than to receive pay for it, and what we should delight to do if the necessities of ourselves and families would admit it.

PAUL TAKES HIS LEAVE
(*vv.* 36–38)

After the parting sermon that Paul preached to the elders of Ephesus, which was very affecting, we have here the parting prayer and tears, which were yet more affecting; we can scarcely read the account here given of them, and meditate upon them with dry eyes.

I. They parted with prayer ·(*v.* 36): *And, when he had thus spoken, he kneeled down, and prayed with them all.* And, no doubt, it was a prayer every way suited to the present mournful occasion. He committed them to God in this prayer, prayed that he would not leave them, but continue his presence with them.

II. They parted with tears, abundance of tears, and most affectionate embraces, *vv.* 37, 38.

III. They *accompanied him unto the ship,* partly to show their respect for him (they would bring him on his way as far as they could), and partly that they might have a little more of his company and conversation. But this was a comfort to both sides, and soon turned this tide of passion, that the presence of Christ both went with him and stayed with them.

CHAPTER TWENTY-ONE
A WARNING FOR PAUL
(*vv.* 1–7)

We may observe here,

I. How much ado Paul had to get clear from Ephesus, intimated in the first words of the chapter, *after we had gotten from them,* that is, were drawn from them as by violence. It was a force put upon both sides; Paul was loth to leave them, and they were loth to part with him, and yet there was no remedy, but so it must be.

II. What a prosperous voyage they had thence. Without any difficulty, *they came with a straight course*, by direct sailing, *to Coos*, a famous Grecian island,—*the next day to Rhodes*, talked of for the Colossus there,—*thence to Patara*, a famous port, the metropolis of Lycia (*v.* 1); here they very happily *found a ship sailing over into Phenicia*, the very course they were steering, *v.* 2. This ship that was bound for Phenicia (that is, Tyre) they took the convenience of, *went on board, and set sail* for Tyre. In this voyage *they discovered Cyprus*, the island that Barnabas was of, and which he took care of, and therefore Paul did not visit it, but *we left it on the left hand* (*v.* 3), *sailed* upon the coast of *Syria, and* at length *landed at Tyre*, that celebrated mart of the nations, so it had been, but was now reduced; yet something of a trade it had still, *for there the ship was to unlade her burden*, and did so.

III. The halt that Paul made at Tyre.

1. *At Tyre he found disciples*, some that had embraced the gospel, and professed the Christian faith.

2 Paul, *finding those disciples at Tyre, tarried there seven days*, they urging him to stay with them as long as he could.

3. The disciples at Tyre were endowed with such gifts that they could by the Spirit foretell the troubles Paul would meet with at Jerusalem; for *the Holy Ghost witnessed it in every city, ch.* xx. 23.

Therefore they said to him, *by the Spirit, that he should not go up*, because they concluded it would be most for the glory of God that he should continue at liberty; and it was not at all their fault to think so, and consequently to dissuade him; but it was their mistake, for his trial would be for the glory of God and the furtherance of the gospel, and he knew it; and the importunity that was used with him, to dissuade him from it, renders his pious and truly heroic resolution the more illustrious.

4. The disciples of Tyre, though they were none of Paul's converts, yet showed a very great respect to Paul, whose usefulness in the church they had heard so much of when he departed from Tyre.

5. They parted with prayer, as Paul and the Ephesian elders had done, *ch.* xx. 36. Thus Paul has taught us by example, as well as rule, to pray always, to pray without ceasing.

6. They parted at last (*v.* 6):*When we had taken our leave one of another*, with the most affectionate embraces and expressions of love and grief, *we took ship* to be gone, and *they returned home again*, each complaining that this is a parting world.

IV. Their arrival at Ptolemais, which was not far from Tyre (*v.* 7). Paul begged leave to go ashore there, *to salute the brethren,* to enquire of their state, and to testify his good will to them.

A SECOND WARNING
(*vv.* 8–14)

We have here Paul and his company arrived at length at Cæsarea, where he designed to make some stay, it being the place where the gospel was first preached to the Gentiles, and *the Holy Ghost fell upon them*, *ch.* x. 1, 44. Now here we are told,

I. Who it was that entertained Paul and his company *at Cæsarea*. He seldom had occasion to go to a public house, but, wherever he came, some friend or other took him in, and bade him welcome. Now at Cæsarea,

1. They were entertained by Philip the evangelist, whom we left at Cæsarea many years ago, after he had baptized the eunuch (*ch.* viii. 40), and there we now find him again.

2. This Philip *had four maiden daughters, who did prophesy*, *v.* 9. It intimates that they prophesied of Paul's troubles at Jerusalem, as others had done, and dissuaded him from going; or perhaps they prophesied for his comfort and encouragement, in reference to the difficulties that were before him. Here was a further accomplishment of that prophecy, Joel ii. 28, of such a plentiful pouring out of the Spirit upon all flesh that their *sons and their daughters should prophesy*, that is, foretell things to come.

II. A plain and full prediction of the sufferings of Paul, by a noted prophet, *vv.* 10, 11. *Agabus took Paul's girdle*, when he laid it by, or perhaps took it from about him, and with it *bound* first *his own hands, and then his own feet*, or perhaps bound his hands and feet together; this was designed both to confirm the prophecy (it was as sure to be done as if it were done already) and to affect those about him with

it, because that which we see usually makes a greater impression upon us than that which we only hear of. *Thus saith the Holy Ghost*, the Spirit of prophecy, *So shall the Jews at Jerusalem bind the man that owneth this girdle, and*, as they dealt with his Master (Matt. xx. 18, 19), *shall deliver him into the hands of the Gentiles*, as the Jews in other places had all along endeavoured to do, by accusing him to the Roman governors.

III. The great importunity which his friends used with him to dissuade him from going forward to Jerusalem, *v.* 12.

IV. The holy bravery and intrepidity with which Paul persisted in his resolution, *v.* 13.

1. He reproves them for dissuading him. Here is a quarrel of love on both sides, and very sincere and strong affections clashing with each other. They love him dearly, and therefore oppose his resolution; he loves them dearly, and therefore chides them for opposing it: *What mean you to weep and to break my heart?* They were an offence to him, as Peter was to Christ, when, in a like case, he said, *Master, spare thyself*. Their weeping about him *broke his heart*.

2. He repeats his resolution to go forward, notwithstanding. Now, (1) See how far his resolution extends: You are told that I must be bound at Jerusalem, and you would have me keep away for fear of this. I tell you, *I am ready not only to be bound, but*, if the will of God be so, *to die at Jerusalem*; not only to lose my liberty, but to lose my life." (2) See what it is that carries him out thus, that makes him willing

to suffer and die: it is *for the name of the Lord Jesus.* All that a man has will he give for his life; but life itself will Paul give for the service and honour of the name of Christ.

V. The patient acquiescence of his friends in his resolution, *v.* 14. 1. They submitted to the wisdom of a good man. They had carried the matter as far as they could with decency; but, "*when he would not be persuaded, we ceased* our importunity." They submitted to the will of a good God: *We ceased,* saying, *The will of the Lord be done.* They did not resolve his resolution into his stubbornness, but into his willingness to suffer, and God's will that he should.

PAUL ARRIVES AT JERUSALEM (*vv.* 15–26)

In these verses we have,

I. Paul's journey to Jerusalem from Cæsarea, and the company that went along with him.

II. Paul's welcome at Jerusalem. 1. Many of the brethren there *received him gladly, v.* 17. They *gladly received his word.* 2. They paid a visit to James and the elders of the church, at a church-meeting (*v.* 18). Paul saluted them all, paid his respects to them, enquired concerning their welfare, and gave them the right hand of fellowship.

III. The account they had from him of his ministry among the Gentiles, and their satisfaction in it. 1. He gave them a narrative of the success of the gospel in those countries where he had been employed, knowing it would be very acceptable to them to hear of the enlarging of Christ's kingdom. Observe how modestly he speaks, not what

things he had wrought (he was but the instrument), but what God had wrought by his ministry. It was *not I, but the grace of God which was with me.* He planted and watered, but God gave the increase. 2. Hence they took occasion to give praise to God (*v.* 20): *When they heard it, they glorified the Lord.* Paul ascribed it all to God, and to God they gave the praise of it.

IV. The request of James and the elders of the church at Jerusalem to Paul, or their advice rather, that he would gratify the believing Jews by showing some compliance with the ceremonial law, and appearing publicly in the temple to offer sacrifice, which was not a thing in itself sinful. It was dead, but not buried; dead, but not yet deadly. And, being not sinful, they thought it was a piece of prudence in Paul to conform thus far.

1. They desired him to take notice of the great numbers there were of the Jewish converts. The number of the names at first was but one hundred and twenty, yet now many thousands. Let none therefore despise the day of small things; for, though the beginning be small, God can make the latter end greatly to increase.

2. They informed him of a prevailing infirmity these believing Jews laboured under, of which they could not yet be cured: *They are all zealous of the law.* They believe in Christ as the true Messiah, they rest upon his righteousness and submit to his government; but they know the law of Moses was of God, they have found spiritual benefit in their attendance on the institutions of it, and therefore they can by no

means think of parting with it, no, nor of growing cold to it. This was a great weakness and mistake, to be so fond of the shadows when the substance was come, to keep their necks under a yoke of bondage when Christ had come to make them free. But see, (1) The power of education and long usage, and especially of a ceremonial law. (2) The charitable allowance that must be made in consideration of these. Their being zealous of the law was capable of a good construction, which charity would put upon it; and it was capable of a good excuse, considering what they were brought up in, and among whom they lived.

3. They gave him to understand that these Jews, who were so zealous of the law, were ill-affected to him, *v.* 21. Now, (1) It was true that Paul preached the abrogation of the law of Moses, taught them that it was impossible to be justified by it, and therefore we are not bound up any longer to the observance of it. But, (2) It was false that he taught them to forsake Moses; for the religion he preached tended not to destroy the law, but to fulfil it. He preached Christ (*the end of the law for righteousness*), and repentance and faith, in the exercise of which we are to make great use of the law.

4. They therefore desired Paul that he would by some public act, now that he had come to Jerusalem, make it appear that the charge against him was false, and that he did not teach people to forsake Moses and to break the customs of the Jewish church, for he himself retained the use of them.

(1) Now something must be done to satisfy them that Paul does not teach the people to forsake Moses, and they think it necessary, [1] For Paul's sake, that his reputation should be cleared. [2] For the people's sake, that they may not continue prejudiced against so good a man, nor lose the benefit of his ministry by those prejudices.

(2) They produce a fair opportunity which Paul might take to clear himself. *We have four men,* Jews who believe, of our own churches, and *they have a vow on them,* a vow of Nazariteship for a certain time; their time has now expired (*v.* 23), and they are to offer their offering according to the law, when they shave the head of their separation, a he-lamb for a burnt-offering, a ewe-lamb for a sin-offering, and a ram for a peace-offering, with other offerings appertinent to them, Num. vi. 13–20. Now Paul having so far of late complied with the law as to take upon him the vow of a Nazarite, and to signify the expiration of it by shaving his head at Cenchrea (*ch.* xviii. 18), according to the custom of those who lived at a distance from the temple, they desire him but to go a little further, and to join with these four in offering the sacrifices of a Nazarite. This, they think, will effectually stop the mouth of calumny, and every one will be convinced that the report was false, that Paul was not the man he was represented to be, did not teach the Jews to forsake Moses, but that he himself, being originally a Jew, walked orderly, and kept the law; and then all would be well.

5. They enter a protestation that this shall be no infringement at all of the decree lately made in favour of the Gentile converts, nor do they intend by this in the least to derogate from the liberty allowed them (*v.* 25).

V. Here is Paul's compliance with it. He was willing to gratify them in this matter. Though he would not be persuaded not to go to Jerusalem, yet, when he was there, he was persuaded to do as they there did, *v.* 26. Now it has been questioned whether James and the elders did well to give Paul this advice, and whether he did well to take it. 1. Some have blamed this occasional conformity of Paul's, as indulging the Jews too much in their adherence to the ceremonial law, and a discouragement of those who stood fast in the liberty wherewith Christ had made them free. But, 2. Others think the advice was prudent and good, and Paul's following it was justifiable enough, as the case stood. It was Paul's avowed principle, *To the Jews became I as a Jew, that I might gain the Jews*, 1 Cor. ix. 20. It is true, this compliance of Paul's sped ill to him, for this very thing by which he hoped to pacify the Jews did but provoke them, and bring him into trouble; yet this is not a sufficient ground to go upon in condemning it: Paul might do well, and yet suffer for it.

PAUL ARRESTED (*vv.* 27–40)

I. We have here Paul seized, and laid hold on.

1. He was seized in the temple, when he was there attending the days of his purifying, and the solemn services of those days, *v.* 27.

2. The informers against him were the Jews of Asia, not those of Jerusalem—the Jews of the dispersion, who knew him best, and who were most exasperated against him.

3. The method they took was to raise the mob, and to incense them against him.

4. The arguments wherewith they exasperated the people against him were popular, but very false and unjust. Note, The enemies of Christianity, since they could never prove it to be an ill thing, have been always very industrious, right or wrong, to put it into an ill name, and so run it down by outrage and outcry.

5. They charge upon him both bad doctrine and bad practice, and both against the Mosaic ritual.

(1) They charge upon him bad doctrine; not only that he holds corrupt opinions himself, but that he vents and publishes them.

(2) They charge upon him bad practices. He *has brought Gentiles also into the temple*, into the inner court of the temple, which none that were uncircumcised were admitted, under any pretence, to come into; there was written upon the wall that enclosed this inner court, in Greek and Latin, *It is a capital crime for strangers to enter.* —Joseph. *Antiq.* lib. xv. cap. 14. They had seen him with him in the city, and therefore they supposed that Paul had brought him with him into the temple, which was utterly false.

II. We have Paul in danger of being pulled in pieces by the rabble.

1. All the city was in an uproar,

v. 30. But God does not reckon himself at all honoured by those whose zeal for him transports them to such irregularities, and who, while they pretend to act for him, act in such a brutish barbarous manner.

2. They drew Paul out of the temple, and shut the doors between the outer and inner court of the temple, or perhaps the doors of the outer court. The officers of the temple shut the doors, either, [1] Lest Paul should find means to get back and take hold of the horns of the altar, and so protect himself by that sanctuary from their rage. Or rather, [2] Lest the crowd should by the running in of more to them be thrust back into the temple, and some outrage should be committed, to the profanation of that holy place.

3. They went about to kill him (v. 31), for they fell a beating him (v. 32), resolving to beat him to death by blows without number, a punishment which the Jewish doctors allowed in some cases (not at all to the credit of their nation), and called *the beating of the rebels*.

III. We have here Paul rescued out of the hands of his Jewish enemies by a Roman enemy.

IV. The provision which the chief captain made, with much ado, to bring Paul to speak for himself.

1. There was no knowing the sense of the people; for when the chief captain enquired concerning Paul, *some cried one thing, and some another*, among the multitude; so that it was impossible for the chief captain to know their mind, when really they knew not either one another's mind or their own, when every one pretended to give the sense of the whole body.

2. There was no quelling the rage and fury of the people; for when *the chief captain commanded that Paul should be carried into the castle*, the tower of Antonia, where the Roman soldiers kept garrison, near the temple, the soldiers themselves had much ado to get him safely thither out of the noise, the people were so violent (v. 35).

3. Paul at length begged leave of the chief captain to speak to him (v. 37).

4. The chief captain tells him what notion he had of him: *Canst thou speak Greek?* I am surprised to hear thee speak a learned language; for, *Art not thou that Egyptian who made an uproar?* The Jews made the uproar, and then would have it thought that Paul had given them occasion for it, by beginning first; for probably some of them whispered this in the ear of the chief captain. It seems, there had lately been an insurrection somewhere in that country, headed by an Egyptian, who took on him to be a prophet. The ringleader of this rebellion, it seems, had made his escape, and the chief captain concluded that one who lay under so great an odium as Paul seemed to lie under, and against whom there was so great an outcry, could not be a criminal of less figure than this Egyptian.

5. Paul rectifies his mistake concerning him, by informing him particularly what he was; not such a vagabond, a scoundrel, a rake, as that Egyptian, who could give no good account of himself. No: *I am a man who is a Jew* originally, and

no Egyptian—a Jew both by nation and religion; *I am of Tarsus, a city of Cilicia,* of honest parents and a liberal education (Tarsus was a university), and, besides that, *a citizen of no mean city.* Whether he means Tarsus or Rome is not certain; they were neither of them mean cities, and he was a freeman of both.

6. He humbly desired a permission from the chief captain, whose prisoner he now was, to speak to the people.

7. He obtained leave to plead his own cause, for he needed not to have counsel assigned him, when the Spirit of the Father was ready to dictate to him, Matt. x. 20. *The chief captain gave him license* (*v.* 40), so that now he could speak with a good grace, and with the more courage; he had, I will not say that favour, but that justice, done him by the chief captain, which he could not obtain from his countrymen the Jews; for they would not hear him, but the captain would, though it were but to satisfy his curiosity. This licence being obtained, (1) The people were attentive to hear. There he *beckoned with the hand unto the people,* made signs to them to be quiet and to have a little patience, for he had something to say to them; and so far he gained his point that every one cried hush to his neighbour, and there was made a profound silence. (2) Paul addressed himself to speak, well assured that he was serving the interest of Christ's kingdom as truly and effectually as if he had been preaching in the synagogue: he *spoke unto them in the Hebrew tongue,* that is, in their own vulgar tongue, which was the language of their country, to which he hereby owned not only an abiding relation, but an abiding respect.

PAUL GAINS A HEARING
(*vv.* 1–2)

Paul had, in the last verse of the foregoing chapter, gained a great point, by commanding so profound a silence after so loud a clamour. Now here observe,

I. With what an admirable composure and presence of mind he addresses himself to speak.

II. What respectful titles he gives even to those who thus abused him, and how humbly he craves their attention.

III. The language he spoke in, which recommended what he said to the auditory. *He spoke in the Hebrew tongue,* that is, the vulgar language of the Jews, which, at this time, was not the pure Old-Testament Hebrew, but the Syriac, a dialect of the Hebrew, or rather a corruption of it, as the Italian of the Latin.

PAUL'S DEFENCE
(*vv.* 3–21)

Paul here gives such an account of himself as might serve not only to satisfy the chief captain that he was not that Egyptian he took him to be, but the Jews also that he was not that enemy to their church and nation, to their law and temple, they took him to be, and that what he did in preaching Christ, and particularly in preaching him to the Gentiles, he did by a divine commission. He here gives them to understand,

I. What his extraction and education were. 1. That he was one of their own nation, *of the stock of Israel, of the seed of Abraham, a Hebrew of the Hebrews*, not of any obscure family, or a renegado of some other nation. 2. That he was born in a creditable reputable place, *in Tarsus, a city of Cilicia*, and was by his birth a freeman of that city. 3. That he had a learned and liberal education. He was not only a Jew, and a gentleman, but a scholar. 4. That he was in his early days a very forward and eminent professor of the Jews' religion; his studies and learning were all directed that way. So far was he from being principled in his youth with any disaffection to the religious usages of the Jews that there was not a young man among them who had a greater and more entire veneration for them than he had, was more strict in observing them himself, or more hot in enforcing them upon others.

II. What a fiery furious persecutor he had been of the Christian religion in the beginning of his time, *vv.* 4, 5. He mentions this to make it the more plainly and evidently to appear that the change which was wrought upon him, when he was converted to the Christian faith, was purely the effect of a divine power.

III. In what manner he was converted, and made what he now was. 1. He was as fully bent upon persecuting the Christians just before Christ arrested him as ever. He *made his journey, and was come nigh to Damascus* (*v.* 6), and had no other thought than to execute the cruel design he was sent upon. 2.

It was *a light from heaven* that first startled him, *a great light*, which *shone suddenly round about him*, and the Jews knew that God is light, and his angels angels of light, and that such a light as this shining at noon, and therefore exceeding that of the sun, must be from God. 3. It was a *voice from heaven* that first begat in him awful thoughts of Jesus Christ, of whom before he had had nothing but hateful spiteful thoughts. By which it appeared that this Jesus of Nazareth, whom they also were now persecuting, was one that spoke from heaven, and they knew it was dangerous resisting one that did so, Heb. xii. 25. 4. Lest it should be objected, "How came this light and voice to work such a change upon him, and not upon those that journeyed with him?" (though, it is very probable, it had a good effect upon them, and that they thereupon became Christians), he observes *that his fellow travellers saw indeed the light, and were afraid* they should be consumed with fire from heaven; but, though the light made them afraid, they heard not the voice of him that spoke to Paul, that is, they did not distinctly hear the words. 5. He assures them that when he was thus startled he referred himself entirely to a divine guidance; he did not hereupon presently cry out, "Well, I will be a Christian," but, *"What shall I do, Lord?* Let the same voice from heaven that has stopped me in the wrong way guide me into the right way, *v.* 10. 6. As a demonstration of the greatness of that light which fastened upon him, he tells them of the immediate effect it had upon his eye-sight (v. 11): *I could not see for the glory of that light.* Those that were with Paul had not the light so directly darted into their faces as Paul had into his, and therefore they were not blinded, as he was; yet, considering the issue, who would not rather have chosen his lot than theirs? They, having their sight, led *Paul by the hand into the city.*

IV. How he was confirmed in the change he had made, and further directed what he should do, by Ananias who lived at Damascus.

Observe, 1. The character here given of Ananias. He was not a man that was any way prejudiced against the Jewish nation or religion, but was himself *a devout man according to the law*; and he conducted himself so well that he had a *good report of all the Jews that dwelt at Damascus.*

2. The cure immediately wrought by him upon Paul's eyes, which miracle was to confirm Ananias's mission to Paul, and to ratify all that he should afterwards say to him.

3. The declaration which Ananias makes to him of the favour, the peculiar favour, which the Lord Jesus designed him above any other.

(1) In the present manifestation of himself to him (v. 14): *The God of our fathers has chosen thee.* This powerful call is the result of a particular choice. *This God of our fathers has chosen thee that thou shouldst,* [1] *Know his will,* the will of his precept that is to be done by thee, the will of his providence that is to be done concerning thee. He hath chosen thee that thou shouldst know it in a more peculiar manner; not of man nor by man, but

immediately by *the revelation of Christ,* Gal. i. 1, 12. [2] *That thou shouldst see that Just One, and shouldst hear the voice of his mouth,* and so shouldst know his will immediately from himself. This was what Paul was, in a particular manner, chosen to above others; it was a distinguishing favour, that he should see Christ here upon earth after his ascension into heaven.

(2) In the after-manifestation of himself by him to others (v. 15). He told them what God had done for his soul, to encourage them to hope that he would do something for their souls.

4. The counsel and encouragement he gave him to join himself to the Lord Jesus by baptism (v. 16): *Arise, and be baptized.*

V. How he was commissioned to go and preach the gospel to the Gentiles. This was the great thing for which they were so angry at him, and therefore it was requisite he should for this, in a special manner, produce a divine warrant; and here he does it. He tells them, 1. That he received his orders to do it when he was at prayer, begging of God to appoint him his work and to show him the course he should steer. Now as Paul's praying in the temple was an evidence, contrary to their malicious suggestion, that he had a veneration for the temple, though he did not make an idol of it as they did; so God's giving him this commission there in the temple was an evidence that the sending him to the Gentiles would be no prejudice to the temple, unless the Jews by their infidelity made it so. 2. He received it in a vision. He fell *into a trance*

127

(*v.* 17), his external senses, for the present, locked up; he was in an ecstasy, as when he was *caught up into the third heaven*, and was not at that time sensible whether he was *in the body or out of the body.* In this trance he saw Jesus Christ, not with the eyes of his body, as at his conversion, but represented to the eye of his mind (*v.* 18): *I saw him saying unto me.* 3. Before Christ gave him a commission to go to the Gentiles, he told him it was to no purpose for him to think of doing any good at Jerusalem; so that they must not blame him, but themselves, if he be sent to the Gentiles. 4. Paul, notwithstanding this, renewed his petition that he might be employed at Jerusalem, because they knew, better than any did, what he had been before his conversion, and therefore must ascribe so great a change in him to the power of almighty grace, and consequently give the greater regard to his testimony; thus he reasoned, both with himself and with the Lord, and thought he reasoned justly (*vv.* 19, 20). 5. Paul's petition for a warrant to preach the gospel at Jerusalem is overruled, and he has peremptory orders to go among the Gentiles (*v.* 21). It is God that appoints his labourers both their day and their place, and it is fit they should acquiesce in his appointment, though it may cross their own inclinations.

PAUL, THE FREEMAN
(*vv.* 22–30)

Paul was going on with this account of himself. But when he speaks of being sent to the Gentiles, though it was what Christ himself said to him, they cannot bear it, not so much as to hear the Gentiles named, such an enmity had they to them, and such a jealousy of them.

I. They interrupted him, by lifting up their voice, to put him into confusion, and that nobody might hear a word he said.

II. They clamoured against him as one that was unworthy of life, much more of liberty. Without weighing the arguments he had urged in his own defence, or offering to make any answer to them, they cried out with a confused noise, "*Away with such a fellow* as this *from the earth*, who pretends to have a commission to preach to the Gentiles; why, *it is not fit that he should live.*" He that was worthy of the greatest honours of life is condemned as not worthy of life itself.

III. They went stark mad against Paul, and against the chief captain for not killing him immediately at their request, or throwing him as a prey into their teeth, that they might devour him (*v.* 23).

IV. The chief captain took care for his safety, by ordering him to be brought into the castle, *v.* 24.

V. He ordered him the torture, to force from him a confession of some flagrant crimes which had provoked the people to such an uncommon violence against him.

VI. Paul pleaded his privilege as a Roman citizen, by which he was exempted from all trials and punishments of this nature (*v.* 25).

VII. The chief captain was surprised at this, and put into a fright. He had taken Paul to be a vagabond Egyptian, and wondered he could speak Greek (*ch.* xxi. 37), but is much more surprised now he finds that he is as good a gentleman as himself. Now, 1. The chief captain would be satisfied of the truth of this from his own mouth (*v.* 27): *"Tell me, art thou a Roman?"* 2. The chief captain very freely compares notes with him upon this matter, and it appears that the privilege Paul had as a Roman citizen was of the two more honourable than the colonel's; for the colonel owns that his was purchased. 3. This put an immediate stop to Paul's trouble. Those that were appointed to examine him by scourging quitted the spot; they *departed from him* (*v.* 29), lest they should run themselves into a snare. 4. The governor, the next day, brought Paul before the sanhedrim, *v.* 30. He first *loosed him from his bands*, and then summoned the chief priests and all their council to come together to take cognizance of Paul's case, for he found it to be a matter of religion, and therefore looked upon them to be the most proper judges of it. Gallio in this case discharged Paul; finding it to be a matter of their law, he drove the prosecutors from the judgment-seat (*ch.* xviii. 16), and would not concern himself at all in it: but this Roman, who was a military man, kept Paul in custody, and appealed from the rabble to the general assembly.

CHAPTER TWENTY-THREE
PAUL BEFORE THE COUNCIL
(*vv.* 1–5)

Here we have,

I. Paul's protestation of his own

integrity. Whether the chief priest put any question to him, or the chief captain made any representation of his case to the court, we are not told; but Paul appeared here,

1. With a good courage. He was not at all put out of countenance upon his being brought before such an august assembly, for which in his youth he had conceived such a veneration; nor did he fear their calling him to an account about the letters they gave him to Damascus, to persecute the Christians there, though (for aught we know) this was the first time he had ever seen them since; but *he earnestly beheld the council.*

2. With a good conscience, and that gave him a good courage. He said, *"Men and brethren, I have lived in all good conscience before God unto this day.* I may be reproached, my heart does not reproach me, but witnesses for me."

II. The outrage of which Ananias the high priest was guilty: he *commanded those that stood by,* the beadles that attended the court, *to smite him on the mouth* (*v.* 2), to give him a dash on the teeth, either with a hand or with a rod. 1. The high priest was highly offended at Paul; some think, because he looked so boldly and earnestly at the council, as if he would face them down; others because he did not address himself particularly to him as president, with some title of honour and respect, but spoke freely and familiarly to them all, as men and brethren. 2. In his rage he ordered him to be smitten, so to put disgrace upon him, and to be smitten on the mouth, as having offended with his lips, and in token of his enjoining him silence.

III. The denunciation of the wrath of God against the high priest for this *wickedness in the place of judgment* (Eccl. iii. 16). Paul did not speak this in any sinful heat or passion, but in a holy zeal against the high priest's abuse of his power, and with something of a prophetic spirit, not at all with a spirit of revenge. 1. He gives him his due character: *Thou whited wall*; that is, thou hypocrite—a mud-wall, trash and dirt and rubbish underneath, but plastered over, or whitewashed. 2. He reads him his just doom: "*God shall smite thee.*" 3. He assigns a good reason for that doom: "For *sittest thou* there as president in the supreme judicature of the church, pretending *to judge me after the law*, to convict and condemn me by the law, and yet *commandest me to be smitten* before any crime is proved upon me, which is *contrary to the law?*"

IV. The offence which was taken at this bold word of Paul's (*v.* 4): *Those that stood by said, Revilest thou God's high priest?*

V. The excuse that Paul made for what he had said, because he found it was a stumbling-block to his weak brethren, and might prejudice them against him in other things. He wished he had not done it; and though he did not beg the high priest's pardon, nor excuse it to him, yet he begs their pardon who took offence at it, because this was not a time to inform them better, nor to say what he could say to justify himself. 1. He excuses it with this, that he did not consider when he said it to whom he spoke (*v.* 5): *I wist not, brethren, that he was the high priest* I see not how we can with any probability think that Paul did not know him to be the high priest, for Paul had been seven days in the temple at the time of the feast, where he could not miss of seeing the high priest; and his telling him that *he sat to judge him after the law* shows that he knew who he was; but, says he, I did not consider it. Yet, 2. He takes care that what he had said should not be drawn into a precedent, to the weakening of the obligation of that law in the least: *For it is written*, and it remains a law in full force, *Thou shalt not speak evil of the ruler of thy people.*

PAUL DIVIDES THE OPPOSITION (*vv.* 6–11)

I. Paul's own prudence and ingenuity stand him in some stead, and contribute much to his escape. The honest policy Paul used here for his own preservation was to divide his judges, and to set them at variance one with another about him; and, by incensing one part of them more against him, to engage the contrary part for him.

1. The great council was made up of Sadducees and Pharisees, and Paul perceived it. Now these differed very much from one another, and yet they ordinarily agreed well enough to do the business of the council together. (1) The Pharisees were bigots, zealous for the ceremonies, not only those which God had appointed, but those which

were enjoined by the tradition of the elders. But at the same time they were very orthodox in the faith of the Jewish church concerning the world of spirits, the resurrection of the dead, and the life of the world to come. (2) The Sadducees were deists—no friends to the scripture, or divine revelation. The books of Moses they admitted as containing a good history and a good law, but had little regard to the other books of the Old Testament; see Matt. xxii. 23. The account here given of these Sadducees is, [1] That they *deny the resurrection*; not only the return of the body to life, but a future state of rewards and punishments. [2] That they denied the existence of angels and spirits, and allowed of no being but matter. They thought that God himself was corporeal, and had parts and members as we have.

2. In this matter of difference between the Pharisees and Sadducees Paul openly declared himself to be on the Pharisees' side against the Sadducees (*v.* 6). Though Paul preached against the traditions of the elders (as his Master had done), and therein opposed the Pharisees, yet he valued himself more upon his preaching the resurrection of the dead, and a future state, in which he concurred with the Pharisees.

3. This occasioned a division in the council. It is probable that the high priest sided with the Sadducees (as he had done *ch.* v. 17, and made it to appear by his rage at Paul, *v.* 2), which alarmed the Pharisees so much the more; but so it was, there arose a *dissension*

between the Pharisees and the Sadducees (*v.* 7), for this word of Paul's made the Sadducees more warm and the Pharisees more cool in the prosecution of him; so that *the multitude was divided.*

4. The Pharisees hereupon (would one think it?) took Paul's part (*v.* 9). Nay, they go further, "*If a spirit or an angel hath spoken to him* concerning Jesus, and put him upon preaching as he does, though we may not be so far satisfied as to give credit to him, yet we ought to be cautioned not to oppose him, *lest we be found fighting against God*;" as Gamaliel, who was himself a Pharisee, had argued, *ch.* v. 39.

II. The chief captain's care and conduct stand him in more stead. 1. See here Paul's danger. Between his friends and his enemies he had like to have been pulled to pieces. 2. His deliverance: *The chief captain ordered his soldiers to go down* from the upper wards, and *to take them by force from among them*, out of that apartment in *the temple* where he had ordered the council to meet, and *to bring him into the castle*, or tower of Antonia; for he saw he could make nothing of them towards the understanding of the merits of his cause.

III. Divine consolations stood him in most stead of all. Then did the Lord Jesus make him a kind visit, and, though at midnight, yet a very seasonable one (*v.* 11). 1. Christ bids him have a good heart upon it: "*Be of good cheer, Paul*; be not discouraged; let not what has happened sadden thee, nor let what may yet be before thee frighten thee." 2. It is a strange argument which he makes use of to encourage him: _As thou hast testified of me in Jerusalem, so must thou bear witness also at Rome._ One would think this was but cold comfort: "As thou hast undergone a great deal of trouble for me so thou must undergo a great deal more;" and yet this was designed to encourage him; for hereby he is given to understand, (1) That he had been serving Christ as a witness for him in what he had hitherto endured. It was for no fault that he was buffeted, and it was not his former persecuting of the church that was now remembered against him, however he might remember it against himself, but he was still going on with his work. (2) That he had not yet finished his testimony, nor was, by his imprisonment, laid aside as useless, but was only reserved for further service.

A PLOT AGAINST PAUL
(vv. 12–35)

We have here the story of a plot against the life of Paul; how it was laid, how it was discovered, and how it was defeated.

I. How this plot was laid. They found they could gain nothing by popular tumult, or legal process, and therefore have recourse to the barbarous method of assassination; they will come upon him suddenly, and stab him, if they can but get him within their reach. Now observe here,

1. Who they were that formed this conspiracy. They were _certain Jews_ that had the utmost degree of indignation against him because he

was the apostle of the Gentiles, _v._ 12. _And they were more than forty_ that were in the design, _v._ 13.

2. When the conspiracy was formed: _When it was day._ In the night Christ appeared to Paul to protect him, and, when it was day, here were forty men appearing against him to destroy him; they were not up so soon but Christ was up before them.

3. What the conspiracy was. These men _banded together_ in a league, perhaps they called it a _holy_ league; they engaged to stand by one another, and every one, to his power, to be aiding and assisting to murder Paul.

4. How firm they made it, as they thought, that none of them might fly off, upon conscience of the horror of the fact, at second thoughts: _They bound themselves under an anathema_, imprecating the heaviest curses upon themselves, their souls, bodies, and families, if they did not kill Paul, and so quickly _that they would not eat nor drink till they had done it._

5. What method they took to bring it about. Having been all day employed in engaging one another to this wickedness, towards evening they come to the principal members of the great sanhedrim, and, though they might have concealed their mean design and yet might have moved them upon some other pretence to send for Paul, they are so confident of their approbation of this villainy, that they are not ashamed nor afraid to own to them _that they have bound themselves under a great curse_, without consulting the priests first whether they might lawfully do it _that they_

will eat nothing the next day *till they have killed Paul.* And yet, vile as the proposal was which was made to them (for aught that appears), the priests and elders consented to it, and at the first word, without boggling at it in the least, promised to gratify them.

II. How the plot was discovered. See here,

1. How it was discovered to Paul, *v.* 16. There was a youth that was related to Paul, *his sister's son,* whose mother probably lived in Jerusalem; and some how or other, we are not told how, *he heard of their lying in wait,* either overheard them talking of it among themselves, or got intelligence from some that were in the plot: and *he went into the castle,* probably, as he used to do, to attend on his uncle, and bring him what he wanted, which gave him a free access to him, and *he told Paul* what he heard.

2. How it was discovered to the chief captain by the young man that told it to Paul. This part of the story is related very particularly, perhaps because the penman was an eye-witness of the prudent and successful management of this affair, and remembered it with a great deal of pleasure.

III. How the plot was defeated: The chief captain resolves to send him away with all speed out of their reach.

1. He orders a considerable detachment of the Roman forces under his command to get ready *to go to Cæsarea* with all expedition, and to bring Paul thither to *Felix the governor,* where he might sooner expect to have justice done him than by the great sanhedrim at Jerusalem. See how justly God brought the Jewish nation under the Roman yoke, when such a party of the Roman army was necessary to restrain them from the most execrable villainies!

2. The chief captain orders, for the greater security of Paul, that he be taken away at *the third hour of the night,* which some understand of three hours after sun-set, that, it being now soon after *the feast of pentecost* (that is, in the midst of summer), they might have the cool of the night to march in. Others understand it of *three hours after midnight, in the third watch, about three in the morning,* that they might have the day before them, and might get out of Jerusalem before Paul's enemies were stirring, and so might prevent any popular tumult, and leave them to roar when they rose, like a lion disappointed of his prey.

3. *He writes a letter to Felix the governor* of this province, by which he discharges himself from any further care about Paul, and leaves the whole matter with Felix.

4. Paul was accordingly conducted to Cæsarea.

5. He was delivered into the hands of Felix, as his prisoner, *v.* 33. (1) He promises him a speedy trial (*v.* 35): "*I will hear thee when thine accusers have come,* and will have an ear open to both sides, as becomes a judge." (2) He ordered him into custody, that he should *be kept* a prisoner *in Herod's judgment-hall,* in some apartment belonging to that palace which was denominated from Herod the Great, who built it.

THE CASE AGAINST PAUL
(*vv.* 1–9)

We must suppose *that Lysias, the chief captain*, when he had *sent away Paul to Cæsarea*, gave notice to the chief priests, and others that had appeared against Paul, that if they had any thing to accuse him of they must follow him to Cæsarea, and there they would find him, and a judge ready to hear them—thinking, perhaps, they would not have given themselves so much trouble; but what will not malice do?

I. We have here the cause followed against Paul, and it is vigorously carried on. 1. Here is no time lost, for they are ready for a hearing *after five days*; all other business is laid aside immediately, to prosecute Paul; so intent are evil men to do evil! 2. Those who had been his judges do themselves appear here as his prosecutors. *Ananias* himself *the high priest*, who had sat to judge him, now stands to inform against him. *The elders* attended him, to signify their concurrence with him, and to invigorate the prosecution; for they could not find any attorneys or solicitors that would follow it with so much violence as they desired.

II. We have here the cause pleaded against Paul. The prosecutors brought *with them a certain orator named Tertullus*, a Roman, skilled in the Roman law and language, and therefore fittest to be employed in a cause before *the Roman governor*, and most likely to gain favour. His speech (or at least an abstract of it, for it appears, by Tully's orations, that the Roman lawyers, on such occasions, used to make long harangues) is here reported, and it is made up of flattery and falsehood; it calls evil good, and good evil.

1. One of the worst of men is here applauded as one of the best of benefactors, only because he was the judge. Felix is represented by the historians of his own nation, as well as by Josephus the Jew, as a very bad man, who, depending upon his interest in the court, allowed himself in all manner of wickedness, was a great oppressor, very cruel, and very covetous, patronising and protecting assassins.—Joseph. *Antiq*. lib. xx. cap. 6. And yet Tertullus here, in the name of the high priest and elders, and probably by particular directions from them and according to the instructions of his brief, compliments him, and extols him to the sky, as if he were so good a magistrate as never was the like.

2. One of the best of men is here accused as one of the worst of malefactors, only because he was the prisoner. Two things Tertullus here complains of to Felix, in the name of the high priest and the elders:

(1) That the peace of the nation was disturbed by Paul.

[1] Paul was a useful man, and a great blessing to his country, a man of exemplary candour and goodness, obliging to all, and provoking to none; and yet he is here called *a pestilent fellow* (*v.* 5).

[2] Paul was a peace-maker, was a preacher of that gospel which has a direct tendency to *slay all*

enmities, and to establish true and lasting peace; he lived peaceably and quietly himself, and taught others to do so too, and yet is here represented as *a mover of sedition among all the Jews throughout all the world*.

[3] Paul was a man of catholic charity, who did not affect to be singular, but made himself the servant of all for their good; and yet he is here charged as being a *ringleader of the sect of the Nazarenes*, a standard-bearer of that sect, so the word signifies. Now it was true that Paul was an active leading man in propagating Christianity. But, *First*, It was utterly false that this was a sect; he did not draw people to a party or private opinion, nor did he make his own opinions their rule. True Christianity establishes that which is of common concern to all mankind, published good-will to men, and shows us God in Christ reconciling the world to himself; and therefore cannot be thought to take its rise from such narrow opinions and private interests as sects owe their origin to. *Secondly*, It is invidiously called *the sect of the Nazarenes*, by which Christ was represented as of Nazareth, whence no good thing was expected to arise; whereas he was of Bethlehem, where the Messiah was to be born. *Thirdly*, It was false that Paul was the author or standard-bearer of this sect; for he did not draw people to himself, but to Christ—did not preach himself, but Christ Jesus.

[4] Paul had a veneration for the temple, as it was the place which God had chosen to put his name there, and had lately himself with reverence attended the temple-service; and yet it is here charged upon him that he went about to *profane the temple*, and that he designedly put contempt upon it, and violated the laws of it, *v.* 6. Their proof of this failed; for what they alleged as matter of fact was utterly false, and they knew it, *ch.* xxi. 29.

(2) That the course of justice against Paul was obstructed by the chief captain. [1] They pleaded that they *took him, and would have judged him according to their law*. [2] They reflected upon the chief captain as having done them an injury in rescuing Paul out of their hands; whereas he therein not only did him justice, but them the greatest kindness that could be, in preventing the guilt they were bringing upon themselves. [3] They referred the matter to Felix and his judgment, yet seeming uneasy that they were under a necessity of doing so, the chief captain having obliged them to it (*v.* 8).

III. The assent of the Jews to this charge which Tertullus exhibited (*v.* 9): *They confirmed it, saying that those things were so*.

PAUL'S DEFENCE (*vv.* 10–21)

We have here Paul's defence of himself, in answer to Tertullus's charge. And here,

I. He addressed himself very respectfully to the governor, and with a confidence that he would do him justice. Here are no such flattering compliments as Tertullus soothed him up with, but, which was more truly respectful, a profession that he *answered for himself cheerfully*, and with good assurance

135

before him, looking upon him, though not as one that was his friend, yet as one that would be fair and impartial. He thus expresses his expectation that he would be so, to engage him to be so.

II. He denies the facts that he was charged with, upon which their character of him was grounded. Now he would have him to understand (and what he said he was ready, if required, to make out by witnesses),

1. That he came up to Jerusalem on purpose to worship God in peace and holiness, so far was he from any design to move sedition among the people, or to profane the temple. He came to keep up his communion with the Jews, not to put any affront upon them.

2. That it was but twelve days since he came up to Jerusalem, and he had been six days a prisoner; he was alone, and it could not be supposed that in so short a time he could do the mischief they charged upon him. And, as for what he had done in other countries, they knew nothing of it but by uncertain report, by which the matter was very unfairly represented.

3. That he had demeaned himself at Jerusalem very quietly and peaceably, and had made no manner of stir. If it had been true (as they alleged) that he was a *mover of sedition among all the Jews*, surely he would have been industrious to make a party at Jerusalem: but he did not do so. (1) He had nothing in him of a contradicting spirit, as the movers of sedition have; he had no disposition to quarrel or oppose. They never found him *dis-puting with any man*. (2) He had nothing in him of a turbulent spirit: "They never found me *raising up the people*, by incensing them against their governors in church or state or suggesting to them fears and jealousies concerning public affairs, nor by setting them at variance one with another or sowing discord among them."

4. That as to what they had charged him with, of moving sedition in other countries, he was wholly innocent, and they could not make good the charge (*v.* 13): *Neither can they prove the things whereof they now accuse me*.

III. He gives a fair and just account of himself, which does at once both clear him from crime and likewise intimate what was the true reason of their violence in prosecuting him.

1. He acknowledges himself to be one whom they looked upon as a heretic, and that was the reason of their spleen against him. I confess that *in the way which they call heresy*—or a *sect, so worship I the God of my fathers*.

2. He vindicates himself from this imputation. They call Paul a heretic, but he is not so; for,

(1) He *worships the God of his fathers*, and therefore is right in the object of his worship.

(2) He *believes all things which are written in the law and the prophets*, and therefore is right in the rule of his worship.

(3) He has his eye upon a future state, and is a believing expectant of that, and therefore is right in the end of his worship.

(4) His way of life is of a piece with his devotion (*v.* 16): *And*

herein do I exercise myself, to have always a conscience void of offence towards God and towards men. Prophets and their doctrine were to be tried by their fruits. Observe, [1] What was Paul's aim and desire: To *have a conscience void of offence.* Either, *First*, "A conscience not offending; not informing me wrong, nor flattering me, nor dealing deceitfully with me, nor in any thing misleading me." Or, *Secondly*, A conscience not offended; it is like Job's resolution, "*My heart shall not reproach me*," that is, I will never give it any occasion to do so. [2] What was his care and endeavour, in pursuance of this: "I make it my constant business, and govern myself by this intention." [3] The extent of this care: *First*, To all times: *To have always a conscience void of offence*, always void of gross offence; for though Paul was conscious to himself that he *had not yet attained perfection*, and the evil that he would not do yet he did, yet he was *innocent from the great transgression. Secondly*, To all things: *Both towards God, and towards man.* His conscientious care extended itself to the whole of his duty, and he was afraid of breaking the law of love either to God or his neighbour. [4] The inducement to it: "Because I look for the resurrection of the dead and the life of the world to come, therefore I thus exercise myself." The consideration of the future state should engage us to be universally conscientious in our present state.

IV. Having made confession of his faith, he gives a plain and faithful account of his case, and of the wrong done him by his persecutors.

(1) It was very hard to accuse him as an *enemy to their nation*, when after long absence from Jerusalem he came to *bring alms to his nation*, money which (though he had need enough himself of it) he had collected among his friends, for the relief of the poor at Jerusalem. (2) It was very hard to accuse him of having profaned the temple when he brought offerings to the temple, and was himself at charges therein (*ch.* xxi. 24), and was found *purifying himself in the temple*, according to the law (*v.* 18), and that in a very quiet decent manner, *neither with multitude nor with tumult.*

2. In the council: "Since the Jews of Asia are not here to prove any thing upon me done amiss in the temple, let *these same* that are *here*, the high priest and the elders, say whether they have *found any evil doing in me*, or whether I was guilty of any misdemeanour *when I stood before the council*, when also they were ready to pull me in pieces, *v.* 20. When I was there, they could not take offence at any thing I said; for all I said was, *Touching the resurrection of the dead I am called in question by you this day* (*v.* 21), which gave no offence to any one but the Sadducees. This I hope was no crime, that I stuck to that which is the faith of the whole Jewish church, excepting those whom they themselves call heretics."

FELIX POSTPONES JUDGMENT (*vv.* 22–27)

We have here the result of Paul's trial before Felix, and what was the consequence of it.

I. Felix adjourned the cause, and took further time to consider of it (*v.* 22). Now, 1. It was a disappointment to the high priest and the elders that Paul was not condemned, or remitted to their judgment, which they wished for and expected. 2. It was an injury to Paul that he was not released. It is a wrong not only to deny justice, but to delay it.

II. He detained the prisoner in custody, and would not take bail for him; else here at Cæsarea Paul had friends enough that would gladly have been his security. The high priest and the elders grudged him his life, but Felix generously allows him a sort of liberty; for he had not those prejudices against him and his way that they had. He also gave orders that none of his friends should be hindered from coming to him; the centurion must not forbid any of his acquaintances from ministering to him; and a man's prison is as it were his own house, if he had but his friends about him.

III. He had frequent conversation with him afterwards in private, once particularly, not long after his public trial, *vv.* 24, 25. Observe.

1. With what design *Felix sent for Paul*. He had a mind to have some talk with him *concerning the faith in Christ*, the Christian religion: he had some knowledge of that way, but he desired to have an account of it from Paul, who was so celebrated a preacher of that faith, above the rest.

2. What the account was which Paul gave him of the Christian religion; by the idea he had of it, he expected to be amused with a mystical divinity, but, as Paul represents it to him, he is alarmed with a practical divinity. Paul, being asked *concerning the faith in Christ, reasoned* (for Paul was always a rational preacher) concerning *righteousness, temperance, and judgment to come*. It is probable that he mentioned the peculiar doctrines of Christianity concerning the death and resurrection of the Lord Jesus, and his being *the Mediator between God and man*; but he hastened to his application, in which he designed to come home to the consciences of his hearers. Felix and Drusilla were such hardened sinners that it was not at all likely they should be brought to repentance by Paul's preaching, especially under such disadvantages; and yet Paul deals with them as one that did not despair of them.

3. What impressions Paul's discourse made upon this great but wicked man. Paul never trembled before him, but he was made to tremble before Paul. See here, (1) The power of the word of God, when it comes with commission; it is searching, it is startling, it can strike a terror into the heart of the most proud and daring sinner, by *setting his sins in order before him*, and showing him *the terrors of the Lord*. (2) The workings of natural conscience; when it is startled and awakened, it fills the soul with horror and amazement at its own deformity and danger.

4. How Felix struggled to get clear of these impressions, and to shake off the terror of his convictions; he did by them as he did by Paul's prosecutors (*v.* 25), *he deferred them*; he said, *Go thy way for this time, when I have a convenient season I will call for thee.*

Note, [1] Many lose all the benefit of their convictions for want of striking while the iron is hot. If Felix, now that he trembled, had but asked, as Paul and the jailer did when they trembled, *What shall I do?* he might have been brought to the faith of Christ, and have been a *Felix* indeed, *happy* for ever; but, by dropping his convictions now, he lost them for ever, and himself with them. [2] In the affairs of our souls, delays are dangerous; nothing is of more fatal consequence than men's putting off their conversion from time to time.

IV. After all, he detained him a prisoner, and left him so, when two years after he was removed from the government, *vv.* 26, 27.

CHAPTER TWENTY-FIVE

PAUL BEFORE FESTUS
(*vv.* 1–12)

We commonly say, "New lords, new laws, new customs;" but here was a new governor, and yet Paul had the same treatment from him that he had from the former, and no better. Festus, like Felix, is not so just to him as he should have been, for he does not release him; and yet not so unjust to him as the Jews would have had him to be, for he will not condemn him to die, nor expose him to their rage. Here is,

I. The pressing application which the high priest and other Jews used with the governor to persuade him to abandon Paul; for to send him to Jerusalem was in effect to abandon him.

II. The governor's resolution that Paul shall take his trial at Cæsarea, where he now is, *vv.* 4, 5. See how he manages the prosecutors. 1. He will not do them the kindness to send for him to Jerusalem; no, he gave orders *that Paul should be kept at Cæsarea.* 2. Yet he will do them the justice to hear what they have to say against Paul, if they will go down to Cæsarea, and appear against him there.

III. Paul's trial before Festus. Festus stayed *at Jerusalem about ten days*, and then *went down to Cæsarea*, and the prosecutors, it is likely, in his retinue. Now here we have, 1. The court set, and the prisoner called to the bar. Festus *sat in the judgment-seat*, as he used to do when any cause was brought before him that was of consequence, and he *commanded Paul to be brought*, and to make his appearance, *v.* 6. 2. The prosecutors exhibiting their charges against the prisoner (*v.* 7): *The Jews stood round about*, which intimates that they were many. They charged him with high crimes and misdemeanors. 3. The prisoner's insisting upon his own vindication, *v.* 8. (1) He had not violated the law of the Jews, not taught any doctrine destructive of it. (2) He had not profaned the temple, nor put any contempt at all upon the temple-service; his helping to set up the gospel temple did not at all offend against that temple which was a type of it. (3) He had not offended against Cæsar, nor his government.

IV. Paul's appeal to the emperor, and the occasion of it. This gave the cause a new turn. Whether he had before designed it, or whether it was a sudden resolve upon the present provocation, does not appear; but God puts it into his heart to do it, for the bringing about of that which he had said to him, *that he must bear witness to Christ at Rome*, for there the emperor's court was, *ch.* xxiii. 11. We have here,

1. The proposal which Festus made to Paul to go and take his trial at Jerusalem, *v.* 9.

2. Paul's refusal to consent to it, and his reasons for it. He knew, if he were removed to Jerusalem, notwithstanding the utmost vigilance of the president, the Jews would find some means or other to be the death of him; and therefore desires to be excused, and pleads, (1) That, as a citizen of Rome, it was most proper for him to be tried, not only by the president, but in that which was properly his court, which sat at Cæsarea: *I stand at Cæsar's judgment-seat, where I ought to be judged*, in the city which is the metropolis of the province. (2) That, as a member of the Jewish nation, he had done nothing to make himself obnoxious to them. (3) That he was willing to abide by the rules of the law, and to let that take its course, *v.* 11.

3. His appealing to court. "*I appeal unto Cæsar.* Rather than be delivered to the Jews" (which Festus seems inclined to consent to) "let me be delivered to Nero."

V. The judgment given upon the whole matter. Paul is neither released nor condemned. 1. The president takes advice upon the matter: *He conferred with the council*—not with the council of the Jews, but with his own counsellors, who were always ready to

assist the governor with their advice. 2. He determines to send him to Rome. Some think Paul meant not an appeal to Cæsar's person, but only to his court, the sentence of which he would abide by, rather than be remitted to the Jew's council, and that Festus might have chosen whether he would have sent him to Rome, or, at least, whether he would have joined issue with him upon the appeal. But it should seem, by what Agrippa said (*ch.* xxvi. 32), that *he might have been set at liberty if he had not appealed to Cæsar*—that, by the course of the Roman law, a Roman citizen might appeal at any time to a superior court, even to the supreme. Festus, therefore, either of choice or of course, comes to this resolution: *Hast thou appealed unto Cæsar? Unto Cæsar thou shalt go.*

PAUL BEFORE AGRIPPA
(*vv.* 13–27)

We have here the preparation that was made for another hearing of Paul before king Agrippa, not in order to his giving judgment upon him, but in order to his giving advice concerning him, or rather only to gratify his curiosity. Here is,

I. The kind and friendly visit which king Agrippa made to Festus, now upon his coming into the government in that province (*v.* 13). Observe,

1. Who the visitants were. (1) King Agrippa, the son of that Herod (surnamed *Agrippa*) who killed James the apostle, and was himself eaten of worms, and great grandson of Herod the Great, under whom Christ was born. (2)

Bernice came with him. She was his own sister, now a widow, the widow of his uncle Herod, king of Chalcis, after whose death she lived with this brother of hers, who was suspected to be too familiar with her, and, after she was a second time married to Polemon king of Cilicia, she got to be divorced from him, and returned to her brother king Agrippa.

2. What the design of this visit was: they *came to salute Festus*, to give him joy of his new promotion, and to wish him joy in it.

II. The account which Festus gave to king Agrippa of Paul and his case.

(1) He found him a prisoner when he came into the government of this province; and therefore could not of his own knowledge give an account of his cause from the beginning.

(2) That the Jewish sanhedrim were extremely set against him. These being great pretenders to religion, and therefore to be supposed men of honour and honesty, Festus thinks he ought to give credit to them; but Agrippa knows them better than he does, and therefore Festus desires his advice in this matter.

(3) That he had insisted upon the Roman law in favour of the prisoner, and would not condemn him unheard (*v.* 16).

(4) That he had brought him upon his trial, according to the duty of his place, *v.* 17. He called a great court on purpose for the trial of Paul, that the sentence might be definitive, and the cause ended.

(5) That he was extremely *disap-pointed* in the charge they brought against him (*vv.* 18, 19): *When he accusers stood up against him*, and opened their indictment, *they brought no accusations of such things as I supposed.*

(6) That therefore he had proposed to Paul that the cause might be adjourned to the Jewish courts, as best able to take cognizance of an affair of this nature (*v.* 20).

(7) That Paul had chosen rather to remove his cause to Rome than to Jerusalem, as expecting fairer play from the emperor than from the priests.

III. The bringing of him before Agrippa, that he might have the hearing of his cause.

1. The king desired it (*v.* 22). Agrippa would not for all the world have gone to a meeting to hear Paul preach, any more than Herod to hear Jesus; and yet they are both glad to have them brought before them, only to satisfy their curiosity.

2. Festus granted it: *To-morrow thou shalt hear him.*

3. Great preparation was made for it (*v.* 23): *The next day* there was a great appearance *in the place of hearing*, Paul and his cause being much talked of, and the more for their being much talked against.

IV. The speech with which Festus introduced the cause, when the court, or rather the audience, was set, which is much to the same purport with the account he had just now given to Agrippa. He could not as yet write *any thing certain* concerning Paul; so confused were the informations that were given in against him, and so inconsistent, that Festus could make nothing at all of them. He therefore desired

Paul might thus be publicly examined, that he might be advised by them what to write.

I. Paul addressed himself with a very particular respect to Agrippa, *vv.* 2, 3. He answered cheerfully before Felix, because he knew he had been *many years a judge to that nation*, ch. xxiv. 10. But his opinion of Agrippa goes further. Observe, 1. Being accused of the Jews, and having many base things laid to his charge, he is glad he has an opportunity of clearing himself; so far is he from imagining that his being an apostle exempted him from the jurisdiction of the civil powers. Magistracy is an ordinance of God, which we have all benefit by, and therefore must all be subject to. 2. Since he is forced to answer for himself, he is glad it is before king Agrippa, who, being himself a proselyte to the Jewish religion, understood all matters relating to it better than the other Roman governors did. 3. He therefore begs that he would *hear him patiently, with long suffering*. Paul designs a long discourse, and begs that Agrippa will hear him out, and not be weary.

II. He professes that though he was hated and branded as an apostate, yet he still adhered to all that good which he was first educated and trained up in; his religion was always built upon the *promise of God made unto the fathers*; and this he still built upon.

See here what his religion is. He has not indeed such a zeal for the ceremonial law as he had in his youth. The sacrifices and offerings appointed by that, he thinks, are superseded by the great sacrifice which they typified; ceremonial pollutions and purifications from them he makes no conscience of, and thinks the Levitical priesthood is honourably swallowed up in the priesthood of Christ; but for the main principles of his religion he is as zealous for them as ever, and more so, and resolves to live and die by them.

(1) His religion is built upon the *promise made of God unto the fathers*. It is built upon divine revelation, which he receives and believes, and ventures his soul upon; it is built upon divine grace, and that grace manifested and conveyed by promise. The promise of God is the guide and ground of his religion, the promise *made to the fathers*, which was more ancient than the ceremonial law, *that covenant which was confirmed before of God in Christ, and which the law, that was not till four hundred and thirty years after, could not disannul*, Gal. iii. 17. Christ and heaven are the two great doctrines of the gospel—that *God has given to us eternal life, and this life is in his Son*. Now these two are the matter of the *promise made unto the fathers*.

(2) His religion consists in the hopes of this promise. He places it not, as they did, in meats and drinks, and the observance of carnal ordinances. Paul had no confidence in the flesh, but in Christ; no expectation at all of great things in this world, but of greater things in the other world than any this

world can pretend to; he had his eye upon a future state.

Herein he concurred with all the pious Jews; his faith was not only according to the scripture, but according to the testimony of the church, which was a support to it. Now all the Israelites profess to believe in this promise, both of Christ and heaven, and hope to come to the benefits of them. They all hope for a Messiah to come, and we that are Christians hope in a Messiah already come; so that we all agree to build upon the same promise. They look for the *resurrection of the dead* and *the life of the world to come*, and this is what I look for.

This was what he was now suffering for—for preaching that doctrine which they themselves, if they did but understand themselves aright, must own.

(5) This was what he would persuade all that heard him cordially to embrace (*v.* 8): *Why should it be thought a thing incredible with you that God should raise the dead?* This seems to come in somewhat abruptly; but it is probable Paul said much more than is here recorded, and that he explained the *promise made to the fathers* to be the promise of the resurrection and eternal life, and proved that he was in the right way of pursuing his hope of that happiness because he believed in Christ who had *risen from the dead*, which was a pledge and earnest of that resurrection which the fathers hoped for.

III. He acknowledges that while he continued a Pharisee he was a bitter enemy to Christians and Christianity, and thought he ought

to be so, and continued so to the moment that Christ wrought that wonderful change in him. This he mentions,

1. To show that his becoming a Christian and a preacher was not the product and result of any previous disposition or inclination that way, or any gradual advance of thought in favour of the Christian doctrine; he did not reason himself into Christianity by a chain of arguments, but was brought into the highest degree of an assurance of it, immediately from the highest degree of prejudice against it, by which it appeared that he was made a Christian and a preacher by a supernatural power.

2. Perhaps he designs it for such an excuse of his prosecutors as Christ made for his, when he said, *They know not what they do.*

PAUL RELATES HIS CONVERSION
(*vv.* 12–23)

Paul here, by a plain and faithful narrative of matters of fact, makes it out to this august assembly that he had an immediate call from heaven to preach the gospel of Christ to the Gentile world, which was the thing that exasperated the Jews against him. He here shows,

I. That he was made a Christian by a divine power, notwithstanding all his prejudices against that way. Two things bring about this surprising change, a vision from heaven and a voice from heaven, which conveyed the knowledge of Christ to him by the two learning senses of seeing and hearing.

1. He saw a heavenly vision, the circumstances of which were such

that it could not be a *delusion*, but it was without doubt a divine appearance.

2. He heard a heavenly voice, an articulate one, *speaking to him*; it is here said to be *in the Hebrew tongue* (which was not taken notice of before), his native language, the language of his religion, to intimate to him that though he must be sent among the Gentiles, yet he must not forget that he was a Hebrew, nor make himself a stranger to the Hebrew language. In what Christ said to him we may observe, (1) That he called him by his name, and repeated it (*Saul, Saul*), which would surprise and startle him; and the more because he was now in a strange place, where he thought nobody knew him. (2) That he convinced him of sin, of that great sin which he was now in the commission of, the sin of persecuting the Christians, and showed him the absurdity of it. (3) That he interested himself in the sufferings of his followers: *Thou persecutest me* (*v.* 14), and again, It is *Jesus whom thou persecutest, v.* 15. (4) That he checked him for his wilful resistance of those convictions: *It is hard for thee to kick against the pricks*, or goads, *as a bullock unaccustomed to the yoke*. (5) That, upon his enquiry, Christ made himself known to him. This convinced him that the doctrine of Jesus was divine and heavenly, and not only not to be opposed, but to be cordially embraced.

II. That he was made a minister by a divine authority: *That the same Jesus that appeared to him in that glorious light* ordered him *to go and preach the gospel to the Gen-*tiles; he did not run without sending, nor was he sent by men like himself, but by him whom the Father sent, John xx. 21. Observe,

1. The office to which Paul is appointed: he is made a minister, to attend on Christ, and act for him, as a witness—to give evidence in his cause, and attest the truth of his doctrine.

2. The matter of Paul's testimony: he must give an account to the world, (1) *Of the things which he had seen*, now at this time, must tell people of Christ's manifesting himself to him by the way, and what he said to him. (2) *Of those things in which he would appear to him.* Christ now settled a correspondence with Paul, which he designed afterwards to keep up, and only told him now that he should hear further from him.

3. The spiritual protection he was taken under, while he was thus employed as Christ's witness: all the powers of darkness could not prevail against him till he had finished his testimony (*v.* 17), *delivering thee from the people of the Jews and from the Gentiles*.

4. The special commission given him to go among the Gentiles, and the errand upon which he is sent to them; it was some years after Paul's conversion before he was *sent to the Gentiles*, or (for aught that appears) knew any thing of his being designed for that purpose (see *ch.* xxii. 21); but at length he is ordered to steer his course that way.

There is a great happiness designed for the Gentiles by this work—*that they may receive forgiveness of sins, and inheritance among those who are sanctified*; they are turned from the darkness of sin to the light of holiness, from the slavery of Satan to the service of God; not that God may be a gainer by them, but that they may be gainers by him.

III. That he had discharged his ministry, pursuant to his commission, by divine aid, and under divine direction and protection. God, who called him to be an apostle, owned him in his apostolical work, and carried him on in it with enlargement and success.

1. God gave him a heart to comply with the call (*v.* 19): *I was not disobedient to the heavenly vision*, for any one would say he ought to be obedient to it.

2. God enabled him to go through a great deal of work, though in it he grappled with a great deal of difficulty, *v.* 20. He applied himself to the preaching of the gospel with all vigour.

3. His preaching was all practical. He showed them, declared it, demonstrated it, that they ought, (1) *To repent of their sins*, to be sorry for them and to confess them, and enter into covenant against them. (2) *To turn to God.* They must not only conceive an antipathy to sin, but they must come into a conformity to God—must not only turn from that which is evil, but turn to that which is good. (3) *To do works meet for repentance.* Those that profess repentance must practise it, must live a life of repentance, must in every thing carry it as becomes penitents. It is not enough to speak penitent words, but we must do works agreeable to those words.

4. The Jews had no quarrel with him but upon this account, that he did all he could to persuade people to be religious, and to bring them to God by bringing them to Christ (*v.* 21): It was for these causes, and no other, *that the Jews caught me in the temple, and went about to kill me*; and let any one judge whether these were crimes worthy of death or of bonds.

5. He had no help but from heaven; supported and carried on by that, he went on in this great work (*v.* 22).

6. He preached no doctrine but what agreed with the scriptures of the Old Testament. These indeed were but what the prophets of the Old Testament had preached; but, besides these, he had preached Christ, and his death, and his resurrection, and this was what they quarrelled with him for, as appears by *ch.* xxv. 19, *that he affirmed Jesus to be alive:* "And so I did," says Paul, "and so I do, but therein also I say *no other than that which Moses and the prophets said should come*; and what greater honour can be done to them than to show that what they foretold is accomplished, and in the appointed season too—that what they said should come is come, and at the time they prefixed?" This also was foretold by the Old-Testament prophets, *that the Gentiles should be brought to the knowledge of God by the Messiah*; and what was there in all this that the Jews could justly be displeased at?

REACTION OF FESTUS
(*vv.* 24–32)

It was a thousand pities that he should be interrupted, as he is here, and that, being permitted to speak for himself (*v.* 1), he should not be permitted to say all he designed.

I. Festus, the Roman governor, is of opinion that the poor man is crazed. Now here observe,

1. What it was that Festus said of him (*v.* 24): *Much learning hath made thee mad*, thou hast cracked thy brains with studying. This he speaks, not so much in anger, as in scorn and contempt.

2. How Paul cleared himself from this invidious imputation. (1) He denies the charge, with due respect indeed to the governor, but with justice to himself, protesting that there was neither ground nor colour for it (*v.* 25). (2) He appeals to Agrippa concerning what he spoke (*v.* 26): *For the king knows of these things*, concerning Christ, and his death and resurrection, and the prophecies of the Old Testament, which had their accomplishment therein. *This thing was not done in a corner*; all the country rang of it; and any of the Jews present might have witnessed for him that they had heard it many a time from others, and therefore it was unreasonable to censure him as a distracted man for relating it, much more for speaking of the death and resurrection of Christ, which was so universally spoken of.

II. Agrippa is so far from thinking him a madman that he thinks he never heard a man argue more strongly, nor talk more to the purpose.

1. Paul applies himself closely to Agrippa's conscience. "*King Agrippa, believest thou the prophets?* Dost thou receive the scriptures of the Old Testament as a divine revelation, and admit them as foretelling good things to come?" He does not stay for an answer, but, in compliment to Agrippa, takes it for granted: *I know that thou believest*; for every one knew that Agrippa professed the Jews' religion, as his fathers had done, and therefore both knew the writings of the prophets and gave credit to them.

2. Agrippa owns there was a great deal of reason in what Paul said (*v.* 28): *Almost thou persuadest me to be a Christian.* Some understand this as spoken ironically, and read it thus, *Wouldest thou in so little a time persuade me to be a Christian?* But, taking it so, it is an acknowledgment that Paul spoke very much to the purpose, and that, whatever others thought of it, to his mind there came a convincing power along with what he said. Others take it as spoken seriously, and as a confession that he was in a manner, or within a little, convinced that Christ was the Messiah; for he could not but own, and had many a time thought so within himself, that the prophecies of the Old Testament had had their accomplishment in him; and now that it is urged thus solemnly upon him he is ready to yield to the conviction, he begins to sound a parley, and to think of rendering. He is as near being persuaded to believe in Christ as Felix, when he trembled, was to leave his sins.

3. Paul, not being allowed time to pursue his argument, concludes with a compliment, or rather a pious wish that all his hearers were Christians, and this wish turned into a prayer.

III. They all agree that Paul is an

146

innocent man, and is wronged in his prosecution. 1. The court broke up with some precipitation (*v.* 30). The king himself found his own heart begin to yield, and durst not trust himself to hear more, but, like Felix, dismissed Paul for this time. 2. They all concurred in an opinion of Paul's innocence, *v.* 31. The court withdrew to consult of the matter; to know one another's minds upon it, and *they talked among themselves*, all to the same purport, *that this man does nothing worthy of death*—he is not a criminal that deserves to die; nay, he *does nothing worthy of bonds*— he is not a dangerous man, whom it is prudent to confine. 3. *Agrippa* gave his judgment *that he might have been set at liberty, if he had not himself appealed to Cæsar* (*v.* 32), but by that appeal he had put a bar in his own door. Some think that by the Roman law this was true. Others think that Agrippa and Festus, being unwilling to disoblige the Jews by setting him at liberty, made this serve for an excuse of their continuing him in custody, when they themselves knew they might have justified the discharging of him.

CHAPTER TWENTY-SEVEN

PAUL'S VOYAGE BEGINS
(*vv.* 1–11)

Here we are told,

I. How Paul was shipped off for Italy: a long voyage, but there is no remedy. He has appealed to Cæsar, and to Cæsar he must go. Now here we are told, 1. Whose custody he was committed to—to *one named Julius, a centurion of*

Augustus's band, as Cornelius was of the Italian band, or legion, *ch.* x. 1. 2. What vessel he embarked in: they went on board a ship of Adramyttium (*v.* 2), a sea-port of Africa, whence this ship brought African goods, and, as it should seem, made a coasting voyage for Syria, where those goods came to a good market. 3. What company he had in this voyage, there were some prisoners who were committed to the custody of the same centurion, and who probably had appealed to Cæsar too, or were upon some other account removed to Rome, to be tried there, or to be examined as witnesses against some prisoners there. But he had also some of his friends with him, Luke particularly, the penman of this book, for he puts himself in all along, *We* sailed into Italy, and, *We* launched, *v.* 2.

II. What course they steered, and what places they touched at, which are particularly recorded for the confirming of the truth of the history to those who lived at that time, and could by their own knowledge tell of their being at such and such a place.

III. What advice Paul gave them with reference to that part of their voyage they had before them—it was to be content to winter where they were, and not to think of stirring till a better season of the year. 1. It was now a bad time for sailing; they had lost a deal of time while they were struggling with contrary winds. Sailing was now dangerous. 2. Paul put them in mind of it, and gave them notice of their danger (*v.* 10): "*I perceive*" (either by notice from God, or by observing their wilful resolution to prosecute the voyage notwithstanding the peril of the season) "that *this voyage will be with hurt and damage*; you that have effects on board are likely to lose them, and it will be a miracle of mercy if our lives be given us for a prey." There were some good men in the ship, and many more bad men: but in things of this nature *all things come alike to all*, and *there is one event to the righteous and to the wicked.* If both be in the same ship, they both are in the same danger. 3. They would not be advised by Paul in this matter, *v.* 11. The centurion gave more regard to the opinion of the master and owner of the ship than to Paul's; for every man is to be credited in his own profession ordinarily: but such a man as Paul, who was so intimate with Heaven, was rather to be regarded in seafaring matters than the most celebrated sailors.

THE STORM BREAKS
(*vv.* 12–19)

In these verses we have,

I. The ship putting to sea again, and pursuing her voyage at first with a promising gale.

II. The ship in a storm presently, a dreadful storm. They looked at second causes, and took their measures from the favourable hints they gave, and imagined that because the south wind now blew softly it would always blow so; in confidence of this, they ventured to sea, but were soon made sensible of their folly in giving more credit to a smiling wind than to the word of God in Paul's mouth, by which they had fair warning given them of a storm. Observe,

1. What their danger and distress was, (1) There *arose against them a tempestuous wind*, which was not only contrary to them, and directly in their teeth, so that they could not get forward, but a violent wind, which raised the waves, like that which was sent forth in pursuit of Jonah, though Paul was following God, and going on in his duty, and not as Jonah running away from God and his duty. This wind the sailors called *Euroclydon*, a northeast wind, which upon those seas perhaps was observed to be in a particular manner troublesome and dangerous.

2. What means they used for their own relief: they betook themselves to all the poor shifts (for I can call them no better) that sailors in distress have recourse to.

3. The despair which at last they were brought to (*v.* 20): *All hope that we should be saved was then taken away.* The storm continued, and they saw no symptoms of its abatement; we have known very blustering weather to continue for some weeks. The means they had used were ineffectual, so that they were at their wits' end; and such was the consternation that this melancholy prospect put them into that they had no heart either to eat or drink. They had provision enough on board (*v.* 38), but such bondage were they under, through fear of death, that they could not admit the supports of life.

SHIPWRECK (*vv.* 21–44)

We have here the issue of the distress of Paul and his fellow-travellers; they escaped with their lives and that was all, and that was for Paul's sake. Now here we have,

I. The encouragement Paul gave them, by assuring them, in the name of God, that their lives should all be saved, even when, in human appearance, all hope that they should be saved was taken away.

1. He reproves them for not taking his advice, which was to stay where they were, in the road of Lasea (*v.* 8). Paul, before administering comfort, will first make them sensible of their sin in no hearkening to him, by upbraiding them with their rashness, and probably, when he tells them of their gaining harm and loss, he reflects upon what they promised themselves by proceeding on their voyage, that they should gain so much time, gain this and the other point: "But," says he, "you have gained nothing but harm and loss; how will you answer it?"

2. He assures them that though they should lose the ship yet they should none of them lose their lives. He tells them, (1) That they must count upon the loss of the ship. But, (2) *Not a life shall be lost*. This would be good news to those that were ready to die for fear of dying, and whose guilty consciences made death look very terrible to them.

3. He tells them what ground he had for this assurance, that it is not a banter upon them, to put them into humour, nor a human conjecture, he has a divine revelation for it, and is as confident of it as that God is true, being fully satisfied that he has his word for it. An angel of God appeared to him in the night, and told him that for his sake they should all be preserved

(*vv.* 23–25), which would double the mercy of their preservation, that they should have it not only by providence, but by promise, and as a particular favour to Paul. Now observe here,

(1) The solemn profession Paul makes of relation to God, the God from whom he had this favourable intelligence: It is he *whose I am, and whom I serve*.

(2) The account he gives of the vision he had: *There stood by me this night an angel of God*, a divine messenger who used formerly to bring him messages from heaven; he *stood by him*, visibly appeared to him, probably when he was awake upon his bed.

(3) The encouragements that were given him in the vision, *v.* 14. [1] He is forbidden to fear. Though all about him are at their wits' end, and lost in despair, yet, *Fear not, Paul*; fear not *their fear, nor be afraid*, Isa. viii. 12. [2] He is assured that for his part he shall come safely to Rome: *Thou must be brought before Cæsar*. [3] That for his sake all that were in the ship with him should be delivered too from perishing in this storm: *God hath given thee all those that sail with thee*.

4. He comforts them with the same comforts wherewith he himself was comforted (*v.* 25): "*Where-fore, Sirs, be of good cheer*, you shall see even this will end well; *for I believe God*, and depend upon his word, *that it shall be even as it was told me*."

5. He gives them a sign, telling them particularly what this tempestuous voyage would issue in (*v.* 26).

II. Their coming at length to an anchor upon an unknown shore, *vv.* 27–29. 1. They had been a full fortnight in the storm, continually expecting death. 2. *About midnight the mariners apprehended that they drew near to some shore,* which confirmed what Paul had told them, that they must be driven upon some island. To try whether it was so or no, *they sounded,* in order to their finding the depth of the water, for the water would be shallower as they drew nearer to shore; by the first experiment *they found they drew twenty fathoms deep of water,* and by *the next fifteen fathoms,* which was a demonstration that they were near some shore. 3. They took the hint, and, fearing rocks near the shore, *they cast anchor, and wished for the day;* they durst not go forward for fear of rocks, and yet would not go back in hope of shelter, but they would wait for the morning, and heartily wished for it; who can blame them when the affair came to a crisis? When they had light, there was no land to be seen; now that there was land near them, they had no light to see it by; no marvel then they wished for day.

III. The defeating of the sailors' attempt to quit the ship; here was a new danger added to their distress, which they narrowly escaped. Observe, 1. The treacherous design of the seamen to leave the sinking ship. 2. Paul's discovery of it, and protestation against it, *v.* 31. *Except these abide in the ship, you cannot be saved.* 3. The effectual defeat of it by the soldiers, *v.* 32. It was no time to stand arguing the case with the seamen, and therefore they made no more ado, *but cut the ropes of the boat.* And now the seamen, being forced to stay in the ship whether they would or no, are forced likewise to work for the safety of the ship as hard as they could, because if the rest perish they must perish with them.

IV. The new life which Paul put into the company, by cheerfully inviting them to take some refreshment, and by the repeated assurances he gave them that they should all of them have their lives given tehm for a prey. *He gave thanks to God in presence of them all.* We have reason to think he had often prayed with Luke and Aristarchus, and what others there were among them that were Christians, that they prayed daily together; but whether he had before this prayed with the whole company is not certain. Now *he gave thanks to God, in presence of them all,* that they were alive, and had been preserved hitherto, and that they had a promise that their lives should be preserved in the imminent peril now before them; he gave thanks for the provision they had, and begged a blessing upon it. He set them a good example: *When he had given thanks, he broke the bread* (it was seabiscuit) and *he began to eat.* It had a happy influence upon them all (*v.* 36): *Then were they all of good cheer.* They then ventured to believe the message God sent them by Paul when they plainly perceived that Paul believed it himself, who was in the same common danger with them.

V. Their putting to shore, and the staving of the ship in the adventure. They made a shift among them *to run the ship aground*, in a shelf or bed of sand, as it should seem, or an isthmus, or neck of land, washed with the sea on both sides, and therefore two seas are said to meet upon it, and *there the forepart stuck fast*; and then, when it had no liberty to play, as a ship has when it rides at anchor, but remained immovable, *the hinder part* would soon be broken of course *by the violence of the waves*. Whether the seamen did not do their part, being angry that they were disappointed in their design to escape, and therefore wilfully ran the ship aground, or whether we may suppose that they did their utmost to save it, but God in his providence overruled, for the fulfilling of Paul's word, *that the ship must be lost (v.* 22), I cannot say; but this we are sure of *that God will confirm the word of his servants, and perform the counsel of his messengers*, Isa. xliv. 26. The ship, that had strangely weathered the storm in the vast ocean, where it had room to roll, is dashed to pieces when it sticks fast.

VI. A particular danger that Paul and the rest of the prisoners were in, besides their share in the common calamity, and their deliverance from it. 1. In this critical moment, when every man hung in doubt of his life, *the soldiers advised the killing of the prisoners* that were committed to their custody, and whom they were to give an account of, *lest any of them should swim out and escape, v.* 42. 2. The centurion, for Paul's sake, quashed this motion presently. Paul, who was his prisoner, had found favour with him, as Joseph with the captain of

the guard. Julius, though he despised Paul's advice *(v.* 11), yet afterwards saw a great deal of cause to respect him, and therefore, being *willing to save Paul*, he prevented the execution of that bloody project.

VII. The saving of the lives of all the persons in the ship, by the wonderful providence of God. When the ship broke under them, surely *there was but a step between them and death*; and yet infinite mercy interposed, and that step was not stepped. Here was an instance of the performance of a particular word of promise which God gave, that all the persons in this ship should be saved for Paul's sake.

CHAPTER TWENTY-EIGHT

PAUL ON MALTA (*vv*. 1–10)

Even stormy winds fulfil God's counsel, and an ill wind indeed it is that blows nobody any good; this ill wind blew good to the island of Melita; for it gave them Paul's company for three months, who was a blessing to every place he came to. Now here we have,

I. The kind reception which the inhabitants of this island gave to the distressed strangers that were shipwrecked on their coast (*v.* 2): *The barbarous people showed us no little kindness. They kindled a fire*, in some large hall or other, and *they received us every one*—made room for us about the fire, and bade us all welcome, without asking either what country we were of or what religion.

II. The further danger that Paul was in by a viper's fastening on his hand, and the unjust construction that the people put upon it. Paul is among strangers, and appears one of the meanest and most contemptible of the company, therefore God distinguishes him, and soon causes him to be taken notice of.

1. When the fire was to be made, and to be made bigger, that so great a company might all have the benefit of it, Paul was as busy as any of them in gathering sticks, *v.* 3.

2. The sticks being old dry rubbish, it happened there was a viper among them, that lay as dead till it came to the heat, and then revived, or lay quiet till it felt the fire, and then was provoked, and flew at him that unawares threw it into the fire, and *fastened upon his hand, v.* 3.

3. The barbarous people concluded that Paul, being a prisoner, was certainly a murderer, who had appealed to Rome, to escape justice in his own country, and that this viper was sent by divine justice to be the avenger of blood; or, if they were not aware that he was a prisoner, they supposed that he was in his flight; and *when they saw the venomous animal hang on his hand*, which it seems he could not, or would not, immediately throw off, but let it hang, they concluded, "*No doubt this man is a murderer*, has shed innocent blood, and therefore, *though he has escaped the sea, yet* divine *vengeance* pursues him, and fastens upon him now that he is pleasing himself with the thoughts of that escape, and will *not suffer him to live.*"

4. When he shook off the viper from his hand, yet they expected that divine vengeance would ratify the censure they had passed, and

that he would have swollen and burst, through the force of the poison, or *that he would have fallen down dead suddenly.*

III. Paul's deliverance from the danger, and the undue construction the people put upon this. The viper's fastening on his hand was a trial of his faith; and it was found to praise, and honour, and glory: for, 1. It does not appear that it put him into any fright or confusion at all. 2. He carelessly *shook off the viper into the fire*, without any difficulty, calling for help, or any means used to loosen its hold; and it is probable that it was consumed in the fire. 3. He was none the worse. Those that thought it would have been his death *looked a great while, but saw no harm at all come to him.* God hereby intended to make him remarkable among these barbarous people, and so to make way for the entertainment of the gospel among them. 4. They then magnified him as much as before they had vilified him: *They changed their minds, and said that he was a god*—an immortal god; for they thought it impossible that a mortal man should have a viper hang on his hand so long and be never the worse.

IV. The miraculous cure of an old gentleman that was ill of a fever, and of others that were otherwise diseased, by Paul. And, with these confirmations of the doctrine of Christ, no doubt there was a faithful publication of it.

V. The grateful acknowledgment which even these barbarous people made of the kindness Paul had done them, in preaching Christ unto them. They were civil to him, and to the other ministers that were with him, who, it is likely, were assisting to him in preaching among them, *v.* 10. They showed them all possible respect; they saw God honoured them, and therefore they justly thought themselves obliged to honour them, and thought nothing too much by which they might testify the esteem they had for them.

PAUL REACHES ROME
(*vv.* 11–16)

We have here the progress of Paul's voyage towards Rome, and his arrival there at length.

We have here,

I. Their leaving Malta. That island was a happy shelter to them, but it was not their home; when they are refreshed they must put to sea again.

II. Their landing in or about Italy, and the pursuing of their journey towards Rome. They came to Puteoli, a sea-port town not far from Naples, now called *Pozzolana.* The ship of Alexandria was bound for that port, and therefore there Paul, and the rest that were bound for Rome, were put ashore, and went the remainder of their way by land. At Puteoli they *found brethren,* Christians. Who brought the knowledge of Christ hither we are not told, but here it was, so wonderfully did the leaven of the gospel diffuse itself. God has many that serve and worship him in places where we little think he has. From Puteoli they went forward towards Rome; whether they travelled on foot, or whether they had beasts provided for them to ride on (as *ch.* xxiii. 24), does not appear; but

to Rome they must go, and this was their last stage.

III. The meeting which the Christians at Rome gave to Paul. It is probable that notice was sent to them by the Christians at Puteoli, as soon as ever Paul had come thither, how long he intended to stay there, and when he would set forward for Rome, which gave an opportunity for this interview. He finds there are those there who love and value him, and whom he may both converse with and consult with as his friends, which will take off much of the tediousness of his imprisonment, and the terror of his appearing before Nero. Note, It is an encouragement to those who are travelling towards heaven to meet with their fellow travellers, who are their *companions in the kingdom and datience of Jesus Christ.*

IV. The delivering of Paul into custody at Rome, *v.* 16. He is now come to his journey's end. And, 1. He is still a prisoner. He had longed to see Rome, but, when he comes there, he is delivered, with other prisoners, to the *captain of the guard,* and can see no more of Rome than he will permit him. 2. Yet he has some favour shown him. He is a prisoner, but not a close prisoner, not in the common jail: *Paul was suffered to dwell by himself,* in some convenient private lodgings which his friends there provided for him, and a soldier was appointed to be his guard, who, we hope, was civil to him, and let him take all the liberty that could be allowed to a prisoner, for he must be very ill-natured indeed that could be so to such a courteous obliging man as Paul. Paul, being suffered to dwell by himself, could the better enjoy himself, and his friends, and his God, than if he had been lodged with the other prisoners.

THE JEWS AT ROME
(vv. 17–22)

Paul, with a great deal of expense and hazard, is brought a prisoner to Rome, and when he has come nobody appears to prosecute him or lay any thing to his charge; but he must call his own cause; and here he represents it to the chief of the Jews at Rome. And here we are told,

I. What he said to them, and what account he gave them of his cause. Now, 1. He professes his own innocency, and that he had not given any just occasion to the Jews to bear him such an ill will as generally they did. 2. He modestly complains of the hard usage he had met with—that, though he had given no offence, yet *he was delivered prisoner from Jerusalem into the hands of the Romans*. 3. He declares the judgment of the Roman governors concerning him, *v*. 18. They examined him, enquired into his case, heard what was to be said against him, and what he had to say for himself. The chief captain examined him, so did Felix, and Festus, and Agrippa, and they could find no cause of death in him; nothing appeared to the contrary but that he was an honest, quiet conscientious, good man, and therefore they would never gratify the Jews with a sentence of death upon him; but, on the contrary, would have let him go, and have let him go on in his work too, and

have given him no interruption, for they all heard him and liked his doctrine well enough. It was for the honour of Paul that those who most carefully examined his case acquitted him, and none condemned him but unheard, and such as were prejudiced against him. 4. He pleads the necessity he was under to remove himself and his cause to Rome; and that it was only in his own defence, and not with any design to recriminate, or exhibit a cross bill against the complainants, (*v*. 19). 5. He puts his sufferings upon the true footing, and gives them such an account of the reason of them as should engage them not only to join with his persecutors against him, but to concern themselves for him, and to do what they could on his behalf (*v*. 20). He carried the mark of his imprisonment about with him, and probably was chained to the soldier that kept him; and it was, (1) Because he preached that the Messiah was come, who was the hope of Israel, he whom Israel hoped for. (2) Because he preached that the resurrection of the dead would come. This also was the hope of Israel; so he had called it, *ch*. xxiii. 6; xxiv. 15; xxvi. 6, 7.

II. What was their reply. They own, 1. That they had nothing to say in particular against him; nor had any instructions to appear as his prosecutors before the emperor, either by letter or word of mouth (*v*. 21). 2. That they desired to know particularly concerning the doctrine he preached, and the religion he took so much pains to propagate in the face of so much opposition (*v*. 22).

PAUL AT ROME (*vv.* 23–29)

We have here a short account of a long conference which Paul had with the Jews at Rome about the Christian religion.

I. We are here told how Paul managed this conference in defence of the Christian religion. The Jews appointed the time, a day was set for this dispute, that all parties concerned might have sufficient notice, *v.* 23. Those Jews seemed well disposed to receive conviction, and yet it did not prove that they all were so. Now when the day came,

1. There were *many got together to Paul*. Though he was a prisoner, and could not come out to them, yet they were willing to come to him to his lodging.

2. He was very large and full in his discourse with them, seeking their conviction more than his own vindication.

3. He was very long; for he continued his discourse, and it should seem to have been a continued discourse, from *morning till evening*; perhaps it was a discourse eight or ten hours long.

II. What was the effect of his discourse. One would have thought that so good a cause as that of Christianity, and managed by such a skilful hand as Paul's could not but carry the day, and that all the hearers would have yielded to it presently; but it did not prove so. 1. *They did not agree among themselves*, *v.* 25. 2. *Some believed the things that were spoken, and some believed not*, *v.* 24. There was the disagreement. Such as this has always been the success of the gospel.

III. The awakening word which Paul said to them at parting.

1. "You will by the righteous judgment of God be sealed up under unbelief."

2. "Your unbelief will justify God in sending the gospel to the Gentile world, which is the thing you look upon with such a jealous eye (*v.* 28): therefore seeing you put the grace of God away from you, and will not submit to the power of divine truth and love, seeing you will not be converted and healed in the methods which divine wisdom has appointed, *therefore be it known unto you that the salvation of God is sent unto the Gentiles*, that salvation which was of the Jews only (John iv. 22), the offer of it is made to them, the means of it afforded to them, and they stand fairer for it than you do; it is sent to them, and they will hear it, and receive it, and be happy in it.

IV. The breaking up of the assembly, as it should seem, in some disorder. They departed, many of them with a resolution never to hear Paul preach again, nor trouble themselves with further enquiries about this matter.

EPILOGUE (*vv.* 30, 31)

We are here taking our leave of the history of blessed Paul; and therefore, since God saw it not fit that we should know any more of him, we should carefully take notice of every particular of the circumstances in which we must here leave him.

I. It cannot but be a trouble to us that we must leave him in bonds for Christ, nay, and that we have no prospect given us of his being set at liberty.

II. Yet it is a pleasure to us (for we are sure it was to him) that, though we leave him in bonds for Christ, yet we leave him at work for Christ, and this made his bonds easy that he was not by them bound out from serving God and doing good. His prison becomes a temple, a church, and then it is to him a palace. His hands are tied, but, thanks be to God, his mouth is not stopped; a faithful zealous minister can better bear any hardship than being silenced. Here is Paul a prisoner, and yet a preacher; he is bound, but the word of th? Lord is not bound. When he wrote his epistle to the Romans, he said *he longed to see them, that he might impart into them some spiritual gift* (Rom. i. 11); he was glad *to see some of them* (*v.* 15), but it would not be half his joy unless he could impart to them some spiritual gift, which here he has an opportunity to do, and then he will not complain of his confinement. Observe,

1. To whom he preached: to all that had a mind to hear him, whether Jews or Gentiles.

2. What he preached. He does not fill their heads with curious speculations, nor with matters of state and politics, but he keeps to his text, minds his business as an apostle. Paul stuck still to his principle—to know and preach *nothing but Christ, and him crucified.*

Ministers, when in their preaching they are tempted to diverge from that which is their main business, should reduce themselves with this question, What does this concern the Lord Jesus Christ? What tendency has it to bring us to him, and to keep us walking in him? *For we preach not ourselves, but Christ.*

3. With what liberty he preached. (1) Divine grace gave him a liberty of spirit. He preached *with all confidence,* as one that was himself well assured of the truth of what he preached—that it was what he durst stand by; and of the worth of it—that it was what he durst suffer for. He was *not ashamed of the gospel of Christ.* (2) Divine Providence gave him a liberty of speech: *No man forbidding him,* giving him any check for what he did or laying any restraint upon him. The Jews that used to forbid him to speak to the Gentiles had no authority here; and the Roman government as yet took no cognizance of the profession of Christianity as a crime. Though it was a very low and narrow sphere of opportunity that Paul was here placed in, compared with what he had been in, yet, such as it was, he was not molested nor disturbed in it. Though it was not a wide door that was opened to him, yet it was kept open, and no man was suffered to shut it; and it was to many an effectual door, so that there were saints even in Cæsar's household, Phil. iv. 22.

THE EPISTLE OF ST. PAUL TO THE

ROMANS

CHAPTER ONE

INTRODUCTION (vv. 1–7)

In this paragraph we have,

I. The person who writes the epistle described (*v.* 1): *Paul, a servant of Jesus Christ*; this is his title of honour, which he glories in. *Called to be an apostle*. Some think he alludes to his old name Saul, which signifies *one called for*, or *enquired after*: Christ sought him to make an apostle of him, Acts ix. 15. *Separated to the gospel of God*. The Pharisees had their name from separation, because they *separated themselves to the study of the law*; such a one Paul had formerly been; but now he had changed his studies, was a gospel Pharisee, separated by the counsel of God (Gal. i. 15), *separated from his mother's womb*, by an immediate direction of the Spirit, and a regular ordination according to that direction (Acts xiii. 2, 3), by a dedication of himself to this work. He was an entire devotee to the gospel of God, the gospel which has God for its author, the origin and extraction of it divine and heavenly.

II. Having mentioned the gospel of God, he digresses, to give us an encomium of it.

1. The antiquity of it. It was *promised before* (*v.* 2); it was no novel upstart doctrine, but of ancient standing in the promises and prophecies of the Old Testament.

2. The subject-matter of it: it is concerning Christ, *vv.* 3, 4. The prophets and apostles all bear witness to him; he is the true treasure hid in the field of the scriptures.

3. The fruit of it (*v.* 5): This apostleship was received *for obedience and faith*, that is, to bring people to that obedience; as Christ, so his ministers, received that they might give.

III. The persons to whom it is written (*v.* 7): *To all that are in Rome, beloved of God, called to be saints*; that is, to all the professing Christians that were in Rome, whether Jews or Gentiles originally, whether high or low, bond or free, learned or unlearned.

IV. The apostolical benediction (*v.* 7): *Grace to you and peace.* This is one of the tokens in every epistle; and it hath not only the affection of a good wish, but the authority of a blessing.

PAUL, THE DEBTOR (vv. 8–15)

We may here observe,

I. His thanksgiving for them (*v.* 8): *First, I thank my God.* In all our thanksgivings, it is good for us to eye God as our God; this makes every mercy sweet, when we can say of God, "He is mine in covenant."—*Through Jesus Christ.* All our duties and performances are pleasing to God only through Jesus Christ, praises as well as prayers.— *For you all.* We must express our love to our friends, not only by praying for them, but by praising God for them. *That your faith is spoken of.* Paul travelled up and down from place to place, and, wherever he came, he heard great commendations of the Christians at Rome, which he mentions, not to make them proud, but to quicken them to answer the general character people gave of them, and the general expectation people had from them. The faith of the Roman Christians came to be thus talked of, not only because it was excelling in itself, but because it was eminent and observable in its circumstances. Rome was a city upon a hill, every one took notice of what was done there.

II. His prayer for them, *v.* 9. From Paul's example here we may learn. 1. Constancy in prayer: *Always without ceasing.* He did himself observe the same rules he gave to others, Eph. vi. 18; 1 Thes. v. 17. 2. Charity in prayer: *I make mention of you.* Though he had no particular acquaintance with them, nor interest in them, yet he prayed for them; not only for all saints in general, but he made express mention of them. *God, whom I serve with my spirit.* Those that serve God with their spirits may, with a humble confidence, appeal to him; hypocrites who rest in bodily exercise cannot. His particular prayer, among many other petitions he put up for them, was that he might have an opportunity of paying them

a visit (*v.* 10): *Making request, if by any means,* &c.

III. His great desire to see them, with the reasons for it, *vv.* 11–15. He had heard so much of them that he had a great desire to be better acquainted with them. Fruitful Christians are as much the joy as barren professors are the grief of faithful ministers. Accordingly, he *often purposed to come, but was let hitherto* (*v.* 13), for man purposeth, but God disposeth. He was hindered by other business that took him off, by his care of other churches, whose affairs were pressing; and Paul was for doing that first, not which was most pleasant (then he would have gone to Rome), but which was most needful. Paul desired to visit these Romans,

1. That they might be edified (*v.* 11): *That I may impart unto you.* He received, that he might communicate.—*To the end you may be established.* Having commended their flourishing he here expresses his desire of their establishment, that as they grew upward in the branches they might grow downward in the root.

2. That he might be comforted, *v.* 12. What he heard of their flourishing in grace was so much a joy to him that it must needs be much more so to behold it. *By the mutual faith both of you and me,* that is, our mutual faithfulness and fidelity. Their edification would be his advantage, it would be fruit abounding to a good account.

3. That he might discharge his trust as the apostle of the Gentiles (*v.* 14): *I am a debtor.* (1) His receivings made him a debtor; for they were talents he was entrusted

with to trade for his Master's honour. (2) His office made him a debtor. He was a debtor as he was an apostle; he was called and sent to work, and had engaged to mind it. Accordingly, we find him paying his debt, both in his preaching and in his writing, doing good *both to Greeks and barbarians*, and suiting his discourse to the capacity of each. For these reasons he was ready, if he had an opportunity, *to preach the gospel at Rome, v.* 15.

THE POWER OF GOD
(vv. 16–18)

Paul here enters upon a large discourse of justification. He was ready to preach the gospel at Rome, though a place where the gospel was run down by those that called themselves the wits; *for*, saith he, *I am not ashamed of it, v.* 16. The reason of this bold profession, taken from the nature and excellency of the gospel, introduces his dissertation.

I. The proposition, *vv.* 16, 17. The excellency of the gospel lies in this, that it reveals to us,

1. The salvation of believers as the end: *It is the power of God unto salvation.* But, (1) *It is through the power of God*; without that power the gospel is but a dead letter. (2) It is to those, and those only, that believe. Believing interests us in the gospel salvation; to others it is hidden. The medicine prepared will not cure the patient if it be not taken.—*To the Jew first. The lost sheep of the house of Israel* had the first offer made them, both by Christ and his apostles.

2. The justification of believers

as the way (*v.* 17): *For therein*, that is, in this gospel, which Paul so much triumphs in, *is the righteousness of God revealed.* This evangelical righteousness, (1) Is called the *righteousness of God*; it is of God's appointing, of God's approving and accepting. (2) it is said to be *from faith to faith*, from the faithfulness of God revealing to the faith of man receiving (so some); from the faith of dependence upon God, and dealing with him immediately, as Adam before the fall, to the faith of dependence upon a Mediator, and so dealing with God (so others); from the first faith, by which we are put into a justified state, to after faith, by which we live, and are continued in that state. *The just shall live by faith. Just by faith*, there is faith justifying us; *live by faith*, there is faith maintaining us; and so *there is a righteousness from faith to faith.* Faith is all in all, both in the beginning and progress of a Christian life.

II. The proof of this proposition. Justification must be either by faith or works. It cannot be by works, which he proves at large by describing the works both of Jews and Gentiles; and therefore he concludes it must be by faith, *ch.* iii. 20, 28. Here is

1. The sinfulness of man described; he reduces it to two heads, *ungodliness and unrighteousness*; ungodliness against the laws of the first table, unrighteousness against those of the second.

2. The cause of that sinfulness, and that is, *holding the truth in unrighteousness.* An unrighteous wicked heart is the dungeon in

which many a good truth is detained and buried.

3. The displeasure of God against it: *The wrath of God is revealed from heaven.*

THE GENTILES (*vv.* 19–32)

In this last part of the chapter the apostle applies what he had said particularly to the Gentile world, in which we may observe,

I. This means and helps they had to come to the knowledge of God. Observe,

1. What discoveries they had: *That which may be known of God is manifest among them*; that is, there were some even among them that had the knowledge of God.

2. Whence they had these discoveries: *God hath shown it to them.* Those common natural notions which they had of God were imprinted upon their hearts by the God of nature himself, who is the *Father of lights.*

3. By what way and means these discoveries and notices which they had were confirmed and improved, namely, by the work of creation (*v.* 20): *For the invisible things of God,* &c.

(1) Observe what they knew: *The invisible things of him, even his eternal power and Godhead.* Though God be not the object of sense, yet he hath discovered and made known himself by those things that are sensible.

(2) How they knew it: *By the things that are made,* which could not make themselves, nor fall into such an exact order and harmony by any casual hits; and therefore must have been produced by some first cause or intelligent agent,

which first cause could be no other than an eternal powerful God. See Ps. xix. 1; Isa. xl. 26; Acts xvii. 24.

II. Their gross idolatry, notwithstanding these discoveries that God made to them of himself; described here, *vv.* 21–23, 25. Observe,

1. The inward cause of their idolatry, *vv.* 21, 22. They are therefore without excuse, in that they did know God, and from what they knew might easily infer that it was their duty to worship him, and him only.

2. The outward acts of their idolatry, *vv.* 23–25. (1) Making images of God (*v.* 23), by which, as much as in them lay, they *changed the glory of the incorruptible God.* Compare Ps. cvi. 20; Jer. ii. 11. They ascribed a deity to the most contemptible creatures, and by them represented God. (2) Giving divine honour to the creature: *Worshipped and served the creature, besides the Creator.* Or, *above* the Creator, paying more devout respect to their inferior deities, stars, heroes, demons, thinking the supreme God inaccessible, or above their worship.

III. The judgments of God upon them for this idolatry. Observe,

1. By whom they were given up. God gave them up, in a way of righteous judgment, as the just punishment of their idolatry—taking off the bridle of restraining grace—leaving them to themselves—letting them alone; for his grace is his own, he is debtor to no man, he may give or withhold his grace at pleasure.

2. To what they were given up.

(1) *To uncleanness and vile affections, vv.* 24, 26, 27. Those who

dishonoured God were given up to dishonour themselves. A man cannot be delivered up to a greater slavery than to be given up to his own lusts.

(2) To a reprobate mind in these abominations, *v.* 28.

[1] They *did not like to retain God in their knowledge*. The blindness of their understandings was caused by the wilful aversion of their wills and affections.

[2] Answerable to this wilfulness of theirs, in gainsaying the truth, God gave them over to a wilfulness in the grossest sins, here called a *reprobate mind*, a mind void of all sense and judgment to discern things that differ, so that they could not distinguish their right hand from their left in spiritual things.

First, Sins against the first table: *Haters of God*. Here is the devil in his own colours, sin appearing sin.

Secondly, Sins against the second table. These are especially mentioned, because in these things they had a clearer light. (2) They knew the penalty; so it is explained here: They knew *that those who commit such things were worthy of death*, eternal death; their own consciences could not but suggest this to them, and yet they ventured upon it.

Now lay all this together, and then say whether the Gentile world, lying under so much guilt and corruption, could be justified before God by any works of their own

CHAPTER TWO
GOD'S PERFECT JUSTICE
(*vv.* 1–16)

In the former chapter the apostle had represented the state of the Gentile world to be as bad and black as the Jews were ready enough to pronounce it. And now, designs to show that the state of the Jews was very bad too, and their sin in many respects more aggravated.

I. He arraigns them for their censoriousness and self-conceit (*v.* 1): *Thou art inexcusable, O man, whosoever thou art that judgest*. The Jews were generally a proud sort of people, that looked with a great deal of scorn and contempt upon the poor Gentiles, as not worthy to be set with the dogs of their flock; while in the mean time they were themselves as bad and immoral— though not idolaters, as the Gentiles, yet sacrilegious, *v.* 22. *Therefore thou art inexcusable*.

II. He asserts the invariable justice of the divine government *vv.* 2, 3. To drive home the conviction, he here shows what a righteous God that is with whom we have to do, and how just in his proceedings.

III. He draws up a charge against them (*vv.* 4, 5) consisting of two branches:

1. Slighting the goodness of God (*v.* 4), *the riches of his goodness*. This is especially applicable to the Jews, who had singular tokens of the divine favour. Means are mercies, and the more light we sin against the more love we sin against.

2. Provoking the wrath of God, *v.* 5. The rise of this provocation is a *hard and impenitent heart*; and the ruin of sinners is their walking after such a heart, being led by it.

IV. He describes the measures by which God proceeds in his judgment.

1. He will *render to every man according to his deeds* (*v.* 6), a truth often mentioned in scripture, to prove that the Judge of all the earth does right.

(1) In dispensing his favours; and this is mentioned twice here, both in *v.* 7 and *v.* 10. For he delights to show mercy.

(2) In dispensing his frowns (*vv.* 8, 9). Observe, [1] The objects of his frowns. In general those that do evil, more particularly described to be *such as are contentious and do not obey the truth.* Contentious against God. Every wilful sin is a quarrel with God, it is *striving with our Maker* (Isa. xlv. 9), the most desperate contention. [2] The products or instances of these frowns: *Indignation and wrath, tribulation and anguish.* These are the wages of sin. *Indignation and wrath* the causes—*tribulation and anguish* the necessary and unavoidable effects.

2. *There is no respect of persons with God, v.* 11. As to the spiritual state, there is a respect of persons; but not as to outward relation or condition. Jews and Gentiles stand upon the same level before God. This was Peter's remark upon the first taking down of the partition-wall (Acts x. 34), that God is no respecter of persons; and it is explained in the next words, that *in every nation he that fears God, and works righteousness, is accepted of him.*

V. He proves the equity of his proceedings with all, when he shall actually come to Judge them (*vv.* 12–16), upon this principle, that that which is the rule of man's obedience is the rule of God's judgment. Three degrees of light are revealed to the children of men:

1. The light of nature. This the Gentiles have, and by this they shall be judged. They had that within them which approved and commended what was well done and which reproached them for what was done amiss. So that the guilty Gentiles are left without excuse. God is justified in condemning them. They cannot plead ignorance, and therefore are likely to perish if they have not something else to plead.

2. The light of the law. This the Jews had, and by this they shall be judged (*v.* 12). It was a great privilege that they had the law, but not a saving privilege, unless they lived up to the law they had, which it is certain the Jews did not, and therefore they had need of a righteousness wherein to appear before God.

3. The light of the gospel: and according to this those that enjoyed the gospel shall be judged (*v.* 16): *According to my gospel.* As many as are under that dispensation shall be judged according to that dispensation, Mark xvi. 16.

A TRUE JEW (*vv.* 17–29)

In the latter part of the chapter the apostle directs his discourse more closely to the Jews, and shows what sins they were guilty of, notwithstanding their profession and vain pretensions. He had said (*v.* 13) that not the hearers but the doers of the law are justified; and he here applies that great truth to the Jews. Observe,

I. He allows their profession (*vv.* 17–20) and specifies their particular pretensions and privileges in which they prided themselves, that they might see he did not condemn them out of ignorance of what they had to say for themselves; no, he knew the best of their cause.

1. They were a peculiar people, separated and distinguished from all others by their having the written law and the special presence of God among them.

2. They were a knowing people (v. 18). They did not only know the truth of God, but the will of God, that which he would have them do. The Jews, having the touchstone of the law ready at hand, were, or at least thought they were, able to distinguish, to cleave the hair in doubtful cases.

3. They were a teaching people, or at least thought themselves so (vv. 19, 20): *And art confident that thou thyself art a guide of the blind.* Apply it, (1) To the Jews in general. They thought themselves guides to the poor blind Gentiles that sat in darkness, were very proud of this, that whoever would have the knowledge of God must be beholden to them for it. (2) To their rabbis, and doctors, and leading men among them, who were especially those that judged others, v. 1.

II. He aggravates their provocations (vv. 21–24) from two things:

1. That they sinned against their knowledge and profession, did that themselves which they taught others to avoid: *Thou that teachest another, teachest thou not thyself?*

2. That they dishonoured God by their sin, vv. 23, 24. While God and his law were an honour to them, which they boasted of and prided themselves in, they were a dis-

honour to God and his law, by their sin.

III. He asserts the utter insufficiency of their profession to clear them from the guilt of these provocations (vv. 25–29). Further to illustrate this,

1. He shows that the uncircumcised Gentiles, if they live up to the light they have, stand upon the same level with the Jews; if *they keep the righteousness of the law* (v. 26), *fulfil the law* (v. 27); that is, by submitting sincerely to the conduct of natural light, perform the matter of the law.

2. He describes the true circumcision, vv. 28, 29. (1). It is *not that which is outward in the flesh and in the letter.* To be Abraham's children is to do the works of Abraham, John viii. 39, 40. (2) It is *that which is inward, of the heart, and in the spirit.* It is the heart that God looks at, the circumcising of the heart that renders us acceptable to him. See Deut. xxx. 6. This is *the circumcision that is not made with hands,* Col. ii. 11, 12. (3) The praise thereof, though it be *not of men,* who judge according to outward appearance, yet it is *of God,* that is, God himself will own and accept and crown this sincerity; for *he seeth not as man seeth.*

CHAPTER THREE

JEWS' ADVANTAGES
(vv. 1–18)

I. Here the apostle answers several objections, which might be made, to clear his way.

Object. 1. If Jew and Gentile stand so much upon the same level before God, *what advantage then hath the Jew?*

Answer. The door is open to the Gentiles as well as the Jews, but the Jews have a fairer way up to this door, by reason of their church-privileges, which are not to be undervalued, though many that have them perish eternally for not improving them. The Jews had the means of salvation, but they had not the monopoly of salvation.

Object 2. To what purpose were the oracles of God committed to them, when so many of them, notwithstanding these oracles, continued strangers to Christ, and enemies to his gospel? *Some did not believe, v.* 3.

Answer. It is very true that some, nay most of the present Jews, do not believe in Christ; *but shall their unbelief make the faith of God without effect?* The apostle startles at such a thought: *God forbid!* The infidelity and obstinacy of the Jews could not invalidate the overthrow those prophecies of the Messiah which were contained in the oracles committed to them. Christ will be glorious, *though Israel be not gathered,* Isa. xlix. 5. God's words shall be accomplished, his purposes performed, and all his ends answered, though there be a generation that by their unbelief go about to make God a liar. *Let God be true but every man a liar;* let us abide by this principle, that God is true to every word which he has spoken, and will let none of his oracles fall to the ground, though thereby we give the lie to man; better question and overthrow the credit of all the men in the world than doubt of the faithfulness of God.

Object. 3. Now it may be suggested, If all our sin be so far from overthrowing God's honour that it commends it, and his ends are secured, so that there is no harm done, it is not unjust for God to punish our sin and unbelief so severely?

Answer. God forbid; far be it from us to imagine such a thing. Suggestions that reflect dishonour upon God and his justice and holiness are rather to be startled at than parleyed with. The sin has never the less of malignity and demerit in it though God bring glory to himself out of it. It is only accidentally that sin commends God's righteousness. No thanks to the sinner for that, who intends no such thing.

Object. 4. The former objection is repeated and prosecuted (*vv* 7, 8). *Let us do evil that good may come* is oftener in the heart than in the mouth of sinners, so justifying themselves in their wicked ways.

Answer. He says no more by way of confutation but that, whatever they themselves may argue, the damnation of those is just. Those who deliberately do evil that good may come of it will be so far from escaping, under the shelter of that excuse, that it will rather justify their damnation, and render them the more inexcusable; for sinning upon such a surmise, and in such a confidence, argues a great deal both of the wit and of the will in the sin —a wicked will deliberately to choose the evil, and a wicked wit to palliate it with the pretence of good arising from it.

II. Paul, having removed these objections, next revives his assertion of the general guilt and corruption of mankind in common, both of Jews and Gentiles, *vv.* 9–18. They *are all under sin*. Under the guilt of sin: under it as under a sentence;—under it as under a bond, by which they are bound over to eternal ruin and damnation; —under it as under a burden (Ps. xxxviii. 4) that will sink them to the lowest hell: we are guilty before God, *v.* 19. He who, when he himself had made all, looked upon every thing that he had made, and behold all was very good, now that man had marred all, looked, and behold all was very bad. Let us take a view of the particulars. Observe,

1. That which is habitual, which is twofold:

(1) An habitual defect of every thing that is good. [1] *There is none righteous*, none that has an honest good principle of virtue, or is governed by such a principle, none that retains any thing of that image of God, consisting in righteousness, wherein man was created; *no, not one*; implying that, if there had been but one, God would have found him out. [2] *There is none that understandeth, v.* 11. The fault lies in the corruption of the understanding; that is blinded, depraved, perverted. [3] *None that seeketh after God*, that is, none that has any regard to God, any desire after him. [4] *They are together become unprofitable, v.* 12. Those that have forsaken God soon grow good for nothing, useless burdens of the earth. [5] *There is none that doeth good;* no, not a just man upon the earth, that doeth good, and sinneth not, Eccl. vii. 23.

(2) An habitual defection to every thing that is evil: *They are all gone out of the way*. No wonder that those miss the right way who do not seek after God, the highest end. God made man in the way, set him in right, but he hath forsaken it. The corruption of mankind is an apostasy.

2. That which is actual. And what good can be expected from such a degenerate race? He instances,

(1) In their words (*vv.* 13, 14), in three things particularly: [1] Cruelty: *Their throat is an open sepulchre*, ready to swallow up the poor and innocent. These passages are borrowed from Ps. v. 9 and cxl. 3. [2] Cheating: *With their tongues they have used deceit*. [3] Cursing: reflecting upon God, and blaspheming his holy name; wishing evil to their brethren: *Their mouth is full of cursing and bitterness*.

(2) In their ways (*vv.* 15–17): *Their feet are swift to shed blood*; that is, they are very industrious to compass any cruel design, ready to lay hold of all such opportunities.

(3) The root of all this we have: *There is no fear of God before their eyes, v.* 18. The fear of God is here put for all practical religion, which consists in an awful and serious regard to the word and will of God as our rule, to the honour and glory of God as our end.

SIN AND JUSTIFICATION
(*vv.* 19–31)

From all this Paul infers that it is in vain to look for justification by the works of the law, and that it is to be had only by faith, which is the point he has been all along proving, from *ch.* i. 17, and which he lays down (*v.* 28) as the summary of his discourse.

I. He argues from man's guiltiness, to show the folly of expecting justification by the works of the law. Now concerning the guiltiness of man,

1. He fastens it particularly upon the Jews; for they were the men that made their boast of the law, and set up for justification by it.

2. He extends it in general to all the world: *That all the world may become guilty before God. For all have sinned* (*v.* 23); all are sinners by nature, by practice, and *have come short of the glory of God*—have failed of that which is the chief end of man. *Come short*, as the archer comes short of the mark, as the runner comes short of the prize; so come short, as not only not to win, but to be great losers.

3. Further to drive us off from expecting justification by the law, he ascribes this conviction to the law (*v.* 20): *For by the law is the knowledge of sin.* That law which convicts and condemns us can never justify us.

II. He argues from God's glory to prove that justification must be expected only by faith in Christ's righteousness. There is no justification by the works of the law. Must guilty man then remain eternally under wrath? Is there no hope? Is the wound become incurable because of transgression? No, blessed be God, it is not (*vv.* 21, 22); there is another way laid open for us, *the righteousness of God without the law is manifested* now under the gospel.

1. Now concerning this righteousness of God observe, (1) That it is manifested. The gospel-way of justification is a high-way, a plain way, it is laid open for us. (2) It is *without the law.* Here he obviates the method of the judaizing Christians, who would needs join Christ and Moses together. (3) Yet *it is witnessed by the law and the prophets;* that is, there were types, and prophecies, and promises, in the Old Testament, that pointed at this. (4) It is by the *faith of Jesus Christ,* that faith which hath Jesus Christ for its object—an *anointed Saviour,* so Jesus Christ signifies. (5) It is *to all, and upon all, those that believe.* In this expression he inculcates that which he had been often harping upon, that Jews and Gentiles, if they believe, stand upon the same level, and are alike welcome to God through Christ; *for there is no difference.*

2. But now how is this for God's glory?

(1) It is for the glory of his grace (*v.* 24). It comes freely to us, but Christ bought it, and paid dearly for it, which yet is so ordered as not to derogate from the honour of free grace.

(2) It is for the glory of his justice and righteousness (*vv.* 25, 26): *Whom God hath set forth to be a propitiation,* &c. Note, [1] Jesus Christ is the great propitiation, or propitiatory sacrifice, typified by the *mercy-seat,* under the law. He is all in all in our reconciliation, not only the maker, but the matter of it—our priest, our sacrifice, our altar, our all. [2] *God hath set him forth* to be so. See Matt. iii. 17, and xvii. 5. [3] That *by faith in his blood*

we become interested in this propitiation. Christ is the propitiation; there is the healing plaster provided. Faith is the applying of this plaster to the wounded soul. [4] That all who by faith are interested in this propitiation have *the remission of their sins that are past. Through the forbearance of God.* Divine patience has kept us out of hell, that we might have space to repent, and get to heaven. [5] That God does in all this *declare his righteousness. First,* In the propitiation itself. Never was there such a demonstration of the justice and holiness of God as there was in the death of Christ. *Secondly,* In the pardon upon that propitiation; so it follows, by way of explanation: *That he might be just, and the justifier of him that believeth.* It would not comport with his justice to demand the debt of the principal when the surety has paid it and he has accepted that payment in full satisfaction. See I John i. 9.

(3) It is for God's glory; for boasting is thus excluded, *v.* 27. God will have the great work of the justification and salvation of sinners carried on from first to last in such a way as to exclude boasting, that no flesh may glory in his presence, 1 Cor. i. 29–31.

From all this he draws this conclusion (*v.* 28): *That a man is justified by faith without the deeds of the law.*

III. In the close of the chapter he shows the extent of this privilege of justification by faith, and that it is not the peculiar privilege of the Jews, but pertains to the Gentiles also; for he had said (*v.* 22) that there is no difference.

CHAPTER FOUR

THE CASE OF ABRAHAM
(*vv.* 1–8)

I. If he had been justified by works, room would have been left for boasting, which must for ever be excluded. If so, *he hath whereof to glory* (*v.* 2), which is not to be allowed. "But," might the Jews say, "was not his name made great (Gen. xii. 2), and then might not he glory?" Yes, but not before God; he might deserve well of men, but he could never merit of God.

II. It is expressly said that Abraham's faith was counted to him for righteousness. *What saith the scripture? v.* 3. It is mentioned in Genesis, upon occasion of a very signal and remarkable act of faith concerning the promised seed, and is the more observable in that it followed upon a grievous conflict he had had with unbelief; his faith was now a victorious faith, newly returned from the battle. It is not the perfect faith that is required to justification (there may be acceptable faith where there are remainders of unbelief), but the prevailing faith, the faith that has the upper hand of unbelief.

III. If he had been justified by works, the reward would have been *of debt, and not of grace,* which is not to be imagined. This is his argument (*vv,* 4, 5): Abraham's reward was God himself; so he had told him but just before (Gen. xv. 1), *I am thy exceeding great reward.* Now, if Abraham had merited this by the perfection of his obedience, it had not been an act of grace in God, but Abraham might have demanded it with as much confidence as ever any labourer in the vineyard demanded the penny he had earned. But this cannot be; it is impossible for man, much more guilty man, to make God a debtor to him, Rom. xi. 35.

IV. He further illustrates this by a passage out of the Psalms, where David speaks of the remission of sins, the prime branch of justification, as constituting the happiness and blessedness of a man, pronouncing blessed, not the man who has no sin, or none which deserved death (for then, while man is so sinful, and God so righteous, where would be the blessed man?) but *the man to whom the Lord imputeth not sin*, who though he cannot plead, Not guilty, pleads the act of indemnity, and his plea is allowed. It is quoted from Ps. xxxii. 1, 2.

ABRAHAM JUSTIFIED
(vv. 9–17)

St. Paul observes in this paragraph when and why Abraham was thus justified; for he has several things to remark upon that. It was before he was circumcised, and before the giving of the law; and there was a reason for both.

I. It was before he was circumcised, *v.* 10. Abraham was pardoned and accepted in uncircumcision, a circumstance which, as it might silence the fears of the poor uncircumcised Gentiles, so it might lower the pride and conceitedness of the Jews, who gloried in their circumcision, as if they had the monopoly of all happiness. Here are two reasons why Abraham was justified by faith in circumcision:

1. That circumcision might be *a seal of* the *righteousness of faith, v.*

11. The tenor of the covenants must first be settled before the seal can be annexed. Sealing supposes a previous bargain, which is confirmed and ratified by that ceremony.

2. *That he might be the father of all those that believe.* Abraham was the father of believers, because to him particularly the *magna charta* was renewed. (1) The father of believing Gentiles, *though they be not circumcised.* Zaccheus, a publican, if he believe, is reckoned a son of Abraham, Luke xix. 9. (2) The father of believing Jews, not merely as circumcised, and of the seed of Abraham according to the flesh, but because believers, because they *are not of the circumcision only* (that is, are not only circumcised), *but walk in the steps of that faith*—have not only the sign, but the thing signified—not only are of Abraham's family, but follow the example of Abraham's faith.

II. It was before the giving of the law, *vv.* 13–16. Now observe,

1. What that promise was—*that he should be the heir of the world,* that is, of the land of Canaan, the choicest spot of ground in the world,—or the father of many nations of the world, who sprang from him, besides the Israelites,— or the heir of the comforts of the life which now is.

2. How it was made to him: *Not through the law, but through the righteousness of faith. Not through the law,* for that was not yet given: but it was upon that believing which was counted to him for righteousness; it was upon his trusting God, in his leaving his own country when God commanded

him, Heb. xi. 8. Now, being by faith, it could not be by the law, which he proves by the opposition there is between them (*vv.* 14, 15).

3. Why the promise was made to him by faith; for three reasons, *v.* 16. (1) *That it might be by grace*, that grace might have the honour of it. (2) *That the promise might be sure*. The first covenant, being a covenant of works, was not sure. (3) *That it might be sure to all the seed*. If it had been *by the law*, it had been limited to the Jews, *to whom pertained the glory, and the covenants, and the giving of the law* (*ch.* ix. 4); but therefore it was by faith that Gentiles as well as Jews might become inteested in it, the spiritual as well as the natural seed of faithful Abraham.

ABRAHAM'S FAITH
(*vv.* 17–22)

Having observed when Abraham was justified by faith, and why, for the honour of Abraham and for example to us who call him father, the apostle here describes and commends the faith of Abraham, where observe,

I. Whom he believed: *God who quickeneth*. It is God himself that faith fastens upon: *other foundation can no man lay*.

II. How he believed. 1. *Against hope, he believed in hope*, *v.* 18. There was a hope against him, a natural hope. All the arguments of sense, and reason, and experience, which in such cases usually beget and support hope, were against him; no second causes smiled upon him, nor in the least favoured his hope. But, against all those inducements to the contrary, he believed;

for he had a hope for him: *He believed in hope*, which arose, as his faith did, from the consideration of God's all-sufficiency. 2. *Being not weak in faith, he considered not his own body*, *v.* 19. It is mere weakness of faith that makes a man lie poring upon the difficulties and seeming impossibilities that lie in the way of a promise. Though it may seem to be the wisdom and policy of carnal reason, yet it is the weakness of faith, to look into the bottom of all the difficulties that arise against the promise. 3. *He staggered not at the promise of God through unbelief* (*v.* 20), and he therefore staggered not because he considered not the frowns and discouragements of second causes. Unbelief is at the bottom of all our staggerings at God's promises. It is not the promise that fails, but our faith that fails when we stagger. 4. He *was strong in faith, giving glory to God*. The strength of his faith appeared in the victory it won over his fears. And hereby he gave glory to God. 5. He was *fully persuaded that what God had promised he was able to perform*. Such was his full persuasion, and it was built on the omnipotence of God: *He was able*.

A UNIVERSAL TRUTH
(*vv.* 23–25)

In the close of the chapter, he applies all to us; and, having abundantly proved that Abraham was justified by faith, he here concludes that his justification was to be the pattern or sampler of ours: *It was not written for his sake alone*. The accounts we have of the Old-Testament saints were not intended for histories only, barely to inform and divert us, but for precedents to direct us, for examples (1 Cor. x. 11) for *our learning*, *ch.* xv. 4.

JUSTIFIED BY FAITH
(*vv.* 1–5)

The precious benefits and privileges which flow from justification are exceedingly precious.

I. *We have peace with God*, *v.* 1. Justification takes away the guilt, and so makes way for peace. By faith we lay hold of God's arm and of his strength, and so are at peace, Isa. xxvii, 4, 5. There is more in this peace than barely a cessation of enmity, there is friendship and loving-kindness, for God is either the worst enemy or the best friend.

II. *We have access by faith into this grace wherein we stand*, *v.* 2. Now into this grace we have access, *an introduction*, which implies that we were not born in this state; we are *by nature children of wrath*, and *the carnal mind is enmity against God*; but we are brought into it. *By whom we have access by faith*. By Christ as the author and principal agent, by faith as the means of this access. *Wherein we stand*. Not only wherein we are, but wherein we stand, a posture that denotes our discharge from guilt; *we stand in the judgment* (Ps. i. 5), not cast, as convicted criminals, but our dignity and honour secured, not thrown to the ground, as abjects. The phrase denotes also our progress; while we stand, we are going. We must not lie down, as if we had already attained, but stand as those that are pressing forward, stand as

servants attending on Christ our master.

III. *We rejoice in hope of the glory of God*. Besides the happiness in hand, there is a happiness in hope, *the glory of God*, the glory which God will put upon the saints in heaven, glory which will consist in the vision and fruition of God.

IV. *We glory in tribulations also*. How come we to glory in tribulations? Why, because tribulations, by a chain of causes, greatly befriend hope, which he shows in the method of its influence. 1. *Tribulation worketh patience*, not in and of itself, but the powerful grace of God working in and with the tribulation. 2. *Patience experience*, *v.* 4. It works an experience of God, and the songs he gives in the night; the patient sufferers have the greatest experience of the divine consolations, which abound as afflictions abound. 3. *Experience hope*. Experience of God is a prop to our hope; he that hath delivered doth and will. Experience of ourselves helps to evidence our sincerity. 4. This *hope maketh not ashamed*; that is, it is a hope that will not deceive us. Nothing confounds more than disappointment. Sense of God's love to us will make us not ashamed, either of our hope in him or our sufferings for him.

THE SECOND ADAM
(*vv.* 6–21)

The apostle here describes the fountain and foundation of justification, laid in the death of the Lord Jesus.

I. The character we were under when Christ died for us.

1. *We were without strength (v.*

6), in a sad condition; and, which is worse, altogether unable to help ourselves out of that condition. God's time to help and save is when those that are to be saved are without strength, that his own power and grace may be the more magnified, Deut. xxxii. 36.

2. *He died for the ungodly*; not only helpless creatures, and therefore likely to perish, but guilty sinful creatures, and therefore deserving to perish. *While we were yet sinners*, implying that we were not to be always sinners, there should be a change wrought; for he died to save us, not in our sins, but from our sins; but we were yet sinners when he died for us. Nay, which is more, *we were enemies* (*v.* 10). And that for such as these Christ should die is such a mystery, such a paradox, such an unprecedented instance of love, that it may well be our business to eternity to adore and wonder at it.

II. The precious fruits of his death.

1. Justification and reconciliation are the first and primary fruit of the death of Christ: *We are justified by his blood* (*v.* 9), *reconciled by his death*, *v.* 10. Sin is pardoned, the sinner accepted as righteous, the quarrel taken up, the enmity slain, an end made of iniquity, and an everlasting righteousness brought in.

2. Hence results salvation from wrath: *Saved from wrath* (*v.* 9), *saved by his life*, *v.* 10. When that which hinders our salvation is taken away, the salvation must needs follow. Nay, the argument holds very strongly; if God justified and reconciled us when we were

enemies, and put himself to so much charge to do it, much more will he save us when we are justified and reconciled. He that has done the greater, which is of enemies to make us friends, will certainly do the less, which is when we are friends to use us friendly and to be kind to us.

3. All this produces, as a further privilege, our *joy in God*, *v.* 11. *And not only so*, there is more in it yet, a constant stream of favours; we not only go to heaven, but go to heaven triumphantly; not only get into the harbour, but come in with full sail: *We joy in God*, not only saved from his wrath, but solacing ourselves in his love. To *receive the atonement* is, (1) To give our consent to the atonement, approving of, and agreeing to, those methods which Infinite Wisdom has taken of saving a guilty world by the blood of a crucified Jesus, being willing and glad to be saved in a gospel way and upon gospel terms. (2) To take the comfort of the atonement, which is the fountain and the foundation of our joy in God.

III. The parallel that the apostle runs between the communication of sin and death by the first Adam and of righteousness and life by the second Adam (*v.* 12, to the end). Now, for the opening of this, observe,

1. A general truth laid down as the foundation of his discourse— that Adam was a type of Christ (*v.* 14): *Who is the figure of him that was to come.* Christ is therefore called the *last Adam*, 1 Cor. xv. 45. Compare *v.* 22.

2. A more particular explanation of the parallel, in which observe,

(1) How Adam, as a public person, communicated sin and death to all his posterity (*v.* 12): *By one man sin entered.* [1] By him *sin entered.* When God pronounced all very good (Gen. i. 31) there was no sin in the world; it was when Adam ate forbidden fruit that sin made its entry. Now Adam acted thus as a public person, by the sovereign ordination and appointment of God, and yet that founded upon a natural necessity; for God, as the author of nature, had made this the law of nature, that man should beget in his own likeness, and so the other creatures. In Adam therefore, as in a common receptacle, the whole nature of man was reposited, from him to flow down in a channel to his posterity; for all mankind are made *of one blood* (Acts xvii. 26). Adam therefore sinning and falling, the nature became guilty and corrupt, and is so derived. Thus in him all have sinned. [2] *Death by sin,* for death is the wages of sin. Sin, when it is finished, brings forth death. When sin came, of course death came with it. Death is here put for all that misery which is the due desert of sin, temporal, spiritual, eternal death. *Death reigned, v.* 14. He speaks of death as a mighty prince, and his monarchy the most absolute, universal, and lasting monarchy. None are exempted from its sceptre; it is a monarchy that will survive all other earthly rule, authority, and power, for it is the last enemy, 1 Cor. xv. 26.

Further, to clear this, he shows that sin did not commence with the law of Moses, but was *in the world until,* or *before,* that law; therefore that law of Moses is not the only rule of life, for there was a rule, and that rule was transgressed, before the law was given. It likewise intimates that we cannot be justified by our obedience to the law of Moses, any more than we were condemned by and for our disobedience to it.

(2) How, in correspondence to this, Christ, as a public person, communicates righteousness and life to all true believers, who are his spiritual seed. Observe,

[1] Wherein the resemblance holds. This is laid down most fully, *vv.* 18, 19.

First, By the offence and disobedience of one many were made sinners, and judgment came upon all men to condemnation.

Secondly, In like manner, *by the righteousness and obedience of one* (and that one is Jesus Christ, the second Adam), *are many made righteous,* and so the *free gift comes upon all.* It is observable how the apostle inculcates this truth, and repeats it again and again, as a truth of very great consequence. Here observe, 1. The nature of Christ's righteousness, how it is brought in; it is by his obedience. The disobedience of the first Adam ruined us, the obedience of the second Adam saves us. 2. The fruit of it. (1) There is a *free gift come upon all men,* that is, it is made and offered promiscuously to all. (2) *Many shall be made righteous*—many compared with one, or as many as belong to the election of grace, which, though but a few as they are scattered up and down in the world, yet will be a great many when they come all together.

[2] Wherein the communication of grace and love by Christ goes beyond the communication of guilt and wrath by Adam; and this he shows, *vv*. 15–17. His expressions are a little intricate, but this he seems to intend: *First*, If guilt and wrath be communicated, much more shall grace and love; for it is agreeable to the idea we have of the divine goodness to suppose that he should be more ready to save upon an imputed righteousness than to condemn upon an imputed guilt. *Secondly*, If there was so much power and efficacy, as it seems there was, in the sin of a man, who was of the earth, earthy, to condemn us, much more are there power and efficacy in the righteousness and grace of Christ, who is the Lord from heaven, to justify and save us.

IV. In the last two verses the apostle seems to anticipate an objection which is expressed, Gal. iii. 19, *Wherefore then serveth the law?* Answer, 1. *The law entered that the offence might abound.* Not to make sin to abound the more in itself, otherwise than as sin takes occasion by the commandment, but to discover the abounding sinfulness of it. 2. *That grace might much more abound*—that the terrors of the law might make gospel-comforts so much the sweeter.

CHAPTER SIX
FREEDOM FROM SIN
(*vv*. 1–23)

The apostle is very full in pressing the necessity of holiness in this chapter, which may be reduced to two heads: His exhortations to holiness, which show the nature of it; and his motives or arguments to enforce those exhortations, which show the necessity of it.

I. For the first, we may hence observe the nature of sanctification, what it is, and wherein it consists. In general it has two things in it, mortification and vivification—dying to sin and living to righteousness, elsewhere expressed by putting off the old man and putting on the new, ceasing to do evil and learning to do well.

1. Mortification, putting off the old man; several ways this is expressed. (1) We must *live no longer in sin* (*v*. 2), we must not be as we have been nor do as we have done. The time past of our life must suffice, 1 Peter iv. 3. Though there are none that live without sin, yet, blessed be God, there are those that do not live in sin, do not live in it as their element, do not make a trade of it: this is to be sanctified. (2) *The body of sin must be destroyed*, *v*. 6. The corruption that dwelleth in us is the body of sin, consisting of many parts and members, as a body. This is the root to which the axe must be laid. (3) *We must be dead indeed unto sin*, *v*. 11. As the death of the oppressor is a release, so much more is the death of the oppressed, Job iii. 17, 18. Death makes a mighty change; such a change doth sanctification make in the soul, it cuts off all correspondence with sin. (4) *Sin must not reign in our mortal bodies that we should obey it*, *v*. 12. Though sin may remain as an outlaw, though it may oppress as a tyrant, yet let it not reign as a king. (5) We must not *yield our members as instruments of un-*

righteousness, *v.* 13. The members of the body are made use of by the corrupt nature as tools, by which the wills of the flesh are fulfilled; but we must not consent to that abuse.

2. Vivification, or living to righteousness; and what is that? (1) It is to *walk in newness of life*, *v.* 4. Newness of life supposes newness of heart, for out of the heart are the issues of life, and there is no way to make the stream sweet but by making the spring so. (2) Is is to be *alive unto God through Jesus Christ our Lord*, *v.* 11. The love of God reigning in the heart is the life of the soul towards God. (3) It is to *yield ourselves to God, as those that are alive from the dead*, *v.* 13. The very life and being of holiness lie in the dedication of ourselves to the Lord, giving our own selves to the Lord, 2 Cor. viii. 5. (4) It is to yield *our members as instruments of righteousness to God*. The members of our bodies, when withdrawn from the service of sin, are not to lie idle, but to be made use of in the service of God.

II. The motives or arguments here used to show the necessity of sanctification.

1. He argues from our sacramental conformity to Jesus Christ. Our baptism, with the design and intention of it, carries in it a great reason why we should die to sin, and live to righteousness. Thus we must improve our baptism as a bridle of restraint to keep us in from sin, as a spur of constraint to quicken us to duty. Observe this reasoning.

(1) In general, we are *dead to sin*, that is, in profession and in obliga-

tion. Our baptism signifies our cutting off from the kingdom of sin. We profess to have no more to do with sin. All this is in vain if we persist in sin; we contradict a profession, violate an obligation, return to that to which we were dead, like walking ghosts, than which nothing is more unbecoming and absurd. For (*v.* 7) *he that is dead is freed from sin*; that is, he that is dead to it is freed from the rule and dominion of it, as the servant that is dead is freed from his master, Job iii. 19.

(2) In particular, being *baptized into Jesus Christ, we were baptized into his death*, *v.* 3. Baptism binds us to Christ, it binds us apprentice to Christ as our teacher, it is our allegiance to Christ as our sovereign.

[1] Our conformity to the death of Christ obliges us to die unto sin; thereby we know the *fellowship of his sufferings*, Phil. iii. 10. *First, Our old man is crucified with him*, *v.* 6. The death of the cross was a slow death; the body, after it was nailed to the cross, gave many a throe and many a struggle: but it was a sure death, long in expiring, but expired at last; such is the mortification of sin in believers. *Secondly*, We are dead with Christ, *v.* 8. Christ was obedient to death: when he died, we might be said to die with him, as our dying to sin is an act of conformity both to the design and to the example of Christ's dying for sin. Baptism signifies and seals our union with Christ, our engrafting into Christ; so that we are dead with him, and engaged to have no more to do with sin than he had. *Thirdly, We are buried with him by*

baptism, v. 4. Our conformity is complete. We are in profession quite cut off from all commerce and communion with sin, as those that are buried are quite cut off from all the world; not only not of the living, but no more among the living, have nothing more to do with them. Thus must we be, as Christ was, separate from sin and sinners.

[2] Our conformity to the resurrection of Christ obliges us to rise again to newness of life. This is *the power of his resurrection* which Paul was so desirous to know, Phil. iii. 10.

2. He argues from the precious promises and privileges of the new covenant, *v.* 14. God's promises to us are more powerful and effectual for the mortifying of sin than our promises to God. Sin may struggle in a believer, and may create him a great deal of trouble, but it shall not have dominion; it may vex him, but shall not rule over him.

3. He argues from the evidence that this will be of our state, making for us, or against us (*v.* 16): *To whom you yield yourselves servants to obey, his servants you are.* All the children of men are either the servants of God, or the servants of sin; these are the two families. Now, if we would know to which of these families we belong, we must enquire to which of these masters we yield obedience.

4. He argues from their former sinfulness, *vv.* 17–21, where we may observe,

(1) What they had been and done formerly. We have need to be often reminded of our former state. Paul frequently remembers it con-

cerning himself, and those to whom he writes.

(2) How the blessed change was made, and wherein it did consist.

[1] *You have obeyed from the heart that form of doctrine which was delivered to you, v.* 17. This describes conversion, what it is; it is our conformity to, and compliance with, the gospel which was delivered to us by Christ and his ministers.

[2] *Being made free from sin, you became servants of righteousness* (*v.* 18), *servants to God, v.* 22. Conversion is, *First,* A freedom from the service of sin; it is the shaking off of that yoke, resolving to have no more to do with it. *Secondly,* A resignation of ourselves to the service of God and righteousness, to God as our master, to righteousness as our work.

(3) What apprehensions they now had of their former work and way. He appeals to themselves (*v.* 21), whether they had not found the service of sin, [1] An unfruitful service. The present pleasure and profit of sin do not deserve to be called fruit; they are but chaff, ploughing iniquity, sowing vanity, and reaping the same. [2] It is an unbecoming service; it is that of which we *are now ashamed*—ashamed of the folly, ashamed of the filth, of it.

5. He argues from the end of all these things. (1) The end of sin is death (*v.* 21): *The end of those things is death.* Though the way may seem pleasant and inviting, yet the end is dismal: at the last it bites; it will be bitterness in the latter end. *The wages of sin is death, v.* 23. (2) If the fruit be unto

holiness, if there be an active principle of true and growing grace the end will be everlasting life—a, very happy end!—Though the way be up-hill, though it be narrow, and thorny, and beset, yet everlasting life at the end of it is sure. So, *v.* 23, *The gift of God is eternal life.* The death is the wages of sin, it comes by desert; but the life is a gift it comes by favour. Sinners merit hell, but saints do not merit heaven. And this gift is *through Jesus Christ our Lord.* It is Christ that purchased it, prepared it, prepares us for it, preserves us to it; he is *the Alpha and Omega*, All in all in our salvation.

CHAPTER SEVEN

NOT UNDER LAW

(*vv.* 1–6)

Among other arguments used in the foregoing chapter to persuade us against sin, and to holiness, this was one (*v.* 14), that *we are not under the law*; and this argument is here further insisted upon and explained (*v.* 6): *We are delivered from the law.* What is meant by this? And how is it an argument why sin should not reign over us, and why we should walk in newness of life? 1. We are delivered from that power of the law which curses and condemns us for the sin committed by us. The sentence of the law against us is vacated and reversed, by the death of Christ, to all true believers. The law saith, *The soul that sins shall die*; but we are delivered from the law. 2. We are delivered from that power of the law which irritates and provokes the sin that dwelleth in us.

This the apostle seems especially to refer to (*v.* 5): *The motions of sins which were by the law.* The law, by commanding, forbidding, threatening, corrupt and fallen man, but offering no grace to cure and strengthen, did but stir up the corruption.

The difference between a law-state and a gospel-state he had before illustrated by the similitude of rising to a new life, and serving a new master; now here he speaks of it under the similitude of being married to a new husband.

I. Our first marriage was to the law, which, according to the law of marriage, was to continue only during the life of the law. The law of marriage is binding till the death of one of the parties, no matter which, and no longer. The death of either discharges both. Thus were we married to the law (*v.* 5): *When we were in the flesh,* that is, in a carnal state, under the reigning power of sin and corruption—in the flesh as in our element—then *the motions of sins which were by the law did work in our members,* we were carried down the stream of sin, and the law was but as an imperfect dam, which made the stream to swell the higher, and rage the more. Our desire was towards sin, as that of the wife towards her husband, and sin ruled over us. And this continues during life, while the law is alive to us, and we are alive to the law.

II. Our second marriage is to Christ: and how comes this about? Why,

1. We are freed, by death, from our obligation to the law as a covenant, as the wife is from her

obligation to her husband, *v.* 3. This resemblance is not very close, nor needed it to be. *You are become dead to the law, v.* 4.

2. We are married to Christ. The day of our believing is the day of our espousals to the Lord Jesus. We enter upon a life of dependence on him and duty to him: *Married to another, even to him who is raised from the dead*, a periphrasis of Christ very pertinent here; for as our dying to sin and the law is in conformity to the death of Christ, and the crucifying of his body, so our devotedness to Christ in newness of life is in conformity to the resurrection of Christ. We are married to the raised exalted Jesus, a very honourable marriage. Compare 2 Cor. xi. 2; Eph. v. 29. Now we are thus married to Christ, (1) *That we should bring forth fruit unto God, v.* 4. As our old marriage to sin produced fruit unto death, so our second marriage to Christ produces fruit unto God, fruits of righteousness. (2) *That we should serve in newness of spirit, and not in the oldness of the letter, v.* 6. Being married to a new husband, we must change our way. Still we must serve, but it is a service that is perfect freedom, whereas the service of sin was a perfect drudgery. We are under the dispensation of the Spirit, and therefore must be spiritual, and serve in the spirit. Compare with this 2 Cor. iii. 3, 6, &c.

THE LAW IS GOOD
(*vv.* 7–14)

To what he had said in the former paragraph, the apostle here raises an objection, which he answers very fully: *What shall we say then? Is the law sin?* Observe in particular,

I. The great excellency of the law in itself. Far be it from Paul to reflect upon the law; no, he speaks honourably of it. 1. It is *holy, just, and good, v.* 12. The law in general is so, and every particular commandment is so. Laws are as the law-makers are. God, the great lawgiver, is holy, just, and good, therefore his law must needs be so. 2. *The law is spiritual* (*v.* 14), not only in regard to the effect of it, as it is a means of making us spiritual, but in regard to the extent of it; it reaches our spirits, it lays a restraint upon, and gives a direction to, the motions of the inward man; *it is a discerner of the thoughts and intents of the heart*, Heb. iv. 12.

II. The great advantage that he had found by the law. 1. It was discovering: *I had not known sin but by the law, v.* 7. As that which is straight discovers that which is crooked, as the looking-glass shows us our natural face with all its spots and deformities, so there is no way of coming to that knowledge of sin which is necessary to repentance, and consequently to peace and pardon, but by comparing our hearts and lives with the law. Particularly he came to the knowledge of the sinfulness of lust by the law of the tenth commandment. By lust he means sin dwelling in us, sin in its first motions and workings, the corrupt principle. This he came to know when the law said, *Thou shalt not covet.* The law spoke in other language than the scribes and Pharisees made it to speak in; it spoke in the spiritual sense and meaning of it. 2. It was humbling (*v.* 9): *I was alive.* He thought himself in a very good condition; he was alive in his own opinion and apprehension, very secure and confident of the goodness of his state. He had the letter of the law, but he had not the spiritual meaning of it—the shell, but not the kernel. He had the law in his hand and in his head, but he had it not in his heart; the notion of it, but not the power of it. *But when the commandment came,* came in the power of it (not to his eyes only, but to his heart), *sin revived,* as the dust in a room rises (that is, appears) when the sun-shine is let into it. Paul then saw that in sin which he had never seen before: sin in its consequences, sin with death at the heels of it, sin and the curse entailed upon it. "Thus sin revived, and then I died; I lost that good opinion which I had had of myself, and came to be of another mind." Of this excellent use is the law; it is a lamp and a light; it converts the soul, opens the eyes, prepares the way of the Lord in the desert, rends the rocks, levels the mountains, makes ready a people prepared for the Lord.

III. The ill use that his corrupt nature made of the law notwithstanding. 1. *Sin, taking occasion by the commandment, wrought in me all manner of concupiscence, v.* 8. The restraint of the law actually provoked him to sin. *Without the law sin was dead,* as a snake in winter, which the sunbeams of the law quicken and irritate. 2. It *deceived me.* Sin puts a cheat upon the sinner, and it is a fatal cheat, *v.* 11. *By it* (by the commandment) *slew me.*

There being in the law no such express threatening against sinful lustings, sin, that is, his own corrupt nature, took occasion thence to promise him impunity, and to say, as the serpent to our first parents, *You shall not surely die.* Thus it deceived and slew him. 3. It *wrought death in me by that which is good, v.* 13. That which works concupiscence works death for sin bringeth forth death. Now in this sin appears sin. The worst thing that sin does, and most like itself, is the perverting of the law, and taking occasion from it to be so much the more malignant. Thus the commandment, which was ordained to life, was intended as a guide in the way to comfort and happiness, proved unto death, through the corruption of nature, *v.* 10.

THE INNER CONFLICT
(*vv.* 14–25)

Here is a description of the conflict between grace and corruption in the heart, between the law of God and the law of sin. And it is applicable two ways: 1. To the struggles that are in a convinced soul, but yet unregenerate, in the person of whom it is supposed, by some, that Paul speaks. 2. To the struggles that are in a renewed sanctified soul, but yet in a state of imperfection; as others apprehend. And a great controversy there is of which of these we are to understand the apostle here.

I. Apply it to the struggles that are felt in a convinced soul, that is yet in a state of sin, knows his Lord's will, but does it not, approves the things that are more excellent, being instructed out of the law, and yet lives in the constant breach of it, *ch.* ii. 17–23. Though he has that within him that witnesses against the sin he commits, and it is not without a great deal of reluctancy that he does commit it, the superior faculties striving against it, natural conscience warning against it before it is committed and smiting for it afterwards, yet the man continues a slave to his reigning lusts. It is not thus with every unregenerate man, but with those only that are convinced by the law, but not changed by the gospel. The law may discover sin, and convince of sin, but it cannot conquer and subdue sin, witness the predominancy of sin in many that are under very strong legal convictions. It discovers the defilement, but will not wash it off.

II. It seems rather to be understood of the struggles that are maintained between grace and corruption in sanctified souls. That there are remainders of indwelling corruption, even where there is a living principle of grace, is past dispute; that this corruption is daily breaking forth in sins of infirmity (such as are consistent with a state of grace) is no less certain. If we say that we have no sin, we deceive ourselves, 1 John, i. 8, 10. That true grace strives against these sins and corruptions, does not allow of them, hates them, mourns over them, groans under them as a burden, is likewise certain (Gal. v. 17). These are the truths which, I think, are contained in this discourse of the apostle. Understanding it thus, we may observe here,

1. What he complains of—the remainder of indwelling corruptions, which he here speaks of, to show that the law is insufficient to justify even a regenerate man, that the best man in the world hath enough in him to condemn him, if God should deal with him according to the law. Observe the particulars of this complaint. (1) *I am carnal, sold under sin, v.* 14. He speaks of the Corinthians as carnal, 1 Cor. iii. 1. Even where there is spiritual life there are remainders of carnal affections. (2) *What I would, that I do not; but what I hate, that do I, v.* 15. And to the same purport, *vv.* 19, 21, *When I would do good, evil is present with me.* Such was the strength of corruptions, that he could not attain that perfection in holiness which he desired and breathed after. (3) *In me, that is in my flesh, dwelleth no good, v.* 18. As the new nature, as far as that goes, cannot commit sin (1 John iii. 9), so the flesh, the old nature, as far as that goes, cannot perform a good duty. How should it? For the flesh serveth the law of sin (*v.* 25), it is under the conduct and government of that law; and, while it is so, it is not likely to do any good. The corrupt nature is elsewhere called flesh (Gen. vi. 3, John iii. 6); and, though there may be good things dwelling in those that have this flesh, yet, as far as the flesh goes, there is no good, the flesh is not a subject capable of any good. (4) *I see another law in my members warring against the law of my mind, v.* 23. The corrupt and sinful inclination is here compared to a law, because it controlled and checked him in his good motions. It is said to be seated in

his members, because, Christ having set up his throne in his heart, it was only the rebellious members of the body that were the instruments of sin. (5) His general complaint we have *v.* 24, *O wretched man that I am! who shall deliver me from the body of this death?* The thing he complains of is a body of death; either the body of flesh, which is a mortal dying body (while we carry this body about with us, we shall be troubled with corruption; when we are dead, we shall be freed from sin, and not before), or the body of sin, the old man, the corrupt nature, which tends to death, that is, to the ruin of the soul. This made him cry out, *O wretched man that I am!* A man that had learned in every state to be content yet complains thus of his corrupt nature. *Who shall deliver me?* The remainders of indwelling sin are a very grievous burden to a gracious soul.

2. What he comforts himself with. The case was sad, but there were some allays. Three things comforted him:

(1) That his conscience witnessed for him that he had a good principle ruling and prevailing in him, notwithstanding. [1] *I consent unto the law that it is good*, *v.* 16. Here is the approbation of the judgment. Wherever there is grace there is not only a dread of the severity of the law, but a consent to the goodness of the law. [2] *I delight in the law of God after the inward man*, *v.* 22. All that are savingly regenerate or born again do truly delight in the law of God, delight to know it, to do it—cheerfully submit to the authority of it, and take a com-

placency in that submission, never better pleased than when heart and life are in the strictest conformity to the law and will of God. *After the inward man.* The new man is called the *inner man* (Eph. iii. 16), the *hidden man of the heart*, 1 Pet. iii. 4. Paul, as far as he was sanctified, had a delight in the law of God. [3] *With the mind I myself serve the law of God*, *v.* 52. It is not enough to consent to the law, and to delight in the law, but we must serve the law; our souls must be entirely delivered up into the obedience of it. Thus it was with Paul's mind.

(2) That the fault lay in that corruption of his nature which he did really bewail and strive against: *It is no more I that do it, but sin that dwelleth in me.* This he mentions twice (*vv.* 17, 20), not as an excuse for the guilt of his sin (it is enough to condemn us, if we were under the law, that the sin which does the evil dwelleth in us), but as a salvo for his evidences, that he might not sink in despair, but take comfort from the covenant of grace, which accepts the willingness of the spirit, and has provided pardon for the weakness of the flesh.

(3) His great comfort lay in Jesus Christ (*v.* 25): *I thank God, through Jesus Christ our Lord.* In the midst of his complaints he breaks out into praises. *Who shall deliver me?* says he (*v.* 24), as one at a loss for help. At length he finds an all-sufficient friend, even Jesus Christ. If it were not for Christ, this iniquity that dwells in us would certainly be our ruin. He is our advocate with the Father, and

through him God pities, and spares, and pardons, and lays not our iniquities to our charge.

THE SPIRIT OF LIFE
(*vv.* 1–9)

I. The apostle here begins with one signal privilege of true Christians, and describes the character of those to whom it belongs: *There is there-ore now no condemnation to those that are in Christ Jesus, v.* 1. 1. It is the unspeakable privilege and comfort of all those that are in Christ Jesus that there is therefore now no condemnation to them. He does not say, "There is no accusation against them," for this there is; but the accusation is thrown out, and the indictment quashed. Now this arises from their being in Christ Jesus; by virtue of their union with him through faith they are thus secured. They are in Christ Jesus, as in their city of refuge, and so are protected from the avenger of blood. 2. It is the undoubted character of all those who are so in Christ Jesus as to be freed from condemnation that *they walk not after the flesh but after the Spirit.* Observe, The character is given from their walk, not from any one particular act, but from their course and way.

II. This great truth, thus laid down, he illustrates in the following verses; and shows how we come by this great privilege, and how we may answer this character.

1. How comes it about?

(1) The law could not do it, *v.* 3. It could neither justify nor sanctify, neither free us from the guilt nor from the power of sin, having not the promises either of pardon or grace. The law made nothing perfect: *It was weak.*

(2) *The law of the Spirit of life in Christ Jesus* does it, *v.* 2. The covenant of grace made with us in Christ is a treasury of merit and grace, and thence we receive pardon and a new nature, *are freed from the law of sin and death,* that is, both from the guilt and power of sin—from the course of the law, and the dominion of the flesh. We are under another covenant, another master, another husband, under the *law of the Spirit,* the law that gives the Spirit, spiritual life to qualify us for eternal. Observe, [1] How Christ appeared *In the like-ness of sinful flesh.* Not sinful, for he was holy, harmless, undefiled; but in the likeness of that flesh which was sinful. [2] What was done by this appearance of his: Sin *was condemned,* that is, God did therein more than ever manifest his hatred of sin; and not only so, but for all that are Christ's both the damning and the domineering power of sin is broken and taken out of the way. [3] The happy effect of this upon us (*v.* 4): *That the righteousness of the law might be fulfilled in us.* Both in our justifica-tion and in our sanctification, the righteousness of the law is fulfilled. Now,

2. Observe how we may answer to this character, *v.* 5, &c.

(1) By looking to our minds. The man is as the mind is. The mind is the forge of thoughts. *As he thinketh in his heart, so is he,* Prov. xxiii. 7. Now, to caution us against this carnal-mindedness, he

shows the great misery and malignity of it, and compares it with the unspeakable excellency and comfort of spiritual-mindedness. [1] It is death, v. 6. It is spiritual death, the certain way to eternal death. [2] It is enmity to God (v. 7), and this is worse than the former. The former speaks the carnal sinner a dead man, which is bad; but this speaks him a devil of a man. It is not only an enemy, but enmity itself. Hence he infers (v. 8), *Those that are in the flesh cannot please God.* We may know our state and character,

(2) By enquiring whether we have the Spirit of God and Christ, or not (v. 9): *You are not in the flesh, but in the Spirit.* This expresses states and conditions of the soul vastly different. All the saints have flesh and spirit in them; but to be in the flesh and to be in the Spirit are contrary. It denotes our being overcome and subdued by one of these principles. As we say, A man is *in love,* or *in drink,* that is, overcome by it. Now the great question is whether we are in the flesh or in the Spirit; and how may we come to know it? Why, by enquiring whether the Spirit of God dwell in us. The Spirit dwelling in us is the best evidence of our being in the Spirit, for the indwelling is mutual (1 John iv. 16): *Dwelleth in God, and God in him.*

THE LIFEGIVING SPIRIT
(vv. 10–16)

In these verses the apostle represents two more excellent benefits, which belong to true believers.

I. Life. Now we are here told what becomes of the bodies and souls of those in whom Christ is.

1. We cannot say but that *the body is dead*; it is a frail, mortal, dying body, and it will be dead shortly; it is a house of clay, whose foundation is in the dust.

2. But the spirit, the precious soul, that is life; it is now spiritually alive, nay, it is life. Grace in the soul is its new nature; the life of the saint lies in the soul, while the life of the sinner goes no further than the body. When the body dies, and returns to the dust, *the spirit is life*; not only living and immortal, but swallowed up of life.

3. There is a life reserved too for the poor body at last: *He shall also quicken your mortal bodies,* v. 11. Two great assurances of the resurrection of the body are mentioned: (1) The resurrection of Christ: He *that raised up Christ from the dead shall also quicken.* Christ rose as the head, and first-fruits, and forerunner of all the saints, 1 Cor. xv. 20. (2) The indwelling of the Spirit. The same Spirit that raiseth the soul now will raise the body shortly: *By his Spirit that dwelleth in you.* Hence the apostle by the way infers how much it is our duty to walk not after the flesh, but after the Spirit, vv. 12, 13. Let not our life be after the wills and motions of the flesh. Two motives he mentions here: [1] We are not debtors to the flesh, neither by relation, gratitude, nor any other bond or obligation. [2] Consider the consequences, what will be at the end of the way. Here are life and death, blessing and cursing, set before us. *If you live after the flesh, you shall die*; that is, die eternally. But, on the other hand, *You shall live,* live and be happy to eternity; that is

the true life: *If you through the Spirit mortify the deeds of the body*.

II. The *Spirit of adoption* is another privilege belonging to those that are in Christ Jesus, *vv*. 14–16.

1. All that are Christ's are taken into the relation of children to God, *v*. 14. *They are the sons of God*, received into the number of God's children by adoption, owned and loved by him as his children.

2. And those that are the sons of God have the Spirit,

(1) To work in them the disposition of children.

[1] *You have not received the spirit of bondage again to fear*, *v*. 15. Understand it, *First*, Of that spirit of bondage which the Old-Testament church was under, by reason of the darkness and terror of that dispensation. The veil signified bondage, 2 Cor. iii. 15. Compare *v*. 17. *Secondly*, Of that spirit of bondage which many of the saints themselves were under at their conversion, under the convictions of sin and wrath set home by the Spirit; as those in Acts ii. 37, the jailer (Acts xvi. 30), Paul, Acts ix. 6. Then the Spirit himself was to the saints a spirit of bondage: "But," says the apostle, "with you this is over."

[2] But you *have received the Spirit of adoption*. Men may give a charter of adoption; but it is God's prerogative, when he adopts, to give a spirit of adoption—the nature of children. *Whereby we cry, Abba, Father*. Now, the Spirit teaches us in prayer to come to God as a Father, with a holy humble confidence, emboldening the soul in that duty.

(2) To witness to the relation of

children, *v*. 16. The former is the work of the Spirit as a Sanctifier; this as a Comforter. *Beareth witness with our spirit*. The Spirit witnesses to none the privileges of children who have not the nature and disposition of children.

THE REDEMPTION OF THE BODY (*vv*. 17–25)

In these words the apostle describes a fourth illustrious branch of the happiness of believers, namely, a title to the future glory. 1. *Heirs of God*. The Lord himself is the portion of the saints' inheritance (Ps. xvi. 5), a goodly heritage, *v*. 6. 2. *Joint-heirs with Christ*. Christ, as Mediator, is said to be the heir of all things (Heb. i. 2), and true believers, by virtue of their union with him, *shall inherit all things*, Rev. xxi. 7. Now this future glory is further spoken of as the reward of present sufferings and as the accomplishment of present hopes.

I. As the reward of the saints' present sufferings; and it is a rich reward: *If so be that we suffer with him* (*v*. 17), or *forasmuch as we suffer with him*. See the gains of suffering for Christ; though we may be losers for him, we shall not, we cannot, be losers by him in the end. This the gospel is filled with the assurances of. Now, that suffering saints may have strong supports and consolations from their hopes of heaven, he holds the balance (*v*. 18), in a comparison between the two, which is observable. 1. In one scale he puts the *sufferings of this present time*. The sufferings of the saints are but sufferings of this present time, strike no deeper than the things of time, last no longer than the present time (2 Cor. iv. 17), light affliction, and but for a moment. 2. In the other scale he puts the glory, and finds that a weight, an exceeding and eternal weight: *Glory that shall be revealed.* In our present state we come short, not only in the enjoyment, but in the knowledge of that glory (1 Cor. ii. 9; 1 John iii. 2): it shall be revealed. It surpasses all that we have yet seen and known. 3. He concludes the sufferings *not worthy to be compared with the glory.* They cannot merit that glory; and, if suffering for Christ will not merit, much less will doing.

II. As the accomplishment of the saints' present hopes and expectations, *v.* 19, &c. Now he observes an expectation of this glory,

1. In the creatures *vv.* 19–22. That must needs be a great, a transcendent glory, which all the creatures are so earnestly expecting and longing for. The sense of the apostle in these four verses we may take in the following observations: (1) That there is a present vanity to which the creature, by reason of the sin of man, is made subject, *v.* 20. *Under the bondage of corruption, v.* 21. There is an impurity, deformity, and infirmity, which the creature has contracted by the fall of man. They are thus captivated, not for any sin of their own, which they had committed, but for man's sin: *By reason of him who hath subjected the same.* (2) That the creatures *groan and travail in pain* together under this vanity and corruption, *v.* 22. It is a figurative expression. (3) That the creature, that is now thus burdened, shall,

at the time of the restitution of all things, be *delivered from this bondage into the glorious liberty of the children of God* (*v.* 21)—they shall no more be subject to vanity and corruption, and the other fruits of the curse; but, on the contrary, this lower world shall be renewed: when there will be new heavens there will be a new earth (2 Pet. iii. 13; Rev. xxi. 1). (4) That the creature doth therefore earnestly expect and wait for the *manifestation of the children of God, v.* 19. Observe, At the second coming of Christ there will be a manifestation of the children of God. Now the saints are God's hidden ones, the wheat seems lost in a heap of chaff; but then they shall be manifested. It does not yet appear what we shall be (1 John iii. 2), but then the glory shall be revealed.

2. In the saints, who are new creatures, *vv.* 23–25. Observe, (1) The grounds of this expectation in the saints. It is our having received *the first-fruits of the Spirit,* which both quickens our desires and encourages our hopes, and both ways raises our expectations. *We groan within ourselves,* which denotes the strength and secrecy of these desires. (2) The object of this expectation. What is it we are thus desiring and waiting for? What would we have? *The adoption, to wit, the redemption of our body.* The resurrection is here called *the redemption of the body.* It shall then be rescued from the power of death and the grave, and the bondage of corruption; and, though a vile body, yet it shall be refined and beautified, and made like that glorious body of Christ, Phil. iii.

21; 1 Cor. xv. 42. This is called *the adoption*. (3) The agreeableness of this to our present state, *vv.* 24, 25. Our happiness is not in present possession: *We are saved by hope.*

THE SPIRIT INTERCEDES
(*vv.* 26–28)

The apostle here suggests two privileges more to which true Christians are entitled:

I. The help of the Spirit in prayer. Now observe,

1. Our weakness in prayer: *We know not what we should pray for as we ought.* If so great a saint as Paul knew not what to pray for, what little reason have we to go forth about that duty in our own strength!

2. The assistances which the Spirit gives us in that duty. He *helps our infirmities*, meant especially for our praying infirmities, which most easily beset us in that duty, against which the Spirit helps. The Spirit in the word helps; many rules and promises there are in the word for our help. The Spirit in the heart helps, dwelling in us, working in us, as a Spirit of grace and supplication. Why, the *Spirit itself makes intercession for us*, dictates our requests, indites our petitions, draws up our plea for us. Christ intercedes for us in heaven, the Spirit intercedes for us in our hearts. Now this intercession which the Spirit makes is, (1) *With groanings that cannot be uttered.* There may be praying in the Spirit where there is not a word spoken; as Moses prayed (Exod. xiv. 15), and Hannah, 1 Sam. i. 13. (2) *According to the will of God, v.*

27. The Spirit in the heart never contradicts the Spirit in the word.

3. The sure success of these intercessions: *He that searches the heart knoweth what is the mind of the Spirit, v.* 27. He knows what we have need of before we ask, Matt. vi. 8. He knows what is the mind of his own Spirit in us.

II. The concurrence of all providences for the good of those that are Christ's, *v.* 28. Observe here.

1. The character of the saints, who are interested in this privilege; they are here described by such properties as are common to all that are truly sanctified. (1) *They love God.* (2) *They are the called according to his purpose*, effectually called according to the eternal purpose.

2. The privilege of the saints, that *all things work together for good to them*, that is, all the providences of God that concern them. All that God performs he performs for them, Ps. lvii. 2. Either directly or indirectly, every providence has a tendency to the spiritual good of those that love God, breaking them off from sin, bringing them nearer to God, weaning them from the world, fitting them for heaven.

PREDESTINATION (*vv.* 29, 30)

The apostle, having reckoned up so many ingredients of the happiness of true believers, comes here to represent the ground of them all, which he lays in predestination. There are four links of it:

I. *Whom he did foreknow he also did predestinate to be conformed to the image of his Son.* All that God designed for glory and happiness as the end he decreed to grace and holiness as the way. Not, whom he did foreknow to be holy those he predestinated to be so. The counsels and decrees of God do not truckle to the frail and fickle will of men; no, God's foreknowledge of the saints is the same with that everlasing love wherewith he is said to have loved them, Jer. xxxi. 3. God's knowing his people is the same with his owning them, Ps. i. 6; John x. 14; 2 Tim. ii. 19. See *ch.* xi. 2.

II. *Whom he did predestinate those he also called,* not only with the external call (so many are called that were not chosen, Matt. xx. 16; xxii. 14), but with the internal and effectual call. The former comes to the ear only, but this to the heart. All that God did from eternity predestinate to grace and glory he does, in the fulness of time, effectually call.

III. *Whom he called those he also justified.* All that are effectually called are justified, absolved from guilt, and accepted as righteous through Jesus Christ.

IV. *Whom he justified those he also glorified.* The power of corruption being broken in effectual calling, and the guilt of sin removed in justification, all that which hinders is taken out of the way, and nothing can come between that soul and glory.

THE BELIEVER'S TRIUMPH
(*vv.* 31–39)

The apostle closes this excellent discourse upon the privileges of believers with a holy triumph, in the name of all the saints. More particularly.

I. We have supplies ready in all our wants (*v.* 32): *He that spared,* & c. Who can be against us, to strip us, to deprive us of our comforts? 1. Observe what our God has done for us, on which our hopes are built: *He spared not his own Son.* When he was to undertake our salvation, the Father was willing to part with him, did not think him too precious a gift to bestow for the salvation of poor souls. 2. What we may therefore expect he will do: He will *with him freely give us all things.* Can it be imagined that he should do the greater and not do the less? that he should give so great a gift for us when we were enemies, and should deny us any good thing, now that through him we are friends and children?

II. We have an answer ready to all accusations and a security against all condemnations (*vv.* 33, 34): *Who shall lay any thing?* Doth the law accuse them? Do their own consciences accuse them? Is the devil, the accuser of the brethren, accusing them before our God day and night? This is enough to answer all those accusations, *It is God that justifieth.* It is by virtue of our interest in Christ, our relation to him, and our union with him, that we are thus secured. 1. His death: *It is Christ that died.* By the merit of his death he paid our debt; and the surety's payment is a good plea to an action of debt. It is Christ, an able all-sufficient Saviour. 2. His resurrection: *Yea, rather, that has risen again.* This is a much greater encouragement, for it is a convincing evidence that divine justice was satisfied by the merit of his death. 3. His sitting at the right hand of God: He is *even at the right hand of*

God—a further evidence that he has done his work, and a mighty encouragement to us in reference to all accusations, that we have a friend, such a friend, in court. 4. The intercession which he makes there. He is there, not unconcerned about us, not forgetful of us, but *making intercession*. He is agent for us there, an advocate for us, to answer all accusations, to put in our plea, and to prosecute it with effect, to appear for us and to present our petitions.

III. We have good assurance of our preservation and continuance in this blessed state, *v.* 35, to the end. We have here from the apostle,

1. A daring challenge to all the enemies of the saints to separate them, if they could, from the love of Christ. *Who shall?* None shall, *vv.* 35-37. Observe here,

(1) The present calamities of Christ's beloved ones supposed. Can a case be supposed more black and dismal? It is illustrated (*v.* 36) by a passage quoted from Ps. xliv. 22, *For thy sake we are killed all the day long*, which intimates that we are not to think strange, no not concerning the fiery bloody trial.

(2) The inability of all these things to separate us from the love of Christ. Shall they, can they, do it? No, by no means. All this will not cut the bond of love and friendship that is between Christ and true believers.

(3) The triumph of believers in this (*v.* 37): *Nay, in all these things we are more than conquerors.*

[1] We are conquerors: though killed all the day long, yet conquerors. A strange way of conquering,

but it was Christ's way; thus he triumphed over principalities and powers in his cross.

[2] We are more than conquerors. In our patiently bearing these trials we are not only conquerors, but more than conquerors, that is, triumphers.

[3] It is only *through Christ that loved us*, the merit of his death taking the sting out of all these troubles, the Spirit of his grace strengthening us, and enabling us to bear them with holy courage and constancy, and coming in with special comforts and supports. Thus we are conquerors, not in our own strength, but in the grace that is in Christ Jesus.

2. A direct and positive conclusion of the whole matter: *For I am persuaded*, *vv.* 38, 39. It denotes a full, and strong, and affectionate persuasion, arising from the experience of the strength and sweetness of the divine love. And here he enumerates all those things which might be supposed likely to separate between Christ and believers, and concludes that it could not be done.

CHAPTER NINE

THE ISRAELITES (*vv.* 1-5)

We have here the apostle's solemn profession of a great concern for the nation and people of the Jews—that he was heartily troubled that so many of them were enemies to the gospel, and out of the way of salvation.

I. He asserts it with a solemn protestation (*v.* 1): *I say the truth in Christ*, "I speak it as a Christian."

II. He backs it with a very

serious imprecation, which he was ready to make, out of love to the Jews. He would be willing to undergo the greatest misery to do them good.

III. He gives us the reason of this affection and concern.

1. Because of their relation to them: *My brethren, my kinsmen, according to the flesh*. We ought to be in a special manner concerned for the spiritual good of our relations, our brethren and kinsmen.

2. Especially because of their relation to God (vv. 4, 5): *Who are Israelites*, the seed of Abraham, God's friend, and of Jacob his chosen, taken into the covenant of peculiarity, dignified and distinguished by visible church-privileges, many of which are here mentioned.

THE PROMISE STANDS
(vv. 6–13)

Now the difficulty is to reconcile the rejection of the unbelieving Jews with the word of God's promise, and the external tokens of the divine favour, which had been conferred upon them.

In this paragraph the apostle explains the true meaning and intention of the promise. When we mistake the word, and misunderstand the promise, no marvel if we are ready to quarrel with God about the accomplishment; and therefore the sense of this must first be duly stated. Now he here makes it out that, when God said he would be *a God to Abraham, and to his seed* (which was the famous promise made unto the fathers), he did not mean it of all his seed according to the flesh, as if it were a necessary concomitant of the blood of Abraham; but that he intended it with a limitation only to such and such. And as from the beginning it was appropriated to Isaac and not to Ishmael, to Jacob and not to Esau, and yet for all this the word of God was not made of no effect; so now the same promise is appropriated to believing Jews that embrace Christ and Christianity, and, though it throws off multitudes that refuse Christ, yet the promise is not therefore defeated and invalidated, any more than it was by the typical rejection of Ishmael and Esau.

GOD IS SOVEREIGN
(vv. 14–24)

Now this part of his discourse is in answer to two objections.

I. It might be objected, *Is there unrighteousness with God?* If God, in dealing with the children of men, do thus, in an arbitrary manner, choose some and refuse others, may it not be suspected that there is unrighteousness with him? This the apostle startles at the thought of: *God forbid!* He denies the consequences, and proves the denial.

1. In respect of those to whom he shows mercy, vv. 15, 16. He quotes that scripture to show God's sovereignty in dispensing his favours (Exod. xxxiii. 19): *I will be gracious to whom I will be gracious*. God is a competent judge, even in his own case. Whatsoever God does, or is resolved to do, is both by the one and the other proved to be just.

2. In respect of those who perish, v. 17. God's sovereignty, manifested

in the ruin of sinners, is here discovered in the instance of Pharaoh; it is quoted from Exod. ix. 16,

II. It might be objected, *Why doth he yet find fault? For who hath resisted his will? v.* 19. If God, while he gives effectual grace to some, denies it to others, why doth he find fault with those to whom he denies it? If he hath rejected the Jews, and hid from their eyes the things that belong to their peace, why doth he find fault with them for their blindness? This objection he answers at large,

1. By reproving the objector (*v.* 20): *Nay but, O man.* This is not an objection fit to be made by the creature against his Creator, by man against God.

2. By resolving all into the divine sovereignty. We are the thing formed, and he is the former; and it does not become us to challenge or arraign his wisdom in ordering and disposing of us into this or that shape of figure. The rude and unformed mass of matter hath no right to this or that form, but is shaped at the pleasure of him that formeth it. God's sovereignty over us is fitly illustrated by the power that the potter hath over the clay; compare Jer. xviii. 6, where, by a like comparison, God asserts his dominion over the nation of the Jews, when he was about to magnify his justice in their destruction by Nebuchadnezzar.

THE REMNANT (*vv.* 25–29)

Now he shows how this, which was so uneasy to them, was spoken of in the scripture.

I. By the prophet Hosea, who speaks of the taking in of a great many of the Gentiles, Hos. ii. 23 and Hos. i. 10.

II. By the prophet Isaiah, who speaks of the casting off of many of the Jews, in two places:

1. One is Isa. x. 22, 23, which speaks of the saving of a remnant, that is, but a remnant, which, though in the prophecy it seems to refer to the preservation of a remnant from the destruction and desolation that were coming upon them by Sennacherib and his army, yet is to be understood as looking further, and sufficiently proves that it is no strange thing for God to abandon to ruin a great many of the seed of Abraham, and yet maintain his word of promise to Abraham in full force and virtue.

2. Another is quoted from Isa. i. 9, where the prophet is showing how in a time of general calamity and destruction God would preserve a seed. This is to the same purport with the former; and the scope of it is to show that it was no strange thing for God to leave the greatest part of the people of the Jews to ruin, and to reserve to himself only a small remnant: so he had done formerly, as appears by their own prophets; and they must not wonder if he did so now.

THE STUMBLING STONE
(*vv.* 30–33)

The apostle comes here at last to fix the true reason of the reception of the Gentiles, and the rejection of the Jews. There was a difference in the way of their seeking, and therefore there was that different success, though still it was the free grace of God that made them differ.

I. Concerning the Gentiles observe, 1. How they had been alienated from righteousness: they followed not after it; they knew not their guilt and misery, and therefore were not at all solicitous to procure a remedy. In their conversion preventing grace was greatly magnified: God was *found of those that sought him not*, Isa. lxv. 1. 2. How they attained to righteousness, notwithstanding: *By faith;* not by being proselyted to the Jewish religion, and submitting to the ceremonial law, but by embracing Christ, and believing in Christ, and submitting to the gospel.

II. Concerning the Jews observe, 1. How they missed their end: they *followed after the law of righteousness* (*v.* 31)—they talked much of justification and holiness, seemed very ambitious of being the people of God and the favourites of heaven, but they did not attain to it, that is, the greatest part of them did not. 2. How they mistook their way, which was the cause of their missing the end, *vv.* 32, 33. They sought, but not in the right way, not in the humbling way, not in the instituted appointed way. *Not by faith.* But still there is a remnant that do believe on him; and they *shall not be ashamed*, that is, their hopes and expectations of justification by him shall not be disappointed, as theirs are who expect it by the law. So that, upon the whole, the unbelieving Jews have no reason to quarrel with God for rejecting them; they had a fair offer of righteousness, and life, and salvation, made to them upon gospel terms, which they did not like, and would not come up to; and

therefore, if they perish, they may thank themselves—their blood is upon their own heads.

THE JEWS' MISTAKE
(*vv.* 1–11)

The scope of the apostle in this part of the chapter is to show the vast difference between the righteousness of the law and the righteousness of faith, and the great pre-eminence of the righteousness of faith above that of the law; that he might induce and persuade the Jews to believe in Christ, aggravate the folly of sin and those that refused, and justify God in the rejection of such refusers.

I. Paul here professes his good affection to the Jews, with the reason of it (*vv.* 1, 2), where he gives them a good wish, and a good witness.

I bear them record that they have a zeal of God. Their opposition to the gospel is from a principle of respect to the law, which they know to have come from God. There is such a thing as a blind misguided zeal: such was that of the Jews, who, when they hated Christ's people and ministers, and cast them out, said, *Let the Lord be glorified* (Isa. lxvi. 5); nay, they killed them, and thought they did God good service, John xvi. 2.

II. He here shows the fatal mistake that the unbelieving Jews were guilty of, which was their ruin. Their zeal was *not according to knowledge.* This he shows further, *v.* 3, where we may observe,

1. The nature of their unbelief. They *have not submitted themselves*

to the righteousness of God, that is, they have not yielded to gospel-terms, nor accepted the tender of justification by faith in Christ, which is made in the gospel.

2. The causes of their unbelief, and these are two: (1) Ignorance of God's righteousness. They did not understand, and believe, and consider, the strict justice of God, in hating and punishing sin, and demanding satisfaction. (2) A proud conceit of their own righteousness: *Going about to establish their own*—a righteousness of their own devising, and of their own working out, by the merit of their works, and by their observance of the ceremonial law.

III. He here shows the folly of that mistake, and what an unreasonable thing it was for them to be seeking justification by the works of the law, now that Christ had come, and had brought in an everlasting righteousness; considering,

1. The subserviency of the law to the gospel (*v.* 4): *Christ is the end of the law for righteousness*. The design of the law was to lead people to Christ.

2. The excellency of the gospel above the law. This he proves by showing the different constitution of these two.

(1) What is the righteousness which is of the law? This he shows, *v.* 5. The tenour of it is, *Do, and live*. The doing supposed must be perfect and sinless, without the least breach or violation. Now, was it not extreme folly in the Jews to adhere so closely to this way of justification and salvation, which was in itself so hard, and by the corruption of nature now become

impossible, when there was a new and a living way opened?

(2) What is that righteousness which is of faith, *v.* 6, &c. This he describes in the words of Moses, in Deuteronomy xxx. 11–14, and shows,

[1] That it is not at all hard or difficult. The way of justification and salvation has in it no such depths or knots as may discourage us, no insuperable difficulties attending it; but, as was foretold, it is a high-way, Isa. xxxv. 8.

[2] But it is very plain and easy: *The word is nigh thee*. When we speak of looking upon Christ, and receiving Christ, and feeding upon Christ, it is not Christ in heaven, nor Christ in the deep, that we mean; but Christ in the promise, Christ exhibited to us, and offered, in the word. Christ is nigh thee, for the word is nigh thee: nigh thee indeed: it is *in thy mouth, and in thy heart*; there is no difficulty in understanding, believing, and owning it. Now what is this word faith We have the tenour of it, *vv.* 9, 10, the sum of the gospel, which is plain and easy enough. Observe,

First, What is promised to us: *Thou shalt be saved*.

Secondly, Upon what terms.

a. Two things are required as conditions of salvation: (*a*) *Confessing the Lord Jesus*—openly professing relation to him and dependence on him, as our prince and Saviour. (*b*) *Believing in the heart that God raised him from the dead*. The profession of faith with the mouth, if there be not the power of it in the heart, is but a mockery.

b. This is further illustrated (*v.* 10), and the order inverted, because there must first be faith in the heart before there can be an acceptable confession with the mouth. (*a*) Concerning faith: It is *with the heart that man believeth*, which implies more than an assent of the understanding, and takes in the consent of the will, an inward, hearty, sincere, and strong consent. (*b*) Concerning profession: It is with *the mouth that confession is made*—confession to God in prayer and praise (*ch*. xv. 6), confession to men by owning the ways of God before others, especially when we are called to it in a day of persecution. So that we have here a brief summary of the terms of salvation, and they are very reasonable; in short this, that we must devote, dedicate, and give up, to God, our souls and our bodies—our souls in believing with the heart, and our bodies in confessing with the mouth. This do, and thou shalt live. For this (*v* 11) he quotes Isa. xxviii. 16, *Whosoever believeth on him shall not be ashamed*.

PREACHING THE GOSPEL
(*vv*. 12–21)

In Jesus Christ there is neither Greek nor Jew, Col. iii. 11. *There is no difference*. For the proof of this he urges two arguments:

I. That God is the same to all: *The same Lord over all is rich unto all*. There is not one God to the Jews who is more kind, and another to the Gentiles who is less kind; but he is the same to all, a common father to all mankind.

II. That the promise is the same to all (*v*. 13): *Whoever shall call*—one as well as another, without

exception. For the further illustration of this he observes,

1. How necessary it was that the gospel should be preached to the Gentiles, *vv*. 14, 15. This was what the Jews were so angry with Paul for, that he was the apostle of the Gentiles, and preached the gospel to them. Now he shows how needful it was to bring them within the reach of the forementioned promise, an interest in which they should not envy any of their fellow-creatures. (1) *They cannot call on him in whom they have not believed*. (2) *They cannot believe in him of whom they have not heard*. Some way or other the divine revelation must be made known to us, before we can receive it and assent to it; it is not born with us. (3) *They cannot hear without a preacher;* how should they? Somebody must tell them what they are to believe. (4) *They cannot preach except they be sent*, except they be both commissioned and in some measure qualified for their preaching work.

2. How welcome the gospel ought to be to those to whom it was preached, because it showed the way to salvation, *v*. 15. For this he quotes Isa. lii. 7.

3. He answers an objection against all this, which might be taken from the little success which the gospel had in many places (*v*. 16): *But they have not all obeyed the gospel*. All the Jews have not, all the Gentiles have not; far the greater part of both remain in unbelief and disobedience. In answer to this,

(1) He shows that the word preached is the ordinary means of working faith (*v*. 17): though many

that hear do not believe, yet those that believe have first heard. *Faith cometh by hearing*. It is the summary of what he had said before, v. 14.

(2) That those who would not believe the report of the gospel, yet, having heard it, were thereby left inexcusable, and may thank themselves for their own ruin, v. 18, *to the end*.

Many that will not accept of a good proposal will yet acknowledge that they have nothing to say against it: but the Jews who believed not rested not there, but contradicted and blasphemed. God's patience with them was a very great aggravation of their disobedience, and rendered it the more exceedingly sinful; as their disobedience advanced the honour of God's patience and rendered it the more exceedingly gracious. It is a wonder of mercy in God that his goodness is not overcome by man's badness; and it is a wonder of wickedness in man that his badness is not overcome by God's goodness.

CHAPTER ELEVEN

THE FUTURE OF THE JEWS
(*vv.* 1–32)

The apostle proposes here a plausible objection, which might be urged against the divine conduct in casting off the Jewish nation (*v.* 1): *"Hath God cast away his people?* Is the rejection total and final?"

I. The Jews, it is true, were many of them cast off, but not all. The supposition of this he introduces with a *God forbid*. He will by no means endure such a suggestion.

God had made a distinction between some of them and others.

1. There was a chosen remnant of believing Jews, that obtained righteousness and life by faith in Jesus Christ, *vv.* 1–7. Now,

(1) He shows that he himself was one of them.

(2) He suggests that as in Elijah's time, so now, this chosen remnant was really more and greater than one would think it was, which intimates likewise that it is no new nor unusual thing for God's grace and favour to Israel to be limited and confined to a remnant of that people; for so it was in Elijah's time. They were the persons whom God had in his eye in the counsels of his love; they are the election; they are God's choice. Such was the favour of God to the chosen remnant. But,

2. *The rest were blinded, v.* 7. Some are chosen and called, and the call is made effectual. But others are left to perish in their unbelief; nay, they are made worse by that which should have made them better. The gospel, which to those that believed was the savour of life unto life, to the unbelieving was the savour of death unto death. The same sun softens wax and hardens clay. Blindness and hardness are expressive of the same senselessness and stupidity of spirit. They shut their eyes, and would not see; this was their sin: and then God, in a way of righteous judgment, blinded their eyes, that they could not see; this was their punishment.

II. Another thing which qualified this doctrine of the rejection of the Jews was that though they were

193

cast off and unchurched, yet the Gentiles were taken in (*v.* 11-14), which he applies by way of caution to the Gentiles, *vv.* 17-22.

1. The rejection of the Jews made room for the reception of the Gentiles. The Jews' leavings were a feast for the poor Gentiles (*v.* 11).

2. The use that the apostle makes of this doctrine concerning the substitution of the Gentiles in the room of the Jews.

(1) As a kinsman to the Jews, here is a word of excitement and exhortation to them, to stir them up to receive and embrace the gospel-offer. This God intended in his favour to the Gentiles, to provoke the Jews to jealousy (*v.* 11), and Paul endeavours to enforce it accordingly (*v.* 14): *If by any means I might provoke to emulation those who are my flesh.*

(2) As an apostle to the Gentiles, here is a word of caution for them: "*I speak to you Gentiles.* You believing Romans, you hear what riches of salvation are come to you by the fall of the Jews, but take heed lest you do any thing to forfeit it." Now two things he exhorts the Gentiles to, with reference to the rejected Jews:

[1] To have a respect for the Jews, notwithstanding, and to desire their conversion.

[2] To take heed to themselves, lest they should stumble and fall, as the Jews had done, *vv.* 17-22.

III. Another thing that qualifies this doctrine of the Jews' rejection is that, though for the present they are cast off, yet the rejection is not final; but, when the fulness of time is come, they will be taken in again. They are not cast off for ever, but

mercy is remembered in the midst of wrath. The Jews shall continue in blindness, till God hath performed his whole work among the Gentiles, and then their turn will come next to be remembered. This was the purpose and ordination of God, for wise and holy ends; things should not be ripe for the Jews' conversion till the church was replenished with the Gentiles, that it might appear that God's taking them again was not because he had need of them, but of his own free grace.

THE WISDOM OF GOD
(*vv.* 33-36)

Here the apostle does with great affection and awe adore,

1. The secrecy of the divine counsels: *O the depth!* in these proceedings towards the Jews and Gentiles; or, in general, the whole mystery of the gospel, which we cannot fully comprehend.

II. The sovereignty of the divine counsels. In all these things God acts as a free agent, does what he will, because he will, and gives not account of any of his matters (Job xxiii. 13; xxxiii. 13), and yet there is no unrighteousness with him.

REASONABLE SERVICE
(*vv.* 1-21)

We may observe here the apostle's exhortations,

I. Concerning our duty to God, We see what is godliness.

1. It is to surrender ourselves to God, and so to lay a good foundation. We must first give our own selves unto the Lord, 2 Cor. viii. 5.

This is here pressed as the spring of all duty and obedience, *vv.* 1, 2. Man consists of body and soul, Gen. ii. 7; Eccl. xii. 7.

The mind must be renewed for God. This is pressed (*v.* 2): "*Be you transformed by the renewing of your mind;* see to it that there be a saving change wrought in you, and that it be carried on.*" Conversion and sanctification are the renewing of the mind, a change not of the substance, but of the qualities of the soul.

[1] What is the great enemy to this renewing, which we must avoid; and that is, conformity to this world: *Be not conformed to this world.* All the disciples and followers of the Lord Jesus must be nonconformists to this world. We must not conform to the things of the world; they are mutable, and the fashion of them is passing away.

[2] What is the great effect of this renewing, which we must labour after: *That you may prove what is that good, and acceptable, and perfect will of God.* By the will of God here we are to understand his revealed will concerning our duty, what the Lord our God requires of us. *First,* The will of God is *good, and acceptable, and perfect*; three excellent properties of a law. It is good (Mic. vi. 8); it is exactly consonant to the eternal reason of good and evil. It is good in itself. It is good for us. It is acceptable, it is pleasing to God; that and that only is so which is prescribed by him. The only way to attain his favour as the end is to conform to his will as the rule. It is perfect, to which nothing can be added. *Secondly,* That it concerns Christians to

prove what is that will of God which is good, and acceptable, and perfect; that is, to know it with judgment and approbation, to know it experimentally, to know the excellency of the will of God by the experience of a conformity to it.

2. When this is done, to serve him in all manner of gospel obedience. Some hints of this we have here (*vv.* 11, 12), *Serving the Lord.* How? (1) We must make a business of it, and not be slothful in that business. *Not slothful in business.* There is the business of the world, that of our particular calling, in which we must not be slothful, 1 Thess, iv. 11. But this seems to be meant of the business of serving the Lord, our Father's business, Luke ii. 49. (2) We must be *fervent in spirit, serving the Lord.* God must be served with the spirit (*ch.* i. 9; John iv. 24), under the influences of the Holy Spirit. And there must be fervency in the spirit—a holy zeal, and warmth, and ardency of affection in all we do, as those that love God not only with the heart and soul, but with all our hearts and with all our souls. (3) *Rejoicing in hope.* God is worshipped and honoured by our hope and trust in him, especially when we rejoice in that hope, take a complacency in that confidence, which argues a great assurance of the reality and a great esteem of the excellency of the good hoped for. (4) *Patient in tribulation.* Thus also God is served, not only by working for him when he calls us to work, but by sitting still quietly when he calls us to suffer. (5) *Continuing instant in prayer.* It signifies both fervency and perseverance in prayer. We

should not be cold in the duty, nor soon weary of it, Luke xviii. 1; 1 Thess. v. 17; Eph. vi. 18; Col. iv. 2. This is our duty which immediately respects God.

II. Concerning our duty which respects ourselves; this is sobriety.

1. A sober opinion of ourselves, *v.* 3. Pride is a sin that is bred in the bone of all of us, and we have therefore each of us need to be cautioned and armed against it. Now the reasons why we must have such a sober opinion of ourselves, our own abilities and attainments, are these:

(1) Because whatever we have that is good, *God hath dealt* it to us; every good and perfect gift *comes from above*, James i. 17. What have we that we have not received? And, if we have received it, why then do we boast? 1 Cor. iv. 7.

(2) Because God deals out his gifts in a certain measure: According to *the measure of faith*. Now faith, and other spiritual gifts with it, are dealt by measure, according as Infinite Wisdom sees meet for us. Christ had the Spirit given him without measure, John iii. 34. But the saints have it by measure; see Eph. iv. 7.

(3) Because God has dealt out gifts to others as well as to us: *Dealt to every man*. This reasoning he illustrates by a comparison taken from the members of the natural body (as 1 Cor. xii. 12; Eph. iv. 16): *As we have many members in one body*, &c. *vv.* 4, 5. We stand in relation one to another; we are engaged to do all the good we can one to another, and to act in conjunction for the common benefit. See this illustrated

at large, 1 Cor. xii. 14, &c. Therefore we must not be puffed up with a conceit of our own attainments, because, whatever we have, as we received it, so we received it not for ourselves, but for the good of others.

2. A sober use of the gifts that God hath given us. As we must not on the one hand be proud of our talents　so on the other hand we must not bury them. *Having then gifts*. The following induction of particulars supplies the sense of this general. *Having gifts*, let us use them. Authority and ability for the ministerial work are the gift of God. —*Gifts differing*. There were in the primitive church extraordinary gifts of tongues, of discerning, of healing; but he speaks here of those that are ordinary. Compare 1 Cor. xii. 4; 1 Tim. iv. 14; 1 Pet. iv. 10. Seven particular gifts he specifies (*vv.* 6–8), which seem to be meant of so many distinct offices, used by the prudential constitution of many of the primitive churches, especially the larger. There are two general ones here expressed by prophesying and ministering, the former the work of the bishops, the latter the work of the deacons, which were the only two standing officers, Phil. i. 1.

(1) *Prophecy. Whether prophecy, let us prophesy according to the proportion of faith.* It is not meant of the extraordinary gifts of foretelling things to come, but the ordinary office of preaching the word: so *prophesying* is taken, 1 Cor. xiv. 1–3, &c.; xi. 4; 1 Thess. v. 20.

(2) *Ministry.* If a man hath *the office of a deacon*, or assistant to the

pastor and teacher, let him use that office well. Particularly, [1] *He that giveth, let him do it with simplicity* Those church-officers that were the stewards of the church's alms, collected money, and distributed it according as the necessities of the poor were. Let them do it *liberally* and faithfully. Some understand it in general of all almsgiving: He that hath wherewithal, let him give, and give plentifully and liberally; so the word is translated, 2 Cor. viii. 2; ix. 13. God loves a cheerful bountiful giver. [2] *He that ruleth with diligence.* The word denotes both care and industry to discover what is amiss, to reduce those that go astray, to reprove and admonish those that have fallen, to keep the church pure. [3] *He that showeth mercy with cheerfulness.* A pleasing countenance in acts of mercy is a great relief and comfort to the miserable; when they see it is not done grudgingly and unwillingly, but with pleasant looks and gentle words, and all possible indications of readiness and alacrity.

III. Concerning that part of our duty which respects our brethren, of which we have many instances, in brief exhortations. Now all our duty towards one another is summed up in one word, and that a sweet word, *love*. More particularly, there is a love owing to our friends, and to our enemies. He specifies both.

1. To our friends. He that hath friends must show himself friendly. There is a mutual love that Christians owe, and must pay.

(1) An affectionate love (*v.* 10): *Be kindly affectioned one to another, with brotherly love*—it signifies not only love, but a readiness and inclination to love, the most genuine and free affection, kindness flowing out as from a spring.

(2) A respectful love: *In honour preferring one another.* Instead of contending for superiority, let us be forward to give to others the pre-eminence. This is explained, Phil. ii. 3, *Let each esteem other better than themselves.*

(3) A liberal love (*v.* 13): *Distributing to the necessities of saints.* It is but a mock love which rests in the verbal expressions of kindness and respect, while the wants of our brethren call for real supplies, and it is in the power of our hands to furnish them. We must be ready, as we have ability and opportunity, to relieve any that are in want; but we are in a special manner bound to communicate to the saints. There is a common love owing to our fellow-creatures, but a special love owing to our fellow christians (Gal. vi. 10), *Especially to those who are of the household of faith.* He mentions another branch of this bountiful love: *Given to hospitality.* Those who have houses of their own should be ready to entertain those who go about doing good, or who, for fear of persecution, are forced to wander for shelter.

(4) A sympathizing love (*v.* 15): *Rejoice with those that do rejoice, and weep with those that weep.* Where there is a mutual love between the members of the mystical body, there will be such a fellow-feeling. See 1 Cor. xii. 26. True love will interest us in the sorrows and joys of one another, and teach us to make them our own.

(5) A united love: "*Be of the same mind one towards another* (*v.* 16), endeavour to be all one, not affecting to clash, and contradict, and thwart one another; but keep the unity of the Spirit in the bond of peace, Phil, ii. 2; iii. 15. 16; 1 Cor. i. 10.

(6) A condescending love: *Mind not high things, but condescend to men of low estate, v.* 16. True love cannot be without lowliness, Eph. iv. 1, 2; Phil. ii. 3. *Condescend;* that is, suit yourselves to them, stoop to them, stoop to them for their good; as Paul, 1 Cor. ix. 19, &c. Some think the original word is a metaphor taken from travellers, when those that are stronger and swifter of foot say for those that are weak and slow, make a halt, and take them with them; thus must Christians be tender towards their fellow travellers. We are members one of another, depend upon one another, are obliged to one another; and therefore, *Be not wise by yourselves*, remembering it is the merchandise of wisdom that we profess; now merchandise consists in commerce, receiving and returning.

(7) A love that engages us, as much as lies in us, *to live peaceably with all men, v.* 18. Observe how the exhortation is limited. It is not expressed so as to oblige us to impossibilities: *If it be possible, as much as lies in you.* Thus Heb. xii. 14, *Follow peace.* Eph. iv. 3, *Endeavouring to keep.* Study the things that make for peace. — *If it be possible.* It is not possible to preserve the peace when we cannot do it without offending God and wounding conscience.

2. To our enemies. Since men became enemies to God, they have been found very apt to be enemies one to another. Now Christianity teaches us how to behave towards our enemies; and in this instruction it quite differs from all other rules and methods, which generally aim at victory and dominion; but this at inward peace and satisfaction. Whoever are our enemies, that wish us ill and seek to do us ill, our rule is to do them no hurt, but all the good we can.

(1) To do them no hurt (*v.* 17): *Recompense to no man evil for evil*, for that is a brutish recompence, and befitting only those animals which are not conscious either of any being above them or of any state before them. To the same purport, *v.* 19, *Dearly beloved, avenge not yourselves.* Would you pacify a brother offended? Call him dearly beloved. Such a soft word, fitly spoken, may be effectual to turn away wrath. *Avenge not yourselves;* that is, when any body has done you any ill turn, do not desire nor endeavour to bring the like mischief or inconvenience upon him. This is a hard lesson to corrupt nature; and therefore he subjoins, [1] A remedy against it: *Rather give place unto wrath.* Not to our own wrath; to give place to this is to give place to the devil, Eph. iv. 26, 27. We must resist, and stifle, and smother, and suppress this; but, *First*, To the wrath of our enemy. "Give place to it, that is, be of a yielding temper." When others are angry, let us be calm; this is a remedy against revenge, and seems to be the genuine sense. But, *Secondly*, Many apply it to the wrath of God: "Give place to this,

make room for him to take the throne of judgment, and let him alone to deal with thine adversary." [2] A reason against it: *For it is written, Vengeance is mine.* We find it written, Deut. xxxii. 35. God is the sovereign King, the righteous Judge, and to him it belongs to administer justice.

[2] We must not only not do hurt to our enemies, but our religion goes higher, and teaches us to do them all the good we can. It is a command peculiar to Christianity, and which does highly commend it: *Love your enemies*, Matt. v. 44. We are here taught to show that love to them both in word and deed.

[1] In word: *Bless those who persecute you, v.* 14. It has been the common lot of God's people to be persecuted, either with a powerful hand or with a spiteful tongue. Now we are here taught to bless those that so persecute us.

[2] In deed (*v.* 20). It is said of archbishop Cranmer that the way for a man to make him his friend was to do him an ill turn. The precept is quoted from Prov. xxv. 21, 22; so that, high as it seems to be, the Old Testament was not a stranger to it. *Thou shalt heap coals of fire on his head;* that is, "Thou shalt either," 1. "Melt him into repentance and friendship, and mollify his spirit towards thee" or 2. "It will aggravate his condemnation, and make his malice against thee the more inexcusable. Thou wilt hereby hasten upon him the tokens of God's wrath and vengeance." Not that this must be our intention in showing him kindness, but, for our encouragement, such will be the effect. (1) *Be not over-*

come of evil. He that cannot quietly bear an injury is perfectly conquered by it. (2) *But overcome evil with good*, with the good of patience and forbearance, nay, and of kindness and beneficence to those that wrong you.

3. To conclude, there remain two exhortations yet untouched, which are general, and which recommend all the rest as good in themselves, and of good report.

(1) As good in themselves (*v.* 9): *Abhor that which is evil, cleave to that which is good.* God hath shown us what is good: these Christian duties are enjoined; and that is evil which is opposite to them.

(2) As of good report (*v.* 17): "*Provide things honest in the sight of all men;* that is, not only do, but study and forecast and take care to do, that which is amiable and creditable, and recommends religion to all with whom you converse." See Phil. iv. 8.

CHAPTER THIRTEEN

CHRISTIANS AND THE STATE (*vv.* 1–6)

We are here taught to conduct ourselves towards magistrates, and those that are in authority over us, called here the *higher powers.* Observe,

I. The duty enjoined: *Let every soul be subject.* Not that our consciences are to be subjected to the will of any man. It is God's prerogative to make laws immediately to bind conscience, and we must render to God the things that are God's. But it intimates that our subjection must be free and voluntary, sincere and hearty. "They are *higher powers*; be content they should be so, and submit to them accordingly." Now there was good reason for the pressing of this duty of subjection to civil magistrates, 1. Because of the reproach which the Christian religion lay under in the world, as an enemy to public peace, order, and government, as a sect that turned the world upside down, and the embracers of it as enemies to Cæsar, and the more because the leaders were Galileans—an old slander. 2. Because of the temptation which the Christians lay under to be otherwise affected to civil magistrates, some of them being originally Jews, and so leavened with a principle that it was unmeet for any of the seed of Abraham to be subject to one of another nation—their king just be of their brethren, Deut. xvii. 15. Besides, the civil powers were persecuting powers; the body of the law was against them.

II. The reasons to enforce this duty. Why must we be subject?

1. For *wrath's sake*. Because of the danger we run ourselves into by resistance. Magistrates bear the sword, and to oppose them is to hazard all that is dear to us in this world; for it is to no purpose to contend with him that bears the sword. This is a good argument, but it is low for a Christian.

2. We must be subject, *not only for wrath, but for conscience' sake*. Now to oblige conscience to this subjection he argues, *vv.* 1–4, 6.

(1) From the institution of magistracy: *There is no power but of God*. God as the ruler and governor of the world hath appointed the ordinance of magistracy, so that all civil power is derived from him as from its original, and he hath by his providence put the administration into those hands, whatever they are that have it. By him kings reign, Prov. viii. 15. Hence it follows (*v.* 2) that whosoever *resisteth the power resisteth the ordinance of God*. Magistrates are therefore called gods (Ps. lxxxii. 6), because they bear the image of God's authority. And those who spurn at their power reflect upon God himself. Magistrates are here again and again called God's ministers. He is the *minister of God*, *v.* 4, 6. Magistrates are in a more peculiar manner God's servants; the dignity they have calls for duty. Though they are lords to us, they are servants to God, have work to do for him, and an account to render to him.

(2) From the intention of magistracy: *Rulers are not a terror to good works, but to the evil*, &c. Magistracy was designed to be,

[1] A terror to evil works and evil workers. They bear the sword; not only the sword of war, but the sword of justice. Hence it appears that laws with penalties for the lawless and disobedient (1 Tim. i. 9) must be constituted in Christian nations, and are agreeable with, and not contradictory to, the gospel.

[2] A praise to those that do well. Those that keep in the way of their duty shall have the commendation and protection of the civil powers, to their credit and comfort. Never did sovereign prince pervert the

ends of government as Nero did, and yet to him Paul appealed, and under him had the protection of the law and the inferior magistrates more than once. Better a bad government than none at all.

(3) From our interest in it: "He is *the minister of God to thee for good.* Thou hast the benefit and advantage of the government, and therefore must do what thou can'st to preserve it, and nothing to disturb it." Protection draws allegiance.

PAYING TAXES (*vv.* 7–10)

We are here taught a lesson of justice and charity.

I. Of justice (*v.* 7): *Render therefore all their dues,* especially to magistrates, for this refers to what goes before; and likewise to all with whom we have to do. He specifies, 1. Due taxes: *Tribute to whom tribute is due, custom to whom custom.* Many, who in other things seem to be just, yet make no conscience of this, but pass it off with a false ill-favoured maxim, that it is no sin to cheat the state, directly contrary to Paul's rule, *Tribute to whom tribute is due.* 2. Due respect: *Fear to whom fear, honour to whom honour.* This sums up the duty which we owe not only to magistrates, but to all superiors, parents, masters, all that are over us in the Lord, according to the fifth commandment; *Honour thy father and mother.*

II. Of charity: *Owe no man any thing; you do owe* no man any thing; so some read it: "Whatever you owe to any relation, or to any with whom you have to do, it is

eminently summed up and included in this debt of love. But to *love one another,* this is a debt that must be always in the paying, and yet always owing." Love is a debt. The law of God and the interest of mankind make it so. Now, to prove that love is the fulfilling of the law, he gives us, 1. An induction of particular precepts, *v.* 9. He specifies the last five of the ten commandments, which he observes to be all summed up in this royal law, *Thou shalt love thy neighbour as thyself*— with an *as* of quality, not of equality—"with the same sincerity that thou lovest thyself, though not in the same measure and degree." 2. A general rule concerning the nature of brotherly love: *Love worketh no ill* (*v.* 10)—he that walks in love, that is actuated and governed by a principle of love, *worketh no ill*; he neither practises nor contrives any ill *to his neighbour,* to any one that he has any thing to do with. Love is a living active principle of obedience to the whole law. The whole law is written in the heart, if the law of love be there.

TIME TO AWAKE
(*vv.* 11–14)

We are here taught a lesson of sobriety and godliness in ourselves.

I. When to awake: *Now it is high time to awake* (*v.* 11), to awake out of the sleep of sin (for a sinful condition is a sleeping condition), out of the sleep of carnal security, sloth and negligence, out of the sleep of spiritual death, and out of the sleep of spiritual deadness; both the wise and foolish virgins slumbered and slept, Matt. xxv. 5. Considering, 1. The time we are cast into: *Knowing the time.* Consider what time of day it is with us, and you will see it is high time to awake. It is gospel time, it is the accepted time, it is working time; it is a time when more is expected than was in the times of that ignorance which God winked at, when people sat in darkness. It is high time to awake; for the sun has been up a great while, and shines in our faces. Have we this light to sleep in? See 1 Thess. v. 5, 6. 2. The salvation we are upon the brink of: *Now is our salvation nearer than when we believed*—than when we first believed, and so took upon us the profession of Christianity.

II. How to dress ourselves. This is the next care, when we are awake and up. Observe then,

1. What we must put off; put off our night-clothes, which it is a shame to appear abroad in: *Cast off the works of darkness.* Sinful works are works of darkness; they come from the darkness of ignorance and mistake, they covet the darkness of privacy and concealment, and they end in the darkness of hell and destruction.

2. "What we must put on." (1) *Put on the armour of light.* Christians are soldiers in the midst of enemies, and their life a warfare, therefore their array must be armour, that they may stand upon their defence—the *armour of God,* to which we are directed, Eph. vi. 13, &c. (2) *Put on the Lord Jesus Christ, v.* 14. This stands in opposition to a great many base lusts, mentioned *v.* 13. *Rioting and drunkenness* must be cast off: one

would think it should follow, but "Put on sobriety, temperance, chastity," the opposite virtues: no, "*Put on Christ,* this includes all. Put him on as Lord to rule you, as Jesus to save you, and in both as Christ, anointed and appointed by the Father to this ruling saving work.

III. How to walk. When we are up and dressed, we are not to sit still in an affected closeness and privacy. What have we good clothes for, but to appear abroad in them?—*Let us walk.* Christianity teaches us how to walk so as to please God, whose eye is upon us: 1 Thess. iv. 1 *Walk honestly as in the day.* Compare Eph. v. 8, *Walk as children of light.*

IV. What provision to make (*v.* 14): *Make not provision for the flesh.* Be not anxious about the body. The necessities of the body must be considered, but the lusts of it must not be gratified. Natural desires must be answered, but wanton appetites must be checked and denied.

CHAPTER FOURTEEN
AVOIDING DIVISION
(*vv.* 1–23)

We have in this chapter,

I. An account of the unhappy contention which had broken out in the Christian church.

1. There was a difference among them about the distinction of meats and days; these are the two things specified. The case was this: The members of the Christian church at Rome were some of them originally Gentiles, and others of them Jews.

Now those that had been Jews were trained up in the observance of the ceremonial appointments touching meats and days. This, which had been bred in the bone with them, could hardly be got out of the flesh even after they turned Christians. While other Christians that understood themselves better, and knew their Christian liberty, made no such difference. (1) Concerning meats (*v.* 2): *One believeth that he may eat all things*—he is well satisfied that the ceremonial distinction of meats into clean and unclean is no longer in force, but that every creature of God is good, and nothing to be refused; nothing *unclean of itself, v.* 14. On the other hand, *another, who is weak*, is dissatisfied in this point, is not clear in his Christian liberty, but rather inclines to think that the meats forbidden by the law remain still unclean; and therefore, to keep at a distance from them, he will eat no flesh at all, but *eateth herbs*, contenting himself with only the fruits of the earth. (2) Concerning days, *v.* 5. Those who thought themselves still under some kind of obligation by the ceremonial law esteemed *one day above another*— kept up a respect to the times of the passover, pentecost, new moons, and fast of tabernacles. Those who knew that all these things were abolished and done away by Christ's coming esteemed every day alike.

2. It was not so much the difference itself that did the mischief as the mismanagement of the difference, making it a bone of contention. Well, this was the disease, and we see it remaining in the church to this day; the like differences, in like manner mismanaged, are still the disturbers of the church's peace. But,

II. We have proper directions and suggestions laid down for allaying this contention, and preventing the ill consequences of it. Let us observe the rules he gives, some to the strong and some to the weak, and some to both, for they are interwoven; and reduce the reasons to their proper rules.

1. Those who are weak must be *received but not to doubtful disputations, v.* 1. Take this for a general rule; spend your zeal in those things wherein you and all the people of God are agreed, and do not dispute about matters that are doubtful.

2. Those who are strong must by no means despise the weak; nor those who are weak judge the strong, *v.* 3. This is levelled directly against the fault of each party. It is seldom that any such contention exists but there is a fault on both sides, and both must mend. He argues against both these jointly: we must not despise nor judge our brethren.

(1) Because God hath received them; and we reflect upon him if we reject those whom he hath received.

(2) Because they are servants to their own master (*v.* 4): *Who art thou that judgest another man's servant?* We reckon it a piece of ill manners to meddle with other people's servants, and to find fault with them and censure them. Weak and strong Christians are indeed our brethren, but they are not our servants.

[3] Because both the one and the other, if they be true believers, and are right in the main, have an eye to God, and do approve themselves to God in what they do, *v.* 6. Observe his description of true Christians, taken from their end and aim (*vv.* 7, 8), and the ground of it, *v.* 9.

[1] Our end and aim: not self, but the Lord. As the particular end specifies the action, so the general scope and tendency specify the state. If we would know what way we walk in, we must enquire what end we walk towards. *First*, Not to self. We have learned to deny ourselves; this was our first lesson: *None of us liveth to himself. Secondly*, But *to the Lord* (*v.* 8), to the Lord Christ, to whom all power and judgment are committed, and in whose name we are taught, as Christians, to do every thing we do (Col. iii. 17), with an eye to the will of Christ as our rule, to the glory of Christ as our end, Phil. i. 21. This is true Christianity, which makes Christ all in all. So that, *whether we live or die, we are the Lord's*, devoted to him, depending on him, designed and designing for him.

[2] The ground of this, *v.* 9. It is grounded upon Christ's absolute sovereignty and dominion, which were the fruit and end of his death and resurrection. *To this end he both died, and rose, and revived* (he, having risen, entered upon a heavenly life, the glory which he had before) *that he might be Lord both of dead and living*—that he might be universal monarch, Lord of all (Acts x. 36), all the animate and inanimate creatures; for he

is head over all things to the church.

(4) Because both the one and the other must shortly give an account, *vv.* 10–12. A believing regard to the judgment of the great day would silence all these rash judgings: *Why dost thou* that art weak *judge thy brother* that is strong? And *why dost thou* that art strong *set at nought thy brother* that is weak? Why is all this clashing, and contradicting, and censuring, among Christians? *We shall all stand before the judgment-seat of Christ*, 2 Cor. v. 10.

(5) Because the stress of Christianity is not to be laid upon these things, nor are they at all essential to religion, either on the one side or on the other. This is his reason (*vv.* 17, 18), which is reducible to this branch of exhortation. Why should you spend your zeal either for or against those things which are so minute and inconsiderable in religion?

3. Another rule here given is this, that in these doubtful things every one not only may, but must, walk according to the light that God hath given him. This is laid down *v.* 5, *Let every man be fully persuaded in his own mind.* To this purport he argues, *vv.* 14 and 23, which two verses explain this, and give us a rule not to act against the dictates,

(1) Of a mistaken conscience, *v.* 14. If a thing be indifferent, so that it is not in itself a sin not to do it, if we really think it a sin to do it it is to us a sin, though not to others, because we act against our consciences, though mistaken and misinformed.

(2) Nor must we act against the dictates of a doubting conscience. In those indifferent things were we are sure it is no sin not to do, and yet are not clear that it is lawful to do them, we must not do them while we continue under those doubts; for he *that doubteth is damned if he eat* (*v.* 23), that is, it turns into sin to him. *He is condemned* of his own conscience, because he *eateth not of faith*, because he does that which he is not fully persuaded he may lawfully do.

4. Another rule here prescribed is to those who are clear in these matters, and know their Christian liberty, yet to take heed of using it so as to give offence to a weak brother. This is laid down *v.* 13, *Let us not judge one another any more.* We must take heed of saying or doing any thing which may occasion our brother to stumble or fall; the one signifies a less, the other a greater degree of mischief and offence—that which may be an occasion,

(1) Of grief to our brother. Christians should take heed of grieving one another, and of saddening the hearts of Christ's little ones. See Matt. xviii. 6, 10.

(2) Of guilt to our brother. The former is a *stumbling-block*, that gives our brother a great shake, and is a hindrance and discouragement to him; but this is an *occasion to fall.* It is a generous piece of self-denial, for which we have Paul's example (1 Cor. viii. 13), *If meat make my brother to offend*; he does not say, *I will eat no meat*, that is to destroy himself; but *I will eat no flesh*, that is to deny himself, *while*

the world stands. This is to be extended to all such indifferent things whereby thy brother stumbleth, or is offended, is involved either in sin or in trouble: or *is made weak*—his graces weakened, his comforts weakened, his resolutions weakened. Observe the motives to enforce this caution.

[1] Consider the royal law of Christian love and charity, which is hereby broken (*v.* 15).

[2] Consider the design of Christ's death: *Destroy not him with thy meat for whom Christ died*, *v.* 15. Thou pleadest that it is thy own meat, and thou mayest do what thou wilt with it; but remember that, though the meat is thine, the brother offended by it is Christ's, and a part of his purchase.

[3] Consider the work of God (*v.* 20): "*For meat destroy not the work of God*—the work of grace, particularly the work of faith in thy brother's soul."

[4] Consider the evil of giving offence, and what an abuse it is of our Christian liberty. He grants that *all things indeed are pure.* We may lawfully eat flesh, even those meats which were prohibited by the ceremonial law; but, if we abuse this liberty, it turns into sin to us: *It is evil to him that eats with offence.*

5. There is one rule more laid down here; and it is general: *Let us therefore follow after the things which make for peace, and things wherewith one may edify another*, *v.* 19. Here is the sum of our duty towards our brethren. None so strong but they may be edified; none so weak but may edify; and, while we edify others, we benefit ourselves.

THE CHRISTIAN'S DUTY
(vv. 1–4)

The apostle here lays down two precepts, with reasons to enforce them, showing the duty of the strong Christian to consider and condescend to the weakest.

I. We must *bear the infirmities of the weak. v.* 1. We all have our infirmities; but the weak are more subject to them than others—the weak in knowledge or grace, the bruised reed and the smoking flax. We must consider these; not trample upon them, but encourage them, and bear with their infirmities.

II. We must not please ourselves, but our neighbour, *vv.*1, 2.

1. Christians must not please themselves. We must not make it our business to gratify all the little appetites and desires of our own heart; it is good for us to cross ourselves sometimes, and then we shall the better bear others crossing of us.

2. Christians must please their brethren. How amiable and comfortable a society would the church of Christ be if Christians would study to please one another, as now we see them commonly industrious to cross, and thwart, and contradict one another?—*Please his neighbour*, not in every thing, it is not an unlimited rule; but *for his good*, especially for the good of his soul: not please him by serving his wicked wills, and humouring him in a sinful way, or consenting to his enticements, or suffering sin upon him; this is a base way of pleasing our neighbour to the ruin of his soul: if we thus please men, we are

not the servants of Christ; but please him for his good; not for our own secular good, or to make a prey of him, but for his spiritual good. Observe,

(1) That Christ pleased not himself. His whole life was a self-denying self-displeasing life. He bore the *infirmities of the weak,* Heb. iv. 15.

(2) That herein the scripture was fulfilled: *As it is written, The reproaches of those that reproached thee fell on me.* This is quoted out of Ps. lxix. It is quoted to show that Christ was so far from pleasing himself that he did in the highest degree displease himself. He preferred our benefit before his own ease and pleasure.

(3) That therefore we must go and do likewise: *For whatsoever things were written aforetime were written for our learning.* [1] That which is written of Christ, concerning his self-denial and sufferings, is *written for our learning*; he hath left us an example. [2] That which is written in the scriptures of the Old Testament in the general is written for our learning. What David had said in his own person Paul had just now applied to Christ. Now lest this should look like a straining of the scripture, he gives us this excellent rule in general, that all the scriptures of the Old Testament (much more those of the New) were written for our learning, and are not to be looked upon as of private interpretation. *That we through patience and comfort of the scriptures might have hope.* That hope which hath eternal life for its object is here proposed as the end of scripture-learning. The scripture

was written that we might know what to hope for from God, and upon what grounds, and in what way. This should recommend the scripture to us that it is a special friend to Christian hope. Now the way of attaining this hope is *through patience and comfort of the scripture.* The more patience we exercise under troubles the more hopefully we may look through our troubles; nothing more destructive to hope than impatience. And the *comfort of the scriptures,* that comfort which springs from the word of God (that is the surest and sweetest comfort) is likewise a great stay to hope, as it is an earnest in hand of the good hoped for.

CHRISTIAN UNITY (*vv.* 5, 6)

The apostle, having delivered two exhortations, before he proceeds to more, intermixes here a prayer for the success of what he had said. Faithful ministers water their preaching with their prayers, because, whoever sows the seed, it is God that gives the increase. We can but speak to the ear; it is God's prerogative to speak to the heart. Observe,

I. The title he gives to God: *The God of patience and consolation,* who is both the author and the foundation of all the patience and consolation of the saints, from whom it springs and on whom it is built.

II. The mercy be begs of God: *Grant you to be like-minded one towards another, according to Christ Jesus.* 1. The foundation of Christian love and peace is laid in like-mindedness, a consent in judgment

as far as you have attained, or at least a concord and agreement in affection. 2. This like-mindedness must be *according to Christ Jesus,* according to the precept of Christ, the royal law of love, according to the pattern and example of Christ, which he had propounded to them for their imitation, *v.* 3.

III. The end of his desire: that God may be glorified, *v.* 6. The unity of Christians glorifies *God as the Father of our Lord Jesus Christ,* because it is a kind of counter-part or representation of the oneness that is between the Father and the Son.

THE DESTINY OF THE GENTILES
(*vv.* 7–12)

The apostle here returns to his exhortation to Christians. What he says here (*v.* 7) is to the same purport with the former; but the repetition shows how much the apostle's heart was upon it. Those that have received Christ by faith must receive all Christians by brotherly love. Now the reason why Christians must receive one another is taken, as before, from the condescending love of Christ to us: *As Christ also received us, to the glory of God.*

I. Christ hath received us to the glory of God. The end of our reception by Christ is that we might glorify God in this world, and be glorified with him in that to come.

II. We must receive one another to the glory of God. This must be our great end in all our actions, that God may be glorified; and nothing more conduces to this than the mutual love and kindness of those that profess religion; compare *v.* 6, *That you may with one mind and one mouth glorify God.*

1. He received the Jews, *v.* 8. Let not any think hardly or scornfully therefore of those that were originally Jews, and still, through weakness, retain some savour of their old Judaism; for, (1) Jesus Christ was a *minister of the circumcision.* (2) He was so for the truth of God. That which he preached to them was the truth; for he came into the world to bear witness to the truth, John xviii. 37. And he is himself the truth, John xiv. 6.

2. He received the Gentiles likewise. This he shows, *vv.* 9–12.

(1) Observe Christ's favour to the Gentiles, in taking them in to praise God—the work of the church on earth and the wages of that in heaven. One design of Christ was that the Gentiles likewise might be converted, that they might be one with the Jews in Christ's mystical body. A good reason why they should not think the worse of any Christian for his having been formerly a Gentile; for Christ has received him.

(2) The fulfilling of the scriptures in this. The favour of God to the Gentiles was not only mercy, but truth. Though there were not promises directly given to them, as to the fathers of the Jews, yet there were many prophecies concerning them, which related to the calling of them, and the embodying of them in the church, some of which he mentions because it was a thing that the Jews were hardly persuaded to believe.

A PRAYER (*v.* 13)

Here is another prayer directed to God, as the God of hope; and it is, as the former (*vv.* 5, 6), for spiritual blessings: these are the best blessings, and to be first and chiefly prayed for.

1. Observe how he addresses himself to God, as the *God of hope.* It is good in prayer to fasten upon those names, titles, and attributes of God, which are most suitable to the errand we come upon, and will best serve to encourage our faith concerning it.

II. What he asks of God, not for himself, but for them.

1. *That they might be filled with all joy and peace in believing.* Joy and peace are two of those things in which the kingdom of God consists, *ch.* xiv. 17. Joy in God, peace of conscience, both arising from a sense of our justification; see *ch.* v. 1, 2.

2. That they might *abound in hope through the power of the Holy Ghost.* The joy and peace of believers arise chiefly from their hopes. What is laid out upon them is but little, compared with what is laid up for them; therefore the more hope they have the more joy and peace they have.

PAUL'S APOSTOLIC MINISTRY I (*vv.* 14–16)

Here, I. He commends these Christians with the highest characters that could be. 1. That they *were full of goodness*; therefore the more likely to take in good part what he had written, and to account it a kindness; and not only so, but to comply with it, and to put it in practice, especially that which relates to their union and to the healing of their differences. A good understanding of one another, and a good will to one another, would soon put an end to strife. 2. *Filled with all knowledge.* Goodness and knowledge together! A very rare and an excellent conjunction; the head and the heart of the new man. 3. *Able to admonish one another.* To this there is a further gift requisite, even the gift of utterance. Those that have goodness and knowledge should communicate what they have for the use and benefit of others. Would to God that all the Lord's people were prophets. But that which is every body's work is nobody's work; and therefore,

II. He clears himself from the suspicion of intermeddling needlessly with that which did not belong to him, *v.* 15. But then consider,

1. He did it only as their remembrancer: *As putting you in mind.*

2. He did it as the apostle of the Gentiles. It was in pursuance of his office: *Because of the grace* (that is, the *apostleship, ch.* i. 5) *given to me of God,* to be the minister *of Jesus Christ to the Gentiles, v.* 16. Observe here, (1) Whose minister he was: the *minister of Jesus Christ,* 1 Cor. iv. 1. He is our Master; his we are, and him we serve. (2) To whom: to the Gentiles. So God had appointed him, Acts xxii. 21. So Peter and he had agreed, Gal. ii. 7–9. (3) What he ministered: the *gospel of God;—ministering as about holy things* (so the word signifies), executing the office of a Christian priest, more spiritual, and therefore more excellent, than the

Levitical priesthood. (4) For what end: *that the offering up* (or sacrificing) *of the Gentiles might be acceptable—*that God might have the glory which would redound to his name by the conversion of the Gentiles. And it is an acceptable offering, *being sanctified by the Holy Ghost.* Paul preached to them, and dealt with them; but that which made them sacrifices to God was their sanctification; and this was not his work, but the work of the Holy Ghost. None are acceptably offered to God but those that are sanctified: unholy things can never be pleasing to the holy God.

PAUL'S APOSTOLIC MINISTRY II (*vv.* 17–21)

The apostle here gives some account of himself and of his own affairs.

I. His unwearied diligence and industry in his work. He was one that laboured *more abundantly than they all.*

1. He preached in many places: *From Jerusalem,* whence the law went forth as a lamp that shineth, and *round about unto Illyricum,* many hundred miles distant from Jerusalem. We have in the book of the Acts an account of Paul's travels. Now it might be suspected that if Paul undertook so much work, surely he did it by the halves. "No," says he, "*I have fully preached the Gospel of Christ—*have given them a full account of the truth and terms of the gospel, have not shunned to declare the whole counsel of God (Acts xx. 27), have kept back nothing that was necessary for them to know."

2. He preached in places that had

not heard the gospel before, *vv.* 20, 21. He broke up the fallow ground, laid the first stone in many places, and introduced Christianity where nothing had reigned for many ages but idolatry and witchcraft, and all sorts of diabolism. He was in care not to *build upon another man's foundation*, lest he should thereby disprove his apostleship, and give occasion to those who sought occasion to reflect upon him. He quotes a scripture for this out of Isa. lii. 15, *To whom he was not spoken of, they shall see.*

II. The great and wonderful success that he had in his work: It was effectual to *make the Gentiles obedient*. The design of the gospel is to bring people to be *obedient*; it is not only a truth to be believed, but a law to be obeyed. It is the Spirit's operation that makes the difference. Paul himself, as great a preacher as he was, with all his mighty signs and wonders, could not make one soul obedient further than the power of the Spirit of God accompanied his labours.

PAUL'S APOSTOLIC MINISTRY III (*vv.* 22–29)

St. Paul here declares his purpose to come and see the Christians at Rome.

I. He excuses it that he never came yet. Observe how careful Paul was to keep in with his friends, and to prevent or anticipate any exceptions against him; not as one that lorded it over God's heritage.

II. He promised to come and see them shortly, *vv.* 23, 24, 29. *Having no more place in these parts*, namely, in Greece, where he then was. The whole of that country being more or less leavened with the savour of the gospel, churches being planted in the most considerable towns and pastors settled to carry on the work which Paul had begun, he had little more to do there. Observe,

1. How he forecasted his intended visit. His project was to see them in his way to Spain. It appears by this that Paul intended a journey into Spain, to plant Christianity there. Observe his prudence. It is wisdom for every one of us to order our affairs so that we may do the most work in the least time. Observe how doubtfully he speaks: *I trust to see you:* not, "I am resolved I will," but, "I hope I shall." we must purpose all our purposes and make all our promises in like manner with a submission to the divine providence; not boasting ourselves of to-morrow, because we know not what a day may bring forth, Prov. xxvii. 1; James iv. 13–15.

2. What he expected in his intended visit. (1) What he expected from them. He expected they would bring him on his way towards Spain. (2) What he expected in them: to *be somewhat filled with their company*. That which Paul desired was their company and conversation. The good company of the saints is very desirable and delightful. (3) What he expected from God with them, *v.* 29. He expected to come *in the fulness of the blessing of the gospel of Christ*. When ministers are fully prepared to give out, and people fully prepared to receive, this blessing, both are happy. Many have the gospel who have not the blessing of the gospel, and so they have it in vain.

The gospel, and so they have it in vain. The gospel will not profit, unless God bless it to us; and it is our duty to wait upon him for that blessing, and for the fulness of it.

III. He gives them a good reason why he could not come and see them now, because he had other business upon his hands, which required his attendance, upon which he must first make a journey to Jerusalem, *vv.* 25–28. He gives a particular account of it, to show that the excuse was real. He was going to Jerusalem, as the messenger of the church's charity to the poor saints there. Ministering to the saints is good work, and is not below the greatest apostles. This Paul had undertaken, and therefore he resolves to go through with it, before he fell upon other work (*v.* 28): *When I have sealed to them this fruit.* He calls the alms *fruit,* for it is one of the fruits of righteousness; it sprang from a root of grace in the givers, and redounded to the benefit and comfort of the receivers. And his sealing it intimates his great care about it, that what was given might be kept entire, and not embezzled, but disposed of according to the design of the givers.

A REQUEST FOR PRAYER
(*vv.* 30–33)

Here we have, I. St. Paul's desire of a share in the prayers of the Romans for him, expressed very earnestly, *vv.* 30–32.

1. Observe why they must pray for him. (1) *"For the Lord Jesus Christ's sake.* He is my Master, I am going about his work, and his glory is interested in the success of

it: if you have any regard to Jesus Christ, and to his cause and kingdom, pray for me. You love Christ, and own Christ; for his sake then do me this kindness." (2) *"For the love of the Spirit.* As a proof and instance of that love which the Spirit works in the hearts of believers one to another, pray for me; as a fruit of that communion which we have one with another by the Spirit though we never saw one another."

2. How they must pray for him: *That you strive together.* (1) That *you strive in prayer.* We must put forth all that is within us in that duty; pray with fixedness, faith, and fervency; wrestle with God, as Jacob did. (2) That you strive together with me. When he begged their prayers for him, he did not intend thereby to excuse his praying for himself. Those who beg the prayers of others must not neglect to pray for themselves.

3. What they must beg of God for him. He mentions particulars; for, in praying both for ourselves and for our friends, it is good to be particular. (1) The dangers which he was exposed to: *That I may be delivered from those that do not believe in Judea.* (2) His services: *Pray that my service which I have for Juersalem may be accepted of the saints.* Why, was there any danger that it would not be accepted? Can money be otherwise than acceptable to the poor? Yes, there was some ground of suspicion in this case; for Paul was the apostle of the Gentiles, and as the unbelieving Jews looked spitefully at him, which was their wickedness, so those that believed were shy of him upon that

account, which was their weakness.
(3) His journey to them. To engage
their prayers for him, he interests
them in his concerns (*v.* 32): *That
I may come unto you with joy.*

II. Here is another prayer of the
apostle for them (*v.* 33): *Now the
God of peace be with you all, Amen.*
The Lord of hosts, the God of
battle, is the God of peace, the
author and lover of peace. Those
who are united in the blessing of
God should be united in affection
one to another.

<h3 style="text-align:center">CHAPTER SIXTEEN
PERSONAL GREETINGS
(vv. 1–16)</h3>

Such remembrances as these are
usual in letters between friends;
and yet Paul, by the savouriness of
his expressions, sanctifies these
common compliments.

I. Here is the recommendation of
a friend, by whom (as some think)
this epistle was sent—one *Phebe,
vv.* 1, 2. It should seem that she
was a person of quality and estate,
who had business which called her
to Rome, where she was a stranger;
and therefore Paul recommends her
to the acquaintance of the Christians there: an expression of his
true friendship to her. Paul was as
well skilled in the art of obliging as
most men. True religion, rightly
received, never made any man
uncivil. Courtesy and Christianity
agree well together.

II. Here are commendations to
some particular friends among
those to whom he wrote, more than
in any other of the epistles. Though
the care of all the churches came
upon Paul daily, enough to distract

an ordinary head, yet he could
retain the remembrance of so
many; and his heart was so full of
love and affection as to send salutations to each of them with particular characters of them, and
expressions of love to them and
concern for them. *Greet* them,
salute them. "Let them know that
I remember them, and love them,
and wish them well."

Lastly, He concludes with the
recommendation of them to the
love and embraces one of another:
Salute one another with a holy kiss.
Mutual salutations, as they express
love, so they increase and strengthen
love, and endear Christians one to
another: therefore Paul here encourages the use of them, and only
directs that they may be holy—a
chaste kiss, in opposition to that
which is wanton and lascivious; a
sincere kiss, in opposition to that
which is treacherous and dissembling, as Judas's, when he betrayed
Christ with a kiss. He adds, in the
close, a general salutation to them
all, in the name of the churches of
Christ (*v.* 16): "*The churches of
Christ salute you*; that is, the
churches which I am with, and
which I am accustomed to visit
personally, as knit together in the
bonds of the common Christianity,
desire me to testify their affection
to you and good wishes for you."
This is one way of maintaining the
communion of saints.

<h3 style="text-align:center">SOME WARNINGS
(vv. 17–20)</h3>

The apostle having endeavoured
by his endearing salutations to
unite them together, it was not
improper to subjoin a caution to

take heed of those whose principles and practices were destructive to Christian love. And we may observe,

I. The caution itself, which is given in the most obliging manner that could be: *I beseech you, brethren.* He teaches them, 1. To see their danger: *Mark those who cause divisions and offences.* Our Master had himself foretold that divisions and offences would come, but had entailed a woe on those by whom they come (Matt. xviii. 7), and against such we are here cautioned. 2. To shun it: "*Avoid them.* Shun all unnecessary communion and communication with them, lest you be leavened and infected by them. Do not strike in with any dividing interests, nor embrace any of those principles or practices which are destructive to Christian love and charity, or to the truth which is according to godliness. — *Their word will eat as doth a canker.*"

II. The reasons to enforce this caution.

1. Because of the pernicious policy of these seducers, *v.* 18. The worse they are, the more need we have to watch against them. Now observe his description of them, in two things: (1) The master they serve: not *our Lord Jesus Christ.* Though they call themselves Christians, they do not serve Christ; do not aim at his glory, promote his interest, nor do his will, whatever they pretend. But they *serve their own belly*—their carnal, sensual, secular interests. (2) The method they take to compass their design: *By good words and fair speeches they deceive the hearts of the simple.*

2. Because of the peril we are in,

through our proneness and aptness to be inveigled and ensnard by them. And, (1) These seducing teachers would be the more apt to assault them. The devil and his agents have a particular spite against flourishing churches and flourishing souls. (2) They were in danger from these seducers. This Paul suggests with a great deal of modesty and tenderness; not as one suspicious of them, but as one solicitous for them: "Your *obedience has come abroad unto all men*; we grant this and rejoice in it: *I am glad therefore on your behalf.*" Thus does he insinuate their commendation, the better to make way for the caution. A holy jealousy of our friends may very well comport with a holy joy in them. "You think yourselves a very happy people, and so do I too: but for all that you must not be secure: *I would have you wise unto that which is good, and simple concerning evil.* You are a willing good-natured people, but you had best take heed of being imposed upon by those seducers."

3. Because of the promise of God, that we shall have victory at last, which is given to quicken and encourage, not to supersede, our watchful cares and vigorous endeavours. It is a very sweet promise (*v.* 20): *The God of peace shall bruise Satan under your feet.* When Satan seems to have prevailed, and we are ready to give up all for lost, then will the God of peace cut the work short in righteousness. If the grace of Christ be with us, who can be against us so as to prevail? *Be strong therefore in the grace which is in Christ Jesus.* Paul, not only as a

friend, but as a minister and an apostle, who had received grace for grace, thus with authority blesses them with this blessing, and repeats it, *v.* 24.

MORE GREETINGS
(*vv.* 21–24)

As the apostle had before sent his own salutations to many of this church, and that of the churches round him to them all, he here adds an affectionate remembrance of them from some particular persons who were now with him, the better to promote acquaintance and fellowship among distant saints, and that the subscribing of these worthy names, known to them, might the more recommend this epistle. He mentions, 1. Some that were his particular friends, and probably known to the Roman Christians: *Timotheus my workfellow.* Paul sometimes calls Timothy his son, as an inferior; but here he styles him his work-fellow, as one equal with him, such a respect does he put upon him: and *Lucius*, probably Lucius of Cyrene, a noted man in the church of Antioch (Acts xiii. 1), as Jason was at Thessalonica, where he suffered for entertaining Paul (Acts xvii. 5, 6): and *Sosipater*, supposed to be the same with Sopater of Berea, mentioned Acts xx. 4. These Paul calls his kinsmen; not only more largely, as they were Jews, but as they were in blood or affinity nearly allied to him. It seems, Paul was of a good family, that he met with so many of his kindred in several places. It is a very great comfort to see the holiness and usefulness of our kindred.

2. One that was Paul's amanuensis (*v.* 22): *I Tertius, who wrote this epistle.* Paul made use of a scribe, not out of state nor idleness, but because he wrote a bad hand, which was not very legible, which he excuses, when he writes to the Galatians with his own hand (Gal. vi. 11).

FINAL PRAYER (*vv.* 25–27)

Here the apostle solemnly closes his epistle with a magnificent ascription of glory to the blessed God, as one that terminated all in the praise and glory of God, and studied to return all to him, seeing all is of him and from him. He does, as it were, breathe out his soul to these Romans in the praise of God, choosing to make that the end of his epistle which he made the end of his life. Observe here,

I. A description of the gospel of God, which comes in in a parenthesis; having occasion to speak of it as the means by which the power of God establishes souls, and the rule of that establishment: *To establish you according to my gospel.* Paul calls it his gospel, because he was the preacher of it and because he did so much glory in it.

1. It is the *preaching of Jesus Christ.* Christ was the preacher of it himself; it began to be spoken by the Lord, Heb. ii. 3. We preach not ourselves, says Paul, but Christ Jesus the Lord. That which establishes souls is the plain preaching of Jesus Christ.

2. *It is the revelation of the mystery which was kept secret since the world began, and by the scriptures of the prophets made known.*

The subject-matter of the gospel is a mystery. Our redemption and salvation by Jesus Christ, in the foundation, method, and fruits of it, are, without controversy, a great mystery of godliness, 1 Tim. iii. 16. And yet, blessed be God, there is as much of this mystery made plain as will suffice to bring us to heaven, if we do not wilfully neglect so great salvation.

II. A doxology to that God whose gospel it is, ascribing glory to him for ever (v. 27), acknowledging that he is a glorious God, and adoring him accordingly, with the most awful affections, desiring and longing to be at this work with the holy angels, where we shall be doing it to eternity. This is praising God, ascribing glory to him for ever.

CORINTHIANS

CHAPTER ONE
PREFACE (vv. 1–9)

We have here the apostle's preface to his whole epistle, in which we may take notice,

I. Of the inscription, in which, according to the custom of writing letters then, the name of the person by whom it was written and the persons to whom it was written are both inserted. The persons to whom this epistle was directed were *the church of God that was at Corinth, sanctified in Christ Jesus, and called to be saints.* All Christians are thus far sanctified in Christ Jesus, that they are by baptism dedicated and devoted to him, they are under strict obligations to be holy, and they make profession of real sanctity. If they be not truly holy, it is their own fault and reproach.

II. Of the apostolical benediction. *Grace be to you, and peace, from God our Father, and from the Lord Jesus Christ.* An apostle of the prince of peace must be a messenger and minister of peace.

III. Of the apostle's thanksgiving to God on their behalf. Paul begins most of his epistles with thanksgiving to God for his friends and prayer for them. He gives thanks, 1. For their conversion to the faith of Christ: *For the grace which was given you through Jesus Christ, v.*

4. 2. For the abundance of their spiritual gifts. This the church of Corinth was famous for. They did not come behind any of the churches in any gift, *v.* 7. He specifies *utterance and knowledge, v.* 5. Where God has given these two gifts, he has given great capacity for usefulness. Many have the flower of utterance that have not the root of knowledge, and their converse is barren. Many have the treasure of knowledge, and lack utterance to employ it for the good of others, and then it is in a manner wrapped up in a napkin. But, where God gives both, a man is qualified for eminent usefulness.

IV. Of the encouraging hopes the apostle had of them for the time to come, founded on the power and love of Christ, and the faithfulness of God, *vv.* 8, 9. He who had begun a good work in them, and carried it on thus far, would not leave is unfinished.

PARTY SPIRIT (vv. 10–13)

Here the apostle enters on his subject.

I. He exhorts them to unity and brotherly love, and reproves them for their divisions. He had received an account from some that wished them well of some unhappy differences among them.

II. He hints at the origin of these contentions. Pride lay at the bottom, and this made them factious. *Only of pride cometh contention*, Prov. xiii. 10. They quarrelled about their ministers. Paul and Apollos were both faithful ministers of Jesus Christ, and helpers of their faith and joy: but those who were disposed to be contentious broke into parties, and set their ministers at the head of their several factions: some cried up Paul, perhaps as the most sublime and spiritual teacher; others cried up Apollos, perhaps as the most eloquent speaker; some Cephas, or Peter, perhaps for the authority of his age, or because he was the apostle of the circumcision; and some were for none of them, but Christ only. So liable are the best things in the world to be corrupted, and the gospel and its institutions, which are at perfect harmony with themselves and one another, to be made the engines of variance, discord, and contention.

III. He expostulates with them upon their discord and quarrels: "*Is Christ divided?*" No, there is but one Christ, and therefore Christians should be of one heart. Ministers, however instrumental they are of good to us, are not to be put in Christ's stead. And happy were it for the churches if there were no name of distinction among them, as Christ is not divided.

TRUE WISDOM (*vv.* 14–31)

Here the apostle gives an account of his ministry among them. He thanks God he had baptized but a few among them, *Crispus*, who had been a ruler of a synagogue at Corinth (Acts xviii. 8), *Gaius, and the household of Stephanas*, besides whom, he says, he did not remember that he had baptized any. But how was this a proper matter for thankfulness? He is not to be understood in such a sense as if he were thankful for not having baptized at all, but for not having done it in present circumstances, lest it should have had this very bad construction put upon it—that he had baptized in his own name, made disciples for himself, or set himself up as the head of a sect.

We have here,

I. The manner in which Paul preached the gospel, and the cross of Christ: *Not with the wisdom of words* (*v.* 17), *the enticing words of man's wisdom* (*ch.* ii. 4), the flourish of oratory, or the accuracies of philosophical language, upon which the Greeks so much prided themselves, and which seem to have been the peculiar recommendations of some of the heads of the faction in this church that most opposed this apostle. He did not preach the gospel in this manner, lest *the cross of Christ should be of no effect*, lest the success should be ascribed to the force of art, and not of truth; not to the plain doctrine of a crucified Jesus, but to the powerful oratory of those who spread it, and hereby the honour of the cross be diminished or eclipsed.

II. We have the different effects of this preaching: To those who perish it is foolishness, *but to those who are saved it is the power of God, v.* 18. *It is to the Jews a stumbling-block, and to the Greeks foolishness; but unto those who are called, both Jews and Greeks, Christ the power of God and the wisdom of*

God, *vv.* 23, 24. 1. Christ crucified is a stumbling-block to the Jews. They could not get over it. They despised him, and looked upon him as execrable, because he was hanged on a tree, and because he did not gratify them with a sign to their mind, though his divine power shone out in innumerable miracles. The Jews require a sign, *v.* 22. See Matt. xii. 38. 2. He was to the Greeks foolishness. They laughed at the story of a crucified Saviour, and despised the apostles' way of telling it. They sought for wisdom. They were men of wit and reading, men that had cultivated arts and sciences, and had, for some ages, been in a manner the very mint of knowledge and learning. There was nothing in the plain doctrine of the cross to suit their taste, nor humour their vanity, nor gratify a curious and wrangling temper: they entertained it therefore with scorn and contempt. 3. To those who are called and saved *he is the wisdom of God, and the power of God.* Those who are called and sanctified, who receive the gospel, and are enlightened by the Spirit of God, discern more glorious discoveries of God's wisdom and power in the doctrine of Christ crucified than in all his other works.

III. We have here the triumphs of the cross over human wisdom, according to the ancient prophecy (Isa. xxix. 14). All the valued learning of this world was confounded, baffled, and eclipsed, by the Christian revelation and the glorious triumphs of the cross. The heathen politicians and philosophers, the Jewish rabbis and doctors, the curious searchers into the secrets of nature, were all baffled. All the boasted science of the heathen world did not, could not, effectually bring home the world to God.

1. The thing preached was foolishness in the eyes of worldly-wise men. Our living through one who died, our being blessed by one who was made a curse, our being justified by one who was himself condemned, was all folly and inconsistency to men blinded with self-conceit and wedded to their own prejudices and the boasted discoveries of their reason and philosophy.

2. The manner of preaching the gospel was foolishness to them too. None of the famous men for wisdom or eloquence were employed to plant the church or propagate the gospel. A few fishermen were called out, and sent upon this errand. But God seeth not as man seeth. He hath chosen the foolish things of the world, the weak things of the world, the base and despicable things of the world, men of mean birth, of low rank, of no liberal education, to be the preachers of the gospel and planters of the church.

IV. We have an account how admirably all is fitted, 1. To beat down the pride and vanity of men. The gospel dispensation is a contrivance to humble man. But, 2. It is as admirably fitted to glorify God. Though the ministers were poor and unlearned, and the converts generally of the meanest rank, yet the hand of the Lord went along with the preachers, and was mighty in the hearts of the hearers;

and Jesus Christ was made both to ministers and Christians what was truly great and honourable. He is made of God to us *wisdom, righteousness, sanctification, and redemption* (v. 30): all we need, or can desire. Man is humbled, and God glorified and exalted, by the whole scheme.

CHAPTER TWO
PAUL AT CORINTH
(vv. 1–5)

In this passage the apostle pursues his design, and reminds the Corinthians how he acted when he first preached the gospel among them.

I. As to the matter or subject he tells us (v. 2), *He determined to know nothing among them but Jesus Christ and him crucified*—to make a show of no other knowledge than this, to preach nothing, to discover the knowledge of nothing, but Jesus Christ, and him crucified.

II. The manner wherein he preached Christ is here also observable. 1. Negatively. *He came not among them with excellency of speech or wisdom, v.* 1. *His speech and preaching were not with enticing words of man's wisdom, v.* 4. Neither his speech, nor the wisdom he taught, savoured of human skill: he learnt both in another school. Divine wisdom needed not to be set off with such human ornaments. 2. Positively. He came among them *declaring the testimony of God, v.* 1. He published a divine revelation; and there he left the matter. *He was also among them in weakness and fear, and in much trembling;* and yet *his speech and preaching were in demonstration of the Spirit*

and of power, v. 3, 4. He acted in his office with much modesty, concern, and care. He behaved with great humility among them; not as one grown vain with the honour and authority conferred on him, but as one concerned to approve himself faithful, and fearful of himself, lest he should mismanage in his trust. But, though Paul managed with this modesty and concern, yet he spoke with authority: *In the demonstration of the Spirit and of power.* He preached the truths of Christ in their native dress, with plainness of speech.

III. Here is the end mentioned for which he preached Christ crucified in this manner: *That your faith should not stand in the wisdom of man, but the power of God (v.* 5)—that they might not be drawn by human motives, nor overcome by mere human arguments, lest it should be said that either rhetoric or logic had made them Christians. But, when nothing but Christ crucified was plainly preached, the success must be entirely attributed to a divine power accompanying the word. Their faith must be founded, not on human wisdom, but divine evidence and operation. The gospel was so preached that God might appear and be glorified in all.

THE SPIRIT AS INTERPRETER
(vv. 6–16)

In this part of the chapter the apostle shows them that though he had not come to them with the excellency of human wisdom, with any of the boasted knowledge and literature of the Jews or Greeks, yet he had communicated to them a treasure of the truest and the highest wisdom: *We speak wisdom among those who are perfect (v. 6)*, among those who are well instructed in Christianity, and come to some maturity in the things of God. Now, concerning this wisdom, observe,

I. The rise and origin of it: *It was ordained of God, before the world, to our glory, v. 7.* It was ordained of God; he had determined long ago to reveal and make it known, from many ages past, from the beginning, nay, from eternity; and that to our glory, *the glory of us*, either us apostles or us Christians.

II. The ignorance of the great men of the world about it: *Which none of the princes of this world knew (v. 8)*, the principal men in authority and power, or in wisdom and learning.

III. It is such wisdom as could not have been discovered without a revelation, according to what the prophet Isaiah says (Isa. lxiv. 4), *Eye hath not seen, nor ear heard, nor have entered into the heart of man the things which God hath prepared for those that love him—for him that waiteth for him*, that waiteth for his mercy, so the LXX. It was a testimony of love to God in the Jewish believers to live in expectation of the accomplishment of evangelical promises. Waiting upon God is an evidence of love to him. *Lo, this is our God, we have waited for him*, Isa. xxv. 9.

IV. We here see by whom this wisdom is discovered to us: *God hath revealed them to us by his Spirit, v. 10.* The scripture is given by inspiration of God. *Holy men spoke of old as they were moved by*

the Holy Ghost, 2 Pet. i. 21. And the apostles spoke by inspiration of the same Spirit, as he taught them, and gave their utterance. Here is a proof of the divine authority of the holy scriptures.

V. We see here in what manner this wisdom was taught or communicated: *Which things we speak, not in the words which man's wisdom teaches, but which the Holy Ghost teaches, v. 13.* They had received the wisdom they taught, not from the wise men of the world, not from their own enquiry nor invention, but from the Spirit of God. Nor did they put a human dress on it, but plainly declared the doctrine of Christ, in terms also taught them by the Holy Spirit. The language of the Spirit of God is the most proper to convey his meaning.

VI. We have an account how this wisdom is received.

1. *The natural man receiveth not the things of God, for they are foolishness to him, neither can he know them, because they are spiritually discerned, v. 14.* The *natural man, the animal man.* Revelation is not with him a principle of science; he looks upon it as delirium and dotage, the extravagant thought of some deluded dreamer. It is no way to wisdom among the famous masters of the world; and for that reason he can have no knowledge of things revealed, because they are only spiritually discerned, or made known by the revelation of the Spirit, which is a principle of science or knowledge that he will not admit.

2. *But he that is spiritual judgeth all things, yet he himself is judged*, or discerned, *of no man, v. 15.* He does

not lose the power of reasoning, nor renounce the principles of it, by founding his faith and religion on revelation. But *he himself is judged of no man*—can be judged, so as to be confuted, by no man; nor can any man who is not spiritual (see *ch*. xiv. 37), or not founding his faith on a divine revelation, discern or judge whether what he speaks be true or divine, or not. In short, he who founds all his knowledge upon principles of science, and the mere light of reason, can never be a judge of the truth or falsehood of what is received by revelation. *For who hath known the mind of the Lord, that he may instruct him* (*v.* 16), that is, the *spiritual man?* He only is the person to whom God immediately communicates the knowledge of his will. And who can inform or instruct him in the mind of God who is so immediately under the conduct of his own Spirit? Very few have known any thing of the mind of God by a natural power. *But*, adds the apostle, *we have the mind of Christ*: and the mind of Christ is the mind of God. He is God, and the principal messenger and prophet of God. And the apostles were empowered by his Spirit to make known his mind to us. And in the holy scriptures the mind of Christ, and the mind of God in Christ, are fully revealed to us.

CHAPTER THREE
SPIRITUAL INFANTS
(*vv.* 1–4)

Here, I. Paul blames the Corinthians for their weakness and non-proficiency. The apostle tells *them*

he could not speak to them as unto spiritual men, *but as unto carnal* men, *as to babes in Christ*, *v.* 1. They were still mere babes in Christ. They had received some of the first principles of Christianity, but had not grown up to maturity of understanding in them, or of faith and holiness; and yet it is plain, from several passages in this epistle, that the Corinthians were very proud of their wisdom and knowledge. The apostle assigns their little proficiency in the knowledge of Christianity as a reason why he had communicated no more of the deep things of it to them. They could not bear such food, they needed to be fed with milk, not with meat, *v.* 2.

II. He blames them for their carnality, and mentions their contention and discord about their ministers as evidence of it: *For you are yet carnal; for whereas there are among you envyings, and strifes, and divisions, are you not carnal, and walk as men?* *v.* 3. They had mutual emulations, and quarrels, and factions among them, upon the account of their ministers, *while one said, I am of Paul; and another, I am of Apollos, v.* 4. These were proofs of their being carnal, that fleshly interest and affections too much swayed them.

WORKERS TOGETHER
(*vv.* 5–10)

Here the apostle instructs them how to cure this failing, and rectify what was amiss among them upon this head,

I. By reminding them that the ministers about whom they contended were but ministers: *Who then is Paul, and who is Apollos, but*

ministers by whom you believed?
Even as the Lord gave to every man,
v. 5. They are but ministers, mere
instruments used by the God of all
grace. *Paul had planted and Apollos
had watered*, v. 6. Both were useful,
one for one purpose, the other for
another. Note, The success of the
ministry must be derived from the
divine blessing: *Neither he that
planteth is any thing, nor he that
watereth, but God who giveth the
increase*, v. 7. Even apostolical
ministers are nothing of themselves, can do nothing with efficacy
and success unless God give the
increase.

II. By representing to them the
unanimity of Christ's ministers: *He
that planteth and he that watereth
are one* (v. 8), employed by one
Master, entrusted with the same
revelation, busied in one work, and
engaged in one design—in harmony
with one another, however they
may be set in opposition to each
other by factious party-makers.
They have their different gifts from
one and the same Spirit, for the
very same purposes; and they
heartily carry on the same design.
Planters and waterers are but
fellow-labourers in the same work.
They are working together with
God, in promoting the purposes of
his glory, and the salvation of
precious souls; and he who knows
their work will take care they do
not labour in vain.

THE TRUE FOUNDATION
(vv. 11–15)

Here the apostle informs us what
foundation he had laid at the
bottom of all his labours among
them—*even Jesus Christ, the chief*
corner-stone, Eph. ii. 20. Upon this
foundation all the faithful ministers
of Christ build. Upon this rock all
Christians found their hopes. Those
that build their hopes of heaven on
any other foundation build upon
the sand. *Other foundation can no
man lay besides what is laid—even
Jesus Christ*. But of those that hold
the foundation, and embrace the
general doctrine of Christ's being
the mediator between God and
man, there are two sorts:

I. Some build upon this foundation *gold, silver, and precious stones*
(v. 12), namely, those who receive
and propagate the pure truths of
the gospel, who hold nothing but
the *truth as it is in Jesus*, and preach
nothing else. This is building well
upon a good foundation.

II. Others *build wood, hay, and
stubble*, on this foundation; that is,
though they adhere to the foundation, they depart from the mind of
Christ in many particulars, substitute their own fancies and
inventions in the room of his
doctrines and institutions, and
build upon the good foundation
what will not abide the test when
the day of trial shall come, and the
fire must make it manifest, as wood,
hay, and stubble, will not bear the
trial by fire, but must be consumed
in it. There is a time coming when
a discovery will be made of what
men have built on this foundation:
*Every man's work shall be made
manifest*. In that day, 1. Some men's
works will *abide the trial*—will be
found standard. It will appear that
they not only held the foundation,
but that they built regularly and
well upon it—that they laid on
proper materials, and in due form

and order. 2. There are others *whose works shall be burnt* (*v.* 15), whose corrupt opinions and doctrines, or vain inventions and usages in the worship of God, shall be discovered, disowned, and rejected, in that day—shall be first manifested to be corrupt, and then disapproved of God and rejected. He shall be saved, *yet so as by fire,* saved out of the fire. He himself shall be snatched out of that flame which will consume his work. This intimates that it will be difficult for those that corrupt and deprave Christianity to be saved. God will have no mercy on their works, though he may pluck them as brands out of the burning.

THE TEMPLE OF GOD
(*vv.* 16, 17)

Here the apostle resumes his argument and exhortation, founding it on his former allusion, *You are God's building,* *v.* 9, and here, *Know you not that you are the temple of God, and the Spirit of God dwelleth in you? If any man defile* (corrupt and destroy) *the temple of God, him shall God destroy* (the same word is in the original in both clauses); *for the temple of God is holy, which temple you are.* It may be undersood of the church of Corinth collectively, or of every single believer among them; Christian churches are temples of God. He dwells among them by his Holy Spirit. *They are built together for a habitation of God through the Spirit,* Eph. ii. 22. Every Christian is a living temple of the living God. God dwelt in the Jewish temple, took possession of it, and resided in it, by that glorious cloud that was the token of his presence with that people. So Christ by his Spirit dwells in all true believers. If we are the temples of God, we must do nothing that shall alienate ourselves from him, or corrupt and pollute ourselves, and thereby unfit ourselves for his use; and we must hearken to no doctrine nor doctor that would seduce us to any such practices.

THE WORLD'S WISDOM
(*vv.* 18–20)

Here he prescribes humility, and a modest opinion of themselves, for the remedy of the irregularities in the church of Corinth, the divisions and contests among them: "*Let no man deceive himself, v.* 18. Do not be led away from the truth and simplicity of the gospel by pretenders to science and eloquence, by a show of deep learning, or a flourish of words, by rabbis, orators, or philosophers." But *he who seems to be wise must become a fool that he may be wise.* He just be aware of his own ignorance, and lament it; he must distrust his own understanding, and not lean on it. The thoughts of the wisest men in the world have a great mixture of vanity, of weakness and folly, in them; and before God their wisest and best thoughts are very vanity, compared, I mean, with his thoughts of things. And should not all this teach us modesty, diffidence in ourselves, and a deference to the wisdom of God, make us thankful for his revelations, and willing to be taught of God, and not be led away by specious pretences to human wisdom and skill, from the simplicity of Christ, or a regard to his heavenly doctrine? Note, He who would be wise indeed must learn of God, and not set his own wisdom up in competition with God's.

GLORYING IN MEN (*vv.* 21–23)

Here the apostle founds an exhortation against over-valuing their teachers on what he had just said, and on the consideration that they had an equal interest in all their ministers: *Therefore let no man glory in men* (*v.* 21)—forget that their ministers are men, or pay that defence to them that is due only to God. All faithful ministers are serving one Lord and pursuing one purpose. They were appointed of Christ, for the common benefit of the church: "*Paul, and Apollos, and Cephas, are all yours.* One is not to be set up against another, but all are to be valued and used for your own spritual benefit." Upon this occasion also he gives in an inventory of the church's possessions, the spiritual riches of a true believer: "*All is yours*—ministers of all ranks, ordinary and extraordinary. Nay, the world itself is yours." Not that saints are proprietors of the world, but it stands for their sake, they have as much of it as Infinite Wisdom sees to be fit for them, and they have all they have with the divine blessing. But it must be remembered, at the same time, *that we are Christ's,* the subjects of his kingdom, his property. He is Lord over us, and we must own his dominion, and cheerfully submit to his command and yield themselves to his pleasure, if we would have all things minister to our advantage. All things are ours, upon no other ground than

our being Christ's. *And Christ is God's.* He is the Christ of God, anointed of God, and commissioned by him, to bear the office of a Mediator, and to act therein for the purposes of his glory.

CHAPTER FOUR
APOSTOLIC STEWARDSHIP
(*vv.* 1–6)

Here, I. The apostle challenges the respect due to him on account of his character and office, in which many among them had at least very much failed: *Let a man so account of us as of the ministers of Christ, and stewards of the mysteries of God* (*v.* 1), though possibly others might have valued them too highly, by setting him up as the head of a party, and professing to be his disciples. In our opinion of ministers, as well as all other things, we should be careful to avoid extremes. They did not set up for master, but they deserved respect and esteem in this honourable service. Especially,

II. When they did their duty in it, and approved themselves faithful: *It is required in stewards that a man be found faithful* (*v.* 2), trustworthy. They must be true to the interest of their Lord, and consult his honour.

III. The apostle takes occasion hence to caution the Corinthians against censoriousness—the forward and severe judging of others: *Therefore judge nothing before the time, until the Lord come, v.* 5. There is a time coming when *the Lord will bring to light the hidden things of darkness, and make manifest the counsels of the hearts—*

deeds of darkness that are now done in secret, and all the secret inclinations, purposes, and intentions, of the hidden man of the heart. *The day shall declare it*. The Judge will bring these things to light. The Lord Jesus Christ will manifest the counsels of the heart, of all hearts.

IV. The apostle here lets us into the reason why he had used his own name and that of Apollos in this discourse of his. He had done *it in a figure*, and *he had done it for their sakes*. He chose rather to mention his own name, and the name of a faithful fellow-labourer, than the names of any heads of factions among them, that hereby he might avoid what would provoke, and so procure for his advice the greater regard.

FOOLS FOR CHRIST (vv. 7–13)

I. Paul cautions them against pride and self-conceit by this consideration, that all the distinction made among them was owing to God: *Who maketh thee to differ? And what hast thou that thou didst not receive? v. 7.* Here the apostle turns his discourse to the ministers who set themselves at the head of these factions, and did but too much encourage and abet the people in those feuds. What had they to glory in, when all their peculiar gifts were from God? They had received them, and could not glory in them as their own, without wronging God.

II. He presses the duty of humility upon them by a very smart irony, or at least reproves them for their pride and self-conceit: "*You are full, you are rich, you have reigned as kings without us.*" See how apt pride is to overrate benefits and overlook the benefactor, so swell upon its possessions and forget from whom they come; nay, it is apt to behold them in a magnifying-glass: "*You have reigned as kings,*" says the apostle, "that is, in your own conceit; and *I would to God you did reign, that we also might reign with you.* I wish you had as much of the true glory of a Christian church upon you as you arrogate to yourselves. I should come in then for a share of the honour: *I should reign with you*; I should not be overlooked by you as now I am, but valued and regarded as a minister of Christ, and a very useful instrument among you."

III. He comes to set forth his own circumstances and those of the other apostles, and compares them with theirs. 1. To set forth the case of the apostles: *For I think it hath pleased God to set forth us the apostles last, as it were appointed to death. For we are made a spectacle to the world, and to angels, and to men.* Paul and his fellow-apostles were exposed to great hardships. Never were any men in this world so hunted and worried. They carried their lives in their hands: *God hath set forth us the apostles last, as it were appointed to death, v. 9.* The general meaning is that the apostles were exposed to continual danger of death, and that of the worst kinds, in the faithful discharge of their office. God had set them forth, brought them into view, as the Roman emperors brought their combatants into the arena, the place of show, though not for the same purposes. They did it to please the populace, and humour their own vanity, and sometimes a much worse principle. The apostles were shown to manifest the power of divine grace, to confirm the truth of their mission and doctrine, and to propagate religion in the world. 2. He compares his own case with that of the Corinthians: *"We are fools for Christ's sake, but you are wise in Christ; we are weak, but you are strong; you are honourable, but we are despised, v.* 10. *We are fools for Christ's sake*; such in common account, and we are well content to be so accounted. We can pass for fools in the world, and be despised as such, so that the wisdom of God and the honour of the gospel may by this means be secured and displayed." *"But you are wise in Christ.* You have the fame of being wise and learned Christians, and you do not a little value yourselves upon it." The Corinthians may think themselves, and be esteemed by others, as wiser and stronger men in Christ than the apostles themselves. But O! how gross is the mistake!

IV. He enters into some particularities of their sufferings: *Even to this present hour;* that is, after all the service we have been doing among you and other churches, *we hunger and thirst, and are naked, and are buffeted, and have no certain dwelling-place, and labour, working with our own hands, vv.* 11, 12. Nay, they were *made as the filth of the world, and the off-scouring of all things, v.* 13. They were forced to labour with their own hands to get subsistence, and had so much, and

so much greater, business to mind, that they could not attend enough to this, to get a comfortable livelihood, but were exposed to hunger, thirst, and nakedness—many times wanted meat, and drink, and clothes. They were driven about the world, without having any fixed abode, any stated habitation. Poor circumstances indeed, for the prime ministers of our Saviour's kingdom to have no house nor home, and to be destitute of food and raiment! But yet no poorer than his who had not *where to lay his head,* Luke ix. 58. They were the common-sewer into which all the reproaches of the world were to be poured. To be the off-scouring of any thing is bad, but what is it to be the off-scouring of all things! How much did the apostles resemble their Master, *and fill up that which was behind of his afflictions, for his body's sake, which is the church!* Col. i. 24.

V. We have here the apostles' behaviour under all; and the return they made for this maltreatment: *Being reviled, we bless; being persecuted, we suffer it; being defamed, we entreat, vv.* 12, 13. They returned blessings for reproaches, and entreaties and kind exhortations for the rudest slanders and defamation, and were patient under the sharpest persecutions.

THEIR SPIRITUAL FATHER
(*vv.* 14–16)

Here Paul challenges their regard to him as their father. He tells them, 1. That what he had written was not for their reproach, but admonition; not with the gall of an enemy, but the bowels of a father (*v.* 14): *I* write not to shame you, but as my beloved children I warn you. 2. He shows them upon what foundation he claimed paternal relation to them, and called them his sons. They might have other pedagogues or instructors, but he was their father; *for in Christ Jesus he had begotten them by the gospel, v.* 15. They were made Christians by his ministry. 3. We have here the special advice he urges on them: *Wherefore I beseech you be you followers of me, v.* 16. This he elsewhere explains and limits (*ch.* xi. 1): "*Be you followers of me, as I also am of Christ.* Follow me as far as I follow Christ."

PAUL'S AUTHORITY
(vv. 17–21)

Here, I. He tells them of his having sent Timothy to them, *to bring them into remembrance of his ways in Christ, as he taught every where in every church (v.* 17)—to remind them of his ways in Christ, to refresh their memory as to his preaching and practice, what he taught, and how he lived among them.

II. He rebukes the vanity of those who imagined he would not come to them, by letting them know this was his purpose, though he had sent Timothy: "*I will come to you shortly,* though some of you are so vain as to think I will not." But he adds, *if the Lord will.* It seems, as to the common events of life, apostles knew no more than other men, nor were they in these points under inspiration.

III. He lets them know what would follow upon his coming to

them: *I will know, not the speech of those that are puffed up, but the power, v.* 19. He would bring the great pretenders among them to a trial, would know what they were, not by their rhetoric or philosophy, but by the authority and efficacy of what they taught, whether they could confirm it by miraculous operations, and whether it was accompanied with divine influences and saving effects on the minds of men. For, adds he, *the kingdom of God is not in word, but in power.*

IV. He puts it to their choice how he should come among them, *whether with a rod or in love and the spirit of meekness (v.* 21); that is, according as they were they would find him. If they continued perverse among themselves and with him, it would be necessary to come with a rod. But this is far from being desirable, if it may be prevented. And therefore the apostle adds that it was in their own option whether he should come with a rod or in a quite different disposition and manner: *Or in love and the spirit of meekness.*

CHAPTER FIVE
SIN IN THE CHURCH
(vv. 1–6)

Here the apostle states the case; and,

I. Lets them know what was the common or general report concerning them, that one of their community was guilty of fornication, *v.* 1. This was not a common instance of fornication, but *such as was not so much as named among* the Gentiles, *that a man should have his father's wife*—either marry her while his father was alive, or keep her as his concubine, either when he was dead or while he was alive. Yet such a horrible wickedness was committed by one in the church of Corinth, and, as is probable, a leader of one of the factions among them, a principal man.

II. He greatly blames them for their own conduct hereupon: *They were puffed up* (v. 2), *they gloried*, 1. Perhaps on account of this very scandalous person. He might be a man of great eloquence, of deep science, and for this reason very greatly esteemed, and followed, and cried up, by many among them. They were proud that they had such a leader. Instead of mourning for his fall, and their own reproach upon his account, and renouncing him and removing him from the society, they continued to applaud him and pride themselves in him. Or else, 2. It may intimate to us that some of the opposite party were puffed up. They were proud of their own standing, and trampled upon him that fell.

III. We have the apostle's direction to them how they should now proceed with this scandalous sinner. He would have him excommunicated and delivered to Satan (*vv.* 3–5); *as absent in body, yet present in spirit, he had judged already as if he had been present*; that is, he had, by revelation and the miraculous gift of discerning vouchsafed him by the Spirit, as perfect a knowledge of the case, and had hereupon come to the following determination, not without special authority from the Holy Spirit. He says this to let them know that, though he was at a distance, he did not pass an unrighteous sentence, nor judge without having as full cognizance of the case as if he had been on the spot. Paul had judged that *he should be delivered to Satan* (*v.* 5), and this was to be done *in the name of Christ*, with the power of Christ, and in a full assembly, where the apostle would be also present in spirit, or by his spiritual gift of discerning at a distance. Some think that this is to be understood of a mere ordinary excommunication, and that delivering him to Satan for the destruction of the flesh is only meant of disowning him, and casting him out of the church, that by this means he might be brought to repentance, and his flesh might be mortified. Others think the apostle is not to be understood of mere excommunication, but of a miraculous power or authority they had of delivering a scandalous sinner into the power of Satan, to have bodily diseases inflicted, and to be tormented by him with bodily pains, which is the meaning of the *destruction of the flesh*. In this sense the destruction of the flesh has been a happy occasion of the salvation of the spirit. It is probable that this was a mixed case.

IV. He hints the danger of contagion from this example: *Your glorying is not good. Know you not that a little leaven leaveneth the whole lump?* The bad example of a man in rank and reputation is very mischievous, spreads the contagion far and wide. It did so, probably, in this very church and case: see 2 Cor. xii. 21.

CHRIST, OUR PASSOVER
(vv. 7, 8)

Here the apostle exhorts them to purity, by purging out the old leaven. In this observe,

I. The advice itself, addressed either, 1. To the church in general; and so purging out the old leaven, that they might be a new lump, refers to the *putting away from themselves that wicked person*, v. 13. Or, 2. To each particular member of the church. And so it implies that they should purge themselves from all impurity of heart and life, especially from this kind of wickedness, to which the Corinthians were addicted to a proverb.

II. The reason with which this advice is enforced: *For Christ our passover is sacrificed for us*, v. 7. This is the great doctrine of the gospel. The Jews, after they had killed the passover, kept the feast of unleavened bread. So must we; not for seven days only, but all our days. We should die with our Saviour to sin, be planted into the likeness of his death by mortifying sin, and into the likeness of his resurrection by rising again to newness of life, and that internal and external. We must have new hearts and new lives.

SHUN BAD COMPANY
(vv. 9–13)

Here the apostle advises them to shun the company and converse of scandalous members. Consider,

I. The advice itself: *I wrote to you in a letter not to company with fornicators*, v. 9. Some think this was an epistle written to them before, which is lost. Some think it is to be understood of this very epistle, that he had written this advice before he had full information of their whole case, but thought it needful now to be more particular. And therefore on this occasion he tells them that if any man called a brother, any one professing Christianity, and being a member of a Christian church, were *a fornicator, or covetous, or an idolator, or a railer*, that they should not *keep company with him, nor so much as eat with such a one*.

II. How he limits this advice. He does not forbid Christians the like commerce with scandalously wicked heathens. He does not forbid their eating nor conversing with the *fornicators of this world*, &c. They know no better. They profess no better. Note, Christians may and ought to testify more respect to loose worldlings than to loose Christians.

III. The reason of this limitation is here assigned. It is impossible the one should be avoided. Christians must have gone out of the world to avoid the company of loose heathens. But this was impossible, as long as they had business in the world. While they are minding their duty, and doing their proper business, God can and will preserve them from contagion. But the dread of sin wears off by familiar converse with wicked Christians. Our own safety and preservation are a reason of this difference. But, besides, heathens were such as Christians had nothing to do to judge and censure, and avoid upon a censure passed; for *they are without* (v. 12), and must be left to *God's judgment*, v. 13. But, as to members of the church, they are within, are professedly bound by the laws and rules of Christianity, and not only liable to the judgment of God, but to the censures of those who are set over them, and the fellow-members of the same body, when they transgress those rules. Every Christian is bound to judge them unfit for communion and familiar converse.

IV. How he applies the argument to the case before him: *"Therefore put away from among yourselves that wicked person," v. 13.*

<h3 style="text-align:center">CHAPTER SIX</h3>

GOING TO LAW (vv. 1–8)

Here the apostle reproves them for going to law with one another before heathen judges for little matters; and therein blames all *vexatious law-suits,* concerning which observe,

I. The fault he blames them for: it was going to law. Not but that *the law is good, if a man use it lawfully.* But, 1. *Brother went to law with brother (v.* 6), one member of the church with another. The near relation could not preserve peace and good understanding. The bonds of fraternal love were broken through. 2. They brought the matter before the heathen magistrates: *they went to law before the unjust, not before the saints (v.* 1), brought the controversy before unbelievers *(v.* 6), and did not compose it among themselves, Christians and saints, at least in profession. This tended much to the reproach of Christianity.

II. He lays before them the aggravations of their fault: *Do you not know that the saints shall judge the world (v.* 2), *shall judge angels? v.* 3. And are they unworthy *to judge the smallest matters, the things of this life?* It was a dishonour to their Christian character, a forgetting of their real dignity, as saints, for them to carry little matters, about the things of life, before heathen magistrates.

III. He puts them on a method to remedy this fault. And this twofold: 1. By referring it to some to make it up: *"Is it so that there is no wise man among you, no one able to judge between his brethren? v.* 5. 2. By suffering wrong rather than taking this method to right themselves: *It is utterly a fault among you to go to law in this matter*: it is always a fault of one side to go to law, except in a case where the title is indeed dubious, and there is a friendly agreement of both parties to refer it to the judgment of those learned in the law to decide it. And this is referring it, rather than contending about it, which is the thing the apostle here seems chiefly to condemn: *Should you not rather take wrong, rather suffer yourselves to be defrauded?*

EVILS TO BE AVOIDED (vv. 9–11)

Here he takes occasion to warn them against many heinous evils, to which they had been formerly addicted.

1. He puts it to them as a plain truth, of which they could not be ignorant, that such sinners should not inherit the kingdom of God.

II. Yet he warns them against deceiving themselves: *Be not deceived.* Those who cannot but know the fore-mentioned truth are but too apt not to attend to it. Men are very much inclined to flatter themselves that *God is such a one as themselves*, and that they may live in sin and yet die in Christ, may lead the life of the devil's children and yet go to heaven with the children of God. But this is all a gross cheat.

III. He puts them in mind what a change the gospel and grace of God had made in them: *Such were some of you* (v. 11), such notorious sinners as he had been reckoning up.

FORNICATION (vv. 12–20)

The twelfth verse and former part of the thirteenth seem to relate to that early dispute among Christians about the distinction of meats, and yet to be prefatory to the caution that follows against fornication. The connection seems plain enough if we attend to the famous determination of the apostles, Acts xv., where the prohibition of certain foods was joined with that of fornication. Now some among the Corinthians seem to have imagined that they were as much at liberty in the point of fornication as of meats, especially because it was not a sin condemned by the laws of their country. They were ready to say, even in the case of fornication, *All things are lawful for me*. This pernicious conceit Paul here sets himself to oppose.

I. The body is not for fornication, but for the Lord. This is the first argument he uses against this sin, for which the heathen inhabitants of Corinth were infamous, and the converts to Christianity retained too favourable an opinion of it. It is making things to cross their intention and use. The *body is not for fornication*; it was never formed for any such purpose, *but for the Lord*, for the service and honour of God. And *the Lord is for the body*, that is, as some think, Christ is to be Lord of the body, to have property in it and dominion over it, having assumed a body and been made to partake of our nature, that he might be head of his church, and head over all things, Heb. ii. 5, 18.

II. Some understand this last passage, *The Lord is for the body*, thus: He is for its resurrection and glorification, according to what follows, v. 14, which is a second argument against this sin, the honour intended to be put on our bodies: *God hath both raised up our Lord, and will raise us up by his power* (v. 14), by the power of him who *shall change our vile body, and make it like to his glorious body by that power whereby he is able to subdue all things to himself*, Phil. iii. 21. It is an honour done to the body that Jesus Christ was raised from the dead: and it will be an honour to our bodies that they will be raised. Let us not abuse those bodies by sin, and make them vile, which, if they be kept pure, shall, notwithstanding their present vileness, be made like to *Christ's glorious body*.

III. A third argument is the honour already put on them: *Know you not that your bodies are the members of Christ?* v. 15. If the soul be united to Christ by faith, the whole man is become a member of his mystical body. *But now*, says the apostle, *shall I take the members of Christ, and make them the members of a harlot? God forbid.* Or, *take away* the members of Christ? Would not this be a gross abuse, and the most notorious injury? Would it not be dishonouring Christ, and dishonouring ourselves to the very last degree? What, make Christ's members the members of a harlot, prostitute them to so vile a purpose! The thought is to be abhorred. God forbid. *Know you not that he who is joined to a harlot is one body* with hers? *For two*, says he, *shall be one flesh. But he who is joined to the Lord is one spirit*, vv. 16, 17. Now shall one in so close a union with Christ as to be one spirit with him yet be so united to a harlot as to become one flesh with her? Were not this a vile attempt to make a union between Christ and harlots? And can a greater indignity be offered to him or ourselves? Can any thing be more inconsistent with our profession or relation?

IV. A fourth argument is that it is a sin against our own bodies. *Every sin that a man does is without the body; he that committeth fornication sinneth against his own body* (v. 18); every sin, that is, every other sin, every external act of sin besides, is outside the body. Nor does it give the power of the body to another person. This sin is in a peculiar manner styled uncleanness, especially in a Christian. He sins against his own body; he defiles it, he degrades it, making it one with the body of that vile creature with whom he sins. He casts vile reproach on what his Redeemer has dignified to the last degree

by taking it into union with himself.

V. The fifth argument against this sin is that the bodies of Christians are *the temples of the Holy Ghost which is in them, and which they have of God*, v. 19. He that is joined to Christ is one spirit. He is yielded up to him, is consecrated thereby, and set apart for his use, and is hereupon possessed, and occupied, and inhabited, by his Holy Spirit. And shall we desecrate his temple, defile it, prostitute it, and offer it up to the use and service of a harlot? Horrid sacrilege!

VI. The apostle argues from the obligation we are under *to glorify God both with our body and spirit, which are his*, v. 20. He made both, he bought both, and therefore both belong to him and should be used and employed for him, and therefore should not be defiled, alienated from him, and prostituted by us. No, they must be kept as vessels fitted for our Master's use.

CHAPTER SEVEN
RULES ABOUT MARRIAGE I
(vv. 1–9)

The apostle comes now, as a faithful and skilful casuist, to answer some cases of conscience which the Corinthians had proposed to him. He tells them in general,

I. That it was good, in that juncture of time at least, to abstain from marriage altogether: *It is good for a man not to touch a woman* (not to take her to wife). Yet,

II. He informs them that marriage, and the comforts and satisfactions of that state, are by divine wisdom prescribed for preventing fornication (*v.* 2). To avoid these, *Let every man*, says he, *have his own wife, and every woman her own husband*; that is, marry, and confine themselves to their own mates. And, when they are married, let each render the other *due benevolence* (*v.* 3), render conjugal duty, which is owing to each other. For, as the apostle argues (*v.* 4), in the married state neither person has power of his own body, but has delivered it into the power of the other, the wife hers into the power of the husband, the husband his into the power of the wife.

III. The apostle limits what he had said about *every man's having his own wife*, &c. (*v.* 2): *I speak this by permission, not of command.* He did not lay it as an injunction upon every man to marry without exception. Any man might marry. No law of God prohibited the thing. But, on the other hand, no law bound a man to marry so that he sinned if he did not; I mean, unless his circumstances required it for preventing the lust of uncleanness. No, he *could wish all men were as himself* (*v.* 7), that is, single, and capable of living continently in that state. There were several conveniences in it, which at that season, if not at others, made it more eligible in itself. Paul could wish all men were as himself, but *all men cannot receive such a saying, save those to whom it is given,* Matt. xix. 11.

IV. He sums up his sense on this head (*vv.* 9, 10): *I say therefore to the unmarried and widows*, to those in a state of virginity or widowhood, *It is good for them if they abide even as I*. There are many conveniences, and especially at this juncture, in a single state, to render it preferable to a married one. It is convenient therefore *that the unmarried abide as I*, which plainly implies that Paul was at that time unmarried. *But, if they cannot contain, let them marry; for it is better to marry than to burn.* This is God's remedy for lust. The fire may be quenched by the means he has appointed. And marriage, with all its inconveniences, is much better than to burn with impure and lustful desires. *Marriage is honourable in all;* but it is a duty in those who cannot contain nor conquer those inclinations.

RULES ABOUT MARRIAGE II
(*vv.* 10–16)

In this paragraph the apostle gives them direction in a case which must be very frequent in that age of the world, especially among the Jewish converts; I mean whether they were to live with heathen relatives in a married state. Concerning this matter the apostle here gives direction. And,

I. In general, he tells them that marriage, by Christ's command, is for life; and therefore those who are married must not think of separation. The wife *must not depart from the husband* (*v.* 10), nor the *husband put away his wife, v.* 11. This *I command*, says the apostle; *yet not I, but the Lord.*

II. He brings the general advice home to the case of such as had an unbelieving mate (*v.* 12): *But to the rest speak I, not the Lord;* that is, the Lord had not so expressly spoken to this case as to the former divorce. But, having thus prefaced his advice, we may attend,

1. To the advice itself, which is that if an unbelieving husband or wife were pleased to dwell with a Christian relative, the other should not separate. The believer is not by faith in Christ loosed from matrimonial bonds to an unbeliever, but is at once bound and made apt to be a better relative. But, though a believing wife or husband should not separate from an unbelieving mate, yet, if the unbelieving relative desert the believer, and no means can reconcile to a cohabitation, in such *a case a brother or sister is not in bondage* (*v.* 15), not bound servilely to follow or cleave to the malicious deserter, or not bound to live unmarried after all proper means for reconciliation have been tried, at least if the deserter contract another marriage or be guilty of adultery, which was a very easy supposition, because a very common instance among the heathen inhabitants of Corinth.

2. We have here the reasons of this advice. (1) Because the relation or state is sanctified by the holiness of either party: *For the unbelieving husband is sanctified by the wife, and the unbelieving wife by the husband* (*v.* 14), or *hath been sanctified.* The relation itself, and the conjugal use of each other, are sanctified to the believer. He is sanctified for the wife's sake. She is sanctified for the husband's sake. Both are one flesh. He is to be reputed clean who is one flesh with her that is holy, and *vice versa*: *Else were your children unclean, but now are they holy* (*v.* 14), that is, they would be heathen, out of the pale of the church and covenant of God. They would not be of the holy seed (as the Jews are called, Isa. vi. 13), but common and unclean, in the same sense as heathens in general were styled in the apostle's vision, Acts x. 28. (2) Another reason is that *God hath called Christians to peace, v.* 15. The Christian religion obliges us to act peaceably in all relations, natural and civil. (3) A third reason is that it is possible for the believing relative to be an instrument of the other's salvation (*v.* 16): *What knowest thou, O wife, whether thou shalt save thy husband?* Note, It is the plain duty of those in so near a relation to seek the salvation of those to whom they are related.

CHRISTIAN CONTENTMENT (*vv.* 17–24)

Here the apostle takes occasion to advise them to continue in the state and condition in which Christianity found them, and in which they became converts to it. And here,

I. He lays down this rule in general—*as God hath distributed to every one.* Note, Our states and circumstances in this world are distributions of divine Providence.

II. He specifies particular cases; as, 1. That of circumcision. *Is any man called being circumcised? Let him not be uncircumcised. Is any man called being uncircumcised? Let him not be circumcised.* 2. That of servitude and freedom. It was common in that age of the world for many to be in a state of slavery, bought and sold for money, and so the property of those who purchased them. "Now," says the apostle, "*art thou called being a servant? Care not for it.* Be not over-solicitous about it. It is not inconsistent with thy duty, profession, or hopes, as a Christian. *Yet, if thou mayest be made free, use it rather,*" v. 21.

III. He sums up his advice: *Let every man wherein he is called abide therein with God,* v. 24. This is to be understood of the state wherein a man is converted to Christianity. No man should make his faith or religion an argument to break through any natural or civil obligations. He should quietly and comfortably abide in the condition in which he is; and this he may well do, when he may abide therein with God.

ADVICE FOR SPINSTERS
(vv. 25–35)

The apostle here resumes his discourse, and gives directions to virgins how to act, concerning which we may take notice,

I. Of the manner wherein he introduces them: "*Now concerning virgins I have no commandment of the Lord,* v. 25. I have no express and universal law delivered by the Lord himself concerning celibacy; but *I give my judgment, as one who hath obtained mercy of the Lord to be faithful,*" namely, in the apostleship.

II. The determination he gives, which, considering the present distress, was that a state of celibacy was preferable: *It is good for a man so to be,* that is, *to be single. I suppose,* says the apostle, or it is my opinion. It is worded with modesty,

but delivered, notwithstanding, with apostolical authority.

III. Notwithstanding he thus determines, he is very careful to satisfy them that he does not condemn marriage in the gross, nor declare it unlawful. And therefore, though he says, "If thou *art loosed from a wife* (in a single state, whether bachelor or widower, virgin or widow) *do not seek a wife,* do not hastily change conditions;" yet he adds, "*If thou art bound to a wife, do not seek to be loosed.* It is thy duty to continue in the married relation, and do the duties of it." Marrying is not in itself a sin, but marrying at that time was likely to bring inconvenience upon them, and add to the calamities of the times; and therefore he thought it advisable and expedient that such as could contain should refrain from it.

IV. He takes this occasion to give general rules to all Christians to carry themselves with a holy indifference towards the world, and every thing in it. 1. *As to relations:* Those *that had wives must be as though they had none*; that is, they must not set their hearts too much on the comforts of the relation; they must be as though they had none. 2. As to afflictions: *Those that weep must be as though they wept not*; that is, we must not be dejected too much with any of our afflictions, nor indulge ourselves in the sorrow of the world, but keep up a holy joy in God in the midst of all our troubles, so that even in sorrow the heart may be joyful, and the end of our grief may be gladness. 3. As to worldly enjoyments: *Those that rejoice should be as though they rejoiced not*; that is, they should not take too great a complacency in any of their comforts. 4. As to worldly traffic and employment: *Those that buy must be as though they possessed not.* Those that prosper in trade, increase in wealth, and purchase estates, should hold these possessions as though they held them not. It is but setting their hearts on that which is not (Prov. xxiii. 5) to do otherwise. 5. As to all worldly concerns: *Those that use this world as not abusing it, v. 31.* The world may be used, but must not be abused. It is abused when it is not used to those purposes for which it is given, to honour God and do good to men.

V. He enforces these advices with two reasons: 1. *The time is short, v. 29.* We have but little time to continue in this world; but a short season for possessing and enjoying worldly things. Possess what you must shortly leave without suffering yourselves to be possessed by it. 2. *The fashion of this world passeth away* (*v.* 31), *the habit*, figure, appearance, of the world, passeth away. It is daily changing countenance. It is in a continual flux. All is show, nothing solid in it; and it is transient show too, and will quickly be gone. How proper and powerful an argument is this to enforce the former advice! How irrational is it to be affected with the images, the fading and transient images, of a dream!

VI. He presses his general advice by warning them against the embarrassment of worldly cares: *But I would have you without carefulness, v. 32.* Indeed to be careless is

a fault; a wise concern about worldly interests is a duty; but to be careful, full of care, to have an anxious and perplexing care about them, is a sin. Now the married state at that time (if not at all times) did bring most worldly care along with it. *He that is married careth for the things of the world, that he may please his wife, v. 33. And she that is married careth for the things of the world, how she may please her husband.* But the unmarried man and woman mind the things of the Lord, that they may please the Lord, and be holy both in body and spirit, *vv.* 32, 34. Not but the married person may be holy both in body and spirit too. Celibacy is not in itself a state of greater purity and sanctity than marriage; but the unmarried would be able to make religion more their business at that juncture, because they would have less distraction from worldly cares.

ACT WISELY (*vv.* 36–38)

In this passage the apostle is commonly supposed to give advice about the disposal of children in marriage, upon the principle of his former determination. In this view the general meaning is plain. If a man has determined in himself to keep his daughter a virgin, and stands to this determination, and is under no necessity to dispose of her in marriage, but is at liberty, with her consent, to pursue his purpose, he does well in keeping her a virgin. In short, he that gives her in marriage does well; but he that keeps her single, if she can be easy and innocent in such a state, does what is better; that is, more convenient for her in the present state of things, if not at all times and seasons."

But I think the apostle is here continuing his former discourse, and advising unmarried persons, who are at their own disposal, what to do. The general meaning of the apostle is the same, that it was no sin to marry, if a man thought there was a necessity upon him, to avoid popular reproach, much less to avoid the hurrying fervours of lust. But he that was in his own power, stood firm in his purpose, and found himself under no necessity to marry, would, at that season, and in the circumstances of Christians at that time, at least, make a choice every way most for his own conveniency, ease, and advantage, as to his spiritual concerns.

WIDOWS (*vv.* 39, 40)

The whole is here closed up with advice to widows: *As long as the husband liveth the wife is bound by the law*, confined to one husband, and bound to continue and cohabit with him. *But, the husband being dead, she is at liberty to marry whom she will.* There is no limitation by God's law to be married only for such a number of times. It is certain, from this passage, that second marriages are not unlawful. But the apostle asserts she has such a liberty, when her husband is dead, only with a limitation that *she marry in the Lord*. In our choice of relations, and change of conditions, we should always have an eye to God. *But she is happier*, says the apostle, *if she so abide* (that is, continue a widow) *in my judgment;*

and I think I have the Spirit of God, v. 40. At this juncture, at least, if not ordinarily, it will be much more for the peace and quiet of such, and give them less hindrance in the service of God, to continue unmarried. And this, he tells them, was by inspiration of the Spirit.

THINGS OFFERED TO IDOLS (*vv.* 1–3)

The apostle comes here to the case of things that had been offered to idols, concerning which some of them sought satisfaction. For the better understanding of it, it must be observed that it was a custom among the heathens to make feasts on their sacrifices, and not only to eat themselves, but invite their friends to partake with them. These were usually kept in the temple, where the sacrifice was offered (*v.* 10), and, if any thing was left when the feast ended, it was usual to carry away a portion to their friends; what remained, after all, belonged to the priests, who sometimes sold it in the markets. See *ch.* x. 25. In this circumstance of things, while Christians lived among idolaters, had many relations and friends that were such, with whom they must keep up acquaintance and maintain good neighbourhood, and therefore have occasion to eat at their tables, what should they do if any thing that had been sacrificed should be set before them? What, if they should be invited to feast with them in their temples? It seems as if some of the Corinthians had imbibed an opinion that even this might be done, be-

237

cause they knew an idol was nothing in the world, *v.* 4.

IDOLS ARE NOTHING
(*vv.* 4–6)

In this passage he shows the vanity of idols: *As to the eating of things that have been sacrificed to idols, we know that an idol is nothing in the world*; or, there is no idol in the world; or, an idol can do nothing in the world; for the form of expression in the original is elliptical. The meaning in the general is, that heathen idols have no divinity in them; and therefore in the Old Testament they are commonly called *lies* and *vanities*, or *lying vanities*. All their divinity and mediation were imaginary. For, 1. *To us there is but one God*, says the apostle, *the Father, of whom are all things, and we in or for him*. We Christians are better informed; we well know there is but one God, the fountain of being, the author of all things, maker, preserver, and governor of the whole world, of whom and for whom are all things. 2. There is to us but one Lord, one Mediator between God and men, even Jesus Christ. Not many mediators, as the heathen imagined, but one only, by whom all things were created and do consist, and to whom all our hope and happiness are owing—the man Christ Jesus; but a man in personal union with the divine Word, or God the Son. This very man hath God made both Lord and Christ, Acts ii. 36.

ABUSE OF LIBERTY
(*vv.* 7–13)

The apostle, having granted, and indeed confirmed, the opinion of some among the Corinthians, that idols were nothing. He does not indeed here so much insist upon the unlawfulness of the thing in itself as the mischief such freedom might do to weaker Christians, persons that had not the same measure of knowledge with these pretenders. And here,

I. He informs them that every Christian man, at that time, was not so fully convinced and persuaded that an idol was nothing. Note, We should be careful to do nothing that may occasion weak Christians to defile their consciences.

II. He tells them that mere eating and drinking had nothing in them virtuous nor criminal, nothing that could make them better nor worse, pleasing nor displeasing to God.

III. He cautions them against abusing their liberty, the liberty they thought they had in this matter. For that they mistook this matter, and had no allowance to sit at meat in the idol's temple, seems plain from *ch.* x. 20, &c. But the apostle argues here that, even upon the supposition that they had such power, they must be cautious how they use it; it might be a *stumbling-block to the weak* (*v.* 9), it might occasion their falling into idolatrous actions, perhaps their falling off from Christianity and revolting again to heathenism.

IV. He enforces all with his own example (*v.* 13): *Wherefore if meat make my brother to offend I will eat no flesh while the world standeth, lest I make my brother to offend.* He does not say that he will never eat more. This were to destroy himself, and to commit a heinous sin, to prevent the sin and fall of a brother. Such evil must not be done that good may come of it. But, though it was necessary to eat, it was not necessary to eat flesh. And therefore, rather than occasion sin in a brother, he would abstain from it as long as he lived.

CHAPTER NINE

THE APOSTLE'S RIGHTS
(vv. 1–14)

Having asserted his apostolical authority (vv. 1, 2) Paul proceeds to claim the rights belonging to his office, especially that of being maintained by it.

I. These he states, vv. 3–6. "*My answer to those that do examine me* (that is, enquire into my authority, or the reasons of my conduct, if I am an apostle) is this: *Have we not power to eat and drink* (v. 4), or a right to maintenance? *Have we not power to lead about a sister, a wife, as well as other apostles, and the brethren of the Lord, and Cephas*; and, not only to be maintained ourselves, but have them maintained also? Though Paul was at that time single, he had a right to take a wife when he pleased, and to lead her about with him, and expect a maintenance for her, as well as himself, from the churches. In short, the apostle here claims a maintenance from the churches, both for him and his. This was due from them, and what he might claim.

II. He proceeds, by several arguments, to prove his claim. 1. From the common practice and expectations of mankind. Those who addict and give themselves up to any way of business in the world expect to live out of it. 2. He argues it out of the Jewish law: *Say I these things as a man? Or saith not the law the same also? v. 8.* God had therein ordered that the ox should not be muzzled while he was treading out the corn, nor hindered from eating while he was preparing the corn for man's use, and treading it out of the ear. *Those who plough should plough in hope; and those who thresh in hope should be partakers of their hope, v.* 10. The law saith this about oxen for our sakes. 3. He argues from common equity: *If we have sown unto you spiritual things, is it a great thing if we shall reap your carnal things?* What they had sown was much better than they expected to reap. They had taught them the way to eternal life, and laboured heartily to put them in possession of it. It was no great matter, surely, while they were giving themselves up to this work, to expect a support of their own temporal life. 4. He argues from the maintenance they afforded others: "*If others are partakers of this power over you, are not we rather?* You allow others this maintenance, and confess their claim just; but who has so just a claim as I from the church of Corinth? Who has given greater evidence of the apostolical mission? Who has laboured so much for your good, or done like service among you?" 5. He argues from the old Jewish establishment: "*Do you not know that those who minister about holy things live of the things of the temple, and those who wait at the altar are partakers with the altar? v.* 13. And, if the Jewish priesthood was maintained out of the holy things that were then offered, shall not Christ's ministers have a maintenance out of their ministry? He asserts it to be the institution of Christ: "*Even so hath the Lord ordained that those who preach the gospel should live of the gospel* (v. 14), should have a right to a maintenance, though not bound to demand it, and insist upon it."

A PRIVILEGE WAIVED
(vv. 15–18)

Here he tells them that he had, notwithstanding, waived his privilege, and lays down his reason for doing it.

I. He tells them that he had neglected to claim his right in times past: *I have used none of these things*, v. 15. Nor did he write this to make his claim now. Though he here asserts his right, yet he does not claim his due; but denies himself for their sakes, and the gospel.

II. We have the reason assigned of his exercising this self-denial. He would not have his glorying made void: *It were better for him to die than that any man should make his glorying void*, v. 15. It was a singular pleasure to him to preach the gospel without making it burdensome; and he was resolved that among them he would not lose this satisfaction.

III. He shows that this self-denial was more honourable in itself, and yielded him much more content and comfort, than his preaching did: "*Though I preach the gospel, I have nothing whereof to glory; for necessity is laid upon me; yea, woe is unto me, if I preach not the gospel*, v. 16. It is my charge, my business;

it is the work for which I am constituted an apostle, *ch.* i. 17. This is a duty expressly bound upon me. It is not in any degree a matter of liberty. *Necessity is upon me.* I am false and unfaithful to my trust, I break a plain and express command, and *woe be to me, if I do not preach the gospel*." Note, It is a high attainment in religion to renounce our own rights for the good of others; this will entitle to a peculiar reward from God. For,

IV. The apostle here informs us that doing our duty with a willing mind will meet with a gracious recompence from God: *If I do this thing*, that is, either preach the gospel or take no maintenance, *willingly, I have a reward*. Indeed, it is willing service only that is capable of reward from God. It is not the bare doing of any duty, but the doing of it heartily (that is, willingly and cheerfully) that God has promised to reward.

V. The apostle sums up the argument, by laying before them the encouraging hope he had of a large recompence for his remarkable self-denial: *What is my reward then? v.* 18. What is it I expect a recompence from God for? *That when I preach the gospel I may make it without charge, that I abuse not my power in the gospel.*

ALL THINGS TO ALL MEN
(vv. 19–23)

The apostle takes occasion from what he had before discoursed to mention some other instances of his self-denial and parting with his liberty for the benefit of others.

I. He asserts his liberty (v. 19): *Though I be free from all men.* He was free-born, a citizen of Rome. He made himself a servant, that they might be made free.

II. He specifies some particulars wherein he made himself a servant to all. He accommodated himself to all sorts of people. 1. *To the Jews, and those under the law, he became a Jew,* and as under the law, to gain them. Though he looked on the ceremonial law as a yoke taken off by Christ, yet in many instances he submitted to it, that he might work upon the Jews, remove their prejudices, prevail with them to hear the gospel, and win them over to Christ. 2. *To those that are without the law as without law* that is, to the Gentiles, whether converted to the Christian faith or not. In innocent things he could comply with people's usages or humours for their advantage. He would reason with the philosophers in their own way. And, as to converted Gentiles, he behaved among them as one that was not under the bondage of the Jewish laws, but as one who was bound by the laws of Christ. 3. *To the weak he became as weak, that he might gain the weak, v.* 22. He was willing to make the best of them. He did not despise nor judge them, but became as one of them, forbore to use his liberty for their sake, and was careful to lay no stumbling-block in their way.

III. He assigns his reason for acting in this manner (*v.* 23): *This I do for the gospel's sake, and that I may be partaker thereof with you*; that is, for the honour of Christ, whose gospel is, and for the salvation of souls, for which it was designed.

THE CHRISTIAN RACE
(*vv.* 24–27)

In these verses the apostle hints at the great encouragement he had to act in this manner. He had a glorious prize, an incorruptible crown, in view. Upon this head he compares himself to the racers and combatants in the Isthmian games, an allusion well known to the Corinthians, because they were celebrated in their neighbourhood: "*Know you not that those who run in a race run all, but one obtaineth the prize? v.* 24. All run at your games, but only one gets the race and wins the crown." And here,

I. He excites them to their duty: "*So run that you may obtain.* It is quite otherwise in the Christian race than in your races; only one wins the prize in them. You may all run so as to obtain."

II. He directs them in their course, by setting more fully to view his own example, still carrying on the allusion. 1. Those that ran in their games were kept to a set diet: "*Every man that strives for the mastery is temperate in all things, v.* 23." They do not indulge themselves, but restrain themselves from the food they eat and so from the liberties they use on other occasions. 2. They were not only temperate, but inured themselves to hardships. Christians must fight, not as those that beat the air, but must strive against their enemies with all their might. One enemy the apostle here mentions, namely, the body; this must be kept under, beaten black and blue, as the combatants were in these Grecian games, and thereby brought into subjection. By the body we are to understand fleshly appetites and inclinations.

III. The apostle presses this advice on the Corinthians by proper arguments drawn from the same contenders. 1. They take pains, and undergo all those hardships, *to obtain a corruptible crown* (*v.* 25), *but we an incorruptible*. Those who conquered in these games were crowned only with the withering leaves or boughs of trees, of olive, bays, or laurel. But Christians have an incorruptible crown in view, a crown of glory that never fadeth away, an inheritance incorruptible, reserved in heaven for them. 2. The racers in these games run at uncertainty. All run, but one receives the prize, *v.* 24. Every racer, therefore, is at a great uncertainty whether he shall win it or no. But the Christian racer is at no such uncertainty. Every one may run here so as to obtain; but then he must run within the lines, he must keep to the path of duty prescribed, which, some think, is the meaning of *running not as uncertainly*, *v.* 26. He who keeps within the limits prescribed, and keeps on in his race, will never miss his crown, though others may get theirs before him. 3. He sets before himself and them the danger of yielding to fleshly inclinations, and pampering the body and its lusts and appetites: *I keep my body under, lest that by any means, when I have preached to others, I myself should be a castaway* (*v.* 27), *rejected, disapproved*. one to whom *the judge* or *umpire* of the race, will not decree the crown. The allusion to the games runs through the whole sentence.

CHAPTER TEN
WARNINGS (*vv.* 1–5)

In order to dissuade the Corinthians from communion with idolaters, and security in any sinful course, he sets before them the example of the Jews, the church under the Old Testament. They enjoyed great privileges, but, having been guilty of heinous provocations, they fell under very grievous punishments. In these verses he reckons up their privileges, which, in the main, were the same with ours.

I. He prefaces this discourse with a note of regard: "*Moreover, brethren, I would not that you should be ignorant*." I would not have you without the knowledge of this matter; it is a thing worthy both of your knowledge and attention.

II. He specifies some of their privileges. He begins, 1 With their deliverance from Egypt. They were very dear to God, and much in his favour, when he would work such miracles for their deliverance, and take them so immediately under his guidance and protection. 2. They had sacraments like ours. (1) *They were all baptized unto Moses in the cloud, and in the sea* (*v.* 2), or into Moses, that is, brought under obligation to Moses's law and covenant, as we are by baptism under the Christian law and covenant. It was to them a typical baptism. (2) *They did all eat of the same spiritual meat, and drink of the same spiritual drink*, that we do. The manna on which they fed was a type of Christ crucified, the bread which came down from heaven, which whoso eateth shall live for ever. Their drink was a stream fetched from a rock which followed them in all their journeyings in the wilderness; and this rock was Christ, that is, in type and figure. These were great privileges. One would think that this should have saved them; that all who ate of that spiritual meat and drank of that spiritual drink, should have been holy and acceptable to God. Yet was it otherwise: *With many of them God was not well pleased; for they were overthrown in the wilderness, v.* 5. Note, Men may enjoy many and great spiritual privileges in this world, and yet come short of eternal life.

TEMPTATIONS (*vv.* 6–14)

The apostle, having recited their privileges, proceeds here to an account of their faults and punishments, their sins and plagues, which are left upon record for an example to us, a warning against the like sins, if we would escape the like punishments. We must not do as they did, lest we suffer as they suffered.

I. Several of their sins are specified as cautions to us; as, 1. We should shun inordinate desires after carnal objects: *Not lust after evil things, as they lusted, v.* 6. God fed them with manna, but they must have flesh, Num. xi. 4. They had food for their supply, but, not content with this, they asked *meat for their lusts*, Ps. cvi. 14. Carnal desires get head by indulgence, and therefore should be observed and checked in their first rise. 2. He warns against idolatry (*v.* 7): *Neither be you idolaters, as were some of them; as it is written, The*

people sat down to eat and drink, and rose up to play. The sin of the golden calf is referred to, Exod. xxxii. 6. 3. He cautions against fornication, a sin to which the inhabitants of Corinth were in a peculiar manner addicted. 4. He warns us against *tempting Christ* (*as some of them tempted, and were destroyed of serpents, v.* 9), or provoking him to jealousy, *v.* 22. He was with the church in the wilderness; he was the angel of the covenant, who went before them. 5. He warns against murmuring: *Neither murmur you as some of them also murmured, and were destroyed of the destroyer* (*v.* 10), by a destroying angel, an executioner of divine vengeance. They quarrelled with God, and murmured against Moses his minister, when any difficulties pressed them.

II. The apostle subjoins to these particular cautions a more general one (*v.* 11): *All these things happened to them for ensamples, and were written for our admonition.* Not only the laws and ordinances of the Jews, but the providences of God towards them, were typical. Their sins against God, and backslidings from him, were typical of the infidelity of many under the gospel. God's judgments on them were types of spiritual judgments now. Upon this hint the apostle grounds a caution (*v.* 12): *Let him that thinketh he standeth take heed lest he fall.* Note, The harms sustained by others should be cautions to us.

III. But to this word of caution he adds a word of comfort, *v.* 13. Though it is displeasing to God for us to presume, it is not pleasing to him for us to despair. For, 1.

"*No temptation,*" says the apostle, "*hath yet taken you, but such as is common to man.*" Note, The trials of common Christians are but common trials: others have the like burdens and the like temptations; what they bear up under, and break through, we may also. 2. *God is faithful.* Though Satan be a deceiver, God is true. Men may be false, and the world may be false; but God is faithful, and our strength and security are in him. 3. He is wise as well as faithful, and will proportion our burden to our strength. *He will not suffer us to be tempted above what we are able.* He knows what we can bear, and what we can bear up against; and he will, in his wise providence, either proportion our temptations to our strength or make us able to grapple with them.

IV. And upon this argument he grounds another caution against idolatry: *Wherefore, my dearly beloved, flee from idolatry.* Note, We have all the encouragement in the world to flee sin and prove faithful to God. We cannot fall by a temptation if we cleave fast to him.

RULES FOR COMMUNION
(vv. 15–22)

In this passage the apostle urges the general caution against idolatry, in the particular case of eating the heathen sacrifices as such, and out of any religious respect to the idol to whom they were sacrificed.

I. He prefaces his argument with an appeal to their own reason and judgment: "*I speak to wise men, judge you what I say, v.* 15. You are great pretenders to wis-

dom, to close reasoning and argument; I can leave it with your own reason and conscience whether I do not argue justly."

II. He lays down his argument from the Lord's supper: *The cup which we bless, is it not the communion of the blood of Christ? The bread which we break, is it not the communion of the body of Christ?* Is not this sacred rite an instrument of communion with God? Do we not therein profess to be in friendship, and to have fellowship, with him? Is it not a token whereby we professedly hold communion with Christ, whose body was broken, and blood shed, to procure remission of our sins, and the favour of God? And can we be in alliance with Christ, or friendship with God, without being devoted to him? In short, the Lord's supper is a feast on the sacrificed body and blood of our Lord. And to eat of the feast is to partake of the sacrifice, and so to be his guests to whom the sacrifice was offered, and this in token of friendship with him. *Because the bread is one, we, being many, are one body, for we are made partakers of one bread,* or loaf (*v.* 17), which I think is thus more truly rendered: "By partaking of one broken loaf, the emblem of our Saviour's broken body, who is the only true bread that came down from heaven, we coalesce into one body, become members of him and one another." Those who truly partake by faith have this communion with Christ, and one another; and those who eat the outward elements make profession of having this communion, of belonging to God and the blessed fraternity of his people and worshippers. This is the true meaning of this holy rite.

III. He confirms this from the Jewish worship and customs: *Behold Israel after the flesh: are not those who eat of the sacrifices partakers of the altar*, that is, of the sacrifice offered upon it? Those who were admitted to eat of the offerings were reckoned to partake of the sacrifice itself, as made for them, and to be sanctified thereby; and therefore surely to worship God, and be in alliance or covenant with him, even the God of Israel, to whom the sacrifice was made: this was a symbol or token of holding communion with him.

IV. He applies this to the argument against feasting with idolaters on their sacrifices, and to prove those that do so idolaters. This he does, 1. By following the principle on which they would argue it to be lawful, namely, that an idol was nothing. Many of them were nothing at all, none of them had any divinity in them. Now the apostle allows that the food was not changed as to its nature, was as fit to be eaten as common food, where it was set before any who knew not of its having been offered to an idol. But, 2. He proves that the eating of it as a part of a heathen sacrifice was, (1) A partaking with them in their idolatry. *It was having fellowship with devils*, because what the Gentiles sacrificed they sacrificed to devils. (2) It was a virtual renouncing of Christianity: *You cannot drink the cup of the Lord, and the cup of devils: you cannot be partakers of the Lord's table, and the table of devils, v.* 21.

To partake of this Christian feast was to have communion with Christ: to partake of the feasts made in honour of the heathen idols, and made of things sacrificed to them, was to have communion with devils. Now this was to compound contraries; it was by no means consistent.

V. He warns them, upon the whole, against such idolatry, by signifying to them that God is a jealous God (*v.* 22): *Do we provoke the Lord to jealousy? Are we stronger than he?* It is very probable that many among the Corinthians made light of being at these heathen feasts, and thought there was no harm in it. But the apostle bids them beware.

LAW AND CONSCIENCE
(*vv.* 23–33)

In this passage the apostle shows in what instances, notwithstanding, Christians might lawfully eat what had been sacrificed to idols. But,

I. He gives a caution against abusing our liberty in lawful things. That may be lawful which is not expedient, which will not edify.

II. He tells them that what was *sold in the shambles they might eat without asking questions.* The priest's share of heathen sacrifices was thus frequently offered for sale, after it had been offered in the temple. Now the apostle tells them they need not be so scrupulous as to ask the butcher in the market whether the meat he sold had been offered to an idol? It was there sold as common food, and as such might be bought and used; *for the earth is the Lord's, and the fulness thereof* (*v.* 26), and the fruit and products of the earth were designed by him, the great proprietor, for the use and subsistence of mankind, and more especially of his own children and servants.

III. He adds that if they were invited by any heathen acquaintances to a feast, *they might go, and eat what was set before them, without asking questions* (*v.* 27), *nay, though* they knew things sacrificed to idols were served up at such entertainments, as well as sold in the shambles. Note, The apostle does not prohibit their going to a feast upon the invitation of those that believed not. There is a civility owing even to infidels and heathens. Christianity does by no means bind us up from the common offices of humanity, nor allow us an uncourteous behaviour to any of our own kind, however they may differ from us in religious sentiments or practices. And when Christians were invited to feast with infidels they were not to ask needless questions about the food set before them, but eat without scruple.

IV. Yet, even at such an entertainment, he adds, if any should say it was a thing that had been offered to idols, they should refrain: *Eat not, for his sake that showed it, and for conscience' sake.* Whether it were the master of the feast or any of the guests, whether it were spoken in the hearing of all or whispered in the ear, they should refrain for his sake who suggested this to them, whether he were an infidel or an infirm Christian; and for conscience' sake, out of regard to conscience, that they might show a regard to it in themselves, and keep up a regard to it in others.

V. He urges them to refrain where they will give offence, while yet he allows it lawful to eat what was set before them as common food, though it had been offered in sacrifice.

VI. The apostle takes occasion from this discourse to lay down a general rule for Christians' conduct, and apply it to this particular case (*vv.* 31, 32), namely, that in eating and drinking, and in all we do, we should aim at the glory of God, at pleasing and honouring him. This is the fundamental principle of practical godliness. Our own humour and appetite must not determine our practice, but the honour of God and the good and edification of the church. We should not so much consult our own pleasure and interest as the advancement of the kingdom of God among men.

VII. He presses all upon them by his own example: *Even as I please all men* (or study to do it) *in all things* (that I lawfully can), *not seeking my own profit, but that of many, that they may be saved, v.* 33.

CHAPTER ELEVEN

REDRESS OF GRIEVANCES
(*vv.* 1–16)

Paul, having answered the cases put to him, proceeds in this chapter to the redress of grievances. He reprehends and reforms an indecency among them, of which the women were more especially guilty, concerning which observe,

I. How he prefaces it. He begins

with a commendation of what was praiseworthy in them (*v.* 2): *I praise you, that you remember me in all things, and keep the ordinances as I delivered them to you.*

II. How he lays the foundation for his reprehension by asserting the superiority of the man over the woman: *I would have you know that the head of every man is Christ, and the head of the woman is the man, and the head of Christ is God.* Christ, in his mediatorial character and glorified humanity, is at the head of mankind. And as God is the head of Christ, and Christ the head of the whole human kind, so the man is the head of the two sexes: not indeed with such dominion as Christ has over the kind or God has over the man Christ Jesus; but a superiority and headship he has, and the woman should be in subjection and not assume or usurp the man's place. This is the situation in which God has placed her; and for that reason she should have a mind suited to her rank, and not do any thing that looks like an affectation of changing places. Something like this the women of the church of Corinth seem to have been guilty of, who were under inspiration, and prayed and prophesied even in their assemblies, *v.* 5. It is indeed an apostolical canon, that the women *should keep silence in the churches* (*ch.* xiv. 34; 1 Tim. ii. 12), which some understand without limitation, as if a woman under inspiration also must keep silence, which seems very well to agree with the connection of the apostle's discourse, *ch.* xiv. Others with a limitation: though a woman might not

from her own abilities pretend to teach, or so much as question and debate any thing in the church, yet when under inspiration the case was altered, she had liberty to speak. Or, though she might not preach even by inspiration (because teaching is the business of a superior), yet she might pray or utter hymns by inspiration, even in the public assembly. She did not show any affectation of superiority over the man by such acts of public worship. It is plain the apostle does not in this place prohibit the thing, but reprehend the manner of doing it.

III. The thing he reprehends is the woman's praying or prophesying uncovered, or the man's doing either covered *vv.* 4, 5. To understand this, it must be observed that it was a signification either of shame or subjection for persons to be veiled, or covered, in the eastern countries, contrary to the custom of ours, where the being bareheaded betokens subjection, and being covered superiority and dominion. And this will help us the better to understand,

IV. The reasons on which he grounds his reprehension. *The man that prays or prophesies with his head covered dishonoureth his head,* namely, Christ, the head of every man (*v.* 3), by appearing in a habit unsuitable to the rank in which God has placed him. *The woman,* on the other hand, *who prays or prophesies with her head uncovered dishonoureth her head,* namely, the man, *v.* 3. She appears in the dress of her superior, and throws off the token of her subjection. It was doing a thing which, in that age of the world, betokened superiority, and therefore a tacit claim of what did not belong to them but the other sex. Note, The sexes should not affect to change places.

V. He thinks fit to guard his argument with a caution lest the inference be carried too far (*vv.* 11, 12): *Nevertheless, neither is the man without the woman, nor the woman without the man in the Lord.* They were made for one another. *It is not good for him to be alone* (Gen. ii. 18), and therefore was a woman made, and made for the man; and the man was intended to be a comfort, and help, and defence, to the woman, though not so directly and immediately made for her. They were made to be a mutual comfort and blessing, not one a slave and the other a tyrant.

VI. He sums up all by referring those who were contentious to the usages and customs of the churches, *v.* 16. Custom is in a great measure the rule of decency. And the common practice of the churches is what he would have them govern themselves by.

REVERENCE AT WORSHIP
(*vv.* 17–22)

In this passage the apostle sharply rebukes them for much greater disorders than the former, in their partaking of the Lord's supper, which was commonly done in the first ages, as the ancients tell us, with a love-feast annexed, which gave occasion to the scandalous disorders which the apostle here reprehends, concerning which observe,

I. The manner in which he introduces his charge: "*Now in this that*

I declare to you I praise you not, v. 17." I cannot commend, but must blame and condemn you.

II. He enters upon his charge against them in more particulars than one. 1. He tells them that, upon coming together, they fell into *divisions, schisms.* 2. He charges them not only with discord and division, but with scandalous disorder: *For in eating every one taketh before the other his own supper; and one is hungry, and another is drunken, v.* 21. Heathens used to drink plentifully at their feasts upon their sacrifices. Many of the wealthier Corinthians seem to have taken the same liberty at the Lord's table, or at least at their *love-feasts,* that were annexed to the supper. They would not stay for one another; the rich despised the poor, and ate and drank up the provisions they themselves brought, before the poor were allowed to partake; and thus some wanted, while others had more than enough. This was profaning a sacred institution, and corrupting a divine ordinance, to the last degree.

III. The apostle lays the blame of this conduct closely on them, 1. By telling them that their conduct perfectly destroyed the purpose and use of such an institution: *This is not to eat the Lord's supper, v.* 20. Thus to eat the outward elements was not to eat Christ's body. 2. Their conduct carried in it a contempt of God's house, or of the church, *v.* 22. If they had a mind to feast, they might do it at home in their own houses; but to come to the Lord's table, and quarrel, and keep the poor from their share of the provision there made for them as well as the rich, was such an abuse of the ordinance, and such a contempt of the poorer members of the church more especially, as merited a very sharp rebuke.

THE PURPOSE OF THE LORD'S SUPPER
(*vv.* 23–34)

To rectify these gross corruptions and irregularities, the apostle sets the sacred institution here to view. This should be the rule in the reformation of all abuses.

I. He tells us how he came by the knowledge of it. He was not among the apostles at the first institution; but *he had received from the Lord what he delivered to them, v.* 23. He had the knowledge of this matter by revelation from Christ: and what he had received he communicated, without varying from the truth a tittle, without adding or diminishing.

II. He gives us a more particular account of the institution than we meet with elsewhere. We have here an account,

1. Of the author—our Lord Jesus Christ. The king of the church only has power to institute sacraments.

2. The time of the institution: *It was the very night wherein he was betrayed*; just as he was entering on his sufferings which are therein to be commemorated.

3. The institution itself. Our Saviour took bread, and when he had given thanks, or *blessed* (as it is in Matt. xxvi. 26), *he broke, and said, Take, eat; this is my body, broken for you; this do in remembrance of me. And in like manner he took the cup, when he had supped,* saying, *This cup is the New Testament in my blood; this do, as oft as you drink it, in remembrance of me, vv.* 24, 25. Here observe,

(1) The materials of this sacrament; both, [1] As to the visible signs: these are bread and the cup. [2] The things signified by these outward signs: they are Christ's body and blood, his body broken, his blood shed, together with all the benefits which flow from his death and sacrifice: *it is the New Testament in his blood.*

(2) We have here the sacramental actions, the manner in which the materials of the sacrament are to be used. [1] Our Saviour's actions, which are taking the bread and cup, giving thanks, breaking the bread, and giving about both the one and the other. [2] The actions of the communicants, which were to take the bread and eat, to take the cup and drink, and both in remembrance of Christ.

(3) We have here an account of the ends of this institution. [1] It was appointed to be done *in remembrance of Christ*, to keep fresh in our minds an ancient favour, his dying for us, as well as to remember an absent friend, even Christ interceding for us, in virtue of his death, at God's right hand. [2] It was *to show forth Christ's death*, to declare and publish it. It is not barely in remembrance of Christ, of what he has done and suffered, that this ordinance was instituted; but to commemorate, to celebrate, his glorious condescension and grace in our redemption. We set it in view of our own faith, for our own comfort and quickening: and we own before the world, by this very

service, that we are the disciples of Christ, who trust in him alone for salvation and acceptance with God.

(4) It is moreover hinted here, concerning this ordinance, [1] That it should be frequent: *As often as you eat this bread*, &c. [2] That it must be perpetual. It is to be celebrated *till the Lord shall come*; till he shall come the second time, without sin, for the salvation of those that believe, and to judge the world.

III. He lays before the Corinthians the danger of receiving unworthily, of prostituting this institution as they did, and using it to the purposes of feasting and faction. 1. It is great guilt which such contract. They shall *be guilty of the body and blood of the Lord* (*v.* 27), of violating this sacred institution, of despising his body and blood. 2. It is a great hazard which they run: *They eat and drink judgment to themselves*, *v.* 29. They provoke God, and are likely to bring down punishment on themselves. The Corinthians came to the Lord's table as to a common feast, *not discerning the Lord's body*—not making a difference or distinction between that and common food, but setting both on a level.

IV. He points out the duty of those who would come to the Lord's table. 1. In general: *Let a man examine himself* (*v.* 28), try and approve himself. Let him consider the sacred intention of this holy ordinance, its nature, and use, and compare his own views in attending on it and his disposition of mind for it; and, when he has approved himself to his own conscience in the

sight of God, then let him attend. 2. The duty of those who were yet unpunished for their profanation of this ordinance: *If we would judge ourselves, we should not be judged*, *v.* 31. If we would thoroughly search and explore ourselves, and condemn and correct what we find amiss, we should prevent divine judgments.

V. He closes all with a caution against the irregularities of which they were guilty (*vv.* 33, 34), charging them to avoid all indecency at the Lord's table. Holy things are to be used in a holy manner, or else they are profaned. What else was amiss in this matter, he tells them, he would rectify when he came to them.

CHAPTER TWELVE

SPIRITUAL GIFTS (*vv.* 1–11)

The apostle comes now to treat of spiritual gifts, which abounded in the church of Corinth, but were greatly abused.

I. The apostle tells them he would not have them ignorant either of their original or use.

II. He puts them in mind of the sad state out of which they had been recovered: *You were Gentiles, carried away to dumb idols, even as you were led*, *v.* 2. While they were so, they could have no pretensions to be spiritual men, nor to have spiritual gifts. If they well understood their former condition, they could not but know that all true spiritual gifts were from God. Now concerning this observe, 1. Their former character: they *were Gentiles*. Not God's peculiar people, but of the nations whom he had in a manner abandoned. 2. The conduct they were under: *Carried away to these dumb idols, even as you were led.* They were hurried upon the grossest idolatry, the worship even of stocks and stones, through the force of a vain imagination, and the fraud of their priests practising on their ignorance, for, whatever were the sentiments of their philosophers, this was the practice of the herd.

III. He shows them how they might discern those gifts that were from the Spirit of God, true spiritual gifts: *No man, speaking by the Spirit, calls Jesus accursed.* Now the apostle tells them none could act under the influence, nor by the power, of the Spirit of God, who disowned and blasphemed Christ: for the Spirit of God bore uncontrollable witness to Christ by prophecy, miracles, his resurrection from the dead, the success of his doctrine among men, and its effect upon them; and could never so far contradict itself as to declare him accursed. And on the other hand *no man could say Jesus was the Lord* (that is, live by this faith, and work miracles to prove it), *but it must be by the Holy Ghost.* To own this truth before men, and maintain it to the death, and live under the influence of it, could not be done without the sanctification of the Holy Ghost. He adds,

IV. These spiritual gifts, though proceeding from the same Spirit, are yet various. They have one author and original, but are themselves of various kinds. A free cause may produce variety of effects; and the same giver may bestow various

gifts, *v.* 4. However different they may be in themselves, in this they agree; all are from God. And several of the kinds are here specified, *vv.* 8–10. Different persons had their distinct gifts, some one, some another, all from and by the same Spirit. To one was given the *word of wisdom*; that is, say some, a knowledge of the mysteries of the gospel, and ability to explain them, an exact understanding of the design, nature, and doctrines, of the Christian religion. Some confine this word of wisdom to the revelations made to and by the apostles.—*To another the word of knowledge, by the same Spirit*; that is, say some, the knowledge of mysteries (*ch.* ii. 13): wrapped up in the prophecies, types, and histories of the Old Testament: say others, a skill and readiness to give advice and counsel in perplexed cases.—*To another faith, by the same Spirit*; that is, the faith of miracles, or a faith in the divine power and promise, whereby they were enabled to work miracles; or an extraordinary impulse from above, whereby they were enabled to trust God in any emergency, and go on in the way of their duty, and own and profess the truths of Christ, whatever was the difficulty or danger.—*To another the gift of healing, by the same Spirit*; that is, healing the sick, either by laying on of hands, or anointing with oil, or with a bare word.—*To another the working of miracles*; the efficacies of powers, such as raising the dead, restoring the blind to sight, giving speech to the dumb, hearing to the deaf, and the use of limbs to the lame.—*To another prophecy*, that is, ability to foretell future events, which is the more usual sense of prophecy; or to explain scripture by a peculiar gift of the Spirit. See *ch.* xiv. 24.—*To another the discerning of Spirits*, power to distinguish between true and false prophets, or to discern the real and internal qualifications of any person for an office, or to discover the inward workings of the mind by the Holy Ghost, as Peter did those of Ananias, Acts v. 3.—*To another divers kinds of tongues*, or ability to speak languages by inspiration.— *To another the interpretation of tongues*, or ability to render foreign languages readily and properly into their own. With such variety of spiritual gifts were the first ministers and churches blessed.

V. The end for which these gifts were bestowed: *The manifestation of the Spirit is given to every man to profit withal, v.* 7. The Spirit was manifested by the exercise of these gifts; his influence and interest appeared in them. But they were not distributed for the mere honour and advantage of those who had them, but for the benefit of the church, to edify the body, and spread and advance the gospel.

VI. The measure and proportion in which they are given: *All these worketh one and the same Spirit, dividing to every man as he will.* It is according to the sovereign pleasure of the donor. What more free than a gift? And shall not the Spirit of God do what he will with his own?

THE UNITY OF THE BODY
(*vv.* 12–26)

The apostle here makes out the truth of what was above asserted,

and puts the gifted men among the Corinthians in mind of their duty, by comparing the church of Christ to a human body.

I. By telling us that one body may have many members, and that the many members of the same body make but one body (*v.* 12): *As the body is one, and hath many members, and all the members of that one body, being many, are one body, so also is Christ*; that is, Christ mystical, as divines commonly speak. Christ and his church making one body, as head and members, this body is made up of many parts or members, yet but one body; for all the members are *baptized into the same body, and made to drink of the same Spirit, v.* 13.

II. Each member has its particular form, place, and use. 1. The meanest member makes a part of the body. The foot and ear are less useful, perhaps, than the hand and eye; but because one is not a hand, and the other an eye, shall they say, therefore, that they do not belong to the body? *vv.* 15, 16. So every member of the body mystical cannot have the same place and office; but what then? 2. There must be a distinction of members in the body: *Were the whole body eye, where were the hearing? Were the whole ear, where were the smelling? v.* 17. *If all were one member, where were the body? v.* 19. *They are many members,* and for that reason must have distinction among them, *and yet are but one body, v.* 20. Variety in the members of the body contributes to the beauty of it. So it is for the beauty and good appearance of the church that there should be diversity of gifts and offices in it. 3. The disposal of members in a natural body, and their situation, are as God pleases: *But now hath God set the members, every one of them, in the body, as it hath pleased him*, v. 18. We may plainly perceive the divine wisdom in the distribution of the members; but it was made according to the counsel of his will; he distinguished and distributed them as he pleased. So is it also in the members of Christ's body: they are chosen out to such stations, and endued with such gifts, as God pleases. 4. All the members of the body are, in some respect, useful and necessary to each other: (vv. 21, 22); God has so fitted and tempered them together that they are all necessary to one another, and to the whole body; there is no part redundant and unnecessary. None should despise and envy another, seeing God has made the distinction between them as he pleased, yet so as to keep them all in some degree of mutual dependence, and make them valuable to each other, and concerned for each other, because of their mutual usefulness. 5. Such is the man's concern for his whole body that *on the less honourable members more abundant honour is bestowed, and our uncomely parts have more abundant comeliness.* Those parts which are not fit, like the rest, to be exposed to view, which are either deformed or shameful, we most carefully clothe and cover; whereas the comely parts have no such need. So should the members of Christ's body behave towards their fellow-members: instead of despising them, or

reproaching them, for their infirmities, they should endeavour to cover and conceal them, and put the best face upon them that they can. 6. Divine wisdom has contrived and ordered things in this manner that the members of the body should not be schismatics, divided from each other and acting upon separate interests, but well affected to each other, tenderly concerned for each other, having a fellow-feeling of each other's griefs and a communion in each other's pleasures and joys, vv. 25, 26.

VARIETY IN THE BODY
(vv. 27–31)

I. Here the apostle sums up the argument, and applies this similitude to the church of Christ, concerning which observe,

1. The relation wherein Christians stand to Christ and one another. The church, or whole collective body of Christians, in all ages, is his body. Every Christian is a member of his body, and every other Christian stands related to him as a fellow-member (v. 27): *Now you are the body of Christ, and members in particular*, or particular members.

2. The variety of offices instituted by Christ, and gifts or favours dispensed by him (v. 28). Concerning all these observe, (1) The plenteous variety of these gifts and offices. What a multitude are they! A good God was free in his communications to the primitive church; he was no niggard of his benefits and favours. (2) Observe the order of these offices and gifts. They are here placed in their proper ranks.

Those of most value have the first place. What holds the last and lowest rank in this enumeration is diversity of tongues. It is by itself the most useless and insignificant of all these gifts. Healing diseases, relieving the poor, helping the sick, have their use: but how vain a thing is it to speak languages, if a man does it merely to amuse or boast himself! This may indeed raise the admiration, but cannot promote the edification, of the hearers, nor do them any good. And yet it is manifest from *ch.* xiv. that the Corinthians valued themselves exceedingly on this gift. (3) The various distribution of these gifts, not all to one, nor to every one alike. All members and officers had not the same rank in the church, nor the same endowments (*vv.* 29, 30). We must be content with our own rank and share, if they be lower and less than those of others. We must not be conceited of ourselves, and despise others, if we are in the higher rank and have greater gifts.

II. He closes this chapter with an advice (as the generality read it) and a hint. 1. An advice to covet the best gifts, either the most valuable in themselves or the most serviceable to others; and these are, in truth, most valuable in themselves, though men may be apt to esteem those most that will raise their fame and esteem highest. 2. By giving them the hint of a more excellent way, namely, of charity, of mutual love and good-will. This was the only right way to quiet and cement them, and make their gifts turn to the advantage and edification of the church.

CHAPTER THIRTEEN
THE VALUE OF LOVE
(*vv.* 1–3)

Here the apostle shows what more excellent way he meant, or had in view, in the close of the former chapter, namely, *charity*, or, as it is commonly elsewhere rendered, *love*. Without this the most glorious gifts are nothing, of no account to us, of no esteem in the sight of God. He specifies, 1. The gift of tongues. Could a man speak all the languages on earth, and that with the greatest propriety, elegance, and fluency, could he talk like an angel, and yet be without charity, it would be all empty noise, mere unharmonious and useless sound, that would neither profit nor delight. 2. Prophecy, and the understanding of mysteries, and all knowledge. This without charity is as nothing, *v.* 2. It is not great knowledge that God sets a value upon, but true and hearty devotion and love. 3. Miraculous faith, the faith of miracles, or the faith by which persons were enabled to work miracles. The most wonder-working faith, to which nothing is in a manner impossible, is itself nothing without charity. 4. The outward acts of charity: *Bestowing his goods to feed the poor, v.* 3. Should all a man has be laid out in this manner, if he had no charity, it would profit him nothing. Our doing good to others will do none to us, if it be not well done, namely, from a principle of devotion and charity, love to God, and good-will to men. 5. Even sufferings, and even those of the most grievous kind: *If we give our bodies to be burnt, without charity, it profiteth nothing, v.* 3. Should we sacrifice our lives for the faith of the gospel, and be burnt to death in maintenance of its truth, this will stand us in no stead without charity, unless we be animated to these sufferings by a principle of true devotion to God, and sincere love to his church and people, and good-will to mankind.

THE QUALITY OF LOVE
(*vv.* 4–7)

The apostle gives us in these verses some of the properties and effects of charity. As,

I. *It is long suffering.* It can endure evil, and injury, and provocation, without being filled with resentment, indignation, or revenge.

II. *It is kind.* It is benign, bountiful; it is courteous and obliging. *The law of kindness is in her lips;* her heart is large, and her hand open. She is ready to show favours and to do good.

III. Charity suppresses envy: *It envieth not*; it is not grieved at the good of others; neither at their gifts nor at their good qualities, their honours nor their estates. If we love our neighbour we shall be so far from envying his welfare, or being displeased with it, that we shall share in it and rejoice at it.

IV. Charity subdues pride and vain-glory: *It vaunteth not itself, is not puffed up*, is not bloated with self-conceit, does not swell upon its acquisitions, nor arrogate to itself that honour, or power, or respect, which does not belong to it.

V. Charity is careful not to pass the bounds of decency; *it behaveth not unseemly*; it does nothing indecorous, nothing that in the common account of men is base or vile.

VI. Charity is an utter enemy to selfishness: *Seeketh not its own*, does not inordinately desire nor seek its own praise, or honour, or profit, or pleasure. It often neglects its own for the sake of others; prefers their welfare, and satisfaction, and advantage, to its own.

VII. It tempers and restrains the passions, *is not exasperated.* It corrects a sharpness of temper, sweetens and softens the mind, so that it does not suddenly conceive, nor long continue, a vehement passion.

VIII. Charity *thinks no evil.* It cherishes no malice, nor gives way to revenge; so some understand it. It does not suspect evil of others, *it does not reason out* evil, charge guilt upon them by inference and *innuendo*, when nothing of this sort appears open.

IX. The matter of its joy and pleasure is here suggested: 1. Negatively: *It rejoiceth not in iniquity.* It takes no pleasure in doing injury or hurt to any. 2. Affirmatively: *It rejoiceth in the truth*, is glad of the success of the gospel, commonly called *the truth*, by way of emphasis, in the New Testament; and rejoices to see men moulded into an evangelical temper by it, and made good.

X. *It beareth all things, it endureth all things.* Some read the first, *covers all things.* So the original also signifies. *Charity will cover a multitude of sins*, 1 Pet. iv. 8. It will draw a veil over them, as far as it can consistently with duty· Or, it *beareth all things*, — will pass by and put up with injuries, without indulging anger or cherishing revenge, will be patient upon provocation, and long patient, holds firm, though it be much shocked, and borne hard upon; sustains all manner of injury and ill usage, and bears up under it.

XI. Charity believes and hopes well of others: *Believeth all things; hopeth all things.* Indeed charity does by no means destroy prudence, and, out of mere simplicity and silliness, believe every word, Prov. xiv. 15. Wisdom may dwell with love, and charity be cautious. But it is apt to believe well of all, to entertain a good opinion of them when there is no appearance to the contrary; nay, to believe well when there may be some dark appearances, if the evidence of ill be not clear.

LOVE NEVER ENDS (*vv.* 8–13)

Here the apostle goes on to commend charity, and show how much it is preferable to the gifts on which the Corinthians were so apt to pride themselves, to the utter neglect, and almost extinction, of charity. This he makes out,

I. From its longer continuance and duration: *Charity never faileth.* It is a permanent and perpetual grace, lasting as eternity; whereas the extraordinary gifts on which the Corinthians valued themselves were of short continuance. *Prophecy must fail*, that is, either the prediction of things to come (which is its most common sense) or the interpretation of scripture by immediate inspiration. *Tongues will cease*, that is, the miraculous power of speaking languages without learning them. There will be but one langu-

age in heaven. There is no confusion of tongues in the region of perfect tranquillity. And *knowledge will vanish away.* Not that, in the perfect state above, holy and happy souls shall be unknowing, ignorant: it is a very poor happiness that can consist with utter ignorance. The apostle is plainly speaking of miraculous gifts, and therefore of knowledge to be had out of the common way (see *ch.* xiv. 6), a knowledge of mysteries supernaturally communicated. Such knowledge was to vanish away.

II. He hints that these gifts are adapted only to a state of imperfection: *We know in part, and we prophesy in part, v.* 9. Our best knowledge and our greatest abilities are at present like our condition, narrow and temporary.

III. He takes occasion hence to show how much better it will be with the church hereafter than it can be here. A state of perfection is in view (*v.* 10): *When that which is perfect shall come, then that which is in part shall be done away.* When the end is once attained, the means will of course be abolished. There will be no need of tongues, and prophecy, and inspired knowledge, in a future life, because then the church will be in a state of perfection, complete both in knowledge and holiness. The difference between these two states is here pointed at in two particulars: 1. The present state is a state of childhood, the future that of manhood: *When I was a child, I spoke as a child* (that is, as some think, spoke with tongues), *I understood as a child; I thought*, or reasoned, *as a child; but, when I became a man, I put away childish things.* Such is the difference between earth and heaven. 2. Things are all dark and confused now, in comparison of what they will be hereafter: *Now we see through a glass darkly (in a riddle), then face to face; now we know in part, but then we shall know as we are known.* God is to be seen *face to face*; and we *are to know him* as *we are known by him*; not indeed as perfectly, but in some sense in the same manner.

IV. To sum up the excellences of charity, he prefers it not only to gifts, but to other graces, to faith and hope (*v.* 13): *And now abide faith, hope, and charity; but the greatest of these is charity.* True grace is much more excellent than any spiritual gifts whatever. And faith, hope, and love, are the three principal graces, of which charity is the chief, being the end to which the other two are but means. When faith and hope are at an end, true charity will burn for ever with the brightest flame.

CHAPTER FOURTEEN
SPEAKING IN TONGUES
(*vv.* 1–5)

The apostle, in the foregoing chapter, had himself preferred, and advised the Corinthians to prefer, Christian charity to all spiritual gifts. Here he teaches them, among spiritual gifts, which they should prefer, and by what rules they should make comparison. He begins the chapter,

I. With an exhortation to charity (*v.* 1): *Follow after charity,* pursue it. It is an exhortation to obtain charity, to get this excellent disposition of mind upon any terms, whatever pains or prayers it may cost.

II. He directs them with spiritual gift to prefer, from a principle of charity: "*Desire spiritual gifts, but rather that you may prophesy,* or chiefly that you may prophesy." Note, Gifts are fit objects of our desire and pursuit, in subordination to grace and charity. That should be sought first and with the greatest earnestness which is most worth.

III. He assigns the reasons of this preference. And it is remarkable here that he only compares prophesying with speaking with tongues. It seems, this was the gift on which the Corinthians principally valued themselves. This was more ostentatious than the plain interpretation of scripture, more fit to gratify pride, but less fit to pursue the purposes of Christian charity; it would not equally edify nor do good to the souls of men. For, 1. He that spoke with tongues must wholly speak between God and himself; for, whatever mysteries might be communicated in his language, none of his own countrymen could understand them, because they did not understand the language, *v.* 2. 2. He that speaks with tongues may edify himself, *v.* 4. He may understand and be affected with what he speaks; and so every minister should; and he that is most edified himself is in the disposition and fitness to do good to others by what he speaks; but he that speaks with tongues, or language unknown, can only edify himself; others can reap no benefit from his speech. 3. Indeed, no gift is to be despised, but the best gifts are to be preferred. *I could wish*, says the apostle, *that you all spoke with tongues, but rather that you prophesied*, v. 5. Every gift of God is a favour from God, and may be improved for his glory, and as such is to be valued and thankfully received; but then those are to be most valued that are most useful. *Greater is he that prophesieth than he that speaketh with tongues, unless he interpret, that the church may receive edifying*, v. 5. Greater is he who interprets scripture to edify the church than he who speaks tongues to recommend himself. And what other end he who spoke with tongues could have, unless he interpreted what he spoke, is not easy to say.

THE NECESSITY OF INTERPRETATION (vv. 6–14)

An apostle, with all his furniture, could not edify, unless he spoke to the capacity of his hearers.

I. He illustrates this by several allusions. 1. To a pipe and a harp playing always in one tone. Of what use can this be to those who are dancing? If there be no distinction of sounds, how should they order their steps or motions? Unintelligible language is like piping or harping without distinction of sounds. 2. To a trumpet giving an *uncertain sound*, a sound not manifest; either not the proper sound for the purpose, or not distinct enough to be discerned from every other sound. 3. He compares the speaking in an unknown tongue to the gibberish of barbarians. There are, as he says (v. 10), many kinds of voices in the world, none of

which is without its proper signification. But whatever proper signification the words of any language may have in themselves, and to those who understand them, they are perfect gibberish to men of another language, who understand them not. In this case, speaker and hearers are barbarians to each other (v. 11), they talk and hear only sounds without sense. To speak in the church in an unknown tongue is to talk gibberish; it is to play the barbarian; it is to confound the audience, instead of instructing them; and for this reason is utterly vain and unprofitable.

II. Having thus established his point, in the two next verses he applies it, 1. By advising them to be chiefly desirous of those gifts that were most for the church's edification, v. 12. This is the great rule he gives, which, 2. He applies to the matter in hand, that, if they did speak a foreign language, they should beg of God the gift of interpreting it, v. 13. That these were different gifts, see *ch*. xii. 10. 3. He enforces this advice with a proper reason, that, if *he prayed in an unknown tongue, his spirit might pray*, that is, a spiritual gift might be exercised in prayer, or his own mind might be devoutly engaged, *but his understanding would be unfruitful* (v. 14), that is, the sense and meaning of his words would be unfruitful, he would not be understood, nor therefore would others join with him in his devotions.

PRAYING WITH UNDERSTANDING (vv. 15–20)

The apostle here sums up the argument hitherto, and,

I. Directs them how they should sing and pray in public (*v.* 15): *What is it then? I will pray with the spirit, and I will pray with the understanding also. I will sing with the spirit*, &c. He does not forbid their praying or singing under a divine *afflatus*, or when they were inspired for this purpose, or had such a spiritual gift communicated to them; but he would have them perform both so as to be understood by others, that others might join with them.

II. He enforces the argument with several reasons.

1. That otherwise the unlearned could not say Amen to their prayers or thanksgivings, could not join in the worship, for they did not understand it, *v.* 16.

2. He alleges his own example, to make the greater impression, concerning which observe, (1) That he did not come behind any of them in this spiritual gift: "*I thank my God, I speak with tongues more than you all* (*v.* 18); not only more than any single person among you, but more than all together." Yet, (2) He had rather *speak five words with understanding*, that is, so as to be understood, and instruct and edify others, *than ten thousand words in an unknown tongue*, *v.* 19.

3. He adds a plain intimation that the fondness then discovered for this gift was but too plain an indication of the immaturity of their judgment: *Brethren, be not children in understanding; in malice be you children, but in understanding be men*, *v.* 20. Children are apt to be struck with novelty and strange appearances. They are taken with an outward show, without enquir-

ing into the true nature and worth of things. Do not you act like them, and prefer noise and show to worth and substance; show a greater ripeness of judgment, and act a more manly part; be like children in nothing but an innocent and inoffensive disposition.

THE VALUE OF PROPHECY
(*vv.* 21–25)

In this passage the apostle pursues the argument, and reasons from other topics; as,

I. Tongues, as the Corinthians used them, were rather a token of judgment from God than mercy to any people (*v.* 21): *In the law* (that is, the Old Testament) *it is written, With men of other tongues and other lips will I speak to this people; and yet for all this will they not hear me, saith the Lord*, Isa. xxviii. 11. Compare Deut. xxviii. 46, 49.

II. Tongues were rather a sign to unbelievers than to believers, *v.* 22. They were a spiritual gift, intended for the conviction and conversion of infidels, that they might be brought into the Christian church; but converts were to be built up in Christianity by profitable instructions in their own language.

III. The credit and reputation of their assemblies among unbelievers required them to prefer prophesying before speaking with tongues. For, 1. If, when they were all assembled for Christian worship, their ministers, or all employed in public worship, should talk unintelligible language, and infidels should drop in, they would conclude them to be mad, to be no better than a parcel of wild fanatics. Who in their right senses could carry on religious worship in such a manner? Or what sort of religion is that which leaves out sense and understanding? But, on the other hand, 2. If, instead of speaking with tongues, those who minister plainly interpret scripture, or preach, in language intelligible and proper, the great truths and rules of the gospel, a heathen or unlearned person, coming in, will probably be convinced, and become a convert to Christianity (*vv.* 24, 25).

RULES FOR GATHERINGS
(*vv.* 26–33)

In this passage the apostle reproves them for their disorder, and endeavours to correct and regulate their conduct for the future.

I. He blames them for the confusion they introduced into the assembly, by ostentation of their gifts (*v.* 26).

II. He corrects their faults, and lays down some regulations for their future conduct. 1. As to speaking in an unknown tongue, he orders that no more than two or three should do it at one meeting, and this not altogether, but successively, one after another. And even this was not to be done unless there were some one to interpret (*vv.* 27, 28), some other interpreter besides himself, who spoke; for to speak in an unknown tongue what he himself was afterwards to interpret could only be for ostentation. But, if there were none to interpret, he was to be silent in the church, and only exercise his gift between God and himself (*v.* 28), that is (as I think) in private, at home; for all who are present at public worship should join in it, and not be at their private devotions in public assemblies. 2. As to prophesying he orders, (1) That two or three only should speak at one meeting (*v.* 20), and this successively, not all at once; and that the other should examine and judge what he delivered, that is, discern and determine concerning it, whether it were of divine inspiration or not. (2) He orders that, if any assistant prophet had a revelation, while another was prophesying, the other should hold his peace, be silent (*v.* 30), before the inspired assistant uttered his revelation. *That all might prophesy, one by one,* or one after another, which might easily be if he who was afterwards inspired forbore to deliver his new revelation till the former prophet had finished what he had to say. And, to confirm this sense, the apostle quickly adds, *The spirits of the prophets are subject to the prophets* (*v.* 33); that is, the spiritual gifts they have leave them still possessed of their reason, and capable of using their own judgment in the exercise of them. The man inspired by the Spirit of God may still act the man, and observe the rules of natural order and decency in delivering his revelations.

III. The apostle gives the reasons of these regulations. As, 1. That they would be for the church's benefit, their instruction and consolation. It is that *all may learn, and all may be comforted or exhorted,* that the prophets were to speak in the orderly manner the apostle advises. 2. He tells them, *God is not the God of confusion, but of peace and good order,* *v.* 33. Therefore divine inspiration should by no means throw Christian assemblies into confusion, and break through all rules of common decency. 3. He adds that things were thus orderly managed in all the other churches: *As in all the churches of the saints* (v. 33); they kept to these rules in the exercise of their spiritual gifts, which was a manifest proof that the church of Corinth might observe the same regulations.

WOMEN IN CHURCH
(vv. 34, 35)

Here the apostle, 1. Enjoins silence on their women in public assemblies, and to such a degree that they must not ask questions for their own information in the church, but ask their husbands at home. They were not ordinarily to teach, nor so much as to debate and ask questions in the church, but learn in silence there; and, if difficulties occurred, *ask their own husbands at home.* 2. We have here the reason of this injunction: It is God's law and commandment that they should be under obedience (v. 34); they are placed in subordination to the man, and it is a shame for them to do any thing that looks like an affectation of changing ranks, which speaking in public seemed to imply, at least in that age, and among that people, as would public teaching much more: so that the apostle concludes it was a shame for women to speak in the church, in the assembly.

DECENTLY AND IN ORDER
(vv. 36–40)

In these verses the apostle closes his argument, 1. With a just rebuke

of the Corinthians for their extravagant pride and self-conceit: they so managed with their spiritual gifts as no church did like them; they behaved in a manner by themselves, and would not easily endure control nor regulation. 2. He lets them know that what he said to them was the command of God; nor durst any true prophet, any one really inspired, deny it (v. 37): "*If any man think himself a prophet, or spiritual, let him acknowledge,* &c., nay, let him be tried by this very rule. If he will not own what I deliver on this head to be the will of Christ, he himself never had the Spirit of Christ. 3. He sums up all in two general advices: (1) That though they should not despise the gift of tongues, nor altogether disuse it, under the regulations mentioned, yet they should prefer prophesying. This is indeed the scope of the whole argument. It was to be preferred to the other, because it was the more useful gift. (2) He charges them to let all things be done decently and in order (v. 40), that is, that they should avoid every thing that was manifestly indecent and disorderly.

CHAPTER FIFTEEN
THE GOSPEL MESSAGE
(vv. 1–11)

It is the apostle's business in this chapter to assert and establish the doctrine of the resurrection of the dead, which some of the Corinthians flatly denied, v. 12. He begins with an epitome or summary of the gospel, what he had preached among them, namely, the death and resurrection of Christ. Upon this foundation the doctrine of the resurrection of the dead is built. Now concerning the gospel observe,

I. What a stress he lays upon it (*vv.* 1, 2): *Moreover, brethren, I declare unto you the gospel which I preached to you.* 1. It was what he constantly preached. Truth is in its own nature invariable; and the infallible teachers of divine truth could never be at variance with themselves or one another. 2. It was what they had received; they had been convinced of the faith, believed it in their hearts, or at least made profession of doing so with their mouths. 3. It was that alone by which they could hope for salvation (*v.* 2), for there is *no salvation in any other name; no name given under heaven by which we may be saved, but by the name of Christ.* And there is no salvation in his name, but upon supposition of his death and resurrection. Now concerning these saving truths observe, (1) They must be retained in mind, they must be held fast (so the word is translated, Heb. x. 23): *Let us hold fast the profession of our faith.* They will not save us, if we do not attend to them, and yield to their power, and continue to do so to the end. (2) We believe in vain, unless we continue and persevere in the faith of the gospel. And in vain is it to profess Christianity, or our faith in Christ, if we deny the resurrection.

II. Observe what this gospel is, on which the apostle lays such stress. That Christ died for our sins, and was buried, and rose again.

III. Observe how this truth is confirmed,

1. By Old-Testament predictions. He died for our sins, according to the scriptures; he was buried, and rose from the dead, according to the scriptures, according to the scripture-prophecies, and scripture-types. Such prophecies as Ps. xvi. 10; Isa. liii. 4–6; Dan. ix. 26, 27; Hos. vi. 2.

2. By the testimony of many eyewitnesses, who saw Christ after he had risen from the dead. He reckons up five several appearances, beside that to himself. He *was seen of Cephas, or Peter, then of the twelve,* called so, though Judas was no longer among them, because this was their usual number; then he was *seen of above five hundred brethren at once,* many of whom were living when the apostle wrote this epistle, though some had fallen asleep. This was in Galilee, Matt. xxviii. 10. After that, he was seen of James singly, and then by all the apostles when he was taken up into heaven. This was on mount Olivet, Luke xxiv. 50. Compare Acts i. 2, 5–7. Even Paul himself was last of all favoured with the sight of him. It was one of the peculiar offices of an apostle to be a witness of our Saviour's resurrection (Luke xxiv. 48); and, when Paul was called to the apostolical office, he was made an evidence of this sort; the Lord Jesus appeared to him by the way to Damascus, Acts ix. 17. Having mentioned this favour, Paul takes occasion from it to make a humble digression concerning himself. He was highly favoured of God, but he always endeavoured to keep up a mean opinion of himself, and to express it.

After this digression, the apostle

returns to his argument, and tells them (*v.* 11) that he not only preached the same gospel himself at all times, and in all places, but that all the apostles preached the same: *Whether it were they or I, so we preached, and so you believed.* All the apostles agreed in this testimony; all Christians agree in the belief of it. By this faith they live. In this faith they die.

THE NECESSITY OF THE RESURRECTION (*vv.* 12–19)

Having confirmed the truth of our Saviour's resurrection, the apostle goes on to refute those among the Corinthians who said there would be none: *If Christ be preached that he rose from the dead, how say some among you that there is no resurrection of the dead?* *v.* 12. It seems from this passage, and the course of the argument, there were some among the Corinthians who thought the resurrection an impossibility. This was a common sentiment among the heathens. But against this the apostle produces an incontestable fact, namely, the resurrection of Christ; and he goes on to argue against them from the absurdities that must follow from their principle. As,

I. *If there be* (can be) *no resurrection of the dead, then Christ has not risen* (*v.* 13); and again, "*If the dead rise not,* cannot be raised or recovered to life, *then is Christ not raised,*" *v.* 16.

II. It would follow hereupon that the preaching and faith of the gospel would be vain: *If Christ be not risen, then is our preaching vain, and your faith vain, v.* 14. This

supposition admitted, would destroy the principal evidence of Christianity; and so, 1. Make preaching vain. If Christ be not raised, the gospel is a jest; it is chaff and emptiness. 2. This supposition would make the faith of Christians vain, as well as the labours of ministers: *If Christ be not raised, your faith is vain; you are yet in your sins* (*v.* 17), yet under the guilt and condemnation of sin, because it is through his death and sacrifice for sin alone that forgiveness is to be had.

III. Another absurdity following from this supposition is that *those who have fallen asleep in Christ have perished.* If there be no resurrection, they cannot rise, and therefore are lost, even those who have died in the Christian faith, and for it. And this,

IV. Would infer that Christ's ministers and servants were *of all men most miserable,* as having *hope in him in this life only* (*v.* 19), which is another absurdity that would follow from asserting no resurrection. Their condition who hope in Christ would be worse than that of other men. Note, It were a gross absurdity in a Christian to admit the supposition of no resurrection or future state. It would leave no hope beyond this world, and would frequently make his condition the worst in the world.

THE LAST ENEMY (*vv.* 20–34)

In this passage the apostle establishes the truth of the resurrection of the dead, the holy dead, the dead in Christ,

I. On the resurrection of Christ.

1. Because he is indeed *the first-fruits of those that slept*, *v.* 20. The whole body of Christ, all that are by faith united to him, are by his resurrection assured of their own. As he has risen, they shall rise; just as the lump is holy because the first-fruits are so. He has not risen merely for himself, but as head of the body, the church; and *those that sleep in him God will bring with him*, 1 Thess. iv. 14. This is the first argument used by the apostle in confirmation of the truth; and it is, 2. Illustrated by a parallel between the first and second Adam. For, since by man came death, it was every way proper that by man should come deliverance from it, or, which is all one, a resurrection, *v.* 21. All who die die through the sin of Adam; all who are raised, in the sense of the apostle, rise through the merit and power of Christ. But the meaning is not that, as all men died in Adam, so all men, without exception, shall be made alive in Christ; for the scope of the apostle's argument restrains the general meaning. Christ rose as the first-fruits; therefore *those that are Christ's* (*v.* 23) shall rise too. Hence it will not follow that all men without exception shall rise too. 3. Before he leaves the argument he states that there will be an order observed in their resurrection. What that precisely will be we are nowhere told, but in the general only here that there will be order observed.

II. He argues from the continuance of the mediatorial kingdom till all Christ's enemies are destroyed, the last of which is death, *vv.* 24–26.

1. This argument implies in it all these particulars: (1) That our Saviour rose from the dead to have all power put into his hands, and have and administer a kingdom, as Mediator. (3) That it is not to have an end till all opposing power be put down, and all enemies brought to his feet, *vv.* 24, 25. (4) That, among other enemies, death must be destroyed (*v.* 26) or abolished; its powers over its members must be disannulled. Thus far the apostle is express; but he leaves us to make the inference that therefore the saints must rise, else death and the grave would have power over them, nor would our Saviour's kingly power prevail against the last enemy of his people and annul its power.

2. The apostle drops several hints in the course of it which it will be proper to notice: as, (1) That our Saviour, as man and mediator between God and man, has a delegated royalty, a kingdom given: *All things are put under him, he excepted that did put all things under him*, *v.* 27. (2) That this delegated royalty must at length *be delivered up to the Father*, from whom it was received (*v.* 24); for it is a power received for particular ends and purposes, a power to govern and protect his church till all the members of it be gathered in, and the enemies of it for ever subdued and destroyed (*vv.* 25, 26), and when these ends shall be obtained the power and authority will not need to be continued. (3) The Redeemer shall certainly reign till the last enemy of his people be destroyed, till death itself be abolished, till his saints revive and

recover perfect life, never to be in fear and danger of dying any more. (4) When this is done, *and all things are put under his feet, then shall the Son become subject to him that put all things under him, that God may be all in all, v.* 28. The meaning of this I take to be that then the man Christ Jesus, who hath appeared in so much majesty during the whole administration of his kingdom, shall appear upon giving it up to be a subject of the Father.

III. He argues for the resurrection, from the case of those who were baptized for the dead (*v.* 29). But what is this baptism for the dead? It is as easy an explication of the phrase as any I have met with, and as pertinent to the argument, to suppose *the dead* to mean some among the Corinthians, who had been taken off by the hand of God. We read that *many were sickly among them, and many slept* (*ch.* xi. 30), because of their disorderly behaviour at the Lord's table. These executions might terrify some into Christianity; as the miraculous earthquake did the jailer, Acts xvi. 29, 30, &c. Persons baptized on such an occasion might be properly said to be baptized for the dead, that is, on their account. "Now," says he, "what shall they do, and why were they baptized, if the dead rise not? You have a general persuasion that these men have done right, and acted wisely, and as they ought, on this occasion; but why, if the dead rise not, seeing they may perhaps hasten their death, by provoking a jealous God, and have no hopes beyond it?" But whether this be the meaning, or whatever else be, doubtless

the apostle's argument was good and intelligible to the Corinthians. And his next is as plain to us.

IV. He argues from the absurdity of his own conduct and that of other Christians upon this supposition,·

1. It would be a foolish thing for them to run so many hazards (*v.* 30): "*Why stand we in jeopardy every hour?*" Note, Christianity were a foolish profession if it proposed no hopes beyond this life, at least in such hazardous times as attended the first profession of it; it required men to risk all the blessings and comforts of this life, and to face and endure all the evils of it, without any future prospects.

2. It would be a much wiser thing to take the comforts of this life: *Let us eat and drink, for to-morrow we die* (*v.* 32); let us turn epicures. Thus this sentence means in the prophet, Isa. xxii. 13. Let us even live like beasts, if we must die like them. This would be a wiser course, if there were no resurrection, no after-life or state, than to abandon all the pleasures of life, and offer and expose ourselves to all the miseries of life, and live in continual peril of perishing by savage rage and cruelty.

V. The apostle closes his argument with a caution, exhortation, and reproof. 1. A caution against the dangerous conversation of bad men, men of loose lives and principles: *Be not deceived,* says he; *evil communications corrupt good manners, v.* 33. Possibly, some of those who said that there was no resurrection of the dead were men of loose lives, and endeavoured to countenance their vicious practices by so corrupt a principle; and had that speech often in their mouths, *Let us eat and drink, for to-morrow we die*. 2. Here is an exhortation to break off their sins, and rouse themselves, and lead a more holy and righteous life (*v.* 34): *Awake to righteousness*, or *awake righteously, and sin not*, or sin no more. The disbelief of a future state destroys all virtue and piety. 3. Here is a reproof, and a sharp one, to some at least among them: *Some of you have not the knowledge of God; I speak this to your shame*. Note, It is a shame in Christians not to have the knowledge of God. Note, Real atheism lies at the bottom of men's disbelief of a future state. Those who own a God and a providence, and observe how unequal the distributions of the present life are, and how frequently the best men fare worst, can hardly doubt an after state, where every thing will be set to rights.

THE RESURRECTION OF THE BODY (*vv.* 35–50)

The apostle comes now to answer a plausible and principal objection against the doctrine of the resurrection of the dead, concerning which observe the proposal of the objection: *Some man will say, How are the dead raised up? And with what body do they come? v.* 35. The objection is plainly two-fold. *How are they raised up?* that is, "By what means?" The other part of the objection is about the quality of their bodies, who shall rise: "*With what body will they come?* Will it be with the same body, with like shape, and form, and stature,

and members, and qualities, or various?" The former objection is that of those who opposed the doctrine, the latter the enquiry of curious doubters.

I. To the former the apostle replies by telling them this was to be brought about by divine power, that very power which they had all observed to do something very like it, year after year, in the death and revival of the corn; and therefore it was an argument of great weakness and stupidity to doubt whether the resurrection of the dead might not be effected by the same power: *Thou fool! that which thou sowest is not quickened unless it die, v.* 36. It must first corrupt, before it will quicken and spring up. It not only sprouts after it is dead, but it must die that it may live. And why should any be so foolish as to imagine that the man once dead cannot be made to live again, by the same power which every year brings the dead grain to life? This is the substance of the apostle's answer to the first question.

II. But he is longer in replying to the second enquiry.

1. He begins by observing that there is a change made in the grain that is sown: It is *not that body which shall be* that is sown, but *bare grain*, of wheat or barley, &c.; but God gives it such a body as he will, and in such way as he will, only so as to distinguish the kinds from each other.

2. He proceeds hence to observe that there is a great deal of variety among other bodies, as there is among plants.

3. To speak directly to the point: *So also*, says he, *is the resurrection*

of the dead; so (as the plant growing out of the putrefied grain), so as no longer to be a terrestrial but a celestial body, and varying in glory from the other dead, who are raised, as one star does from another. But he specifies some particulars: as, (1) *It is sown in corruption, it is raised in incorruption.* Our bodies, which are sown, are corruptible, liable to putrefy and moulder, and crumble to dust; but, when we rise, they will be out of the power of the grave, and never more be liable to corruption. (2) *It is sown in dishonour, it is raised in glory.* Ours is at present a vile body, Phil. iii. 21. But at the resurrection a glory will be put upon it; it will be made like the glorious body of our Saviour. (3) *It is sown in weakness, it is raised in power.* It is laid in the earth, a poor helpless thing. But when we arise our bodies will have heavenly life and vigour infused into them. (4) *It is sown a natural*, or *animal* body, a body fitted to the low condition and sensitive pleasures and enjoyments of this life, which are all gross in comparison of the heavenly state and enjoyments. But when we rise it will be quite otherwise; our body will rise spiritual.

4. He illustrates this by a comparison of the first and second Adam: *There is an animal body*, says he, *and there is a spiritual body*; and then goes into the comparison in several instances. As surely therefore as we have had natural bodies, we shall have spiritual ones. The dead in Christ shall not only rise, but shall rise thus gloriously changed.

5. He sums up this argument by assigning the reason of this change (*v.* 50): *Now this I say that flesh and blood cannot inherit the kingdom of God; nor doth corruption inherit incorruption.* The natural body is flesh and blood; and, as such, it is of a corruptible frame and form, liable to dissolution, to rot and moulder. But no such thing shall inherit the heavenly regions; for this were for corruption to inherit incorruption, which is little better than a contradiction in terms. The heavenly inheritance is incorruptible, and never fadeth away, 1 Pet. i. 4.

DEATH DEFEATED
(*vv.* 51–58)

To confirm what he had said of this change,

I. He here tells them what had been concealed from or unknown to them till then—that all the saints would not die, but all would be changed. Those that are alive at our Lord's coming will be caught up into the clouds, without dying, 1 Thess. iv. 11. But it is plain from this passage that it will not be without changing from corruption to incorruption. The frame of their living bodies shall be thus altered, as well as those that are dead; and this *in a moment, in the twinkling of an eye, v.* 52.

II. He assigns the reason of this change (*v.* 53): *For this corruptible must put on incorruption, and this mortal must put on immortality.* How otherwise could the man be a fit inhabitant of the incorruptible regions, or be fitted to possess the eternal inheritance? How can that which is corruptible and mortal enjoy what is incorruptible, permanent, and immortal?

III. He lets us know what will follow upon this change of the living and dead in Christ: *Then shall be brought to pass that saying, Death is swallowed up in victory*; or, *He will swallow up death in victory*, Isa. xxv. 8. For *mortality shall be then swallowed up of life* (2 Cor. v. 4), and death perfectly subdued and conquered, and saints for ever delivered from its power. And upon this destruction of death will they break out into a song of triumph.

1. They will glory over death as a vanquished enemy, and insult this great and terrible destroyer: "*O death! where is thy sting?*"

2. The foundation for this triumph is here intimated, (1) In the account given whence death had its power to hurt: *The sting of death is sin.* Sin unpardoned, and nothing else, can keep any under his power. And the *strength of sin is the law*; it is the divine threatening against the transgressors of the law, the curse there denounced, that gives power to sin. Note, Sin is the parent of death, and gives it all its hurtful power. (2) In the account given of the victory saints obtain over it through Jesus Christ, *v.* 56. *The sting of death is sin*; but Christ, by dying, has taken out this sting. He has made atonement for sin; he has obtained remission of it. It may hiss therefore, but it cannot hurt. (3) If this triumph of the saints over death should issue in thanksgiving to God: *Thanks be to God, who giveth us the victory through Christ Jesus, our Lord, v.* 57. The way to sanctify all our joy

is to make it tributary to the praise of God. Note, How many springs of joy to the saints and thanksgiving to God are opened by the death and resurrection, the sufferings and conquests, of our Redeemer!

In verse 58 we have the improvement of the whole argument, in an exhortation, enforced by a motive resulting plainly from it. 1. That they should be steadfast—firm, fixed in the faith of the gospel, that gospel which he had preached and they had received. 2. He exhorts them to be *immovable*, namely, in their expectation of this great privilege of being raised incorruptible and immortal. Christians should not be moved away from this hope of the gospel (Col. i. 23), this glorious and blessed hope. 3. He exhorts them *to abound in the work of the Lord*, and that *always*, in the Lord's service, in obeying the Lord's commands. They should be diligent and persevering herein, and going on towards perfection; they should be continually making advances in true piety, and ready and apt for every good work. The most cheerful duty, the greatest diligence, the most constant perseverance, become those who have such glorious hopes.

II. The motive resulting from the former discourse is that their *labour shall not be in vain in the Lord*; nay, they know it shall not. They have the best grounds in the world to build upon: they have all the assurance that can rationally be expected: as surely as Christ is risen, they shall rise; and Christ is as surely risen as the scriptures are true, and the word of God.

THE COLLECTION (*vv.* 1–4)

In this chapter Paul begins with directing them about a charitable collection on a particular occasion, the distresses and poverty of Christians in Judea, which at this time were extraordinary, partly through the general calamities of that nation and partly through the particular sufferings to which they were exposed. Now concerning this observe,

I. How he introduces his direction. It was not a peculiar service which he required of them; he had given similar *orders to the churches of Galatia*, v. 1. He desired them only to conform to the same rules which he had given to other churches on a similar occasion.

II. The direction itself, concerning which observe,

1. The manner in which the collection was to be made: *Every one was to lay by in store* (v. 2), have a treasury, or fund, with himself, for this purpose. The meaning is that he should lay by as he could spare from time to time, and by this means make up a sum for this charitable purpose.

2. Here is the measure in which they are to lay by: *As God hath prospered them*; as he has been prospered, namely, by divine Providence, as God has been pleased to bless and succeed his labours and business. The more they had, through God's blessing, gained by their business or labour, their traffic or work, the more they were to lay by.

3. Here is the time when this is to be done: *The first day of the*

week, the Lord's day, the Christian holiday, when public assemblies were held and public worship was celebrated, and the Christian institutions and mysteries (as the ancients called them) were attended upon; then let every one lay by him.

4. We have here the disposal of the collections thus made: the apostle would have every thing ready against he came, and therefore gave direction as before: *That there be no gatherings when I come*, v. 2. But, when he came, as to the disposal of it, he would leave it much to themselves. The charity was theirs, and it was fit they should dispose of it in their own way, so it answered its end, and was applied to the right use.

PAUL'S PLANS (*vv.* 5–9)

In this passage the apostle notifies and explains his purpose of visiting them, concerning which, observe, 1. His purpose: he intended to pass out of Asia, where he now was (*vide vv.* 8, 19) and to go through Macedonia into Achaia, where Corinth was, and to stay some time with them, and perhaps the winter, *vv.* 5, 6. 2. His excuse for not seeing them now, because it would be *only by the way* (v. 7), *it would only be a transient visit*. He would not see them because he could not stay with them. Such a visit would give neither him nor them any satisfaction or advantage. 3. We have the limitation of this purpose: *I trust to tarry awhile with you, if the Lord permit*, v. 7. Though the apostles wrote under inspiration, they did not know thereby how God would dispose of them. But, 5. We have the reason given for his staying at

Ephesus for the present: *Because a great door, and effectual, was opened to him, and there were many adversaries, v.* 9. A great door and effectual was opened to him; many were prepared to receive the gospel at Ephesus, and God gave him great success among them; he had brought over many to Christ, and he had great hope of bringing over many more. For this reason he determined to stay awhile at Ephesus. And there were many adversaries, because a great door, and an effectual, was opened. Note, Great success in the work of the gospel commonly creates many enemies.

TIMOTHY AND APOLLOS
(vv. 10–12)

In this passage,

I. He recommends Timothy to them, in several particulars. As, 1. He bids them take care that he should *be among them without fear, v.* 10. Timothy was sent by the apostle to correct the abuses which had crept in among them; and not only to direct, but to blame, and censure, and reprove, those who were culpable. They should not fly out into resentment at his reproof. 2. He warns them against despising him, *v.* 11. He was but a young man, and alone, as Œcumenius observes. He had no one to back him, and his own youthful face and years commanded but little reverence; and therefore the great pretenders to wisdom among them might be apt to entertain contemptuous thoughts of him. "Now," says the apostle, "guard against this." 3. He tells them they should give him all due encourage-

ment, use him well while he was with them; and, as an evidence of this, they should send him away in friendship, and well prepared for his journey back again to Paul.

II. He assigns the reasons why they should behave thus towards Timothy. 1. Because he was employed in the same work as Paul, and acted in it by the same authority, *v.* 10. 2. Another reason is implied; as they were to esteem him for his work's sake, so also for Paul's sake, who had sent him to Corinth; not of his own errand indeed, but to work the work of the Lord.

III. He informs them of Apollos's purpose to see them. 1. He himself had greatly desired him to come to them, *v.* 12. 2. Apollos could not be prevailed on for the present to come, but would at a more convenient season. Perhaps their feuds and factions might render the present season improper.

RESPECT YOUR LEADERS
(vv. 13–18)

In this passage the apostle gives,

I. Some general advices; as, 1. That they should watch (*v.* 13), be wakeful and upon their guard. A Christian is always in danger, and therefore should ever be on the watch; but the danger is greater at some times and under some circumstances. 2. He advises them to *stand fast in the faith,* to keep their ground, adhere to the revelation of God, and not give it up for the wisdom of the world, nor suffer it to be corrupted by it—stand for the faith of the gospel, and maintain it even to death; and stand in it, so as to abide in the profession of it, and feel and yield to its influence. 3,

He advises them to act like men, and be strong. Note, Christians should be manly and firm in all their contests with their enemies, in defending their faith, and maintaining their integrity. 4. He advises them to do every thing in charity, *v.* 14. Our zeal and constancy must be consistent with charity.

II. Some particular directions how they should behave towards some that had been eminently serviceable to the cause of Christ among them (*vv.* 15–18).

FINAL GREETINGS
(*vv.* 19–24)

The apostle closes his epistle,

I. With salutations to the church of Corinth, first from those of Asia, from *Priscilla* and *Aquila* (who seem to have been at this time inhabitants of Ephesus, *vid.* Acts xviii. 26), *with the church in their house* (*v.* 19), and from *all the brethren* (*v.* 20) at Ephesus, where, it is highly probable at least, he then was. All these saluted the church at Corinth, by Paul. Note, Christianity does by no means destroy civility and good manners.

II. With a very solemn warning to them: *If any man love not the Lord Jesus Christ, let him be Anathema, Maran-atha, v.* 22. We sometimes need words of threatening, that we may fear. Here observe, 1. The person described, who is liable to this doom: *He that loveth not the Lord Jesus Christ.* But, 2. We have here the doom of the person described: "*Let him be Anathema, Maran-atha,* lie under the heaviest and most dreadful curse. Let him be separated from the people of God, from the favour of God, and delivered up to his final, irrevocable, and inexorable vengeance." *Maran-atha* is a Syriac phrase, and signifies *The Lord cometh.* That very Lord whom they do not love, to whom they are inwardly and really disaffected whatever outward profession they make, is coming to execute judgment. And to be exposed to his wrath, to be divided to his left hand, to be condemned by him, how dreadful!

III. With his good wishes for them and expressions of good-will to them. 1. With his good wishes: *The grace of our Lord Jesus Christ be with you, v.* 23. The grace of our Lord Jesus Christ comprehends in it all that is good, for time or eternity. To wish our friends may have this grace with them is wishing them the utmost good. And this we should wish all our friends and brethren in Christ. 2. With the declaration of his love to them in Christ Jesus: *My love be with you all, in Christ Jesus, Amen, v.* 24. He had dealt very plainly with them in this epistle, and told them of their faults with just severity; but, to show that he was not transported with passion, he parts with them in love, makes solemn profession of his love to them, nay, to them all in Christ Jesus, that is, for Christ's sake. He tells them that his heart was with them, that he truly loved them; but lest this, after all, should be deemed flattery and insinuation, he adds that his affection was the result of his religion, and would be guided by the rules of it.

CORINTHIANS

CHAPTER ONE
INTRODUCTION (vv. 1, 2)

This is the introduction to this epistle, in which we have,

I. The inscription; and therein, 1. The person from whom it was sent, namely, Paul, who calls himself *an apostle of Jesus Christ by the will of God.* The apostleship itself was ordained by Jesus Christ, according to the will of God; and Paul was called to it by Jesus Christ, according to the will of God. He joins Timothy with himself in writing this epistle. 2. The persons to whom this epistle was sent, namely, *the church of God at Corinth*: and not only to them, but also *to all the saints in all Achaia*, that is, to all the Christians who lived in the region round about.

II. The salutation or apostolical benediction, which is the same as in his former epistle; and therein the apostle desires the two great and comprehensive blessings, grace and peace, for those Corinthians.

GOD'S GOODNESS
(vv. 3–6)

After the foregoing preface, the apostle begins with the narrative of God's goodness to him and his fellow-labourers in their manifold tribulations, which he speaks of by way of thanksgiving to God, and to advance the divine glory (vv.

3–6); and it is fit that in all things, and in the first place, God be glorified. Note, (1) What favours God bestows on us are intended not only to make us cheerful ourselves, but also that we may be useful to others (v. 4). (2) If we do imitate the faith and patience of good men in their afflictions, we may hope to partake of their consolations here and their salvation hereafter (vv. 5, 6).

PAUL'S TROUBLES
(vv. 7–11)

In these verses the apostle speaks for the encouragement and edification of the Corinthians; and tells them (v. 7) of his persuasion or stedfast hope that they should receive benefit by the troubles he and his companions in labour and travel had met with, that their faith should not be weakened, but their consolations increased. In order to this he tells them, 1. What their sufferings had been (v. 8): *We would not have you ignorant of our trouble.* It was convenient for the churches to know what were the sufferings of their ministers. 2. What they did in their distress: *They trusted in God.* And they were brought to this extremity in order *that they should not trust in themselves but in God, v.* 9. 3. What the deliverance was that they had obtained. God had delivered them, and did still deliver them, *v.* 10. *Having obtained help of God, they continued to that day*, Acts xxvi. 22. 4. What use they made of this deliverance: *We trust that he will yet deliver us* (*v.* 10), that God will deliver to the end, and *preserve to his heavenly kingdom*. 5. What was desired of the Corinthians upon this account: *That they would help together by prayer for them* (*v.* 11), by social prayer, agreeing and joining together in prayer on their behalf.

THEIR INTEGRITY
(*vv.* 12–14)

Here,

I. Paul appeals to the testimony of conscience with rejoicing (*v.* 12), in which observe, 1. The witness appealed to, namely, conscience, which is instead of a thousand witnesses. This is God's deputy in the soul, and the voice of conscience is the voice of God. 2. The testimony this witness gave. And here take notice, Conscience witnessed, (1) Concerning their conversation, their constant course and tenor of life: by that we may judge of ourselves, and not by this or that single act. (2) Concerning the nature or manner of their way of life; that it was in simplicity and godly sincerity. (3) Concerning the principle they acted from in all their conversation, both in the world and towards these Corinthians; and that was not fleshly wisdom, nor carnal politics and worldly views, but it was the grace of God, a vital gracious principle in their hearts, that cometh from God, and tendeth to God.

II. He appeals to the knowledge of the Corinthians with hope and confidence, *vv.* 13, 14. Their behaviour did in part fall under the observation of the Corinthians; and these knew how they behaved themselves, *how holily, and justly, and unblamably*.

THEIR CONSISTENCY
(*vv.* 15–24)

The apostle here vindicates himself from the imputation of levity and inconstancy, in that he did not hold his purpose of coming to them at Corinth. Now, for his justification,

I. He avers the sincerity of his intention (*vv.* 15–17), and he does this in confidence of their good opinion of him, and that they would believe him, when he assured them he *was minded*, or did really intend, *to come* to them, and that with the design, not that he might receive, but that they might receive a *second benefit*, that is, a further advantage by his ministry.

II. He would not have the Corinthians to infer that his gospel was false or uncertain, nor that it was contradictory in itself, nor unto truth, *vv.* 18, 19. For if it had been so, that he had been fickle in his purposes, or even false in the promises he made of coming to them, yet it would not follow that the gospel preached not only by him, but also by others in full agreement with him, was either false or doubtful. For *God is true*, and *the Son of God, Jesus Christ*, is true. Jesus Christ, whom the apostle preached, is not *yea* and *nay*, but in him was *yea* (*v.* 19), nothing but infallible truth. And the promises of God in Christ are not yea and nay, but yea and amen, *v.* 20. There is an inviolable constancy and unquestionable sincerity and certainty in all the parts of the gospel of Christ.

III. The apostle gives a good reason why he did not come to Corinth, as was expected, *v.* 23. It was that he might spare them. They ought therefore to own his kindness and tenderness.

CHAPTER TWO
PAUL'S ANGUISH
(*vv.* 1–4)

In these verses, 1. The apostle proceeds in giving an account of the reason why he did not come to Corinth, as was expected; namely, because he was unwilling to grieve them, or be grieved by them, *vv.* 1, 2. 2. He tells them it was to the same intent that he wrote his former epistle, *vv.* 3, 4. He had *written with tears, that they might know his abundant love to them.*

ATTITUDES TOWARDS THE OFFENDER (*vv.* 5–11)

In these verses the apostle treats concerning the incestuous person who had been excommunicated, which seems to be one principal cause of his writing this epistle. Here observe, 1. He tells them that the crime of that person had grieved him *in part*; and that he was grieved also with a part of them, who, notwithstanding this scandal had been found among them, were *puffed up and had not mourned*, 1 Cor. v. 2. However, he was unwilling to lay too heavy a charge upon the whole church, especially seeing they had cleared

themselves in that matter by observing the directions he had formerly given them. 2. He tells them that the punishment which had been inflicted upon this offender was sufficient, *v.* 6. The desired effect was obtained, for the man was humbled, and they had shown the proof of their obedience to his directions. 3. He therefore directs them, with all speed, to restore the excommunicated person, or to receive him again to their communion, *vv.* 7, 8. 4. He uses several weighty arguments to persuade them to do thus. (1) The case of the penitent called for this; for he was in danger of being *swallowed up with over-much sorrow, v.* 7. (2) They had shown obedience to his directions in passing a censure upon the offender and now he would have them comply with his desire to restore him, *v.* 9. (3) He mentions his readiness to forgive this penitent, and concur with them in this matter. (4) He gives another weighty reason (*v.* 11): *Lest Satan get an advantage against us.* Not only was there danger lest Satan should get an advantage against the penitent, by driving him to despair; but against the churches also, and the apostles or ministers of Christ, by representing them as too rigid and severe.

PAUL'S TRAVELS
(*vv.* 12–17)

After these directions concerning the excommunicated person the apostle makes a long digression, to give the Corinthians an account of his travels and labours for the furtherance of the gospel, and what success he had therein, declaring at

the same time how much he was
concerned for them in their affairs,
how he *had no rest in his spirit*,
when he found not Titus at Troas
(*v.* 13), as he expected, from whom
he hoped to have understood more
perfectly how it fared with them.
And we find afterwards (*ch.* vii.
5–7) that when the apostle had
come into Macedonia he was
comforted by the coming of Titus,
and the information he gave him
concerning them. So that we may
look upon all that we read from
this second chapter, *v*, 12, to *ch.*
vii. 5, as a kind of parenthesis.
Here observe,

I. The different success of the
gospel, and its different effects upon
several sorts of persons to whom it
is preached. The success is different;
for some are saved by it, while
others perish under it. Nor is this
to be wondered at, considering the
different effects the gospel has. For,
(1) Unto some it is a *savour of
death unto death.* Those who are
willingly ignorant, and wilfully
obstinate, disrelish the gospel, as
men dislike an ill savour, and therefore they are blinded and hardened
by it: it stirs up their corruptions,
and exasperates their spirits. (2)
Unto others the gospel is a *savour
of life unto life.* To humble and
gracious souls the preaching of the
word is most delightful and
profitable.

II. The awful impressions this
matter made upon the mind of the
apostle, and should also make upon
our spirits: *Who is sufficient for
these things?* v. 16. Who is able to
perform such a difficult work, that
requires so much skill and industry? The work is great and our

strength is small; yea, of ourselves
we have no strength at all; *all our
sufficiency is of God.*

III. The comfort which the
apostle had under this serious consideration, (1) Because faithful
ministers shall be accepted of God,
whatever their success be. (2) Because his conscience witnessed to his
faithfulness, *v.* 17. Though many
did corrupt the word of God, yet
the apostle's conscience witnessed
to his fidelity.

CHAPTER THREE
HUMAN LETTERS
(*vv.* 1–5)

In these verses,

I. The apostle makes an apology
for seeming to commend himself.
And he tells them, 1. That he
neither needed nor desired any
verbal commendation to them, nor
letters testimonial from them, as
some others did, meaning the false
apostles or teachers, *v.* 1. 2. The
Corinthians themselves were his
real commendation, and a good
testimonial for him, that God was
with him of a truth, that he was
sent of God: *You are our epistle,
v.* 2.

II. The apostle is careful not to
assume too much to himself, but
to ascribe all the praise to God.
Therefore, 1. He says they were the
epistle of Christ, v. 3. This epistle
was not written with *ink, but with
the Spirit of the living God*; nor was
it written in *tables of stone*, as the
law of God given to Moses, but
on the *heart*; and that heart not a
stony one, but a heart of flesh,
upon the *fleshy tables of the heart*,
that is, upon hearts that are softened

and renewed by divine grace. 2. He utterly disclaims the taking of any praise to themselves, and ascribes all the glory to God: "*We are not sufficient of ourselves*," *v*. 5.

A MORE GLORIOUS MINISTRY (*vv*. 6–11)

Here the apostle makes a comparison, between the Old Testament and the New, the law of Moses and the gospel of Jesus Christ, and values himself and his fellow-labourers by this, that *they were able ministers of the New Testament*, that God had made them so, *v*. 6. This he does in answer to the accusations of false teachers, who magnify greatly the law of Moses.

I. He distinguishes between the letter and the spirit even of the New Testament, *v*. 6. As able ministers of the New Testament, they were ministers not merely of the letter, to read the written word, or to preach the letter of the gospel only, but they were ministers of the Spirit also; the Spirit of God did accompany their ministrations.

II. He shows the difference between the Old Testament and the New, and the excellency of the gospel above the law. For, 1. The Old-Testament dispensation was the *ministration of death* (*v*. 7), whereas that of the New Testament is the *ministration of life*. 2. The law was the *ministration of condemnation*, for that condemned and cursed every one who *continued not in all things written therein to do them*; but the gospel is the *ministration of righteousness*: therein the righteousness of God by faith is revealed. 3. The law is done away,

but the gospel does and shall *remain*, *v*. 11.

THE VEIL (*vv*. 12–18)

In these verses the apostle draws two inferences from what he had said about the Old and New Testament:

I. Concerning the duty of the ministers of the gospel to use great plainness or clearness of speech. They ought not, like Moses, to put a veil upon their faces, or obscure and darken those things which they should make plain.

II. Concerning the privilege and advantage of those who enjoy the gospel, above those who lived under the law. For, 1. Those who lived under the legal dispensation had their minds blinded (*v*. 14), and there was a *veil upon their hearts*, *v*. 15. Nevertheless, the apostle tells us, there is a time coming when this *veil also shall be taken away*, and *when it* (the body of that people) *shall turn to the Lord*, *v*. 16. Or, when any particular person is converted to God, then the veil of ignorance is taken away; the blindness of the mind, and the hardness of the heart, are cured. 2. The condition of those who enjoy and believe the gospel is much more happy. For, (1) They have liberty: *Where the Spirit of the Lord is*, and where he worketh, as he does under the gospel-dispensation, *there is liberty* (*v*. 17), freedom from the yoke of the ceremonial law, and from the servitude of corruption; liberty of access to God, and freedom of speech in prayer. (2) They have *light*; for with *open face we behold the glory of the Lord*, *v*. 18. The

Israelites saw the glory of God in a cloud, which was dark and dreadful; but Christians see the glory of the Lord as in a glass, more clearly and comfortably.

CHAPTER FOUR

TRUE MINISTRY (*vv.* 1–7)

The apostle had, in the foregoing chapter, been *magnifying his office*, upon the consideration of the excellency or glory of that gospel about which he did officiate; and now in this chapter his design is to vindicate their ministry from the accusation of false teachers.

I. Two things in general we have an account of: Their constancy and sincerity in their work and labour, concerning which observe, 1. Their constancy and perseverance in their work are declared. 2. Their sincerity in their work is avouched (*v.* 2) in several expressions: *We have renounced the hidden things of dishonesty.* They had no base and wicked designs covered with fair and specious pretences of something that was good. Nor did they in their preaching *handle the word of God deceitfully*; but, as he said before, they used *great plainness of speech*, and did not make their ministry serve a turn, or truckle to base designs. And all this they did *as in the sight of God*, desirous thus to commend themselves to God, and to the consciences of men, by their undisguised sincerity.

II. An objection is obviated, which might be thus formed: "If it be thus, how then does it come to pass, that the gospel is hid, and proves ineffectual, as to some who

hear it?" To which the apostle answers by showing that this was not the fault of the gospel, nor of the preachers thereof. But the true reasons of this are, 1. *Those are lost souls* to whom the gospel is hid, or is ineffectual, *v.* 3. 2. *The god of this world hath blinded their minds*, *v.* 4. They are under the influence and power of the devil, who is here called *the god of this world*, and elsewhere *the prince of this world*. The design of the devil is to keep men in ignorance; and, when he cannot keep the light of the gospel out of the world, he makes it his great business to keep it out of the hearts of men.

III. A proof of their integrity is given, *v.* 5. They made it their business to preach Christ, and not themselves: *We preach not ourselves.* Self was not the matter nor the end of the apostles' preaching: they did not give their own notions and private opinions, nor their passions and prejudices, for the word and will of God; nor did they seek themselves, to advance their own secular interest or glory. But they *preached Christ Jesus the Lord*; and thus it did become them and behove them to do, as being Christ's servants. And there was good reason, 1. Why they should preach Christ. For by gospel light we have the *knowledge of the glory of God*, which shines in the *face of Jesus Christ*, *v.* 6. And the light of this *Sun of righteousness* is more glorious than that light which God commanded to shine out of darkness. 2. Why they should not preach themselves: because they were but earthen vessels, things of little or no worth or value. And

God has so ordered it that the weaker the vessels are the stronger his power may appear to be, that the treasure itself should be valued the more.

SUFFERING AND SUPPORT
(*vv.* 8–18)

In these verses the apostle gives an account of their courage and patience under all their sufferings, where observe,

I. How their sufferings, and patience under them, are declared, *vv.* 8–12. The apostles were great sufferers; therein they followed their Master: Christ had told them *that in the world they should have tribulation*, and so they had; yet they met with wonderful support, great relief, and many allays of their sorrows. Still they were preserved, and kept their heads above water. Note, Whatever condition the children of God may be in, in this world, they have a "*but not*" to comfort themselves with; their case sometimes is bad, very bad, but not so bad as it might be. The apostle speaks of their sufferings as constant, and as a counterpart of the sufferings of Christ, *v.* 10. So great were the sufferings of the apostles that, in comparison with them, other Christians were, even at this time, in prosperous circumstances: *Death worketh in us; but life in you*, *v.* 12.

II. What it was that kept them from sinking and fainting under their sufferings, *vv.* 13–18.

1. Faith kept them from fainting: *We have the same spirit of faith* (*v.* 13), that faith which is of the operation of the Spirit; the same

faith by which the saints of old did and suffered such great things.

2. Hope of the resurrection kept them from sinking, *v.* 14. They knew that Christ was raised, and that his resurrection was an earnest and assurance of theirs.

3. The consideration of the glory of God and the benefit of the church, by means of their sufferings, kept them from fainting, *v.* 15. Their sufferings were for the church's advantage (*ch.* i. 6), and thus did redound to God's glory.

4. The thoughts of the advantage their souls would reap by the sufferings of their bodies kept them from fainting: *Though our outward man perish, our inward man is renewed day by day*, *v.* 16. Here note, (1) We have every one of us an outward and an inward man, a body and a soul. (2) If the outward man perish, there is no remedy, it must and will be so, it was made to perish. (3) It is our happiness if the decays of the outward man do contribute to the renewing of the inward man.

5. The prospect of eternal life and happiness kept them from fainting, and was a mighty support and comfort. As to this observe, (1) The apostle and his fellow-sufferers saw their afflictions working towards heaven, and that they would end at last (*v.* 17), whereupon they weighed things aright in the balance of the sanctuary; they did as it were put the heavenly glory in one scale and their earthly sufferings in the other; and, pondering things in their thoughts, they found afflictions to be light, and the glory of heaven to be *a far more exceeding weight*. (2) Their faith enabled them to make this right

judgment of things: *We look not at the things which are seen, but at the things which are not seen, v.* 18. It is by faith that we see God, who is invisible (Heb. xi. 27), and by this we look to an unseen heaven and hell, and faith is the *evidence of things not seen.*

CHAPTER FIVE
HEREAFTER (*vv.* 1–11)

The apostle in these verses pursues the argument of the former chapter, concerning the grounds of their courage and patience under afflictions. And,

I. He mentions their expectation, and desire, and assurance, of eternal happiness after death, *vv.* 1–5. Observe particularly,

1. The believer's expectation of eternal happiness after death, *v.* 1. Note, [1] That the body, this earthly house, is but a tabernacle, that must be dissolved shortly; and then the body will return to dust as it was. [2] When this comes to pass, then comes the house not made with hands. The spirit returns to God who gave it; and such as have walked with God here shall dwell with God for ever.

2. The believer's earnest desire after this future blessedness, which is expressed by this word, *groan,* which denotes, (1) A groaning of sorrow under a heavy load; so believers groan under the burden of life. The body of flesh is a heavy burden, the calamities of life are a heavy load. (2) There is a groaning of desire after the happiness of another life; and thus believers groan: *Earnestly desiring to be clothed upon our house which is*

from heaven (*v.* 2), to obtain a blessed immortality, *that mortality might be swallowed up of life* (*v.* 4), *that being found clothed, we may not be naked* (*v.* 3).

3. The believer's assurance of his interest in this future blessedness, on a double account: (1) From the experience of the grace of God, in preparing and making him meet for this blessedness. (2) The *earnest of the Spirit* gave them this assurance: for an earnest is part of payment, and secures the full payment.

II. The apostle deduces an inference for the comfort of believers in their present state and condition in this world, *vv.* 6–8. True Christians, if they duly considered the prospect faith gives them of another world, and the good reasons of their hope of blessedness after death, would be comforted under the troubles of life, and supported in the hour of death.

III. He proceeds to deduce an inference to excite and quicken himself and others to duty, *vv.* 9–11. Here observe, 1. What it was that the apostle was thus ambitious of—*acceptance with God.* This they coveted as the greatest favour and the highest honour: it was the summit of their ambition. 2. What further quickening motives they had to excite their diligence, from the consideration of the judgment to come, *vv.* 10, 11. The apostle calls this awful judgment *the terror of the Lord* (*v.* 11), and, by the consideration thereof, was excited to persuade men to repent, and live a holy life, that, when Christ shall appear, they may appear before him comfortably.

CONSTRAINT OF LOVE
(vv. 12–15)

Here observe, I. The apostle makes an apology for seeming to commend himself and his fellow-labourers (v. 13), and tells them, 1. It was not to commend themselves, nor for their own sakes, that he had spoken of their fidelity and diligence in the former verses; nor was he willing to suspect their good opinion of him. But, 2. The true reason was this, to put an argument in their mouths wherewith to answer his accusers, who made vain boastings, and gloried in appearances only.

II. He gives good reasons for their great zeal and diligence. The apostle tells them, 1. It was for the glory of God, and the good of the church, that he was thus zealous and industrious. For, 2. *The love of Christ constrained them*, v. 14. They were under the sweetest and strongest constraints to do what they did.

AMBASSADORS FOR CHRIST
(vv 16–21)

In these verses the apostle mentions two things that are necessary for our living to Christ, both of which are the consequences of Christ's dying for us; namely, regeneration and reconciliation.

I. Regeneration, which consists of two things; namely, 1. Weanedness from the world: "*Henceforth we know no man after the flesh*," v. 16. *Yea, though we have known Christ after the flesh, yet*, says the apostle, *we know him no more*. It is questioned whether Paul had seen Christ in the flesh. However, the rest of the apostles had, and so might some among those he was now writing to. However, he would not have them value themselves upon that account; for even the bodily presence of Christ is not to be desired nor doted upon by his disciples. We must live upon his spiritual presence, and the comfort it affords. 2. A thorough change of the heart: *For if any man be in Christ*, if any man be a Christian indeed, and will approve himself such, *he is*, or he must be, *a new creature*, v. 17. Some read it, *Let him be a new creature*.

II. Reconciliation, which is here spoken of under a double notion:

1. As an unquestionable privilege, vv. 18, 19. Reconciliation supposes a quarrel, or breach of friendship; and sin has made a breach, it has broken the friendship between God and man. Yet, behold, there may be a reconciliation; the offended Majesty of heaven is willing to be reconciled.

2. Reconciliation is here spoken of as our indispensable duty, v. 20. As God is willing to be reconciled to us, we ought to be reconciled to God. Faithful ministers are Christ's ambassadors, sent to treat with sinners on peace and reconciliation: they come in God's name, with his entreaties, and act in Christ's stead, doing the very thing he did when he was upon this earth, and what he wills to be done now that he is in heaven. And for our encouragement so to do the apostle subjoins what should be well known and duly considered by us (v. 21), namely (1) The purity of the Mediator: *He knew no sin*. (2) The sacrifice he offered: *He was made*

sin; not a sinner, but *sin*, that is, a sin-offering, a sacrifice for sin. (3) The end and design of all this: that *we might be made the righteousness of God in him*, might be justified freely by the grace of God through the redemption which is in Christ Jesus.

WORKERS WITH GOD
(*vv.* 1–10)

In these verses we have an account of the apostle's general errand and exhortation to all to whom he preached in every place where he came, with the several arguments and methods he used. Observe,

I. The errand or exhortation itself, namely, to comply with the gospel offers of reconciliation— that, being favoured with the gospel, they would not receive this *grace of God in vain*, *v.* 1.

II. The arguments and method which the apostle used. And here he tells them,

1. The present time is the only proper season to accept of the grace that is offered, and improve that grace which is afforded: *Now is the accepted time*. NOW *is the day of salvation*, *v.* 2.

2. What caution they used not to give offence that might hinder the success of their preaching: *Giving no offence in any thing*, *v.* 3. He was careful, in all his words and actions, not to give offence, or occasion of guilt or grief.

3. Their constant aim and endeavour in all things to approve themselves faithful, as became the ministers of God, *v.* 4. (1) By much patience in afflictions. (2) By

acting from good principles. The apostle went by a good principle in all he did, and tells them what his principles were (*vv.* 6, 7); namely, pureness; and there is no piety without purity. (3) By a due temper and behaviour under all the variety of conditions in this world, *vv.* 8–10. They were despised as poor, upon the account of their poverty in this world; and yet they made many rich, by preaching the unsearchable riches of Christ. Such a paradox is a Christian's life, and through such a variety of conditions and reports lies our way to heaven; and we should be careful in all these things to approve ourselves to God.

NO COMPROMISE (*vv.* 11–18)

The apostle proceeds to address himself more particularly to the Corinthians, and cautions them against mingling with unbelievers. Here observe,

I. How the caution is introduced with a profession of the most tender affection to them, *even like that of a father to his children*, *vv.* 11–13.

II. The caution or exhortation itself, not to mingle with unbelievers, not to be *unequally yoked* with them, *v.* 14. Either,

1. In stated relations. Those relations that are our choice must be chosen by rule; and it is good for those who are themselves the children of God to join with those who are so likewise; for there is more danger that the bad will damage the good than hope that the good will benefit the bad.

2. In common conversation. We should not yoke ourselves in friendship and acquaintance with wicked men and unbelievers. Though we

cannot wholly avoid seeing, and hearing, and being with such, yet we should never choose them for our bosom-friends.

3. Much less should we join in religious communion with them. The apostle gives several good reasons against this corrupt mixture. (1) It is a very great absurdity, *vv.* 14, 15. It is an unequal yoking of things together that will not agree together. (2) It is a dishonour to the Christian's profession (*v.* 16); for Christians are by profession, and should be in reality, the *temples of the living God*—dedicated to, and employed for, the service of God. Now there can be no agreement between *the temple of God and idols.* Idols are rivals with God for his honour, and God is a jealous God, and will not give his glory to another. (3) There is a great deal of danger in communicating with unbelievers and idolaters, danger of being defiled and of being rejected; therefore the exhortation is (*v.* 17) *to come out from among them,* and keep at a due distance, *to be separate.* (4) It is base ingratitude to God for all the favours he has bestowed upon believers and promised to them, *v.* 18.

CHAPTER SEVEN
PROGRESSIVE HOLINESS
(*vv.* 1–4)

These verses contain a double exhortation:

I. To make a progress in holiness, or *to perfect holiness in the fear of God, v.* 1. The promises of God are strong inducements to sanctification, in both the branches thereof; namely, 1. The dying unto sin, or

mortifying our lusts and corruptions: we must *cleanse ourselves from all filthiness of flesh and spirit.* 2. The living unto righteousness and holiness. If we hope God is our Father, we must endeavour to be *partakers of his holiness,* to be holy as he is holy, and perfect as our Father in heaven is perfect.

II. To show a due regard to the ministers of the gospel: *Receive us, v.* 2. If the ministers of the gospel are thought contemptible because of their office, there is danger lest the gospel itself be contemned also. He tells them, 1. He had done nothing to forfeit their esteem and good-will, but was cautious not to do any thing to deserve their ill-will (*v.* 2). 2. He did not herein reflect upon them for want of affection to him, *vv.* 3, 4. So tenderly and cautiously did the apostle deal with the Corinthians, among whom there were some who would be glad of any occasion to reproach him, and prejudice the minds of others against him.

GODLY SORROW (*vv.* 5–11)

There seems to be a connection between *ch.* ii. 13 (where the apostle said he had no rest in his spirit when he found not Titus at Troas) and the fifth verse of this chapter: and so great was his affection to the Corinthians, and his concern about their behaviour in relation to the incestuous person, that, in his further travels, he still had no rest till he heard from them. And now he tells them,

I. How he was distressed, *v.* 5. He was troubled when he did not meet with Titus and, besides this, they met with other troubles, with incessant storms of persecutions; there were *fightings without*, or continual contentions with, and opposition from, Jews and Gentiles; and there were *fears within*, and great concern for such as had embraced the Christian faith, lest they should be corrupted or seduced, and give scandal to others, or be scandalized.

II. How he was comforted, *vv*. 6, 7. Here observe, 1. The very coming of Titus was some comfort to him. It was matter of joy to see him, whom he long desired and expected to meet with.

III. How greatly he rejoiced at their repentance, and the evidences thereof. The apostle was sorry that he had grieved them, but now he rejoiced, when he found they had *sorrowed to repentance, v.* 9. Their sorrow in itself was not the cause of his rejoicing; but the nature of it, and the effect of it (*repentance unto salvation, v.* 10), made him rejoice. Observe here,

1. The antecedent of true repentance is godly sorrow; this worketh repentance. It is not repentance itself, but it is a good preparative to repentance, and in some sense the cause that produces repentance.

2. The happy fruits and consequences of true repentance are mentioned (*v.* 11); and those *fruits that are meet for repentance* are the best evidences of it. Where the heart is changed, the life and actions will be changed too.

BOASTING COME TRUE
(*vv*. 12–16)

In these verses the apostle endeavours to comfort the Corinthians, upon whom his admonitions had had such good effect. And in order thereto, 1. He tells them he had a good design in his former epistle, which might be thought severe, *v.* 12. It was not chiefly *for his cause that did the wrong*, not only for his benefit, much less merely that he should be punished; nor was it merely *for his cause that suffered wrong*, namely, the injured father, and that he might have what satisfaction could be given him; but it was also to manifest his great and sincere concern and *care for them*, for the whole church, lest that should suffer by letting such a crime, and the scandal thereof, remain among them without due remark and resentment. 2. He acquaints them with the joy of Titus as well as of himself upon the account of their repentance and good behaviour. 3. He concludes this whole matter with expressing the entire confidence he had in them.

THE GENEROUS MACEDONIANS
(*vv*. 1–6)

Observe here,

I. The apostle takes occasion from the good example of the churches of Macedonia, that is, of Philippi, Thessalonica, Berea, and others in the region of Macedonia, to exhort the Corinthians and the Christians in Achaia to the good work of charity. And,

1. He acquaints them with their great liberality, which he calls *the grace of God bestowed on the churches, v.* 1. Some think the words should be rendered, *the gift of God given in or by the churches*.

He certainly means the charitable gifts of these churches, which are called the grace or gifts of God.

2. He commends the charity of the Macedonians, and sets it forth with good advantage. He tells them, (1) They were but in a low condition, and themselves in distress, yet they contributed to the relief of others. (2) They gave very largely, with *the riches of liberality* (v. 2), that is, as liberally as if they had been rich. It was a large contribution they made, all things considered; it was *according to*, yea *beyond, their power* (v. 3), as much as could well be expected from them, if not more. (3) They were very ready and forward to this good work. *They were willing of themselves* (v. 3), and were so far from needing that Paul should urge and press them with many arguments that they *prayed him with much entreaty to receive the gift*, v. 4. (4) Their charity was founded in true piety, and this was the great commendation of it. They performed this good work in a right method: *First they gave themselves to the Lord, and then* they gave unto us their contributions, *by the will of God* (v. 5), that is, according as it was the will of God they should do, or to be disposed of as the will of God should be, and for his glory.

II. The apostle tells them that Titus was desired to go and make a collection among them (v. 6), and Titus, he knew, would be an acceptable person to them.

MOTIVES FOR GIVING
(vv. 7–15)

In these verses the apostle uses several cogent arguments to stir up the Corinthians to this good work of charity.

I. He urges upon them the consideration of their eminence in other gifts and graces, and would have them excel in this of charity also, v. 7. Great address and much holy art are here used by the apostle.

II. Another argument is taken from the consideration of the grace of our Lord Jesus Christ. He was born in poor circumstances, lived a poor life, and died in poverty; and this was for our sakes, that we thereby might be made rich, rich in the love and favour of God, rich in the blessings and promises of the new covenant, rich in the hopes of eternal life, being heirs of the kingdom. This is a good reason why we should be charitable to the poor out of what we have, because we ourselves live upon the charity of the Lord Jesus Christ.

III. Another argument is taken from their good purposes, and their forwardness to begin this good work. As to this he tells them, 1. It was expedient for them to perform what they purposed, and finish what they had begun, vv. 10, 11. For, 2. This would be acceptable to God. *This willing mind is accepted* (v. 12), when accompanied with sincere endeavours. When men purpose that which is good, and endeavour, according to their ability, to perform also, God will accept of what they have, or can do, and not reject them for what they have not, and what is not in their power to do.

IV. Another argument is taken from the discrimination which the divine Providence makes in the distribution of the things of this world, and the mutability of human affairs, *vv.* 13–15. The force of the arguing seems to be this: It is the will of God that, by our mutually supplying one another, there should *be some sort of equality*; not an *absolute* equality indeed, or such a levelling as would destroy property, for in such a case there could be no exercise of charity. But as in works of charity there should be an equitable proportion observed, that the burden should not lie too heavy on some, while others are wholly eased, so all should think themselves concerned to supply those who are in want. Note, Such is the condition of men in this world that we mutually depend on one another, and should help one another.

PAUL'S MESSENGERS
(*vv.* 16–24)

In these verses the apostle commends the brethren who were sent to them to collect their charity; and, as it were, gives them letters credential, that, if they *were enquired after* (*v.* 23), if any should be inquisitive or suspicious concerning them, it might be known who they were and how safely they might be trusted.

I. He commends Titus, 1. For his earnest care and great concern of heart for them, and desire in all things to promote their welfare. 2. For his readiness to this present service.

II. He commends another brother, who was sent with Titus. It is generally thought that this was Luke. He is commended, 1. As a man whose *praise was in the gospel through all the churches*, *v.* 18. His ministerial services of several kinds were well known, and he had approved himself praiseworthy in what he had done. 2. As one chosen of the churches (*v.* 19) and joined with the apostle in his ministration.

III. He commends also another brother who was joined with the two former in this affair. This brother is thought to be Apollos.

IV. He concludes this point with a general good character of them all (*v.* 23), as *fellow-labourers with him* for their welfare; as the *messengers of the churches*; as the *glory of Christ*, who were to him for a name and a praise, who brought glory to Christ as instruments and had obtained honour from Christ to be counted faithful and employed in his service.

BE GENEROUS! (*vv.* 1–5)

In these verses the apostle speaks very respectfully to the Corinthians, and with great skill; and, while he seems to excuse his urging them so earnestly to charity, still presses them thereto, and shows how much his heart was set upon this matter.

I. He tells them it was needless to press them with further arguments to afford relief to their poor brethren (*v.* 1), being satisfied he had said enough already to prevail with those of whom he had so good an opinion. Note, Christians should consult the reputation of their profession, and endeavour to *adorn the doctrine of God our Saviour.*

GOD'S GIFT (*vv.* 6–15)

Here we have,

I. Proper directions to be observed about the right and acceptable manner of bestowing charity; and it is of great concernment that we not only do what is required, but do it as is commanded. Now, as to the manner in which the apostle would have the Corinthians give, observe, 1. It should be bountifully; this was intimated, *v.* 5, that a liberal contribution was expected, a matter of bounty, not what savoured of covetousness; and he offers to their consideration that men who expect a good return at harvest are not wont to pinch and spare in sowing their seed, for the return is usually proportionable to what they sow, *v.* 6. 2. It should be deliberately. *Every man, according as he purposes in his heart, v.* 7. Works of charity, like other good works, should be done with thought and design. 3. It should be freely, whatever we give, be it more or less: *Not grudgingly, nor of necessity*, but cheerfully, *v.* 7.

II. Good encouragement to perform this work of charity in the manner directed. Here the apostle tells the Corinthians,

1. They themselves would be no losers by what they gave in charity. For, (1) God loveth a cheerful giver (*v.* 7), and what may not those hope to receive who are the objects of the divine love? (2) God is able to make our charity redound to our advantage, *v.* 8. (3) The apostle puts up a prayer to God in their behalf that they might be gainers, and not losers, *vv.* 10, 11.

2. While they would be no losers, the poor distressed saints would be gainers; for this service would *supply their wants, v.* 12.

3. This would redound to the praise and glory of God. Many thanksgivings would be given to God on this account, by the apostle, and by those who were employed in this ministration, *v.* 11.

4. Those whose wants were supplied would make the best return they were able, by sending up many prayers to God for those who had relieved them, *v.* 14.

Lastly, The apostle concludes this whole matter with this doxology, *Thanks be to God for his unspeakable gift, v.* 15. It should seem that he means Jesus Christ, who is indeed the unspeakable gift of God unto this world, a gift we have all reason to be very thankful for.

CHAPTER TEN

THE CHRISTIAN'S WEAPONS
(*vv.* 1–6)

Here we may observe,

I. The mild and humble manner in which the blessed apostle addresses the Corinthians. 1. He addresses them in a very mild and humble manner: *I Paul myself beseech you, v.* 1.

2. He is desirous that no occasion may be given to use severity, *v.* 2. Hereupon,

II. He asserts the power of his preaching and his power to punish offenders.

1. The power of his preaching, *vv.* 3, 5. Here observe, (1) The work of the ministry is a warfare, not *after the flesh* indeed, for it is a spiritual warfare, with spiritual

enemies and for spiritual purposes. (2) The doctrines of the gospel and discipline of the church are the weapons of this warfare; and these are not carnal: outward force, therefore, is not the method of the gospel, but strong persuasions, by the power of truth and the meekness of wisdom.

2. The apostle's power to punish offenders (and that in an extraordinary manner) is asserted in *v.* 6. The apostle speaks not of personal revenge, but of punishing disobedience to the gospel, and disorderly walking among church-members by inflicting church-censures.

PAUL'S BODILY PRESENCE
(*vv.* 7–11)

In these verses the apostle proceeds to reason the case with the Corinthians, in opposition to those who despised him, judged him, and spoke hardly of him: "*Do you,*" says he, "*look on things after the outward appearance?*" *v.* 7. In outward appearance, Paul was mean and despicable with some; he did not make a figure, as perhaps some of his competitors might do: but this was a false rule to make a judgment by. It should seem that some boasted mighty things of themselves, and made a fair show. But there are often false appearances. A man may seem to be learned who has not learned Christ, and appear virtuous when he has not a principle of grace in his heart. However, the apostle asserts two things of himself:

I. His relation to Christ: *If any man trust to himself that he is Christ's, even so are we Christ's,* *v.* 7.

II. His authority from Christ as an apostle. This he had mentioned before (*v.* 6), and now he tells them that he might speak of it again, and that with some sort of boasting, seeing it was a truth, that the *Lord had given it to him,* and it was more than his adversaries could justly pretend to.

SELF-COMMENDATION NO VIRTUE
(*vv.* 12–18)

In these verses observe,

I. The apostle refuses to justify himself, or to act by such rules as the false apostles did, *v.* 12.

II. He fixes a better rule for his conduct, namely, *not to boast of things without his measure,* which was the measure *God had distributed* to him, *v.* 13. His meaning is, either that he would not boast of more gifts or graces, or power and authority, than God had really bestowed on him; or, rather, that he would not act beyond his commission as to persons or things, nor go beyond the line prescribed to him, which he plainly intimates the false apostles did, while they *boasted of other men's labours.* The apostle's resolution was to keep within his own province, and that compass of ground which God had marked out for him.

III. He acted according to this rule: *We stretch not ourselves beyond our measure,* *v.* 14.

IV. He declares his success in observing this rule. His hope was that their faith was increased, and that others beyond them, even in the remoter parts of Achaia, would embrace the gospel also; and in all this he exceeded not his commission, nor acted in another man's line.

V. He seems to check himself in this matter, as if he had spoken too much in his own praise. 1. *He that glorieth should glory in the Lord, v.* 17. 2. *Not he that commendeth himself is approved, but he whom the Lord commendeth, v.* 18.

CHAPTER ELEVEN

GODLY JEALOUSY (vv. 1–4)

Here we may observe, 1. The apology the apostle makes for going about to commend himself. It is no pleasure to a good man to speak well of himself, yet in some cases it is lawful, namely, when it is for the advantage of others, or for our own necessary vindication; as thus it was here. For, 2. We have the reasons for what the apostle did. (1) To preserve the Corinthians from being corrupted by the insinuations of the false apostles, *vv.* 2, 3. (2) To vindicate himself against the false apostles, forasmuch as they could not pretend they had another Jesus, or another Spirit, or another gospel, to preach to them, *v.* 4.

FALSE APOSTLES (vv. 5–15)

After the foregoing preface to what he was about to say, the apostle in these verses mentions,

1. His equality with the other apostles—that *he was not a whit behind the very chief of the apostles, v.* 5. The apostleship, as an office, was equal in all the apostles; but

the apostles, like other Christians, differed one from another.

II. His equality with the false apostles in this particular—the preaching of the gospel unto them freely, without wages. This the apostle largely insists on, and shows that, as they could not but own him to be a minister of Christ, so they ought to acknowledge he had been a good friend to them. For, 1. He had preached the gospel to them freely, *vv.* 7–10. He says he himself had *taken wages of other churches* (*v.* 8), so that he had a right to have asked and received from them: yet he waived his right, and chose rather to abase himself, by working with his hands in the trade of tent-making to maintain himself, than be burdensome to them, that they might *be exalted*, or encouraged to receive the gospel, which they had so cheaply. 2. He informs them of the reason of this his conduct among them. It was not because *he did not love them* (*v.* 11), but it was to avoid offence, that *he might cut off occasion from those that desired occasion.* He would not give occasion for any to accuse him of worldly designs in preaching the gospel.

III. The false apostles are charged *as deceitful workers* (*v.* 13), and that upon this account, because they would *transform themselves* into the likeness of the apostles of Christ, and, though they were the ministers of Satan, would seem to be the *ministers of righteousness.* But it follows, *Their end is according to their works* (*v.* 15); the end will discover them to be deceitful workers, and their work will end in ruin and destruction.

THE RELUCTANT
BOASTER I (*vv.* 16–21)

Here we have a further excuse that the apostle makes for what he was about to say in his own vindication. 1. He would not have them think he was guilty of folly, in saying what he said to vindicate himself: *Let no man think me a fool, v.* 16. Ordinarily, indeed, it is unbecoming a wise man to be much and often speaking in his own praise. Boasting of ourselves is usually not only a sign of a proud mind, but a mark of folly also. However, says the apostle, yet *as a fool receive me*; that is, if you count it folly in me to *boast a little*, yet give due regard to what I shall say. 2. He mentions a caution, to prevent the abuse of what he should say, telling them that what he spoke, *he did not speak after the Lord, v.* 17. He would not have them think that boasting of ourselves, or glorying in what we have, is a thing commanded by the Lord in general unto Christians. 3. He gives a good reason why they should suffer him to boast a little; namely, because they suffered others to do so who had less reason. *You suffer fools gladly, seeing you yourselves are wise* (*v.* 19), may be ironical, and then the meaning is this: "Notwithstanding all your wisdom, you willingly suffer yourselves to be *brought into bondage* under the Jewish yoke, or suffer others to tyrannize over you."

THE RELUCTANT BOASTER
(*vv.* 22–33)

Here the apostle gives a large account of his own qualifications, labours, and sufferings (not out of pride or vain-glory, but to the honour of God, who had enabled him to do and suffer so much for the cause of Christ). Observe,

I. He mentions the privileges of his birth (*v.* 22), which were equal to any they could pretend to.

II. He makes mention also of his apostleship, that he was more than an ordinary minister of Christ, *v.* 23.

III. He chiefly insists upon this, that he had been an extraordinary sufferer for Christ; and this was what he gloried in, or rather he gloried in the grace of God that had enabled him to be more *abundant in labours*, and to endure very great sufferings, such as *stripes above measure, frequent imprisonments*, and *often* the dangers of *death, v.* 23.

CHAPTER TWELVE
THORN IN THE FLESH
(*vv.* 1–10)

Here we may observe,

I. The narrative the apostle gives of the favours God had shown him, and the honour he had done him; for doubtless he himself is the man in Christ of whom he speaks. Concerning this we may take notice, 1. Of the honour itself which was done to the apostle: he was *caught up into the third heaven, v.* 2. The apostle does not mention what he saw in the third heaven or paradise, but tells us that *he heard unspeakable words*, such as it is not possible for a man to utter—such are the sublimity of the matter and our unacquaintedness with the language of the upper world: nor was it lawful to utter those words, because, while we are here in this world, we have a more sure word of prophecy than such visions and revelations. 2 Pet. i. 19. 2. The modest and humble manner in which the apostle mentions this matter is observable. One would be apt to think that one who had had such visions and revelations as these would have boasted greatly of them; but, says he, *It is not expedient for me doubtless to glory*, v. 1.

II. The apostle gives an account of the methods God took to keep him humble, and to prevent his *being lifted up above measure*; and this he speaks of to balance the account that was given before of the visions and revelations he had had. Here observe,

1. The apostle was pained with a thorn in the flesh, and buffeted with a messenger of Satan, v. 7. We are much in the dark what this was, whether some great trouble or some great temptation. Some think it was an acute bodily pain or sickness; others think it was the indignities done him by the false apostles, and the opposition he met with from them, particularly on the account of his speech, which was contemptible.

2. The design of this was to keep the apostle humble: *Lest he should be exalted above measure*, v. 7. If God love us, he will hide pride from us, and keep us from being exalted above measure; and spiritual burdens are ordered, to cure spiritual pride. This thorn in the flesh is said to be a messenger of Satan, which he did not send with a good design, but, on the contrary, with ill intentions, to discourage the apostle (who had been

so highly favoured of God) and hinder him in his work. But God designed this for good, and he overruled it for good, and made this messenger of Satan to be so far from being a hindrance that it was a help to the apostle.

3. The apostle prayed earnestly to God for the removal of this sore grievance.

4. We have an account of the answer given to the apostle's prayer, that, although the trouble was not removed, yet an equivalent should be granted: *My grace is sufficient for thee*. Note, (1) Though God accepts the prayer of faith, yet he does not always answer it in the letter; as he sometimes grants in wrath, so he sometimes denies in love. (2) When God does not remove our troubles and temptations, yet, if he gives us grace sufficient for us, we have no reason to complain, nor to say that he deals ill by us.

III. Here is the use which the apostle makes of this dispensation: *He gloried in his infirmities* (v. 9), and took pleasure in them, v. 10. And the reason of his glory and joy on account of these things was this —they were fair opportunities for Christ to manifest the power and sufficiency of his grace resting upon him, by which he had so much experience of the strength of divine grace that he could say, *When I am weak then am I strong*. This is a Christian paradox: when we are weak in ourselves, then we are strong in the grace of our Lord Jesus Christ.

APOSTOLIC SIGNS (vv. 11–21)

In these verses the apostle addresses

himself to the Corinthians two ways:

I. He blames them for what was faulty in them; namely, that they had not stood up in his defence as they ought to have done, and so made it the more needful for him to insist so much on his own vindication. They in a manner compelled him to commend himself, who *ought to have been commended of them, v.* 11.

II. He gives a large account of his behaviour and kind intentions towards them, in which we may observe the character of a faithful minister of the gospel. 1. He was not willing to be burdensome to them, nor did he seek theirs, but them. 2. He would gladly spend and be spent for them (*v.* 15); that is, he was willing to take pains and to suffer loss for their good. 3. He did not abate in his love to them, notwithstanding their unkindness and ingratitude to him. 4. He was careful not only that he himself should not be burdensome, but that none he employed should. This seems to be the meaning of what we read, *vv.* 16–18. 5. He was a man who did all things for edifying, *v.* 19. This was his great aim and design, to do good, to lay the foundation well, and then with care and diligence to build the superstructure. 6. He would not shrink from his duty for fear of displeasing them, though he was so careful to make himself easy to them. 7. He was grieved at the apprehension that he should find scandalous sins among them not duly repented of. This, he tells them, would be the cause of great humiliation and lamentation.

CHAPTER THIRTEEN
OBSTINACY REPROVED
(*vv.* 1–6)

In these verses observe,

I. The apostle threatens to be severe against obstinate sinners when he should come to Corinth, having now sent to them a first and second epistle, with proper admonitions and exhortations, in order to reform what was amiss among them. Concerning this we may notice, 1. The caution with which he proceeded in his censures: he was not hasty in using severity, but gave a first and second admonition. 2. The threatening itself: *That if* (or when) *he came again* (in person) *he would not spare* obstinate sinners, and such as were impenitent, in their scandalous enormities. He would not spare such, but would inflict church-censures upon them, which are thought to have been accompanied in those early times with visible and extraordinary tokens of divine displeasure.

II. The apostle assigns a reason why he would be thus severe, namely, for *a proof of Christ's speaking in him*, which they *sought after, v.* 3. *Examine yourselves*, &c. Hereby he intimates that, if they could prove their own Christianity, this would be a proof of his apostleship; for if they were in the faith, if Jesus Christ was in them, this was a proof that Christ spoke in him, because it was by his ministry that they did believe.

AIM AT PERFECTION
(*vv.* 7–10)

Here we have,

I. The apostle's prayer to God

on the behalf of the Corinthians, that they might *do no evil*, *v.* 7. We are more concerned to pray that we may not do evil than that we may not suffer evil.

II. The reasons why the apostle put up this prayer to God on behalf of the Corinthians. Observe, he tells them, 1. It was not so much for his own personal reputation as for the honour of religion: "*Not that we should appear approved, but that you should do that which is honest*, or decent, and for the credit of religion, though we should be reproached and vilified, and accounted as reprobates," *v.* 7. 2. Another reason was this: that they might be free from all blame and censure when he should come to them. This is intimated in *v.* 8, *We can do nothing against the truth, but for the truth.* "*We are glad,*" says he (*v.* 9), "*when we are weak and you are strong*; that is, that we have no power to censure those who are strong in faith and fruitful in good works." For, 3. He desired their perfection (*v.* 9); that

is, that they might be sincere, and aim at perfection (sincerity is our gospel-perfection), or else he wished there might be a thorough reformation among them.

A LAST WORD (*vv.* 11–14)

Thus the apostle concludes this epistle with,

I. A valediction. He gives them a parting farewell, and takes his leave of them for the present, with hearty good wishes for their spiritual welfare.

II. The apostolical benediction (*v.* 14): *The grace of the Lord Jesus Christ, and the love of God, and the communion of the Holy Ghost, be with you all.* Thus the apostle concludes his epistle, and thus it is usual and proper to dismiss worshipping assemblies. This plainly proves the doctrine of the gospel, and is an acknowledgment that Father, Son, and Spirit, are three distinct persons, yet but one God; and herein the same, that they are the fountain of all blessings to men.

THE EPISTLE OF ST. PAUL TO THE

GALATIANS

CHAPTER ONE
INTRODUCTION (vv. 1–5)

In these verses we have the preface
or introduction to the epistle,
where observe,

I. The person or persons from
whom this epistle is sent—from Paul
an apostle, &c., *and all the brethren
that were with him.*

II. To whom this epistle is sent—
to the churches of Galatia. There
were several churches at that time
in the country, and it should seem
that all of them were more or less
corrupted through the arts of those
seducers who had crept in among
them; and therefore Paul, on whom
came daily the care of all the churches,
being deeply affected with their
state, and concerned for their
recovery to the faith and establishment in it, writes this epistle to
them. He directs it to all of them,
as being all more or less concerned
in the matter of it; and he gives
them the name of *churches*, though
they had done enough to forfeit it,
for corrupt churches are never
allowed to be churches: no doubt
there were some among them who
still continued in the faith, and he
was not without hope that others
might be recovered to it.

III. The apostolical benediction,
v. 3. Herein the apostle, and the
brethren who were with him, wish
these churches *grace and peace from
God the Father, and from the Lord
Jesus Christ*. This is the usual
blessing wherewith he blesses the
churches in the name of the Lord—
grace and peace. Having mentioned
the Lord Jesus Christ, he cannot
pass without enlarging upon his
love; and therefore adds (*v.* 4),
*Who gave himself for our sins, that
he might deliver*, &c. Jesus Christ
gave himself for our sins, as a great
sacrifice to make atonement for us;
this the justice of God required, and
to this he freely submitted for our
sakes. One great end hereof was *to
deliver us from this present evil
world*; not only to redeem us from
the wrath of God, and the curse of
the law, but also to recover us from
the corruption that is in the world.

ANOTHER GOSPEL (vv. 6–9)

Here the apostle comes to the body
of the epistle; and he begins it with
a more general reproof of these
churches for their unsteadiness in
the faith, which he afterwards, in
some following parts of it, enlarges
more upon. Here we may observe,

I. How much he was concerned
at their defection: *I marvel*, &c. It
filled him at once with the greatest
surprise and sorrow. Their sin and
folly were that they did not hold
fast the doctrine of Christianity as
it had been preached to them, but
suffered themselves to be removed
from the purity and simplicity of it.

They were removed to *another gospel, which yet was not another.* Thus the apostle represents the doctrine of these judaizing teachers; he calls it another gospel, because it opened a different way of justification and salvation from that which was revealed in the gospel, namely, by works, and not by faith in Christ. And yet he adds, "*Which is not another*—you will find it to be no gospel at all—not really another gospel, but the perverting of the gospel of Christ, and the overturning of the foundations of that"—whereby he intimates that those who go about to establish any other way to heaven than what the gospel of Christ has revealed are guilty of a gross perversion of it, and in the issue will find themselves wretchedly mistaken.

II. How confident he was that the gospel he had preached to them was the only true gospel. He was so fully persuaded of this that he pronounced an anathema upon those who pretended to preach any other gospel (*v.* 8), and, to let them see that this did not proceed from any rashness or intemperate zeal in him, he repeated it, *v.* 9.

PAUL'S TESTIMONY
(*vv.* 10–24)

Paul here sets himself to prove the divinity both of his mission and doctrine, that thereby he might wipe off the aspersions which his enemies had cast upon him, and recover these Christians into a better opinion of the gospel he had preached to them. This he gives sufficient evidence of,

I. From the scope and design of his ministry, which was *not to persuade men, but God,* &c. The meaning of this may be either that in his preaching the gospel he did not act in obedience to men, but God, who had called him to this work and office; or that his aim therein was to bring persons to the obedience, not of men, but of God.

II. From the manner wherein he received the gospel which he preached to them, concerning which he assures them (*vv.* 11,12) that he had it not by information from others, but by revelation from heaven. This he was concerned to make out, to prove himself an apostle: and to this purpose,

1. He tells them what his education was, and what, accordingly, his conversation in time past had been, *vv.* 13, 14. Particularly, he acquaints them that he had been brought up in the Jewish religion, and *that he had profited in it above many his equals of his own nation*—that *he had been exceedingly zealous of the traditions of the elders. He had beyond measure persecuted the church of God, and wasted it.*

2. In how wonderful a manner he was turned from the error of his ways, brought to the knowledge and faith of Christ, and appointed to the office of an apostle, *vv.* 15, 16. This was not done in an ordinary way, nor by ordinary means, but in an extraordinary manner; for, (1) God had *separated him hereunto from his mother's womb*: the change that was wrought in him was in pursuance of a divine purpose concerning him, whereby he was appointed to be a Christian and an apostle, before he came into the world, or had done either good or

evil. (2) He was *called by his grace*. All who are savingly converted are called by the grace of God; their conversion is the effect of his good pleasure concerning them, and is effected by his power and grace in them. (3) He had Christ *revealed in him*. He was not only revealed to him, but in him. It pleased God *to reveal his Son in him*, to bring him to the knowledge of Christ and his gospel by special and immediate revelation. And, (4) It was with this design, that he should preach him among the heathen; not only that he should embrace him himself, but preach him to others; so that he was both a Christian and an apostle by revelation.

3. He acquaints them how he behaved himself hereupon, from *v.* 16, to the end. Being thus called to this work and office, *he conferred not with flesh and blood*. This may be taken more generally, and so we may learn from it that, when God calls us by his grace, we must not consult flesh and blood. But the meaning of it here is that he did not consult men; he did not apply to any others for their advice and direction; *neither did he go up to Jerusalem, to those that were apostles before him*, as though he needed to be approved by them, or to receive any further instructions or authority from them: but, instead of that, he steered another course, and *went into Arabia*, either as a place of retirement proper for receiving further divine revelations, or in order to preach the gospel there among the Gentiles, being appointed to be the apostle of the Gentiles; and thence *he returned again to Damascus*, where he had

first begun his ministry, and whence he had with difficulty escaped the rage of his enemies, Acts ix. It was not till *three years after* his conversion that *he went up to Jerusalem, to see Peter*; and when he did so he made but a very short stay with him, no more than *fifteen days*; nor, while he was there, did he go much into conversation; for *others of the apostles he saw none, but James, the Lord's brother*. So that it could not well be pretended that he was indebted to any other either for his knowledge of the gospel or his authority to preach it; but it appeared that both his qualifications for, and his call to, the apostolic office were extraordinary and divine. After this he acquaints them that *he came into the regions of Syria and Cilicia*: having made this short visit to Peter, he returns to his work again. He had no communication at that time with the *churches of Christ in Judea*, they had not so much as *seen his face; but, having heard that he who persecuted them in times past now preached the faith which he once destroyed, they glorified God* because of him; thanksgivings were rendered by many unto God on that behalf; the very report of this mighty change in him, as it filled them with joy, so it excited them to give glory to God on the account of it.

CHAPTER TWO
PAUL AT JERUSALEM
(*vv.* 1-10)

In these verses Paul informs us of another journey which he took to Jerusalem, and of what passed between him and the other apostles there, *vv.* 1–10. Here he acquaints us,

I. With some circumstances relating to this his journey thither. As particularly, 1. With the time of it: that it was not till *fourteen years* after the former (mentioned *ch.* i. 18), or, as others choose to understand it, from his conversion, or from the death of Christ.

II. He gives us an account of his behaviour while he was at Jerusalem, which was such as made it appear that he was not in the least inferior to the other apostles, but that both his authority and qualifications were every way equal to theirs. He particularly acquaints us,

1. That *he there communicated the gospel to them, which he preached among the Gentiles, but privately*, &c. Here we may observe both the faithfulness and prudence of our great apostle. (1) His faithfulness in giving them a free and fair account of the doctrine which he had all along preached among the Gentiles, and was still resolved to preach—that of pure Christianity, free from all mixtures of Judaism. And yet, (2) He uses prudence and caution herein, for fear of giving offence.

2. That in his practice he firmly adhered to the doctrine which he had preached. Paul was a man of resolution, and would adhere to his principles; and therefore, though he had Titus with him, who was a Greek, yet he would not suffer him to be circumcised, because he would not betray the doctrine of Christ, as he had preached it to the Gentiles. It does not appear that the apostles at all insisted upon

this; for, though they connived at the use of circumcision among the Jewish converts, yet they were not for imposing it upon the Gentiles. But there were others who did, whom the apostle here calls *false brethren*, and concerning whom he informs us that they were *unawares brought in*, that is, into the church, or into their company, and that they came only to *spy out their liberty which they had in Christ Jesus*, or to see whether Paul would stand up in defence of that freedom from the ceremonial law which he had taught as the doctrine of the gospel, and represented as the privilege of those who embraced the Christian religion. Their design herein was *to bring them into bondage*, which they would have effected could they have gained the point they aimed at.

3. That, though he conversed with the other apostles, yet he did not receive any addition to his knowledge or authority from them, *v.* 6.

4. That the issue of this conversation was that the other apostles were fully convinced of his divine mission and authority, and accordingly acknowledged him as their fellow-apostle, *vv.* 7–10.

CRUCIFIED WITH CHRIST
(*vv.* 11–21)

I. To give the greater weight to what he had already said, and more fully to fortify them against the insinuations of the judaizing teachers, he acquaints them with another interview which he had with the apostle Peter at Antioch, and what passed between them there, *vv.* 11–14.

Peter and the other apostles had both acknowledged Paul's commission and approved his doctrine, and they parted very good friends. But in this Paul finds himself obliged to oppose Peter, for *he was to be blamed.* Here we may observe,

1. Peter's fault. When he came among the Gentile churches, he complied with them, and did eat with them, though they were not circumcised, agreeably to the instructions which were given in particular to him (Acts x.), when he was warned by the heavenly vision *to call nothing common or unclean.* But, when there came some Jewish Christians from Jerusalem, he grew more shy of the Gentiles, only to humour those of the circumcision and for fear of giving them offence, which doubtless was to the great grief and discouragement of the Gentile churches. Then *he withdrew, and separated himself.* His fault herein had a bad influence upon others, for *the other Jews also dissembled with him.* And (would you think it?) Barnabas himself, one of the apostles of the Gentiles, and one who had been instrumental in planting and watering the churches of the Gentiles, *was carried away with their dissimulation.*

2. The rebuke which Paul gave him for his fault. Notwithstanding Peter's character, yet, when he observes him thus behaving himself to the great prejudice both of the truth of the gospel and the peace of the church, he is not afraid to reprove him for it.

II. Paul having thus established his character and office, and sufficiently shown that he was not inferior to any of the apostles, no, not to Peter himself, from the account of the reproof he gave him he takes occasion to speak of that great fundamental doctrine of the gospel—That justification is only by faith in Christ, and not by the works of the law. Now concerning this Paul aquaints us,

1. With the practice of the Jewish Christians themselves. If it would be wrong in us who are Jews by nature to return to the law, and expect justification by it, would it not be much more so to require this of the Gentiles, who were never subject to it, since *by the works of the law no flesh shall be justified?* To give the greater weight to this he adds (*v.* 17), "*But if, while we seek to be justified by Christ, we ourselves also are found sinners, is Christ the minister of sin?*" If, while we seek justification by Christ alone, and teach others to do so, we ourselves are found giving countenance or indulgence to sin, or rather are accounted sinners of the Gentiles, and such as it is not fit to have communion with, unless we also observe the law of Moses, *is Christ the minister of sin?* Will it not follow that he is so, if he engage us to receive a doctrine that gives liberty to sin? Thus does the apostle argue for the great doctrine of justification by faith without the works of the law from the principles and practice of the Jewish Christians themselves, and from the consequences that would attend their departure from it, whence it appeared that Peter and the other Jews were much in the wrong in refusing to communicate with the Gentile Christians, and endeavour-

ing to bring them under the bondage of the law.

2. He acquaints us what his own judgment and practice were. (1) That he was dead to the law. (2) That, as he was dead to the law, so he was alive unto God through Jesus Christ (v. 20): *I am crucified with Christ*, &c. And here in his own person he gives us an excellent description of the mysterious life of a believer. [1] He is crucified, and yet he lives; the old man is crucified (Rom. vi. 6), but the new man is living; he is dead to the world, and dead to the law, and yet alive to God and Christ; sin is mortified, and grace quickened. [2] *He lives, and yet not he*. This is strange: *I live, and yet not I*; he lives in the exercise of grace; he has the comforts and the triumphs of grace; and yet that grace is not from himself, but from another. Believers see themselves living in a state of dependence. [3] *He is crucified with Christ*, and yet *Christ lives in him*; This results from his mystical union with Christ, by means of which he is interested in the death of Christ, so as by virtue of that to die unto sin; and yet interested in the life of Christ, so as by virtue of that to live unto God. [4] *He lives in the flesh*, and yet *lives by faith*; to outward appearance he lives as other people do, his natural life is supported as others are; yet he has a higher and nobler principle that supports and actuates him, that of faith in Christ, and especially as eyeing the wonders of his love in giving himself for him.

Lastly, The apostle concludes this discourse with acquainting us that by the doctrine of justification by faith in Christ, without the works of the law (which he asserted, and others opposed), he avoided two great difficulties, which the contrary opinion was loaded with: 1. *That he did not frustrate the grace of God*, which the doctrine of justification by the works of the law did; for, as he argues (Rom. xi. 6), *If it be of works, it is no more of grace*. 2. That he did not frustrate the death of Christ; whereas, *if righteousness come by* the law, then it must follow *that Christ has died in vain*; for, if we look for salvation by the law of Moses, then we render the death of Christ needless: for to what purpose should he be appointed to die, if we might have been saved without it?

CHAPTER THREE

GOING ON IN FAITH
(*vv.* 1–5)

The apostle is here dealing with those who, having embraced the faith of Christ, still continued to seek for justification by the works of the law.

He reproves them, and the reproof is very close and warm: he calls them *foolish Galatians, v.* 1. Several things proved and aggravated the folly of these Christians.

1. *Jesus Christ had been evidently set forth as crucified among them*; that is, they had had the doctrine of the cross preached to them, and the sacrament of the Lord's supper administered among them, in both which Christ crucified had been set before them.

2. He appeals to the experiences they had had of the working of the

Spirit upon their souls (*v.* 2); he puts them in mind that, upon their becoming Christians, *they had received the Spirit*, that many of them at least had been made partakers not only of the sanctifying influences, but of the miraculous gifts, of the Holy Spirit. To convince them of the folly of their departing from this doctrine, he desires to know how they came by these gifts and graces: Was it *by the works of the law*, that is, the preaching of the necessity of these in order to justification? Or was it by the *hearing of faith*, that is, the preaching of the doctrine of faith in Christ as the only way of justification?

3. He calls upon them to consider their past and present conduct, and thence to judge whether they were not acting very weakly and unreasonably (*vv.* 3, 4): he tells them that *they had begun in the Spirit*, but now were seeking *to be made perfect by the flesh*.

4. He puts them in mind that they had had ministers among them (and particularly himself) who came with a divine seal and commission; for they had *ministered the Spirit to them, and wrought miracles among them*: and he appeals to them whether they did it *by the works of the law or by the hearing of faith*.

THE EXAMPLE OF ABRAHAM (*vv.* 6–18)

The apostle having reproved the Galatians for not obeying the truth, and endeavoured to impress them with a sense of their folly herein, in these verses he largely proves the doctrine which he had reproved them for rejecting, namely, that of justification by faith without the works of the law. This he does several ways.

I. From the example of Abraham's justification. This argument the apostle uses, Rom. iv. *Abraham believed God, and that was accounted to him for righteousness* (*v.* 6); that is, his faith fastened upon the word and promise of God, and upon his believing he was owned and accepted of God as a righteous man: as on this account he is represented as the father of the faithful, so the apostle would have us to know *that those who are of faith are the children of Abraham* (*v.* 7).

II. He shows that we cannot be justified but by faith fastening on the gospel, because the law condemns us. A strange method it was which Christ took to redeem us from the curse of the law; it was *by his being himself made a curse for us*. Being made sin for us, he was made a curse for us. Hence it appeared that it was not by putting themselves under the law, but by faith in Christ, that they became the people of God and heirs of the promise.

III. To prove that justification is by faith, and not by the works of the law, the apostle alleges the express testimony of the Old Testament, *v.* 11. The place referred to is Habak. ii. 4, where it is said, *The just shall live by faith*; it is again quoted, Rom. i. 17, and Heb. x. 38. The design of it is to show that those only are just or righteous who do truly live, who are freed from death and wrath, and restored into a state of life in the favour of God; and that it is only through faith that persons become righteous, and as such obtain this life and happiness

—that they are accepted of God, and enabled to live to him now, and are entitled to an eternal life in the enjoyment of him hereafter.

IV. To this purpose the apostle urges the stability of the covenant which God made with Abraham, which was not vacated nor disannulled by the giving of the law to Moses, *vv.* 15, &c. Faith had the precedence of the law, for Abraham was justified by faith. It was a promise that he built upon, and promises are the proper objects of faith.

THE LAW'S PURPOSE
(*vv.* 19–22)

It might be asked, "If that promise be sufficient for salvation, wherefore then serveth the law? Or, Why did God give the law by Moses?" To this he answers,

I. The law *was added because of transgressions, v.* 19. The Israelites, though they were chosen to be God's people, were sinners as well as others, and therefore the law was given to convince them of their sin, and of their obnoxiousness to the divine displeasure on the account of it; *for by the law is the knowledge of sin* (Rom. iii. 20), and *the law entered that sin might abound,* Rom. v. 20.

The apostle adds that the law was given for this purpose *till the seed should come to whom the promise was made*; that is, either till Christ should come (the principal seed referred to in the promise, as he had before shown), or till the gospel dispensation should take place, when Jews and Gentiles, without distinction, should, upon believing, become the seed of Abraham.

As a further proof that the law was not designed to vacate the promise, the apostle adds, *It was ordained by angels in the hand of a mediator.* Whereas the promise was given immediately by God himself, the law was given *by the ministry of angels, and the hand of a mediator.* Hence it appeared that the law could not be designed to set aside the promise; for (*v.* 20), *A mediator is not a mediator of one,* of one party only; *but God is one,* but one party in the promise or covenant made with Abraham: and therefore it is not to be supposed that by a transaction which passed only between him and the nation of the Jews he should make void a promise which he had long before made to Abraham and all his spiritual seed, whether Jews or Gentiles.

II. The law was given to convince men of the necessity of a Saviour. *For the scripture hath concluded all under sin* (*v.* 22), or declared that all, both Jew and Gentile, are in a state of guilt, and therefore unable to attain to righteousness and justification by the works of the law.

III. The law was designed for *a schoolmaster, to bring men to Christ, v.* 24. It was their schoolmaster, to instruct and govern them in their state of minority to lead and conduct them to Christ (as children were wont to be led to school by those servants who had the care of them; that they might be more fully instructed by him as their schoolmaster, in the true way of justification and salvation, which is only by faith in him, and of which he was appointed to give the fullest and clearest discoveries.

Having shown for what intent the law was given, in the close of the chapter he acquaints us with our privilege by Christ, where he particularly declares,

(1) That *we are the children of God by faith in Christ Jesus*, *v.* 26. And here we may observe, [1] The great and excellent privilege which real Christians enjoy under the gospel: *They are the children of God.* [2] How they come to obtain this privilege, and that is *by faith in Christ Jesus.* And this faith in Christ, whereby they became the children of God, he reminds us (*v.* 27), was what they professed in baptism; for he adds, *As many of you as have been baptized into Christ have put on Christ.*

(2) That this privilege of being the children of God, and of being by baptism devoted to Christ, is now enjoyed in common by all real Christians. The law indeed made a difference between Jew and Greek, giving the Jews on many accounts the pre-eminence. But it is not so now; they all stand on the same level, *and are all one in Christ Jesus*: All who sincerely believe on Christ, of what nation, or sex, or condition, soever they be, are accepted of him, and become the children of God through faith in him.

(3) That, *being Christ's, we are Abraham's seed, and heirs according to the promise.* Their judaizing teachers would have them believe that they must be circumcised and keep the law of Moses, or they could not be saved: "No," says the apostle, "there is no need of that; for *if you be Christ's*, if you sincerely believe on him, who is the promised seed, in whom all the

nations of the earth were to be blessed, you therefore become the true *seed of Abraham*, the father of the faithful, and as such *are heirs according to the promise*, and consequently are entitled to the great blessings and privileges of it."

CHAPTER FOUR
SONS OF GOD (*vv.* 1–7)

Here,

I. He acquaints us with the state of the Old-Testament church: it was like a child under age, and it was used accordingly, being kept in a state of darkness and bondage, in comparison of the greater light and liberty which we enjoy under the gospel.

II. He acquaints us with the much happier state of Christians under the gospel-dispensation, *vv.* 4–7. *When the fulness of time had come*, the time appointed of the Father, when he would put an end to the legal dispensation, and set up another and a better in the room of it, *he sent forth his Son*, &c. The person who was employed to introduce this new dispensation was no other than the Son of God himself, the only-begotten of the Father, who, as he had been prophesied of and promised from the foundation of the world, so in due time he was manifested for this purpose. He, in pursuance of the great design he had undertaken, submitted to be *made of a woman*—there is his incarnation; and to be *made under the law*—there is his subjection. He who was truly God for our sakes became man; and he who was Lord of all consented to come into a state of subjection and to take upon him

301

the form of a servant; and one great end of all this was *to redeem those that were under the law*—to save us from that intolerable yoke and to appoint gospel ordinances more rational and easy. For he was sent to redeem us, *that we might receive the adoption of sons*—that we might no longer be accounted and treated as servants, but as sons grown up to maturity, who are allowed greater freedoms, and admitted to larger privileges, than while they were under tutors and governors. Now, under the gospel, particular believers receive the adoption; and, as an earnest and evidence of it, they have together therewith the Spirit of adoption, putting them upon the duty of prayer, and enabling them in prayer to eye God as a Father (*v.* 6). From what the apostle says in these verses, we may observe,

1. The wonders of divine love and mercy towards us.

2. The great and invaluable advantages which Christians enjoy under the gospel; for, (1) We receive *the adoption of sons*. Whence note, It is the great privilege which believers have through Christ that they are adopted children of the God of heaven. (2) We receive *the Spirit of adoption*. All who are received into the number partake of the nature of the children of God; for he will have all his children to resemble him.

BACK TO BONDAGE?
(*vv.* 8–11)

In these verses the apostle puts them in mind of what they were before their conversion to the faith of Christ, and what a blessed

change their conversion had made upon them; and thence endeavours to convince them of their great weakness in hearkening to those who would bring them under the bondage of the law of Moses.

I. He reminds them of their past state and behaviour, and what they were before the gospel was preached to them. Then *they knew not God*; for *they did service to those which by nature were no gods*, they were employed in a great number of superstitious and idolatrous services.

II. He calls upon them to consider the happy change that was made in them by the preaching of the gospel among them. Now *they had known God or rather were known of God*; this happy change in their state, whereby they were turned from idols to the living God, and through Christ had received the adoption of sons, was not owing to themselves, but to him.

III. Hence he infers the unreasonableness and madness of their suffering themselves to be brought again into a state of bondage. What they suffered themselves to be brought into bondage to were but *weak and beggarly elements*, such things as had no power in them to cleanse the soul, nor to afford any solid satisfaction to the mind. And therefore their weakness and folly were the more aggravated, in submitting to them, and in symbolizing with the Jews in observing their various festivals, here signified by *days, and months, and times, and years*.

IV. Hereupon he expresses his fears concerning them, *lest he had bestowed on them labour in vain*.

THEIR REJECTION OF PAUL
(vv. 12–16)

That these Christians might be the more ashamed of their defection from the truth of the gospel which Paul had preached to them, he here reminds them of the great affection they formerly had for him and his ministry, and puts them upon considering how very unsuitable their present behaviour was to what they then professed. And here we may observe,

I. How affectionately he addresses himself to them.

II. How he magnifies their former affection to him, that hereby they might be the more ashamed of their present behaviour towards him.

III. How earnestly he expostulates with them hereupon: *Where is then*, says he, *the blessedness you spoke of?* What has become of that pleasure they used to take in communion with God, and in the company of his servants? The more to impress upon them a just shame of their present conduct, he again asks (v. 16), *"Am I become your enemy, because I tell you the truth?"*

SLAVERY OR FREEDOM?
(vv. 17–31)

He here gives them the character of those false teachers who made it their business to draw them away from it, which if they would attend to, they might soon see how little reason they had to hearken to them: whatever opinion they might have of them, he tells them they were designing men, who were aiming to set up themselves, and who, under their specious pretences, were more consulting their own interest than theirs (vv. 17, 18). They were too ready to account him their enemy, but he assures them that he was their friend; nay, not only so, but that he had the feelings of a parent towards them. He calls them *his children*, as he justly might, since he had been the instrument of their conversion to the Christian faith. *He travailed in birth for them* (v. 19): and the great thing which he was in so much pain about, and which he was so earnestly desirous of, was not so much that they might affect him as *that Christ might be formed in them*, that they might become Christians indeed, and be more confirmed and established in the faith of the gospel.

In verses 21–31 the apostle illustrates the difference between believers who rested in Christ only and those judaizers who trusted in the law, by a comparison taken from the story of Isaac and Ishmael. 1. Here he represents the different state and condition of these two sons of Abraham—that the one, Ishmael, *was by a bond-maid*, and the other, Isaac, *by a free-woman*; and that whereas the former *was born after the flesh*, or by the ordinary course of nature, the other *was by promise*, when in the course of nature there was no reason to expect that Sarah should have a son. 2. He acquaints them with the meaning and design of this history, or the use which he intended to make of it (vv. 24–27): *These things*, says he, *are an allegory*, wherein, besides the literal and historical sense of the words, the Spirit of God might design to signify something further to us,

303

and that was, That these two, Agar and Sarah, *are the two covenants*, or were intended to typify and prefigure the two different dispensations of the covenant. The former, Agar, represented that which was given from mount Sinai, and *which gendereth to bondage*; that is, it justly represents the present state of the Jews, who, continuing in their infidelity and adhering to that covenant, are still in bondage with their children. But the other, Sarah, was intended to prefigure Jerusalem which is above, or the state of Christians under the new and better dispensation of the covenant, which is free both from the curse of the moral and the bondage of the ceremonial law, and *is the mother of us all*—a state into which all, both Jews and Gentiles, are admitted, upon their believing in Christ. 3. He applies the history thus explained to the present case (*v.* 28): *Now we, brethren*, says he, *as Isaac was, are the children of the promise.* We Christians, who have accepted Christ, and rely upon him, and look for justification and salvation by him alone, as hereby we become the spiritual, though we are not the natural, seed of Abraham, so we are entitled to the promised inheritance and interested in the blessings of it.

CIRCUMCISION (*vv.* 1–12)

It is our duty to *stand fast in this liberty*, constantly and faithfully to adhere to the gospel and to the liberty of it, and not to suffer ourselves, upon any consideration, *to be again entangled in the yoke of bondage*, nor persuaded to return back to the law of Moses. This is the general caution or exhortation, which in the following verses the apostle enforces by several reasons or arguments. As,

I. That their submitting to circumcision, and depending on the works of the law for righteousness, were an implicit contradiction of their faith as Christians and a forfeiture of all their advantages by Jesus Christ, *vv.* 2–4.

II. To persuade them to stedfastness in the doctrine and liberty of the gospel, he sets before them his own example, and that of other Jews who had embraced the Christian religion, and acquaints them what their hopes were, namely, That *through the Spirit they were waiting for the hope of righteousness by faith.* Here we may observe, 1. What it is that Christians are waiting for: it is *the hope of righteousness*, by which we are chiefly to understand the happiness of the other world. 2. How they hope to obtain this happiness, namely, by faith, that is, in our Lord Jesus Christ, not by the works of the law, or any thing they can do to deserve it, but only by faith, receiving and relying upon him as the Lord our righteousness. And, 3. Whence it is that they are thus waiting for the hope of righteousness: it is *through the Spirit.* Herein they act under the direction and influence of the Holy Spirit.

III. He argues from the nature and design of the Christian institution, which was to abolish the difference between Jew and Gentile, and to establish faith in Christ as the way of our acceptance with

God. He tells them (*v.* 6) that *in Christ Jesus*, or under the gospel dispensation, *neither circumcision availeth any thing nor uncircumcision.* Christ, who is *the end of the law*, having come, now it was neither here nor there whether a man were circumcised or uncircumcised; he was neither the better for the one nor the worse for the other, nor would either the one or the other recommend him to God.

IV. To recover them from their backslidings, and engage them to greater stedfastness for the future, he puts them in mind of their good beginnings, and calls upon them to consider whence it was that they were so much altered from what they had been, *v.* 7.

1. He tells them that *they did run well*, at their first setting out in Christianity. Therefore,

2. He asks them, and calls upon them to ask themselves, *Who did hinder you?* He very well knew who they were, and what it was that hindered them; but he would have them to put the question to themselves, and seriously consider whether they had any good reason to hearken to those who gave them this disturbance, and whether what they offered was sufficient to justify them in their present conduct.

V. He argues for their stedfastness in the faith and liberty of the gospel from the ill rise of that persuasion whereby they were drawn away from it (*v.* 8): *This persuasion*, says he, *cometh not of him that calleth you.* The opinion or persuasion of which the apostle here speaks was no doubt that of the necessity of their being circumcised, and keeping the law of Mo-

ses, or of their mixing the works of the law with faith in Christ, in the business of justification.

VI. The danger there was of the spreading of this infection, and the ill influence it might have upon others, are a further argument which the apostle urges against their complying with their false teachers in what they would impose on them. *A little leaven leaveneth the whole lump*—the whole lump of Christianity may be tainted and corrupted by one such erroneous principle.

VII. That he might conciliate the greater regard to what he had said, he expresses the hopes he had concerning them (*v.* 10): *I have confidence in you*, says he, *through the Lord, that you will be none otherwise minded.* Herein he teaches us that we ought to hope the best even of those concerning whom we have cause to fear the worst.

VIII. Their judaizing teachers had misrepresented him, that they might the more easily gain their ends upon them. When he says (*v.* 11), *And I brethren, if I yet preach circumcision*, it plainly appears that they had reported him to have done so, and that they had made use of this as an argument to prevail with the Galatians to submit to it. To prove the injustice of that charge upon him, he offers such arguments as, if they would allow themselves to consider, could not fail to convince them of it. 1. If he would have preached circumcision, he might have avoided persecution. 2. If he had yielded to the Jews herein, *then would the offence of the cross have ceased.* They would not have taken so much offence against the doctrine of Christianity as they did, nor would he and others have been exposed to so much suffering on the account of it as they were.

FLESH AND SPIRIT (*vv.* 13–25)

In the latter part of this chapter the apostle comes to exhort these Christians to serious practical godliness, as the best antidote against the snares of the false teachers. Two things especially he presses upon them:

I. That they should not strive with one another, but love one another. *But*, says he, if instead of serving one another in love, and therein fulfilling the law of God, *you bite and devour one another, take heed that you be not consumed one of another.* If, instead of acting like men and Christians, they would behave themselves more like brute beasts, in tearing and rending one another, they could expect nothing as the consequence of it, but that they would be consumed one of another; and therefore they had the greatest reason not to indulge themselves in such quarrels and animosities.

II. That they should all strive against sin. To excite Christians hereunto, and to assist them herein, the apostle shows,

1. That there is in every one a struggle between the flesh and the spirit (*v.* 17).

2. That it is our duty and interest in this struggle to side with the better part, to side with our convictions against our corruptions and with our graces against our lusts. This the apostle represents as our duty, and directs us to the most effectual means of success in it.

3. The apostle specifies the works of the flesh, which must be watched against and mortified, and the fruits of the Spirit, which must be cherished and brought forth (*vv.* 19, &c.); and by specifying particulars he further illustrates what he is here upon. (1) He begins with *the works of the flesh*, which, as they are many, so they are manifest. The particulars he specifies are of various sorts; some are sins against the seventh commandment, such as *adultery, fornication, uncleanness, lasciviousness*, by which are meant not only the gross acts of these sins, but all such thoughts, and words, and actions, as have a tendency towards the great transgression. Some are sins against the first and second commandments, as *idolatry* and *witchcraft*. Others are sins against our neighbour, and contrary to the royal law of brotherly love, such as *hatred, variance, emulations, wrath, strife*, which too often occasion *seditions, heresies, envyings*, and sometimes break out into *murders*, not only of the names and reputation, but even of the very lives, of our fellow-creatures. Others are sins against ourselves, such as *drunkenness and revellings*. These are sins which will undoubtedly shut men out of heaven, unless they be first *washed and sanctified, and justified in the name of our Lord Jesus, and by the Spirit of our God,* 1 Cor. vi. 11. (2) He specifies the fruits of the Spirit, or the renewed nature, which as Christians we are concerned to bring forth, *vv.* 22, 23. He particularly recommends to us, *love*, to

God especially, and to one another for his sake,—*joy*, by which may be understood cheerfulness in conversation with our friends, or rather a constant delight in God,—*peace*, with God and conscience, or a peaceableness of temper and behaviour towards others,—*long-suffering*, patience to defer anger, and a contentedness to bear injuries,—*gentleness*, such a sweetness of temper, and especially towards our inferiors, as disposes us to be affable and courteous, and easy to be entreated when any have wronged us,—*goodness* (kindness, beneficence), which shows itself in a readiness to do good to all as we have opportunity,—*faith*, fidelity, justice, and honesty, in what we profess and promise to others,—*meekness*, wherewith to govern our passions and resentments, so as not to be easily provoked, and, when we are so, to be soon pacified,—and *temperance*, in meat and drink, and other enjoyments of life, so as not to be excessive and immoderate in the use of them. Concerning these things, or those in whom these fruits of the Spirit are found, the apostle says, *There is no law against them*, to condemn and punish them. *And those that are Christ's*, says he, *have crucified the flesh with the affections and lusts.* Our Christianity obliges us not only to die unto sin, but to live unto righteousness; not only to oppose the works of the flesh, but to bring forth the fruits of the Spirit too.

4. The apostle concludes this chapter with a caution against pride and envy, *v.* 26. Note, (1) The glory which comes from men is vain-glory, which, instead of being desirous of, we should be dead to. (2) An undue regard to the approbation and applause of men is one great ground of the unhappy strifes and contentions that exist among Christians.

GOD IS NOT MOCKED
(*vv.* 1–10)

I. We are here taught to deal tenderly with those who are overtaken in a fault, *v.* 1. He puts a common case: *If a man be overtaken in a fault*, that is, be brought to sin by the surprise of temptation. *Those who are spiritual*, by whom is meant, not only the ministers (as if none but they were to be called spiritual persons), but other Christians too, especially those of the higher form in Christianity; these must *restore such a one with the spirit of meekness. Considering thyself, lest thou also be tempted.* We ought to deal very tenderly with those who are overtaken in sin, because we none of us know but it may some time or other be our own case.

II. We are here directed *to bear one another's burdens*, *v.* 2. To excite us hereunto, the apostle adds, by way of motive, that so we shall *fulfil the law of Christ.* This is to act agreeably to the law of his precept, which is the law of love, and obliges us to a mutual forbearance and forgiveness, to sympathy with and compassion towards each other; and it would also be agreeable to his pattern and example, which have the force of a law to us.

III. We are advised every one to test his own work, *v.* 4. By our own work is chiefly meant our own actions or behaviour. These the apostle directs us to prove, that is, seriously and impartially to examine them by the rule of God's word, to see whether or no they are agreeable to it, and therefore such as God and conscience do approve. That we may be persuaded to this necessary and profitable duty of proving our own work, the apostle urges two considerations very proper for this purpose:

1. This is the way to *have rejoicing in ourselves alone*. If we set ourselves in good earnest to *prove our own work*, and, upon the trial, can approve ourselves to God, as to our sincerity and uprightness towards him, then may we expect to have comfort and peace in our own souls, having the testimony of our own consciences for us (as 2 Cor. i. 12), and this, he intimates, would be a much better ground of joy and satisfaction than to be able to rejoice *in another*.

2. The other argument which the apostle uses to press upon us this duty of proving our own work is that every man shall bear his own burden (*v.* 5), the meaning of which is that at the great day every one shall be reckoned with according as his behaviour here has been.

IV. Christians are here exhorted to be free and liberal in maintaining their ministers (*v.* 6): *Let him that is taught in the word communicate to him that teacheth, in all good things*.

V. Here is a caution to take heed of mocking God, or of deceiving ourselves, by imagining that he can be imposed upon by mere pretensions or professions (*v.* 7): *Be not deceived, God is not mocked*. Our present time is seed-time: in the other world there will be a great harvest; and, as the husbandman reaps in the harvest according as he sows in the seedness, so we shall reap then as we sow now. And he further informs us (*v.* 8) that, as there are two sorts of seedness, sowing to the flesh and sowing to the Spirit, so accordingly will the reckoning be hereafter: *If we sow to the flesh, we shall of the flesh reap corruption*. If we sow the wind, we shall reap the whirlwind.

VI. Here is a further caution given us, *not to be weary in well doing*, *v.* 9. As we should not excuse ourselves from any part of our duty, so neither should be grow weary in it.

VII. Here is an exhortation to all Christians to do good in their places (*v.* 10): *As we have therefore an opportunity*, &c. It is not enough that we be good ourselves, but we must do good to others, if we would approve ourselves to be Christians indeed.

FINAL APPEAL (*vv.* 11–18)

The apostle, having at large established the doctrine of the gospel, and endeavoured to persuade these Christians to a behaviour agreeable to it, seems as if he intended here to have put an end to the epistle, especially when he had acquainted them that, as a particular mark of his respect for them, he had written this large letter with his own hand. But such is his affection to them that he cannot break off till he has once again given them the true character of those teachers.

I. He gives them the true character of those teachers who were industrious to seduce them, in several particulars. As, 1. They were men who *desired to make a fair show in the flesh*, v. 12. 2. They were men who were afraid of suffering, for they constrained the Gentile Christians to be circumcised, *only lest they should suffer persecution for the cross of Christ*. And, 3. Another part of their character was that they were men of a party spirit, and who had no further zeal for the law than as it subserved their carnal and selfish designs; for they desired to have these Christians circumcised, *that they might glory in their flesh* (v. 13).

II. He acquaints us, on the other hand, with his own temper and behaviour, or makes profession of his own faith, hope, and joy; particularly,

1. That his principal glory was in the cross of Christ: *God forbid*, says he, *that I should glory, save in the cross of our Lord Jesus Christ*, v. 14.

2. That he was dead to the world. By Christ, or by the cross of Christ, *the world was crucified to him, and he to the world*; he had experienced the power and virtue of it in weaning him from the world, and this was one great reason of his glorying in it.

3. That he did not lay the stress of his religion on one side or the other of the contesting interests, but on sound Christianity, v. 15. Here he instructs us both wherein real religion does not and wherein it does consist. It does not consist in circumcision or uncircumcision, in our being in this or the other denomination of Christians; but it consists in our being new creatures; not in having a new name, or putting on a new face, but in our being renewed in the spirit of our minds and having Christ formed in us. *And as many as walk according to this rule peace be upon them, and mercy upon the Israel of God*, by whom he means all sincere Christians, whether Jews or Gentiles.

4. That he had cheerfully suffered persecution for the sake of Christ and Christianity, v. 17.

III. The apostle, having now finished what he intended to write for the conviction and recovery of the churches of Galatia, concludes the epistle with his apostolical benediction, v. 18.

EPHESIANS

CHAPTER ONE

INTRODUCTION (vv. 1, 2)

Here is, 1. The title St. Paul takes to himself, as belonging to him— *Paul, an apostle of Jesus Christ*, &c. 2. The persons to whom this epistle is sent: *To the saints who are at Ephesus*, that is, to the Christians who were members of the church at Ephesus, the metropolis of Asia.

CHOSEN IN CHRIST (vv. 3–14)

He begins with thanksgivings and praise, and enlarges with a great deal of fluency and copiousness of affection upon the exceedingly great and precious benefits which we enjoy by Jesus Christ.

I. In general he blesses God for *spiritual blessings*, v. 3, where he styles him *the God and Father of our Lord Jesus Christ*.

II. The particular spiritual blessings with which we are blessed in Christ, and for which we ought to bless God, are (many of them) here enumerated and enlarged upon. 1. Election and predestination, which are the secret springs whence the others flow, vv. 4, 5, 11. We have here the date of this act of love: it was *before the foundation of the world*; not only before God's people had a being, but before the world had a beginning; for they were chosen in the counsel of God from all eternity. *All is of God, and*

from him, and through him, and therefore all must be to him, and centre in his praise. 2. The next spiritual blessing the apostle takes notice of is acceptance with God through Jesus Christ: *Wherein*, or by which grace, *he hath made us accepted in the beloved*, v. 6. Jesus Christ is the beloved of his Father (Matt. iii. 17), as well as of angels and saints. It is our great privilege to be accepted of God, which implies his love to us and his taking us under his care and into his family. 3. Remission of sins, and redemption through the blood of Jesus, v. 7. No remission without redemption. It was by reason of sin that we were captivated, and we cannot be released from our captivity but by the remission of our sins. This redemption we have in Christ, and this remission through his blood. 4. Another privilege which the apostle here blesses God for is divine revelation—that God hath *made known to us the mystery of his will* (v. 9), that is, so much of his good-will to men, which had been concealed for a long time, and is still concealed from so great a part of the world: this we owe to Christ, who, having lain in the bosom of the Father from eternity, came to declare his will to the children of men. 5. Union in and with Christ is a great privilege, a spiritual blessing, and the foundation of many others. *He gathers together in one and all things in Christ, v.* 10. All the lines of divine revelation meet in Christ; all religion centres in him. 6. The eternal inheritance is the great blessing with which we are blessed in Christ: *In whom also we have obtained an inheritance, v.* 11. Heaven is the inheritance, the happiness of which is a sufficient portion for a soul: it is conveyed in the way of an inheritance, being the gift of a Father to his children. *If children, then heirs.* 7. The seal and earnest of the Spirit are of the number of these blessings. We are said to be *sealed with that Holy Spirit of promise, v.* 13. The earnest is part of payment, and it secures the full sum: so is the gift of the Holy Ghost; all his influences and operations, both as a sanctifier and a comforter, are heaven begun, glory in the seed and bud.

THE LORDSHIP OF CHRIST
(vv. 15–23)

We have come to the last part of this chapter, which consists of Paul's earnest prayer to God in behalf of these Ephesians. The graces and comforts of the Spirit are communicated to the soul by the enlightening of the understanding. In this way he gains and keeps possession. Observe,

I. Whence this knowledge must come from *the God of our Lord Jesus Christ, v.* 17. The Lord *is a God of knowledge*, and there is no sound saving knowledge but what comes from him. This knowledge is first in the understanding. He prays that *the eyes of their understanding may be enlightened, v.* 18.

II. What it is that he more particularly desires they should grow in the knowledge of. 1. *The hope of his calling, v.* 18. Christianity is our calling. God has called us to it, and on that account it is said to be his calling. There is a hope in this calling; for those who deal with God deal upon trust. And it is a desirable thing to know what this hope of our calling is. 2. *The riches of the glory of his inheritance in the saints.* Besides the heavenly inheritance prepared for the saints, there is a present inheritance in the saints; for grace is glory begun, and holiness is happiness in the bud. 3. *The exceeding greatness of God's power towards those who believe, v.* 19. The practical belief of the all-sufficiency of God, and of the omnipotence of divine grace, is absolutely necessary to a close and steady walking with him. Many understand the apostle here as speaking of that *exceeding greatness of power* which God will exert for raising the bodies of believers to eternal life, even the same *mighty power which he wrought in Christ when he raised him*, &c. And how desirable a thing must it be to become at length acquainted with that power, by being raised out of the grave thereby unto eternal life!

Having said something of Christ and his resurrection, the apostle digresses a little from the subject he is upon to make some further honourable mention of the Lord Jesus and his exaltation. He sits at the Father's *right hand in the heavenly places*, &c. vv. 20, 21. Jesus Christ is advanced above all, and he is set in authority over all, they being made subject to him. All the glory of the upper world, and all the powers of both worlds, are entirely devoted to him. The Father *hath put all things under his feet* (*v.* 22), according to the promise, Ps. cx. 1. Jesus Christ filleth all in all; he supplies all defects in all his members, filling them with his Spirit, and even with *the fulness of God*, ch. iii. 19. And yet the church is said to be his fulness, because Christ as Mediator would not be complete if he had not a church. How could he be a king if he had not a kingdom? This therefore comes in to the honour of Christ, *as Mediator, that the church is his fulness.*

CHAPTER TWO
LIFE FROM DEATH (*vv.* 1–3)

The miserable condition of the Ephesians by nature is here in part described. Observe, 1. Unregenerate souls are dead in trespasses and sins. Sin is the death of the soul. 2. A state of sin is a state of conformity to this world, *v.* 2. 3. We are by nature bond-slaves to sin and Satan. Those who walk in trespasses and sins, and according to the course of this world, walk *according to the prince of the power of the air*. The devil, or the prince of devils, is thus described. See Matt. xii. 24, 26. 4. We are by nature drudges to the flesh, and to our corrupt affections, *v.* 3. 5. We are *by nature the children of wrath, even as others*. All men, being naturally children of disobedience, are also by nature children of wrath: God is angry with the wicked every day.

SAVED BY GRACE (*vv.* 4–10)

Here the apostle begins his account of the glorious change that was wrought in them by converting grace, where observe,

I. By whom, and in what manner, it was brought about and effected. 1. Negatively: *Not of yourselves, v.* 8. Our faith, our conversion, and our eternal salvation, are not the mere product of any natural abilities, nor of any merit of our own. 2. Positively: *But God, who is rich in mercy,* &c. *v.* 4. God himself is the author of this great and happy change, and his great love is the spring and fontal cause of it; hence he resolved to show mercy. And then *by grace you are saved* (*v.* 5), and *by grace are you saved through faith—it is the gift of* God, *v.* 8. The grace that saves them is the free undeserved goodness and favour of God; and he saves them, not *by the works of the law*, but through faith in Christ Jesus, by means of which they come to partake of the great blessings of the gospel. Observe,

II. Wherein this change consists, in several particulars, answering to the misery of our natural state, some of which are enumerated in this section, and others are mentioned below. 1. We who were dead are quickened (*v.* 5), we are saved from the death of sin and have a principle of spiritual life implanted in us. 2. We who were buried are raised up, *v.* 6. When he raised Christ from the dead, he did in effect raise up all believers together with him, he being their common head.

III. Observe what is the great

design and aim of God in producing and effecting this change: And this, 1. With respect to others: *That in the ages to come he might show*, &c. (*v. 7*), that he might give a specimen and proof of his great goodness and mercy, for the encouragement of sinners in future time. 2. With respect to the regenerated sinners themselves: *For we are his workmanship, created in Christ Jesus unto good works*, &c. *v. 10*. It appears that all is of grace, because all our spiritual advantages are from God. *We are his workmanship*; he means in respect of the new creation; not only as men, but as saints. The new man is a new creature; and God is its Creator. *Unto good works*, &c. The apostle having before ascribed this change to divine grace in exclusion of works, lest he should seem thereby to discourage good works, he here observes that though the change is to be ascribed to nothing of that nature (*for we are the workmanship of God*), yet God, in his new creation, has designed and prepared us for good works: *Created unto good works*, with a design that we should be fruitful in them.

ALIENS WELCOMED
(*vv.* 11–13)

In these verses the apostle proceeds in his account of the miserable condition of these Ephesians by nature. "*At that time*, while you were Gentiles, and in an unconverted state, you were," 1. "In a Christless condition, without the knowledge of the Messiah, and without any saving interest in him or relation to him." 2. *Aliens from the commonwealth of Israel*; they

did not belong to Christ's church, and had no communion with it, that being confined to the Israelitish nation. 3. *They are strangers from the covenants of promise*. The covenant of grace has ever been the same for substance, though, having undergone various additions and improvements in the several ages of the church, it is called covenants; and the covenants of promise, because it is made up of promises, and particularly contains the great promise of the Messiah, and of eternal life through him. Now the Ephesians, in their gentilism, were strangers to this covenant, having never had any information nor overture of it; and all unregenerate sinners are strangers to it, as they have no interest in it. 4. They had no hope, that is, beyond this life—no well-grounded hope in God, no hope of spiritual and eternal blessings.

The apostle proceeds (*v.* 13) further to illustrate the happy change that was made in their state: *But now, in Christ Jesus, you who sometimes were far off*, &c. They were far off from Christ, from his church, from the promises, from the Christian hope, and from God himself. They were brought home to God, received into the church, taken into the covenant, and possessed of all other privileges consequent upon these.

CHRIST THE RECONCILER
(*vv.* 14–22)

Between the Jews and the Gentiles there had been a great enmity; so there is between God and every unregenerate man. Now Jesus Christ is our peace, *v.* 14. He made peace by the sacrifice of himself; and came to reconcile, 1. Jews and Gentiles to each other. He *made both one*, by reconciling these two divisions of men, who were wont to malign, to hate, and to reproach each other before. He *broke down the middle wall of partition*, the ceremonial law, that made the great feud, and was the badge of the Jews' peculiarity, called *the partition-wall* by way of allusion to the partition in the temple, which separated the court of the Gentiles from that into which the Jews only had liberty to enter. Thus *he abolished in his flesh the enmity*, v. 15. 2. There is an enmity between God and sinners, whether Jews or Gentiles; and Christ came to slay that enmity, and to reconcile them both to God, *v.* 16. Sin breeds a quarrel between God and men. Christ came to take up the quarrel, and to bring it to an end, by reconciling both Jew and Gentile, now collected and gathered into one body, to a provoked and an offended God: and this *by the cross*, or by the sacrifice of himself upon the cross, *having slain the enmity thereby*. He, being slain or sacrificed, slew the enmity that there was between God and poor sinners. Now the effect of this peace is the free access which both Jews and Gentiles have unto God (*v.* 18): *For through him*, in his name and by virtue of his mediation, *we both have access* or admission into the presence of God, who has become the common reconciled Father of both. The Ephesians, upon their conversion, having such an access to God, as well as the Jews, and by the same Spirit, the apostle tells

them, *Now therefore you are no more strangers and foreigners, v.* 19. In *v.* 20 the church is compared to a building. The apostles and prophets are *the foundation* of that building. They may be so called in a secondary sense, Christ himself being the primary foundation; but we are rather to understand it of the doctrine delivered by the prophets of the Old Testament and the apostles of the New. It follows, *Jesus Christ himself being the chief corner-stone.* In him both Jews and Gentiles meet, and constitute one church; and Christ supports the building by his strength: *In whom all the building, fitly framed together*, &c. *v.* 21.

CHAPTER THREE
THE WISDOM OF GOD
(*vv.* 1–12)

Here we have the account which Paul gives the Ephesians concerning himself, as he was appointed by God the apostle of the Gentiles.

I. We may observe that he acquaints them with the tribulations and sufferings which he endured in the discharge of that office, *v.* 1.

II. The apostle informs them of God's appointing him to the office, and eminently fitting and qualifying him for it, by a special revelation that he made unto him. 1. God appointed him to the office: *If you have heard of the dispensation of the grace of God, which is given me to you-ward, v.* 2. 2. As God appointed him to the office, so he eminently qualified him for it, by a special revelation that he made unto him. He makes mention both of the mystery that was revealed and of the revelation of it. (1) The mystery revealed is *that the Gentiles should be fellow-heirs, and of the same body, and partakers of his promise in Christ, by the gospel* (*v.* 6). (2) Of the revelation of this truth he speaks, *vv.* 3–5. Here we may observe that the coalition of Jews and Gentiles in the gospel church was a mystery, a great mystery, what was designed in the counsel of God before all worlds, but what could not be fully understood for many ages, till the accomplishment expounded the prophecies of it. And it is called the mystery of Christ because it was revealed by him (Gal. i. 12), and because it relates so very much to him.

III. The apostle informs them how he was employed in this office, and that with respect to the Gentiles, and to all men.

1. With respect to the Gentiles, he *preached* to them *the unsearchable riches of Christ, v.* 8. Observe, in this verse, how humbly he speaks of himself, and how highly he speaks of Jesus Christ. (1) How humbly he speaks of himself: *I am less than the least of all saints*. (2) How highly he speaks of Jesus Christ: *The unsearchable riches of Christ*. And they are unsearchable riches, which we cannot find the bottom of, which human sagacity could never have discovered, and men could no otherwise attain to the knowledge of them but by revelation.

2. With respect to all men, *v.* 9. His business and employment were *to make all men see* (to publish and make known to the whole world) *what is the fellowship of the mystery*

(that the Gentiles who have hitherto been strangers to the church, shall be admitted into communion with it) *which from the beginning of the world hath been hid in God* (kept secret in his purpose), *who created all things by Jesus Christ*. And this is *according to the eternal purpose which he purposed in Christ Jesus our Lord, v.* 11: the whole of what he has done in the great affair of man's redemption being in pursuance of his eternal decree about that matter. The apostle, having mentioned our Lord Jesus Christ, subjoins concerning him, *In whom we have boldness and access with confidence by the faith of him* (*v.* 12). We may come with humble boldness to hear from God, knowing that the terror of the curse is done away; and we may expect to hear from him good words and comfortable. We may have access with confidence to speak to God, knowing that we have such a Mediator between God and us, and such an Advocate with the Father.

THE LOVE OF CHRIST
(*vv.* 14–21)

We now come to the second part of this chapter, which contains Paul's devout and affectionate prayer to God for his beloved Ephesians. Observe,

I. To whom he prays—to God, as *the Father of our Lord Jesus Christ*, of which see *ch.* i. 3.

II. His outward posture in prayer, which was humble and reverent: *I bow my knees*.

III. What the apostle asks of God for these his friends—spiritual blessings, which are the best blessings, and the most earnestly to be sought and prayed for by every one of us, both for ourselves and for our friends. 1. Spiritual strength for the work and duty to which they were called, and in which they were employed. 2. The indwelling of Christ in their hearts, *v.* 17. Christ is said to dwell in his people, as he is always present with them by his gracious influences and operations. 3 The fixing of pious and devout affections in the soul: *That you being rooted and grounded in love*, stedfastly fixed in your love to God, the Father of our Lord Jesus Christ, and to all the saints, the beloved of our Lord Jesus Christ. In order to do this he prays, 4. For their experimental acquaintance with the love of Jesus Christ. The more intimate acquaintance we have with Christ's love to us, the more our love will be drawn out to him, and to those who are his, for his sake. 5. He prays that they may *be filled with all the fulness of God*. We are not to understand it of his fulness as God in himself, but of his fulness as a God in covenant with us, as a God to his people: such a fulness as God is ready to bestow, who is willing to fill them all to the utmost of their capacity, and that with all those gifts and graces which he sees they need.

The apostle closes the chapter with a doxology, *vv.* 20, 21. It is proper to conclude our prayers with praises.

CHAPTER FOUR

EXHORTATIONS (*vv.* 1–16)

This is a general exhortation to walk as becomes our Christian profession. We have here the petition of a poor prisoner, one of Christ's prisoners: "*I therefore, the prisoner of the Lord, beseech you,* &c." Observe, Christians ought to accommodate themselves to the gospel by which they are called, and to the glory to which they are called; both are their vocation.

There follows an exhortation to mutual love, unity, and concord, with the proper means and motives to promote them. Observe,

I. The means of unity: *Lowliness and meekness, long-suffering, and forbearing one another in love, v.* 2. By lowliness we are to understand humility, entertaining mean thoughts of ourselves, which is opposed to pride. By *meekness*, that excellent disposition of soul which makes men unwilling to provoke others, and not easily to be provoked or offended with their infirmities; and it is opposed to angry resentments and peevishness. *Long-suffering* implies a patient bearing of injuries, without seeking revenge. *Forbearing one another in love* signifies bearing their infirmities out of a principle of love, and so as not to cease to love them on the account of these.

II. The nature of that unity which the apostle prescribes: it is *the unity of the Spirit, v.* 3. This unity of heart and affection may be said to be of the Spirit of God; it is wrought by him, and is one of the fruits of the Spirit. This we should endeavour to keep. *Endeavouring* is a gospel word. We must do our utmost.

III. The motives proper to promote this Christian unity and concord. The apostle urges several, to persuade us thereto.

1. Consider how many unities there are that are the joy and glory of our Christian profession. There should be one heart; for *there is one body, and one Spirit, v.* 4. Two hearts in one body would be monstrous. *Even as you are called in one hope of your calling.* Hope is here put for its object, the thing hoped for, the heavenly inheritance, to the hope of which we are called. All Christians are called to the same hope of eternal life. There is one Christ that they all hope in, and one heaven that they are all hoping for; and therefore they should be of one heart. *One Lord* (*v.* 5), that is, Christ, the head of the church, to whom, by God's appointment, all Christians are immediately subject. *One faith,* that is, the gospel, containing the doctrine of the Christian faith. *One baptism,* by which we profess our faith, being baptized in the name of the Father, Son, and Holy Ghost; and so the same sacramental covenant, whereby we engage ourselves to the Lord Christ. *One God and Father of all, v.* 6. One God, who owns all the true members of the church for his children; for he is the Father of all such by special relation, as he is the Father of all men by creation.

2. Consider the variety of gifts that Christ has bestowed among Christians: *But unto every one of us is given grace according to the measure of the gift of Christ.* David prophesied of the ascension of Christ; and the apostle descants upon it here, and in the three following verses. *When he ascended up on high.* Christ, when he ascended into heaven, as a triumphant conqueror, *led captivity captive.* It is a phrase used in the Old Testament to signify a conquest over enemies, especially over such as formerly had led others captive; see Judges v. 12. *And he gave gifts unto men*: in the psalm it is, *He received gifts for men.* He received for them, that he might give to them, a large measure of gifts and graces; particularly, he enriched his disciples with the gift of the Holy Ghost. He descended to the earth in his incarnation. He descended into the earth in his burial, *that he might fill all things,* all the members of his church, with gifts and graces suitable to their several conditions and stations. Observe, Our Lord humbled himself first, and then he was exalted. *He gave some apostles,* &c. *v.* 11. The gift of the ministry is the fruit of Christ's ascension. And ministers have their various gifts, which are all given them by the Lord Jesus. The officers which Christ gave to his church were of two sorts—*extraordinary* ones advanced to a higher office in the church: such were *apostles, prophets,* and *evangelists.* The apostles were chief. The prophets seem to have been such as expounded the writings of the Old Testament, and foretold things to come. The evangelists were ordained persons (2 Tim. i. 6) whom the apostles took for their companions in travel (Gal. ii. 1), and sent them out to settle and establish such churches as the apostles themselves had planted (Acts xix. 22), and, not being fixed to any particular place, they were to continue till recalled, 2 Tim. iv. 9.

and then there are *ordinary* ministers, employed in a lower and narrower sphere; as *pastors* and *teachers*. Some take these two names to signify one office, implying the duties of ruling and teaching belonging to it. We see here that it is Christ's prerogative to appoint what officers and offices he pleases in his church.

3. The gifts of Christ were intended for the good of his church, and in order to advance his kingdom and interest among men. All are *for the perfecting of the saints* (v. 12); that is, according to the import of the original, to bring into an orderly spiritual state and frame those who had been as it were dislocated and disjointed by sin, and then to strengthen, confirm, and advance them therein, that so each, in his proper place and function, might contribute to the good of the whole. All are designed to prepare us for heaven: *Till we all come*, &c., v. 13. *Unto a perfect man*, to our full growth of gifts and graces, free from those childish infirmities that we are subject to in the present world. — *Unto the measure of the stature of the fulness of Christ*, so as to be Christians of a full maturity and ripeness in all the graces derived from Christ's fulness. The apostle further shows, in the following verses, what was God's design in his sacred institutions, and what effect they ought to have upon us. As, (1) *That we henceforth be no more children*, &c. (v. 14); that is, that we may be no longer children in knowledge, weak in the faith, and inconstant in our judgments, easily yielding to every temptation. (2) *That we should speak the truth in*

love (v. 15), or follow the truth in love, or be sincere in love to our fellow-christians. (3) That we should *grow up into Christ in all things*. Into Christ, so as to be more deeply rooted in him. In all things; in knowledge, love, faith, and all the parts of the new man. We should grow up towards maturity, which is opposed to being children. (4) We should be assisting and helpful one to another, as members of the same body, v. 16. Observe, Particular Christians receive their gifts and graces from Christ for the sake and benefit of the whole body. *Unto the edifying of itself in love.* We may understand this two ways: Either that all the members of the church may attain to a greater measure of love to Christ and to one another; or that they are moved to act in the manner mentioned from love to Christ and to one another.

PURITY AND HOLINESS
(vv. 17–32)

The apostle having gone through his exhortation to mutual love, unity, and concord, in the foregoing verses, there follows in these an exhortation to Christian purity and holiness of heart and life, and that both more general (vv. 17–24) and in several particular instances, vv. 25–32. Consider,

I. The more general exhortation to purity and holiness of heart and life.

II. The apostle proceeds to some things more particular. 1. Take heed of lying, and be ever careful to speak the truth (v. 25). 2. "Take heed of anger and ungoverned passions. *Be you angry, and sin not,"* v. 26. This is borrowed from the LXX. translation of Ps. iv. 4, where we render it, *Stand in awe, and sin not.* Here is an easy concession; for as such we should consider it, rather than as a command. 3. We are here warned against the sin of stealing, the breach of the eighth commandment, and advised to honest industry and to beneficence: *Let him that stole steal no more,* v. 28. It is a caution against all manner of wrong-doing, by force or fraud. 4. We are here warned against corrupt communication; and directed to that which is useful and edifying, v. 29. The great use of speech is to edify those with whom we converse. 5. Here is another caution against wrath and anger, with further advice to mutual love and kindly dispositions towards each other, vv. 31, 32. By *bitterness, wrath,* and *anger,* are meant violent inward resentment and displeasure against others: and, by *clamour,* big words, loud threatenings, and other intemperate speeches, by which bitterness, wrath, and anger, vent themselves. The contrary to all this follows: *Be you kind one to another.* This implies the principle of love in the heart, and the outward expression of it, in an affable, humble, courteous behaviour. *Tender-hearted*; that is, merciful, and having a tender sense of the distresses and sufferings of others, so as to be quickly moved to compassion and pity. *Forgiving one another.* Occasions of difference will happen among Christ's disciples; and therefore they must be placable, and ready to forgive, therein resembling God himself, who *for Christ's sake hath*

forgiven them, and that more than they can forgive one another.

In the midst of these exhortations and cautions the apostle interposes that general one, *And grieve not the Holy Spirit of God,* v. 30. By looking to what precedes, and to what follows, we may see what it is that grieves the Spirit of God. It is a good reason why we should not grieve him that *by him we are sealed unto the day of redemption.* There is to be a day of redemption; the body is to be redeemed from the power of the grave at the resurrection-day, and then God's people will be delivered from all the effects of sin, as well as from all sin and misery, which they are not till rescued out of the grave: and then their full and complete happiness commences.

CHAPTER FIVE
CHILDREN OF LIGHT
(vv. 1–20)

Here we have the exhortation to mutual love, or to Christian charity. And those only are God's dear children who imitate him in these. It follows, *And walk in love,* v. 2. This godlike grace should conduct and influence our whole conversation, which is meant by walking in it. *As Christ also hath loved us.* Here the apostle directs us to the example of Christ, whom Christians are obliged to imitate, and in whom we have an instance of the most free and generous love that ever was, that great love wherewith he hath loved us.

I. To fortify us against the sins of uncleanness, &c., the apostle urges several arguments, and prescribes several remedies, in what follows,

1. He urges several arguments, As, (1) Consider that these are sins which shut persons out of heaven: *For this you know*, &c., *v.* 5. They knew it, being informed of it by the Christian religion. (2) These sins bring the wrath of God upon those who are guilty of them: "*Let no man deceive you with vain words*, &c.," *v.* 6. *Be not you therefore partakers with them*, *v.* 7. "Do not partake with them in their sins, that you may not share in their punishment." We partake with other men in their sins, not only when we live in the same sinful manner that they do, and consent and comply with their temptations and solicitations to sin, but when we encourage them in their sins, prompt them to sin, and do not prevent and hinder them, as far as it may be in our power to do so. (3) Consider what obligations Christians are under to live at another rate than such sinners do: *For you were sometimes darkness, but now*, &c., *v.* 8. Sinners, like men in the dark, are going they know not whither, and doing they know not what. But the grace of God had produced a mighty change in their souls: *Now are you light in the Lord*, savingly enlightened by the word and the Spirit of God. *Now*, upon your believing in Christ, and your receiving the gospel. *Walk as children of light*.

2. The apostle prescribes some remedies against them. As, (1) If we would not be entangled by the lusts of the flesh, we must bring forth *the fruits of the Spirit*, *v.* 9. (2) We must have no fellowship with sin nor sinners, *v.* 11. Sinful works are works of darkness: they come from the darkness of ignorance, they seek the darkness of concealment, and they lead to the darkness of hell. We must therefore *have no fellowship* with these unfruitful works; as we must not practise them ourselves, so we must not countenance others in the practice of them. But, rather than have fellowship with them, we must *reprove them*, implying that if we do not reprove the sins of others we have fellowship with them. One reason given is, *For it is a shame even to speak of those things*, &c., *v.* 12. They are so filthy and abominable that it is a shame to mention them, except in a way of reproof, much more must it be a shame to have any fellowship with them. Christ, by his ministers, who preach the everlasting gospel, is continually calling upon sinners to this effect: *Awake, thou that sleepest, and arise from the dead*. When God calls upon them to awake, and to arise, his meaning is that they would break off their sins by repentance, and enter on a course of holy obedience, and he encourages them to essay and do their utmost that way, by that gracious promise, *And Christ shall give thee light*; or *Christ shall enlighten thee*, or *shall shine upon thee*. (3) Another remedy against sin is circumspection, care, or caution (*v.* 15): *See then*, &c. This may be understood either with respect to what immediately precedes, or else we nave here another remedy or rather preservative from the before-mentioned sins; and this I take to be the design of the apostle, it being im-

possible to maintain purity and holiness of heart and life without great circumspection and care. It follows, *redeeming the time* (v. 16), literally, *buying the opportunity*. It is a metaphor taken from merchants and traders who diligently observe and improve the seasons for merchandise and trade. It is a great part of Christian wisdom to redeem the time. The reason given is *because the days are evil*, either by reason of the wickedness of those who dwell in them, or rather "as they are troublesome and dangerous times to you who live in them."

II. In the three following verses the apostle warns against some other particular sins, and urges some other duties. 1. He warns against the sin of drunkenness: *And be not drunk with wine*, v. 18. 2. Instead of being filled with wine, he exhorts them to *be filled with the Spirit*. Those who are full of drink are not likely to be full of the Spirit; and therefore this duty is opposed to the former sin. The meaning of the exhortation is that men should labour for a plentiful measure of the graces of the Spirit, that would fill their souls with great joy, strength, and courage, which things sensual men expect their wine should inspire them with. 3. To sing unto the Lord, v. 19. Drunkards are wont to sing obscene and profane songs. The heathens, in their Bacchanalia, used to sing hymns to Bacchus, whom they called the god of wine. Thus they expressed their joy; but the joy of Christians should express itself in songs of praise to their God. In these they should *speak to themselves* in their assemblies and

meetings together, for mutual edification. 4. Thanksgiving is another duty that the apostle exhorts to, v. 20. We are appointed to sing psalms, &c., for the expression of our thankfulness to God; but, though we are not always singing, we should be *always giving thanks*; that is, we should never want a disposition for this duty, as we never want matter for it.

HUSBANDS AND WIVES
(vv. 21–33)

Here the apostle begins his exhortation to the discharge of relative duties. As a general foundation for these duties, he lays down that rule v. 21. There is a mutual submission that Christians owe one to another, condescending to bear one another's burdens: not advancing themselves above others, nor domineering over one another and giving laws to one another.

I. The duty prescribed to wives is submission to their husbands in the Lord (v. 22), which submission includes the honouring and obeying of them, and that from a principle of love to them. They must do this in compliance with God's authority, who has commanded it, which is doing it *as unto the Lord*. There is a resemblance of Christ's authority over the church in that superiority and headship which God has appointed to the husband. The apostle adds, *and he is the Saviour of the body*. Christ's authority is exercised over the church for the saving of her from evil, and the supplying of her with every thing good for her. In like manner should the husband be

321

employed for the protection and comfort of his spouse; and therefore she should the more cheerfully submit herself unto him. So it follows, *Therefore as the church is subject unto Christ* (v. 24), with cheerfulness, with fidelity, with humility, *so let the wives be to their own husbands in every thing*—in every thing to which their authority justly extends itself, in every thing lawful and consistent with duty to God.

II. The duty of husbands (on the other hand), is to love their wives (v. 25); for without this they would abuse their superiority and headship, and, wherever this prevails as it ought to do, it will infer the other duties of the relation, it being a special and peculiar affection that is required in her behalf. The love of Christ to the church is proposed as an example of this, which love of his is a sincere, a pure, an ardent, and a constant affection, and that notwithstanding the imperfections and failures that she is guilty of. The greatness of his love to the church appeared in his giving himself unto the death for it. *For this cause* (because they are one, as Christ and his church are one) *shall a man leave his father and mother*; the apostle refers to the words of Adam, when Eve was given to him for a meet help, Gen. ii. 24. *And they two shall be one flesh*, that is, by virtue of the matrimonial bond. *This is a great mystery*, v. 32. Those words of Adam, just mentioned by the apostle, are spoken literally of marriage; but they have also a hidden mystical sense in them, relating to the union between Christ and his church, of which the con-

jugal union between Adam and the mother of us all was a type: though not instituted or appointed by God to signify this, yet it was a kind of natural type, as having a resemblance to it: *I speak concerning Christ and the church.*

After this, the apostle concludes this part of his discourse with a brief summary of the duty of husbands and wives, v. 33. "*Nevertheless* (though there be such a secret mystical sense, yet the plain literal sense concerns you) *let every one of you in particular so love his wife even as himself*, with such a sincere, peculiar, singular, and prevailing affection as that is which he bears to himself. *And the wife see that she reverence her husband.*" Reverence consists of love and esteem, which produce a care to please, and of fear, which awakens a caution lest just offence be given. That the wife thus reverence her husband is the will of God and the law of the relation.

CHAPTER SIX
DUTIES OF CHILDREN
(vv. 1–9)

Here we have further directions concerning relative duties, in which the apostle is very particular.

I. The great duty of children is to obey their parents (v. 1), parents being the instruments of their being, God and nature having given them an authority to command, in subserviency to God.

II. The duty of parents: *And you fathers*, v. 4. Or, you parents, 1. "*Do not provoke your children to wrath.* Though God has given you power, you must not abuse that power, remembering that your children are, in a particular manner, pieces of yourselves, and therefore ought to be governed with great tenderness and love." 2. "*Bring them up* well, *in the nurture and admonition of the Lord*, in the discipline of proper and of compassionate correction, and in the knowledge of that duty which God requires of them and by which they may become better acquainted with him."

III. The duty of servants. This also is summed up in one word, which is, *obedience*. He is largest on this article, as knowing there was the greatest need of it. These servants were generally slaves. Civil servitude is not inconsistent with Christian liberty. Those may be the Lord's freemen who are slaves to men.

IV. The duty of masters: "*And you masters, do the same things unto them*" (*v.* 9); that is, act after the same manner. Be just to them, as you expect they should be to you: show the like good-will and concern for them, and be careful herein to approve yourselves to God."

THE ARMOUR OF GOD
(*vv.* 10–18)

Here is a general exhortation to constancy in our Christian course, and to courage in our Christian warfare.

I. They must see that they be stout-hearted. This is prescribed here: *Be strong in the Lord*, &c. Be strong in the Lord, either in his cause and for his sake or rather in his strength. We have no sufficient strength of our own.

II. They must be well armed:

"*Put on the whole armour of God*" (*v.* 11). This the apostle enlarges upon here, and shows,

1. What our danger is, and what need we have to put on this whole armour, considering what sort of enemies we have to deal with—the devil and all the powers of darkness: *For we wrestle not against flesh and blood*, &c. *v.* 12. (1) We have to do with a subtle enemy, an enemy who uses wiles and stratagems, as *v.* 11. (2) He is a powerful enemy: *Principalities*, and *powers*, and *rulers*. They are numerous, they are vigorous; and rule in those heathen nations which are yet in darkness. (3) They are spiritual enemies: *Spiritual wickedness in high places*, or wicked spirits, as some translate it.

2. What our duty is: to take and put on the whole armour of God, and then to stand our ground, and withstand our enemies.

(1) We must *withstand, v.* 13. We must not yield to the devil's allurements and assaults, but oppose them.

(2) We must stand our ground: *And, having done all, to stand*. We must resolve, by God's grace, not to yield to Satan. Resist him, and he will flee. If we give back, he will get ground.

(3) We must stand armed; and this is here most enlarged upon. Here is a Christian in complete armour: and the armour is divine. [1] Truth or sincerity is our girdle, *v.* 14. God desires truth, that is, sincerity, in the inward parts. [2] Righteousness must be our breast-plate. The breast-plate secures the vitals, shelters the heart. The righteousness of Christ imput-

ed to us is our breast-plate against the arrows of divine wrath. [3] Resolution must be as the greaves to our legs: *And their feet shod with the preparation of the gospel of peace*, v. 15. *The preparation of the gospel of peace* signifies a prepared and resolved frame of heart, to adhere to the gospel and abide by it, which will enable us to walk with a steady pace in the way of religion, notwithstanding the difficulties and dangers that may be in it. [4] Faith must be our shield: *Above all*, or chiefly, *taking the shield of faith*, v. 16. This is more necessary than any of them. Faith is all in all to us in an hour of temptation. The devil is here called *the wicked one*. He is wicked himself, and he endeavours to make us wicked. His temptations are called *darts*, because of their swift and undiscerned flight, and the deep wounds that they give to the soul; *fiery darts*, by way of allusion to the poisonous darts which were wont to inflame the parts which were wounded with them, and therefore were so called, as the serpents with poisonous stings are called fiery serpents. Faith is the shield with which we must quench these fiery darts, wherein we should receive them, and so render them ineffectual, that they may not hit us, or at least that they may not hurt us. [5] Salvation must be our helmet (v. 17); that is, *hope*, which has salvation for its object; so 1 Thess. v. 8. The helmet secures the head. A good hope of salvation, well founded and well built, will both purify the soul and keep it from being defiled by Satan, and it will comfort the soul and keep it from being troubled

and tormented by Satan. [6] The word of God is the sword of the Spirit. The sword is a very necessary and useful part of a soldier's furniture. It is called *the sword of the Spirit*, because it is of the Spirit's inditing and he renders it efficacious and powerful, and *sharper than a two-edged sword*. [7] Prayer must buckle on all the other parts of our Christian armour, v. 18. We must join prayer with all these graces, for our defence against these spiritual enemies, imploring help and assistance of God, as the case requires: and we must pray always. And we must pray *with supplication*, not for ourselves only, but *for all saints*; for we are members one of another.

CONCLUSION (vv. 19–24)

Here, I. He desires their prayers for him, v. 19. Having mentioned *supplication for all saints*, he puts himself into the number. We must pray for all saints, and particularly for God's faithful ministers. Observe what it is he would have them pray for in his behalf: "*That utterance may be given unto me*; that I may be enlarged from my present restraints, and so have liberty to propagate the faith of Christ; that I may have ability to express myself in a suitable and becoming manner; *and that I may open my mouth boldly*, that is, that I may deliver the whole counsel of God, without any base fear, shame, or partiality." *To make known the mystery of the gospel*. The whole gospel was a mystery, till made known by divine revelation; and it is the work of Christ's ministers to publish it. Having thus desired their prayers,

II. He recommends Tychicus unto them, *vv.* 21, 22. He was a sincere Christian, and so a brother in Christ: he was a faithful minister in the work of Christ, and he was very dear to Paul, which makes Paul's love to these Christian Ephesians the more observable, in that he should now part with so good and dear a friend for their sakes.

III. He concludes with his good wishes and prayers for them, and not for them only, but for all the brethren, *vv.* 23, 24. His usual benediction was, *Grace and peace*; here it is, *Peace be to the brethren, and love with faith.*

PHILIPPIANS

CHAPTER ONE

GREETINGS AND THANKS
(vv. 1–11)

We have here the inscription and benediction. Observe,

I. The persons writing the epistle —*Paul and Timothy*.

II. The persons to whom it is directed. 1. To *all the saints in Christ who are at Philippi*. 2. It is directed to the ministers, or church-officers—*with the bishops and deacons*, the bishops or elders, in the first place, whose office it was to teach and rule, and the deacons, or overseers of the poor, who took care of the outward business of the house of God.

III. Here is the apostolical benediction: *Grace be unto you, and peace, from God our Father, and from the Lord Jesus Christ, v. 2*. This is the same, almost word for word, in all the epistles.

The apostle proceeds after the inscription and benediction to thanksgiving for the saints at Philippi. He tells them what it was he thanked God for, upon their account. Observe here,

IV. Paul remembered them: he bore them much in his thoughts; and though they were out of sight, and he was at a distance from them, yet they were not out of his mind.

V. He remembered them with joy. At Philippi he was maltreated; there he was scourged and put into the stocks, and for the present saw little of the fruit of his labour; and yet he remembers Philippi with joy.

VI. He remembered them in prayer: *Always in every prayer of mine for you all, v. 4*. The best remembrance of our friends is to remember them at the throne of grace.

VII. He thanked God upon every joyful remembrance of them.

VIII. As in our prayers, so in our thanksgiving, we must eye God as our God: *I thank my God*. But what is the matter of this thanksgiving? 1. He gives thanks to God for the comfort he had in them: for *your fellowship in the gospel, from the first day until now, v. 5*. 2. For the confidence he had concerning them (*v. 6*): *Being confident of this very thing, &c. That he who has begun a good work in you will perform it unto the day of Jesus Christ*. He who hath planted Christianity in the world will preserve it as long as the world stands. Christ will have a church till the mystery of God shall be finished and the mystical body completed.

IX. The apostle expresses the ardent affection he had for them, and his concern for their spiritual welfare: *I have you in my heart, v. 7*.

He loved them as his own soul, and they lay near his heart. He thought much of them, and was in care about them. Having them in his heart, he longed after them; either he longed to see them, longed to hear from them, or he longed for their spiritual welfare and their increase and improvement in knowledge and grace. For this he appeals to God: *God is my record.* It was an inward disposition of mind that he expressed towards them, to the sincerity of which God only was witness, and therefore to him he appeals. "Whether you know it or not, or are sensible of it, God, who knows the heart, knows it."

X. He prayed, 1. That they might be a loving people, and that good affections might abound among them: *That your love might abound yet more and more.* He means it of their love to God, and one another, and all men. 2. That they might be a knowing and judicious people: that love might abound *in knowledge and in all judgment.* 3. That they might be a discerning people. This would be the effect of their knowledge and judgment: *That you may approve the things which are excellent* (*v.* 10). 4. That they might be an honest upright-hearted people: *That you may be sincere.* 5. That they might be an inoffensive people: that you may be *without offence until the day of Christ*; not apt to take offence; and very careful not to give offence to God or their brethren, to *live in all good conscience before God* (Acts xxiii. 1). 6. That they might be a fruitful useful people (*v.* 11): *Being filled with the fruits of righteousness,* &c.

PRISON AND PRAISE
(*vv.* 12–20)

Paul was now a prisoner at Rome; this might be a stumbling-block to those who had received the gospel by his ministry. Now to take off the offence of the cross, he expounds this dark and hard chapter of his sufferings, and makes it very easy and intelligible, and reconcilable to the wisdom and goodness of God who employed him.

I. He suffered by the sworn enemies of the gospel, who laid him in prison, and aimed at taking away his life; but they should not be stumbled at this, for good was brought out of it, and it tended to the furtherance of the gospel (*v.* 12). But how was this?

1. It alarmed those who were outside (*v.* 13): "*My bonds in Christ, or for Christ, are manifest in all the palace and in all other places.*"

2. It emboldened those who were within. As his enemies were startled at his sufferings, so his friends were encouraged by them. *Many of the brethren in the Lord waxing confident by my bonds, v.* 14.

II. He suffered from false friends as well as from enemies (*vv.* 15, 16): *Some preach Christ even of envy and strife. The one preach Christ of contention, not sincerely.* However, there were others who were animated by Paul's sufferings to preach Christ the more vigorously: *Some also of good will, and love.*

III. It is very affecting to see how easy he was in the midst of all: *Notwithstanding every way, whether in pretence or in truth, Christ is* preached; and I therein do rejoice, yea, and I will rejoice, *v.* 18. Note, The preaching of Christ is the joy of all who wish well to his kingdom among men. Two things made the apostle rejoice in the preaching of the gospel:

1. Because it tended to the salvation of the souls of men: *I know that this shall turn to my salvation, v.* 19.

2. Because it would turn to the glory of Christ, *v.* 20, where he takes occasion to mention his own entire devotedness to the service and honour of Christ.

LIVING OR DYING (*vv.* 21–26)

We have here an account of the life and death of blessed Paul: his life was Christ, and his death was gain. Observe, 1. It is the undoubted character of every good Christian that to him to live is Christ. 2. All those to whom to live is Christ to them to die *will be gain*: it is great gain, a present gain, everlasting gain. It might be thought, if death were gain to him, he would be weary of life, and impatient for death. No, says he,

I. *If I live in the flesh, this is the fruit of my labour* (*v.* 22), that is, Christ is. He reckoned his labour well bestowed, if he could be instrumental to advance the honour and interest of the kingdom of Christ in the world. Here we have him reasoning with himself upon the matter.

1. His inclination was for death (*v.* 23).

2. His judgment was rather to live awhile longer in this world, for the service of the church (*v.* 24):

Nevertheless to abide in the flesh is more needful for you.

II. *And, having this confidence, I know that I shall abide and continue with you all for your furtherance and joy of faith, v.* 25. Observe here,

1. What a great confidence Paul had in the divine Providence, that it would order all for the best to him. 2. Whatsoever is best for the church, we may be sure God will do. 3. Observe what ministers are continued for: *For our furtherance and joy of faith*, our further advancement in holiness and comfort. 4. What promotes our *faith and joy of faith* is very much for our furtherance in the way to heaven.

III. *That your rejoicing may be more abundant in Jesus Christ for me, by my coming to you again, v.* 26. They rejoiced in the hope of seeing him, and enjoying his further labours among them.

CHRISTIAN BEHAVIOUR (*vv.* 27–30)

The apostle concludes the chapter with two exhortations:

I. He exhorts them to strictness of behaviour (*v.* 27): *Only let your conversation be as becometh the gospel of Christ.* Observe, Those who profess the gospel of Christ should behave as becomes the gospel, or in a suitableness and agreeableness to it.

II. He exhorts them to courage and constancy in suffering: *And in nothing terrified by your adversaries, v.* 28. Our great care must be to keep close to our profession, and be constant to it: whatever oppositions we meet with, we must not be frightened at them, considering that the condition of the persecuted is much better and more desirable than the condition of the persecutors; for persecuting is an *evident token of perdition. For to you it is given on the behalf of Christ not only to believe, but also to suffer for his name, v.* 29. Here are two precious gifts given, and both on the behalf of Christ: 1. To believe in him. 2. To suffer for the sake of Christ is a valuable gift too: it is a great honour and a great advantage; for we may be very serviceable to the glory of God, which is the end of our creation, and encourage and confirm the faith of others.

CHAPTER TWO
THE HUMILITY OF CHRIST
(*vv.* 1–11)

The apostle proceeds in this chapter where he left off in the last, with further exhortations to Christian duties. Here we may observe,

I. The great gospel precept pressed upon us; that is, to love one another. This is the law of Christ's kingdom, the lesson of his school, the livery of his family. This he represents (*v.* 2) by being *likeminded, having the same love, being of one accord, of one mind.*

2. He proposes some means to promote it. (1) *Do nothing through strife and vain glory, v.* 3. There is no greater enemy to Christian love than pride and passion. (2) We must *esteem others in lowliness of mind better than ourselves.* (3) We must interest ourselves in the concerns of others, not in a way of curiosity and censoriousness, or as *busy-bodies in other men's matters,* but in Christian love and sympathy. A selfish spirit is destructive of Christian love.

II. Here is a gospel pattern proposed to our imitation, and that is the example of our Lord Jesus Christ: *Let this mind be in you which was also in Christ Jesus, v.* 5. Observe, Christians must be of Christ's mind. Now what was the mind of Christ? He was eminently humble, and this is what we are peculiarly to learn of him.

1. Here are the two natures of Christ: his divine nature and his human nature. (1) Here is his divine nature: *Who being in the form of God* (*v.* 6), partaking of the divine nature, as the eternal and only begotten Son of God. *He thought it no robbery to be equal with God*; did not think himself guilty of any invasion of what did not belong to him, or assuming another's right. He said, *I and my Father are one,* John x. 30. (2) His human nature: He was *made in the likeness of men,* and *found in fashion as a man.* He was really and truly man, *took part of our flesh and blood,* appeared in the nature and habit of man. And he voluntarily assumed human nature; it was his own act, and by his own consent. Herein he *emptied himself,* divested himself of the honours and glories of the upper world, and of his former appearance, to clothe himself with the rags of human nature. *He was in all things like to us,* Heb. ii. 17.

2. Here are his two estates, of humiliation and exaltation. (1) His estate of humiliation. He not only took upon him the likeness and fashion of a man, but the *form of a servant,* that is, a man of mean

estate. But the lowest step of his humiliation was his dying the death of the cross. *He became obedient to death, even the death of the cross*, a cursed, painful, and shameful death,—a death accursed by the law. Such was the condescension of the blessed Jesus. (2) His exaltation: *Wherefore God also hath highly exalted him*. His exaltation was the reward of his humiliation. Because he humbled himself, God exalted him; and he *highly exalted him*, raised him to an exceeding height. He exalted his whole person, the human nature as well as the divine; for he is spoken of as being in the form of God as well as in the fashion of man. His exaltation here is made to consist in honour and power. In honour; so *he had a name above every name*, a title of dignity above all the creatures, men and angels. And in power: *Every knee must bow to him*. The whole creation must be in subjection to him: *things in heaven, and things in earth, and things under the earth*, the inhabitants of heaven and earth, the living and the dead. *At the name of Jesus*; not at the sound of the word, but the authority of Jesus; all should pay a solemn homage. And that *every tongue should confess that Jesus Christ is Lord*—every nation and language should publicly own the universal empire of the exalted Redeemer, and that *all power in heaven and earth is given to him*, Matt. xxviii. 18.

GOD WORKING IN US
(*vv.* 12, 13)

I. He exhorts them to diligence and seriousness in the Christian course: *Work out your own salvation*. Observe, It concerns us above all things to secure the welfare of our souls: whatever becomes of other things, let us take care of our best interests. We are required to *work out our salvation*. The word signifies *working thoroughly* at a thing, and taking *true pains*. He adds, *With fear and trembling*, that is, with great care and circumspection.

II. He urges this from the consideration of their readiness always to obey the gospel. They were not merely awed by the apostle's presence, but did it even *much more in his absence*. "And because *it is God who worketh in you*, do you work out your salvation. Work, for he worketh." It should encourage us to do our utmost, because our *labour shall not be in vain*.

THE WORD OF LIFE
(*vv.* 14–18)

The apostle exhorts them in these verses to adorn their Christian profession by a suitable temper and behaviour, in several instances. 1. By a cheerful obedience to the commands of God (*v.* 14). 2. By peaceableness and love one to another. 3. By blameless behaviour towards all men (*v.* 15). *Among whom you shine as lights in the world*. Christ is the light of the world, and good Christians are lights in the world. They must shine as well as be sincere.—*Holding forth the word of life*, *v.* 16. The gospel is called the word of life because it reveals and proposes to us eternal life through Jesus Christ. *Life and immortality are brought to light by the gospel*, 2 Tim. i. 10. He would have them think his pains well bestowed, and that *he had not run in vain, nor laboured in vain.*

If I be offered, or *poured* out as the wine of the *drink-offerings,* 2 Tim. iv. 6, *I am now ready to be offered.* He could rejoice to seal his doctrine with his blood (*v.* 18): *For the same cause also do you joy and rejoice with me.* It is the will of God that good Christians should be much in rejoicing.

TWO GOOD MINISTERS
(*vv.* 19–30)

Paul takes particular notice of two good ministers; for though he was himself a great apostle, and *laboured more abundantly than they all,* yet he took all occasions to speak with respect of those who were far his inferiors.

I. He speaks of Timothy, whom he intended to send to the Philippians, that he might have an account of their state. Timothy was a man who had been tried, and had made *full proof of his ministry* (2 Tim. iv. 5), and was faithful in all that befell him. All the churches with whom he had acquaintance knew the proof of him.

II. Concerning Epaphroditus, whom he calls *his brother, and companion in labour, and fellow-soldier,* his Christian brother, to whom he bore a tender affection,— his companion in the work and sufferings of the gospel, who submitted to the same labours and hardships with himself,—and their messenger, one who was sent by them to him, probably to consult him about some affairs relating to their church, or to bring a present from them for his relief for he adds,

and *who ministered to my wants.* Observe, (1) Those who truly love Christ, and are hearty in the interests of his kingdom, will think it very well worth their while to hazard their health and life to do him service, and promote the edification of his church. (2) They were to receive him with joy, as newly recovered from sickness. It is an endearing consideration to have our mercies restored to us after danger of removal, and should make them the more valued and improved. What is given us in answer to prayer should be received with great thankfulness and joy.

A WARNING (*vv.* 1–3)

I. He exhorts them to *rejoice in the Lord* (*v.* 1), to rest satisfied in the interest they had in him and the benefit they hoped for by him.

II. He cautions them to take heed of those false teachers: *To write the same thing to you to me indeed is not grievous, but for you it is safe*; that is, the same things which I have already preached to you; as if he had said, "What has been presented to your ears shall be presented to your eyes: what I have spoken formerly shall now be written; to show that I am still of the same mind."

III. He describes true Christians, who are indeed the circumcision, the spiritual circumcision, the peculiar people of God, who are in covenant with him, as the Old-Testament Israelites were. Here are three characters: 1. They worshipped in the spirit, in opposition to the carnal ordinances of the Old

Testament, which consist in meats, and drinks, and divers washings, &c. 2. They *rejoice in Christ Jesus*, and not in the peculiar privileges of the Jewish church, or what answers to them in the Christian church—mere outward enjoyments and performances. 3. They have no *confidence in the flesh*, in those carnal ordinances and outward performances.

PAUL, THE EXAMPLE
(*vv.* 4–8)

The apostle here proposes himself for an example of trusting in Christ only, and not in his privileges as an Israelite.

I. He shows what he had to boast of as a Jew and a Pharisee. But,

II. The apostle tells us here how little account he made of these, in comparison of his interest in Christ and his expectations from him: *But what things were gain to me those have I counted loss for Christ* (*v.* 7); that is, those things which he had counted gain while he was a Pharisee, and which he had before reckoned up, *these he counted loss for Christ*. The apostle explains himself. 1. He tells us what it was that he was ambitious of and reached after: it was the knowledge of Christ Jesus his Lord, a believing experimental acquaintance with Christ as Lord; not a merely notional and speculative, but a practical and efficacious knowledge of him. 2. He shows how he had quitted his privileges as a Jew and a Pharisee. He had spoken before of *those things*, his Jewish privileges: here he speaks of *all things*, all worldly enjoyments and mere out-

ward privileges whatsoever, things of a like kind or any other kind which could stand in competition with Christ for the throne in his heart, or pretend to merit and desert. Nay, he not only counted them loss, but dung, *offals* thrown to dogs; they are not only less valuable than Christ, but in the highest degree contemptible, when they come in competition with him.

PRESSING TO THE MARK
(*vv.* 9–14)

We have heard what the apostle renounced; let us now see what he laid hold on, and resolved to cleave to, namely, Christ and heaven. He had his heart on these two great peculiarities of the Christian religion.

I. The apostle had his heart upon Christ as his righteousness. This is illustrated in several instances. 1. He desired to win Christ; and an unspeakable gainer he would reckon himself if he had but an interest in Christ and his righteousness, and if Christ became his Lord and his Saviour. 2. That he *might be found in him* (*v.* 9). There is a righteousness provided for us in Jesus Christ, and it is a complete and perfect righteousness. Observe, The apostle was as ambitious of being sanctified as he was of being justified. 4. That he might be conformable unto him, and this also is meant of his sanctification. We are then made conformable to his death when we die to sin, as Christ died for sin, when we are crucified with Christ, the flesh and affections of it mortified, and the *world is crucified to us*, and *we to the world, by virtue of the cross of*

Christ. This is our conformity to his death.

II. The apostle had his heart upon heaven as his happiness: *If by any means I might attain to the resurrection of the dead, v. 11.*

1. The happiness of heaven is here called the resurrection of the dead, because, though the souls of the faithful, when they depart, are immediately with Christ, yet their happiness will not be complete till the general resurrection of the dead at the last day.

2. This joyful resurrection the apostle pressed towards. He was willing to do any thing, or suffer any thing, that he might attain that resurrection. Observe,

(1) He looks upon himself to be in a state of imperfection and trial: *Not as though I had already attained, or were already perfect, v. 12.*

(2) What the apostle's actings were under this conviction. Considering that he had not already attained, and had not apprehended, he pressed forward (*v. 12*). He adds further (*v. 13*): *This one thing I do* (this was his great care and concern), *forgetting those things which are behind, and reaching forth to those things which are before.* There is a sinful forgetting of past sins and past mercies, which ought to be remembered for the exercise of constant repentance and thankfulness to God. But Paul forgot the things which were behind so as not to be content with present measures of grace: he was still for having more and more.

(3) The apostle's aim in these actings: *I press towards the mark, for the prize of the high calling of God in Christ Jesus, v. 14.* He

pressed towards the mark. As he who runs a race never takes up short of the end, but is still making forwards as fast as he can, so those who have heaven in their eye must still be pressing forward to it in holy desires and hopes, and constant endeavours and preparations. Heaven is called here the mark, because it is that which every good Christian has in his eye; as the archer has his eye fixed upon the mark he designs to hit. *For the prize of the high calling.* Observe, A Christian's calling is a high calling: it is from heaven, as its original; and it is to heaven in its tendency.

TRANSFORMATION
(*vv.* 15-21)

We see here how he was minded; let us be like-minded, and set our hearts upon Christ and heaven, as he did. 1. He shows that this was the thing wherein all good Christians were agreed, to make Christ all in all, and set their hearts upon another world. 2. That this is a good reason why Christians who differ in smaller matters should yet bear with one another, because they are agreed in the main matter.

Paul then closes the chapter with warnings and exhortations.

I. He warns them against following the examples of seducers and evil teachers (*vv.* 18, 19): *Many walk, of whom I have told you often, and now tell you weeping, that they are the enemies of the cross of Christ.* Observe,

1. There are many called by Christ's name who are enemies to Christ's cross, and the design and intention of it.

2. He gives us the characters of

those who were the enemies of the cross of Christ. (1) Whose God is their belly. They minded nothing but their sensual appetites. (2) They glory in their shame. They not only sinned, but boasted of it and gloried in that of which they ought to have been ashamed. (3) They mind earthly things. Christ came by his cross to *crucify the world to us and us to the world*; and those who mind earthly things act directly contrary to the cross of Christ, and this great design of it. (4) Whose end is destruction. Their way seems pleasant, but death and hell are at the end of it.

II. He proposes himself and his brethren for an example, in opposition to these evil examples: *Brethren, be followers together of me, and mark those who walk as you have us for an example, v.* 17. Mark them out for your pattern. He explains himself (*v.* 20) by their regard to Christ and heaven: *For our conversation is in heaven.*

1. Because we look for the Saviour from heaven (*v.* 20).

2. Because at the second coming of Christ we expect to be happy and glorified there. There is a glory reserved for the bodies of the saints, which they will be instated in at the resurrection. Observe, (1) The example of this change, and that is, the glorious body of Christ; when he was transfigured upon the mount, *his face did shine as the sun, and his raiment was white as the light*, Matt. xvii. 2. (2) The power by which this change will be wrought: *According to the working whereby he is able even to subdue all things unto himself.* There is an efficacy of power, an *exceeding*

greatness of power, and the *working of mighty power,* Eph. i. 19.

THE PEACE OF GOD (*vv.* 1–9)

The apostle begins the chapter with exhortations to divers Christian duties.

I. To stedfastness in our Christian profession, *v.* 1. Observe here,

1. The compellations are very endearing: *My brethren, dearly beloved and longed for, my joy and crown*; and again, *My dearly beloved.*

2. The exhortation itself: *So stand fast in the Lord.* Being in Christ, they must stand fast in him, be even and steady in their walk with him, and close and constant unto the end.

II. He exhorts them to unanimity and mutual assistance (*vv.* 2, 3): *I beseech Euodias and Syntyche that they be of the same mind in the Lord.* This is directed to some particular persons. Then he exhorts to mutual assistance (*v.* 3), and this exhortation he directs to particular persons: *I entreat thee also, true yoke-fellow.* Who this person was whom he calls true yoke-fellow is uncertain. Some think Epaphroditus, who is supposed to have been one of the pastors of the church of the Philippians.

III. He exhorts to holy joy and delight in God: *Rejoice in the Lord always, and again I say, Rejoice, v.* 4. All our joy must terminate in God; and our thoughts of God must be delightful thoughts.

IV. We are here exhorted to candour and gentleness, and good temper towards our brethren: "*Let your moderation be known to all men, v. 5.* The reason is, *the Lord is at hand.* The consideration of our Master's approach, and our final account, should keep us from smiting our fellow-servants, support us under present sufferings, and moderate our affections to outward good.

V. Here is a caution against disquieting perplexing care (*v.* 6): *Be careful for nothing*: the same expression with that Matt. vi: 25, *Take no thought for your life*; that is, avoid anxious care and distracting thought in the wants and difficulties of life.

VI. As a sovereign antidote against perplexing care he recommends to us constant prayer: *In every thing by prayer and supplication, with thanksgiving, let your requests be made known to God.* Not that God needs to be told either our wants or desires; for he knows them better than we can tell him: but he will know them from us, and have us show our regards and concern, express our value of the mercy and sense of our dependence on him. 4. The effect of this will be the *peace of God keeping our hearts, v.* 7. The *peace of God,* that is, the comfortable sense of our reconciliation to God and interest in his favour, and the hope of the heavenly blessedness, and enjoyment of God hereafter, *which passeth all understanding,* is a greater good than can be sufficiently valued or duly expressed.

VII. We are exhorted to get and keep a good name, a name for good things with God and good men: *Whatsoever things are true and honest (v.* 8), *just and pure,*—

agreeable to the rules of justice and righteousness in all our dealings with men, and without the impurity or mixture of sin. Whatsoever things are *lovely and of good report,* that is, amiable; that will render us beloved, and make us well spoken of, as well as well thought of, by others. *If there is any virtue, if there is any praise*—any thing really virtuous of any kind and worthy of commendation.

In these things he proposes himself to them for an example (*v.* 9). Observe, Paul's doctrine and life were of a piece.

ALL NEEDS MET (*vv.* 10–19)

In these verses we have the thankful grateful acknowledgment which the apostle makes of the kindness of the Philippians in sending him a present for his support, now that he was a prisoner at Rome. And here,

I. He takes occasion to acknowledge their former kindnesses to him, and to make mention of them, *vv.* 15, 16.

II. He excuses their neglect of late. It seems, for some time they had not sent to enquire after him, or sent him any present; but *now at last their care of him flourished again (v.* 10), like a tree in the spring, which seemed all the winter to be quite dead.

III. He commends their present liberality: *Notwithstanding, you have well done that you did communicate with my affliction, v.* 14.

IV. He takes care to obviate the bad use some might make of his taking so much notice of what was sent him. It did not proceed either from discontent and distrust (*v.* 11) or from covetousness and love of the world, *v.* 12. 1. It did not come from discontent, or distrust of Providence: *Not that I speak in respect of want* (*v.* 11); not in respect of any want he felt, nor of any want he feared. *For I have learned, in whatsoever state I am, therewith to be content.* He had learnt to be content; and that was the lesson he had as much need to learn as most men, considering the hardships and sufferings with which he was exercised. *I know both how to be abased and I know how to abound, v.* 12. This is a special act of grace, to accommodate ourselves to every condition of life, and carry an equal temper of mind through all the varieties of our state. But how must we learn it? *I can do all things through Christ who strengthens me, v.* 13. We have need of strength from Christ, to enable us to perform not only those duties which are purely Christian, but even those which are the fruit of moral virtue. 2. It did not come from covetousness, or an affection to worldly wealth: "*Not because I desired a gift* (*v.* 17); that is, I welcome your kindness, not because it adds to my enjoyments, but because it adds to your account." They sent him a small token, and he desired no more; he was not solicitous for a present superfluity, or a future supply.

V. The apostle assures them that God did accept, and would recom-

pense, their kindness to him. 1. He did accept it: *It is an odour of a sweet smell, a sacrifice acceptable, well-pleasing to God.* Not a sacrifice of atonement, for none makes atonement for sin but Christ; but a sacrifice of acknowledgment, and *well-pleasing to God.* 2. He would recompense it: *But my God shall supply all your wants according to his riches in glory by Christ Jesus, v.* 19. He does as it were draw a bill upon the exchequer in heaven, and leaves it to God to make them amends for the kindness they had shown him.

CONCLUSION (*vv.* 20–23)

The apostle concludes the epistle in these verses,

1. With praises to God: *Now unto God and our Father be glory for ever and ever, Amen, v.* 20.

2. With salutations to his friends at Philippi.

3. He sends salutations from those who were at Rome. *Chiefly those who are of Cæsar's household;* the Christian converts who belonged to the emperor's court. Observe, There were saints in Cæsar's household. Though Paul was imprisoned at Rome, for preaching the gospel, by the emperor's command, yet there were some Christians in his own family.

4. The apostolical benediction, as usual.

COLOSSIANS

INTRODUCTION (vv. 1–8)

After the usual greetings, Paul proceeds to the body of the epistle, and begins with thanksgiving to God for what he had heard concerning them, though he had no personal acquaintance with them, and knew their state and character only by the reports of others.

I. He gave thanks to God for them, that they had embraced the gospel of Christ, and given proofs of their fidelity to him. Observe, 1. What he gives thanks to God for —for the graces of God in them, which were evidences of the grace of God towards them.

II. Having blessed God for these graces, he blesses God for the means of grace which they enjoyed: *Wherein you heard before in the word of the truth of the gospel.* They had heard in the word of the truth of the gospel concerning this *hope laid up for them in heaven.* Observe, 1. The gospel is the word of truth, and what we may safely venture our immortal souls upon. 2. It is a great mercy to hear this word of truth; for the great thing we learn from it is the happiness of heaven.

III. He takes this occasion to mention the minister by whom they believed (vv. 7, 8): *As you also learned of Epaphras, our dear fellow-servant, who is for you a faithful minister of Christ.* He mentions him with great respect, to engage their love to him.

HIS PRAYER (vv. 9–11)

The apostle proceeds in these verses to pray for them. Observe what it is that he begs of God for them,

I. That they might be knowing intelligent Christians: *filled with the knowledge of his will, in all wisdom and spiritual understanding.*

II. That their behaviour might be good. Good knowledge without a good life will not profit. Our understanding is then a spiritual understanding when we exemplify it in our way of living. Good words will not do without good works.

III. That they might be strengthened: *Strengthened with all might, according to his glorious power* (v. 11), fortified against the temptations of Satan and furnished for all their duty. The word of God is the means of it, by which he conveys it; and it must be fetched in by prayer. The special use of this strength was for suffering work: *That you may be strengthened unto all patience and long-suffering with joyfulness.* He prays not only that they may be *supported* under their troubles, but *strengthened* for them: the reason is there is work to be done even when we are suffering.

CHRIST IN YOU (*vv.* 12–29)

Here is a summary of the doctrine of the gospel concerning the great work of our redemption by Christ. The order and connection of the apostle's discourse may be considered in the following manner:

I. He speaks concerning the operations of the Spirit of grace upon us. We must give thanks for them, because by these we are qualified for an interest in the mediation of the Son: *Giving thanks to the Father*, &c. *vv.* 12, 13. Now what is it which is wrought for us in the application of redemption? 1. "He hath *delivered us from the power of darkness*, *v.* 13." They are *called out of darkness*, 1 Pet. ii. 9. 2. "He hath *translated us into the kingdom of his dear Son*." Those were made willing subjects of Christ who were the slaves of Satan. 3. "He hath not only done this, but hath *made us meet to partake of the inheritance of the saints in light*, *v.* 12. He hath prepared us for the eternal happiness of heaven, as the Israelites divided the promised land by lot; and has given us the earnest and assurance of it.

II. Concerning the person of the Redeemer, Glorious things are here said of him; for blessed Paul was full of Christ, and took all occasions to speak honourably of him. He speaks of him distinctly as God, and as Mediator. 1. As God he speaks of him, *vv.* 15–17. (1) He is the *image of the invisible God*. Not as man was made *in the image of God* (Gen. i. 27), in his natural faculties and dominion over the creatures: no, he is the *express image of his person*, Heb. i. 3. (2) He is the *first-born of every creature*. Not that he is himself a creature. It signifies his dominion over all things, as the first-born in a family is heir and lord of all, so he is the *heir of all things*, Heb. i. 2. (3) He is so far from being himself a creature that he is the Creator: *For by him were all things created, which are in heaven and earth, visible and invisible*, *v.* 16. (4) He *was before all things*. He not only had a being before he was born of the virgin, but he had a being before all time. (5) *By him all things consist*. They not only subsist in their beings, but consist in their order and dependences. He not only created them all at first, but it is by the word of his power that they are still upheld, Heb. i. 3.

2. The apostle next shows what he is as Mediator, *vv.* 18, 19. (1) He is the *head of the body the church*. (2) He is the *beginning, the first-born from the dead*, the principle of our resurrection, as well as the first-born himself. All our hopes and joys take their rise from him who is the author of our salvation. (3) He hath in *all things the pre-eminence*. It was the will of the Father that he should have *all power in heaven and earth*, that he might be preferred above angels and all the powers in heaven. He has the pre-eminence in the hearts of his people above the world and the flesh; and by giving him the pre-eminence we comply with the Father's will, That *all men should honour the Son even as they honour the Father*, John v. 23. (4) All fulness dwells in him, and it pleased the Father it should do so (*v.* 19); a

fulness of merit and righteousness, of strength and grace.

III. Concerning the work of redemption.

1. Wherein it consists. It is made to lie in two things: (1) In the remission of sin: *In whom we have redemption, even the forgiveness of sins, v.* 14. It was sin which sold us, sin which enslaved us: if we are redeemed, we must be redeemed from sin; and this is by forgiveness, or remitting the obligation to punishment. (2) In reconciliation to God. God by him *reconciled all things to himself, v.* 20. He is the Mediator of reconciliation, who procures peace as well as pardon for sinners.

2. How the redemption is procured: *it is through his blood* (*v.* 14); he has *made peace through the blood of his cross* (*v.* 20), and it is *in the body of his flesh through death, v.* 22. It was the *blood which made an atonement, for the blood is the life; and without the shedding of blood there is no remission,* Heb. ix. 22.

IV. Concerning the preaching of this redemption. Here observe,

1. To whom it was preached: *To every creature under heaven* (*v.* 23), that is, it was ordered to be preached to every creature, Mark xvi. 15.

2. By whom it was preached: *Whereof I am made a minister.* Paul was a great apostle; but he looks upon it as the highest of his titles of honour to be a minister of the gospel of Jesus Christ.

3. The gospel which was preached. We have an account of this: *Even the mystery which hath been hid from ages, and from generations,* but is now made manifest to his saints, vv.* 26, 27. The meanest saint under the gospel understands more than the greatest prophets under the law. And what is this mystery? It is the riches of God's glory among the Gentiles, the breaking down of the partition-wall between the Jew and Gentile, and preaching the gospel to the Gentile world, and making those partakers of the privileges of the gospel state who before lay in ignorance and idolatry.

4. The duty of those who are interested in this redemption: *If you continue in the faith, grounded and settled, and be not moved away from the hope of the gospel which you have heard, v.* 23. We must continue in the faith grounded and settled, and not be moved away from the hope of the gospel; that is, we must be so well fixed in our minds as not to be moved from it by any temptations.

CHAPTER TWO

THE TREASURES OF CHRIST
(vv. 1–3)

We may observe here the great concern which Paul had for these Colossians and the other churches which he had not any personal knowledge of.

I. What was it that the apostle desired for them? *That their hearts may be comforted, being knit together in love,* &c., *v.* 2. It was their spiritual welfare about which he was solicitous.

1. *To understand the mystery,* either what was before concealed, but is now made known concerning the Father and Christ, or the

mystery before mentioned, of calling the Gentiles into the Christian church. This is what we should labour after, and then the soul prospers.

2. When our faith grows to a full assurance, or a well-settled judgment, upon their proper evidence, of the great truths of the gospel. This is called the *riches of the full assurance of understanding*.

3. *That their hearts might be comforted.* The soul prospers when it is filled with joy and peace (Rom. xv. 13), and has a satisfaction within which all the troubles without cannot disturb, and is able to joy in the Lord when all other comforts fail, Hab. iii. 17, 18.

4. *Being knit together in love.* Holy love knits the hearts of Christians one to another; and faith and love both contribute to our comfort.

II. His concern for them is repeated (v. 5): *Though I am absent in the flesh, yet am I with you in the spirit, joying, and beholding your order, and the stedfastness of your faith in Christ.*

WALKING IN CHRIST
(vv. 4–12)

The apostle cautions the Colossians against deceivers (v. 4). Observe,

I. A sovereign antidote against seducers (vv. 6, 7): *As you have therefore received Christ Jesus the Lord, so walk you in him, rooted and built up*, &c. Here note, 1. All Christians have, in profession at least, *received Jesus Christ the Lord*, consented to him, taken him for ours in every relation and every capacity, and for all the purposes and uses of them. 2. The great concern of those who have received Christ is *to walk in him*—to make their practices conformable to their principles and their behaviour agreeable to their engagements. 3. The more closely we walk with Christ the more we are *rooted and established in the faith*. If we walk in him, we shall be rooted in him; and the more firmly we are rooted in him the more closely we shall walk in him.

II. The fair warning given us of our danger: *Beware lest any man spoil you through philosophy and vain deceit, after the tradition of men, after the rudiments of the world, and not after Christ, v.* 8. There is a philosophy which is vain and deceitful, which is prejudicial to religion, and sets up the wisdom of man in competition with the wisdom of God, and while it pleases men's fancies ruins their faith. Those who pin their faith on other men's sleeves, and walk in the way of the world, have turned away from following after Christ.

Now here the apostle shows,

1. That we have in Christ the substance of all the shadows of the ceremonial law; for example, (1) Had they then the Shechinah, or special presence of God, called the glory, from the visible token of it? So have we now in Jesus Christ (v. 9). The fulness of the Godhead dwells in Christ really, and not figuratively; for he is both God and man. (2) Had they circumcision, which was the seal of the covenant? In Christ we are *circumcised with the circumcision made without hands* (v. 11), by the work of regeneration in us, which is the spiritual or Christian circumcision.

2. We have communion with Christ in his whole undertaking (*v.* 12): *Buried with him in baptism, wherein also you have risen with him.* The thing signified by our baptism is that we are buried with Christ, as baptism is the seal of the covenant and an obligation to our dying to sin; and that we are raised with Christ, as it is a seal and obligation to our living to righteousness, or newness of life.

CHRISTIAN PRIVILEGES
(*vv.* 13–15)

The apostle here represents the privileges we Christians have above the Jews, which are very great.

I. Christ's death is our life: *And you, being dead in your sins and the uncircumcision of your flesh, hath he quickened together with him, v.* 13. A state of sin is a state of spiritual death. Those who are in sin are dead in sin. Now through Christ we, who were dead in sins, are quickened. Christ's death was the death of our sins; Christ's resurrection is the quickening of our souls.

II. Through him we have the remission of sin: *Having forgiven you all the trespasses.* This is our quickening. The pardon of the crime is the life of the criminal.

III. Whatever was in force against us is taken out of the way. He has obtained for us a legal discharge from the *hand-writing of ordinances, which was against us* (*v.* 14), which may be understood, 1. Of that obligation to punishment in which consists the guilt of sin. Or rather, 2. It must be understood of the ceremonial law, the *hand-writing of ordinances*, which was a yoke to the

Jews and a partition-wall to the Gentiles. The Lord Jesus *took it out of the way, nailed it to his cross*; that is, disannulled the obligation of it, that all might see and be satisfied that it was no more binding.

IV. He has obtained a glorious victory for us over the powers of darkness: *And, having spoiled principalities and powers, he made a show of them openly, triumphing over them in it, v.* 15. The devil and all the powers of hell were conquered and disarmed by the dying Redeemer. He *spoiled them*, broke the devil's power, and conquered and disabled him, and *made a show of them openly*—exposed them to public shame, and made a show of them to angels and men.

WILL-WORSHIP (*vv.* 16–23)

The apostle concludes the chapter with exhortations to proper duty, which he infers from the foregoing discourse.

I. Here is a caution to take heed of judaizing teachers, or those who would impose upon Christians the yoke of the ceremonial law: *Let no man therefore judge you in meat nor in drink,* &c. *v.* 16.

II. He cautions them to take heed of those who would introduce the worship of angels as mediators between God and them, as the Gentile philosophers did: *Let no man beguile you of your reward, in a voluntary humility and worshipping of angels, v.* 18. It is the highest disparagement to Christ, who is the head of the church, for any of the members of it to make use of any intercessors with God but him.

III. He takes occasion hence to

warn them again: "*Wherefore, if you be dead with Christ from the rudiments of the world, why, as though living in the world, are you subject to ordinances? v.* 20. If as Christians you are dead to the observances of the ceremonial law, why are you subject to them? Such observances as, *Touch not, taste not, handle not,*" *vv.* 21, 22.—*Which things have indeed a show of wisdom in will-worship and humility.* They thought themselves wiser than their neighbours, in observing the law of Moses together with the gospel of Christ, that they might be sure in the one, at least, to be in the right; but, alas! it was but a show of wisdom, a mere invention and pretence.

CHAPTER THREE
THE RISEN LIFE (*vv.* 1–4)

The apostle, having described our privileges by Christ in the former part of the epistle, and our discharge from the yoke of the ceremonial law, comes here to press upon us our duty as inferred thence.

I. He explains this duty (*v.* 2): *Set your affections on things above, not on things on the earth.* Observe, To seek heavenly things is to set our affections upon them, to love them and let our desires be towards them.

II. He assigns three reasons for this, *vv.* 3, 4.

1. That we are dead; that is, to present things, and as our portion. We are so in profession and obligation; for we are *buried with Christ, and planted into the likeness of his death.*

2. Our true life lies in the other world: *You are dead, and your life is hid with Christ in God, v.* 3. The new man has its livelihood thence. It is born and nourished from above; and the perfection of its life is reserved for that state. It is *hid with Christ:* not hid from us only, in point of secrecy, but hid for us, denoting security.

3. Because at the second coming of Christ we hope for the perfection of our happiness. If we live a life of Christian purity and devotion now, *when Christ, who is our life, shall appear, we shall also appear with him in glory, v.* 4.

PUTTING SIN TO DEATH (*vv.* 5–7)

The apostle exhorts the Colossians to the mortification of sin, the great hindrance to seeking the things which are above. He specifies,

I. The lusts of the flesh, for which they were before so very remarkable.

II. The love of the world: *And covetousness, which is idolatry;* that is, an inordinate love of present good and outward enjoyments, which proceeds from too high a value in the mind. He proceeds to show how necessary it is to mortify sins, *v.* 6, 7. 1. Because, if we do not kill them, they will kill us: *For which things' sake the wrath of God cometh on the children of disobedience, v.* 6. 2. We should mortify these sins because they have lived in us: *In which you also walked some time, when you lived in them, v.* 7.

PUT OFF EVIL (*vv.* 8–11)

As we are to mortify inordinate appetites, so we are to mortify inordinate passions (*v.* 8): *But now you also put off all these, anger, wrath, malice*; for these are contrary to the design of the gospel, as well as grosser impurities; and, though they are more spiritual wickedness, have not less malignity in them. Seeing *you have put off the old man with his deeds, and have put on the new man, v.* 10. Those who have put off the old man have put it off with its deeds; and those who have put on the new man must put on all its deeds — not only espouse good principles but act them in a good way of life. The new man is said to be *renewed in knowledge*, because an ignorant soul cannot be a good soul. Without knowledge the heart cannot be good, Prov. xix. 2. In the privilege and duty of sanctification *there is neither Greek nor Jew, circumcision nor uncircumcision, Barbarian, Scythian, bond nor free, v.* 11. There is now no difference arising from different country or different condition and circumstance of life: it is as much the duty of the one as of the other to be holy, and as much the privilege of the one as of the other to receive from God the grace to be so.

PUT ON GOOD
(*vv.* 12–17)

The apostle proceeds to exhort to mutual love and compassion.

I. The argument here used to enforce the exhortation is very affecting: *Put on, as the elect of God, holy and beloved.* (1) Compassion towards the miserable: *Bowels of mercy*, the tenderest mercies. Those who owe so much to mercy ought to be merciful to all who are proper objects of mercy. (2) *Kindness* towards our friends, and those who love us. (3) *Humbleness of mind*, in submission to those above us, and condescension to those below us. (4) *Meekness* towards those who have provoked us, or been any way injurious to us. (5) *Long-suffering* towards those who continue to provoke us. (6) Mutual forbearance, in consideration of the infirmities and deficiencies under which we all labour: *Forbearing one another*. (7) A readiness to forgive injuries: *Forgiving one another, if any man have a quarrel against any.*

II. In order to do all this, we are exhorted here to several things: 1. To clothe ourselves with love (*v.* 14): *Above all things put on charity: over all things.* Let this be the upper garment, the robe, the livery, the mark of our dignity and distinction. 2. To submit ourselves to the government of the *peace of God* (*v.* 15): *Let the peace of God rule in your hearts.* "Let this peace *rule in your heart* — prevail and govern there, or as an umpire decide all matters of difference among you." — *To which you are called in one body.* We are called to this peace, to peace with God as our privilege and peace with our brethren as our duty. 3. To let the *word of Christ dwell in us richly, v.* 16. The gospel is the word of Christ, which has come to us; but that is not enough, it must dwell in us, or *keep house*, not as a servant in a family, who is under another's control, but as a master, who has a right to prescribe to and direct all under his roof. 4. We must *admonish one another in psalms and hymns.*

Observe, Singing of psalms is a gospel ordinance — the Psalms of David, and spiritual hymns and odes, collected out of the scripture, and suited to special occasions. But, when we sing psalms, we make no melody unless we sing with grace in our hearts. 5. All must be done in the name of Christ (v. 17): *And whatsoever you do in word or deed, do all in the name of the Lord Jesus,* according to his command and in compliance with his authority, by strength derived from him, with an eye to his glory, and depending upon his merit for the acceptance of what is good and the pardon of what is amiss, *Giving thanks to God and the Father by him.*

FAMILY DUTIES (vv. 18–25)

The apostle concludes the chapter with exhortations to relative duties, as before in the epistle to the Ephesians.

I. He begins with the duties of wives and husbands (v. 18): *Wives, submit yourselves unto your own husbands, as it is fit in the Lord.* Submission is the duty of wives. It is agreeable to the order of nature and the reason of things, as well as the appointment and will of God. On the other hand, *husbands must love their wives, and not be bitter against them, v. 19.* They must love them with tender and faithful affection, as Christ loved the church, and as their own bodies, and even as themselves (Eph. v. 25, 28, 33), with a love peculiar to the nearest relation and the greatest comfort and blessing of life.

II. The duties of children and parents: *Children, obey your parents in all things, for this is well-*pleasing unto the Lord, v. 20.* They must be willing to do all their lawful commands, and be at their direction and disposal; as those who have a natural right and are fitter to direct them than themselves. And parents must be tender, as well as children obedient (v. 21): *"Fathers, provoke not your children to anger, lest they be discouraged."* The bad temper and example of imprudent parents often prove a great hindrance to their children and a stumbling-block in their way; see Eph. vi. 4.

III. Servants and masters: *Servants, obey your masters in all things according to the flesh, v. 22.* Servants must do the duty of the relation in which they stand, and obey their master's commands in *all things* which are consistent with their duty to God their heavenly Master. *Not with eye-service, as men-pleasers* — not only when their master's eye is upon them, but when they are from under their master's eye. "And *whatsoever you do, do it heartily* (v. 23), with diligence, not idly and slothfully:" or, "Do it cheerfully, not discontented at the providence of God which put you in that relation."— *As to the Lord, and not as to men.* It sanctifies a servant's work when it is done as unto God — with an eye to his glory and in obedience to his command, and not merely as unto men, or with regard to them only.

MASTERS (v. 1)

The apostle proceeds with the duty of masters to their servants, which might have been joined to the foregoing chapter, and is a part of that discourse. Here observe, 1. Justice is required of them: *Give unto your servants that which is just and equal* (v. 1), not strict justice, but equity and kindness. 2. A good reason for this regard: "*Knowing that you also have a Master in heaven.*" Deal with your servants as you expect God should deal with you, and as those who believe they must give an account.

ADVICE FOR CHRISTIANS
(vv. 2–6)

If this be considered as connected with the foregoing verse, then we may observe that it is part of the duty which masters owe their servants to pray with them, and to pray daily with them, or *continue in prayer. — With thanksgiving*, or solemn acknowledgment of the mercies received. Thanksgiving must have a part in every prayer.— *Withal praying also for us*, v. 3. The people must pray particularly for their ministers, and bear them upon their hearts at all times at the throne of grace. *That God would open to us a door of utterance*, that is, either afford opportunity to preach the gospel (so he says, *a great door and effectual is opened to me*, 1 Cor. xvi. 9), or else give me ability and courage, and enable me with freedom and faithfulness; so Eph. vi. 19.

The apostle exhorts them further to a prudent and decent conduct towards all those with whom they conversed, towards the heathen world, or those out of the Christian church among whom they lived (v. 5): *Walk in wisdom towards those who are without.* "*Let your speech be always with grace, v. 6.*" Let all your discourse be as becomes Christians, suitable to your profession — savoury, discreet, seasonable. Though it be not always of grace, it must be always with grace; and, though the matter of our discourse be that which is common, yet it must be in a Christian manner: *seasoned with salt.* Grace is the salt which seasons our discourse, makes it savoury, and keeps it from corrupting. *That you may know how to answer every man.* One answer is proper for one man, and another for another man Prov. xxvi. 4, 5. We have need of a great deal of wisdom and grace.

SUNDRY GREETINGS
(vv. 7–18)

In the close of this epistle the apostle does several of his friends the honour to leave their names upon record, with some testimony of his respect, which will be spoken of wherever the gospel comes, and last to the end of the world.

I. Concerning Tychicus, *v.* 7. By him this epistle was sent.

II. Concerning Onesimus (*v.* 9): *With Onesimus, a faithful and beloved brother, who is one of you.* He was sent back from Rome along with Tychicus. This was he whom Paul had begotten in his bonds, Philem. 10.

III. *Aristarchus, a fellow-prisoner.* Those who join in services and sufferings whould be thereby engaged to one another in holy love.

IV. *Marcus, sister's son to Barnabas.* This is supposed to be the same who wrote the gospel which bears his name.

V. Here is one who is called *Jesus*, which is the Greek name for the Hebrew *Joshua*.

VI. *Epaphras* (*v.* 12), the same with *Epaphroditus*. He is *one of you*, one of your church; *he salutes you*, or sends his service to you, and his best affections and wishes.

VII. *Luke* is another here mentioned, whom he calls the *beloved physician*. This is he who wrote the Gospel and Acts, and was Paul's companion.

VIII. *Demas*. Whether this was written before the second epistle to Timothy or after is not certain. There we read (2 Tim. iv. 10), *Demas hath forsaken me, having loved this present world.*

IX. The *brethren in Laodicea* are here mentioned, as living in the neighbourhood of Colosse: and Paul sends salutations to them, and orders that this epistle should be read in the church of the Laodiceans (*v.* 16).

X. *Nymphas* is mentioned (*v.* 15) as one who lived at Colosse, and had a church in his house; that is, either a religious family, where the several parts of worship were daily performed; or some part of the congregation met there, when they had no public places of worship allowed, and they were forced to assemble in private houses for fear of their enemies.

XI. Concerning *Archippus*, who was one of their ministers at Colosse.

XII. Concerning himself (*v.* 18): *The salutation of me Paul. Remember my bonds.* He had a scribe to write all the rest of the epistle, but these words he wrote with his own hand: *Remember my bonds.*

THE FIRST EPISTLE OF ST. PAUL TO THE

THESSALONIANS

CHAPTER ONE
INTRODUCTION AND THANKS (vv. 1-5)

In this introduction we have,

I. The inscription, where we have,
1. The persons from whom this epistle came, or by whom it was written. Paul was the inspired apostle and writer of this epistle. 2. The persons to whom this epistle is written, namely, the church of the Thessalonians, the converted Jews in Thessalonica.

II. The salutation or apostolical benediction.

III. The apostle then begins with thanksgiving to God. The apostle gave thanks not only for those who were his most intimate friends, or most eminently favoured of God, but for them all.

II. He joined prayer with his praise or thanksgiving. Note, As there is much that we ought to be thankful for on the behalf of ourselves and our friends, so there is much occasion of constant prayer for further supplies of good.

III. He mentions the particulars for which he was so thankful to God; namely,

1. The saving benefits bestowed on them.

2. He also takes notice, (1) Of the object and efficient cause of these graces, namely, our Lord Jesus Christ. (2) Of the sincerity of them:

being in the *sight of God even our Father*. (3) He mentions the fountain whence these graces flow, namely, God's electing love: *Knowing, brethren beloved, your election of God*, v. 4. Thus he runs up these streams to the fountain, and that was God's eternal election.

3. Another ground or reason of the apostle's thanksgiving is the success of his ministry among them. He was thankful on his own account as well as theirs, that he had not laboured in vain. Their *faith was the evidence of things not seen*; and the Thessalonians thus knew what manner of men the apostle and his fellow-labourers were among them, and what they did for their sake, and with what good success.

EVIDENCES OF THEIR FAITH (vv. 6-10)

In these words we have the evidence of the apostle's success among the Thessalonians, which was notorious and famous in several places. For,

I. They were careful in their holy conversation to imitate the good examples of the apostles and ministers of Christ, v. 6.

II. Their zeal prevailed to such a degree that they were themselves examples to all about them, vv. 7, 8. The word of the Lord, or its wonderful effects upon the Thessalonians, sounded, or was famous and well known, in the regions round about that city, and *in every place*. The effects of their faith were famous. (1) They quitted their idolatry; they turned from their idols, and abandoned all the false worship they had been educated in. (2) They gave themselves up to God, to the living and true God, and devoted themselves to his service. (3) They set themselves to wait for the Son of God from heaven, *v.* 10.

CHAPTER TWO

STRAIGHT TALKING
(*vv.* 1–6)

Here we have an account of Paul's manner of preaching, and his comfortable reflection upon his entrance in among the Thessalonians. He had no sinister or worldly design in his preaching, which he puts them in mind to have been,

I. With courage and resolution: *We were bold in our God to speak unto you the gospel of God, v.* 2.

II. With great simplicity and godly sincerity: *Our exhortation was not of deceit, nor of uncleanness, nor in guile, v.* 3. The apostle not only asserts his sincerity, but subjoins the reasons and evidences thereof. The reasons are contained, *v.* 4.

1. They were stewards, *put in trust* with the gospel: and it is required of a steward that he be faithful.

2. Their design was to please God and not men. God is a God of truth, and requires truth in the inward parts; and, if sincerity be wanting, all that we do cannot please God.

3. They acted under the consider-

ation of God's omniscience, as in the sight of him who *tries our hearts*. This is indeed the great motive to sincerity, to consider that God not only seeth all that we do, but knoweth our thoughts afar off, and searcheth the heart. The evidences of the apostle's sincerity follow; and they are these: (1) He avoided flattery: *Neither at any time used we flattering words, as you know, v.* 5. (2) He avoided covetousness. He did not make the ministry *a cloak*, or a covering, for *covetousness, as God was witness, v.* 5. His design was not to enrich himself by preaching the gospel. (3) He avoided ambition and vain-glory: *Nor of men sought we glory, neither of you nor yet of others, v.* 6.

PAUL'S WAY OF LIFE
(*vv.* 7–12)

In these words the apostle reminds the Thessalonians of the manner of his conversation among them. And,

I. He mentions the gentleness of their behaviour: *We were gentle among you, v.* 7.

II. He mentions their faithful discharge of the work and office of the ministry, *vv.* 11, 12. Concerning this also he could appeal to them as witnesses.

THE EFFECTIVE WORD
OF GOD (*vv.* 13–16)

Here observe, I. The apostle makes mention of the success of his ministry among these Thessalonians (*v.* 13), which is expressed,

1. By the manner of their receiving the word of God: *When you received the word of God, which you heard of us, you received it, not as the word of men, but (as it is in*

348

truth) *the word of God.* Such was the word the apostles preached by divine inspiration, and such is that which is left upon record, written in the scriptures by divine inspiration; and such is that word which in our days is preached, being either contained, or evidently founded on, or deduced from, these sacred oracles.

2. By the wonderful operation of this word they received: *It effectually worketh in those that believe,* v. 13. Those who by faith receive the word find it profitable. *It does good to those that walk uprightly,* and by its wonderful effects evidences itself to be the word of God.

II. He mentions the good effects which his successful preaching had,

1. Upon himself and fellow-labourers. It was a constant cause of thankfulness: *For this cause thank we God without ceasing,* v. 13.

2. Upon them. The word wrought effectually in them, not only to be examples unto others in faith and good works (which he had mentioned before), but also in constancy and patience under sufferings and trials for the sake of the gospel: *You became followers of the churches of God, and have suffered like things as they have done* (v. 14), and with like courage and constancy, with like patience and hope. The apostle mentions the sufferings of the churches of God, which *in Judea were in Christ Jesus.* Those in Judea first heard the gospel, and they first suffered for it: for the Jews were the most bitter enemies Christianity had, and were especially enraged against their countrymen who embraced Christianity. In every city where the apostles went to preach the gospel the Jews stirred up the inhabitants against them. They were the ringleaders of persecution in all places. They had *an implacable enmity to the Gentiles,* and envied them the offers of the gospel: *Forbidding the apostles to speak to the Gentiles, that they might be saved.* The means of salvation had long been confined to the Jews. And they were envious against the Gentiles, and angry that they should be admitted to share in the means of salvation. For the sake of these things *wrath has come upon them to the uttermost*; that is, wrath was determined against them, and would soon overtake them. It was not many years after this that Jerusalem was destroyed, and the Jewish nation cut off by the Romans.

CROWN OF JOY (*vv.* 17–20)

In these words the apostle apologizes for his absence. Here observe,

1. He tells them they were involuntarily forced from them: *We, brethren, were taken from you,* v. 17.

2. Though he was absent in body, yet he was present in heart. 3. Even his bodily absence was but for a short time, the time of an hour. 4. He earnestly desired and endeavoured to see them again: *We endeavoured more abundantly to see your face with great desire,* v. 17.

5. He tells them that Satan hindered his return (v. 18), that is, either some enemy or enemies, or the great enemy of mankind. 6. He assures them of his affection and high esteem for them, though he was not able, as yet, to be present with them according to his desire.

The apostle here puts the Thessalonians in mind that though he could not come to them as yet, and though he should never be able to come to them, yet our Lord Jesus Christ will come, nothing shall hindred this. And further, when he shall come, all must appear in his presence, or before him.

CHAPTER THREE

TIMOTHY SENT TO THESSALONICA

(vv. 1–5)

In these words the apostle gives an account of his sending Timothy to the Thessalonians. Observe,

I. The character he gives of Timothy (v. 2): *We sent Timotheus, our brother.* He calls him also a minister of God. He calls him also his fellow-labourer in the gospel of Christ.

II. The end and design why Paul sent Timothy: *To establish you and to comfort you concerning your faith, v.* 2. Paul had converted them to the Christian faith, and now he was desirous that they might be confirmed and comforted, that they might be confirmed in the choice they had made of the Christian religion, and be comforted in the profession and practice of it.

III. The motive inducing Paul to send Timothy for this end, namely, a godly fear or jealousy, lest they should be moved from the faith of Christ, v. 3.

1. He apprehended there was danger, and feared the consequence.

(1) There was danger, [1] By reason of *affliction* and persecution for the sake of the gospel, v. 3. [2] By reason of the tempter's subtlety and malice.

(2) The consequence the apostle

feared was lest his labour should be in vain.

2. To prevent this danger, with its bad consequence, the apostle tells them what care he took in sending Timothy, (1) To put them in mind of what he had told them before concerning suffering tribulation (v. 4), he says (v. 3), *We are appointed thereunto*, that is, unto afflictions. So is the will and purpose of God that *through many afflictions we must enter into his kingdom.* Their troubles and persecutions did not come by chance, not merely from the wrath and malice of the enemies of religion, but by the *appointment of God.* (2) To know their faith, that so he might inform the apostles whether they remained stedfast under all their sufferings, whether their faith failed or not, because, if their faith did not fail, they would be able to stand their ground against the tempter and all his temptations: their faith would be a *shield, to defend them against all the fiery darts of the wicked,* Eph. vi. 16.

STAND FAST (vv. 6–10)

Here we have Paul's great satisfaction upon the return of Timothy with good tidings from the Thessalonians, in which we may observe,

I. The good report Timothy made concerning them, v. 6. *Concerning their faith*, that is, concerning their stedfastness in the faith, that they were not shaken in mind, nor turned aside from the profession of the gospel. *Their love* also continued; their love to the gospel, and the ministers of the gospel.

II. The great comfort and satisfaction the apostle had in this good report concerning them (*vv.* 7, 8): *Therefore, brethren, we were comforted in all our affliction and distress.*

III. The effects of this were thankfulness and prayer to God on their behalf. Observe, 1. How thankful the apostle was, *v.* 9. He was full of joy, and full of praise and thanksgiving. 2. He prayed for them night and day (*v.* 10), evening and morning, or very frequently, in the midst of the business of the day or slumber of the night lifting up his heart to God in prayer. Thus we should pray always. And Paul's prayer was fervent prayer. He prayed exceedingly, and was earnest in his supplication.

ABOUNDING IN LOVE
(*vv.* 11–13)

In these words we have the earnest prayer of the apostle. Observe,

I. Whom he prays to, namely, God and Christ. Prayer is a part of religious worship, and all religious worship is due unto God only.

II. What he prays for, with respect to himself and his fellow-labourers, and on behalf of the Thessalonians

1. He prays that himself and fellow-labourers might have a prosperous journey to them by the will of God, that their way might be directed to them, *v.* 11.

2. He prays for the prosperity of the Thessalonians. Whether he should have an opportunity of coming to them or not, yet he earnestly prayed for the prosperity of their souls. (1) That they might increase and abound in love (*v.* 12), in love to one another and in love to all men. (2) That they might be established unblamable in holiness,

v. 13. This spiritual benefit is mentioned as an effect of increasing and abounding love: *To the end that he* (the Lord) *may establish your hearts.*

ABOUNDING IN HOLINESS
(*vv.* 1–8)

Here we have,

I. An exhortation to abound in holiness, to *abound more and more* in that which is good, *vv.* 1, 2. We may observe,

1. The manner in which the exhortation is given—very affectionately.

2. The matter of his exhortation —that they would abound more and more in holy walking, or excel in those things that are good, in good works.

3. The arguments with which the apostle enforces his exhortation. (1) They had been informed of their duty. They knew their Master's will, and could not plead ignorance as an excuse. (2) Another argument is that the apostle taught and exhorted them in the name, or by the authority, of the Lord Jesus Christ. He was Christ's minister and ambassador, declaring to them what was the will and command of the Lord Jesus. (3) Another argument is this. Herein they would please God. Holy walking is most pleasing to the holy God, *who is glorious in holiness.* (4) The rule according to which they ought to walk and act—*the commandments they had given them by the Lord Jesus Christ.*

II. A caution against uncleanness, this being a sin directly contrary to sanctification, or that holy walking to which he so earnestly exhorts them. This caution is expressed, and also enforced by many arguments.

1. It is expressed in these words: *That you should abstain from fornication* (*v.* 3), by which we are to understand all uncleanness whatsoever, either in a married or unmarried state.

2. There are several arguments to enforce this caution. As, (1) This branch of sanctification in particular is the will of God, *v.* 3. It is the will of God in general that we should be holy, because *he that called us is holy*, and because we are *chosen unto salvation through the sanctification of the Spirit*. (2) This will be greatly for our honour: so much is plainly implied, *v.* 4. Whereas the contrary will be a great dishonour. (3) To indulge the lust of concupiscence is to live and act like heathens. (4) The sin of uncleanness, especially adultery, is a great piece of injustice that God will be the avenger of; so we may understand those words, *That no man go beyond or defraud his brother* (*v.* 6) *in any matter*—in *this* matter of which the apostle is speaking, in the preceding and following verses, namely, the sin of uncleanness. (5) The sin of uncleanness is contrary to the nature and design of our Christian calling: *For God hath called us not unto uncleanness, but unto holiness, v.* 7. (6) The contempt therefore of God's law and gospel is the contempt of God himself: *He that despises despises God, not man* only.

HONEST WORK (*vv.* 9–12)

In these words the apostle mentions the great duties,

I. Of brotherly love. This he exhorts them to increase in yet more and more.

II. Of quietness and industry in their callings. Observe, 1. The apostle exhorts to these duties: that they should *study to be quiet, v.* 11. It is the most desirable thing to have a calm and quiet temper, and to be of a peaceable and quiet behaviour. It follows, *Do your own business*. Those who are busy-bodies, meddling in other men's matters, generally have but little quiet in their own minds and cause great disturbances among their neighbours; at least they seldom mind the other exhortation, to be diligent in their own calling, *to work with their own hands*; and yet this was what the apostle commanded them, and what is required of us also. Christianity does not discharge us from the work and duty of our particular callings, but teaches us to be diligent therein. 2. The exhortation is enforced with a double argument; namely, (1) So we shall live creditably. Thus we shall walk honestly, or decently and creditably, towards those that are without, *v.* 12. (2) We shall live comfortably, and have lack of nothing, *v.* 12. Such as are diligent in their own business live comfortably and have lack of nothing. They earn their own bread, and have the greatest pleasure in so doing.

THE CHRISTIAN DEAD
(*vv.* 13–18)

In these words the apostle comforts the Thessalonians who mourned for the death of their relations and friends that died in the Lord.

Yet we must not be immoderate in our sorrows, because,

I. This looks as if we had no hope, *v.* 13. This hope is more than enough to balance all our griefs upon account of any of the crosses of the present time.

II. This is an effect of ignorance concerning those who are dead, *v.* 13. There are some things concerning those especially who die in the Lord that we need not, and ought not, to be ignorant of; and, if these things be really understood and duly considered, they will be sufficient to allay our sorrow concerning them.

1. They sleep in Jesus. They are asleep, *v.* 13. They have *fallen asleep in Christ,* 1 Cor. xv. 18. Death does not annihilate them. It is but a sleep to them. It is their rest, and undisturbed rest. Their souls are in his presence, and their dust is under his care and power; so that they are not lost, nor are they losers, but great gainers by death, and their removal out of this world is into a better.

2. They shall be raised up from the dead, and awakened out of their sleep, for *God will bring them with him,* *v.* 14. The doctrine of the resurrection and the second coming of Christ is a great antidote against the fear of death and inordinate sorrow for the death of our Christian friends; and this doctrine we have a full assurance of, because we *believe that Jesus died and rose again,* *v.* 14.

3. Their state and condition shall be glorious and happy at the second coming of Christ. This the apostle informs the Thessalonians of *by the word of the Lord* (*v.* 15), by divine

revelation from the Lord Jesus. By this word of the Lord we know, (1) That the Lord Jesus will come down from heaven in all the pomp and power of the upper world (*v.* 16): *The Lord himself shall descend from heaven with a shout.* For, (2) The dead shall be raised: *The dead in Christ shall rise first* (*v.* 16), before those who are *found alive at Christ's coming shall be changed*; and so it appears that those who shall then *be found alive shall not prevent those that are asleep,* *v.* 15. The first care of the Redeemer in that day will be about his dead saints; he will raise them before the great change passes on those that shall be found alive: so that those who did not sleep in death will have no greater privilege or joy at that day than those who fell asleep in Jesus. (3) Those that shall be found alive will then be changed. They shall *be caught up together with them in the clouds, to meet the Lord in the air,* *v.* 17. At, or immediately before, this rapture into the clouds, those who are alive will undergo a mighty change, which will be equivalent to dying. This change is so mysterious that we cannot comprehend it: we know little or nothing of it, 1 Cor. xv. 51. Only, in the general, *this mortal must put on immortality,* and these bodies will be made fit to inherit the kingdom of God, which flesh and blood in its present state are not capable of. And those who are raised, and thus changed, shall meet together in the clouds, and there meet with their Lord. (4) Here is the bliss of the saints at that day: they shall *be ever with the Lord,* *v.* 17. It will be some part of their felicity that all the saints shall meet together, and remain together for ever; but the principal happiness of heaven is this, *to be with the Lord*, to see him, live with him, and enjoy him, for ever. And the apostle would have us *comfort one another with these words*, v. 18.

CHAPTER FIVE

THE DAY OF THE LORD
(*vv.* 1–5)

In these words observe,

I. The apostle tells the Thessalonians it was needless or useless to enquire about the particular time of Christ's coming: *Of the times and seasons you need not that I write unto you*, v. 1. The thing is certain that Christ will come, and there is a certain time appointed for his coming; but there was no need that the apostle should write about this, and therefore he had no revelation given him.

II. He tells them that the coming of Christ would be sudden, and a great surprise to most men, *v.* 2.

III. He tells them how terrible Christ's coming would be to the ungodly, *v.* 3. It will be to their destruction in that day of the Lord. 1. It will be sudden. It will overtake them, and fall upon them, in the midst of their carnal security and jollity, when they say in their hearts, *Peace and safety*. 2. It will be unavoidable destruction too: *They shall not escape*; they shall in no wise escape.

IV. He tells them how comfortable this day will be to the righteous, *vv.* 4, 5. They are not in darkness; they are the children of the light, &c. This was the happy condition of the Thessalonians as it is of all true Christians. They were not in a state of sin and ignorance as the heathen world. They were *some time darkness, but were made light in the Lord*. They were favoured with the divine revelation of things that are unseen and eternal, particularly concerning the coming of Christ, and the consequences thereof.

WATCH AND BE SOBER
(*vv.* 6–10)

On what had been said, the apostle grounds seasonable exhortations to several needful duties.

I. To watchfulness and sobriety, *v.* 6. 1. Then *let us not sleep as do others, but let us watch*; we must not be secure and careless, nor indulge spiritual sloth and idleness.

II. To be well armed as well as watchful: to put on the whole armour of God. 1. We must live by faith, and this will keep us watchful and sober. 2. We must get a heart inflamed with love; and this also will be our defence. 3. We must make salvation our hope, and should have a lively hope of it. This good hope, through grace, of eternal life, will be as a helmet to defend the head. Our hopes are to be grounded, (1) Upon God's appointment: because *God hath not appointed us to wrath, but to obtain salvation*, v. 9. (2) Upon Christ's merit and grace, and that salvation is by our Lord Jesus Christ, who died for us. Our salvation therefore is owing to, and our hopes of it are grounded on, Christ's atonement as well as God's appointment.

SOME WARNINGS (*vv.* 11-15)

In these words the apostle exhorts the Thessalonians to several duties.

I. Towards those who were nearly related one to another. Such should comfort themselves, or exhort one another, and edify one another, *v.* 11.

II. He shows them their duty towards their ministers, *vv.* 12, 13. The apostle here exhorts them to observe,

1. How the ministers of the gospel are described by the work of their office. (1) Ministers must labour among their people, labour with diligence, and unto weariness (so the word in the original imports); *they must labour in the word and doctrine*, 1 Tim. v. 17. And, (2) Ministers are to rule their people also, so the word is rendered, 1 Tim. v. 17. They must rule, not with rigour, but with love. (3) They must also admonish the people, and that not only publicly, but privately, as there may be occasion.

2. What the duty of the people is towards their ministers. There is a mutual duty between ministers and people. If ministers should labour among the people, then, (1) The people must know them. As the shepherd should know his flock, so the sheep must know their shepherd. (2) They must esteem their ministers highly in love; they should greatly value the office of the ministry, honour and love the persons or their ministers, and show their esteem and affection in all proper ways, and this for their work's sake.

III. He gives various other exhortations touching the duty Christians owe to one another. 1. *To be at peace among themselves, v.* 13. Ministers and people should avoid everything that tends to alienate their affections one from another. 2. *To warn the unruly, v.* 14. Such should be put in mind of what they should do, and be reproved for doing otherwise. 3. *To comfort the feebleminded, v.* 14. By these are intended the timorous and faint-hearted, or such as are dejected and of a sorrowful spirit. 4. *To support the weak, v.* 14. Some are not well able to perform their work, nor bear up under their burdens; we should therefore support them, help their infirmities, and lift at one end of the burden, and so help to bear it. 5. *To be patient towards all men, v.* 14. We must bear and forbear. We must not be high in our expectations and demands, nor harsh in our resentments, nor hard in our impositions, but endeavour to make the best we can of every thing, and think the best we can of every body. 6. *Not to render evil for evil to any man, v.* 15. If others do us an injury, this will not justify us in returning it, in doing the same, or the like, or any other injury to them. 7. *Ever to follow that which is good, v.* 15. In general, we must study to do what is our duty, and pleasing to God, in all circumstances, whether men do us good turns or ill turns; whatever men do to us, we must do good to others.

INSTRUCTIONS (*vv.* 16-28)

Here we have divers short exhortations, that will not burden our memories, but will be of great use to direct the motions of our hearts and lives. 1. *Rejoice evermore, v.* 16. This must be understood of spiritual joy; for if we rejoice in God, we may do that evermore. 2. *Pray without ceasing, v.* 17. Note, The way to rejoice evermore is to pray without ceasing. We should rejoice more if we prayed more. 3. *In every thing give thanks, v.* 18. If we pray without ceasing, we shall not want matter for thanksgiving *in every thing.* 4. *Quench not the Spirit* (*v.* 19), for it is this Spirit of grace and supplication that helpeth our infirmities, that assisteth us in our prayers and thanksgivings. 5. *Despise not prophesyings* (*v.* 20); for, if we neglect the means of grace, we forfeit the Spirit of grace. By *prophesyings* here we are to understand the preaching of the word, the interpreting and applying of the scriptures. 6. *Prove all things, but hold fast that which is good, v.* 21. This is a needful caution, to test all things; for, though we must put a value on preaching, we must not take things upon trust from the preacher, but try them by the law and the testimony. 7. *Abstain from all appearance of evil, v.* 22. This is a good means to prevent our being deceived with false doctrines, or unsettled in our faith; for our Saviour has told us (John vii. 17), *If*

a man will do his will, he shall know of the doctrine whether it be of God. Corrupt affections indulged in the heart, and evil practices allowed of in the life, will greatly tend to promote fatal errors in the mind.

In *vv.* 23–28, which conclude this epistle, observe,

I. Paul's prayer for them, *v.* 23. He had told them, in the beginning of this epistle, that he always made mention of them in his prayers; and, now that he is writing to them, he lifts up his heart to God in prayer for them.

II. His comfortable assurance that God would hear his prayer: *Faithful is he who calleth you, who will also do it, v.* 24.

III. His request of their prayers: *Brethren, pray for us, v.* 25. We should pray for one another; and brethren should thus express brotherly love.

IV. His salutation: *Greet all the brethren with a holy kiss, v.* 26. Thus the apostle sends a friendly salutation from himself.

V. His solemn charge for the reading of this epistle, *v.* 27. This is not only an exhortation, but an adjuration by the Lord.

VI. The apostolical benediction that is usual in other epistles; *v.* 28.

THESSALONIANS

CHAPTER ONE
GREETINGS (vv. 1-4)

Here we have,

I. The introduction (vv. 1, 2) in the same words as in the former epistle.

II. The apostle's expression of the high esteem he had for them.

1. How his esteem of them is expressed. (1) He glorified God on their behalf: *We are bound to thank God always for you, brethren, as it is meet, v. 3.* (2) He also *glories in them before the churches of God, v. 4.* The apostle never flattered his friends, but he took pleasure in commending them, and speaking well of them, to the glory of God and for the excitement and encouragement of others.

2. For what he esteemed them and thanked God; namely, the increase of their faith, and love, and patience. The matter of the apostle's thanksgiving and glorifying on behalf of the Thessalonians was, (1) That their faith grew exceedingly, *v.* 3. (2) Their charity abounded (*v.* 3), their love to God and man. (3) Their patience as well as faith increased in all their persecutions and tribulations.

GOD'S VENGEANCE (vv. 5-10)

I. He tells them of the present happiness and advantage of their sufferings, *v.* 5. Their faith being thus tried, and patience exercised, they were improved by their sufferings, insomuch that they were *counted worthy of the kingdom of God.*

II. He tells them next of the future recompense that shall be given to persecutors and persecuted.

1. In this future recompense there will be, (1) A punishment inflicted on persecutors: God will *recompense tribulation to those that trouble you, v.* 6. (2) A reward for those that are persecuted: God will recompense their trouble with rest, *v.* 7. There is a rest that remains for the people of God, a rest from sin and sorrow.

2. Concerning this future recompence we are further to observe,

(1) The certainty of it, proved by the righteousness and justice of God: *It is a righteous thing with God (v.* 6) to render to every man according to his works.

(2) The time when this righteous recompense shall be made: *When the Lord Jesus shall be revealed from heaven, v.* 7. As,

[1] That the Lord Jesus will in that day appear from heaven.

[2] He will be revealed with his mighty angels (*v.* 7), or the angels of his power. They will summon the criminals to his tribunal, and gather in the elect, and be employed in executing his sentence.

[3] He will come in flaming fire,

v. 8. A fire goeth before him, which shall consume his enemies.

[4] The effects of this appearance will be terrible to some and joyful to others.

First, They will be terrible to some; for he will then take vengeance on the wicked. 1. On those that sinned against the principles of natural religion, and rebelled against the light of nature, *that knew not God* (*v.* 8), though the invisible things of him are manifested in the things that are seen. 2. On those that rebel against the light of revelation, that *obey not the gospel of our Lord Jesus Christ.* And this is the condemnation, that light is come into the world, and men love darkness rather than light. Their punishment will be no less than destruction, not of their being, but of their bliss; not that of the body alone, but both as to body and soul. This destruction shall come from the *presence of the Lord*, that is, immediately from God himself.

Secondly, It will be a joyful day to some, even to the saints, to those that believe and obey the gospel. In that bright and blessed day, 1. Christ Jesus will be glorified and admired by his saints. 2. Christ will be glorified and admired in them.

THE WORK OF FAITH
(*vv.* 11, 12)

In these verses the apostle again tells the Thessalonians of his earnest and constant prayer for them. Observe,

I. What the apostle prayer for, *v.* 11. 1. That God would begin his good work of grace in them; so we may understand this expression: *That our God would count you* (or, as it might be read, *make you*) *worthy of this calling.* 2. That God would carry on the good work that is begun, and *fulfil all the good pleasure of his goodness.* The good pleasure of God denotes his gracious purposes towards his people, which flow from his goodness, and are full of goodness towards them; and it is thence that all good comes to us.

II. Why the apostle prayed for these things (*v.* 12); *That the name of the Lord Jesus may be glorified*; this is the end we should aim at in every thing we do and desire, that God and Christ in all things may be glorified.

CHAPTER TWO
THE COMING OF CHRIST
(*vv.* 1–12)

From *vv.* 1–3 it appears that some among the Thessalonians had mistaken the apostle's meaning, in what he had written in his former epistle about the coming of Christ, by thinking that it was near at hand, —that Christ was just ready to appear and come to judgment. Or, it may be, some among them pretended that they had the knowledge of this by particular revelation from the Spirit, or from some words they had heard from the apostle, when he was with them, or some letter he had written or they pretended he had written to them or some other person: and hereupon the apostle is careful to rectify this mistake, and to prevent the spreading of this error.

The apostle confutes the error against which he had cautioned them, and gives the reasons why they should not expect the coming of Christ as just at hand. There were several events previous to the second coming of Christ; in particular, he tells them there would be

I. A general apostasy, *there would come a falling away first*, v. 3. And let us observe that no sooner was Christianity planted and rooted in the world than there began to be a defection in the Christian church.

II. A revelation of that man of sin, that is (v. 3), antichrist would take his rise from this general apostasy. The apostle afterwards speaks of the revelation of that wicked one (v. 8), intimating the discovery which should be made of his wickedness; here he seems to speak of his rise, which should be occasioned by the general apostasy he had mentioned, and to intimate that all sorts of false doctrines and corruptions should centre in him.

The apostle further describes the reign and rule of this man of sin (vv. 9–11). Here we are to observe, (1) The manner of his coming, or ruling, and working: in general, that it is after the example of Satan, the grand enemy of souls, the great adversary of God and man. (2) The persons are described who are his willing subjects, or most likely to become such, v. 10. They are such as *love not the truth that they may be saved*. And of these persons it is said that they perish or are lost; they are in a lost condition, and in danger to be lost for ever. For,

6. We have the *sin and ruin of the subjects* of antichrist's kingdom declared, vv. 11, 12. (1) Their sin is this: *They believed not the truth, but had pleasure in unrighteousness.*

(2) Their ruin is thus expressed: *God shall send them strong delusions, to believe a lie.* Thus he will punish men for their unbelief, and for their dislike of the truth and love to sin and wickedness; not that God is the author of sin, but in righteousness he sometimes withdraws his grace from such sinners as are here mentioned.

HOLD THE TRADITIONS
(vv. 13–17)

Here observe, I. The consolation the Thessalonians might take against the terrors of this apostasy, vv. 13, 14. For they were chosen to salvation, and called to the obtaining of glory. This preservation of the saints is owing,

1. To the stability of the election of grace, v. 13. Therefore were they beloved of the Lord, because God had chosen them from the beginning.

2. To the efficacy of the gospel call, v. 14. As they were chosen to salvation, so they were called thereunto by the gospel. Whom he did predestinate those he also called, Rom. viii. 30. Hereupon there follows,

II. An exhortation to stedfastness and perseverance: *Therefore, brethren, stand fast*, v. 15. The Thessalonians are exhorted to stedfastness in their Christian profession, to *hold fast the traditions which they had been taught*, or the doctrine of the gospel, which had been delivered by the apostle, by word or epistle.

III. In vv. 16, 17 we have the apostle's earnest prayer for them, in which observe,

1. To whom he prays: *Our Lord*

Jesus Christ himself, and God, even our Father. We may and should direct our prayers, not only to God the Father, through the mediation of our Lord Jesus Christ, but also *to our Lord Jesus himself*; and should pray in his name unto God, not only as his Father but as our Father in and through him.

2. From what he takes encouragement in his prayer—from the consideration of what God had already done for him and them.

3. What it is that he asks of God for them—that *he would comfort their hearts, and establish them in every good word and work, v.* 17. We must be established in every good word and work, in the word of truth and the work of righteousness: Christ must be honoured by our good works and good words.

CHAPTER THREE
CHRISTIAN CONFIDENCE
(*vv.* 1–5)

In these words observe,

I. The apostle desires the prayers of his friends: *Finally, brethren, pray for us, v.* 1. He always remembered them in his prayers and would not have them forget him and his fellow-labourers, but bear them on their hearts at the throne of grace. Observe, further, what they are desired and directed to pray for; namely, (1) For the success of the gospel ministry: *That the word of the Lord may have free course, and be glorified, v.* 1. He desired that the word of the Lord might run (so it is in the original), that it might get ground, that the interest of religion in the world might go forward and not backward, and not only go

forward, but go apace. (2) For the safety of gospel ministers. He asks their prayers, not for preferment, but for preservation: *That we may be delivered from unreasonable and wicked men, v.* 2.

II. He encourages them to trust in God. We should not only pray to God for his grace, but also place our trust and confidence in his grace, and humbly expect what we pray for, *vv.* 3, 4.

III. He makes a short prayer for them, *v.* 5. It is a prayer for spiritual blessings. Two things of the greatest importance the apostle prays for: 1. That their hearts may be brought into the love of God, to be in love with God as the most excellent and amiable Being, the best of all beings. 2. That a *patient waiting for Christ* may be joined with this love of God. There is no true love of God without faith in Jesus Christ.

DISORDERLY CONDUCT
(*vv.* 6–15)

Observe,

I. That which was amiss among the Thessalonians, which is expressed,

1. More generally. There were some who *walked disorderly, not after the tradition they received* from the apostle, *v.* 6. They did not live regularly, nor govern themselves according to the rules of Christianity, nor agreeably to their profession of religion.

2. In particular, there were among them some *idle persons and busybodies, v.* 11. (1) There were some among them who were idle, *not working at all,* or doing nothing. It is probable that these persons had a

notion (by misunderstanding some passages in the former epistle) concerning the near approach of the coming of Christ, which served them for a pretence to leave off the work of their callings, and live in idleness. (2) There were busybodies among them: and it should seem, by the connection, that the same persons who were idle were busy-bodies also.

II. The good laws which were occasioned by these evil manners, concerning which we may take notice,

1. Whose laws they are: they are commands of the apostles of our Lord, given in the name of their Lord and ours, that is, the commands of our Lord himself. *We command you, brethren, in the name of the Lord Jesus Christ, v.* 6. Again, *We command and exhort you by our Lord Jesus Christ, v.* 12.

2. What the good laws and rules are.

(1) His commands and directions to the whole church regard, [1] Their behaviour towards the disorderly persons who were among them, which is thus expressed

(*v.* 6), to *withdraw themselves from such,* and afterwards to *mark that man, and have no company with him, that he may be ashamed; yet not to count him as an enemy, but to admonish him as a brother.* [2] Their general conduct and behaviour ought to be according to the good example the apostle and those who were with him had given them: *Yourselves know how you ought to follow us, v.* 7.

(2) He commands and directs those that lived idle lives to reform, and set themselves to their business. It was a proverbial speech among the Jews, *He who does not labour does not deserve to eat.*

(3) He exhorts *those that did well not* to be *weary in well-doing* (*v.* 13); as if he had said, "Go on and prosper. It will be time enough to rest when you come to heaven, that *everlasting rest which remains for the people of God.*"

BLESSING (*vv.* 16–18)

In this conclusion of the epistle we have the apostle's benediction and prayers for these Thessalonians.

THE FIRST EPISTLE OF ST. PAUL TO

TIMOTHY

CHAPTER ONE
INSCRIPTION (vv. 1-4)

Here is, I. The inscription of the epistle, from whom it is sent: *Paul an apostle of Jesus Christ*, constituted an apostle *by the commandment of God our Saviour, and Lord Jesus Christ*. He calls Timothy his own son, because he had been an instrument of his conversion, and because he had been a son that served him, served with him in the gospel, Phil. ii. 22.

II. The benediction is, *grace, mercy, and peace, from God our Father*.

III. Paul tells Timothy what was the end of his appointing him to this office: *I besought thee to abide at Ephesus*. Though he might assume an authority to command him, yet for love's sake he chose rather to beseech him. Observe, 1. Ministers must not only be charged to preach the true doctrine of the gospel, but charged to preach no other doctrine. 2. In the times of the apostles there were attempts made to corrupt Christianity, otherwise this charge to Timothy might have been spared. 3. He must not only see to it that he did not preach any other doctrine, but he must charge others that they might not add any thing of their own to the gospel, or take any thing from it, but that they preach it pure and uncorrupt.

THOSE WHO DEVIATE
(vv. 5-11)

Here the apostle instructs Timothy how to guard against the judaizing teachers, or others who mingled fables and endless genealogies with the gospel.

I. He shows the end and uses of the law: it is intended to promote love, *for love is the fulfilling of the law*, Rom. xiii. 10.

1. *The end of the commandment is charity*, or love, Rom. xiii. 8. The main scope and drift of the divine law are to engage us to the love of God and one another. Now some who set up for teachers of the law swerved from the very end of the commandment: they set up for disputers, but their disputes proved vain jangling; they set up for teachers, but they pretended to teach others what they themselves did not understand.

2. The use of the law (v. 8): *The law is good, if a man use it lawfully*. The abuse which some have made of the law does not take away the use of it; but when a divine appointment has been abused, call it back to its right use and take away the abuses, for the law is still very useful as a rule of life. It is the grace of God that changes men's hearts; but the terrors of the law may be of use to tie their hands and restrain their tongues. In this black roll of

362

sinners, he particularly mentions breaches of the second table, duties which we owe to our neighbour.

II. He shows the glory and grace of the gospel. Paul's epithets are expressive and significant; and frequently every one is a sentence: as here (*v.* 11), *According to the glorious gospel of the blessed God.* Paul reckoned it a great honour put upon him, and a great favour done him, that this glorious gospel was committed to his trust; that is, the preaching of it, for the framing of it is not committed to any man or company of men in the world. The settling of the terms of salvation in the gospel of Christ is God's own work; but the publishing of it to the world is committed to the apostles and ministers.

MINISTRY AND MERCY
(*vv.* 12–17)

Here the apostle, I. Returns thanks to Jesus Christ for putting him into the ministry. Observe, 1. It is Christ's work to put men into the ministry, Acts xxvi. 16, 17. He *counted me faithful*; and none are counted faithful but those whom he makes so.

II. The more to magnify the grace of Christ in putting him into the ministry, he gives an account of his conversion.

1. What he was before his conversion: *A blasphemer, a persecutor, and injurious.*

2. The great favour of God to him: *But I obtained mercy.*

(1) If Paul had persecuted the Christians wilfully, knowing them to be the people of God, for aught I know he had been guilty of the

unpardonable sin; but, because he did it ignorantly and in unbelief, he obtained mercy.

(2) Here he takes notice of the abundant grace of Jesus Christ, *v.* 14. *This is a faithful saying, &c.* Here we have the sum of the whole gospel, *that Jesus Christ came into the world.* His errand into the world was to seek and find, and so save, *those that were lost,* Luke xix. 10. The ratification of this is *that it is a faithful saying, and worthy of all acceptation.* It is good news, worthy of all acceptation; and yet not too good to be true, for it is a faithful saying. In the close of the verse Paul applies it to himself: *Of whom I am chief.* Paul was a sinner of the first rank; so he acknowledges himself to have been, for he breathed out threatenings and slaughter against the disciples of the Lord, &c., Acts ix. 1, 2.

(3) The mercy which Paul found with God, notwithstanding his great wickedness before his conversion, he speaks of,

[1] For the encouragement of others to repent and believe (*v.* 16).

[2] He mentions it to the glory of God, having spoken of the mercy he had found with God, he could not go on with his letter without inserting a thankful acknowledgment of God's goodness to him: *Now unto the King eternal, immortal, invisible, the only wise God, be honour and glory for ever and ever. Amen.*

HOLD THE FAITH (*vv.* 18–20)

Here is the charge he gives to Timothy to proceed in his work with resolution, *v.* 18. Observe, 1. The ministry is a warfare, it is a good warfare against sin and Satan: and under the banner of the Lord Jesus, who is the Captain of our salvation (Heb. ii. 10), and in his cause, and against his enemies, ministers are in a particular manner engaged. 2. Ministers must war this good warfare, must execute their office diligently and courageously, notwithstanding oppositions and discouragements. 3. The prophecies which went before concerning Timothy are here mentioned as a motive to stir him up to a vigorous and conscientious discharge of his duty; so the good hopes that others have entertained concerning us should excite us to our duty: *That thou by them mightest war a good warfare.* 4. We must hold both faith and a good conscience: *Holding faith and a good conscience,* v. 19. Those that put away a good conscience will soon make shipwreck of faith. As for those who had made shipwreck of the faith, he specifies two, *Hymeneus and Alexander,* who had made a profession of the Christian religion, but had quitted that profession; and Paul had delivered them to Satan.

CHAPTER TWO
DIRECTIONS FOR PRAYER
(vv. 1–8)

Here is, I. A charge given to Christians to pray for all men in general, and particularly for all in authority. We must pray for them, and we must give thanks for them, pray for their welfare and for the welfare of their kingdoms, and therefore must not plot against them, that in the peace thereof we may have peace, and give thanks

for them and for the benefit we have under their government, that *we may lead a quiet and peaceable life in all godliness and honesty.*

II. As a reason why we should in our prayers concern ourselves for all men, he shows God's love to mankind in general, v. 4.

1. One reason why all men are to be prayed for is because there is one God, and that God bears a good will to all mankind. There is one God (v. 5), and one only, there is no other, there can be no other, for there can be but one infinite. This one God *will have all men to be saved*; he desires not the death and destruction of any (Ezek. xxxiii. 11), but the welfare and salvation of all. Not that he has decreed the salvation of all, for then all men would be saved; but he has a good will to the salvation of all, and none perish but by their own fault, Matt. xxiii. 37.

2. There is one Mediator, and that Mediator gave himself a ransom for all. *He gave himself a ransom.* Observe, The death of Christ was a ransom, a counterprice. We deserved to have died. Christ died for us, to save us from death and hell. He died to work out a common salvation: to do this, he put himself into the office of Mediator between God and man. A mediator supposes a controversy. Sin had made a quarrel between us and God; Jesus Christ is a Mediator who undertakes to make peace, to bring God and man together.

III. A direction how to pray, v. 8. 1. *Pray every where.* We must pray in our closets, pray in our families, pray at our meals, pray when we are on journeys, and pray in the solemn assemblies, whether more public or private. 2. It is the will of God that in prayer we should lift up holy hands: *Lifting up holy hands*, or pure hands, pure from the pollution of sin, washed in the fountain opened for sin and uncleanness. 3. We must pray in charity: *Without wrath*, or malice, or anger at any person. 4. We must pray in faith *without doubting* (Jam. i. 6), or, as some read it, *without disputing*, and then it falls under the head of charity.

THE ROLE OF WOMEN
(vv. 9–15)

I. Here is a charge, that women who profess the Christian religion should be modest, sober, silent, and submissive, as becomes their place. 1. They must be very modest in their apparel, not affecting gaudiness, gaiety, or costliness. 2. Women must learn the principles of their religion, learn Christ, learn the scriptures; they must not think that their sex excuses them from that learning which is necessary to salvation. 3. They must be silent, submissive, and subject, and not usurp authority. The reason given is because *Adam was first formed, then Eve* out of him, to denote her subordination to him and dependence upon him; and that she was made for him, to be a help-meet for him.

II. Here observe, Women are to profess godliness as well as men; for they are baptized, and thereby stand engaged to exercise themselves to godliness; and, to their honour be it spoken, many of them were eminent professors of Christianity in the days of the apostles,

as the book of Acts will inform us. *Notwithstanding she shall be saved,* &c. Though in sorrow, yet she shall bring forth, and be a living mother of living children; with this proviso, that they continue in faith, and charity, and holiness with sobriety: and women, under the circumstance of child-bearing should by faith lay hold of this promise for their support in the needful time.

CHAPTER THREE
QUALIFICATIONS FOR LEADERSHIP (vv. 1–7)

Here we have the character of a gospel minister, whose office it is to preside in a particular congregation of Christians. Observe,

I. The ministry is a work. However the office of a bishop may be now thought a good preferment, then it was thought a good work. 1. The office of a scripture-bishop is an office of divine appointment, and not of human invention. 2. This office of a Christian bishop is a work, which requires diligence and application. 3. It is a good work, a work of the greatest importance, and designed for the greatest good. 4. There ought to be an earnest desire of the office in those who would be put into it; if a man desire, he should earnestly desire it for the prospect he has of bringing greater glory to God, and of doing the greatest good to the souls of men by this means.

II. To discharge this office, this work, the workman must be duly qualified. 1. A minister must be blameless, he must not lie under any scandal. 2. He must be the husband of one wife. 3. He must be vigilant and watchful against Satan, that subtle enemy; he must watch over himself, and the souls of those who are committed to his charge, of whom having taken the *oversight*, he must improve all opportunities of doing them good. 4. He must be sober, temperate, moderate in all his actions, and in the use of all creature-comforts. 5. He must be of good behaviour, composed and solid, and not light, vain, and frothy. 6. He must be given to hospitality. 7. Apt to teach. Therefor this is a preaching bishop whom Paul describes, one who is both able and willing to communicate to others the knowledge which God has given him. 8. No drunkard: *Not given to wine*. 9. No striker; one who is not quarrelsome, nor apt to use violence to any, but does every thing with mildness, love, and gentleness. 10. One who is not greedy of filthy lucre, who is dead to the wealth of this world. 11. He must be patient, and not a brawler, of a mild disposition. 12. Not covetous. Covetousness is bad in any, but it is worst in a minister, whose calling leads him to converse so much with another world. 13. He must be one who keeps his family in good order: *That rules well his own house. For, if a man know not how to rule his own house, how shall he take care of the church of God.* 14. He must not be a novice, not one newly brought to the Christian religion: the more ignorant men are the more proud they are: *Lest, being lifted up with pride, he fall into the condemnation of the devil.* 15. He must be of good reputation among his neighbours.

DEACONS (*vv.* 8–13)

We have here the character of deacons: these had the care of the temporal concerns of the church, that is, the maintenance of the ministers and provision for the poor: they served tables, while the ministers or bishops gave themselves only to the ministry of the word and prayer, Acts vi. 2, 4. They must be *grave*. Gravity becomes all Christians, but especially those who are in office in the church. *Not double-tongued*; that will say one thing to one and another thing to another, according as their interest leads them: a double tongue comes from a double heart; flatterers and slanderers are double-tongued. *Not given to much wine*; for this is a great disparagement to any man, especially to a Christian, and one in office, unfits men for business, opens the door to many temptations. *Not greedy of filthy lucre*; this would especially be bad in the deacons, who were entrusted with the church's money, and, if they were covetous and greedy of filthy lucre, would be tempted to embezzle it, and convert that to their own use which was intended for the public service. *Holding the mystery of faith in a pure conscience, v.* 9. The practical love of truth is the most powerful preservative from error and delusion. Their wives likewise must have a good character (*v.* 11). And the reason why the deacons must be thus qualified is (*v.* 13) because, though the office of a deacon be of an inferior degree, yet it is a step towards the higher degree; and those who had served tables well the church might see cause afterwards to discharge from that service, and prefer to serve in preaching the word and in prayer.

GROUND OF TRUTH
(vv. 14–16)

He concludes the chapter with a particular direction to Timothy. Observe,

I. Those who are employed in the house of God must see to it that they behave themselves well, lest they bring reproach upon the house of God, and that worthy name by which they are called.

II. It is the great support of the church that it is the church of the living *God*, the true God in opposition to false gods, dumb and dead idols.

1. As the church of God, it is *the pillar and ground of truth*; that is, either, (1) The church itself is the pillar and ground of truth. The church holds forth the scripture and the doctrine of Christ, as the pillar to which a proclamation is affixed holds forth the proclamation. (2) Others understand it of Timothy. He, not he himself only, but he as an evangelist, he and other faithful ministers, are the pillars and ground of truth; it is their business to maintain, hold up, and publish, the truths of Christ in the church.

2. But what is the truth which the churches and ministers are the pillars and grounds of? Observe,

(1) Christianity is a mystery, a mystery that could not have been found out by reason or the light of nature, and which cannot be comprehended by reason, because it is above reason, though not contrary

thereto. It is a mystery, not of philosophy or speculation; but of godliness, designed to promote godliness; and herein it exceeds all the mysteries of the Gentiles. But,

(2) What is the mystery of godliness? It is Christ; and here are six things concerning Christ, which make up the mystery of godliness. [1] That he is God manifest in the flesh: *God was manifest in the flesh.* This proves that he is God, the eternal Word, that was made flesh and was manifest in the flesh. [2] He is *justified in the Spirit*. That is, it was made to appear that his sacrifice was accepted, and so he rose again for our justification, as he was delivered for our offences, Rom. iv. 25. He was put to death in the flesh, but quickened by the Spirit, 1 Pet. iii. 18. [3] He was *seen of angels*. They worshipped him (Heb. i. 6); they attended his incarnation, his temptation, his agony, his death, his resurrection, his ascension. [4] He is *preached unto the Gentiles*. This is a great part of the mystery of godliness, that Christ was offered to the Gentiles a Redeemer and Saviour. [5] That he was *believed on in the world*, so that he was not preached in vain. [6] He was *received up into glory*, in his ascension. This indeed was before he was believed on in the world; but it is put last, because it was the crown of his exaltation.

CHAPTER FOUR
APOSTASY FORETOLD
(vv. 1–5)

We have here a prophecy of the apostasy of the latter times, which he had spoken of as a thing expected and taken for granted among Christians, 2 Thess. ii.

I. The prophecies concerning antichrist, as well as the prophecies concerning Christ, came from the Spirit. The Spirit in both spoke expressly of a general apostasy from the faith of Christ and the pure worship of God. This should come in the *latter times*, during the Christian dispensation, for these are called the latter days; in the following ages of the church, for the mystery of iniquity now began to work. *Some shall depart from the faith*, or there shall be an apostasy from the faith. Some, not all; for in the worst of times God will have a remnant, according to the election of grace. *Giving heed to seducing spirits*, men who pretended to the Spirit, but were not really guided by the Spirit. Now here observe,

(1) It will be done by hypocrisy of those that speak lies, the agents and emissaries of Satan, who promote these delusions by lies and forgeries and pretended miracles, *v.* 2. This respects also the hypocrisy of those who have *their consciences seared with a red-hot iron*, who are perfectly lost to the very first principles of virtue and moral honesty. (2) Another part of their character is that they forbid to marry, and speak very reproachfully of marriage, though an ordinance of God; and that they command *to abstain from meats*, and place religion in such abstinence at certain times and seasons, only to exercise a tyranny over the consciences of men.

II. Having mentioned their hypocritical fastings, the apostle takes occasion to lay down the doctrine of the Christian liberty, which we enjoy under the gospel, of using God's good creatures, —that, whereas under the law there was a distinction of meats between clean and unclean (such sorts of flesh they might eat, and such they might not eat), all this is now taken away; and we are to call nothing common or unclean, Acts x. 15.

AN EXAMPLE TO THE BELIEVERS (*vv.* 6–16)

I. Godliness is here pressed upon him and others: *Refuse profane and old wives' sayings*, *vv.* 7, 8. The Jewish traditions, which some people fill their heads with, have nothing to do with them. *But exercise thyself rather unto godliness*; that is, mind practical religion. Those who would be godly must exercise themselves unto godliness; it requires a constant exercise. The reason is taken from the gain of godliness; *bodily exercise profits little*, or for a little time. Abstinence from meats and marriage, and the like, though they pass for acts of mortification and self-denial, yet profit little, · they turn to little account.

II. The encouragement which we have to proceed in the ways of godliness. Here is another of Paul's faithful sayings, worthy of all acceptation—that all our labours and losses in the service of God and the work of religion will be abundantly recompensed, so that though we lose for Christ we shall not lose by him. *Therefore we labour and suffer reproach, because we trust in the living God*, *v.* 10.

God is the general Saviour of all

men, as he has put them into a savable state; but he is in a particular manner the Saviour of true believers; there is then a general and a special redemption.

III. He concludes the chapter with an exhortation to Timothy,

1. To *command and teach these things* that he had now been teaching him.

2. To conduct himself with that gravity and prudence which might gain him respect, notwithstanding his youth.

3. To confirm his doctrine by a good example: *Be thou an example of the believers*, &c. Observe, Those who teach by their doctrine must teach by their life, else they pull down with one hand what they build up with the other: they must be examples both *in word and conversation*.

4. He charges him to study hard: *Till I come give attendance to reading, to exhortation, to doctrine, to meditation upon these things*, v. 13. Though Timothy had extraordinary gifts, yet he must use ordinary means.

5. He charges him to beware of negligence: *Neglect not the gift that is in thee*, v. 14. The gifts of God will wither if they be neglected. It was an extraordinary gift that we read of elsewhere as being conferred on him by the laying on of Paul's hands, but he was invested in the office of the ministry by the laying on of the hands of the presbytery.

6. Having this work committed to him, he must *give himself wholly* to it: "Be wholly in those things, *that thy profiting may appear*." He was a wise knowing man, and yet must still be profiting, and make it

appear that he improved in knowledge.

7. He presses it upon him to be very cautious: "*Take heed to thyself and to the doctrine*, consider what thou preachest; *continue in them*, in the truths that thou hast received; and this will be the way to *save thyself, and those that hear thee*."

CHAPTER FIVE

HANDLING PEOPLE (vv. 1–16)

Here the apostle gives rules to Timothy, and in him to other ministers, in reproving. A great difference is to be made in our reproofs, according to the age, quality, and other circumstances, of the persons rebuked; thus, an elder in age or office must be entreated as a father; *on some have compassion, making a difference*, Jude 22. The younger must be rebuked as brethren, with love and tenderness; The elder women must be reproved, when there is occasion, as mothers. The younger women must be reproved, but reproved as *sisters, with all purity*.

In *vv.* 3–16 directions are given concerning the taking of widows into the number of those who were employed by the church and had maintenance from the church.

I. It is appointed that those widows only should be relieved by the charity of the church who were pious and devout, and not wanton widows that *lived in pleasure*, vv. 5, 6. She is to be reckoned a widow indeed, and fit to be maintained at the church's charge, who, being *desolate, trusteth in God*.

II. Another rule he gives is that the church should not be charged with the maintenance of those widows who had relations of their own that were able to maintain them.

III. He gives directions concerning the characters of the widows that were to be taken into the number to receive the church's charity: not under sixty years old, nor any who have divorced their husbands or been divorced from them and have married again; she must have been *the wife of one man*, such as had been a housekeeper, had a good name for hospitality and charity, *well reported of for good works*. Here are instances of such good works as are proper to be done by good wives: *If she have brought up children. If she have lodged strangers*, and *washed the saints' feet*; if she have been ready to give entertainment to good Christians and good ministers, when they were in their travels for the spreading of the gospel.

IV. He cautions them to take heed of admitting into the number those who are likely to be no credit to them (*v.* 11): *The younger widows refuse*; they will be weary of their employments in the church, and of living by rule, as they must do; so they *will marry, and cast off their first faith*. Besides, the apostle here advises the younger widows to marry (*v.* 14), which he would not if hereby they must have broken their vows.

SUPPORTING THE MINISTRY (*vv.* 17–25)

Here are directions,

I. Concerning the supporting of ministers. Care must be taken that they be honourably maintained

(*v.* 17). Here we have, 1. The work of ministers; it consists principally in two things: ruling well and labouring in the word and doctrine. This was the main business of elders or presbyters in the days of the apostles. 2. The honour due to those who were not idle, but laborious in this work; they were worthy of double honour, esteem, and maintenance. He quotes a scripture to confirm this command concerning the maintenance of ministers that we might think foreign; but it intimates what a significancy there was in many of the laws of Moses, and particularly in this, *Thou shalt not muzzle the ox that treads out the corn*, Deut. xxv. 4. The beasts that were employed in treading out the corn (for that way they took instead of threshing it) were allowed to feed while they did the work, so that the more work they did the more food they had; therefore let the elders that labour in the word and doctrine be well provided for; *for the labourer is worthy of his reward* (Matt. x. 10).

II. Concerning the accusation of ministers (*v.* 19): *Against an elder receive not an accusation, but before two or three witnesses*. Here is the scripture-method of proceeding against an elder, when accused of any crime. Observe, (1) Public scandalous sinners must be rebuked publicly: as their sin has been public, and committed before many, or at least come to the hearing of all, so their reproof must be public, and before all. (2) Public rebuke is designed for the good of others, that they may fear, as well as for the good of the party rebuked.

III. Concerning the ordination of ministers (v. 22): *Lay hands suddenly on no man*; it seems to be meant of the ordaining of men to the office of the ministry, which ought not to be done rashly and inconsiderately, and before due trial made of their gifts and graces, their abilities and qualifications for it.

IV. Concerning absolution, to which *vv.* 24, 25, seem to refer: *Some men's sins are open beforehand, going before to judgment, and some follow after*, &c. Observe, Ministers have need of a great deal of wisdom, to know how to accommodate themselves to the variety of offences and offenders that they have occasion to deal with. Some men's sins are so plain and obvious, and not found by secret search, that there is no dispute concerning the bringing of them under the censures of the church; they *go before to judgment*, to lead them to censure.—*Others they follow after*; that is, their wickedness does not presently appear, nor till after a due search has been made concerning it.

V. Concerning Timothy himself. 1. Here is a charge to him to be careful of his office; and a solemn charge it is: *I charge thee before God, as thou wilt answer it to God before the holy and elect angels, observe these things without partiality*, v. 21. 2. He charges him to take care of his health: *Drink no longer water*, &c. It seems, Timothy was a mortified man to the pleasures of sense; he drank water, and he was a man of no strong constitution of body, and for this reason Paul advises him to use wine for the

helping of his stomach and the recruiting of his nature.

DUTY OF SERVANTS
(*vv.* 1–5)

I. Here is the duty of servants. They must respect their masters, *count them worthy of all honour* (because they are their masters), of all the respect, observance, compliance, and obedience, that are justly expected from servants to their masters. Or suppose the master were a Christian, and a believer, and the servant a believer too, would not this excuse him, because *in Christ there is neither bond nor free?* No, by no means, for Jesus Christ did not come to dissolve the bond of civil relation, but to strengthen it: *Those that have believing masters, let them not despise them because they are brethren.* Timothy is appointed to *teach and exhort these things*. Ministers must preach not only the general duties of all, but the duties of particular relations.

II. Paul here warns Timothy to withdraw from those who corrupted the doctrine of Christ, and made it the subject of strife, debate, and controversy. But he that does not consent to the words of Christ *is proud* (v. 4) and contentious, ignorant, and does a great deal of mischief to the church, knowing nothing. When men are not content with the words of the Lord Jesus Christ, and the doctrine which is according to godliness, but will frame notions of their own and impose them, and that too in their own words, which man's wisdom teaches, and not in the words which the Holy Ghost teaches (1 Cor. ii. 13), they sow the seeds of all mischief in the church. Hence come *perverse disputings of men of corrupt minds* (*v.* 5), disputes that are all subtlety, and no solidity. From such as these Timothy is warned to withdraw himself.

CONTENTMENT (*vv.* 6–12)

From the mention of the abuse which some put upon religion, making it to serve their secular advantages, the apostle,

I. Takes occasion to show the excellency of contentment and the evil of covetousness.

1. The excellency of contentment, *vv.* 6–8.

(1) The truth he lays down is that *godliness with contentment is great gain.* Godliness is itself great gain, it is profitable to all things; and, wherever there is true godliness, there will be contentment; but those that have arrived at the highest pitch of contentment with their godliness are certainly the easiest happiest people in this world.

(2) The reason he gives for it is, *For we brought nothing with us into this world, and it is certain we can carry nothing out, v.* 7. This is a reason why we should be content with a little. [1] Because we can challenge nothing as a debt that is due to us, for we came naked into the world. [2] We shall carry nothing with us out of this world. Why should we not be content with a little, because, how much soever we have, we must leave it behind us? Eccl. v. 15, 16.

(3) Hence he infers, *having food*

and raiment, let us be therewith content, v. 8. Observe, If God give us the necessary supports of life, we ought to be content therewith, though we have not the ornaments and delights of it.

2. The evil of covetousness. *Those that will be rich* (that set their hearts upon the wealth of this world, and are resolved, right or wrong, they will have it) *fall into temptation and a snare, v.* 9. It is not said, those that are rich, but those that will be rich, that is, that place their happiness in worldly wealth, that covet it inordinately, and are eager and violent in the pursuit of it.

(2) The apostle affirms that *the love of money is the root of all evil, v.* 10. Observe, [1] What is the root of all evil; the love of money; people may have money, and yet not love it; but, if they love it inordinately, it will push them on to all evil. [2] Covetous persons will quit the faith, if that be the way to get money: *Which while some coveted after, they have erred from the faith.*

II. Hence he takes occasion to caution Timothy, and to counsel him to keep in the way of God and his duty, and particularly to fulfil the trust reposed in him as a minister. He addresses himself to him as *a man of God.* 1. He charges Timothy to take heed of the love of money, which had been so pernicious to many: *Flee these things.* 2. To arm him against the love of the world, he directs him to follow that which is good. *Follow after righteousness, godliness, faith, love, patience, meekness.* 3. He exhorts him to do the part of a soldier: *Fight the good fight of faith.* Note,

Those who will get to heaven must fight their way thither. There must be a conflict with corruption and temptations, and the opposition of the powers of darkness. Observe, It is a good fight, it is a good cause, and it will have a good issue. It is the fight of faith; we do not war after the flesh, for the weapons of our warfare are not carnal, 2 Cor. x. 3, 4. 4. He exhorts him to *lay hold on eternal life*. Observe, (1) Eternal life is the crown proposed to us, for our encouragement to war, and to fight the good fight of faith, the good warfare. (2) This we must lay hold on, as those that are afraid of coming short of it and losing it.

SOLEMN CHARGES
(*vv.* 13–21)

The apostle here charges Timothy *to keep this commandment* (that is, the whole work of his ministry, all the trust reposed in him, all the service expected from him) *without spot, unrebukable*; he must conduct himself so in his ministry that he might not lay himself open to any blame nor incur any blemish. What are the motives to move him to this?

I. He gives him a solemn charge: *I give thee charge in the sight of God that thou do this*. He charges him as he will answer it at the great day to that God whose eyes are upon us all, who sees what we are and what we do. Observe, Christ died not only as a sacrifice, but as a martyr; and he witnessed a good confession when he was arraigned before Pilate (John xviii. 36, 37).

II. He reminds him of the confession that he himself had made: *Thou hast professed a good profes-sion before many witnesses* (*v.* 12), namely, when he was ordained by the laying on of the hands of the presbytery.

III. He reminds him of Christ's second coming. Keep it with an eye to his second coming, when we must all give an account of the talents we have been entrusted with," Luke xvi. 2. Observe,

1. Concerning Christ and God the Father the apostle here speaks great things. (1) That God is the only Potentate; the powers of earthly princes are all derived from him, and depend upon him. (2) He is the blessed and the only Potentate, infinitely happy, and nothing can in the least impair his happiness. (3) He is King of kings, and Lord of lords. (4) He only has immortality. He only is immortal in himself, and has immortality as he is the fountain of it, for the immortality of angels and spirits is derived from him. (5) He dwells in inaccessible light, *light which no man can approach unto*: no man can get to heaven but those whom he is pleased to bring thither, and admit into his kingdom. (6) He is invisible: *Whom no man hath seen, nor can see*. It is impossible that mortal eyes should bear the brightness of the divine glory. No man can see God and live.

2. Having mentioned these glorious attributes, he concludes with a doxology: *To him be honour and power everlasting. Amen*. God having all power and honour to himself, it is our duty to ascribe all power and honour to him.

IV. The apostle adds, by way of postscript, a lesson for rich people, *vv.* 17–19.

1. Timothy must charge those that are rich to beware of the temptations, and improve the opportunities, of their prosperous estate.

2. Hence we may observe, (1) Ministers must not be afraid of the rich; be they ever so rich, they must speak to them, and charge them. (2) They must caution them against pride, and vain confidence in their riches. (3) This is the way for the rich to lay up in store for themselves for the time to come, that they may lay hold on eternal life. 3. That science which opposes the truth of the gospel is falsely so called, it is not true science, for if it were it would approve of the gospel and consent to it (v. 20). Those who are so fond of such science are in great danger of erring concerning the faith; those who are for advancing reason above faith are in danger of leaving faith.

V. Our apostle concludes with a solemn prayer and benediction: *Grace be with thee. Amen.*

THE SECOND EPISTLE OF ST. PAUL TO

TIMOTHY

CHAPTER ONE
GREETINGS (vv. 1–5)

Here is, I. The inscription of the epistle. He calls Timothy his *beloved son*. Paul felt the warmest affection for him both because he had been an instrument of his conversion and because as a son with his father he had served with him in the gospel.

II. Paul's thanksgiving to God for Timothy's faith and holiness: he thanks God that he remembered Timothy in his prayers. He thanks God that Timothy kept up the religion of his ancestors, *v.* 5. Observe, The entail of religion descended upon Timothy by the mother's side; he had a good mother, and a good grandmother: they believed, though his father did not, Acts xvi. 1. It is a comfortable thing when children imitate the faith and holiness of their godly parents, and tread in their steps, 3 John 4.

HOLD FAST (vv. 6–14)

Here is an exhortation and excitation of Timothy to his duty (*v.* 6): *I put thee in remembrance.*

I. He exhorts him to stir *up the gift of God* that was *in him.* Stir it up as fire under the embers. It is meant of all the gifts and graces that God had given him, to qualify him for the work of an evangelist.

Observe, 1. The great hindrance of usefulness in the increase of our gifts is slavish fear. Paul therefore warns Timothy against this: *God hath not given us the spirit of fear,* *v.* 7. God hath delivered us from the spirit of fear, and hath given us the spirit *of power, and of love, and of a sound mind.* The spirit of power, or of courage and resolution to encounter difficulties and dangers; the spirit of love to God, which will carry us through the opposition we may meet with; the spirit of love to God will set us above the fear of man, and all the hurt that man can do us; and the spirit of a sound mind, or quietness of mind, a peaceable enjoyment of ourselves. 2. The spirit God gives to his ministers is not a fearful, but a courageous spirit; it is a spirit of power, for they speak in his name who has all power, both in heaven and earth; and it is a spirit of love, for love to God and the souls of men must inflame ministers in all their service; and it is a spirit of a sound mind, for they speak the words of truth and soberness.

II. He exhorts him to count upon afflictions, and get ready for them. Observe,

1. The gospel of Christ is what we have none of us reason to be ashamed of. We must not be ashamed of those who are suffering for the gospel of Christ. *Be partaker*

of the afflictions of the gospel;" or, as it may be read, *Do thou suffer with the gospel.*

2. Mentioning God and the gospel, he takes notice what great things God has done for us by the gospel, *vv.* 9, 10. To encourage him to suffer, he urges two considerations:

(1) The nature of that gospel which he was called to suffer for, and the glorious and gracious designs and purposes of it. It is usual with Paul, when he mentions Christ, and the gospel of Christ, to digress from his subject, and enlarge upon them; so full was he of that which is all our salvation, and ought to be all our desire. Let us value the gospel more than ever, as it is that whereby life and immortality are brought to light, for herein it has the pre-eminence above all former discoveries.

(2) Consider the example of blessed Paul, *vv.* 11, 12. He was appointed to teach the Gentiles. He thought it a cause worth suffering for, and why should not Timothy think so too? No man needs to be afraid nor ashamed to suffer for the cause of the gospel: *I am not ashamed,* says Paul, *for I know whom I have believed, and am persuaded that he is able to keep that which I have committed unto him against that day.* There is a day coming, and it will be a very solemn and awful day, when we must give an account of our stewardship (Luke xvi. 2), give an account of our souls: now, if by an active obedient faith we commit it to Jesus Christ, we may be sure he is able to keep it, and it shall be forthcoming to our comfort in that day.

III. He exhorts him to *hold fast the form of sound words,* v. 13. Adhere to it in opposition to all heresies and false doctrine, which corrupt the Christian faith. Hold that fast *which thou hast heard of me.* But how must it be held fast? *In faith and love;* that is, we must assent to it as *a faithful saying,* and bid it welcome as *worthy of all acceptation.* Faith and love must go together; it is not enough to believe the sound words, and to give an assent to them, but we must love them, believe their truth and love their goodness, and we must propagate the form of sound words in love; speaking the truth in love, Eph. iv. 15. To the same purport is that (*v.* 14), *That good thing which was committed unto thee keep by the Holy Ghost, which dwelleth in us.* That good thing was the form of sound words, the Christian doctrine, which was committed to Timothy in his baptism and education as he was a Christian, and in his ordination as he was a minister.

APOSTASY AND LOYALTY
(*vv.* 15–18)

Having (*vv.* 13, 14) exhorted Timothy to hold fast,

I. He mentions the apostasy of many from the doctrine of Christ, *v.* 15. He does not say that they had turned away from the doctrine of Christ (though it should seem they had) but they had turned away from him, and disowned him in the time of his distress.

II. He mentions the constancy of one that adhered to him, namely, Onesiphorus: *For he often refreshed me, and was not ashamed of my chain*, v. 16. He repays him with his prayers: *The Lord give mercy to Onesiphorus*.

III. He prays for Onesiphorus himself, as well as for his house: *That he may find mercy in that day*, in the day of death and of judgment, when Christ will account all the good offices done to his poor members as done to himself.

CHAPTER TWO
PERSEVERANCE (*vv.* 1–7)

Here Paul encourages Timothy to constancy and perseverance in his work: *Be strong in the grace that is in Christ Jesus*, v. 1. Observe,

I. Timothy must count upon sufferings, even unto blood, and therefore he must train up others to succeed him in the ministry of the gospel, v. 2. Two things he must have an eye to in ordaining ministers: Their fidelity or integrity ("Commit them to *faithful men*"), and also their ministerial ability. They must not only be knowing themselves, but be able to teach others also, and be apt to teach. Here we have, 1. The things Timothy was to commit to others—what he had heard of the apostle among many witnesses; he must not deliver any thing besides, and what Paul delivered to him and others he had received of the Lord Jesus Christ. 2. He was to commit them as a trust, as a sacred deposit, which they were to keep, and to transmit pure and uncorrupt unto others. 3. Those to whom he was to commit these things must be faithful, that is, trusty men, and who were skilful to teach others.

II. He must *endure hardness* (v. 3): *Thou therefore*, &c. 1. All Christians, but especially ministers, *are soldiers of Jesus Christ*. 2. The soldiers of Jesus Christ must approve themselves good soldiers, faithful to their captain, resolute in his cause. 3. Those who would approve themselves good soldiers of Jesus Christ must endure hardness; that is, we must expect it and count upon it in this world.

III. He must not entangle himself in the affairs of this world, v. 4. A soldier, when he has enlisted, leaves his calling, and all the business of it, that he may attend his captain's orders. If we have given up ourselves to be Christ's soldiers, we must sit loose to this world.

IV. He must see to it that in carrying on the spiritual warfare he went by rule, that he observed the laws of war (v. 5): *If a man strive for masteries, yet is he not crowned, except he strive lawfully*. We are striving for mastery, to get the mastery of our lusts and corruptions, to excel in that which is good, but we cannot expect the prize unless we observe the laws. In doing that which is good we must take care that we do it in a right manner, that our good may not be evil spoken of.

V. He must be willing to wait for a recompense (v. 6): *The husbandman that laboureth must be first partaker of the fruits*. Or, as it should be read, *The husbandman labouring first must partake of the fruits*, as appears by comparing it with Jam. v. 7. If we would be partakers of the fruits, we must labour; if we would gain the prize, we must run the race.

CHRIST'S FAITHFULNESS
(vv. 8–13)

I. To encourage Timothy in suffering, the apostle puts him in mind of the resurrection of Christ (*v.* 8). The incarnation and resurrection of Jesus Christ, heartily believed and rightly considered, will support a Christian under all sufferings in the present life.

II. Another thing to encourage him in suffering was that he had Paul for an example.

Good ministers may and should encourage themselves in the hardest services and the hardest sufferings, with this, that God will certainly bring good to his church, and benefit to his elect, out of them.

III. Another thing with which he encourages Timothy is the prospect of a future state.

1. Those who faithfully adhere to Christ and to his truths and ways, whatever it cost them, will certainly have the advantage of it in another world: *If we be dead with him, we shall live with him, v.* 11.

2. It is at our peril if we prove unfaithful to him: *If we deny him, he also will deny us.* If we deny him before man, he will deny us before his Father, Matt. x. 33. If we be faithful to Christ, he will certainly be faithful to us. If we be false to him, he will be faithful to his threatenings: *he cannot deny himself,* cannot recede from any word that he hath spoken, for he is yea, and amen, the faithful witness.

WARNINGS AGAINST ERROR (vv. 14–18)

Having thus encouraged Timothy to suffer, he comes in the next place to direct him in his work.

I. He must make it his business to edify those who were under his charge, *to put them in remembrance* of those things which they did already know.—*Study to show thyself approved unto God, v.* 15. Ministers must be workmen; they have work to do, and they must take pains in it. And what is their work? It is *rightly to divide the word of truth.* Not to invent a new gospel, but rightly to divide the gospel that is committed to their trust.

II. He must take heed of that which would be a hindrance to him in his work, *v.* 16. He must take heed of error: *Shun profane and vain babblings.* Upon this occasion the apostle mentions some who had lately advanced erroneous doctrines: *Hymeneus and Philetus.* They have *erred concerning the truth,* or concerning one of the fundamental articles of the Christian religion, which is truth. The resurrection of the dead is one of the great doctrines of Christ. Now see the subtlety of the serpent and the serpent's seed. They did not deny the resurrection (for that had been boldly and avowedly to confront the word of Christ), but they put a corrupt interpretation upon that true doctrine, saying that the resurrection was past already, that what Christ spoke concerning the resurrection was *to be understood mystically* and by way of allegory, that it must be meant of a spiritual resurrection only. It is true, there is a spiritual resurrection, but to infer thence that there will not be a true and real resurrection of the body at the last day is to dash one truth of

Christ in pieces against another. By this they *overthrow the faith of some.*

GOOD VESSELS (*vv.* 19–21)

Here we see what we may comfort ourselves with, in reference to this, and the little errors and heresies that both infect and infest the church, and do mischief.

I. It may be a great comfort to us that the unbelief of men cannot make the promise of God of no effect. The prophets and apostles, that is, the doctrines of the Old and New Testament, are still firm; and they have a seal with two mottoes upon it, one on the one side, and the other one the other, as is usual in a broad seal. 1. One expresses our comfort—that *the Lord knows those that are his,* and those that are not; knows them, that is, he owns them, so knows them that he will never lose them. 2. Another declares our duty—that every one who names the name of Christ must depart from iniquity. Those who would have the comfort of the privilege must make conscience of the duty.

II. Another thing that may comfort us is that though there are some whose faith is overthrown, yet there are others who keep their integrity, and hold it fast (*v.* 20). Now we should see to it that we be vessels of honour: we must *purge ourselves from these corrupt opinions,* that we may be sanctified for our Master's use.

THINGS TO AVOID (*vv.* 22–26)

I. Paul here exhorts Timothy to beware of *youthful lusts, v.* 22.

Though he was a holy good man, very much mortified to the world, yet Paul thought it necessary to caution him against youthful lusts. He prescribes an excellent remedy against youthful lusts: *Follow right-eousness, faith, charity, peace,* &c.

II. He cautions him against contention, and, to prevent this (*v.* 23), against *foolish and unlearned questions,* that tend to no benefit, strifes of words. Those who advanced them, and doted upon them, thought themselves wise and learned; but Paul calls them foolish and unlearned. The mischief of these is that they *gender strifes,* that they breed debates and quarrels among Christians and ministers.—*The servant of the Lord must not strive, v.* 24. Nothing worse becomes the servant of the Lord Jesus, who himself did not strive nor cry (Matt. xii. 19). The servant of the Lord must be *gentle to all men,* and thereby show that he is himself subject to the commanding power of that holy religion which he is employed in preaching and propagating.—*Apt to teach.* Those are unapt to teach who are apt to strive, and are fierce and froward. Ministers must have in their eyes, in instructing those who oppose themselves, their recovery: *If God, peradventure, will give them repentance to the acknowledging of the truth.*

REPROBATES (*vv.* 1–9)

1. Timothy must know that in the *last days* (*v.* 1), in gospel times, there would *come perilous times.* These would be difficult times,

wherein it would be difficult for a man to keep a good conscience.

II. Paul tells Timothy what would be the occasion of making these times perilous, or what shall be the marks and signs whereby these times may be known, *vv.* 2, &c. 1. Self-love will make the times perilous. Men love to gratify their own lusts, and make provision for them, more than to please God and to do their duty. 2. Covetousness. Observe, Self-love brings in a long train of sins and mischiefs. When men are lovers of themselves, no good can be expected from them, as all good may be expected from those who love God with all their hearts. 3. Pride and vain-glory. The times are perilous when men, being proud of themselves, are *boasters and blasphemers*. 4. When children are disobedient to their parents, they make the times perilous; for what wickedness will those stick at who will be abusive to their own parents and rebel against them? 5. Unthankfulness and unholiness make the times perilous, and these two commonly go together. 6. The times are perilous when men will not be held by the bonds either of nature or common honesty, when they are *without natural affection*, and *truce-breakers*, *v.* 3. 7. The times are perilous when men are *false accusers* one of another, having no regard to the good name of others, or to the religious obligations of an oath, but thinking themselves at liberty to say and do what they please, Ps. xii. 4. 8. When men have no government of themselves and their own appetites, they are soon fired, upon the least provocation. 9. When that which is good

and ought to be honoured is generally despised and looked upon with contempt. 10. When men are generally treacherous, wilful, and haughty, the times are perilous (*v.* 4)—when men are *traitors, heady, high-minded.* 11. When men are generally *lovers of pleasure more than lovers of God.* When there are more epicures than true Christians, then the times are bad indeed. 12. When, notwithstanding all this, they *have the form of godliness* (*v.* 5), are called by the Christian name, baptized into the Christian faith, and make a show of religion; but, how plausible soever their form of godliness is, they deny the power of it.

III. Here Paul warns Timothy to take heed of certain seducers, not only that he might not be drawn away by them himself, but that he might arm those who were under his charge against their seduction. Though the spirit of error may be let loose for a time, God has it in a chain. Satan can deceive the nations and the churches no further and no longer than God will permit him: *Their folly shall be manifest*, it shall appear that they are impostors, and every man shall abandon them.

THE INSPIRED SCRIPTURES
(*vv.* 10–17)

Here the apostle, to confirm Timothy in that way wherein he walked,

I. Sets before him his own example, which Timothy had been an eye-witness of, having long attended Paul (*v.* 10): *Thou hast fully known my doctrine.* The more fully we know the doctrine of

Christ and the apostles, the more closely we shall cleave to it; the reason why many sit loose to it is because they do not fully know it.

II. He warns Timothy of the fatal end of seducers, as a reason why he should stick closely to the truth as it is in Jesus: *But evil men and seducers shall wax worse and worse*, &c. v. 13.

III. He directs him to keep close to a good education, and particularly to what he had learned out of the holy scriptures (*vv.* 14, 15): *Continue thou in the things which thou hast learned.*

1. It is a great happiness to know the certainty of the things wherein we have been instructed (Luke i. 4); not only to know what the truths are, but to know that they are of undoubted certainty, for certainty in religion is of great importance and advantage: *Knowing*, (1) "That thou hast had good teachers. Consider of *whom thou hast learned them.*" (2) Knowing especially the firm foundation upon which thou has built, namely, that of the scripture (*v.* 15): *That from a child thou hast known the holy scriptures.*

2. Those who would acquaint themselves with the things of God, and be assured of them, must know the holy scriptures, for these are the summary of divine revelation.

3. It is a great happiness to know the holy scriptures from our childhood; and children should betimes get the knowledge of the scriptures.

4. The scriptures we are to know are the holy scriptures; they come from the holy God, were delivered by holy men, contain holy precepts, treat of holy things, and were designed to make us holy and to lead us in the way of holiness to happiness. Now here observe,

(1) What is the excellency of the scripture. It is *given by inspiration of God* (*v.* 16), and therefore is his word. It is a divine revelation, which we may depend upon as infallibly true. The same Spirit that breathed reason into us breathes revelation among us.

(2) What use it will be of to us. [1] *It is able to make us wise to salvation*; that is, it is a sure guide in our way to eternal life. [2] It is *profitable* to us for all the purposes of the Christian life, *for doctrine, for reproof, for correction, for instruction in righteousness.* It answers all the ends of divine revelation. It instructs us in that which is true, reproves us for that which is amiss, directs us in that which is good. [3] *That the man of God may be perfect, v.* 17. The Christian, the minister, is the man of God. That which finishes a man of God in this world is the scripture. By it we are *thoroughly furnished for every good work*. There is that in the scripture which suits every case.

(3) On the whole we here see, [1] That the scripture has various uses, and answers divers ends and purposes: *It is profitable for doctrine, for reproof, for correction* of all errors in judgment and practice, and *for instruction in righteousness.* [2] The scripture is a perfect rule of faith and practice, and was designed for the man of God, the minister as well as the Christian who is devoted to God, for it is *profitable for doctrine*, &c. [3] If we consult the scripture, which was given by inspiration of God, and

follow its directions, we shall be made men of God, *perfect, and thoroughly furnished to every good work.*

PAUL'S CHARGE (*vv.* 1–8)

Observe, I. How awfully this charge is introduced (*v.* 1): *I charge thee before God, and the Lord Jesus Christ, who shall judge the quick and the dead at his appearing and his kingdom.* Observe, The best of men have need to be awed into the discharge of their duty.

II. What is the matter of the charge, *vv.* 2–5. He is charged,

1. To *preach the word.* This is ministers' business; a dispensation is committed to them.

2. To urge what he preached, and to press it with all earnestness upon his hearers: "*Be instant in season and out of season, reprove, rebuke, exhort.*" We must do it in season, that is, let slip no opportunity; and do it out of season, that is, not shift off the duty, under pretence that it is out of season.

3. He must tell people of their faults: "*Reprove them, rebuke them.*"

4. He must direct, encourage, and quicken those who began well. "*Exhort them* (persuade them to hold on, and endure to the end) and this *with all long-suffering and doctrine.*" (1) He must do it very patiently: *With all long-suffering.* (2) He must do it rationally, not with passion, but *with doctrine.*

5. He must *watch in all things.* "Seek an opportunity of doing them a kindness; let no fair occasion slip, through thy negligence.

6. He must count upon afflictions, and endure them, make the best of them.

7. He must remember his office, and discharge its duties: *Do the work of an evangelist.* The office of the evangelist was, as the apostles' deputies, to water the churches that they planted. They were not settled pastors, but for some time resided in, and presided over, the churches that the apostles had planted, till they were settled under a standing ministry. This was Timothy's work.

8. He must fulfil his ministry: *Make full proof of it.* It was a great trust that was reposed in him, and therefore he must answer it, and perform all the parts of his office with a diligence and care.

III. The reasons to enforce the charge.

1. Because errors and heresies were likely to creep into the church, by which the minds of many professing Christians would be corrupted (*vv.* 3, 4): "*For the time will come when they will not endure sound doctrine.*" They will *turn away their ears from the truth*; they will grow weary of the old plain gospel of Christ, and then they will be greedy of fables, and take pleasure in them, and God will give them up to those strong delusions, because they received not the truth in the love of it, 2 Thess. ii. 11, 12.

2. Because Paul for his part had almost done his work: *Do thou make full proof of thy ministry, for I am now ready to be offered, v.* 6. Observe,

[1] With what pleasure he speaks of dying. He calls it his departure; though it is probable that he fore-

saw he must die a violent bloody death, yet he calls it his departure, or his release.

[2] With what pleasure he looks back upon the life he had lived (*v.* 7): *I have fought a good fight, I have finished my course,* &c. He did not fear death, because he had the testimony of his conscience that by the grace of God he had in some measure answered the ends of living.

[3] With what pleasure he looks forward to the life he was to live hereafter (*v.* 8): *Henceforth there is laid up for me a crown of righteousness,* &c. He had lost for Christ, but he was sure he should not lose by him, Phil. iii. 8.

DIRECTIONS (*vv.* 9–15)

Here are particular matters which Paul mentions to Timothy, now at the closing of the epistle. 1. He bids him hasten to him, if possible (*v.* 9): *Do thy diligence to come shortly to me.* Paul wanted Timothy's company and help; and the reason he gives is because several had left him (*v.* 10); one from an ill principle, namely, *Demas,* who abides under an ill name for it: *Demas hath forsaken me, having loved this present world. Crescens* had gone one way and *Titus* another way. *Luke* however remained with Paul (*vv.* 11, 12), and was not this enough? Paul did not think it so; he loved the company of his friends. 2. He speaks respectfully concerning *Mark*: *He is profitable to me for the ministry.* It is supposed that this Mark was he about whom Paul and Barnabas had contended, Acts xv. 39. By this it appears that Paul was not reconciled to Mark, and

had a better opinion of him than he had had formerly. 3. Paul orders Timothy to come to him, bids him as he came through Troas to bring with him thence those things which he had left behind him there (*v.* 13), the cloak he had left there, which, it may be, Paul had the more occasion for in a cold prison. Paul was guided by divine inspiration, and yet he would have his books with him. 4. He mentions *Alexander*, and the mischief that he had done him, *vv.* 14, 15. This is he who is spoken of Acts xix. 33. He cautions Timothy to take heed of him: "*Of whom be thou aware also,* that he do not, under pretence of friendship, betray thee to mischief." It is dangerous having any thing to do with those who would be enemies to such a man as Paul.

CONCLUSION (*vv.* 16–22)

Here, I. He gives Timothy an account of his own present circumstances.

1. He had lately been called to appear before the emperor, upon his appeal to Cæsar; and then *no man stood with him* (*v.* 16), to plead his cause, to bear testimony for him, or so much as to keep him in countenance, but *all men forsook him.*

2. *Notwithstanding this God stood by him* (*v.* 17), gave him extraordinary wisdom and courage, to enable him to speak so much the better himself. *And that all the Gentiles might hear*; the emperor himself and the great men who would never have heard Paul preach if he had not been brought before them. *And I was delivered out of the mouth of the lion,* that is, of Nero (as some

think) or some other judge. *And the Lord shall deliver me from every evil work.* See how Paul improved his experiences: "*He that hath delivered doth deliver, and we trust he will yet deliver*, will deliver me *from every evil work*, from any ill done to me by others. *And shall preserve me to his heavenly kingdom*." And for this he gives glory to God, rejoicing in hope of the glory of God.

II. He sends salutations to *Aquila, and Priscilla, and the household of Onesiphorus, v.* 19. He mentions his leaving *Trophimus sick at Miletus* (*v.* 20), by which it appears that though the apostles healed all manner of diseases miraculously, for the confirmation of their doctrine, yet they did not exert that power upon their own friends, lest it should have looked like a collusion.

III. He hastens Timothy to *come to him before winter* (*v.* 21), because he longed to see him, and because in the winter the journey or voyage would be more dangerous.

IV. He sends commendations to him from *Eubulus, Pudens, Linus, Claudia*, and all the *brethren.*

V. He concludes with a prayer, that the *Lord Jesus would be with his spirit.*

TITUS

CHAPTER ONE

GREETINGS (vv. 1–5)

Here is the preface to the epistle, showing,

I. The writer. *Paul*, a Gentile name taken by the apostle of the Gentiles, Acts xiii. 9, 46, 47.

II. The person written to, who is described, 1. By his name, *Titus*, a Gentle Greek, yet called both to the faith and ministry. Observe, the grace of God is free and powerful. What worthiness or preparation was there in one of heathen stock and education? 2. By his spiritual relation to the apostle: *My own* (or *my genuine*) *son*, not by natural generation, but by supernatural regeneration. *I have begotten you through the gospel*, said he to the Corinthians, 1 Cor. iv. 15. "*My own son after the common faith*, that faith which is common to all the regenerate, and which thou hast in truth, and expressest to the life." This might be said to distinguish Titus from hypocrites and false teachers, and to recommend him to the regard of the Cretans, as being among them a lively image of the apostle himself, in faith, and life, and heavenly doctrine.

III. The salutation and prayer, wishing all blessings to him: *Grace, mercy, and peace, from God the Father, and the Lord Jesus Christ our Saviour.*

Thus far is the preface to the epistle; then follows the entrance into the matter, by signifying the end of Titus's being left in Crete:

I. More generally: *For this cause left I thee in Crete, that thou shouldst set in order the things that are wanting.* Titus was to go on in settling what the apostle himself had not time for, in his short stay there.

II. In special: *To ordain elders in every city*, that is, ministers, who were mostly out of the elder and most understanding and experienced Christians; or, if younger in years, yet such as were grave and solid in their deportment and manners. These were to be set where there was any fit number of Christians, as in larger towns and cities was usually the case; though villages, too, might have them where there were Christians enough for it. These presbyters or elders were to have the ordinary and stated care and charge of the churches; to feed and govern them, and perform all pastoral work and duty in and towards them.

III. The rule of his proceeding: *As I had appointed thee*, probably when he was going from him, and in the presence and hearing of others, to which he may now refer, not so much for Titus's own sake as for the people's, that they might the more readily yield obedience to Titus.

385

ORDINATION (*vv.* 6–16)

The apostle here gives Titus directions about ordination, showing whom he should ordain, and whom not.

I. Of those whom he should ordain. He points out their qualifications and virtues; such as respect their life and manners, and such as relate to their doctrine: the former in the sixth, seventh, and eighth verses, and the latter in the ninth.

1. Their qualifications respecting their life and manners are,

(1) More general: *If any be blameless.* The meaning is, He must be one who lies not under an ill character; but rather must have a good report.

(2) More particularly.

[1] There is his relative character. In his own person, he must be of conjugal chastity: *The husband of one wife.* And, as to his children, *having faithful children,* obedient and good, brought up in the true Christian faith, and living according to it, at least as far as the endeavours of the parents can avail. *Not accused of riot, nor unruly,* not justly so accused, as having given ground and occasion for it, for otherwise the most innocent may be falsely so charged; they must look to it therefore that there be no colour for such censure. The ground of this qualification is shown from the nature of his office (*v.* 7): *For a bishop must be blameless, as the steward of God.* Those before termed presbyters, or elders, are in this verse styled bishops; and such they were, having no ordinary fixed and standing officers above them.

[2] The more absolute ones are expressed, *First*, Negatively, showing what an elder or bishop must not be: *Not self-willed. Not soon angry, not one of a hasty angry temper,* soon and easily provoked and inflamed. *Not given to wine;* there is no greater reproach on a minister than to be a wine-bibber, one who loves it, and gives himself undue liberty this way who *continues at the wine or strong drink till it inflames him.* Seasonable and moderate use of this, as of the other good creatures of God, is not unlawful. But excess therein is shameful in all, especially in a minister. *No striker,* in any quarrelsome or contentious manner, not injuriously nor out of revenge, with cruelty or unnecessary roughness. *Not given to filthy lucre;* not greedy of it (as 1 Tim. iii. 3). But, *Secondly,* Positively: he must be (*v.* 8) *a lover of hospitality,* as an evidence that he is not given to filthy lucre. *A lover of good men,* or of *good things;* ministers should be exemplary in both; this will evince their open piety, and likeness to God and their Master Jesus Christ. *Holy* in what concerns religion; one who reverences and worships God, and is of a spiritual and heavenly conversation. *Temperate;* it comes from a word that signifies *strength,* and denotes one who has power over his appetite and affections, or, in things lawful, can, for good ends, restrain and hold them in.

2. As to doctrine,

(1) Here is his duty: *Holding fast the faithful word, as he has been taught,* keeping close to the doctrine of Christ, *the word of his grace.*

(2) Here is the end: *That he may be able, by sound doctrine, both to exhort, and to convince the gainsayers*, to persuade and draw others to the true faith, and to convince the contrary-minded.

II. The apostle's directory shows whom he should reject or avoid.

1. From bad teachers. (1) Those false teachers are described. They were *unruly*, headstrong and ambitious of power. (2) Here is the apostle's direction how to deal with them (*v.* 11): *Their mouths must be stopped*; not by outward force (Titus had no such power, nor was this the gospel method), but by confutation and conviction, showing them their error, *not giving place to them even for an hour*.

III. In reference to their people or hearers, who are described from ancient testimony given of them.

1. Here is the witness (*v.* 12): *One of themselves, even a prophet of their own*, that is, one of the Cretans, not of the Jews, Epimenides a Greek poet, likely to know and unlikely to slander them.

2. Here is the matter of his testimony: *The Cretans are always liars, evil beasts, slow bellies*. Even to a proverb, they were infamous for falsehood and lying.

3. Here is the verification of this by the apostle himself: *v.* 13. This witness is true.

4. He instructs Titus how to deal with them: *Wherefore rebuke them sharply*. When Paul wrote to Timothy he bade him instruct with meekness; but now, when he writes to Titus, he bids him rebuke them sharply. The Cretans' sins and corruptions were many, great, and habitual; therefore they must be rebuked sharply. But that such direction might not be misconstrued,

5. Here is the end of it noted: *That they may be sound in the faith* (*v.* 14), *not giving heed to Jewish fables, and commandments of men, that turn from the truth*.

6. He gives the reasons of this, from the liberty we have by the gospel from legal observances, and the evil and mischief of a Jewish spirit under the Christian dispensation in the last two verses. To good Christians that are sound in the faith and thereby purified *all things are pure*.

CHAPTER TWO

GENERAL DUTIES (*vv.* 1–10)

Now here he exhorts him,

I. Generally, to a faithful discharge of his own office: and then,

II. Specially and particularly, he instructs him to apply this sound doctrine to several sorts of persons, from *vv.* 2–10.

1. To the aged men. By aged men some understand elders by office, including deacons, &c. But all old disciples of Christ must conduct themselves in every thing agreeably to the Christian doctrine.

2. To the aged women. These also must be instructed and warned. They must *be in behaviour as becometh holiness*: both men and women must accommodate their behaviour to their profession.

3. There are lessons for young women also, whom the aged women must teach, instructing and advising them in the duties of religion according to their years. These young women the more aged must

teach, (1) To bear a good personal character: *To be sober and discreet.* (2) *To love their husbands, and to be obedient to them*: and where there is true love this will be no difficult command. (3). *And to love their children*, not with a natural affection only, but a spiritual, a love springing from a holy sanctified heart and regulated by the word. The reason is added: *That the word of God may not be blasphemed.* Failures in such relative duties would be greatly to the reproach of Christianity.

4. Here is the duty of young men. They are apt to be eager and hot, thoughtless and precipitant; therefore they must be earnestly called upon and exhorted to be considerate; not rash; advisable and submissive, not wilful and headstrong; humble and mild, not haughty and proud; for there are more young people ruined by pride than by any other sin.

5. With these instructions to Titus, the apostle inserts some directions to himself. He could not expect so successfully to teach others, if he did not conduct himself well both in his conversation and preaching. (1) Here is direction for his manner of life: *In all things showing thyself a pattern of good works, v.* 7. Without this, he would pull down with one hand what he built with the other. And here is direction, (2) For his teaching and doctrine, as well as for his life: *In doctrine showing uncorruptness, gravity, sincerity, sound speech, that cannot be condemned, vv.* 7, 8. They must make it appear that the design of their preaching is purely to advance the honour of God, the interest of Christ and his kingdom, and the welfare and happiness of souls.

6. The directions respecting servants. Servants must know and do their duty to their earthly masters, but with an eye to their heavenly one: and Titus must not only instruct and warn earthly masters of their duties, but servants also of theirs, both in his public preaching and private admonitions.

THE DESIGN OF THE GOSPEL (*vv.* 11–15)

Here we have the grounds or considerations upon which all the foregoing directions are urged, taken from the nature and design of the gospel, and the end of Christ's death.

I. This is the very aim and business of Christianity, to instruct, and help, and form persons, under all distinctions and relations, to a right frame and conduct. For this,

1. They are put under the dispensation of *the grace of God*, so the gospel is called, Eph. iii. 2. Now grace is obliging and constraining to goodness.

2. This gospel grace *brings salvation* (reveals and offers it to sinners and ensures it to believers)— salvation from sin and wrath, from death and hell. Hence it is called *the word of life.*

3. *It hath appeared*, or shone out more clearly and illustriously than ever before. For,

4. It hath appeared *to all men*; not to the Jews only, but gospel grace is open to all, and all are invited to come and partake of the benefit of it, Gentiles as well as Jews.

5. This gospel revelation is to *teach*. For it teaches us,

(1) To abandon sin: *Denying ungodliness and worldly lusts*; to renounce and have no more to do with these. And then,

(2) To make conscience of that which is good: *To live soberly, righteously, and godly*, &c. Religion is not made up of negatives only; there must be doing good as well as eschewing evil; in these conjunctly is sincerity proved and the gospel adorned.

(3) To look for the glories of another world, to which a sober, righteous, and godly life in this is preparative: *Looking for that blessed hope, and the glorious appearing of the great God and our Saviour Jesus Christ*. And herewith is connected another ground, namely,

II. From the end of Christ's death: *Who gave himself for us, that he might redeem us from all iniquity, and purify unto himself a peculiar people, zealous of good works, v.* 14. To bring us to holiness and happiness was the end of Christ's death, as well as the scope of his doctrine.

CHAPTER THREE

GOOD WORKS (vv. 1–8)

Here is the fourth thing in the matter of the epistle. The apostle had directed Titus in reference to the particular and special duties of several sorts of persons; now he bids him exhort to what concerned them more in common, namely, to quietness and submission to rulers, and readiness to do good, and to equitable and gentle behaviour towards all men—things comely and ornamental of religion; he must therefore put them in mind of such things. Here are the duties themselves, and the reasons of them.

I. The duties themselves, which they were to be reminded of. 1. *Put them in mind to be subject to principalities and powers, to obey magistrates*. Magistracy is God's ordinance for the good of all, and therefore must be regarded and submitted to by all; not for wrath and by force only, but willingly and for conscience' sake. And, 2. *To be ready to every good work*. The precept regards doing good in all kinds, and on every occasion that may offer, whether respecting God, ourselves, or our neighbour—What may bring credit to religion in the world. And, 3. *To speak evil of no man: to revile*, or *curse*, or *blaspheme none*: or (as our translation more generally) *to speak evil of none*, unjustly and falsely. If no good can be spoken, rather than speak evil unnecessarily, say nothing. And, 4. *To be no brawlers; no fighters*, either with hand or tongue, no quarrelsome contentious persons, apt to give or return ill and provoking language. Wherefor it follows, 5. *But gentle; equitable and just*, or candid and fair in constructions of things, not taking words or actions in the worst sense; and for peace sometimes yielding somewhat of strict right. And, 6. *Showing all meekness to all men*. We must be of a mild disposition, and not only have meekness in our hearts, but show it in our speech and conduct. Thus of the duties themselves, which Titus was to put people in mind of: for which,

II. He adds the reasons, which are derived

1. From their own past condition. Consideration of men's natural condition is a great means and ground of equity and gentleness, and all meekness, towards those who are yet in such a state. This has a tendency to abate pride and work pity and hope in reference to those who are yet unconverted. And he reasons,

2. From their present state. "We are delivered out of that our miserable condition by no merit nor strength of our own; but only by the mercy and free grace of God, and merit of Christ, and operation of his Spirit. Therefore we have no ground, in respect of ourselves, to contemn those who are yet unconverted, but rather to pity them, and cherish hope concerning them, that they, though in themselves as unworthy and unmeet as we were, yet may obtain mercy, as we have: and so upon this occasion the apostle again opens the causes of our salvation, *vv.* 4–7.

(1) We have here the prime author of our salvation—God the Father, therefore termed here *God our Saviour.*

(2) The spring and rise of it—the divine *philanthropy*, or *kindness and love of God to man.* By grace we are saved from first to last.

(3) Here is the means, or instrumental cause—the shining out of this love and grace of God in the gospel, *after it appeared*, that is, in the word.

(4) False grounds and motives are here removed: *Not by works of righteousness which we have done, but according to his mercy, he saved us*; not for foreseen works of ours, but his own free grace and mercy alone.

(5) Here is the formal cause of salvation, or that wherein it lies, the beginnings of it at least—in regeneration or spiritual renewing, as it is here called.

(6) Here is the outward sign and seal thereof in baptism, called therefore *the washing of regeneration.* The work itself is inward and spiritual; but it is outwardly signified and sealed in this ordinance.

(7) Here is the principal efficient, namely, the Spirit of God; it is the *renewing of the Holy Ghost.*

(8) Here is the manner of God's communicating this Spirit in the gifts and graces of it; not with a scanty and niggardly hand, but most freely and plentifully: *Which he shed on us abundantly.*

(9) Here is the procuring cause of all, namely, Christ: *Through Jesus Christ our Saviour.* He it is who purchased the Spirit and his saving gifts and graces. All come through him, and through him as a Saviour, whose undertaking and work it is to bring to grace and glory.

(10) Here are the ends why we are brought into this new spiritual condition, namely, justification, and heirship, and hope of eternal life: *That, being justified by his grace, we should be made heirs according to the hope of eternal life.*

III. The apostle, having opened the duties of Christians in common, with the reasons respecting themselves, adds another from their goodness and usefulness to men. These things are good in themselves, and the teaching of them useful to mankind, making persons a common good in their places.

CONCLUSION (*vv.* 9–15)

Here is the fifth and last thing in the matter of the epistle: what Titus should avoid in teaching; how he should deal with a heretic; with some other directions. Observe,

1. That the apostle's meaning might be more clear and full, and especially fitted to the time and state of things in Crete, and the many judaizers among them, he tells Titus what, in teaching, he should shun, *v.* 9. Idle and foolish enquiries, tending neither to God's glory nor the edification of men, must be shunned. — *And genealogies* (of the gods, say some, that the heathen poets made such noise about; or rather those that the Jews were so curious in). — *And contentions, and strivings about the law.* There were those who were for the Mosaic rites and ceremonies, and would have them continued in the church, though by the gospel

and the coming of Christ they were superseded and done away. Titus must give no countenance to these, but avoid and oppose them.

II. But because, after all, there will be *heresies* and *heretics* in the church, the apostle next directs Titus what to do in such a case, and how to deal with such, *v.* 10. "Admonish him once and again, that, if possible, he may be brought back, and thou mayest gain thy brother; but, if this will not reduce him, that others be not hurt, cast him out of the communion, and warn all Christians to avoid him. — *Knowing that he that is such is subverted* (turned off from the foundation) *and sinneth* grievously, being *self-condemned.*

III. The apostle subjoins some further directions, *vv.* 12, 13.

IV. The apostle concludes with salutations and benedictions, *v.* 5. Though perhaps not personally known (some of them at least), yet all by Paul testify their love and good wishes to Titus, owning him thereby in his work, and stimulating him to go on therein.

PHILEMON

CHAPTER ONE

GREETINGS (*vv.* 1–7)

I. In the first two verses of the preface we have the persons from and to whom it is written.

1. The persons writing: Paul, the principal, who calls himself *a prisoner of Jesus Christ*, that is, for Jesus Christ, and Timothy. What could be denied to two such petitioners?

2. The persons written to are *Philemon and Apphia*, and with them Archippus, and the church in Philemon's house. Philemon, the master of Onesimus, a slave, was the principal, to whom the letter is inscribed, the head of the family, in whom were the authority and power of taking in or shutting out, and whose property Onesimus was: with him therefore chiefly lay the business. Next to this inscription is,

II. The apostle's salutation of those named by him (*v.* 3): *Grace to you and peace from God our Father and the Lord Jesus Christ*.

III. He expresses the singular affection he had for him, by thanksgiving and prayer to God in his behalf, and the great joy for the many good things he knew and heard to be in him, *vv.* 4–7. The apostle's thanksgiving and prayer for Philemon are here set forth by the object, circumstance, and mat-

ter of them, with the way whereby much of the knowledge of Philemon's goodness came to him.

1. Here is the object of Paul's praises and prayers for Philemon: *I thank my God, making mention of thee in my prayers, v.* 4.

2. Here is the circumstance: *Always making mention of thee. Always*—usually, not once or twice only, but frequently.

3. Here is the matter both of his praises and prayers, in reference to Philemon.

(1) Of his praises. [1] He thanks God for the love which he heard Philemon had towards the Lord Jesus. [2] For his faith in Christ also. Love to Christ, and faith in him, are prime Christian graces, for which there is great ground of praise to God, where he has blessed any with them. [3] He praises God likewise for Philemon's love to all the saints. These two must go together; for he who *loveth him that begat must and* will *love those also that are begotten of him*. Mere external differences are nothing here. Paul calls a poor converted slave *his bowels*. We must love, as God does, all saints.

(2) The apostle joins prayer with his praises, that the fruits of Philemon's faith and love might be more and more conspicuous, so that the communication of them might constrain others to the

acknowledgment of the all good things that were in him and in his house towards Christ Jesus.

4. He adds a reason, both of his prayer and his praises (*v.* 7): *For "we have great joy and consolation in thy love, because the bowels of the saints are refreshed by thee, brother."*

PAUL'S PLEA (*vv.* 8–25)

We have here,

I. The main business of the epistle, which was to plead with Philemon on behalf of Onesimus, that he would receive him and be reconciled to him. Many arguments Paul urges for this purpose, *vv.* 8–21. The

1st Argument is taken from what was before noted: "Seeing so much good is reported of thee and found in thee, especially thy love to all saints, now let me see it on a fresh and further occasion; *refresh the bowels of Onesimus and mine also*, in forgiving and receiving him, who is now a convert, and so a saint indeed, and meet for thy favour and love." The

2nd Argument is from the authority of him that was now making this request to him: *I might be very bold in Christ to enjoin thee that which is convenient, v.* 8. The apostles had under Christ great power in the church over the ordinary ministers, as well as the members of it, for edification; they might require of them what was fit, and were therein to be obeyed, which Philemon should consider. This was a matter within the compass of the apostle's power to require, though he would not in this

instance act up to it. Wherefore this may be a

3rd Argument, Waiving the authority which yet he had to require, he chooses to entreat it of him (*v.* 9): *Yet for love's sake I rather beseech thee.* And especially, which may be a

4th Argument, When any circumstance of the person pleading gives additional force to his petition, as here: *Being such a one as Paul the aged, and now also a prisoner of Jesus Christ.* The request of an aged apostle, and now suffering for Christ and his gospel, should be tenderly considered. He makes also a

5th Argument. From the spiritual relation now between Onesimus and himself: *I beseech thee for my son Onesimus, whom I have begotten in my bonds, v.* 10. Paul makes an argument to Philemon from this dear relation that now was between Onesimus and him, his son begotten in his bonds. And a

6th Argument is from Philemon's own interest: *Who in time past was to thee unprofitable, but now profitable to thee and to me, v.* 11. There seems an allusion to the name Onesimus, which signifies *profitable.* Now he will answer to his name. This then is the argument here urged: "It will now be for thy advantage to receive him: thus changed, as he is, thou mayest expect him to be a dutiful and faithful servant, though in time past he was not so." Whereupon,

7th Argument, He urges Philemon from the strong affection that he had to Onesimus. He had mentioned the spiritual relation before, *My son begotten in my bonds*; and now he signifies how dear he was to him: *Thou therefore receive him, that is my own bowels, v.* 12. And again, an

8*th Argument* is from the apostle's denying himself in sending back Onesimus: though he might have presumed upon Philemon's leave to detain him longer, yet he would not, *vv.* 13, 14. And he further urges,

9*th Argument,* That such a change was now wrought in Onesimus that Philemon needed not fear his ever running from him, or injuring him any more. And, besides interest, a

10*th Argument* is taken from the capacity under which Onesimus now would return, and must be received by Philemon (*v.* 16): "*Not now as a servant* (that is, not merely or so much), *but above a servant* (in a spiritual respect), *a brother beloved,* one to be owned as a brother in Christ, and to be beloved as such, upon account of this holy change that is wrought in him, and one therefore who will be useful unto thee upon better principles and in a better manner than before, who will love and promote the best things in thy family, be a blessing in it, and help to keep up the church that is in thy house." This argument is strengthened by another, the

11*th Argument,* From the communion of saints: *If thou count me therefore a partner, receive him as myself, v.* 17. There is a fellowship among saints; they have interest one in another, and must love and act accordingly. The answer to this makes a

12*th Argument,* A promise of satisfaction to Philemon: *If he hath*

wronged thee, or oweth thee aught, &c., vv.* 18, 19. Here are three things:

(1) A confession of Onesimus's debt to Philemon: *If he hath wronged thee, or oweth thee aught.* It is not an *if* of doubting, but of concession; *seeing he hath wronged thee,* and thereby has become indebted to thee; such as *if* as Col. iii. 1 and 2 Pet. ii. 4, &c. And,

(2) Paul here engages for satisfaction: *Put that on my account; I Paul have written it with my own hand, I will repay it.* It was much that Paul, who lived on contributions himself, would undertake to make good all loss by an evil servant to his master; but hereby he expresses his real and great affection for Onesimus, and his full belief of the sincerity of his conversion; and he might have hope that, notwithstanding this generous offer, Philemon would not insist on it, but freely remit all, considering,

(3) The reason of things between him and Philemon: "*Albeit, I do not say to thee how thou owest unto me even thy own self besides*; thou wilt remember, without my reminding thee, that thou art on other accounts more in debt to me than this comes to." Modesty in self-praises is true praise. Further, a

13*th Argument* is from the joy and comfort the apostle hereby would have on Philemon's own account, as well as on Onesimus's in such a seasonable and acceptable fruit of Philemon's faith and obedience: *Yea, brother, let me have joy of thee in the Lord: refresh my bowels in the Lord, v.* 20. And, once more, his last, which is the

14*th Argument,* Lies in the good

hope and opinion which he expresses of Philemon: *Having confidence in thy obedience, I wrote unto thee, knowing that thou wilt also do more than I say, v.* 21. Good thoughts and expectations of us more strongly move and engage us to do the things expected from us.

Thus far is the substance and body of the epistle. We have,

II. The conclusion, where,

1. He signifies his good hope of deliverance, through their prayers, and that shortly he might see them, desiring Philemon to make provision for him.

2. He sends salutations from one who was his fellow-prisoner, and four more who were his fellow-labourers, *vv.* 23, 24.

3. Here is the apostle's closing prayer and benediction, *v.* 25.

HEBREWS

CHAPTER ONE

SPOKEN THROUGH A SON
(*vv*. 1–3)

Here the apostle begins with a general declaration of the excellency of the gospel dispensation above that of the law. Observe,

I. The way wherein God communicated himself and his will to men under the Old Testament. We have here an account, 1. Of the persons by whom God delivered his mind under the Old Testament; they were *the prophets*. 2. The persons to whom God spoke by the prophets: *To the fathers*, to all the Old-Testament saints who were under that dispensation. 3. The order in which God spoke to men in those times that went before the gospel, those past times: he spoke to his ancient people *at sundry times and in divers manners*.

II. God's method of communicating his mind and will under the New-Testament dispensation. There was first the natural revelation; then the patriarchal, by dreams, visions, and voices; then the Mosaic, in the law given forth and written down; then the prophetic, in explaining the law, and giving clearer discoveries of Christ: but now we must expect no new revelation, but only more of the Spirit of Christ to help us better to understand what is already re-

vealed. Now the excellency of the gospel revelation above the former consists in two things:

1. It is the final, the finishing revelation, given forth in the last days of divine revelation, to which nothing is to be added, but the canon of scripture is to be settled and sealed.

2. It is a revelation which God has made by his Son, the most excellent messenger that was ever sent into the world. And here we have an excellent account of the glory of our Lord Jesus Christ.

(1) The glory of his office, and that in three respects: [1] God hath appointed him to be heir of all things. [2] By him God made the worlds, both visible and invisible, the heavens and the earth; not as an instrumental cause, but as his essential word and wisdom. [3] He upholds all things by the word of his power: he keeps the world from dissolving. *By him all things consist.*

(2) Hence the apostle passes to the glory of the person of Christ, who was able to execute such an office: *He was the brightness of his Father's glory, and the express image of his person, v.* 3. [1] He is, in person, the Son of God, the only-begotten Son of God, and as such he must have the same nature. [2] The person of the Son is the glory of the Father, shining forth

with a truly divine splendour. [3] The person of the Son is the true image and character of the person of the Father; being of the same nature, he must bear the same image and likeness.

(3) From the glory of the person of Christ he proceeds to mention the glory of his grace; his condescension itself was truly glorious. The sufferings of Christ had this great honour in them, to be a full satisfaction for the sins of his people: *By himself he purged away our sins.*

(4) From the glory of his sufferings we are at length led to consider the glory of his exaltation: *When by himself he had purged away our sins, he sat down at the right hand of the Majesty on high*, at his Father's right hand.

Now it was by no less a person than this that God in these last days spoke to men; and, since the dignity of the messenger gives authority and excellency to the message, the dispensations of the gospel must therefore exceed, very far exceed, the dispensation of the law.

BETTER THAN THE ANGELS
(*vv.* 4–14)

Here observe,

I. The superior nature of Christ is proved from his superior name. The scripture does not give high and glorious titles without a real foundation and reason in nature.

II. Here are several passages of scripture cited, in which those things are said of Christ that were never said of the angels.

1. It was said of Christ, *Thou art*

my Son, this day have I begotten thee (Ps. ii. 7), which may refer to his eternal generation, or to his resurrection, or to his solemn inauguration into his glorious kingdom at his ascension and session at the right hand of the Father. Now this was never said concerning the angels, and therefore by inheritance he has a more excellent nature and name than they.

2. It is said concerning Christ, but never concerning the angels, *I will be to him a Father, and he shall be to me a Son*; taken from 2 Sam. vii. 14.

3. It is said of Christ, *When God bringeth his First-begotten into the world, let all the angels of God worship him.* God will not suffer an angel to continue in heaven who will not be in subjection to Christ, and pay adoration to him.

4. God has said concerning Christ, *Thy throne, O God, is for ever and ever*, &c., *vv.* 8–12. But of the angels he has only said that *he hath made them spirits, and his ministers a flame of fire, v.* 7. Now, upon comparing what he here says of the angels with what he says to Christ, the vast inferiority of the angels to Christ will plainly appear.

(1) What does God say here of the angels? *He maketh his angels spirits, and his ministers a flame of fire.* This we have in Ps. civ. 4. But observe,

(2) How much greater things are said of Christ by the Father. Here two passages of scripture are quoted.

[1] One of these is out of Ps. xlv. 6, 7, where God declares of Christ, *First*, His true and real divinity, and that with much pleasure and

affection, not grudging him that glory: *Thy throne, O God. Secondly*, God declares his dignity and dominion, as having a throne, a kingdom, and a sceptre of that kingdom. *Thirdly*, God declares the eternal duration of the dominion and dignity of Christ, founded upon the divinity of his person: *Thy throne, O God, is for ever and ever. Fourthly*, God declares of Christ the perfect equity of his administration, and of the execution of his power, through all the parts of his government. *Fifthly*, God declares of Christ how he was qualified for the office of Mediator, and how he was installed and confirmed in it (*v.* 9): *Therefore God, even thy God, hath anointed thee with the oil of gladness above thy fellows.*

[2] The other passage of scripture in which is the superior excellence of Christ to the angels is taken out of Ps. cii. 25–27, and is recited in *vv.* 10–12, where the omnipotence of the Lord Jesus Christ, is declared as it appears both in creating the world and in changing it.

First, In creating the world (*v.* 10): *And thou, Lord, in the beginning hast laid the foundation of the earth, and the heavens are the work of thy hands.* The Lord Christ had the original right to govern the world, because he made the world in the beginning.

Secondly, In changing the world that he has made; and here the mutability of this world is brought in to illustrate the immutability of Christ. Christ is immutable and immortal: his years shall not fail. This may comfort us under all decays of nature that we may observe in ourselves or in our

friends, though our flesh and heart fail and our days are hastening to an end.

III. The superiority of Christ to the angels appears in this, that God never said to the angels what he has said to Christ, *vv*, 13, 14.

1. What has God said to Christ? He has said, "*Sit thou at my right hand, till I make thy enemies thy footstool*, Ps. cx. 1. Receive thou glory, dominion, and rest; and remain in the administration of thy mediatorial kingdom until all thy enemies shall either be made thy friends by conversion or thy footstool."

2. What has God said to the angels? He never said to them, as he said to Christ, *Sit you at my right hand*; but he has said of them here that *they are ministering spirits, sent forth to minister for those who shall be the heirs of salvation.* Angels are ministering spirits under the blessed Trinity, to execute the divine will and pleasure; they are the ministers of divine Providence.

CHAPTER TWO

DANGER OF NEGLECT

(*vv*. 1–4)

He now comes to apply this doctrine both by way of exhortation and argument.

I. By way of exhortation: *Therefor we ought to give the more diligent heed to the things which we have heard, v.* 1. This is the first way by which we are to show our esteem of Christ and of the gospel.

II. By way of argument, he adds strong motives to enforce the exhortation.

1. From the great loss we shall sustain if we do not take this earnest heed to the things which we have heard: *We shall let them slip.*

2. Another argument is taken from the dreadful punishment we shall incur if we do not do this duty, a more dreadful punishment than those fell under who neglected and disobeyed the law, *vv.* 2, 3. Here observe, (1) How the law is described: it was the *word spoken by angels, and declared to be stedfast.* It was the word spoken by angels, because given by the ministration of angels, they sounding the trumpet, and perhaps forming the words according to God's direction. (2) How the gospel is described. It is salvation, a great salvation; so great salvation that no other salvation can compare with it. (3) How sinning against the gospel is described: it is declared to be a *neglect of this great salvation*; it is a contempt put upon the saving grace of God in Christ, making light of it, not caring for it. Let us all take heed that we be not found among those wretched sinners who neglect the grace of the gospel. (4) How the misery of such sinners is described: it is declared to be unavoidable (*v.* 3): *How shall we escape?*

3. Another argument to enforce the exhortation is taken from the dignity and excellency of the person by whom the gospel began to be spoken (*v.* 3): *It began at first to be spoken by the Lord.* This great Lord of all was the first who began to speak it plainly and clearly, without types and shadows as it was before he came.

4. Another argument is taken from the character of those who were witnesses to Christ and the gospel (*vv.* 3, 4): *It was confirmed to us by those that heard him, God also bearing them witness.* It was the will of God that we should have sure footing for our faith, and a strong foundation for our hope in receiving the gospel. As at the giving forth of the law there were signs and wonders, by which God testified the authority and excellency of it, so he witnessed to the gospel by more and greater miracles, as to a more excellent and abiding dispensation.

THE SON OF MAN (*vv.* 5–9)

The apostle, having made this serious application of the doctrine of the personal excellency of Christ above the angels, now returns to that pleasant subject again, and pursues it further (*v.* 5): *For to the angels hath he not put in subjection the world to come, whereof we speak.*

I. Here the apostle lays down a negative proposition, including a positive one—That the state of the gospel-church, which is here called *the world to come*, is *not subjected to the angels*, but under the special care and direction of the Redeemer himself.

II. We have a scripture-account of that blessed Jesus to whom the gospel world is put into subjection. It is taken from Ps. viii. 4–6, *But one in a certain place testified, saying, What is man, that thou art mindful of him? or the Son of man, that thou visitest him?* &c. These words are to be considered both as applicable to mankind in general, and as applied here to the Lord Jesus Christ.

1. As applicable to mankind in general, (1) In remembering them, or being mindful of them, when yet they had no being but in the counsels of divine love. (2) In visiting them. God's purpose of favours for men is productive of gracious visits to them; he comes to see us, how it is with us, what we ail, what we want, what dangers we are exposed to, what difficulties we have to encounter; and by his visitation our spirit is preserved. (3) In making man the head of all the creatures in this lower world. (4) In crowning him with glory and honour, the honour of having noble powers and faculties of soul, whereby he is allied to both worlds, capable of serving the interests of both worlds, and of enjoying the happiness of both. (5) In giving him right to and dominion over the inferior creatures.

2. As applied to the Lord Jesus Christ, and the whole that is here said can be applied only to him, vv. 8, 9. God crowned the human nature of Christ with glory and honour, in his being perfectly holy, and having the Spirit without measure, and by union with the divine nature in the second person of the Trinity, the fulness of the Godhead dwelling in him bodily.

CAPTAIN OF SALVATION
(vv. 10–13)

Having mentioned the death of Christ, the apostle here proceeds to prevent and remove the scandal of the cross; and this he does by show-ing both how it became God that Christ should suffer and how much man should be benefited by those sufferings.

I. How it became God that Christ should suffer, v. 10. Here,

1. God is described as the final end and first cause of all things, and as such it became him to secure his own glory in all that he did.

2. He is declared to have acted up to this glorious character in the work of redemption, as to the choice both of the end and of the means.

(1) In the choice of the end; and that was to bring many sons to glory, to present glory in enjoying the glorious privileges of the gospel, and to future glory in heaven, which will be glory indeed, an exceeding eternal weight of glory.

(2) In the choice of the means. [1] In finding out such a person as should be the captain of our salvation; those that are saved must come to that salvation under the guidance of a captain and leader sufficient for that purpose. [2] In making this captain of our salvation perfect through sufferings. That is, he perfected the work of our redemption by shedding his blood, and was thereby perfectly qualified to be a Mediator between God and man. He found his way to the crown by the cross, and so must his people too.

II. He shows how much they would be benefited by the cross and sufferings of Christ. Hereby they are brought into a near union with Christ, and into a very endearing relation.

1. Into a near union (v. 11): *Both he that sanctifieth and those that are*

sanctified are all of one. How? Why,
(1) They are all of one heavenly
Father, and that is God. (2) They
are of one earthly father, Adam.
Christ and believers have the same
human nature. (3) Of one spirit,
one holy and heavenly disposition;
the same mind is in them that was
in Christ, though not in the same
measure; the same Spirit informs
and actuates the head and all the
members.

2. Into an endearing relation.
This results from the union.

(1) He declares what this relation
is: he and believers being all of one,
he therefore is not ashamed to call
them *brethren*.

(2) He illustrates this from three
texts of scripture.

[1] The first is out of Ps. xxii. 22.
Now here it is foretold, *First*, That
Christ should have a church or
congregation in the world, a company of volunteers, freely willing to
follow him. *Secondly*, That these
should not only be brethren to one
another, but to Christ himself.
Thirdly, That he would declare his
Father's name to them, that is, his
nature and attributes, his mind and
will. *Fourthly*, That Christ would
sing praise to his Father in the
church.

[2] The second scripture is
quoted from Ps. xviii. 2, *And again,
I will put my trust in him*. He suffered
and trusted as our head and president. His brethren must suffer and
trust too.

[3] The third scripture is taken
from Isa. viii. 18, *Behold, I and the
children which God hath given me*.
this proves Christ really and truly
man, for parents and children are
of the same nature.

A FAITHFUL HIGH PRIEST
(*vv.* 14–18)

Here the apostle proceeds to assert
the incarnation of Christ, as taking
upon him not the nature of angels,
but the seed of Abraham; and he
shows the reason and design of his
so doing.

I. The incarnation of Christ is
asserted (*v.* 16). Now Christ resolving to recover the seed of Abraham
and raise them up from their fallen
state, he took upon him the human
nature from one descended from
the loins of Abraham, that the same
nature that had sinned might suffer,
to restore human nature to a state
of hope and trial.

II. The reasons and designs of
the incarnation of Christ are
declared.

1. *Because the children were partakers of flesh and blood, he must
take part of the same, and be made
like his brethren*, *vv.* 14, 15. For no
higher nor lower nature than man's
that had sinned could so suffer for
the sin of man as to satisfy the
justice of God.

2. He became man that he might
die; as God he could not die, and
therefore he assumed another
nature and state.

3. That *through death he might
destroy him that had the power of
death, that is, the devil*, *v.* 14. Now
Christ has so far destroyed him who
had the power of death that he can
keep none under the power of
spiritual death; nor can he draw
any into sin, nor execute the sentence upon any but those who
choose and continue to be his willing
slaves, and persist in their enmity
to God.

4. That he might deliver his own people from the slavish fear of death to which they are often subject. Christ became man, and died, to deliver them from those perplexities of soul, by letting them know that death is not only a conquered enemy, but a reconciled friend, not sent to hurt the soul, or separate it from the love of God, but to put an end to all their grievances and complaints, and to give them a passage to eternal life and blessedness; so that to them death is not now in the hand of Satan, but in the hand of Christ.

5. Christ must be made like unto his brethren, that he might be a merciful and faithful high priest in things pertaining to the justice and honour of God and to the support and comfort of his people. He must be faithful to God and merciful to men. Christ is ready and willing to succour those who under their temptations apply to him; and he became man, and was tempted, that he might be every way qualified to succour his people.

CHAPTER THREE

A SON IN HIS HOUSE
(vv. 1–6)

In these verses we have the application of the doctrine laid down in the close of the last chapter concerning the priesthood of our Lord Jesus Christ. And observe,

I. In how fervent and affectionate a manner the apostle exhorts Christians to have this high priest much in their thoughts. That this exhortation might be made the more effectual, observe,

1. The honourable compellation used towards those to whom he wrote: *Holy brethren, partakers of the heavenly calling.*

2. The titles he gives to Christ, whom he would have them consider, (1) As the apostle of our profession, a messenger and a principal messenger sent of God to men, upon the most important errand. (2) Not only the apostle, but the high priest too, of our profession, upon whose satisfaction and intercession we profess to depend for pardon of sin, and acceptance with God. (3) As Christ, the Messiah, anointed and every way qualified for the office both of apostle and high priest.

II. We have the duty we owe to him who bears all these high and honourable titles, and that is to consider him as thus characterized. Consider what he is in himself, what he is to us, and what he will be to us hereafter and for ever.

III. We have several arguments drawn up to enforce this duty of considering Christ the apostle and high priest of our profession.

1. The first is taken from his fidelity, *v.* 2. He was faithful to him that appointed him, as Moses was in all his house.

2. Another argument is taken from the superior glory and excellence of Christ above Moses *(vv.* 3–6); therefore they were more obliged to consider Christ. (1) Christ was a maker of the house, Moses but a member in it. (2) Christ was the master of this house, as well as the maker, *vv.* 5, 6. This house is styled his house, as the Son of God.

We have here a direction what those must do who would partake of the dignity and privileges of the household of Christ. *First*, They must take the truths of the gospel into their heads and hearts. *Secondly*, They must build their hopes of happiness upon those truths. *Thirdly*, They must make an open profession of those truths. *Fourthly*, They must so live up to them as to keep their evidences clear, that they may rejoice in hope, and then they must in all persevere to the end.

HARDENED HEARTS
(*vv.* 7–19)

Here the apostle proceeds in pressing upon them serious counsels and cautions to the close of the chapter; and he recites a passage out of Ps. xcv. 7, &c. where observe,

I. What he counsels them to do— to give a speedy and present attention to the call of Christ.

II. What he cautions them against—hardening their hearts, turning the deaf ear to the calls and counsels of Christ.

III. Whose example he warns them by—that of the Israelites their fathers in the wilderness.

IV. What use the apostle makes of their awful example, *vv.* 12, 13, &c. He gives the Hebrews a proper caution, and enforces it with an affectionate compellation.

1. He gives the Hebrews a proper caution; the word is, *Take heed, look to it.*

2. He enforces the admonition with an affectionate compellation: *Take heed, brethren, lest there be in any of you an evil heart of unbelief in departing from the living God.*

Here observe, (1) A heart of unbelief is an evil heart. Unbelief is a great sin, it vitiates the heart of man. (2) An evil heart of unbelief is at the bottom of all our sinful departures from God.

3. He subjoins good counsel to the caution, and advises them to that which would be a remedy against this evil heart of unbelief— that they should *exhort one another daily, while it is called to-day, v.* 13.

4. He comforts those who not only set out well, but hold on well, and hold out to the end (*v.* 14).

5. The apostle resumes what he had quoted before from Ps. xcv. 7, &c., and he applies it closely to those of that generation, *vv.* 15, 16, &c. While it is said, *To-day if you will hear,* &c.; as if he should say, "What was recited before from that scripture belonged not only to former ages, but to you now, and to all who shall come after you; that you take heed you fall not into the same sins, lest you fall under the same condemnation."

6. The apostle puts some queries upon what had been before mentioned, and gives proper answers to them (*vv.* 17–19). Whence observe, (1) God is grieved only with those of his people who sin against him, and continue in sin. (2) God is grieved and provoked most by sins publicly committed by the generality of a nation. (3) Though God grieves long, and bears long, when pressed with the weight of general and prevailing wickedness, yet he will at length ease himself of public offenders by public judgments. (4) Unbelief (with rebellion which is the consequent of it) is the great damning sin of the world.

CHAPTER FOUR

THE PERFECT REST (*vv.* 1–10)

Here, I. The apostle declares that our privileges by Christ under the gospel are not only as great, but greater than those enjoyed under the Mosaic law. He specifies this, that we have a promise left us of entering into his rest; that is, of entering into a covenant-relation to Christ, and a state of communion with God through Christ, and of growing up therein, till we are made perfect in glory.

II. He demonstrates the truth of his assertion, that we have as great advantages as they. For says he (*v.* 2), *To us was the gospel preached as well as unto them.*

III. He again assigns the reason why so few of the ancient Jews profited by that dispensation of the gospel which they enjoyed, and that was their want of faith: *The word preached did not profit them because it was not mixed with faith in those that heard him, v.* 2.

IV. On these considerations the apostle grounds his repeated and earnest caution and counsel that those who enjoy the gospel should maintain a holy fear and jealousy over themselves, lest latent unbelief should rob them of the benefit of the word, and of that spiritual rest which is discovered and tendered in the gospel.

V. The apostle confirms the happiness of all those who truly believe the gospel; and this he does,

1. By asserting so positively the truth of it, from the experience of himself and others: "*We, who have believed, do enter into rest, v.* 3."

2. He illustrates and confirms it

that those who believe are thus happy, and do enter into rest. (1) From God's finishing his work of creation, and so entering into his rest (*vv.* 3, 4), appointing our first parents to rest the seventh day, to rest in God. (2) From God's continuing the observance of the sabbath, after the fall, and the revelation of a Redeemer. (3) From God's proposing Canaan as a typical rest for the Jews who believed: and as those who did believe, Caleb and Joshua, did actually enter into Canaan; so those who now believe shall enter into rest. (4) From the certainty of another rest besides that seventh day of rest instituted and observed both before and after the fall. For the Psalmist has spoken of another day and another rest, whence it is evident that there is a more spiritual and excellent sabbath remaining for the people of God than that into which Joshua led the Jews (*vv.* 6–9). Every true believer hath ceased from his own works of sin, from relying on his own works of righteousness, and from the burdensome works of the law, as God and Christ have ceased from their works of creation and redemption.

VI. The apostle confirms the misery of those who do not believe; they shall never enter into this spiritual rest, either of grace here or glory hereafter.

A COMPASSIONATE PRIEST
(*vv.* 11–16)

In this latter part of the chapter the apostle concludes, first, with a serious repeated exhortation, and then with proper and powerful motives.

I. Here we have a serious exhortation: *Let us labour therefore to enter into that rest*, v. 11.

II. Here we have proper and powerful motives to make the advice effectual, which are drawn,

1. From the dreadful example of those who have already perished by unbelief: *Lest any man fall after the same example of unbelief.*

2. From the great help and advantage we may have from the word of God to strengthen our faith, and excite our diligence, that we may obtain this rest: *The word of God is quick and powerful*, v. 12. Now of this word it is said, (1) That it is *quick*; it is very lively and active, in all its efforts, in seizing the conscience of the sinner, in cutting him to the heart, and in comforting him and binding up the wounds of the soul. (2) It is *powerful*. When God sets it home by his Spirit, it convinces powerfully, converts powerfully, and comforts powerfully. (3) It is *sharper than any two-edged sword*; it cuts both ways; it is *the sword of the Spirit*, Eph. vi. 17. It is the two-edged sword that cometh out of the mouth of Christ, Rev. i. 16. It is sharper than any two-edged sword, for it will enter where no other sword can, and make a more critical dissection. (4) It is *a discerner of the thoughts and intents of the heart*, even the most secret and remote thoughts and designs. It will uncover to men the variety of their thoughts and purposes. The word will turn the inside of a sinner out, and let him see all that is in his heart.

3. From the perfections of the Lord Jesus Christ, both of his person and office.

(1) His person, particularly his omniscience: *Neither is there any creature that is not manifest in his sight*, v. 13. We shall have to do with him as one who will determine our everlasting state. This omniscience of Christ, and the account we owe of ourselves to him, should engage us to persevere in faith and obedience till he has perfected all our affairs.

(2) We have an account of the excellency and perfection of Christ, as to his office, and this particular office of our high priest.

[1] What kind of high priest Christ is (*v.* 14): *Seeing we have such a high priest*; that is, *First*, A great high priest, much greater than Aaron, or any of the priests of his order. The greatness of our high priest is set forth, 1. By his having passed into the heavens. The high priest under the law, once a year, went out of the people's sight within the veil, into the holiest of all, where were the sacred signals of the presence of God; but Christ once for all has passed into the heavens, to take the government of all upon him. 2. The greatness of Christ is set forth by his name, *Jesus*—a physician and a Saviour, and one of a divine nature, the Son of God by eternal generation; and therefore having divine perfection, able to save to the uttermost all who come to God by him. *Secondly*, He is not only a great, but a gracious high priest, merciful, compassionate, and sympathizing with his people: *We have not a high priest who cannot be touched with the feeling of our infirmities*, v. 15. *Thirdly*, He is a sinless high priest: *He was in all things tempted as we*

are, yet without sin. He was tempted by Satan, but he came off without sin. He was holy, harmless, and undefiled; and such a high priest became us. Having thus told us what a one our high priest is, the apostle proceeds to show us,

[2] How we should demean ourselves towards him. *First,* Let us hold fast our profession of faith in him, *v.* 14. Let us never deny him, never be ashamed of him before men. *Secondly,* We should encourage ourselves, by the excellency of our high priest, to come boldly to the throne of grace, *v.* 16. The office of Christ, as being our high priest, and such a high priest, should be the ground of our confidence in all our approaches to the throne of grace. Had we not a Mediator, we could have no boldness in coming to God; for we are guilty and polluted creatures. We must either go in the hand of a Mediator or our hearts and hopes will fail us. We have boldness to enter into the holiest by the blood of Jesus.

CHAPTER FIVE
THE OBEDIENT SON (*vv.* 1–9)

We have here an account of the nature of the priestly office in general, though with an accommodation to the Lord Jesus Christ. We are told,

I. Of what kind of beings the high priest must be. He must be taken from among men; he must be a man, one of ourselves, bone of our bone, flesh of our flesh, and spirit of our spirits, a partaker of our nature, and a standard-bearer among ten thousand. This implies, 1. That man had sinned. 2. That God would not admit sinful man to come to him immediately and alone, without a high priest, who must be taken from among men. 3. That God was pleased to take one from among men, by whom they might approach God in hope, and he might receive them with honour. 4. That every one shall now be welcome to God that comes to him by this his priest.

II. For whom every high priest is ordained: *For men in things pertaining to God,* for the glory of God and the good of men, that he might come between God and man.

III. For what purpose every high priest was ordained: *That he might offer both gifts and sacrifices for sin.*

1. This intimates, (1) That all we bring to God must be free and not forced; it must be a gift; it must be given and not taken away again. (2) That all we bring to God must go through the high priest's hands, as the great agent between God and man.

2. That he might offer sacrifices for sin; that is, the offerings that were appointed to make atonement, that sin might be pardoned and sinners accepted. Thus Christ is constituted a high priest for both these ends.

IV. How this high priest must be qualified, *v.* 2.

1. He must be one that can have compassion on two sorts of persons: (1) *On the ignorant,* or those that are guilty of sins of ignorance. (2) *On those that are out of the way,* out of the way of truth, duty, and happiness; and he must be one who

406

has tenderness enough to lead them back from the by-paths of error, sin, and misery.

2. He must also be compassed with infirmity; and so be able from himself feelingly to consider our frame, and to sympathize with us. Thus Christ was qualified.

V. How the high priest was to be called of God. He must have both an internal and external call to his office: *For no man taketh this honour to himself* (v. 4), that is, no man ought to do it, no man can do it legally; if any does it, he must be reckoned a usurper, and treated accordingly.

VI. How this is brought home and applied to Christ: *So Christ glorified not himself*, v. 5.

VII. The apostle prefers Christ before Aaron, both in the manner of his call and in the holiness of his person. 1. In the manner of his call, in which God said unto him, *Thou art my Son, this day have I begotten thee* (quoted from Ps. ii. 7), referring to his eternal generation as God. Now God never said thus to Aaron. Another expression that God used in the call of Christ we have in Ps. cx. 4, *Thou art a priest for ever, after the order of Melchisedec*, v. 6. God the Father appointed him a priest of a higher order than that of Aaron. The priesthood of Aaron was to be but temporary; the priesthood of Christ was to be perpetual: the priesthood of Aaron was to be successive, descending from the fathers to the children; the priesthood of Christ, after the order of Melchisedec, was to be personal, and the high priest immortal as to his office, without descent, having neither beginning

of days nor end of life, as it is more largely described in the seventh chapter, and will be opened there. 2. Christ is here preferred to Aaron in the holiness of his person. Other priests were to offer up sacrifices, as for the *sins of others, so for themselves*, v. 3. But Christ needed not to offer for sins for himself, *for he had done no violence*, neither was there *any deceit in his mouth*, Isa. liii. 9. And such a high priest became us.

VIII. We have an account of Christ's discharge of this his office, and of the consequences of that discharge, vv. 7–9.

1. The discharge of his office of the priesthood (v. 7): *Who in the days of his flesh, when he had offered up prayers and supplications*, &c.

2. The consequences of this discharge of his office, vv. 8, 9, &c.

(1) By these his sufferings *he learned obedience, though he was a Son*, v. 8. Here observe, [1] The privilege of Christ: *He was a Son*; the only-begotten of the Father. [2] Christ made improvement by his sufferings. By his passive obedience, he learned active obedience; that is, he practised that great lesson, and made it appear that he was well and perfectly learned in it. We need affliction, to teach us submission.

(2) By these his sufferings he was made perfect, and became the author of eternal salvation to all who obey him, v. 9. To those who obey him, devoting themselves to him, denying themselves, and taking up their cross, and following him, he will be the author, the grand cause of their salvation, and they shall own him as such for ever.

TRUE TEACHING (*vv.* 10-14)

Here the apostle returns to what he had in *v.* 6 cited out of Ps. cx., concerning the peculiar order of the priesthood of Christ, that is, the order of Melchisedec. And here,

I. He declares he had many things which he could say to them concerning this mysterious person called Melchisedec, whose priesthood was eternal, and therefore the salvation procured thereby should be eternal also. We have a more particular account of this Melchisedec in *ch.* vii.

II. He assigns the reason why he did not say all those things concerning Christ, our Melchisedec, that he had to say, and what it was that made it so difficult for him to utter them, namely, the dullness of the Hebrews to whom he wrote: *You are dull of hearing.* Dull hearers make the preaching of the gospel a difficult thing.

III. He insists upon the faultiness of this infirmity of theirs. It was not a mere natural infirmity, but it was a sinful infirmity, and more in them than others, by reason of the singular advantages they had enjoyed for improving in the knowledge of Christ.

IV. The apostle shows how the various doctrines of the gospel must be dispensed to different persons. There are in the church babes and persons of full age (*vv.* 12-14), and there are in the gospel milk and strong meat. The deeper mysteries of religion belong to those that are of a higher class in the school of Christ, who have learned the first principles and well improved them.

CHAPTER SIX
FIRST PRINCIPLES (*vv.* 1-8)

We have here the apostle's advice to the Hebrews—that they would grow up from a state of childhood to the fulness of the stature of the new man in Christ.

I. The apostle mentions several foundation-principles, which must be well laid at first, and then built upon; neither his time nor theirs must be spent in laying these foundations over and over again. These foundations are six:

1. Repentance from dead works, that is, conversion and regeneration, repentance from a spiritually dead state and course.

2. Faith towards God, a firm belief of the existence of God, of his nature, attributes, and perfections, the trinity of persons in the unity of essence, the whole mind and will of God as revealed in his word, particularly what relates to the Lord Jesus Christ.

3. The doctrine of baptisms, that is, of being baptized by a minister of Christ with water, in the name of the Father, and of the Son, and of the Holy Ghost, as the initiating sign or seal of the covenant of grace. And the doctrine of an inward baptism, that of the Spirit sprinkling the blood of Christ upon the soul, for justification, and the graces of the Spirit for sanctification.

4. Laying on of hands, on persons passing solemnly from their initiated state by baptism to the confirmed state, by returning the answer of a good conscience towards God, and sitting down at the Lord's table. Or by this may be

meant ordination of persons to the ministerial office.

5. The resurrection of the dead, that is, of dead bodies; and their re-union with their souls.

6. Eternal judgment, determining the soul of every one, when it leaves the body at death, and both soul and body at the last day, to their eternal state.

II. The apostle declares his readiness and resolution to assist the Hebrews in building themselves up on these foundations till they arrive at perfection: *And this we will do, if God permit*, v. 3.

III. He shows that this spiritual growth is the surest way to prevent that dreadful sin of apostasy from the faith. And here,

1. He shows how far persons may go in religion, and, after all, fall away, and perish for ever, vv. 4, 5. (1) They may be *enlightened*. Some of the ancients understand this of their being baptized; but it is rather to be understood of notional knowledge and common illumination, of which persons may have a great deal, and yet come short of heaven. (2) They may *taste of the heavenly gift*, feel something of the efficacy of the Holy Spirit in his operations upon their souls. (3) They may be *made partakers of the Holy Ghost*, that is, of his extraordinary and miraculous gifts. (4) They may *taste of the good word of God*; they may have some relish of gospel doctrines. (5) They may have *tasted of the powers of the world to come*; they may have been under strong impressions concerning heaven and hell. Now hence observe, [1] These great things are spoken here of those who may fall way; yet it is

not here said of them that they were truly converted, or that they were justified; there is more in true saving grace than in all that is here said of apostates. [2] This therefore is no proof of the final apostasy of true saints. These indeed may fall frequently and foully, but yet they will not totally nor finally from God.

2. The apostle describes the dreadful case of such as fall away after having gone so far in the profession of religion. (1) The greatness of the sin of apostasy. It is *crucifying the Son of God afresh, and putting him to open shame*. They do what in them lies to represent Christ and Christianity as a shameful thing, and would have him to be a public shame and reproach. This is the nature of apostasy. (2) The great misery of apostates. [1] It is impossible to renew them again unto repentance. God can renew them to repentance, but he seldom does it; and with men themselves it is impossible. [2] Their misery is exemplified by a proper similitude, taken from the ground that after much cultivation brings forth nothing but briers and thorns.

I. He freely and openly declares the good hope he had concerning them, that they would endure to the end: *But beloved, we are persuaded better things of you*, v. 9.

II. He proposes arguments and encouragements to them to go on in the way of their duty. 1. That God had wrought a principle of holy love and charity in them, which had discovered itself in suitable works that would not be forgotten of God: *God is not unrighteous to forget your labour of love*, v. 10. 2. Those who expect a gracious reward for the labour of love must continue in it as long as they have ability and opportunity. 3. Those who persevere in a diligent discharge of their duty shall attain to the full assurance of hope in the end.

III. He proceeds to set before them caution and counsel how to attain this full assurance of hope to the end. 1. That they should not be slothful. 2. That they would follow the good examples of those who had gone before, *v.* 12.

IV. The apostle closes the chapter with a clear and full account of the assured truth of the promises of God, *v.* 13, *to the end.* They are all confirmed by the oath of God, and they are all founded in the eternal counsel of God, and therefore may be depended upon.

1. They are all confirmed by the oath of God. Now, if God would condescend to take an oath to his people, he will surely remember the nature and design of it.

2. The promises of God are all founded in his eternal counsel; and this counsel of his is an immutable counsel.

3. The promises of God, which are founded upon these immutable counsels of God, and confirmed by the oath of God, may safely be depended upon; for here we have two immutable things, the counsel and the oath of God, in which it is impossible for God to lie, contrary to his nature as well as to his will. Gospel hope is our anchor (*v.* 19). It is sure and stedfast, or else it could not keep us so. *First,* It is sure in its own nature; for it is the special work of God in the soul. *Secondly,* It is stedfast as to its object; it is an anchor that has taken good hold, it enters that which is within the veil; it is an anchor that is cast upon the rock, the Rock of ages.

CHAPTER SEVEN

MELCHISEDEC, THE PRIEST
(*vv.* 1–10)

The foregoing chapter ended with a repetition of what had been cited once and again before out of Ps. cx. 4, *Jesus, a high priest for ever, after the order of Melchisedec.*

I. The great question that first offers itself is, Who was this Melchisedec? All the account we have of him in the Old Testament is in Gen. xiv. 18, &c., and in Ps. cx. 4. Indeed we are much in the dark about him; God has thought fit to leave us so, that this Melchisedec might be a more lively type of him whose generation none can declare.

1. Many Christian writers have thought him to be Jesus Christ himself, appearing by a special dispensation and privilege to Abraham in the flesh, and who was known to Abraham by the name *Melchisedec,* which agrees very well to Christ, and to what is said, John viii. 56, *Abraham saw* his *day and rejoiced.* Much may be said for this opinion, and what is said in *v.* 3 does not seem to agree with any mere man; but then it seems strange to make Christ a type of himself. The most general opinion is that he was a Canaanite king, who reigned in Salem, and kept up religion and the worship of the true God; that he was raised to be a type of Christ, and was honoured by Abraham as such.

2. But we shall leave these conjectures, and labour to understand, as far as we can, what is here said of him by the apostle, and how Christ is represented thereby, *vv.* 1–3. (1) Melchisedec was a king, and so is the Lord Jesus—a king of God's anointing. (2) That he was *king of righteousness*: his name signifies *the righteous king*. Jesus Christ is a rightful and a righteous king—rightful in his title, righteous in his government. (3) He was king of Salem, that is, king of peace; first king of righteousness, and after that king of peace. So is our Lord Jesus. (4) He was *priest of the most high God*, qualified and anointed in an extraordinary manner to be his priest among the Gentiles. So is the Lord Jesus. (5) He was *without father, without mother, without descent, having neither beginning of days nor end of life, v.* 3. This must not be understood according to the letter. His priesthood is without descent, did not descend to him from another, nor from him to another, but is personal and perpetual. (6) That he *met Abraham returning from the slaughter of the kings, and blessed him.* The incident is recorded Gen. xiv. 18, &c. He brought forth bread and wine to refresh Abraham and his servants when they were weary; he gave as a king, and blessed as a priest. Thus our Lord Jesus meets his people in their spiritual conflicts, refreshes them, renews their strength, and blesses them. (7) That *Abraham gave him a tenth part of all* (*v.* 2), that is, as the apostle explains it, of all *the spoils.* And thus are we obliged to make all possible returns of love and gratitude to the

Lord Jesus for all the rich and royal favours we receive from him. (8) That this Melchisedec was *made like unto the Son of God, and abideth a priest continually.* He bore the image of God in his piety and authority, and stands upon record as an immortal high priest; the ancient type of him who is the eternal and only-begotten of the Father, who abideth a priest for ever.

II. Let us now consider (as the apostle advises) how great this Melchisedec was, and how far his priesthood was above that of the order of Aaron (*vv.* 4, 5, &c.): *Now consider how great this man was,* &c. The greatness of this man and his priesthood appears, 1. From Abraham's paying the tenth of the spoils unto him. 2. From Melchisedec's blessing of Abraham, *who had the promises; and, without contradiction, the less is blessed of the greater, vv.* 6, 7. (2) Melchisedec's greater honour—in that it was his place and privilege to bless Abraham; and it is an incontested maxim *that the less is blessed of the greater, v.* 7. He who gives the blessing is greater than he who receives it.

A GREATER PRIEST
(*vv.* 11–28)

Here,

I. It is asserted that perfection could not come by the Levitical priesthood and the law.

II. That therefore another priest must be raised up, after the order of Melchisedec, by whom, and his law of faith, perfection might come to all who obey him.

III. It is asserted that the priesthood being changed there must of necessity be a change of the law; there being so near a relation between the priesthood and the law, the dispensation could not be the same under another priesthood; a new priesthood must be under a new regulation, managed in another way, and by rules proper to its nature and order.

IV. It is not only asserted, but proved, that the priesthood and law are changed, *vv.* 13, 14. The priesthood and law by which perfection could not come are abolished, and a priest has arisen, and a dispensation is now set up, by which true believers may be made perfect (*vv.* 15–21). Observe the description we have of the personal holiness of Christ expressed in various terms, all of which some learned divines consider as relating to his perfect purity. [1] He is holy, perfectly free from all the habits or principles of sin, not having the least disposition to it in his nature; no sin dwells in him, though it does in the best of Christians, not the least sinful inclination. [2] He is harmless, perfectly free from all actual transgression, has done no violence, nor is there any deceit in his mouth, never did the least wrong to God or man. [3] He is undefiled, he was never accessory to other men's sins. [4] He is separate from sinners, not only in his present state, but in his personal purity. Christ was, by his ineffable conception in the virgin, separate from sinners; though he took a true human nature, yet the miraculous way in which it was conceived set him upon a separate footing from

all the rest of mankind. [5] He is made higher than the heavens. Most expositors understand this concerning his state of exaltation in heaven, at the right hand of God, to perfect the design of his priesthood. But Dr. Goodwin thinks this may be very justly referred to the personal holiness of Christ, which is greater and more perfect than the holiness of the hosts of heaven.

CHAPTER EIGHT

CHRIST'S PRIESTHOOD
(*vv.* 1–5)

Here is, I. A summary recital of what had been said before concerning the excellency of Christ's priesthood, showing what we have in Christ, where he now resides, and what sanctuary he is the minister of, *vv.* 1, 2.

II. The apostle sets before the Hebrews the necessary parts of Christ's priesthood, or what it was that belonged to that office, in conformity to what every high priest is ordained to, *vv*, 3, 4. 1. *Every high priest is ordained to offer gifts and sacrifices.* It necessarily belongs to the priesthood of Christ that he should have somewhat to offer; and he, as the antitype, had himself to offer, his human nature upon the altar of his divine nature, as the great atoning sacrifice that finished transgression, and made an end of sin once for all. 2. Christ must now execute his priesthood in heaven, in the holy of holies, the true tabernacle which the Lord hath fixed. For, (1) *If Christ were on earth, he would not be a priest* (*v.* 4), that is, not according to the Levitical law, as not being of the

line of that priesthood; and so long
as that priesthood continued there
must be a strict regard paid to the
divine institution in every thing.
(2) All the services of the priest,
under the law, as well as every
thing in that tabernacle which was
framed according to the pattern in
the mount, were only exemplars
and shadows of heavenly things,
v. 5.

THE NEW COVENANT
(*vv.* 6–13)

Now observe,

I. What is here said of the old
covenant, or rather of the old dispensation of the covenant of grace:
of this it is said, 1. That it was made
with the fathers of the Jewish
nation at mount Sinai (*v.* 9), and
Moses was the Mediator of that
covenant. 2. That this covenant
was not found faultless (*vv.* 7, 8); it
was a dispensation of darkness and
dread, tending to bondage, and only
a schoolmaster to bring us to
Christ; it was perfect in its kind,
and fitted to answer its end, but
very imperfect in comparison of the
gospel. 3. That it was not sure or
stedfast; *for the Jews continued not
in that covenant, and the Lord
regarded them not, v.* 9. God will
regard those who remain in his
covenant, but will reject those who
cast away his yoke from them.
4. That it is decayed, grown old,
and vanisheth away, *v.* 13.

II. What is here said of the New-
Testament dispensation, to prove
the superior excellency of Christ's
ministry. It is said,
1. That it is a better covenant
(*v.* 6), without fault, well ordered in

all things. It requires nothing but
what it promises grace to perform.
2. That it is established upon
better promises, more clear and
express, more spiritual, more absolute.
3. It is a new covenant, even that
new covenant that God long ago
declared he would make with the
house of Israel, that is, all the
Israel of God; this was promised in
Jer. xxxi. 31, 32, and accomplished
in Christ.
4. Here,
(1) God articles with his people
*that he will put his laws into their
minds and write them in their
hearts, v.* 10. He once wrote his
laws to them, now he will write his
laws in them.
(2) He articles with them to take
them into a near and very honourable relation to himself.
(3) He articles with them that
they shall grow more acquainted
with their God (*v.* 11): *They shall
all know me from the least to the
greatest,* insomuch that there shall
not be so much need of one neighbour teaching another the knowledge of God.
(4) God articles with them about
the pardon of their sins, as what
always accompanies the true knowledge of God (*v.* 12): *For I will be
merciful to their unrighteousness,*
&c.

CHAPTER NINE
THE TABERNACLE (*vv.* 1–7)

Here, I. The apostle gives an account of the tabernacle, that place
of worship which God appointed to
be pitched on earth.
II. From the description of the

place of worship in the Old-Testament dispensation, the apostle proceeds to speak of the duties and services performed in those places, *v.* 6. When the several parts and furniture of the tabernacle were thus settled, then what was to be done there?

1. The ordinary priests went always into the first tabernacle, to accomplish the service of God.

2. Into the second, the interior part, went the high priest alone, *v.* 7. This part was an emblem of heaven, and Christ's ascension thither.

A GREATER TABERNACLE
(*vv.* 8–14)

Now here are several things mentioned as the things that the Holy Ghost signified and certified to his people in the tabernacle.

I. That the way into the holiest of all was not yet made manifest, while the first tabernacle was standing, *v.* 8.

II. That the first tabernacle was only a figure for the time then present, *v.* 9.

III. That none of the gifts and sacrifices there offered could make the offerers perfect as pertaining to conscience (*v.* 9). He could not be saved by them from sin or hell, as all those are who believe in Christ.

IV. The Holy Ghost hereby signifies that the Old-Testament institutions were but external carnal ordinances imposed upon them until the time of reformation, *v.* 10.

V. The Holy Ghost signifies to us hereby that we never make the right use of types but when we apply them to the antitype. For,

1. *Christ is a high priest of good things to come*, by which may be understood, (1) All the good things that were to come during the Old Testament, and now have come under the New. (2) All the good things yet to come and to be enjoyed in a gospel state, when the promises and prophecies made to the gospel church in the latter days shall be accomplished. (3) Of all the good things to come in the heavenly state, which will perfect both the Testaments.

2. Christ is a high priest *by a greater and more perfect tabernacle* (*v.* 11), *a tabernacle not made with hands, that is to say, not of this building*, but his own body, or rather human nature, conceived by the Holy Ghost overshadowing the blessed virgin. This was a new fabric, a new order of building, infinitely superior to all earthly structures, not excepting the tabernacle of the temple itself.

3. Christ, our high priest, has entered into heaven, not as their high priest entered into the holiest, with the blood of bulls and of goats, but by his own blood, typified by theirs, and infinitely more precious. And this,

4. Not for one year only, which showed the imperfection of that priesthood, that it did but typically obtain a year's reprieve or pardon. But our high priest entered into heaven *once for all*, and has obtained not a yearly respite, but eternal redemption.

5. The Holy Ghost further signified and showed what was the efficacy of the blood of the Old-Testament sacrifices, and thence is inferred the much greater efficacy

of the blood of Christ. (1) The efficacy of the blood of the legal sacrifices extended to the purifying of the flesh (*v.* 13): it freed the outward man from ceremonial uncleanness and from temporal punishment. (2) He infers very justly hence the far greater efficacy of the blood of Christ (*v.* 14): *How much more shall the blood of Christ*, &c. For, *First*, It is sufficient to purge the conscience from dead works, it reaches to the very soul and conscience, the defiled soul, defiled with sin, which is a dead work, proceeds from spiritual death, and tends to death eternal. *Secondly*, It is sufficient to enable us to serve the living God, not only by purging away that guilt which separates between God and sinners, but by sanctifying and renewing the soul through the gracious influences of the Holy Spirit, purchased by Christ for this purpose, that we might be enabled to serve the living God in a lively manner.

PURGED WITH BLOOD
(*vv.* 15–22)

In these verses the apostle considers the gospel under the notion of a will or testament, the new or last will and testament of Christ, and shows the necessity and efficacy of the blood of Christ to make this testament valid and effectual.

I. The gospel is here considered as a testament, the new and last will and testament of our Lord and Saviour Jesus Christ. It is observable that the solemn transactions that pass between God and man are sometimes called a covenant, here a testament. A testament is a voluntary act and deed of a single person, duly executed and witnessed, bestowing legacies on such legatees as are described and characterized by the testator, and which can only take effect upon his death.

II. To make this New Testament effectual, it was necessary that Christ should die; the legacies accrue by means of death. The method taken by Moses, according to the direction he had received from God, is here particularly related. (1) Moses spoke every precept to all the people, according to the law, *v.* 19. He published to them the tenour of the covenant, the duties required, the rewards promised to those who did their duty, and the punishment threatened against the transgressors, and he called for their consent to the terms of the covenant; and this in an express manner. (2) Then he took the blood of calves and of goats, with water, and scarlet wool, and hyssop, and applied this blood by sprinkling it. Now with these Moses sprinkled, [1] The book of the law and covenant, to show that the covenant of grace is confirmed by the blood of Christ and made effectual to our good. [2] The people, intimating that the shedding of the blood of Christ will be no advantage to us if it be not applied to us. [3] He sprinkled the tabernacle and all the utensils of it, intimating that all the sacrifices offered up and services performed there were accepted only through the blood of Christ, which procures the remission of that iniquity that cleaves to our holy things, which could not have been remitted but by that atoning blood.

415

ONE SACRIFICE FOR EVER
(*vv.* 23–28)

In this last part of the chapter, the apostle goes on to tell us what the Holy Ghost has signified to us by the legal purifications of the patterns of the things in heaven, inferring thence the necessity of better sacrifices to consecrate the heavenly things themselves.

I. The necessity of purifying the patterns of the things in heaven, *v.* 23.

II. The necessity that the heavenly things themselves should be purified with better sacrifices than of bulls and goats. Now it is very evident that the sacrifice of Christ is infinitely better than those of the law, 1. From the places in which the sacrifices under the law, and that under the gospel, were offered. Christ's sacrifice, though offered upon earth, was by himself carried up into heaven, and is there presented in a way of daily intercession; for he appears in the presence of God for us. 2. From the sacrifices themselves, *v.* 26. Those under the law were the lives and blood of other creatures of a different nature from the offerers; but the sacrifice of Christ was the oblation of himself; he offered his own blood, truly called, by virtue of the hypostatical union, *the blood of God*; and therefore of infinite value. 3. From the frequent repetition of the legal sacrifices. This showed the imperfection of that law. It is the honour and perfection of Christ's sacrifice that, being once offered, it was sufficient to all the ends of it. 4. From the inefficacy of the legal sacrifices, and the efficacy of Christ's sacrifice.

III. The apostle illustrates the argument from the appointment of God concerning men (*vv.* 27, 28), and observes something like it in the appointment of God concerning Christ.

1. The appointment of God concerning men contains in it two things: (1) That they must once die, or, at least, undergo a change equivalent to death. (2) It is appointed to men that after death they shall come to judgment, to a particular judgment immediately after death.

2. The appointment of God concerning Christ, bearing some resemblance to the other. (1) He must be once offered, to bear the sins of many, of all the Father had given to him, of all who should believe in his name. (2) It is appointed that Christ shall appear the second time without sin, to the salvation of those who look for him.

INEFFECTIVE SACRIFICES
(*vv.* 1–6)

Here the apostle, by the direction of the Spirit of God, sets himself to lay low the Levitical dispensation. As,

I. That the law had a shadow, and but a shadow, of good things to come; and who would dote upon a shadow, though of good things, especially when the substance has come?

II. That the law was not the very image of the good things to come. The law did not go so far, but was only a shadow. The law was a very rough draught of the great design of divine grace, and therefore not to be so much doted on.

III. The legal sacrifices, being offered year by year, could never make the comers thereunto perfect; for then there would have been an end of offering them, *vv.* 1, 2.

IV. As the legal sacrifices did not of themselves take away sin, so it was impossible they should, *v.* 4. There was an essential defect in them. 1. They were not of the same nature with us who sinned. 2. They were not of sufficient value to make satisfaction for the affronts offered to the justice and government of God. 3. The beasts offered up under the law could not consent to put themselves in the sinner's room and place. The atoning sacrifice must be one capable of consenting, and must voluntarily substitute himself in the sinner's stead: Christ did so.

V. There was a time fixed and foretold by the great God, and that time had now come, when these legal sacrifices would be no longer accepted by him nor useful to men.

THE OFFERING OF CHRIST
(*vv.* 7–18)

Here the apostle raises up and exalts the Lord Jesus Christ, as high as he had laid the Levitical priesthood low. He recommends Christ to them as the true high priest, the true atoning sacrifice, the antitype of the rest: and this he illustrates,

I. From the purpose and promise of God concerning Christ, which are frequently recorded in the volume of the book of God, *v.* 7.

II. From what God had done in preparing a body for Christ (that is, a human nature), that he might be qualified to be our Redeemer and Advocate.

III. From the readiness and willingness that Christ discovered to engage in this work, when no other sacrifice would be accepted, *vv.* 7–9.

IV. From the errand and design upon which Christ came; and this was to do the will of God, not only as a prophet to reveal the will of God, not only as a king to give forth divine laws, but as a priest to satisfy the demands of justice, and to fulfil all righteousness.

V. From the perfect efficacy of the priesthood of Christ (*v.* 14): *By one offering he hath for ever perfected those that are sanctified*; he has delivered and will perfectly deliver those that are brought over to him, from all the guilt, power, and punishment of sin, and will put them into the sure possession of perfect holiness and felicity.

VI. From the place to which our Lord Jesus is now exalted, the honour he has there, and the further honour he shall have: *This man, after he had offered one sacrifice for sins, for ever sat down at the right hand of God, henceforth expecting till his enemies be made his footstool, vv.* 12, 13. The Father acquiesces and is satisfied in him; he is satisfied in his Father's will and presence; this is his rest for ever; here he will dwell, for he has both desired and deserved it.

VII. The apostle recommends Christ from the witness the Holy Ghost has given in the scriptures concerning him; this relates chiefly to what should be the happy fruit and consequence of his humiliation and sufferings, which in general is that new and gracious covenant that is founded upon his satisfaction, and sealed by his blood (*v.* 15).

THE CONSECRATED WAY
(*vv.* 19–39)

I. Here the apostle sets forth the dignities of the gospel state. The privileges are, 1. Boldness to enter into the holiest. 2. A high priest over the house of God, even this blessed Jesus, who presides over the church militant, and every member thereof on earth, and over the church triumphant in heaven.

II. The apostle tells us the way and means by which Christians enjoy such privileges, and, in general, declares it to be *by the blood of Jesus*, by the merit of that blood which he offered up to God as an atoning sacrifice. Now the apostle, having given this general account of the way by which we have access to God, enters further into the particulars of it, *v.* 20. As, 1. It is the only way; there is no way left but this. 2. It is a new way, both in opposition to the covenant of works and to the antiquated dispensation of the Old Testament; *the last way* that will ever be opened to men. 3. It is a living way. It would be death to attempt to come to God in the way of the covenant of works; but this way we may come to God, and live. 4. It is a way that Christ has consecrated for us through the veil, that is, his flesh. Our way to heaven is by a crucified Saviour; his death is to us the way of life. To those who believe this he will be precious.

III. He proceeds to show the Hebrews the duties binding upon them on account of these privi-

leges, which were conferred in such an extraordinary way, *vv.* 22, 23, &c.

1. They must draw near to God, and that in a right manner. (1) With a true heart, without any allowed guile or hypocrisy. (2) In full assurance of faith, with a faith grown up to a full persuasion that when we come to God by Christ we shall have audience and acceptance. And, (3) Having our hearts sprinkled from an evil conscience, by a believing application of the blood of Christ to our souls. (4) Our bodies washed with pure water, that is, with the water of baptism, or with the sanctifying virtue of the Holy Spirit.

2. The apostle exhorts believers to hold fast the profession of their faith, *v.* 23. The motive or reason enforcing this duty: *He is faithful that hath promised*. God has made great and precious promises to believers, and he is a faithful God, true to his word; there is no falseness nor fickleness with him, and there should be none with us.

IV. We have the means prescribed for preventing our apostasy, and promoting our fidelity and perseverance, *vv.* 24, 25. &c. He mentions several; as, 1. That we should *consider one another, to provoke to love and to good works*. Christians ought to have a tender consideration and concern for one another. 2. *Not to forsake the assembling of ourselves together*, *v.* 25. It is the will of Christ that his disciples should assemble together, sometimes more privately for conference and prayer, and in public for hearing and joining in all the ordinances of gospel worship. There were in the apostles' times, and should be in every age, Christian assemblies for the worship of God, and for mutual edification. 3. To exhort one another, to exhort ourselves and each other, to warn ourselves and one another of the sin and danger of backsliding, to put ourselves and our fellow-christians in mind of our duty, of our failures and corruptions, to watch over one another, and be jealous of ourselves and one another with a godly jealousy. 4. That we should observe the approaching of times of trial, and be thereby quickened to greater diligence: *So much the more, as you see the day approaching.*

V. Having mentioned these means of establishment, the apostle proceeds, in the close of the chapter, to enforce his exhortations to perseverance, and against apostasy, by many very weighty considerations, *vv.* 26, 27, &c.

1. From the description he gives of the sin of apostasy. It is *sinning wilfully after we have received the knowledge of the truth,* sinning wilfully against that truth of which we have had convincing evidence. It is total apostasy.

2. From the dreadful doom of such apostates. (1) There remains no more sacrifice for such sins, no other Christ to come to save such sinners; they sin against the last resort and remedy. (2) There remains for them only a certain fearful looking for of judgment, *v.* 27.

3. From the methods of divine justice with those who despised Moses's law, that is, sinned presumptuously, despising his authority, his threatenings and his power.

Here he refers to their own consciences, to judge how much sorer punishment the despisers of Christ (after they have professed to know him) are likely to undergo; and they may judge of the greatness of the punishment by the greatness of the sin. How dreadful is the case when not only the justice of God, but his abused grace and mercy call for vengeance!

4. From the description we have in the scripture of the nature of God's vindictive justice, *v.* 30. Vindictive justice is a glorious, though terrible attribute of God; it belongs to him, and he will use and execute it upon the heads of such sinners as despise his grace; he will avenge himself, and his Son, and Spirit, and covenant, upon apostates. And how dreadful then will their case be!

5. He presses them to perseverance by putting them in mind of their former sufferings for Christ: *But call to mind the former days, in which, after you were illuminated, you endured a great fight of afflictions, v.* 32. In the early days of the gospel there was a very hot persecution raised up against the professors of the Christian religion, and the believing Hebrews had their share of it.

What was it that enabled them to bear up under their sufferings? They knew in themselves that they had in heaven a better and a more enduring substance.

6. He presses them to persevere, from that recompence of reward that waited for all faithful Christians (*v.* 35): *Cast not away therefore your confidence, which hath great recompence of reward.* Observe, The

greatest part of the saints' happiness is in promise. They must first do the will of God before they receive the promise; and, after they have done the will of God, they have need of patience to wait for the time when the promise shall be fulfilled; they have need of patience to live till God calls them away. The Christian's present conflict may be sharp, but it will be soon over.

7. He presses them to perseverance, by telling them that this is their distinguishing character and will be their happiness; whereas apostasy is the reproach, and will be the ruin, of all who are guilty of it (*vv*. 38, 39): *Now the just shall live by faith*, &c. The apostle concludes with declaring his good hope concerning himself and these Hebrews, that they should not forfeit the character and happiness of the just, and fall under the brand and misery of the wicked (*v*. 39): *But we are not*, &c.

CHAPTER ELEVEN

NATURE OF FAITH (*vv*. 1–3)

Here we have, I. A definition or description of the grace of faith in two parts. 1. It *is the substance of things hoped for*. Faith and hope go together; and the same things that are the object of our hope are the object of our faith. It is a firm persuasion and expectation that God will perform all that he has promised to us in Christ. 2. It is *the evidence of things not seen*. Faith demonstrates to the eye of the mind the reality of those things that cannot be discerned by the eye of the body.

II. An account of the honour it reflects upon all those who have lived in the exercise of it (*v*. 2): *By it the elders obtained a good report*— the ancient believers, who lived in the first ages of the world.

III. We have here one of the first acts and articles of faith, which has a great influence on all the rest, and which is common to all believers in every age and part of the world, namely, the creation of the *worlds by the word of God*, not out of pre-existent matter, but out of nothing, *v*. 3. By faith we understand much more of the formation of the world than ever could be understood by the naked eye of natural reason. Now what does faith give us to understand concerning *the worlds*, that is, the upper, middle, and lower regions of the universe? 1. *That these worlds were* not eternal, nor did they produce themselves, but they were made by another. 2. That the maker of the worlds is God; he is the maker of all things; and whoever is so must be God. 3. That he made the world with great exactness. 4. That God made the world by his word, that is, by his essential wisdom and eternal Son, and by his active will, saying, *Let it be done, and it was done*, Ps. xxxiii. 9. 5. That the world was thus framed out of nothing, out of no pre-existent matter. These things we understand by faith.

EXAMPLES OF FAITH
(*vv*. 4–31)

The apostle, having given us a more general account of the grace of faith, now proceeds to set before us some illustrious examples of it in the Old-Testament times, and these may be divided into two classes: 1. Those whose names are mentioned, and the particular exercise and actings of whose faith are specified. 2. Those whose names are barely mentioned, and an account given in general of the exploits of their faith, which it is left to the reader to accommodate, and apply to the particular persons from what he gathers up in the sacred story. We have here those whose names are not only mentioned, but the particular trials and actings of their faith are subjoined.

1. The leading instance and example of faith here recorded is that of Abel, one of the first saints, and the first martyr for religion, of all the sons of Adam, one who lived by faith, and died for it, and therefore a fit pattern for the Hebrews to imitate.

II. Of the faith of Enoch, *v.* 5. He is the second of those elders that through faith have a good report. Observe,

1. What is here reported of him. In this place (and in Gen. v. 22, &c.) we read, (1) *That he walked with God*, that is, that he was really, eminently, actively, progressively, and perseveringly religious in his conformity to God, communion with God, and complacency in God. (2) *That he was translated, that he should not see death*, nor any part of him be found upon earth; for God took him, soul and body, into heaven, as he will do those of the saints who shall be found alive at his second coming. (3) *That before his translation he had this testimony, that he pleased God.* He

had the evidence of it in his own conscience, and the Spirit of God witnessed with his spirit.

2. What is here said of his faith, *v.* 6. It is said that *without* this *faith it is impossible to please God*, without such a faith as helps us to walk with God, an active faith, and that we cannot come to God unless we *believe that he is, and that he is a rewarder of those that diligently seek him.*

III. The faith of Noah, *v.* 7. Observe,

1. The ground of Noah's faith—a warning he had received from God of things as yet not seen.

2. The actings of Noah's faith, and the influence it had both upon his mind and practice. (1) Upon his mind; it impressed his soul with a fear of God's judgment: he was *moved with fear.* (2) His faith influenced his practice. His fear, thus excited by believing God's threatening, moved him to prepare an ark, in which, no doubt, he met with the scorns and reproaches of a wicked generation.

3. The blessed fruits and rewards of Noah's faith. (1) Hereby himself and his house were saved, when a whole world of sinners were perishing about them. (2) Hereby he judged and condemned the world; his holy fear condemned their security and vain confidence; his faith condemned their unbelief; his obedience condemned their contempt and rebellion. (3) Hereby *he became an heir of the righteousness which is by faith.* [1] He was possessed of a true justifying righteousness; he was *heir to it*: and, [2] This his right of inheritance was through faith in Christ, as *a*

member of Christ, *a child of God,* and, if a child, then an heir.

IV. The faith of Abraham, the friend of God, and father of the faithful, in whom the Hebrews boasted, and from whom they derived their pedigree and privileges; and therefore the apostle, that he might both please and profit them, enlarges more upon the heroic achievements of Abraham's faith than of that of any other of the patriarchs; and in the midst of his account of the faith of Abraham he inserts the story of Sarah's faith, whose daughters those women are that continue to do well. Observe,

1. The ground of Abraham's faith, the call and promise of God, *v* 8.

2. The exercise of Abraham's faith: he yielded an implicit regard to the call of God. (1) *He went out, not knowing whither he went.* (2) *He sojourned in the land of promise as in a strange country.* This was an exercise of his faith.

3. The supports of Abraham's faith (*v.* 10): *He looked for a city that hath foundations, whose builder and maker is God.* It was a support to him under all the trials of his sojourning state, helped him patiently to bear all the inconveniences of it, and actively to discharge all the duties of it, persevering therein unto the end.

V. In the midst of the story of Abraham, the apostle inserts an account of the faith of Sarah. Here observe,

1. The difficulties of Sarah's faith, which were very great.

2. The actings of her faith. Her unbelief is pardoned and forgotten, but her faith prevailed and is recorded: *She judged him faithful, who had promised, v.* 11.

3. The fruits and rewards of her faith. (1) *She received strength to conceive seed.* (2) *She was delivered of a child,* a man-child, a child of the promise, the comfort of his parents' advanced years, and the hope of future ages. (3) From them, by this son, sprang a numerous progeny of illustrious persons, *as the stars of the sky* (*v.* 12)—a great, powerful, and renowned nation.

VI. The apostle proceeds to make mention of the faith of the other patriachs, Isaac and Jacob, and the rest of his happy family, *v.* 13.

VII. Now after the apostle has given this account of the faith of others, with Abraham, he returns to him again, and gives us an instance of the greatest trial and act of faith that stands upon record, either in the story of the father of the faithful or of any of his spiritual seed; and this was his offering up Isaac: *By faith Abraham, when he was tried, offered up Isaac; and he that had received the promises offered up his only-begotten son, v.* 17.

VIII. Of the faith of Isaac, *v.* 20. Something of him we had before interwoven with the story of Abraham; here we have something of a distinct nature—that by faith he blessed his two sons, Jacob and Esau, *concerning things to come.* Here observe,

1. The actings of his faith: He *blessed Jacob and Esau concerning things to come.* He blessed them; that is, he resigned them up to God in covenant.

2. The difficulties Isaac's faith struggled with. (1) He seemed to

have forgotten how God had determined the matter at the birth of these his sons, Gen. xxv. 23. (2) He acted in this matter with some reluctance. We now go on to,

IX. The faith of Jacob (*v.* 21), who, *when he was dying, blessed both the sons of Joseph, and worshipped, leaning upon the top of his staff.* There were a great many instances of the faith of Jacob; his life was a life of faith, and his faith met with great exercise.

X. The faith of Joseph, *v.* 22. And here also we consider,

1. What he did by his faith: *He made mention of the departing of the children of Israel, and gave commandment concerning his bones.* The passage is out of Gen. l. 24, 25.

2. When it was that the faith of Joseph acted after this manner; namely, as in the case of Jacob, when he was dying.

XI. The faith of the parents of Moses, which is cited from Exod. ii. 3, &c.

XII. The faith of Moses himself (*vv.* 24, 25, &c.), here observe,

1. An instance of his faith in conquering the world.

(1) He *refused to be called the son of Pharaoh's daughter,* whose foundling he was, and her fondling too; she had adopted him for her son, and he refused it.

(2) He chose *rather to suffer affliction with the people of God than to enjoy the pleasures of sin for a season, v.* 25. He was willing to take his lot with the people of God here, though it was a suffering lot, that he might have his portion with them hereafter, rather than to enjoy all the sensual sinful pleasures of Pharaoh's court, which would be

but for a season, and would then be punished with everlasting misery.

(3) He accounted *the reproaches of Christ greater riches than the treasures of Egypt, v.* 26. See how Moses weighed matters: in one scale he put the worst of religion— *the reproaches of Christ,* in the other scale the best of the world—*the treasures of Egypt*; and in his judgment, directed by faith, the worst of religion weighed down the best of the world.

2. The circumstance of time is taken notice of, when Moses by his faith gained this victory over the world, in all its honours, pleasures, and treasures: *When he had come to years (v.* 24). It was not the act of a child, that prefers counters to gold, but it proceeded from mature deliberation.

3. What it was that supported and strengthened the faith of Moses to such a degree as to enable him to gain such a victory over the world: *He had respect unto the recompence of reward,* that is, say some, the deliverance out of Egypt; but doubtless it means much more— the glorious reward of faith and fidelity in the other world.

4. We have another instance of the faith of Moses, namely, in forsaking Egypt: *By faith he forsook Egypt, not fearing the wrath of the king, v.* 27.

5. We have yet another instance of the faith of Moses, in keeping *the passover and sprinkling of blood, v.* 28. The account of this we have in Exod. xii. 13–23. Though all Israel kept this passover, yet it was by Moses that God delivered the institution of it; and, though it was a great mystery, Moses by faith

both delivered it to the people and kept it that night in the house where he lodged.

XIII. The next instance of faith is that of the Israelites passing through the Red Sea under the conduct of Moses their leader, *v.* 29. The story we have in Exodus, *ch.* xiv. Observe,

1. The preservation and safe passage of the Israelites through the Red Sea, when there was no other way to escape from Pharaoh and his host, who were closely pursuing them.

2. The destruction of the Egyptians. They, presumptuously attempting to follow Israel through the Red Sea, being thus blinded and hardened to their ruin, were all drowned. Their rashness was great, and their ruin was grievous.

XIV. The next instance of faith is that of the Israelites, under Joshua their leader, before the walls of Jericho. The story we have Josh. vi. 5, &c. God can and will in his own time and way cause all the powerful opposition that is made to his interest and glory to fall down, and the grace of faith is mighty through God for the pulling down of strong-holds; he will make Babylon fall before the faith of his people, and, when he has some great thing to do for them, he raises up great and strong faith in them.

XV. The next instance is the faith of Rahab, *v.* 31. Among the noble army of believing worthies, bravely marshalled by the apostle, Rahab comes in the rear, to show *that God is no respecter of persons.* Here consider,

1. Who this Rahab was. (1) She was a Canaanite, a *stranger to the commonwealth of Israel*, and had but little help for faith, and yet she was a believer; the power of divine grace greatly appears when it works without the usual means of grace. (2) She was a harlot, and lived in a way of sin; and yet she believed that the greatness of sin, if truly repented of, shall be no bar to the pardoning mercy of God.

2. What she did by her faith: *She received the spies in peace*, the men that Joshua had sent to spy out Jericho, Josh. ii. 6, 7.

3. What she gained by her faith. She escaped perishing with those that believed not. Singular faith, when the generality are not only unbelievers, but against believers, will be rewarded with singular favours in times of common calamity.

THE HEROES OF FAITH
(*vv.* 32–40)

The apostle now concludes his narrative with a more summary account of another set of believers, where the particular acts are not ascribed to particular persons by name, but left to be applied by those who are well acquainted with the sacred story; and, like a divine orator, he prefaces this part of the narrative with an elegant expostulation: *What shall I say more? Time would fail me.*

I. In this summary account the apostle mentions,

1. Gideon, whose story we have in Judges vi. 11, &c.

2. Barak, another instrument raised up to deliver Israel out of the hand of Jabin, king of Canaan, Judg. iv.

3. Samson, another instrument that God raised up to deliver Israel from the Philistines: his story we have in Judges xiii., xiv., xv., and xvi., and from it we learn that the grace of faith is the strength of the soul for great service.

4. Jephthah, whose story we have, Judg. xi., before that of Samson. He was raised up to deliver Israel from the Ammonites.

5. David, that great man after God's own heart. Few ever met with greater trials, and few ever discovered a more lively faith.

6. Samuel, raised up to be a most eminent prophet of the Lord to Israel, as well as a ruler over them. God revealed himself to Samuel when he was but a child, and continued to do so till his death.

7. To Samuel he adds, *and of the prophets*, who were extraordinary ministers of the Old-Testament church. Now a true and strong faith was very requisite for the right discharge of such an office as this.

II. Having done naming particular persons, he proceeds to tell us what things were done by their faith.

1. *By faith they subdued kingdoms*, *v.* 33. The interests and powers of kings and kingdoms are often set up in oppositin to God and his people.

2. They *wrought righteousness*, both in their public and personal capacities.

3. They *obtained promises*, both general and special. It is faith that gives us an interest in the promises; it is by faith that we have the comfor of the promises; and it is by faith that we are prepared to wait for the promises, and in due time to receive them.

4. They *stopped the mouths of lions*; so did Samson, Judg. xiv. 5, 6, and David, 1 Sam. xvii. 34, 35, and Dan. vi. 22.

5. They *quenched the violence of the fire*, *v.* 34. So Moses, by the prayer of faith, quenched the fire of God's wrath that was kindled against the people of Israel, Num. xi. 1, 2. So did the three children, or rather mighty champions, Dan. III. 17–27.

6. They *escaped the edge of the sword*. The swords of men are held in the hand of God, and he can blunt the edge of the sword, and turn it away from his people against their enemies when he pleases.

7. *Out of weakness they were made strong*. From national weakness, into which the Jews often fell by their unbelief. From bodily weakness; thus Hezekiah (Isa. xxxviii. 15, 16). And it is the same grace of faith that from spiritual weakness helps men to recover and renew their strength.

8. They *grew valiant in fight*. True faith gives truest courage and patience, as it discerns the strength of God, and thereby the weakness of all his enemies. And they were not only valiant, but successful.

9. *Women received their dead raised to life again*, *v.* 35. So did the widow of Zarepath (1 Kings xvii. 23), and the Shunamite, 2 Kings iv. 36.

III. The apostle tells us what these believers endured by faith. 1. They *were tortured, not accepting deliverance*, *v.* 35. 2. They endured *trials of cruel mockings and scourgings, and bonds and imprisonment*, *v.* 36. 3. They were put to death in the most cruel manner. 4. Those who escaped death were used so ill that death might seem more eligible than such a life. Such sufferings as these they endured then for their faith; and such they endured through the power of the grace of faith.

IV. What they obtained by their faith. 1. A most honourable character and commendation from God, the true Judge and fountain of honour—that *the world was not worthy* of such men; the world did not deserve such blessings; they did not know how to value them, nor how to use them. 2. They *obtained a good report* (*v.* 39) of all good men, and of the truth itself, and have the honour to be enrolled in this sacred calendar of the Old-Testament worthies, God's witnesses. 3. They obtained an interest in the promises, though not the full possession of them. They had a title to the promises, though they received not the great things promised. He tells the Hebrews that God had *provided some better things for* them (*v.* 40), and therefore they might be assured that he expected at least as good things from them; and that since the gospel is the end and perfection of the Old Testament, which had no excellency but in its reference to Christ and the gospel, it was expected that their faith should be as much more perfect than the faith of the Old-Testament saints.

CHAPTER TWELVE

LOOKING TO JESUS (*vv.* 1–3)

Here observe what is the great duty which the apostle urges upon the Hebrews, and which he so much desires they would comply with,

and that is, to *lay aside every weight, and the sin that did so easily beset them, and run with patience the race set before them.* The duty consists of two parts, the one preparatory, the other perfective.

I. Preparatory: *Lay aside every weight, and the sin,* &c. 1. *Every weight*, that is, all inordinate affection and concern for the body, and the present life and world. 2. *The sin that doth so easily beset us*; the sin that has the greatest advantage against us, by the circumstances we are in, our constitution, our company.

II. Perfective: *Run with patience the race that is set before us.* The apostle speaks in the gymnastic style, taken from the Olympic and other exercises.

1. Christians have a race to run, a race of service and a race of sufferings, a course of active and passive obedience.

2. This race is set before them; it is marked out unto them, both by the word of God and the examples of the faithful servants of God, that cloud of witnesses with which they are compassed about.

3. This race must be run with patience and perseverance.

4. Christians have a greater example to animate and encourage them in their Christian course than any or all who have been mentioned before, and that is the Lord Jesus Christ: *Looking unto Jesus, the author and finisher of our faith, v.* 2. Here observe,

(1) What our Lord Jesus is to his people: he is *the author and finisher of* their *faith*—the beginning, perfecter, and rewarder of it.

(2) What trials Christ met with in

his race and course. [1] He *endured the contradiction of sinners against himself* (v. 3); he bore the opposition that they made to him, both in their words and behaviour. [2] He *endured the cross*—all those sufferings that he met with in the world. [3] He *despised the shame*. All the reproaches that were cast upon him, both in his life and at his death, he despised.

(3) What it was that supported the human soul of Christ under these unparalleled sufferings; and that was *the joy that was set before him*. He had something in view under all his sufferings, which was pleasant to him. This was the joy that was set before him.

(4) The reward of his suffering: he *has sat down at the right hand of the throne of God*.

(5) What is our duty with respect to this Jesus. We must, [1] Look unto him; that is, we must set him continually before us as our example, and our great encouragement; we must look to him for direction, for assistance, and for acceptance, in all our sufferings. [2] We must consider him, meditate much upon him, and reason with ourselves from his case to our own.

(6) The advantage we shall reap by thus doing: it will be a means to prevent our weariness and fainting (v. 3).

CHASTENING (vv. 4–17)

Here the apostle presses the exhortation to patience and perseverance by an argument taken from the gentle measure and gracious nature of those sufferings which the believing Hebrews endured in their Christian course.

I. From the gentle and moderate degree and measure of their sufferings: *You have not yet resisted unto blood, striving against sin*, v. 4. Observe,

1. He owns that they had suffered much, they had been striving to an agony against sin.

2. He puts them in mind that they might have suffered more, that they had not suffered as much as others; for they had *not yet resisted unto blood*, they had not been called to martyrdom as yet, though they knew not how soon they might be.

II. He argues from the peculiar and gracious nature of those sufferings that befall the people of God. Observe,

1. Those afflictions which may be truly persecution as far as men are concerned in them are fatherly rebukes and chastisements as far as God is concerned in them.

2. God has directed his people how they ought to behave themselves under all their afflictions; they must avoid the extremes that many run into. (1) They must not despise the chastening of the Lord. Those who make light of affliction make light of God and make light of sin. (2) They must not faint when they are rebuked; they must not despond and sink under their trial, nor fret and repine, but bear up with faith and patience. (3) If they run into either of these extremes, it is a sign they have forgotten their heavenly Father's advice and exhortation, which he has given them in true and tender affection.

3. Afflictions, rightly endured, though they may be the fruits of God's displeasure, are yet proofs of his paternal love to his people

and care for them (*vv.* 6, 7): *Whom the Lord loveth he chasteneth, and scourgeth every sin whom he receiveth.*

4. Those that are impatient under the discipline of their heavenly Father behave worse towards him than they would do towards earthly parents, *vv.* 9, 10.

5. The children of God, under their afflictions, ought not to judge of his dealings with them by present sense, but by reason, and faith, and experience: *No chastening for the present seemeth to be joyous, but grievous; nevertheless afterwards it yieldeth the peaceable fruits of righteousness, v.* 11.

6. Where afflictions and sufferings for the sake of Christ are not considered by men as the chastisement of their heavenly Father, and improved as such, they will be a dangerous snare and temptation to apostasy, which every Christian should most carefully watch against (*vv.* 15, 16): *Looking diligently lest any man fail of the grace of God,* &c.

[2] The apostle backs the caution with an awful example, and that is, that of Esau, who though born within the pale of the church, and having the birthright as the eldest son, and so entitled to the privilege of being prophet, priest, and king, in his family, was so profane as to despise these sacred privileges, and to sell his birthright for a morsel of meat. Where observe, *First*, Esau's sin. He profanely despised and sold the birthright, and all the advantages attending it. So do apostates, who to avoid persecution, and enjoy sensual ease and pleasure, though they bore the character of the children of God, and had a visible right to the blessing and inheritance, give up all pretensions thereto. *Secondly*, Esau's punishment, which was suitable to his sin. His conscience was convinced of his sin and folly, when it was too late: *He would afterwards have inherited the blessing,* &c. His punishment lay in two things: 1. He was condemned by his own conscience; he now saw that the blessing he had made so light of was worth the having, worth the seeking, though with much carefulness and many tears. 2. He was rejected of God: *He found no place of repentance* in God nor in his father; the blessing was given to another, even to him to whom he sold it for a mess of pottage. Esau, in his great wickedness, had made the bargain, and God, in his righteous judgment, ratified and confirmed it, and would not suffer Isaac to reverse it.

We may hence learn, [1] That apostasy from Christ is the fruit of preferring the gratification of the flesh to the blessing of God and the heavenly inheritance [2] Sinners will not always have such mean thoughts of the divine blessing and inheritance as now they have. [3] When the day of grace is over (as sometimes it may be in this life), they will find no place for repentance: they cannot repent aright of their sin; and God will not repent of the sentence he has passed upon them for their sin.

THE EARTH SHAKEN
(*vv.* 18–29)

Here the apostle goes on to engage the professing Hebrews to perseverance in their Christian course and conflict, and not to relapse again into Judaism.

1. He shows how much the gospel church differs from the Jewish church, and how much it excels. And here we have a very particular description of the state of the church under the Mosaic dispensation, *vv.* 18–21. 1. It was a gross sensible state. Mount Sinai, constituted, was a *mount that might be touched* (*v.* 18), a gross palpable place; so was the dispensation. 2. It was a dark dispensation. Upon that mount there were blackness and darkness, and that church-state was covered with dark shadows and types. 3. It was a dreadful and terrible dispensation; the Jews could not bear the terror of it. 4. It was a limited dispensation; all might not approach to that mount, but only Moses and Aaron. 5. It was a very dangerous dispensation. The mount burned with fire, and whatever man or beast touched the mount must *be stoned, or thrust through with a dart, v.* 20.

II. He shows how much the gospel church represents the church triumphant in heaven, what communication there is between the one and the other. The gospel church is called *mount Zion, the heavenly Jerusalem, which is free,* in opposition to mount Sinai, which tendeth to bondage, Gal. iv. 24. Now, in coming to mount Zion, believers come into heavenly places, and into a heavenly society.

1. Into heavenly places. (1) *Unto the city of the living God.* God has taken up his gracious residence in the gospel church, which on that account is an emblem of heaven.

(2) To *the heavenly Jerusalem* as born and bred there, as free denizens there. Here believers have clearer views of heaven, plainer evidences for heaven, and a greater meetness and more heavenly temper of soul.

2. To a heavenly society. (1) *To an innumerable company of angels,* who are of the same family with the saints, under the same head, and in a great measure employed in the same work. (2) *To the general assembly and church of the firstborn, that are written in heaven,* that is, to the universal church, however dispersed. (3) *To God the Judge of all,* that great God who will judge both Jew and Gentile according to the law they are under. (4) *To the spirits of just men made perfect.* Believers have union with departed saints in one and the same head and Spirit, and a title to the same inheritance, of which those on earth are heirs, those in heaven possessors. (5) *To Jesus the Mediator of the new covenant, and to the blood of sprinkling, that speaketh better things than that of Abel.* This is none of the least of the many encouragements there are to perseverance in the gospel state, since it is a state of communion with Christ the Mediator of the new covenant, and of communication of his blood, that speaketh better things than the blood of Abel. This is speaking blood, and it speaks better things than that of Abel. *First,* It speaks to God in behalf of sinners; it pleads not for vengeance, as the blood of Abel did on him who shed it, but for mercy. *Secondly,* To sinners, in the name of God. It speaks pardon to their

sins, peace to their souls; and bespeaks their strictest obedience and highest love and thankfulness.

III. The apostle, having thus enlarged upon the argument to perseverance taken from the heavenly nature of the gospel church state, closes the chapter by improving the argument in a manner suitable to the weight of it (*vv* 25, &c.): *See then that you refuse not him that speaketh*—that speaketh by his blood; and not only speaketh after another manner than the blood of Abel spoke from the ground, but than God spoke by the angels, and by Moses spoke on mount Sinai; then he spoke on earth, now he speaks from heaven.

And hence the apostle justly concludes, [1] How necessary it is for us to obtain *grace from God, to serve him acceptably*: if we be not accepted of God under this dispensation, we shall never be accepted at all; and we lose all our labour in religion if we be not accepted of God. [2] We cannot worship God acceptably, unless we worship him with *godly reverence and fear*. As faith, so holy fear, is necessary to acceptable worship. [3] It is only the grace of God that enables us to worship God in a right manner: nature cannot come up to it. [4] God is the same just and righteous God under the gospel that he appeared to be under the law.

CHAPTER THIRTEEN
VARIOUS DUTIES (*vv*. 1–17)

Now the apostle calls the believing Hebrews to the performance of many excellent duties, in which it becomes Christians to excel.

I. To brotherly love (*v*. 1), by which he does not only mean a general affection to all men, as our brethren by nature, nor that more limited affection which is due to those who are of the same immediate parents, but that special and spiritual affection which ought to exist among the children of God. Christians should always love and live as brethren, and the more they grow in devout affection to God their heavenly Father the more they will grow in love to one another for his sake.

II. To hospitality: *Be not forgetful to entertain strangers for his sake, v.* 2. We must add to brotherly kindness charity. Here observe, 1. The duty required—*to entertain strangers*, both those that are strangers to the commonwealth of Israel, and strangers to our persons. Though we know not who they are, nor whence they come, yet, seeing they are without any certain dwelling place, we should allow them room in our hearts and in our houses, as we have opportunity and ability. 2. The motive: *Thereby some have entertained angels unawares*; so Abraham did (Gen. xviii.), and Lot (Gen. xix.), and one of those that Abraham entertained was the Son of God; and, though we cannot suppose this will ever be our case, yet what we do to strangers, in obedience to him, he will reckon and reward as done to himself. Matt. xxv. 35, *I was a stranger, and you took me in.*

III. To Christian sympathy: *Remember those that are in bonds, v.* 3. Here observe,

1. The duty—to *remember those that are in bonds* and in *adversity*.

2. The reason of the duty: *As being yourselves in the body*; not only in the body natural, and so liable to the like sufferings, and you should sympathise with them now that others may sympathise with you when your time of trial comes; but in the same mystical body, under the same head, *and if one member suffer all the rest suffer with it*, 1. Cor. xii. 26.

IV. To purity and chastity, *v.* 4. Here you have, 1. A recommendation of God's ordinance of marriage, that it *is honourable in all*, and ought to be so esteemed by all, and not denied to those to whom God has not denied it. 2. A dreadful but just censure of impurity and lewdness: *Whoremongers and adulterers God will judge.*

V. To Christian contentment, *vv.* 5, 6. Here observe, 1. The sin that is contrary to this grace and duty—*covetousness*, an over eager desire of the wealth of this world, envying those who have more than we. 2. The duty and grace that is contrary to covetousness—being satisfied and pleased *with such things as we have.* 3. What reason Christians have to be contented with their lot. (1) *God hath said, I will never leave thee, nor forsake thee, vv.* 5, 6. (2) From this comprehensive promise they may assure themselves of help from God: *So that we may boldly say, The Lord is my helper; I will not fear what man shall do unto me, v.* 6. Men can do nothing against God, and God can make all that men do against his people to turn to their good.

VI. To the duty Christians owe to their ministers, and that both to

those that are dead and to those that are yet alive.

1. To those that are dead: *Remember those that have had the rule over you, v.* 7. Here observe,

(1) The description given of them. They were such as had the rule over them, and had spoken to them the word of God; their guides and governors, who had spoken to them the word of God.

(2) The duties owing to them, even when they were dead.

[1] "*Remember them*—their preaching, their praying, their private counsel, their example."

[2] "*Follow* their *faith*; be stedfast in the profession of the faith they preached to you, and labour after the grace of faith by which they lived and died so well." Now this duty of following the same true faith in which they had been instructed the apostle enlarges much upon, and presses them earnestly to it, not only from the remembrance of their faithful deceased guides, but from several other motives.

First, From the immutability and eternity of the Lord Jesus Christ.

Secondly, From the nature and tendency of those erroneous doctrines that they were in danger of falling in with.

Observe,

(*a*) The Christian church has its altar. It was objected against the primitive Christians that their assemblies were destitute of an altar; but this was not true. *We have an altar*, not a material altar, but a personal one, and that is Christ; he is both our altar, and our sacrifice; he sanctifies the gift.

(*b*) This altar furnishes out a feast for true believers, a feast upon the sacrifice, spiritual strength and growth, and holy delight and pleasure.

(c) Those who adhere to the tabernacle or the Levitical dispensation, or return to it again, exclude themselves from the privileges of this altar, from the benefits purchased by Christ.

VII. To improve this argument (vv. 13–15) in suitable advices. *First, Let us go forth therefore unto him without the camp*; go forth from the ceremonial law, from sin, from the world, from ourselves, our very bodies, when he calls us. *Secondly,* Let us be willing to *bear his reproach,* be willing to be accounted the offscouring of all things, not worthy to live, not worthy to die a common death. *Thirdly,* Let us make a right use of this altar; not only partake of the privileges of it, but discharge the duties of the altar, as those whom Christ has made priests to attend on this altar.

2. Having thus told us the duty Christians owe to their deceased ministers, which principally consists in following their faith and not departing from it, the apostle tells us what is the duty that people owe to their living ministers (v. 17) and the reasons of that duty: (1) The duty—to obey them, and submit themselves to them. (2) The motives to this duty. [1] They have the rule over the people; their office, though not magisterial, yet is truly authoritative. [2] They watch for the souls of the people,

not to ensnare them, but to save them. [3] They must give an account how they have discharged their duty, and what has become of the souls committed to their trust, whether any have been lost through their neglect, and whether any of them have been brought in and built up under their ministry. [4] They would be glad to give a good account of themselves and their hearers. [5] If they give up their account with grief, it will be the people's loss as well as theirs.

CONCLUSION (vv. 18–25)

Here, I. The apostle recommends himself, and his fellow-sufferers, to the prayers of the Hebrew believers (v. 18): "*Pray for us*; for me and Timothy" (mentioned v. 23), "and for all those of us who labour in the ministry of the gospel."

II. He offers up his prayers to God for them, being willing to do for them as he desired they should do for him: *Now the God of peace,* &c., v. 20.

III. He gives the Hebrews an account of Timothy's liberty and his hopes of seeing them with him in a little time, v. 23. It seems, Timothy had been a prisoner, doubtless for the gospel, but now he was set at liberty.

IV. Having given a brief account of this his letter, and begged their attention to it (v. 22), he closes with salutations, and a solemn, though short benediction.

JAMES

CHAPTER ONE
FAITH AND PATIENCE
(vv. 1–12)

Here is an apostle writing to the scattered; an epistle from God to them, when driven away from his temple, and seemingly neglected by him. It was the desire of this apostle's heart that those who were scattered might be comforted — that they might do well and fare well, and be enabled to rejoice even in their distresses.

We now come to consider the matter of this epistle. In this paragraph we have the following things to be observed:

I. The suffering state of Christians in this world is represented. 1. It is implied that troubles and afflictions may be the lot of the best Christians, even of those who have the most reason to think and hope well of themselves. 2. These outward afflictions and troubles are temptations to them. The devil endeavours by sufferings and crosses to draw men to sin and to deter them from duty, or unfit them for it. 3. These temptations may be numerous and various: *Divers temptations*, as the apostle speaks. 4. The trials of a good man are such as he does not create to himself, nor sinfully pull upon himself; but they are such as he is said to fall into.

II. The graces and duties of a state of trial and affliction are here pointed out to us.

1. One Christian grace to be exercised is joy: *Count it all joy*, *v.* 2. We must not sink into a sad and disconsolate frame of mind, which would make us faint under our trials.

2. Faith is a grace that one expression supposes and another expressly requires: *Knowing this, that the trial of your faith*, *v.* 3; and then in *v.* 6, *Let him ask in faith*. There must be a sound believing of the great truths of Christianity, and a resolute cleaving to them, in times of trial.

3. There must be patience: *The trial of faith worketh patience*. The trying of one grace produces another; and the more the suffering graces of a Christian are exercised the stronger they grow. *Tribulation worketh patience*, Rom. v. 3.

4. Prayer is a duty recommended also to suffering Christians; and here the apostle shows, (1) What we ought more especially to pray for — wisdom: *If any lack wisdom, let him ask of God*. We should not pray so much for the removal of an affliction as for wisdom to make a right use of it. (2) In what way this is to be obtained — upon our petitioning or asking for it. Let us confess our want of wisdom to God and daily ask it of him. (3) We have the greatest encouragement to do

this: *he giveth to all men liberally, and upbraideth not.* Yea, it is expressly promised that *it shall be given, v.* 5. But, (4) There is one thing necessary to be observed in our asking, namely, that we do it with a believing, steady mind: *Let him ask in faith, nothing wavering, v.* 6.

5. That oneness, and sincerity of intention, and a steadiness of mind, constitute another duty required under affliction: *He that wavereth is like a wave of the sea, driven with the wind, and tossed.* Now, for the cure of a wavering spirit and a weak faith, the apostle shows the ill effects of these, (1) In that the success of prayer is spoiled hereby: *Let not that man think that he shall receive any thing of the Lord, v.* 7. (2) A wavering faith and spirit has a bad influence upon our conversations. *A double-minded man is unstable in all his ways, v.* 8.

III. The holy humble temper of a Christian, both in advancement and debasement, is described: and both poor and rich are directed on what grounds to build their joy and comfort, *vv.* 9–11. Here we may observe, 1. Those of low degree are to be looked upon as brethren: *Let the brother of low degree,* &c. Poverty does not destroy the relation among Christians. 2. Good Christians may be rich in the world, *v.* 10. 3. Both these are allowed to rejoice. No condition of life puts us out of a capacity of rejoicing in God. 4. Observe what reason rich people have, notwithstanding their riches, to be humble and low in their own eyes, because both they and their riches are passing away: *As the flower of the grass he shall*

pass away. He, and his wealth with him, *v.* 11.

IV. A blessing is pronounced on those who endure their exercises and trials, as here directed: *Blessed is the man that endureth temptation, v.* 12. The crown of life is promised not only to great and eminent saints, but to all those who have the love of God reigning in their hearts.

TEMPTATION (*vv.* 13–18)

I. We are here taught that God is not the author of any man's sin. Whoever they are who raise persecutions against men, and whatever injustice and sin they may be guilty of in proceeding against them, God is not to be charged with it. As God cannot be tempted with evil himself, so neither can he be a tempter of others.

II. We are taught where the true cause of evil lies, and where the blame ought to be laid (*v.* 14): *Every man is tempted* (in an ill sense) *when he is drawn away of his own lust, and enticed.* In other scriptures the devil is called *the tempter,* and other things may sometimes concur to tempt us; but neither the devil nor any other person or thing is to be blamed so as to excuse ourselves; for the true original of evil and temptation is in our own hearts.

III. We are taught yet further that, while we are the authors and procurers of all sin and misery to ourselves, *God is the Father and fountain of all good, vv.* 16, 17. We must own God as the author of all the powers and perfections that are in the creature, and the giver of all the benefits which we have in and by those powers and perfections: but none of their darknesses, their imperfections, or their ill actions are to be charged on the Father of lights; from him proceeds every good and perfect gift, both pertaining to this life and that which is to come. As every good gift is from God, so particularly the renovation of our natures, our regeneration, and all the holy happy consequences of it, must be ascribed to him (*v.* 18): *Of his own will begat he us with the word of truth.* The end and design of God's giving renewing grace is here laid down: *That we should be a kind of first-fruits of his creatures* — that we should be God's portion and treasure, and a more peculiar property to him, as the first-fruits were; and that we should become holy to the Lord, as the first-fruits were consecrated to him.

DOERS OF THE WORD
(*vv.* 19–27)

In this part of the chapter we are required,

I. To restrain the workings of passion. *Wherefore, my beloved brethren, let every man be swift to hear, slow to speak, slow to wrath, v.* 19. Instead of censuring God under our trials, let us open our ears and hearts to hear what he will say to us. People are often stiff in their own opinions because they are not willing to hear what others have to offer against them: whereas we should be swift to hear reason and truth on all sides, and be slow to speak any thing that should prevent this: and, when we do speak, there should be nothing of wrath; for a soft answer turneth away wrath.

II. A very good reason is given for suppressing anger: *For the wrath of man worketh not the righteousness of God, v.* 20. *Wrath* is a human thing, and the wrath of man stands opposed to the righteousness of God.

III. We are called upon to suppress other corrupt affections, as well as rash anger: *Lay aside all filthiness and superfluity of naughtiness, v.* 21. The word here translated *filthiness* signifies those lusts which have the greatest turpitude and sensuality in them; and the words rendered *superfluity of naughtiness* may be understood of the overflowings of malice or any other spiritual wickednesses. Observe, from the foregoing parts of this chapter, the laying aside of all filthiness is what a time of temptation and affliction calls for, and is necessary to the avoiding of error, and the right receiving and improving of the word of truth: for,

IV. We are here fully, though briefly, instructed concerning hearing the word of God.

1. We are required to prepare ourselves for it (*v.* 21), to get rid of every corrupt affection and of every prejudice and prepossession, and to lay aside those sins which pervert the judgment and blind the mind.

2. We are directed how to hear it: *Receive with meekness the engrafted word, which is able to save your souls.* (1) In hearing the word of God, we are to receive it — assent to the truths of it — consent to the laws of it. (2) We must therefore yield ourselves to the word of God, with most submissive, humble, and tractable tempers: this is to *receive it with meekness.* (3) In all our

hearing we should aim at the salvation of our souls.

3. We are taught what is to be done after hearing (*v.* 22): *But be you doers of the word, and not hearers only, deceiving your own selves.* Observe here, (1) Hearing is in order to do; the most attentive and the most frequent hearing of the word of God will not avail us, unless we be also doers of it. Observe, (2) Bare hearers are self-deceivers; the original word signifies men's arguing sophistically to themselves; their reasoning is manifestly deceitful and false when they would make one part of their work discharge them from the obligation they lie under to another.

4. The apostle shows what is the proper use of the word of God, who they are that do not use it as they ought, and who they are that do make a right use of it, *vv.* 23–25. Let us consider each of these distinctly. (1) The use we are to make of God's word may be learnt from its being compared to a glass, in which a man may *behold his natural face*. As a looking-glass shows us the spots and defilements upon our faces, that they may be remedied and washed off, so the word of God shows us our sins, that we may repent of them and get them pardoned; it shows us what is amiss, that it may be amended. (2) We have here an account of those who do not use this glass of the word as they ought: *He that beholds himself, and goes his way, and straightway forgets what manner of man he was, v.* 24. This is the true description of one who hears the word of God and does it not. (3) Those also are described, and

pronounced blessed, who hear aright, and who use the glass of God's word as they should do (*v.* 25): *Whoso looketh into the perfect law of liberty, and continueth therein,* &c. Observe here, [1] The gospel is a law of liberty, or, as Mr. Baxter expresses it, *of liberation,* giving us deliverance from the Jewish law, and from sin and guilt, and wrath and death. [2] It is a perfect law; nothing can be added to it. [3] In hearing the word, we look into this perfect law; we consult it for counsel and direction; we look into it, that we may thence take our measures. [4] Then only do we look into the law of liberty as we should when we *continue therein.* [5] Those who thus do, and *continue in the law and word of God,* are, and *shall be, blessed in their deed; blessed in all their ways,* according to the first psalm, to which, some think, James here alludes.

V. The apostle next informs us how we may distinguish between a vain religion and that which is pure and approved of God. Here it is plainly and peremptorily declared,

1. What is a vain religion: *If any man among you seemeth to be religious, and bridleth not his tongue, but deceives his own heart, this man's religion is vain.* The man who has a detracting tongue cannot have a truly humble gracious heart. He who delights to injure his neighbour in vain pretends to love God; therefore a reviling tongue will prove a man a hypocrite.

2. It is here plainly and peremptorily declared wherein true religion consists: *Pure religion and undefiled before God and the Father is this, v.* 27. *Visiting the fatherless and*

widows in their affliction. Visiting is here put for all manner of relief which we are capable of giving to others; and fatherless and widows are here particularly mentioned, because they are generally most apt to be neglected or oppressed: but by them we are to understand all who are proper objects of charity, all who are in affliction. It is very remarkable that if the sum of religion be drawn up in two articles this is one—to be charitable and relieve the afflicted. Observe, (4) An unspotted life must accompany an unfeigned love and charity: *To keep himself unspotted from the world.* The world is apt to spot and blemish the soul, and it is hard to live in it, and have to do with it, and not be defiled; but this must be our constant endeavour. Herein consists pure and undefiled religion. The very things of the world too much taint our spirits, if we are much conversant with them; but the sins and lusts of the world deface and defile them very woefully indeed. James comprises *all that is in the world,* which we are not to love, under three heads: *the lust of the flesh, the lust of the eyes, and the pride of life*; and to keep ourselves unspotted from all these is to keep ourselves unspotted from the world. May God by his grace keep both our hearts and lives clean from the love of the world, and from the temptations of wicked worldly men.

CHAPTER TWO
SNOBBERY REBUKED (*vv.* 1–7)

The apostle is here reproving a very corrupt practice. He shows how much mischief there is in the sin of *respect of persons.* Here we have,

I. A caution against this sin laid down in general: *My brethren, have not the faith of our Lord Jesus Christ, the Lord of glory, with respect of persons, v.* 1. You should not make men's outward and worldly advantages the measure of your respect. In professing the faith of our Lord Jesus Christ, we should not show respect to men, so as to cloud or lessen the glory of our glorious Lord.

II. We have this sin described and cautioned against, by an instance or example of it (*vv.* 2, 3): *For if there come into your assembly a man with a gold ring,* &c. In matters of religion, rich and poor stand upon a level; no man's riches set him in the least nearer to God, nor does any man's poverty set him at a distance from God. *With the Most High there is no respect of persons,* and therefore in matters of conscience there should be none with us. All undue honouring of worldly greatness and riches should especially be watched against in Christian societies.

III. We have the greatness of this sin set forth, *vv.* 4, 5. It is great partiality, it is injustice, and it is to set ourselves against God, who has chosen the poor, and will honour and advance them (if good), let who will despise them. Again, take notice that many poor of the world are rich in faith; thus the poorest may become rich; and this is what they ought to be especially ambitious of. It is expected from those who have wealth and estates that they be rich in good works, because the more they have the more they have to do good with; but it is expected from the poor in the world that they be rich in faith, for the less they have here the more they may, and should, live in the believing expectation of better things in a better world. After such considerations as these, the charge is cutting indeed: *But you have despised the poor*, v. 6. "*Do not rich men oppress you, and draw you before the judgment-seat? Do not they blaspheme that worthy name by which you are called?* v. 7. Consider how commonly riches are the incentives of vice and mischief, of blasphemy and persecution: consider how many calamities you yourselves sustain, and how great reproaches are thrown upon your religion and your God by men of wealth, and power, and worldly greatness; and this will make your sin appear exceedingly sinful and foolish.

THE ROYAL LAW (*vv.* 8–13)

Here,

I. We have the law that is to guide us in all our regards to men set down in general. *If you fulfil the royal law, according to the scripture, Thou shalt love thy neighbour as thyself, you do well*, v. 8. Observe hence, 1. The rule for Christians to walk by is settled in the scriptures: *If according to the scriptures*, &c. 2. The scripture gives us this as a law, to love our neighbour as ourselves. 3. This law is a royal law, it comes from the King of kings. 4. A pretence of observing this royal law, when it is interpreted with partiality, will not excuse men in any unjust proceedings.

II. This general law is to be con-

sidered together with a particular law: "*If you have respect to persons, you commit sin, and are convinced of the law as transgressors*," v. 9. The very royal law itself, rightly explained, would serve to convict them, because it teaches them to put themselves as much in the places of the poor as in those of the rich, and so to act equitably towards one as well as the other. Hence he proceeds,

III. To show the extent of the law, and how far obedience must be paid to it. They must fulfil the royal law, have a regard to one part as well as another, otherwise it would not stand them in stead, when they pretended to urge it as a reason for any particular actions: *For whosoever shall keep the whole law, and yet offend in one point, is guilty of all*, v. 10.

IV. James directs Christians to govern and conduct themselves more especially by the law of Christ. *So speak and so do as those that shall be judged by the law of liberty*, v. 12. This will teach us, not only to be just and impartial, but very compassionate and merciful to the poor; and it will set us perfectly free from all sordid and undue regards to the rich. The consideration of our being judged by the gospel should engage us more especially to be merciful in our regards to the poor (v. 13): *For he shall have judgment without mercy that hath shown no mercy; and mercy rejoiceth against judgment.*

FAITH AND WORKS(*vv.* 14–26)

It is here proved at large that a man is justified, not by faith only, but by works. Now,

I. Upon this arises a very great question, namely, how to reconcile Paul and James. Paul, in his epistles to the Romans and Galatians, seems to assert the directly contrary thing to what James here lays down, saying it often, and with a great deal of emphasis, *that we are justified by faith only, and not by the works of the law.* Many ways might be mentioned which have been invented among learned men to make the apostles agree; but it may be sufficient only to observe these few things following: 1. When Paul says that *a man is justified by faith, without the deeds of the law* (Rom. iii. 28), he plainly speaks of another sort of work than James does, but not of another sort of faith. Paul speaks of works wrought in obedience to the law of Moses, and before men's embracing the faith of the gospel. But James speaks of works done in obedience to the gospel, and as the proper and necessary effects and fruits of sound believing in Christ Jesus. 2. Paul not only speaks of different works from those insisted on by James, but he speaks of a quite different use that was made of good works from what is here urged and intended. Paul had to do with those who depended on the merit of their works in the sight of God, and thus he might well make them of no manner of account. James had to do with those who cried up faith, but would not allow works to be used even as evidences; they depended upon a bare profession, as sufficient to justify them. 3. The justification of which Paul speaks is different from that spoken of by James; the one speaks of our persons being justified before God, the other speaks of our faith being justified before men.

II. Having thus cleared this part of scripture from every thing of a contradiction to other parts of it, let us see what is more particularly to be learnt from this excellent passage of James; we are taught,

1. That faith without works will not profit, and cannot save us. *What doth it profit, my brethren, if a man say he hath faith, and have not works? Can faith save him?* For a man to have faith, and to say he has faith, are two different things; the apostle does not say, *If a man have faith without works,* for that is not a supposable case; the drift of this place of scripture is plainly to show that an opinion, or speculation, or assent, without works, is not faith; but the case is put thus, *If a man say he hath faith,* &c.

2. "*If a brother or a sister be naked, and destitute of daily food, and one of you say unto them, Depart in peace, be you warmed and filled, notwithstanding you give them not those things which are needful to the body, what doth it profit?* vv.* 15–17. What will such a charity as this, that consists in bare words, avail either you or the poor? Will you come before God with such empty shows of charity as these? "*Even so faith, if it hath not works, is dead, being alone,*" *v.* 17. We are too apt to rest in a bare profession of faith, and to think that this will save us; it is a cheap and easy religion to say, "We believe the articles of the Christian faith;" but it is a great delusion to imagine that this is enough to bring us to heaven.

3. We are taught to compare a

faith boasting of itself without works and a faith evidenced by works, by looking on both together, to try how this comparison will work upon our minds. And this is the evidence according to which Christ will proceed at the day of judgment. *The dead were judged according to their works*, Rev. xx. 12. How will those be exposed then who boast of that which they cannot evidence, or who go about to evidence their faith by any thing but works of piety and mercy!

4. We are taught to look upon a faith of bare speculation and knowledge as the faith of devils: *Thou believest that there is one God; thou doest well; the devils also believe, and tremble, v.* 19. They tremble, not out of reverence, but hatred and opposition to that one God on whom they believe. To rehearse that article of our creed, therefore, *I believe in God the Father Almighty*, will not distinguish us from devils at last, unless we now give up ourselves to God as the gospel directs, and love him, and delight ourselves in him, and serve him, which the devils do not, cannot do.

5. We are taught that he who boasts of faith without works is to be looked upon at present as a foolish condemned person. *But wilt thou know, O vain man, that faith without works is dead? v.* 20. Faith without works is said to be *dead*, not only as void of all those operations which are the proofs of spiritual life, but as unavailable to eternal life: such believers as rest in a bare profession of faith *are dead while they live*.

6. We are taught that a justifying faith cannot be without works, from two examples, Abraham and Rahab.

(1) The first instance is that of Abraham, the father of the faithful, and the prime example of justification, to whom the Jews had a special regard (*v.* 21). Paul, on the other hand, says (in *ch.* iv. of the epistle to the Romans) that Abraham *believed, and it was counted to him for righteousness*. But these are well reconciled, by observing what is said in Heb. xi., which shows that the faith both of Abraham and Rahab was such as to produce those good works of which James speaks, and which are not to be separated from faith as justifying and saving. By what Abraham did, it appeared that he truly believed.

(2) The second example of faith's justifying itself and us with and by works is Rahab: *Likewise also was not Rahab the harlot justified by works, when she had received the messengers, and had sent them out another way? v.* 25. The former instance was of one renowned for his faith all his life long. This is of one noted for sin, whose faith was meaner and of a much lower degree; so that the strongest faith will not do, nor the meanest be allowed to go without works. This Rahab believed the report she had heard of God's powerful presence with Israel; but that which proved her faith sincere was, that, to the hazard of her life, she *received the messengers, and sent them out another way*.

7. And now, upon the whole matter, the apostle draws this conclusion, *As the body without the spirit is dead, so faith without works*

is dead also, v. 26. These words are read differently; some reading them, *As the body without the breath is dead, so is faith without works*: and then they show that works are the companions of faith, as breathing is of life. Others read them, *As the body without the soul is dead, so faith without works is dead also*: and then they show that as the body has no action, nor beauty, but becomes a loathsome carcase, when the soul is gone, so a bare profession without works is useless, yea, loathsome and offensive. Let us then take heed of running into extremes in this case.

CHAPTER THREE
THE TONGUE (*vv.* 1–12)

Those who set up faith in the manner the former chapter condemns are most apt to run into those sins of the tongue which this chapter condemns. And indeed the best need to be cautioned against a dictating, censorious, mischievous use of their tongues. We are therefore taught,

I. Not to use our tongues so as to lord it over others: *My brethren, be not many masters*, &c., *v.* 1. These words do not forbid doing what we can to direct and instruct others in the way of their duty or to reprove them in a Christian way for what is amiss; but we must not affect to speak and act as those who are continually assuming the chair, we must not prescribe to one another, so as to make our own sentiments a standard by which to try all others, because God gives various gifts to men, and expects from each according to that measure of light which he gives.

II. We are taught to govern our tongue so as to prove ourselves perfect and upright men, as such as have an entire government over ourselves: *If any man offend not in word, the same is a perfect man, and able also to bridle the whole body*. It is here implied that he whose conscience is affected by tongue-sins, and who takes care to avoid them, is an upright man, and has an undoubted sign of true grace. But, on the other hand, *if a man seemeth to be religious* (as was declared in the first chapter) *and bridleth not his tongue*, whatever profession he makes, *that man's religion is vain*. Further, he that offends not in word will not only prove himself a sincere Christian, but a very much advanced and improved Christian. For the wisdom and grace which enable him to rule his tongue will enable him also to rule all his actions. This we have illustrated by two comparisons: 1. The governing and guiding of all the motions of a horse, by the bit which is put into his mouth. 2. The governing of a ship by the right management of the helm.

III. We are taught to dread an unruly tongue as one of the greatest and most pernicious evils. It is compared to a little fire placed among a great deal of combustible matter, which soon raises a flame and consumes all before it: *Behold, how great a matter a little fire kindleth! And the tongue is a fire, a world of iniquity*, &c., *vv.* 5, 6.

IV. We are next taught how very difficult a thing it is to govern the tongue: *For every kind of beasts, and of birds, and of serpents, and of things in the sea, is tamed, and hath been tamed, of mankind. But the tongue can no man tame, vv.* 7, 8. The apostle does not intend to represent it as a thing impossible, but as a thing extremely difficult, which therefore will require great watchfulness, and pains, and prayer, to keep it in due order.

V. We are taught to think of the use we make of our tongues in religion and in the service of God, and by such a consideration to keep it from cursing, censuring, and every thing that is evil on other occasions. How absurd is it that those who use their tongues in prayer and praise should ever use them in cursing, slandering, and the like!

WISDOM FROM ABOVE
(*vv.* 13–18)

I. We have here some account of true wisdom, with the distinguishing marks and fruits of it: *Who is a wise man, and endued with knowledge among you? Let him show out of a good conversation his works with meekness of wisdom, v.* 13. Now where this is the happy case of any there will be these following things: 1. A good way of life. If we are wiser than others, this should be evidenced by the goodness of our behaviour, not by the roughness or vanity of it. 2. True wisdom may be known by its works. The conversation here does not refer only to words, but to the whole of men's practice. 3. True wisdom may be known by the meekness of the spirit and temper: *Let him show with meekness,* &c. It is a great instance of wisdom prudently to bridle our

own anger, and patiently to bear the anger of others.

II. We have the glorying of those taken away who are of a contrary character to that now mentioned, and their wisdom exposed in all its boasts and productions: "*If you have bitter envying and strife in your hearts, glory not,* &c., *vv.* 14–16. Pretend what you will, and think yourselves ever so wise, yet you have abundance of reason to cease your glorying, if you run down love and peace, and give way to bitter envying and strife. For observe, whence such wisdom cometh: *It descendeth not from above,* but ariseth from beneath; and, to speak plainly, it is *earthly, sensual, devilish, v.* 15.

III. We have the lovely picture of that wisdom which is from above more fully drawn, and set in opposition to this which is from beneath: *But the wisdom that is from above is first pure, then peaceable,* &c., *vv.* 17, 18. It consists of these several things: 1. It is pure, without mixture of maxims or aims that would debase it. 2. The wisdom that is from above is peaceable. Peace follows purity, and depends upon it. 3. It is gentle, not standing upon extreme right in matters of property; not being rude and overbearing in conversation, nor harsh and cruel in temper. 4. Heavenly wisdom is *easy to be entreated,* it is very *persuadable,* either to what is good or from what is evil. 5. Heavenly wisdom is full of mercy and good fruits, inwardly disposed to every thing that is kind and good. 6. Heavenly wisdom is without partiality. The wisest men are least apt to be censurers. 7. That wisdom which is from above is without hypocrisy. It has no disguises nor deceits.

CHAPTER FOUR
CAUSES OF WAR (*vv.* 1–10)

I. The apostle here reproves the Jewish Christians for their wars, and for their lusts as the cause of them: *Whence come wars and fightings among you? Come they not hence, even of your lusts that war in your members, v.* 1. Hereupon, our apostle informs them that the origin of their wars and fightings was not (as they pretended) a true zeal for their country, and for the honour of God, but that their prevailing lusts were the cause of all. Impetuous passions and desires first war in their members, and then raise feuds in their nation. Apply this to private cases, and may we not then say of fightings and strifes among relations and neighbours that they come from those lusts which war in the members? Sinful desires and affections generally exclude prayer, and the working of our desires towards God: "*You fight and war, yet you have not, because you ask not.*" You fight, and do not succeed, because you do not pray: you do not consult God in your undertakings, whether he will allow of them or not. Let us learn hence, in the management of all our worldly affairs and in our prayers to God for success in them, to see that our ends be right.

II. We have fair warning to avoid all criminal friendships with this world: *You adulterers and adulteresses, know you not that the friendship of the world is enmity with God? v.* 4. Worldly people are here called adulterers and adulteresses, because of their perfidiousness to God, while they give their best affections to the world. *You cannot serve God and mammon*, Matt. vi. 24. Hence arise wars and fightings, even from this adulterous idolatrous love of the world, and serving of it; for what peace can there be among men, so long as there is enmity towards God? or who can fight against God, and prosper?

III. We are taught to observe the difference God makes between pride and humility. *God resisteth the proud, but giveth grace unto the humble, v.* 6. Grace, as opposed to disgrace, is honour; this God gives to the humble; and, where God gives grace to be humble, there he will give all other graces, and, as in the beginning of this sixth verse, he will *give more grace.*

IV. We are taught to submit ourselves entirely to God: *Submit yourselves therefore to God. Resist the devil, and he will flee from you, v.* 7. Christians should forsake the friendship of the world, and watch against that envy and pride which they see prevailing in natural men, and should by grace learn to glory in their submissions to God. If we basely yield to temptations, the devil will continually follow us; but if we *put on the whole armour of God*, and stand it out against him, he will be gone from us. Resolution shuts and bolts the door against temptation.

V. We are directed how to act towards God, in our becoming submissive to him, *vv.* 8–10. 1. *Draw nigh to God.* The heart that has rebelled must be brought to the foot of God; the spirit that was distant and estranged from a life of communion and converse with God must become acquainted with him. 2. *Cleanse your hands.* He who comes unto God must have clean hands. Paul therefore directs to *lift up holy hands without wrath and doubting* (1 Tim. ii. 8), hands free from blood, and bribes, and every thing that is unjust or cruel, and free from every defilement of sin: he is not subject to God who is a servant of sin. 3. The hearts of the double-minded must be purified. Those who halt between God and the world are here meant by *the double-minded.* To *purify the heart* is to be sincere, and to act upon this single aim and principle, rather to please God than to seek after any thing in this world. 4. *Be afflicted, and mourn, and weep.* This may be taken either as a prediction of sorrow or a prescription of seriousness. 5. "*Humble yourselves in the sight of the Lord.* Let the inward acts of the soul be suitable to all those outward expressions of grief, affliction, and sorrow, before mentioned."

VI. We have great encouragement to act thus towards God: *He will draw nigh to those that draw nigh to him* (*v.* 8), *and he will lift up* those who humble themselves in his sight, *v.* 10.

WARNING AGAINST OVER-CONFIDENCE
(*vv.* 11–17)

In this part of the chapter,

I. We are cautioned against the sin of evil-speaking: *Speak not evil one of another, brethren, v.* 11. He who is guilty of the sin here cautioned against is not a doer of the law, but a judge; he assumes an office and a place that do not belong to him, and he will be sure to suffer for his presumption in the end. God, the Lawgiver, has reserved the power of passing the final sentence on men wholly to himself.

II. We are cautioned against a presumptuous confidence of the continuance of our lives, and against forming projects thereupon with assurance of success, *vv.* 13, 14. We can fix the hour and minute of the sun's rising and setting tomorrow, but we cannot fix the certain time of a vapour's being scattered; such is our life: *it appears but for a little time, and then vanisheth away.*

III. We are taught to keep up a constant sense of our dependence on the will of God for life, and all the actions and enjoyments of it: *You ought to say, If the Lord will, we shall live, and do this, or that, v.* 15. The apostle, having reproved them for what was amiss, now directs them how to be and do better. All our actions and designs are under the control of Heaven. Therefore both our counsels for action and our conduct in action should be entirely referred to God; all we design and all we do should be with a submissive dependence on God.

IV. We are directed to avoid vain boasting, and to look upon it not only as a weak, but a very evil thing. *You rejoice in your boastings; all such rejoicing is evil, v.* 16. They promised themselves life and prosperity, and great things in the world, without any just regard to God; and then they boasted of these things. If we rejoice in our own vain confidences and presumptuous boasts, this is evil: it is an evil carefully to be avoided by all wise and good men.

V. We are taught, in the whole of our conduct, to act up to our own convictions, and, whether we have to do with God or men, to see that we never go contrary to our own knowledge (*v.* 17).

CHAPTER FIVE

WARNING TO THE RICH
(*vv.* 1–11)

The apostle is here addressing first sinners and then saints.

I. Let us consider the address to sinners; and here we find James seconding what his great Master had said: *Woe unto you that are rich; for you have received your consolation,* Luke vi. 24.

1. He foretells the judgments of God that should come upon them, *vv.* 1–3). Their misery shall arise from the very things in which they placed their happiness. "Corruption, decay, rust, and ruin, will come upon all your goodly things: *Your riches are corrupted and your garments are motheaten, v.* 2. They think to heap up treasure for their latter days, to live plentifully upon when they come to be old; but, alas! they are only heaping up treasures to become a prey to others (as the Jews had all taken from them by the Romans), and treasurers that will prove at last to be only treasures of wrath, *in the day of the revelation of the righteous judgment of God.*

2. The apostle shows what those sins are which should bring such miseries. (1) Covetousness is laid to the charge of this people; they laid by their garments till they bred moths and were eaten; they hoarded up their gold and silver till they were rusty and cankered. God gives us our worldly possessions that we may honour him and do good with them; but if, instead of this, we sinfully hoard them up, through an undue affection towards them, or a distrust of the providence of God for the future, this is a very heinous crime. (2) Another sin charged upon those against whom James writes is oppression: *Behold, the hire of the labourers, who have reaped down your fields, which is of you kept back by fraud, crieth, &c., v.* 4. Those who have wealth in their hands get power into their hands, and then they are tempted to abuse that power to oppress such as are under them. This is a crying sin, an iniquity that cries so as to reach the ears of God; and, in this case, God is to be considered as *the Lord of sabaoth,* or *the Lord of hosts,* a phrase often used in the Old-Testament, when the people of God were defenceless and wanted protection, and when their enemies were numerous and powerful. (3) Another sin here mentioned is sensuality and voluptuousness. *You have lived in pleasure on the earth, and been wanton, v.* 5. God does not forbid us to use pleasure; but to live in them as if we lived for nothing else is a very provoking sin. (4) Another sin here charged on the rich is persecution: *You have condemned and killed the just, and he*

doth not resist you, v. 6. This fills up the measure of their iniquity. They oppressed and acted very unjustly, to get estates; when they had them, they gave way to luxury and sensuality, till they had lost all sense and feeling of the wants or afflictions of others; and then they persecute and kill without remorse.

II. We have next subjoined an address to saints.

1. Attend to your duty: *Be patient* (v. 7), *establish your hearts* (v. 8), *grudge not one against another, brethren*, v. 9. Consider well the meaning of these three expressions: (1) "*Be patient*—bear your afflictions without murmuring, your injuries without revenge; and, though God should not in any signal manner appear for you immediately, wait for him. (2) "*Establish your hearts*—let your faith be firm, without wavering, your practice of what is good constant and continued, without tiring, and your resolutions for God and heaven fixed, in spite of all sufferings or temptations." (3) *Grudge not one against another*. Those who are in the midst of common enemies, and in any suffering circumstances, should be more especially careful not to grieve nor to groan against one another, otherwise judgments will come upon them as well as others; and the more such grudgings prevail the nearer do they show judgment to be.

2. Consider what encouragement here is for Christians to be patient, to establish their hearts, and not to grudge one against another. And, (1) "Look to the example of the husbandman: *He waits for the precious fruit of the earth, and hath long patience for it, until he receive the early and latter rain*." (2) "Think how short your waiting time may possibly be: *The coming of the Lord draweth nigh*, v. 8; *behold, the Judge standeth before the door*, v. 9. (3) The danger of our being condemned when the Judge appears should excite us to mind our duty as before laid down; *Grudge not, lest you be condemned*. (4) We are encouraged to be patient by the example of the prophets (v. 10). Those who were the greatest examples of suffering affliction were also the best and greatest examples of patience. (5) Job also is proposed as an example for the encouragement of the afflicted. In the case of Job you have an instance of a variety of miseries, and of such as were very grievous; but under all he could bless God, and, as to the general bent of his spirit, he was patient and humble: and what came to him in the end? Why, truly, God accomplished and brought about those things for him which plainly prove that *the Lord is very pitiful, and of tender mercy.*

PRAYER THAT WORKS
(*vv.* 12–20)

I. The sin of swearing is cautioned against: *But above all things, my brethren, swear not*, &c., v. 12. All customary needless swearing is undoubtedly forbidden, and all along in scripture condemned, as a very grievous sin.

2. *But let your yea be yea, and your nay nay; lest you fall into condemnation*; that is, let it be known that you keep to truth, and

are firm to your word, and by this means you will find there is no need to swear to what you say.

II. As Christians we are taught to suit ourselves to the dispensations of Providence (*v.* 13): *Is any among you afflicted? Let him pray. Is any merry? Let him sing psalms.* Our condition in this world is various; and our wisdom is to submit to its being so, and to behave as becomes us both in prosperity and under affliction.

III. We have particular directions given as to sick persons, and *healing pardoning mercy promised* upon the observance of those directions. *If any be sick,* they are required, 1. To *send for the elders, the presbyters,* pastors or ministers *of the church, vv.* 14, 15. It lies upon sick people as a duty to send for ministers, and to desire their assistance and their prayers. 2. It is the duty of ministers to pray over the sick, when thus desired and called for. 3. In the times of miraculous healing, the *sick were to be anointed with oil in the name of the Lord,* and some have thought that it should not be wholly laid aside in any age, but that where there are extraordinary measures of faith in the person anointing, and in those who are anointed, an extraordinary blessing may attend the observance of this direction for the sick. However that be, there is one thing carefully to be observed here, that the saving of the sick is not ascribed to the *anointing with oil,* but to prayer: *The prayer of faith shall save the sick,* &c., *v.* 15. So that, 4. Prayer over the sick must proceed from, and be accompanied with, a lively faith. 5. We

should observe the success of prayer. The Lord shall raise up; that is, if he be a person capable and fit for deliverance, and if God have any thing further for such a person to do in the world. *And, if he have committed sins, they shall be forgiven him;* that is, where sickness is sent as a punishment for some particular sin, that sin shall be pardoned, and in token thereof the sickness shall be removed.

IV. Christians are directed to *confess their faults one to another, and so to join in their prayers with and for one another, v.* 16. Some expositors connect this with *v.* 14. As if when sick people send for ministers to pray over them they should then confess their faults to them. Indeed, where any are conscious that their sickness is a vindictive punishment of some particular sin, and they cannot look for the removal of their sickness without particular applications to God for the pardon of such a sin, there it may be proper to acknowledge and tell his case, that those who pray over him may know how to plead rightly for him. But the confession here required is that of Christians to one another, and not to a priest. Where persons have injured one another, acts of injustice must be confessed to those against whom they have been committed.

V. The great advantage and efficacy of prayer are declared and proved: *The effectual fervent prayer of a righteous man availeth much,* whether he pray for himself or for others: witness the example of Elijah, *vv.* 17, 18. He who prays must be a righteous man; not righteous in an absolute sense (for this Elias was not, who is here made a pattern to us), but righteous in a gospel sense; not loving nor approving of any known iniquity. *If I regard iniquity in my heart, the Lord will not hear my prayer*, Ps. lxvi. 18. Further, the prayer itself must be a fervent, in-wrought, well-wrought prayer. It must be a pouring out of the heart to God; and it must proceed from a faith unfeigned. Such prayer avails much. The power of prayer is here proved from the success of Elijah. This may be encouraging to us even in common cases, if we consider that Elijah was *a man of like passions with us*.

VI. This epistle concludes with an exhortation to do all we can in our places to promote the conversion and salvation of others, *vv.* 19, 20. It is no mark of a wise or a holy man to boast of his being free from

error, or to refuse to acknowledge when he is in an error. But if any do err, be they ever so great, you must not be afraid to show them their error; and, be they ever so weak and little, you must not disdain to make them wiser and better. If they err from the truth, that is, from the gospel (the great rule and standard of truth), whether it be in opinion or practice, you must endeavour to bring them again to the rule. He who thus converteth a sinner from the error of his ways *shall save a soul from death*. There is a soul in the case; and what is done towards the salvation of the soul shall certainly turn to good account. And then, by such conversion of heart and life, a *multitude of sins shall be hid*. Those that turn many to righteousness, and those who help to do so, *shall shine as the stars for ever and ever.*

THE FIRST EPISTLE GENERAL OF

PETER

CHAPTER ONE

GREETINGS AND BLESSINGS (vv. 1–5)

In this inscription we have three parts:

I. The author of it, described, 1. By his name—*Peter*. His first name was *Simon*, and Jesus Christ gave him the surname of *Peter*, which signifies *a rock*, as a commendation of his faith, and to denote that he should be an eminent pillar in the church of God, Gal. ii. 9. 2. By his office—*an apostle of Jesus Christ*.

II. The persons to whom this epistle was addressed, and they are described, –

1. By their external condition— *Strangers dispersed throughout Pontus, Galatia, &c.* They were chiefly Jews.

2. They are described by their spiritual condition: *Elect according to the foreknowledge of God the Father*, &c. These poor strangers, who were oppressed and despised in the world, were nevertheless in high esteem with the great God, and in the most honourable state that any person can be in during this life; for they were,

III. The salutation follows: *Grace unto you, and peace be multiplied.* The blessings desired for them are *grace and peace*. The increase of grace and peace is from

God. Where he gives true grace he will give more grace.

Next we have,

IV. A congratulation of the dignity and happiness of the state of these believers, brought in under the form of a thanksgiving to God. Other epistles begin in like manner, 2. Cor. i. 3; Eph. i. 3. Here we have,

1. The duty performed, which is blessing God. A man blesses God by a just acknowledgment of his excellency and blessedness.

2. The object of this blessing described by his relation to Jesus Christ: *The God and Father of our Lord Jesus Christ.* Here are three names of one person, denoting his threefold office. (1) He is *Lord*, a universal king or sovereign. (2) *Jesus*, a priest or Saviour. (3) *Christ*, a prophet, anointed with the Spirit and furnished with all gifts necessary for the instruction, guidance, and salvation of his church.

3. The reasons that oblige us to this duty of blessing God, which are comprised in *his abundant mercy*.

V. Having congratulated these people on their new birth, and the hope of everlasting life, the apostle goes on to describe that life under the notion of *an inheritance*, a most proper way of speaking to these people; for they were poor and persecuted, perhaps turned out of their inheritances to which they were born; to allay this grievance, he tells them they were new-born to a new inheritance, infinitely better than what they had lost. Here note,

1. Heaven is the undoubted inheritance of all the children of God. This inheritance is not our purchase, but our Father's gift; not wages we merit, but the effect of grace.

2. The incomparable excellencies of this inheritance, which are four: (1) It is incorruptible, in which respect it is like its Maker, who is called the *incorruptible God*, Rom. i. 23. (2) This inheritance is undefiled, like the great high priest that is now in possession of it, who is *holy, harmless, and undefiled*, Heb. vii. 26. (3) It fadeth not away, but always retains its vigour and beauty. (4) "*Reserved in heaven for you.*" This inheritance is preserved for them, and none but them; all the rest will be shut out for ever.

VI. This inheritance being described as future, and distant both in time and place, the apostle supposes some doubt or uneasiness yet to remain upon the minds of these people, whether they might not possibly fall short by the way. To this he answers that they should be safely guarded and conducted thither; they should be kept and preserved from all such destructive temptations and injuries as would prevent their safe arrival at eternal life. The blessing here promised is preservation: You *are kept*; the author of it is *God*; the means in us made use of for that end are our own *faith* and care; the end to which we are preserved is *salvation*; and the time when we shall see the

safe end and issue of all is *the last time*.

FAITH ON TRIAL (*vv.* 6–9)

The first word, *wherein*, refers to the apostle's foregoing discourse about the excellency of their present state, and their grand expectations for the future.

I. The apostle grants they were in great affliction, and propounds several things in mitigation of their sorrows. 1. Every sound Christian has always something wherein he may greatly rejoice. 2. The chief joy of a good Christian arises from things spiritual and heavenly, from his relation to God and to heaven. 3. The best Christians, those who have reason greatly to rejoice, may yet be in great heaviness through manifold temptations. 4. The afflictions and sorrows of good people are but for a little while, they are but for a season; though they may be smart, they are but short. 5. Great heaviness is often necessary to a Christian's good: *If need be, you are in heaviness*. God does not afflict his people willingly, but acts with judgment, in proportion to our needs.

II. He expresses the end of their afflictions and the ground of their joy under them, *v.* 7. The end of good people's afflictions is *the trial of their faith*. As to the nature of this trial, it is *much more precious than of gold that perisheth, though it be tried with fire*. The effect of the trial is this, it will *be found unto praise, honour, and glory at the appearing of Jesus Christ*.

III. He particularly commends the faith of these primitive Christians upon two accounts:

1. The excellency of its object, the unseen Jesus.

2. On account of two notable productions or effects of their faith, *love* and *joy*, and this joy so great as to be above description: *You rejoice with joy unspeakable, and full of glory.* Learn,

(1) The faith of a Christian is properly conversant about things revealed, but not seen.

(2) True faith is never alone, but produces a strong love to Jesus Christ.

(3) Where there are true faith and love to Christ there is, or may be, *joy unspeakable and full of glory.* This joy is inexpressible, it cannot be described by words; the best discovery is by an experimental taste of it; it is *full of glory*, full of heaven. Well might these primitive Christians rejoice with joy unspeakable, since they were every day *receiving the end of their faith, the salvation of their souls v.* 4.

THE AUTHORITY OF THE PROPHETS (*vv.* 10–12)

Because they were Jews, and had a profound veneration for the Old Testament, he produces the authority of the prophets to convince them that the doctrine of salvation by faith in Jesus Christ was no new doctrine, but the same which the old prophets did enquire and search diligently into. Note,

I. Who made this diligent search —*the prophets*, who were persons inspired by God either to do or to say things extraordinary, above the reach of their own studies and abilities, as foretelling things to come, and revealing the will of God, by the direction of the Holy Spirit.

II. The object of their search, which was *salvation*, and *the grace of God which should come unto you.*

III. The manner of their enquiry: they *enquired and searched diligently.*

IV. The particular matters which the ancient prophets chiefly searched into, which are expressed in *v.* 11. Jesus Christ was the main subject of their studies; and, in relation to him, they were most inquisitive into,

1. His humiliation and death, and the glorious consequences of it.

2. The time, and the manner of the times, wherein the Messiah was to appear. The works here ascribed to the Holy Ghost prove him to be God. He *did signify*, discover, and manifest to the prophets, many hundred years *beforehand, the sufferings of Christ*, with a multitude of particular circumstances attending them; and he did also *testify*, or give proof and evidence beforehand, of the certainty of that event, by inspiring the prophets to reveal it, to work miracles in confirmation of it, and by enabling the faithful to believe it.

V. The success with which their enquiries were crowned. They were informed that these things should not come to pass in their time, but yet all was firm and certain, and should come to pass in the times of the apostles. The mysteries of the gospel, and the methods of man's salvation, are so glorious that the blessed angels earnestly desire to look into them; they are curious, accurate, and industrious in prying into them; they consider the whole scheme of man's redemption with deep attention and admiration, particularly the points the apostle had been discoursing of: *Which things the angels desire to* stoop down and *look into*, as *the cherubim* did continually *towards the mercy-seat*.

TRUE HOLINESS (*vv*. 13–23)

Here the apostle begins his exhortations to those whose glorious state he had before described.

I. He exhorts them to sobriety and holiness.

1. *Wherefore gird up the loins of your mind*, &c., *v*. 13. As if he had said, You have a journey to go, a race to run, a warfare to accomplish, and a great work to do; as the traveller, the racer, the warrior, and the labourer, gather in, and gird up, their long and loose garments, that they may be more ready, prompt, and expeditious in their business, so do you by your minds, your inner man, and affections seated there." *Be sober*, be vigilant against all your spiritual dangers and enemies. Be sober-minded also in opinion, as well as in practice, and humble in your judgment of yourselves." *And hope to the end, for the grace that is to be brought to you at the revelation of Jesus Christ*. Hope perfectly, trust without doubting to that grace which is now offered to you by the gospel.

2. *As obedient children*, &c., *v*. 14. These words may be taken as a rule of holy living, which is both positive—"You ought to live *as obedient children*, as those whom God hath adopted into his family, and regenerated by his grace;" and negative—"You must *not fashion yourselves according to the former lusts, in your ignorance*." Or the words may be taken as an argument to press them to holiness from the consideration of what they now are, children of obedience, and what they were when they lived in lust and ignorance.

3. *But as he who hath called you*, &c., *vv*. 15, 16. Here is a noble rule enforced by strong arguments: *Be you holy in all manner of conversation*. Who is sufficient for this? And yet it is required in strong terms, and enforced by three reasons, taken from the grace of God in calling us, —from his command, *it is written*, —and from his example. *Be you holy, for I am holy*.

4. *If you call on the Father*, &c., *v*. 17. The apostle does not there express any doubt at all whether these Christians would call upon their heavenly Father, but supposes they would certainly do it, and from this argues with them to *pass the time of their sojourning here in fear*: "If you own the great God as a Father and a Judge, you ought to live the time of your sojourning here in his fear." The judgment of God will be without respect of persons: *According to every man's work*. We are obliged to faith, holiness, and obedience, and our works will be an evidence whether we have complied with our obligations or not.

5. The apostle having exhorted them to *pass the time of their sojourning in the fear of God* from this consideration, that they *called on the Father*, he adds (*v*. 18) a second argument: *Because* or *forasmuch as you were not redeemed with corruptible things*, &c. Herein he puts them in mind, (1) That they were redeemed, or brought back

again, by a ransom paid to the Father. (2) What the price paid for their redemption was: *Not with corruptible things, as silver and gold, but with the precious blood of Christ.* (3) From what they were redeemed: *From a vain conversation received by tradition.* (4) They knew this: *Forasmuch as you know*, and cannot pretend ignorance of this great affair.

6. Having mentioned the price of redemption, the apostle goes on to speak of some things relating both to the Redeemer and the redeemed, *vv.* 20, 21. (1) The Redeemer is further described, not only as a Lamb without spot, but as one, [1] That was *fore-ordained before the foundation of the world*, fore-ordained or foreknown. When prescience is ascribed to God, it implies more than bare prospect or speculation. It imports an act of the will, a resolution that the thing shall be, Acts ii. 23. [2] That was *manifested in these last days for them.* He was manifested or demonstrated to be that Redeemer whom God had fore-ordained. [3] That was raised from the dead by the Father, who gave him glory.

(2) The redeemed are also described here by their faith and hope, the cause of which is Jesus Christ: "*You do by him believe in God*—by him as the author, encourager, support, and finisher of your faith; your faith and hope now may be in God, as reconciled to you by Christ the Mediator."

(3) From all this we learn, [1] The decree of God to send Christ to be a Mediator was from everlasting, and was a just and merciful decree, which yet does not at all excuse man's sin in crucifying him, Acts ii. 23. God had purposes of special favour towards his people long before he made any manifestations of such grace to them [2] Great is the happiness of the last times in comparison with what the former ages of the world enjoyed. [3] The redemption of Christ belongs to none but true believers.

II. He exhorts them to brotherly love.

1. He supposes that the gospel had already had such an effect upon them as to purify their souls while they obeyed it through the Spirit, and that it had produced at least an *unfeigned love of the brethren*; and thence he argues with them to proceed to a higher degree of affection, to love one another with a pure heart fervently, *v.* 22.

2. He further presses upon Christians the duty of loving one another with a pure heart fervently from the consideration of their spiritual relation; they are all *born again, not of corruptible seed, but incorruptible*, &c. Hence we may learn, (1) That all Christians are born again. (2) The word of God is the great means of regeneration, Jam. i. 18. The grace of regeneration is conveyed by the gospel. (3) This new and second birth is much more desirable and excellent than the first. (4) Those that are regenerate should love one another with a pure heart fervently.

A WORD FOR EVER
(*vv.* 24, 25)

The apostle having given an account of the excellency of the renewed spiritual man as born again, not of corruptible but incorruptible seed, he now sets before us the vanity of the natural man, taking him with all his ornaments and advantages about him: *For all flesh is as grass, and all the glory of man as the flower of grass*; and nothing can make him a solid substantial being but the being born again of the incorruptible seed, the word of God, which will transform him into a most excellent creature, whose glory will not fade like a flower, but shine like an angel; and this word is daily set before you in the preaching of the gospel.

CHAPTER TWO
THE MILK OF THE WORD
(*vv.* 1–3)

The holy apostle pursues his discourse, and very properly comes in with this necessary advice, *Wherefore laying aside all malice*, &c.

I. His advice is to lay aside or put off what is evil, as one would do an old rotten garment: "Cast it away with indignation never put it on more."

II. The apostle goes on to direct to wholesome and regular food, that they may grow thereby. The duty exhorted to is a strong and constant desire for the *word of God*, which word is here called *reasonable milk*, only, this phrase not being proper English, our translators rendered it *the milk of the word*, by which we are to understand food proper for the soul, or a reasonable creature, whereby the mind, not the body, is nourished and strengthened. This milk of the word must be *sincere*, not adulter-

ated by the mixtures of men, who often corrupt the word of God, 2 Cor. ii. 17. The manner in which they are to desire this sincere milk of the word is stated thus: *As newborn babes*. He puts them in mind of their regeneration. A new life requires suitable food. They, being newly born, must desire the milk of the word.

III. He adds an argument from their own experience: *If so be*, or *since that*, or *forasmuch as*, *you have tasted that the Lord is gracious*, *v.* 3. The apostle does not express a doubt, but affirms that these good Christians had tasted the goodness of God, and hence argues with them. "You ought to lay aside these vile sins (*v.* 1); you ought to desire the word of God; you ought to grow thereby, since you cannot deny but that you have tasted that the Lord is gracious."

THE PEOPLE OF GOD
(*vv.* 4–12)

I. The apostle here gives us a description of Jesus Christ as a living stone.

1. In this metaphorical description of Jesus Christ, he is called a stone, to denote his invincible strength and everlasting duration, and to teach his servants that he is their protection and security, the foundation on which they are built, and a rock of offence to all their enemies. He is the living stone, having eternal life in himself, and being the prince of life to all his people.

2. Having described Christ as the foundation, the apostle goes on to speak of the superstructure, the materials built upon him: *You also,*

as living stones, are built up, v. 6.
Christ, the foundation, is a living
stone. Christians are lively stones,
and these make a spiritual house,
and they are a holy priesthood; and,
though they have no bloody sacrifices of beasts to offer, yet they have
much better and more acceptable,
and they have an altar too on
which to present their offerings; for
they offer spiritual sacrifices, acceptable to God by Jesus Christ.

II. He confirms what he had
asserted of Christ being a *living
stone*, &c., from Isa. xxviii. 16. The
constituting of Christ Jesus head of
the church is an eminent work of
God: *I lay in Zion*. Jesus Christ is
the chief corner-stone that God
hath laid in his spiritual building.
The corner-stone stays inseparably
with the building, supports it,
unites it, and adorns it. So does
Christ by his holy church, his
spiritual house.

III. He deduces an important
inference, v. 7. Jesus Christ is said
to be the chief corner-stone. Hence
the apostle infers with respect to
good men, "To you therefore who
believe he is precious, or he is an
honour. Christ is the crown and
honour of a Christian; you who
believe will be so far from being
ashamed of him that you will boast
of him and glory in him for ever."
As to wicked men, the disobedient
will go on to disallow and reject
Jesus Christ; but God is resolved
that he shall be, in despite of all
opposition, the head of the corner.

IV. The apostle adds a further
description, still preserving the
metaphor of a stone, v. 8. The
words are taken from Isa. viii. 13,
14. Observe,

1. The builders, the chief-priests,
refused him, and the people
followed their leaders; and so
Christ became to them *a stone of
stumbling, and a rock of offence*, at
which they stumbled and hurt
themselves; and in return he fell
upon them as a mighty stone or
rock, and punished them with
destruction. Matt. xxi. 44, *Whosoever shall fall on this stone shall be
broken; but on whomsoever it shall
fall it will grind him to powder*.

2. Those who received him were
highly privileged, v. 9. The Jews
were exceedingly tender of their
ancient privileges, of being the only
people of God, taken into a special
covenant with him, and separated
from the rest of the world. "Now,"
say they, "if we submit to the
gospel-constitution, we shall lose
all this, and stand upon the same
level with the Gentiles."

(1) To this objection the apostle
answers, that if they did not submit
they were ruined (*vv.* 7, 8), but that
if they did submit they should lose
no real advantage, but continue
still what they desired to be, *a
chosen generation, a royal priesthood*, &c. Learn, [1] All true
Christians *are a chosen generation*;
they all make one family, a sort and
species of people distinct from the
common world, of another spirit,
principle, and practice, which they
could never be if they were not
chosen in Christ to be such, and
sanctified by his spirit. [2] All the
true servants of Christ are a royal
priesthood, separated from sin and
sinners, consecrated to God, and
offering to God spiritual services
and oblations, acceptable to God
through Jesus Christ. [3] All

Christians, wheresoever they be, compose one holy nation, collected under one head, agreeing in the same manners and customs, and governed by the same laws; and they are a holy nation, because consecrated and devoted to God, renewed and sanctified by his Holy Spirit. [4] It is the honour of the servants of Christ that they are God's peculiar people. They are the people of his acquisition, choice, care, and delight.

(2) To make this people content, and thankful for the great mercies and dignities brought unto them by the gospel, the apostle advises them to compare their former and their present state. Time was when they were not a people, nor had they obtained mercy, but they were solemnly disclaimed and divorced (Jer. iii. 8; Hos. i. 6, 9); but now they are taken in again to be the people of God, and have obtained mercy.

V. He warns them to beware of fleshly lusts, *v.* 11. The duty is to abstain from, and to suppress, the first inclination or rise of fleshly lusts. These Christians ought to avoid, considering, 1. The respect they have with God and good men: They are *dearly beloved*. 2. Their condition in the world: *They are strangers and pilgrims*. 3. The mischief and danger these sins do: *"They war against the soul*; and therefore your souls ought to war against them."

VI. He exhorts them further to adorn their profession by an honest manner of life. Their behaviour in every turn, every instance, and every action of their lives, ought to be honest; that is,

good, lovely, decent, amiable, and without blame.

SUBMISSION (vv. 13–25)

I. The case of subjects. Christians were not only reputed innovators in religion, but disturbers of the state; it was highly necessary, therefore, that the apostle should settle the rules and measures of obedience to the civil magistrate, which he does here, where,

1. The duty required is submission, which comprises loyalty and reverence to their persons, obedience to their just laws and commands, and subjection to legal penalties.

2. The persons or objects to whom this submission is due are described, (1) More generally: *Every ordinance of man.* (2) Particularly: *To the king, as supreme.*

3. The reasons to enforce this duty are,

(1) For the Lord's sake, who has ordained magistracy for the good of mankind, who has required obedience and submission (Rom. xiii.), and whose honour is concerned in the dutiful behaviour of subjects to their sovereigns.

(2) From the end and use of the magistrate's office, which are, to punish evil-doers, and to praise and encourage all those that do well.

(3) Another reason why Christians should submit to the civil magistrate is because it *is the will of God*, and consequently their duty; and because it is the way to put to silence the malicious slanders of ignorant and foolish men, *v.* 15.

(4) He reminds them of the spiritual nature of Christian liberty. They were free spiritually from the

bondage of sin and Satan, and the ceremonial law; but they must not make their Christian liberty a cloak or covering for any wickedness, or for the neglect of any duty towards God or towards their superiors, but must still remember they were *the servants of God.*

4. The apostle concludes his discourse concerning the duty of subjects with four admirable precepts: (1) *Honour all men.* A due respect is to be given to all men. (2) *Love the brotherhood.* All Christians are a fraternity, united to Christ the head. (3) *Fear God* with the highest reverence, duty, and submission. (4) *Honour the king* with that highest honour that is peculiarly due to him above other men.

II. The case of servants wanted and apostolical determination as well as that of subjects, for they imagined that their Christian liberty set them free from their unbelieving and cruel masters; to this the apostle answers, *Servants, be subject, v.* 18. Observe,

I. He orders them to *be subject,* to do their business faithfully and honestly, to conduct themselves with reverence and affection, and to submit patiently to hardships and inconveniences.

2. Having charged them to be subject, he condescends to reason with them about it.

(1) If they were patient under their hardships, while they suffered unjustly, and continued doing their duty to their unbelieving and untoward masters, this would be acceptable to God, and he would reward all that they suffered for conscience towards him; but to be patient when they were justly chastised would deserve no commendation at all; it is only *doing well, and suffering patiently for that, which is acceptable with God, vv.* 19, 20.

(2) More reasons are given to encourage Christian servants to patience under unjust sufferings, *v.* 21. [1] From their Christian calling and profession: *Hereunto were you called.* [2] From the example of Christ, who *suffered for us,* and so became our *example, that we should follow his steps,* whence learn,

3. The example of Christ's subjection and patience is here explained and amplified: *Christ suffered,* (1) Wrongfully, and without cause; for he *did no sin, v.* 22. (2) Patiently: *When he was reviled, he reviled not again* (*v.* 23). *But committed* both *himself* and his cause *to God that judgeth righteously,* who would in time clear his innocency, and avenge him on his enemies.

4. Lest any should think, from what is said, *vv.* 21–23, that Christ's death was designed merely for an example of patience under sufferings, the apostle here adds a more glorious design and effect of it: *Who his own self,* &c., where note, (1) The person suffering—Jesus Christ: *His own self—in his own body.* (2) The sufferings he underwent were *stripes,* wounds, and death, *the death of the cross*— servile and ignominious punishments! (3) The reason of his sufferings: He *bore our sins,* which teaches, [1] That Christ, in his sufferings, stood charged with our sins, as one who had undertaken to put them away by *the sacrifice of*

himself, Isa. liii. 6. [2] That he bore the punishment of them, and thereby satisfied divine justice. [3] That hereby he takes away our sins, and removes them away from us. (4) Christ was bruised and crucified as an expiatory sacrifice, and *by his stripes we are healed*.

5. The apostle concludes his advice to Christian servants, by putting them in mind of the difference between their former and present condition, *v*. 25. They *were as sheep going astray, but are now returned*. The word is passive, and shows that the return of a sinner is the effect of divine grace.

CHAPTER THREE

HUSBANDS AND WIVES
(vv. 1–7)

The apostle having treated of the duties of subjects to their sovereigns, and of servants to their masters, proceeds to explain the duty of husbands and wives.

I. Lest the Christian matrons should imagine that their conversion to Christ, and their interest in all Christian privileges, exempted them from subjection to their pagan or Jewish husbands, the apostle here tells them,

1. In what the duty of wives consists.

(1) In *subjection*, or an affectionate submission to the will, and obedience to the just authority, of *their own husbands*.

(2) In *fear*, or reverence to their husbands, Eph. v. 33.

(3) In a *chaste conversation*, which their unbelieving husbands would accurately observe and attend to.

(4) In preferring the ornaments of the mind to those of the body.

2. The duties of Christian wives being in their nature difficult, the apostle enforces them by the example, (1) Of the holy women of old, who trusted in God, *v*. 5. (2) Of Sara, who obeyed her husband, and followed him when he went from Ur of the Chaldeans, *not knowing whither he went*, and *called him lord*.

II. The husband's duty to the wife comes next to be considered.

1. The particulars are, (1) *Cohabitation*, which forbids unnecessary separation, and implies a mutual communication of goods and persons one to another, with delight and concord. (2) *Dwelling with the wife according to knowledge*; not according to lust, as brutes; nor according to passion, as devils; but according to knowledge, as wise and sober men, who know the word of God and their own duty. (3) *Giving honour to the wife*—giving due respect to her.

2. The reasons are, Because she is *the weaker vessel* by nature and constitution, and so ought to be defended. They are *heirs together of the grace of life*, of all the blessings of this life and another, and therefore should live peaceably and quietly one with another, and, if they do not, their prayers one with another and one for another will be hindered, so that often "you will not pray at all, or, if you do, you will pray with a discomposed ruffled mind, and so without success."

FRIENDS AND ENEMIES
(vv. 8–15)

The apostle here passes from special to more general exhortations.

I. He teaches us how Christians and friends should treat one another. He advises Christians to *be all of one mind*, to be unanimous in the belief of the same faith, and the practice of the same duties of religion; and, whereas the Christians at that time were many of them in a suffering condition, he charges them to *have compassion one of another*, to *love as brethren*, to *pity* those who were in distress, and to *be courteous* to all.

II. He instructs us how to behave towards enemies. The apostle knew that Christians would *be hated* and evil-entreated *of all men for Christ's sake*; therefore,

1. He warns them not to return *evil for evil*, *nor railing for railing*; but, on the contrary, "when they rail at you, do you bless them; when they give you evil words, do you give them good ones; for Christ has both by his word and example called you to bless those that curse you, and has settled a blessing on you as your everlasting inheritance, though you were unworthy."

2. He gives an excellent prescription for a comfortable happy life in this quarrelsome ill-natured world (*v.* 10): it is quoted from Ps. xxxiv. 12–14. Avoid doing any real damage or hurt to your neighbour, but be ever ready to do good, and to overcome evil with good; seek peace with all men, and pursue it, though it retire from you.

3. He shows that Christians need not fear that such patient inoffensive behaviour as is prescribed will invite and encourage the cruelty of their enemies, for God will thereby be engaged on their side: *For the eyes of the Lord are over the righteous* (*v.* 12).

4. This patient humble behaviour of Christians is further recommended and urged from two considerations: (1) This will be the best and surest way to prevent suffering; for *who is he that will harm you? v.* 13. (2) This is the way to improve sufferings. "*If you be followers of that which is good*, and yet *suffer*, this is suffering for righteousness' sake (*v.* 14), and will be your glory and your happiness, as it entitles you to the blessing promised by Christ (Matt. v. 10). When this principle is laid deeply into your hearts, the next thing, as to men, is to be always ready, that is, able and willing, *to give an answer*, or make an apology or defence, of the faith you profess, and that *to every man that asketh a reason of your hope*, what sort of hope you have, for which you suffer such hardships in the world. These confessions of our faith ought to be made *with meekness and fear*; apologies for our religion ought to be made with modesty and meekness, in the fear of God, with jealousy over ourselves, and reverence to our superiors.

OUR SUFFERINGS AND CHRIST'S (*vv.* 16–20)

The confession of a Christian's faith cannot credibly be supported but by the two means here specified —*a good conscience* and a *good conversation.* Conscience is good when it does its office well, when it is kept pure and uncorrupt, and clear from guilt; then it will justify you, though men accuse you. *A good conversation in Christ* is a holy life, according to the doctrine and example of Christ.

Then, I. The example of Christ is proposed as an · argument for patience under sufferings. In the case of our Lord's suffering, it was the just that suffered for the unjust; he substituted himself in our room and stead, and bore our iniquities. He that knew no sin suffered instead of those that knew no righteousness. The merit and perfection of Christ's sacrifice were such that for him to suffer once was enough. The legal sacrifices were repeated from day to day, and from year to year; but the sacrifice of Christ, once offered, purgeth away sin, Heb. vii. 27; ix. 26, 28; x. 10, 12, 14. If he once suffered, and then entered into glory, shall not we be patient under trouble, since it will be but a little time and we shall follow him to glory?

II. The apostle passes from the example of Christ to that of the old world, and sets before the Jews, to whom he wrote, the different event of those who believed and obeyed Christ preaching by Noah, from those that continued disobedient and unbelieving, intimating to the Jews that they were under a like sentence.

1. For the explication of this we may notice, (1) The preacher— Christ Jesus, who has interested himself in the affairs of the church and of the world ever since he was first promised to Adam, Gen. iii. 15. (2) The hearers. Because they were dead and disembodied when the apostle speaks of them, therefore he properly calls them spirits now *in prison*; not that they were *in prison when Christ preached to them*. (3) The sin of these people: They were *disobedient*, that is, *rebellious*, *unpersuadable*, and *unbelieving*, as the word signifies; this their sin is aggravated from the patience and *long-suffering of God* (which *once waited* upon them for 120 years together, *while Noah was preparing the ark*, and by that, as well as by his preaching, giving them fair warning of what was coming upon them. (4) The event of all: Their bodies were drowned, and their spirits cast into hell, which is called a prison (Matt. v. 25; 2 Pet. ii. 4, 5); but Noah and his family, who believed and were obedient, *were saved in the ark*.

2. From the whole we learn that, (1) God takes exact notice of all the means and advantages that people in all ages have had for the salvation of their souls; it is put to the account of the old world that Christ offered them his help, sent his Spirit, gave them fair warning by Noah, and waited a long time for their amendment. (2) Though the patience of God wait long upon sinners, yet it will expire at last; it is beneath the majesty of the great God always to wait upon man in vain. (3) The spirits of disobedient sinners, as soon as they are out of their bodies, are committed to the prison of hell, whence there is no redemption. (4) The way of the most is neither the best, the wisest, nor the safest way to follow.

BAPTISM'S MEANING
(*vv.* 21, 22)

Noah's salvation in the ark upon the water prefigured the salvation of all good Christians in the church by baptism.

I. Peter declares what he means by saving baptism; not the outward ceremony of washing with water, which, in itself, does no more than put away the filth of the flesh, but it is that baptism wherein there is a faithful answer or restipulation of a resolved good conscience, engaging to believe in, and be entirely devoted to, God, the Father, Son, and Holy Ghost, renouncing at the same time the flesh, the world, and the devil.

II. The apostle shows that the efficacy of baptism to salvation depends not upon the work done, but upon the resurrection of Christ, which supposes his death, and is the foundation of our faith and hope, to which we are rendered conformable by dying to sin, and rising again to holiness and newness of life.

III. The apostle, having mentioned the death and resurrection of Christ, proceeds to speak of his ascension, and sitting at the right hand of the Father, as a subject fit to be considered by these believers for their comfort in their suffering condition, *v.* 22.

CHAPTER FOUR

CEASING FROM SIN (*vv.* 1–3)

The apostle here draws a new inference from the consideration of Christ's sufferings. As he had before made use of it to persuade to patience in suffering, so here to mortification of sin. Observe,

I. How the exhortation is expressed. The supposition is *that Christ had suffered* for us in the flesh, or in his human nature. The consequent or inference is, "*Arm* and fortify *yourselves likewise with the same mind*, courage, and resolution." The word flesh in the former part of the verse signifies Christ's human nature, but in the latter part it signifies man's corrupt nature. So the sense is, "As Christ suffered in his human nature, do you, according to your baptismal vow and profession, make your corrupt nature suffer, by putting to death the body of sin by self-denial and mortification; for, if you do thus suffer, you will be conformable to Christ in his death and resurrection, and will *cease from sin.*"

II. How it is further explained, *v.* 2. The apostle explains what he means by being dead to sin, and ceasing from sin, both negatively and positively. Negatively, a Christian ought *no longer to live the rest of his time in the flesh*, to the sinful lusts and corrupt desires of carnal wicked men; but, positively, he ought to conform himself to the revealed will of the holy God.

III. How it is enforced (*v.* 3): *For the time past of our life may suffice us to have wrought the will of the Gentiles*, &c. Here the apostle argues from equity. "It is but just, equal, and reasonable, that as you have hitherto all the former part of your life served sin and Satan, so you should now serve the living God."

A VISIBLE CHANGE (*vv.* 4–6)

I. Here you have the visible change wrought in those who in the foregoing verse were represented as having been in the former part of their life very wicked. They no longer run on in the same courses, or with the same companions, as they used to do. Hereupon observe the conduct of their wicked acquaintance towards them. 1. *They think it strange*, they are surprised and wonder at it, as at something new and unusual, that their old friends should be so much altered. 2. *They speak evil of them.* Their surprise carries them to blasphemy. They speak evil of their persons, of their way, their religion, and their God.

II. For the comfort of the servants of God, it is here added,

1. That all wicked people, especially those who speak evil of such as are not as bad as themselves, shall *give an account.*

2. That *for this cause was the gospel preached also to those that are dead, that they might be judged according to men in the flesh, but live according to God in the Spirit*, *v.* 6. Some understand this difficult place thus: *For this cause was the gospel preached* to all the faithful of old, who are now dead in Christ, that thereby they might be taught and encouraged to bear the unrighteous judgments and persecutions which the rage of men put upon them *in the flesh, but might live in the Spirit unto God.* Others take the expression, *that they might be judged according to men in the flesh*, in a spiritual sense, thus: The gospel was preached to them, to judge them, condemn them, and reprove them, for the corruption of their natures, and the viciousness of their lives, while they lived after the manner of the heathen or the mere natural man; and that, having thus mortified their sins, they might live according to God, a new and spiritual life.

GOOD STEWARDS (*vv.* 7–11)

We have here an awful position or doctrine, and an inference drawn from it. The position is that the *end of all things is at hand.* The inference from this comprises a series of exhortations.

1. To sobriety and watchfulness: *Be you therefore sober, v.* 7.

2. To charity: *And above all things have fervent charity among yourselves, v.* 8. Here is a noble rule in Christianity. Christians ought to love one another, which implies an affection to their persons, a desire of their welfare, and a hearty endeavour to promote it.

3. To hospitality, *v.* 9. The hospitality here required is a free and kind entertainment of strangers and travellers.

4. To the improvement of talents, *v.* 11.

(1) The rule is that whatever gift, ordinary or extraordinary, whatever power, ability, or capacity of doing good is given to us, we should minister, or do service, with the same *one to another*, accounting ourselves not masters, but only *stewards of the manifold grace*, or the various gifts, of God.

(2) The apostle exemplifies his direction about gifts in two particulars—speaking and ministering, concerning which he gives these rules: [1] *If any man*, whether a minister in public or a Christian in private conference, *speak* or teach, he must do it *as the oracles of God*, which direct us as to the matter of our speech. [2] *If any man minister*, either as a deacon, distributing the alms of the church and taking care of the poor, or as a private person,

by charitable gifts and contributions, *let him do it as of the ability which God giveth*. He who has received plenty and ability from God ought to minister plentifully, and according to his ability.

SUFFERING AS A CHRISTIAN (*vv.* 12–19)

The frequent repetition of counsel and comfort to Christians, considered as sufferers, in every chapter of this epistle, shows that the greatest danger these new converts were in arose from the persecutions to which their embracing Christianity exposed them. An unmortified spirit is very unfit to bear trials. Observe,

I. The apostle's kind manner of address to these poor despised Christians: they were his *beloved*, *v.* 9.

II. His advice to them, relating to their sufferings, which is,

1. That they should not think them strange, nor be surprised at them, as if some unexpected event befell them; for,

(1) Though they be sharp and fiery, yet they are designed only to try, not to ruin them, to try their sincerity, strength, patience, and trust in God.

(2) From the fiery trial the apostle descends to a lower degree of persecution — that of the tongue by slander and reproach, *v.* 14. He supposes that this sort of suffering would fall to their lot: they would be reviled, evil-spoken of, and slandered for the name or sake of Christ. In such case he asserts, *Happy are you*. By your patience and fortitude in suffering, by your dependence upon the promises of

God, and adhering to the word which the Holy Spirit hath revealed, *he is on your part glorified*; but by the contempt and reproaches cast upon you *the Spirit itself* is evil-spoken of and blasphemed."

2. That they should take care they did not suffer justly, as evildoers, *v.* 15. One would think such a caution as this needless to such an excellent set of Christians as these were. But their enemies charged them with these and other foul crimes; therefore the apostle, when he was settling the rules of the Christian religion, thought these cautions necessary, forbidding every one of them to hurt the life or the estate and property of any one, or to do any sort of evil, or, without call and necessity, to play the *bishop in another man's charge*, or busy himself *in other men's matters*. To this caution he adds a direction, *that if any man suffer* for the cause of Christianity, and with a patient Christian spirit, he ought not to account it a shame, but an honour to him; and ought to glorify God who hath thus dignified him, *v.* 16.

3. That their trials were now at hand, and they should stand prepared accordingly, *vv.* 17, 18.

(1) He tells them that the time had come when *judgment must begin at the house of God*. The usual method of Providence has been this: When God brings great calamities and sore judgments upon whole nations, he generally begins with his own people, Isa. x. 12; Jer. xxv. 29; Ezek. ix. 6. "Such a time of universal calamity is now at hand, which was foretold by our Saviour, Matt. xxiv, 9, 10. This renders all the foregoing exhorta-

tions to patience necessary for you."

(2) He intimates the irremediable doom of the wicked: *If the righteous scarcely be saved, where shall the ungodly and sinner appear*, *v.* 18. This whole verse is taken from Prov. xi. 31.

4. That when called to suffer, *according to the will of God*, they should look chiefly to the safety of their souls, which are put into hazard by affliction, and cannot be kept secure otherwise than by *committing them to God*, who will undertake the charge, if we commit them to him in well-doing; for he is their Creator, and has out of mere grace made many kind promises to them of eternal salvation, in which he will show himself faithful and true, *v.* 19.

CHAPTER FIVE

ADVICE TO ELDERS (*vv.* 1–4)

Here we may observe,

I. The persons to whom this exhortation is given—to the presbyters, pastors, and spiritual guides of the church, elders by office, rather than by age, ministers of those churches to whom he wrote this epistle.

II. The person who gives this exhortation—the apostle Peter: *I exhort*; and, to give force to this exhortation, he tells them he was their brother-presbyter or fellow-elder, and so puts nothing upon them but what he was ready to perform himself. He was also *a witness of the sufferings of Christ*, being with him in the garden, attending him to the palace of the high-priest, and very likely being a spectator of his suffering upon the

cross, at a distance among the crowd, Acts iii. 15. He adds that he was also *a partaker of the glory* that was in some degree revealed at the transfiguration (Matt. xvii. 1–3), and shall be completely enjoyed at the second coming of Jesus Christ.

III. The pastor's duty described, and the manner in which that duty ought to be performed. The pastoral duty is three-fold: 1. *To feed the flock*, by preaching to them the sincere word of God, and ruling them according to such directions and discipline as the word of God prescribes. 2. The pastors of the church must *take the oversight thereof*. 3. They must be *examples to the flock*, and practise the holiness, self-denial, mortification, and all other Christian duties, which they preach and recommend to their people.

IV. In opposition to that filthy lucre which many propose to themselves as their principal motive in undertaking and discharging the pastoral office, the apostle sets before them the crown of glory designed by the great shepherd, Jesus Christ, for all his faithful ministers.

HUMILITY (*vv.* 5–7)

Having settled and explained the duty of the pastors or spiritual guides of the church, the apostle comes now to instruct the flock,

I. How to behave themselves to their ministers and to one another. He exhorts those that are younger and inferior to *submit themselves to the elder*, to give due respect and reverence to their persons, and to yield to their admonitions, reproof, and authority, enjoining and commanding what the word of God requires, Heb. xiii. 17. As to one another, the rule is that they should all *be subject one to another*, so far as to receive the reproofs and counsels one of another, and be ready to *bear one another's burdens*, and perform all the offices of friendship and charity one to another. He advises them to *be clothed with humility*. Observe, Humility is the great preserver of peace and order in all Christian churches and societies, consequently pride is the great disturber of them, and the cause of most dissensions and breaches in the church.

II. The apostle, knowing that these Christians were already under very hard circumstances, rightly supposes that what he had foretold of greater hardships yet coming might excite in them abundance of care and fear about the event of these difficulties. His advice is to *cast all their care*, or *all care of themselves, upon God*. Learn, 1. The best of Christians are apt to labour under the burden of anxious and excessive care; the apostle calls it, *all your care*, intimating that the cares of Christians are various and of more sorts than one: personal cares, family cares, cares for the present, cares for the future, cares for themselves, for others, and for the church. The best remedy against immoderate care is to *cast our care upon God*, and resign every event to his wise and gracious determination.

RESISTING THE DEVIL
(*vv.* 8, 9)

Here the apostle does three things:
I. He shows them their danger

from an enemy more cruel and restless than even the worst of men, whom he describes.

1. By his characters and names.
2. By his business: *He walks about, seeking whom he may devour*; his whole design is to devour and destroy souls.

II. Hence he infers that it is their duty, 1. To *be sober*, and to govern both the outward and the inward man by the rules of temperance, modesty, and mortification. 2. To *be vigilant*; not secure or careless, but rather suspicious of constant danger from this spiritual enemy, and, under that apprehension, to be watchful and diligent to prevent his designs and save our souls. 3. To resist him *stedfast in the faith*.

III. He tells them that their care was not singular, for they knew that the like afflictions befell their brethren in all parts of the world, and that all the people of God were their fellow-soldiers in this warfare.

PRAYER (*vv.* 10–14)

We now come to the conclusion of this epistle, which,

I. The apostle begins with a most weighty prayer, which he addresses to God as *the God of all grace*, the author and finisher of every heavenly gift and quality, acknowledging, on their behalf, that God had already called them to be partakers of that eternal glory, which, being his own, he had promised and settled upon them, through the merit and intercession of Jesus Christ.

II. He recapitulates the design of his writing this epistle to them (*v.* 12), which was, 1. To testify, and in the strongest terms to assure them, that the doctrine of salvation, which he had explained and they had embraced, was the true account of the grace of God, foretold by the prophets and published by Jesus Christ. 2. To exhort them earnestly that, as they had embraced the gospel, they would continue stedfast in it, notwithstanding the arts of seducers, or the persecutions of enemies.

III. He recommends *Silvanus*, the person by whom he sent them this brief epistle, as a brother whom he esteemed faithful and friendly to them, and hoped they would account him so, though he was a minister of the uncircumcision.

IV. He closes with salutations and a solemn benediction. He exhorts them to fervent love and charity one towards another, and to express this by giving *the kiss of peace* (*v.* 14), according to the common custom of those times and countries, and so concludes with a benediction, which he confines to those *that are in Christ Jesus*, united to him by faith and sound members of his mystical body.

PETER

CHAPTER ONE
GREETINGS (vv. 1–4)

The apostle Peter, being moved by the Holy Ghost to write once more to those who from among the Jews were turned to faith in Christ, begins this second epistle with an introduction, wherein the same persons are described and the same blessings are desired that are in the preface to his former letter. Observe, (1) The fountain of all spiritual blessings is the divine power of Jesus Christ, who could not discharge all the office of Mediator, unless he was God as well as man. (2) All things that have any relation to, and influence upon, the true spiritual life, the life and power of godliness, are from Jesus Christ; *in him all fulness dwells*, and it is from him that we receive, *and grace for grace* (John i. 16). (3) Knowledge of God, and faith in him, are the channel whereby all spiritual supports and comforts are conveyed to us; but then we must own and acknowledge God as the author of our effectual calling, for so he is here described: *Him that hath called us to glory and virtue.* (4) In the fourth verse the apostle goes on to encourage their faith and hope in looking for an increase of grace and peace, because the same glory and virtue are employed and evidenced in giving the promises of the gospel that are exercised in our effectual calling.

ADDITIONS TO FAITH
(vv. 5–11)

In these words the apostle comes to the chief thing intended in this epistle—to excite and engage them to advance in grace and holiness.

I. Here we cannot but observe how the believer's way is marked out step by step. 1. He must get *virtue*, by which some understand *justice*; and then the *knowledge, temperance, and patience* that follow, being joined with it, the apostle may be supposed to put them upon pressing after the four cardinal virtues, or the four elements that go to the making up of every virtue or virtuous action. 2. The believer must add *knowledge* to his virtue, prudence to his courage. Every believer must labour after the knowledge and wisdom that are profitable to direct, both as to the proper method and order wherein all Christian duties are to be performed and as to the way and manner of performing them. 3. We must add *temperance* to our knowledge. We must be sober and moderate in our love to, and use of, the good things of this life. 4. Add to temperance *patience*, which must *have its perfect work*, or we cannot be *perfect and entire, wanting nothing*

(Jam. i. 4). 5. To patience we must add *godliness*, and this is the very thing which is produced by patience, for that works experience, Rom. v. 4. Hereby they are brought to the child-like fear and reverential love wherein true godliness consists: to this, 6. We must add *brotherly-kindness*, a tender affection to all our fellow-christians. 7. *Charity*, or a love of good-will to all mankind, must be added to the love of delight which we have for those who are the children of God.

II. All the forementioned graces must be had, or we shall not be *thoroughly furnished for all good works*—for the duties of the first and second table, for active and passive obedience, and for those services wherein we are to imitate God as well as for those wherein we only obey him—and therefore to engage us to an industrious and unwearied pursuit of them, the apostle sets forth the advantages that redound to all who successfully labour so as to get these things to *be and abound in them*, *vv.* 8–11.

THE PRESENT TRUTH
(*vv.* 12–15)

I. The importance and advantage of progress and perseverance in grace and holiness made the apostle to be very diligent in doing the work of a minister of Christ, that he might thereby excite and assist them to be diligent in the duty of Christians.

II. The apostle, being set upon the work, tells us (*v.* 14) what makes him earnest in this matter, even the knowledge he had, not only that he must certainly, but also that he must shortly, *put off this tabernacle*.

THE HOLY MOUNT
(*vv.* 16–18)

Here we have the reason of giving the foregoing exhortation, and that with so much diligence and seriousness. These things are not idle tales, or a vain thing, but of undoubted truth and vast concern. The gospel is not a *cunningly devised fable*. 1. The preaching of the gospel is a making known the power of Christ, that he is able to save to the uttermost all who come to God by him. He is the mighty God, and therefore can save from both the guilt and the filth of sin. 2. The coming of Christ also is made known by the preaching of the gospel. 3. And though this gospel of Christ has been blasphemously called a *fable*, yet our apostle proves that it is of the greatest certainty and reality, inasmuch as during our blessed Saviour's abode here on earth, when he took on him the form of a servant and was found in fashion as a man, he sometimes manifested himself to be God, and particularly to our apostle and the two sons of Zebedee, who *were eye-witnesses of his divine majesty, when he was transfigured before them*. This Peter, James, and John, were eye-witnesses of, and therefore might and ought to attest; and surely their testimony is true, when they witness what they have seen with their eyes, yea, and heard with their ears: for, besides the visible glory that Christ was invested with here on earth, there was an audible voice from heaven.

A SURE WORD (*vv.* 19–21)

Here note,

I. The description that is given of the scriptures of the Old Testament: they are called *a more sure word of prophecy. Moses and the prophets* more powerfully persuade than even miracles themselves, Luke xvi. 31. How firm and sure should our faith be, who have such a firm and sure word to rest upon! All the prophecies of the Old Testament are more sure and certain to us who have the history of the most exact and minute accomplishment of them.

II. The encouragement the apostle gives us to search the scriptures. He tells us, *We do well if we take heed to them*; that is, apply our minds to understand the sense, and our hearts to believe the truth, of this sure word, yea, bend ourselves to it, that we may be moulded and fashioned by it. When the light of the scripture is darted into the blind mind and dark understanding by the Holy Spirit of God, then the *spiritual day dawns and the day-star arises in that soul.*

III. The apostle lays down one thing as previously necessary to our giving heed to, and getting good by, the scriptures, and that is the knowing that all prophecy is of divine origin. Now this important truth he not only asserts, but proves. 1. Observe, No scripture prophecy is of private interpretation (or a man's own proper opinion, an explication of his own mind), but the revelation of the mind of God. This was the difference between the prophets of the Lord and the false prophets who have been in the world. 2. This important truth of the divine origin of the scriptures (that what is contained in them is the mind of God and not of man) is to be known and owned by all who will give heed to the sure word of prophecy. 3. The divinity of the scriptures must be known and acknowledged in the first place, before men can profitably use them, before they can give good heed to them.

IV. Seeing it is so absolutely necessary that persons be fully persuaded of the scripture's divine origin, the apostle (*v.* 21) tells us how the Old Testament came to be compiled, and that, 1. Negatively: *It came not by the will of man.* Neither the things themselves that are recorded, and make up the several parts of the Old Testament, are the opinions of men, nor was the will of any of the prophets or penmen of the scriptures the rule or reason why any of those things were written which make up the canon of the scripture. 2. Affirmatively: *Holy men of God spoke as they were moved by the Holy Ghost.* So that the very words of scripture are to be accounted the words of the Holy Ghost, and all the plainness and simplicity, all the power and virtue, all the elegance and propriety, of the very words and expressions are to be regarded by us as proceeding from God.

CHAPTER TWO

FALSE TEACHERS (*vv.* 1–3)

I. In all ages of the church, and under all dispensations, when God sends true prophets, the devil sends some to seduce and deceive, false prophets in the Old Testament, and false Christs, false apostles, and seducing teachers, in the New.

II. He proceeds, in the second verse, to tell us the consequence with respect to others; and here we may learn, 1. Corrupt leaders seldom lack many to follow them; though the way of error is a pernicious way, yet many are ready to walk therein. 2. The spreading of error will bring up an evil report on the way of truth; that is, the way of salvation by Jesus Christ, who is *the way, the truth, and the life*.

III. Observe, in the next place, the method seducers take to draw disciples after them: they use *feigned words*; they flatter, and by good words and fair speeches deceive the hearts of the simple.

THE JUDGMENT OF GOD
(*vv.* 3–6)

I. See how God dealt with the angels who sinned. Observe, 1. No excellency will exempt a sinner from punishment. 2. By how much the more excellent the offender, by so much the more severe the punishment. 3. Sin debases and degrades the persons who commit it. 4. Those who rebel against the God of heaven shall all be sent down to hell. 5. Sin is the work of darkness, and darkness is the wages of sin. 6. As sin binds men over to punishment, so misery and torment hold men under punishment. 7. The last degree of torment is not till the day of judgment.

II. See how God dealt with the old world, even in much the same way that he dealt with the angels.

He spared not the old world. Observe what was the procuring cause of this: *it was a world of ungodly men*. Ungodliness puts men out of the divine protection, and exposes them to utter destruction.

III. See how God dealt with Sodom and Gomorrah; though they were situated in a country like the garden of the Lord, yet, if in such a fruitful soil they abound in sin, God can soon turn a fruitful land into barrenness and a well-watered country into dust and ashes. Let us take warning by all the instances of God's taking vengeance, which are recorded for our admonition, and to prevent our promising ourselves impunity, though we go on in a course of sin.

DELIVERANCE (*vv.* 7–9)

Here observe, 1. The character given of Lot; he is called *a just man*. And here is a just man in the midst of a most corrupt and profligate generation universally gone off from all good. 2. The impression the sins of others made upon this righteous man. Though the sinner takes pleasure in his wickedness, it is a grief and vexation to the soul of the righteous. 3. Here is particular mention of the duration and continuance of this good man's grief and vexation: it was *from day to day*. It is here presupposed that the righteous must have their temptations and trials. The devil and his instruments will thrust sore at them, that they may fall; and, if we will get to heaven, it must be through many tribulations. It is therefore our duty to reckon upon and prepare for them.

DANGERS OF APOSTASY AND ERROR (*vv.* 10–22)

But why will God thus deal with these false teachers? This he shows in what follows.

I. *These walk after the flesh*; they follow the devices and desires of their own hearts, they give up themselves to the conduct of their own fleshly mind, refusing to make their reason stoop to divine revelation, and to *bring every thought to the obedience of Christ*; they, in their lives, act directly contrary to God's righteous precepts, and comply with the demands of corrupt nature.

II. This he aggravates, by setting forth the very different conduct of more excellent creatures, even the *angels*. Let us, who pray that God's *will may be done on earth as it is in heaven*, imitate the angels in this particular; if we complain of wicked men, let it be to God, and that not with rage and reviling, but with compassion and composedness of mind, that may evidence that we belong to him who is meek and merciful.

III. The apostle, having shown (*v.* 11) how unlike seducing teachers are to the most excellent creatures, proceeds (*v.* 12) to show how they are to the most inferior: they are *like the horse and mule, which have no understanding*; they are *as natural brute beasts, made to be taken and destroyed*.

IV. The apostle (*vv.* 15, 16) proves that they are *cursed children*, even such covetous persons as *the Lord abhors*, by showing, 1. They *have forsaken the right way*; and it cannot be but such self-seekers must be out of the right way, which is a self-denying way. 2. They have gone into a wrong way: they have erred and strayed from the way of life, and gone over into the path which leads to death, and takes hold of hell; and this he makes out by showing it to be *the way of Balaam, the son of Bosor*. Balaam was indeed restrained from actually *cursing the people*, but he had so strong a desire after the honours and riches that were promised him that he went as far as he could, and did his utmost to get from under the restraint that was upon him.

V. The apostle proceeds (*v.* 17) to a further description of seducing teachers, whom he sets forth,

1. As *wells*, or fountains, *without water*. In vain then are all our expectations of being fed and filled with knowledge and understanding by those who are themselves ignorant and empty.

2. As *clouds carried with a tempest*. When we see a cloud we expect a refreshing shower from it; but these are clouds which yield no rain, for they are driven with the wind, but not of the Spirit, but the stormy wind or tempest of their own ambition and covetousness. To prevent these men's gaining proselytes, he tells us that, in the midst of all their talk of liberty, they themselves are the vilest slaves, for they are the servants of corruption; their own lusts have got a complete victory over them, and they are actually in bondage to them, making *provision for the flesh*, to satisfy its cravings, comply with its directions, and obey its commands. Their minds and hearts

are so far corrupted and depraved that they have neither power nor will to refuse the task that is imposed on them. They are conquered and captivated by their spiritual enemies, and yield their members servants of unrighteousness: and what a shame it is to be overcome and commanded by those who are themselves _the servants of corruption, and slaves to their own lusts!_

VI. The apostle, in the last two verses of the chapter, sets himself to prove that a state of apostasy is worse than a state of ignorance; for it is a _condemning of the way of righteousness_, after they have had some knowledge of it, and expressed some liking to it; it carries in it a declaring that they have found some iniquity in the way of righteousness and some falsehood in the word of truth.

THE LAST DAYS (_vv._ 1–7)

That the apostle might the better reach his end in writing this epistle, which is to make them steady and constant in a fiducial and practical remembrance of the doctrine of the gospel, he, 1. Expresses his special affection and tenderness for them, by calling them _beloved_. 2. He evinces a sincere love to them, and hearty concern for them, by writing the same thing to them, though in other words. 3. The better to recommend the matter, he tells them that what he would have them to remember are, (1) _The words spoken by the holy prophets_, who were divinely inspired, both en-

lightened and sanctified by the Holy Ghost. (2) _The commandments of the apostles of the Lord and Saviour_; and therefore the disciples and servants of Christ ought to regard what those who are sent by him have declared unto them to be the will of their Lord.

To quicken and excite us to a serious minding and firm adhering to what God has revealed to us by the prophets and apostles, we are told that there will be _scoffers_, men who will _make a mock of sin_, and of salvation from it. Now to prevent the true Christian's being overcome, when attacked by these scoffers, we are told,

I. What sort of persons they are: they _walk after their own lusts_, they follow the devices and desires of their own hearts, and carnal corrupt affections, not the dictates and directions of right reason and an enlightened well-informed judgment.

II. We also are forewarned how far they will proceed: they will attempt to shake and unsettle us, even as to our belief of Christ's second coming; they will scoffingly say, _Where is the promise of his coming?_ _v._ 4.

III. We are also forewarned of the method of their reasoning, for while they laugh they will pretend to argue too. To this purpose they add that _since the fathers fell asleep all things continue as they were from the beginning of the creation_, _v._ 4. This is a subtle, though not a solid way of reasoning; it is apt to make impressions upon weak minds, and especially upon wicked hearts. _Because sentence against them is not speedily executed_, therefore they flatter themselves that it never will.

IV. Here is the falsehood of their argument detected. Whereas they confidently had said there had not been any change *from the beginning of the creation*, the apostle puts us in remembrance of a change already past, which, in a manner, equals that which we are called to expect and look for, which was the drowning of the world in the days of Noah. He mentions the one as what God has done, to convince and persuade us the rather to believe that the other both may be and will be.

1. We begin with the apostle's account of the destruction which has once already come upon the world (*vv.* 5, 6).

2. What the apostle says of the destructive change which is yet to come upon it: *The heavens and the earth, which now are, by the same word are kept in store, reserved unto fire against the day of judgment and perdition of ungodly men, v.* 7. Here we have an awful account of the final dissolution of the world, and which we are yet more nearly concerned in. Let therefore the scoffers, who laugh at the coming of our Lord to judgment, at least consider that it *may be*. There is nothing said of it in the word of God but what is within reach of the power of God. Now that which he has said, and which he will certainly make good, is that *the heavens and the earth which now are kept in store*, not to be, what earthly minds would wish to have them, treasures for us, but to be what God will have them, in his treasury, securely lodged and kept safely for his purposes. It follows, they are *reserved unto fire*.

A DAY—OR A THOUSAND YEARS (*v.* 8)

Here we may observe,

1. The truth which the apostle asserts—*that with the Lord one day is as a thousand years, and a thousand years are as one day.* Though, in the account of men, there is a great deal of difference between a day and a year, and a vast deal more between one day and a thousand years, yet in the account of God, who inhabits eternity, in which there is no succession, there is no difference; for all things past, present, and future, are ever before him, and the delay of a thousand years cannot be so much to him as the deferring of any thing for a day or an hour is to us.

II. The importance of this truth. If men have no knowledge or belief of the eternal God, they will be very apt to think him such a one as themselves. Yet how hard is it to conceive of eternity! It is therefore not very easy to attain such a knowledge of God as is absolutely necessary.

THE DAY OF THE LORD (*vv.* 9–10)

We are here told that *the Lord is not slack*—he does not delay beyond the appointed time. But the apostle assures us,

I. That what men count slackness is truly *long-suffering*, and that *to us-ward*; it is giving more time to his own people, *whom he has chosen before the foundation of the world*, many of whom are not as yet converted; and those who are in a state of grace and favour with God are to advance in knowledge and holiness.

II. *The day of the Lord will come as a thief in the night*, v. 10. Here we may observe, 1. The certainty of the day of the Lord. 2. The suddenness of this day: It *will come as a thief in the night*, at a time when men are sleeping and secure, and have no manner of apprehension or expectation of the day of the Lord, any more than men have of a thief when they are in a deep sleep, in the dark and silent night.

NEW HEAVEN, NEW EARTH
(vv. 11–18)

The apostle, having instructed them in the doctrine of Christ's second coming,

I. Takes occasion thence to exhort them to purity and godliness in their whole conversation: all the truths which are revealed in scripture should be improved for our advancement in practical godliness: this is the effect that knowledge must produce, or we are never the better for it. Here we must take notice, 1. What true Christians look for: *new heavens and a new earth*, in which a great deal more of the wisdom, power and goodness of our great God and Saviour Jesus Christ will be clearly discerned than we are able to discover in what we now see. 2. What is the ground and foundation of this expectation and hope—*the promise of God*. To look for any thing which God has not promised is presumption; but if our expectations are according to the promise, both as to the things we look for

and the time and way of their being brought about, we cannot meet with a disappointment.

II. As in *v.* 11 he exhorts to holiness from the consideration that *the heavens and the earth shall be dissolved*, so in *v.* 14 he resumes his exhortation from the consideration that they shall be again renewed. Get ready to *appear before the judgment-seat of Christ*: and see to it,

1. "That you be *found of him in peace*, in a state of peace and reconciliation with God through Christ, in whom alone God is *reconciling the world to himself*."

2. That you be *found of Christ without spot, and blameless. Follow after holiness* as well as peace.

III. He mentions Paul as one who had an uncommon measure of wisdom given unto him. But the apostle Peter proceeds to tell us that in those things which are to be met with in Paul's epistles there are some things hard to be understood. Among the variety of subjects treated of in scripture, some are not easy to be understood because of their own obscurity, such are prophecies; others cannot be so easily understood because of their excellency and sublimity, as the mysterious doctrines; and others are with difficulty taken in because of the weakness of men's minds, such are the things of the Spirit of God, mentioned 1 Cor. ii. 14. And here the unlearned and unstable make wretched work; for they wrest and torture the scriptures, to make them speak what the Holy Ghost did not intend.

IV. The apostle gives them a word of caution, *vv.* 17, 18, where,

1. He intimates that the knowledge we have of these things should make us very wary and watchful.

2. That we may the better avoid being led away, the apostle directs us what to do, *v.* 18. And, (1) We must *grow in grace.* (2) We must grow *in the knowledge of our Lord Jesus Christ. To him be glory both now and for ever. Amen.*

THE FIRST EPISTLE GENERAL OF

JOHN

CHAPTER ONE

THE APOSTOLIC TESTIMONY
(*vv.* 1–4)

The apostle begins,

I. With an account or character of the Mediator's person, 1. *As the Word of life, v.* 1. In the gospel these two are disjoined, and he is called first *the Word*, John i. 1, and afterwards *Life. In him was life, and that life was* (efficiently and objectively) *the light of men*, John i. 4. Here both are conjoined: *The Word of life*, the vital Word. 2. *As eternal life*. His duration shows his excellency. He was from eternity; and so is, in scripture-account, necessary, essential, uncreated life. 3. *As life manifested (v.* 2), manifested in the flesh, manifested to us. The eternal life would assume mortality, would put on flesh and blood (in the entire human nature), and so dwell among us and converse with us, John i. 14.

II. With the evidences and assurances that the apostle and his brethren had of the Mediator's presence in this world. *The life, the word of life, the eternal life*, as such, could not be seen and felt; but the life manifested might be, and was so. The divine life, or Word incarnate, presented and evinced itself to the very senses of the apostles. As, 1. To their ears: *That which we have heard, vv.* 1, 3. 2. To their eyes: *That which we have seen with our eyes, vv.* 1–3. 3. To their internal sense, to the eyes of their mind; for so (possibly) may the next clause be interpreted: *Which we have looked upon.* 4. To their hands and sense of feeling: *And our hands have handled* (touched and felt) *of the Word of life*. This surely refers to the full conviction our Lord afforded his apostles of the truth, reality, solidity, and organization of his body, after his resurrection from the dead.

III. With a solemn assertion and attestation of these grounds and evidences of the Christian truth and doctrine. The apostles publish these assurances for our satisfaction: *We bear witness, and show unto you, v.* 2. *That which we have seen and heard declare we unto you, v.* 3.

IV. With the reason of the apostle's exhibiting and asserting this summary of sacred faith. This reason is twofold:

1. That the believers of it may be advanced to the same happiness with them (with the apostles themselves): *That which we have seen and heard declare we unto you, that you may have fellowship with us, v.* 3. We see there is a fellowship or communion that runs through the whole church of God. There may be some personal distinctions and peculiarities, but there is a communion (or common participation of privilege and dignity) belonging

476

to all saints, from the highest apostle to the lowest believer. *And truly our fellowship* (or communion) *is with the Father and his Son Jesus Christ.*

2. That believers may be enlarged and advanced in holy joy: *And these things write we unto you that your joy may be full*, v. 4. The gospel dispensation is not properly a dispensation of fear, sorrow, and dread, but of peace and joy.

TRUE FELLOWSHIP (*vv.* 5–7)

I. Here is the message or report that the apostle avers to come from the Lord Jesus: *This then is the message which we have heard of him* (*v.* 5), of his Son Jesus Christ. What was communicated to them they were solicitous to impart: *This then is the message which we have heard of him, and declare unto you. — That God is light, and in him is no darkness at all*, v. 5. This report asserts the excellency of the divine nature. He is all that beauty and perfection that can be represented to us by light. There is no defect or imperfection, no mixture of any thing alien or contrary to absolute excellency, no mutability or capacity of any decay in him: *In him is no darkness at all*, v. 5.

II. There is a just conclusion to be drawn from this message and report. This conclusion issues into two branches: 1. For the conviction of such as have no true fellowship with God: *If we say we have fellowship with him, and walk in darkness, we lie, and do not the truth.* It is known that to walk, in scripture account, is to order and frame the course and actions of the moral life, that is, of the life so far as it is

capable of subjection to the divine law. *To walk in darkness* is to live and act according to such ignorance, error, and erroneous practice, as are contrary to the fundamental dictates of our holy religion. Now there may be those who may pretend to great attainments and enjoyments in religion; they may profess to have communion with God; and yet their lives may be irreligious, immoral, and impure. To such the apostle would not fear to give the lie: *They lie, and do not the truth.* 2. For the conviction and consequent satisfaction of those that are near to God: *But, if we walk in the light, we have fellowship one with another, and the blood of Jesus Christ his Son cleanseth us from all sin.* Those that so walk show that they know God, that they have received of the Spirit of God, and that the divine impress or image is stamped upon their souls. *Then we have fellowship one with another*, they with us and we with them, and both with God, in his blessed communications to us. And this is one — that his Son's blood or death is applied or imputed to us: *The blood of Jesus Christ his Son cleanseth us from all sin.* His blood applied to us discharges us from the guilt of all sin, both original and actual, inherent and committed: and so far we stand righteous in his sight.

CONFESSION (*vv.* 8–10)

Here, I. The apostle, having supposed that even those of this heavenly communion have yet their sin, proceeds here to justify that supposition, and this he does by showing the dreadful consequences of denying it, and that in two particulars: 1. *If we say, We have no sin, we deceive ourselves, and the truth is not in us, v.* 8. We must beware of deceiving ourselves in denying or excusing our sins. 2. *If we say, We have not sinned, we make him a liar, and his word is not in us, v.* 10. The denial of our sin not only deceives ourselves, but reflects dishonour upon God. It challenges his veracity. He has abundantly testified of, and testified against, the sin of the world.

II. The apostle then instructs the believer in the way to the continued pardon of his sin. Here we have, 1. His duty in order thereto: *If we confess our sins, v.* 9. Penitent confession and acknowledgment of sin are the believer's business, and the means of his deliverance from his guilt. And, 2. His encouragement thereto, and assurance of the happy issue. This is the veracity, righteousness, and clemency of God, to whom he makes such confession: *He is faithful and just to forgive us our sins, and to cleanse us from all unrighteousness, v.* 9. God is faithful to his covenant and word, wherein he has promised forgiveness to penitent believing confessors.

CHAPTER TWO
OUR ADVOCATE (*vv.* 1, 2)

These verses relate to the concluding subject of the foregoing chapter, in which the apostle proceeds upon the supposition of the real Christian's sin. And here he gives them both dissuasion and support.

I. Dissuasion. He would leave no room for sin: "*My little children,*

these things write I unto you, that you sin not, v. 1. The design or purport of this letter, the design of what I have just said concerning communion with God and the overthrow of it by an irreligious course, is to dissuade and drive you from sin.*" But, if a man sin,* he may know his help and cure. And so we see,

II. The believer's support and relief in case of sin: *And* (or *but*) *if any man sin* (any of us, or of our foresaid communion), *we have we an Advocate with the Father, &c., v.* 1. Believers themselves, those that are advanced to a happy gospel-state, have yet their sins. And this must be the support, satisfaction, and refuge of believers (or real Christians) in or upon their sins: *We have an Advocate.* The original name is sometimes given to the Holy Ghost, and then it is rendered, *the Comforter.* He acts within us; he puts pleas and arguments into our hearts and mouths; and so is our advocate, by teaching us to intercede for ourselves. But here is an advocate outside us, in heaven and with the Father. The proper office and business of an advocate is with the judge; with him he pleads the client's cause. The Judge with whom our advocate pleads is the Father, his Father and ours. *And he is the propitiation for our sins, v.* 2. He is the expiatory victim, the propitiatory sacrifice that has been offered to the Judge for all our offences against his majesty, and law, and government. The Mediator of intercession, the Advocate for us, is the Mediator of redemption, the propitiation for our sins. It is his propitiation that he pleads. *He is the propitiation for our sins; and not for ours only* (not only for the sins of us Jews, us that are Abraham's seed according to the flesh), *but also for those of the whole world* (*v.* 2); not only for the past, or us present believers, but for the sins of all who shall hereafter believe on him or come to God through him.

ABIDING IN HIM (*vv.* 3–6)

These verses may seem to relate to the seventh verse of the former chapter. Here now succeeds the trial or test of our light and of our love.

I. The trial of our light: *And hereby we do know that we know him, if we keep his commandments, v.* 3. A careful conscientious obedience to his commands shows that the apprehension and knowledge of these things are graciously impressed upon the soul; and therefore it must follow in the reverse that *he that saith, I know him, and keepeth not his commandments, is a liar, and the truth is not in him, v.* 4.

II. The trial of our love: *But whoso keepeth his word in him verily is the love of God perfected*; *hereby know we that we are in him, v.* 5. To keep the word of God, or of Christ, is sacredly to attend thereto in all the conduct and motion of life; in him that does so is the love of God perfected.

BROTHERLY LOVE (*vv.* 7–11)

The precept of fraternal love is recommended,

I. As an old one: *I write no new commandment unto you, but an old commandment, which you had from the beginning, v.* 7. In the state of

sin and promised recovery, they must love one another as related to God their Maker, as related to each other by blood, and as partners in the same hope.

II. As a new one: "*Again, a new commandment I write unto you.*" We should see that that grace or virtue which was true in Christ be true also in us; we should be conformable to our head. 1. He who wants such love in vain pretends his light: *He that saith he is in the light, and hateth his brother, is in darkness even until now, v.* 9. 2. He who is governed by such love approves his light to be good and genuine: *He that loveth his brother* (as his brother in Christ) *abideth in the light, v.* 10. He sees the foundation and reason of Christian love; he discerns the weight and value of the Christian redemption; he sees how meet it is that we should love those whom Christ hath loved; and then the consequence will be that *there is no occasion of stumbling in him* (*v.* 10); he will be no scandal, *no stumbling-block, to his brother.* 3. Hatred is a sign of spiritual darkness: *But he that hateth his brother is in darkness, v.* 11. Spiritual light is instilled by the Spirit of grace, and one of *the first-fruits of that Spirit is love*; he then who is possessed with malignity towards a Christian brother must needs be destitute of spiritual light; consequently *he walks in darkness* (*v.* 11).

LOVE OF THE WORLD (*vv.* 12–17)

I. We have the address itself made to the various forms and ranks in the church of Christ. In this distribution the apostle addresses,

1. The lowest in the Christian school: *I write unto you, little children, v.* 12. He addresses *the children* in Christianity upon two accounts: (1) *Because their sins were forgiven them for his name's sake, v.* 12. The youngest sincere disciple is pardoned. (2) Because of their knowledge of God: *I write unto you, little children, because you have known the Father, v.* 13. Children are wont to know none so soon as their father. Next he addresses,

2. Those of the highest station and stature, to the seniors in Christianity, to whom he gives an honourable appellation: *I write unto you, fathers (vv.* 13, 14), *unto you old disciples,* Acts xxi. 16. Those that are of longest standing in Christ's school have need of further advice and instruction; none are too old to learn. He writes to them upon the account of their knowledge: *I write unto you, fathers, because you have known him that is from the beginning, vv.* 13, 14. Then,

3. To the middle age of Christians, to those who are in their bloom and flower: *I write unto you, young men, vv.* 13, 14. There are the adult in Christ Jesus, those that have arrived at the strength of spirit and sound sense and can discern between good and evil. The apostle applies to them upon these accounts: (1) Upon the account of their martial exploits. Dexterous soldiers they are in the camp of Christ: *Because you have overcome the wicked one, v.* 13. (2) Upon the account of their strength, discovered in this their achievement: *Because you are strong, and you have overcome the wicked one, v.* 14. (3) Because of their acquain-

tance with the word of God: *And the word of God abideth in you, v.* 14.

II. We have a caution fundamental to vital practical religion: "*Love not the world, neither the things that are in the world, v.* 15. Be crucified to the world, be mortified to the things, to the affairs and enticements, of it." The several degrees of Christians should unite in this, in being dead to the world. These reasons are taken,

1. From the inconsistency of this love with the love of God: *If any man love the world, the love of the Father is not in him, v.* 15.

2. From the prohibition of worldly love or lust; it is not ordained of God: *It is not of the Father, but is of the world, v.* 16.

3. From the vain and vanishing state of earthly things and the enjoyment of them. *And the world passeth away, and the lust thereof, v.* 17.

4. From the immortality of the divine lover, the lover of God: *But he that doeth the will of God,* which must be the character of the lover of God, in opposition to this lover of the world, *abideth for ever, v.* 17.

ANTICHRISTS (*vv.* 18, 19)

Here is, I. A moral prognostication of the time; the end is coming: *Little children, it is the last time, v.* 18. It is meet that the disciples should be warned of the haste and end of time, and apprised as much as may be of the prophetic periods of time.

II. The sign of this last time: *Even now there are many antichrists* (*v.* 18), many that oppose the person, doctrine, and kingdom of Christ. Let the prediction that we see there has been of seducers arising in the Christian world fortify us against their seduction.

III. Some account of these seducers or antichrists. 1. More positively. They were once entertainers or professors of apostolical doctrine: *"They went out from us* (*v.* 19), from our company and communion." 2. More privatively. "They were not inwardly such as we are: *But they were not of us*; they had not *from the heart obeyed the form of sound doctrine delivered to them*; they were not of our union with Christ the head." *But* this was done (or *they went out*) *that they might be made manifest that they were not all of us, v.* 19. The church knows not well who are its vital members and who are not; and therefore the church, considered as internally sanctified, may well be styled *invisible*.

THE ANOINTING (*vv.* 20–17)

Here, I. The apostle encourages the disciples (to whom he writes) in these dangerous times, in this hour of seducers; he encourages them in the assurance of their stability in this day of apostasy: *But you have an unction from the Holy One, and you know all* things. We see, 1. The blessing wherewith they were enriched—an unguent from heaven: *You have an unction.* 2. From whom this blessing comes—*from the Holy One*, either from the Holy Ghost or from the Lord Christ. 3. The effect of this unction—it is a spiritual eye-salve; it enlightens and strengthens the eyes of the understanding.

II. The apostle indicates to them the mind and meaning with which he wrote to them. 1. By way of

negation; not as suspecting their knowledge, or supposing their ignorance in the grand truths of the gospel. 2. By way of assertion and acknowledgment, as relying upon their judgment in these things: *But because you know it* (you know *the truth in Jesus*), *and that no lie is of the truth.*

III. The apostle further arraigns these seducers who had newly arisen. 1. They are *liars*, egregious opposers of sacred truth: *Who is a liar*, or the liar, the notorious liar of the time and age in which we live, *but he that denieth that Jesus is the Christ?* 2. They are direct enemies to God as well as to the Lord Christ; *He is antichrist who denieth the Father and the Son, v.* 22. He that opposes Christ denies the witness and testimony of the Father, and the seal that he hath given to his Son; *for him hath God the Father sealed*, John vi. 27.

IV. Hereupon the apostle advises and persuades the disciples to continue in the old doctrine at first communicated to them: *Let that therefore abide in you which you have heard from the beginning, v.* 24. Truth is older than error. True Christians have an inward confirmation of the divine truth they have imbibed: the Holy Spirit has imprinted it on their minds and hearts. The unction, the pouring out of the gifts of grace upon sincere disciples, is a seal to the truth and doctrine of Christ, since none giveth that seal but God. It is better than human instruction: *"And you need not that any man teach you, v.* 27." The divine unction does not supersede ministerial teaching, but surmount it.

It teaches you to abide in Christ; and, as it teaches you, it secures you; it lays a restraint upon your minds and hearts, that you may not revolt from him.

ABIDE IN HIM (*vv.* 28, 29)

From the blessing of the sacred unction the apostle proceeds in his advice and exhortation to constancy in and with Christ: *And now, little children, abide in him, v.* 28. This duty of perseverance and constancy in trying times is strongly urged by the two following considerations: 1. From the consideration of his return at the great day of account: *That when he shall appear we may have confidence, and not be ashamed before him at his coming, v.* 28. At his public appearance he will shame all those who have abandoned him, by professing before men and angels that he is ashamed of them, Mark viii. 38. To the same advice and exhortation he proceeds, 2. From the consideration of the dignity of those who still adhere to Christ and his religion: *If you know that he is righteous, you know that every one that doeth righteousness is born of him, v.* 29. He that doeth righteousness may here be justly enough assumed as another name for him that abideth in Christ. For he that abideth in Christ abideth in the law and love of Christ, and consequently in his allegiance and obedience to him.

CHAPTER THREE
THE PURE HOPE (*vv.* 1–3)

The apostle, having shown the dignity of Christ's faithful followers, that they are born of him and thereby nearly allied to God, now here,

I. Breaks forth into the admiration of that grace that is the spring of such a wonderful vouchsafement. Thence the apostle,

II. Infers the honour of believers above the recognition of the world. Unbelievers know little of them. *Therefore* (or wherefore, upon this score) *the world knoweth us not, v.* 1. Little does the world perceive the advancement and happiness of the genuine followers of Christ. Then the apostle,

III. Exalts these persevering disciples in the prospect of the certain revelation of their state and dignity. *But we know that when he shall appear we shall be like him.* When the head of the church, the only-begotten of the Father, shall appear, his members, the adopted of God, shall appear and be manifested together with him. *We shall be like him, for we shall see him as he is.* Their likeness will be the cause of that sight which they shall have of him. Their likeness shall enable them to see him as the blessed do in heaven. Then the apostle,

IV. Urges the engagement of these sons of God to the prosecution of holiness: *And every man that hath this hope in him purifies himself even as he is pure, v.* 3. The sons of God know that their Lord is holy and pure; he is of purer heart and eyes than to admit any pollution or impurity to dwell with him. Those then who hope to live with him must study the utmost purity from the world, and flesh, and sin; they must grow in grace and holiness.

MARKS OF GOD'S PEOPLE
(*vv.* 4–10)

The apostle now proceeds to fill his own mouth and the believer's mind with multiplied arguments against sin. And so he reasons and argues,

I. From the nature of sin and the intrinsic evil of it. It is contrary to the divine law: *Whosoever committeth sin transgresseth also* (or *even*) *the law; for sin is the transgression of the law*, or is lawlessness, *v.* 4. The current commission of sin now is the rejection of the divine law, and this is the rejection of the divine authority, and consequently of God himself.

II. From the design and errand of the Lord Jesus in and to this world, which was to remove sin: *And you know that he was manifested to take away our sins, and in him is no sin, v.* 5. Those that expect communion with Christ above should study communion with him here in the utmost purity.

III. From the opposition between sin and a real union with or adhesion to the Lord Christ: *Whosoever abideth in him sinneth not, v.* 6. To sin here is the same as to commit sin (*vv.* 8, 9), and to commit sin is to practise sin. He that abideth in Christ continues not in the practice of sin.

IV. From the connection between the practice of righteousness and a state of righteousness, intimating that the practice of sin and a justified state are inconsistent.

V. From the relation between the sinner and the devil. 1. As elsewhere sinners and saints are distinguished, *so to commit sin* is here

so to practise it as sinners do, that are distinguished from saints, to live under the power and dominion of it; and he who does so *is of the devil*. And thereupon we must see how he argues, 2. From the design and office of the Lord Christ against the devil: *For this purpose the Son of God was manifested, that he might destroy the works of the devil, v.* 8. Let not us serve or indulge what the Son of God came to destroy.

VI. From the connection between regeneration and the relinquishment of sin: *Whosoever is born of God doth not commit sin. Such a one committeth not sin*, does not work iniquity nor practise disobedience, which is contrary to his new nature and the regenerate complexion of his spirit; for, as the apostle adds, *his seed remaineth in him*, either the word of God in its light and power *remaineth in him* (as 1 Pet. i. 23), or, *that which is born of the Spirit is spirit*; the spiritual seminal principle of holiness remaineth in him. *He therefore cannot sin*, in the sense in which the apostle says, *he cannot commit sin*. He cannot continue in the course and practice of sin. He cannot so sin as to denominate him a sinner in opposition to a saint or servant of God. Again, he cannot sin comparatively, as he did before he was born of God, and as others do that are not so. And the reason is *because he is born of God*, which will amount to all this inhibition and impediment.

VII. From the discrimination between the children of God and the children of the devil. They have their distinct characters. *In this the children of God are manifest and the children of the devil, v.* 10.

LOVING ONE ANOTHER
(*vv.* 11–13)

The apostle, having intimated that one mark of the devil's children is hatred of the brethren, takes occasion thence,

I. To recommend fraternal Christian love, and that from the excellence, or antiquity, or primariness of the injunction relating thereto.

II. To dissuade from what is contrary thereto, all ill-will towards the brethren, and that by the example of Cain. His envy and malignity should deter us from harbouring the like passion. And then,

III. To infer that it is no wonder that good men are so served now: *Marvel not, my brethren, if the world hate you, v.* 13. The serpentine nature still continues in the world.

THE MARK OF LOVE
(*vv.* 14–19)

The beloved apostle can scarcely touch upon the mention of sacred love, but he must enlarge upon the enforcement of it, as here he does by divers arguments and incentives thereto; as,

I. That it is a mark of our evangelical justification, of our transition into a state of life: *We know that we have passed from death to life, because we love the brethren, v.* 14. But this love,

1. Supposes a general love to mankind: the law of Christian love, in the Christian community, is founded on the catholic law, in the society of mankind, *Thou shalt love thy neighbour as thyself.*

2. It includes a peculiar love to the Christian society, to the catholic church, and that for the sake of her head, as being his body, as being redeemed, justified, and sanctified in and by him.

II. The hatred of our brethren is, on the contrary, a sign of our deadly state, of our continuance under the legal sentence of death: *He that loveth not his brother* (his brother in Christ) *abideth in death, v.* 14. He yet stands under the curse and condemnation of the law.

III. The example of God and Christ should inflame our hearts with this holy love: *Hereby perceive we the love of God, because he laid down his life for us; and we ought to lay down our lives for the brethren, v.* 16. Surely we should love those whom God hath loved, and so loved; and we shall certainly do so if we have any love for God.

IV. The apostle, having proposed this flaming constraining example of love, and motive to it, proceeds to show us what should be the temper and effect of this our Christian love. And, 1. It must be, in the highest degree, so fervent as to make us willing to suffer even to death for the good of the church, for the safety and salvation of the dear brethren: *And we ought to lay down our lives for the brethren* (*v.* 16). 2. It must be, in the next degree, compassionate, liberal, and communicative to the necessities of the brethren: For *whoso hath this world's good, and seeth his brother have need, and shutteth up his bowels of compassion from him, how dwelleth the love of God in him? v.* 17.

V. This love will evince our sincerity in religion, and give us hope towards God: *And hereby we know that we are of the truth, and shall assure our hearts before him, v.* 19.

CONSCIENCE AND CONFIDENCE (*vv.* 20–22)

The apostle, having intimated that there may be, even among us, such a privilege as an assurance or sound persuasion of heart towards God, proceeds here,

I. To establish the court of conscience, and to assert the authority of it: *For, if our heart condemn us, God is greater than our heart, and knoweth all things, v.* 20. Our heart here is our self-reflecting judicial power. This power can act as witness, judge, and executioner of judgment; it either accuses or excuses, condemns or justifies; it is set and placed in this office by God himself. 1. If conscience condemn us, God does so too: *For, if our heart condemn us, God is greater than our heart, and knoweth all things, v.* 20. Or, 2. If conscience acquit us, God does so too: *Beloved, if our heart condemn us not, then have we confidence towards God* (*v.* 21), then have we assurance that he accepts us now, and will acquit us in the great day of account.

II. To indicate the privilege of those who have a good conscience towards God. They have interest in heaven and in the court above; their suits are heard there: *And whatsoever we ask we receive of him, v.* 22.

HIS COMMANDMENT (*vv.* 23, 24)

The apostle, having mentioned keeping the commandments, and pleasing God, as the qualification of effectual petitioners in and with Heaven, here suitably proceeds.

I. To represent to us what those commandments primarily and summarily are; they are comprehended in this double one: *And this is his commandment, That we should believe on the name of his Son Jesus Christ, and love one another, as he gave us commandment, v.* 23.

II. To represent to us the blessedness of obedience to these commands. The obedient enjoy communion with God: *And he that keepeth his commandments,* and particularly those of faith and love, *dwelleth in him, and he in him, v.* 24.

CHAPTER FOUR
TEST THE SPIRITS (*vv.* 1–3)

The apostle, having said that God's dwelling in and with us may be known by *the Spirit that he hath given us,* intimates that that Spirit may be discerned and distinguished from other spirits that appear in the world; and so here,

I. He calls the disciples, to whom he writes, to caution and scrutiny about the spirits and spiritual professors that had now risen. A reason is given for this trial: *Because many false prophets have gone out into the world, v.* 1. It should not seem strange to us that false teachers set themselves up in the church: it was so in the apostles' times; fatal is the spirit of delusion, sad that men should vaunt themselves for prophets and inspired preachers that are by no means so!

II. He gives a test whereby the disciples may try these pretending spirits. These spirits set up for prophets, doctors, or dictators in religion, and so they were to be tried by their doctrine; and the test whereby in that day, or in that part of the world where the apostle now resided (for in various seasons, and in various churches, tests were different), must be this: *Hereby know you the Spirit of God, Every spirit that confesseth that Jesus Christ has come in the flesh* (or *that confesseth Jesus Christ that came in the flesh) is of God, v.* 2. Jesus Christ is to be confessed as the Son of God, the eternal life and Word, that was with the Father from the beginning; as the Son of God that came into, and came in, our human mortal nature, and therein suffered and died at Jerusalem. He who confesses and preaches this, by a mind supernaturally instructed and enlightened therein, does it by the Spirit of God, or God is the author of that illumination. On the contrary, *"Every spirit that confesseth not that Jesus Christ has come in the flesh* (or *Jesus Christ that came in the flesh) is not of God, v.* 3.

TRUTH AND ERROR
(*vv.* 4–6)

In these verses the apostle encourages the disciples against the fear and danger of this seducing antichristian spirit, and that by such methods as these: 1. He assures them of a more divine principle in them: *"You are of God, little children, v.* 4. *You are God's little children. We are of God, v.* 6. 2. He gives them hope of victory: *"And have overcome them, v.* 4. You have hitherto overcome these deceivers and their temptations, and there is good ground of hope that you will do so still, and that upon these two

accounts:"—(1) "There is a strong preserver within you: *Because greater is he that is in you than he that is in the world," v.* 4. (2) You are not of the same temper with these deceivers. The Spirit of God hath framed your mind for God and heaven; *but they are of the world.* Then, 3. He represents to them that though their company might be the smaller, yet it was the better; they had more divine and holy knowledge: *"He that knoweth God heareth us."* As, on the contrary, *"He that is not of God heareth not us.* He who knows not God regards not us. He that is not *born of God* (walking according to his natural disposition) walks not with us."

GOD IS LOVE (*vv.* 7–13)

As *the Spirit of truth* is known by doctrine (thus spirits are to be tried), it is known by love likewise; and so here follows a strong fervent exhortation to holy Christian love: *Beloved, let us love one another, v.* 7. This exhortation is pressed and urged with variety of argument: as,

I. From the high and heavenly descent of love: *For love is of God.* He is the fountain, author, parent, and commander of love; it is the sum of his law and gospel: *And every one that loveth* (whose spirit is framed to judicious holy love) *is born of God, v.* 7. The Spirit of God is the Spirit of love. Love comes down from heaven.

II. Love argues a true and just apprehension of the divine nature: *He that loveth knoweth God, v.* 7. *He that loveth not knoweth not God, v.* 8. What attribute of the divine Majesty so clearly shines in all the world as his communicative goodness, which is love. His love must needs shine among his primary brightest perfections; *for God is love* (*v.* 8), his nature and essence are love, his will and works are primarily love. Then,

III. Divine love to the brethren should constrain ours: *Beloved* (I would adjure you by your interest in my love to remember), *if God so loved us, we ought also to love one another, v.* 11. This should be an invincible argument.

IV. The Christian love is an assurance of the divine inhabitation: *If we love one another, God dwelleth in us, v.* 12.

V. Herein the divine love attains a considerable end and accomplishment in us: *"And his love is perfected in us," v.* 12. It has obtained its completion in and upon us. God's love is not perfected in him, but in and with us.

DIVINE LOVE (*vv.* 14–16)

Since faith in Christ works love to God, and love to God must kindle love to the brethren, the apostle here confirms the prime article of the Christian faith as the foundation of such love. Here,

I. He proclaims the fundamental article of the Christian religion, which is so representative of the love of God: *And we have seen, and do testify, that the Father sent the Son to be the Saviour of the world, v.* 14. Thereupon,

II. The apostle states the excellency, or the excellent privilege attending the due acknowledgment of this truth: *Whosoever shall confess that Jesus is the Son of God, God dwelleth in him, and he in God,*

v. 15. This confession seems to include faith in the heart as the foundation of it, acknowledgment with the mouth to the glory of God and Christ, and profession in the life and conduct, in opposition to the flatteries or frowns of the world. Then,

III. The apostle applies this to the excitation of holy love. God's love is thus seen and exerted in Christ Jesus; *and* thus *have we known and believed the love that God hath to us, v.* 16. Hence we may learn,

1. That *God is love* (*v.* 16); he is essential boundless love.

2. That hereupon *he that dwelleth in love dwelleth in God, and God in him, v.* 16. There is great communion between the God of love and the loving soul.

PERFECT LOVE (*vv.* 17–21)

The apostle, having thus excited and enforced sacred love from the great pattern and motive of it, proceeds to recommend it further by other considerations; and he recommends it in both the branches of it, both as love to God, and love to our brother or Christian neighbour.

I. As love to God. Love to God seems here to be recommended on these accounts: 1. It will give us peace and satisfaction of spirit in the day when it will be most needed, or when it will be the greatest pleasure and blessing imaginable: *Herein is our love made perfect, that we may have boldness in the day of judgment, v.* 17. Possibly here by the love of God may be meant our *love to God*, which is *shed abroad upon our hearts by the Holy Ghost*;

this is the foundation of our hope, or of our assurance that our hope will hold good at last. He will give the crown of righteousness to all that love his appearing. And we have this boldness towards Christ because of our conformity to him: *Because as he is so are we in this world*, v. 17. 2. It prevents or removes the uncomfortable result and fruit of servile fear: *There is no fear in love* (v. 18); so far as love prevails, fear ceases. There is a being afraid of God, which arises from a sense of guilt, and a view of his vindictive perfections; in the view of them, God is represented as a consuming fire; and so fear here may be rendered *dread: There is no dread in love*. Love considers its objects as good and excellent, and therefore amiable, and worthy to be beloved. Those who perfectly love God are, from his nature, and counsel, and covenant, perfectly assured of his love, and consequently are perfectly free from any dismal dreadful suspicions of his punitive power and justice, as armed against them; they well know that God loves them, and they thereupon triumph in his love. 3. From the source and rise of it, which is the antecedent love of God: *We love him, because he first loved us*, v. 19. His love is the incentive, the motive, and moral cause of ours.

II. As love to our brother and neighbour in Christ; such love is argued and urged on these accounts: 1. As suitable and consonant to our Christian profession. How shall the hater of a visible image of God pretend to love the unseen original, the invisible God himself? 2. As suitable to the express law of God, and the just reason of it: *And this commandment have we from him, that he who loveth God love his brother also*, v. 21.

THE VICTORY OF FAITH
(vv. 1–5)

I. The apostle having, in the conclusion of the last chapter, as was there observed, urged Christian love upon those two accounts, as suitable to Christian profession and as suitable to the divine command, here adds a third: Such love is suitable, and indeed demanded, by their eminent relation; our Christian brethren or fellow-believers are nearly related to God; they are his children: *Whosoever believeth that Jesus is the Christ is born of God*, v. 1.

II. The apostle shows, 1. How we may discern the truth, or the true evangelical nature of our love to the regenerate. The ground of it must be our love to God, whose they are: *By this we know that we love the children of God, when we love God*, v. 2. 2. How we may learn the truth of our love to God—it appears in our holy obedience: *When we love God, and keep his commandments*, v. 2. 3. What is and ought to be the result and effect of regeneration—an intellectual spiritual conquest of this world: *For* whatsoever *is born of God*, or, as in some copies, whosoever *is born of God, overcometh the world*, v. 4. He that is born of God is born *for* God, and consequently for another world. Faith is the cause of victory, the means, the instrument, the spiritual armour and artillery by which we overcome.

III. The apostle concludes that it is the real Christian that is the true conqueror of the world: *Who is he* then *that overcometh the world, but he that believeth that Jesus is the Son of God? v.* 5. It is the world that lies in our way to heaven, and is the great impediment to our entrance there. But he who believes that Jesus is the Son of God believes therein that Jesus came from God to be the Saviour of the world, and powerfully to conduct us from the world to heaven, and to God, who is fully to be enjoyed there. And he who so believes must needs by this faith overcome the world.

THE THREE WITNESSES
(vv. 6–9)

The Lord Jesus brings his credentials along with him, and he brings them in the way by which he came and in the witness that attends him.

I. In the way and manner by which he came; not barely by which he came into the world, but by and with which he came, and appeared, and acted, as a Saviour in the world: *This is he that came by water and blood. Jesus Christ came with water and blood,* as the notes and signatures of the true effectual Saviour of the world; and he came by water and blood as the means by which he would heal and save us. (1) Inwardly, from the power and pollution of sin in our nature. For our cleansing from this we need spiritual water; such as can reach the soul and the powers of it. Accordingly, there is in and by Christ Jesus *the washing of regeneration and the renewing of the Holy Ghost.* (2) We are defiled outwardly, by the guilt and condemning power of sin upon our persons. From this we must be purged by atoning blood. It is the law or determination in the court of heaven *that without shedding of blood there shall be no remission,* Heb. ix. 22. The Saviour from sin therefore must come with blood. He who comes by water and blood is an accurate perfect Saviour. And this is he who comes by water and blood, even Jesus Christ! But we see his credentials also.

II. In the witness that attends him, and that is, the divine Spirit, that Spirit to whom the perfecting of the works of God is usually attributed: *And it is the Spirit that beareth witness, v.* 6. *Because* (or for) *there are three that bear record in heaven, the Father, the Word, and the Holy Ghost, and these three are one.*

To these there is opposed, though with them joined, a trinity of witnesses on earth, such as continue here below: *And there are three that bear witness on earth, the spirit, the water, and the blood; and these three agree in one, v.* 8. [1] Of these witnesses the first is the *spirit.* This must be distinguished from the person of the Holy Ghost, who is in heaven. We must say then, with the Saviour (according to what is reported by this apostle), *that which is born of the Spirit is spirit,* John iii. 6. The regeneration or renovation of souls is a testimony to the Saviour. It is his actual though initial salvation. It is a testimony on earth, because it continues with the church here, and is not performed in that conspicuous astonishing manner in which signs from heaven are accomplished. To this Spirit belong not only the regeneration and conversion of the church, but its progressive sanctification, victory over the world, her peace, and love, and joy, and all that grace by which she is made meet for the inheritance of the saints in light. [2] The second is the *water*. This was before considered as a means of salvation, now as a testimony to the Saviour himself, and intimates his purity and purifying power. [3] The third witness is the blood; this he shed, and this was our ransom. This testifies for Jesus Christ, *First*, In that it sealed up and finished the sacrifices of the Old Testament, *Christ, our Passover, was sacrificed for us*. *Secondly*, In that it confirmed his own predictions, and the truth of all his ministry and doctrine, John xviii. 37. *Thirdly*, In that it showed unparalleled love to God, in that he would die a sacrifice to his honour and glory, in making atonement for the sins of the world, John xiv. 30, 31. *Fourthly*, In that it demonstrated unspeakable love to us; and none will deceive those whom they entirely love, John xiv. 13–15. *Fifthly*, In that it demonstrated the disinterestedness of the Lord Jesus as to any secular interest and advantage. No impostor and deceiver ever proposes to himself contempt and a violent cruel death, John xviii. 36. *Sixthly*, In that it lays obligation on his disciples to suffer and die for him. *Seventhly*, The benefits accruing and procured by his blood (well understood) must immediately demonstrate that he is indeed the Saviour of the world. And then, *Eighthly*, These are signified and sealed in the institution of his own supper: *This is my blood of the New Testament* (which ratifies the New Testament), *which is shed for many, for the remission of sins*, Matt. xxiv. 28. Such are the witnesses on earth.

III. The apostle justly concludes, *If we receive the witness of men, the witness of God is greater; for this is the witness of God, that he hath testified of his Son*, v. 9. *God, that cannot lie*, hath given sufficient assurance to the world that Jesus Christ is his Son, the Son of his love, and Son by office, to reconcile and recover the world unto himself; he testified therefore the truth and divine origin of the Christian religion, and that it is the sure appointed way and means of bringing us to God.

CHRISTIAN ASSURANCE
(*vv.* 10–13)

In these words we may observe,

I. The privilege and stability of the real Christian: *He that believeth on the Son of God*, hath been prefailed with unfeignedly to cleave to him for salvation, *hath the witness in himself*, v. 10.

II. The aggravation of the unbeliever's sin, the sin of unbelief: *He that believeth not God hath made him a liar*. He does, in effect, give God the lie, *because he believeth not the record that God gave of his Son*, v. 10.

III. The matter, the substance, or contents of all this divine testimony concerning Jesus Christ: *And this is the record, that God hath given to us eternal life, and this life is in his Son, v.* 11. This is the sum of the gospel. This is the sum and epitome of the whole record given us by all the aforesaid six witnesses.

IV. The end and reason of the apostle's preaching this to believers. 1. For their satisfaction and comfort: *These things have I written unto you that believe on the name of the Son of God, that you may know that you have eternal life, v.* 13. These believers may come to know that they have eternal life, and should be quickened, encouraged, and comforted, in the prospect of it. 2. For their confirmation and progress in their holy faith: *And that you may believe on the name of the Son of God* (*v.* 13), may go on believing. Believers must persevere, or they do nothing.

MORTAL SIN (*vv.* 14–17)

Here we have,

I. A privilege belonging to faith in Christ, namely, audience in prayer: *This is the confidence that we have in him, that, if we ask any thing according to his will, he heareth us, v.* 14. The Lord Christ emboldens us to come to God in all circumstances, with all our supplications and requests. It is not fit that we should ask what is contrary either to his majesty and glory or to our own good, who are his and dependent on him. And then we may have confidence that the prayer of faith shall be heard in heaven.

II. The advantage accruing to us by such privilege: *If we know that he heareth us, whatsoever we ask, we know that we have the petitions that we desired of him, v.* 15. Great are the deliverances, mercies, and blessings, which the holy petitioner needs.

III. Direction in prayer in reference to the sins of others: *If any man see his brother sin a sin which is not unto death, he shall ask, and he shall give him life for those that sin not unto death. There is a sin unto death: I do not say that he shall pray for it, v.* 16. Here we may observe, 1. We ought to pray for others as well as for ourselves. 2. There is a great distinction in the heinousness and guilt of sin: *There is a sin unto death* (*v.* 16), *and there is a sin not unto death, v.* 17. (1) *There is a sin unto death.* All sin, as to the merit and legal sentence of it, is unto death. But there is a sin unto death in opposition to such sin as is here said *not to be unto death.* There is therefore, (2) *A sin not unto death.* This surely must include all such sin as by divine or human constitution may consist with life; in the human constitution with temporal or corporal life, in the divine constitution with corporal or with spiritual life. There are sins which, by divine constitution, are inconsistent with spiritual and evangelical life, with spiritual life in the soul and with an evangelical right to life above. Such are total impenitence and unbelief for the present. Final impenitence and unbelief are infallibly to death eternal, as also a blaspheming of the Spirit of God in the testimony that he has given to Christ and his gospel, and a total apostasy from the light and convictive evidence of the truth of the Christian religion. These are sins involving the guilt of everlasting death. Then comes,

IV. The application of the direction for prayer according to the different sorts of sin thus distinguished. The prayer is supposed to be for life: *He shall ask, and he* (God) *shall give them life.* Life is to be asked of God. In the case of a brother's sin, which is not (in the manner already mentioned) unto death, we may in faith and hope pray for him; and particularly for the life and soul and body. But, in case of the sin unto death in the forementioned ways, we have no allowance to pray.

CONCLUSION (*vv.* 18–21)

Here we have,

I. A recapitulation of the privileges and advantages of sound Christian believers. 1. They are secured against sin, against the fulness of its dominion or the fulness of its guilt: *We know that whosoever is born of God* (and the believer in Christ is born of God, *v.* 1) *sinneth not* (*v.* 18). 2. They are fortified against the devil's destructive attempts: *He that is begotten of God keepeth himself,* that is, is enabled to guard himself, *and the wicked one toucheth him not* (*v.* 18), that is, that the wicked one may not touch him, namely, to death. 3. They are on God's side and interest, in opposition to the state of the world: *And we know that we are of God, and the whole world lieth in wickedness, v.* 19. Mankind are divided

into two great parties or dominions, that which belongs to God and that which belongs to wickedness or to the wicked one. The Christian believers belong to God. 4. They are enlightened in the knowledge of the true eternal God: "*And we know that the Son of God has come, and has given us an understanding, that we may know him that is true, v.* 20. 5. They have a happy union with God and his Son: "*And we are in him that is true,* even (or and) *in his Son Jesus Christ," v.* 20. The Son leads us to the Father, and we are in both, in the love and favour of both, in covenant and federal alliance with both, in spiritual conjunction with both by the inhabitation and operation of their Spirit: and, that you may know how great a dignity and felicity this is, you must remember that this true one is *the true God and eternal life.* Then we have,

II. The apostle's concluding monition: "*Little children*" (dear children, as it has been interpreted), "*keep yourselves from idols, v.* 21. Since you know the true God, and are in him, let your light and love guard you against all that is advanced in opposition to him, or competition with him. Flee from the false gods of the heathen world. They are not comparable to the God whose you are and whom you serve."

THE SECOND EPISTLE OF

JOHN

SALUTATION (vv. 1–4)

Ancient epistles began, as here, with salutation and good wishes: religion consecrates, as far as may be, old forms, and turns compliments into real expressions of life and love. Here we have, as usually.

I. The saluter, not expressed by name, but by a chosen character: *The elder.*

II. The saluted—a noble Christian matron, and her children: *To the elect lady and her children.* This *lady and her children* are further notified by the respect paid them, and that, 1. By the apostle himself: *Whom I love in the truth,* or in truth, whom I sincerely and heartily love. 2. By all her Christian acquaintance, all the religious who knew her: *And not I only, but also all those that have known the truth.*

III. The salutation, which is indeed an apostolical benediction: *Grace be with you, mercy, and peace, from God the Father and from the Lord Jesus Christ, the Son of the Father, in truth and love, v. 3.* Sacred love pours out blessings upon this honourable Christian family; to those who have shall more be given.

IV. The congratulation upon the prospect of the exemplary behaviour of other children of this excellent lady. Happy parent, who was blessed with such a numerous religious offspring! *I rejoiced greatly that I found of thy children walking in the truth, as we have received commandment from the Father, v. 4.* We see here also the rule of true walking: *the commandment of the Father.* Then is our walk true, our converse right, when it is managed by the word of God.

TRUE LOVE (vv. 5, 6)

We come now more into the design and substance of the epistle; and here we have,

I. The apostle's request: *Now, I beseech thee, lady.*

1. This love is recommended, (1) From the obligation thereto—*the commandment.* Divine command should sway our mind and heart. (2) From the antiquity of the obligation: *Not as though I wrote a new commandment unto thee, but that which we had from the beginning, v. 5.*

2. Then this love is illustrated from the fruitful nature of it: *And this is love, that we walk after his commandments, v. 5.* This is the test of our love to God, our obedience to him.

DECEIVERS (vv. 7–9)

In this principal part of the epistle we find,

I. The ill news communicated to the lady—seducers are abroad: *For many deceivers have entered into the world.* Now here is, 1. The description of the deceiver and his deceit—he *confesses not that Jesus Christ has come in the flesh* (v. 7); he brings some error or other concerning the person of the Lord Jesus. 2. The aggravation of the case—such a one is *a deceiver and an antichrist* (v. 7); he deludes souls and undermines the glory and kingdom of the Lord Christ.

II. The counsel given to this elect household hereupon. Now care and caution are needful: *Look to yourselves,* v. 8. Two things they must beware of: 1. *That they lose not what they have wrought* (v. 8), what they have done or what they have gained. 2. That they lose not their reward, none of it, no portion of that honour, or praise, or glory that they once stood fair for.

III. The reason of the apostle's counsel, and of their care and caution about themselves, which is twofold: 1. The danger and evil of departure from gospel light and revelation; it is in effect and reality a departure from God himself: *Whosoever transgresseth* (transgresseth at this dismal rate), *and abideth not in the doctrine of Christ, hath not God.* 2. The advantage and happiness of firm adherence to Christian truth; it unites us to Christ (the object or subject-matter of that truth), and thereby to the Father also; for they are one.

A WARNING (*vv.* 10–13)

Here, I. Upon due warning given concerning seducers, the apostle gives direction concerning the treatment of such. They are not to be entertained as the ministers of Christ. The Lord Christ will distinguish them from such, and so would he have his disciples. The direction is negative. 1. Support them not. These deceivers might possibly expect the same reception with others, or with the best who came there (as the blind are often bold enough), but the apostle allows it not: "Do not welcome them into your family." 2. Bless not their enterprises: *Neither bid him God speed.* Attend not their service with your prayers and good wishes. Then,

II. Here is the reason of such direction, forbidding the support and patronage of the deceiver: *For he that biddeth him God speed is partaker of his evil deeds.* Favour and affection partake of the sin.

The apostle concludes this letter with an adjournment of many things to personal conference: *Having many things to write unto you I would not write with paper and ink; but I trust to come unto you, and speak face to face, that our joy may be full.* Here it is supposed that some things are better spoken than written.

JOHN

SALUTATION (*vv.* 1, 2)

Here we see, I. The sacred penman who writes and sends the letter; not here indeed notified by his name, but a more general character: *The elder*.

II. The person saluted and honoured by the letter. The former is directed to an elect lady, this to a choice gentleman; such are worthy of esteem and value. He is notified, 1. By his name, — *Gaius*. Then, 2. By the kind expressions of the apostle to him: *The well-beloved*, and *whom I love in the truth*.

III. The salutation or greeting, containing a prayer, introduced by an affectionate compellation — *Beloved*, thou beloved one in Christ. Grace and health are two rich companions; grace will improve health, health will employ grace.

THE FAITHFUL MAN
(*vv.* 3–8)

In these verses we have,

I. The good report that the apostle had received concerning this friend of his: *The brethren came and testified of the truth that is in thee* (*v.* 3), *who have borne witness of thy charity before the church, v.* 6.

II. The report the apostle himself gives of him, introduced by an endearing appellation again: *Be-*
loved, thou doest faithfully whatso-ever thou doest to the brethren, and to strangers, v. 5. 1. He was hospitable, good to the brethren, even to strangers; it was enough to recommend them to Gaius's house that they belonged to Christ. 2. He seems to have been of a catholic spirit; he could overlook the petty differences among serious Christians, and be communicative to all who bore the image and did the work of Christ. And, 3. He was conscientious in what he did.

III. The apostle's joy therein, in the good report itself, and the good ground of it: *I rejoiced greatly when the brethren came and testified*, &c., *v.* 3. *I have no greater joy than to hear that my children walk in the truth*, in the prescripts of the Christian religion. The best evidence of our having the truth is our *walking in the truth*.

IV. The direction the apostle gives his friend concerning further treatment of the brethren that were with him: *Whom if thou bring forward on their journey, after a godly sort, thou shalt do well*. It seems to have been customary in those days of love to attend travelling ministers and Christians, at least some part of their road, 1 Cor. xvi. 6.

V. The reasons of this directed conduct; these are two: 1. *Because that for his name's sake these brethren went forth, taking nothing of the Gentiles.* It appears thus that these were ministerial brethren. 2. *We ought therefore to receive such, that we may be fellow-helpers to the truth,* to true religion. The institution of Christ is the true religion; it has been attested by God. Those that are true in it and true to it will earnestly desire, and pray for, and contribute to, its propagation in the world.

A MALICIOUS ENEMY
(*vv.* 9–11)

I. Here is a very different example and character, an officer, a minister in the church, less generous, catholic, and communicative than the private Christians. In reference to this minister, we see,

1. His name—a Gentile name: *Diotrephes,* attended with an unchristian spirit.

2. His temper and spirit— full of pride and ambition: *He loves to have the pre-eminence.*

3. His contempt of the apostle's authority, and letter, and friends. (1) Of his authority: *The deeds which he doeth* contrary to our appointment, *prating against us with malicious words.* Malice and ill-will in the heart will be apt to vent themselves by the lips. The heart and mouth are both to be watched. (2) Of his letter: "*I wrote to the church* (*v.* 9), namely, in recommendation of such and such brethren. *But Diotrephes receiveth us not,* admits not our letter and testimony therein." This seems to be the church of which Gaius was a member. (3) Of his friends, the brethren he recommended: *Neither doth he himself receive the brethren, and forbiddeth those that would, and casteth them out of the church, v.* 10. Many are cast out of the church who should be received there with satisfaction and welcome. But woe to those who cast out the brethren whom the Lord Christ will take into his own communion and kingdom!

4. The apostle's menace of this proud domineerer: *Wherefore, if I come, I will remember his deeds which he doeth* (*v.* 10), will remember to censure them.

II. Here is counsel upon that different character, dissuasion from copying such a pattern, and indeed any evil at all: *Beloved, follow not that which is evil, but that which is good, v.* 11.

CONCLUSION (*vv.* 12–14)

Here we have, I. The character of another person, one *Demetrius,* not much known otherwise. But here his name will live. It is well for those who are commended when those who commend them can appeal to the consciences of those who knew them most.

II. The conclusion of the epistle, in which we may observe, 1. The referring of some things to personal interview: *I have many things to write, but I will not with ink and pen, but I trust I shall shortly see thee, vv.* 13, 14. 2. The benediction: *Peace be to you;* all felicity attend you. 3. The public salutation sent to Gaius: *Our friends salute thee.* 4. The apostle's particular salutation of the Christians in Gaius's church or vicinity: *Greet the friends by name.*

JUDE

GREETINGS (*vv* 1, 2)

Here we have the preface or introduction, in which,

I. We have an account of the penman of this epistle, *Jude*, or *Judas*, or Judah. He was an apostle, a faithful servant of Jesus Christ.

II. We are here informed to whom this epistle is directed; namely, to all those *who are sanctified by God the Father, and preserved in Jesus Christ, and called*.

III. We have the apostolical benediction: *Mercy to you*, &c. From the mercy, peace, and love of God all our comfort flows, all our real enjoyment in this life, all our hope of a better.

BEWARE OF INFILTRATORS (*vv*. 3–7)

We have here, I. The design of the apostle in writing this epistle to the lately converted Jews and Gentiles; namely, to establish them in the Christian faith. Here observe, 1. The gospel salvation is a common salvation, that is, in a most sincere offer and tender of it to all mankind to whom the notice of it reaches: for so the commission runs (Mark xvi. 15, 16). 2. This common salvation is the subject-matter of the faith of all the saints. It is the faith once, *or at once, once for all, delivered to the saints*, to which nothing can be added, from which nothing

may be detracted, in which nothing more or less should be altered. 3. The apostles and evangelists all wrote to us of this common salvation. 4. Those who preach or write of the common salvation should give all diligence to do it well: they should not allow themselves to offer to God or his people that which costs them nothing, or next to nothing, little or no pains or thought, 2 Sam. xxiv. 24. This were to treat God irreverently, and man unjustly. 5. Those who have received the doctrine of this common salvation must contend earnestly for it. *Earnestly*, not *furiously*. Those who strive for the Christian faith, or in the Christian course, must strive lawfully, or they lose their labour, and run great hazard of losing their crown, 2 Tim. ii. 5.

II. The occasion the apostle had to write to this purport. As evil manners give rise to good laws, so dangerous errors often give just occasion to the proper defence of important truths. Here observe, 1. Ungodly men are the great enemies of the faith of Christ and the peace of the church. 2. Those are *the worst of ungodly men who turn the grace of God into lasciviousness*, who take encouragement to sin more boldly because the grace of God has abounded, and still abounds, so wonderfully, who are hardened in their impieties by the extent and fulness of gospel grace, the design of which is to reduce men from sin, and bring them unto God. 3. Those who turn the grace of God into lasciviousness do in effect *deny the Lord God, and our Lord Jesus Christ*; that is, they deny both natural and revealed religion. 4. Those who turn the grace of God into lasciviousness are ordained unto condemnation. They sin against the last, the greatest, and most perfect remedy; and so are without excuse. 5. We ought to contend earnestly for the faith, in opposition to those who would corrupt or deprave it, such as have *crept in unawares*. Whoever may attempt to corrupt the faith, we ought to contend earnestly against them.

III. The fair warning which the apostle, in Christ's name, gives to those who, having professed his holy religion, do afterwards desert and prove false to it, *vv.* 5–7. We have here a recital of the former judgments of God upon sinners, with design to awaken and terrify those to whom warning is given in this epistle.

Now what are these things which we Christians need to be put in remembrance of?

1. The destruction of the unbelieving Israelites in the wilderness, *v.* 5.

2. We are here put in remembrance of the fall of the angels, *v.* 6. There were a great number of the angels who *left their own habitation*; that is, who were not pleased with the posts and stations the supreme Monarch of the universe had assigned and allotted to them. Thus they quitted their post, and rebelled against God, their Creator and sovereign Lord. But God did not spare them (high and great as they were). There is, undoubtedly there is, a judgment to come; the fallen angels are *reserved to the judgment of the great day*; and shall fallen men escape it? Surely not.

3. The apostle here calls to our remembrance the destruction of Sodom and Gomorrah, *v.* 7. *Even as*, &c. Their ruin is a particular warning to all people to take heed of, and fly *from, fleshly lusts that war against the soul*, 1 Pet. ii. 11.

WARNINGS FROM THE PAST
(*vv.* 8–15)

The apostle here exhibits a charge against deceivers who were now seducing the disciples of Christ from the profession and practice of his holy religion. Here,

I. The character of these deceivers is described.

1. They *defile the flesh*. The flesh or body is the immediate seat, and often the irritating occasion, of many horrid pollutions.

2. They *despise dominion, and speak evil of dignities*, are of a disturbed mind and a seditious spirit, forgetting that *the powers that be are ordained of God*, Rom. xiii. 1.

On this occasion the apostle brings in *Michael the archangel*, &c., *v.* 9. Interpreters are at a loss what is here meant by *the body of Moses*. Some think that the devil contended that Moses might have a public and honourable funeral, that the place where he was interred might be generally known, hoping thereby to draw the Jews, so naturally prone thereto, to a new and fresh instance of idolatry. Dr.

Scott thinks that by the body of Moses we are to understand the Jewish church, whose destruction the devil strove and contended for, as the Christian church is called the body of Christ in the New-Testament style. Others bring other interpretations, which I will not here trouble the reader with. Though this contest was mightily eager and earnest, and Michael was victorious in the issue, yet he would not *bring a railing accusation against the devil himself*; he knew a good cause needed no such weapons to be employed in its defence. Truth needs no supports from falsehood or scurrility. So the lesson hence is that we ought to stand up in defence of those whom God owns, how severe soever Satan and his instruments may be in their censures of them and their conduct.

3. *They speak evil of the things which they know not*, &c., *v.* 10. Observe, Those who speak evil of religion and godliness *speak evil of the things which they know not*; for, if they had known them, they would have spoken well of them.

4. In *v.* 11 the apostle represents them as followers *of Cain*, and in *vv.* 12, 13, as atheistical and profane people, who thought little, and perhaps believed not much, of God or a future world—as greedy and covetous, who, so they could but gain present worldly advantages, cared not what came next—rebels against God and man, who, like Core, ran into attempts in which they must assuredly perish, as he did. Of such the apostle further says, (1) *These are spots in your feasts of charity*—the *love-feasts*, so much spoken of by the ancients.

They happened, by whatever means or mischance, to be admitted among them, but were spots in them, defiled and defiling. (2) *When they feast with you, they feed themselves without fear*. Arrant gluttons, no doubt, they were; such as minded only the gratifying of their appetites with the daintiness and abundance of their fare; they had no regard to Solomon's caution, Prov. xxiii. 2. (3) *Clouds they are without water*, which promise rain in time of drought, but perform nothing of what they promise. (4) *Trees whose fruit withereth*, &c. Trees they are, for they are planted in the Lord's vineyard, yet fruitless ones. (5) *Raging waves of the sea*, boisterous, noisy, and clamorous; full of talk and turbulency, but with little (if any) sense or meaning. (6) *Wandering stars*, planets that are erratic in their motions, keep not that steady regular course which the fixed ones do, but shift their stations, that one has sometimes much ado to know where to find them.

II. The doom of this wicked people is declared: *To whom is reserved the blackness of darkness for ever*.

Of the prophecy of Enoch (*vv.* 14, 15) we have no mention made in any other part or place of scripture; yet now it is scripture that there was such prophecy. Observe, 1. Christ's coming to judgment was prophesied of as early as the middle of the patriarchal age, and was therefore even then a received and acknowledged truth.—*The Lord cometh with* his holy myriads, including both angels and the spirits of just men made perfect.

2. It was spoken of then, so long ago, as a thing just at hand.

ENCOURAGEMENT
(vv. 16–25)

Here, I. The apostle enlarges further on the character of these evil men and seducers: they *are murmurers, complainers*, &c., *v.* 16. Observe, A murmuring complaining temper, indulged and expressed, lays men under a very bad character; such are very weak at least, and for the most part very wicked.

II. He proceeds to caution and exhort those to whom he is writing, *vv.* 17–23. Here,

1. He calls them to remember how they had been forewarned: *But, beloved, remember*, &c., *v.* 17.

2. He guards them against seducers by a further description of their odious character: *These are those who separate*, &c., *v.* 19. Observe, (1) Sensualists are the worst separatists. They separate themselves from God, and Christ, and his church, to the devil, the world, and the flesh, by their ungodly courses and vicious practices. (2) Sensual men have not the Spirit, that is, of God and Christ, the Spirit of holiness, which whoever *has not, is none of Christ's*, does not belong to him, Rom. viii. 9. (3) The worse others are the better should we endeavour and approve ourselves to be.

3. He exhorts them to persevering constancy in truth and holiness.

(1) *Building up yourselves in your most holy faith*, *v.* 20. Observe, The way to hold fast our profession is to hold on in it. Having laid our foundation well in a sound faith,

and a sincere upright heart, we must build upon it, make further progress continually.

(2) *Praying in the Holy Ghost*. Observe, [1] Prayer is the nurse of faith; the way to *build up ourselves in our most holy faith* is to *continue instant in prayer*, Rom. xii. 12. [2] Our prayers are then most likely to prevail when we *pray in the Holy Ghost*, that is, under his guidance and influence.

(3) *Keep yourselves in the love of God*, *v.* 21. [1] "Keep up the grace of love to God in its lively vigorous actings and exercises in your souls." [2] "Take heed of throwing yourselves out of the love of God to you, or its delightful, cheering, strengthening manifestations; keep yourselves in the way of God, if you would continue in his love."

(4) *Looking for the mercy*, &c. [1] Eternal life is to be looked for only through *mercy*; mercy is our only plea, not merit. [2] It is said, not only through the mercy of God as our Creator, but through the mercy *of our Lord Jesus Christ* as Redeemer; all who come to heaven must come thither through our Lord Jesus Christ. [3] A believing expectation of eternal life will arm us against the snares of sin (2 Pet. iii. 14); a lively faith of the blessed hope will help us to mortify our cursed lusts.

4. He directs them how to behave towards erring brethren: *And of some have compassion*, &c., *vv.* 22, 23. Observe, (1) We ought to do all we can to rescue others out of the snare of the devil, that they may be saved from (or recovered, when entangled therein, out of) dangerous errors, or pernicious

practices. (2) This must be done with *compassion, making a difference.* How is that? We must distinguish between the weak and the wilful. *Others save with fear,* urging upon them *the terrors of the Lord. Hating even the garment spotted with the flesh,* that is, keeping yourselves at the utmost distance from what is or appears evil, and designing and endeavouring that others may do so too.

III. The apostle concludes this epistle with a solemn ascription of glory to the great God, *vv.* 24, 25. Note, 1. Whatever is the subject or argument we have been treating of, ascribing glory to God is fittest for us to conclude with. 2. God is able, and he is as willing as able, *to keep us from falling, and to present us faultless before the presence of his glory*; not as those who never have been faulty, but as those whose faults shall not be imputed, to their ruin, which, but for God's mercy and a Saviour's merits they might most justly have been.

THE
REVELATION OF ST. JOHN
THE DIVINE

CHAPTER ONE
THE FAITHFUL WITNESS
(vv. 1–8)

Our Lord Jesus is the great trustee of divine revelation; it is to him that we owe the knowledge we have of what we are to expect from God and what he expects from us. This revelation Christ *sent and signified by his angel*. Observe here the admirable order of divine revelation. God gave it to Christ, and Christ employed an angel to communicate it to the churches. The angels *signified it to the apostle John*. John was the apostle chosen for this service. Some think he was the only one surviving, the rest having sealed their testimony with their blood. This was to be the last book of divine revelation; and therefore notified to the church by the last of the apostles. John was the beloved disciple.

The evangelists give us an account of the things that are past; prophecy gives us an account of things to come. These future events are shown, not in the clearest light in which God could have set them, but in such a light as he saw most proper, and which would best answer his wise and holy purposes. We have in this revelation a general idea of the methods of divine providence and government in and about the church, and many good lessons may be learned hereby. These events (it is said) were such as should come to pass not only *surely*, but *shortly*; that is, they would begin to come to pass very shortly, and the whole would be accomplished in a short time. For now the last ages of the world had come.

We have here an apostolic benediction on those who should give a due regard to this divine revelation; and this benediction is given more generally and more especially.

I. More generally, to all who either read or hear the words of the prophecy.

II. The apostolic benediction is pronounced more especially and particularly to the seven Asian churches, *v.* 4. These seven churches are named in *v.* 11, and distinct messages sent to each of them respectively in the chapters following. Observe the particular account we have here of Christ, *v.* 5. [1] He *is the faithful witness*; he was from eternity a witness to all the counsels of God (John i. 18), and he was in time a faithful witness to the revealed will of God, who has now spoken to us by his Son. [2] He is the first-begotten or first-born from the dead, or the first parent

502

and head of the resurrection. [3] He is the prince of the kings of the earth. This is good news to the church, and it is good evidence of the Godhead of Christ, who is King of kings and Lord of lords. [4] He is the great friend of his church and people. He has loved them, and, in pursuance of that everlasting love, he has, *First, Washed them from their sins in his own blood*. Sins leave a stain upon the soul, a stain of guilt and of pollution. Nothing can fetch out this stain but the blood of Christ. *Secondly*, He has *made them kings and priests to God and his Father*. Having justified and sanctified them, he makes them kings to his Father; that is, in his Father's account, with his approbation, and for his glory. He hath made them priests, given them access to God, enabled them to enter into the holiest and to offer spiritual and acceptable sacrifices, and has given them an unction suitable to this character; and for these high honours and favours they are bound to ascribe to him dominion and glory for ever. [5] He will be the Judge of the world: *Behold, he cometh, and every eye shall see him, v.* 7. This book, the Revelation, begins and ends with a prediction of the second coming of the Lord Jesus Christ. He will come publicly: *Every eye shall see him*, the eye of his people, the eye of his enemies, every eye, yours and mine. [6] This account of Christ is ratified and confirmed by himself, *v.* 8. Here our Lord Jesus justly challenges the same honour and power that is ascribed to the Father, *v.* 4. He is the beginning and the end; all

things are from him and for him; he is the Almighty; he is the same eternal and unchangeable one. And surely whoever presumes to blot out one character of this name of Christ deserves to have his name blotted out of the book of life. Those that honour him he will honour; but those who despise him shall be lightly esteemed.

VISION OF CHRIST (*vv*. 9–20)

We have now come to that glorious vision which the apostle had of the Lord Jesus Christ, when he came to deliver this revelation to him, where observe,

I. The account given of the person who was favoured with this vision. He describes himself, 1. By his present state and condition. He was *the brother and companion of these churches in tribulation, and in the kingdom and patience of Christ*. He was, at their time, as the rest of true Christians were, a persecuted man, banished, and perhaps imprisoned, for his adherence to Christ. 2. By the place where he was when he was favoured with this vision: he was in *the isle Patmos*. 3. The day and time in which he had this vision: it was *the Lord's day*, the day which Christ had separated and set apart for himself, as the eucharist is called *the Lord's supper*. Surely this can be no other than the Christian sabbath, the first day of the week, to be observed in remembrance of the resurrection of Christ. 4. The frame that his soul was in at this time: *He was in the Spirit*. He was not only in a rapture when he received the vision, but before he received it; he was in a serious, heavenly, spiritual frame, under the blessed gracious influences of the Spirit of God. God usually prepares the souls of his people for uncommon manifestations of himself, by the quickening sanctifying influences of his good Spirit.

II. The apostle gives an account of what he heard when thus in the Spirit. An alarm was given as with the sound of a trumpet, and then *he heard a voice*, the voice of Christ applying to himself the character before given, *the first and the last*, and commanding the apostle to commit to writing the things that were now to be revealed to him, and to send it immediately *to the seven Asian churches*, whose names are mentioned.

III. We have also an account of what he saw. *He turned to see the voice*, whose it was and whence it came; and then a wonderful scene of vision opened itself to him.

1. He saw a representation of the church under the emblem of *seven golden candlesticks*, as it is explained in the last verse of the chapter. The churches are compared to candlesticks, because they hold forth the light of the gospel to advantage.

2. He saw a representation of the Lord Jesus Christ in the midst of the golden candlesticks; for he has promised to be with his churches always to the end of the world, filling them with light, and life, and love, for he is the very animating informing soul of the church. And here we observe,

(1) The glorious form in which Christ appeared in several particulars. [1] He was *clothed with a garment down to the foot*, a princely end priestly robe, denoting righteousness and honour. [2] *He was girt about with a golden girdle*, the breast-plate of the high priest, on which the names of his people are engraven; he was ready girt to do all the work of a Redeemer. [3] *His head and hairs were white like wool or snow*. He was the Ancient of days; his hoary head was no sign of decay, but was indeed a crown of glory. [4] *His eyes were as a flame of fire*, piercing and penetrating into the very hearts and reins of men, scattering terrors among his adversaries. [5] *His feet were like unto fine burning brass*, strong and stedfast, supporting his own interest, subduing his enemies, and treading them to powder. [6] *His voice was as the sound of many waters*, of many rivers falling in together. He can and will make himself heard to those who are afar off as well as to those who are near. [7] *He had in his right hand seven stars*, that is, the ministers of the seven churches, who are under his direction, have all their light and influence from him, and are secured and preserved by him. [8] *Out of his mouth went a two-edged sword*, his word, which both wounds and heals, strikes at sins on the right hand and on the left, [9] *His countenance was as the sun shining*, its strength too bright and dazzling for mortal eyes to behold.

(2) The impression this appearance of Christ made upon the apostle John (*v.* 17): *He fell at the feet of Christ as dead*; he was overpowered with the greatness of the lustre and glory in which Christ appeared.

He laid his hand upon him, v. 17. He raised him up; he did not plead against him with his great power, but he put strength into him, he spoke kind words to him. And here he acquaints him, *First,* With his divine nature: *The first and the last. Secondly,* With his former sufferings: *I was dead;* the very same that his disciples saw upon the cross dying for the sins of men. *Thirdly,* With his resurrection and life: "*I live, and am alive for evermore,* have conquered death and opened the grave, and am partaker of an endless life." *Fourthly,* With his office and authority: *I have the keys of hell and of death,* a sovereign dominion in and over the invisible world. *Fifthly,* With his will and pleasure: *Write the things which thou hast seen, and the things which are, and which shall be hereafter. Sixthly,* With the meaning of the seven stars, that *they are the ministers of the churches;* and of the seven candlesticks, that *they are the seven churches,* to whom Christ would now send by him particular and proper messages.

CHAPTER TWO
MESSAGE FOR EPHESUS
(*vv.* 1–7)

We have here,

I. The inscription, where observe, 1. To whom the first of these epistles is directed: *To the church of Ephesus,* a famous church planted by the apostle Paul (Acts xix.), and afterwards watered and governed by John, who had his residence very much there.

II. The contents of the epistle, in which, as in most of those that follow, we have,

1. The commendation Christ gave this church, ministers and members, which he always brings in by declaring that he knows their works, and therefore both his commendation and reprehension are to be strictly regarded; for he does not in either speak at a venture: he knows what he says. Now the church of Ephesus is commended, (1) For their diligence in duty: *I know thy works, and thy labour, v.* 2. (2) For their patience in suffering: *Thy labour and thy patience, v.* 2. It is not enough that we be diligent, but we must be patient, and endure hardness as good soldiers of Christ. (3) For their zeal against what was evil: *Thou canst not bear those that are evil, v.* 2.

2. The rebuke given to this church: *Nevertheless, I have somewhat against thee, v.* 4. The sin that Christ charged this church with was their decay and declension in holy love and zeal: *Thou hast left thy first love;* not left and forsaken the object of it, but lost the fervent degree of it that at first appeared.

3. The advice and counsel given them from Christ: *Remember therefore whence thou hast fallen, and repent,* &c. (1) Those that have lost their first love *must remember whence they have fallen;* they must compare their present with their former state, and consider how much better it was with them then than now. (2) They must repent. They must be inwardly grieved and ashamed for their sinful declension and judge and condemn themselves for it. (3) They must return and do their first works. They must

endeavour to revive and recover their first zeal, tenderness, and seriousness, and must pray as earnestly, and watch as diligently, as they did when they first set out in the ways of God.

4. This good advice is enforced and urged, (1) By a severe threatening, if it should be neglected: *I will come unto thee quickly, and remove thy candlestick out of its place.* (2) By an encouraging mention that is made of what was yet good among them: *This thou hast, that thou hatest the deeds of the Nicolaitans, which I also hate, v.* 6. The Nicolaitans were a loose sect who sheltered themselves under the name of Christianity. They held hateful doctrines, and they were guilty of hateful deeds, hateful to Christ and to all true Christians; and it is mentioned to the praise of the church of Ephesus that they had a just zeal and abhorrence of those wicked doctrines and practices.

III. We have the conclusion of this epistle, in which, as in those that follow, we have,

1. A call to attention: *He that hath an ear, let him hear what the Spirit saith unto the churches.*

2. A promise of great mercy to those who overcome.

SMYRNA (vv. 8–11)

We now proceed to the second epistle sent to another of the Asian churches, where, as before, observe,

I. The superscription, telling us to whom it was more expressly and immediately directed: *To the angel of the church in Smyrna,* a place well known at this day by our merchants, a city of great trade and wealth,

perhaps the only city of all the seven that is still known by the same name.

II. The subject-matter of this epistle to Smyrna, where, after the common declaration of Christ's omniscience, and the perfect cognizance he has of all the works of men and especially of his churches, he takes notice,

1. Of the improvement they had made in their spiritual state. This comes in in a short parenthesis; yet it is very emphatic: *But thou art rich (v.* 9), poor in temporals, but rich in spirituals—poor in spirit, and yet rich in grace.

2. Of their sufferings: *I know thy tribulation and thy poverty*—the persecution they underwent, even to the spoiling of their goods.

3. He knows the wickedness and the falsehood of their enemies: *I know the blasphemy of those that say they are Jews, but are not*; that is, of those who pretend to be the only peculiar covenant-people of God, as the Jews boasted themselves to be, even after God had rejected them; or of those who would be setting up the Jewish rites and ceremonies, which were now not only antiquated, but abrogated; these may say that they only are the church of God in the world, when indeed *they are the synagogue of Satan.*

4. He foreknows the future trials of his people, and forewarns them of them, and fore-arms them against them. (1) He forewarns them of future trials: *The devil shall cast some of you into prison, and you shall have tribulation, v.* 10. (2) Christ fore-arms them against these approaching troubles, [1] By his

counsel: *Fear none of these things.*
[2] By showing them how their
sufferings would be alleviated and
limited. *First,* They should not be
universal. It would be some of
them, not all, who should be cast
into prison, those who were best
able to bear it and might expect to
be visited and comforted by the
rest. *Secondly,* They were not to be
perpetual, but for a set time, and a
short time: *Ten days.* It should not
be everlasting tribulation. *Thirdly,*
It should be to try them, not to
destroy them, that their faith, and
patience, and courage, might be
proved and improved, might be found
to honour and glory. [3] By proposing and promising a glorious
reward to their fidelity: *Be thou
faithful to death, and I will give thee
a crown of life.* The life so worn out
in his service, or laid down in his
cause, shall be rewarded with
another and a much better life that
shall be eternal.

III. The conclusion of this message, and that, as before, 1. With a
call to universal attention, that all
men, all the world, should hear
what passes between Christ and his
churches. 2. With a gracious
promise to the conquering Christian: *He that overcometh shall not
be hurt of the second death, v.* 11.
The second death shall have no
power over those who are *partakers
of the first resurrection*: the first
death shall not hurt them, and the
second death shall have no power
over them.

PERGAMOS (*vv.* 12–17)

Here also we are to consider,

I. To whom it was sent: *To the
angel of the church of Pergamos.*

Whether this was a city raised up
out of the ruins of old Troy, or
some other city of the same name,
is neither certain nor material. It
was a place where Christ had called
and constituted a gospel church, by
the preaching of the gospel and the
grace of his Spirit making the word
effectual. The church of Pergamos
was infested with men of corrupt
minds, who did what they could to
corrupt both the faith and manners
of the church; and Christ, being
resolved to fight against them by
the sword of his word, takes the
title of him that *hath the sharp
sword with two edges.*

II. From the inscription we
proceed to the contents of the
epistle, in which the method is
much the same as is observed in the
rest. Here,

1. Christ takes notice of the trials
and difficulties this church encountered with: *I know thy works,
and where thou dwellest,* &c. *v.* 13.
Some think that the Roman
governor in this city was a most
violent enemy to the Christians;
and the seat of persecution is
Satan's seat.

2. He commends their stedfastness: *Thou holdest fast my name,
and hast not denied my faith.* These
two expressions are much the same
in sense; the former may, however,
signify the effect and the latter the
cause or means.

3. He reproves them for their
sinful failures (*v.* 14): *But I have a
few things against thee, because thou
hast there those that hold the doctrine of Balaam,* &c., and *those that
hold the doctrine of the Nicolaitans,
which thing I hate.* There were some
who taught that it was lawful to eat

things sacrificed to idols, and that simple fornication was no sin; they, by an impure worship, drew men into impure practices, as Balaam did the Israelites.

4. He calls them to repentance: *Repent, or else I will come unto thee quickly*, &c., *v.* 16. The word of God will take hold of sinners, sooner or later, either for their conviction or their confusion.

III. We have the conclusion of this epistle, where, after the usual demand of universal attention, there is the promise of great favour to those that overcome. They shall *eat of the hidden manna, and have the new name, and the white stone, which no man knoweth, saving he that receiveth it, v.* 17. The stone alludes to the ancient custom of giving a white stone to those acquitted on trial and a black stone to those condemned.

THYATIRA (vv. 18–29)

I. To whom it is directed: *To the angel of the church of Thyatira*, a city of the proconsular Asia, bordering upon Mysia on the north and Lydia on the south, a town of trade. *The Son of God* is here described as having *eyes like a flame of fire, and feet like as fine brass*. His general title is here, *the Son of God*, that is, the eternal and only-begotten Son of God. The description we have here of him is in two characters: (1) That his eyes are like a flame of fire, signifying his piercing, penetrating, perfect knowledge. (2) That his feet are like fine brass, that the outgoings of his providence are steady, awful, and all pure and holy.

II. The contents or subject-matter of this epistle, which, as the rest, includes,

1. The honourable character and commendation Christ gives of this church. Now in this church Christ makes honourable mention, (1) Of their *charity*, either more general, a disposition to do good to all men, or more special, to the household of faith: there is no religion where there is no charity. (2) Their *service*, their ministration; this respects chiefly the officers of the church, who had laboured in the word and doctrine. (3) Their *faith*, which was the grace that actuated all the rest, both their charity and their service. (4) Their *patience*. (5) Their growing fruitfulness: their last works were better than the first.

2. A faithful reproof for what was amiss. This is not so directly charged upon the church itself as upon some wicked seducers who were among them; the church's fault was that she connived too much at them.

(1) These wicked seducers are compared to Jezebel, and called by her name. The sin of these seducers was that they attempted to draw the servants of God into fornication, and to offer sacrifices to idols.

(2) Now why should the wickedness of this Jezebel be charged upon the church of Thyatira? Because that church suffered her to seduce the people of that city. But how could the church help it? They had not, as a church, civil power to banish or imprison her; but they had ministerial power to censure and to excommunicate her: and it is probable that neglecting to use the power they had made them sharers in her sin.

3. The punishment of this seducer, this Jezebel, *vv.* 22, 23, in which is couched a prediction of the fall of Babylon. (1) *I will cast her into a bed*, into a bed of pain. (2) *I will kill her children with death*; that is, the second death, which does the work effectually, and leaves no hope of future life.

4. The design of Christ in the destruction of these wicked seducers, and this was the instruction of others, especially of his churches.

5. The encouragement given to those who keep themselves pure and undefiled: *But to you I say, and unto the rest*, &c., *v.* 24. Christ is coming to put an end to all the temptations of his people; and, if they hold fast faith and a good conscience till he come, all the difficulty and danger will be over.

III. We now come to the conclusion of this message, *vv.* 26–29. Here we have, 1. The promise of an ample reward to the persevering victorious believer, in two parts: (1) Very great power and dominion over the rest of the world: *Power over the nations*, which may refer either to the time when the empire should turn Christian, or to the other world, when believers shall sit down with Christ on his throne of judgment. (2) Knowledge and wisdom, suitable to such power and dominion: *I will give him the morning-star*. Christ is the morning-star. He brings day with him into the soul, the light of grace and of glory; and he will give his people that perfection of light and wisdom. 2. This epistle ends with the usual demand of attention: *He that hath an ear let him hear what the Spirit saith unto the churches*.

CHAPTER THREE

THE CHURCH OF SARDIS
(*vv.* 1–6)

Here is, I. To whom this letter is directed: *To the angel of the church of Sardis*, an ancient city of Lydia, on the banks of the mountain Tmolus, said to have been the chief city of Asia the Less, and the first city in that part of the world that was converted by the preaching of John; and, some say, the first that revolted from Christianity, and one of the first that was laid in its ruins, in which it still lies, without any church or ministry. The Lord Jesus here assumes the character of him *that hath the seven spirits of God, and the seven stars*, taken out of *ch.* i. 4, where *the seven spirits are said to be before the throne*.

II. The body of this epistle. There is this observable in it, that whereas in the other epistles Christ begins with commending what is good in the churches, and then proceeds to tell them what is amiss, in this (and in the epistle to Laodicea) he begins,

1. With a reproof, and a very severe one: *I know thy works, that thou hast a name that thou livest, and art dead*. Hypocrisy, and a lamentable decay in religion, are the sins charged upon this church, by one who knew her well, and all her works.

2. Our Lord proceeds to give this degenerate church the best advice: *Be watchful, and strengthen the things*, &c., *v.* 2. (1) He advises them to be upon their watch. The cause of their sinful deadness and declension was that they had let down their watch. (2) To strengthen

the things that remain, and that are ready to die. Some understand this of persons; there were some few who had retained their integrity, but they were in danger of declining with the rest. Or it may be understood of practices, as it follows: *I have not found thy works perfect before God*, not filled up; there is something wanting in them. (3) To recollect themselves, and *remember how they have received and heard* (*v.* 3); not only to remember what they had received and heard, but how they had received and heard, what impressions the mercies of God had made upon their souls at first. (4) To hold fast what they had received, that they might not lose all, *and repent* sincerely that they had lost so much of the life of religion, and had run the risk of losing all.

3. Christ enforces his counsel with a dreadful threatening in case it should be despised: *I will come unto thee as a thief, and thou shalt not know the hour, v.* 3.

4. Our blessed Lord does not leave this sinful people without some comfort and encouragement: *In the midst of judgment he remembers mercy* (*v.* 4), and here, (1) He makes honourable mention of the faithful remnant in Sardis, though but small. (2) He makes a very gracious promise to them: *They shall walk with me in white, for they are worthy*—in the *stola*, the white robes of justification, and adoption, and comfort, or in the white robes of honour and glory in the other world.

III. We now come to the conclusion of this epistle, in which, as before, we have,

1. A great reward promised to the conquering Christian (*v.* 5), and it is very much the same with what has been already mentioned: *He that overcometh shall be clothed in white raiment*. Now to this is added another promise very suitable to the case: *I will not blot his name out of the book of life, but will confess his name before my Father, and before his angels*.

2. The demand of universal attention finishes the message.

PHILADELPHIA (*vv.* 7–13)

Observe,

I. For whom the letter was more immediately designed: *The angel of the church of Philadelphia*; this also was a city in Asia Minor, seated upon the borders of Mysia and Lydia, and had its name from that brotherly love for which it was eminent.

2. By whom this letter was signed; even by the same Jesus who is alone the universal head of all the churches; and here observe by what title he chooses to represent himself to this church: *He that is holy, he that is true, he that hath the key of David*, &c. Observe, (1) The acts of his government. [1] He opens. He opens a door of opportunity to his churches; he opens a door of utterance to his ministers; he opens a door of entrance, opens the heart; he opens a door of admission into the visible church, laying down the terms of communion; and he opens the door of admission into the church triumphant, according to the terms of salvation fixed by him. [2] He shuts the door. When he pleases, he shuts the door of opportunity and the

door of utterance, and leaves obstinate sinners shut up in the hardness of their hearts; he shuts the door of church-fellowship against unbelievers and profane persons; and he shuts the door of heaven against the foolish virgins who have slept away their day of grace, and against the workers of iniquity, how vain and confident soever they may be. (2) The way and manner in which he performs these acts, and that is absolute sovereignty, independent upon the will of men, and irresistible by the power of men.

II. The subject-matter of this epistle, where,

1. Christ puts them in mind of what he had done for them: *I have set before thee an open door, and no man can shut it*, v. 8. I have set it open, though there be many adversaries.

2. This church is commended: *Thou hast a little strength, and hast kept my word, and hast not denied my name*, v. 8. In this there seems to be couched a gentle reproof. True grace, though weak, has the divine approbation; but, though Christ accepts a little strength, yet believers should not rest satisfied in a little, but should strive to grow in grace, to be *strong in faith, giving glory to God*.

3. Here is a promise of the great favour God would bestow on this church, *vv.* 9, 10. This favour consists in two things:

(1) Christ would make this church's enemies subject to her. [1] Those enemies are described to be such as *said they were Jews*, but lied in saying so—pretended to be the only and peculiar people of

God, but were really *the synagogue of Satan*. [2] Their subjection to the church is described: *They shall worship at thy feet*; not pay a religious and divine honour to the church itself, nor to the ministry of it, but shall be convinced that they have been in the wrong, that this church is in the right and is beloved of Christ.

(2) Another instance of favour that Christ promises to this church is persevering grace in the most trying times (*v.* 10), and this as the reward of their past fidelity. *To him that hath shall be given*.

4. Christ calls the church to that duty which he before promised he would enable her to do, and that is, to persevere, *to hold fast that which she had*.

III. The conclusion of this epistle, *vv.* 12, 13. Here,

1. After his usual manner, our Saviour promises a glorious reward to the victorious believer, in two things: (1) He shall be a monumental *pillar in the temple of God*; not a pillar to support the temple (heaven needs no such props), but a monument of the free and powerful grace of God. (2) On this monumental pillar there shall be an honourable inscription, as in those cases is usual.

2. The epistle is closed up with the demand of attention: *He that hath an ear, let him hear what the Spirit saith unto the churches*, how Christ loves and values his faithful people, how he commends, and how he will crown their fidelity.

LAODICEA (*vv.* 14–22)

We now come to the last and worst of all the seven Asian churches, the reverse of the church of Philadelphia; for, as there was nothing reproved in that, here is nothing commended in this, and yet this was one of *the seven golden candlesticks*, for a corrupt church may still be a church. Here we have, as before,

I. To whom: *To the angel of the church of Laodicea.* This was a once famous city near the river Lycus, had a wall of vast compass, and three marble theatres, and, like Rome, was built on seven hills. 2. From whom this message was sent. Here our Lord Jesus styles himself *the Amen, the faithful and true witness, the beginning of the creation of God. The beginning of the creation of God*, either of the first creation, and so he is the beginning, that is, the first cause, the Creator, and the Governor of it; or of the second creation, the church; and so he is the head of that body, the first-born from the dead, as it is in *ch. i. 5*, whence these titles are taken.

II. The subject-matter, in which observe,

1. The heavy charge drawn up against this church, ministers and people, by one who knew them better than they knew themselves: *Thou art neither cold nor hot*, but worse than either; *I would thou wert cold or hot*, *v.* 15. Lukewarmness or indifference in religion is the worst temper in the world. If religion is a real thing, it is the most excellent thing, and therefore we should be in good earnest in it.

2. A severe punishment threatened: *I will spue thee out of my mouth.* He is sick of them, and cannot long bear them.

3. We have one cause of this

indifference and inconsistency in religion assigned, and that is self-conceitedness or self-delusion. They thought they were very well already, and therefore they were very indifferent whether they grew better or no: *Because thou sayest, I am rich, and increased with goods*, &c., *v.* 17.

4. We have good counsel given by Christ to this sinful people, and that is that they drop their vain and false opinion they had of themselves, and endeavour to be that really which they would seem to be: *I counsel thee to buy of me*, &c., *v.* 18. How can those that are poor buy gold? Just as they may buy of Christ wine and milk, that is, *without money and without price*, Isa. lv. 1. These people were naked; Christ tells them where they might have clothing, and such as would cover the shame of their nakedness. They were blind; and he *counsels them to buy of him eye-salve, that they might see*, to give up their own wisdom and reason, which are but blindness in the things of God, and resign themselves to his word and Spirit, and their eyes shall be opened to see their way and their end, their duty and their true interest.

5. Here is added great and gracious encouragement to this sinful people to take the admonition and advice well that Christ had given them, *vv.* 19, 20. He tells them, (1) It was given them in true and tender affection: "*Whom I love, I rebuke and chasten.*" (2) If they would comply with his admonitions, he was ready to make them good to their souls: *Behold, I stand at the door and knock*, &c., *v.* 20. Here observe, [1] Christ is gra-

ciously pleased by his word and Spirit to come to the door in the heart of sinners; he draws near to them in a way of mercy, ready to make them a kind visit. [2] He finds this door shut against him; the heart of man is by nature shut up against Christ by ignorance, unbelief, sinful prejudices. [3] When he finds the heart shut, he does not immediately withdraw, but he waits to be gracious. [4] He uses all proper means to awaken sinners, and to cause them to open to him: he calls by his word, he knocks by the impulses of his Spirit upon their conscience. [5] Those who open to him shall enjoy his presence, to their great comfort and advantage.

III. We now come to the conclusion of this epistle; and here we have as before,

1. The promise made to the overcoming believer. *They shall sit down with me on my throne, as I also overcame, and have sat down with my Father on his throne, v.* 21.

2. All is closed up with the general demand of attention (*v.* 22). Thus end the messages of Christ to the Asian churches, the epistolary part of this book. We now come to the prophetical part.

CHAPTER FOUR

VISION OF HEAVEN (*vv.* 1–8)

We have here an account of a second vision with which the apostle John was favoured. Observe,

I. The preparation made for the apostle's having this vision.

1. *A door was opened in heaven.* Hence we learn, (1) Whatever is transacted on earth is first designed and settled in heaven. (2) We can know nothing of future events but what God is pleased to discover to us. But, (3) So far as God reveals his designs to us we may and ought to receive them, and not pretend to be wise above what is revealed.

2. To prepare John for the vision, a trumpet was sounded, and he was called up into heaven, to have a sight there of the things which were to be hereafter. He was called into the third heavens.

3. To prepare for this vision, *the apostle was in the Spirit.* He was in a rapture, as before (*ch.* i. 10), whether in the body or out of the body we cannot tell. Now observe,

II. The vision itself. It begins with the strange sights that the apostle saw, and they were such as these: 1. He saw *a throne set in heaven,* the seat of honour, and authority, and judgment. 2. He saw a glorious one upon the throne. This throne was not empty; there was one in it who filled it, and that was God, who is here described by those things that are most pleasant and precious in our world: *His countenance was like a jasper and a sardine-stone;* he is not described by any human features, so as to be represented by an image, but only by his transcendant brightness. 3. He saw *a rainbow about the throne, like unto an emerald, v.* 3. The rainbow was the seal and token of the covenant of providence that God made with Noah and his posterity with him, and is a fit emblem of that covenant of promise that God had made with Christ as the head of the church. 4. He saw *four-and-twenty seats* round about the throne, not empty, but filled with *four-and-twenty elders*, presbyters, representing, very probably, the whole church of God, both in the Old-Testament and in the New-Testament state. *They are clothed in white raiment*, the righteousness of the saints, both imputed and inherent; *they had on their heads crowns of gold*, signifying the honour and authority given them of God, and the glory they have with him. 5. He perceived lightnings and voices proceeding out of the throne; that is, the awful declarations that God makes to his church of his sovereign will and pleasure. 6. He saw *seven lamps of fire burning before the throne*, which are explained to be *the seven Spirits of God* (*v*. 5), the various gifts, graces, and operations of the Spirit of God in the churches of Christ. 7. He saw *before the throne a sea of glass, like unto crystal*. In the gospel church the sea or laver for purification is the blood of the Lord Jesus Christ, who cleanses from all sin, even from sanctuary-sins. In this all those must be washed that are admitted into the gracious presence of God on earth or his glorious presence in heaven. 8. He saw *four animals*, living creatures, between the throne and the circle of the elders (as seems most probable), standing between God and the people; these seem to signify the ministers of the gospel.

WORSHIP IN HEAVEN
(*vv*. 8–11)

We have considered the sights that the apostle saw in heaven: now let us observe the songs that he heard.

I. He heard the song of the four living creatures, of the ministers of the church, which refers to the prophet Isaiah's vision, *ch*. vi. And here, 1. They adore one God, and one only, *the Lord God Almighty*, unchangeable and everlasting. 2. They adore three holies in this one God, the Holy Father, the Holy Son, and the Holy Spirit; and these are one infinitely holy and eternal Being, who sits upon the throne, *and lives for ever and ever*. In this glory the prophet saw Christ, and spoke of him.

II. He heard the adorations of the *four-and-twenty elders*, that is, of the Christian people represented by them; the ministers led, and the people followed, in the praises of God, *vv*. 10, 11.

THE SEALED BOOK (*vv*. 1–5)

Hitherto the apostle had seen only the great God, the governor of all things, now,

I. He is favoured with a sight of the model and methods of his government, as they are all written down in a book which he holds in his hand; and this we are now to consider as shut up and sealed in the hand of God. *Known unto God*, and to him alone, *are all his works, from the beginning of the world*; but it is his glory to conceal the matter as he pleases.

II. He heard a proclamation made concerning this sealed book. The cry or challenge proclaimed was, "*Who is worthy to open the book, and to loose the seals thereof?*" *v*. 2. None in heaven or earth could accept the challenge and undertake the task: none *in heaven*, none of the glorious holy angels, though before the throne of God, and the ministers of his providence; they with all their wisdom cannot dive into the decrees of God: none *on earth*, no man, the wisest or the best of men, none of the magicians and soothsayers, none of the prophets of God, any further than he reveals his mind to them: *none under the earth*, none of the fallen angels, none of the spirits of men departed, though they should return to our world, can open this book. Satan himself, with all his subtlety, cannot do it; the creatures cannot open it, nor look on it; they cannot read it. God only can do it.

III. He felt a great concern in himself about this matter: the apostle *wept much*; it was a great disappointment to him.

IV. The apostle was comforted and encouraged to hope this sealed book would yet be opened. Here observe, Who it was that would do the thing—the Lord Jesus Christ, called *the lion of the tribe of Judah*, according to his human nature, alluding to Jacob's prophecy (Gen. xlix. 10), and *the root of David* according to his divine nature, though a branch of David according to the flesh. He who is a middle person, God and man, and bears the office of Mediator between God and man, is fit and worthy to open and execute all the counsels of God towards men.

THE LAMB WITH THE MARKS OF DEATH (*vv.* 6–14)

Here, I. The apostle beholds this book taken into the hands of the Lord Jesus Christ, in order that it might be unsealed and opened by him. Here Christ is described, 1. By

his place and station: *In the midst of the throne, and of the four beasts, and of the elders.* 2. The form in which he appeared. Before he is called *a lion*; here he appears *as a lamb slain*. He appears with the marks of his sufferings upon him, to show that he intercedes in heaven in the virtue of his satisfaction. He appears as a *lamb, having seven horns and seven eyes*, perfect power to execute all the will of God and perfect wisdom to understand it all and to do it in the most effectual manner; *for he hath the seven Spirits of God.* 3. He is described by his act and deed: *He came, and took the book out of the right hand of him that sat on the throne* (*v.* 7), not by violence, nor by fraud, but he prevailed to do it (as *v.* 5), he prevailed by his merit and worthiness, he did it by authority and by the Father's appointment.

II. The apostle observes the universal joy and thanksgiving that filled heaven and earth upon this transaction.

1. The church begins the doxology, as being more immediately concerned in it (*v.* 8), the four living creatures, and *the four-and-twenty elders*, the Christian people, under their minister, lead up the chorus.

2. The doxology, thus begun by the church, is carried on by the angels; they take the second part, in conjunction with the church, *v.* 11.

3. This doxology, thus begun by the church, and carried on by the angels, is resounded and echoed by the whole creation, *v.* 13. Heaven and earth ring with the high praises of the Redeemer. Thus we have seen this sealed book passing with

great solemnity from the hand of the Creator into the hand of the Redeemer.

CHAPTER SIX

THE WHITE HORSE (vv. 1, 2)

Here, 1. Christ, the Lamb, opens the first seal; he now enters upon the great work of opening and accomplishing the purposes of God towards the church and the world. 2. One of the ministers of the church calls upon the apostle, with a voice like thunder, to come near, and observe what then appeared. 3. We have the vision itself, v. 2. (1) The Lord Jesus appears riding on *a white horse*. He rides on the white horse of a pure but despised gospel, with great swiftness through the world. (2) *He had a bow* in his hand. This bow, in the hand of Christ, abides in strength, and, like that of Jonathan, *never returns empty*. (3) *A crown was given him*, importing that all who receive the gospel must receive Christ as a king, and must be his loyal and obedient subjects. (4) *He went forth conquering, and to conquer.* As long as the church continues militant Christ will be conquering.

THE RED HORSE (vv. 3–8)

I. Upon opening the second seal, to which John was called to attend, *another horse* appears, of a different colour from the former, *a red horse*, v. 4. This signifies the desolating judgment of war; he that sat upon this red horse had *power to take peace from the earth, and that* the inhabitants of *the earth should kill one another*.

II. Upon opening the third seal, which John was directed to observe, another horse appears, different from the former, *a black horse*, signifying famine, that terrible judgment; *and he that sat on the horse had a pair of balances in his hand* (v. 5), signifying that men must now eat their bread by weight, as was threatened (Lev. xxvi. 26).

III. Upon opening the fourth seal, which John is commanded to observe, there appears another horse, of a pale colour. Here observe, 1. The name of the rider— *Death*, the king of terrors; the pestilence, which is death in its empire, death reigning over a place or nation, death on horseback, marching about, and making fresh conquests every hour. 2. The attendants or followers of this king of terrors—*hell*, a state of eternal misery to all those who die in their sins; and, in times of such a general destruction, multitudes go down unprepared into the valley of destruction.

IV. After the opening of these seals of approaching judgments, and the distinct account of them, we have this general observation, that God *gave power to them over the fourth part of the earth, to kill with the sword, and with hunger, and with death, and with the beasts of the earth*, v. 8. He gave them power, that is, those instruments of his anger, or those judgments themselves. To the three great judgments of war, famine, and pestilence, is here added *the beasts of the earth*, another of God's sore judgments, mentioned Ezek. xiv. 21, and mentioned here the last, because, when a nation is depopulated by the sword, famine, and pestilence, the small remnant that continue in a waste and howling wilderness encourage the wild beasts to make head against them, and they become an easy prey.

THE DAY OF WRATH
(vv. 9–17)

In the remaining part of this chapter we have the opening of the fifth and the sixth seals.

I. The fifth seal. Here observe,

1. The sight this apostle saw at the opening of the fifth seal; it was a very affecting sight (v. 9): *I saw under the altar the souls of those that were slain for the word of God, and for the testimony which they held.* He saw the souls of the martyrs. Here observe, (1) Where he saw them—*under the altar*; at the foot of the altar of incense, in the most holy place; he saw them in heaven, at the foot of Christ. (2) What was the cause in which they suffered— *the word of God and the testimony which they held*, for believing the word of God, and attesting or confessing the truth of it; this profession of their faith they held fast without wavering, even though they died for it.

2. The cry he heard: *How long, O Lord, holy and true, dost thou not judge and avenge our blood on those that dwell on the earth?* v. 10. Observe, Even *the spirits of just men made perfect* retain a proper resentment of the wrong they have sustained by their cruel enemies; and though they die in charity, praying, as Christ did, that God would forgive them, yet they are desirous that God will take a just revenge upon the sin of persecution,

even while he pardons and saves the persecutors.

3. He observed the kind return that was made to this cry (v. 11), both what was given to them and what was said to them. (1) What was given to them—*white robes*, the robes of victory and of honour; their present happiness was an abundant recompence of their past sufferings. (2) What was said to them—that they should be satisfied, and easy in themselves, for it would not be long ere the number of their fellow-sufferers *should be fulfilled.*

II. We have here the sixth seal opened, v. 12. Some refer this to the great revolutions in the empire at Constantine's time, the downfall of paganism; others, with great probability, to the destruction of Jerusalem, as an emblem of the general judgment, and destruction of the wicked, at the end of the world. Here observe,

1. The tremendous events that were hastening; and here are several occurrences that contribute to make that day and dispensation very dreadful: (1) *There was a great earthquake.* (2) *The sun became black as sackcloth of hair*, either naturally, by a total eclipse, or politically, by the fall of the chief rulers and governors of the land. (3) *The moon* should *become as blood*; the inferior officers, or their military men, should be all wallowing in their own blood. (4) *The stars of heaven shall fall to the earth* (v. 13), and that *as a fig-tree casteth her untimely figs, when she is shaken of a mighty wind.* The stars may signify all the men of note and influence among them, though in lower spheres of activity; there

should be a general desolation. (5) *The heaven* should *depart as a scroll when it is rolled together*. This may signify that their ecclesiastical state should perish and be laid aside for ever. (6) *Every mountain and island shall be moved out of its place*. This leads to,

2. The dread and terror that would seize upon all sorts of men in that great and awful day, *v.* 15. When that day shall come, the most stout-hearted sinners will not be able to stand before him: all these terrors actually fell upon the sinners in Judea and Jerusalem in the day of their destruction, and they will all, in the utmost degree, fall upon impenitent sinners, at the general judgment of the last day.

CHAPTER SEVEN

BEFORE THE THRONE
(*vv.* 1–12)

Here we have, I. An account of the restraint laid upon the winds. By these winds we suppose are meant those errors and corruptions in religion which would occasion a great deal of trouble and mischief to the church of God.

II. An account of the sealing of the servants of God, where observe, 1. To whom this work was committed—to an angel, *another angel*. 2. How they were distinguished—the seal of God was set upon their foreheads, a seal known to him, and as plain as if it appeared in their foreheads; by this mark they were set apart for mercy and safety in the worst of times. 3. The number of those that were sealed, where observe, (1) A particular account of those that were

sealed of the twelve tribes of Israel—twelve thousand out of every tribe, the whole sum amounting to *a hundred and forty-four thousand*. Some take these to be a select number of the Jews who were reserved for mercy at the destruction of Jerusalem; others think that time was past, and therefore it is to be more generally applied to God's chosen remnant in the world. (2) A general account of those who were saved out of other nations (*v.* 9): *A great multitude, which no man could number, of all nations, and kindreds, and people, and tongues*. Though these are not said to be sealed, yet they were selected by God out of all nations, and brought into his church, and there stood before the throne.

III. We have the songs of saints and angels on this occasion, *vv.* 9–12, where observe,

1. The praises offered up by the saints (and, as it seems to me, by the Gentile believers) for the care of God in reserving so large a remnant of the Jews, and saving them from infidelity and destruction. Here observe, (1) The posture of these praising saints: they *stood before the throne, and before the Lamb*, before the Creator and the Mediator. (2) Their habit: they were *clothed with white robes, and had palms in their hands*; they were invested with the robes of justification, holiness, and victory, and had palms in their hands, as conquerors used to appear in their triumphs. (3) Their employment: they *cried with a loud voice, saying, Salvation to our God who sitteth upon the throne, and to the Lamb*.

2. Here is the song of the angels (*vv.* 11, 12). Here, [1] They acknowledge the glorious attributes of God—his wisdom, his power, and his might. [2] They declare that for these his divine perfections he ought to be blessed, and praised, and glorified, to all eternity; and they confirm it by their *Amen.*

THOSE IN WHITE (*vv.* 13–17)

Here we have a description of the honour and happiness of those who have faithfully served the Lord Jesus Christ, and suffered for him. Observe,

I. A question asked by one of the elders, not for his own information, but for John's instruction.

II. The answer returned by the apostle, in which he tacitly acknowledges his own ignorance, and sues to this elder for information: *Thou knowest.*

III. The account given to the apostle concerning that noble army of martyrs who stood *before the throne of God in white robes*, with palms of victory in their hands: and notice is taken here of, 1. The low and desolate state they had formerly been in. 2. The means by which they had been prepared for the great honour and happiness they now enjoyed: they had *washed their robes, and made them white in the blood of the Lamb, v.* 14. 3. The blessedness to which they are now advanced, being thus prepared for it. (1) They are happy in their station, for *they are before the throne of God night and day*; and he *dwells among them*; they are in that presence where there is fulness of joy. (2) They are happy in their employment, for they serve God

continually, and that without weakness, drowsiness, or weariness. Heaven is a state of service, though not of suffering; it is a state of rest, but not of sloth; it is a praising delightful rest. (3) They are happy in their freedom from all the inconveniences of this present life. This should moderate the Christian's sorrow in his present state, and support him under all the troubles of it.

CHAPTER EIGHT

THE SEVEN TRUMPETS
(*vv.* 1–6)

In these verses we have the prelude to the sounding of the trumpets in several parts.

I. The opening of the last seal. This was to introduce a new set of prophetical events.

II. A profound *silence in heaven for the space of half an hour*.

III. The trumpets were delivered to the angels who were to sound them.

IV. To prepare for this, another angel must first offer incense, *v.* 3. It is very probable that this other angel is the Lord Jesus, the high priest of the church, who is here described in his sacerdotal office, having a golden censer and much incense, a fulness of merit in his own glorious person, and this incense he was to offer up, *with the prayers of all the saints, upon the golden altar* of his divine nature. These prayers that were thus accepted in heaven produced great changes upon earth in return to them; the same angel that in his censer offered up the prayers of the saints in the same censer *took of the fire of the altar, and cast it into the earth*, and this presently caused strange commotions, *voices, and thunderings, and lightnings, and an earthquake*; these were the answers God gave to the prayers of the saints, and tokens of his anger against the world and that he would do great things to avenge himself and his people of their enemies; and now, all things being thus prepared, the angels discharge their duty.

WORMWOOD (*vv.* 7–13)

Observe, I. *The first angel sounded* the first trumpet, and the events which followed were very dismal: *There followed hail and fire mingled with blood*, &c., *v.* 7. There was a terrible storm; but whether it is to be understood of a storm of heresies, a mixture of monstrous errors falling on the church (for in that age Arianism prevailed), or a storm or tempest of war falling on the civil state, expositors are not agreed.

II. *The second angel sounded*, and the alarm was followed, as in the first, with terrible events: *A great mountain burning with fire was cast into the sea; and the third part of the sea became blood*, *v.* 8. By this mountain some understand the leader or leaders of the heretics; others the city of Rome, which was five times sacked by the Goths and Vandals, within the compass of 137 years.

III. *The third angel sounded*, and the alarm had the like effects as before: *There fell a great star from heaven*, &c., *v.* 10. Some take this to be a political star, some eminent governor. Others take it to be an ecclesiastical star, some eminent person in the church, compared to a *burning lamp*, and they fix it upon Pelagius, who proved about this time a falling star, and greatly corrupted the churches of Christ.

IV. *The fourth angel sounded*, and the alarm was followed with further calamities. Observe, 1. The nature of this calamity; it was darkness; it fell therefore upon the great luminaries of the heaven, that give light to the world—*the sun, and the moon, and the stars*, either the guides and governors of the church, or of the state, who are placed in higher orbs than the people, and are to dispense light and benign influences to them. 2. The limitation: it was confined to a third part of these luminaries; there was some light both of the sun by day, and of the moon and stars by night, but it was only a third part of what they had before.

V. Before the other three trumpets are sounded here is solemn warning given to the world how terrible the calamities would be that should follow them, and how miserable those times and places would be on which they fell, *v.* 13.

CHAPTER NINE
THE FIFTH ANGEL (*vv.* 1–12)

Upon the sounding of this trumpet, the things to be observed are, 1. *A star falling from heaven to the earth* Some think this star represents some eminent bishop in the Christian church, some angel of the church. 2. To this fallen star *was given the key of the bottomless pit*. Having now ceased to be a minister of Christ, he becomes the antichrist, the minister of the devil; and by the permission of Christ, who had taken from him the keys of the church, he becomes the devil's turnkey, to let loose the powers of hell against the churches of Christ. 3. Upon the opening of the bottomless pit *there arose a great smoke*, which darkened the sun and the air. The devils are the powers of darkness; hell is the place of darkness. 4. Out of this dark smoke there came a swarm of locusts, one of the plagues of Egypt, the devil's emissaries headed by antichrist, all the rout and rabble of antichristian orders, to promote superstition, idolatry, error, and cruelty; and these had, by the just permission of God, power to hurt those who had not the mark of God in their foreheads. 5. The hurt they were to do them was not a bodily, but a spiritual hurt. 6. They had no power so much as to hurt those who had the seal of God in their foreheads. 7. The power given to these factors for hell is limited in point of time: *five months*, a certain season, and but a short season, though how short we cannot tell. 8. Though it would be short, it would be very sharp. 9. These locusts were of a monstrous size and shape, *vv.* 7, 8, &c. The king and commander of this hellish squadron is here described, [1] As an angel; so he was by nature, an angel, once one of the angels of heaven. [2] *The angel of the bottomless pit*; an angel still, but a fallen angel, fallen into the bottomless pit, vastly large, and out of which there is no recovery. [3] In these infernal regions he is a sort of prince and governor, and has the powers of darkness under

his rule and command. [4] His true name is *Abaddon, Apollyon—a destroyer*, for that is his business, his design, and employment.

THE SIXTH ANGEL (*vv.* 13–21)

Here let us consider the preface to this vision, and then the vision itself.

I. The preface to this vision: *A voice was heard from the horns of the golden altar, vv.* 13, 14. These four messengers of divine judgment lay bound in the river Euphrates, a great way from the European nations. Here the Turkish power had its rise, which seems to be the story of this vision.

II. The vision itself: *And the four angels that had been bound in the great river Euphrates were now loosed, vv.* 15, 16. And here observe, 1. The time of their military operations and executions is limited to *an hour, and a day, and a month, and a year*. God will make the wrath of man praise him, and the remainder of wrath he will restrain. 2. The army that was to execute this great commission is mustered, and the number found to be of horsemen *two hundred thousand thousand*; but we are left to guess what the infantry must be. In general, it tells us, the armies of the Mahomedan empire should be vastly great; and so it is certain they were. 3. Their formidable equipage and appearance, *v.* 17. 4. The vast havoc and desolation that they made in the Roman empire, which had now become antichristian: a third part of them were killed; they went as far as their commission suffered them, and they could go no further. 5.

Their artillery, by which they made such slaughter, described *by fire, smoke, and brimstone*, issuing out of the mouths of their horses, and the stings that were in their tails. 6. Observe the impenitency of the antichristian generation under these dreadful judgments (*v.* 20).

III. From this sixth trumpet we learn, 1. God can make one enemy of the church to be a scourge and plague to another. 2. He who is the Lord of hosts has vast armies at his command, to serve his own purposes. 3. The most formidable powers have limits set them, which they cannot transgress.

CHAPTER TEN

SEVEN THUNDERS (*vv.* 1–7)

Here we have an account of another vision the apostle was favoured with, between the sounding of the sixth trumpet and that of the seventh. And we observe,

I. The person who was principally concerned in communicating this discovery to John—an angel from heaven, *another mighty angel*, who is so set forth as would induce one to think it could be no other than our Lord and Saviour Jesus Christ!

II. His station and posture: *He set his right foot upon the sea and his left foot upon the earth*, to show the absolute power and dominion he had over the world. *And he held in his hand a little book opened*, probably the same that was before sealed, but was now opened, and gradually fulfilled by him.

III. His awful voice: *He cried aloud, as when a lion roareth* (*v.* 3), and his awful voice was echoed by *seven thunders*, seven solemn and

terrible ways of discovering the mind of God.

IV. The prohibition given to the apostle, that he should not publish, but conceal what he had learned from the seven thunders, *v.* 4.

V. The solemn oath taken by this mighty angel. 1. The manner of his swearing: *He lifted up his hand to heaven, and swore by him that liveth for ever*, by himself, as God often has done, or by God as God, to whom he, as Lord, Redeemer, and ruler of the world, now appeals. 2. The matter of the oath: that *there shall be time no longer*; either, (1) That there shall be now no longer delay in fulfilling the predictions of this book. Or, (2) That when this mystery of God is finished time itself shall be no more.

THE LITTLE BOOK (*vv.* 8–11)

Here we have, I. A strict charge given to the apostle, which was, 1. That he should *go and take the little book* out of the hands of that mighty angel mentioned before. 2. To eat the book; this part of the charge was given by the angel himself, hinting to the apostle that before he should publish what he had discovered he must more thoroughly digest the predictions, and be in himself suitably affected with them.

II. An account of the taste and relish which this little book would have, when the apostle had taken it in; at first, while *in his mouth, sweet*. All persons feel a pleasure in looking into future events, and in having them foretold; and all good men love to receive a word from God, of what import soever it be. But, when this book of prophecy was more thoroughly digested by the apostle, the contents would be bitter; these were things so awful and terrible, such grievous persecutions of the people of God, and such desolation made in the earth, that the foresight and foreknowledge of them would not be pleasant, but painful to the mind of the apostle: thus was Ezekiel's prophecy to him, *ch*. iii. 3.

III. The apostle's discharge of the duty he was called to (*v*. 10): *He took the little book out of the angel's hand, and ate it up*, and he found the relish to be as was told him.

IV. The apostle is made to know that this book of prophecy, which he had now taken in, was not given him merely to gratify his own curiosity, or to affect him with pleasure or pain, but to be communicated by him to the world.

CHAPTER ELEVEN

MEASUREMENTS OF THE TEMPLE (*vv*. 1, 2)

This prophetical passage about measuring the temple is a plain reference to what we find in Ezekiel's vision, Ezek. xl. 3, &c. But how to understand either the one or the other is not so easy. It should seem the design of measuring the temple in the former case was in order to the rebuilding of it, and that with advantage; the design of this measurement seems to be either, 1. For the preservation of it in those times of public danger and calamity that are here foretold; or, 2. For its trial; that it may be seen how far it agrees with the

standard, or pattern, in the mount; or, 3. For its reformation; that what is redundant, deficient, or changed, may be regulated according to the true model. Observe,

I. How much was to be measured. 1. *The temple*; the gospel church in general, whether it be so built, so constituted, as the gospel rule directs, whether it be too narrow or too large, the door too wide or too strait. 2. *The altar*. That which was the place of the most solemn acts of worship may be put for religious worship in general. 3. The worshippers too must be measured, whether they make God's glory their end and his word their rule, in all their acts of worship; and whether they come to God with suitable affections, and whether their *conversation be as becomes the gospel*.

II. What was not to be measured (*v*. 2), and why it should be left out. 1. What was not to be measured: *The court which is without the temple measure it not*. 2. Why was not the outer court measured? This was no part of the temple, according to the model either of Solomon or Zerubbabel, and therefore God would have no regard to it. Those who worship in the outer court are either such as worship in a false manner or with hypocritical hearts; and these are rejected of God, and will be found among his enemies.

THE TWO WITNESSES (*vv*. 3–13)

In this time of treading down, God has reserved to himself his faithful witnesses, who will not fail to attest the truth of his word and worship, and the excellency of his ways. Here observe,

I. The number of these witnesses: it is but a small number and yet it is sufficient. Christ sent out his disciples two by two, to preach the gospel. Some think these two witnesses are Enoch and Elijah, who are to return to the earth for a time: others, the church of the believing Jews and that of the Gentiles: it should rather seem that they are God's eminent faithful ministers, who shall not only continue to profess the Christian religion, but to preach it, in the worst of times.

II. The time of their prophesying, or bearing their testimony for Christ. *A thousand two hundred and threescore days*; that is (as many think), to the period of the reign of antichrist; and, if the beginning of that interval could be ascertained, this number of prophetic days, taking a day for a year, would give us a prospect when the end shall be.

III. Their habit, and posture: they prophesy in sackcloth, as those that are deeply affected with the low and distressed state of the churches and interest of Christ in the world.

IV. How they were supported and supplied during the discharge of their great and hard work: they stood before the God of the whole earth, and he gave them power to prophesy.

V. Their security and defence during the time of their prophesying: *If any attempted to hurt them, fire proceeded out of their mouths, and devoured them, v. 5.* God has ordained his arrows for the persecutors, and is often plaguing them while they are persecuting his people; they find it hard work to *kick against the pricks*.

VI. The slaying of the witnesses. To make their testimony more strong, they must seal it with their blood. Here observe, 1. The time when they should be killed. *When they have finished their testimony.* They are immortal, they are invulnerable, till their work be done. 2. The enemy that should overcome and slay them—*the beast that ascendeth out of the bottomless pit.* Antichrist, the great instrument of the devil, should make war against them, not only with the arms of subtle and sophistical learning, but chiefly with open force and violence; and God would permit his enemies to prevail against his witnesses for a time. 3. The barbarous usage of these slain witnesses; the malice of their enemies was not satiated with their blood and death, but pursued even their dead bodies.

VII. The resurrection of these witnesses, and the consequences thereof. Observe, 1. The time of their rising again; after they had lain dead *three days and a half* (v. 11), a short time in comparison of that in which they had prophesied. 2. The power by which they were raised: *The spirit of life from God entered into them, and they stood upon their feet.* God put not only life, but courage into them.

VIII. The ascension of the witnesses into heaven and the consequences thereof, vv. 12, 13. Observe, 1. Their ascension. By heaven we may understand either some more eminent station in the church, the kingdom of grace in this world, or a high place in the kingdom of glory above. 2. The consequences of their ascension—a mighty shock and convulsion in the antichristian empire and the fall of *a tenth part of the city*. Thus, when God's work and witnesses revive, the devil's work and witnesses fall before him.

THE LAST TRUMPET
(*vv.* 14–19)

We have here the sounding of the seventh and last trumpet, which is ushered in by the usual warning and demand of attention: *The second woe is past, and, behold, the third woe cometh quickly. Then the seventh angel sounded.* Here observe the effects and consequences of this trumpet, thus sounded.

I. Here were loud and joyful acclamations of the saints and angels in heaven. Observe, 1. The manner of their adorations: they rose from their seats, *and fell upon their faces, and worshipped God*; they did it with reverence and humility. 2. The matter of their adorations. (1) They thankfully recognise the right of our God and Saviour to rule and reign over all the world: *The kingdoms of this world have become the kingdoms of our Lord and of his Christ, v.* 15. They were always so in title, both by creation and purchase. (2) They thankfully observe his actual possession of them, and reign over them. (3) They rejoice that this his reign shall never end: *He shall reign for ever and ever*, till all enemies be put under his feet; none shall ever wrest the sceptre out of his hand.

II. Here were angry resentments in the world at these just appearances and actings of the power of God (*v.* 18). *The nations were angry*; not only had been so, but were so still: their hearts rose up against God; they met his wrath with their own anger.

III. Another consequence was the opening of the temple of God in heaven. By this may be meant that here is now a more free communication between heaven and earth, prayer and praises more freely and frequently ascending and graces and blessings plentifully descending. But it rather seems to intend the church of God on earth, a heavenly temple. So, during the power of antichrist, the temple of God seemed to be shut up, and was so in a great degree; but now it was opened again.

CHAPTER TWELVE
THE WOMAN AND THE DRAGON (*vv.* 1–11)

Here we see that early prophecy eminently fulfilled in which God said he would *put enmity between the seed of the woman and the seed of the serpent*, Gen. iii. 15. You will observe,

I. The attempts of Satan and his agents to prevent the increase of the church, by devouring her offspring *as soon as it was born*: of this we have a very lively description in the most proper images.

1. We see how the church is represented in this vision. (1) As a *woman*, the weaker part of the world, but the spouse of Christ, and the mother of the saints. (2) As *clothed with the sun*, the imputed righteousness of the Lord Jesus Christ. (3) As having *the moon under her feet* (that is, the world);

she stands upon it, but lives above it. (4) As having on her head *a crown of twelve stars*, that is, the doctrine of the gospel preached by the twelve apostles, which is a crown of glory to all true believers. (5) As in travail, crying out, and *pained to be delivered*.

2. How the grand enemy of the church is represented. (1) As a *great red dragon*—a dragon for strength and terror—a red dragon for fierceness and cruelty. (2) As *having seven heads*, that is, placed on seven hills, as Rome was; and therefore it is probable that pagan Rome is here meant. (3) As having *ten horns*, divided into ten provinces, as the Roman empire was by Augustus Cæsar. (4) As having *seven crowns upon his head*, which is afterwards expounded to be seven kings, *ch.* xvii. 10. (5) As drawing with his tail a *third part of the stars in heaven*, and *casting them down to the earth*, turning the ministers and professors of the Christian religion out of their places and privileges and making them as weak and useless as he could. (6) As standing *before the woman, to devour her child as soon as it should be born*, very vigilant to crush the Christian religion in its birth and entirely to prevent the growth and continuance of it in the world.

II. The unsuccessfulness of these attempts against the church; for, 1. She was safely delivered of a *man-child* (*v.* 5), by which some understand Christ, others Constantine, but others, with greater propriety, a race of true believers, strong and united. 2. Care was taken of this child: it *was caught up to God, and to his throne*; that is,

taken into his special, powerful, and immediate protection. 3. Care was taken of the mother as well as of the child, *v.* 6. She *fled into the wilderness, a place prepared* both for her safety and her sustenance.

III. The attempts of the dragon not only proved unsuccessful against the church, but fatal to his own interests; for, upon his endeavour to devour the man-child, he engaged all the powers of heaven against him (*v.* 7): *There was war in heaven. Heaven* will espouse the quarrel of the church. Here observe,

1. The seat of this war—*in heaven*, in the church, which is *the kingdom of heaven* on earth, under the care of heaven and in the same interest.

2. The parties—*Michael and his angels* on one side, and *the dragon and his angels* on the other: Christ, the great Angel of the covenant, and his faithful followers; and Satan and all his instruments.

3. The success of the battle: *The dragon and his angels fought and prevailed not*; there was a great struggle on both sides, but the victory fell to Christ and his church.

4. The triumphant song that was composed and used on this occasion, *vv.* 10, 11. The servants of God overcame Satan, [1] *By the blood of the Lamb*, as the meritorious cause. [2] *By the word of their testimony*, as the great instrument of war, *the sword of the Spirit, which is the word of God*,—by a resolute powerful preaching of the everlasting gospel.

THE DRAGON'S WAR
(*vv.* 12–17)

We have here an account of this war, so happily finished in heaven, or in the church, as it was again renewed and carried on in the wilderness, the place to which the church had fled, and where she had been for some time secured by the special care of her God and Saviour. Observe,

I. The warning given of the distress and calamity that should fall upon the inhabitants of the world in general, through the wrath and rage of the devil.

II. His second attempt upon the church now in the wilderness: *He persecuted the woman who brought forth the man-child*, *v.* 13. Her obscurity could not altogether protect her; the old subtle serpent, which at first lurked in paradise, now follows the church into the wilderness, and *casts out a flood of water after her, to carry her away.* This is thought to be meant of a flood of error and heresy. *The earth helped the woman, and opened her mouth, and swallowed up the flood*, *v.* 16. Some think that we are to understand the swarms of Goths and Vandals that invaded the Roman empire, and found work for the Arian rulers, who otherwise would have been as furious persecutors as the pagan had been, and had exercised great cruelties already. The devil, being thus defeated in his designs upon the universal church, now turns his rage against particular persons and places; his malice against the woman pushes him on to *make war with the remnant of her seed.* Their fidelity to God and Christ, in doctrine, worship, and practice, was that which exposed them to the rage of Satan and his instruments; and such fidelity will expose men still,

less or more, to the end of the world, when *the last enemy shall be destroyed.*

CHAPTER THIRTEEN
THE FIRST BEAST (*vv.* 1–10)

We have here an account of the rise, figure, and progress of the first beast; and observe, 1. From what situation the apostle saw this monster. He seemed to himself to stand upon *the sea-shore*, though it is probable he was still in a rapture. 2. Whence this beast came—*out of the sea*; and yet, by the description of it, it would seem more likely to be a land-monster. 3. What was the form and shape of this beast. It was for the most part *like a leopard*, but its *feet were like the feet of a bear and its mouth as the mouth of a lion*; it had *seven heads, and ten horns, and upon its heads the name of blasphemy*: a most horrid and hideous monster! 4. The source and spring of his authority—*the dragon; he gave him his power, and seat, and great authority.* He was set up by the devil, and supported by him to do his work and promote his interest; and the devil lent him all the assistance he could. 5. A dangerous wound given him, and yet unexpectedly healed, *v.* 3. 6. The honour and worship paid to this infernal monster: *All the world wondered after the beast.* So great were the darkness, degeneracy, and madness of the world! 7. How he exercised his infernal power and policy: He had *a mouth, speaking great things, and blasphemies; he blasphemed God, the name of God, the tabernacle of God, and all those that dwell in heaven; and he made war with the saints, and overcame them*, and gained a sort of universal empire in the world. Thus the malice of the devil shows itself against heaven and the blessed inhabitants of heaven. These are above the reach of his power. All he can do is to blaspheme them; but the saints on earth are more exposed to his cruelty, and he sometimes is permitted to triumph over them and trample upon them. 8. The limitation of the devil's power and success, and that both as to time and persons. He is limited in point of time; his reign is *to continue forty-and-two months* (v. 5), suitable to the other prophetical characters of the reign of antichrist. He is also limited as to the persons and people that he shall entirely subject to his will and power; it will be only those *whose names are not written in the Lamb's book of life*.

THE SECOND BEAST
(*vv.* 11–18)

Here observe,

I. The form and shape of this second beast: *He had two horns like a lamb*, but a mouth that *spoke like the dragon*. All agree that this must be some great impostor, who, under a pretence of religion, shall deceive the souls of men.

II. The power which he exercises: *All the power of the former beast* (v. 12); he promotes the same interest, pursues the same design in substance, which is, to draw men off from worshipping the true God to worship those who by nature are no gods, and subject the souls and consciences of men to the will and authority of men, in opposition to the will of God.

III. The methods by which this second beast carried on his interests and designs; they are of three sorts: 1. Lying wonders, pretended miracles, by which they should be deceived. 2. Excommunications, anathemas, severe censures, by which they pretend to cut men off from Christ, and cast them into the power of the devil, but do indeed deliver them over to the secular power, that they may be put to death; and thus, notwithstanding their vile hypocrisy, they are justly charged with killing those whom they cannot corrupt. 3. By disfranchisement, allowing none to enjoy natural, civil, or municipal rights, who will not worship the beast.

IV. We have here *the number of the beast*, given in such a manner as shows the infinite wisdom of God, and will sufficiently exercise all the wisdom and accuracy of men: *The number* is *the number of a man*, computed after the usual manner among men, and it is 666. Only this we know, God has written *Mene Tekel* upon all his enemies; he has numbered their days, and they shall be finished, but his own kingdom shall endure for ever.

CHAPTER FOURTEEN
FOLLOWERS OF THE LAMB (*vv.* 1–5)

Here we have one of the most pleasing sights that can be viewed in this world—the Lord Jesus Christ at the head of his faithful adherents and attendants. Here observe, 1. How Christ appears: as a Lamb standing upon *mount Zion*.

Mount Zion is the gospel church. Christ is with his church and in the midst of her in all her troubles, and therefore she is not consumed. 2. How his people appear: very honourably. (1) As to the numbers, they are many, even all who were sealed. (2) Their distinguishing badge: they had *the name of God written in their foreheads*; they made a bold and open profession of their faith in God and Christ, and, this being followed by suitable actings, they are known and approved. (3) Their congratulations and songs of praise, which were peculiar to the redeemed (*v* 3). (4) Their character and description. [1] They are described by their chastity and purity: *They are virgins.* They had not defiled themselves either with corporal or spiritual adultery. [2] By their loyalty and stedfast adherence to Christ: *They follow the Lamb whithersoever he goes.* [3] By their former designation to this honour: *These were redeemed from among men, being the first-fruits to God, and to the Lamb, v.* 4. Here is plain evidence of a special redemption. [4] By their universal integrity and conscientiousness: *There was no guile found in them,* and *they were without fault before the throne of God.*

THE THREE ANGELS
(*vv.* 6–12)

In this part of the chapter we have three angels or messengers sent from heaven to give notice of the fall of Babylon, and of those things that were antecedent and consequent to that great event.

I. The first angel was sent on an errand antecedent to it, and that was *to preach the everlasting gospel, vv.* 6, 7.

II. The second angel follows the other and proclaims the actual fall of Babylon. By Babylon is generally understood Rome, which was before called *Sodom* and *Egypt,* for wickedness and cruelty, and is now first called *Babylon,* for pride and idolatry.

III. A third angel follows the other two, and gives warning to all of that divine vengeance which would overtake all those that obstinately adhered to the antichristian interest after God had thus proclaimed its downfall, *vv.* 9, 10.

THE HARVEST (*vv.* 13–20)

Here we have the vision of the harvest and vintage, introduced with a solemn preface. Observe,

I. The preface, *v.* 13. Here observe, (1) The description of those that are and shall be blessed—such as die in the Lord. (2) The demonstration of this blessedness: *They rest from their labours, and their works do follow them.* [1] They are blessed in their rest; they rest from all sin, temptation, sorrow, and persecution. [2] They are blessed in their recompence: *Their works follow them*; they do not go before them as their title, or price of purchase, but follow them as their evidence of having lived and died in the Lord. [3] They are happy in the time of their dying, when they have lived to see the cause of God reviving.

II. We have the vision itself, represented by a harvest and a vintage.

1. By a harvest (*vv.* 14, 15), an

529

emblem that sometimes signifies the cutting down of the wicked, when ripe for ruin, by the judgments of God, and sometimes the gathering in of the righteous, when ripe for heaven, by the mercy of God. This seems rather to represent God's judgments against the wicked.

2. By a vintage, *v.* 17. Some think that these two are only different emblems of the same judgment; others that they refer to distinct events of providence before the end of all things. Perhaps this great event has not yet had its accomplishment, but *the vision is for an appointed time*; and therefore, though it may seem to tarry, we are to wait for it. *But who shall live when the Lord does this?*

CHAPTER FIFTEEN
THE SEVEN VIALS (*vv.* 1–4)

Here we have the preparation of matters for the pouring out of the seven vials, which was committed to seven angels; and observe how these angels appeared to the apostle—*in heaven*; it was in a wonderful manner, and that upon account, 1. Of the work they had to do, which was to finish the destruction of antichrist. 2. The spectators and witnesses of this their commission: all *that had gotten the victory over the beast*, &c. (1) They extol the greatness of God's works, and the justice and truth of his ways, both in delivering his people and destroying their enemies. (2) They call upon all nations to render unto God their fear, glory, and worship, due to such a discovery of his truth and justice: *Who shall not fear thee? v.* 4.

SEVEN PLAGUES (*vv.* 5–8)

Observe, I. How these angels appeared—coming out of heaven to execute their commission: *The temple of the tabernacle of the testimony in heaven was opened, v.* 5.

II. How they were equipped and prepared for their work. Observe, 1. Their array: They were *clothed with pure and white linen*, and had *their breasts girded with golden girdles, v.* 6. This was the habit of the high priests when they went in to enquire of God, and came out with an answer from him. 2. Their artillery was *seven vials filled with the wrath of God*; they were armed with the wrath of God against his enemies. Now from whom did the angels receive these vials? From one of the four living creatures, one of the ministers of the true church, that is, in answer to the prayers of the ministers and people of God, and to avenge their cause, in which the angels are willingly employed.

III. The impressions these things made upon all who stood near the temple. God himself was now preaching to the church and to all the world, by terrible things in righteousness; but, when this work was done, then the churches would have rest, the temple would be opened, and the solemn assemblies gathered, edified, and multiplied.

CHAPTER SIXTEEN
PLAGUES ON LAND AND SEA (*vv.* 1–7)

We had in the foregoing chapter the great and solemn preparation that was made for the pouring out of the vials; now we have the performance of that work. Here observe,

I. That, though every thing was made ready before, yet nothing was to be put in execution without an immediate positive order from God; and this he gave out of the temple, answering the prayers of his people, and avenging their quarrel.

II. No sooner was the word of command given than it was immediately obeyed; no delay, no objection made. Now we proceed to,

(1) The first angel who poured out his vial, *v.* 2. Observe, [1] Where it fell—*upon the earth.* [2] What it produced—*noisome and grievous sores on all who had the mark of the beast.*

(2) *The second angel poured out his vial;* and here we see, [1] Where it fell—*upon the sea.* [2] What it produced: It turned the sea into blood, *as the blood of a dead man, and every living soul died in the sea.*

(3) The next angel poured out his vial; and we are told, [1] Where it fell—*upon the rivers, and upon the fountains of waters.* [2] What effect it had upon them: *It turned them into blood.* The instrument that God makes use of in this work is here called *the angel of the waters,* who extols the righteousness of God in this retaliation: *They have shed the blood of thy saints, and thou hast given them blood to drink, for they are worthy,* to which another angel answered by full consent, *v.* 7.

HEAT AND DARKNESS
(*vv.* 8–11)

In these verses we see the work going on in the appointed order.

The fourth angel poured out his vial, and that fell upon the sun. That sun which before cherished them with warm and benign influences shall now grow hot against these idolaters, and shall scorch them. The fifth angel poured out his vial, *v.* 10. And observe, 1. Where this fell—*upon the seat of the beast,* upon Rome itself, the mystical Babylon, the head of the antichristian empire. 2. What effect it had there: The whole kingdom of the beast *was full of darkness* and distress.

THE FINAL PLAGUES
(*vv.* 12–16)

The sixth angel poured out his vial; and observe,

I. Where it fell—*upon the great river Euphrates.* Some take it literally, for the place where the Turkish power and empire began. Others take it for the river Tiber; for, as Rome is mystical Babylon, Tiber is mystical Euphrates. And when Rome shall be destroyed her river and merchandise must suffer with her.

II. What did this vial produce? 1. The drying up of the river, which furnished the city with wealth, provisions, and all sorts of accommodations. 2. A way is hereby prepared *for the kings of the east.* There will be a more open communication between the western and eastern nations, which may facilitate the conversion of the Jews, and of *the fulness of the Gentiles.* 3. The last effort of the great dragon; he is resolved to have another push for it, that, if possible, he may retrieve the ruinous posture of his affairs in the world. He is now rallying his forces, recollecting all his spirits, to make one desperate sally before all be lost. This is occasioned by the pouring out of the sixth vial. Here observe, (1) The instruments he makes use of to engage the powers of the earth in his cause and quarrel: *Three unclean spirits like frogs* come forth, one *out of the mouth of the dragon*, another *out of the mouth of the beast, and* a third *out of the mouth of the false prophet.* (2) The means these instruments would use to engage the power of earth in this war. They would work pretended miracles, the old stratagem of him *whose coming is after the working of Satan, with all power, and signs, and lying wonders, and with all deceivableness of unrighteousness*, 2 Thess. ii. 9, 10. (3) The field of battle—a place called *Armageddon*; that is, say some, the mount of Megiddo. This battle required time to prepare for it, and therefore the further account of it is suspended till we come to the nineteenth chapter, *vv.* 19, 20. (4) The warning which God gives of this great and decisive trial, to engage his people to prepare for it, *v.* 15.

'IT IS DONE' (*vv.* 17–21)

Here we have an account of the seventh and last angel pouring forth his vial, contributing his part towards the accomplishment of the downfall of Babylon, which was the finishing stroke. And here, as before, observe,

I. Where this plague fell—*on the air*, upon the prince of the power of the air, that is, the devil.

II. What it produced, 1. A thankful voice from heaven, pronouncing that now the work was done. 2. A

mighty commotion on the earth— an earthquake, so great as never was before, shaking the very centre, and this ushered in by the usual concomitants of thunder and lightnings. 3. The fall of Babylon, which was divided into three parts, *called the cities of the nations* (*v.* 19).

III. How the antichristian party were affected with it. Though it fell upon them as a dreadful storm, as if the stones of the city, tossed up into the air, came down upon their heads, like hailstones of a talent weight each, yet they were so far from repenting that they blasphemed that God who thus punished them. Here was a dreadful plague of the heart, a spiritual judgment more dreadful and destructive than all the rest.

CHAPTER SEVENTEEN

FALL OF BABYLON (*vv.* 1–6)

Here we have a new vision, not as to the matter of it, for that is contemporary with what came under the three last vials; but as to the manner of description, &c. Observe, 1. The invitation given to the apostle to take a view of what was here to be represented: *Come hither, and I will show thee the judgment of the great whore*, &c., *v.* 1. Now in this observe, (1) She is named from her place of residence—*Babylon the great*. But, that we might not take it for the old Babylon literally so called, we are told there is a mystery in the name; it is some other great city resembling the old Babylon. (2) She is named from her infamous way and practice; not only a harlot, but a mother of harlots, breeding up harlots, and nursing and training them up to idolatry, and all sorts of lewdness and wickedness—the parent and nurse of all false religion and filthy conversation. 5. Her diet: she satiated herself with *the blood of the saints and martyrs of Jesus*.

VISION EXPLAINED (*vv.* 7–13)

Here we have the mystery of this vision explained. 1. This beast *was, and is not, and yet is*; that is, it *was* a seat of idolatry and persecution; *and is not*, that is, not in the ancient form, which was pagan; *and yet it is*, it is truly the seat of idolatry and tyranny, though of another sort and form. *It ascends out of the bottomless pit* (idolatry and cruelty are the issue and product of hell), and it shall return thither and go into perdition. 2. *This beast has seven heads*, which have a double signification. (1) *Seven mountains*—the seven hills on which Rome stands; and, (2) *Seven kings*—seven sorts of government. This beast makes an eighth governor, and sets up idolatry again. 3. This beast had ten horns; which are said to be *ten kings which have as yet received no kingdoms*.

DOWNFALL OF BABYLON (*vv.* 14–18)

Here we have some account of the downfall of Babylon, to be more fully described in the following chapter.

I. Here is a war begun between the beast and his followers, and the Lamb and his followers.

II. Here is a victory gained by the Lamb: *The Lamb shall overcome.*

III. Here is the ground or reason of the victory assigned; and this is

taken, 1. From the character of the Lamb: *He is King of kings and Lord of lords*. 2. From the character of his followers: *They are called, and chosen, and faithful.*

IV. The victory is justly aggrandised. 1. By the vast multitude who paid obedience and subjection to the beast and to the whore. 2. By the powerful influence which God hereby showed he had over the minds of great men.

CHAPTER EIGHTEEN
THE SIN OF BABYLON
(*vv.* 1–8)

The downfall and destruction of Babylon form an event so fully determined in the counsels of God, and of such consequence to his interests and glory, that the visions and predictions concerning it are repeated. 1. Here is another angel sent from heaven, attended with great power and lustre, *v.* 1. 2. This angel publishes the fall of Babylon, as a thing already come to pass. 3. the reason of this ruin is declared (*v.* 3). The wickedness of Babylon had been very great; for she had not only forsaken the true God herself, and set up idols, but had with great art and industry drawn all sorts of men into the spiritual adultery, and by her wealth and luxury had retained them in her interest. 4. Fair warning is given to all that expect mercy from God, that they should not only *come out of her*, but be assisting in her destruction, *vv.* 4, 5.

LAMENT FOR BABYLON
(*vv.* 9–24)

Here we have,

I. A doleful lamentation made by

Babylon's friends for her fall; and here observe,

1. Who are the mourners, namely, those who had been bewitched by her fornication, those who had been sharers in her sensual pleasures, and those who had been gainers by her wealth and trade.

2. What was the manner of their mourning. (1) They stood afar off, they durst not come nigh her. (2) They made a grievous outcry: *Alas! alas! that great city, Babylon, that mighty city!* (3) They wept, and *cast dust upon their heads, v.* 19. The pleasures of sin are but for a season, and they will end in dismal sorrow.

3. What was the cause of their mourning; not their sin, but their punishment.

II. An account of the joy and triumph there was both in heaven and earth at the irrecoverable fall of Babylon: while her own people were bewailing her, the servants of God were called to *rejoice over her, v.* 20. This enemy should never molest them any more, and of this they were assured by a remarkable token (*v.* 21): An *angel* from heaven *took up a stone like a great millstone, and cast it into the sea, saying,* "*Thus shall Babylon be thrown down with violence, and be found no more at all*; the place shall be no longer habitable by man, no work shall be done there, no comfort enjoyed, no light seen there, but utter darkness and desolation, as the reward of her great wickedness, first in *deceiving the nations with her sorceries,* and secondly in destroying and murdering those whom she could not deceive," *v.* 24. Such abominable sins deserved so great a ruin.

CHAPTER NINETEEN

PRAISE IN HEAVEN (*vv.* 1–10)

The fall of Babylon being fixed, finished, and declared to be irrecoverable in the foregoing chapter, this begins with a holy triumph over her, in pursuance of the order given forth: *Rejoice over her, thou heaven, and you holy apostles and prophets,* ch. xviii. 20.

The triumphant song being ended, an epithalamium, or marriage-song, begins, *v.* 6. Here observe,

I. The concert of heavenly music. The chorus was large and loud, *as the voice of many waters and of mighty thunderings.*

II. The occasion of this song; and that is the reign and dominion of that omnipotent God who has *redeemed his church by his own blood,* and is now in a more public manner betrothing her to himself: *The marriage of the Lamb has come, v.* 7. Some think this refers to the conversion of the Jews, which they suppose will succeed the fall of Babylon; others, to the general resurrection: the former seems more probable. Now, 1. You have here a description of the bride, how she appeared; not in the gay and gaudy dress of the mother of harlots, but *in fine linen, clean and white,* which *is the righteousness of saints*; in the robes of Christ's righteousness, both imputed for justification and imparted for sanctification. 2. The marriage-feast, which, though not particularly described (as Matt. xxii. 4), yet is declared to be such as would make all those happy who were called to it, so called as to accept the invitation, a feast made up of the promises of the gospel, *the true sayings of God*, v. 9. 3. The transport of joy which the apostle felt in himself at this vision. Here observe, (1) What honour he offered to the angel: *He fell at his feet, to worship him*. (2) How the angel refused it, and this was with some resentment: "*See thou do it not*; have a care what thou doest, thou art doing a wrong thing." (3) He gave a very good reason for his refusal: "*I am thy fellow-servant, and of thy brethren which have the testimony of Jesus—*I am a creature, thine equal in office, though not in nature."

THE WORD OF GOD
(vv. 11–21)

No sooner was the marriage solemnized between Christ and his church by the conversion of the Jews than the glorious head and husband of the church is called out to a new expedition, which seems to be the great battle that was to be fought at Armageddon, foretold *ch.* xvi. 16. And here observe,

I. The description of the great Commander, 1. By the seat of his empire; and that is *heaven*; his throne is there, and his power and authority are heavenly and divine. 2. His equipage: he is again described as sitting *on a white horse*, to show the equity of the cause, and certainty of success. 3. His attributes: he is *faithful and true* to his covenant and promise. 4. His armour; and that is *a vesture dipped in blood*, either his own blood, by which he purchased this mediatorial power, or the blood of his enemies, over whom he has always prevailed. 5. His name: *The Word of God*, a name that none fully

knows but himself, only this we know, that this *Word was God manifest in the flesh*; but his perfections are incomprehensible by any creature.

II. The army which he commands (v. 14), a very large one, made up of many armies; angels and saints followed his conduct, and resembled him in their equipage, and in their armour of purity and righteousness—chosen, and called, and faithful.

III. The weapons of his warfare —*a sharp sword* proceeding from *his mouth* (v. 15), with which *he smites the nations*, either the threatenings of the written word, which now he is going to execute, or rather his word of command calling on his followers to take a just revenge on his and their enemies, who are now put into the winepress of the wrath of God, to be trodden under foot by him.

IV. The ensigns of his authority, his coat of arms—*a name written on his vesture and thigh, King of kings, and Lord of lords*, asserting his authority and power, and the cause of the quarrel, *v.* 16.

V. An invitation given *to the fowls of heaven*, that they should come and see the battle, and share in the spoil and pillage of the field (vv. 17, 18).

VI. The battle joined. The enemy falls on with great fury, headed by *the beast, and the kings of the earth*; the powers of earth and hell gathered, to make their utmost effort, *v.* 19.

VII. The victory gained by the great and glorious head of the church: *The beast and the false prophet*, the leaders of the army, are taken prisoners, both he who led them by power and he who led them by policy and falsehood; these are taken and *cast into the burning lake*, made incapable of molesting the church of God any more; and their followers, whether officers or common soldiers, are given up to military execution, and made a feast for *the fowls of heaven*.

CHAPTER TWENTY

THE MILLENNIUM (*vv*. 1–10)

We have here, I. A prophecy of *the binding of Satan* for a certain term of time, in which he should have much less power and the church much more peace than before. Observe, 1. To whom this work of binding Satan is committed—to *an angel from heaven*. 2. The means he makes use of in this work: he has a *chain* and a *key, a great chain* to bind Satan, and *the key of the* prison in which he was to be confined. 3. The execution of this work, *vv*. 2, 3. (1) *He laid hold on the dragon, that old serpent, which is the devil, and Satan*. And, (2) He *cast him into the bottomless pit*, cast him down with force, and with a just vengeance, to his own place and prison, from which he had been permitted to break out, and disturb the churches, and deceive the nations; now he is brought back to that prison, and there laid in chains. (3) He is *shut up, and a seal set upon him*. (4) We have the term of this confinement of Satan—*a thousand years*, after which he was to *be loosed* again for *a little season*. The church should have a considerable time of peace and pros-

perity, but all her trials were not yet over.

II. An account of the reign of the saints for the same space of time in which Satan continued bound (*vv*. 4–6), and here observe,

1. Who those were that received such honour—those who had suffered for Christ, and all who had faithfully adhered to him.

2. The honour bestowed upon them. (1) They were raised from the dead, and restored to life. (2) *Thrones*, and power of *judgment, were given to them*; they were possessed of great honour, and interest, and authority, I suppose rather of a spiritual than of a secular nature. (3) *They reigned with Christ a thousand years*. Those who suffer with Christ shall reign with Christ.

3. The happiness of these servants of God is declared. (1) They are *blessed and holy*, v. 6. None can be blessed but those that are holy. (2) They are secured from the power of the second death. We know something of what the first death is, and it is awful; but we know not what this second death is. It must be much more dreadful; it is the death of the soul, eternal separation from God.

III. An account of the return of the church's troubles, and another mighty conflict, very sharp, but short and decisive. No sooner is Satan let loose than he falls to his old work, *deceiving the nations*, and so stirring them up to make a war with the saints and servants of God, which they would never do if he had not first deceived them. The power now permitted to him seems to be more unlimited than before.

God would, in an extraordinary and more immediate manner, fight this last and decisive battle for his people, that the victory might be complete and the glory redound to himself.

THE GREAT WHITE THRONE
(*vv.* 11–15)

The utter destruction of the devil's kingdom very properly leads to an account of the day of judgment, which will determine every man's everlasting state. Here we have a description of it, where observe, 1. We behold *the throne*, and tribunal of judgment, *great* and *white*, very glorious and perfectly just and righteous. 2. The appearance of the Judge, and that is the Lord Jesus Christ, who then puts on such majesty and terror that *the earth and the heaven flee from his face, and there is no place found for them*; there is a dissolution of the whole frame of nature, 2 Pet. iii. 10. 3. The persons to be judged (*v.* 12): *The dead, small and great*; that is, young and old, low and high, poor and rich, 4. The rule of judgment settled: *The books were opened.* What books? The book of God's omniscience, who is greater than our consciences, and knows all things (there is a book of remembrance with him both for good and bad); and the book of the sinner's conscience, which, though formerly secret, will now be opened. *And another book* shall be *opened*—the book of the scriptures, the statute-book of heaven, the rule of life. 5. The cause to be tried; and that is, *the works of men*, what they have done and whether it be good or evil. 6. The issue of the trial and judg-ment; and this will be according to the evidence of fact, and rule of judgment.

CHAPTER TWENTY-ONE

NEW JERUSALEM (*vv.* 1–8)

We have here a more general account of the happiness of the church of God in the future state, by which it seems most safe to understand the heavenly state.

I. A new world now opens to our view (*v.* 1): *I saw a new heaven and a new earth*; that is, a new universe; for we suppose the world to be made up of heaven and earth. By the new earth we may understand a new state for the bodies of men, as well as a heaven for their souls.

II. In this new world the apostle *saw the holy city, the new Jerusalem, coming down from heaven*, not locally, but as to its original: this new Jerusalem is the church of God in its new and perfect state, *prepared as a bride adorned for her husband*, beautified with all perfection of wisdom and holiness, meet for the full fruition of the Lord Jesus Christ in glory.

III. The blessed presence of God with his people is here proclaimed and admired: *I heard a great voice out of heaven, saying, Behold, the tabernacle of God is with men*, &c., *v.* 3.

IV. This new and blessed state will be free from all trouble and sorrow; for, 1. All the effects of former trouble shall be done away. 2. All the causes of future sorrow shall be for ever removed.

V. The truth and certainty of this blessed state are ratified by the word and promise of God, and ordered to be committed to writing, as matter of perpetual record, *vv.* 5, 6.

VI. The greatness of this future felicity is declared and illustrated, 1. By the freeness of it—it is the free gift of God: *He gives of the water of life freely*; this will not make it less but more grateful to his people. 2. The fulness of it. The people of God then lie at the fountain-head of all blessedness: they *inherit all things* (*v.* 7); enjoying God, they enjoy all things. He is all in all. 3. By the tenure and title by which they enjoy this blessedness—by right of inheritance, as *the sons of God.* 4. By the vastly different state of the wicked. Their misery helps to illustrate the glory and blessedness of the saints, and the distinguishing goodness of God towards them, *v.* 8. Thus the misery of the damned will illustrate the blessedness of those that are saved, and the blessedness of the saved will aggravate the misery of those that are damned.

THE GLORIES OF HEAVEN
(*vv.* 9–27)

We have already considered the introduction to the vision of the new Jerusalem in a more general idea of the heavenly state; we now come to the vision itself, where observe,

I. The person that opened the vision to the apostle—*one of the seven angels, that had the seven vials full of the seven last plagues, v.* 9. God has a variety of work and employment for his holy angels.

II. The place from which the apostle had this glorious view and prospect. He was taken, in ecstasy, into *a high mountain.*

III. The subject-matter of the vision—*the bride, the Lamb's wife* (*v.* 10); that is, the church of God in her glorious, perfect, triumphant state, under the resemblance of Jerusalem, having the glory of God shining in its lustre.

1. The exterior part of the city—*the wall* and *the gates*, the wall for security and the gates for entrance.

(1) The wall for security. Heaven is a safe state; those that are there are enclosed with a wall, that separates them and secures them from all evils and enemies. The foundations are described by their number and by their matter; by their number—*twelve*, alluding to the twelve apostles (*v.* 14), whose gospel doctrines are the foundations upon which the church is built, *Christ himself being the chief corner-stone*; and, as to the matter of these foundations, it was various and precious, set forth by twelve sorts of precious stones, denoting the variety and excellency of the doctrines of the gospel, or of the graces of the Holy Spirit, or the person excellencies of the Lord Jesus Christ.

(2) The gates for entrance. Heaven is not inaccessible; there is a way opened into the holiest of all; there is a free admission to all those that are sanctified; they shall not find themselves shut out. Now, as to these gates, observe, [1] Their number—*twelve gates*, answering to the twelve tribes of Israel. [2] Their guards which were placed upon them—*twelve angels*, to admit and receive the several tribes of the spiritual Israel and to keep out others. [3] The inscription on the gates—*the names of the twelve*

tribes, to show that they have a right to the tree of life, and to enter through the gates into the city. [4] The situation of the gates. As the city had four equal sides, answering to the four quarters of the world, east, west, north, and south, so on each side there were three gates, signifying that from all quarters of the earth there shall be some who shall get safely to heaven and be received there.

2. The interior part of the new Jerusalem, *vv.* 22–27. We have seen its strong wall, and stately gates, and glorious guards; now we are to be led through the gates into the city itself; and the first thing which we observe there is the street of the city, *which is of pure gold, like transparent glass, v.* 21. The saints in heaven tread upon gold. Observe,

(1) The temple of the new Jerusalem, which was no material temple, made with men's hands, as that of Solomon and Zerubbabel, but a temple altogether spiritual and divine.

(2) The light of this city. Where there is no light, there can be no lustre nor pleasure. Heaven is *the inheritance of the saints in light.* But what is that light? There is no sun nor moon shining there, *v.* 23. There is no want of the light of the sun, *for the glory of God lightens that city, and the Lamb is the light thereof.*

(3) The inhabitants of this city. They are described here several ways. [1] By their numbers— whole nations of saved souls; some out of all nations, and many out of some nations. [2] By their dignity— some of the kings and princes of the

earth: great kings. God will have some of all ranks and degrees of men to fill the heavenly mansions, high and low; and when the greatest kings come to heaven they will see all their former honour and glory swallowed up of this heavenly glory that so much excels. [3] Their continual accession and entrance into this city: *The gates shall never be shut.* There is no night, and therefore no need of shutting up the gates.

(4) The accommodations of this city: All the *glory and honour of the nations shall be brought into it.* Whatever is excellent and valuable in this world shall be there enjoyed in a more refined kind, and to a far greater degree.

(5) The unmixed purity of all who belong to the new Jerusalem, *v.* 27. [1] There the saints shall have no impure thing remaining in them. [2] There the saints shall have no impure persons admitted among them.

CHAPTER TWENTY-TWO
THE THRONE OF GOD
(*vv.* 1–5)

The heavenly state which was before described as a city, and called the new Jerusalem, is here described as a paradise. And here observe,

I. The river of paradise. The earthly paradise was well watered: no place can be pleasant or fruitful that is not so. This river is described, 1. By its fountain-head—*the throne of God and the Lamb.* 2. By its quality—*pure and clear as crystal.*

II. The tree of life, in this paradise. Such a tree there was in the earthly paradise, Gen. ii. 9. This far excels it. And now, as to this tree, observe, 1. The situation of it —*in the midst of the street, and on either side the river*; or, as it might have been better rendered, *in the midst between the terrace-walk and the river*. This tree of life is fed by the pure waters of the river that comes from the throne of God. 2. The fruitfulness of this tree. (1) It brings forth many sorts of fruit— *twelve sorts*, suited to the refined taste of all the saints. (2) It brings forth fruit at all times—*yields its fruit every month*. This tree is never empty, never barren; there is always fruit upon it. (3) The fruit is not only pleasant, but wholesome.

III. The perfect freedom of this paradise from every thing that is evil (*v.* 3): *There shall be no more curse*; no *accursed one*—no serpent there, as there was in the earthly paradise. Here is the great excellency of this paradise.

IV. The supreme felicity of this paradisaical state. 1. There the saints shall see the face of God; there they shall enjoy the beatific vision. 2. God will own them, as having his seal and name on their foreheads. 3. *They shall reign with him for ever*; their service shall be not only freedom but honour and dominion. 4. All this shall be with perfect knowledge and joy.

DIVINE CONFIRMATION
(*vv.* 6–19)

We have here a solemn ratification of the contents of this book, and particularly of this last vision (though some think it may not only refer to the whole book, but to the whole New Testament, yea, to the whole Bible, completing and confirming the canon of scripture); and here, 1. This is confirmed by the name and nature of that God who gave out these discoveries: he is *the Lord God, faithful and true*, and so are all his sayings. 2. By the messengers he chose, to reveal these things to the world; the holy angels showed them to holy men of God; and God would not employ his saints and angels in deceiving the world. 3. They will soon be confirmed by their accomplishment: they are things that must shortly be done; Christ will make haste, *he will come quickly*, and put all things out of doubt; and then those will prove the wise and happy men who have believed and kept his words. 4. By the integrity of that angel who had been the apostle's guide and interpreter in these visions. 5. By the order given to leave the book of the prophecy open, to be perused by all, that they might labour to understand it, that they might make their objections against it, and compare the prophecy with the events. God here deals freely and openly with all; he does not speak in secret, but calls every one to witness to the declarations here made, *v.* 10. 6. By the effect this book, thus kept open, will have upon men; those that are filthy and unjust will take occasion thence to be more so, but it will confirm, strengthen, and further sanctify those that are upright with God. 7. It will be Christ's rule of judgment at the great day; he will dispense rewards and punishments to men according as their works agree or disagree with the word of God.

8. It is the word of him who is the author, finisher, and rewarder of the faith and holiness of his people, *vv.* 13, 14. He is *the first and the last*, and the same from first to last, and so is his word too. 9. It is a book that condemns and excludes from heaven all wicked, unrighteous persons, and particularly *those that love and make lies* (*v.* 15), and therefore can never be itself a lie. 10. It is confirmed by *the testimony of Jesus, which is the Spirit of prophecy*. 11. It is confirmed by an open and general invitation to all to come and partake of the promises and privileges of the gospel, those streams of the water of life; these are tendered to all who feel in their souls a thirst which nothing in this world can quench. 12. It is confirmed by the joint testimony of the Spirit of God, and that gracious Spirit that is in all the true members of the church of God; *the Spirit and the bride* join in testifying the truth and excellency of the gospel. 13. It is confirmed by a most solemn sanction, condemning and cursing all who should dare to corrupt or change the word of God, either by adding to it or taking from it, *vv.* 18, 19.

FINAL PRAYER (*vv.* 20, 21)

We have now come to the conclusion of the whole, and that in three things:

I. Christ's farewell to his church. He seems now, after he has been discovering these things to his people on earth, to take leave of them, and return to heaven; but he parts with them in great kindness, and assures them it shall not be long before he comes again to them: *Behold, I come quickly.*

II. The church's hearty echo to Christ's promise, 1. Declaring her firm belief of it: *Amen, so it is*, so it shall be. 2. Expressing her earnest desire of it: *Even so, come, Lord Jesus; make haste, my beloved, and be thou like a roe, or like a young hart on the mountains of spices.* What comes from heaven in a promise should be sent back to heaven in a prayer.

III. The apostolical benediction, which closes the whole: *The grace of our Lord Jesus Christ be with you all, Amen.*